FOUNDATIONS
SERIES

Prentice Hall

Algebra 1

Randall I. Charles
Basia Hall
Dan Kennedy
Allan E. Bellman
Sadie Chavis Bragg
William G. Handlin
Siegfried Haenisch
Stuart J. Murphy
Grant Wiggins

PEARSON

Boston, Massachusetts • Chandler, Arizona • Glenview, Illinois • Upper Saddle River, New Jersey

Acknowledgments appear on page 913, which constitutes an extension of this copyright page.

ISBN-13: 978-0-7854-6917-9
ISBN-10: 0-7854-6917-6
15 V057 15

Contents *in Brief*

Welcome to Pearson's *Prentice Hall Algebra 1* student book. Throughout this textbook, you will find content that has been developed to cover all of the American Diploma Project's (ADP) math benchmarks. The End-of-Course Assessment is modeled after the ADP Algebra 1 test and can serve as practice before taking the actual ADP test.

Series *Authors*

Randall I. Charles, Ph.D., is Professor Emeritus in the Department of Mathematics and Computer Science at San Jose State University, San Jose, California. He began his career as a high school mathematics teacher, and he was a mathematics supervisor for five years. Dr. Charles has been a member of several NCTM committees and is the former Vice President of the National Council of Supervisors of Mathematics (NCSM). Much of his writing and research has been in the area of problem solving. He has authored more than 75 mathematics textbooks for kindergarten through college.

Dan Kennedy, Ph.D., is a classroom teacher and the Lupton Distinguished Professor of Mathematics at the Baylor School in Chattanooga, Tennessee. A frequent speaker at professional meetings on mathematics education reform, Dr. Kennedy has conducted numerous workshops and institutes for high school teachers. He is coauthor of calculus and precalculus textbooks, and, from 1990 to 1994, he chaired the College Board's AP Calculus Development Committee. He is a 1992 Tandy Technology Scholar and a 1995 Presidential Award winner.

Basia Hall is currently Manager of Instructional Programs for the Houston Independent School District. Ms. Hall has been a department chair, instructional supervisor, school improvement facilitator, and professional development trainer. She has developed curricula for high school mathematics and co-developed the Texas state mathematics standards. A 1992 Presidential Awardee, Ms. Hall is past president of the Texas Association of Supervisors of Mathematics and is a state representative for NCSM.

Consulting *Authors*

Stuart J. Murphy is a visual learning author and consultant. He is the author of *MathStart*, a series of children's books that presents mathematical concepts in the story contexts. A graduate of the Rhode Island School of Design, Mr. Murphy has worked extensively in educational publishing and has been on the authorship teams of a number of mathematics programs. He is a frequent presenter at meetings of the National Council of Teachers of Mathematics and the International Reading Association.

Grant Wiggins, Ed.D., is the President of Authentic Education in Hopewell, New Jersey. Dr. Wiggins consults with schools, districts, and state education departments on reform matters; organizes conferences and workshops; and develops materials on curricular change. With Jay McTighe, he is co-author of *Understanding by Design* and *The Understanding by Design Handbook*, published by ASCD. His work has been supported by the Pew Charitable Trusts, the Geraldine R. Dodge Foundation, and the National Science Foundation.

Siegfried Haenisch, Ed.D., has taught mathematics from elementary to graduate school, most recently as Professor in the Department of Mathematics and Statistics at the College of New Jersey. Dr. Haenisch was the site director for the training of teachers in the New Jersey Algebra Project. Dr. Haenisch currently serves as a mathematics curriculum consultant to school districts. The Mathematical Association of America granted him the 1995 Award for Distinguished Teaching of Mathematics.

Program *Authors*

Algebra 1 and Algebra 2

Allan E. Bellman, Ph.D., is a Lecturer/Supervisor in the School of Education at the University of California, Davis. Before coming to Davis, he was a mathematics teacher for 31 years in Montgomery County, Maryland. He has been an instructor for both the Woodrow Wilson National Fellowship Foundation and the T^3 program. He has been involved in the development of many products from Texas Instruments. Dr. Bellman has a particular expertise in the use of technology in education and speaks frequently on this topic. He was a 1992 Tandy Technology Scholar and has twice been listed in Who's Who Among America's Teachers.

Sadie Chavis Bragg, Ed.D., is Senior Vice President of Academic Affairs at the Borough of Manhattan Community College of the City University of New York. A former professor of mathematics, she is a past president of the American Mathematical Association of Two-Year Colleges (AMATYC), co-director of the AMATYC project to revise the standards for introductory college mathematics before calculus, and an active member of the Benjamin Banneker Association. Dr. Bragg has coauthored more than 50 mathematics textbooks for kindergarten through college.

William G. Handlin, Sr., is a classroom teacher and Department Chairman of Technology Applications at Spring Woods High School in Houston, Texas. Awarded Life Membership in the Texas Congress of Parents and Teachers for his contributions to the well-being of children, Mr. Handlin is also a frequent workshop and seminar leader in professional meetings throughout the world.

Geometry

Laurie E. Bass is a classroom teacher at the 9–12 division of the Ethical Culture Fieldston School in Riverdale, New York. A classroom teacher for more than 30 years, Ms. Bass has a wide base of teaching experience, ranging from Grade 6 through Advanced Placement Calculus. She was the recipient of a 2000 Honorable Mention for the Radio Shack National Teacher Awards. She has been a contributing writer for a number of publications, including software-based activities for the Algebra 1 classroom. Among her areas of special interest are cooperative learning for high school students and geometry exploration on the computer. Ms. Bass is a frequent presenter at local, regional, and national conferences.

Art Johnson, Ed.D., is a professor of mathematics education at Boston University. He is a mathematics educator with 32 years of public school teaching experience, a frequent speaker and workshop leader, and the recipient of a number of awards: the Tandy Prize for Teaching Excellence, the Presidential Award for Excellence in Mathematics Teaching, and New Hampshire Teacher of the Year. He was also profiled by the Disney Corporation in the American Teacher of the Year Program. Dr. Johnson has contributed 18 articles to NCTM journals and has authored over 50 books on various aspects of mathematics.

Reviewers *National*

Tammy Baumann
K-12 Mathematics Coordinator
School District of the City
of Erie
Erie, Pennsylvania

Sandy Cowgill
Mathematics Department Chair
Muncie Central High School
Muncie, Indiana

Kari Egnot
Mathematics Teacher
Newport News High School
Newport News, Virginia

Sheryl Ezze
Mathematics Chairperson
DeWitt High School
Lansing, Michigan

Dennis Griebel
Mathematics Coordinator
Cherry Creek School District
Aurora, Colorado

Bill Harrington
Secondary Mathematics
Coordinator
State College School District
State College, Pennsylvania

Michael Herzog
Mathematics Teacher
Tucson Small School Project
Tucson, Arizona

Camilla Horton
Secondary Instruction Support
Memphis School District
Memphis, Tennessee

Gary Kubina
Mathematics Consultant
Mobile County School System
Mobile, Alabama

Sharon Liston
Mathematics Department Chair
Moore Public Schools
Oklahoma City, Oklahoma

Ann Marie Palmeri Monahan
Mathematics Supervisor
Bayonne Public Schools
Bayonne, New Jersey

Indika Morris
Mathematics Department Chair
Queen Creek School District
Queen Creek, Arizona

Jennifer Petersen
K-12 Mathematics Curriculum
Facilitator
Springfield Public Schools
Springfield, Missouri

Tammy Popp
Mathematics Teacher
Mehlville School District
St. Louis, Missouri

Mickey Porter
Mathematics Teacher
Dayton Public Schools
Dayton, Ohio

Steven Sachs
Mathematics Department Chair
Lawrence North High School
Indianapolis, Indiana

John Staley
Secondary Mathematics
Coordinator
Office of Mathematics, PK-12
Baltimore, Maryland

Robert Thomas, Ph.D.
Mathematics Teacher
Yuma Union High School
District #70
Yuma, Arizona

Linda Ussery
Mathematics Consultant
Alabama Department of
Education
Tuscumbia, Alabama

Denise Vizzini
Mathematics Teacher
Clarksburg High School
Montgomery County,
Maryland

Marcia White
Mathematics Specialist
Academic Operations,
Technology and Innovations
Memphis City Schools
Memphis, Tennessee

Merrie Wolf
Mathematics Department Chair
Tulsa Public Schools
Tulsa, Oklahoma

From the *Authors*

Welcome

Math is a powerful tool with far-reaching applications throughout your life. We have designed a unique and engaging program that will enable you to tap into the power of mathematics and mathematical reasoning.

Developing mathematical skills and problem-solving strategies is an ongoing process—a journey both inside and outside the classroom. This course is designed to help make sense of the mathematics you encounter in and out of class each day.

You will learn important mathematical principles. You will also learn how the principles are connected to one another and to what you already know. You will learn to solve problems and learn the reasoning that lies behind your solutions.

Each chapter begins with the "big ideas" of the chapter and some essential questions that you will learn to answer. Through this question-and-answer process you will develop your ability to analyze problems independently and solve them in different applications.

Your skills and confidence will increase through practice and review. Work the examples so you understand the concepts and methods presented and the thinking behind them. Then do your homework. Ask yourself how new concepts relate to old ones. Make the connections!

Everyone needs help sometimes. You will find that this program has built-in opportunities, both in this text and online, to get help whenever you need it.

This course will also help you succeed on the tests you take in class and on other tests like the SAT, ACT, and state exams. The practice problems in each lesson will prepare you for the format and content of such tests. No surprises!

The reasoning habits and problem-solving skills you develop in this program will serve you in all your studies and in your daily life. They will prepare you for future success not only as a student, but also as a member of a changing technological society.

Best wishes,

Power_Algebra_.com

Welcome to Algebra 1. _Prentice Hall Algebra 1_ is part of an integrated digital and print environment for the study of high school mathematics. Take some time to look through the features of our mathematics program, starting with **PowerAlgebra.com,** the site of the digital features of the program.

Hi, I'm Darius. My friends and I will be showing you the great features of the Prentice Hall Algebra 1 program.

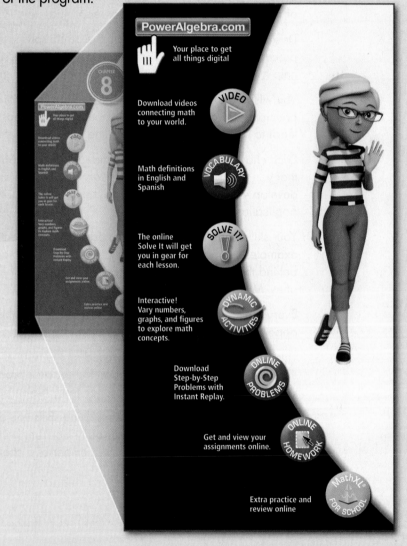

In each chapter opener, you will be invited to visit the **PowerAlgebra.com** site to access these online features. Look for these buttons throughout the lessons.

Big *Ideas*

We start with **Big Ideas.** Each chapter is organized around Big Ideas that convey the key mathematics concepts you will be studying in the program. Take a look at the Big Ideas on pages xx and xxi.

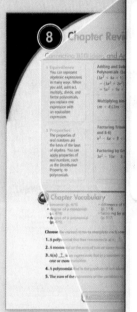

BIGideas

1 Equivalence

Essential Question Can two algebraic expressions that appear to be different be equivalent?

2 Properties

Essential Question How are the properties of real numbers related to polynomials?

The **Big Ideas** are organizing ideas for all of the lessons in the program. At the beginning of each chapter, we'll tell you which Big Ideas you'll be studying. We'll also present an **Essential Question** for each Big Idea.

1 Equivalence

You can represent algebraic expressions in many ways. When you add, subtract, multiply, divide, and factor polynomials, you replace one expression with an equivalent expression.

2 Properties

The properties of real numbers are the basis of the laws of algebra. You can apply properties of real numbers, such as the Distributive Property, to polynomials.

In the **Chapter Review** at the end of the chapter, you'll find the answers to the Essential Question for each Big Idea. We'll also remind you of the lesson(s) where you studied the concepts that support the Big Ideas.

Exploring *Concepts*

The lessons offer many opportunities to explore concepts in different contexts and through different media.

Hi, I'm Serena. I never have to power down when I am in math class now.

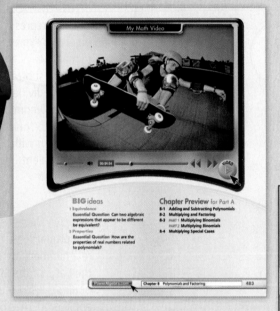

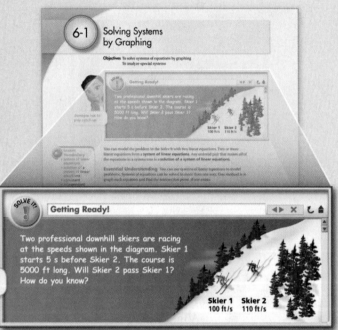

For each chapter, there is a video that you can access at **PowerAlgebra.com.** The video presents concepts in a real-life context. And you can contribute your own math video.

Here's another cool feature. Each lesson opens with a **Solve It,** a problem that helps you connect what you know to an important concept in the lesson. Do you notice how the Solve It frame looks like it comes from a computer? That's because all of the Solve Its can be found at **PowerAlgebra.com.**

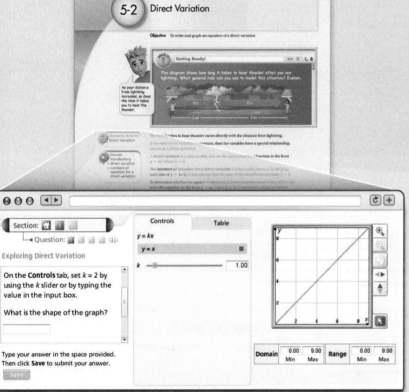

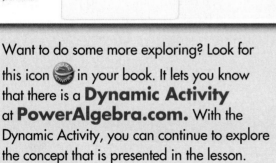

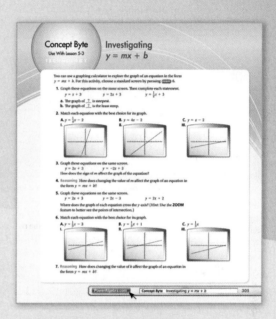

Try a **Concept Byte!** In a Concept Byte, you might explore technology, do a hands-on activity, or try a challenging extension.

Want to do some more exploring? Look for this icon in your book. It lets you know that there is a **Dynamic Activity** at **PowerAlgebra.com.** With the Dynamic Activity, you can continue to explore the concept that is presented in the lesson.

Thinking *Mathematically*

Mathematical reasoning is the key to solving problems and making sense of math. Throughout the program you'll learn strategies to develop mathematical reasoning habits.

Hello, I'm Tyler. These plan boxes will help me figure out where to start.

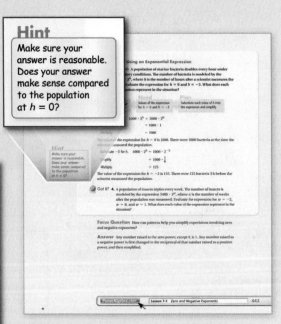

Hint

Make sure your answer is reasonable. Does your answer make sense compared to the population at $h = 0$?

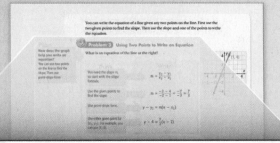

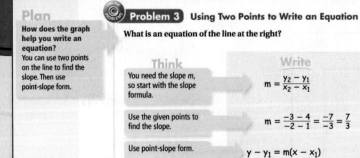

Plan

How does the graph help you write an equation?
You can use two points on the line to find the slope. Then use point-slope form.

Problem 3 Using Two Points to Write an Equation

What is an equation of the line at the right?

Think	Write
You need the slope *m*, so start with the slope formula.	$m = \dfrac{y_2 - y_1}{x_2 - x_1}$
Use the given points to find the slope.	$m = \dfrac{-3 - 4}{-2 - 1} = \dfrac{-7}{-3} = \dfrac{7}{3}$
Use point-slope form.	$y - y_1 = m(x - x_1)$
Use either given point for (x_1, y_1). For example, you can use (1, 4).	$y - 4 = \dfrac{7}{3}(x - 1)$

The worked-out problems include call-outs that reveal the strategies and reasoning behind the solution. Look for the boxes labeled **Plan** and **Think.**

The **Think-Write** problems model the thinking behind each step of a solution.

Other example problems include **Hints**, to help you remember a skill you already know or to point you to a different strategy.

Got It? **5. a.** In Problem 5, suppose the store charged $15 for each movie. What equation describes the numbers of songs and movies you can purchase for $60?

b. Reasoning What domain and range are reasonable for the equation in part (a)? Explain.

Concept Summary Linear Equations

You can describe any line using one or more of these forms of a linear equation. Any two equations for the same line are equivalent.

Graph

Forms

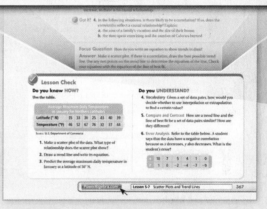

Causation is when a change in one quantity causes a change in a second quantity. A correlation between quantities does not always imply causation.

Focus Question How do you write an equation to show trends in data?

Answer Make a scatter plot. If there is a correlation, draw the best possible trend line. Use any two points on the trend line to determine the equation of the line. Check your equation with the equation of the line of best fit.

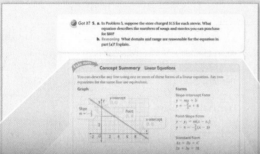

take note

Concept Summary   Linear Equations

You can describe any line using one or more of these forms of a linear equation. Any two equations for the same line are equivalent.

Graph

y-intercept (0, 6)

Slope $m = -\frac{2}{3}$

Point (3, 4)

x-intercept (9, 0)

Forms

Slope-Intercept Form
$y = mx + b$
$y = -\frac{2}{3}x + 6$

Point-Slope Form
$y - y_1 = m(x - x_1)$
$y - 4 = -\frac{2}{3}(x - 3)$

Standard Form
$Ax + By = C$
$2x + 3y = 18$

A **Take Note** box highlights key concepts in a lesson. You can use these boxes to review concepts throughout the year.

Part of Thinking Mathematically is figuring out the main reason behind learning a new concept. The **Focus Questions** and **Answers** help you get there.

Active *Learning*

Through active learning, you become a successful, independent problem solver. The **Student Companion** has graphic organizers and other tools to help you master skills and problem solving.

Hello, I'm Maya. I always review my work in the Student Companion when I'm studying.

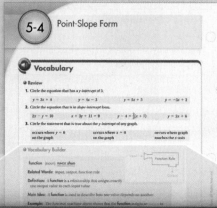

Think	Write
I start with the function form of direct variation.	$y = \boxed{} \cdot x$
Then I substitute 10 for y and -2 for $\boxed{}$.	$10 = \boxed{} \cdot (-2)$
Now I divide each side by $\boxed{}$ to solve for k.	$\boxed{} = \boxed{}$
Next, I write an equation by substituting $\boxed{}$ for k.	$y = \boxed{} \cdot x$
Finally, I determine the value of y when $x = -15$.	$y = \boxed{} \cdot \boxed{} = \boxed{}$

Vocabulary Builder

function (noun) FUNGK shun

Related Words: input, output, function rule

Definition: A **function** is a relationship that assigns exactly one output value to each input value.

Main Idea: A **function** is used to describe how one value depends on another.

Example: The function machine above shows that the **function** assigns an output to every input according to a specified rule.

Input → Function Rule → Output

The **Think-Write** format allows you to organize your thinking in order to solve a problem.

The Companion has a **Vocabulary Builder** for each lesson. After reading the definitions, examples and nonexamples in the Vocabulary Builder, you use the vocabulary in realistic contexts.

Got It? Reasoning Write the equation from Exercise 16 in slope-intercept form. What does the *y*-intercept represent?

17. Write the equation in point-slope form from Exercise 16. Use it to write the equation in slope-intercept form.

18. What does the *y*-intercept in your answer to Exercise 17 represent?

_____

_____

Lesson Check • **Do you UNDERSTAND?**

Reasoning Can any equation in point-slope form also be written in slope-intercept form? Give an example to explain.

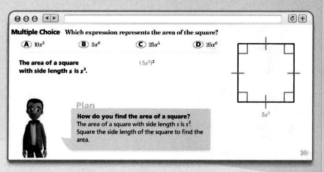

Not sure you "got it" yet? Try out the **Online Problems** at **PowerAlgebra.com.** You will find some problems with stepped-out solutions as well as some helpful math tools, such as the graphing utility.

Use the **Got Its** and **Lesson Checks** to actively participate in the presentation of a lesson. These will help you make sure you understand a lesson before you do your homework.

Practice *Makes Perfect*

Ask any professional and you'll be told that the one requirement for becoming an expert is practice, practice, practice.

Hello, I'm Anya. I can leave my book at school and still get my homework done. All of the lessons are at PowerAlgebra.com

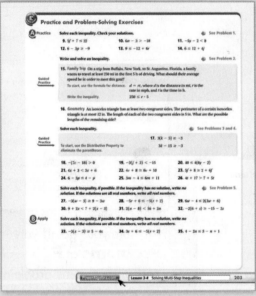

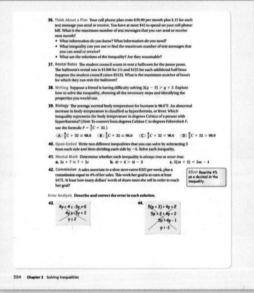

We give you lots of practice! There are **Practice** exercises for each concept or skill. Having difficulty with any of them? The green arrow tells you what problem with a worked-out solution to revisit in the lesson. The blue arrow of the guided practice points to information to help you get started on an exercise.

In the **Apply** section, you apply the concepts or skills to different situations or contexts. Be on the lookout for hints to exercises here.

You can test your knowledge using the **Self-Quiz** for each lesson at **PowerAlgebra.com**.

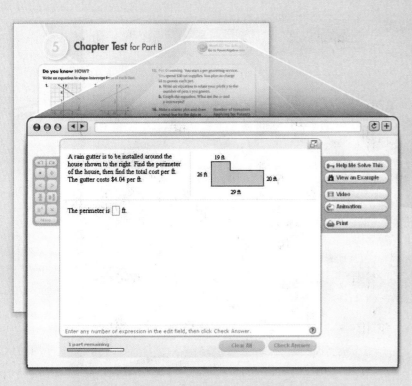

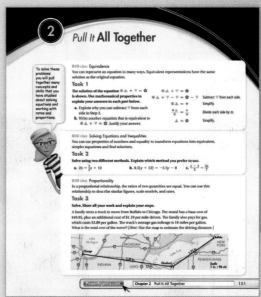

Want more practice? Look for this icon in your book. Check out all of the opportunities in **MathXL® for School.** Your teacher can assign you some practice exercises or you can choose some on your own. And you'll know right away if you got the right answer!

But the best practice occurs when you **Pull It All Together** — understanding of concepts, mathematical thinking, and problem solving — to solve interesting problems. And look: there are those Big Ideas again.

Pearson *Video Challenge*

Be inspired by **My Math Video** and make your own math video. Show math concepts in action. Enter your video in Pearson's Video Challenge! If selected, your video will be added to our library of math videos.

Acing *the Test*

Doing well on tests, whether they are chapter tests or state assessments, depends on a good understanding of math concepts, skill at solving problems, and, just as important, good test-taking skills.

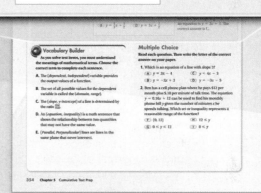

TIPS FOR SUCCESS

Some questions on standardized tests ask you to use a graph. Read the sample question at the right. Then follow the tips to answer it.

TIP 1
Identifying the y-intercept may help eliminate some possibilities.

What is an equation of the line shown below?

(A) $y = \frac{1}{3}x - 1$ (C) $y = 3x - 1$

(B) $y = \frac{1}{3}x + \frac{1}{2}$ (D) $y = 3x + \frac{1}{2}$

TIP 2
Find the slope by using the point that represents the y-intercept and another point on the line.

Think It Through
You can see from the graph that the y-intercept is −1. So you can eliminate choices B and D. To get from (0, −1) to (1, 2), move 3 units up and 1 unit to the right. The slope is $\frac{3}{1} = 3$. So an equation is $y = 3x - 1$. The correct answer is C.

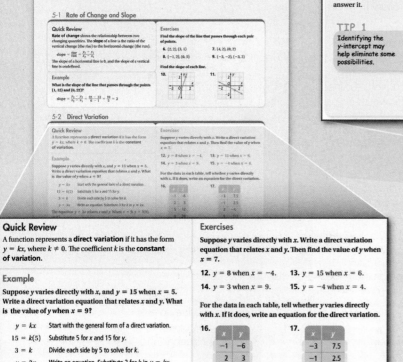

Quick Review

A function represents a **direct variation** if it has the form $y = kx$, where $k \neq 0$. The coefficient k is the **constant of variation**.

Example

Suppose y varies directly with x, and $y = 15$ when $x = 5$. Write a direct variation equation that relates x and y. What is the value of y when $x = 9$?

$y = kx$ Start with the general form of a direct variation.

$15 = k(5)$ Substitute 5 for x and 15 for y.

$3 = k$ Divide each side by 5 to solve for k.

$y = 3x$ Write an equation. Substitute 3 for k in $y = kx$.

The equation $y = 3x$ relates x and y. When $x = 9$, $y = 3(9)$, or 27.

Exercises

Suppose y varies directly with x. Write a direct variation equation that relates x and y. Then find the value of y when $x = 7$.

12. $y = 8$ when $x = -4$.   **13.** $y = 15$ when $x = 6$.

14. $y = 3$ when $x = 9$.   **15.** $y = -4$ when $x = 4$.

For the data in each table, tell whether y varies directly with x. If it does, write an equation for the direct variation.

16.

x	y
−1	−6
2	3
5	12
9	24

17.

x	y
−3	7.5
−1	2.5
2	−5
5	−12.5

At the end of the chapter or the chapter part, you'll find a **Quick Review** of concepts and a few examples and exercises so you can check your skill at solving problems related to the concepts.

In the Cumulative Test Prep at the end of the chapter, you'll also find **Tips for Success** to strengthen your test-taking skills. We include problems of all different formats and types so you can feel comfortable with any test item on your state assessment.

BIGideas

These Big Ideas are the organizing ideas for the study of important areas of mathematics: algebra, geometry, and statistics.

Stay connected! These Big Ideas will help you understand how the math you study in high school fits together.

Algebra

Properties
- In the transition from arithmetic to algebra, attention shifts from arithmetic operations (addition, subtraction, multiplication, and division) to use of the *properties* of these operations.
- All of the facts of arithmetic and algebra follow from certain properties.

Variable
- Quantities are used to form expressions, equations, and inequalities.
- An expression refers to a quantity but does not make a statement about it. An equation (or an inequality) is a statement about the quantities it mentions.
- Using variables in place of numbers in equations (or inequalities) allows the statement of relationships among numbers that are unknown or unspecified.

Equivalence
- A single quantity may be represented by many different expressions.
- The facts about a quantity may be expressed by many different equations (or inequalities).

Solving Equations & Inequalities
- Solving an equation is the process of rewriting the equation to make what it says about its variable(s) as simple as possible.
- Properties of numbers and equality can be used to transform an equation (or inequality) into equivalent, simpler equations (or inequalities) in order to find solutions.
- Useful information about equations and inequalities (including solutions) can be found by analyzing graphs or tables.
- The numbers and types of solutions vary predictably, based on the type of equation.

Proportionality
- Two quantities are *proportional* if they have the same ratio in each instance where they are measured together.
- Two quantities are *inversely proportional* if they have the same product in each instance where they are measured together.

Function
- A function is a relationship between variables in which each value of the input variable is associated with a unique value of the output variable.
- Functions can be represented in a variety of ways, such as graphs, tables, equations, or words. Each representation is particularly useful in certain situations.
- Some important families of functions are developed through transformations of the simplest form of the function.
- New functions can be made from other functions by applying arithmetic operations or by applying one function to the output of another.

Modeling
- Many real-world mathematical problems can be represented algebraically. These representations can lead to algebraic solutions.
- A function that models a real-world situation can be used to make estimates or predictions about future occurrences.

Statistics and Probability

Data Collection and Analysis

- Sampling techniques are used to gather data from real-world situations. If the data are representative of the larger population, inferences can be made about that population.
- Biased sampling techniques yield data unlikely to be representative of the larger population.
- Sets of numerical data are described using measures of central tendency and dispersion.

Data Representation

- The most appropriate data representations depend on the type of data—quantitative or qualitative, and univariate or bivariate.
- Line plots, box plots, and histograms are different ways to show distribution of data over a possible range of values.

Probability

- Probability expresses the likelihood that a particular event will occur.
- Data can be used to calculate an experimental probability, and mathematical properties can be used to determine a theoretical probability.
- Either experimental or theoretical probability can be used to make predictions or decisions about future events.
- Various counting methods can be used to develop theoretical probabilities.

Geometry

Visualization

- Visualization can help you see the relationships between two figures and help you connect properties of real objects with two-dimensional drawings of these objects.

Transformations

- Transformations are mathematical functions that model relationships with figures.
- Transformations may be described geometrically or by coordinates.
- Symmetries of figures may be defined and classified by transformations.

Measurement

- Some attributes of geometric figures, such as length, area, volume, and angle measure, are measurable. Units are used to describe these attributes.

Reasoning & Proof

- Definitions establish meanings and remove possible misunderstanding.
- Other truths are more complex and difficult to see. It is often possible to verify complex truths by reasoning from simpler ones using deductive reasoning.

Similarity

- Two geometric figures are similar when corresponding lengths are proportional and corresponding angles are congruent.
- Areas of similar figures are proportional to the squares of their corresponding lengths.
- Volumes of similar figures are proportional to the cubes of their corresponding lengths.

Coordinate Geometry

- A coordinate system on a line is a number line on which points are labeled, corresponding to the real numbers.
- A coordinate system in a plane is formed by two perpendicular number lines, called the x- and y-axes, and the quadrants they form. The coordinate plane can be used to graph many functions.
- It is possible to verify some complex truths using deductive reasoning in combination with the distance, midpoint, and slope formulas.

1 Foundations for Algebra

2 Solving Equations

Visual See It!

Reasoning Try It!

Practice Do It!

3

Solving Inequalities

An Introduction to Functions

Visual **See It!**

Reasoning **Try It!**

Practice **Do It!**

5

Linear Functions

Systems of Equations and Inequalities

Visual **See It!**

Reasoning **Try It!**

Practice **Do It!**

7

Exponents and Exponential Functions

Polynomials and Factoring

Visual See It!

Reasoning Try It!

Practice Do It!

9

Quadratic Functions and Equations

Radical Expressions and Equations

Visual See It!

Reasoning Try It!

Practice Do It!

11 Rational Expressions

Data Analysis and Probability

Visual See It!

Reasoning Try It!

Practice Do It!

Entry-Level Assessment

Multiple Choice

Read each question. Then write the letter of the correct answer on your paper.

1. Sophia had $50 she put into a savings account. If she saves $15 per week for one year, how much will she have saved altogether?

    (A) $50   (C) $780

    (B) $65   (D) $830

2. Which set below is the domain of $\{(2, -3), (-1, 0), (0, 4), (-1, 5), (4, -2)\}$?

    (F) $\{-3, 0, 4, 5, -2\}$ (H) $\{2, -1, 4\}$

    (G) $\{-3, 4, 5, -2\}$ (I) $\{2, -1, 0, 4\}$

3. Which ordered pair is the solution of the system of equations graphed below?

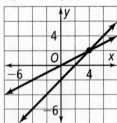

    (A) $(4, 1)$ (C) $(4, 2)$

    (B) $(1, 4)$ (D) $(2, 4)$

4. The Martins keep goats and chickens on their farm. If there are 23 animals with a total of 74 legs, how many of each type of animal are there?

    (F) 14 chickens, 9 goats

    (G) 19 chickens, 4 goats

    (H) 9 chickens, 14 goats

    (I) 4 chickens, 19 goats

5. Which equation represents the phrase "six more than twice a number is 72"?

    (A) $6 + x = 72$ (C) $2 + 6x = 72$

    (B) $2x = 6 + 72$ (D) $6 + 2x = 72$

6. Which of the following graphs best represents a person walking slowly and then speeding up?

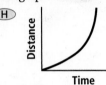
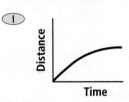
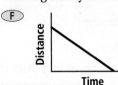
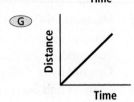

7. The graph below shows the time it takes Sam to get from his car to the mall door.

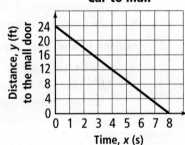

Walking From Car to Mall

Which of the following best describes the x-intercept?

    (A) Sam's car was parked 24 ft from the mall door.

    (B) After 24 s, Sam reached the mall door.

    (C) Sam's car was parked 8 ft from the mall door.

    (D) After 8 s, Sam reached the mall door.

8. What is 23.7×10^4 written in standard notation?

    (F) 0.00237

    (G) 0.0237

    (H) 237,000

    (I) 2,370,000

9. What equation do you get when you solve $2x + 3y = 12$ for y?

(A) $y = -\frac{2}{3}x + 4$

(B) $y = -\frac{2}{3}x + 12$

(C) $y = -2x + 12$

(D) $y = 12 - 2x$

10. The formula for the circumference of a circle is $C = 2\pi r$. What is the formula solved for r?

(F) $r = C \cdot 2\pi$

(G) $r = \frac{C}{2\pi}$

(H) $r = 2\pi$

(I) $r = \frac{C\pi}{2}$

11. Which table of values was used to make the following graph?

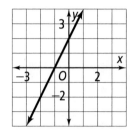

(A)

x	−3	−1	0	1
y	−2	−1	2	4

(B)

x	−3	−2	0	1
y	4	2	2	4

(C)

x	−3	−1	0	1
y	−4	0	2	4

(D)

x	−3	−2	0	1
y	−3	−2	2	4

12. A jewelry store marks up the price of a topaz ring 215%. The store paid $70 for the ring. For how much is the store selling the ring?

(F) $91.50

(G) $150.50

(H) $161.50

(I) $220.50

13. What is the solution of $-3p + 4 < 22$?

(A) $p < -6$

(B) $p > -6$

(C) $p < 18$

(D) $p > 18$

14. Which of the graphs below shows the solution of $-5 + x > 8$?

(F) [number line: 2 4 6 8 10 12 14]

(G) [number line: 2 4 6 8 10 12 14]

(H) [number line: 2 4 6 8 10 12 14]

(I) [number line: 2 4 6 8 10 12 14]

15. Between which two whole numbers does $\sqrt{85}$ fall?

(A) 8 and 9

(B) 9 and 10

(C) 41 and 42

(D) 42 and 43

16. What is the simplified form of $\frac{6 + 3^2}{(2^3)(3)}$?

(F) $\frac{1}{3}$

(G) $\frac{1}{2}$

(H) $\frac{5}{8}$

(I) $\frac{5}{6}$

17. Which of the following expressions is equivalent to $\frac{4^3}{4^6}$?

(A) $\frac{1}{4^3}$

(B) $\frac{1}{4^2}$

(C) 4^2

(D) 4^3

18. What is 40,500,000 written in scientific notation?

(F) 4.05×10^7

(G) 4.05×10^6

(H) 4.05×10^{-6}

(I) 4.05×10^{-7}

19. There are $3\frac{3}{4}$ c of flour, $1\frac{1}{2}$ c of sugar, $\frac{2}{3}$ c of brown sugar, and $\frac{1}{4}$ c of oil in a cake mix. How many cups of ingredients are there in all?

(A) $4\frac{1}{2}$ c

(B) $5\frac{1}{6}$ c

(C) $5\frac{1}{2}$ c

(D) $6\frac{1}{6}$ c

20. Cathy ran for 30 min at a rate of 5.5 mi/h. Then she ran for 15 min at a rate of 6 mi/h. How many miles did she run in all?

    F 2.75 mi   **H** 4.25 mi

    G 4.375 mi   **I** 5.75 mi

21. A 6-ft-tall man casts a shadow that is 9 ft long. At the same time, a tree nearby casts a 48 ft shadow. How tall is the tree?

    A 32 ft   **C** 45 ft

    B 36 ft   **D** 72 ft

22. Triangle *ABC* is similar to triangle *DEF*. What is *x*?

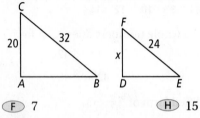

    F 7   **H** 15

    G 12   **I** 27

23. Which side lengths given below can form a right triangle?

    A 12, 13, 17

    B 3.2, 5.6, 6.4

    C 14, 20, 24

    D 10, 24, 26

24. The formula $F = \frac{9}{5}C + 32$ converts temperatures in degrees Celsius *C* to temperatures in degrees Fahrenheit *F*. What is 35°C in degrees Fahrenheit?

    F 20°F   **H** 95°F

    G 67°F   **I** 120°F

25. A bowling ball is traveling at 15 mi/h when it hits the pins. How fast is the bowling ball traveling in feet per second? (*Hint:* 1 mi = 5280 ft)

    A 11 ft/s

    B 88 ft/s

    C 22 ft/s

    D 1320 ft/s

26. What is the median of the tree height data displayed in the box-and-whisker plot below?

Tree Height (ft)

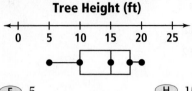

    F 5   **H** 15

    G 10   **I** 20

27. Helena tracked the number of hours she spent working on a science experiment each day in the scatter plot below.

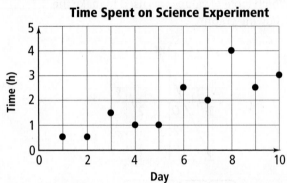

Between which two days was there the greatest increase in the number of hours Helena spent working on her science experiment?

    A Day 2 and 3

    B Day 7 and 8

    C Day 5 and 6

    D Day 9 and 10

28. Your grades on four exams are 78, 85, 97, and 92. What grade do you need on the next exam to have an average of 90 on the five exams?

    F 71   **H** 98

    G 92   **I** 100

29. The number of points scored by a basketball team during the first 8 games of the season are shown below.

    65 58 72 74 82 67 75 71

How much will their average game score increase by if the team scores 93 points in the next game?

    A 2.5   **C** 11.6

    B 10.5   **D** 19.5

Get Ready!

Skills Handbook Page 784

Factors

Find the greatest common factor of each set of numbers.

1. 12, 18   **2.** 25, 35   **3.** 13, 20   **4.** 40, 80, 100

Skills Handbook Page 784

Least Common Multiple

Find the least common multiple of each set of numbers.

5. 5, 15   **6.** 11, 44   **7.** 8, 9   **8.** 10, 15, 25

Skills Handbook Page 785

Using Estimation

Estimate each sum or difference.

9. $956 - 542$ **10.** $1.259 + 5.312 + 1.7$ **11.** $\$14.32 + \$1.65 + \$278.05$

Skills Handbook Page 786

Simplifying Fractions

Write in simplest form.

12. $\frac{12}{15}$ **13.** $\frac{20}{28}$ **14.** $\frac{8}{56}$ **15.** $\frac{48}{52}$

Skills Handbook Page 787

Fractions and Decimals

Write each fraction as a decimal. Round to the nearest hundredth.

16. $\frac{7}{10}$ **17.** $\frac{3}{5}$ **18.** $\frac{13}{20}$ **19.** $\frac{93}{100}$ **20.** $\frac{7}{15}$

Skills Handbook Page 788

Adding and Subtracting Fractions

Find the sum or difference.

21. $\frac{4}{7} + \frac{3}{14}$ **22.** $6\frac{2}{3} + 3\frac{4}{5}$ **23.** $\frac{9}{10} - \frac{4}{5}$ **24.** $8\frac{3}{4} - 4\frac{5}{6}$

 ## Looking Ahead Vocabulary

25. Several expressions may have the same meaning. For actors, the English *expression* "break a leg" means "good luck." In math, what is another *expression* for $5 \cdot 7$?

26. A beginning guitarist learns to play using *simplified* guitar music. What does it mean to write a *simplified* math expression as shown at the right?

$5 \cdot 7 \div 5 = 7$

27. A study *evaluates* the performance of a hybrid bus to determine its value. What does it mean to *evaluate* an expression in math?

Foundations for Algebra

These sky divers are falling very
fast! You can use positive and
negative numbers to describe all
kinds of things, such as changes
in elevation. In this chapter, you'll
learn to use different kinds of
numbers to describe real-world
situations and perform operations.

Vocabulary for Part A

English/Spanish Vocabulary Audio Online:

English	Spanish
algebraic expression, *p. 4*	expresión algebraica
base, *p. 11*	base
counterexample, *p. 28*	contraejemplo
deductive reasoning, *p. 28*	razonamiento deductivo
equivalent expressions, *p. 26*	ecuaciones equivalentes
evaluate, *p. 15*	evaluar
integers, *p. 21*	números enteros
irrational number, *p. 21*	número irracional
order of operations, *p. 12*	orden de las operaciones
real number, *p. 21*	número real
set, *p. 20*	conjunto
simplify, *p. 11*	simplificar
variable, *p. 4*	variable

My Math Video

00:04:04

VIDEO

BIGideas

- **Variable**
  Essential Question How can you represent quantities, patterns, and relationships?

- **Properties**
  Essential Question How are properties related to algebra?

1-1 Variables and Expressions

Objective To write algebraic expressions

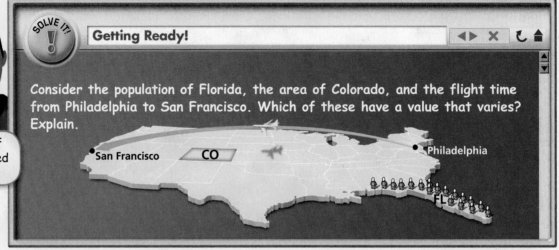

Can the number of states in the United States vary?

A mathematical **quantity** is anything that can be measured or counted. Some quantities remain constant, change, or vary. They are called *variable quantities*.

Focus Question How is an algebraic expression different from a numerical expression? Algebra uses symbols to represent quantities that are unknown or that vary.

A **variable** is a symbol, usually a letter, that represents the value(s) of a variable quantity. An **algebraic expression** is a mathematical phrase that includes one or more variables. A **numerical expression** is a mathematical phrase involving numbers and operation symbols, but no variables. To translate word phrases into algebraic expressions, look for words that describe mathematical operations.

take note

Summary Word Phrases

Operation	Algebraic Expression	Word Phrases
Addition sum, plus, more than, total, increased by	$5 + x$	the sum of 5 and a number x 5 more than a number x 5 increased by a number x
Subtraction difference, minus, less than, decreased by	$n - 7$	the difference of a number n and 7 7 less than n a number n minus 7
Multiplication product, times, multiplied by, of	$4 \cdot y, 4 \times y, 4y$	the product of 4 and y 4 times a number y
Division quotient, divided by	$\frac{n}{2}, n \div 2$	the quotient of n and 2 n divided by 2

Problem 1 Writing Expressions With Addition and Subtraction

Plan

How can a diagram help you write an algebraic expression?
Models like the ones shown can help you to visualize the relationships described by the word phrases.

What is an algebraic expression for the word phrase?

Word Phrase	Model	Expression
A 32 more than a number n		$n + 32$
	n \ \ \ 32	
B 58 less than a number n		$n - 58$
	? \ \ \ 58	

Got It? 1. What is an algebraic expression for 18 more than a number n?

Problem 2 Writing Expressions With Multiplication and Division

Think

Is there more than one way to write an algebraic expression with multiplication?
Yes. Multiplication can be represented using a dot or parentheses or an ×.

What is an algebraic expression for the word phrase?

Word Phrase	Model	Expression
A 8 times a number n	?	$8 \times n, 8 \cdot n, 8n$
	n \ n \ n \ n \ n \ n \ n \ n	
B the quotient of a number n and 5	n	$n \div 5, \dfrac{n}{5}$
	? \ ? \ ? \ ? \ ?	

Got It?

2. What is an algebraic expression for each word phrase?

    a. 6 times a number n **b.** the quotient of 18 and a number n

Problem 3 Writing Expressions With Two Operations

Plan

How can I represent the phrases visually?
Draw a diagram. You can represent the phrase in Problem 3, part (A), as shown below.

⊢- - - - - ? - - - - - ⊣
| 3 | x | x |

9 less than n means $n - 9$, not $9 - n$.

What is an algebraic expression for the word phrase?

Word Phrase			Expression		
A 3 more than twice a number x	3	more than	twice a number x		
	3	+	$2x$		
			$3 + 2x$		
B 9 less than the quotient of 6 and a number x	9	less than	the quotient of 6 and a number x		
	$\frac{6}{x}$	–	9		
			$\frac{6}{x} - 9$		
C the product of 4 and the sum of a number x and 7	the product of	4	and the sum of a number x and 7		
	4	·	$(x + 7)$		
			$4(x + 7)$		

Got It? **3.** What is an algebraic expression for each word phrase?

 a. 8 less than the product of a number x and 4

 b. twice the sum of a number x and 8

You can translate algebraic expressions into word phrases.

 Problem 4 **Using Words for an Expression**

Think

Is there only one way to write the expression in words?
No. The operation performed on 3 and x can be described by different words like "multiply," "times," and "product."

What word phrase can you use to represent the algebraic expression $3x$?

Expression

$3x$ — A number and a variable side by side indicate a product.

$3 \cdot x$

Words three times a number x or   the product of 3 and a number x

 Got It? **4.** What word phrase can you use to represent the algebraic expression?

 a. $x + 8.1$ **b.** $10x + 9$ **c.** $\frac{n}{3}$ **d.** $5x - 1$

You can use words or an algebraic expression to write a mathematical rule that describes a real-life pattern.

 Problem 5 **Writing a Rule to Describe a Pattern**

Hobbies The table below shows how the height above the floor of a house of cards depends on the number of levels. What is a rule for the height? Give the rule in words and as an algebraic expression.

House of Cards

Number of Levels	Height (in.)
2	$(3.5 \cdot 2) + 24$
3	$(3.5 \cdot 3) + 24$
4	$(3.5 \cdot 4) + 24$
n	?

3.5 in.

24 in.

Know **Need** **Plan**

Numerical expressions for the height given several different numbers of levels

A rule for finding the height given a house with any number of levels n

Look for a pattern in the table. Describe the pattern in words. Then use the words to write an algebraic expression.

Rule in Words   Multiply the number of levels by 3.5 and add 24.

Rule as an Algebraic Expression   The variable n represents the number of levels in the house of cards.

$3.5n + 24$ — This expression lets you find the height for any number of levels n.

Got It? **5.** Suppose you draw a segment from any one vertex of a regular polygon to the other vertices. A sample for a regular hexagon is shown below. Use the table to find a pattern. What is a rule for the number of nonoverlapping triangles formed? Give the rule in words and as an algebraic expression.

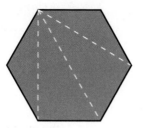

Triangles in Polygons

Number of Sides of Polygon	Number of Triangles
4	4 − 2
5	5 − 2
6	6 − 2
n	■

Focus Question How is an algebraic expression different from a numerical expression?

Answer An algebraic expression uses variables, numbers, and operation symbols. A numerical expression uses only numbers and operation symbols.

 ## Lesson Check

Do you know HOW?

1. Is each expression *algebraic* or *numerical*?

   a. $7 \div 2$ **b.** $4m + 6$ **c.** $2(5 - 4)$

2. What is an algebraic expression for each phrase?

   a. the product of 9 and a number t

   b. the difference of a number x and $\frac{1}{2}$

   c. the sum of a number m and 7.1

   d. the quotient of 207 and a number n

Use words to describe each algebraic expression.

3. $6c$ **4.** $x - 1$

5. $\frac{t}{2}$ **6.** $3t - 4$

Do you UNDERSTAND?

7. Vocabulary Explain the difference between numerical expressions and algebraic expressions.

8. Reasoning Use the table to decide whether $49n + 0.75$ or $49 + 0.75n$ represents the total cost to rent a truck that you drive n miles.

Truck Rental Fees

Number of Miles	Cost
1	$49 + ($.75 × 1)
2	$49 + ($.75 × 2)
3	$49 + ($.75 × 3)
n	■

Practice and Problem-Solving Exercises

Ⓐ Practice Write an algebraic expression for each word phrase. ◀ **See Problems 1-3.**

Guided Practice ➡

To start, draw a model.

9. 12 fewer than n

12	?

$\vdash\text{-------- } n \text{ --------}\dashv$

10. y minus 12

11. 4 more than p

12. the product of 15 and c

13. the quotient of n and 8

14. the quotient of 17 and k

15. 23 less than x

16. the sum of v and 3

17. a third of a number n

18. a number t divided by 82

19. 2 more than twice a number w

20. the sum of 13 and twice a number h

21. 9 more than the difference of 17 and k

22. 6.7 more than the product of 5 and n

23. 9.85 less than the product of 37 and t

24. 7 minus the quotient of 3 and v

25. 15 plus the quotient of 60 and w

Write a word phrase for each algebraic expression. ◀ **See Problem 4.**

26. $q + 5$

27. $3 - t$

28. $\frac{y}{5}$

29. $12x$

30. $14.1 - w$

31. $49 + m$

32. $9n + 1$

33. $62 + 7h$

34. $\frac{z}{8} - 9$

35. $13p + 0.1$

36. $15 - \frac{1.5}{d}$

37. $2(5 - n)$

Write a rule in words and as an algebraic expression to model the relationship in each table.

38. Sightseeing While on vacation, you rent a bicycle. You pay $9 for each hour you use the bicycle. It costs $5 to rent a helmet while you use the bicycle.

Bike Rental

Number of Hours	Rental Cost
1	($9 × 1) + $5
2	($9 × 2) + $5
3	($9 × 3) + $5
n	■

Guided Practice

To start, describe the pattern in the table using words. Multiply the number of hours by 9 and add 5.

39. Sales At a shoe store, a salesperson earns a weekly salary of $150. A salesperson is also paid $2.00 for each pair of shoes he or she sells during the week.

Shoe Sales

Pairs of Shoes Sold	Total Earned
5	$150 + ($2 × 5)
10	$150 + ($2 × 10)
15	$150 + ($2 × 15)
n	■

Ⓑ Apply

Write an algebraic expression for each word phrase.

40. 8 minus the product of 9 and r

41. the sum of 15 and x, plus 7

42. 4 less than three sevenths of y

43. the quotient of 12 and the product of 5 and t

44. Error Analysis A student writes the word phrase "the quotient of n and 5" to describe the expression $\frac{5}{n}$. Describe and correct the student's error.

45. Think About a Plan The table at the right shows the number of bagels a shop gives you per "baker's dozen." Write an algebraic expression that gives the rule for finding the number of bagels in any number b of baker's dozens.

- What is the pattern of increase in the number of bagels?
- What operation can you perform on b to find the number of bagels?

Bagels

Baker's Dozens	Number of Bagels
1	13
2	26
3	39
b	■

46. Volunteering Serena and Tyler are wrapping gift boxes at the same pace. Serena starts first, as shown in the diagram. Write an algebraic expression that represents the number of boxes Tyler will have wrapped when Serena has wrapped x boxes.

47. Multiple Choice Which expression gives the value in dollars of d dimes?

  Ⓐ $0.10d$ Ⓑ $0.10 + d$ Ⓒ $\dfrac{0.10}{d}$ Ⓓ $10d$

Standardized Test Prep

SAT/ACT

48. What is an algebraic expression for *2 less than the product of 3 and a number x*?

  Ⓐ $3x - 2$ Ⓑ $(3 - 2)x$ Ⓒ $3 - 2x$ Ⓓ $2 - 3x$

49. Which word phrase can you use to represent the algebraic expression $n \div 8$?

  Ⓕ the product of a number n and 8   Ⓗ the difference of a number n and 8

  Ⓖ the quotient of a number n and 8   Ⓘ the quotient of 8 and a number n

50. A state park charges an entrance fee plus $18 for each night of camping. The table shows this relationship. Which algebraic expression describes the total cost of camping for n nights?

  Ⓐ $20n + 18$ Ⓒ $18n + 20n$

  Ⓑ $18n + 20$ Ⓓ $18n - 20$

Camping

Nights	Total Cost
1	($18 × 1) + $20
2	($18 × 2) + $20
3	($18 × 3) + $20
n	▪

Mixed Review

Find each sum or difference. Write each answer in simplest form.

◀ See p. 788.

51. $\dfrac{1}{4} + \dfrac{1}{2}$ **52.** $\dfrac{9}{14} - \dfrac{2}{7}$ **53.** $\dfrac{2}{5} + \dfrac{3}{10}$ **54.** $\dfrac{5}{6} - \dfrac{2}{3}$

Get Ready!   **To prepare for Lesson 1-2, do Exercises 55–58.**

Find the greatest common factor of each pair of numbers.

◀ See p. 784.

55. 3 and 6   **56.** 12 and 15   **57.** 7 and 11   **58.** 8 and 12

Order of Operations and Evaluating Expressions

Objectives To simplify expressions involving exponents
To use the order of operations to evaluate expressions

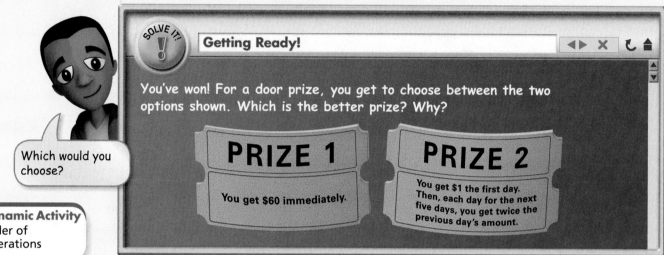

SOLVE IT!

Getting Ready!

You've won! For a door prize, you get to choose between the two options shown. Which is the better prize? Why?

PRIZE 1

You get $60 immediately.

PRIZE 2

You get $1 the first day. Then, each day for the next five days, you get twice the previous day's amount.

Which would you choose?

Dynamic Activity
Order of Operations

Lesson Vocabulary
- power
- exponent
- base
- simplify

Focus Question How does simplifying an expression with an exponent involve multiplication?

You can use *powers* to shorten how you represent repeated multiplication, such as $2 \cdot 2 \cdot 2 \cdot 2 \cdot 2 \cdot 2$.

A **power** has two parts, a *base* and an *exponent*. The **exponent** tells you how many times to use the **base** as a factor. You read the power 2^3 as "two to the third power" or "two cubed." You read 5^2 as "five to the second power" or "five squared."

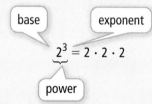

base   exponent

$$2^3 = 2 \cdot 2 \cdot 2$$

power

You **simplify** a numerical expression when you replace it with its single numerical value. For example, the simplest form of $2 \cdot 8$ is 16. To simplify a power, you replace it with its simplest name. For example, the simplest form of 2^3 is 8.

Problem 1 Simplifying Powers

Think

What does the exponent indicate?
It shows the number of times you use the base as a factor.

What is the simplified form of each expression?

A 10^7

Write the expression using repeated multiplication. $10^7 = 10 \cdot 10 \cdot 10 \cdot 10 \cdot 10 \cdot 10 \cdot 10$

Simplify. $= 10,000,000$

B $\left(\frac{1}{2}\right)^3$

Write the expression using repeated multiplication. $\left(\frac{1}{2}\right)^3 = \frac{1}{2} \cdot \frac{1}{2} \cdot \frac{1}{2}$

Simplify. $= \frac{1}{8}$

C $(0.2)^2$

Write the expression using repeated multiplication. $(0.2)^2 = 0.2 \cdot 0.2$

Simplify. $= 0.04$

 Got It? **1.** What is the simplified form of each expression?

a. 3^4 **b.** $\left(\frac{2}{3}\right)^3$ **c.** $(0.5)^3$

Focus Question Why is it necessary to use the order of operations to evaluate an expression?

When simplifying an expression, you need to perform operations in the correct order.

You might think about simplifying the expression $2 + 3 \times 5$ in two ways:

Add first.

Multiply first.

$2 + 3 \times 5 = 5 \times 5 = 25$ ✗ $2 + 3 \times 5 = 2 + 15 = 17$ ✔

Both results may seem sensible, but only the second result is considered correct. This is because the second way uses the order of operations that mathematicians have agreed to follow. Always use the following order of operations:

take note

Key Concept Order of Operations

1. Perform any operation(s) inside grouping symbols, such as parentheses ( ) and brackets [ ]. A fraction bar also acts as a grouping symbol.
2. Simplify powers.
3. Multiply and divide from left to right.
4. Add and subtract from left to right.

What is the simplified form of each expression?

A $(6 - 2)^2 \div 2$

Subtract inside parentheses. $(6 - 2)^2 \div 2 = 4^2 \div 2$

Simplify the power. $= 16 \div 2$

Divide. $= 8$

B $\dfrac{2^4 - 1}{5}$

Simplify the power. $\dfrac{2^4 - 1}{5} = \dfrac{16 - 1}{5}$

Subtract. $= \dfrac{15}{5}$

Divide. $= 3$

 Got It? **2.** What is the simplified form of each expression?

a. $5 \cdot 7 - 4^2 \div 2$ **b.** $12 - \dfrac{25}{5}$ **c.** $(5 - 2)^3 \div 3$

Focus Question How does simplifying an expression with an exponent involve multiplication?

Answer An exponent tells you how many times to multiply the base times itself.

Focus Question Why is it necessary to use the order of operations to evaluate an expression?

Answer Follow the agreed upon order of operations to get the correct answer.

 Lesson Check

Do you know HOW?

What is the simplified form of each expression?

1. 5^2

2. 2^3

3. $\left(\dfrac{3}{4}\right)^2$

4. 0.1^3

5. $(4 - 1)^2 - 5$

6. $75 \div (3^3 - 2)$

Do you UNDERSTAND?

7. Vocabulary Identify the exponent and the base in 4^3.

8. Error Analysis A student simplifies an expression as shown below. Find the error and simplify the expression correctly.

$$23 - 8 \cdot 2 + 3^2 = 23 - 8 \cdot 2 + 9$$
$$= 15 \cdot 2 + 9$$
$$= 30 + 9$$
$$= 39 \quad ✗$$

Practice and Problem-Solving Exercises

A Practice

Simplify each expression.

See Problem 1.

Guided Practice

To start, write the expression using repeated multiplication.

9. 3^5

$3^5 = 3 \cdot 3 \cdot 3 \cdot 3 \cdot 3$

10. 4^3 **11.** 2^4 **12.** 10^8

13. $\left(\frac{2}{3}\right)^3$ **14.** $\left(\frac{1}{2}\right)^4$ **15.** $(0.4)^6$

16. 7^4 **17.** $(0.5)^3$ **18.** $\left(\frac{3}{4}\right)^2$

Simplify each expression.

See Problem 2.

Guided Practice

To start, simplify the power.

19. $20 - 2 \cdot 3^2$

$20 - 2 \cdot 3^2 = 20 - 2 \cdot 9$

20. $27 \cdot 2 \div 3^2$ **21.** $6 + 4 \div 2 + 3$

22. $(6^2 - 3^3) \div 2$ **23.** $5 \cdot 2^2 \div 2 + 8$

24. $80 - (4 - 1)^3$ **25.** $52 + 8^2 - 3(4 - 2)^3$

26. $\dfrac{6^4 \div 3^2}{9}$ **27.** $\dfrac{2 \cdot 7 + 4}{9 \div 3}$

B Apply

Simplify each expression.

28. $2[(8 - 4)^5 \div 8]$ **29.** $3[(4 - 2)^5 - 20]$ **30.** $10 - (2^3 + 4) \div 3 - 1$

31. $\dfrac{22 + 1^3 + (3^4 - 7^2)}{2^3}$ **32.** $3[42 - 2(10^2 - 9^2)]$ **33.** $\dfrac{2[8 - (67 - 2^6)^3]}{9}$

34. Writing Consider the expression $(1 + 5)^2 - (18 \div 3)$. Can you perform the operations in different orders and still get the correct answer? Explain.

35. Find the value of $14 + 5 \cdot 3 - 3^2$. Then change two operation signs so that the value of the expression is 8.

1-2
PART 2

Order of Operations and Evaluating Expressions

Objective To use the order of operations to evaluate expressions

In Part 1 of this lesson, you simplified numerical expressions with exponents.

Connect to What You Know

Here, you will evaluate algebraic expressions for given values of the variable.

Lesson Vocabulary
• evaluate

Focus Question How is evaluating an algebraic expression different from evaluating a numerical expression?

You **evaluate** an algebraic expression by replacing each variable with a given number. Then simplify the expression using the order of operations.

Problem 3 Evaluating Algebraic Expressions

ONLINE PROBLEMS

Plan

How is this Problem like ones you've seen before?
You begin by substituting numbers for the variables. After substituting, you have numerical expressions just like the ones in Problem 2.

What is the value of the expression for $x = 5$ and $y = 2$?

A $x^2 + x - 12 \div y^2$

Substitute 5 for x and 2 for y.	$x^2 + x - 12 \div y^2 = 5^2 + 5 - 12 \div 2^2$
Simplify powers.	$= 25 + 5 - 12 \div 4$
Divide.	$= 25 + 5 - 3$
Add and subtract from left to right.	$= 27$

B $(xy)^2$

Substitute 5 for x and 2 for y.	$(xy)^2 = (5 \cdot 2)^2$
Multiply inside parentheses.	$= 10^2$
Simplify the power.	$= 100$

Got It? **3.** What is the value of each expression when $a = 3$ and $b = 4$ in parts (a) and (b)?

a. $3b - a^2$ **b.** $2b^2 - 7a$

c. Reasoning Find the value of xy^2 for $x = 5$ and $y = 2$. Compare your results to $(xy)^2$ in Problem 3. What can you conclude?

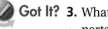

Problem 4 **Evaluating a Real-World Expression**

Banking What is an expression for the spending money you have left after depositing $\frac{2}{5}$ of your wages in savings? Evaluate the expression for weekly wages of $40, $50, $75, and $100.

Know	Need	Plan
• Savings equals $\frac{2}{5}$ of wages. • Various weekly wages	• Expression for spending money • Amount of spending money for various weekly wages	Write an algebraic expression and evaluate it for each amount of weekly wages. Use a table to organize your results.

Think

How can a model help you write the expression?

This model shows that spending money equals your wages w minus the amount you save: $\frac{2}{5}w$.

Relate spending money equals

wages minus $\frac{2}{5}$ of wages

Define Let w = your wages.

Write w — $\frac{2}{5} \cdot w$

The expression $w - \frac{2}{5} \cdot w$ represents the amount of money you have left after depositing $\frac{2}{5}$ of your wages in savings.

Spending Money

Wages (w)	$w - \frac{2}{5}w$	Total Spending Money ($)
40	$40 - \frac{2}{5}(40)$	24
50	$50 - \frac{2}{5}(50)$	30
75	$75 - \frac{2}{5}(75)$	45
100	$100 - \frac{2}{5}(100)$	60

 Got It? **4.** The shipping cost for an order at an online store is $\frac{1}{10}$ the cost of the items you order. What is an expression for the total cost of a given order? What are the total costs for orders of $43, $79, $95, and $103?

Focus Question How is evaluating an algebraic expression different from evaluating a numerical expression?

Answer You replace each variable in an algebraic expression with a given number.

Lesson Check

Do you know HOW?

Evaluate each expression for $x = 3$ and $y = 4$.

1. $x^2 + 2(x + y)$

2. $(xy)^3$

3. $4x^2 - 3xy$

Do you UNDERSTAND?

4. Vocabulary Explain how to evaluate an algebraic expression.

5. Reasoning Show that the expressions $2xy^2$ and $x^5 + 8y$ are equal when $x = 2$ and $y = 4$.

Practice and Problem-Solving Exercises

A Practice   Evaluate each expression for $s = 4$ and $t = 8$.

See Problem 3.

Guided Practice

To start, substitute 4 for s and 8 for t.

6. $(s + t)^3$

$(s + t)^3 = (4 + 8)^3$

7. $s^4 + t^2 + s \div 2$

8. $(st)^2$

9. $3st^2 \div (st) + 6$

10. $(t - s)^5$

11. $(2s)^2 t$

12. $2st^2 - s^2$

13. $2s^2 - t^3 \div 16$

14. $\dfrac{(3s)^3 t + t}{s}$

15. Write an expression for the amount of change you will receive after buying an item for price p using a \$20 bill. Make a table to find the amounts of change you will receive for items with prices of \$11.59, \$17.50, \$19.00, and \$20.00.

See Problem 4.

Guided Practice

To start, describe the situation in words.   20 dollars minus price p

16. An object's momentum is defined as the product of its mass m and velocity v. Write an expression for the momentum of an object. Make a table to find the momentums of a vehicle with a mass of 1000 kg moving at a velocity of 15 m/s, 20 m/s, and 25 m/s.

B Apply

17. Geometry The expression $\pi r^2 h$ represents the volume of a cylinder with radius r and height h.

   a. What is the volume, to the nearest tenth of a cubic inch, of the juice can at the right? Use 3.14 for π.

   b. Reasoning About how many cubic inches, to the nearest tenth of a cubic inch, does a fluid ounce of juice fill?

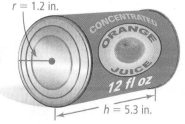

$r = 1.2$ in.

$h = 5.3$ in.

12 fl oz

18. Think About a Plan The snack bar at your school has added sushi to its menu. The ingredients for one roll include sushi rice, seaweed sheets, cucumbers, cream cheese, and 3 oz of smoked salmon. One roll can be cut into 8 servings. Write an expression for the amount of salmon needed to make s servings of sushi. How much salmon is needed to make 16 servings? 24 servings? 80 servings? 100 servings?

- What operations are needed in your calculations?
- Use a table to help you organize your results. What will you use for the column headings in your table?

19. Salary You earn \$10 for each hour you work at a canoe rental shop. Write an expression for your salary for working the number of hours h. Make a table to find how much you earn after working 10 h, 20 h, 30 h, and 40 h.

Evaluate each expression for the given values of the variables.

20. $3(s - t)^2$; $s = 4, t = 1$

21. $2x - y^2$; $x = 7, y = 3.5$

22. $3m^2 - n$; $m = 2, n = 6$

23. $(2a + 2b)^2$; $a = 3, b = 4$

24. $2p^2 + (2q)^2$; $p = 4, q = 3$

25. $(4c - d + 0.2)^2 - 10c$; $c = 3.1, d = 4.6$

26. $\dfrac{3g + 6}{h}$; $g = 5, h = 7$

27. $\dfrac{2w + 3v}{v^2}$; $v = 6, w = 1$

28. A student wrote the expressions shown and claimed that they were equal for all values of x and y.

$(x + y)^2$
$x^2 + y^2$

  a. Evaluate each expression for $x = 1$ and $y = 0$.

  b. Evaluate each expression for $x = 1$ and $y = 2$.

  c. Open-Ended Choose another pair of values for x and y. Evaluate each expression for those values.

  d. Writing Is the student's claim correct? Justify your answer.

Standardized Test Prep

SAT/ACT

29. What is the simplified form of $4 + 10 \div 4 + 6$?

 Ⓐ 4 Ⓑ 9.5 Ⓒ 12.5 Ⓓ 24

30. What is the value of $(2a)^2b - 2c^2$ for $a = 2, b = 4$, and $c = 3$?

 Ⓕ 14 Ⓖ 28 Ⓗ 32 Ⓘ 46

31. A shirt is on sale for $25 at the local department store. The sales tax equals $\frac{1}{25}$ of the shirt's price. What is the total cost of the shirt including sales tax?

 Ⓐ $17 Ⓑ $26 Ⓒ $27 Ⓓ $33

32. You can find the distance, in feet, that an object falls in t seconds using the expression $16t^2$. If you drop a ball from a tall building, how far does the ball fall in 3 s?

 Ⓕ 16 ft Ⓖ 48 ft Ⓗ 96 ft Ⓘ 144 ft

Mixed Review

Write an algebraic expression for each word phrase.

See Lesson 1-1.

33. 4 more than p

34. 5 minus the product of y and 3

35. the quotient of m and 10

36. 3 times the difference of 7 and d

Tell whether each number is *prime* or *composite*.

See p. 783.

37. 17 **38.** 33 **39.** 43 **40.** 91

Get Ready! **To prepare for Lesson 1-3, do Exercises 41–48.**

Write each fraction as a decimal and each decimal as a fraction.

See p. 787.

41. $\frac{3}{5}$ **42.** $\frac{7}{8}$ **43.** $\frac{2}{3}$ **44.** $\frac{4}{7}$

45. 0.7 **46.** 0.07 **47.** 4.25 **48.** 0.425

1-3 Real Numbers and the Number Line

Objectives To classify, graph, and compare real numbers
To find and estimate square roots

This problem involves a special group of numbers.

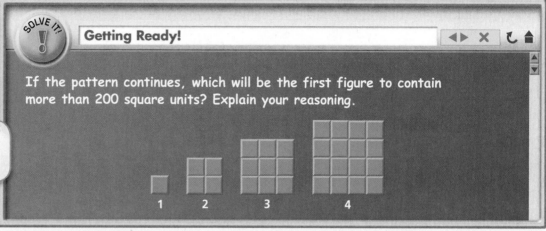

Getting Ready!

If the pattern continues, which will be the first figure to contain more than 200 square units? Explain your reasoning.

1   2   3   4

Dynamic Activity
Exploring Square Roots
The Real Number Line

Lesson Vocabulary
- square root
- radicand
- radical
- perfect square
- set
- element of a set
- subset
- rational numbers
- natural numbers
- whole numbers
- integers
- irrational numbers
- real numbers
- inequality

The diagrams in the Solve It model what happens when you multiply a number by itself to form a product. When you do this, the original number is called a *square root* of the product.

Focus Question What is the difference between finding the square root of a perfect square and the square root of a nonperfect square?

Key Concept   Square Root

Algebra A number a is a **square root** of a number b if $a^2 = b$.

Example $7^2 = 49$, so 7 is a square root of 49.

You can use the definition above to find the exact square roots of some nonnegative numbers. You can approximate the square roots of other nonnegative numbers.

The radical symbol $\sqrt{\ }$ indicates a nonnegative square root, that is also called a *principal square root*. The expression under the radical symbol is called the **radicand.**

$$\text{radical symbol} \rightarrow \sqrt{a} \leftarrow \text{radicand}$$

Together, the radical symbol and radicand form a **radical.** You will learn about negative square roots in Lesson 1-6.

Think

How can you find a square root?
Find a number that you can multiply by itself to get a product that is equal to the radicand.

 Problem 1 Simplifying Square Root Expressions

What is the simplified form of each expression?

A $\sqrt{81} = 9$ $\qquad$ $9^2 = 81$, so 9 is a square root of 81.

B $\sqrt{\frac{9}{16}} = \frac{3}{4}$ $\qquad$ $\left(\frac{3}{4}\right)^2 = \frac{9}{16}$, so $\frac{3}{4}$ is a square root of $\frac{9}{16}$.

 Got It? **1.** What is the simplified form of each expression?

$\qquad$ **a.** $\sqrt{64}$ $\qquad$ **b.** $\sqrt{25}$ $\qquad$ **c.** $\sqrt{\frac{1}{36}}$ $\qquad$ **d.** $\sqrt{\frac{81}{121}}$

The square of an integer is called a **perfect square.** For example, 49 is a perfect square because $7^2 = 49$. When a radicand is not a perfect square, you can estimate the square root of the radicand.

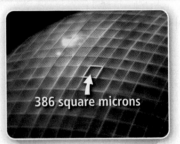
386 square microns

 Problem 2 Estimating a Square Root

Biology Lobster eyes are made of tiny square regions. Under a microscope, the surface of the eye looks like graph paper. A scientist measures the area of one of the squares to be 386 square microns. What is the approximate side length of the square to the nearest micron?

Plan

How can you get started?
The square root of the area of a square is equal to its side length. So, find $\sqrt{386}$.

Method 1 Estimate $\sqrt{386}$ by finding the two closest perfect squares.

The perfect squares closest to 386 are 361 and 400.
$19^2 = 361$
$\qquad \longleftarrow 386$
$20^2 = 400$

386 is closer to 400, so $\sqrt{386} \approx 20$.
The side length is about 20 microns.

Method 2 Estimate $\sqrt{386}$ using a calculator.

Use the square root function on your calculator. $\sqrt{386} \approx 19.6$

The side length of the square is about 20 microns.

 Got It? **2.** What is the value of $\sqrt{34}$ to the nearest integer?

Focus Question Why is it helpful to classify, graph, and compare numbers?

You can classify numbers using *sets*. A **set** is a well-defined collection of objects. Each object is called an **element of the set.** A **subset** of a set consists of elements from the given set. You can list the elements of a set within braces { }.

A **rational number** is any number that you can write in the form $\frac{a}{b}$, where a and b are integers and $b \neq 0$. A rational number in decimal form is either a terminating decimal such as 5.45 or a repeating decimal, such as $0.41666\ldots$, which you can write as $0.41\overline{6}$. Each graph below shows a subset of the rational numbers on a number line.

Natural numbers $\{1, 2, 3, \ldots\}$

Whole numbers $\{0, 1, 2, 3, \ldots\}$

Integers $\{\ldots -2, -1, 0, 1, 2, 3, \ldots\}$

An **irrational number** cannot be represented as the quotient of two integers. In decimal form, irrational numbers do not terminate or repeat. Here are some examples.

$$0.1010010001\ldots \qquad\qquad \pi = 3.14159265\ldots$$

Some square roots are rational numbers and some are irrational numbers. If a whole number is not a perfect square, its square root is irrational.

Rational $\sqrt{4} = 2$ $\sqrt{25} = 5$

Irrational $\sqrt{3} = 1.73205080\ldots$ $\sqrt{10} = 3.16227766\ldots$

Rational numbers and irrational numbers form the set of **real numbers.**

Problem 3 **Classifying Real Numbers**

ONLINE PROBLEMS

Think

What clues can you use to classify real numbers?
Look for negative signs, fractions, decimals that do or do not terminate or repeat, and radicands that are not perfect squares.

To which subsets of the real numbers does each number belong?

A **15** natural numbers, whole numbers, integers, rational numbers

B $\frac{4}{5}$ rational numbers

C **−1.4583** rational numbers (since −1.4583 is a terminating decimal)

D $\sqrt{57}$ irrational numbers (since 57 is not a perfect square)

Got It? **3.** To which subsets of the real numbers does each number belong?

   a. $\sqrt{9}$ **b.** $\frac{3}{10}$ **c.** -0.45 **d.** $\sqrt{12}$

take note

Concept Summary   **Real Numbers**

Real Numbers

Rational Numbers	Integers	Whole Numbers	Natural Numbers	Irrational Numbers
$\frac{-2}{3}$	-3	0	$\sqrt{25}$	$\sqrt{10}$ $-\sqrt{123}$
$0.\overline{3}$	$-\frac{10}{5}$		$\frac{4}{2}$ 7	$0.1010010001\ldots$
$\sqrt{0.25}$	$-\sqrt{16}$			π

An **inequality** is a mathematical sentence that compares the values of two expressions using an inequality symbol. The symbols are:

$<$, less than $\leq$, less than or equal to

$>$, greater than $\geq$, greater than or equal to

Problem 4   Comparing Real Numbers

Plan

How can you compare numbers?
Write the numbers in the same form, such as decimal form.

What is an inequality that compares the numbers $\sqrt{17}$ and $4\frac{1}{3}$?

Write the square root as a decimal. $\sqrt{17} = 4.12310\ldots$

Write the fraction as a decimal. $4\frac{1}{3} = 4.\overline{3}$

Compare the decimals. $4.12310\ldots < 4.33333\ldots$

Compare using an inequality symbol. $\sqrt{17} < 4\frac{1}{3}$

Got It?   4. a. What is an inequality that compares the numbers $\sqrt{129}$ and 11.52?

    b. **Reasoning** In Problem 4, is there another inequality you can write that compares the two numbers? Explain.

You can graph and order all real numbers using a number line.

Problem 5   Graphing and Ordering Real Numbers

Multiple Choice What is the order of $\sqrt{4}$, 0.4, $-\frac{2}{3}$, $\sqrt{2}$, and -1.5 from least to greatest?

Ⓐ $-\frac{2}{3}$, 0.4, -1.5, $\sqrt{2}$, $\sqrt{4}$

Ⓒ -1.5, $-\frac{2}{3}$, 0.4, $\sqrt{2}$, $\sqrt{4}$

Ⓑ -1.5, $\sqrt{2}$, 0.4, $\sqrt{4}$, $-\frac{2}{3}$

Ⓓ $\sqrt{4}$, $\sqrt{2}$, 0.4, $-\frac{2}{3}$, -1.5

Know	Need	Plan
Five real numbers	Order of numbers from least to greatest	Graph the numbers on a number line.

Think

Why is it useful to rewrite numbers in decimal form?
It allows you to compare numbers that have values that are close, like $\frac{1}{4}$ and 0.26.

First, write the numbers that are not in decimal form as decimals: $\sqrt{4} = 2$, $-\frac{2}{3} \approx -0.67$, and $\sqrt{2} \approx 1.41$. Then graph all five numbers on the number line to order the numbers, and read the graph from left to right.

$$-1.5 \quad -\frac{2}{3} \quad 0.4 \quad \sqrt{2} \; \sqrt{4}$$

number line marked from -2 to 3

From least to greatest, the numbers are -1.5, $-\frac{2}{3}$, 0.4, $\sqrt{2}$, and $\sqrt{4}$. The correct answer is C.

 Got It?   5. Graph 3.5, -2.1, $\sqrt{9}$, $-\frac{7}{2}$, and $\sqrt{5}$ on a number line. What is the order of the numbers from least to greatest?

Focus Question What is the difference between finding the square root of a perfect square and the square root of a nonperfect square?

Answer For perfect squares, find a number times itself that equals the perfect square. For nonperfect squares, estimate the square root by finding the two closest perfect squares.

Focus Question Why is it helpful to classify, graph, and compare numbers?

Answer Since there are many types of numbers, it is helpful to classify them. In real life situations, you may need to compare different types of real numbers by graphing them on a number line.

Lesson Check

Do you know HOW?

Name the subset(s) of the real numbers to which each number belongs.

1. $\sqrt{11}$ **2.** -7

3. Order $\frac{47}{10}$, 4.1, -5, and $\sqrt{16}$ from least to greatest.

4. A square card has an area of 15 in.^{2}. What is the approximate side length of the card?

Do you UNDERSTAND?

5. Vocabulary What are the two subsets of the real numbers that form the set of real numbers?

6. Vocabulary Give an example of a rational number that is not an integer.

Reasoning Tell whether each square root is *rational* or *irrational*. Explain.

7. $\sqrt{100}$ **8.** $\sqrt{0.29}$

Practice and Problem-Solving Exercises

Ⓐ Practice

Simplify each expression.

                                              ◀ See Problem 1.

9. $\sqrt{36}$ **10.** $\sqrt{169}$ **11.** $\sqrt{16}$

12. $\sqrt{900}$ **13.** $\sqrt{\frac{36}{49}}$ **14.** $\sqrt{\frac{25}{81}}$

15. $\sqrt{\frac{1}{9}}$ **16.** $\sqrt{\frac{121}{16}}$ **17.** $\sqrt{0.25}$

Estimate the square root. Round to the nearest integer.   **◀ See Problem 2.**

Guided Practice

To start, find the two perfect squares closest to 17.

18. $\sqrt{17}$

      $4^2 = 16$ $5^2 = 25$

19. $\sqrt{35}$ **20.** $\sqrt{242}$ **21.** $\sqrt{61}$ **22.** $\sqrt{320}$

Find the approximate side length of each square figure to the nearest whole unit.

23. a mural with an area of 18 m^2

24. a game board with an area of 160 in.^{2}

25. a helicopter launching pad with an area of 3000 ft^2

Name the subset(s) of the real numbers to which each number belongs ◀ **See Problem 3.**

26. $\frac{2}{3}$

27. 13

28. -1

29. $-\frac{19}{100}$

30. π

31. -2.38

32. $\sqrt{144}$

33. $\sqrt{113}$

34. $\frac{59}{2}$

Compare the numbers in each exercise using an inequality symbol. ◀ **See Problem 4.**

Guided Practice

35. $5\frac{2}{3}, \sqrt{29}$

To start, write the square root as a decimal. $\sqrt{29} = 5.38516\ldots$

36. $-3.1, -\frac{16}{5}$

37. $\frac{4}{3}, \sqrt{2}$

38. $9.6, \sqrt{96}$

39. $-\frac{7}{11}, -0.63$

40. $\sqrt{115}, 10.72104\ldots$

41. $-\frac{22}{25}, -0.\overline{8}$

Order the numbers in each exercise from least to greatest. ◀ **See Problem 5.**

42. $\frac{1}{2}, -2, \sqrt{5}, -\frac{7}{4}, 2.4$

43. $-3, \sqrt{31}, \sqrt{11}, 5.5, -\frac{60}{11}$

44. $-6, \sqrt{20}, 4.3, -\frac{59}{9}$

45. $\frac{10}{3}, 3, \sqrt{8}, 2.9, \sqrt{7}$

46. $-\frac{13}{6}, -2.1, -\frac{26}{13}, -\frac{9}{4}$

47. $-\frac{1}{6}, -0.3, \sqrt{1}, -\frac{2}{13}, \frac{7}{8}$

B **Apply**

48. Think About a Plan A stage designer paid \$4 per square foot for flooring to be used in a square room. If the designer spent \$600 on the flooring, about how long is a side of the room? Round to the nearest foot.
  • How is the area of a square related to its side length?
  • How can you estimate the length of a side of a square?

Tell whether each statement is *true* or *false*. Explain.

49. All negative numbers are integers.

50. All integers are rational numbers.

51. All square roots are irrational numbers.

52. No positive number is an integer.

53. Reasoning A restaurant owner is going to panel a square portion of the restaurant's ceiling. The portion to be paneled has an area of 185 ft². The owner plans to use square tin ceiling panels with a side length of 2 ft. What is the first step in finding out whether the owner will be able to use a whole number of panels?

Show that each number is rational by writing it in the form $\frac{a}{b}$, where a and b are integers.

54. 417

55. 0.37

56. 2.01

57. 2.1

58. 3.06

59. Error Analysis A student says that $\sqrt{7}$ is a rational number because you can write $\sqrt{7}$ as the quotient $\frac{\sqrt{7}}{1}$. Is the student correct? Explain.

60. Construction A contractor is tiling a square patio that has the area shown at the right. What is the approximate side length of the patio? Round to the nearest foot.

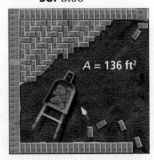

$A = 136$ ft²

61. Open-Ended You are tutoring a younger student. How would you explain rational numbers, irrational numbers, and how they are different?

62. **Geometry** The irrational number π, equal to $3.14159\ldots$, is the ratio of a circle's circumference to its diameter. In the sixth century, the mathematician Brahmagupta estimated the value of π to be $\sqrt{10}$. In the thirteenth century, the mathematician Fibonacci estimated the value of π to be $\frac{864}{275}$. Which is the better estimate? Explain.

63. **Home Improvement** If you lean a ladder against a wall, the length of the ladder should be $\sqrt{(x)^2 + (4x)^2}$ ft to be considered safe. The distance x is how far the ladder's base is from the wall. Estimate the desired length of the ladder when the base is positioned 5 ft from the wall. Round your answer to the nearest tenth.

64. **Writing** Is there a greatest integer on the real number line? A least fraction? Explain.

65. **Reasoning** Choose three intervals on the real number line that contain both rational and irrational numbers. Do you think that any given interval on the real number line contains both rational and irrational numbers? Explain.

Standardized Test Prep

SAT/ACT

66. A square picture has an area of 225 in.^{2}. What is the side length of the picture?

   (A) 5 in.   (B) 15 in.   (C) 25 in.   (D) 225 in.

67. To simplify the expression $9 \cdot (33 - 5^2) \div 2$, what do you do first?

   (F) Divide by 2.   (G) Subtract 5.   (H) Multiply by 9.   (I) Square 5.

68. The table at the right shows the number of pages you can read per minute. Which algebraic expression gives a rule for finding the number of pages read in any number of minutes m?

   (A) m (C) $2m$

   (B) $m + 2$ (D) $\frac{m}{2}$

Reading

Minutes	Pages Read
1	2
2	4
3	6
m	■

Mixed Review

Evaluate each expression for the given values of the variables.   ◀ See Lesson 1-2.

69. $(r - t)^2; r = 11, t = 7$ 70. $3m^2 + n; m = 5, n = 3$ 71. $(2x)^2 y; x = 4, y = 8$

Write an algebraic expression for each word phrase.   ◀ See Lesson 1-1.

72. the sum of 14 and x

73. 4 multiplied by the sum of y and 1

74. 3880 divided by z

75. the product of t and the quotient of 19 and 3

Get Ready!   **To prepare for Lesson 1-4, do Exercises 76–79.**

Simplify each expression.   ◀ See Lesson 1-2.

76. $4 + 7 \cdot 2$ 77. $(7 + 1)9$ 78. $2 + 22 \cdot 20$ 79. $6 + 18 \div 6$

1-4 Properties of Real Numbers

Objective To identify and use properties of real numbers

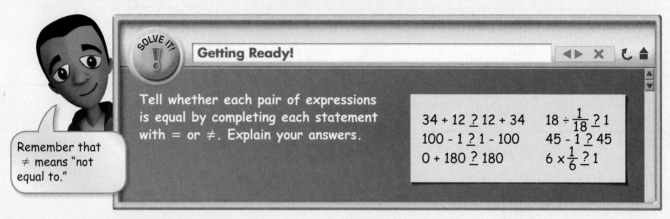

Getting Ready!

Tell whether each pair of expressions is equal by completing each statement with = or ≠. Explain your answers.

Remember that ≠ means "not equal to."

$34 + 12 \underline{?} 12 + 34$ $18 \div \frac{1}{18} \underline{?} 1$

$100 - 1 \underline{?} 1 - 100$ $45 - 1 \underline{?} 45$

$0 + 180 \underline{?} 180$ $6 \times \frac{1}{6} \underline{?} 1$

The Solve It illustrates numerical relationships that are always true for real numbers.

Lesson Vocabulary
• equivalent expressions
• deductive reasoning
• counterexample

Focus Question Why are the properties of real numbers, such as the commutative and associative properties, useful?

Relationships that are always true for real numbers are called *properties*. Properties are rules used to rewrite and compare expressions.

Two algebraic expressions are **equivalent expressions** if they have the same value for all values of the variable(s). The following properties show expressions that are equivalent for all real numbers.

---

take note

Properties   Properties of Real Numbers

Let *a*, *b*, and *c* be any real numbers.

Commutative Properties of Addition and Multiplication
Changing the order of the addends does not change the sum. Changing the order of the factors does not change the product.

	Algebra	**Example**
Addition	$a + b = b + a$	$18 + 54 = 54 + 18$
Multiplication	$a \cdot b = b \cdot a$	$12 \cdot \frac{1}{2} = \frac{1}{2} \cdot 12$

Associative Properties of Addition and Multiplication
Changing the grouping of the addends does not change the sum. Changing the grouping of the factors does not change the product.

Addition	$(a + b) + c = a + (b + c)$	$(23 + 9) + 4 = 23 + (9 + 4)$
Multiplication	$(a \cdot b) \cdot c = a \cdot (b \cdot c)$	$(7 \cdot 9) \cdot 10 = 7 \cdot (9 \cdot 10)$

Properties Properties of Real Numbers

Let a be any real number.

Identity Properties of Addition and Multiplication
The sum of any real number and 0 is the original number. The product of any real number and 1 is the original number.

	Algebra	Example
Addition	$a + 0 = a$	$5\frac{3}{4} + 0 = 5\frac{3}{4}$
Multiplication	$a \cdot 1 = a$	$67 \cdot 1 = 67$

Zero Property of Multiplication
The product of a and 0 is 0. $a \cdot 0 = 0$ $18 \cdot 0 = 0$

Multiplication Property of −1
The product of −1 and a is $-a$. $-1 \cdot a = -a$ $-1 \cdot 9 = -9$

Problem 1 Identifying Properties

Think

What math symbols give you clues about the properties?
Parentheses, operation symbols, and the numbers 0 and 1 may indicate certain properties.

What property is illustrated by each statement?

A $42 \cdot 0 = 0$ Zero Property of Multiplication

B $(y + 2.5) + 28 = y + (2.5 + 28)$ Associative Property of Addition

C $10x + 0 = 10x$ Identity Property of Addition

 Got It? **1.** What property is illustrated by each statement?

a. $4x \cdot 1 = 4x$ **b.** $x + (\sqrt{y} + z) = x + (z + \sqrt{y})$

You can use properties to help you solve some problems using mental math.

Problem 2 Using Properties for Mental Calculations

Plan

How can you make the addition easier?
Look for numbers having decimal parts you can add easily, such as 0.75 and 0.25.

Movies A movie ticket costs $7.75. A drink costs $2.40. Popcorn costs $1.25. What is the total cost for a ticket, a drink, and popcorn? Use mental math.

Use the Commutative Property of Addition.	$(7.75 + 2.40) + 1.25 = (2.40 + 7.75) + 1.25$
Use the Associative Property of Addition.	$= 2.40 + (7.75 + 1.25)$
Simplify inside parentheses.	$= 2.40 + 9$
Add.	$= 11.40$

The total cost is $11.40.

 Got It? **2.** A can holds 3 tennis balls. A box holds 4 cans. A case holds 6 boxes. How many tennis balls are in 10 cases? Use mental math.

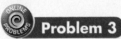 **Problem 3** **Writing Equivalent Expressions**

Simplify each expression.

A $5(3n)$

Know	Need	Plan
An expression	Groups of numbers that can be simplified	Use properties to group or reorder parts of the expression.

Write the original expression. $\qquad$ $5(3n)$

Use the Associative Property of Multiplication. $\quad 5(3n) = (5 \cdot 3)n$

Simplify. $\qquad\qquad\qquad\qquad\qquad = 15n$

B $(4 + 7b) + 8$

Write the original expression. $\qquad\qquad$ $(4 + 7b) + 8$

Use the Commutative Property of Addition. $\quad (4 + 7b) + 8 = (7b + 4) + 8$

Use the Associative Property of Addition. $\qquad\qquad = 7b + (4 + 8)$

Simplify. $\qquad\qquad\qquad\qquad\qquad\qquad\qquad = 7b + 12$

C $\dfrac{6xy}{y}$

Write the original expression. $\qquad\qquad\qquad\qquad\qquad\qquad\qquad \dfrac{6xy}{y}$

Rewrite the denominator using the Identity Property of Multiplication. $\quad \dfrac{6xy}{y} = \dfrac{6x \cdot y}{1 \cdot y}$

Use the rule for multiplying fractions: $\dfrac{a}{b} \cdot \dfrac{c}{d} = \dfrac{ac}{bd}$. $\qquad = \dfrac{6x}{1} \cdot \dfrac{y}{y}$

$x \div 1 = x$ and $y \div y = 1$. $\qquad\qquad\qquad\qquad\qquad = 6x \cdot 1$

Use the Identity Property of Multiplication. $\qquad\qquad\qquad = 6x$

 Got It? **3.** Simplify each expression.

    a. $2.1(4.5x)$ **b.** $6 + (4h + 3)$ **c.** $\dfrac{8m}{12mn}$

In Problem 3, reasoning and properties were used to show that two expressions are equivalent. This is an example of *deductive reasoning*. **Deductive reasoning** is the process of reasoning logically from given facts to a conclusion.

To show that a statement is *not* true, find an example for which the statement is not true. An example showing that a statement is false is a **counterexample.** You need only one counterexample to prove that a statement is false.

Problem 4 Using Deductive Reasoning and Counterexamples

Is the statement *true* or *false*? If it is false, give a counterexample.

Ⓐ For all real numbers a and b, $a \cdot b = b + a$.

False. $5 \cdot 3 \neq 3 + 5$ is a counterexample.

Ⓑ For all real numbers a, b, and c, $(a + b) + c = b + (a + c)$.

True. Use the properties of real numbers to show that the expressions are equivalent.

Use the Commutative Property of Addition. $(a + b) + c = (b + a) + c$

Use the Associative Property of Addition. $= b + (a + c)$

Plan

Look for a counterexample to show the statement is false. If you don't find one, try to use properties to show that it is true.

 Got It? **4. Reasoning** Is each statement in parts (a) and (b) *true* or *false*? If it is false, give a counterexample. If true, use the properties of real numbers to show that the expressions are equivalent.

a. For all real numbers j and k, $j \cdot k = (k + 0) \cdot j$.

b. For all real numbers m and n, $m(n + 1) = mn + 1$.

c. Is the statement in part (A) of Problem 4 false for *every* pair of real numbers a and b? Explain.

Focus Question Why are the properties of real numbers, such as the commutative and associative properties, useful?

Answer The properties of real numbers allow you to write equivalent equations so that you can solve equations.

 ## Lesson Check

Do you know HOW?

Name the property that each statement illustrates.

1. $x + 12 = 12 + x$

2. $5 \cdot (12 \cdot x) = (5 \cdot 12) \cdot x$

3. You buy a sandwich for \$2.95, an apple for \$.45, and a bottle of juice for \$1.05. What is the total cost?

4. Simplify $\frac{24cd}{c}$.

Do you UNDERSTAND?

5. Vocabulary Tell whether the expressions in each pair are equivalent.

a. $5x \cdot 1$ and $1 + 5x$

b. $1 + (2t + 1)$ and $2 + 2t$

6. Justify each step.

$$\begin{aligned} 3 \cdot (10 \cdot 12) &= 3 \cdot (12 \cdot 10) \\ &= (3 \cdot 12) \cdot 10 \\ &= 36 \cdot 10 \\ &= 360 \end{aligned}$$

 ## Practice and Problem-Solving Exercises

Ⓐ Practice   Name the property that each statement illustrates.   ◆ See Problem 1.

7. $75 + 6 = 6 + 75$ **8.** $\frac{7}{9} \cdot 1 = \frac{7}{9}$ **9.** $h + 0 = h$

10. $389 \cdot 0 = 0$ **11.** $27 \cdot \pi = \pi \cdot 27$ **12.** $9 \cdot (-1 \cdot x) = 9 \cdot (-x)$

Mental Math Simplify each expression.

See Problem 2.

13. $21 + 6 + 9$

14. $10 \cdot 2 \cdot 19 \cdot 5$

15. $0.1 + 3.7 + 5.9$

16. $4 \cdot 5 \cdot 13 \cdot 5$

17. $55.3 + 0.2 + 23.8 + 0.7$

18. $0.25 \cdot 12 \cdot 4$

Guided Practice

19. Fishing Trip The sign at the right shows the costs for a deep-sea fishing trip. How much will the total cost be for 1 adult, 2 children, and 1 senior citizen to go on a fishing trip? Use mental math.

To start, list what you know.
cost of 1 adult ticket = \$33
cost of 2 children's tickets = $2 \cdot \$25 = 50$
cost of 1 senior citizen's ticket = \$27

Write an expression for the cost. Use the Commutative Property of Addition to write an equivalent expression.
$33 + 50 + 27 = 50 + 33 + 27$

Simplify each expression. Justify each step.

See Problem 3.

Guided Practice

To start, use the Commutative Property of Addition to write an equivalent expression.

20. $8 + (9t + 4)$
$8 + (9t + 4) = 8 + (4 + 9t)$

21. $9(2x)$

22. $(4 + 105x) + 5$

23. $(10p)11$

24. $(12 \cdot r) \cdot 13$

25. $(2 + 3x) + 9$

26. $4 \cdot (x \cdot 6.3)$

27. $1.1 + (7d + 0.1)$

28. $\dfrac{56ab}{b}$

29. $\dfrac{13p}{pq}$

Use deductive reasoning to tell whether each statement is *true* or *false*. If it is false, give a counterexample. If true, use properties of real numbers to show that the expressions are equivalent.

See Problem 4.

30. For all real numbers r, s, and t, $(r \cdot s) \cdot t = t \cdot (s \cdot r)$.

31. For all real numbers p and q, $p \div q = q \div p$.

32. For all real numbers x, $x + 0 = 0$.

33. For all real numbers a and b, $-a \cdot b = a \cdot (-b)$.

 Apply

34. Error Analysis Your friend shows you the problem at the right. He says that the Associative Property allows you to change the order in which you complete two operations. Is your friend correct? Explain.

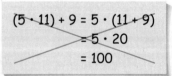

35. Travel The distance from Tulsa, Oklahoma, to Dallas, Texas is 258 mi. The distance from Dallas, Texas to Houston, Texas, is 239 mi.
a. What is the total distance of a trip from Tulsa to Dallas to Houston?
b. What is the total distance of a trip from Houston to Dallas to Tulsa?
c. Explain how you can tell whether the distances described in parts (a) and (b) are equal by using reasoning.

Tell whether the expressions in each pair are equivalent.

36. $2 + h + 4$ and $2 \cdot h \cdot 4$

37. $9y \cdot 0$ and 1

38. $3x$ and $3x \cdot 1$

39. $m(1 - 1)$ and 0

40. $(9 - 7) + \pi$ and 2π

41. $(3 + 7) + m$ and $m + 10$

42. $\frac{63ab}{7a}$ and $9ab$

43. $\frac{11x}{(2 + 5 - 7)}$ and $11x$

44. $\frac{7t}{4 - 8 + \sqrt{9}}$ and $7t$

45. Think About a Plan Hannah makes a list of possible gifts for Mary, Jared, and Michael. She has two plans and can spend a total of $75 for all gifts. Which plan(s) can Hannah afford?

- What property can you use to make it easier to find the total cost of different gifts?
- What number do you compare to the total cost of each plan to decide whether it is affordable?

46. Writing Suppose you are mixing red and blue paint in a bucket. Do you think the final color of the mixed paint will be the same whether you add the blue paint or the red paint to the bucket first? Relate your answer to a property of real numbers.

Standardized Test Prep

47. What is the simplified form of $(1.2 + 0) + 4.6 + 3.8$?

    Ⓐ 1.2   Ⓑ 8.0   Ⓒ 8.4   Ⓓ 9.6

48. Which expression is equal to $3 \cdot 3 \cdot 8 \cdot 8 \cdot 3$?

    Ⓕ $3 \cdot 8$ Ⓖ 3^8 Ⓗ $3^3 \cdot 8^2$ Ⓘ $3 \cdot 3 + 2 \cdot 8$

49. There are four points plotted on the number line below.

Which expression represents the greatest amount?

    Ⓐ $M \div L$ Ⓑ $M - L$ Ⓒ $J + K$ Ⓓ $L - K$

Mixed Review

Order the numbers in each exercise from least to greatest. ◀ See Lesson 1-3.

50. $-6, 6^3, 1.6, \sqrt{6}$

51. $\frac{8}{5}, 1.4, -17, 10^2$

52. $1.75, -4.5, \sqrt{4}, 14^1$

Get Ready! **To prepare for Lesson 1-5, do Exercises 53–56.**

Find each sum or difference. ◀ See p. 788.

53. $3 + 11$

54. $\frac{3}{8} + \frac{5}{8}$

55. $9.7 - 8.6$

56. $\frac{5}{9} - \frac{5}{10}$

Chapter Review for Part A

Chapter Vocabulary

- algebraic expression (p. 4)
- base (p. 11)
- counterexample (p. 28)
- deductive reasoning (p. 28)
- element of a set (p. 20)
- equivalent expressions (p. 26)
- evaluate (p. 15)
- exponent (p. 11)
- inequality (p. 22)
- integers (p. 21)
- irrational number (p. 21)
- natural number (p. 21)
- numerical expression (p. 4)
- order of operations (p. 12)
- perfect square (p. 20)
- power (p. 11)
- quantity (p. 4)
- radical (p. 19)
- radicand (p. 19)
- rational number (p. 21)
- real number (p. 21)
- set (p. 20)
- simplify (p. 11)
- square root (p. 19)
- subset (p. 20)
- variable (p. 4)
- whole number (p. 21)

Choose the correct term to complete each sentence.

1. Real numbers that you cannot represent as a quotient of two integers are __?__ numbers.

2. You __?__ a numerical expression when you replace it with its single numerical value.

3. A __?__ has two parts, a base and an exponent.

4. You __?__ an algebraic expression by replacing each variable with a given number and performing all operations.

5. An __?__ is a mathematical sentence that compares the values of two expressions using an inequality symbol.

6. The expression under the radical symbol is called the __?__.

7. The square of an integer is called a __?__.

8. A __?__ is a well-defined collection of objects.

9. An example showing that a statements is false is a __?__.

10. A __?__ is a symbol, usually a letter, that represents the value(s) of a variable quantity.

1-1 Variables and Expressions

Quick Review

A **variable** is a symbol, usually a letter, that represents values of a variable quantity. For example, d often represents distance. An **algebraic expression** is a mathematical phrase that includes one or more variables. A **numerical expression** is a mathematical phrase involving numbers and operation symbols, but there are no variables.

Example

What is an algebraic expression for the word phrase *3 less than half a number x*?

You can represent "half a number x" as $\frac{x}{2}$. Then subtract 3 to get $\frac{x}{2} - 3$.

Exercises

Write an algebraic expression for each word phrase.

11. the product of a number w and 737

12. the difference of a number q and 8

13. the sum of a number x and 84

14. 9 more than the product of 51 and a number t

15. 14 less than the quotient of 63 and a number h

16. a number b less the quotient of a number k and 5

Write a word phrase for each algebraic expression.

17. $12 + a$ **18.** $r - 31$

19. $19t$ **20.** $b \div 3$

21. $7c - 3$ **22.** $2 + \frac{x}{8}$

23. $\frac{y}{11} - 6$ **24.** $21d + 13$

1-2 Order of Operations and Evaluating Expressions

Quick Review

To **evaluate** an algebraic expression, substitute a given number for each variable. Then simplify the numerical expression using the order of operations.

1. Do operation(s) inside grouping symbols.
2. Simplify powers.
3. Multiply and divide from left to right.
4. Add and subtract from left to right.

Example

A student studies with a tutor for 1 hour each week and studies alone for h hours each week. What is an expression for the total hours spent studying each week? Evaluate the expression for $h = 5$.

The expression is $h + 1$. To evaluate the expression for $h = 5$, substitute 5 for h: $(5) + 1 = 6$.

Exercises

Simplify each expression.

25. 9^2 **26.** 5^3 **27.** $\left(\frac{1}{6}\right)^2$

28. $7^2 \div 5$ **29.** $(2^4 - 6)^2$ **30.** $(3^3 - 4) + 5^2$

Evaluate each expression for $c = 3$ and $d = 5$.

31. $d^3 \div 15$ **32.** $(2 + d)^2 - 3^2$

33. $cd^2 + 4$ **34.** $(3c^2 - 3d)^2 - 21$

35. The expression $6s^2$ represents the surface area of a cube with edges of length s.

     a. What is the cube's surface area when $s = 6$?

     b. Reasoning Explain how a cube's surface area changes if you divide s by 2 in the expression $6s^2$.

36. A race car travels at 205 mi/h. How far does the car travel in 3 h?

1-3 Real Numbers and the Number Line

Quick Review

The rational numbers and irrational numbers form the **set of real numbers.**

A **rational number** is any number that you can write as $\frac{a}{b}$, where a and b are integers and $b \neq 0$. The rational numbers include all positive and negative integers, as well as fractions, mixed numbers, and terminating and repeating decimals. **Irrational numbers** cannot be represented as the quotient of two integers. Irrational numbers include the square roots of all positive integers that are not perfect squares.

Example

Is the number rational or irrational?

Ⓐ -5.422 rational

Ⓑ $\sqrt{7}$ irrational

Exercises

Tell whether each number is rational or irrational.

37. π **38.** $-\frac{1}{2}$

39. $\sqrt{\frac{2}{3}}$ **40.** $0.\overline{57}$

Estimate each square root. Round to the nearest integer.

41. $\sqrt{99}$ **42.** $\sqrt{48}$ **43.** $\sqrt{30}$

Name the subset(s) of the real numbers to which each number belongs.

44. -17 **45.** $\frac{13}{62}$ **46.** $\sqrt{94}$

47. $\sqrt{100}$ **48.** 4.288 **49.** $1\frac{2}{3}$

Order the numbers in each exercise from least to greatest.

50. $-1\frac{2}{3}, 1.6, -1\frac{4}{5}$ **51.** $\frac{7}{9}, -0.8, \sqrt{3}$

1-4 Properties of Real Numbers

Quick Review

You can use the properties below to simplify and evaluate expressions.

Commutative Properties $-2 + 7 = 7 + (-2)$

                              $3 \times 4 = 4 \times 3$

Associative Properties $2 \times (14 \times 3) = (2 \times 14) \times 3$

                              $3 + (12 + 2) = (3 + 12) + 2$

Identity Properties $-6 + 0 = -6$

                       $21 \times 1 = 21$

Zero Property of Multiplication $-7 \times 0 = 0$

Multiplication Property of −1 $6 \cdot (-1) = -6$

Example

Use an identity property to simplify $-\frac{7ab}{a}$.

$-\frac{7ba}{a} = -7b \cdot \frac{a}{a} = -7b \cdot 1 = -7b$

Exercises

Simplify each expression. Justify each step.

52. $-8 + 9w + (-23)$

53. $\frac{6}{5} \cdot (-10 \cdot 8)$

54. $\left(\frac{4}{3} \cdot 0\right) \cdot (-20)$

55. $53 + (-12) + (-4t)$

56. $\frac{6 + 3}{9}$

Tell whether the expressions in each pair are equivalent.

57. $(5 - 2)c$ and $c \cdot 3$

58. $41 + z + 9$ and $41 \cdot z \cdot 9$

59. $\frac{81xy}{3x}$ and $9xy$

60. $\frac{11t}{(5 + 7 - 11)}$ and t

Do you know HOW?

Write an algebraic expression for each phrase.

1. a number n divided by 4

2. 2 less than the product of 5 and n

3. The table shows how the total cost of a field trip depends on the number of students. What is a rule for the total cost of the tickets? Give the rule in words and as an algebraic expression.

Field Trip

Number of Students	Total Cost
20	$(12 \cdot 20) + 150$
40	$(12 \cdot 40) + 150$
60	$(12 \cdot 60) + 150$

4. The sign shows the costs associated with a whitewater rafting trip. Write an expression to determine the cost of 3 children and 1 adult renting equipment for a whitewater rafting trip that lasts h hours.

Whitewater Tours

Adult Ticket	$53
Child Ticket	$32
Equipment Rental	$5 per hour

Simplify each expression.

5. $24 \div (3 + 2^2)$

6. $\sqrt{144}$

Evaluate each expression for the given values of the variables.

7. $3x \cdot 2 \div y$; $x = 3$ and $y = 6$

8. $(4a)^3 \div (b - 2)$; $a = 2$ and $b = 4$

9. Name the subset(s) of real numbers to which each number belongs. Then order the numbers from least to greatest.
$$\sqrt{105}, \ -4, \ \tfrac{4}{3}$$

10. Estimate $\sqrt{14}$ to the nearest integer.

11. What property is shown in the following equation?
$$(5 + 8) + 11 = 5 + (8 + 11)$$

12. Use the table below. Find the total cost of 2 salads, 1 sandwich, and 2 drinks. Use mental math.

Lunch Menu

Salad	$6.25
Sandwich	$5.50
Drink	$2.75

Do you UNDERSTAND?

13. What word phrases represent the expressions $-2 + 3x$ and $3x + (-2)$? Are the two expressions equivalent? Explain.

14. Use grouping symbols to make the following equation true.
$$4^2 + 2 \cdot 3 = 54$$

15. Choose the correct word to complete the following sentence: A natural number is (*always, sometimes, never*) a whole number.

16. How many natural numbers are in the set of numbers from -10 to 10 inclusive? Explain.

17. What is the simplified form of $\frac{3abc}{abc}$, when $abc \neq 0$? Explain using the properties of real numbers.

18. **Reasoning** Are the associative properties true for all integers? Explain.

19. Use the Commutative Property of Multiplication to rewrite the expression $(x \cdot y) \cdot z$ in two different ways.

Foundations for Algebra

In Part A, you built a foundation with the order of operations and the properties of real numbers. Now you will learn to add, subtract, multiply, and divide real numbers, and you will explore patterns in basic equations.

Vocabulary for Part B

English/Spanish Vocabulary Audio Online:

English	Spanish
absolute value, *p. 38*	valor absoluto
additive inverse, *p. 39*	inverso aditivo
coefficient, *p. 57*	coeficiente
constant, *p. 57*	constante
equation, *p. 61*	ecuación
inductive reasoning, *p. 71*	razonamiento inductivo
like terms, *p. 57*	términos semejantes
multiplicative inverse, *p. 47*	inverso multiplicativo
open sentence, *p. 61*	ecuación abierta
opposite, *p. 39*	opuestos
reciprocal, *p. 48*	recíproco
term, *p. 57*	término

BIG ideas

1 Variable
Essential Question How can you represent quantities, patterns, and relationships?

2 Properties
Essential Question How are properties related to algebra?

Chapter Preview for Part B

1-5 Adding and Subtracting Real Numbers

Objective To find sums and differences of real numbers

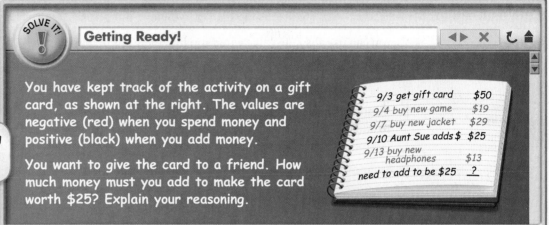

SOLVE IT!

Getting Ready!

You have kept track of the activity on a gift card, as shown at the right. The values are negative (red) when you spend money and positive (black) when you add money.

You want to give the card to a friend. How much money must you add to make the card worth $25? Explain your reasoning.

You may find using a number line helpful here.

9/3 get gift card	$50
9/4 buy new game	$19
9/7 buy new jacket	$29
9/10 Aunt Sue adds $	$25
9/13 buy new headphones	$13
need to add to be $25	?

Focus Question What are two methods for finding sums and differences of real numbers?

You can add or subtract any real numbers using a number line model.

Lesson Vocabulary
• absolute value
• opposites
• additive inverses

Think

How do you know which direction to move along the number line?
If the number added is positive, move to the right. If the number added is negative, move to the left.

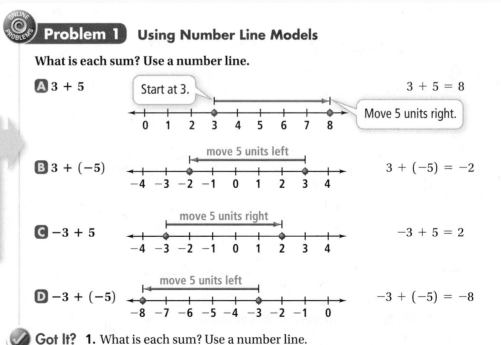

Problem 1 **Using Number Line Models**

What is each sum? Use a number line.

Ⓐ $3 + 5$ Start at 3.   Move 5 units right. $3 + 5 = 8$

Ⓑ $3 + (-5)$ move 5 units left $3 + (-5) = -2$

Ⓒ $-3 + 5$ move 5 units right $-3 + 5 = 2$

Ⓓ $-3 + (-5)$ move 5 units left $-3 + (-5) = -8$

Got It? **1.** What is each sum? Use a number line.

a. $8 + 4$ **b.** $8 + (-4)$ **c.** $-8 + 4$ **d.** $-8 + (-4)$

You can also add or subtract real numbers using rules involving absolute value.

The **absolute value** of a number is its distance from 0 on a number line. Absolute value is always nonnegative since distance is always nonnegative.

For example, the absolute value of 4 is 4 and the absolute value of -4 is 4. You can write this as $|4| = 4$ and $|-4| = 4$.

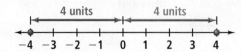

You can use absolute value when you find the sums of real numbers.

Key Concept   Adding Real Numbers

Adding Numbers With the Same Sign

To add two numbers with the same sign, add their absolute values. The sum has the same sign as the addends.

Examples $3 + 4 = 7$ $-3 + (-4) = -7$

Adding Numbers With Different Signs

To add two numbers with different signs, subtract their absolute values. The sum has the same sign as the addend with the greater absolute value.

Examples $-3 + 4 = 1$ $3 + (-4) = -1$

Problem 2   Adding Real Numbers

What is each sum?

Plan

What is the first step in finding each sum?
Identify whether the addends have the same sign or different signs. Then choose the appropriate rule to use.

A $-12 + 7$

The difference of the absolute values is 5. The negative addend has the greater absolute value. The sum is negative.

$$-12 + 7 = -5$$

B $-18 + (-2)$

The addends have the same sign (negative), so add their absolute values. The sum is negative.

$$-18 + (-2) = -20$$

C $-4.8 + 9.5$

The difference of the absolute values is 4.7. The positive addend has the greater absolute value. The sum is positive.

$$-4.8 + 9.5 = 4.7$$

D $\frac{3}{4} + \left(-\frac{5}{6}\right)$

Find the least common denominator.

The difference of the absolute values is $\frac{1}{12}$. The negative addend has the greater absolute value. The sum is negative.

$$\frac{3}{4} + \left(-\frac{5}{6}\right) = \frac{9}{12} + \left(-\frac{10}{12}\right)$$
$$= -\frac{1}{12}$$

 Got It? 2. What is each sum?

a. $-16 + (-8)$ **b.** $-11 + 9$ **c.** $9.2 + (-11.3)$ **d.** $-\frac{2}{3} + \left(-\frac{1}{4}\right)$

Two numbers that are the same distance from 0 on a number line but lie in opposite directions are **opposites.**

−3 and 3 are the same distance from 0. So −3 and 3 are opposites.

A number and its opposite are called **additive inverses.** To find the sum of a number and its opposite, you can use the **Inverse Property of Addition.**

take note

Property   Inverse Property of Addition

For every real number a, there is an additive inverse $-a$ such that
$a + (-a) = -a + a = 0$.

Examples $14 + (-14) = 0$ $-14 + 14 = 0$

You can use opposites (additive inverses) to subtract real numbers. To see how, look at the number line below, which models $3 - 5$ and $3 + (-5)$.

Start at 3 and move 5 units left.

$3 - 5$ and $3 + (-5)$ are equivalent expressions, illustrating the rule below.

take note

Property   Subtracting Real Numbers

To subtract a real number, add its opposite: $a - b = a + (-b)$.

Examples $3 - 5 = 3 + (-5) = -2$ $3 - (-5) = 3 + 5 = 8$

Problem 3   Subtracting Real Numbers

Think

Why rewrite subtraction as addition?
You can simplify expressions using the rules for adding real numbers that you learned earlier in this lesson.

What is each difference?

Ⓐ $-8 - (-13)$

The opposite of −13 is 13. So add 13. $= -8 + 13$
Use rules for addition. $= 5$

Ⓑ $3.5 - 12.4$

The opposite of 12.4 is −12.4. So add −12.4. $= 3.5 + (-12.4)$
Use rules for addition. $= -8.9$

Ⓒ $9 - 9$

The opposite of 9 is −9. So add −9. $= 9 + (-9)$
Use the Inverse Property of Addition. $= 0$

Got It? **3. a.** What is $4.8 - (-8.7)$?
 b. Reasoning For what values of a and b does $a - b = b - a$?

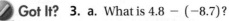

All of the addition properties of real numbers that you learned in Lesson 1-4 apply to both positive and negative numbers. You can use these properties to reorder and simplify expressions.

 Problem 4 Adding and Subtracting Real Numbers

Scuba Diving A reef explorer dives 25 ft to photograph brain coral and then rises 16 ft to travel over a ridge before diving 47 ft to survey the base of the reef. Then the diver rises 29 ft to see an underwater cavern. What is the location of the cavern in relation to sea level?

Know	Need	Plan
Distance and direction for each change in location	Location in relation to sea level after changes	Represent the diver's trip with an expression. Reorder the values to make your calculations easier.

Think

How do you represent the problem with an expression?
Start your expression with zero to represent sea level. Subtract for dives, and add for rises.

Write an expression.	$0 - 25 + 16 - 47 + 29$
Use the rule for subtracting real numbers.	$= 0 + (-25) + 16 + (-47) + 29$
Use the Commutative Property of Addition.	$= 0 + 16 + 29 + (-25) + (-47)$
Group addends with the same sign.	$= 0 + (16 + 29) + [(-25) + (-47)]$
Add inside grouping symbols.	$= 0 + 45 + (-72)$
Use the Identity Property of Addition.	$= 45 + (-72)$
Use the rule for adding numbers with different signs.	$= -27$

The cavern is at -27 ft in relation to sea level.

 Got It? **4.** A robot submarine dives 803 ft to the ocean floor. It rises 215 ft as the water gets shallower. Then the submarine dives 2619 ft into a deep crevice. Next, it rises 734 ft to photograph a crack in the wall of the crevice. What is the location of the crack in relation to sea level?

Focus Question What are two methods for finding sums and differences of real numbers?

Answer You can use a number line, or you can use rules involving absolute value.

 Lesson Check

Do you know HOW?

Use a number line to find each sum.

1. $-5 + 2$ **2.** $-2 + (-1)$

Find each sum or difference.

3. $-12 + 9$ **4.** $-4 + (-3)$

5. $-3 - (-5)$ **6.** $1.5 - 8.5$

Do you UNDERSTAND?

7. Vocabulary What is the sum of a number and its opposite?

8. Compare and Contrast How is subtraction related to addition?

9. Error Analysis Your friend says that since $-a$ is the opposite of a, the opposite of a number is always negative. Describe and correct the error.

Practice and Problem-Solving Exercises

 Practice   Use a number line to find each sum.   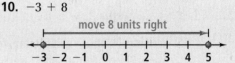 **See Problem 1.**

Guided Practice

10. $-3 + 8$

To start, plot a point at -3 on the number line. Then move 8 units right to add 8.

move 8 units right

$$-3 \quad -2 \quad -1 \quad 0 \quad 1 \quad 2 \quad 3 \quad 4 \quad 5$$

11. $-4 + 7$ **12.** $4 + (-3)$ **13.** $1 + (-6)$

14. $-6 + 9$ **15.** $-6 + (-8)$ **16.** $-9 + (-3)$

Find each sum.   **See Problem 2.**

17. $11 + 9$ **18.** $17 + (-28)$ **19.** $12 + (-9)$ **20.** $-2 + 7$

21. $-14 + (-10)$ **22.** $-9 + (-2)$ **23.** $3.2 + 1.4$ **24.** $5.1 + (-0.7)$

25. $-2.2 + (-3.8)$ **26.** $\frac{1}{2} + \left(-\frac{7}{2}\right)$ **27.** $-\frac{2}{3} + \left(-\frac{3}{5}\right)$ **28.** $\frac{7}{9} + \left(-\frac{5}{12}\right)$

Find each difference.   **See Problem 3.**

Guided Practice

29. $5 - 15$

To start, add -15 because the opposite of 15 is -15.

$$5 - 15 = 5 + (-15)$$

30. $-13 - 7$ **31.** $36 - (-12)$ **32.** $-29 - (-11)$

33. $-7 - (-5)$ **34.** $8.5 - 7.6$ **35.** $-2.5 - 17.8$

36. $3.5 - 1.9$ **37.** $\frac{1}{8} - \frac{3}{4}$ **38.** $\frac{7}{16} - \left(-\frac{1}{2}\right)$

39. Bird Watching An eagle starts flying at an elevation of 42 ft. Elevation is the    **See Problem 4.**
distance above sea level. The diagram below shows the elevation changes during
the eagle's flight. Write an expression representing the eagle's flight. What is the
elevation at the brook?

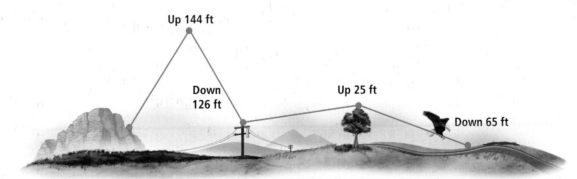

Up 144 ft

Down 126 ft

Up 25 ft

Down 65 ft

40. Stock Market A stock's starting price per share is $51.47 at the beginning of the
week. During the week, the price changes by gaining $1.22, then losing $3.47,
then losing $2.11, then losing $.98, and finally gaining $2.41. What is the ending
stock price?

Evaluate each expression for $a = -2$, $b = -4.1$, and $c = 5$.

41. $a - b + c$ **42.** $-c + b - a$ **43.** $-a + (-c)$

44. Error Analysis Describe and correct the error in finding the difference shown at the right.

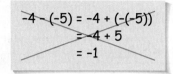

45. Writing Without calculating, tell which is greater, the sum of -135 and 257 or the sum of 135 and -257. Explain your reasoning.

Simplify each expression.

46. $1 - \frac{1}{2} - \frac{1}{3} - \frac{1}{4}$ **47.** $7 + (2^3 - 3^2)$ **48.** $-2.1 - [2.3 - (3.5 - (-1.9))]$

49. Think About a Plan In golf, the expected number of strokes is called "par." When the number of strokes taken is more than par, your score is positive. When the number of strokes is less than par, your score is negative. The lowest score wins.

The scorecard shows par and one golfer's score for the first four holes played on a nine-hole golf course. The golfer's scores on the remaining five holes are $-1, 0, -1, +1,$ and 0. Par for the nine holes is 36. What is the golfer's total number of strokes for the nine holes?

* Can you solve the problem by adding the strokes taken on each hole?
* How is the sum of the golfer's scores related to the total number of strokes taken?

Golf Scorecard

Par	Number of Strokes	Score
4	6	+2
4	3	−1
3	3	0
5	3	−2

Reasoning Use reasoning to determine whether the value of each expression is *positive* or *negative*. Do not calculate the exact answers.

50. $-225 + 318$ **51.** $-\frac{7}{8} + \frac{1}{3}$ **52.** $34.5 + 12.9 - 50$

53. Temperature Scales The Kelvin temperature scale is related to the degrees Celsius (°C) temperature scale by the formula $x = 273 + y$, where x is the number of kelvins and y is the temperature in degrees Celsius. What is each temperature in kelvins?

a. $-22°C$ **b.** $0°C$ **c.** $-32°C$

54. Writing Explain how you can tell without calculating whether the sum of a positive number and a negative number will be positive, negative, or zero.

Decide whether each statement is true or false. Explain your reasoning.

55. The sum of a positive number and a negative number is always negative.

56. The difference of two numbers is always less than the sum of those two numbers.

57. A number minus its opposite is twice the number.

58. Meteorology Weather forecasters use a barometer to measure air pressure and make weather predictions. Suppose a standard mercury barometer reads 29.8 in. The mercury rises 0.02 in. and then falls 0.09 in. The mercury falls again 0.18 in. before rising 0.07 in. What is the final reading on the barometer?

59. Multiple Choice Which expression is equivalent to $x - y$?

(A) $y - x$ (B) $x - (-y)$ (C) $x + (-y)$ (D) $y + (-x)$

60. Chemistry Atoms contain particles called protons and electrons. Each proton has a charge of $+1$ and each electron has a charge of -1. A certain sulfur ion has 18 electrons and 16 protons. The charge on an ion is the sum of the charges of its protons and electrons. What is the sulfur ion's charge?

Standardized Test Prep

SAT/ACT

61. What is the value of $-b - a$ when $a = -4$ and $b = 7$?

(A) -11 (B) -3 (C) 3 (D) 11

62. Which expression is equivalent to $19 - 41$?

(F) $|19 - 41|$ (G) $|19 + 41|$ (H) $-|19 - 41|$ (I) $-|19 + 41|$

63. Which equation illustrates the Identity Property of Multiplication?

(A) $x \cdot 0 = 0$ (B) $x \cdot 1 = x$ (C) $x(yz) = (xy)z$ (D) $x \cdot y = y \cdot x$

64. What is an algebraic expression for the perimeter of the triangle?

(F) $8 + x$ (H) 8

(G) $4x$ (I) $4 + x$

65. Which point on the number line below is the best estimate for $\sqrt{8}$?

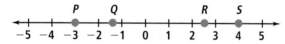

(A) P (B) Q (C) R (D) S

Mixed Review

Tell whether the expressions in each pair are equivalent.   ◀ See Lesson 1-4.

66. $\frac{3}{4} \cdot d \cdot 4$ and $3d$ **67.** $(2.1 \cdot h) \cdot 3$ and $6.3 + h$ **68.** $(6 + b) + a$ and $6 + (a + b)$

Name the subset(s) of real numbers to which each number belongs.   ◀ See Lesson 1-3.

69. $\frac{1}{3}$ **70.** -5.333 **71.** $\sqrt{16}$ **72.** 82.0371 **73.** $\sqrt{21}$

Get Ready!   **To prepare for Lesson 1-6, do Exercises 74–76.**

Evaluate each expression for $a = 2$, $h = 5$, and $w = 8$.   ◀ See Lesson 1-2.

74. $4h - 5a \div w$ **75.** $a^2w - h^2 + 2h$ **76.** $(w^2h - a^2) + 12 \div 3a$

Concept Byte

Use With Lesson 1-5

ACTIVITY

Always, Sometimes, or Never

A statement can be always, sometimes, or never true. For each activity, work with a group of 4 students. Take turns predicting each answer. If the predictor gives a correct answer, he or she scores 1 point. Otherwise, the person who proves the predictor incorrect scores 1 point. Whoever has the most points at the end of an activity wins.

Activity 1

Is each description *always, sometimes,* or *never* true about the members of your group?

1. takes an algebra class

2. lives in your state

3. plays a musical instrument

4. is less than 25 years old

5. speaks more than one language

6. is taller than 5 m

Activity 2

Suppose each member of your group takes one of the four cards at the right. Will a group member chosen at random *always, sometimes,* or *never* have a number that fits each description?

7. greater than 2

8. greater than 25

9. even

10. irrational number

11. prime number

12. rational number

Activity 3

Each member of your group substitutes any integer for x in each statement. Will a group member chosen at random *always, sometimes,* or *never* have a true statement?

13. $x - 2$ is greater than x.

14. $|x|$ is less than x.

15. $7 + x = x + 7$

16. $13 - x = x - 13$

17. $x + 0 = x$

18. $-4 + (3 + x) = x + (-4 + 3)$

19. $x \div 5$ is less than x.

20. $x \cdot 0 = 0$

21. $x + 9$ is less than x.

22. $|x|$ is greater than x.

1-6 Multiplying and Dividing Real Numbers

Objective To find products and quotients of real numbers

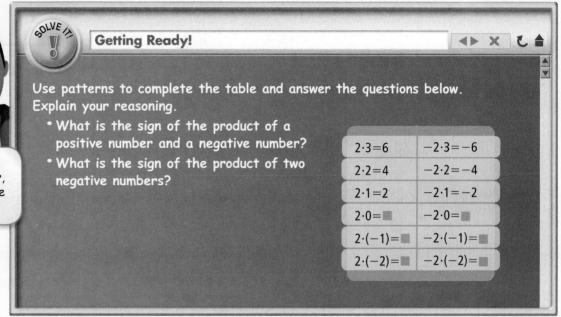

SOLVE IT!

Getting Ready!

Use patterns to complete the table and answer the questions below. Explain your reasoning.
- What is the sign of the product of a positive number and a negative number?
- What is the sign of the product of two negative numbers?

2·3=6	−2·3=−6
2·2=4	−2·2=−4
2·1=2	−2·1=−2
2·0=■	−2·0=■
2·(−1)=■	−2·(−1)=■
2·(−2)=■	−2·(−2)=■

You might not know the answer, but you can make a conjecture.

Lesson Vocabulary
- multiplicative inverse
- reciprocal

The patterns in the Solve It suggest rules for multiplying real numbers.

Focus Question How do the rules for finding the product of real numbers compare to the rules for finding the product of integers?

The rules for multiplying real numbers are related to the properties of real numbers and the definitions of operations.

You know that the product of two positive numbers is positive. For example, $3(5) = 15$. You can think about the product of a positive number and a negative number in terms of groups of numbers. For example, $3(−5)$ means 3 groups of $−5$. So, $3(−5) = (−5) + (−5) + (−5)$, or $3(−5) = −15$.

You can also derive the product of two negative numbers, such as $−3(−5)$.

Start with the product $3(−5) = −15$.	$3(−5) = −15$
The opposites of two equal numbers are equal.	$−[3(−5)] = −(−15)$
Multiplication Property of −1	$−1[3(−5)] = −(−15)$
Associative Property of Multiplication	$[−1(3)](−5) = −(−15)$
Multiplication Property of −1	$−3(−5) = −(−15)$
The opposite of −15 is 15.	$−3(−5) = 15$

These discussions illustrate the following rules for multiplying real numbers.

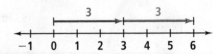

Key Concept Multiplying Real Numbers

Words The product of two real numbers with different signs is negative.

Examples $2(-3) = -6$ $-2 \cdot 3 = -6$

Model $2(-3) = -6$

Words The product of two real numbers with the same sign is positive.

Examples $2 \cdot 3 = 6$ $-2(-3) = 6$

Model $2 \cdot 3 = 6$

Plan

What is your first step in finding a product of real numbers?
Identify the signs of the factors. Then determine the sign of the product.

 Problem 1 **Multiplying Real Numbers**

What is each product?

A $12(-8) = -96$ The product of two numbers with different signs is negative.

B $24(0.5) = 12$ The product of two numbers with the same sign is positive.

C $-\frac{3}{4} \cdot \frac{1}{2} = -\frac{3}{8}$ The product of two numbers with different signs is negative.

D $(-3)^2 = (-3)(-3) = 9$ The product of two numbers with the same sign is positive.

✓ **Got It?** **1.** What is each product?

     a. $6(-15)$ **b.** $12(0.2)$ **c.** $-\frac{7}{10}\left(\frac{3}{5}\right)$ **d.** $(-4)^2$

Notice that $(-3)^2 = 9$ in part (d) of Problem 1. Recall from Lesson 1-3 that a is a square root of b if $a^2 = b$. So, -3 is a square root of 9. A negative square root is represented by $-\sqrt{}$. Every positive real number has a positive and a negative square root. The symbol $\pm$ in front of the radical indicates both square roots.

Think

How can you find a negative square root?
Look for a negative number that you can multiply by itself to get a product that is equal to the radicand.

 Problem 2 **Simplifying Square Root Expressions**

What is the simplified form of each expression?

A $-\sqrt{25} = -5$ $(-5)^2 = 25$, so $-\sqrt{25} = -5$.

B $\pm\sqrt{\frac{4}{49}} = \pm\frac{2}{7}$ $\left(\frac{2}{7}\right)^2 = \frac{4}{49}$ and $\left(-\frac{2}{7}\right)^2 = \frac{4}{49}$, so $\pm\sqrt{\frac{4}{49}} = \pm\frac{2}{7}$.

✓ **Got It?** **2.** What is the simplified form of each expression?

     a. $\sqrt{100}$ **b.** $\pm\sqrt{16}$ **c.** $-\sqrt{121}$ **d.** $\pm\sqrt{\frac{1}{36}}$

Focus Question How do the rules for finding the sign of a product compare to the rules for finding the sign of a quotient?

Rules for dividing real numbers are related to the rules for multiplying real numbers.

For any real numbers a, b, and c where $a \neq 0$, if $a \cdot b = c$, then $b = c \div a$. For instance, $-8(-2) = 16$, so $-2 = 16 \div (-8)$. Similarly $-8(2) = -16$, so $2 = -16 \div (-8)$. These examples illustrate the following rules.

Key Concept   Dividing Real Numbers

Words	The quotient of two real numbers with *different* signs is *negative*.
Examples	$-20 \div 5 = -4$ $20 \div (-5) = -4$
Words	The quotient of two real numbers with the *same* sign is *positive*.
Examples	$20 \div 5 = 4$ $-20 \div (-5) = 4$

Division Involving 0

Words	The quotient of 0 and any nonzero real number is 0. The quotient of any real number and 0 is undefined.
Examples	$0 \div 8 = 0$ $8 \div 0$ is undefined.

Problem 3   Dividing Real Numbers

Sky Diving A sky diver's elevation changes by -3600 ft in 4 min after the parachute opens. What is the average change in the sky diver's elevation each minute?

The numbers have different signs, so the quotient is negative. $-3600 \div 4 = -900$

The sky diver's average change in elevation is -900 ft per minute.

 Got It? 3. You make five withdrawals of equal amounts from your bank account. The total amount you withdraw is $360. What is the change in your account balance each time you make a withdrawal?

Think

How is dividing similar to multiplying?
You find the sign of a quotient using the signs of the numbers you're dividing, just as you find the sign of a product using the signs of the factors.

The Inverse Property of Multiplication describes the relationship between a number and its multiplicative inverse.

Property   Inverse Property of Multiplication

Words	For every nonzero real number a, there is a **multiplicative inverse** $\frac{1}{a}$ such that $a\left(\frac{1}{a}\right) = 1$.
Examples	The multiplicative inverse of -4 is $-\frac{1}{4}$ because $-4\left(-\frac{1}{4}\right) = 1$.

The **reciprocal** of a nonzero real number of the form $\frac{a}{b}$ is $\frac{b}{a}$. The product of a number and its reciprocal is 1, so the reciprocal of a number is its multiplicative inverse. This suggests a rule for dividing fractions.

Here's Why It Works Let a, b, c, and d be nonzero integers.

Write the expression as a fraction.
$$\frac{a}{b} \div \frac{c}{d} = \frac{\frac{a}{b}}{\frac{c}{d}}$$

Multiply the numerator and denominator by $\frac{d}{c}$.
Since this is equivalent to multiplying by 1,
it does not change the quotient.
$$= \frac{\frac{a}{b} \cdot \frac{d}{c}}{\frac{c}{d} \cdot \frac{d}{c}}$$

Use the Inverse Property of Multiplication.
$$= \frac{\frac{a}{b} \cdot \frac{d}{c}}{1}$$

Simplify.
$$= \frac{a}{b} \cdot \frac{d}{c}$$

This shows that dividing by a fraction is equivalent to multiplying by the reciprocal of the fraction.

Problem 4   **Dividing Fractions**

Multiple Choice What is the value of $\frac{x}{y}$ when $x = -\frac{3}{4}$ and $y = -\frac{2}{3}$?

Ⓐ $-\frac{9}{8}$ Ⓑ $-\frac{1}{2}$ Ⓒ $\frac{1}{2}$ Ⓓ $\frac{9}{8}$

Think

Rewrite the expression.

Substitute $-\frac{3}{4}$ for x and $-\frac{2}{3}$ for y.

Multiply by the reciprocal of $-\frac{2}{3}$.

Simplify. Since both factors are negative, the product is positive.

Write

$$\frac{x}{y} = x \div y$$

$$= -\frac{3}{4} \div \left(-\frac{2}{3}\right)$$

$$= -\frac{3}{4} \cdot \left(-\frac{3}{2}\right)$$

$$= \frac{9}{8}$$

The correct answer is D.

 Got It? 4. a. What is the value of $\frac{3}{4} \div \left(-\frac{5}{2}\right)$?

   b. Reasoning Is $\frac{3}{4} \div \left(-\frac{5}{2}\right)$ equivalent to $-\left(\frac{3}{4} \div \frac{5}{2}\right)$? Explain.

Focus Question How do the rules for finding the product of real numbers compare to the rules for finding the product of integers?

Answer The rules are the same.

Focus Question How do the rules for finding the sign of a product compare to the rules for finding the sign of a quotient?

Answer The rules are the same.

Lesson Check

Do you know HOW?

Find each product. Simplify, if necessary.

1. $-3(-12)$ **2.** $\frac{5}{8}\left(-\frac{2}{8}\right)$

Find each quotient. Simplify, if necessary.

3. $-48 \div 3$ **4.** $-\frac{9}{10} \div \left(-\frac{4}{5}\right)$

Do you UNDERSTAND?

5. Vocabulary What is the reciprocal of $-\frac{1}{5}$?

6. Reasoning Use a number line to explain why $-15 \div 3 = -5$.

7. Reasoning Determine how many real square roots each number has. Explain your answers.

     a. 49   **b.** 0

Practice and Problem-Solving Exercises

 Practice

Find each product. Simplify, if necessary.   See Problem 1.

8. $-8(12)$ **9.** $8(12)$ **10.** $7(-9)$ **11.** $5 \cdot 4.1$

12. $-7 \cdot 1.1$ **13.** $10(-2.5)$ **14.** $6\left(-\frac{1}{4}\right)$ **15.** $-\frac{1}{9}\left(-\frac{3}{4}\right)$

16. $-\frac{3}{7} \cdot \frac{9}{10}$ **17.** $-\frac{2}{11}\left(-\frac{11}{2}\right)$ **18.** $\left(-\frac{2}{9}\right)^2$ **19.** $(-1.2)^2$

Simplify each expression.   See Problem 2.

Guided Practice

To start, find a number multiplied by itself that equals 400.

20. $\sqrt{400}$

$20^2 = 400$

21. $\sqrt{169}$ **22.** $-\sqrt{16}$ **23.** $-\sqrt{900}$

24. $\sqrt{\frac{36}{49}}$ **25.** $-\sqrt{\frac{25}{81}}$ **26.** $-\sqrt{\frac{1}{9}}$

27. $-\sqrt{\frac{121}{16}}$ **28.** $\pm\sqrt{1.96}$ **29.** $\pm\sqrt{0.25}$

Find each quotient. Simplify, if necessary.   See Problem 3.

30. $48 \div 3$ **31.** $-84 \div 14$ **32.** $-39 \div (-13)$

33. $\frac{63}{-21}$ **34.** $-46 \div (-2)$ **35.** $-8.1 \div 9$

36. $\frac{-121}{11}$ **37.** $75 \div (-0.3)$ **38.** $121 \div 1.1$

39. Scuba Diving A scuba diver's vertical position in relation to the surface of the water changes by -90 ft in 3 min. What is the average change in the diver's vertical position each minute?

40. Part-Time Job You earn the same amount each week at your part-time job. The total amount you earn in 4 weeks is $460. How much do you earn per week?

Find each quotient. Simplify, if necessary.

◆ See Problem 4.

41. $20 \div \frac{1}{4}$

42. $-5 \div \left(-\frac{5}{3}\right)$

43. $-\frac{12}{13} \div \frac{12}{13}$

Find the value of the expression $\frac{x}{y}$ for the given values of x and y. Write your answer in the simplest form.

Guided Practice →

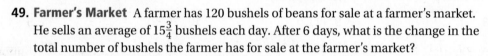

44. $x = -\frac{2}{3}, y = -\frac{1}{4}$

To start, rewrite the expression.

Then substitute for x and y.

$\frac{x}{y} = x \div y$

$= -\frac{2}{3} \div \left(-\frac{1}{4}\right)$

45. $x = -\frac{5}{6}; y = \frac{3}{5}$

46. $x = \frac{2}{7}; y = -\frac{20}{21}$

47. $x = \frac{3}{8}; y = \frac{3}{4}$

Ⓑ Apply

48. Think About a Plan A lumberjack cuts 7 pieces of equal length from a log, as shown at the right. What is the change in the log's length after 7 cuts?
- What operation can you use to find the answer?
- Will your answer be a positive value or a negative value? How do you know?

$2\frac{1}{4}$ ft

49. Farmer's Market A farmer has 120 bushels of beans for sale at a farmer's market. He sells an average of $15\frac{3}{4}$ bushels each day. After 6 days, what is the change in the total number of bushels the farmer has for sale at the farmer's market?

50. Stocks The price per share of a stock changed by $-\$4.50$ on each of 5 consecutive days. If the starting price per share was $\$67.50$, what was the ending price?

Open-Ended Write an algebraic expression that uses x, y, and z and simplifies to the given value when $x = -3$, $y = -2$, and $z = -1$. The expression should involve only multiplication or division.

51. -16

52. 1

53. 12

54. History The Rhind Papyrus is one of the best known examples of Egyptian mathematics. One problem solved on the Rhind Papyrus is $100 \div 7\frac{7}{8}$. What is the solution of this problem?

Evaluate each expression for $m = -5$, $n = \frac{3}{2}$, and $p = -8$.

55. $-7m - 10n$

56. $-3mnp$

57. $8n \div (-6p)$

58. $2p^2(-n) \div m$

59. Look for a Pattern Extend the pattern in the diagram to six factors of -2. What rule describes the sign of the product based on the number of negative factors?

-2(-2) = 4
-2(-2)(-2) = -8
-2(-2)(-2)(-2) = 16

60. **Temperature** The formula $F = \frac{9}{5}C + 32$ changes a temperature reading from the Celsius scale C to the Fahrenheit scale F. What is the temperature measured in degrees Fahrenheit when the Celsius temperature is $-25°C$?

61. **Reasoning** Suppose a and b are integers. Describe what values of a and b make the statement true.
    a. Quotient $\frac{a}{b}$ is positive. **b.** Quotient $\frac{a}{b}$ is negative.
    c. Quotient $\frac{a}{b}$ is equal to 0. **d.** Quotient $\frac{a}{b}$ is undefined.

62. **Writing** Explain how to find the quotient of $-1\frac{2}{3}$ and $-2\frac{1}{2}$.

63. **Reasoning** Do you think a negative number raised to an even power will be positive or negative? Explain.

64. **Error Analysis** Describe and correct the error in dividing the fractions at the right.

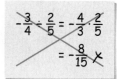

65. **Reasoning** You can derive the rule for division involving 0 shown on page 47.
    a. Suppose $0 \div x = y$ where $x \neq 0$. Show that $y = 0$. (*Hint*: If $0 \div x = y$, then $x \cdot y = 0$ by the definition of division.)
    b. If $x \neq 0$, show that there is no value of y such that $x \div 0 = y$. (*Hint*: Suppose there is a value of y such that $x \div 0 = y$. What would this imply about x?)

Standardized Test Prep

66. Which expression does NOT have the same value as $-11 + (-11) + (-11)$?
    Ⓐ -33 Ⓑ $3(-11)$ Ⓒ $(-11)^3$ Ⓓ $33 - 66$

67. Miguel measured the area of a piece of carpet and figured out that the approximate error was $3|-0.2|$. What is the decimal form of $3|-0.2|$?
    Ⓕ -0.6 Ⓖ -0.06 Ⓗ 0.06 Ⓘ 0.6

68. What is the perimeter of the triangle shown?
    Ⓐ $6y + 24$ Ⓒ $15y + 15$
    Ⓑ $21y + 9$ Ⓓ $30y$

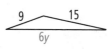

Mixed Review

Find each difference.   ◀ See Lesson 1-5.

69. $46 - 16$ 70. $34 - 44$ 71. $-37 - (-27)$

Get Ready!   To prepare for Lesson 1-7, do Exercises 72–74.

Name the property that each statement illustrates.   ◀ See Lesson 1-4.

72. $-x + 0 = -x$ 73. $13(-11) = -11(13)$ 74. $-5 \cdot (m \cdot 8) = (-5 \cdot m) \cdot 8$

1-7
PART 1

The Distributive Property

Objective To use the Distributive Property to simplify expressions

There's more than one way to figure this out.

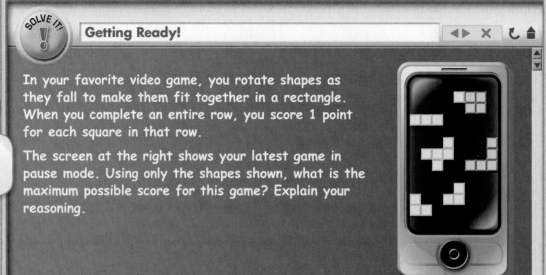

Getting Ready!

In your favorite video game, you rotate shapes as they fall to make them fit together in a rectangle. When you complete an entire row, you score 1 point for each square in that row.

The screen at the right shows your latest game in pause mode. Using only the shapes shown, what is the maximum possible score for this game? Explain your reasoning.

To solve problems in mathematics, it is often useful to rewrite expressions in simpler forms. The **Distributive Property,** illustrated by the area model below, is another property of real numbers that helps you to simplify expressions.

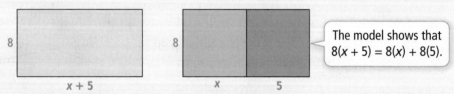

The model shows that $8(x + 5) = 8(x) + 8(5)$.

Focus Question How does the Distributive Property work?

You can use the Distributive Property to simplify the product of a number and a sum or the product of a number and a difference.

Here's Why It Works

$$8(x + 5) = (x + 5) + (x + 5) + (x + 5) + (x + 5)$$
$$+ (x + 5) + (x + 5) + (x + 5) + (x + 5)$$
$$= x + x + x + x + x + x + x + x$$
$$+ 5 + 5 + 5 + 5 + 5 + 5 + 5 + 5$$
$$= 8x + 8(5)$$

Property Distributive Property

Let a, b, and c be real numbers.

Algebra

$a(b + c) = ab + ac$
$(b + c)a = ba + ca$
$a(b - c) = ab - ac$
$(b - c)a = ba - ca$

Examples

$4(20 + 6) = 4(20) + 4(6)$
$(20 + 6)4 = 20(4) + 6(4)$
$7(30 - 2) = 7(30) - 7(2)$
$(30 - 2)7 = 30(7) - 2(7)$

Think

How do you read expressions like $3(x + 8)$?
Read an expression inside parentheses as "the quantity." Read $3(x + 8)$ as "3 times the quantity x plus 8."

 Problem 1 Simplifying Expressions

What is the simplified form of each expression?

Ⓐ $3(x + 8)$

Use the Distributive Property. $3(x + 8) = 3(x) + 3(8)$

Simplify. $= 3x + 24$

Ⓑ $(-7)(5b - 4)$

Use the Distributive Property. $(-7)(5b - 4) = (-7)(5b) + (-7)(-4)$

Simplify. $= -35b + 28$

✓ **Got It? 1.** What is the simplified form of each expression?

a. $5(x + 7)$ **b.** $(-y)(2y - 1)$

Recall that a fraction bar may act as a grouping symbol. A fraction bar indicates division. Any fraction $\frac{a}{b}$ can also be written as $a \cdot \frac{1}{b}$. You can use this fact and the Distributive Property to rewrite some fractions as sums or differences.

Think

How can you get started?
Think of division as multiplying by the reciprocal. So change the division by 5 to multiplication by $\frac{1}{5}$.

 Problem 2 Rewriting Fraction Expressions

What sum or difference is equivalent to $\frac{7x + 2}{5}$?

Write division as multiplication. $\frac{7x + 2}{5} = \frac{1}{5}(7x + 2)$

Use the Distributive Property. $= \frac{1}{5}(7x) + \frac{1}{5}(2)$

Simplify. $= \frac{7}{5}x + \frac{2}{5}$

✓ **Got It? 2.** What sum or difference is equivalent to $\frac{4 - 2x}{8}$?

The Multiplication Property of -1 states that $-1 \cdot x = -x$. To simplify an expression, such as $-(x + 6)$, you can rewrite the expression as $-1(x + 6)$.

 Problem 3 **Using the Multiplication Property of -1**

Multiple Choice What is the simplified form of $-(2y - 3x)$?

Ⓐ $2y + 3x$ Ⓑ $-2y + (-3x)$ Ⓒ $-2y + 3x$ Ⓓ $2y - 3x$

Use the Multiplication Property of -1. $-(2y - 3x) = -1(2y - 3x)$

Use the Distributive Property. $= (-1)(2y) + (-1)(-3x)$

Simplify. $= -2y + 3x$

The correct choice is C.

Think

What does the negative sign in front of the parentheses mean?
It indicates the opposite of the entire expression inside the parentheses.

 Got It? 3. What is the simplified form of $-(6m - 9n)$?

Focus Question How does the Distributive Property work?

Answer Multiply the expression outside the parentheses by each expression inside the parentheses.

 Lesson Check

Do you know HOW?

1. What is the simplified form of each expression? Use the Distributive Property.

  a. $7(j + 2)$ **c.** $-(4 - c)$

  b. $-8(x - 3)$ **d.** $-(11 + 2b)$

Do you UNDERSTAND?

2. Vocabulary Does each equation demonstrate the Distributive Property? Explain.

  a. $-2(x + 1) = -2x - 2$

  b. $(s - 4)8 = 8(s - 4)$

  c. $5n - 45 = 5(n - 9)$

 Practice and Problem-Solving Exercises

 Practice   Use the Distributive Property to simplify each expression.    **See Problem 1.**

Guided Practice

To start, use the Distributive Property.

3. $6(a + 10)$

$6(a + 10) = 6(a) + 6(10)$

4. $8(4 + x)$ **5.** $(5 + w)5$ **6.** $(2t + 3)11$

7. $10(9 - t)$ **8.** $12(2j - 6)$ **9.** $16(7b + 6)$

10. $(1 + 3d)9$ **11.** $(3 - 8c)1.5$ **12.** $(5w - 15)2.1$

13. $\frac{1}{4}(4f - 8)$ **14.** $6\left(\frac{1}{3}h + 1\right)$ **15.** $(-8z - 10)(-1.5)$

16. $0(3.7x - 4.21)$ **17.** $1\left(\frac{3}{11} - \frac{7d}{17}\right)$ **18.** $\frac{1}{2}\left(\frac{1}{2}y - \frac{1}{2}\right)$

Write each fraction as a sum or difference.

See Problem 2.

To start, rewrite division as multiplication.

19. $\dfrac{2x + 7}{5}$

$\dfrac{2x + 7}{5} = \dfrac{1}{5}(2x + 7)$

20. $\dfrac{17 + 5n}{4}$

21. $\dfrac{8 - 9x}{3}$

22. $\dfrac{4y - 12}{2}$

23. $\dfrac{25 - 8t}{5}$

24. $\dfrac{18x + 51}{17}$

25. $\dfrac{22 - 2n}{2}$

26. $\dfrac{42w + 14}{7}$

27. $\dfrac{16 + 36b}{9}$

28. $\dfrac{-5c + 32}{12}$

29. $\dfrac{19 - 24h}{8}$

B Apply

Write a word phrase for each expression. Then simplify each expression.

30. $3(t - 1)$

31. $4(d + 7)$

32. $\dfrac{1}{3}(6x - 1)$

33. $5(2m + 1)$

34. $\dfrac{1}{2}(n - 3)$

35. $-12\left(k - \dfrac{1}{4}\right)$

36. Error Analysis Identify and correct the error shown below.

$4(x+5) = (4\cdot x)(4\cdot 5)$
$= 80x$

37. Error Analysis A friend uses the Distributive Property to simplify $4(2b - 5)$ and gets $8b - 5$ as the result. Describe and correct the error.

38. Reasoning The Distributive Property also applies to division, as shown.

$$\dfrac{a + b}{c} = \dfrac{a}{c} + \dfrac{b}{c}$$

Use the Distributive Property of Division to rewrite $\dfrac{9 + 12n}{3}$. Then simplify.

39. Open-Ended Suppose you used the Distributive Property to get the expression $3m - 6n - 15$. With what expression could you have started?

40. Writing Your friend uses the order of operations to find the value of $11(39 - 3)$. Would you prefer to use the Distributive Property instead? Explain.

1-7
PART 2

The Distributive Property

Objective   To use the Distributive Property to simplify expressions

In Part 1 of this lesson, you learned to use the Distributive Property to simplify algebraic expressions.	**Connect to What You Know**	Here, you will use the Distributive Property to make mental math calculations and to combine like terms.

You can use the Distributive Property and mental math to make calculations easier. You can think of some numbers as simple sums or differences.

 Problem 4   **Using the Distributive Property for Mental Math**

Eating Out   Deli sandwiches cost $4.95 each. What is the total cost of 8 sandwiches? Use mental math.

Know	**Need**	**Plan**
• Sandwiches cost $4.95. • You are buying 8 sandwiches.	Total cost of 8 sandwiches	Express $4.95 as a difference and use the Distributive Property.

The total cost is the product of the number of sandwiches you buy, 8, and the cost per sandwich, $4.95.

Think

How can you express decimals as simple sums and differences?

Think of a decimal as the sum or difference of its whole number portion and its decimal portion.

Think of 4.95 as $5 - 0.05$.	$8(4.95) = 8(5 - 0.05)$
Use the Distributive Property.	$= 8(5) - 8(0.05)$
Multiply mentally.	$= 40 - 0.4$
Subtract mentally.	$= 39.6$

The total cost for 8 sandwiches is $39.60.

Got It?   **4.** Julia commutes to work on the train 4 times each week. A round-trip ticket costs $7.25. What is her weekly cost for tickets? Use mental math.

Focus Question How can you simplify an algebraic expression with terms that are alike?

An algebraic expression may have one or more *terms*. In an algebraic expression, a **term** is a number, a variable, or the product of a number and one or more variables. A **constant** is a term that has no variable. A **coefficient** is a numerical factor of a term. Rewrite expressions as sums to identify these parts of an expression.

$6a^2$, $-5ab$, $3b$, and -12 are terms.

$$6a^2 - 5ab + 3b - 12 = 6a^2 + (-5ab) + 3b + (-12)$$

coefficients   constant

In the algebraic expression $6a^2 - 5ab + 3b - 12$, the terms have coefficients of 6, -5, and 3. The term -12 is a constant.

Like terms have the same variable factors. To identify like terms, compare the variable factors of the terms, as shown below.

Terms	$7a$ and $-3a$	$4x^2$ and $12x^2$	$6ab$ and $-2a$	xy^2 and x^2y
Variable Factors	a and a	x^2 and x^2	ab and a	xy^2 and x^2y
Like Terms?	yes	yes	no	no

You can simplify an algebraic expression by combining the parts of the expression that are alike. An algebraic expression in simplest form has no like terms or parentheses.

Not Simplified	**Simplified**
$2(3x - 5 + 4x)$	$14x - 10$

You can use the Distributive Property to help combine like terms. Think of the Distributive Property as $ba + ca = (b + c)a$.

Problem 5 Combining Like Terms

Plan

What terms can you combine?
You can combine any terms that have exactly the same variables with exactly the same exponents.

What is the simplified form of each expression?

A $8x^2 + 2x^2$

Use the Distributive Property. $8x^2 + 2x^2 = (8 + 2)x^2$

Simplify. $= 10x^2$

B $5x - 3 - 3x + 6y + 4$

Rewrite as a sum. $5x - 3 - 3x + 6y + 4 = 5x + (-3) + (-3x) + 6y + 4$

Use the Commutative Property. $= 5x + (-3x) + 6y + (-3) + 4$

Use the Distributive Property. $= (5 - 3)x + 6y + (-3) + 4$

Simplify. $= 2x + 6y + 1$

Got It? 5. What is the simplified form of each expression in parts (a) and (b)?

　　　　a. $-7mn^4 - 5mn^4$　　　　　　**b.** $n + 5 - 17n + 3$

Focus Question How can you simplify an algebraic expression with terms that are alike?

Answer Combine the terms that are alike using either addition or subtraction.

Lesson Check

Do you know HOW?

Rewrite each expression as a sum.

1. $-8x^2 + 3xy - 9x - 3$

2. $2ab - 5ab^2 - 9a^2b$

Tell whether the terms are like terms.

3. $3a$ and $-5a$ **4.** $2xy^2$ and $-x^2y$

Do you UNDERSTAND?

5. Mental Math How can you express 499 to find the product 499×5 using mental math? Explain.

6. Reasoning Is each expression in simplified form? Justify your answer.

  a. $4xy^3 + 5x^3y$

  b. $-(y - 1)$

  c. $5x^2 + 12xy - 3yx$

Practice and Problem-Solving Exercises

A Practice

Simplify each expression.

    ◀ **See Problem 3.**

  7. $-(20 + d)$ **8.** $-(-5 - 4y)$

  9. $-(9 - 7c)$ **10.** $-(-x + 15)$

  11. $-(18a - 17b)$ **12.** $-(2.1c - 4d)$

  13. $-(-m + n + 1)$ **14.** $-(x + 3y - 3)$

Use mental math to find each product.

    ◀ **See Problem 4.**

Guided Practice

15. 5.1×8

To start, rewrite 5.1 as an addition expression.

$5.1 = 5 + 0.1$

  16. 3×7.25 **17.** 299×3

  18. 4×197 **19.** 3.9×6

  20. 5×2.7 **21.** 6×9.1

22. You buy 50 of your favorite songs from a Web site that charges $.99 for each song. What is the cost of 50 songs? Use mental math.

23. The perimeter of a baseball diamond is about 360 ft. If you run 12 laps around the diamond, what is the total distance you run? Use mental math.

24. One hundred and five students see a play. Each ticket costs $45. What is the total amount that the students spend for tickets? Use mental math.

25. Suppose the distance you travel to school is 5 mi. What is the total distance for 197 one-way trips from home to school? Use mental math.

Simplify each expression by combining like terms.

See Problem 5.

Guided Practice

To start, use the Distributive Property.

26. $5t - 7t$

$5t - 7t = t(5 - 7)$

27. $11x + 9x$

28. $8y - 7y$

29. $-n + 4n$

30. $5w^2 + 12w^2$

31. $-4y^2 + 9y^2$

32. $6c - 4 + 2c - 7$

33. $5 - 3x + y + 6$

34. $2n + 1 - 4m - n$

35. $10ab + 2ab^2 - 9ab$

B Apply

36. Exercise The recommended heart rate for exercise, in beats per minute, is given by the expression $0.8(200 - y)$ where y is a person's age in years. Rewrite this expression using the Distributive Property. What is the recommended heart rate for a 20-year-old person? For a 50-year-old person? Use mental math.

Geometry Write an expression in simplified form for the area of each rectangle.

37.

11

$3x + 2$

38.

$5 + 2y$

5

39.

7

$5n - 9$

40. Think About a Plan You are replacing your regular shower head with a water-saving shower head. These shower heads use the amount of water per minute shown. If you take an 8-min shower, how many gallons of water will you save?
- Which would you use to represent water saved each minute, an expression involving addition or an expression involving subtraction?
- How can you use the Distributive Property to find the total amount of water saved?

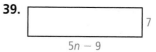

New

2.5 gallons per minute

7 gallons per minute

Simplify each expression.

41. $6yz + 2yz - 8yz$

42. $-2ab + ab + 9ab - 3ab$

43. $-9m^3n + 4m^3n + 5mn$

44. $3(-4cd - 5)$

45. $12x^2y - 8x^2y^2 + 11x^2y - 4x^3y^2 - 9xy^2$

46. $a - \frac{a}{4} + \frac{3}{4}a$

47. Lawn Game You play a game where you throw a pair of connected balls at a structure, as shown at the right. When a pair wraps around a bar, you earn the points shown. You toss 3 pairs, and all of them wrap around a bar. Which expression could represent your total score if a pairs of balls wrap around the blue bar?

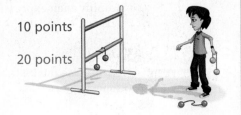

10 points

20 points

Ⓐ $30 + 10a$

Ⓑ $20a + 3 - 10a$

Ⓒ $10a + 20(3 - a)$

Ⓓ $30a + 10$

Standardized Test Prep

SAT/ACT

48. What is the simplified form of the expression $2(7c - 1)$?

Ⓐ $14c - 1$ Ⓑ $9c - 3$ Ⓒ $14c - 2$ Ⓓ $9c - 1$

49. You have already traveled 2.3 mi in a canoe. You continue to travel 0.1 mi each minute. The expression $0.1m + 2.3$ gives the distance traveled, in miles, after m minutes. What is your distance traveled after 25 min?

Ⓕ 2.5 mi   Ⓖ 2.55 mi   Ⓗ 4.8 mi   Ⓘ 27.3 mi

50. The table, at the right, shows the depth that several submersible vehicles can reach. Which of the submersibles are capable of diving to 12,500 ft?

Ⓐ *Clelia* and *Pisces* V

Ⓑ *Alvin, Clelia,* and *Pisces* V

Ⓒ *Alvin* and *Mir* I

Ⓓ *Mir* I

Depth of Submersibles

Submersible	Depth (ft)
Alvin	14,764
Clelia	1000
Mir I	20,000
Pisces V	6280

Source: National Oceanic and Atmospheric Administration

51. Which expression gives the value in dollars of n nickels?

Ⓕ $0.05n$ Ⓖ $0.05 + n$ Ⓗ $0.5n$ Ⓘ $5n$

Mixed Review

Find each product.

See Lesson 1-6.

52. -5^2

53. $\left(-\frac{3}{4}\right)^2$

54. $(-1.2)^2$

Get Ready!   **To prepare for Lesson 1-8, do Exercises 55–57.**

Write a word phrase for each algebraic expression.

See Lesson 1-1.

55. $x - 10$

56. $5x - 18$

57. $\frac{7}{y} + 12$

1-8 An Introduction to Equations

Objective To solve equations using tables and mental math

You can use a pattern to solve this problem, but there's another way.

Dynamic Activity
Using Algebraic Equations

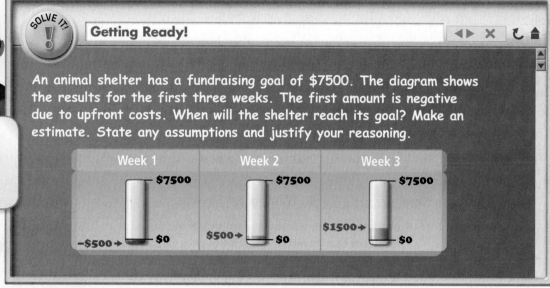

SOLVE IT!

Getting Ready!

An animal shelter has a fundraising goal of $7500. The diagram shows the results for the first three weeks. The first amount is negative due to upfront costs. When will the shelter reach its goal? Make an estimate. State any assumptions and justify your reasoning.

Week 1	Week 2	Week 3
$7500	$7500	$7500
–$500 → $0	$500 → $0	$1500 → $0

You can model the problem in the Solve It by an equation. An **equation** is a mathematical sentence that uses an equal sign (=).

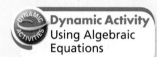

Lesson Vocabulary
• equation
• open sentence
• solution of an equation

Focus Question How do you solve an equation using a table and mental math?

An equation is true if the expressions on either side of the equal sign are equal $(1 + 1 = 2, x + x = 2x)$. An equation is false if the expressions on either side of the equal sign are not equal $(1 + 1 = 3, x + x = 3x)$. An equation is an **open sentence** if it contains one or more variables and may be true or false depending on the values of its variables.

Plan

How do you classify an equation?

If an equation contains only numbers, simplify the expression on each side to determine if the expressions are equal. If there is a variable in the equation, it is open.

Problem 1 Classifying Equations

Is the equation *true*, *false*, or *open*? Explain.

Ⓐ $24 + 18 = 20 + 22$ True, because both expressions equal 42.

Ⓑ $7 \cdot 8 = 54$ False, because $7 \cdot 8 = 56$ and $56 \neq 54$.

Ⓒ $2x - 14 = 54$ Open, because there is a variable.

 **Got It?** **1.** Is the equation *true*, *false*, or *open*? Explain.
   a. $3y + 6 = 5y - 8$ **b.** $16 - 7 = 4 + 5$ **c.** $32 \div 8 = 2 \cdot 3$

A **solution of an equation** containing a variable is a value of the variable that makes the equation true.

Problem 2 Identifying Solutions of an Equation

Plan

How can you tell whether a number is a solution of an equation?
Substitute the number for the variable in the equation. Simplify each side to see whether you get a true statement.

Is $x = 6$ a solution of the equation $32 = 2x + 12$?

$$32 = 2x + 12$$

Substitute 6 for x.　　$32 \stackrel{?}{=} 2(6) + 12$

Simplify.　　　　　　$32 \neq 24$

No, $x = 6$ is not a solution of the equation $32 = 2x + 12$.

 Got It? 2. Is $m = \frac{1}{2}$ a solution of the equation $6m - 8 = -5$?

In real-world problems, the word *is* can indicate equality. You can represent some real-world situations using an equation.

Problem 3 Writing an Equation

Multiple Choice An art student wants to make a model of the Mayan Great Ball Court in Chichén Itzá, Mexico. The length of the court is 2.4 times its width. The length of the student's model is 54 in. What should the width of the model be?

Ⓐ 2.4 in.　　　　Ⓒ 22.5 in.

Ⓑ 11.25 in.　　　Ⓓ 129.6 in.

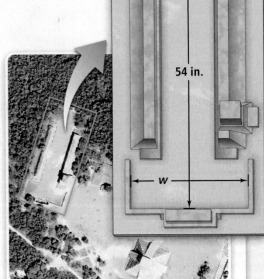

54 in.

w

Satellite view of Chichén Itzá

Plan

Why do you need to test each answer choice?
You should test each answer choice in case you made a calculation error. If you get two correct answers, then you know you need to double-check your work.

Relate　　The length　is　2.4　times　the width

Define　Let　w　= the width of the model.

Write　　54　=　2.4　·　w

Test each answer choice in the equation to find whether it is a solution.

Check A:	Check B:	Check C:	Check D:
$54 = 2.4w$	$54 = 2.4w$	$54 = 2.4w$	$54 = 2.4w$
$54 \stackrel{?}{=} 2.4(2.4)$	$54 \stackrel{?}{=} 2.4(11.25)$	$54 \stackrel{?}{=} 2.4(22.5)$	$54 \stackrel{?}{=} 2.4(129.6)$
$54 \neq 5.76$	$54 \neq 27$	$54 = 54$ ✔	$54 \neq 311.04$

The correct answer is C.

 Got It? 3. The length of the ball court at La Venta is 14 times the height of its walls. Write an equation that you can use to find the height of a model that has a length of 49 cm.

Problem 4 Using Mental Math to Find Solutions

Plan

How can you find the solution of an equation?
You can use mental math to find a value that makes the equation true.

What is the solution of each equation? Use mental math.

		Think	Solution	Check
A $x + 8 = 12$		What number plus 8 equals 12?	4	$4 + 8 = 12$ ✔
B $\frac{a}{8} = 9$		What number divided by 8 equals 9?	72	$\frac{72}{8} = 9$ ✔

 Got It? 4. What is the solution of $12 - y = 3$? Use mental math.

 Problem 5 Using a Table to Find a Solution

Think

How can you start?
You can use mental math to quickly check values like 0, 1, and 10. Use these results to choose a reasonable starting value for your table.

What is the solution of $5n + 8 = 48$? Use a table.

Make a table of values. Choose a starting value using mental math. $5(1) + 8 = 13$ and $5(10) + 8 = 58$, so 1 is too low and 10 is too high.

Try $n = 5$ and $n = 6$.

n	$5n + 8$	Value of $5n + 8$
5	$5(5) + 8$	33
6	$5(6) + 8$	38
7	$5(7) + 8$	43
8	$5(8) + 8$	48

The value of $5n + 8$ increases as n increases, so try greater values of n.

When $n = 8$, $5n + 8 = 48$. So the solution is 8.

 Got It? 5. a. What is the solution of $25 - 3p = 55$? Use a table.
    b. What is a reasonable starting value to solve part (a)? Explain your reasoning.

 Problem 6 Estimating a Solution

What is an estimate of the solution of $-9x - 5 = 28$? Use a table.

To estimate the solution, find the integer values of x between which the solution must lie. Start by substituting $x = 0$ and $x = 1$: $-9(0) - 5 = -5$ and $-9(1) - 5 = -14$. If you try values of $x > 1$, the value of $-9x - 5$ gets farther from 28.

Think

Can identifying a pattern help you make an estimate?
Yes. Identify how the value of the expression changes as you substitute for the variable. Use the pattern you find to work *toward* the desired value.

Try lesser values, such as $x = -1$ and $x = -2$.

x	$-9x - 5$	Value of $-9x - 5$
-1	$-9(-1) - 5$	4
-2	$-9(-2) - 5$	13
-3	$-9(-3) - 5$	22
-4	$-9(-4) - 5$	31

Now the values of $-9x - 5$ are getting closer to 28.

28 is between 22 and 31, so the solution is between -3 and -4.

 Got It? 6. What is an estimate of the solution of $3x + 3 = -22$? Use a table.

Focus Question How do you solve an equation using a table and mental math?

Answer Use mental math to test values so that you choose a reasonable value to start a table. Then use the table to find the value that makes the expressions in the equation equal.

Lesson Check

Do you know HOW?

1. Is $y = -9$ a solution of $y + 1 = 8$?

2. What is the solution of $x - 3 = 12$? Use mental math.

3. **Reading** You can read 1.5 pages for every page your friend can read. Write an equation that relates the number of pages p that you can read and the number of pages n that your friend can read.

Do you UNDERSTAND?

4. **Vocabulary** Give an example of an equation that is true, an equation that is false, and an open equation.

5. **Open-Ended** Write an open equation using one variable and division.

6. **Compare and Contrast** Use two different methods to find the solution of the equation $x + 4 = 13$. Which method do you prefer? Explain.

Practice and Problem-Solving Exercises

 Practice
Tell whether each equation is *true, false,* or *open.* Explain.

See Problem 1.

7. $85 + (-10) = 95$

8. $225 \div t - 4 = 6.4$

9. $29 - 34 = -5$

10. $-8(-2) - 7 = 14 - 5$

11. $4(-4) \div (-8)6 = -3 + 5(3)$

12. $91 \div (-7) - 5 = 35 \div 7 + 3$

13. $4a - 3b = 21$

14. $14 + 7 + (-1) = 21$

15. $5x + 7 = 17$

Tell whether the given number is a solution of each equation.

See Problem 2.

Guided Practice

To start, substitute 3 for x.

16. $8x + 5 = 29; 3$

$8(3) + 5 \stackrel{?}{=} 29$

17. $5b + 1 = 16; -3$

18. $6 = 2n - 8; 7$

19. $2 = 10 - 4y; 2$

20. $9a - (-72) = 0; -8$

21. $14 = \frac{1}{3}x + 5; 27$

22. $\frac{3}{2}t + 2 = 4; \frac{2}{3}$

Write an equation for each sentence.

See Problem 3.

23. The sum of $4x$ and -3 is 8.

24. The product of 9 and the sum of 6 and x is 1.

25. **Training** An athlete trains for 115 min each day for as many days as possible. Write an equation that relates the number of days d that the athlete spends training when the athlete trains for 690 min.

26. **Salary** The manager of a restaurant earns $2.25 more each hour than the host of the restaurant. Write an equation that relates the amount h that the host earns each hour when the manager earns $11.50 each hour.

Use mental math to find the solution of each equation.

◀ See Problem 4.

27. $x - 3 = 10$

28. $4 = 7 - y$

29. $18 + d = 24$

30. $\frac{x}{7} = 5$

31. $20a = 100$

32. $13c = 26$

Use a table to find the solution of each equation.

◀ See Problem 5.

33. $2t - 1 = 11$

To start, estimate the value of t using mental math.

$2(2) - 1 = 3$ and $2(10) - 1 = 19$.
So, t must be between 2 and 10.

Make a table of values starting with $t = 4$.

t	$2t - 1$	Value of $2t - 1$
4	$2(4) - 1$	7
5	$2(5) - 1$	■
6	$2(6) - 1$	■
7	$2(7) - 1$	■

34. $5x + 3 = 23$

35. $0 = 4 + 2y$

36. $8a - 10 = 38$

37. $12 = 6 - 3b$

38. $8 - 5w = -12$

39. $\frac{1}{2}x - 5 = -1$

Use a table to find two consecutive integers between which the solution lies.

◀ See Problem 6.

40. $6x + 5 = 81$

41. $3.3 = 1.5 - 0.4y$

42. $-115b + 80 = -489$

B Apply

43. Bicycle Sales In the United States, the number y (in millions) of bicycles sold with wheel sizes of 20 in. or greater can be modeled by the equation $y = 0.3x + 15$, where x is the number of years since 1981. In what year were about 22 million bicycles sold?

44. Error Analysis A student checked whether $d = -2$ is a solution of $-3d + (-4) = 2$, as shown. Describe and correct the student's error.

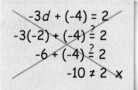

45. Writing What are the differences between an expression and an equation? Does a mathematical expression have a solution? Explain.

46. Basketball A total of 1254 people attend a basketball team's championship game. There are six identical benches in the gymnasium. About how many people would you expect each bench to seat?

Find the solution of each equation using mental math or a table. If the solution lies between two consecutive integers, identify these integers.

47. $x + 4 = -2$

48. $4m + 1 = 9$

49. $-3 + t = 19$

50. $5a - 4 = -16$

51. $9 = 4 + (-y)$

52. $17 = 6 + 2x$

53. Think About a Plan Polar researchers drill into an ice sheet. The drill is below the surface at the location shown. The drill advances at a rate of 67 m/h. About how many hours will it take the drill to reach a depth of 300m?
- What equation models this situation?
- What integers do you need?

54. Deliveries The equation $25 + 0.25p = c$ gives the cost c in dollars that a store charges to deliver an appliance that weighs p pounds. Use the equation and a table to find the weight of an appliance that costs $55 to deliver.

Standardized Test Prep

SAT/ACT

55. Which equation is false?

Ⓐ $\frac{2}{3} + 1 \cdot \frac{1}{2} = \frac{7}{6}$ Ⓑ $84 - 25 = 59$ Ⓒ $51 - (-57) = -6$ Ⓓ $3(-3) + 3 = -6$

56. Which equation has a solution of 4?

Ⓕ $0 = 8 + 2y$ Ⓖ $5x + 3 = 23$ Ⓗ $8a - 10 = 42$ Ⓘ $2t - 1 = 9$

57. At 7 P.M., the temperature is 6.8°C. Over the next 4 h, the temperature changes by the amounts shown in the table. What is the final temperature?

Ⓐ −12.6°C   Ⓒ 3.9°C

Ⓑ 1°C   Ⓓ 5.8°C

Temperature Changes

Time	Change in Temperature
8 P.M.	−0.4°C
9 P.M.	−1.2°C
10 P.M.	−1.3°C
11 P.M.	−2.9°C

58. Monique has ordered 32 pizzas to serve at the student government picnic. If each person will get $\frac{1}{4}$ of a pizza, how many people will she be able to serve?

Ⓕ 8   Ⓖ 32

Ⓗ 64   Ⓘ 128

Mixed Review

Use the Distributive Property to simplify each expression.   🔊 See Lesson 1-7.

59. $7(4 + 2y)$ **60.** $-6(3b + 11)$ **61.** $(8 + 2t)(-2.1)$ **62.** $(-1 + 5x)5$

Evaluate each expression for $m = 4$, $n = -1$, and $p = -\frac{1}{2}$.   🔊 See Lesson 1-6.

63. $2m - 2n$ **64.** $pm - n$ **65.** $6mp$ **66.** $7m \div (-4n)$

67. $8p - (-5n)$ **68.** $-2m - n$ **69.** $-1.5m \div 6p$ **70.** $3n^2 \cdot (-10p^2)$

Get Ready! **To prepare for Lesson 1-9, do Exercises 71–74.**

Use a table to find the solution of each equation.   🔊 See Lesson 1-8.

71. $4x - 1 = 7$ **72.** $0 = 10 + 10y$ **73.** $5\frac{1}{2} = 7 - \frac{1}{2}b$ **74.** $3t - (-5.4) = 5.4$

Using Tables to Solve Equations

You can solve equations by making a table using a graphing calculator.

Activity

A raft floats down river at 9 mi/h. The distance y the raft travels can be modeled by the equation $y = 9x$, where x is the number of hours. Make a table on a graphing calculator to find how long it takes the raft to travel 153 mi.

Step 1 Enter the equation $y = 9x$ into a graphing calculator.

• Press (y=). The cursor appears next to Y_1.

• Press 9 (x,t,θ,n) to enter $y = 9x$.

Step 2 Access the table setup feature.

• Press (2nd) (window).

• TblStart represents the starting value in the table. Enter 1 for TblStart.

• $\triangle$Tbl represents the change in the value of x as you go from row to row. Enter 1 for $\triangle$Tbl.

Step 3 Display the table and find the solution.

• Press (2nd) (graph). Use ▽, to scroll through the table until you find the x-value for which $y = 153$. This x-value is 17. It takes the raft 17 h to travel 153 mi.

Exercises

Solve each problem by making a table on a graphing calculator.

1. A town places 560 T of waste in a landfill each month. The amount y of waste in the landfill can be modeled by the equation $y = 560x$, where x is the number of months. How many months will it take to accumulate 11,200 T of waste in the landfill?

2. A coupon gives $15 off a customer's purchase. The total amount y of the customer's purchase can be modeled by $y = x - 15$, where x is the amount of the purchase before the coupon is used. A customer using the coupon pays $17 for a shirt. What was the original price of the shirt?

Graphing in the Coordinate Plane

Two number lines that intersect at right angles form a **coordinate plane.** The horizontal axis is the **x-axis** and the vertical axis is the **y-axis.** The axes intersect at the **origin** and divide the coordinate plane into four sections called **quadrants.**

An **ordered pair** of numbers names the location of a point in the plane. These numbers are the **coordinates** of the point. Point B has coordinates $(-3, 4)$.

| The first coordinate is the x-coordinate. | $(-3, 4)$ | The second coordinate is the y-coordinate. |

To reach the point (x, y), you use the x-coordinate to tell how far to move right (positive) or left (negative) from the origin. Then you use the y-coordinate to tell how far to move up (positive) or down (negative).

Activity

Play against a partner using two number cubes and a coordinate grid. One cube represents positive numbers and the other cube represents negative numbers.

- During each turn, a player rolls both cubes and adds the numbers to find an x-coordinate. Both cubes are rolled a second time, and the numbers are added to find the y-coordinate. The player graphs the resulting ordered pair on the grid.

- The two players take turns, with each player using a different color to graph points. If an ordered pair has already been graphed, the player does not graph a point, and the turn is over.

- Play ends after each player has completed 10 turns. The player with the most points graphed in a quadrant scores 1 for Quadrant I, 2 for Quadrant II, and so on. Points graphed on either axis do not count. If both players graph an equal number of points in a quadrant, both players score 0 for that quadrant.

Exercises

Describe a pair of number cube rolls that would result in a point plotted at the given location.

1. $(-3, 4)$ **2.** $(4, -3)$ **3.** Quadrant III   **4.** the origin

1-9 Patterns, Equations, and Graphs

Objective To use tables, equations, and graphs to describe relationships

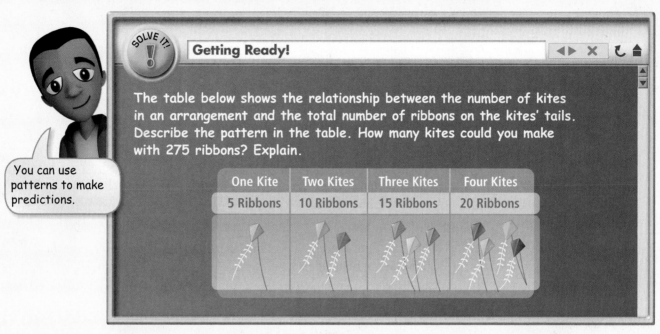

SOLVE IT!

Getting Ready!

The table below shows the relationship between the number of kites in an arrangement and the total number of ribbons on the kites' tails. Describe the pattern in the table. How many kites could you make with 275 ribbons? Explain.

One Kite	Two Kites	Three Kites	Four Kites
5 Ribbons	10 Ribbons	15 Ribbons	20 Ribbons

You can use patterns to make predictions.

Lesson Vocabulary
- solution of an equation
- inductive reasoning

In the Solve It, you may have described the pattern using words. You can also use an equation or a graph to describe a pattern.

Focus Question Why is it useful to describe a relationship using a table, an equation, and a graph?

Sometimes the value of one quantity can be found if you know the value of another quantity. You can represent the relationship between the quantities in different ways, including tables, equations, and graphs.

You can use an equation with two variables to represent the relationship between two varying quantities. A **solution of an equation** with two variables x and y is any ordered pair (x, y) that makes the equation true.

Plan

How can you tell whether an ordered pair is a solution?
Replace x with the first value in the ordered pair and y with the second value in the ordered pair. Is the resulting equation true?

Problem 1 Identifying Solutions of a Two-Variable Equation

Is (3, 10) a solution of the equation $y = 4x$?

Write the equation.	$y = 4x$
Substitute 3 for x and 10 for y.	$10 \stackrel{?}{=} 4 \cdot 3$
So, (3, 10) is not a solution of $y = 4x$.	$10 \neq 12$

Got It? 1. Is the ordered pair a solution of the equation $y = 4x$?
    a. (5, 20)   **b.** $(-20, -5)$

You can represent the same relationship between two variables in several different ways.

Problem 2 Using a Table, an Equation, and a Graph

Ages Both Carrie and her sister Kim were born on October 25, but Kim was born 2 years before Carrie. How can you represent the relationship between Carrie's age and Kim's age in different ways?

Know
Kim was born 2 years before Carrie.

Need
Different ways to represent the relationship

Plan
Use a table, an equation, and a graph.

Step 1 Make a table.

Carrie's and Kim's Ages (years)										
Carrie's Age	1	2	3	4	5	6	7	8	9	10
Kim's Age	3	4	5	6	7	8	9	10	11	12

Step 2 Write an equation.

Let x = Carrie's age. Let y = Kim's age. From the table, you can see that y is always 2 greater than x.

So $y = x + 2$.

Think

Why does it make sense to connect the points on the graph?
A person's age can be any positive real number, and the ages of the girls are always 2 years apart. So every point on the line makes sense in this situation.

Step 3 Draw a graph.

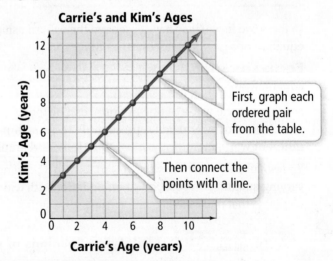

Carrie's and Kim's Ages

First, graph each ordered pair from the table.

Then connect the points with a line.

Got It? 2. a. Will runs 6 laps before Megan joins him at the track. Then they run together at the same pace. How can you represent the relationship between the number of laps Will runs and the number of laps Megan runs in different ways? Use a table, an equation, and a graph.

b. Reasoning Describe how the graph in Problem 2 above would change if the difference in ages were 5 years instead of 2 years.

Inductive reasoning is the process of reaching a conclusion based on an observed pattern. You can use inductive reasoning to predict values.

 Problem 3 Extending a Pattern

The table shows the relationship between the number of blue tiles and the total number of tiles in each figure. Extend the pattern. What is the total number of tiles in a figure with 8 blue tiles?

Tiles

Number of Blue Tiles, x	Total Number of Tiles, y
1	9
2	18
3	27
4	36
5	45

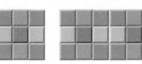 

Think

Should you connect the points on the graph with a solid line?
No. The number of tiles must be a whole number. Use a dotted line to see the trend.

Method 1 Draw a graph.

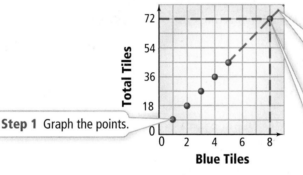

Number of Tiles

Step 1 Graph the points.

Step 2 The points fall on a line. Extend the pattern with a dashed line.

Step 3 Find the point on the line with x-coordinate 8. The y-coordinate of this point is 72.

The total number of tiles is 72.

Method 2 Write an equation.

The total number of tiles is 9 times the number of blue tiles. $y = 9x$

Substitute 8 for x. $= 9(8)$

Simplify. $= 72$

The total number of tiles is 72.

Got It? **3.** Use the tile figure from Problem 3.
  a. Make a table showing the number of orange tiles and the total number of tiles in each figure. How many tiles in all will be in a figure with 24 orange tiles?
  b. Make a table showing the number of blue tiles and the number of yellow tiles in each figure. How many yellow tiles will be in a figure with 24 blue tiles?

Focus Question Why is it useful to describe a relationship using a table, an equation, and a graph?

Answer You can calculate the x- and y-values that make the relationship true using an equation and a table. A graph lets you see the relationship visually.

Lesson Check

Do you know HOW?

1. Is $(2, 4)$ a solution of the equation $y = x - 2$?

2. Is $(-3, -9)$ a solution of the equation $y = 3x$?

3. Drinks at the fair cost $2.50. Use a table, an equation, and a graph to represent the relationship between the number of drinks bought and the cost.

4. **Exercise** On a treadmill, you burn 11 Cal in 1 min, 22 Cal in 2 min, 33 Cal in 3 min, and so on. How many Calories do you burn in 10 min?

Do you UNDERSTAND?

5. **Vocabulary** Describe the difference between inductive reasoning and deductive reasoning.

6. **Compare and Contrast** How is writing an equation to represent a situation involving two variables similar to writing an equation to represent a situation involving only one variable? How are they different?

7. **Reasoning** Which of $(3, 5)$, $(4, 6)$, $(5, 7)$, and $(6, 8)$ are solutions of $y = x + 2$? What is the pattern in the solutions of $y = x + 2$?

Practice and Problem-Solving Exercises

Ⓐ Practice Tell whether the given equation has the ordered pair as a solution. ◀ See Problem 1.

Guided Practice

8. $y = 1 - x; (2, 1)$

To start, substitute 2 for x and 1 for y.

$1 = 1 - 2$

9. $y = x + 6; (0, 6)$

10. $y = -x + 3; (4, 1)$

11. $y = 6x; (3, 16)$

12. $-x = y; (-3.1, 3.1)$

13. $y = -4x; (-2, 8)$

14. $\frac{x}{5} = y; (-10, -2)$

Use a table, an equation, and a graph to represent each relationship. ◀ See Problem 2.

15. Ty is 3 years younger than Bea.

16. The number of checkers is 24 times the number of checkerboards.

17. The number of triangles is $\frac{1}{3}$ the number of sides.

18. Gavin makes $8.50 for each lawn he mows.

Use the table to draw a graph and answer the question. ◀ See Problem 3.

19. The table shows the height in inches of stacks of tires. Extend the pattern. What is the height of a stack of 7 tires?

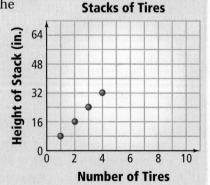

Stacks of Tires

Number of Tires, x	Height of Stack, y
1	8
2	16
3	24
4	32

Guided Practice

To start, plot the points in the table.

Use the table to write an equation and answer the question.

20. The table shows the length in centimeters of a scarf you are knitting. Suppose the pattern continues. How long is the scarf after 8 days?

Knitted Scarf

Number of Days, x	Length of Scarf, y
1	12.5
2	14.5
3	16.5
4	18.5

21. The table shows the heights, in inches, of trees after they have been planted. What is the height of a tree after it has been planted that is 64 in. tall in its pot?

Tree Height

Height in Pot, x	Height Without Pot, y
30	18
36	24
42	30
48	36

22. Patterns Make a table and draw a graph to show the relationship between the number of houses and the number of windows. What is the number of windows in 9 houses?

B **Apply**

Tell whether the given ordered pair is a solution of the equation.

23. $y = 2x + 7; (-2, 3)$

24. $y = -4x - 3; (0, 3)$

25. $y = 5x - 8; (2, -2)$

26. $y = 9 - 2x; (-2, 5)$

27. $-\frac{1}{4}x + 6 = y; (2, 4)$

28. $y = 3 - \frac{x}{5}; \left(\frac{1}{2}, \frac{1}{10}\right)$

29. $y = 11 - 2x; (5, 1)$

30. $1.9x - 4 = y; (2, 0.2)$

31. $y = -1.2x - 2.6; (3.5, 6.8)$

32. Think About a Plan The table shows how long it takes Kayla to learn new songs. How many hours does Kayla need to practice to learn 9 songs?

Kayla's Piano Practice

Hours, h	Songs Learned, s
1.5	1
3.0	2
4.5	3
6.0	4

- From row to row, how much does the number of hours h increase? How much does the number of songs s increase?
- By how many rows would you need to extend the table to solve the problem?

33. Error Analysis A student reasons that $(4, 1)$ is a solution of $y = 3x + 1$ because $x = 1$ when $y = 4$. Explain and correct the student's error.

34. Reasoning Savannah looks at the table shown and says the equation $y = x - 6$ represents the pattern. Mary says $y = x + (-6)$ represents the pattern. Who is correct? Explain.

x	y
0	−6
1	−5
2	−4
3	−3

35. Open-Ended Think of a real-world pattern. Describe the pattern using words and an equation with two variables. Define the variables.

36. Air Travel Use the table below. How long will the jet take to travel 5390 miles?

Passenger Jet Travel				
Hours, h	1	2	3	4
Miles, m	490	980	1470	1960

Standardized Test Prep

SAT/ACT

37. Use the graph. What is the total price for 4 bags of seeds?

  Ⓐ $.50   Ⓒ $4.00

  Ⓑ $2.00   Ⓓ $8.00

38. What is the simplified form of the expression $-5(n - 2)$?

  Ⓕ $-7n$ Ⓗ $-5n + 10$

  Ⓖ $-5n - 2$ Ⓘ $n + 10$

39. If $a = 3$ and $b = -2$, what does $-2b - a$ equal?

  Ⓐ -9 Ⓑ -7 Ⓒ -1 Ⓓ 1

40. What is the value of -3^4?

  Ⓕ -81 Ⓖ -12 Ⓗ 12 Ⓘ 81

Mixed Review

Tell whether the given number is a solution of each equation.   ◀ See Lesson 1-8.

41. $3x + 7 = 10; 0$ **42.** $80 = 4a; 20$ **43.** $10 = -5t; -2$

Give an example that illustrates each property.   ◀ See Lesson 1-4.

44. Commutative Property of Addition   **45.** Associative Property of Multiplication

46. Identity Property of Multiplication   **47.** Zero Property of Addition

Get Ready! **To prepare for Lesson 2-1, do Exercises 48–55.**   ◀ See Lesson 1-5.

Find each sum or difference.

48. $12 + (-3)$ **49.** $-7 + 4$ **50.** $-8 + (-6)$ **51.** $-42 + 15$

52. $32 - (-8)$ **53.** $-18 - 12$ **54.** $-15 - (-14)$ **55.** $-76 - 5$

Pull It **All Together**

BIG idea Variable

You can use variables to represent quantities that are unknown or vary and to write expressions and equations.

Task 1

Solve. Show all of your work and explain your steps.

A riding-stable manager is planning a nutritional diet for 6 horses. The manager finds the table below in a guide about horse health. The cost of 1000 Calories of horse feed is $.15. What is the cost per day to feed the 6 horses? (*Hint:* First, try writing an expression for the number of daily Calories needed for h horses.)

Calories Needed				
Number of Horses	1	2	3	4
Daily Calories Needed	15,000	30,000	45,000	60,000

Task 2

Use the table at the right to complete each part.

- **a.** Copy the table. Extend the table by writing expressions for y when $x = 5, 6$, and 7.
- **b.** Simplify each expression for y in your table from part (a). What pattern do you notice in the simplified expressions?
- **c.** Write an equation that relates x and y. Use your equation to find the value of y when $x = 15$.

x	y
1	1
2	$1 + 2$
3	$1 + 2 + 4$
4	$1 + 2 + 4 + 8$

BIG idea Properties

The properties of real numbers describe relationships that are always true. The properties of real numbers are true in both arithmetic and algebra. You can use them to rewrite expressions.

Task 3

Solve. Show all of your work and explain your steps.

You are buying gifts for 10 people. You decide to buy each person either a CD or a DVD. A CD costs $12 and a DVD costs $20.

- **a.** Let $c =$ the number of CDs you decide to buy. What is an expression in terms of c for the number of DVDs you buy?
- **b.** What is an expression in terms of c for the cost of the CDs? For the cost of the DVDs?
- **c.** Write and simplify an expression in terms of c for the *total* cost of all the gifts you buy. What properties of real numbers did you use to simplify the expression?

Connecting **BIG** ideas and Answering the Essential Questions

1 Variable
You can use variables to represent quantities and to write algebraic expressions and equations.

Variables and Expressions (Lesson 1-1)
a number n plus 3
$n + 3$

$\vdash$----- ? -----$\dashv$

| n | 3 |

Patterns and Equations (Lessons 1-8 and 1-9)
1 variable: $x + 3 = 5$
2 variables: $y = 2x$

2 Properties
The properties of real numbers describe relationships that are always true. You can use them to rewrite expressions.

Operations With Real Numbers (Lessons 1-2, 1-5, and 1-6)
2^5 $0 \cdot 3$ $2 + (-5)$ $7(-3)$

Properties (Lessons 1-4 and 1-7)
$a \cdot b = b \cdot a$
$(a \cdot b) \cdot c = a \cdot (b \cdot c)$
$a(b + c) = ab + ac$

Chapter Vocabulary

- absolute value (p. 38)
- additive inverse (p. 39)
- coefficient (p. 57)
- constant (p. 57)
- Distributive Property (p. 52)

- equation (p. 61)
- inductive reasoning (p. 71)
- like terms (p. 57)

- multiplicative inverse (p. 47)
- open sentence (p. 61)
- opposite (p. 39)
- reciprocal (p. 48)

- solution of an equation (pp. 62, 69)
- term (p. 57)

Choose the correct term to complete each sentence.

1. The sum of a number and its __?__ equals zero.

2. You can simplify an expression by combining __?__ .

3. __?__ is a number's distance from zero on a number line.

4. When you make conclusions based on patterns you observe, you use __?__ .

5. A number and its opposite are called __?__ .

6. __?__ have the same variable factors.

7. An equation that contains one or more variables is called an __?__ .

8. A __?__ is a numerical factor of a term.

1-5 and 1-6 Operations with Real Numbers

Quick Review

To add numbers with different signs, find the difference of their **absolute values**. Then use the sign of the addend with the greater absolute value.

$$3 + (-4) = -(4 - 3) = -1$$

To subtract, add the opposite.

$$9 - (-5) = 9 + 5 = 14$$

The product or quotient of two numbers with the same sign is positive: $5 \cdot 5 = 25 \qquad (-5) \cdot (-5) = 25$

The product or quotient of two numbers with different signs is negative: $6 \cdot (-6) = -36 \qquad -36 \div 6 = -6$

Example

Cave explorers descend to a site that has an elevation of -1.3 mi. (Negative elevation means below sea level.) The explorers descend another 0.6 mi before they stop to rest. What is the elevation at their resting point?

$$-1.3 + (-0.6) = -1.9$$

The elevation at their resting point is -1.9 mi.

Exercises

Find each sum. Use a number line.

9. $1 + 4$ **10.** $3 + (-8)$ **11.** $-2 + (-7)$

Simplify each expression.

12. $-5.6 + 7.4$ **13.** -12^2

14. $-5(-8)$ **15.** $4.5 \div (-1.5)$

16. $-13 + (-6)$ **17.** $-9 - (-12)$

18. $(-2)(-2)(-2)$ **19.** $-54 \div (-0.9)$

Evaluate each expression for $p = 5$ and $q = -3$.

20. $-3q + 7$ **21.** $-(4q)$ **22.** $q - 8$

23. $5p - 6$ **24.** $-(2p)^2$ **25.** $q + p$

26. $7q - 7p$ **27.** $(pq)^2$ **28.** $2q \div (4p)$

1-7 The Distributive Property

Quick Review

Terms with exactly the same variable factors are **like terms**. You can combine like terms and use the Distributive Property to simplify expressions.

Distributive Property $a(b + c) = ab + ac$

$a(b - c) = ab - ac$

Example

Simplify $7t + (3 - 4t)$.

Use the Commutative Property. $7t + (3 - 4t) = 7t + (-4t + 3)$

Use the Associative Property. $= (7t + (-4t)) + 3$

Use the Distributive Property. $= (7 + (-4))t + 3$

Simplify. $= 3t + 3$

Exercises

Simplify each expression.

29. $-2(7 - a)$ **30.** $(-j + 8)\frac{1}{2}$ **31.** $3v^2 - 2v^2$

32. $2(3y - 3)$ **33.** $(6y - 1)\frac{1}{4}$ **34.** $(24 - 24y)\frac{1}{4}$

35. $6y - 3 - 5y$ **36.** $\frac{1}{3}y + 6 - \frac{2}{3}y$ **37.** $-ab^2 - ab^2$

38. Music Each of the 95 members of the jazz club pay $30 to go see a jazz performance. What is the total cost of tickets? Use mental math.

39. Reasoning Are $8x^2y$ and $-5yx^2$ like terms? Explain.

1-8 An Introduction to Equations

Quick Review

An **equation** can be true or false, or it can be an **open sentence** with a variable. A **solution** of an equation is the value (or values) of the variable that makes the equation true.

Example

Is $c = 6$ a solution of the equation $25 = 3c - 2$?

Write the original equation. $25 = 3c - 2$

Substitute 6 for c. $25 \stackrel{?}{=} 3 \cdot 6 - 2$

Simplify. $25 \neq 16$

No, $c = 6$ is not a solution of the equation $25 = 3c - 2$.

Exercises

Tell whether the given number is a solution of each equation.

40. $17 = 37 + 4f; f = -5$ **41.** $-3a^2 = 27; a = 3$

42. $3b - 9 = 21; b = -10$ **43.** $-2b + 4 = 3; b = \frac{1}{2}$

Use a table to find or estimate the solution of each equation.

44. $x + (-2) = 8$ **45.** $3m - 13 = 24$

46. $4t - 2 = 9$ **47.** $6b - 3 = 17$

1-9 Patterns, Equations, and Graphs

Quick Review

You can represent the relationship between two varying quantities in different ways, including tables, equations, and graphs. A **solution of an equation** with two variables is an **ordered pair** (x, y) that makes the equation true.

Example

Bo makes $15 more per week than Sue. How can you represent this relationship with an equation and a table?

First write an equation. Let $b =$ Bo's earnings. Let $s =$ Sue's earnings. Bo makes $15 more than Sue, so $b = s + 15$. You can use the equation to make a table for $s = 25, 50, 75,$ and 100.

Sue's Earnings (s)	25	50	75	100
Bo's Earnings (b)	40	65	90	115

Exercises

Tell whether the given ordered pair is a solution of each equation.

48. $3x + 5 = y; (1, 8)$

49. $y = -2(x + 3); (-6, 0)$

50. $y = (x - 1.2)(-3); (0, 1.2)$

51. $10 - 5x = y; (-4, 10)$

52. Describe the pattern in the table using words, an equation, and a graph. Extend the pattern for $x = 5, 6,$ and 7.

x	y
1	15
2	25
3	35
4	45

Chapter Test for Part B

Do you know HOW?

1. Write an algebraic expression for the phrase *the quotient of n and 6.*

2. Write a word phrase for $-12t + 2$.

3. Evaluate the expression $-(pq)^2 \div (-8)$ for $p = 2$ and $q = 4$.

4. **Dance** The table shows how the total cost of dance classes at a studio depends on the number of classes you take. Write a rule in words and as an algebraic expression to model the relationship.

Dance Classes

Number of Classes	Total Cost
1	$(1 \times 15) + 20$
2	$(2 \times 15) + 20$
3	$(3 \times 15) + 20$

Simplify each expression.

5. $-20 - (-5) \cdot (-2^2)$

6. $\left(-\frac{1}{4}\right)^3$

7. $-\frac{7ab}{a}, a \neq 0$

8. $-|-25|$

9. $\sqrt{\frac{16}{25}}$

10. Is each statement true or false? If false, give a counterexample.

    a. For all real numbers a and b, $a \cdot b$ is equivalent to $b \cdot a$.

    b. For all real numbers a and b, $a(b \cdot c) = ab \cdot ac$

11. Is the ordered pair $(2, -5)$ a solution to the equation $4 + 3x = -2y$? Show your work.

12. Order the numbers $-\frac{7}{8}, \frac{7}{4}, -1\frac{4}{5}$, and $-\frac{13}{16}$ from least to greatest.

13. **Soccer** There are t teams in a soccer league. Each team has 11 players. Make a table, write an equation, and draw a graph to describe the total number of players, p, in the league. How many players are on 17 teams?

Simplify each expression.

14. $5x^2 - x^2$

15. $12 \div \left(-\frac{3}{4}\right)$

16. $-(-2 + 6t)$

17. $-3[b - (-7)]$

18. Name the subset(s) of the real numbers to which each number belongs.

    a. -2.324 b. $\sqrt{46}$

19. Identify each property.

    a. $a(b + c) = ab + ac$

    b. $(a + b) + c = a + (b + c)$

Do you UNDERSTAND?

20. Is the set of positive integers the same as the set of nonnegative integers? Explain.

21. **Error Analysis** Find and correct the error in the work shown at the right.

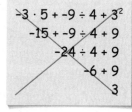

22. Is the following statement true or false? If the product of three numbers is negative, then all the numbers are negative. If false, give a counterexample.

23. **Reasoning** You notice that $10°C = 50°F$, $20°C = 68°F$, and $30°C = 86°F$. Use inductive reasoning to predict the value in degrees Fahrenheit of $40°F$.

24. **Reasoning** When is the absolute value of a difference equal to the difference of the absolute values? Explain.

TIPS FOR SUCCESS

Some test questions ask you to enter a numerical answer on a grid. In this textbook, you will record answers on a grid like the one shown below.

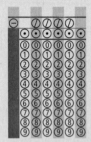

TIP 1

An answer may be either a fraction or a decimal. If an answer is a mixed number, rewrite it as an improper fraction or as a decimal.

What is the value of $\frac{1}{2} + \frac{3}{4}$?

Solution

$\frac{1}{2} + \frac{3}{4} = \frac{2}{4} + \frac{3}{4} = \frac{5}{4} = 1\frac{1}{4}$

Record the answer as $\frac{5}{4}$ or 1.25.

Do not record the answer as $1\frac{1}{4}$ because the test-scoring computer will read it as $\frac{11}{4}$.

TIP 2

You do not have to simplify a fraction unless the question asks for simplest form or the fraction does not fit on the grid.

Think It Through

You can add the fractions as shown in the solution on the left, or you can convert the fractions to decimals and add.

$\frac{1}{2} + \frac{3}{4} = 0.5 + 0.75 = 1.25$

Record the decimal answer on the grid.

Vocabulary Builder

As you solve test items, you must understand the meanings of mathematical terms. Select the correct term to complete each sentence.

A. An algebraic (*expression, equation*) is a mathematical sentence with an equal sign.

B. A (*coefficient, constant*) is a numerical factor of a term.

C. The (*exponent, base*) of a power tells how many times a number is used as a factor.

D. To (*simplify, evaluate*) an algebraic expression, you substitute a given number for each variable.

E. A(n) (*rational, irrational*) number is any number that you can write in the form $\frac{a}{b}$, where a and b are integers, and $b \neq 0$.

Multiple Choice

Read each question. Then write the letter of the correct answer on your paper.

1. If $x = -2$, $y = 3$, and $z = 4$, which expression has the greatest value?

   Ⓐ $z(x - y)$ Ⓒ $z(x - y)^3 + x$

   Ⓑ $z(x - y)^2 - x$ Ⓓ $\frac{z}{x} - xy$

2. What is the solution of the equation $7d + 7 = 14$?

   Ⓕ -3 Ⓗ 1

   Ⓖ -1 Ⓘ 3

3. What is the value of the expression $8(-9) - 6(-3)$?

   Ⓐ -90 Ⓒ 54

   Ⓑ -54 Ⓓ 90

4. What is the order of the numbers $\sqrt{10}$, 3.3, $\frac{8}{3}$, and $\sqrt{9}$ from least to greatest?

   (F) $\sqrt{10}$, 3.3, $\frac{8}{3}$, $\sqrt{9}$

   (G) $\frac{8}{3}$, $\sqrt{9}$, 3.3, $\sqrt{10}$

   (H) 3.3, $\sqrt{10}$, $\sqrt{9}$, $\frac{8}{3}$

   (I) $\frac{8}{3}$, $\sqrt{9}$, $\sqrt{10}$, 3.3

5. You ship an 8-lb care package to your friend at college. It will cost you $.85 per pound, plus a flat fee of $12, to ship the package. How much will you pay to ship the package?

   (A) $6.92   (C) $12.85

   (B) $10.20   (D) $18.80

6. Which ordered pair is NOT a solution of the equation $y = x - 3$?

   (F) $(-4, -7)$ (H) $(0, -3)$

   (G) $(12, 9)$ (I) $(-8, 11)$

7. Which property does the equation $4 + x + 7 = 4 + 7 + x$ illustrate?

   (A) Identity Property of Addition

   (B) Distributive Property

   (C) Commutative Property of Addition

   (D) Associative Property of Addition

8. Bill has a $10 coupon for a party store. He needs to buy some balloons for a birthday party. If each balloon costs $2, and Bill uses his coupon, what is an equation that gives the total cost, y, of his purchase?

   (F) $y = 2x$

   (G) $y = 2x - 10$

   (H) $y = 2x + 10$

   (I) $y = 10 - 2x$

9. Which expression is equivalent to $2.5(k - 3.4)$?

   (A) $k - 0.9$ (C) $2.5k - 3.4$

   (B) $k - 5.9$ (D) $2.5k - 8.5$

10. What is the value of $2 + |x + 4|$ for $x = -5$?

   (F) -7 (H) 3

   (G) 1   (I) 11

11. You own 100 shares of Stock A and 30 shares of Stock B. On Monday, Stock A decreased by $.40 per share, and Stock B increased by $.25 per share. What was the total change in value of your shares?

   (A) $-$32.50   (C) $-$.15

   (B) $-$21.20   (D) $12

12. The table shows the relationship between the number of laps x you swim in a pool and the distance, in meters, y, that you swim. Which equation describes the pattern in the table?

Laps, x	2	4	5	8
Distance (m), y	100	200	250	400

   (F) $y = 50x$ (H) $y = x + 50$

   (G) $y = 100x$ (I) $y = x + 100$

13. Which expression does NOT equal 9?

   (A) $|-4 - 5|$ (C) $-|9|$

   (B) $|-9|$ (D) $|9|$

14. A store is having a sale on cases of juice. The first two cases of juice cost $8 each. Any additional cases of juice cost $6 each. What is the cost of 9 cases of juice?

   (F) $54   (H) $58

   (G) $68   (I) $72

15. Which statement about real numbers is true?

Real Numbers

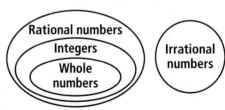

   (A) Every rational number is an integer.

   (B) Every real number is a rational number.

   (C) Every integer is a rational number.

   (D) Every irrational number is an integer.

16. Chris spends $3 per square foot on carpet for a square room. If he spends about $430 on carpet, what is the approximate length, in feet, of a side of the room?

   F   12 ft   **H**   72 ft

   G   36 ft   **I**   215 ft

17. To make 12 muffins, you need $1\frac{1}{4}$ cups of milk. You want to make 36 muffins, and you have $2\frac{1}{3}$ cups of milk. How many cups of milk do you still need?

   A $1\frac{1}{2}$ cups   **C** $2\frac{1}{3}$ cups

   B $1\frac{5}{12}$ cups   **D** $3\frac{3}{4}$ cups

18. A blank CD can hold 80 min of music. You have m minutes of music to burn onto the CD. Which expression models the amount of time t that is left on the CD?

   F $t = 80 - m$ **H** $t = 80 + m$

   G $t = m - 80$ **I** $t = 80m$

19. Which expression is equivalent to $3(2n + 1) + 4(n - 2)$?

   A $10n + 1$ **C** $10n - 7$

   B $10n - 1$ **D** $10n - 5$

20. A clock originally costs x dollars. After you apply a $3 discount, the clock costs y dollars. Which graph models this situation?

   F 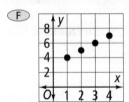   **H**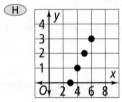

   G 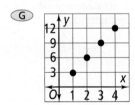   **I**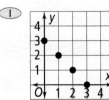

21. The expression 2^5 represents the number of cells in a petri dish after a single cell has gone through several stages of cell division. How many cells are in the petri dish after cell division?

   A   10   **C**   32

   B   16   **D**   64

22. To order movie tickets online, John has to pay $10 per ticket plus a $2 handling fee. If John buys three tickets, how much money will he spend?

   F $12   **H** $32

   G $30   **I** $36

23. What is the value of $(7 - 3)^2 + 3(8)$?

   A   32   **C**   64

   B   40   **D**   152

GRIDDED RESPONSE

Record your answers in a grid.

24. Marlee orders a window blind. She measures the window's length at three locations and displays her results in the table below. The length of the blind should be the same as the greatest length measured. What should be the length, in inches, of the blind?

Location	Left side	Center	Right side
Length (in.)	$53\frac{1}{2}$	$53\frac{3}{4}$	$53\frac{3}{8}$

25. Cole has $15 to spend on notebooks. Each notebook costs $3.99. What is the greatest amount, in dollars, that Cole can spend on notebooks?

26. What is the value of $-\frac{1}{5} + \frac{9}{10}$?

27. Tom auditions for a music school. For his piano audition, he will select two pieces from the table below. He can play for no more than 10 min.

Piano Piece	Time
Prelude	4 min, 13 s
Étude	5 min, 24 s
Waltz	4 min, 52 s

What is the greatest amount of time, in seconds, that he can play for his audition?

Get Ready!

Lesson 1-4

Describing a Pattern

Describe the relationship shown in each table below using words and using an equation.

1.

Number of Lawns Mowed	Money Earned
1	$7.50
2	$15.00
3	$22.50
4	$30.00

2.

Number of Hours	Pages Read
1	30
2	60
3	90
4	120

Lesson 1-5

Adding and Subtracting Real Numbers

Simplify each expression.

3. $6 + (-3)$ **4.** $-4 - 6$ **5.** $-5 - (-13)$ **6.** $-7 + (-1)$

7. $-4.51 + 11.65$ **8.** $8.5 - (-7.9)$ **9.** $\frac{3}{10} - \frac{3}{4}$ **10.** $\frac{1}{5} + \left(-\frac{2}{3}\right)$

Lesson 1-6

Multiplying and Dividing Real Numbers

Simplify each expression.

11. $-85 \div (-5)$ **12.** $7\left(-\frac{6}{14}\right)$ **13.** $4^2(-6)^2$ **14.** $22 \div (-8)$

Lesson 1-7

Combining Like Terms

Simplify each expression.

15. $14k^2 - (-2k^2)$ **16.** $4xy + 9xy$ **17.** $6t + 2 - 4t$ **18.** $9x - 4 + 3x$

 Looking Ahead Vocabulary

19. If you say that two shirts are *similar,* what does that mean about the shirts? What would you expect *similar* to mean if you are talking about two similar triangles?

20. A model ship is a type of *scale model.* What is the relationship of a model ship to the actual ship that it models?

Solving Equations

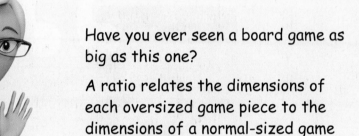

Have you ever seen a board game as big as this one?

A ratio relates the dimensions of each oversized game piece to the dimensions of a normal-sized game piece.

You'll find out how ratios and models are related using proportions in this chapter.

 Vocabulary for Part A

English/Spanish Vocabulary Audio Online:

English	Spanish
equivalent equations, p. 87	ecuaciones equivalentes
formula, p. 118	fórmula
inverse operations, p. 88	operaciones inversas
literal equation, p. 117	ecuación literal

My Math Video

00:04:04

VIDEO

BIG ideas

1 Equivalence

Essential Question Can equations that appear to be different be equivalent?

2 Solving Equations and Inequalities

Essential Question How can you solve equations?

3 Proportionality

Essential Question What kinds of relationships can proportions represent?

Chapter Preview for Part A

Modeling One-Step Equations

Algebra tiles can help you understand how to solve one-step equations in one variable. You can use the algebra tiles shown below to model equations. Notice that the yellow tile is positive and the red tile is negative. Together, they form a zero pair, which represents 0.

Unit tiles

 = +1   ■ = −1

■ + ☐ = 0

Variable tiles

 = a variable, such as *x*

Activity

Model and solve $x - 2 = 4$.

Equation	Algebra tiles	Step
$x - 2 = 4$		Model the equation using tiles.
$x - 2 + 2 = 4 + 2$		The green tile represents *x*. To get the green tile by itself on one side of the equation, add two yellow tiles to each side. Remember, a yellow tile and a red tile form a zero pair. Remove all zero pairs.
$x = 6$		The green tile equals six yellow tiles. This represents $x = 6$. The solution of $x - 2 = 4$ is 6.

Exercises

Write the equation modeled by the algebra tiles.

1.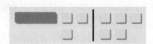

2.

Use algebra tiles to model and solve each equation.

3. $x - 3 = 2$

4. $x - 4 = 7$

5. $x + 1 = 5$

6. $x + 4 = 7$

7. $1 + x = -3$

8. $5 + x = -3$

9. $x - 4 = -3$

10. $-4 + x = -8$

2-1 Solving One-Step Equations

Objective To solve one-step equations in one variable

In a fair game, all players start out equal.

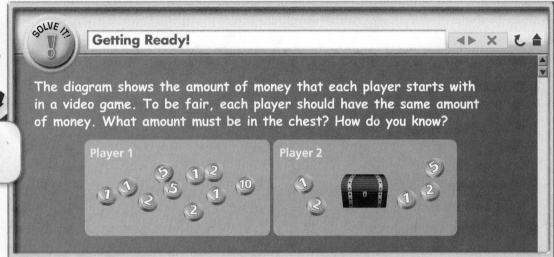

SOLVE IT!

Getting Ready!

The diagram shows the amount of money that each player starts with in a video game. To be fair, each player should have the same amount of money. What amount must be in the chest? How do you know?

Player 1

Player 2

Dynamic Activity
One-Step Equations

Lesson Vocabulary
- equivalent equations
- Addition Property of Equality
- Subtraction Property of Equality
- isolate
- inverse operations
- Multiplication Property of Equality
- Division Property of Equality

In the Solve It, you may have used reasoning to find the amount of money in the chest. In this lesson, you will learn to solve problems like the one above by using equations.

Focus Question How can you solve a one-step equation?

Equivalent equations are equations that have the same solution(s). You can apply the same operation to each side of an equation to get an equivalent equation.

Property Addition and Subtraction Properties of Equality

Addition Property of Equality Adding the same number to each side of an equation produces an equivalent equation.

Algebra	**Example**
For any real numbers a, b, and c,	$x - 3 = 2$
if $a = b$, then $a + c = b + c$.	$x - 3 + 3 = 2 + 3$

Subtraction Property of Equality Subtracting the same number from each side of an equation produces an equivalent equation.

Algebra	**Example**
For any real numbers a, b, and c,	$x + 3 = 2$
if $a = b$, then $a - c = b - c$.	$x + 3 - 3 = 2 - 3$

To solve an equation, you must **isolate** the variable. You do this by getting the variable alone on one side of the equation.

You can isolate a variable using the properties of equality and inverse operations. An **inverse operation** undoes another operation. For example, subtraction is the inverse of addition. You undo the addition of a number by subtracting the same number from each side of an equation.

Problem 1   Solving an Equation Using Subtraction

What is the solution of $x + 13 = 27$?

Plan

How can you visualize the equation?
You can *draw a diagram*. Use a model like the one below to help you visualize an equation. A model for the equation $x + 13 = 27$ is

| ⊢ ------- 27 ------- ⊣ |
| x | 13 |

Think

You need to isolate x. Start by writing the equation.

Undo addition by subtracting the same number from each side.

Simplify each side of the equation.

Substitute your answer into the original equation to check your answer.

Write

$$x + 13 = 27$$

$$x + 13 - 13 = 27 - 13$$

$$x = 14$$

$$x + 13 = 27$$
$$14 + 13 \stackrel{?}{=} 27$$
$$27 = 27 ✔$$

 Got It? **1.** What is the solution of $y + 2 = -6$? Check your answer.

Problem 2   Solving an Equation Using Addition

What is the solution of $-7 = b - 3$?

Plan

How can a model help you solve the equation?
The model below shows that the expressions -7 and $b - 3$ are equal. This relationship can help you choose the operation to use to solve the equation.

| ⊢ ------- −7 ------- ⊣ |
| b | −3 |

Write the original equation.	$-7 = b - 3$
Undo subtraction by adding 3 to each side.	$-7 + 3 = b - 3 + 3$
Simplify.	$-4 = b$

Check

Write the original equation.	$-7 = b - 3$
Substitute -4 for b.	$-7 \stackrel{?}{=} -4 - 3$
Simplify. The solution is correct.	$-7 = -7 ✔$

 Got It? **2.** What is the solution of each equation? Check your answer using substitution.

    a. $m - 8 = -14$ **b.** $\frac{1}{2} = y - \frac{3}{2}$

You can use the Multiplication and Division Properties of Equality to solve equations. Division is the inverse of multiplication.

Property   Multiplication and Division Properties of Equality

Multiplication Property of Equality Multiplying each side of an equation by the same nonzero number produces an equivalent equation.

Algebra

For any real numbers a, b, and c,
if $a = b$, then $a \cdot c = b \cdot c$.

Example

$$\frac{x}{3} = 2$$

$$\frac{x}{3} \cdot 3 = 2 \cdot 3$$

Division Property of Equality Dividing each side of an equation by the same nonzero number produces an equivalent equation.

Algebra

For any real numbers a, b, and c, such
that $c \neq 0$, if $a = b$, then $\frac{a}{c} = \frac{b}{c}$.

Example

$$5x = 20$$

$$\frac{5x}{5} = \frac{20}{5}$$

Plan

How can a model help you solve the equation?
The model tells you that you must divide 12 by 4 in order to solve the equation $4x = 12$.

Problem 3   Solving an Equation Using Division   GRIDDED RESPONSE

What is the solution of $4x = 12$?

Write the original equation.	$4x = 12$
Undo multiplication by dividing each side by 4.	$\frac{4x}{4} = \frac{12}{4}$
Simplify.	$x = 3$

Got It? 3. What is the solution of each equation? Does your solution make the equation true?

    a. $10 = -15x$ **b.** $3.2z = 14$

Plan

How can a model help you solve the equation?
The model tells you that you must multiply -9 by 4 in order to solve the equation $\frac{x}{4} = -9$.

Problem 4   Solving an Equation Using Multiplication

What is the solution of $\frac{x}{4} = -9$?

Write the original equation.	$\frac{x}{4} = -9$
Undo division by multiplying each side by 4.	$\frac{x}{4} \cdot 4 = -9 \cdot 4$
Simplify.	$x = -36$

Got It? 4. What is the solution of each equation? Check your answer.

    a. $19 = \frac{r}{3}$ **b.** $\frac{x}{-9} = 8$

Sometimes the coefficient of the variable in an equation is a fraction. You can use the reciprocal of the fraction to solve the equation.

 Problem 5 Solving Equations Using Reciprocals

What is the solution of $\frac{4}{5}m = 28$?

Think

Why multiply by the reciprocal?
You want the coefficient of m to be 1. The product of a number and its reciprocal is 1, so multiply by the reciprocal.

Write the original equation.	$\frac{4}{5}m = 28$
The reciprocal of $\frac{4}{5}$ is $\frac{5}{4}$. Multiply each side by $\frac{5}{4}$.	$\frac{5}{4}\left(\frac{4}{5}m\right) = \frac{5}{4}(28)$
Simplify.	$m = 35$

Got It? 5. a. What is the solution of $12 = \frac{3}{4}x$? Check your answer.
 b. Reasoning Are the equations $m = 18$ and $\frac{2}{3}m = 12$ equivalent? How do you know?

 Problem 6 Using a One-Step Equation as a Model

Biology Toucans and blue-and-yellow macaws are both tropical birds. The length of an average toucan is about two thirds of the length of an average blue-and-yellow macaw. Toucans are about 24 in. long. What is the length of an average blue-and-yellow macaw?

Relate [length of toucan] is $\frac{2}{3}$ of [length of blue-and-yellow macaw]

Define Let ℓ = the length of an average blue-and-yellow macaw.

Write [24] $= \frac{2}{3} \cdot$ [ℓ]

Plan

Does the problem tell you which operation to use in the equation?
Yes. The phrase *two thirds of* means that you should use multiplication.

Write the original equation.	$24 = \frac{2}{3}\ell$
Multiply each side by $\frac{3}{2}$.	$\frac{3}{2}(24) = \frac{3}{2}\left(\frac{2}{3}\ell\right)$
Simplify.	$36 = \ell$

An average blue-and-yellow macaw is 36 in. long.

Check	$24 = \frac{2}{3}\ell$
Substitute 36 for ℓ.	$24 \overset{?}{=} \frac{2}{3}(36)$
Simplify. The solution checks.	$24 = 24$ ✔

Got It? 6. An online DVD rental company offers gift certificates that you can use to purchase rental plans. You have a gift certificate for $30. The plan you select costs $5 per month. How many months can you purchase with the gift certificate?

Focus Question   How can you solve a one-step equation?

Answer   You can use the properties of equality and inverse operations to isolate the variable.

Lesson Check

Do you know HOW?

Solve each equation. Check your answer.

1. $x + 7 = 3$

2. $9 = m - 4$

3. $5y = 24$

4. Books You have already read 117 pages of a book. You are one third of the way through the book. Write and solve an equation to find the number of pages in the book.

Do you UNDERSTAND?

Vocabulary Which property of equality would you use to solve each equation? Why?

5. $3 + x = -34$ **6.** $2x = 5$

7. $x - 4 = 9$ **8.** $\frac{x}{7} = 9$

9. Reasoning Write a one-step equation. Then write two equations that are equivalent to your equation. How can you prove that all three equations are equivalent?

Practice and Problem-Solving Exercises

 Practice   Solve each equation using addition or subtraction. Check your answer.   ◀ **See Problems 1 and 2.**

Guided Practice

To start, undo addition by subtracting 2 from each side.

10. $6 = x + 2$
        $6 - 2 = x + 2 - 2$

11. $27 + n = 46$ **12.** $4 = q + 13$ **13.** $f + 9 = 20$

14. $-5 + a = 21$ **15.** $5.5 = -2 + d$ **16.** $c + 4 = -9$

17. $67 = w - 65$ **18.** $23 = b - 19$ **19.** $g - 3.5 = 10$

20. $y - 19 = 37$ **21.** $-2.5 = p + 7.1$ **22.** $j - 3 = -7$

Solve each equation using multiplication or division. Check your answer.   ◀ **See Problems 3 and 4.**

Guided Practice

To start, undo multiplication by dividing each side by -8.

23. $-8n = -64$
       $\dfrac{-8n}{-8} = \dfrac{-64}{-8}$

24. $-7y = 28$ **25.** $5b = 145$ **26.** $6a = 0.96$

27. $-96 = 4c$ **28.** $11 = 2.2t$ **29.** $7r = -\frac{7}{2}$

30. $\frac{m}{7} = 12$ **31.** $35 = \frac{j}{5}$ **32.** $-39 = \frac{q}{3}$

33. $14 = \frac{z}{2}$ **34.** $\frac{q}{-9} = -9$ **35.** $\frac{k}{4} = -\frac{17}{2}$

Solve each equation. Check your answer.

◀ See Problem 5.

36. $\frac{2}{3}q = 18$

37. $\frac{3}{4}x = 9$

38. $\frac{3}{5}m = -15$

39. $\frac{1}{5}x = \frac{2}{7}$

40. $36 = \frac{4}{9}d$

41. $-6 = \frac{3}{7}n$

Define a variable and write an equation for each situation. Then solve.

◀ See Problem 6.

42. Music You have a rack that can hold 30 CDs. You can fit 7 more CDs on the rack before the rack is full. How many CDs are in the rack?

43. Population In a 3-year period, a city's population decreased by 7525 to about 581,600. What was the city's population at the beginning of the 3-year period?

44. Writing If a one-step equation includes addition, should you expect to solve it by using addition? Why or why not?

45. Think About a Plan Costumes for a play at a community theater cost $1500, which is one third of the total budget. What is the total budget for the play?
- How can the model at the right help you solve the problem?
- How does the model tell you which operation to use in the equation?

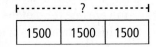

	?	
1500	1500	1500

46. Entertainment On a quiz show, a contestant was penalized 250 points for an incorrect answer, leaving the contestant with 1050 points. How many points did the contestant have before the penalty?

47. Picnics At a party of 102 people, 17 lb of potato salad is served.
- **a.** Write and solve an equation to find how many people each pound of potato salad serves.
- **b.** Write and solve an equation to find the average number of pounds of potato salad that each person is served. Round your answer to the nearest hundredth.

Solve each equation. Check your answer.

48. $\frac{2}{7} = \frac{1}{3} + a$

49. $z - 4\frac{2}{3} = 2\frac{2}{3}$

50. $6\frac{1}{4} = \frac{r}{5}$

51. $h + 2.8 = -3.7$

52. $\frac{3}{2}f = \frac{1}{2}$

53. $-4 = \frac{2}{9}d$

54. $4d = -2.4$

55. $-5.3 + z = 8.9$

56. $5b = 8.5$

57. Error Analysis Describe and correct the error in solving the equation at the right.

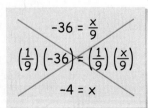

$$-36 = \frac{x}{9}$$
$$\left(\frac{1}{9}\right)(-36) = \left(\frac{1}{9}\right)\left(\frac{x}{9}\right)$$
$$-4 = x$$

58. U.S. History Between 1788 and 2008, the U.S. Constitution was amended 27 times. How many years have passed on average between one amendment and the next, to the nearest tenth of a year?

59. Volleyball In volleyball, players serve the ball to the opposing team. If the opposing team fails to hit the ball, the service is called an ace. A player's ace average is the number of aces served divided by the number of games played. A certain player has an ace average of 0.3 and has played in 70 games this season. How many aces has the player served?

Standardized Test Prep

60. Luis helped raise money for his school by jogging in the school jog-a-thon. The total amount of money he raised can be represented by the expression $1.75m$, where m is the number of miles he jogged. If Luis raised a total of $21, how many miles did he jog?

(A) 12   (B) 19.25   (C) 22.75   (D) 36.75

61. What operation should you use to solve $14 + c = 39$?

(F) squaring   (G) subtraction   (H) multiplication   (I) division

62. Sonya is checking orders at the fabric store where she works. Some of the orders are in decimals and some are in fractions. Which of the following statements is *not* true?

(A) $\frac{10}{4} = 2.5$ (B) $1.3 = 1\frac{1}{3}$ (C) $0.03 = \frac{3}{100}$ (D) $\frac{6}{5} = 1.2$

Mixed Review

63. If the pattern shown in the table continues, what is the total amount the group will raise by Week 5?

Scholarship Funds				
Week	0	1	2	3
Amount (thousands)	0	2	4	6

See Lesson 1-9.

Simplify each expression. Justify each step.

See Lesson 1-4.

64. $4(13x)$ **65.** $2.2 + (3.8 - x)$ **66.** $(m + 4.5) - 0.5$

Get Ready!   **To prepare for Lesson 2-2, do Exercises 67–69.**

Simplify each expression.

See Lesson 1-2.

67. $2[2 - (2 - 3) - 2]$ **68.** $\left(\frac{1}{2} + \frac{1}{3}\right)^2$ **69.** $-1 + 2 \cdot 3 - 4$

2-2 Solving Two-Step Equations

Objective To solve two-step equations in one variable

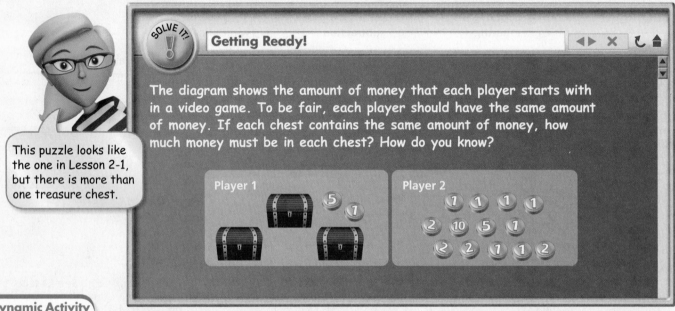

SOLVE IT!

Getting Ready!

The diagram shows the amount of money that each player starts with in a video game. To be fair, each player should have the same amount of money. If each chest contains the same amount of money, how much money must be in each chest? How do you know?

This puzzle looks like the one in Lesson 2-1, but there is more than one treasure chest.

Player 1

Player 2

Dynamic Activity
Solving Two-Step Equations

The problem in the Solve It can be modeled by the equation $3t + 6 = 30$. The equation is different from the equations in Lesson 2-1 because it requires two steps to solve.

Focus Question How can you solve a two-step equation?

A two-step equation, like the one shown below, involves two operations.

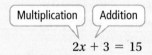

Multiplication   Addition

$$2x + 3 = 15$$

To solve a two-step equation, work backward to undo operations. Reverse the order of operations. For example, to solve $2x + 3 = 15$, you can use subtraction first to undo the addition, and then use division to undo the multiplication.

 **Problem 1** **Solving a Two-Step Equation**

A What is the solution of $2x + 3 = 15$?

Write the original equation.	$2x + 3 = 15$
Undo addition by subtracting 3 from each side.	$2x + 3 - 3 = 15 - 3$
Simplify.	$2x = 12$
Undo multiplication by dividing each side by 2.	$\frac{2x}{2} = \frac{12}{2}$
Simplify.	$x = 6$

Check Write the original equation. $2x + 3 = 15$

       Substitute 6 for x. $2(6) + 3 \stackrel{?}{=} 15$

       Simplify. The solution is correct. $15 = 15$

B What is the solution of $\frac{x}{8} - 4 = 2$?

Write the original equation.	$\frac{x}{8} - 4 = 2$
Undo subtraction by adding 4 to each side.	$\frac{x}{8} - 4 + 4 = 2 + 4$
Simplify.	$\frac{x}{8} = 6$
Undo division by multiplying each side by 8.	$8 \cdot \frac{x}{8} = 8 \cdot 6$
Simplify.	$x = 48$

Check Write the original equation. $\frac{x}{8} - 4 = 2$

       Substitute 48 for x. $\frac{48}{8} - 4 = 2$

       Simplify. The solution is correct. $2 = 2$ ✔

 Got It? **1.** What is the solution of each equation?

     a. $3x + 1 = 16$ **b.** $2 + 3x = 17$ **c.** $5 = \frac{t}{2} - 3$

You can solve a two-step equation that represents a real-world situation using the properties of equality.

 Problem 2 **Using an Equation as a Model**

Community Service You are making a bulletin board to advertise community service opportunities in your town. You plan to use half a sheet of construction paper for each ad. You need 5 sheets of construction paper for a title banner. You have 18 sheets of construction paper. How many ads can you make?

Know
- Paper per ad: $\frac{1}{2}$ sheet
- Paper for banner: 5 sheets
- Total paper: 18 sheets

Need
The number of ads you can make

Plan
Write and solve an equation. Let the variable represent the unknown.

Think

How can a model help you write the equation?
The model shows that a half of a sheet per ad plus 5 sheets for the title banner is equal to 18 sheets.

|←-------- 18 --------→|
| $\frac{1}{2}a$ | 5 |

Let $a =$ the number of ads you can make.

Write the equation.	$\frac{1}{2}a + 5 = 18$
Use the reverse order of operations. Undo addition by subtracting 5 from each side.	$\frac{1}{2}a + 5 - 5 = 18 - 5$
Simplify.	$\frac{1}{2}a = 13$
Multiply each side by 2, the reciprocal of $\frac{1}{2}$.	$2\left(\frac{1}{2}a\right) = 2(13)$
Simplify.	$a = 26$

You can make 26 community service advertisements for the bulletin board.

 Got It? 2. Suppose you used one quarter of a sheet of paper for each ad and four full sheets for the title banner in Problem 2. How many ads could you make?

Sometimes one side of an equation is a fraction with more than one term in the numerator. You can still undo division by multiplying each side by the denominator.

 Problem 3 **Solving With Two Terms in the Numerator**

What is the solution of $\frac{x - 7}{3} = -12$?

Plan

What operation should you perform first?
Multiplication. When you multiply by the denominator of the fraction in the equation, you get a one-step equation. So, multiplying first gets rid of the fraction.

Write the original equation.	$\frac{x - 7}{3} = -12$
Multiply each side by 3, the denominator of the fraction.	$3\left(\frac{x - 7}{3}\right) = 3(-12)$
Simplify.	$x - 7 = -36$
Add 7 to each side.	$x - 7 + 7 = -36 + 7$
Simplify.	$x = -29$

Got It? 3. a. What is the solution of $6 = \frac{x - 2}{4}$?

Hint

deductive reasoning
Deductive reasoning is a process of reasoning logically from given facts to a conclusion.

Think

Why isn't −t = −5 the solution?
When you solve for a variable, the coefficient must be 1, not −1.

When you use deductive reasoning, you must state your steps and your reason for each step using properties, definitions, or rules. In Problem 4, you will provide a reason for each step of the problem.

 Problem 4 Using Deductive Reasoning

What is the solution of $-t + 8 = 3$? Justify each step.

Steps	Reasons
$-t + 8 = 3$	This is the original equation.
$-t + 8 - 8 = 3 - 8$	Subtraction Property of Equality
$-t = -5$	Use subtraction to simplify.
$-1t = -5$	Multiplicative Property of -1
$\dfrac{-1t}{-1} = \dfrac{-5}{-1}$	Division Property of Equality
$t = 5$	Use division to simplify.

 Got It? 4. What is the solution of $\frac{x}{3} - 5 = 4$? Justify each step.

Focus Question How can you solve a two-step equation?

Answer You can use the reverse order of operations and properties of equality.

 Lesson Check

Do you know HOW?

Solve each equation. Check your answer.

1. $5x + 12 = -13$ **2.** $6 = \frac{m}{7} - 3$

3. $\frac{y - 1}{4} = -2$ **4.** $-x - 4 = 9$

5. Fundraising The junior class is selling granola bars to raise money. They purchased 1250 granola bars and paid a delivery fee of $25. The total cost, including the delivery fee, was $800. What was the cost of each granola bar?

Do you UNDERSTAND?

What properties of equality would you use to solve each equation? What operation would you perform first? Explain.

6. $-8 = \frac{s}{4} + 3$ **7.** $2x - 9 = 7$

8. $\frac{x}{3} - 8 = 4$ **9.** $-4x + 3 = -5$

10. Reasoning Can you solve the equation $\frac{d - 3}{5} = 6$ by adding 3 before multiplying by 5? Explain.

Practice and Problem-Solving Exercises

 Practice

Guided Practice

Solve each equation. Check your answer.

See Problem 1.

11. $2 + \frac{a}{4} = -1$

To start, undo addition by subtracting 2 from each side.

$2 - 2 + \frac{a}{4} = -1 - 2$

Simplify.

$\frac{a}{4} = -3$

12. $3n - 4 = 11$

13. $-1 = 7 + 8x$

14. $\frac{y}{5} + 2 = -8$

15. $4b + 6 = -2$

16. $10 = \frac{x}{4} - 8$

17. $10 + \frac{h}{3} = 1$

18. $-14 = -5 + 3c$

19. $26 = \frac{m}{6} + 5$

20. $\frac{a}{5} - 18 = 2$

Define a variable and write an equation for each situation. Then solve.

See Problem 2.

21. Maximum Capacity A delivery person uses a service elevator to bring boxes of books up to an office. The delivery person weighs 160 lb and each box of books weighs 50 lb. The maximum capacity of the elevator is 1000 lb. How many boxes of books can the delivery person bring up at one time?

22. Shopping You have $16 and a coupon for a $5 discount at a local supermarket. A bottle of olive oil costs $7. How many bottles of olive oil can you buy?

23. Rentals Two friends rent an apartment. They owe two months' rent and a $500 security deposit when they sign the lease. They pay the landlord $2800. What is the rent for one month?

Solve each equation. Check your answer.

See Problem 3.

24. $\frac{y - 4}{2} = 10$

25. $7 = \frac{x - 8}{3}$

26. $\frac{z + 10}{9} = 2$

27. $7\frac{1}{2} = \frac{x + 3}{2}$

28. $\frac{b + 3}{5} = -1$

29. $-2 = \frac{d - 7}{7}$

Solve each equation. Justify each step.

See Problem 4.

Guided Practice

30. $14 - b = 19$

To start, undo addition by subtracting 14 from each side.

$14 - 14 - b = 19 - 14$

Simplify.

$-b = 5$

31. $20 - 3h = 2$

32. $3 - \frac{x}{2} = 6$

33. $-1 = 4 + \frac{x}{3}$

Solve each equation. Check your answer.

34. $\dfrac{2 + y}{3} = -1$

35. $-24 = -10t + 3$

36. $\dfrac{1}{2} = \dfrac{1}{2}c - 2$

37. $9.4 = -d + 5.6$

38. $2.4 + 10m = 6.89$

39. $\dfrac{1}{5}t - 3 = 17$

40. Error Analysis Describe and correct the error in finding the solution of the equation below.

$$2x - 4 = 8$$
$$2x = 4$$
$$x = 2$$

41. Writing Without solving the equation $-3x + 5 = 44$, tell whether the value of x is positive or negative. How do you know?

42. a. Solve the equation $2x - 1 = 7$ by undoing subtraction first.
   b. Solve the equation in part (a) by undoing multiplication first. Do you get the same answer you got in part (a)?
   c. Reasoning Which method from parts (a) and (b) do you prefer? Explain.

43. Think About a Plan A Web site allows musicians to post their songs online. Then people using the Web site can buy any of the posted songs. Suppose each musician must pay a one-time fee of $5 to use the Web site. Each musician earns $.09 every time a particular song of his or hers is downloaded. If a musician earned a profit of $365 for a particular song, how many times was the song downloaded?
   • How can the model at the right help you solve the problem?
   • How does the model tell you which operations to use in the equation?

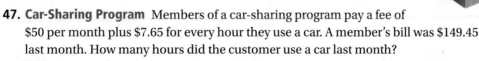

|← - - - - - - - - 365 - - - - - - - - →|
| 0.09x | −5 |

44. Open-Ended Write a real-world problem that you can model with the two-step equation $8b + 6 = 38$. Then solve the problem.

45. Earth Science The air temperature beneath Earth's surface increases by about $10°C$ per kilometer. The surface temperature and the air temperature at the bottom of a mine are shown. How many kilometers below Earth's surface is the bottom of the mine?

Surface: 18°C

Bottom of mine: 38°C
Not drawn to scale

46. Home Improvement A contractor is adding a back porch onto a house. The porch needs to hold 20 people and furniture that weighs 250 lb. The contractor calculates that the porch needs to hold 3750 lb to meet that specification. What value did the contractor use for the weight of a person?

47. Car-Sharing Program Members of a car-sharing program pay a fee of $50 per month plus $7.65 for every hour they use a car. A member's bill was $149.45 last month. How many hours did the customer use a car last month?

Standardized Test Prep

SAT/ACT

48. William's age w and Jamie's age j are related by the equation $w = 2j - 12$. When William is 36.5 years old, how old is Jamie?

49. Dominique paints faces at an annual carnival. Her goal this year is to earn $100. She spends $15 on supplies and will work for 2.5 h. How much will she need to earn in dollars per hour in order to reach her goal?

50. The cost of a gallon of milk m is $.50 more than five times the cost of a gallon of water w. If a gallon of milk costs $3.75, what is the cost of a gallon of water?

Mixed Review

Solve each equation.   ◀ **See Lesson 2-1.**

51. $-5x = -25$ **52.** $7 = 3.2 + y$ **53.** $\frac{y}{4} = 36$ **54.** $z - 2 = 4.5$

Tell whether each statement is *true* or *false*. If it is false, give a counterexample.   ◀ **See Lesson 1-4.**

55. The difference of the absolute value of two numbers is the same as the difference of the two numbers themselves.

56. Adding 1 to a number always increases its absolute value.

Get Ready! To prepare for Lesson 2-3, do Exercises 57–60.

Simplify each expression.   ◀ **See Lesson 1-7.**

57. $7(5 - t)$ **58.** $-2(-2x + 5)$ **59.** $-3(2 - b)$ **60.** $5(2 - 5n)$

Solving Multi-Step Equations

Objective To solve multi-step equations in one variable

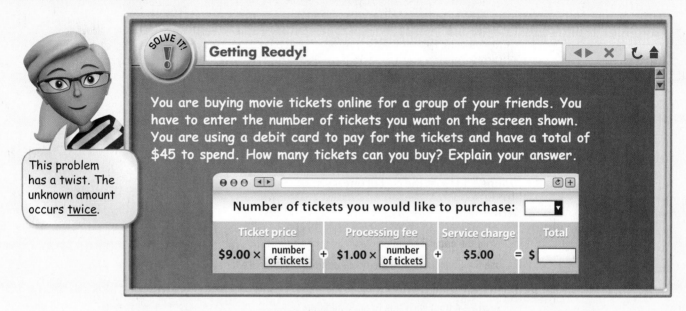

SOLVE IT!

Getting Ready!

You are buying movie tickets online for a group of your friends. You have to enter the number of tickets you want on the screen shown. You are using a debit card to pay for the tickets and have a total of $45 to spend. How many tickets can you buy? Explain your answer.

Number of tickets you would like to purchase: [   ]

Ticket price		Processing fee		Service charge	Total
$9.00 × number of tickets	+	$1.00 × number of tickets	+	$5.00	= $ [ ]

This problem has a twist. The unknown amount occurs _twice_.

Focus Question How is solving a multi-step equation similar to solving a two-step equation?

Think

How is this equation different from equations you've seen before?
The variable occurs in _two_ terms. You can simplify the equation by grouping like terms and combining them.

Problem 1 Combining Like Terms

What is the solution of $5 = 5m - 23 + 2m$?

Write the original equation.	$5 = 5m - 23 + 2m$
Use the Commutative Property of Addition to gather like terms.	$5 = 5m + 2m - 23$
Combine like terms.	$5 = 7m - 23$
Add 23 to each side.	$5 + 23 = 7m - 23 + 23$
Simplify.	$28 = 7m$
Divide each side by 7.	$\dfrac{28}{7} = \dfrac{7m}{7}$
Simplify.	$4 = m$

Check Write the original equation. $\quad 5 = 5m - 23 + 2m$

Substitute 4 for m. $\quad 5 \overset{?}{=} 5(4) - 23 + 2(4)$

Simplify. The solution checks. $\quad 5 = 5$ ✓

Got It? **1.** What is the solution of each equation? Check each answer.

    a. $11m - 8 - 6m = 22$ **b.** $-2y + 5 + 5y = 14$

Problem 2 Solving a Multi-Step Equation

Concert Merchandise Martha takes her niece and nephew to a concert. She buys T-shirts and bumper stickers for them. The bumper stickers cost $1 each. Martha's niece wants 1 shirt and 4 bumper stickers, and her nephew wants 2 shirts but no bumper stickers. If Martha's total is $67, what is the cost of one shirt?

Know
- Bumper stickers cost $1
- Niece's items: 1 shirt, 4 bumper stickers
- Nephew's items: 2 shirts
- Total spent: $67

Need
The cost of one shirt

Plan
Write and solve an equation that models the situation.

Think

How can a model help you write the equation?
The model shows that the cost of the niece's items plus the cost of the nephew's items is $67.

```
|-------- 67 --------|
| s + 4  |    2s     |
```

Relate   cost of niece's items (1 shirt and 4 stickers)   plus   cost of nephew's items (2 shirts)   is   total Martha spent

Define   Let s = the cost of one shirt.

Write $(s + 4)$ $+$ $2s$ $=$ 67

Write the original equation.	$(s + 4) + 2s = 67$
Use the Commutative Property of Addition to gather like terms.	$s + 2s + 4 = 67$
Combine like terms.	$3s + 4 = 67$
Subtract 4 from each side to undo addition.	$3s + 4 - 4 = 67 - 4$
Simplify.	$3s = 63$
Divide each side by 3 to undo multiplication.	$\frac{3s}{3} = \frac{63}{3}$
Simplify.	$s = 21$

One shirt costs $21.

 Got It? **2.** Noah buys 2 magazines. Kate buys 2 magazines and a book. The book costs $16. Their total cost is $72. How much is one magazine?

 Problem 3 Solving an Equation Using the Distributive Property

What is the solution of $-8(2x - 1) = 36$?

Think

How can you make the equation easier to solve?
Remove the grouping symbols by using the Distributive Property.

Write the original equation.	$-8(2x - 1) = 36$
Use the Distributive Property.	$-8(2x) + (-8)(-1) = 36$
Simplify.	$-16x + 8 = 36$
Subtract 8 from each side to undo addition.	$-16x + 8 - 8 = 36 - 8$
Simplify.	$-16x = 28$
Divide each side by -16 to undo multiplication.	$\frac{-16x}{-16} = \frac{28}{-16}$
Simplify.	$x = -\frac{7}{4}$

Got It? **3. a.** What is the solution of $18 = 3(2x - 6)$? Check your answer.

   b. Reasoning Can you solve the equation in part (a) by using the Division Property of Equality instead of the Distributive Property? Explain.

Focus Question How is solving a multi-step equation similar to solving a two-step equation?

Answer When solving any equation, the goal is to isolate the variable. Use the Distributive Property and combine like terms until a multi-step equation becomes a two-step equation.

Lesson Check

Do you know HOW?

Solve each equation. Check your answer.

1. $7p + 8p - 16 = 59$

2. $-2(3x + 9) = 24$

3. $5c - 9 - 2c = 6$

4. $4(y - 2) + 6 = 0$

Do you UNDERSTAND?

Explain how you would solve each equation.

5. $7(3x - 4) = 49$ **6.** $-4x - 8 = 14$

7. Reasoning Ben solves the equation $-24 = 5(g + 3)$ by first dividing each side by 5. Amelia solves the equation by using the Distributive Property. Whose method do you prefer? Explain.

Practice and Problem-Solving Exercises

 Practice

Solve each equation. Check your answer.

See Problem 1.

Guided Practice

To start, rewrite the equation as a sum.	**8.** $7 - y - y = -1$ $7 + (-1y) + (-1y) = -1$
Combine like terms.	$7 + (-2y) = -1$

9. $13 = 5 + 3b - 13$ **10.** $6p - 2 - 3p = 16$

11. $x + 2 + x = 22$ **12.** $9t - 6 - 6t = 6$

13. $17 = p - 3 - 3p$ **14.** $-23 = 2a - 10 - a$

Write an equation to model each situation. Then solve the equation.

See Problem 2.

15. Employment You have a part-time job. You work for 3 hours on Friday and 6 hours on Saturday. You also receive an allowance of $20 per week. You earn $92 per week. How much do you earn per hour at your part-time job?

16. Travel A family buys airline tickets online. Each ticket costs $167. The family buys travel insurance that costs $19 per ticket. The Web site charges a fee of $16 for the entire purchase. The family is charged a total of $1132. How many tickets did the family buy?

Solve each equation. Check your answer.

 See Problem 3.

Guided
Practice

17. $64 = 8(r + 2)$

To start, use the Distributive Property. $64 = 8(r) + 8(2)$
Simplify. $64 = 8r + 16$

18. $5(2x - 3) = 15$

19. $5(2 + 4z) = 85$

20. $2(8 + 4c) = 32$

21. $15 = -2(2t - 1)$

22. $26 = 6(5 - 4f)$

23. $n + 5(n - 1) = 7$

B **Apply**

Solve each equation.

24. $25(d - 12) = 4$

25. $-(w + 5) = -14$

26. $8n - (2n - 3) = 12$

27. $4(2 - 3b) = 68$

28. Error Analysis Describe and correct the error in solving the equation below.

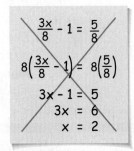

$$\frac{3x}{8} - 1 = \frac{5}{8}$$

$$8\left(\frac{3x}{8} - 1\right) = 8\left(\frac{5}{8}\right)$$

$$3x - 1 = 5$$

$$3x = 6$$

$$x = 2$$

29. Savings You have $85 in your bank account. Each week you plan to deposit $8 from your allowance and $15 from your paycheck. The equation $b = 85 + (15 + 8)w$ gives the amount b in your bank account after w weeks. How many weeks from now will you have $175 in your bank account?

Geometry Find the value of x. (*Hint*: The sum of the angle measures of a quadrilateral is 360°.)

30.

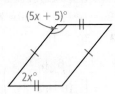

$(5x + 5)°$

$2x°$

31.

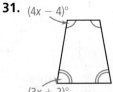

$(4x - 4)°$

$(3x + 2)°$

32.

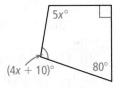

$5x°$

$(4x + 10)°$

$80°$

Objective To solve multi-step equations in one variable

In Part 1 of the lesson, you learned how to solve multi-step equations.

Connect to What You Know

Here you will learn how to solve multi-step equations with fractions and decimals.

Focus Question How can you solve a multi-step equation?

You can solve equations that contain fractions by removing the fractions.

Problem 4 Solving an Equation That Contains Fractions

What is the solution of $\frac{3x}{4} - \frac{x}{3} = 10$?

Write the original equation	$\frac{3x}{4} - \frac{x}{3} = 10.$
Multiply each side by the least common denominator, 12.	$12\left(\frac{3x}{4} - \frac{x}{3}\right) = 12(10)$
Use the Distributive Property.	$12\left(\frac{3x}{4}\right) - 12\left(\frac{x}{3}\right) = 12(10)$
Multiply.	$9x - 4x = 120$
Combine like terms.	$5x = 120$
Divide each side by 5.	$\frac{5x}{5} = \frac{120}{5}$
Simplify.	$x = 24$

 Got It? **4.** What is the solution of each equation?

a. $\frac{2b}{5} + \frac{2}{4} = \frac{5}{2}$

b. $\frac{1}{9} = \frac{5}{6} - \frac{m}{3}$

You can clear decimals from an equation by multiplying by a power of 10. First, find the greatest number of digits to the right of any decimal point. Then multiply by 10 raised to that power.

 Problem 5 **Solving an Equation That Contains Decimals**

What is the solution of $3.5 - 0.02x = 1.24$?

Plan

Count the number of digits to the right of each decimal point. Here, 3.5 has 1 digit , 0.02 has 2 digits, and 1.24 has 2 digits. The greatest number of digits to the right of any decimal point is 2. So, multiply each side of the equation by 10^2, or 100, to clear the decimals.

Think

When you multiply a decimal by 10^n, where n is a positive integer, you can move the decimal point n places to the right. For example, $100(3.5) = 350$.

Write the original equation.	$3.5 - 0.02x = 1.24$
Multiply each side by 10^2, or 100.	$100(3.5 - 0.02x) = 100(1.24)$
Use the Distributive Property.	$350 - 2x = 124$
Subtract 350 from each side.	$350 - 2x - 350 = 124 - 350$
Simplify.	$-2x = -226$
Divide each side by -2.	$\dfrac{-2x}{-2} = \dfrac{-226}{-2}$
Simplify.	$x = 113$

 Got It? 5. What is the solution of $0.5x - 2.325 = 3.95$? Check your answer.

Hint

Start by finding the greatest number of digits to the right of any decimal.

Focus Question How can you solve a multi-step equation?

Answer You can form a series of simpler equivalent equations.

 Lesson Check

Do you know HOW?

Solve each equation. Check your answer.

1. $\dfrac{2m}{7} + \dfrac{3m}{14} = 3$
2. $1.2 = 2.4 - 0.6x$

3. **Gardening** There is a 12-ft fence on one side of a rectangular garden. The gardener has 44 ft of fencing to enclose the other three sides. What is the length of the garden's longer dimension?

Do you UNDERSTAND?

Explain how you would solve each equation.

4. $1.3 + 0.5x = -3.41$
5. $-\dfrac{2}{9}x - 4 = \dfrac{7}{18}$

6. **Reasoning** Suppose you want to solve $-\dfrac{3m}{4} + 5 + \dfrac{2m}{3} = -3$. What would you do as your first step? Explain.

Practice and Problem-Solving Exercises

 Practice

Solve each equation. Check your answer.

⬅ See Problem 4.

Guided Practice

To start, multiply by 13 to remove the fractions.

7. $\frac{b}{13} - \frac{3}{13} = \frac{8}{13}$

$(13)\left(\frac{b}{13} - \frac{3}{13}\right) = (13)\frac{8}{13}$

8. $5y - \frac{3}{5} = \frac{4}{5}$

9. $\frac{n}{5} - 9 = \frac{1}{5}$

10. $\frac{x}{2} - \frac{2x}{16} = \frac{3}{8}$

11. $\frac{2}{3} + \frac{3m}{5} = \frac{31}{15}$

12. $\frac{1}{4} + \frac{4x}{5} = \frac{11}{20}$

13. $\frac{5z}{16} + \frac{7}{8} = \frac{5}{16}$

Solve each equation. Check your answer.

⬅ See Problem 5.

Guided Practice

To start, multiply each side by 10^2, or 100.

14. $1.06g - 3 = 0.71$

$106g - 300 = 71$

15. $0.11k + 1.5 = 2.49$

16. $1.025v + 2.458 = 7.583$

17. $1.12 + 1.25g = 8.62$

18. $25.24 = 5g + 3.89$

 Apply

Solve each equation.

19. $\frac{2}{3}(c - 18) = 7$

20. $\frac{a}{20} + \frac{4}{15} = \frac{9}{15}$

21. $\frac{b}{3} + \frac{1}{8} = 19$

22. Think About a Plan Jillian and Tyson are shopping for knitting supplies. Jillian wants 3 balls of yarn and 1 set of knitting needles. Tyson wants 1 ball of yarn and 2 sets of knitting needles. Each ball of yarn costs $6.25. If their total cost is $34.60, what is the cost of 1 set of knitting needles?
  * How can the model at the right help you solve the problem?
  * How does the model tell you which operations to use in the equation?

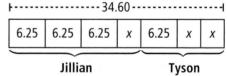

23. Online Video Games Angie and Kenny play online video games. Angie buys 1 software package and 3 months of game play. Kenny buys 1 software package and 2 months of game play. Each software package costs $20. If their total cost is $115, what is the cost of one month of game play?

24. Bowling Three friends go bowling. The cost per person per game is $5.30. The cost to rent shoes is $2.50 per person. Their total cost is $55.20. How many games did they play?

25. Moving Expenses A college student is moving onto campus. The student rents a moving truck for $19.95 plus $.99 per mile. Before returning the truck, the student fills the tank with gasoline, which costs $65.32. The total cost is $144.67. How many miles did the student drive the truck?

Standardized Test Prep

SAT/ACT

26. When a number is increased by 3 and that number is doubled, the result is -8. What was the original number?

    Ⓐ -14 Ⓑ -7 Ⓒ -5.5 Ⓓ -1

27. What is the value of the expression $-3r + 6 + r$ when $r = -2$?

    Ⓕ -2 Ⓖ 0 Ⓗ 10 Ⓘ 12

28. Ray's car gets an average gas mileage of 29 mi/gal. Ray starts his trip with the amount of gas shown. About how many gallons of gas are left at the end of his trip?

    Ⓐ 6 gal   Ⓒ 8 gal

    Ⓑ 7 gal   Ⓓ 10 gal

Mixed Review

Solve each equation.   ◀ See Lesson 2-2.

29. $3y + 5 = -10$ **30.** $4x - 5 = 23$ **31.** $-3a + 21 = 9$

Name the property that each statement illustrates.   ◀ See Lesson 1-4.

32. $4 + (-4) = 0$ **33.** $(5 \cdot 6) \cdot 2 = 5 \cdot (6 \cdot 2)$ **34.** $7 \cdot 0 = 0$

Get Ready!   **To prepare for Lesson 2-4, do Exercises 35–37.**

Simplify each expression.   ◀ See Lesson 1-7.

35. $7y - 4y$ **36.** $4y - 7y$ **37.** $7y - 7y$

Concept Byte

Use With Lesson 2-4

ACTIVITY

Modeling Equations With Variables on Both Sides

Algebra tiles can help you understand how to solve equations with variables on both sides.

Activity

Model and solve $3b - 4 = b + 2$.

Equation	Algebra tiles	Step
$3b - 4 = b + 2$	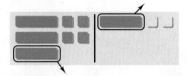	Model the equation using tiles.
$3b - 4 - b = b + 2 - b$ $2b - 4 = 2$	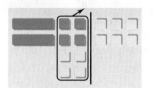	Remove one green tile from each side of the equation so that all remaining green tiles are on one side.
$2b - 4 + 4 = 2 + 4$ $2b = 6$		Add four yellow tiles to each side of the equation to form zero pairs that can be removed.
$\dfrac{2b}{2} = \dfrac{6}{2}$		Notice that two green tiles equal six yellow tiles. You can divide the tiles on each side of the equation into two identical groups, as shown.
$b = 3$		So, one green tile equals three yellow tiles. The solution of $3b - 4 = b + 2$ is $b = 3$. You can substitute 3 for b to check.

Exercises

Write the equation modeled by the algebra tiles.

1.

2.

Use algebra tiles to model and solve each equation.

3. $3x - 5 = x + 3$　　**4.** $6x - 4 = 3x + 2$　　**5.** $5x - 3 = 3x + 1$　　**6.** $4x + 4 = 1 + x$

2-4 Solving Equations With Variables on Both Sides

Objectives To solve equations with variables on both sides
To identify equations that are identities or have no solution

SOLVE IT!

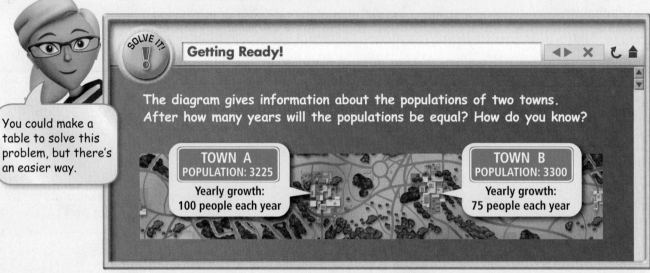

Getting Ready!   ◀▶ ✕ ↻ ⌂

The diagram gives information about the populations of two towns. After how many years will the populations be equal? How do you know?

> You could make a table to solve this problem, but there's an easier way.

TOWN A
POPULATION: 3225
Yearly growth:
100 people each year

TOWN B
POPULATION: 3300
Yearly growth:
75 people each year

Lesson Vocabulary
• Identity

The problem in the Solve It can be modeled by $3225 + 100x = 3300 + 75x$. Notice that this equation has variables on *both* sides.

Focus Question How can you solve equations with variables on both sides?

Plan

How do you get started?
There are variable terms on both sides of the equation. Decide which variable term to add or subtract. The goal is to get the variable on one side of the equation and the numeric terms on the other side.

Problem 1 **Solving an Equation With Variables on Both Sides**

What is the solution of $5x + 2 = 2x + 14$?

Write the original equation.	$5x + 2 = 2x + 14$
Subtract $2x$ from each side. The coefficient 2 is less than the coefficient 5, so it is easier to subtract.	$5x + 2 - 2x = 2x + 14 - 2x$
Simplify. Now there is only one variable term.	$3x + 2 = 14$
Subtract 2 from each side.	$3x + 2 - 2 = 14 - 2$
Simplify.	$3x = 12$
Divide each side by 3.	$\dfrac{3x}{3} = \dfrac{12}{3}$
Simplify.	$x = 4$

Check $5x + 2 = 2x + 14$

Substitute 4 for x. $5(4) + 2 \stackrel{?}{=} 2(4) + 14$

Simplify. The solution checks. $22 = 22$ ✔

Hint

Decide which variable term to add or subtract.

 Got It? **1. a.** What is the solution of $7k + 2 = 4k - 10$?

b. Reasoning Solve the equation in Problem 1 by subtracting $5x$ from each side instead of $2x$. Compare and contrast your solution with the solution in Problem 1.

Dynamic Activity
Solving Equations

Problem 2 Using an Equation With Variables on Both Sides

Graphic Design It takes a graphic designer 1.5 h to make one page of a Web site. Using new software, the designer could complete each page in 1.25 h, but it takes 8 h to learn the software. How many Web pages would the designer have to make in order to save time using the new software?

Know
- Current design time: 1.5 h per page
- Time with new software: 1.25 h per page
- Time to learn software: 8 h

Need
The number of pages the designer needs to make for the new software to save time

Plan
Write and solve an equation that models the situation.

Think

How can a model help you write the equation?
The model shows that the current design time equals the new design time plus the time to learn the new software (8 h).

1.5p	
1.25p	8

Relate $\begin{array}{ccc} \text{current} \\ \text{design time} \end{array} = \begin{array}{c} \text{design time with} \\ \text{new software} \end{array} + \begin{array}{c} \text{time to learn} \\ \text{software} \end{array}$

Define Let $p =$ the number of pages the designer needs to make.

Write $\qquad 1.5p \qquad = \qquad 1.25p \qquad + \qquad 8$

Write the original equation.	$1.5p = 1.25p + 8$
Get the variable terms on the left side. Subtract $1.25p$ from each side.	$1.5p - 1.25p = 1.25p + 8 - 1.25p$
Simplify.	$0.25p = 8$
Divide each side by 0.25.	$\dfrac{0.25p}{0.25} = \dfrac{8}{0.25}$
Simplify.	$p = 32$

It will take the designer the same amount of time to make 32 Web pages using either software. The designer must make 33 pages or more in order to save time using the new software.

Hint

First, find the amount that the monthly electric bill will be reduced.

 Got It? **2.** An office manager spent $650 on a new energy-saving copier. The copier will reduce the monthly electric bill for the office from $112 to $88. In how many months will the copier pay for itself?

 **Problem 3** **Solving an Equation With Grouping Symbols**

What is the solution of $2(5x - 1) = 3(x + 11)$?

Write the original equation.	$2(5x - 1) = 3(x + 11)$
Use the Distributive Property.	$10x - 2 = 3x + 33$
Subtract $3x$ from each side.	$10x - 2 - 3x = 3x + 33 - 3x$
Gather like terms.	$10x - 3x - 2 = 3x - 3x + 33$
Simplify.	$7x - 2 = 33$
Add 2 to each side.	$7x - 2 + 2 = 33 + 2$
Simplify.	$7x = 35$
Divide each side by 7.	$\dfrac{7x}{7} = \dfrac{35}{7}$
Simplify.	$x = 5$

 Got It? 3. What is the solution of each equation?

a. $4(2y + 1) = 2(y - 13)$ **b.** $7(4 - a) = 3(a - 4)$

An equation that is true for every possible value of the variable is an **identity.** You can replace the variable with any value and the expressions on each side are equivalent. For example, $x + 1 = x + 1$ is an identity.

An equation has no solution if there is no value of the variable that makes the equation true. For example, the equation $x + 1 = x + 2$ has no solution.

 Problem 4 **Identities and Equations With No Solution**

What is the solution of each equation?

Ⓐ $10x + 12 = 2(5x + 6)$

Write the original equation.	$10x + 12 = 2(5x + 6)$
Use the Distributive Property.	$10x + 12 = 10x + 12$

Because $10x + 12 = 10x + 12$ is always true, there are infinitely many solutions of the equation. The original equation is an identity.

B $9m - 4 = -3m + 5 + 12m$

Write the original equation.	$9m - 4 = -3m + 5 + 12m$
Gather like terms.	$9m - 4 = -3m + 12m + 5$
Combine like terms.	$9m - 4 = 9m + 5$
Subtract $9m$ from each side.	$9m - 4 - 9m = 9m + 5 - 9m$
Combine like terms.	$-4 = 5$ ✗

Because $-4 \neq 5$, the original equation has no solution.

Hint

While you are solving the equation, look for a variable you can eliminate.

 Got It? **4.** What is the solution of each equation? If the equation is an identity, write *identity*. If the equation has no solution, write *no solution*.

a. $3(4b - 2) = -6 + 12b$ **b.** $2x + 7 = -1(3 - 2x)$

There are a variety of ways to solve equations. The steps below provide a general guideline for solving equations.

Hint

If you see the equation is an identity after step 2, you do not need to continue.

take note

Concept Summary   Solving Equations

Step 1   Use the Distributive Property to remove any grouping symbols. Use properties of equality to clear decimals and fractions.

Step 2   Combine like terms on each side of the equation.

Step 3   Use the properties of equality to get the variable terms on one side of the equation and the constants on the other.

Step 4   Use the properties of equality to solve for the variable.

Step 5   Check your solution in the original equation.

Focus Question   How can you solve equations with variables on both sides?

Answer   You can use the properties of equality and inverse operations to write a series of simpler equivalent equations.

Lesson Check

Do you know HOW?

Solve each equation. Check your answer.

1. $3x + 4 = 5x - 10$ **2.** $5(y - 4) = 7(2y + 1)$

3. $2a + 3 = \frac{1}{2}(6 + 4a)$ **4.** $4x - 5 = 2(2x + 1)$

5. Printing Pristine Printing will print business cards for $.10 each plus a setup charge of $15. The Printing Place offers business cards for $.15 each with a setup charge of $10. What number of business cards costs the same from either printer?

Do you UNDERSTAND?

Vocabulary Match each equation with the appropriate number of solutions.

6. $3y - 5 = y + 2y - 9$ **A.** infinitely many

7. $2y + 4 = 2(y + 2)$ **B.** one solution

8. $2y - 4 = 3y - 5$ **C.** no solution

9. Writing A student solves an equation and eliminates the variable. How would the student know whether the equation is an identity or an equation with no solution?

Practice and Problem-Solving Exercises

Practice   Solve each equation. Check your answer.   ◀ **See Problem 1.**

> **Guided Practice**

To start, subtract x from each side. The coefficient 1 is less than the coefficient 5, so it is easier to subtract. Simplify.	**10.** $\begin{aligned} 5x - 1 &= x + 15 \\ 5x - 1 - x &= x + 15 - x \\ 4x - 1 &= 15 \end{aligned}$

11. $4p + 2 = 3p - 7$ **12.** $3 + 5q = 9 + 4q$ **13.** $8 - 2y = 3y - 2$

14. $2b + 4 = -18 - 9b$ **15.** $-3c - 12 = -5 + c$ **16.** $-n - 24 = 5 - n$

Write and solve an equation for each situation. Check your solution.   ◀ **See Problem 2.**

17. Architecture An architect is designing a rectangular greenhouse. Along one wall is a 7-ft storage area and 5 sections for different kinds of plants. On the opposite wall is a 4-ft storage area and 6 sections for plants. All of the sections for plants are of equal length. What is the length of each wall?

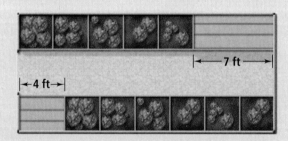

> **Guided Practice**

To start, record what you know.

Wall 1 length: 7 ft + length of 5 sections
Wall 2 length: 4 ft + length of 6 sections
The walls are equal in length because the greenhouse is rectangular.

Describe what you need to find.

The length of a wall

18. Business A hairdresser is deciding where to open her own studio. If the hairdresser chooses Location A, she will pay $1200 per month in rent and will charge $45 per haircut. If she chooses Location B, she will pay $1800 per month in rent and will charge $60 per haircut. How many haircuts would she have to give in one month to make the same profit at either location?

Solve each equation. Check your answer.   See Problem 3.

19. $3(q - 5) = 2(q + 5)$ **20.** $7(6 - 2a) = 5(-3a + 1)$

21. $(g + 4) - 3g = 1 + g$ **22.** $5g + 4(-5 + 3g) = 1 - g$

Determine whether each equation is an *identity* or whether it has *no solution*.   See Problem 4.

23. $2(a - 4) = 4a - (2a + 4)$ **24.** $5y + 2 = \frac{1}{2}(10y + 4)$

25. $k - 3k = 6k + 5 - 8k$ **26.** $2(2k - 1) = 4(k - 2)$

27. $-6a + 3 = -3(2a - 1)$ **28.** $4 - d = -(d - 4)$

 Apply

Solve each equation. If the equation is an identity, write *identity*. If it has no solution, write *no solution*.

29. $3.2 - 4d = 2.3d + 3$ **30.** $3d + 4 = 2 + 3d - \frac{1}{2}$

31. $3a + 1 = -3.6(a - 1)$ **32.** $0.5b + 4 = 2(b + 2)$

33. $-2(-c - 12) = -2c - 12$ **34.** $3(m + 1.5) = 1.5(2m + 3)$

35. Travel Suppose a family drives at an average rate of 60 mi/h on the way to visit relatives and then at an average rate of 40 mi/h on the way back. The return trip takes 1 h longer than the trip there.
   a. Let d be the distance in miles the family traveled to visit their relatives. How many hours did it take to drive there?
   b. In terms of d, how many hours did it take to make the return trip?
   c. Write and solve an equation to determine the distance the family drove to see their relatives. What was the average rate for the entire trip?

36. Think About a Plan Each morning, a deli worker has to make several pies and peel a bucket of potatoes. On Monday, it took the worker 2 h to make the pies and an average of 1.5 min to peel each potato. On Tuesday, the worker finished the work in the same amount of time, but it took 2.5 h to make the pies and an average of 1 min to peel each potato. About how many potatoes are in a bucket?
   • What quantities do you know and how are they related to each other?
   • How can you use the known and unknown quantities to write an equation for this situation?

37. Error Analysis Describe and correct the error in finding the solution of the equation $2x = 6x$.

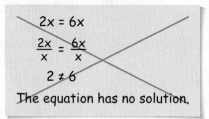

$2x = 6x$

$\dfrac{2x}{x} = \dfrac{6x}{x}$

$2 \neq 6$

The equation has no solution.

38. Skiing A skier is trying to decide whether or not to buy a season ski pass. A daily pass costs $67. A season ski pass costs $350. The skier would have to rent skis with either pass for $25 per day. How many days would the skier have to go skiing in order to make the season pass less expensive than daily passes?

39. Business A small juice company spends $1200 per day on business expenses plus $1.10 per bottle of juice they make. They charge $2.50 for each bottle of juice they produce. How many bottles of juice must the company sell in one day in order to equal its daily costs?

Standardized Test Prep

SAT/ACT

40. What is the solution of $-2(3x - 4) = -2x + 2$?

Ⓐ $-\dfrac{2}{3}$ Ⓑ $\dfrac{3}{2}$ Ⓒ 2   Ⓓ 24

41. Two times a number plus three equals one half of the number plus 12. What is the number?

Ⓕ 3.6   Ⓖ 6   Ⓗ 8   Ⓘ 10

42. Josie's goal is to run 30 mi each week. This week she has already run the distances shown in the table. She wants to have one day of rest and to spread out the remaining miles evenly over the rest of the week. Which equation can she use to find how many miles m per day she must run?

Miles per Day						
M	T	W	T	F	S	S
4	4.5	3.5	■	■	■	■

Ⓐ $4 + 4.5 + 3.5 + 3m = 30$

Ⓑ $4 + 4.5 + 3.5 + 4m = 30$

Ⓒ $30 - (4 + 4.5 + 3.5) = m$

Ⓓ $4 + 4.5 + 3.5 + m = 30$

Mixed Review

Solve each equation.   ◀ See Lesson 2-3.

43. $-2a + 5a - 4 = 11$ **44.** $6 = -3(x + 4)$ **45.** $3\left(c + \dfrac{1}{3}\right) = 4$

46. A carpenter is filling in an open entranceway with a door and two side panels of the same width. The entranceway is 3 m wide. The door will be 1.2 m wide. How wide should the carpenter make the panels on either side of the door so that the two panels and the door will fill the entranceway exactly?   ◀ See Lesson 2-2.

Get Ready! **To prepare for Lesson 2-5, do Exercises 47–49.**

Evaluate each expression for the given values of the variables.   ◀ See Lesson 1-2.

47. $n + 2m$; $m = 12, n = -2$ **48.** $3b \div c$; $b = 12, c = 4$ **49.** xy^2; $x = 2.8, y = 2$

2-5 Literal Equations and Formulas

Objective To rewrite and use literal equations and formulas

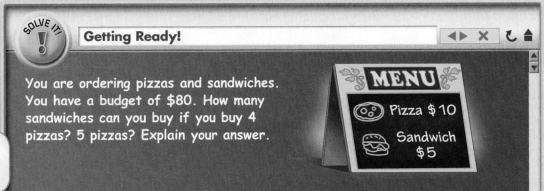

Getting Ready!

You are ordering pizzas and sandwiches. You have a budget of $80. How many sandwiches can you buy if you buy 4 pizzas? 5 pizzas? Explain your answer.

MENU
Pizza $10
Sandwich $5

Hey—there are <u>two</u> variable quantities here!

Dynamic Activity
Solving Formulas for Any Variable

In this lesson, you will learn to solve problems using equations in more than one variable. A **literal equation** is an equation that involves two or more variables.

Focus Question How can you rewrite a literal equation?

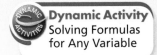

Lesson Vocabulary
• literal equation
• formula

Think

Why should you rewrite the equation?
If you rewrite the equation, you have to isolate y only once. Then substitute for x. If you substitute for x first, you must isolate y twice (once for each x-value).

Problem 1 Rewriting a Literal Equation

The equation $10x + 5y = 80$, where x is the number of pizzas and y is the number of sandwiches, models the problem in the Solve It. How many sandwiches can you buy if you buy 3 pizzas? 6 pizzas?

Step 1 Solve the equation $10x + 5y = 80$ for y.

Write the original equation.	$10x + 5y = 80$
Subtract $10x$ from each side because $10x$ is on the same side as y.	$10x + 5y - 10x = 80 - 10x$
Simplify.	$5y = 80 - 10x$
Divide each side by 5.	$\dfrac{5y}{5} = \dfrac{80 - 10x}{5}$
Simplify.	$y = 16 - 2x$

Step 2 Use the new equation to find y when $x = 3$ and when $x = 6$.

Write the new equation twice.	$y = 16 - 2x$	$y = 16 - 2x$
Substitute 3 for x in the first equation and 6 for x in the second equation.	$y = 16 - 2(3)$	$y = 16 - 2(6)$
Simplify.	$y = 10$	$y = 4$

If you buy 3 pizzas, you can buy 10 sandwiches. If you buy 6 pizzas, you can buy 4 sandwiches.

Got It? **1. a.** Solve the equation $4 = 2m - 5n$ for m. What are the values of m when $n = -2, 0$, and 2?

       b. Reasoning Solve Problem 1 by substituting $x = 3$ and $x = 6$ into the equation $10x + 5y = 80$ and then solving for y in each case. Do you prefer this method or the method shown in Problem 1? Explain.

When you rewrite literal equations, you may have to divide by a variable or variable expression. In this lesson, assume that the variable or variable expression is not equal to zero. Division by zero is not defined.

 Problem 2 **Rewriting a Literal Equation With Only Variables**

ONLINE PROBLEMS

Think

How can you solve a literal equation for a variable?
When a literal equation contains only variables, treat the variables you are *not* solving for as constants.

What equation do you get when you solve $ax + b = c$ for x?

Write the original equation.	$ax + b = c$
Subtract b from each side because it is on the same side as x.	$ax + b - b = c - b$
Simplify.	$ax = c - b$
Divide each side by a.	$\dfrac{ax}{a} = \dfrac{c - b}{a}$
Simplify.	$x = \dfrac{c - b}{a}$

Hint

You might rewrite the equation in part (a) as $px + r = -t$ before you begin.

 Got It? **2. a.** What equation do you get when you solve $-t = r + px$ for x?

       b. What equation do you get when you solve $\dfrac{m - d}{e} = g$ for d?

A **formula** is an equation that states a relationship among quantities. Formulas are special types of literal equations. Some common formulas are given below. Notice that some of the formulas use the same variables, but the definitions of the variables are different.

Formula Name	Formula	Definitions of Variables
Perimeter of a rectangle	$P = 2\ell + 2w$	P = perimeter, ℓ = length, w = width
Circumference of a circle	$C = 2\pi r$	C = circumference, r = radius
Area of a rectangle	$A = \ell w$	A = area, ℓ = length, w = width
Area of a triangle	$A = \frac{1}{2}bh$	A = area, b = base, h = height
Area of a circle	$A = \pi r^2$	A = area, r = radius
Distance traveled	$d = rt$	d = distance, r = rate, t = time
Temperature	$C = \frac{5}{9}(F - 32)$	C = degrees Celsius, F = degrees Fahrenheit

ONLINE PROBLEMS

Problem 3 Rewriting a Geometric Formula

What is the radius of a circle with circumference 64 ft? Round to the nearest tenth. Use 3.14 for π.

Write the appropriate formula.	$C = 2\pi r$
Divide each side by 2π to isolate r, the variable you need to find.	$\dfrac{C}{2\pi} = \dfrac{2\pi r}{2\pi}$
Simplify.	$\dfrac{C}{2\pi} = r$
Substitute 64 for C.	$\dfrac{64}{2\pi} = r$
Simplify. Use 3.14 for π.	$10.2 \approx r$

The radius of the circle is about 10.2 ft.

 Got It? 3. What is the height of a triangle that has an area of 24 in.^{2} and a base with a length of 8 in.?

 ONLINE PROBLEMS

Problem 4 Rewriting a Formula

Biology The monarch butterfly is the only butterfly that migrates annually north and south. The distance that a particular group of monarch butterflies travel is shown. It takes a typical butterfly about 120 days to travel one way. What is the average rate at which a butterfly travels in miles per day? Round to the nearest mile per day.

Write the appropriate formula.	$d = rt$
Divide each side by t.	$\dfrac{d}{t} = \dfrac{rt}{t}$
Simplify.	$\dfrac{d}{t} = r$
Substitute 1700 for d and 120 for t.	$\dfrac{1700}{120} = r$
Simplify.	$14 \approx r$

Indiana

1700 miles

Mexico

The butterflies travel at an average rate of about 14 mi per day.

 Got It? 4. Pacific gray whales migrate annually from the waters near Alaska to the waters near Baja California, Mexico, and back. The whales travel a distance of about 5000 mi each way at an average rate of 91 mi per day. About how many days does it take the whales to migrate one way?

Focus Question How can you rewrite a literal equation?

Answer Use the properties of equality and inverse operations to isolate the variable you choose.

Lesson Check

Do you know HOW?

Solve each equation for the given variable.

1. $-2x + 5y = 12$ for y **2.** $a - 2b = -10$ for b

3. $mx + 2nx = p$ for x **4.** $C = \frac{5}{9}(F - 32)$ for F

5. Gardening Jonah is planting a rectangular garden. The perimeter of the garden is 120 yd, and the width is 20 yd. What is the length of the garden?

Do you UNDERSTAND?

Vocabulary Use the list before Problem 3 to help you classify each equation below as a formula, a literal equation, or both.

6. $c = 2d$ **7.** $y = 2x - 1$

8. $A = \frac{1}{2}bh$ **9.** $P = 2\ell + 2w$

10. Compare and Contrast How is the process of rewriting literal equations similar to the process of solving equations in one variable? How is it different?

Practice and Problem-Solving Exercises

 Practice   Solve each equation for y. Then find the value of y for each value of x.

See Problem 1.

Guided Practice

11. $y + 2x = 5$ when $x = -1, 0, 3$

$y + 2x - 2x = 5 - 2x$

To start, subtract $2x$ from each side because $2x$ is on the same side as y.

12. $2y + 4x = 8$ when $x = -2, 1, 3$ **13.** $3x - 5y = 9$ when $x = -1, 0, 1$

14. $4x = 3y - 7$ when $x = 4, 5, 6$ **15.** $5x = -4y + 4$ when $x = 1, 2, 3$

16. $2y + 7x = 4$ when $x = 5, 10, 15$ **17.** $6x = 7 - 4y$ when $x = -2, -1, 0$

Solve each equation for x.

See Problem 2.

Guided Practice

18. $y = \dfrac{x - v}{b}$

$b(y) = b\left(\dfrac{x - v}{b}\right)$

To start, notice that x is part of a fraction. Multiply each side by b, the denominator.

Simplify.

$by = x - v$

19. $mx + nx = p$ **20.** $S = C + xC$ **21.** $\dfrac{x}{a} = \dfrac{y}{b}$

22. $A = Bxt + C$ **23.** $4x - 4b = x$ **24.** $\dfrac{x + 2}{y} = 2$

Solve each problem. Round to the nearest tenth, if necessary. Use 3.14 for π.

⬤ **See Problem 3.**

25. What is the radius of a circle with circumference 22 m?

26. What is the length of a rectangle with width 10 in. and area 45 in.^{2}?

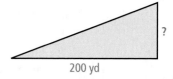

> **Hint** You will find all the formulas you need on the list after Problem 2.

27. A triangle has height 4 ft and area 32 ft^2. What is the length of its base?

28. A rectangle has perimeter 84 cm and length 35 cm. What is its width?

29. Parks A public park is in the shape of a triangle. The side of the park that forms the base of the triangle is 200 yd long, and the area of the park is 7500 yd^2. What is the length of the side of the park that forms the height of the triangle?

?

200 yd

Solve each problem. Round to the nearest tenth, if necessary.

⬤ **See Problem 4.**

30. Travel A vehicle travels on a highway at a rate of 65 mi/h. How long does it take the vehicle to travel 25 mi?

31. Baseball You can use the formula $a = \frac{h}{n}$ to find the batting average a of a batter who has h hits in n times at bat. Solve the formula for h. If a batter has a batting average of .290 and has been at bat 300 times, how many hits does the batter have?

32. Construction Bricklayers use the formula $n = 7\ell h$ to estimate the number n of bricks needed to build a wall of length ℓ and height h, where ℓ and h are in feet. Solve the formula for h. Estimate the height of a wall 28 ft long that requires 1568 bricks.

B Apply

Solve each equation for the given variable.

33. $2m - 2x = x + n$ for x

34. $cd + ed = m$; d

35. $a + 2xy = 14$ for y

36. $V = \frac{1}{3}\pi r^2 h$ for h

37. $A = \left(\frac{f + g}{2}\right)h$ for g

38. $2(x + a) = 4b$ for a

39. Think About a Plan The interior angles of a polygon are the angles formed inside a polygon by two adjacent sides. The sum S of the measures of the interior angles of a polygon with n sides can be found using the formula $S = 180(n - 2)$. The sum of a polygon's interior angle measures is 1260°. How many sides does the polygon have?
- What information are you given in the problem?
- What variable do you need to solve for in the formula?

40. Error Analysis Describe and correct the error made in solving the literal equation below for n.

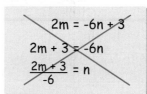

$2m = -6n + 3$

$2m + 3 = -6n$

$\frac{2m + 3}{-6} = n$

41. Weather Polar stratospheric clouds are colorful clouds that form when temperatures fall below $-78°C$. What is this temperature in degrees Fahrenheit?

Polar stratospheric clouds

42. Geometry The formula for the volume of a cylinder is $V = \pi r^2 h$, where r is the cylinder's radius and h is its height. Solve the equation for h. What is the height of a cylinder with volume 502.4 cm^3 and radius 4 cm? Use 3.14 for π.

43. Density The density of an object is calculated using the formula $D = \frac{m}{V}$, where m is the object's mass and V is its volume. Gold has a density of 19.3 g/cm^3. What is the volume of an amount of gold that has a mass of 96.5 g?

44. Open-Ended Write an equation in three variables. Solve the equation for each variable. Show all your steps.

Standardized Test Prep

GRIDDED RESPONSE

SAT/ACT

45. What is the value of the expression $-\frac{3}{4}m + 15$ when $m = 12$?

46. What is the solution of $9p + 6 - 3p = 45$?

47. The formula $F = \frac{n}{4} + 37$ relates the number of chirps n a cricket makes in 1 min to the outside temperature F in degrees Fahrenheit. How many chirps can you expect a cricket to make in 1 min when the outside temperature is $60°F$?

Mixed Review

Solve each equation. If the equation is an *identity*, write *identity*. If it has no solution, write *no solution*.

◀ See Lesson 2-4.

48. $3x - 3 = x + 7$ **49.** $2b - 10 = -3b + 5$ **50.** $4 + 12a = -2(6 - 4a)$

51. $2(y - 4) = -4y + 10$ **52.** $4c - 10 = 2(2c - 5)$ **53.** $5 + 4p = 2(2p + 1)$

Evaluate each expression for $b = 3$ and $c = 7$.

◀ See Lesson 1-2.

54. bc^2 **55.** $b^2 - c^2$ **56.** $(3b)^2 c$ **57.** $(b + c)^2$

Get Ready!   To prepare for Lesson 2-6, do Exercises 58–60.

Simplify each product.

◀ See p. 789.

58. $\frac{35}{25} \times \frac{30}{14}$ **59.** $\frac{99}{108} \times \frac{96}{55}$ **60.** $\frac{21}{81} \times \frac{63}{105}$

Finding Perimeter, Area, and Volume

Composite figures are figures composed of two or more simpler shapes. You can use formulas to find the perimeters and areas of composite figures.

Example 1

The composite figure at the right is made up of a rectangle and half of a circle. What are the perimeter and area of the figure? Use 3.14 for π.

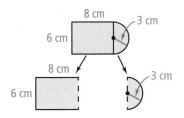

Step 1 The perimeter P is the sum of the lengths of the exterior sides of the rectangle, plus half the circumference of the circle. To find the perimeter, add these measures.

$$P = \ell + \ell + w + \left(\frac{1}{2} \cdot 2\pi r\right)$$
$$= 8 + 8 + 6 + \left(\frac{1}{2} \cdot 2\pi(3)\right)$$
$$\approx 8 + 8 + 6 + \left(\frac{1}{2} \cdot 2(3.14)(3)\right)$$
$$= 31.42 \text{ cm}$$

Step 2 The total area A is the sum of the area A_r of the rectangle and the area A_h of the half circle. Use the appropriate formula to find the area of each shape. Then add to find the total area.

$$A_r = \ell w \qquad\qquad A_h = \frac{1}{2}\pi r^2$$
$$= 8 \cdot 6 \qquad\qquad \approx \frac{1}{2}(3.14)(3)^2$$
$$= 48 \text{ cm}^2 \qquad\qquad = 14.13 \text{ cm}^2$$

$$A = A_r + A_h$$
$$= 48 + 14.13$$
$$= 62.13 \text{ cm}^2$$

The perimeter is 31.42 cm. The area is 62.13 cm^2.

The figures at the right show a rectangular prism with length ℓ, width w, and height h and a cylinder with radius r and height h.

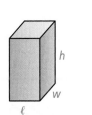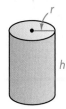

For each figure, the surface area *S.A.* is the sum of the area of the two bases and the lateral area.

Prism: S.A. = $\dfrac{\text{area of}}{\text{bases}}$ + $\dfrac{\text{lateral}}{\text{area}}$
$= 2\ell w + 2\ell h + 2wh$

Cylinder: S.A. = $\dfrac{\text{area of}}{\text{bases}}$ + $\dfrac{\text{lateral}}{\text{area}}$
$= 2\pi r^2 + 2\pi rh$

The volume V of each figure is the area of the base times the height.

Prism: V = **area of base** $\times$ **height**

$\quad = \ell w h$

Cylinder: V = **area of base** $\times$ **height**

$\quad = \pi r^2 h$

Example 2

What are the surface area and volume of each figure? Use 3.14 for π.

Prism

5 in.
3 in.
4 in.

Cylinder

3 cm
8 cm

Step 1 To find the surface area of each figure, use the appropriate formula. Substitute. Then calculate.

S.A. $= 2\ell w + 2\ell h + 2wh$

$\quad = 2(4 \cdot 3) + 2(4 \cdot 5) + 2(3 \cdot 5)$

$\quad = 94$ in.^{2}

The surface area is 94 in.^{2}.

S.A. $= 2\pi r^2 + 2\pi rh$

$\quad \approx 2(3.14)(3)^2 + 2(3.14)(3)(8)$

$\quad = 207.24$ cm^2

The surface area is about 207 cm^2.

Step 2 To find the volume of each figure, use the appropriate formula. Substitute. Then multiply.

$V = \ell wh$

$\quad = 4(3)(5)$

$\quad = 60$ in.^{3}

The volume is 60 in.^{3}.

$V = \pi r^2 h$

$\quad \approx 3.14(3)^2(8)$

$\quad = 226.08$ cm^3

The volume is about 226 cm^3.

Exercises

Find the area and perimeter of each composite figure. Use 3.14 for π. Round your answer to the nearest tenth.

1.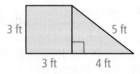
3 ft
5 ft
3 ft
4 ft

2.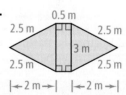
0.5 m
2.5 m
2.5 m
3 m
2.5 m
2.5 m
|←2 m→| |←2 m→|

3.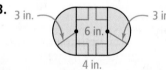
3 in.
3 in.
6 in.
4 in.

Find the surface area and volume of each figure. Use 3.14 for π. Round your answer to the nearest tenth.

4.
6 yd
20 yd

5.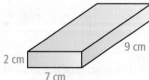
9 cm
2 cm
7 cm

6.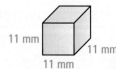
11 mm
11 mm
11 mm

Chapter Vocabulary

- Addition Property of Equality (p. 87)
- Division Property of Equality (p. 89)
- equivalent equations (p. 87)
- formula (p. 118)
- identity (p. 112)
- inverse operations (p. 88)
- isolate (p. 88)
- literal equation (p. 117)
- Multiplication Property of Equality (p. 89)
- Subtraction Property of Equality (p. 87)

Choose the correct term to complete each sentence.

1. Addition and subtraction are examples of ⟨?⟩ because they undo each other.

2. An equation that is true for every value of the variable is a(n) ⟨?⟩.

3. A(n) ⟨?⟩ is an equation that involves two or more variables.

4. ⟨?⟩ are equations that have the same solution(s).

5. To ⟨?⟩ a variable, you get it alone on one side of an equation.

2-1 Solving One-Step Equations

Quick Review

To solve an equation, get the variable by itself on one side of the equation. You can use properties of equality and inverse operations to isolate the variable. Use addition to undo its inverse, subtraction. Use multiplication to undo its inverse, division.

Example

What is the solution of $w - 6 = 15$?

Add to undo subtraction. $w - 6 + 6 = 15 + 6$

Simplify. $w = 21$

Exercises

Solve each equation. Check your answer.

6. $x + 5 = -2$

7. $a - 2.5 = 4.5$

8. $3b = 42$

9. $\frac{n}{5} = 13$

10. $c - 4 = 13.7$

11. $9m = -162$

12. Dining Five friends equally split a restaurant bill that comes to $32.50. How much does each pay?

2-2 Solving Two-Step Equations

Quick Review

To solve a two-step equation, use the reverse of the order of operations to isolate the variable. Continue to use properties of equality and inverse operations to isolate the variable.

Example

What is the solution of $\frac{y}{2} + 5 = 8$?

Subtract to undo addition. $\quad \frac{y}{2} + 5 - 5 = 8 - 5$

Simplify. $\qquad\qquad\qquad\qquad \frac{y}{2} = 3$

Multiply to undo division. $\quad 2 \cdot \frac{y}{2} = 3 \cdot 2$

Simplify. $\qquad\qquad\qquad\qquad y = 6$

Exercises

Solve each equation. Check your answer.

13. $8 + 3m = -7$ **14.** $2k - 7 = -19$

15. $7x - 2 = 22.5$ **16.** $\frac{y}{4} - 3 = -4$

17. $\frac{r + 5}{3} = -16$ **18.** $-\frac{3d}{4} + 5 = 11$

19. Plumbing A plumber charge $55 per hour, plus a $9 service fee. If the plumber earns $255, how many hours did he work?

20. Reasoning Justify each step in solving $4x - 3 = 9$.

$$4x - 3 + 3 = 9 + 3 \qquad \underline{\quad?\quad}$$
$$4x = 12 \qquad \underline{\quad?\quad}$$
$$\frac{4x}{4} = \frac{12}{4} \qquad \underline{\quad?\quad}$$
$$x = 3 \qquad \underline{\quad?\quad}$$

2-3 Solving Multi-Step Equations

Quick Review

To solve some equations, you may need to combine like terms or use the Distributive Property to clear fractions or decimals.

Example

What is the solution of $12 = 2x + \frac{4}{3} - \frac{2x}{3}$?

Multiply by 3. $\quad 3 \cdot 12 = 3\left(2x + \frac{4}{3} - \frac{2x}{3}\right)$

Simplify. $\qquad\qquad 36 = 6x + 4 - 2x$

Combine like terms. $\quad 36 = 4x + 4$

Subtract 4. $\qquad\qquad 36 - 4 = 4x + 4 - 4$

Combine like terms. $\quad 32 = 4x$

Divide each side by 4. $\quad \frac{32}{4} = \frac{4x}{4}$

Simplify. $\qquad\qquad\qquad 8 = x$

Exercises

Solve each equation. Check your answer.

21. $7(s - 5) = 42$ **22.** $3a + 2 - 5a = -14$

23. $-4b - 5 + 2b = 10$ **24.** $3.4t + 0.08 = 11$

25. $10 = \frac{c}{3} - 4 + \frac{c}{6}$ **26.** $\frac{2x}{7} + \frac{4}{5} = 5$

Write an equation to model each situation. Then solve the equation.

27. Earnings You work for 4 h on Saturday and 8 h on Sunday. You also receive a $50 bonus. You earn $164. How much did you earn per hour?

28. Entertainment Online concert tickets cost $37 each, plus a service charge of $8.50 per ticket. The Web site also charges a transaction fee of $14.99 for the purchase. You paid $242.49. How many tickets did you buy?

2-4 Solving Equations With Variables on Both Sides

Quick Review

When an equation has variables on both sides, you can use properties of equality to isolate the variable on one side. An equation has no solution if no value of the variable makes it true. An equation is an **identity** if every value of the variable makes it true.

Example

What is the solution of $3x - 7 = 5x + 19$?

Subtract $3x$.	$3x - 7 - 3x = 5x + 19 - 3x$
Simplify.	$-7 = 2x + 19$
Subtract 19.	$-7 - 19 = 2x + 19 - 19$
Simplify.	$-26 = 2x$
Divide each side by 2.	$\dfrac{-26}{2} = \dfrac{2x}{2}$
Simplify.	$-13 = x$

Exercises

Solve each equation. If the equation is an identity, write *identity*. If it has no solution, write *no solution*.

29. $\frac{2}{3}x + 4 = \frac{3}{5}x - 2$ **30.** $6 - 0.25f = f - 3$

31. $3(h - 4) = -\frac{1}{2}(24 - 6h)$ **32.** $5n = 20(4 + 0.25n)$

33. Architecture Two buildings have the same total height. One building has 8 floors with height h. The other building has a ground floor of 16 ft and 6 other floors with height h. Write and solve an equation to find the height h of these floors.

34. Travel A train makes a trip at 65 mi/h. A plane traveling 130 mi/h makes the same trip in 3 fewer hours. Write and solve an equation to find the distance of the trip.

2-5 Literal Equations and Formulas

Quick Review

A **literal equation** is an equation that involves two or more variables. A **formula** is an equation that states a relationship between quantities. You can use properties of equality to solve a literal equation for one variable in terms of others.

Example

What is the width of a rectangle with area 91 ft² and length 7 ft?

Write the appropriate formula.	$A = \ell w$
Divide each side by ℓ.	$\dfrac{A}{\ell} = w$
Substitute.	$\dfrac{91}{7} = w$
Simplify.	$13 = w$

The width of the rectangle is 13 ft.

Exercises

Solve each equation for x.

35. $ax + bx = -c$ **36.** $\frac{x + r}{t} + 1 = 0$

37. $m - 3x = 2x + p$ **38.** $\frac{x}{p} + \frac{x}{q} = s$

Solve each problem. Round to the nearest tenth, if necessary. Use 3.14 for π.

39. What is the width of a rectangle with length 5.5 cm and area 220 cm² (*Hint*: $A = \ell w$)?

40. What is the radius of a circle with circumference 94.2 mm (*Hint*: $C = 2\pi r$)?

41. A triangle has height 15 in. and area 120 in.². What is the length of its base (*Hint*: $A = \frac{1}{2}bh$)?

Do you know HOW?

Solve each equation. Check your answer.

1. $38 = 2a + 54$

2. $t + 18.1 = 23.9$

3. $18.9 = 2.1x$

4. $\frac{1}{2}(b - 3) = \frac{5}{2}$

Solve each equation. Justify your steps.

5. $9 - 3r = 14$

6. $3 = \frac{1}{2}b + 11$

Solve each equation. If the equation is an identity, write *identity*. If it has no solution, write *no solution*.

7. $8(h - 1) = 6h + 4 + 2h$

8. $\frac{1}{7}(14 - 7p) - 2 = -2\left(\frac{1}{2}p + 3\right) + 6$

9. $\frac{c + 3}{5} = 15$

10. $\frac{2}{3}(x - 4) = \frac{1}{3}(2x - 6)$

11. $1.7m = 10.2$

12. $2 + \frac{1}{3}t = 1 + \frac{1}{4}t$

13. **Geometry** The formula for the area of a triangle is $A = \frac{1}{2}bh$. Solve the formula for h. A triangle has a base of 7 cm and an area of 28 cm^2. What is its height?

14. **Menus** A new pizza shop is going to print new menus. Each menu costs $.50 to produce. The owners have a total budget of $2500 for the new menus. How many menus can the pizza shop print?

15. **Guitars** You paid $600 for a new guitar. Your guitar cost $40 more than twice the cost of your friend's guitar. How much did your friend's guitar cost?

Define a variable and write an equation to model each situation. Then solve.

16. **Concerts** Concert tickets cost $25 each. A college student ordered some tickets online. There was a service charge of $3 per ticket. The total came to $252. How many tickets did the student order?

17. **Gyms** Membership for the Alpine rock-climbing gym costs $25 per month plus a $125 sign-up fee. Membership for Rocco's rock-climbing gym costs $30 per month plus a $50 sign-up fee.

    a. After how many months will the memberships cost the same?

    b. If you only wanted a one-year membership, which gym would you join?

Do you UNDERSTAND?

18. **Vocabulary** Complete: You can use subtraction to undo addition. Subtraction is called the ___?___ of addition.

19. **Reasoning** The equation $\frac{5}{x} = \frac{2}{x} + \frac{3}{x}$ is true for all values of x where $x \neq 0$. Is the equation an identity?

20. **Writing** Would you solve the equation $10 = 4(y - 1)$ by using the Distributive Property or by dividing each side by 4? Explain.

21. **Reasoning** In the process of solving an equation, a student noticed that the variable was eliminated. The student concluded that the equation must be an identity. Is the student correct? Explain.

22. **Reasoning** You are solving the equation $0.02x - 0.004 = 0.028$. Your first step is to multiply both sides by 1000 to clear the decimals. Your classmate starts by dividing both sides by 0.02. Is there any disadvantage to your classmate's method? Explain.

PowerAlgebra.com
Your place to get
all things digital.

CHAPTER
2
PART B

Solving Equations

In Part A, you learned to solve one-step and two-step equations. Now you will apply what you have learned to mathematical contexts involving one-step and two-step equations.

Vocabulary for Part B

English/Spanish Vocabulary Audio Online:

English	Spanish
conversion factor, *p. 131*	factor de conversión
cross products, *p. 137*	productos cruzados
percent change, *p. 157*	cambio porcentual
proportion, *p. 136*	proporción
rate, *p. 130*	tasa
ratio, *p. 130*	razón
scale, *p. 145*	escala
unit analysis, *p. 132*	análisis de unidades

BIG ideas

1 Equivalence
Essential Question Can equations that appear to be different be equivalent?

2 Solving Equations and Inequalities
Essential Question How can you solve equations?

3 Proportionality
Essential Question What kind of relationships can proportions represent?

Chapter Preview for Part B

2-6   **Ratios, Rates, and Conversions**
2-7   **Solving Proportions**
2-8   **Proportions and Similar Figures**
2-9   **Percents**
2-10 **Change Expressed as a Percent**

2-6 Ratios, Rates, and Conversions

Objectives To find ratios and rates
To convert units and rates

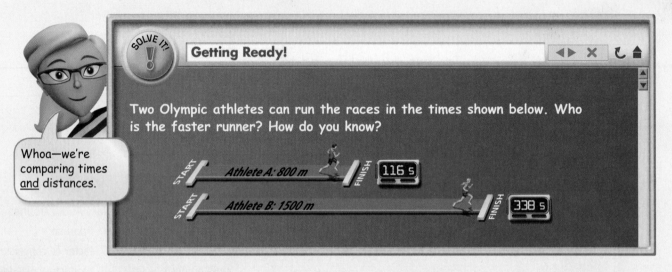

Getting Ready!

Two Olympic athletes can run the races in the times shown below. Who is the faster runner? How do you know?

Whoa—we're comparing times and distances.

Athlete A: 800 m   116 s

Athlete B: 1500 m   338 s

Lesson Vocabulary
- ratio
- rate
- unit rate
- conversion factor
- unit analysis

A **ratio** compares two numbers by division. The ratio of two numbers a and b, where $b \neq 0$, can be written in three ways:

$$\frac{a}{b}, \; a : b, \text{ and } a \text{ to } b.$$

Suppose the ratio of the number of boys to the number of girls in a class is $2 : 1$. The ratio can also be written as $\frac{2}{1}$ or 2 to 1. This means the number of boys is *two times* the number of girls.

Focus Question How can ratios help you compare or convert quantities?

A ratio that compares quantities measured in different units is called a **rate.** A rate with a denominator of 1 unit is a **unit rate.** In the Solve It, speed is the number of meters traveled per 1 second of time. This is an example of a unit rate.

Problem 1 Comparing Unit Rates

Think

How can you compare prices?
You can write all prices as unit rates.

Shopping You are shopping for T-shirts. Which store offers the best deal?

Store A: $25 for 2 shirts   Store B: $45 for 4 shirts   Store C: $30 for 3 shirts

Step 1 Write each price as a ratio.

Step 2 Write each ratio as a unit rate.

Store A $\dfrac{\$25}{2 \text{ shirts}} = \dfrac{\$12.50}{1 \text{ shirt}}$

Store B $\dfrac{\$45}{4 \text{ shirts}} = \dfrac{\$11.25}{1 \text{ shirt}}$

Step 3 Compare unit rates. Store C has the best deal.

Store C $\dfrac{\$30}{3 \text{ shirts}} = \dfrac{\$10}{1 \text{ shirt}}$

Got It? **1.** If Store B lowers its price to $42 for 4 shirts, does the solution to Problem 1 change? Explain.

To convert from one unit to another, such as feet to inches, you use a *conversion factor*. A **conversion factor** is a ratio of two equivalent measures in different units, such as $\dfrac{1 \text{ ft}}{12 \text{ in}}$ or $\dfrac{1 \text{ yd}}{3 \text{ ft}}$. See the table on page 798 for some common equivalent units of measure.

Problem 2 Converting Units

Plan

How do you choose the conversion factor?
Write a conversion factor that has the desired units in the numerator and the original units in the denominator.

What is the given amount converted to the named unit?

A 330 min; hours   **B** 15 kg; grams

Choose a conversion factor and multiply it by the original amount. $330 \text{ min} \cdot \dfrac{1 \text{ h}}{60 \text{ min}}$ $15 \text{ kg} \cdot \dfrac{1000 \text{ g}}{1 \text{ kg}}$

Cross out pairs of matching units on opposite sides of the division bar. $330 \, \cancel{\text{min}} \cdot \dfrac{1 \text{ h}}{60 \, \cancel{\text{min}}}$ $15 \, \cancel{\text{kg}} \cdot \dfrac{1000 \text{ g}}{1 \, \cancel{\text{kg}}}$

Simplify.   5.5 h   15,000 g

C 5 ft 3 in.; inches

Separate parts with different units.   5 ft 3 in. = 5 ft + 3 in.

Choose a conversion factor to convert the units in one part to the units in the other part. $= 5 \, \cancel{\text{ft}} \cdot \dfrac{12 \text{ in.}}{1 \, \cancel{\text{ft}}} + 3 \text{ in.}$

Simplify.   = 60 in. + 3 in.

Combine like terms.   = 63 in.

Hint

If your desired unit is meters, choose a conversion factor with meters in the numerator and centimeters in the denominator.

Got It? **2.** What is the given amount converted to the named unit?
  a. 1250 cm; meters   **b.** 11 lbs; ounces   **c.** 6 h 45 min; hours

In Problem 2, you may notice that calculations show the units for each quantity. This process is called **unit analysis.** You can also convert units from one system to another.

 Problem 3 **Converting Units Between Systems**

Architecture The CN Tower in Toronto, Canada, is about 1815 ft tall. About how many meters tall is the tower? Use the fact that 1 m ≈ 3.28 ft.

Plan

How can you convert units?
Write the conversion factor so that the original units divide out and leave only the desired units.

Multiply by a conversion factor.	$1815 \text{ ft} \cdot \dfrac{1 \text{ m}}{3.28 \text{ ft}}$
Cross out matching units.	$1815 \cancel{\text{ft}} \cdot \dfrac{1 \text{ m}}{3.28 \cancel{\text{ft}}}$
Simplify.	$\approx 553 \text{ m}$

The CN Tower is about 553 m tall.

Check Round 1815 to 1800 and 3.28 to 3. Then divide 1800 by 3. $1800 \div 3 = 600$, and 600 is about 553. So, 553 m is a reasonable answer.

 Got It? **3. a.** The Sears Tower in Chicago, Illinois, is 1450 ft tall. About how many meters tall is the tower? Use the fact that 1 m ≈ 3.28 ft.

  b. Monetary exchange rates change from day to day. On a particular day, the exchange rate for dollars to euros was about 1 dollar = 0.63 euro. About how many euros could you get for \$325 on that day?

You can also convert both of the units in a rate. To change both of the units, you must multiply by two conversion factors.

 Problem 4 **Converting Rates**

A student ran the 50-yd dash in 5.8 s. At what speed did the student run in miles per hour?

Know	Need	Plan
The running speed in yards per second	The running speed in miles per hour	Write the speed as a ratio. Choose conversion factors so that the original units (yards and seconds) divide out, leaving you with the units you need (miles and hours).

Hint

To get matching units, you use the conversion factors $\dfrac{1 \text{ mi}}{1760 \text{ yd}}$ and $\dfrac{3600 \text{ s}}{1 \text{ hr}}$.

Write the speed as a ratio. Use a conversion factor to change yards to miles.	$\dfrac{50 \text{ yd}}{5.8 \text{ s}} \cdot \dfrac{1 \text{ mi}}{1760 \text{ yd}}$
Cross out matching units.	$\dfrac{50 \cancel{\text{yd}}}{5.8 \text{ s}} \cdot \dfrac{1 \text{ mi}}{1760 \cancel{\text{yd}}}$
Use another conversion factor to change seconds to hours.	$\dfrac{50}{5.8 \text{ s}} \cdot \dfrac{1 \text{ mi}}{1760} \cdot \dfrac{3600 \text{ s}}{1 \text{ h}}$
Cross out matching units.	$\dfrac{50}{5.8 \cancel{\text{s}}} \cdot \dfrac{1 \text{ mi}}{1760} \cdot \dfrac{3600 \cancel{\text{s}}}{1 \text{ h}}$
Simplify until only a fraction remains.	$\dfrac{180{,}000 \text{ mi}}{10{,}208 \text{ h}} \approx 17.6 \text{ mi/h}$

The student ran at a speed of about 17.6 mi/h.

Hint

You can use the reciprocal of a conversion factor to divide out common units.

 Got It? **4.** An athlete ran a sprint of 100 ft in 3.1 s. At what speed was the athlete running in miles per hour? Round to the nearest mile per hour.

Focus Question How can ratios help you compare or convert quantities?

Answer You can change rates to unit rates and compare them. To convert quantities, you can multiply by conversion factors, ratios equal to 1.

Lesson Check

Do you know HOW?

1. Which is the better buy, 6 bagels for $3.29 or 8 bagels for $4.15?

2. What is 7 lb 4 oz converted to ounces?

3. Which is longer, 12 m or 13 yd?

4. A car is traveling at 55 mi/h. What is the car's speed in feet per second?

Do you UNDERSTAND?

Vocabulary Tell whether each rate is a unit rate.

5. 20 mi every 3 h

6. 2 dollars per day

7. **Reasoning** Does multiplying by a conversion factor change the amount of what is being measured? How do you know?

8. **Reasoning** If you convert pounds to ounces, will the number of ounces be greater or less than the number of pounds? Explain.

Practice and Problem-Solving Exercises

 Practice Find the best deal.   ◀ **See Problem 1.**

9. $57 for 4 DVDs

 $31 for 2 DVDs

 $75 for 5 DVDs

10. $66 for 3 pairs of jeans

 $81 for 4 pairs of jeans

 $42 for 2 pairs of jeans

Guided Practice ➡

11. **Running** Trisha ran 10 kilometers in 2.5 hours. Jason ran 7.5 kilometers in 2 hours. Olga ran 9.5 kilometers in 2.25 hours. Who had the fastest average speed?

 To start, write a ratio for Trisha's speed. $\dfrac{10 \text{ km}}{2.5 \text{ h}}$

12. **Population** Bellingham, Washington, has an area of 25.4 mi^2 and a population of 74,547 during one year. Bakersfield, California, has an area of 113.1 mi^2 and a population of 295,536 during the same year. Which city has a greater number of people per square mile?

Convert the given amount to the named unit.

See Problems 2 and 3.

13. 63 yd; feet

14. 168 h; days

15. 2.5 lb; ounces

16. 200 cm; meters

17. 4 min; seconds

18. 1500 mL; liters

19. 9 yd; meters

20. 5 kg; pounds

21. 79 dollars; cents

22. Maintenance The janitor at a school discovered a slow leak in a pipe. The janitor found that it was leaking at a rate of 4 fl oz per minute. How fast was the pipe leaking in gallons per hour?

See Problem 4.

To start, write a ratio. Use a conversion factor to change fl oz to gal.

$$\frac{4 \text{ fl oz}}{1 \text{ min}} \cdot \frac{1 \text{ gal}}{128 \text{ fl oz}}$$

23. Shopping Mr. Swanson bought a package of 10 disposable razors for $6.30. He found that each razor lasted for 1 week. What was his shaving cost per day?

B **Apply**

Copy and complete each statement.

24. 7 ft 3 in. = ■ in.

25. 2.2 kg = ■ lb

26. 2.5 h = ■ min

27. 2 qt/min = ■ gal/s

28. 75 cents/h = ■ dollars/day

29. 60 ft/s = ■ km/h

Choose a method Choose paper and pencil, mental math, or a calculator to tell which measurement is greater.

30. 640 ft; 0.5 mi

31. 63 in.; 125 cm

32. 75 g; 5 oz

33. Think About a Plan A college student is considering a subscription to a social-networking Internet site that advertises its cost as "only 87 cents per day." What is the cost of membership in dollars per year?
- How many conversion factors will you need to use to solve the problem?
- How do you choose the appropriate conversion factors?

34. Recipes Recipe A makes 5 dinner rolls using 1 c of flour. Recipe B makes 24 rolls using $7\frac{1}{2}$ c of flour. Recipe C makes 45 rolls using 10 c of flour. Which recipe requires the most flour per roll?

35. Error Analysis Find the mistake in the conversion below. Explain the mistake and convert the units correctly.

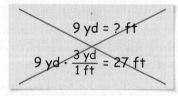

36. Writing Suppose you want to convert kilometers to miles. Which unit should be in the numerator of the conversion factor? Which unit should be in the denominator? Explain how you know.

37. Estimation Five mi is approximately equal to 8 km. Use mental math to estimate the distance in kilometers to a town that is 30 mi away.

38. Reasoning A carpenter is building an entertainment center. She is calculating the size of the space to leave for the television. She wants to leave about a foot of space on either side of the television. Would measuring the size of the television exactly or estimating the size to the nearest inch be more appropriate? Explain.

39. Reasoning A traveler changed $300 to euros for a trip to Germany, but the trip was canceled. Three months later, the traveler changed the euros back to dollars. Would you expect that the traveler got exactly $300 back? Explain.

Standardized Test Prep

SAT/ACT

40. Most mammals take 1 breath for every 4 heartbeats. The heart of a large dog beats about 180 times in 1 min. About how many times does the dog take a breath in 1 min?

(A) 40　　　　　(B) 45　　　　　(C) 90　　　　　(D) 720

41. Which equation best describes the relationship shown in the table?

x	−2	−1	0	1	2
y	−4	−2	0	2	4

(F) $y = x - 2$　　　(G) $y = x - 1$　　　(H) $y = x$　　　(I) $y = 2x$

42. Which expression is equivalent to $-2(3x - 4) - (-2x + 1)$?

(A) $-4x - 7$　　　(B) $-4x - 5$　　　(C) $-4x + 7$　　　(D) $-4x + 9$

Mixed Review

43. What is the height of a triangle with an area of 30 cm^2 and a base length of 12 cm?　　　◀ **See Lesson 2-5.**

44. What is the diameter of a circle with a circumference of 47.1 in.? Use 3.14 for π.

Solve each equation. Check your answer.　　　◀ **See Lesson 2-3.**

45. $2y + 0.5y + 4.5 = 17$

46. $-\frac{2}{3}x - 8 = -12$

47. $-4.8 = -4(2.4d)$

48. $\frac{3a + 1}{5} = 2$

Get Ready! **To prepare for Lesson 2-7, do Exercises 49–51.**

Simplify each expression. Justify each step.　　　◀ **See Lesson 1-4.**

49. $\frac{27x}{x}$

50. $\frac{b}{112b}$

51. $\frac{20mn}{n}$

2-7 Solving Proportions

Objective To solve and apply proportions

You've used ratios to compare. This problem involves <u>equal</u> ratios.

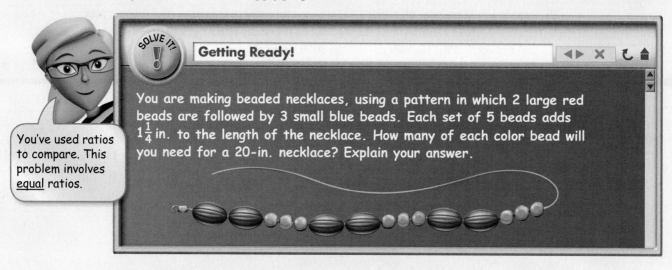

SOLVE IT!

Getting Ready!

You are making beaded necklaces, using a pattern in which 2 large red beads are followed by 3 small blue beads. Each set of 5 beads adds $1\frac{1}{4}$ in. to the length of the necklace. How many of each color bead will you need for a 20-in. necklace? Explain your answer.

In the Solve It, the number of red beads and the number of blue beads are quantities that have a proportional relationship. This means that the ratio of the quantities is constant even though the quantities themselves can change. For example, as you are making the necklace you will have 2 red beads and 3 blue beads, then 4 red beads and 6 blue beads, then 6 red beads and 9 blue beads, and so on. At each stage, the ratio of red beads to blue beads remains $\frac{2}{3}$, a constant.

A proportional relationship can produce an infinite number of equivalent ratios. You can use any two of these to write a proportion. A **proportion** is an equation that states that two ratios are equal. For example, $\frac{a}{b} = \frac{c}{d}$, where $b \neq 0$ and $d \neq 0$, is a proportion. You read this as "a is to b as c is to d."

Focus Question How can you solve a proportion to find an unknown quantity?

Problem 1 Solving a Proportion Using the Multiplication Property

Think

How is this problem related to problems you've solved before? Solving this proportion is similar to solving a one-step equation using multiplication. You can simply multiply by 12 to isolate m.

What is the solution of the proportion $\frac{7}{8} = \frac{m}{12}$?

Write the original proportion. $\qquad \frac{7}{8} = \frac{m}{12}$

Multiply each side by 12 to isolate m. $\qquad 12 \cdot \frac{7}{8} = 12 \cdot \frac{m}{12}$

Simplify. $\qquad \frac{84}{8} = m$

Divide. $\qquad 10\frac{1}{2} = m$, or $10.5 = m$

Check

Write the original proportion. $\qquad \frac{7}{8} = \frac{m}{12}$

Substitute 10.5 for m $\qquad \frac{7}{8} \overset{?}{=} \frac{10.5}{12}$

The solution checks. $\qquad 0.875 = 0.875 \checkmark$

 Got It? **1.** What is the solution of the proportion $\frac{x}{7} = \frac{4}{5}$?

In the proportion $\frac{a}{b} = \frac{c}{d}$, the products ad and bc are **cross products.** You can use the following property of cross products to solve proportions.

take note

Property Cross Products Property of a Proportion

Words The cross products of a proportion are equal.

Algebra If $\frac{a}{b} = \frac{c}{d}$, where $b \neq 0$ and $d \neq 0$, then $ad = bc$.

Example $\frac{3}{4} = \frac{9}{12}$, so $3(12) = 4(9)$, or $36 = 36$.

Here's Why It Works You can use the Multiplication Property of Equality to prove the Cross Products Property.

Assume this equation is true. $\qquad \frac{a}{b} = \frac{c}{d}$

Clear the fractions by multiplying each side by bd. $\qquad bd \cdot \frac{a}{b} = bd \cdot \frac{c}{d}$

Divide the common factors. $\qquad \cancel{b}d \cdot \frac{a}{\cancel{b}} = b\cancel{d} \cdot \frac{c}{\cancel{d}}$

Simplify. $\qquad da = bc$

Use the Commutative Property of Multiplication to order the variables alphabetically. $\qquad ad = bc$

For this proportion, *a* and *d* are the *extremes* of the proportion, and *b* and *c* are the *means* of the proportion. Notice that in the Cross Products Property the product of the means equals the product of the extremes.

$$ad = bc$$

The diagram at the right illustrates the Cross Products Property in another way. The arrows show you can cross-multiply to find each product.

Problem 2 Solving a Proportion Using the Cross Products Property

What is the solution of the proportion $\frac{4}{3} = \frac{8}{x}$?

Think

Which property should you use?
The Cross Products Property can be easier to use when the variable is in the denominator. If you use the Multiplication Property, you must multiply each side by 3*x*.

Write the original proportion.	$\frac{4}{3} = \frac{8}{x}$
Use the Cross Products Property.	$4x = 3(8)$
Multiply.	$4x = 24$
Divide each side by 4 to isolate *x*.	$\frac{4x}{4} = \frac{24}{4}$
Simplify.	$x = 6$

Check $\frac{4}{3} = \frac{8}{6}$ ✓

 Got It? **2. a.** What is the solution of the proportion $\frac{y}{3} = \frac{3}{5}$?

  b. Reasoning Would you rather use the Cross Products Property or the Multiplication Property of Equality to solve $\frac{3}{5} = \frac{13}{b}$? Explain.

Problem 3 Solving a Multi-Step Proportion

Think

How is this proportion different from others you've seen?
This proportion looks more complex, but the Cross Products Property is true for *any* proportion. Treat each numerator as a single variable when you cross-multiply.

What is the solution of the proportion $\frac{b-8}{5} = \frac{b+3}{4}$?

Write the original proportion.	$\frac{b-8}{5} = \frac{b+3}{4}$
Use the Cross Products Property.	$4(b-8) = 5(b+3)$
Use the Distributive Property.	$4b - 32 = 5b + 15$
Get the *b* term on one side by subtracting 4*b* from each side.	$4b - 32 - 4b = 5b + 15 - 4b$
Simplify.	$-32 = b + 15$
Isolate *b* by subtracting 15 from each side.	$-32 - 15 = b + 15 - 15$
Simplify.	$-47 = b$

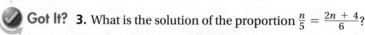 **Got It?** **3.** What is the solution of the proportion $\frac{n}{5} = \frac{2n+4}{6}$?

When you model a real-world situation with a proportion, you must write the proportion so that the numerators have the same units and the denominators have the same units. For example, suppose you travel 100 miles in 2 hours at a constant speed. You write proportion to find the number of miles you will travel in 5 hours.

Correct: $\dfrac{100 \text{ mi}}{2 \text{ h}} = \dfrac{x \text{ mi}}{5 \text{ h}}$ **Incorrect:** $\dfrac{100 \text{ mi}}{2 \text{ h}} = \dfrac{5 \text{ h}}{x \text{ mi}}$

 Problem 4   **Using a Proportion to Solve a Problem**

Music A portable media player has 2 gigabytes of storage and can hold about 500 songs. A similar but larger media player has 80 gigabytes of storage. About how many songs can the larger media player hold?

Know
- Smaller media player has 2 gigabytes and can hold 500 songs
- Larger media player has 80 gigabytes

Need
The number of songs the larger player can hold

Plan
Write a proportion to model the situation. You can set up the proportion so that the numerators have the same units and the denominators have the same units. Then solve the proportion.

Think

Is there only one way to write a proportion?
No. You can write other proportions to solve the problem. For example,
$\dfrac{2 \text{ gigabytes}}{80 \text{ gigabytes}} = \dfrac{500 \text{ songs}}{s \text{ songs}}$
also works.

Write a proportion. $\dfrac{2 \text{ gigabytes}}{500 \text{ songs}} = \dfrac{80 \text{ gigabytes}}{s \text{ songs}}$

Use the Cross Products Property. $2s = 500(80)$

Multiply. $2s = 40{,}000$

Divide each side by 2 to isolate s. $\dfrac{2s}{2} = \dfrac{40{,}000}{2}$

Simplify. $s = 20{,}000$

The larger media player can hold 20,000 songs.

 Got It? **4.** An 8-oz can of orange juice contains about 97 mg of vitamin C. About how many milligrams of vitamin C are there in a 12-oz can of orange juice?

Focus Question How can you solve a proportion to find an unknown quantity?

Answer Use the Multiplication Property of Equality or the Cross Products Property.

Lesson Check

Do you know HOW?

Solve each proportion.

1. $\frac{b}{6} = \frac{4}{5}$

2. $\frac{5}{9} = \frac{15}{x}$

3. $\frac{w+3}{4} = \frac{w}{2}$

4. $\frac{3}{x+1} = \frac{1}{2}$

5. **Music** A band went to a recording studio and recorded 4 songs in 3 h. How many hours would it take the band to record 9 songs if they record at the same rate?

Do you UNDERSTAND?

Vocabulary Use the proportion $\frac{m}{n} = \frac{p}{q}$. Identify the following.

6. the extremes

7. the means

8. the cross products

9. **Reasoning** When solving $\frac{x}{5} = \frac{3}{4}$, Lisa's first step was to write $4x = 5(3)$. Jen's first step was to write $20\left(\frac{x}{5}\right) = 20\left(\frac{3}{4}\right)$. Will both methods work? Explain.

Practice and Problem-Solving Exercises

See Problem 1.

A Practice   Solve each proportion using the Multiplication Property of Equality.

Guided Practice

10. $\frac{q}{8} = \frac{4}{5}$

To start, multiply each side by 8 to isolate q. $8 \cdot \frac{q}{8} = 8 \cdot \frac{4}{5}$

11. $\frac{-3}{4} = \frac{x}{26}$

12. $\frac{3}{4} = \frac{x}{5}$

13. $\frac{m}{7} = \frac{3}{5}$

14. $\frac{3}{16} = \frac{x}{12}$

15. $\frac{x}{120} = \frac{1}{24}$

16. $\frac{2}{15} = \frac{h}{125}$

See Problem 2.

Solve each proportion using the Cross Products Property.

Guided Practice

17. $\frac{3}{v} = \frac{8}{13}$

To start, use the Cross Products Property. $3(13) = 8v$

18. $\frac{15}{a} = \frac{3}{2}$

19. $\frac{2}{7} = \frac{4}{d}$

20. $\frac{-9}{b} = \frac{5}{6}$

21. $\frac{8}{p} = \frac{3}{10}$

22. $\frac{-3}{4} = \frac{m}{22}$

23. $\frac{2}{-5} = \frac{6}{t}$

See Problem 3.

Solve each proportion using any method.

24. $\frac{a-2}{9} = \frac{2}{3}$

25. $\frac{2c}{11} = \frac{c-3}{4}$

26. $\frac{7}{k-2} = \frac{5}{8}$

27. $\frac{3}{3b+4} = \frac{2}{b-4}$

28. $\frac{q+2}{5} = \frac{2q-11}{7}$

29. $\frac{c+1}{c-2} = \frac{4}{7}$

See Problem 4.

30. **Gardening** A gardener is transplanting flowers into a flowerbed. She has been working for an hour and has transplanted 14 flowers. She has 35 more flowers to transplant. If she works at the same rate, how many more hours will it take her?

31. Florists A florist is making centerpieces. He uses 2 dozen roses for every 5 centerpieces. How many dozens of roses will he need to make 20 centerpieces?

32. Picnics If 5 lb of pasta salad serves 14 people, how much pasta salad should you bring to a picnic with 49 people?

 Apply

Solve each proportion. Tell whether you used the Multiplication Property of Equality or the Cross Products Property for your first step. Explain your choice.

33. $\frac{p}{4} = \frac{7}{8}$

34. $\frac{m}{4.5} = \frac{2}{2\frac{2}{5}}$

35. $\frac{9}{14} = \frac{3}{n}$

36. $\frac{1.5}{y} = \frac{2.5}{7}$

37. $\frac{b + 13}{2} = \frac{-5b}{3}$

38. $\frac{3b}{b - 4} = \frac{3}{7}$

39. Statistics Approximately 3 people out of every 25 are left-handed. About how many left-handed people would you expect in a group of 140 people?

40. Think About a Plan Maya runs 100 m in 13.4 s. Amy can run 100 m in 14.1 s. If Amy were to finish a 100-m race at the same time as Maya, how much of a head start, in meters, would Amy need?
- What information do you know? What information is unknown?
- What proportion can you write that will help you solve the problem?

41. Electricity The electric bill for Ferguson's Furniture is shown at the right. The cost of electricity per kilowatt-hour and the total charges for one month are given. How many kilowatt-hours of electricity did Ferguson's Furniture use in that month?

⚡ *Centerville Electric*

Account Name: Ferguson's Furniture
Account Number: 34-14567-89

Cost per kilowatt-hour	$.07
Total charges	$143.32
Previous balance	$.00
Total Amount Due	$143.32

42. Video Downloads A particular computer takes 15 min to download a 45-min TV show. How long will it take the computer to download a 2-hour movie?

43. Error Analysis Describe and correct the error in solving the proportion at the right.

$\frac{8}{3} = \frac{x + 3}{2}$
$16 = 3x + 3$
$13 = 3x$
$\frac{13}{3} = x$

44. Bakery A bakery sells packages of 10 bagels for $3.69. If the bakery starts selling the bagels in packages of 12, how much would you expect a package of 12 to cost?

Ⓐ $3.08

Ⓒ $4.43

Ⓑ $4.32

Ⓓ $4.69

45. Open-Ended Write a proportion that contains a variable. Name the extremes, the means, and the cross products. Solve the proportion. Tell whether you used the Multiplication Property of Equality or the Cross Products Property to solve the proportion. Explain your choice.

46. Biology Many trees have concentric rings that can be counted to determine the tree's age. Each ring represents one year's growth. A maple tree with a diameter of 12 in. has 32 rings. If the tree continues to grow at about the same rate, how many rings will the tree have when its diameter is 20 in.?

Standardized Test Prep

47. A high school soccer team is making trail mix to sell at a fundraiser. The recipe calls for 3 lb of raisins and 2 lb of peanuts. If the team purchases 54 lb of peanuts, how many pounds of raisins will they need?

   (A) 27   (B) 36   (C) 81   (D) 162

48. One day during flu season, $\frac{1}{3}$ of the students in a class were out sick, and only 24 students were left. How many students are in the class?

   (F) 16   (G) 30   (H) 36   (I) 72

49. An art gallery owner is framing a rectangular painting as shown. The owner wants the width of the framed painting to be $38\frac{1}{2}$ in. How wide should each of the vertical sections of the frame be?

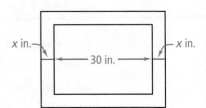

   (A) $4\frac{1}{8}$ in.   (C) $4\frac{1}{2}$ in.

   (B) $4\frac{1}{4}$ in.   (D) $8\frac{1}{2}$ in.

Mixed Review

Copy and complete each statement.   ◀ **See Lesson 2-6.**

50. 6 qt = ■ gal   **51.** 84 in. = ■ ft   **52.** $2\frac{1}{2}$ yd = ■ in.   **53.** 3 min 10 s = ■ s

Solve each equation. If the equation is an identity, write *identity*. If it has no solution, write *no solution*.   ◀ **See Lesson 2-4.**

54. $3x - (x - 4) = 2x$ **55.** $4 + 6c = 6 - 4c$ **56.** $5a - 2 = 0.5(10a - 4)$

Get Ready!   **To prepare for Lesson 2-8, do Exercises 57–60.**

Solve each proportion.   ◀ **See Lesson 2-7.**

57. $\frac{x}{12} = \frac{7}{30}$ **58.** $\frac{y}{12} = \frac{8}{45}$ **59.** $\frac{w}{15} = \frac{12}{27}$ **60.** $\frac{n}{9} = \frac{n+1}{24}$

Proportions and Similar Figures

Objectives To find missing lengths in similar figures
To use similar figures when measuring indirectly

A good model is an exact copy of the thing that it represents. It's just a different size.

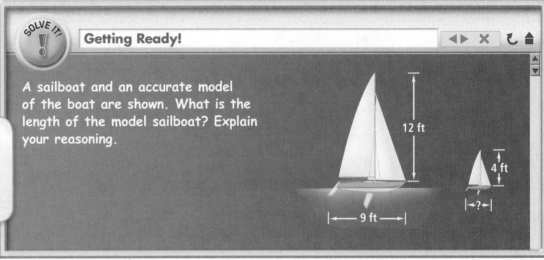

Getting Ready!

A sailboat and an accurate model of the boat are shown. What is the length of the model sailboat? Explain your reasoning.

12 ft

4 ft

9 ft

?

Lesson Vocabulary
- similar figures
- scale drawing
- scale
- scale model

In the Solve It, the sailboats have the same shape but they are different sizes. **Similar figures** have the same shape but not necessarily the same size. Such figures can help you measure real-world distances indirectly.

Focus Question How can you find the missing side lengths in similar figures?

The symbol ~ means *is similar to*. In the diagram, $\triangle ABC \sim \triangle FGH$.

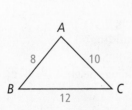

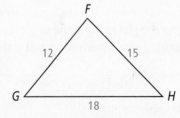

In similar figures, the measures of corresponding angles are equal, and the ratios of corresponding side lengths are equal. You can use the order of the letters in the figure name to match the figures. The names tell which parts of the figures are corresponding parts. So, because $\triangle ABC \sim \triangle FGH$, the following is true.

Hint

A corresponds to F,
B corresponds to G,
and C corresponds to H.

$\angle A \cong \angle F$ $\angle B \cong \angle G$ $\angle C \cong \angle H$ and $\dfrac{AB}{FG} = \dfrac{AC}{FH} = \dfrac{BC}{GH}$

The symbol $\cong$ means "is congruent to."
Congruent angles have the same measure.

The ratios are equal.

Problem 1   Finding the Length of a Side

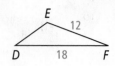

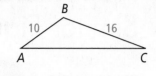

Multiple Choice In the diagram, $\triangle ABC \sim \triangle DEF$. What is *DE*?

(A) 7.5   (C) 21.3

(B) 9.5   (D) 24

Know

- The length of $\overline{AB}$, which corresponds to $\overline{DE}$
- The lengths of two other corresponding sides, $\overline{BC}$ and $\overline{EF}$
- The triangles are similar

Need

The length of $\overline{DE}$

Plan

Write a proportion involving two pairs of corresponding sides: $\overline{AB}$ and $\overline{DE}$, and $\overline{BC}$ and $\overline{EF}$. The length of $\overline{DE}$ is the only unknown, so you can solve for it.

Write a proportion relating the sides.	$\dfrac{BC}{EF} = \dfrac{AB}{DE}$
Substitute the side lengths in the proportion.	$\dfrac{16}{12} = \dfrac{10}{DE}$
Use the Cross Products Property to write an equation.	$16(DE) = 12(10)$
Multiply.	$16DE = 120$
Divide each side by 16 to isolate *DE*.	$\dfrac{16DE}{16} = \dfrac{120}{16}$
Simplify.	$DE = 7.5$

DE is 7.5. The correct answer is A.

Got It? **1.** Use the figures in Problem 1. What is *AC*?

You can use similar figures and proportions to find lengths that you cannot directly measure in the real world.

Problem 2   Applying Similarity

Indirect Measurement The sun's rays strike the building and the girl at the same angle, forming the two similar triangles shown. How tall is the building?

Write a proportion.	$\dfrac{\text{girl's shadow}}{\text{building's shadow}} = \dfrac{\text{girl's height}}{\text{building's height}}$
Substitute known information in the proportion.	$\dfrac{3}{15} = \dfrac{5}{x}$
Use the Cross Products Property to write an equation.	$3x = 15(5)$
Multiply.	$3x = 75$
Divide each side by 3 to isolate *x*.	$\dfrac{3x}{3} = \dfrac{75}{3}$
Simplify.	$x = 25$

The building is 25 ft tall.

Got It? **2.** A 6-ft tall man is standing next to a flagpole. The man's shadow is 3.5 ft. The flagpole's shadow is 17.5 ft. What is the flagpole's height?

A **scale drawing** is a drawing that is similar to an actual object or place. In a scale drawing, the ratio of any length on the drawing to the actual length is always the same. This ratio is called the **scale** of the drawing.

Problem 3 **Interpreting Scale Drawings**

Maps What is the actual distance from Jacksonville to Orlando? Use the ruler to measure the distance from Jacksonville to Orlando on the map below.

Think

What does the scale of the map tell you?
The scale tells you that each inch on the map represents 110 mi of actual distance.

Relate $\text{map scale} = \dfrac{\text{map distance}}{\text{actual distance}}$

Define Let $x =$ the total distance from Jacksonville to Orlando.

Write Write a proportion in words. $\dfrac{\text{map distance}}{\text{actual distance}} = \dfrac{\text{measured distance}}{\text{total distance}}$

Write a proportion in numbers. $\dfrac{1}{110} = \dfrac{1.25}{x}$

Use the Cross Products Property. $1(x) = 110(1.25)$

Multiply. $x = 137.5$

The actual distance from Jacksonville to Orlando is 137.5 mi.

 Got It? **3. a.** The distance from Jacksonville to Gainesville on the map is about 0.6 in. What is the actual distance from Jacksonville to Gainesville?

b. Reasoning If you know that the actual distance between two cities is 250 mi and that the cities are 2 in. apart on a map, how can you find the scale of the map?

A **scale model** is a three-dimensional model that is similar to an actual three-dimensional object. The ratio of a linear measurement of a model to the corresponding linear measurement of the actual object is always the same. This ratio is called the scale of the model.

Problem 4　Using Scale Models

Science A giant model heart on display at the Franklin Institute Science Museum in Philadelphia is shown below. The heart is the ideal size for a person who is 220 ft tall. About what size would you expect the heart of a man who is 6 ft tall to be?

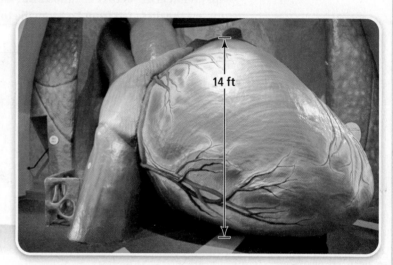

14 ft

6 ft

Think

Is this problem like ones you have seen?
Yes. Scale model problems are like scale drawing problems, so you can write a proportion like you did to find the height of the building in Problem 2.

Write a proportion.

$$\frac{\text{height of giant heart}}{\text{height of man's heart}} = \frac{\text{height of giant person}}{\text{height of man}}$$

Substitute.

$$\frac{14}{x} = \frac{220}{6}$$

Use the Cross Products Property.

$$14(6) = 220x$$

Divide each side by 220 and simplify.

$$0.38 \approx x$$

The size of the man's heart would be about 0.38 ft, or 4.6 in.

 Got It?　4. A scale model of a building is 6 in. tall. The scale of the model is 1 in. : 50 ft. How tall is the actual building?

Focus Question How can you find missing side lengths in similar figures?

Answer You can write and solve a proportion.

Lesson Check

Do you know HOW?

1. **Photocopies** You use a photocopier to enlarge a drawing of a right triangle with a base of 13 cm and a height of 7 cm. The enlarged triangle has a height of 17.5 cm.
   a. What is the base of the enlarged triangle?
   b. What is the scale of the enlargement?

2. **Maps** The scale of a map is 1 cm : 75 km. What is the actual distance between two towns that are 3 cm apart on the map?

Do you UNDERSTAND?

3. **Vocabulary** Suppose $\triangle MNP \sim \triangle RST$. How can you identify corresponding parts?

4. **Reasoning** Suppose $\triangle ABC \sim \triangle TUV$. Determine whether each pair of measures is equal.
   a. the measures of $\angle A$ and $\angle T$
   b. the perimeters of the two triangles
   c. the ratios of the sides $\frac{BC}{UV}$ and $\frac{AC}{TV}$

5. **Reasoning** The scale of a map is 1 in. : 100 mi. Is the actual distance between two towns 100 times the map distance between the two towns? Explain.

Practice and Problem-Solving Exercises

Practice   The figures in each pair are similar. Identify the corresponding sides and angles.   ◀ **See Problem 1.**

6. $\triangle ABC \sim \triangle DEF$

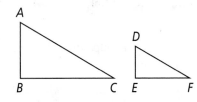

7. $FGHI \sim KLMN$

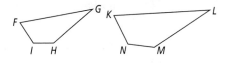

The figures in each pair are similar. Find the missing length.

8.

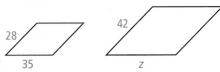

Guided Practice   To start, write a proportion using the ratios for the corresponding side lengths.

$\frac{18}{7.5} = \frac{x}{5}$

9.

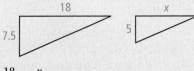

10.

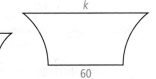

11. Bridges In the diagram of the park, $\triangle ADF \sim \triangle BCF$. The crosswalk at point A is about 20 yd long. A bridge across the pond will be built, from point B to point C. What will be the length of the bridge?

See Problem 2.

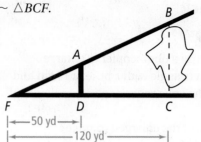

The scale of a map is 1 cm : 15 km. Find the actual distance corresponding to each map distance.

See Problem 3.

12. 2.5 cm   **13.** 0.2 cm   **14.** 15 cm   **15.** 4.6 cm

16. Movies A professional model-maker is building a giant scale model of a housefly to be used in a science fiction film. An actual fly is about 0.2 in. long with a wingspan of about 0.1 in. The model fly for the movie will be 27 ft long. What will its wingspan be?

See Problem 4.

Guided Practice

To start, record what you know.
    Actual fly length: 0.2 in.
    Actual fly wingspan: 0.1 in.
    Model fly length: 27 ft

Describe what you need to find.
    The model fly wingspan

17. Maps Abbottsville and Broken Branch are 175 mi apart. On a map, the distance between the two towns is 2.5 in. What is the scale of the map?

Ⓑ Apply

Architecture An architect is using the blueprint below to remodel a laundry room. The side length of each grid square represents 12 in.

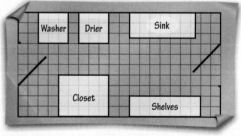

18. Find the actual length and width of the sink.

19. Find the total length and width of the actual room.

20. Model Rockets A particular model rocket kit uses the scale 1 : 144. The actual rocket is 168 ft tall. How tall will the model rocket be when completed?

21. Error Analysis The two figures at the right are similar. A student uses the proportion $\frac{BC}{CJ} = \frac{GH}{FN}$ to find FN.
  a. What mistake did the student make?
  b. What proportion should the student have used instead?

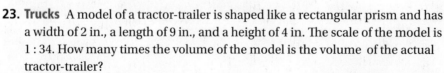

22. Writing Are all squares similar? Explain your answer.

23. Trucks A model of a tractor-trailer is shaped like a rectangular prism and has a width of 2 in., a length of 9 in., and a height of 4 in. The scale of the model is 1 : 34. How many times the volume of the model is the volume of the actual tractor-trailer?

24. Think About a Plan An interior designer sketches a design for a rectangular rug. The dimensions of the sketch are 4 in. by 7.5 in. The dimensions of the actual rug will be ten times the dimensions of the drawing, so the scale of the drawing is 1 : 10. How many times the area of the sketch is the area of the actual rug?

• Which figures in the problem are similar? What are their dimensions?
• How can proportions help you find the dimensions of the actual rug?

25. Eiffel Tower The height of the Eiffel Tower is 324 m. Which scale was used to make the model of the Eiffel Tower shown at the right?

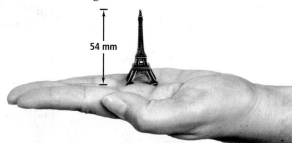

54 mm

Ⓐ 1 mm : 0.9 m   Ⓒ 1 mm : 30 m

Ⓑ 1 mm : 6 m   Ⓓ 1 mm : 324 m

Standardized Test Prep

SAT/ACT

26. The scale of a map is 1 in. : 80 mi. If the actual distance between two cities is 350 mi, how far apart will they be on the map?

Ⓐ $4\frac{1}{4}$ in.   Ⓑ $4\frac{3}{16}$ in.   Ⓒ $4\frac{3}{8}$ in.   Ⓓ $4\frac{1}{2}$ in.

27. The cost c of purchasing r roses from Sandra's Delivery Service is given by the equation $c = 3r + 15$. Luke has $50 to spend on roses. How many roses can he buy?

Ⓕ 11   Ⓖ $11\frac{2}{3}$ Ⓗ 12   Ⓘ 13

28. Which property of addition is illustrated by $a + (b + c) = (a + b) + c$?

Ⓐ Commutative   Ⓑ Associative   Ⓒ Inverse   Ⓓ Identity

29. Tamara and Will set up two booths to sell papayas at the farmer's market. Tamara sold hers for $5 each and Will sold his for $7 each. By noon, Tamara had sold 3 more papayas than Will and together they had earned a total of $147. How many papayas did they sell altogether?

Ⓕ 8   Ⓖ 11   Ⓗ 14   Ⓘ 25

Mixed Review

Solve each proportion.   See Lesson 2-7.

30. $\frac{y}{4} = \frac{17}{2}$ **31.** $\frac{3}{a} = \frac{2}{3}$ **32.** $\frac{20}{14} = \frac{2 - x}{7}$ **33.** $\frac{-3}{m} = \frac{2}{m + 1}$

34. Suppose you add a certain number to 3. The result is the same as if you had multiplied the number by 3. What is the number?   See Lesson 2-4.

Get Ready!   To prepare for Lesson 2-9, do Exercises 35–38.

Simplify each expression.   See Lesson 1-2.

35. $4 + 0.5(8)$ **36.** $0.2(5 - 3)$ **37.** $0.1(5) - 0.25$ **38.** $3 - 0.01(10)$

Objectives To solve percent problems using proportions
To solve percent problems using the percent equation

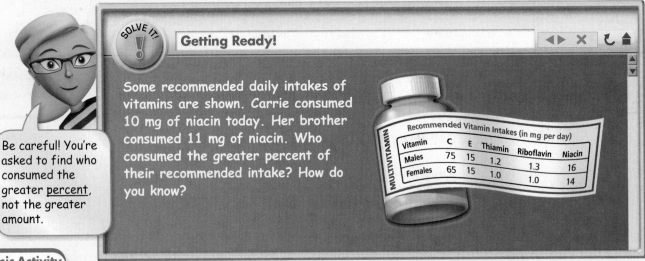

Getting Ready!

Some recommended daily intakes of vitamins are shown. Carrie consumed 10 mg of niacin today. Her brother consumed 11 mg of niacin. Who consumed the greater percent of their recommended intake? How do you know?

Be careful! You're asked to find who consumed the greater <u>percent</u>, not the greater amount.

Recommended Vitamin Intakes (in mg per day)					
Vitamin	C	E	Thiamin	Riboflavin	Niacin
Males	75	15	1.2	1.3	16
Females	65	15	1.0	1.0	14

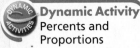

Dynamic Activity
Percents and Proportions

In the Solve It you might convert fractions to percents. Percents are useful because they standardize comparisons to a common base of 100. In this lesson, you will solve percent problems in a variety of ways.

Focus Question How can you solve a problem involving a percent?

take note

Key Concept The Percent Proportion

You can represent "*a* is *p* percent of *b*" using the percent proportion shown below.
In the proportion, *b* in the denominator is the base, and *a* in the numerator is a *part* of base *b*.

Algebra $\frac{a}{b} = \frac{p}{100}$, where $b \neq 0$

Example What percent of 50 is 25?
$$\frac{25}{50} = \frac{p}{100}$$

Model

part   base
↓   ↓

Number → 0   25   50

Percent → 0%   p%   100%

Think

How can a model help you visualize the proportion?

Use a model like the one below to visualize any percent problem. A model for the proportion $\frac{42}{56} = \frac{p}{100}$ is

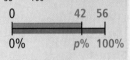

Problem 1   Finding a Percent Using the Percent Proportion

What percent of 56 is 42?

Write the percent proportion.	$\frac{a}{b} = \frac{p}{100}$
Substitute 42 for *a* and 56 for *b*.	$\frac{42}{56} = \frac{p}{100}$
Use the Cross Products Property.	$42(100) = 56p$
Multiply.	$4200 = 56p$
Divide each side by 56 to isolate *p*.	$\frac{4200}{56} = \frac{56}{56}p$
Simplify.	$75 = p$

42 is 75% of 56.

 Got It?   **1.** What percent of 90 is 54?

Here's How It Works   In Problem 1, you used the percent proportion $\frac{a}{b} = \frac{p}{100}$ to find a percent. When you write $\frac{p}{100}$ as $p\%$ and solve for *a*, you get the equation $a = p\% \cdot b$.

Write the proportion.	$\frac{a}{b} = \frac{p}{100}$
Write $\frac{p}{100}$ as $p\%$.	$\frac{a}{b} = p\%$
Multiply each side by *b*.	$b \cdot \frac{a}{b} = p\% \cdot b$
Simplify.	$a = p\% \cdot b$

This equation is called the percent equation. You can use either the percent equation or the percent proportion to solve any percent problem.

take note

Key Concept   The Percent Equation

You can represent "*a* is *p* percent of *b*" using the percent equation shown below. In the equation, *a* is a part of the base *b*.

Algebra $a = p\% \cdot b$, where $b \neq 0$

Example   What percent of 50 is 25?
$$25 = p\% \cdot 50$$

Model

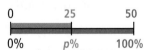

Problem 2   Finding a Percent Using the Percent Equation

Think

Is this problem related to other problems you've seen?
Yes. This problem is related to Problem 1. Both involve finding a percent, but they use different methods.

What percent of 40 is 6?

Write the percent equation.	$a = p\% \cdot b$
Substitute 6 for a and 40 for b.	$6 = p\% \cdot 40$
Divide each side by 40.	$\frac{6}{40} = p\% \cdot \frac{40}{40}$
Write the fraction as a decimal.	$0.15 = p\%$
Write the decimal as a percent.	$15\% = p\%$

6 is 15% of 40.

 Got It?   **2. Reasoning** What percent of 84 is 63? First, solve using the percent equation. Then solve using the percent proportion. Compare your answers.

Problem 3   Finding a Part

Shopping A shirt that costs $38.50 is on sale for 30% off. What is the sale price?

Think

How can a model help you visualize finding a part or base?
Use the model below to help you visualize finding the part in the equation $a = 30\% \cdot 38.50$.

```
0     a        38.50
|-----|----------|
0%  30%       100%
```

Step 1   Use the percent equation to find the amount of discount.

Write the percent equation.	$a = p\% \cdot b$
Substitute 30 for p and 38.50 for b.	$= 30\% \cdot 38.50$
Write the percent as a decimal.	$= 0.30 \cdot 38.50$
Multiply. The discount is a.	$= 11.55$

Step 2   Find the sale price.

Subtract $11.55 from the cost. $38.50 - 11.55 = 26.95$

The sale price of the shirt is $26.95.

 Got It?   **3.** A family sells a car to a dealership for 60% less than they paid for it. They paid $9000 for the car. For what price did they sell the car?

Problem 4   Finding a Base

125% of what number is 17.5?

Think

Will 125% of a number be greater than the number?
Yes. When you multiply a number by a percent greater than 100%, the part will be greater than the base. This is shown in the model below.

```
0         b   17.5
|---------|----|
0%      100% 125%
```

Write the percent equation.	$a = p\% \cdot b$
Substitute 17.5 for a and 125 for p.	$17.5 = 125\% \cdot b$
Write the percent as a decimal.	$17.5 = 1.25 \cdot b$
Divide each side by 1.25.	$14 = b$

125% of 14 is 17.5.

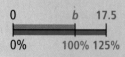 **Got It?**   **4.** 30% of what number is 12.5? Solve the problem using the percent equation. Then solve the problem using the percent proportion.

A common application of percents is simple interest.

Key Concept Simple Interest Formula

The simple interest formula uses the following variables.

I	interest in dollars
P	principal in dollars
r	annual interest rate written as a decimal
t	time in years

Algebra $I = Prt$

Example If you invest $50 at a simple interest rate of 3.5% per year for 3 years, the interest you earn is $I = 50(0.035)(3) = \$5.25$.

Hint

Simple interest the interest earned on the principal in an account.

When you solve problems involving percents, it is helpful to know fraction equivalents for common percents. You can use the fractions to check your answers for reasonableness. Here are some common percents represented as fractions.

$1\% = \frac{1}{100}$ $5\% = \frac{1}{20}$ $10\% = \frac{1}{10}$ $20\% = \frac{1}{5}$ $25\% = \frac{1}{4}$

$33.\overline{3}\% = \frac{1}{3}$ $50\% = \frac{1}{2}$ $66.\overline{6}\% = \frac{2}{3}$ $75\% = \frac{3}{4}$ $100\% = 1$

Problem 5 Using the Simple Interest Formula

Finance You deposited $840 in a savings account that earns a simple interest rate of 4.5% per year. You want to keep the money in the account for 4 years. How much interest will you earn? Check your answer for reasonableness.

Think

This is a simple interest problem, so use the formula for simple interest.

Identify what you know from the problem: $P = 840$, $r = 0.045$, and $t = 4$.

Check for reasonableness by using a common percent. Because 4.5% is about 5%, use 5%.

Write

$I = Prt$

$= 840(0.045)(4)$

$= 151.2$

The account will earn $151.20.

$840 \cdot \frac{1}{20} \cdot 4 = 42 \cdot 4 = \$168$

So, $151.20 is reasonable. ✔

Plan

How can you check the problem for reasonableness?

Because $5\% = \frac{1}{20}$ you can substitute $\frac{1}{20}$ into the formula to check if the answer is reasonable.

Got It? 5. You deposited $125 in a savings account that earns a simple interest rate of 1.75% per year. You earned a total of $8.75 in interest. For how long was your money in the account?

Concept Summary   Solving Percent Problems

Problem Type	Example	Proportion	Equation
Find a percent.	What percent of 6.3 is 3.5?	$\frac{3.5}{6.3} = \frac{p}{100}$	$3.5 = p\% \cdot 6.3$
Find a part.	What is 32% of 125?	$\frac{a}{125} = \frac{32}{100}$	$a = 32\% \cdot 125$
Find a base.	25% of what number is 11?	$\frac{11}{b} = \frac{25}{100}$	$11 = 25\% \cdot b$

Focus Question How can you solve a problem involving a percent?

Answer You can use a proportion or the percent equation.

Lesson Check

Do you know HOW?

1. What percent of 70 is 21?

2. What percent of 50 is 60?

3. What is 35% of 80?

4. 75% of what number is 36?

5. **Finance** How much interest will you earn by investing $1200 at a simple interest rate of 2.5% per year for 6 years?

Do you UNDERSTAND?

6. **Vocabulary** Complete: $p\%$ is equivalent to a fraction with a numerator of p and a denominator of __?__.

7. **Reasoning** You deposited money in a savings account paying 4% simple interest per year. The first year, you earned $75 in interest. How much interest will you earn during the following year?

8. **Open-Ended** Give an example of a percent problem where the part is greater than the base.

Practice and Problem-Solving Exercises

A Practice   Find each percent.    See Problems 1 and 2.

Guided Practice

To start, write the percent proportion.

Substitute 15 for a and 75 for b.

9. What percent of 75 is 15?

$$\frac{a}{b} = \frac{p}{100}$$

$$\frac{15}{75} = \frac{p}{100}$$

10. What percent of 15 is 5?

11. What percent of 16 is 10?

12. What percent of 40 is 32?

13. What percent of 88 is 88?

Find each part. See Problem 3.

Guided Practice

To start, write the percent equation.
Substitute 25 for *p* and 144 for *b*.

14. What is 25% of 144?
$$a = p\% \cdot b$$
$$a = 25\% \cdot 144$$

15. What is 63% of 150?

16. What is 15% of 63?

17. What is 12% of 12.8?

18. What is 1% of 1?

19. Shopping A tennis racket normally costs $65. The tennis racket is on sale for 20% off. What is the sale price of the tennis racket?

20. Hair Care A beauty salon buys bottles of styling gel for $4.50 per bottle and marks up the price by 40%. For what price does the salon sell each bottle?

Find each base. See Problem 4.

21. 20% of what number is 80?

22. 80% of what number is 20?

23. 60% of what number is 13.5?

24. 160% of what number is 200?

25. Finance Suppose you deposit $1200 in a savings account that earns simple interest at a rate of 3% per year. How much interest will you earn after 3 years? See Problem 5.

26. Finance Suppose you deposit $150 in a savings account that earns simple interest at a rate of 5.5% per year. How much interest will you earn after 4 years?

 Apply

Tell whether you are finding a *percent*, a *part*, or a *base*. Then solve.

27. What is 95% of 150?

28. What percent of 30 is 400?

29. 60 is 250% of what number?

Solve using mental math.

30. 20% of 80 is __?__ .

31. 120 is 200% of __?__ .

32. 30 is __?__ % of 40.

Tell which is greater, *A* or *B*. Assume *A* and *B* are positive numbers.

33. *A* is 20% of *B*.

34. 150% of *A* is *B*.

35. *B* is 90% of *A*.

36. Think About a Plan The United States Mint reported at the end of 2006 that the unit cost of producing and distributing a penny was 1.21¢. What percent of the value of a penny is this cost? What can you conclude about the cost of making pennies?
 • How can a model help you to visualize the problem?
 • How can you use a proportion or the percent equation to solve the problem?

37. Error Analysis A teacher asks a student to write and solve a percent problem, so the student writes, "What percent of 1.5 is 3?" and solves it as shown at the right. Describe and correct the error in the student's solution.

$$\frac{a}{b} = \frac{p}{100}$$

$$\frac{1.5}{3} = \frac{p}{100}$$

$$150 = 3p$$

$$50 = p$$

3 is 50% of 1.5.

38. Writing Part of a bottle of water has been consumed. Write the steps needed to determine the percent of water that has been consumed.

39. Finance A savings account earns simple interest at a rate of 6% per year. Last year the account earned $10.86 in interest. What was the balance in the account at the beginning of last year?

40. Furniture A furniture store offers a set of furniture for $990. You can also purchase the set on an installment plan for 24 payments of $45 each. If you choose the installment plan, what percent of the original price will you have paid when you finish? Round to the nearest percent.

Standardized Test Prep

SAT/ACT

41. A rare disease has been discovered that affects 2 out of every 10,000 trees in a forest. What percent of trees are affected?

Ⓐ 0.0002% Ⓑ 0.002% Ⓒ 0.02% Ⓓ 0.2%

42. One kilometer equals about $\frac{5}{8}$ mi. A European racecar driver is driving at 120 km/h. Approximately what is this speed in miles per hour?

Ⓕ 75 mi/h Ⓖ 100 mi/h Ⓗ 160 mi/h Ⓘ 192 mi/h

43. What is the solution of $\frac{x}{2} + \frac{x}{3} - 15 = 0$?

Ⓐ 12 Ⓑ 18 Ⓒ 24 Ⓓ 30

Mixed Review

44. Art A painting 36 cm wide and 22.5 cm tall is going to be reproduced on a postcard. The image on the postcard will be 9 cm tall. How wide will the image be?

◀ See Lesson 2-8.

45. Cats Alexis's cat eats 3 cans of cat food every 5 days. Alexis is going away for 30 days. A friend has offered to feed her cat. How many cans of cat food must Alexis leave for her cat while she is away?

◀ See Lesson 2-7.

46. Taxis A taxi charges $1.75 for the first $\frac{1}{8}$ mi and $.30 for each additional $\frac{1}{8}$ mi. Write an equation that gives the cost c of a taxi ride in terms of the number of miles m. How many miles did you travel if a ride costs $7.75?

◀ See Lesson 2-7.

Get Ready! To prepare for Lesson 2-10, do Exercises 47–49.

Solve each percent problem.

◀ See Lesson 2-9.

47. What percent of 8 is 100? **48.** What is 20% of 3? **49.** 35 is what percent of 20?

2-10 Change Expressed as a Percent

Objectives To find percent change
To find the relative error in linear and nonlinear measurements

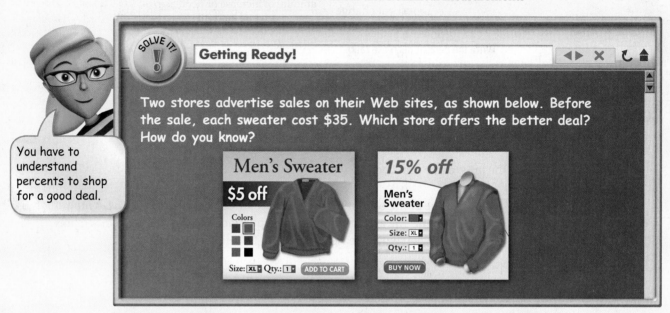

You have to understand percents to shop for a good deal.

Lesson Vocabulary
- percent change
- percent increase
- percent decrease
- relative error
- percent error

In the Solve It, the 15% discount is a percent change in the price of the sweaters. A **percent change** expresses an amount of change as a percent of an original amount.

Focus Question How can you find a percent change?

Suppose you know the original amount and how much it has changed. If the new amount is greater than the original amount, the percent change is called a **percent increase.** If the new amount is less than the original amount, the percent change is a **percent decrease.**

take note

Key Concept   Percent Change

Percent change is the ratio of the amount of change to the original amount.

$$\text{percent change, } p\% = \frac{\text{amount of increase or decrease}}{\text{original amount}}$$

- amount of increase = new amount − original amount
- amount of decrease = original amount − new amount

A common example of a percent decrease is a percent discount. In this lesson, round your answers to the nearest percent, if necessary.

 Problem 1 Finding a Percent Decrease

Clothing A coat is on sale. The original price of the coat is $82. The sale price is $73.80. What is the discount expressed as a percent change?

$$\text{percent change} = \frac{\text{amount of increase or decrease}}{\text{original amount}}$$

Write the percent decrease ratio. $= \dfrac{\text{original amount} - \text{new amount}}{\text{original amount}}$

Substitute known values. $= \dfrac{82 - 73.80}{82}$

Simplify. $= \dfrac{8.2}{82}$

Write the result as a percent. $= 0.1$, or 10%

The price of the coat decreased by 10%.

Got It? **1.** The average monthly precipitation for Chicago, Illinois, peaks in June at 4.1 in. The average monthly precipitation in December is 2.8 in. What is the percent decrease from June to December?

A common example of a percent increase is a percent markup.

 Problem 2 Finding a Percent Increase

Music A store buys an electric guitar for $295. The store then marks up the price of the guitar to $340. What is the markup expressed as a percent change? Round to the nearest percent.

$$\text{percent change} = \frac{\text{amount of increase or decrease}}{\text{original amount}}$$

Write the percent increase ratio. $= \dfrac{\text{new amount} - \text{original amount}}{\text{original amount}}$

Substitute known values. $= \dfrac{340 - 295}{295}$

Simplify. $= \dfrac{45}{295}$

Write the result as a percent. ≈ 0.15 or 15%
Round to the nearest percent.

The price of the guitar increased by about 15%.

Got It? **2.** In one year, the toll for passenger cars to use a tunnel rose from $3 to $3.75. What was the percent increase?

Focus Question How can you use percents to compare estimated or measured values to actual or exact values?

Key Concept   Relative Error

Relative error is the ratio of the absolute value of the difference of a measured (or estimated) value and an actual value compared to the actual value.

$$\text{relative error} = \frac{|\,\text{measured or estimated value} - \text{actual value}\,|}{\text{actual value}}$$

When relative error is expressed as a percent, it is called **percent error.**

 Problem 3

Finding Percent Error

Multiple Choice A decorator estimates that a rectangular rug is 5 ft by 8 ft. The rug is actually 4 ft by 8 ft. What is the percent error in the estimated area?

Think

What does the percent error tell you?
The percent error tells how accurate a measurement or estimate is.

Ⓐ 0.25%	Ⓑ 20%	Ⓒ 25%	Ⓓ 80%

Write the percent error ratio. $\text{percent error} = \dfrac{|\,\text{estimated value} - \text{actual value}\,|}{\text{actual value}}$

Substitute known values. $= \dfrac{|\,5(8) - 4(8)\,|}{4(8)}$

Multiply. $= \dfrac{|\,40 - 32\,|}{32}$

Simplify the absolute value. $= \dfrac{8}{32}$

Write the result as a percent. $= 0.25, \text{ or } 25\%$

The estimated area is off by 25%. The correct answer is C.

✓ **Got It?** **3.** You think that the distance between your house and a friend's house is 5.5 mi. The actual distance is 4.75 mi. What is the percent error in your estimation?

Focus Question How can you find a percent change?

Answer You can write the percent change as a ratio, where the numerator is the amount of change. The denominator is always the original amount.

Focus Question How can you use percents to compare estimated or measured values to actual or exact values?

Answer Find the percent error using a ratio.

Lesson Check

Do you know HOW?

1. **Running** Last year, an athlete's average time to run a mile was 6 min 13 s. This year, the athlete's average time is 6 min 5 s. What is the percent decrease? Round to the nearest percent.

2. **Cars** A used car dealership buys a car for $2800 and then sells it for $4500. What is the percent increase?

Do you UNDERSTAND?

3. **Vocabulary** Determine whether each situation involves a percent increase or a percent decrease.

   a. A hat that originally costs $12 sold for $9.50.

   b. You buy a CD for $10 and sell it for $8.

   c. A store buys glasses wholesale for $2 per glass. The store sells them for $4.50.

4. **Writing** How is calculating percent increase different from calculating percent decrease?

Practice and Problem-Solving Exercises

A Practice   Tell whether each percent change is an increase or decrease. Then find the percent change. Round to the nearest percent.   ◀ **See Problems 1 and 2.**

Guided Practice

To start, decide whether the change from 12 to 18 is an increase or a decrease.

Write the ratio for percent increase.

5. original amount: 12
   new amount: 18

   The original amount, 12, increases to 18, so the percent change is an increase.

   $$\frac{\text{new amount} - \text{original amount}}{\text{original amount}}$$

6. original amount: 9
   new amount: 6

7. original amount: 15
   new amount: 14

8. original amount: 7.5
   new amount: 9.5

9. original amount: 40.2
   new amount: 38.6

10. original amount: 2008
    new amount: 1975

11. original amount: 14,500
    new amount: 22,320

12. **Employment** An employee was hired at a wage of $8 per hour. After a raise, the employee earned $8.75 per hour. What was the percent increase?

13. Climate On June 1, 2007, there were about 18.75 h of daylight in Anchorage, Alaska. On November 1, 2007, there were about 8.5 h of daylight. What was the percent decrease?

Find the percent error in each estimation. Round to the nearest percent.

◀ See Problem 3.

Guided Practice

14. You estimate that your friend's little brother is about 8 years old. He is actually 6.5 years old.

To start, write the percent error equation. $\text{percent error} = \dfrac{|\text{estimated value} - \text{actual value}|}{\text{actual value}}$

Substitute the known values. $= \dfrac{|8 - 6.5|}{6.5}$

15. You estimate that your school is about 45 ft tall. Your school is actually 52 ft tall.

16. You estimate that the volume of a bathtub is 36 ft³ of water. The bathtub is actually 5.5 ft long, 3 ft wide, and 2 ft tall.

B Apply

Find the percent change. Round to the nearest percent.

17. 2 ft to $5\frac{1}{2}$ ft

18. 18 lb to $22\frac{1}{4}$ lb

19. $8.99 to $15.99

20. $168.45 to $234.56

21. Error Analysis A student is trying to find the percent of change when an amount increases from 12 to 18, as shown. Describe and correct the student's error.

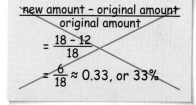

22. Writing How are percent change and percent error similar?

23. Think About a Plan In one season, an average of 6500 fans attended each home game played by the basketball team at Siena College in Londonville, New York, played at home in one. In the next season, the average number of fans per game increased by about 12%. What was the average number of fans per game for that season?
- What is missing — the new amount or the original amount?
- How can a percent change help you find the missing amount?

24. Open-Ended Write a percent change problem that you recently experienced.

25. Student Discounts You show your student identification at a local restaurant in order to receive a 5% discount. You spend $12 for your meal at the restaurant. How much would your meal cost without the discount?

26. Rounding Error Your science class visits an aquarium. In a report on your class's visit, you sketch one of the fish tanks and round the dimensions as shown in the diagram at the right. You use the rounded dimensions to state that the volume of the tank is approximately $(7)(5)(3) = 105$ m³. What is the percent error in your volume calculation due to rounding?

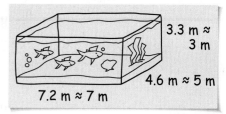

SAT/ACT

27. Marcus bought a shirt that was marked $28, but it was on sale for 15% off the marked price. What is the price of the shirt after the discount?

Ⓐ $4.20   Ⓑ $23.80   Ⓒ $24.80   Ⓓ $32.20

28. What equation do you get when you solve $ax + bx = c$ for x?

Ⓕ $x = c - ab$ Ⓖ $x = c - a - b$ Ⓗ $x = \dfrac{c}{a - b}$ Ⓘ $x = \dfrac{c}{a + b}$

29. A teacher wants to give each student 2 pencils. A store is selling pencils in boxes of 24. If the teacher has a total of 125 students, how many boxes of pencils should he buy?

Ⓐ 5   Ⓑ 6   Ⓒ 10   Ⓓ 11

Mixed Review

Solve each percent problem.   ◀ **See Lesson 2-9.**

30. What percent of 12 is 8?   **31.** What is 35% of 185?   **32.** 20% of what number is 4.2?

Get Ready!   **To prepare for Lesson 3-1, do Exercises 33–36.**

Graph the numbers on the same number line. Then order them from least to greatest.   ◀ **See Lesson 1-3.**

33. -3 **34.** $\dfrac{1}{2}$ **35.** 2 **36.** -2.8

② Pull It **All Together**

To solve these problems you will pull together many concepts and skills that you have studied about solving equations and working with rates and proportions.

BIG idea Equivalence

You can represent an equation in many ways. Equivalent representations have the same solution as the original equation.

Task 1

The solution of the equation ✳▲ + ♥ = ✿ is shown at the right. Use mathematical properties to explain your answers in each part below.

a. Explain why you can subtract ♥ from each side in Step 2.

b. Write another equation that is equivalent to ✳▲ + ♥ = ✿. Justify your answer.

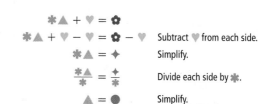

✳▲ + ♥ = ✿

✳▲ + ♥ − ♥ = ✿ − ♥   Subtract ♥ from each side.

✳▲ = ✦   Simplify.

$\dfrac{✳▲}{✳} = \dfrac{✦}{✳}$ Divide each side by ✳.

▲ = ●   Simplify.

BIG idea Solving Equations and Inequalities

You can use properties of numbers and equality to transform equations into equivalent, simpler equations and find solutions.

Task 2

Solve using two different methods. Explain which method you prefer to use.

a. $24 = \frac{2}{3}x + 12$ **b.** $0.5(y + 12) = -2.5y - 8$ **c.** $\frac{x - 3}{5} = \frac{3x}{7}$

BIG idea Proportionality

In a proportional relationship, the ratios of two quantities are equal. You can use this relationship to describe similar figures, scale models, and rates.

Task 3

Solve. Show all your work and explain your steps.

A family rents a truck to move from Buffalo to Chicago. The rental has a base cost of $49.95, plus an additional cost of $1.19 per mile driven. The family also pays for gas, which costs $3.89 per gallon. The truck's average gas mileage is 18 miles per gallon. What is the total cost of the move? (*Hint:* Use the map to estimate the driving distance.)

2 Chapter Review for Part B

Connecting **BIG** ideas and Answering the Essential Questions

1 Equivalence
You can represent an equation in many ways. Equivalent representations have the same solution as the original equation.

→ **Solving Equations (Lessons 2-1, 2-2, 2-3, 2-4)**
Equivalent equations have the same solution(s). To solve a given equation, form a series of simpler equivalent equations that isolate the variable.

2 Solving Equations and Inequalities
You can use properties of numbers and equality to transform equations into equivalent, simpler equations and find solutions.

→ **Solving Equations (Lessons 2-1, 2-2, 2-3, 2-4)**
Use equations to model real-world situations and find unknown quantities.

→ **Literal Equations and Formulas (Lesson 2-5)**
Formulas represent reliable real-world relationships. Use them to solve problems.

3 Proportionality
In a proportional relationship, the ratios of two quantities are equal. You can use this relationship to describe similar figures, scale models, and rates.

→ **Rates, Proportions, and Similar Figures (Lessons 2-6, 2-7, 2-8)**
Use rates to model ideas like growth, speed, and unit prices. Use proportions to interpret scale drawings.

→ **Percents (Lessons 2-9, 2-10)**
Formulas represent reliable real-world relationships. Use them to solve problems.

Chapter Vocabulary

- conversion factor (p. 131)
- cross products (p. 137)
- Cross Products Property (p. 137)
- percent change (p. 157)
- percent error (p. 159)
- percent decrease (p. 157)
- percent increase (p. 157)
- proportion (p. 136)
- rate (p. 130)
- ratio (p. 130)
- relative error (p. 159)
- scale (p. 145)
- scale drawing (p. 145)
- scale model (p. 146)
- similar figures (p. 143)
- unit analysis (p. 132)
- unit rate (p. 130)

Choose the correct term to complete each sentence.

1. A ratio of two equivalent measures given in different units is a(n) __?__ .

2. On a map, information such as "1 in. : 5 mi" is the __?__ of the map.

3. In the proportion $\frac{a}{b} = \frac{c}{d}$, *ad* and *bc* are the __?__ .

4. A(n) __?__ expresses an amount of change as a percent of an original amount.

5. __?__ is the ratio of the absolute value of the difference of a measured value and an actual value compared to the actual value.

2-6 Ratios, Rates, and Conversions

Quick Review

A ratio between numbers measured in different units is called a **rate**. A **conversion factor** is a ratio of two equivalent measures in different units such as $\frac{1\,h}{60\,min}$, and is always equal to 1. To convert from one unit to another, multiply the original unit by a conversion factor that has the original units in the denominator and the desired units in the numerator.

Example

A painting is 17.5 in. wide. What is its width in centimeters? Recall that 1 in. = 2.54 cm.

$$17.5 \text{ in.} \cdot \frac{2.54 \text{ cm}}{1 \text{ in.}} = 44.45 \text{ cm}$$

The painting is 44.45 cm wide.

Exercises

Convert the given amount to the given unit.

6. $6\frac{1}{2}$ ft; in.

7. 4 lb 7 oz; oz

8. 135 s; min

9. 2.25 mi; yd

10. Production A bread slicer runs 20 h per day for 30 days and slices 144,000 loaves of bread. How many loaves per hour are sliced?

11. Pets A gerbil eats about $\frac{1}{4}$ oz of food per day. About how many pounds of food can a gerbil eat in a year?

12. Sports If a baseball travels at 90 mi/h, how many seconds does it take to travel 60 ft?

2-7 and 2-8 Solving Proportions and Using Similar Figures

Quick Review

The **cross products** of a proportion are equal.

If $\frac{a}{b} = \frac{c}{d}$, where $b \neq 0$ and $d \neq 0$, then $ad = bc$.

If two figures are **similar,** then corresponding angles are congruent and corresponding side lengths are in proportion. You can use proportions to find missing side lengths in similar figures and for indirect measurement.

Example

A tree casts a shadow 10 m long. At the same time, a signpost next to the tree casts a shadow 4 m long. The signpost is 2.5 m tall. How tall is the tree?

Write a proportion.	$\frac{x}{10} = \frac{2.5}{4}$
Use the Cross Products Property.	$4x = 10(2.5)$
Simplify.	$4x = 25$
Divide each side by 4.	$x = 6.25$

Exercises

Solve each proportion.

13. $\frac{3}{7} = \frac{9}{x}$

14. $\frac{-8}{10} = \frac{y}{5}$

15. $\frac{6}{15} = \frac{a}{4}$

16. $\frac{3}{-7} = \frac{-9}{t}$

17. $\frac{b+3}{7} = \frac{b-3}{6}$

18. $\frac{5}{2c-3} = \frac{3}{7c+4}$

19. Models An airplane has a wingspan of 25 ft and a length of 20 ft. You are designing a model of the airplane with a wingspan of 15 in. What will the length of your model be?

20. Projections You project a drawing 7 in. wide and $4\frac{1}{2}$ in. tall onto a wall. The projected image is 27 in. tall. How wide is the projected image?

2-9 Percents

Quick Review

A percent is a ratio that compares a number to 100. If you write a percent as a fraction, you can use a proportion to solve a percent problem.

Example

What percent of 84 is 105?

Write the percent proportion.	$\frac{105}{84} = \frac{p}{100}$
Use the Cross Products Property.	$100(105) = 84p$
Simplify.	$10,500 = 84p$
Divide each side by 84.	$125 = p$

105 is 125% of 84.

Exercises

21. What percent of 37 is 111?

22. What is 72% of 150?

23. 60% of what number is 102?

24. Gardening A gardener expects that 75% of the seeds she plants will produce plants. She wants 45 plants. How many seeds should she plant?

25. Fundraising A charity sent out 700 fundraising letters and received 210 contributions in response. What was the percent of response?

26. Surveys In a survey, 60% of students prefer bagels to donuts. If 120 students were surveyed, how many students prefer bagels?

2-10 Change Expressed as a Percent

Quick Review

Percent change $p\%$ is the ratio of the amount of change to the original amount.

$$p\% = \frac{\text{amount of increase or decrease}}{\text{original amount}}$$

You can use the percent change formula to express changes as percents.

Example

A bookstore buys a book for $16 and marks it up to $28. What is the markup expressed as a percent change?

percent of change $=$	$\dfrac{\text{new amount } - \text{ original amount}}{\text{original amount}}$
Substitute.	$= \dfrac{28 - 16}{16}$
Simplify.	$= \dfrac{12}{16}$
Write the result as a percent.	$= 0.75$ or 75%

The price of the book increased by 75%.

Exercises

Tell whether each percent change is an increase or decrease. Then find the percent change. Round to the nearest percent.

27. original amount: 27
new amount: 30

28. original amount: 250
new amount: 200

29. original amount: 873
new amount: 781

30. original amount: 4.7
new amount: 6.2

31. Demographics In 1970, the U.S. population was about 205 million people. In 2007, it was about 301 million. What was the percent increase?

32. Astronomy The time from sunrise to sunset on the shortest day of the year in Jacksonville, Florida, is about 10 h 11 min. On the longest day, the time is 14 h 7 min. What is the percent increase?

Do you know HOW?

Solve each proportion.

1. $\frac{8}{k} = -\frac{12}{30}$

2. $\frac{3}{5} = \frac{y+1}{9}$

Solve each equation. Check your answer.

3. $3w + 2 = w - 4$

4. $\frac{1}{4}(k - 1) = 7$

5. $6y = 12.8$

6. $\frac{5n+1}{8} = \frac{3n-5}{4}$

7. **Bicycling** You are riding your bicycle to prepare for a race. It takes you 12 min to go 2.5 mi. What was your speed in miles per hour?

The figures in each pair are similar. Find the missing length.

8.
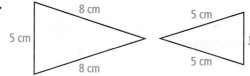

9.
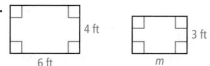

10. **Shadows** In the late afternoon, a 3.5-ft child casts a 60-in. shadow. The child is next to a telephone pole that casts a 50-ft shadow, forming similar triangles. How tall is the telephone pole?

Tell whether each percent change is an increase or decrease. Then find the percent change.

11. original amount: $5000
new amount: $6500

12. original amount: 150 lb
new amount: 135 lb

Define a variable and write an equation to model each situation. Then solve.

13. **Farming** You have 100 ft of fencing to build a circular sheep pen.

 a. What is the diameter of the largest pen you can build? Use 3.14 for π.

 b. What is the area of the largest pen you can fence?

14. **Maps** The scale on a map is 1 in. : 25 mi. You measure 6.5 in. between two towns. What is the actual distance?

15. **Birds** In a bird sanctuary, 30% of the birds are hummingbirds. If there are about 350 birds in the sanctuary at any given time, how many are hummingbirds?

Do you UNDERSTAND?

16. **Reasoning** Explain which is more accurate: measuring to the nearest millimeter or to the nearest eighth of an inch.

17. **Writing** A 30-pack of blank CDs costs $9.50. A 50-pack of blank CDs costs $13. How can you tell which is the better buy?

18. **Error Analysis** Average attendance at a school's basketball games increased from 1000 to 1500 last year. One student said that represented a 150% increase. Explain the student's error. What is the actual percent increase?

Some questions on tests ask you to write a short response. Short response questions in this textbook are usually worth 2 points. To get full credit for an answer, you must give the correct answer (including appropriate units, if applicable) and justify your reasoning or show your work.

TIP 1

If you write the correct expression but make an error when calculating your answer, you might earn one point.

Mandy is selling copies of historic photos to raise money for a class trip. She can order each photo for $2.75 and each frame for $4.25. Mandy plans to sell each photo with a frame for $10.00. Write an expression to represent the total amount of money Mandy will have after selling n framed photos. Evaluate your expression for 12 framed photos. Show your work.

Solution

She makes $3n$ after selling n framed photos.

She earns $3(12) = \$36$ after selling 12 framed photos.

TIP 2

You also might earn one point if you do not write an expression but you show a method for getting to the correct answer.

Think It Through

It costs Mandy $\$2.75 + \$4.25 = \$7$ to make each framed photo. She makes $\$10 - (\$7) = \$3$ after selling one framed photo. So, she makes $3n$ after selling n framed photos. She earns $3(12) = \$36$ after selling 12 framed photos. This answer is complete and earns 2 points.

Vocabulary Builder

As you solve test items, you must understand the meanings of mathematical terms. Match each term with its mathematical meaning.

A. variable

B. similar

C. scale factor

D. perimeter

E. formula

I. the distance around the outside of a figure

II. two figures with the exact same shape, but not necessarily the same size

III. a math sentence that defines the relationship between quantities

IV. a symbol that represents a number or numbers

V. the ratio of the lengths of corresponding sides in similar figures

Multiple Choice

Read each question. Then write the letter of the correct answer on your paper.

1. Which expression is equivalent to $2b - 3a + b + a$?

Ⓐ $b - 2a$ Ⓒ $3b - 4a$

Ⓑ $b - 4a$ Ⓓ $3b - 2a$

2. Belle surveyed her classmates in music class. The ratio of students who prefer playing string instruments to those who prefer wind instruments is $2 : 5$. There are 28 students in Belle's class. How many students prefer playing string instruments?

Ⓕ 5   Ⓗ 20

Ⓖ 8   Ⓘ 25

3. Which equation is equivalent to
$2(3x - 1) - 3(5x - 3) = 4$?

Ⓐ $-3x - 5 = 4$ Ⓒ $-9x - 11 = 4$

Ⓑ $-9x - 4 = 4$ Ⓓ $-9x + 7 = 4$

4. The statement $-2 \cdot (7 \cdot 4) = (-2 \cdot 7) \cdot 4$ is an example of which property?

Ⓕ Commutative Property of Multiplication

Ⓖ Identity Property of Multiplication

Ⓗ Distributive Property

Ⓘ Associative Property of Multiplication

5. Jim uses 3 cups of peaches to yield 4 jars of peach jam. He also makes strawberry-peach jam. He uses equal amounts of strawberries and peaches. How many cups of strawberries does Jim need to yield 10 jars of strawberry-peach jam?

Ⓐ $3\frac{3}{4}$ c   Ⓒ $7\frac{1}{2}$ c

Ⓑ $4\frac{1}{2}$ c   Ⓓ 9 c

6. $3(6x + 2) - 2(5x + 3)$ is equivalent to which of the following expressions?

Ⓕ $8x$ Ⓗ $8x + 9$

Ⓖ $8x + 5$ Ⓘ $8x + 12$

7. Sabrina's car has traveled 28,000 mi. If she drives 36 mi each day, which equation can be used to find the total number of miles m Sabrina's car will have traveled after she drives it for d days?

Ⓐ $d = 36m + 28,000$

Ⓑ $m = 36d + 28,000$

Ⓒ $m + 36d = 28,000$

Ⓓ $d = 28,000m + 36$

8. Which operation should be done first to simplify the expression $12 + 6 \cdot 3 - (35 - 14 \div 7)$?

Ⓕ $12 + 6$ Ⓗ $35 - 14$

Ⓖ $6 \cdot 3$ Ⓘ $14 \div 7$

9. Erica is making feathered caps for her school play. Each cap must have 3 feathers. Which equation represents the number of feathers f Erica needs to make c caps?

Ⓐ $c = 3f$ Ⓒ $c = f + 3$

Ⓑ $f = 3c$ Ⓓ $f = c + 3$

10. Which property is shown by the equation
$8 \times (7 \times 9) = (7 \times 9) \times 8$?

Ⓕ Commutative Property of Multiplication

Ⓖ Associative Property of Multiplication

Ⓗ Identity Property of Multiplication

Ⓘ Closure Property of Multiplication

11. Use the diagram below, which shows similar triangles formed by the shadows of a person and a tree.

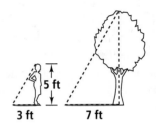

3 ft   7 ft

What is the approximate height of the tree?

Ⓐ 4 ft   Ⓒ 12 ft

Ⓑ 9 ft   Ⓓ 105 ft

12. Which of the following fractions is equivalent to $\frac{36}{153}$?

Ⓕ $\frac{13}{47}$ Ⓗ $\frac{4}{17}$

Ⓖ $\frac{1}{9}$ Ⓘ $\frac{9}{34}$

13. Which product is equal to -36?

Ⓐ $12(2 - 12)$

Ⓑ $6(2 + 12)$

Ⓒ $12(1 - 22)$

Ⓓ $3(10 - 22)$

14. Last year, Conner paid 15% of his earnings in federal taxes. He paid $3000. Jose also paid 15% of his earnings in federal taxes, but he paid $3600. How much more did Jose earn than Conner?

(F) $4000   (H) $20,000

(G) $6000   (I) $24,000

15. The table shows the price of a bus ticket based on the number of miles traveled. Which equation represents the relationship between the ticket price p and the number of miles traveled m?

Miles	Price
100	$50
150	$70
200	$90
250	$110

(A) $p = 2m$

(B) $p = 0.5m$

(C) $p = 2m + 10$

(D) $p = 0.4m + 10$

16. The formula for the volume V of a cone is $V = \frac{1}{3}\pi r^2 h$, where h is the height of the cone and r is the radius of the base. The height of a cone is 5 in. and the radius of the base is 2 in. What is the approximate volume of the cone? Use 3.14 for π.

(F) 2 in.^{3} (H) 15 in.^{3}

(G) 6 in.^{3} (I) 21 in.^{3}

17. During a trip, Josh recorded the amount of time it took him to travel the distances shown in the table below.

Time (hours)	2	5	7	8
Distance (miles)	60	150	210	240

Which equation represents the relationship between distance d and time t?

(A) $d = 30t$

(B) $t = 30d$

(C) $d = 30 + t$

(D) $t = d + 30$

Record your answers in a grid.

18. What is the value of x when $\frac{13}{55} = \frac{x}{10}$? Round your answer to the nearest hundredth.

19. When Paige left middle school and entered high school, her class size increased by 225%. There were 56 students in her middle school class. How many students are in her high school class?

20. The perimeter of a rectangle is given by the equation $2w + 33 = 54$. What is w, the width of the rectangle?

21. Pablo can wash 6 cars in 40 min. At this rate, how many cars can Pablo wash in 4 h?

22. The formula for the time that a certain traffic light remains yellow is $t = \frac{1}{8}s + 1$, where t represents the time in seconds and s represents the speed limit in miles per hour. If the light is yellow for 6 s, what is the speed limit in miles per hour?

Short Response

23. The cost for using a phone card is 35 cents per call plus 25 cents per minute. Write an expression for the cost of a call that is n minutes long. A certain call costs $3.60. How many minutes long was the call? Show your work.

24. Travis sells black and white photos of cities across the country. Each photo's width is half its height. Write an equation to represent the area A of a photo given its height h. Use this equation to find the area of a photo that is 4 in. tall.

25. Carroll has a piece of fabric that is 4 yd long to make curtains. Each curtain requires a piece of fabric that is 16 in. long. How many curtains can Carroll make?

26. A rental car company charges $25.00 per day plus $.30 for every mile the car is driven. Dale rents a car while his own car is being repaired, and he only drives it to and from work each day. Dale drives 7 mi each way to and from work. Write an expression to represent Dale's cost of renting a car for d days. Dale rents the car for 4 days. How much does Dale owe for the rental?

Get Ready!

CHAPTER

3

See Lesson 1-3 ◆ **Ordering Rational Numbers**

Complete each statement with <, =, or >.

1. $-3 \blacksquare -5$ **2.** $7 \blacksquare \frac{14}{2}$ **3.** $-8 \blacksquare -8.4$ **4.** $-\frac{5}{2} \blacksquare 2.5$

See Lesson 1-5 ◆ **Absolute Value**

Simplify each expression.

5. $5 + |4 - 6|$ **6.** $|30 - 28| - 6$ **7.** $|-7 + 2| - 4$

See Lesson 2-1 ◆ **Solving One-Step Equations**

Solve each equation. Check your solution.

8. $x - 4 = -2$ **9.** $b + 4 = 7$ **10.** $-\frac{3}{4}y = 9$

11. $\frac{m}{12} = 2.7$ **12.** $-8 + x = 15$ **13.** $n - 7 = 22.5$

See Lesson 2-2 ◆ **Solving Two-Step Equations**

Solve each equation. Check your solution.

14. $-5 + \frac{b}{4} = 7$ **15.** $4.2m + 4 = 25$ **16.** $-12 = 6 + \frac{3}{4}x$

17. $6 = -z - 4$ **18.** $4m + 2.3 = 9.7$ **19.** $\frac{5}{8}t - 7 = -22$

See Lessons 2-3 and 2-4 ◆ **Solving Multi-Step Equations**

Solve each equation. Check your solution.

20. $4t + 7 + 6t = -33$ **21.** $2a + 5 = 9a - 16$

22. $6(y - 2) = 8 - 2y$ **23.** $n + 3(n - 2) = 10.4$

🔊 Looking Ahead Vocabulary

24. You make a *compound* word, such as houseboat, by joining two words together. Why do you think $-4 < x < 7$ is called a *compound inequality*?

25. The *intersection* of two roads is the place where the roads cross. How would you define the *intersection* of two groups of objects?

Solving Inequalities

I've always wanted to be in a band!
I wonder how they figure out the
maximum number of people who
can come to a concert or what the
shortest length of a song can be.
In this chapter, you'll learn about
inequalities. They can help you in
situations where there is a maximum
or minimum value.

Vocabulary for Part A

English/Spanish Vocabulary Audio Online:

English	Spanish
equivalent inequalities, *p. 184*	desigualdades equivalentes
solution of an inequality, *p. 175*	solución de una desigualdad

00:04:04

VIDEO
▷

BIGideas

1 Variable

Essential Question How do you represent relationships between quantities that are not equal?

2 Equivalence

Essential Question Can inequalities that appear to be different be equivalent?

3 Solving Equations and Inequalities

Essential Question How can you solve inequalities?

Chapter Preview for Part A

Inequalities and Their Graphs

Objective   To write and identify solutions of inequalities

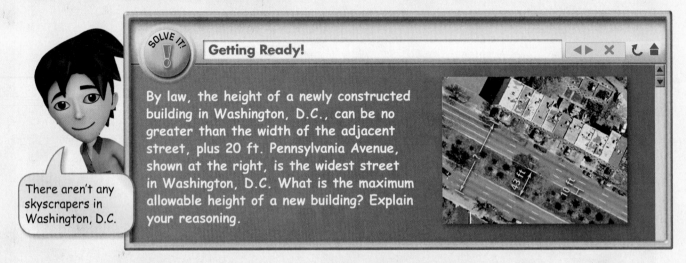

SOLVE IT!

Getting Ready!

By law, the height of a newly constructed building in Washington, D.C., can be no greater than the width of the adjacent street, plus 20 ft. Pennsylvania Avenue, shown at the right, is the widest street in Washington, D.C. What is the maximum allowable height of a new building? Explain your reasoning.

There aren't any skyscrapers in Washington, D.C.

Lesson Vocabulary
• solution of an inequality

The Solve It involves comparing two quantities—the height of a building and the width of the street adjacent to it. You can use an inequality to compare such quantities.

Focus Question   How do you write inequalities?

An inequality is a mathematical sentence that uses an inequality symbol to compare the values of two expressions.

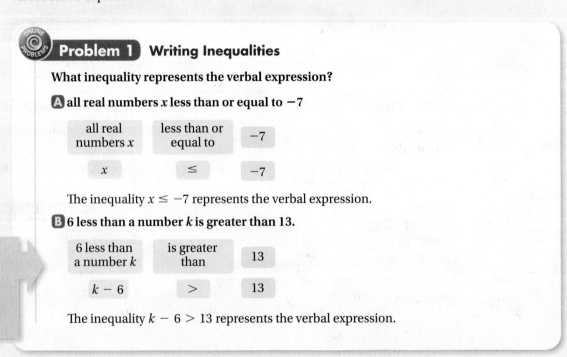

Problem 1   **Writing Inequalities**

What inequality represents the verbal expression?

A all real numbers x less than or equal to -7

all real numbers x	less than or equal to	-7
x	$\leq$	-7

The inequality $x \leq -7$ represents the verbal expression.

B 6 less than a number k is greater than 13.

6 less than a number k	is greater than	13
$k - 6$	$>$	13

The inequality $k - 6 > 13$ represents the verbal expression.

Think

Less than and *is less than* have different meanings. For example, "6 less than k" means $k - 6$, while "6 is less than k" means $6 < k$.

Got It? 1. What is an inequality that represents the verbal expression?
  a. all real numbers p greater than or equal to 1.5
  b. The sum of t and 7 is less than -3.

Focus Question How do you determine if a number is a solution of an inequality?

A **solution of an inequality** is any number that makes the inequality true. The solutions of the inequality $x < 5$ are all real numbers x that are less than 5. You can evaluate an expression to determine whether a value is a solution of an inequality.

ONLINE PROBLEMS **Problem 2** **Identifying Solutions by Evaluating**

Is the number a solution of $2x + 1 > -3$?

A -3

Write the inequality.	$2x + 1 > -3$
Substitute for x.	$2(-3) + 1 \overset{?}{>} -3$
Simplify.	$-6 + 1 \overset{?}{>} -3$
Compare.	$-5 \not> -3$

-3 does not make the original inequality true, so -3 is *not* a solution.

B -1

Write the inequality.	$2x + 1 > -3$
Substitute for x.	$2(-1) + 1 \overset{?}{>} -3$
Simplify.	$-2 + 1 \overset{?}{>} -3$
Compare.	$-1 > -3$

-1 does make the original inequality true, so -1 is a solution.

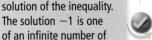 **Got It?** **2. a.** Consider the numbers $-1, 0, 1,$ and 3. Which are solutions of
    $13 - 7y \le 6$?
  b. Reasoning In Problem 2, how is the solution of the related equation
    $2x + 1 = -3$ related to the solutions of the inequality?

Hint

The symbol $\overset{?}{>}$ indicates a question. Is the expression greater than or equal to -3? The symbol $\not>$ means is not greater than -3.

Think

Is -1 the *only* solution to the inequality?
No. *Any* number that makes the original inequality true is a solution of the inequality. The solution -1 is one of an infinite number of solutions.

Focus Question How do you write inequalities?

Answer You can use the symbol $\leq$, $\geq$, $<$, or $>$ to compare two expressions.

Focus Question How do you determine if a number is a solution of an inequality?

Answer You can substitute the number in the inequality and evaluate the inequality to see if you get a true statement.

Lesson Check

Do you know HOW?

1. What algebraic inequality represents all real numbers y that are greater than or equal to 12?

2. Is the number a solution of $6x - 3 \geq 10$?

   a. -1 **b.** 0   **c.** 3   **d.** 4

Do you UNDERSTAND?

3. **Vocabulary** How do you decide whether a number is a solution of an inequality?

4. **Compare and Contrast** What are the differences and similarities between $x > 5$ and $x \geq 5$?

5. **Open-Ended** What are three possible values for b that make the inequality $b \leq -4$ true?

Practice and Problem-Solving Exercises

 Practice   Write an inequality that represents each verbal expression.   ◀ **See Problem 1.**

Guided Practice

To start, break the sentence into parts.

6. v is greater than or equal to 5.

| v | is greater than or equal to | 5 |

7. The product of t and 6 is greater than 12.

8. b is less than 4.

9. 3 less than g is less than or equal to 17.

10. The quotient of k and 9 is greater than $\frac{1}{3}$.

Determine whether each number is a solution of the given inequality.   ◀ **See Problem 2.**

Guided Practice

To start, substitute for m.

11. $8m - 6 \leq 10$ **a.** 2   **b.** 3   **c.** -1

   a. $8(2) - 6 \leq 10$

   b. $8(3) - 6 \leq 10$

   c. $8(-1) - 6 \leq 10$

12. $3y - 8 > 22$	**a.** 2	**b.** 0	**c.** 5
13. $4x + 2 < -6$	**a.** 0	**b.** -2	**c.** 1
14. $6 - n \geq 11$	**a.** -10	**b.** 2	**c.** -4
15. $m(m - 3) < 54$	**a.** -10	**b.** 0	**c.** 9

Apply

16. Error Analysis A student claims that the inequality $3x + 1 > 0$ is always true because multiplying a number by 3 and then adding 1 to the result always produces a number greater than 0. Explain the student's error.

> **Hint** Choose different values for x. Include positive and negative values, and zero.

17. Open-Ended Describe an inequality that you can write to represent all numbers less than or equal to twelve.

Write each inequality in words.

18. $n < 5$

19. $b > 0$

20. $z \geq 25.6$

21. $21 \geq m$

22. $35 \geq w$

23. $a \leq 3$

24. $8 \leq h$

25. $1.2 > k$

Determine whether each number is a solution of the given inequality.

26. $\frac{7a + 4}{2} > 9$ **a.** -2 **b.** 2   **c.** 4

27. $-2p - 3 \leq -1$ **a.** 0.5   **b.** -1 **c.** 1

28. $5k - 16 \geq k$ **a.** -5 **b.** -4 **c.** 4

3-1
PART 2

Inequalities and Their Graphs

Objective To write and graph inequalities

In Part 1 of the lesson, you learned how to write inequalities and identify solutions.

Connect to What You Know

Here you will learn how to show the solutions of an inequality on a number line.

Focus Question How do you graph solutions of inequalities?

You can use a number line to show all of the solutions of an inequality.

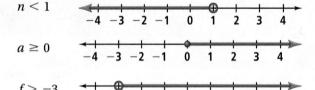

Inequality	Graph	
$n < 1$		The open dot shows that 1 is *not* a solution. Shade to the left of 1.
$a \geq 0$		The closed dot shows that 0 is a solution. Shade to the right of 0.
$f > -3$		The open dot shows that -3 is *not* a solution. Shade to the right of -3.
$-2 \geq x$		The closed dot shows that -2 is a solution. Shade to the left of -2.

You can also write $-2 \geq x$ as $x \leq -2$.

Hint

When you write the variable on the left side of the inequality symbol, the inequality symbol points in the direction of the shaded area.

Problem 3 Graphing an Inequality

What is the graph of $2 \geq a$?

Hint

When the symbol used in the inequality is $<$ or $>$, use an open dot on the graph. When the symbol used in the inequality is $\leq$ or $\geq$, use a closed dot.

Think

If 2 is greater than or equal to a, then a must be less than or equal to 2.

$a \leq 2$ means all real numbers a that are less than or equal to 2. Since 2 is a solution, draw a closed dot at 2.

The numbers less than 2 are to the left of 2 on the number line. Shade to the left of 2.

Write

$a \leq 2$

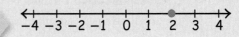

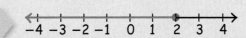

Got It? **3.** What is the graph of each inequality?

    a. $x > -4$ **b.** $c < 0$ **c.** $3 \leq n$

Problem 4 Writing an Inequality From a Graph

What inequality represents the graph?

Plan

How do you know which inequality symbol to use?
Look at the arrow to see whether the solution is for quantities greater than or less than the endpoint. Look at the endpoint to see whether "equal to" is included in the solution.

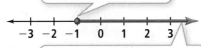

The closed dot means that -1 is a solution.

The open dot means that 4 is *not* a solution.

The number line is shaded to the right of -1, so all numbers greater than -1 are solutions.

The number line is shaded to the left of 4, so all numbers less than 4 are solutions.

The inequality $x \geq -1$ represents the graph.   The inequality $x < 4$ represents the graph.

Got It? **4.** What inequality represents each graph?

    a.

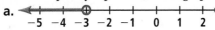

    b.

Problem 5 **Writing Real-World Inequalities**

What inequality describes the situation? Be sure to define a variable.

Plan

How do you know which inequality symbol to use?
The phrase "starting at $19.99" implies that the cost of a trail ride starts at $19.99 and goes up. So the cost is greater than or equal to 19.99.

A

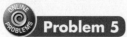

Trail Rides
Starting at
$19.99

Let c = the cost of a trail ride in dollars.

The sign indicates that $c \geq 19.99$.

B

8 M P H

Let s = a legal speed in miles per hour.

The sign indicates that $s \leq 8$.

 Got It? **5. Reasoning** In part (B) of Problem 5, can the speed be *all* real numbers less than or equal to 8? Explain.

---

take note

Concept Summary **Representing Inequalities**

Words	Symbols	Graph
x is less than 3.	$x < 3$	number line: open circle at 3, arrow left; −2 −1 0 1 2 3 4 5 6
x is greater than −2.	$x > -2$	number line: open circle at −2, arrow right; −4 −3 −2 −1 0 1 2 3 4
x is less than or equal to 0.	$x \leq 0$	number line: closed dot at 0, arrow left; −4 −3 −2 −1 0 1 2 3 4
x is greater than or equal to 1.	$x \geq 1$	number line: closed dot at 1, arrow right; −4 −3 −2 −1 0 1 2 3 4

Focus Question How do you graph solutions of inequalities?

Answer You can use a number line to graph an inequality. Draw a dot at the location of the solution to the related equation and draw an arrow to show the other solutions.

 Lesson Check

Do you know HOW?

1. What is the graph of $2 > p$?

2. What inequality represents the graph?

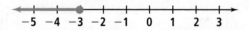
number line: closed dot at −3; −5 −4 −3 −2 −1 0 1 2 3

Do you UNDERSTAND?

3. **Compare and Contrast** What are some situations you could model with $x \geq 0$? How do they differ from situations you could model with $x > 0$?

4. **Open-Ended** What is a real-world situation that you can represent with the following graph?

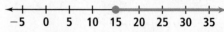
number line: closed dot at 15; −5 0 5 10 15 20 25 30 35

Practice and Problem-Solving Exercises

A Practice   Match each inequality with graph A, B, C, or D.    **See Problem 3.**

5. $x < -1$ **6.** $x \geq -1$

7. $-1 < x$ **8.** $-1 \geq x$

A. ![number line -4 to 4, open dot at -1, shaded right]

C. ![number line -4 to 4, closed dot at -1, shaded right]

B. ![number line -4 to 4, closed dot at -1, shaded left]

D. ![number line -4 to 4, open dot at 0, shaded left]

Graph each inequality.

Guided Practice

9. $y > 2$

To start, decide if 2 is a solution. $y > 2$ means all real numbers y that are greater than 2. Because 2 is not a solution, draw an open dot at 2.

![number line -3 to 3, open dot at 2, shaded right]

10. $t < -4$ **11.** $z \leq -5$ **12.** $v \geq -2$

13. $-3 < f$ **14.** $8 \geq b$ **15.** $5.75 > d$

Write an inequality for each graph.    **See Problem 4.**

16. ![number line -6 to 2, open dot at -4, shaded right]

17. ![number line -4 to 12, closed dot at 8, shaded left]

18. ![number line -4 to 4, closed dot at 2, shaded right]

19. ![number line -10 to -2, open dot at -7, shaded left]

20. ![number line -1 to 7, closed dot at 5, shaded right]

21. ![number line -4 to 4, open dot at 2, shaded left]

Define a variable and write an inequality to model each situation.   **See Problem 5.**

Guided Practice

To start, define a variable.

22. The restaurant can seat at most 172 people.

Let $p =$ the number of people that can be seated at the restaurant.

23. A person must be at least 35 years old to be elected President of the United States.

24. A light bulb can be no more than 75 watts to be safely used in this light fixture.

25. At least 475 students attended the orchestra concert Thursday night.

26. A law clerk has earned more than \$20,000 since being hired.

27. **Ticket Sales** Suppose your school plans a musical. The director's goal is ticket sales of at least $4500. Adult tickets are $7.50 and student tickets are $5.00. Let *a* represent the number of adult tickets and *s* represent the number of student tickets. Which inequality represents the director's goal?

Ⓐ $5a + 7.5s < 4500$

Ⓑ $7.5a + 5s > 4500$

Ⓒ $7.5a + 5s \leq 4500$

Ⓓ $7.5a + 5s \geq 4500$

> **Hint** Rewrite $7.50 and $5.00 without the zero placeholders. Write an expression for the total ticket sales.

28. **Open-Ended** Describe a situation that you can model with $x \geq 25$.

29. **Physics** According to Albert Einstein's special theory of relativity, no object can travel faster than the speed of light, which is approximately 186,000 mi/s. What is an inequality that represents this information?

30. **Basketball** Emily has to make at least two free throws to send the basketball game into overtime. Write an inequality to model the number of free throws she has to make.

31. **Class Party** You are making muffins for a class party. You need 2 cups of flour to make a pan of 12 muffins. You have a 5-lb bag of flour, which contains 18 cups. What is an inequality that represents the possible numbers of muffins you can make?

32. **Writing** Explain what the phrases *no more than* and *no less than* mean when writing inequalities that model real-world situations.

Use the map at the right for Exercises 33 and 34.

33. **Think About a Plan** You plan to go from Portland to Tucson. Let *x* be the distance in miles of any flight between Portland and Tucson. What is a true statement about the mileage of any route from Portland to Tucson? Assume that no route visits the same city more than once and that each route has no more than one layover.
    • How many routes exist between Portland and Tucson? What are they? Which route is the shortest?
    • Can you write an inequality that represents the mileage of any route from Portland to Tucson?

34. **Air Travel** Your travel agent is making plans for you to go from San Diego to Seattle. A direct flight is not available. Option A consists of flights from San Diego to Boise to Seattle. Option B consists of flights from San Diego to Las Vegas to Seattle. What inequality compares the flight distances of these two options?

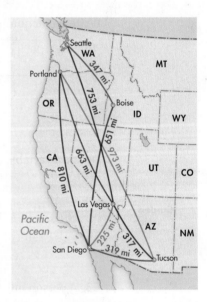

Standardized Test Prep

SAT/ACT

35. Which inequality has the same solutions as $k > 6$?

 Ⓐ $k < -6$ Ⓑ $k < 6$

 Ⓒ $6 < k$ Ⓓ $k > -6$

36. What is the value of the expression $\dfrac{2^3 \cdot 4 - (-3)^2}{(-3)^2 + 4 \cdot 5}$?

 Ⓕ $\dfrac{23}{29}$ Ⓖ $\dfrac{41}{29}$

 Ⓗ $\dfrac{23}{11}$ Ⓘ $\dfrac{41}{11}$

37. Last season, Betsy scored 36 points. This is 8 less than twice the number of points that Amy scored. How many points did Amy score?

 Ⓐ 22   Ⓑ 36

 Ⓒ 44   Ⓓ 72

Short Response

38. At an airport, a runway 1263 ft long is being repaired. The project foreman reports that less than one third of the job is complete. Draw a diagram of the runway that shows how much of it has been repaired. What is an inequality that represents the number of feet f that still need to be repaired?

Mixed Review

Tell whether each percent change is an *increase* or *decrease*. Then find the percent change. Round to the nearest percent.

 **See Lesson 2-10.**

39. original amount: $10
new amount: $12

40. original amount: 20 in.
new amount: 18 in.

41. original amount: 36°
new amount: 12°

Find each product or quotient.

See Lesson 1-6.

42. $-4(-11)$ **43.** $\dfrac{5}{6} \cdot \left(-\dfrac{1}{4}\right)$ **44.** $-3.9 \div 1.3$ **45.** $\dfrac{4}{7} \div \left(-\dfrac{2}{5}\right)$

Get Ready!   To prepare for Lesson 3-2, do Exercises 46–49.

Solve each equation.

See Lesson 2-1.

46. $y - 5 = 6$ **47.** $p - 4 = -6$ **48.** $v + 5 = -6$ **49.** $k + \dfrac{2}{3} = \dfrac{5}{9}$

3-2 Solving Inequalities Using Addition or Subtraction

Objective To use addition or subtraction to solve inequalities

There's a minimum number of states you need to win to get elected president.

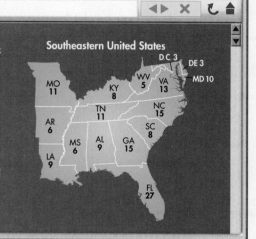

SOLVE IT!

Getting Ready!

In a U.S. presidential election, a candidate must win at least 270 out of 538 total electoral votes to be declared the winner. Suppose a candidate has earned 238 electoral votes in states outside the southeastern U.S.

What is the least number of states in the southeastern U.S. that the candidate could win and still become president? What are these states? Justify your reasoning.

Southeastern United States

Dynamic Activity
Linear Inequalities

Lesson Vocabulary
• equivalent inequalities

You can model the situation in the Solve It with the inequality $238 + x \geq 270$, where x represents the number of electoral votes needed. You can find its solutions using one of the *properties of inequality*.

Focus Question How is solving an inequality with addition or subtraction similar to solving an equation?

Equivalent inequalities are inequalities that have the same solutions. You will use the Addition Property of Inequality, shown below, to produce equivalent inequalities.

Key Concept Addition Property of Inequality

Words
Let a, b, and c be real numbers.
If $a > b$, then $a + c > b + c$.
If $a < b$, then $a + c < b + c$.

This property is also true for $\geq$ and $\leq$.

Diagram
The diagram below illustrates one way to think about this rule.

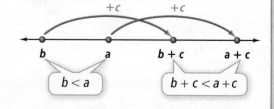

Examples
$5 > 4$, so $5 + 3 > 4 + 3$.
$-2 < 0$, so $-2 + 1 < 0 + 1$.

Think

Do you know how to solve a related problem?
Yes. You know how to solve the related equation $x - 15 = -12$ using the Addition Property of Equality.

Problem 1 Using the Addition Property of Inequality

What are the solutions of $x - 15 > -12$? Graph the solutions.

Write the original inequality.	$x - 15 > -12$
Add 15 to each side to undo subtraction.	$x - 15 + 15 > -12 + 15$
Simplify.	$x > 3$
The solutions of $x > 3$ are all real numbers greater than 3.	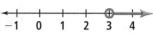

 Got It? 1. What are the solutions of $n - 5 < -3$? Graph the solutions.

To check the solution of an inequality, you need to check at least two values. First, determine if the endpoint is a solution of the related equation. To check the answer to Problem 1, determine if 3 is a solution of the equation $x - 15 = -12$. Then, choose and test a value that falls on the shaded part of the number line. If it makes the inequality true, you know you shaded in the correct direction. For Problem 1, you could test 3.5, 4, 10, or 100. For example, determine if $x - 15 > -12$ is true when $x = 4$.

Problem 2 Solving an Inequality and Checking Solutions

What are the solutions of $10 \geq x - 3$? Graph and check the solutions.

Hint

Recall the steps you used to solve an equality. You will use the same steps to solve an inequality.

Plan

What value should you test?
After you test the endpoint 13, test a value that is on the shaded part of the number line. Try any number less than 13, like 12, 11, or 10.

Think

You need to isolate x. Undo subtraction by adding the same number to each side.

Write

$$10 \geq x - 3$$
$$10 + 3 \geq x - 3 + 3$$
$$13 \geq x$$

The graph of $13 \geq x$ (or $x \leq 13$) contains 13 and all real numbers to the left of 13.

To check the endpoint 13 of $13 \geq x$, make sure that 13 is the solution of the related *equation* $10 = x - 3$.

$$10 = x - 3$$
$$10 \overset{?}{=} 13 - 3$$
$$10 = 10 ✔$$

To check the inequality symbol of $13 \geq x$, make sure that a number *less than* 13 is a solution of the original inequality.

$$10 \geq x - 3$$
$$10 \overset{?}{=} 12 - 3$$
$$10 \geq 9 ✔$$

 Got It? 2. What are the solutions of $m - 11 \geq -2$? Graph and check the solutions.

The Subtraction Property of Inequality is shown below.

take note

Key Concept   Subtraction Property of Inequality

Words

Let a, b, and c be real numbers.
If $a > b$, then $a - c > b - c$.
If $a < b$, then $a - c < b - c$.
This property is also true for $\geq$ and $\leq$.

Diagram

The diagram below illustrates one way to think about this rule.

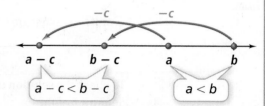

Examples

$-3 < 5$, so $-3 - 2 < 5 - 2$.
$3 > -4$, so $3 - 1 > -4 - 1$.

Problem 3   Using the Subtraction Property of Inequality

What are the solutions of $t + 6 > -4$? Graph the solutions.

Think

How is this inequality different from others you have seen before?
The expression $t + 6$ involves addition, so you have to use subtraction to undo the addition and isolate the variable.

Write the original inequality.	$t + 6 > -4$
Subtract 6 from each side to undo addition.	$t + 6 - 6 > -4 - 6$
Simplify.	$t > -10$

Use an open dot because -10 is not a solution. The solutions of $t > -10$ are all real numbers to the right of -10.

$-10 \quad -8 \quad -6 \quad -4 \quad -2 \quad 0$

Got It? 3. What are the solutions of $-1 \geq y + 12$? Graph the solutions.

Problem 4   Writing and Solving an Inequality

Computers The hard drive on your computer has a capacity of 120 gigabytes (GB). You have used 85 GB. You want to save some home videos to your hard drive. What are the possible sizes of the home video collection you can save?

Think

How do you know which inequality symbol to use?
Words and phrases like *at most*, *no more than*, and *maximum* may indicate that you should use $\leq$.

Relate   current hard drive space used   plus   size of videos   is at most   hard drive capacity

Define   Let v = the size of the video collection.

Write   85   + v $\leq$ 120

Write the inequality.	$85 + v \leq 120$
Subtract 85 from each side.	$85 + v - 85 \leq 120 - 85$
Simplify.	$v \leq 35$

The home video collection can be any size less than or equal to 35 GB.

Got It? **4. a.** A club has a goal to sell at least 25 plants for a fundraiser. Club members sell 8 plants on Wednesday and 9 plants on Thursday. What are the possible numbers of plants the club can sell on Friday to meet their goal?

b. *Reasoning* Can you use the same inequality symbol to represent phrases like *at least, no less than,* and *greater than or equal to*? Explain your reasoning.

Focus Question How is solving an inequality with addition or subtraction similar to solving an equation?

Answer You can use the Addition Property to undo subtraction or the Subtraction Property to undo addition until you isolate the variable.

Lesson Check

Do you know HOW?

Solve each inequality. Graph and check your solutions.

1. $p - 4 < 1$

2. $8 \geq d - 2$

3. $y + 5 < -7$

4. $4 + c > 7$

5. A cyclist takes her bicycle on a chairlift to the top of a slope. The chairlift can safely carry 680 lb. The cyclist weighs 124 lb, and the bicycle weighs 32 lb. What are the possible additional weights the chairlift can safely carry?

Do you UNDERSTAND?

6. *Writing* How can you use the addition and subtraction properties of inequality to produce equivalent inequalities?

7. *Reasoning* What can you do to the first inequality in each pair in order to get the second inequality?

a. $x + 4 \leq 10; x \leq 6$

b. $-6 < y - 2; -4 < y$

8. *Compare and Contrast* Suppose you solve the two inequalities $y + 4 \leq 6$ and $y - 4 \leq 6$. How are your methods of solving the inequalities similar? How are they different?

Practice and Problem-Solving Exercises

A Practice Tell what number you would add to each side of the inequality to solve the inequality.

◀ See Problems 1 and 2.

9. $f - 6 \geq -3$ **10.** $a - 3.3 \geq 2.6$ **11.** $5 > -18 + m$

Solve each inequality. Graph and check your solutions.

Guided Practice

To start, undo subtraction by adding 2 to each side.

12. $y - 2 > 11$

$y - 2 + 2 > 11 + 2$

13. $v - 4 < -3$ **14.** $-6 > c - 2$ **15.** $8 \leq f - 4$

16. $t - 4 \geq -7$ **17.** $s - 10 \leq 1$ **18.** $-3 \geq x - 1$

19. $z - 12 \leq -4$ **20.** $-\frac{3}{4} > r - \frac{3}{4}$ **21.** $y - 1 \geq 1.5$

Tell what number you would subtract from each side of the inequality to solve the inequality.

◀ See Problem 3.

22. $x + 3 > 0$ **23.** $6.8 \geq m + 4.2$ **24.** $\ell + \frac{1}{3} \geq \frac{7}{3}$

Solve each inequality. Graph and check your solutions.

Guided Practice ➡

25. $x + 5 \leq 10$

To start, undo addition by subtracting 5 from each side.

$x + 5 - 5 \leq 10 - 5$

26. $n + 6 > -2$ **27.** $2 < 9 + c$ **28.** $-1 \geq 5 + b$

29. $\frac{1}{4} + a \geq -\frac{3}{4}$ **30.** $\frac{1}{3} < n + 3$ **31.** $3.8 \geq b + 4$

32. Exercise Your goal is to take at least 10,000 steps per day. According to your pedometer, you have walked 5274 steps. Write and solve an inequality to find the possible numbers of steps you can take to reach your goal.

◀ See Problem 4.

Hint Decide what operation(s) you will use to write the inequalities.

33. Fundraising The environmental club is selling indoor herb gardens for Earth Day. Each member is encouraged to sell at least 10 gardens. You sell 3 gardens on Monday and 4 gardens on Tuesday. Write and solve an inequality to find the possible numbers of gardens you can sell to reach your goal.

34. Monthly Budget You earn $250 per month from your part-time job. You are in a kayaking club that costs $20 per month, and you save at least $100 each month. Write and solve an inequality to find the possible amounts you have left to spend each month.

Ⓑ Apply

Tell what you can do to the first inequality in order to get the second.

35. $36 \leq -4 + y$ and $40 \leq y$ **36.** $9 + b > 24$ and $b > 15$

You can draw a model to represent an inequality. For example, the model below represents the inequality $85 + v < 120$. Draw a model to represent each inequality below.

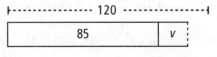

37. $17 + x < 51$ **38.** $12 + y > 18$

Solve each inequality. Justify each step.

39. $z - 1.4 < 3.9$ **40.** $-5 > p - \frac{1}{5}$ **41.** $a + 5.2 < -4.6$

42. $-3.1 > z - 1.9$ **43.** $\frac{5}{8} + v - \frac{7}{16} > 0$ **44.** $5y + 5 - 4y < 8$

45. $9m - 2m + 5 \leq 6$ **46.** $8v - 7v - 3 \geq -6$ **47.** $5 \geq m - \frac{7}{16}$

48. Government The U.S. Senate is composed of 2 senators from each of the 50 states. In order for a treaty to be ratified, at least two thirds of the senators present must approve the treaty. Suppose all senators are present and 48 of them have voted in favor of a treaty. What are the possible numbers of additional senators who must vote in favor of the treaty in order to ratify it?

49. Think About a Plan You want to qualify for a regional diving competition. At today's competition, you must score at least 53 points. Out of a possible 10 points, your scores on each of the first 5 dives are shown at the right. What scores can you earn on the armstand dive that will qualify you for the regional diving competition?
* What information do you know? What information do you need?
* How might writing and solving an inequality help you?
* What does the solution of the inequality mean in terms of the original situation?

OFFICIAL SCORE CARD	
DIVE	**SCORE**
Front Dive	*9.8*
Back Dive	*8.9*
Reverse Dive	*8.4*
Inward Dive	*8.2*
Twisting Dive	*9.4*
Armstand Dive	*?*

50. Qualifying Scores To enter a competition, students must score a total of at least 450 points on five qualifying tests. Each test is worth 100 points. On the first four tests, your scores were 94, 88, 79, and 95. What are three possible scores you can earn on the last test to enter the competition?

Error Analysis Describe and correct the error in solving each inequality or in graphing the solution.

51.

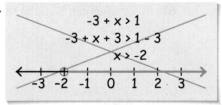

52.

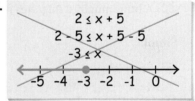

53. a. Open-Ended Use each of the inequality symbols $<$, $\leq$, $>$, and $\geq$ to write four inequalities involving addition or subtraction.

b. Solve each inequality from part (a) and graph your solutions.

54. Geometry Suppose a triangle has side lengths a, b, and c, where c is the length of the longest side. You can use the following equation and inequalities to determine whether the triangle is right, acute, or obtuse.

* If $a^2 + b^2 = c^2$, then the triangle is right.
* If $a^2 + b^2 > c^2$, then the triangle is acute.
* If $a^2 + b^2 < c^2$, then the triangle is obtuse.

> **Hint** An acute angle is less than 90°. An obtuse angle is more than 90°. A right angle equals 90°.

Classify each triangle with the following side lengths as *right*, *acute*, or *obtuse*.
a. 4 in., 5 in., 6 in.   **b.** 3 cm, 4 cm, 5 cm   **c.** 10 m, 15 m, 20 m

55. Banking To avoid a service fee, your checking account balance must be at least $500 at the end of each month. Your current balance is $536.45. You use your debit card to spend $125.19. What possible amounts can you deposit into your account by the end of the month to avoid paying the service fee?

Standardized Test Prep

SAT/ACT

56. What is the solution of $-21 + p > 30$?

    Ⓐ $p < 9$ Ⓑ $p > 9$ Ⓒ $p < 51$ Ⓓ $p > 51$

57. Richard won a 130-mi bike race. He finished in 11 h and 45 min. What was his average speed?

    Ⓕ 11.8 mi/h   Ⓖ 11.4 mi/h   Ⓗ 11.1 mi/h   Ⓘ 10.8 mi/h

58. The variable a is an integer. Which of the following values could NOT equal a^3?

    Ⓐ -27 Ⓑ -8 Ⓒ 16   Ⓓ 64

Short Response

59. The leading scorer in your high school's soccer division finished the season with an average of 4 goals per game for 15 games. As the division's second-leading scorer, you have an average of 4 goals per game for 14 games. You still have to play your last game. How many goals must you score in the final game to overtake the division's leading scorer? Show your work.

Mixed Review

Define a variable and write an inequality to model each situation.   ◀ See Lesson 3-1.

60. A hummingbird migrates more than 1850 mi.   **61.** An octopus can be up to 18 ft long.

Simplify.   ◀ See Lesson 1-2.

62. $7^2 + 23$ **63.** $3(4 - 5)^2 - 4$ **64.** $0.4 + 0.2(4.2 - 3.4)$

Get Ready!   **To prepare for Lesson 3-3, do Exercises 65–67.**

Solve each equation.   ◀ See Lesson 2-1.

65. $10 = \frac{v}{2}$ **66.** $15 = -22y$ **67.** $\frac{3}{4}z = -18$

Solving Inequalities Using Multiplication or Division

Objective To use multiplication or division to solve inequalities

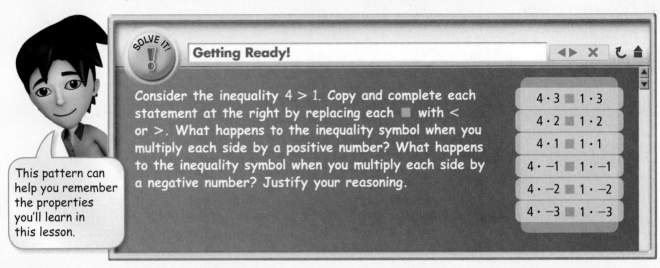

Getting Ready!

Consider the inequality $4 > 1$. Copy and complete each statement at the right by replacing each ▪ with < or >. What happens to the inequality symbol when you multiply each side by a positive number? What happens to the inequality symbol when you multiply each side by a negative number? Justify your reasoning.

$4 \cdot 3$ ▪ $1 \cdot 3$
$4 \cdot 2$ ▪ $1 \cdot 2$
$4 \cdot 1$ ▪ $1 \cdot 1$
$4 \cdot -1$ ▪ $1 \cdot -1$
$4 \cdot -2$ ▪ $1 \cdot -2$
$4 \cdot -3$ ▪ $1 \cdot -3$

This pattern can help you remember the properties you'll learn in this lesson.

Dynamic Activity
Solving Inequalities

In the Solve It, you may have noticed that multiplying both sides of an inequality by a negative number affects the inequality symbol.

Focus Question How is solving an inequality with multiplication or division similar to solving an equation?

take note

Key Concept Multiplication Property of Inequality

Words

Let a, b, and c be real numbers with $c > 0$.

If $a > b$, then $ac > bc$.

If $a < b$, then $ac < bc$.

Diagram

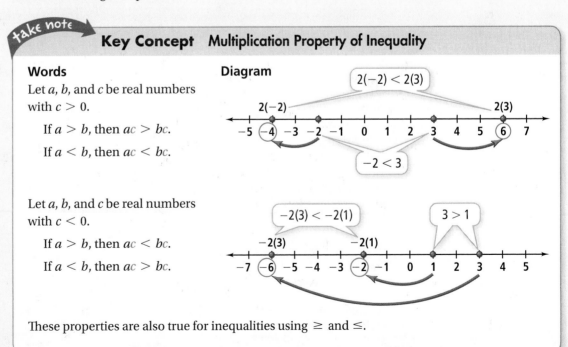

$2(-2) < 2(3)$

$-2 < 3$

Let a, b, and c be real numbers with $c < 0$.

If $a > b$, then $ac < bc$.

If $a < b$, then $ac > bc$.

$-2(3) < -2(1)$

$3 > 1$

These properties are also true for inequalities using $\geq$ and $\leq$.

Here's Why It Works Multiplying or dividing each side of an inequality by a negative number changes the meaning of the inequality. You need to reverse the inequality symbol to make the inequality true. Here is an example:

Write a statement of inequality.	$3 > 1$
Multiply by -2.	$-2(3)$ ■ $-2(1)$
Simplify.	-6 ■ -2
Reverse the inequality symbol to make the inequality true.	$-6 < -2$

 Problem 1 **Multiplying by a Positive Number**

What are the solutions of $\frac{x}{3} < -2$? Graph the solutions.

Think

Why multiply by 3?
You can multiply by any multiple of 3 to remove the fraction. But multiplying by 3 isolates the variable.

Write the original inequality.	$\frac{x}{3} < -2$
Multiply each side by 3 to remove the fraction.	$3\left(\frac{x}{3}\right) < 3(-2)$
Simplify.	$x < -6$
Graph the solutions.	

 Got It? **1.** **a.** What are the solutions of $\frac{x}{5} < 4$? Graph the solutions.

b. What are the solutions of $\frac{c}{8} > \frac{1}{4}$? Graph the solutions.

 Problem 2 **Multiplying by a Negative Number**

What are the solutions of $\frac{w}{-2} \geq 2$? Graph and check the solutions.

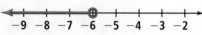

Think

Multiplying by a negative number changes the inequality. Reverse the inequality symbol to make it a true statement.

$$\frac{w}{-2} \geq 2$$

$$-2\left(\frac{w}{-2}\right) \leq -2(2)$$

$$w \leq -4$$

To check the endpoint of $w \leq -4$, make sure that -4 is the solution of the related equation $\frac{w}{-2} = 2$.

$$\frac{w}{-2} = 2$$

$$\frac{-4}{-2} \overset{?}{=} 2$$

$$2 = 2 ✔$$

To check the inequality symbol of $w \leq -4$, make sure a number less than -4 is a solution of the original inequality. Here, -6 is tested.

$$\frac{-6}{-2} \overset{?}{\geq} 2$$

$$3 \geq 2 ✔$$

Got It? 2. a. What are the solutions of $\frac{2}{5}x \geq -4$? Graph the solutions.
  b. What are the solutions of $-\frac{n}{3} < -1$? Graph and check.

Solving inequalities using division is similar to solving inequalities using multiplication. If you divide each side of an inequality by a negative number, you need to reverse the direction of the inequality symbol.

take note

Key Concept Division Property of Inequality

Let a, b, and c be real numbers with $c > 0$.

If $a > b$, then $\frac{a}{c} > \frac{b}{c}$.

If $a < b$, then $\frac{a}{c} < \frac{b}{c}$.

Let a, b, and c be real numbers with $c < 0$.

If $a > b$, then $\frac{a}{c} < \frac{b}{c}$.

If $a < b$, then $\frac{a}{c} > \frac{b}{c}$.

Examples

$6 > 3$, so $\frac{6}{3} > \frac{3}{3}$.

$9 < 12$, so $\frac{9}{3} < \frac{12}{3}$.

$6 > 3$, so $\frac{6}{-3} < \frac{3}{-3}$.

$9 < 12$, so $\frac{9}{-3} > \frac{12}{-3}$.

These properties are also true for inequalities using $\geq$ and $\leq$.

Problem 3 Dividing by a Positive Number

Part-Time Job You walk dogs in your neighborhood after school. You earn $4.50 per dog. How many dogs do you need to walk to earn at least $75?

Relate | cost per dog | times | number of dogs | is at least | amount wanted |

Define Let d = the number of dogs.

Write 4.50 · d $\geq$ 75

Think

What types of solutions make sense for this situation?
Only whole-number solutions make sense because you cannot walk part of a dog.

Write the original inequality. $4.50d \geq 75$

Divide each side by 4.50. $\frac{4.50d}{4.50} \geq \frac{75}{4.50}$

Simplify. $d \geq 16\frac{2}{3}$

However, since d represents the number of dogs, it must be a positive integer. So, you must walk at least 17 dogs to earn at least $75.

 Got It? 3. a. A student club plans to buy food for a soup kitchen. A case of vegetables costs $10.68. The club can spend at most $50 for this project. What are the possible numbers of cases the club can buy?
  b. Reasoning In Problem 3, why do you round to the greater whole number?

 **Problem 4** **Dividing by a Negative Number**

What are the solutions of $-9y \leq 63$? Graph the solutions.

 Think

How is this inequality different from the one in Problem 3?
The coefficient is negative. You can still use the properties of inequality to solve, but pay attention to the direction of the symbol.

Write the original inequality.	$-9y \leq 63$
Divide each side by -9. Reverse the inequality symbol.	$\dfrac{-9y}{-9} \geq \dfrac{63}{-9}$
Simplify each side.	$y \geq -7$
Graph the inequality.	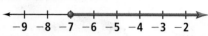

Got It? **4.** What are the solutions of $-5x > -10$? Graph the solutions.

Focus Question How is solving an inequality with multiplication or division similar to solving an equation?

Answer You can use the Multiplication Property to undo division or the Division Property to undo multiplication until you isolate the variable. If there is a fraction in the inequality, you can multiply by its reciprocal.

Lesson Check

Do you know HOW?

Match the inequality with its graph.

1. $x + 2 > -1$ **A.**
2. $-\dfrac{x}{3} < -1$ **B.**
3. $x - 4 \leq -1$ **C.**
4. $-3x \geq 9$ **D.**

Do you UNDERSTAND?

5. Which operation would you use to solve the inequality? Explain.

a. $1 \leq -\dfrac{x}{2}$ **b.** $y - 4 > -5$ **c.** $-6w < -36$

6. **Error Analysis** Describe and correct the error in the solution.

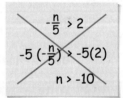

Practice and Problem-Solving Exercises

A **Practice** **Solve each inequality. Graph and check your solution.** ◆ **See Problems 1 and 2.**

Guided Practice

To start, undo division by multiplying each side by 5.

7. $\dfrac{x}{5} \geq -2$

$5\left(\dfrac{x}{5}\right) \geq 5(-2)$

8. $\frac{w}{6} < 1$

9. $4 > \frac{p}{8}$

10. $1 \leq -\frac{5}{4}y$

11. $-\frac{v}{2} \geq 1.5$

12. $-3 < \frac{x}{3}$

13. $-7 \leq \frac{7}{3}x$

14. $0 \leq -\frac{3}{11}m$

15. $-\frac{3}{2}b < 6$

16. $-5 \geq -\frac{5}{9}y$

Solve each inequality. Graph and check your solution.

See Problems 3 and 4.

Guided Practice

To start, undo multiplication by dividing each side by −5. Reverse the inequality symbol.

17. $-30 > -5c$

$$\frac{-30}{-5} < \frac{-5c}{-5}$$

18. $3m \geq 6$

19. $4t < -12$

20. $-4w \leq 20$

21. $11z > -33$

22. $56 < -7d$

23. $18b \leq -3$

24. $-5h < 65$

25. $8t \leq 64$

26. $63 \geq 7q$

B Apply

Write four solutions to each inequality.

27. $\frac{x}{2} \leq -1$

28. $\frac{r}{3} \geq -4$

29. $-1 \geq \frac{r}{3}$

Tell what you can do to the first inequality in order to get the second.

30. $-\frac{c}{4} > 3$; $c < -12$

31. $5z > -25$; $z > -5$

32. $\frac{3}{4}b \leq 3$; $b \leq 4$

Replace each ▦ **with the number that makes the inequalities equivalent.**

33. ▦$s > 14$ and $s < -7$

34. ▦$x \geq 25$ and $x \leq -5$

35. $-2a > $ ▦ and $a < -9$

Determine whether each statement is *always, sometimes,* or *never* true. Justify your answer.

36. If $x > 3$ and $y < 1$, then $xy > 0$.

37. If $x < 0$ and $y < 0$, then $xy > 0$.

38. If $x \geq 0$ and $y > 1$, then $xy > 0$.

39. If $x > 0$ and $y \geq 0$, then $xy > 0$.

40. Text Messages Text messages cost $.15 each. You can spend no more than $10. How many text messages can you send?

41. Aquarium Fish Tetras cost $3.99 each. You can spend at most $25. How many tetras can you buy for your aquarium?

42. Think About a Plan A friend calls you and asks you to meet at the park 2 mi away in 25 min. You set off on your skateboard after the call. At what speeds (in miles per minute) can you ride your skateboard to be at the park in at most 25 min?
- How are the distance you travel, your speed, and time related?
- How can an inequality help you solve the problem?
- How can the model below help you solve the problem?

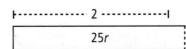

Solve each inequality. Justify each step.

43. $-4.5 > 9p$

44. $-1 \geq \frac{t}{3}$

45. $\frac{3}{4}n < 4$

46. $-8u < 4$

47. $\frac{n}{5} \leq -2$

48. $-12 > 4a$

49. Trip A family is taking a cross-country trip by car. They drive at an average speed of 55 mi/h, and their goal is to travel at least 400 mi/day. How many hours per day do they need to drive?

50. Lunch You have $30. You are going to buy a sandwich and a drink for yourself and two friends from the menu at the right. You will spend the remainder on snacks. What is the least number of snacks you can afford? What is the greatest number of snacks you can afford? Explain.

Drinks	Sandwiches	
Sm $1	Veggie	$4
Med $1.50	Chicken	$5
Lg $2	Roast Beef	$7
Snacks		
Pretzels $1	Ice Cream $2	
Brownie $3		

51. Open-Ended Write an inequality that can be solved by dividing by a negative number and has the solution $x < \frac{1}{3}$.

Standardized Test Prep

52. The mayor of Renee's town chose 160 students from her school to attend a city debate. This amount is no more than $\frac{1}{4}$ of the students in Renee's school. What is the least possible number of students that attend Renee's school?

Ⓐ 40 　　　　Ⓑ 160 　　　　Ⓒ 320 　　　　Ⓓ 640

53. An art teacher has a box of 100 markers. The teacher gives 7 markers to each student in the class and has 16 markers left over. How many students are in the class?

Ⓕ 11 　　　　Ⓖ 12 　　　　Ⓗ 13 　　　　Ⓘ 14

Short Response

54. The width of a rectangle is 3 in. shorter than the length. The perimeter of the rectangle is 18 in. What is the length of the rectangle? Show your work.

Mixed Review

Solve each inequality.

◀ See Lesson 3-2.

55. $x + 5 \leq -6$

56. $y - 4.7 \geq 8.9$

57. $q - 5 < 0$

58. $\frac{1}{2} > \frac{3}{4} + c$

59. $-\frac{2}{3} < b + \frac{1}{3}$

60. $y - 21 \leq 54$

Get Ready! To prepare for Lesson 3-4, do Exercises 61–63.

Solve each equation.

◀ See Lesson 2-3.

61. $-x + 8 + 4x = 14$

62. $-6(2y + 2) = 12$

63. $0.5t + 3.5 - 2.5t = 1.5t$

More Algebraic Properties

The following properties can help you understand algebraic relationships.

Reflexive, Symmetric, and Transitive Properties of Equality

For all real numbers a, b, and c:

Reflexive Property
$a = a$

Examples
$5x = 5x$, $\$1 = \$1$

Symmetric Property
If $a = b$, then $b = a$.

If $15 = 3t$, then $3t = 15$.
If 1 pair $=$ 2 socks, then 2 socks $=$ 1 pair.

Transitive Property
If $a = b$ and $b = c$, then $a = c$.

If $d = 3y$ and $3y = 6$, then $d = 6$.
If 36 in. $=$ 3 ft and 3 ft $=$ 1 yd, then 36 in. $=$ 1 yd.

Transitive Property of Inequality

For all real numbers a, b, and c, if $a < b$ and $b < c$, then $a < c$.

Examples If $8x < 7$ and $7 < y$, then $8x < y$.
If 1 cup $<$ 1 qt and 1 qt $<$ 1 gal, then 1 cup $<$ 1 gal.

Example

Use the property given in parentheses to complete each statement.

A If $7x < y$ and $y < z + 2$, then $7x < \blacksquare$. (Transitive Property of Inequality)
  If $7x < y$ and $y < z + 2$, then $7x < z + 2$.

B If 2000 lb $=$ 1 ton, then 1 ton $=$ __?__ . (Symmetric Property)
  If 2000 lb $=$ 1 ton, then 1 ton $=$ 2000 lb.

Exercises

Name the property that each statement illustrates.

1. If $3.8 = n$, then $n = 3.8$.

2. 6 in. $=$ 6 in.

3. If $x = 7$ and $7 = 5 + 2$, then $x = 5 + 2$.

4. If math class is earlier than art class and art class is earlier than history class, then math class is earlier than history class.

5. Complete the following sentence. If Amy is shorter than Greg and Greg is shorter than Lisa, then Amy is shorter than __?__ .

Modeling Multi-Step Inequalities

Sometimes you need to perform two or more steps to solve an inequality. Models can help you understand how to solve multi-step inequalities.

Activity

Model and solve $2x - 3 < 1$.

Inequality	Model	Think
$2x - 3 < 1$		The tiles model the inequality.
$2x - 3 + 3 < 1 + 3$		Add 3 yellow tiles to each side.
$2x < 4$		Simplify by removing the zero pairs.
$\dfrac{2x}{2} < \dfrac{4}{2}$		Divide each side into two equal groups.
$x < 2$		Each green tile is less than two yellow tiles, so $x < 2$.

Exercises

Write an inequality for each model. Use tiles to solve each inequality.

1.

2.

Use tiles to model and solve each inequality.

3. $2n - 5 \geq 3$

4. $-9 > 4x - 1$

5. $3w + 4 < -5$

6. $z + 6 \leq 2z + 2$

7. $3m + 7 \geq m - 5$

8. $5b + 6 > 3b - 2$

Objective   To solve multi-step inequalities

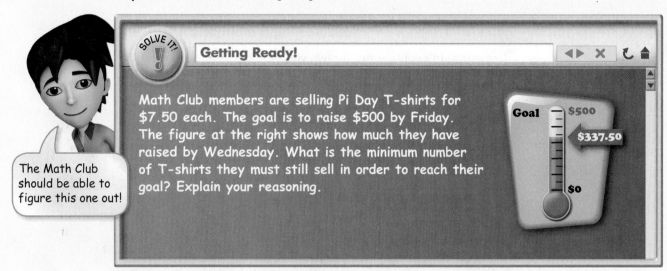

Getting Ready!

Math Club members are selling Pi Day T-shirts for $7.50 each. The goal is to raise $500 by Friday. The figure at the right shows how much they have raised by Wednesday. What is the minimum number of T-shirts they must still sell in order to reach their goal? Explain your reasoning.

Goal $500
$337.50
$0

The Math Club should be able to figure this one out!

You can model the situation in the Solve It with the inequality $337.50 + 7.50x \geq 500$. In this lesson, you will learn how to write and solve multi-step inequalities like this one.

Focus Question   How is solving a multi-step inequality similar to solving a multi-step equation?

 Problem 1   **Using More Than One Step**

What are the solutions of $9 + 4t > 21$? Check the solutions.

Write the original inequality.	$9 + 4t > 21$
Subtract 9 from each side to undo addition.	$9 + 4t - 9 > 21 - 9$
Simplify.	$4t > 12$
Divide each side by 4 to undo multiplication.	$\frac{4t}{4} > \frac{12}{4}$
Simplify.	$t > 3$

Check

Check the endpoint of $t > 3$ by substituting 3 for t in the related equation.	$9 + 4(3) \overset{?}{=} 21$
Simplify.	$21 = 21$ ✔
Check the inequality symbol of $t > 3$ by substituting 4 for t in the original inequality.	$9 + 4(4) \overset{?}{>} 21$
Simplify.	$25 > 21$ ✔

Plan

How can you check the solutions?
Check the endpoint, 3. Then choose a value greater than 3 and check the inequality symbol.

Got It? **1.** What are the solutions of the inequality? Check your solutions.

    a. $-6a - 7 \le 17$ **b.** $-4 < 5 - 3n$ **c.** $50 > 0.8x + 30$

You can adapt familiar formulas to write inequalities. You use the real-world situation to determine which inequality symbol to use.

 Problem 2   **Writing and Solving a Multi-Step Inequality**

Geometry In a community garden, you want to fence in a vegetable garden that is adjacent to your friend's garden. You have at most 42 ft of fence. What are the possible lengths of your garden?

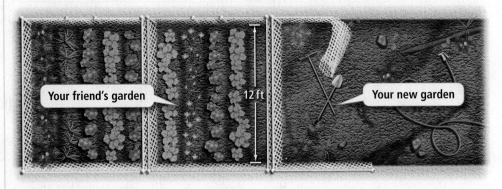

Your friend's garden   12 ft   Your new garden

Relate   Because the fence will surround the garden, you can use the perimeter formula $P = 2\ell + 2w$.

twice the length	plus	twice the width	is at most	the amount of fence

Define   Let $\ell =$ the length of the garden.

Write 2ℓ $+$ $2(12)$ $\le$ 42

Write the original inequality. $2\ell + 2(12) \le 42$

Simplify. $2\ell + 24 \le 42$

Subtract 24 from each side to undo addition. $2\ell + 24 - 24 \le 42 - 24$

Simplify. $2\ell \le 18$

Divide each side by 2 to undo multiplication. $\dfrac{2\ell}{2} \le \dfrac{18}{2}$

Simplify. $\ell \le 9$

The length of the garden must be 9 ft or less.

 Got It? **2.** You want to make a rectangular banner that is 18 ft long. You have no more than 48 ft of trim for the banner. What are the possible widths of the banner?

Think

You can use reasoning and *guess-and-check* to solve the problem. If either −6 or −8 is a solution, at least one other answer choice would also be a solution. So, eliminate −6 and −8 as possible answers. Guess that either −4 or −10 is correct and check your guess.

 Problem 3 Using the Distributive Property

Multiple Choice Which is a solution of $3(t + 1) \geq -9$?

A) −4   B) −6   C) −8   D) −10

Write the original inequality.	$3(t + 1) \geq -9$
Apply the Distributive Property to remove the parentheses.	$3t + 3 \geq -9$
Subtract 3 from each side to undo addition.	$3t + 3 - 3 \geq -9 - 3$
Simplify.	$3t \geq -12$
Divide each side by 3 to undo multiplication.	$\dfrac{3t}{3} \geq \dfrac{-12}{3}$
Simplify.	$t \geq -4$

−4 is a solution of the inequality $t \geq -4$. The correct answer is A. Only one of the solutions is given in the answer choices above. You can use a graph to show all of the solutions.

 Got It? 3. What are the solutions of $38 \leq 2(4m + 7)$? Check your solutions.

Some inequalities have variables on both sides of the inequality symbol. You need to gather the variable terms on one side of the inequality and the constant terms on the other side.

 Problem 4 Solving an Inequality With Variables on Both Sides

What are the solutions of $6n - 1 > 3n + 8$?

Think

Why subtract 3n instead of 6n from each side of the inequality?

You can subtract either 3n or 6n from each side. However, subtracting 3n gives you a variable term with a positive coefficient.

Write the original inequality.	$6n - 1 > 3n + 8$
To gather variables on the left, subtract 3n from each side.	$6n - 1 - 3n > 3n + 8 - 3n$
Simplify.	$3n - 1 > 8$
To gather the constants on the right, add 1 to each side.	$3n - 1 + 1 > 8 + 1$
Simplify.	$3n > 9$
Divide each side by 3 to undo multiplication.	$\dfrac{3n}{3} > \dfrac{9}{3}$
Simplify.	$n > 3$

 Got It? 4. a. What are the solutions of $3b + 12 > 27 - 2b$? Check your solutions.

       b. Reasoning The first step in solving Problem 4 was to subtract 3n from each side of the inequality. What else could have been the first step in solving the inequality? Explain.

Sometimes solving an inequality gives a statement that is *always* true, such as $4 > 1$. In that case, the solutions are all real numbers. If the statement is *never* true, as is $9 \le -5$, then the inequality has no solution.

 Problem 5 Inequalities With Special Solutions

ONLINE PROBLEMS

Think

Is there another way to solve this inequality?
Yes. Instead of using the Distributive Property, you can first divide each side by 2.

Ⓐ What are the solutions of $10 - 8a \ge 2(5 - 4a)$?

Write the original inequality.	$10 - 8a \ge 2(5 - 4a)$
Use the Distributive Property.	$10 - 8a \ge 10 - 8a$
Add $8a$ to each side.	$10 - 8a + 8a \ge 10 - 8a + 8a$
Simplify.	$10 \ge 10$

Because the inequality $10 \ge 10$ is always true, the solutions of $10 - 8a \ge 2(5 - 4a)$ are all real numbers.

Think

Without solving, how can you tell that this inequality has no solution?
The variable terms on each side of the inequality are equal, but -5 is *not* greater than 7.

Ⓑ What are the solutions of $6m - 5 > 7m + 7 - m$?

Write the original inequality.	$6m - 5 > 7m + 7 - m$
Combine like terms.	$6m - 5 > 6m + 7$
Subtract $6m$ from each side.	$6m - 5 - 6m > 6m + 7 - 6m$
Simplify.	$-5 > 7$

Because the inequality $-5 > 7$ is never true, the inequality $6m - 5 > 7m + 7 - m$ has no solution.

 Got It? 5. What are the solutions of each inequality?

    a. $9 + 5n \le 5n - 1$ **b.** $8 + 6x \ge 7x + 2 - x$

Focus Question How is solving a multi-step inequality similar to solving a multi-step equation?

Answer You use the properties of inequality to isolate the variable.

 Lesson Check

Do you know HOW?

Solve each inequality, if possible. If it is not possible, tell why not.

1. $7 + 6a > 19$

2. $2(t + 2) \ge -6$

3. $6z - 15 < 4z + 11$

4. $18x - 5 \le 3(6x - 2)$

5. The perimeter of a rectangle is at most 24 cm. Two opposite sides are each 4 cm long. What are the possible lengths of the other two sides?

Do you UNDERSTAND?

6. Reasoning How can you tell that the inequality $3t + 1 > 3t + 2$ has no solution just by looking at the terms in the inequality?

7. Reasoning Can you solve the inequality $2(x - 3) \le 10$ *without* using the Distributive Property? Explain.

8. Error Analysis Your friend says that the solutions of the inequality $-2(3 - x) > 2x - 6$ are all real numbers. Do you agree with your friend? Explain. What if the inequality symbol were $\ge$?

Practice and Problem-Solving Exercises

Practice

Solve each inequality. Check your solutions.

See Problem 1.

9. $5f + 7 \leq 22$

10. $6n - 3 > -18$

11. $-5y - 2 < 8$

12. $6 - 3p \geq -9$

13. $9 \leq -12 + 6r$

14. $6 \leq 12 + 4j$

Write and solve an inequality.

See Problem 2.

15. Family Trip On a trip from Buffalo, New York, to St. Augustine, Florida, a family wants to travel at least 250 mi in the first 5 h of driving. What should their average speed be in order to meet this goal?

Guided Practice

To start, use the formula for distance. $d = rt$, where d is the distance in mi, r is the rate in mph, and t is the time in h.

Write the inequality. $250 \leq r \cdot 5$

16. Geometry An isosceles triangle has at least two congruent sides. The perimeter of a certain isosceles triangle is at most 12 in. The length of each of the two congruent sides is 5 in. What are the possible lengths of the remaining side?

Solve each inequality.

See Problems 3 and 4.

Guided Practice

17. $3(k - 5) \geq -3$

To start, use the Distributive Property to eliminate the parentheses. $3k - 15 \geq -3$

18. $-(7c - 18) > 0$

19. $-3(j + 3) < -15$

20. $40 \leq 4(6y - 2)$

21. $4x + 3 < 3x + 6$

22. $4v + 8 \geq 6v + 10$

23. $5f + 8 \geq 2 + 6f$

24. $6 - 3p \leq 4 - p$

25. $3m - 4 \leq 6m + 11$

26. $4t + 17 > 7 + 5t$

Solve each inequality, if possible. If the inequality has no solution, write *no solution*. If the solutions are all real numbers, write *all real numbers*.

See Problem 5.

27. $-3(w - 3) \geq 9 - 3w$

28. $-5r + 6 \leq -5(r + 2)$

29. $6w - 4 \leq 2(3w + 6)$

30. $9 + 2x < 7 + 2(x - 3)$

31. $2(n - 8) < 16 + 2n$

32. $-2(6 + s) \geq -15 - 2s$

Apply

Solve each inequality, if possible. If the inequality has no solution, write *no solution*. If the solutions are all real numbers, write *all real numbers*.

33. $-3(x - 3) \geq 5 - 4x$

34. $3s + 6 \leq -5(s + 2)$

35. $4 - 2n \leq 5 - n + 1$

36. **Think About a Plan** Your cell phone plan costs $39.99 per month plus $.15 for each text message you send or receive. You have at most $45 to spend on your cell phone bill. What is the maximum number of text messages that you can send or receive next month?
   • What information do you know? What information do you need?
   • What inequality can you use to find the maximum number of text messages that you can send or receive?
   • What are the solutions of the inequality? Are they reasonable?

37. **Rental Rates** The student council wants to rent a ballroom for the junior prom. The ballroom's rental rate is $1500 for 3 h and $125 for each additional half hour. Suppose the student council raises $2125. What is the maximum number of hours for which they can rent the ballroom?

38. **Writing** Suppose a friend is having difficulty solving $3(q - 5) > q + 3$. Explain how to solve the inequality, showing all the necessary steps and identifying the properties you would use.

39. **Biology** The average normal body temperature for humans is 98.6°F. An abnormal increase in body temperature is classified as hyperthermia, or fever. Which inequality represents the body temperature in degrees Celsius of a person with hyperthermia? (*Hint*: To convert from degrees Celsius C to degrees Fahrenheit F, use the formula $F = \frac{9}{5}C + 32$.)

   Ⓐ $\frac{9}{5}C + 32 \geq 98.6$ Ⓑ $\frac{9}{5}C + 32 \leq 98.6$ Ⓒ $\frac{9}{5}C + 32 < 98.6$ Ⓓ $\frac{9}{5}C + 32 > 98.6$

40. **Open-Ended** Write two different inequalities that you can solve by subtracting 3 from each side and then dividing each side by −5. Solve each inequality.

41. **Mental Math** Determine whether each inequality is *always true* or *never true*.
   a. $5s + 7 \geq 7 + 5s$ **b.** $4t + 6 > 4t - 3$ **c.** $5(m + 2) < 5m - 4$

42. **Commission** A sales associate in a shoe store earns $325 per week, plus a commission equal to 4% of her sales. This week her goal is to earn at least $475. At least how many dollars' worth of shoes must she sell in order to reach her goal?

> **Hint** Rewrite 4% as a decimal in the inequality.

Error Analysis Describe and correct the error in each solution.

43.
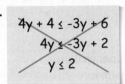

$4y + 4 \leq -3y + 6$
$4y \leq -3y + 2$
$y \leq 2$

44.

$5(p + 3) > 4p + 2$
$5p + 3 > 4p + 2$
$5p > 4p - 1$
$p > -1$

Standardized Test Prep

45. The Science Club hopes to collect at least 200 kg of aluminum cans for recycling during a 21-week semester. The graph shows the first week's results. Let x represent the minimum average mass of cans required per week for the remainder of the semester. What is x?

46. What is the solution of $2x + 8 = 4x + 2$?

47. What is the solution of $-5n - 16 = -7n$?

48. Great Gifts pays its supplier $65 for each box of 12 bells. The owner wants to determine the minimum amount x he can charge his customers per bell in order to make at least a 50% profit per box. What is x? Round to the nearest hundredth if necessary.

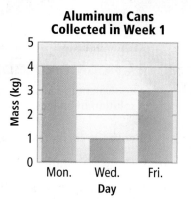

Aluminum Cans Collected in Week 1

Mixed Review

Solve each inequality.

See Lesson 3-3.

49. $-9m \geq 36$

50. $-24 \leq 3y$

51. $\dfrac{y}{5} > -4$

52. $-\dfrac{t}{3} \leq 1$

Get Ready! To prepare for Lesson 3-5, do Exercises 53–55.

Determine whether each set represents the set of *natural numbers, whole numbers,* or *integers.*

See Lesson 1-3.

53. the nonnegative integers

54. the counting numbers

55. $\ldots, -3, -2, -1, 0, 1, 2, 3, \ldots$

3 Chapter Review for Part A

Chapter Vocabulary

- equivalent inequalities (p. 184)
- solution of an inequality (p. 175)

Choose the correct term to complete each sentence.

1. The __?__ is a number that makes the inequality true.

2. Inequalities that have the same solutions are __?__.

3-1 Inequalities and Their Graphs

Quick Review

A **solution of an inequality** is any number that makes the inequality true. You can indicate all the solutions of an inequality on the graph. A closed dot indicates that the endpoint is a solution. An open dot indicates that the endpoint is *not* a solution.

Example

What is the graph of $x \leq -4$?

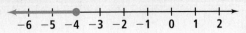

Exercises

Graph each inequality.

3. $x > 5$ 4. $h \leq -1$

5. $10 \geq p$ 6. $r < 3.2$

Write an inequality for each graph.

7.
```
←—+——+——+——+——●——+——+——+——+——→
  -6  -5  -4  -3  -2  -1   0   1   2
```

8.
```
←—+——+——○——+——+——+——+——+——+——→
  -7  -6  -5  -4  -3  -2  -1   0   1
```

3-2 Solving Inequalities Using Addition or Subtraction

Quick Review

You can use the addition and subtraction properties of inequality to transform an inequality into a simpler, equivalent inequality.

Example

What are the solutions of $x + 4 \leq 5$?

Write the original inequality.	$x + 4 \leq 5$
Subtract 4 from each side.	$x + 4 - 4 \leq 5 - 4$
Simplify.	$x \leq 1$

Exercises

Solve each inequality. Graph your solutions.

9. $w + 3 > 9$ 10. $v - 6 < 4$

11. $-4 < t + 8$ 12. $n - \frac{1}{2} \geq \frac{3}{4}$

13. $22.3 \leq 13.7 + h$ 14. $q + 0.5 > -2$

15. **Allowance** You have at most $15.00 to spend. You want to buy a used CD that costs $4.25. Write and solve an inequality to find the possible additional amounts you can spend.

3-3 Solving Inequalities Using Multiplication or Division

Quick Review

You can use the multiplication and division properties of inequality to transform an inequality. When you multiply or divide each side of an inequality by a negative number, you have to reverse the inequality symbol.

Example

What are the solutions of $-3x > 12$?

Write the original inequality. $\qquad -3x > 12$

Divide each side by -3. Reverse the $\quad \frac{-3x}{-3} < \frac{12}{-3}$
inequality symbol.

Simplify. $\qquad\qquad\qquad\qquad x < -4$

Exercises

Solve each inequality. Graph your solutions.

16. $5x < 15$

17. $-6t > 18$

18. $\frac{y}{3} \leq 2$

19. $-\frac{h}{4} < 6$

20. $25.5g > 102$

21. $-\frac{3}{5}n \geq -9$

22. $44 \leq 2d$

23. $-16m < 24$

24. Part-Time Job You earn $7.25 per hour baby-sitting. Write and solve an inequality to find how many full hours you must work to earn at least $200.

3-4 Solving Multi-Step Inequalities

Quick Review

When you solve inequalities, sometimes you need to use more than one step. You need to gather the variable terms on one side of the inequality and the constant terms on the other side.

Example

What are the solutions of $3x + 5 > -1$?

Write the original inequality. $\quad 3x + 5 > -1$

Subtract 5 from each side. $\qquad 3x > -6$

Divide each side by 3. $\qquad\quad x > -2$

Exercises

Solve each inequality.

25. $4k - 1 \geq -3$

26. $6(c - 1) < -18$

27. $3t > 5t + 12$

28. $-\frac{6}{7}y - 6 \geq 42$

29. $4 + \frac{x}{2} > 2x$

30. $3x + 5 \leq 2x - 8$

31. $13.5a + 7.4 \leq 85.7$

32. $42w > 2(w + 7)$

33. Commission A salesperson earns $200 per week plus a commission equal to 4% of her sales. This week her goal is to earn no less than $450. Write and solve an inequality to find the amount of sales she must have to reach her goal.

Do you know HOW?

Write an inequality that represents each verbal expression or graph.

1. all real numbers y greater than or equal to 12

2. 8 more than a number m is less than 5.

3.
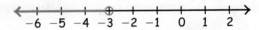

```
←—+——+——+——●——+——+——+——+——→
  −4  −3  −2  −1   0   1   2   3   4
```

4. The product of -3 and t is greater than 11.

5. c less than 7 is less than or equal to -3.

6.
```
←——+——+——+——+——+——+——⊕——+——+——→
   −6  −4  −2   0   2   4   6   8  10
```

7. A cat weighs no more than 8 lb.

Solve each inequality. Graph the solutions.

8. $8d + 2 < 5d - 7$

9. $2n + 1 \geq -3$

10. $-2x + 7 \leq 45$

11. $5s - 3 + 1 < 8$

12. $5(3p - 2) > 50$

13. $\dfrac{y}{2} < -3$

14. $6 \geq -\dfrac{4}{5}n$

15. $-1.5d > 18$

16. A baseball team wants to collect at least 160 cans of food for an upcoming food drive. Team members brought 42 cans of food on Monday and 65 cans of food on Wednesday. Write and solve an inequality to describe how many cans of food the team must collect on Friday to make or exceed their goal.

17. Suppose you earn \$7.25 per hour working part-time for a florist. Write and solve an inequality to find how many *full* hours you must work to earn at least \$125.

Solve each inequality, if possible. If the inequality has no solution, write *no solution*. If the solutions are all real numbers, write *all real numbers*.

18. $7 - 6b \leq 19$

19. $15f + 9 > 3(5f + 3)$

20. $6z - 15 \geq 4z + 11$

21. The cheerleaders are making a rectangular banner for a football game. The length of the banner is 30 ft. The cheerleaders can use no more than 96 ft of trim around the outside of the banner. What are the possible widths of the banner?

Do you UNDERSTAND?

22. a. **Error Analysis** A student claims that the graph below represents the solutions of the inequality $-3 < x$. What error did the student make?

```
←——+——+——+——⊕——+——+——+——+——+——→
   −6  −5  −4  −3  −2  −1   0   1   2
```

   b. What inequality is actually represented by the graph?

Decide whether the two inequalities in each pair are equivalent. Explain.

23. $36 \leq -4 + y$ and $40 \leq y$

24. $9 + b > 24$ and $b > 33$

25. $m - \dfrac{1}{2} < \dfrac{3}{8}$ and $m < \dfrac{7}{8}$

26. **Reasoning** A local gym offers a trial membership for 3 months. It discounts the regular monthly fee x by \$25. If the total cost of the trial membership is less than \$100, you will consider signing up. What inequality can you use to determine whether you should sign up?

Solving Inequalities

In Part A, you learned how to solve inequalities. Now you will look at sets and inequalities involving absolute value.

 Vocabulary for Part B

English/Spanish Vocabulary Audio Online:

English	Spanish
complement of a set, *p. 212*	complemento de un conjunto
compound inequality, *p. 216*	desigualdad compuesta
disjoint sets, *p. 231*	conjuntos ajenos
empty set, *p. 211*	conjunto vacío
intersection, *p. 231*	intersección
roster form, *p. 210*	lista
set-builder notation , *p. 210*	notación conjuntista
union, *p. 230*	unión
universal set, *p. 212*	conjunto universal

BIG ideas

1 Variable
Essential Question How do you represent relationships between quantities that are not equal?

2 Equivalence
Essential Question Can inequalities that appear to be different be equivalent?

3 Solving Equations and Inequalities
Essential Question How can you solve inequalities?

Chapter Preview for Part B

3-5 **Working With Sets**
3-6 **Compound Inequalities**
3-7 PART 1 **Absolute Value Equations and Inequalities**
PART 2 **Absolute Value Equations and Inequalities**
3-8 **Unions and Intersections of Sets**

Working With Sets

Objectives To write sets and identify subsets
To find the complement of a set

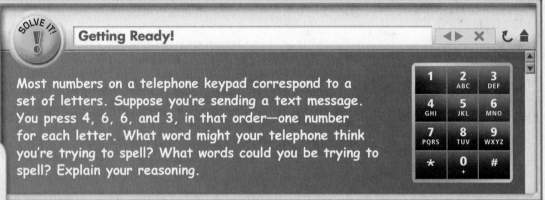

Lesson Vocabulary
- roster form
- set-builder notation
- empty set
- universal set
- complement of a set

Recall from Lesson 1-3 that a *set* is a collection of distinct elements. A *subset* contains elements from a set. For example, the number 6 on the telephone keypad corresponds to the set {M, N, O}. The set {M, O} is one subset of this set.

Focus Question How can you write sets and identify subsets?

Roster form is one way to write sets. Roster form lists the elements of a set within braces, { }. For example, you write the set containing 1 and 2 as {1, 2}, and you write the set of multiples of 2 as {2, 4, 6, 8, . . .}.

Set-builder notation is another way to write sets. It describes the properties an element must have to be included in a set. For example, you can write the set {2, 4, 6, 8, . . . } in set-builder notation as $\{x \mid x$ is a multiple of 2$\}$. You read this as "the set of all real numbers x, such that x is a multiple of 2."

Plan

How are roster form and set-builder notation different?
Roster form *lists* the elements of a set. Set-builder notation *describes* the properties of those elements.

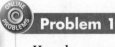 **Problem 1**   **Using Roster Form and Set-Builder Notation**

How do you write "T is the set of natural numbers that are less than 6" in roster form? In set-builder notation?

Roster form	Set-builder notation

Roster form

Write "T is" as "$T =$." | List all natural numbers that are less than 6.

$$T = \{1, 2, 3, 4, 5\}$$

Set-builder notation

Use a variable. | Describe the limits on the variable.

$$T = \{x \mid x \text{ is a natural number, } x < 6\}$$

Got It? **1.** N is the set of even natural numbers that are less than or equal to 12.

 a. How do you write N in roster form?

 b. How do you write N in set-builder notation?

You can use set-builder notation to write the solutions of a linear inequality.

Plan

How is this problem similar to others you've solved?
It requires using properties of inequality to solve a multi-step inequality, as you did in Lesson 3-4.

 Problem 2 **Inequalities and Set-Builder Notation**

Multiple Choice In set-builder notation, how do you write the solutions of $-5x + 7 \le 17$?

 Ⓐ $x \ge -2$ Ⓒ $\{-2, -1, 0, \ldots\}$

 Ⓑ $\{x \mid x \ge -2\}$ Ⓓ $\{x \mid x \le -2\}$

Write the original inequality.	$-5x + 7 \le 17$
Subtract 7 from each side to undo addition.	$-5x + 7 - 7 \le 17 - 7$
Simplify.	$-5x \le 10$
Divide each side by -5 to undo multiplication. Reverse the inequality symbol.	$\dfrac{-5x}{-5} \ge \dfrac{10}{-5}$
Simplify.	$x \ge -2$

In set-builder notation, the solutions are given by $\{x \mid x \ge -2\}$. The answer is B.

 Got It? **2.** In set-builder notation, how do you write the solutions of $9 - 4n > 21$?

Set A is a subset of a set B if each element of A is also an element of B. For example, if $B = \{-2, -1, 0, 1, 2, 3\}$ and $A = \{-1, 0, 2\}$, then A is a subset of B. You can write this relationship as $A \subseteq B$.

The **empty set,** or *null set*, is the set that contains no elements. The empty set is a subset of every set. Use $\emptyset$ or $\{\,\}$ to represent the empty set.

 Problem 3 **Finding Subsets**

What are all the subsets of the set $\{3, 4, 5\}$?

Start with the empty set.	$\emptyset$
List the subsets with one element.	$\{3\}, \{4\}, \{5\}$
List the subsets with two elements.	$\{3, 4\}, \{3, 5\}, \{4, 5\}$
List the original set. It is always considered a subset.	$\{3, 4, 5\}$

Think

Why is the original set considered a subset?
It's a subset because it contains elements from the original set. In this case, it's the subset that contains all three elements.

The eight subsets of $\{3, 4, 5\}$ are $\emptyset$, $\{3\}, \{4\}, \{5\}, \{3, 4\}, \{3, 5\}, \{4, 5\}$, and $\{3, 4, 5\}$.

Got It? **3. a.** What are the subsets of the set $P = \{a, b\}$?

 b. What are the subsets of the set $S = \{a, b, c\}$?

 c. **Reasoning** Let $A = \{x \mid x < -3\}$ and $B = \{x \mid x \le 0\}$. Is A a subset of B? Explain your reasoning.

When working with sets, you call the largest set you are using the **universal set,** or universe. The **complement of a set** is the set of all elements in the universal set that are *not* in the set. You denote the complement of A by A'.

In the Venn diagrams below, U represents the universal set. Notice that $A \subseteq U$ and $A' \subseteq U$.

Set A is shaded.

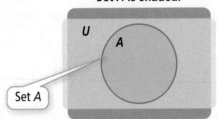

Set A

The complement of set A is shaded.

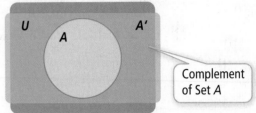

Complement of Set A

Problem 4   **Finding the Complement of a Set**

Universal set $U = \{$king, queen, bishop, knight, rook, pawn$\}$ and set A is the set of chess pieces that move side to side. What is the complement of set A?

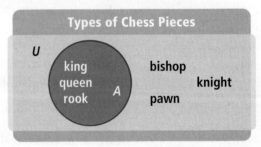

King

Queen

Bishop

Knight

Rook

Pawn

Know	**Need**	**Plan**
• The elements of set U • The elements of set A	• The elements of A'	Use a Venn diagram to find all the elements in set U that are *not* in set A.

The Venn diagram shows the relationship between sets A and U. The elements in set U that are *not* in set A are bishop, knight, and pawn.

So, $A' = \{$bishop, knight, pawn$\}$.

Types of Chess Pieces

U

king
queen
rook A

bishop

knight

pawn

Got It?   **4.** Universal set $U = \{$months of the year$\}$ and set $A = \{$months with exactly 31 days$\}$. What is the complement of set A? Write your answer in roster form.

Focus Question How can you write sets and identify subsets?

Answer You can write sets in roster form or set-builder notation. A subset contains some or all of the elements of another set. Each element of a subset must be in the original set.

Lesson Check

Do you know HOW?

1. How do you write "G is the set of odd natural numbers that are less than 18" in roster form? In set-builder notation?

2. In set-builder notation, how do you write the solutions of $5 + d \leq 8$?

3. What are all the subsets of $\{4, 8, 12\}$?

4. Given the universal set $U = \{$seasons of the year$\}$ and $W = \{$winter$\}$, what is W'?

Do you UNDERSTAND?

5. **Vocabulary** What is the complement of A'? Explain.

6. Is the first set in each pair a subset of the second set? Explain.
   a. $\emptyset$; $\{1, 3, 5\}$ b. $\{1, 3, 5\}$; $\{1, 3\}$ c. $\{3\}$; $\{1, 3, 5\}$

7. **Reasoning** A nonempty set is a set that contains at least one element. Given nonempty sets A and B, suppose that $A \subseteq B$. Is $B \subseteq A$ *always*, *sometimes*, or *never* true?

8. **Error Analysis** A student says sets A and B below are the same. What error did the student make?
   $A = \{x \mid x$ is a whole number less than 5$\}$
   $B = \{1, 2, 3, 4\}$

Practice and Problem-Solving Exercises

A Practice Write each set in roster form and in set-builder notation.

See Problem 1.

9. M is the set of integers that are greater than -1 and less than 4.

10. N is the set of real numbers that are factors of 12.

11. P is the set of natural numbers that are less than 11.

12. R is the set of even natural numbers that are less than 2.

Write the solutions of each inequality in set-builder notation.

See Problem 2.

Guided Practice

13. $4y + 7 \geq 23$
To start, subtract 7 from each side. $4y + 7 - 7 \geq 23 - 7$

14. $5r + 8 < 63$ 15. $13 - 9m < 58$ 16. $7 - 3d \geq 28$

List all the subsets of each set.

See Problem 3.

Guided Practice

17. $\{a, e, i, o\}$
To start, write the empty set. $\emptyset$
Then list the subsets with one element. $\{a\}, \{e\}, \{i\}, \{o\}$

18. $\{$dog, cat, fish$\}$ 19. $\{1\}$ 20. $\{+, -, \times, \div\}$

21. Suppose $U = \{1, 2, 3, 4, 5\}$ is the universal set and $A = \{2, 3\}$. What is A'?   **See Problem 4.**

22. Suppose $U = \{1, 2, 3, 4, 5, 6, 7, 8\}$ is the universal set and $P = \{2, 4, 6, 8\}$. What is P'?

23. Suppose $U = \{\ldots, -3, -2, -1, 0, 1, 2, 3, \ldots\}$ is the universal set and
$R = \{\ldots, -3, -1, 1, 3, \ldots\}$. What is R'?

24. Suppose $U = \{1, 2\}$ is the universal set and $T = \{1\}$. What is T'?

25. Think About a Plan Universal set U and set A are defined below. What are the elements of A'?
$U = \{$days of the week$\}$
$A = \{$days of the week that contain the letter N$\}$
* What are the elements of the universal set?
* What are the elements of set A?
* How can you find the complement of set A?

Suppose $U = \{0, 1, 2, 3, 4, 5, 6\}$, $A = \{2, 4, 6\}$, and $B = \{1, 2, 3\}$. Tell whether each statement is *true* or *false*. Explain your reasoning.

26. $A \subseteq U$ **27.** $U \subseteq B$ **28.** $B \subseteq A$ **29.** $\emptyset \subseteq B$

Write each set in set-builder notation.

30. $B = \{11, 12, 13, 14, \ldots\}$ **31.** $M = \{1, 3, 5, 7, 9, 11, 13, 15, 17, 19\}$

32. $S = \{1, 2, 3, 4, 6, 12\}$ **33.** $G = \{\ldots, -2, -1, 0, 1, 2, \ldots\}$

34. Universal set U and set B are defined below. What are the elements of B'?
$U = \{$states of the United States$\}$
$B = \{$states that do not start with the letter A$\}$

35. Universal set $U = \{$planets in Earth's solar system$\}$ and set $P = \{$planets farther from the sun than Earth is from the sun$\}$. What is the complement of set P? Write your answer in roster form.

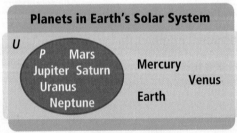

Solve each inequality. Write your solutions in set-builder notation.

36. $2x + 1 > 5$ **37.** $4y - 9 < 11$

38. $-2(3x + 7) > -14$ **39.** $-2(3x + 7) > -14 - 6x$

40. Suppose $U = \{x \mid x$ is a multiple of 2, $x < 18\}$ is the universal set and $C = \{4, 8, 12, 16\}$. What is C'?

41. Suppose $U = \{x \mid x$ is an integer, $x \leq 12\}$ is the universal set and $T = \{x \mid x$ is a natural number, $x \leq 12\}$. What is T'?

42. Open-Ended Write a two-step inequality with solutions that are given by $\{n \mid n > 0\}$.

43. How many elements are in the set $\{x \mid x$ is an even prime number, $x < 100\}$?

SAT/ACT

44. Let the universal set be $U = \{x \mid x$ is a natural number$\}$, and let set $E = \{2, 4, 6, 8, \ldots\}$. What is E'?

    Ⓐ $\{1, 3, 5, 7, \ldots\}$ Ⓒ $\{$all positive integers$\}$

    Ⓑ $\{0, 2, 4, 6, 8, \ldots\}$ Ⓓ $\{2, 4, 6, 8, \ldots\}$

45. Which set represents the solutions of $-9x + 17 \geq -64$?

    Ⓕ $\{x \mid x \leq 9\}$ Ⓖ $\{x \mid x \geq 9\}$ Ⓗ $\left\{x \mid x \leq -\dfrac{47}{9}\right\}$ Ⓘ $\left\{x \mid x \geq -\dfrac{47}{9}\right\}$

46. In the diagram below, $\triangle ABC \sim \triangle EFG$. What is FG?

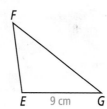

    Ⓐ $3\dfrac{8}{9}$ Ⓑ $6\dfrac{3}{7}$ Ⓒ 11 Ⓓ $12\dfrac{3}{5}$

47. What is the least whole-number solution of $-10n \leq 5$?

    Ⓕ -1 Ⓖ 0 Ⓗ 1 Ⓘ 2

Short Response

48. Mum's Florist sells two dozen roses for $24.60. First Flowers Florist sells 6 roses for $7.50. Which florist has the lower cost per rose? Explain.

Mixed Review

Solve each inequality.   ◀ **See Lesson 3-4.**

49. $3b + 2 > 26$ **50.** $2(t + 2) - 3t \geq -1$ **51.** $6z - 15 < 4z + 11$

Evaluate each expression for the given value of the variable.   ◀ **See Lesson 1-2.**

52. $3n - 6$ when $n = 4$ **53.** $7 - 2b$ when $b = 5$ **54.** $\dfrac{2d - 3}{5}$ when $d = 9$

Get Ready!   **To prepare for Lesson 3-6, do Exercises 55–57.**

Graph each pair of inequalities on one number line.   ◀ **See Lesson 3-1.**

55. $c < 8$ and $c \geq 10$ **56.** $t \geq -2$ and $t \leq -5$ **57.** $m \leq 7$ and $m > 12$

Objectives To solve and graph inequalities containing the word *and*
To solve and graph inequalities containing the word *or*

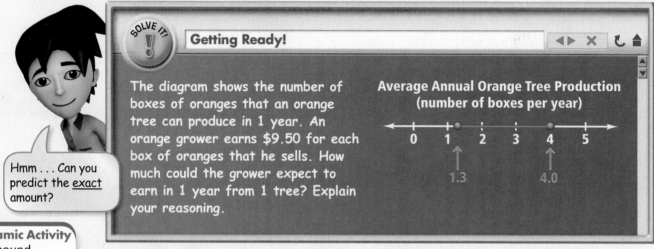

Getting Ready!

The diagram shows the number of boxes of oranges that an orange tree can produce in 1 year. An orange grower earns $9.50 for each box of oranges that he sells. How much could the grower expect to earn in 1 year from 1 tree? Explain your reasoning.

Average Annual Orange Tree Production (number of boxes per year)

Hmm . . . Can you predict the <u>exact</u> amount?

Dynamic Activity
Compound Inequalities

Lesson Vocabulary
• compound inequality

The Solve It involves a value that is between two numbers. You can use a compound inequality to represent this relationship. A **compound inequality** consists of two distinct inequalities joined by the word *and* or the word *or*.

Focus Question How do you solve and graph inequalities containing the word *and* or *or*?

The graph of a compound inequality with the word *and* contains the *overlap* of the graphs of the two inequalities that form the compound inequality.

The graph of a compound inequality with the word *or* contains *each* graph of the two inequalities that form the compound inequality.

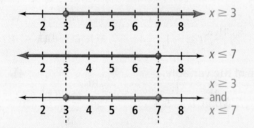

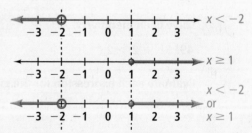

You can rewrite a compound inequality involving *and* as a single inequality. For instance, in the inequality above, you can write $x \geq 3$ and $x \leq 7$ as $3 \leq x \leq 7$. You read this as "*x* is greater than or equal to 3 and less than or equal to 7." Another way to read it is "*x* is between 3 and 7, inclusive." In this example, *inclusive* means the solutions of the inequality include both 3 and 7.

 **Problem 1** Writing a Compound Inequality

What compound inequality represents the phrase? Graph the solutions.

Think

Why can you write an *and* inequality without the word *and*?
The compound inequality $-2 < n$ and $n < 6$ means n is greater than -2 *and* n is less than 6. This means n is between -2 and 6. You write this as $-2 < n < 6$.

A **all real numbers that are greater than -2 and less than 6**

Write each inequality separately.	$n > -2$ and $n < 6$
Rewrite the first inequality so that both statements use $<$.	$-2 < n$ and $n < 6$
Write the solutions as a single inequality.	$-2 < n < 6$

Graph the solutions.

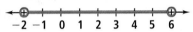

B **all real numbers that are less than 0 or greater than or equal to 5**

Write the inequalities separately.　　$t < 0$ or $t \geq 5$

Graph the solutions.

Got It? **1.** For parts (a) and (b) below, write a compound inequality that represents each phrase. Graph the solutions.
   a. all real numbers that are greater than or equal to -4 and less than 6
   b. all real numbers that are less than or equal to $2\frac{1}{2}$ or greater than 6
   c. **Reasoning** What is the difference between "x is between -5 and 7" and "x is between -5 and 7, inclusive"?

A solution of a compound inequality involving *and* is any number that makes *both* inequalities true. One way you can solve a compound inequality is by separating it into two inequalities.

 Problem 2 Solving a Compound Inequality Involving *And*

What are the solutions of $-3 \leq m - 4 < -1$? Graph the solutions.

Plan

How do you know to join the two inequalities with *and*?
The compound inequality $-3 \leq m - 4 < -1$ means that the quantity $m - 4$ is between -3 and -1, including -3. So use the word *and*.

Write the original inequality.	$-3 \leq m - 4 < -1$
Write the compound inequality as two inequalities joined by the word *and*.	$-3 \leq m - 4$　　　and　　　$m - 4 < -1$
Add 4 to each side of each inequality.	$-3 + 4 \leq m - 4 + 4$ and $m - 4 + 4 < -1 + 4$
Simplify.	$1 \leq m$　　　and　　　$m < 3$
Write the solutions as a single inequality.	$1 \leq m < 3$

Graph the inequality.

Got It? **2.** What are the solutions of $-2 < 3y - 4 < 14$? Graph the solutions.

You can also solve an inequality like $-3 \le m - 4 < -1$ by working on all three parts of the inequality at the same time. You work to isolate the variable between the inequality symbols. This method is used in Problem 3.

Problem 3 Writing and Solving a Compound Inequality

Test Average To earn a B in your algebra course, you must achieve an unrounded test average between 84 and 86, inclusive. You scored 86, 85, and 80 on the first three tests of the grading period. What possible scores can you earn on the fourth and final test to earn a B in the course?

Know	Need	Plan
• Test average must be between 84 and 86, inclusive • First 3 test scores	Possible scores you can earn on the last test to get a B in the course	Write an expression for your test average. Then write and solve a compound inequality.

Think

What is another way to solve this problem?
You can work backward to solve this problem. You can start with the inequality $84 \le x \le 86$, where *x* represents the average of your test scores. Then rewrite the inequality in terms of the sum of your 4 test scores.

Write a compound inequality.
$$84 \le \frac{86 + 85 + 80 + x}{4} \le 86$$

Multiply each part by 4 to remove the fraction.
$$4(84) \le 4\left(\frac{251 + x}{4}\right) \le 4(86)$$

Simplify.
$$336 \le 251 + x \le 344$$

Subtract 251 from each part to isolate *x*.
$$336 - 251 \le 251 + x - 251 \le 344 - 251$$

Simplify.
$$85 \le x \le 93$$

Your score on the fourth test must be between 85 and 93, inclusive.

 Got It? 3. Reasoning Suppose you scored 78, 78, and 79 on the first three tests. Is it possible for you to earn a B in the course? Assume that 100 is the maximum grade you can earn in the course and on the test. Explain.

A solution of a compound inequality involving *or* is any number that makes *either* inequality true. To solve a compound inequality involving *or*, you must solve separately the two inequalities that form the compound inequality.

Plan

How is this inequality different from others you've solved?

It contains the word *or*. Unlike an *and* inequality, it's formed by two inequalities with solutions that do not overlap.

What are the solutions of $3t + 2 < -7$ or $-4t + 5 < 1$? Graph the solutions.

Step 1 First solve $3t + 2 < -7$.

Write the original inequality.	$3t + 2 < -7$
Subtract 2 from each side to undo addition.	$3t + 2 - 2 < -7 - 2$
Simplify.	$3t < -9$
Divide each side by 3 to undo multiplication.	$\frac{3t}{3} < \frac{-9}{3}$
Simplify.	$t < -3$

Step 2 Next solve $-4t + 5 < 1$.

Write the original inequality.	$-4t + 5 < 1$
Subtract 5 from each side to undo addition.	$-4t + 5 - 5 < 1 - 5$
Simplify.	$-4t < -4$
Divide each side by -4 to undo multiplication.	$\frac{-4t}{-4} > \frac{-4}{-4}$
Simplify.	$t > 1$

> Reverse the inequality symbol when you divide by a negative number.

The solutions are given by $t < -3$ or $t > 1$.

Graph the solutions.

Got It? 4. What are the solutions of $-2y + 7 < 1$ or $4y + 3 \le -5$? Graph the solutions.

Focus Question How do you solve and graph inequalities containing the word *and* or *or*?

Answer You can find the solutions to inequalities containing the word *and* or *or* by breaking the inequality into two separate inequalities. If the inequality contains the word *and*, identify where the solution sets of the two inequalities overlap. If the inequality contains the word *or*, combine the solution sets to form a larger solution set.

 Lesson Check

Do you know HOW?

1. What compound inequality represents the phrase "all real numbers that are greater than or equal to 0 and less than 8"? Graph the solutions.

2. What are the solutions of $-4 \le r - 5 < -1$? Graph the solutions.

3. Your test scores in science are 83 and 87. What possible scores can you earn on your next test to have a test average between 85 and 90, inclusive?

Do you UNDERSTAND?

4. **Vocabulary** Which of the following are compound inequalities?

   A. $x > 4$ or $x < -4$ **B.** $x \ge 6$

   C. $8 \le 5x < 30$ **D.** $7x > 42$ or $-5x \le 10$

5. **Reasoning** What are the solutions of $3x - 7 \le 14$ or $4x - 8 > 20$? Write your solutions as a compound inequality and in interval notation.

6. **Writing** Compare the graph of a compound inequality involving *and* with the graph of a compound inequality involving *or*.

Practice and Problem-Solving Exercises

A Practice

Write a compound inequality that represents each phrase. Graph the solutions.   See Problem 1.

7. all real numbers that are between -5 and 7

8. The circumference of a women's basketball must be between 28.5 in. and 29 in., inclusive.

Solve each compound inequality. Graph your solutions.   See Problems 2 and 3.

Guided Practice

To start, subtract 3 from each pair to isolate k.

9. $\quad -4 < k + 3 < 8$
$$-4 - 3 < k + 3 - 3 < 8 - 3$$

10. $5 \le y + 2 \le 11$ **11.** $3 < 4p - 5 \le 15$ **12.** $-3 \le \dfrac{6 - q}{9} \le 3$

Solve each compound inequality. Graph your solutions.   See Problem 4.

Guided Practice

To start, add 1 to each side of the inequality on the left. Subtract 1 from each side of the inequality on the right.

13. $\quad 6b - 1 < -7$ or $2b + 1 > 5$
$$6b - 1 < -7 \qquad \text{or} \qquad 2b + 1 > 5$$
$$6b - 1 + 1 < -7 + 1 \quad \text{or} \quad 2b + 1 - 1 > 5 - 1$$

14. $5 + m > 4$ or $7m < -35$ **15.** $5y + 7 \le -3$ or $3y - 2 \ge 13$ **16.** $5z - 3 > 7$ or $4z - 6 < -10$

B Apply

Solve each inequality.

17. $7 < x + 6 \le 12$ **18.** $-9 < 3m + 6 \le 18$

19. $f + 14 < 9$ or $-9f \le -45$ **20.** $12h - 3 \ge 15h + 1$ or $5 > -0.2h + 10$

Write a compound inequality that each graph could represent.

21. ![number line from -4 -2 0 2 4 6]   **22.** ![number line from -3 -2 -1 0 1 2]   **23.** ![number line from -2 0 2 4 6 8]

Solve each compound inequality. Justify each step.

24. $4r - 3 > 11$ or $4r - 3 \le -11$ **25.** $2 \le 0.75v \le 4.5$

26. $\dfrac{4y + 2}{5} - 5 > 3$ or $\dfrac{4 - 3y}{6} > 4$ **27.** $-112 \le 7w - 63 < 84$

28. Chemistry The acidity of the water in a swimming pool is considered normal if the average of three pH readings is between 7.2 and 7.8, inclusive. The first two readings for a swimming pool are 7.4 and 7.9. What possible values for the third reading p will make the average pH normal?

> **Hint** The average is the sum of the readings divided by the number of readings.

29. Think About a Plan The Triangle Inequality Theorem states that the sum of the lengths of any two sides of a triangle is greater than the length of the third side. The lengths of two sides of a triangle are given. What are the possible lengths x of the third side of the triangle?

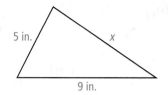

- Is there an upper limit on the value of x? Is there a lower limit?
- How can you use your answers to the previous question to write one or more inequalities involving x?

30. Physics The force exerted on a spring is proportional to the distance the spring is stretched from its relaxed position. Suppose you stretch a spring a distance of d inches by applying a force of F pounds. For your spring, $\frac{d}{F} = 0.8$. You apply forces between 25 lb and 40 lb, inclusive. What inequality describes the distances the spring is stretched?

Standardized Test Prep

SAT/ACT

31. A taxi traveled 5 mi to John's home and then drove him to the airport 10 mi away. Which inequality represents the possible distances d of the taxi from the airport when it started traveling toward John's home?

Ⓐ $5 \le d \le 10$ Ⓑ $5 \le d \le 15$ Ⓒ $0 \le d \le 5$ Ⓓ $0 \le d \le 10$

32. A student must earn at least 24 credits in high school in order to graduate. Which inequality or graph does NOT describe this situation?

Ⓕ $c \le 24$

Ⓖ $c \ge 24$

Ⓗ $24 \le c$

Ⓘ
```
  ←+——+——+——+——+——+●——+——+——+→
   -6  0  6  12 18 24 30 36 42
```

Short Response

33. The County Water Department charges a monthly administration fee of $10.40 plus $.0059 for each gallon of water used, up to, but not including, 7500 gal. What is the minimum and maximum number of gallons of water used by customers whose monthly charge is at least $35 but no more than $50? Express amounts to the nearest gallon.

Mixed Review

Let $A = \{1, 3, 5, 7\}$, let $B = \{4, 8, 12\}$, and let the universal set be $U = \{1, 2, 3, 4, 5, 7, 8, 12, 15\}$.

◀ See Lesson 3-5.

34. What are the subsets of A?   **35.** What is B'?   **36.** Is B' a subset of A?

Solve each inequality.

◀ See Lesson 3-4.

37. $5 < 6b + 3$ **38.** $12n \le 3n + 27$ **39.** $2 + 4r \ge 5(r - 1)$

Get Ready! To prepare for Lesson 3-7, do Exercises 40–42.

Complete each statement with $<$, $=$, or $>$.

◀ See Lesson 1-5.

40. $|3 - 7| \blacksquare 4$ **41.** $|-5| + 2 \blacksquare 6$ **42.** $\left|6 - 2\frac{1}{4}\right| \blacksquare 3\frac{5}{8}$

3-7
PART 1

Absolute Value Equations and Inequalities

Objective To solve equations involving absolute value

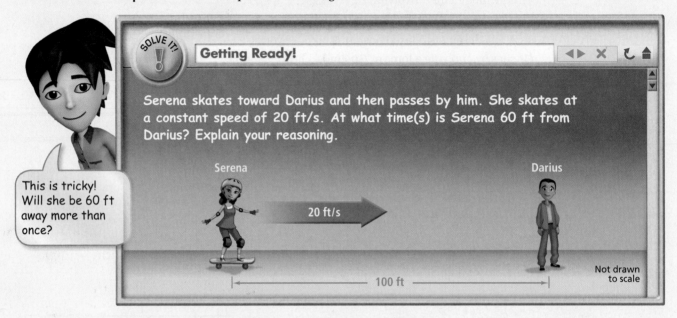

SOLVE IT!

Getting Ready!

Serena skates toward Darius and then passes by him. She skates at a constant speed of 20 ft/s. At what time(s) is Serena 60 ft from Darius? Explain your reasoning.

Serena

Darius

20 ft/s

Not drawn to scale

100 ft

This is tricky! Will she be 60 ft away more than once?

In the Solve It, Serena's distance from Darius decreases and then increases. You can use absolute value to model such changes.

Focus Question How is solving an equation with an absolute value similar to solving other equations?

To solve an absolute value equation, isolate the absolute value expression. Then write two equations, one where the expression inside the absolute value is positive and one where the expression inside the absolute value is negative.

Problem 1 **Solving an Absolute Value Equation**

What are the solutions of $|x| + 2 = 9$? Graph and check the solutions.

Write the original equation.	$|x| + 2 = 9$
Subtract 2 from each side to undo addition.	$|x| + 2 - 2 = 9 - 2$
Simplify.	$|x| = 7$
Use the definition of absolute value to write two equations.	$x = 7$ or $x = -7$

Plot the solutions 7 and −7 on the number line.

$\leftarrow\!|\!-\!-\!|\!-\!-\!|\!-\!-\!|\!-\!-\!|\!-\!-\!|\!-\!-\!|\!-\!-\!|\!-\!-\!|\!\rightarrow$
$-8\ -6\ -4\ -2\ \ 0\ \ 2\ \ 4\ \ 6\ \ 8$

Think

How many solutions does the equation have?
There are two values on a number line that are 7 units from 0: 7 and −7. So the equation has two solutions.

Check Substitute 7 for x. $\quad |7| + 2 \stackrel{?}{=} 9$
Simplify. $\qquad\qquad 7 + 2 = 9$ ✔
Substitute −7 for x. $\quad |-7| + 2 \stackrel{?}{=} 9$
Simplify. $\qquad\qquad 7 + 2 = 9$ ✔

Got It? **1.** What are the solutions of $|n| - 5 = -2$? Graph and check the solutions.

Some equations, such as $|2x - 5| = 13$, have variable expressions within absolute value symbols. The equation $|2x - 5| = 13$ means that the distance on a number line from $2x - 5$ to 0 is 13 units. There are two points that are 13 units from 0, 13 and -13. So to find the values of x, solve the equations $2x - 5 = 13$ and $2x - 5 = -13$. You can generalize this process as follows.

take note

Key Concept Solving Absolute Value Equations

To solve an equation in the form $|A| = b$, where A represents a variable expression and $b > 0$, solve $A = b$ and $A = -b$.

Problem 2 Solving an Absolute Value Equation

Multiple Choice Starting from 100 ft away, your friend skates toward you and then passes by you. She skates at a constant speed of 20 ft/s. Her distance d from you in feet after t seconds is given by $d = |100 - 20t|$. At what times is she 40 ft from you?

   Ⓐ -2 s and 8 s   Ⓑ -3 s and 7 s   Ⓒ 3 s and 7 s   Ⓓ 2 s and 8 s

Plan

What must be true of the expression $100 - 20t$?
Its absolute value is 40, so $100 - 20t$ must equal either 40 or -40. Use this fact to write and solve two equations.

Step 1 Solve the equation $100 - 20t = 40$.

Write the original equation.	$100 - 20t = 40$
Subtract 100 from each side.	$-20t = -60$
Divide each side by -20.	$t = 3$

Step 2 Solve the equation $100 - 20t = -40$.

Write the original equation.	$100 - 20t = -40$
Subtract 100 from each side.	$-20t = -140$
Divide each side by -20.	$t = 7$

The solutions are 3 s and 7 s. The correct answer is C.

Hint

Check the solutions by substituting each value in the original equation.

 Got It? **2.** What are the solutions of $|3x - 1| = 8$? Check the solutions.

Recall that absolute value represents distance from 0 on a number line. Distance is always nonnegative. So any equation that states that the absolute value of an expression is negative has no solutions.

How can you make
the equation look
like one you've
solved before?
Use properties of equality
to isolate the absolute
value expression on one
side of the equal sign.

 Problem 3 **Solving an Absolute Value Equation With No Solution**

What are the solutions of $3|2z + 9| + 12 = 10$**?**

Write the original equation.	$3|2z + 9| + 12 = 10$
Subtract 12 from each side.	$3|2z + 9| = -2$
Divide each side by 3.	$|2z + 9| = -\dfrac{2}{3}$

The absolute value of an expression cannot be negative, so there is no solution.

 Got It? 3. What are the solutions of $|3x - 6| - 5 = -7$?

Focus Question How is solving an equation with an absolute value similar to solving other equations?

Answer You can solve absolute value equations by treating the absolute value bars like parentheses. First, isolate the absolute value expression. Then, remove the absolute value bars and write two equations.

 ## Lesson Check

Do you know HOW?

Solve and graph each equation.

1. $|x| = 5$

2. $|n| - 3 = 4$

3. $|2t| = 6$

Do you UNDERSTAND?

4. Reasoning How many solutions do you expect to get when you solve an absolute value equation? Explain.

5. Writing Explain why the absolute value equation $|3x| + 8 = 5$ has no solution.

Practice and Problem-Solving Exercises

 A Practice   Solve each equation. Graph and check your solutions.   **See Problem 1.**

Guided
Practice

To start, use the definition of absolute
value to write two equations.

6. $|b| = \dfrac{1}{2}$

$b = \dfrac{1}{2}$ or $b = -\dfrac{1}{2}$

7. $4 = |y|$

8. $|n| + 3 = 7$

9. $7 = |s| - 3$

10. $|x| - 10 = -2$

11. $5|d| = 20$

12. $-3|m| = -9$

Solve each equation. If there is no solution, write *no solution*.

See Problems 2 and 3.

Guided Practice

13. $|r - 8| = 5$

To start, use the definition of absolute value to write two equations.

$$r - 8 = 5 \quad \text{or} \quad r - 8 = -5$$

14. $|c + 4| = 6$ **15.** $2 = |g + 3|$ **16.** $3 = |m + 2|$

17. $-2|7d| = 14$ **18.** $3|v - 3| = 9$ **19.** $2|d + 4| = 8$

20. $|3t - 2| + 6 = 2$ **21.** $|-3n| - 2 = 4$ **22.** $-4|k + 1| = 16$

B Apply

Solve each equation. If there is no solution, write *no solution*.

23. $|2d| + 3 = 21$ **24.** $1.2|5p| = 3.6$ **25.** $\left|d + \frac{1}{2}\right| + \frac{3}{4} = 0$

26. $|f| - \frac{2}{3} = \frac{5}{6}$ **27.** $3|5y - 7| - 6 = 24$ **28.** $|t| + 2.7 = 4.5$

29. Biking Starting from 200 ft away, your friend rides his bike toward you and then passes by you at a speed of 18 ft/s. His distance d (in feet) from you t seconds after he started riding his bike is given by $d = |200 - 18t|$. At what time(s) is he 120 ft from you?

30. Error Analysis Find and correct the mistake in solving the equation.

$$|x - 3| = -2$$
$$x - 3 = -2 \quad \text{or} \quad x - 3 = 2$$
$$x = 1 \quad \text{or} \quad x = 5$$

31. Open-Ended Write an absolute value equation that has 2 and 6 as solutions.

32. Polling According to a poll for an upcoming school board election, 40% of voters are likely to vote for the incumbent. The poll shows a margin of error of ± 3 percentage points. Write and solve an absolute value equation to find the least and the greatest percents of voters v likely to vote for the incumbent.

Hint A poll should be reported with an estimate of error called the margin of error. The symbol $\pm$ means plus or minus.

33. Oil Production An oil refinery aims to produce 900,000 barrels of oil per day. The daily production varies by up to 50,000 barrels from this goal, inclusive. What are the minimum and maximum numbers of barrels of oil produced each day?

34. Farm Maintenance For safety, the recommended height of a horse fence is 5 ft. Because of uneven ground surfaces, the actual height of the fence can vary from this recommendation by up to 3 in. Write and solve an absolute value equation to find the maximum and minimum heights of the fence.

Absolute Value Equations and Inequalities

Objective To solve inequalities involving absolute value

In Part 1 of the lesson, you learned how to solve absolute value equations.

Connect to What You Know

Here you will learn how to solve absolute value inequalities.

Focus Question How is solving an absolute value inequality similar to solving an absolute value equation?

Hint

If an absolute value inequality has a < or ≤ symbol (and the absolute value is on the left), write an *and* statement. If an absolute value inequality has a > or ≥ symbol (and the absolute value is on the left), write an *or* statement.

You can write absolute value inequalities as compound inequalities. The graphs below show two absolute value inequalities.

$|n - 1| < 2$

$|n - 1| < 2$ represents all numbers with a distance from 1 that is less than 2 units. So $|n - 1| < 2$ means $-2 < n - 1 < 2$.

$|n - 1| > 2$

$|n - 1| > 2$ represents all numbers with a distance from 1 that is greater than 2 units. The inequality $|n - 1| > 2$ means $n - 1 < -2$ or $n - 1 > 2$. So $n < -1$ and $n > 3$.

take note

Key Concept   Solving Absolute Value Inequalities

To solve an inequality in the form $|A| < b$, where A is a variable expression and $b > 0$, solve the compound inequality $-b < A < b$.

To solve an inequality in the form $|A| > b$, where A is a variable expression and $b > 0$, solve the compound inequality $A < -b$ or $A > b$.

Similar rules are true for $|A| \leq b$ or $|A| \geq b$.

Problem 4 Solving an Absolute Value Inequality Involving ≥

What are the solutions of $|8n| \geq 24$? Graph the solutions.

Think

The inequality says that 8n is at least 24 units from 0 on a number line.

Plan

How can you write the absolute value inequality as a compound inequality?
The inequality $|8n| \geq 24$ has the absolute value on the left and a ≥ symbol, so write an *or* statement.

To be at least 24 units from 0, 8n can be less than or equal to −24 or greater than or equal to 24.

You need to isolate n. Undo multiplication by dividing each side by the same number.

Write

$|8n| \geq 24$

$8n \leq -24 \quad \text{or} \quad 8n \geq 24$

$\dfrac{8n}{8} \leq \dfrac{-24}{8} \quad \text{or} \quad \dfrac{8n}{8} \geq \dfrac{24}{8}$

$n \leq -3 \quad \text{or} \quad n \geq 3$

-4 -3 -2 -1 0 1 2 3 4

Got It? **4.** What are the solutions of $|2x + 4| \geq 5$? Graph the solutions.

Problem 5 Solving an Absolute Value Inequality Involving ≤

Manufacturing A company makes boxes of crackers that should weigh 213 g. A quality-control inspector randomly selects boxes to weigh. Any box that varies from the weight by more than 5 g is sent back. What is the range of allowable weights for a box of crackers?

Relate difference between actual and ideal weights   is at most   5 g

Define Let $w =$ the actual weight in grams.

Think

How else could you write this inequality?
You could break the compound inequality into two parts:
$w - 213 \geq -5$ and
$w - 213 \leq 5$.

Write $|w - 213|$ ≤   5

Write the inequality. $|w - 213| \leq 5$

Write a compound inequality. $-5 \leq w - 213 \leq 5$

Add 213 to each expression. $208 \leq w \leq 218$

The weight of a box of crackers must be between 208 g and 218 g, inclusive.

Got It? **5. a.** A food manufacturer makes 32-oz boxes of pasta. Not every box weighs exactly 32 oz. The allowable difference from the ideal weight is at most 0.05 oz. Write and solve an absolute value inequality to find the range of allowable weights.

b. **Reasoning** In Problem 5, could you have solved the inequality $|w - 213| \leq 5$ by first adding 213 to each side? Explain your reasoning.

Focus Question How is solving an absolute value inequality similar to solving an absolute value equation?

Answer You can solve absolute value inequalities by first isolating the absolute value expression. Then write a pair of linear inequalities.

Lesson Check

Do you know HOW?

Solve and graph each inequality.

1. $|3m| > 12$

2. $|h - 3| < 5$

3. $|x + 2| \geq 1$

Do you UNDERSTAND?

4. **Compare and Contrast** Explain the similarities and differences in solving the equation $|x - 1| = 2$ with solving the inequalities $|x - 1| \leq 2$ and $|x - 1| \geq 2$.

5. **Writing** When does an absolute value inequality have no solution?

Practice and Problem-Solving Exercises

 Practice

Guided Practice

Solve and graph each inequality.

 **See Problems 4 and 5.**

To start, write two inequalities. x can be greater than or equal to 3 or less than or equal to −3.

6. $|x| \geq 3$

$x \geq 3$ or $x \leq -3$

7. $|x| < 5$

8. $|x + 3| < 5$

9. $|y + 8| \geq 3$

10. $|y - 2| \leq 1$

11. $|p - 7| \leq 3$

12. $|3t + 1| > 8$

13. $|5t - 4| \geq 16$

14. $|2v - 1| \leq 9$

15. $|3d - 7| > 28$

Guided Practice

16. **Quality Control** The ideal length of one type of model airplane is 90 cm. The actual length may vary from ideal by at most 0.05 cm. What are the acceptable lengths for the model airplane?

To start, define the variable.   Let x = the actual length in cm.

Write the inequality. $|x - 90| \leq 0.05$

17. **Basketball** The ideal circumference of a women's basketball is 28.75 in. The actual circumference may vary from the ideal by at most 0.25 in. What are the acceptable circumferences for a women's basketball?

 Apply

Solve each inequality. If there is no solution, write *no solution.*

18. $|n| - \frac{5}{4} < 5$

19. $\frac{7}{8} < |c + 7|$

20. $4 - 3|m + 2| > -14$

21. **Think About a Plan** The monthly average temperature T for San Francisco, California, is usually within 7.5°F of 56.5°F, inclusive. What is the monthly average temperature in San Francisco?
- Should you model this situation with an equation or an inequality?
- How can you use the given information to write the equation or inequality?

22. **Biology** A horse's body temperature T is considered to be normal if it is within at least 0.9°F of 99.9°F. Find the range of normal body temperatures for a horse.

23. Error Analysis Find and correct the mistake in solving the inequality.

24. Banking The official weight of a nickel is 5 g, but the actual weight can vary from this amount by up to 0.194 g. Suppose a bank weighs a roll of 40 nickels. The wrapper weighs 1.5 g.

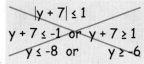

$|y + 7| \leq 1$
$y + 7 \leq -1$ or $y + 7 \geq 1$
$y \leq -8$ or $y \geq -6$

 a. What is the range of possible weights for the roll of nickels?

 b. **Reasoning** If all of the nickels in the roll each weigh the official amount, then the roll's weight is $40(5) + 1.5 = 201.5$ g. Is it possible for a roll to weigh 201.5 g and contain nickels that do not weigh the official amount? Explain.

Write an absolute value inequality that represents each set of numbers.

25. all real numbers less than 4 units from 0

26. all real numbers at most 7 units from 0

27. all real numbers more than 2 units from 6

28. all real numbers at least 2 units from -1

Standardized Test Prep

SAT/ACT

29. The expected monthly rainfall in a certain town is shown for June, July, and, August. The actual rainfall generally varies from the expected amount by up to 0.015 in. What is the maximum amount of rainfall the town can expect to receive in July?

30. What is the solution of the equation $3w + 2 = 4w - 3$?

Expected Monthly Rainfall (inches)		
June	**July**	**August**
4.12	4.25	4.41

31. Jose is purchasing 4 dress shirts that cost $28 each and 2 pairs of pants that cost $38 each. The items are all on sale for 35% off. How much money will Jose save by purchasing them on sale instead of at full price?

32. 75% of what number is 90?

Mixed Review

Write a compound inequality to model each situation.

◀ See Lesson 3-6.

33. The highest elevation in North America is 20,320 ft above sea level at Mount McKinley, Alaska. The lowest elevation in North America is 282 ft below sea level at Death Valley, California.

34. Normal human body temperature T is within 0.3°C of 37.2°C.

Simplify each expression.

◀ See Lesson 1-7.

35. $2(x + 5)$ **36.** $-3(y - 7)$ **37.** $4(\ell + 3) - 7$ **38.** $-(m - 4) + 8$

Get Ready!   To prepare for Lesson 3-8, do Exercises 39–42.

Write each set in set-builder notation.

◀ See Lesson 3-5.

39. $A = \{0, 1, 2, 3, 4, 5, 6, 7, 8, 9\}$ **40.** $B = \{1, 3, 5, 7\}$

Write each set in roster form.

41. $C = \{n \mid n \text{ is an even number between } -15 \text{ and } -5\}$

42. $D = \{k \mid k \text{ is a composite number between 7 and 17}\}$

3-8 Unions and Intersections of Sets

Objective To find the unions and intersections of sets

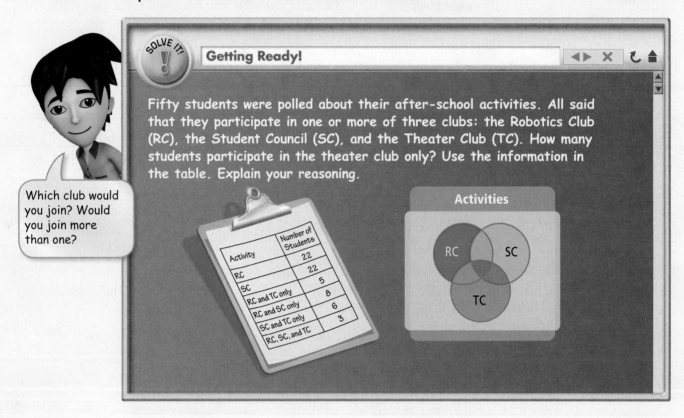

Getting Ready!

Fifty students were polled about their after-school activities. All said that they participate in one or more of three clubs: the Robotics Club (RC), the Student Council (SC), and the Theater Club (TC). How many students participate in the theater club only? Use the information in the table. Explain your reasoning.

Which club would you join? Would you join more than one?

Activity	Number of Students
RC	22
SC	22
RC and TC only	5
RC and SC only	8
SC and TC only	6
RC, SC, and TC	3

Activities

Certain regions of the Venn diagram in the Solve It show *unions* and *intersections* of sets.

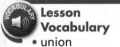

Lesson Vocabulary
• union
• intersection
• disjoint sets

Focus Question What are the union and intersection of sets?

The **union** of two or more sets is the set that contains all elements of the sets. The symbol for union is ∪. To find the union of two sets, list the elements that are in either set, or in both sets. An element is in the union if it belongs to *at least one* of the sets. In the Venn diagram below, $A \cup B$ is shaded.

Hint

The symbol for union ∪ is the first letter of the word *union*.

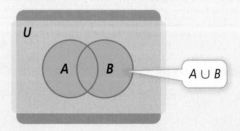

$A \cup B$

Problem 1 Union of Sets

In your left pocket, you have a quarter, a paper clip, and a key. In your right pocket, you have a penny, a quarter, a pencil, and a marble. What is a set that represents the different items in your pockets?

Step 1 Write sets that represent the contents of each pocket.

Left pocket: $L = $ {quarter, paper clip, key}
Right pocket: $R = $ {penny, quarter, pencil, marble}

Step 2 Write the union of the sets, which represents the different items that are in your pockets.

$L \cup R = $ {quarter, paper clip, key, penny, pencil, marble}

Think

What if an item is in both sets?
Sets L and R each contain a quarter, so a quarter is in the union of L and R. You should list it only once, though.

Got It? **1. a.** Write sets P and Q below in roster form. What is $P \cup Q$? *Hint:* Roster form lists the elements of a set within braces { }.
$P = \{x \mid x$ is a whole number less than 5$\}$
$Q = \{y \mid y$ is an even natural number less than 5$\}$

b. Reasoning What is true about the union of two sets if one set is a subset of the other?

Hint

The intersection of two streets is the part where the streets overlap. Similarly, the intersection of two sets is the part where the sets overlap.

The **intersection** of two or more sets is the set of elements that are common to every set. An element is in the intersection if it belongs to *all* of the sets. The symbol for intersection is $\cap$. When you find the intersection of two sets, list only the elements that are in both sets. In the Venn Diagram below, $A \cap B$ is shaded.

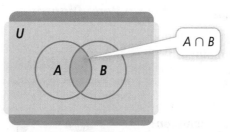

Disjoint sets have no elements in common. The intersection of disjoint sets is the empty set. The diagram below shows two disjoint sets.

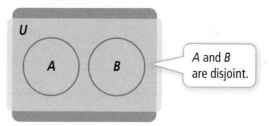

Problem 2 Intersection of Sets

Set $X = \{x \mid x$ is a natural number less than 19$\}$, set $Y = \{y \mid y$ is an odd integer$\}$, and set $Z = \{z \mid z$ is a multiple of 6$\}$.

Ⓐ What is $X \cap Z$?

Natural numbers less than 19: $X = \{1, 2, 3, 4, \ldots, 17, 18\}$

Multiples of 6: $Z = \{6, 12, 18, 24, 30, \ldots\}$

List the elements that are both natural numbers less than 19 and multiples of 6:
$X \cap Z = \{6, 12, 18\}$.

Ⓑ What is $Y \cap Z$?

Odd integers: $Y = \{1, 3, 5, 7, 9, \ldots\}$

Multiples of 6: $Z = \{6, 12, 18, 24, 30, \ldots\}$

List the elements that are both odd integers and multiples of 6. There are no multiples of 6 that are also odd, so Y and Z are disjoint sets. They have no elements in common. $Y \cap Z = \emptyset$, the empty set.

Think

Why are sets Y and Z disjoint?
Every element of Z is a multiple of 6, so every element of Z is *even*. Y contains only *odd* numbers. So no element of Z belongs to Y.

 Got It? **2.** Let $A = \{2, 4, 6, 8\}$, $B = \{0, 2, 5, 7, 8\}$, and $C = \{n \mid n$ is an odd whole number$\}$.
 a. What is $A \cap B$? **b.** What is $A \cap C$? **c.** What is $C \cap B$?

You can draw Venn diagrams to solve problems involving relationships between sets.

Problem 3 Making a Venn Diagram

Camping Three friends are going camping. The items in each of their backpacks form a set. Which items do all three friends have in common?

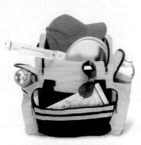

Think

How do you know where in the diagram to place each item?
Items that the friends have in common belong in an intersection. Use the Venn diagram to determine the correct intersection.

Draw a Venn diagram to represent the union and intersection of the sets.

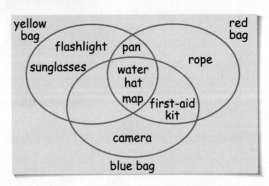

All three friends have a hat, a map, and a bottle of water in their backpacks.

Got It? **3.** Let $A = \{x \mid x$ is one of the first five letters in the English alphabet$\}$, $B = \{x \mid x$ is a vowel$\}$, and $C = \{x \mid x$ is a letter in the word VEGETABLE$\}$. Which letters are in all three sets?

You can also use Venn diagrams to show the *number* of elements in the union or intersection of sets.

Problem 4 **Using a Venn Diagram to Show Numbers of Elements**

Think

The question asks how many commuters take public transportation. This includes the people who take only public transportation, and the people who drive and take public transportation.

Polling Of 500 commuters polled, some drive to work, some take public transportation, and some do both. Two hundred commuters drive to work, and 125 use both types of transportation. How many commuters take public transportation?

Know
- Number who commute: 500
- Number who drive: 200
- Number who drive *and* use public transportation: 125

Need
Number who use public transportation

Plan
- Draw a Venn diagram.
- Calculate the number of commuters who only drive.
- Calculate the number of commuters who only use public transportation.

Step 1 Draw a Venn diagram. Let D = commuters who drive and P = commuters who take public transportation.

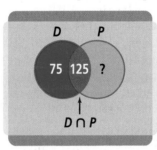

Step 2 The intersection of D and P represents the commuters who use both methods of transportation: $D \cap P$ has 125 commuters.

Step 3 Find the number of commuters who only drive: $200 - 125 = 75$. Enter 75 into the Venn diagram.

Step 4 The total number of commuters is 500. Subtract to find the number of commuters who use only public transportation: $500 - 200 = 300$.

The number of commuters using public transportation is $300 + 125 = 425$.

Hint

Name each set using a capital letter. Define each set using words.

 Got It? **4.** Of 30 students in student government, 20 are honor students and 9 are officers and honor students. All of the students are officers, honor students, or both. How many are officers but not honor students?

Focus Question What are the union and intersection of sets?

Answer The union of sets are the elements that belong to *at least one* of the sets. The intersection of sets are the elements that belong to *all* of the sets.

Lesson Check

Do you know HOW?

Let $X = \{2, 4, 6, 8, 10\}$, $Y = \{1, 2, 3, 4, 5, 6, 7, 8, 9, 10\}$, and $Z = \{1, 3, 5, 7, 9\}$. **Find each union or intersection.**

1. $X \cup Y$　　**2.** $X \cap Y$　　**3.** $X \cap Z$　　**4.** $Y \cup Z$

5. In a survey of 80 people who use their cell phones to take pictures and play games, 49 take pictures and 35 take pictures and play games. How many people only use their cell phones to play games?

Do you UNDERSTAND?

6. Vocabulary Suppose A and B are nonempty sets. Which set contains more elements: $A \cup B$ or $A \cap B$? Explain your reasoning.

7. Compare and Contrast How are unions and intersections of sets different?

Determine whether each statement is *true* or *false*.

8. If x is an element of set A and x is not an element of set B, then x is an element of $A \cup B$.

9. If x is not an element of set A and x is an element of set B, then x is an element of $A \cap B$.

Practice and Problem-Solving Exercises

A Practice 　Find each union or intersection. Let $A = \{1, 3, 4\}$, $B = \{x \mid x$ is an even whole number less than $9\}$, $C = \{2, 5, 7, 10\}$, and $D = \{x \mid x$ is an odd whole number less than $10\}$.

 **See Problems 1 and 2.**

Guided Practice

To start, write the elements in set A and in set B.

10. $A \cup B$

$A = \{1, 3, 4\}$

$B = \{2, 4, 6, 8\}$

11. $B \cup C$　　　　　　**12.** $B \cup D$　　　　　　**13.** $C \cup D$

14. $A \cap B$　　　　　　**15.** $A \cap C$　　　　　　**16.** $A \cap D$

17. $B \cap C$　　　　　　**18.** $B \cap D$　　　　　　**19.** $C \cap D$

Draw a Venn diagram to represent the union and intersection of these sets.  **See Problem 3.**

Guided Practice

20. The letters in the words ALGEBRA, GEOMETRY, and CALCULUS are represented by the sets $V = \{A, L, G, E, B, R\}$, $W = \{G, E, O, M, T, R, Y\}$, and $X = \{C, A, L, U, S\}$, respectively.

To start, draw a Venn diagram with three regions.

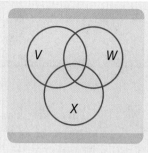

21. Let $E = \{x \mid x$ is a positive, composite number less than 10$\}$, $F = \{1, 2, 4, 5, 6, 8, 9\}$, and $G = \{x \mid x$ is a positive, even number less than or equal to 10$\}$.

> **Hint** A composite number is a whole number greater than 1 with more than two factors.

22. Let $L = \{A, B, C, 1, 2, 3,$ horse, cow, pig$\}$, $M = \{-1, 0, 1, B, Y,$ pig, duck, $\Delta\}$, and $N = \{C, 3,$ duck, $\Delta\}$.

23. Camping Twenty-eight girls went camping. There were two main activities: volleyball and swimming. Fourteen girls went swimming, 5 participated in both activities, and 4 girls did neither. How many girls only played volleyball?    **See Problem 4.**

24. Winter Sports A ski shop owner surveys 200 people who ski or snowboard. If 196 people ski and 154 people do both activities, how many people snowboard?

B Apply Find each union or intersection. Let $W = \{5, 6, 7, 8\}$, $X = \{3, 6, 9\}$, $Y = \{2, 3, 7, 8\}$, and $Z = \{x \mid x$ is an even whole number less than 10$\}$.

25. $W \cup Y \cup Z$ **26.** $X \cap Y \cap Z$ **27.** $W \cap X \cap Z$

28. Writing Let $M = \{x \mid x$ is a multiple of 3$\}$ and $N = \{x \mid x$ is a multiple of 5$\}$. Describe the intersection of M and N.

29. Think About a Plan Blood type is determined partly by which *antigens* a red blood cell has. An antigen is a protein on the surface of a red blood cell. Type A contains the A antigen. Type B contains the B antigen. Type AB contains both A and B antigens. Type O does not have any antigens. A hospital has 25 patients with the A antigen, 17 with the B antigen, 10 with the A and B antigens, and 30 without A or B antigens. How many patients are represented by the data?
- How can a Venn diagram help you solve the problem?
- What strategies can you use to complete the Venn diagram?

30. Sports In a survey of students about favorite sports, the results include 22 who like tennis, 25 who like football, 9 who like tennis and football, 17 who like tennis and baseball, 20 who like football and baseball, 6 who like all three sports, and 4 who like none of the sports. How many students like only tennis and football? How many students like only tennis and baseball? How many students like only baseball and football?

The *cross product* of two sets A and B, denoted by $A \times B$, is the set of all ordered pairs with the first element in A and with the second element in B. In set-builder notation, you write:

$$A \times B = \{(a, b) \mid a \text{ is an element of } A, b \text{ is an element of } B\}$$

For example, suppose $A = \{1, 2\}$ and $B = \{7, 10, 12\}$. Then:

$$A \times B = \{(1, 7), (1, 10), (1, 12), (2, 7), (2, 10), (2, 12)\}$$

Given sets A and B, find $A \times B$.

31. $A = \{1, 2, 3\}, B = (-3, -2, -1, 0\}$

32. $A = \{\pi, 2\pi, 3\pi, 4\pi\}, B = \{2, 4\}$

33. $A = \{\text{grape, apple, orange}\}, B = \{\text{jam, juice}\}$

34. $A = \{\text{reduce, reuse, recycle}\}, B = \{\text{plastic}\}$

35. Reasoning Suppose A and B are sets such that $A \subseteq B$. What is true about $A \cap B$?

Standardized Test Prep

SAT/ACT

36. Set $X = \{x \mid x \text{ is a factor of } 12\}$ and set $Y = \{y \mid y \text{ is a factor of } 16\}$. Which set represents $X \cap Y$?

   Ⓐ $\emptyset$ Ⓑ $\{1, 2, 4\}$ Ⓒ $\{0, 1, 2, 4\}$ Ⓓ $\{1, 2, 3, 4, 6, 8, 12, 16\}$

37. Which compound inequality is equivalent to $-8 < x + 4 < 8$?

   Ⓕ $-12 < x < 4$ Ⓗ $-12 > x > 4$

   Ⓖ $x < -12 \text{ or } x > 4$ Ⓘ $x > -12 \text{ or } x < 4$

Short Response

38. Suppose you earn $80 per week at your summer job. Your employer offers you a $20 raise or a 20% raise. Which should you take? Explain.

Mixed Review

Solve each equation or inequality.   ◀ **See Lesson 3-7.**

39. $|x| = 4$ **40.** $|n| + 7 = 9$ **41.** $4|f - 5| = 12$ **42.** $3|3y + 2| = 18$

43. $|4d| \leq 20$ **44.** $|x - 3| \geq 7$ **45.** $|2w + 6| > 24$ **46.** $2|3x| + 1 = 9$

Tell whether the ordered pair is a solution to the given equation.   ◀ **See Lesson 1-9.**

47. $x + 3 = y; (1, 4)$ **48.** $2x - 5 = y; (-1, 8)$ **49.** $\frac{1}{2}x + 7 = y; (8, 11)$

Get Ready!   **To prepare for Lesson 4-1, do Exercises 50–53.**

Graph each point on the same coordinate grid.   ◀ **See Review p. 68.**

50. $(1, 4)$ **51.** $(-1, -5)$ **52.** $(3, -6)$ **53.** $(-2, 1)$

Pull It **All Together**

3

To solve these problems you will pull together many concepts and skills that you have studied about solving inequalities.

BIG idea Variable

You can use algebraic inequalities to represent relationships between quantities that are not equal.

Task 1

A camping supply store carries tents usually priced from $68 to $119. The store is having a sale. What is the range of possible prices you could pay for a tent?

ALL TENTS ON SALE
10% to 25% Off

▶ Shop Now

BIG idea Equivalence

You can represent an inequality using symbols in an infinite number of ways. Equivalent representations have the same solutions as the original inequality.

Task 2

For each figure, find the values of x such that the area A of the figure satisfies the given condition.

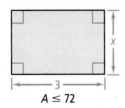

$A \le 72$

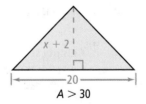

$x + 2$

20

$A > 30$

BIG idea Solving Equations and Inequalities

You can use properties of inequality to transform an inequality into equivalent, simpler inequalities and then find solutions.

Task 3

You have a photograph 12 in. wide and 18 in. long. You surround the photograph with a mat x in. wide, as shown at the right. You want to make a frame for the matted photograph, but you only have an 80-in. length of wood to use for the frame. What are the dimensions of the largest frame you can make?

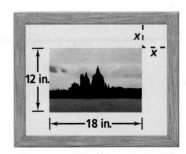

12 in.

18 in.

x

Connecting BIG ideas and Answering the Essential Questions

1 Variable
You can use algebraic inequalities to represent relationships between quantities that are not equal.

Inequalities and Their Graphs
(Lessons 3-1, 3-2, 3-3, 3-4, 3-6, 3-7)

$c \geq -2$

$$\overset{\bullet}{\underset{-3 \quad -2 \quad -1 \quad 0 \quad 1 \quad 2}{\longleftarrow\!\!\mid\!\!\mid\!\!\mid\!\!\mid\!\!\mid\!\!\mid\!\!\longrightarrow}}$$

2 Equivalence
You can represent an inequality in many ways. Equivalent representations have the same solutions as the original inequality.

Solving One-Step Inequalities
(Lessons 3-2, 3-3)

The inequalities in each pair are equivalent.
$$f - 4 \geq -3 \qquad 6y < 24$$
$$f \geq 1 \qquad\quad y < 4$$

3 Solving Equations and Inequalities
You can use properties of inequality to transform an inequality into equivalent, simpler inequalities and then find solutions.

Solving Multi-Step Inequalities
(Lessons 3-4)

$$7z + 10 \leq 24$$
$$7z + 10 - 10 \leq 24 - 10$$
$$7z \leq 14$$
$$\frac{7z}{7} \leq \frac{14}{7}$$
$$z \leq 2$$

Solving Compound and Absolute Value Inequalities
(Lessons 3-6, 3-7)

$$|3m + 2| \leq 14$$
$$-14 \leq \quad 3m + 2 \ \leq 14$$
$$-16 \leq \qquad 3m \quad \leq 12$$
$$-\frac{16}{3} \leq \qquad m \qquad \leq 4$$

Chapter Vocabulary

- complement of a set (p. 212)
- compound inequality (p. 216)
- disjoint sets (p. 231)

- empty set (p. 211)
- intersection (p. 231)
- roster form (p. 210)

- set-builder notation (p. 210)
- union (p. 230)
- universal set (p. 212)

Choose the correct term to complete each sentence.

1. The set $\{5, 10, 15, 20, \ldots\}$ represents the multiples of 5 written in __?__.

2. The __?__ of two or more sets is the set that contains all elements of the sets.

3. The set that contains no elements is the __?__.

3-5 Working With Sets

Quick Review
The **complement** of a set A is the set of all elements in the universal set that are *not* in A.

Example
Suppose $U = \{1, 2, 3, 4, 5, 6\}$ and $Y = \{2, 4, 6\}$. **What is Y'?**

The elements in U that are *not* in Y are 1, 3, and 5.
So $Y' = \{1, 3, 5\}$.

Exercises
List all the subsets of each set.

4. $\{s, t\}$

5. $\{5, 10, 15\}$

6. How do you write "A is the set of even whole numbers that are less than 18" in roster form? How do you write A using set-builder notation?

7. Suppose $U = \{1, 2, 3, 4, 5, 6, 7, 8\}$ and $B = \{2, 4, 6, 8\}$. What is B'?

3-6 Compound Inequalities

Quick Review
Two inequalities that are joined by the word *and* or the word *or* are called **compound inequalities**. A solution of a compound inequality involving *and* makes both inequalities true. A solution of an inequality involving *or* makes either inequality true.

Example
What are the solutions of $-3 \leq z - 1 < 3$?

Write the original inequality. $-3 \leq z - 1 < 3$

Add 1 to each part of the inequality. $-2 \leq z < 4$

Exercises
Solve each compound inequality.

8. $-2 \leq d + \frac{1}{2} < 4\frac{1}{2}$

9. $0 < -8b \leq 12$

10. $2t \leq -4$ or $7t \geq 49$

11. $5m < -10$ or $3m > 9$

12. $-1 \leq a - 3 \leq 2$

13. $9.1 > 1.4p \geq -6.3$

14. Climate A town's high temperature for a given month is 88°F and the low temperature is 65°F. Write a compound inequality to represent the range of temperatures for the given month.

3-7 Absolute Value Equations and Inequalities

Quick Review

Solving an equation or inequality that contains an absolute value expression is similar to solving other equations and inequalities. You will need to write two equations or inequalities using positive and negative values. Then solve the equations.

Example

What is the solution of $|x| - 7 = 3$?

Write the original inequality.	$	x	- 7 = 3$
Add 7 to each side.	$	x	= 10$
Use the definition of absolute value.	$x = 10$ or $x = -10$

Exercises

Solve each equation or inequality. If there is no solution, write *no solution*.

15. $|y| = 3$

16. $|n + 2| = 4$

17. $4 + |r + 2| = 7$

18. $|x + 3| = -2$

19. $|5x| \le 15$

20. $|3d + 5| < -2$

21. $|2x - 7| - 1 > 0$

22. $4|k + 5| > 8$

23. Manufacturing The ideal length of a certain nail is 20 mm. The actual length can vary from the ideal by at most 0.4 mm. Find the range of acceptable lengths of the nail.

3-8 Unions and Intersections of Sets

Quick Review

The **union** of two or more sets is the set that contains all elements of the sets. The **intersection** of two or more sets is the set of elements that are common to all the sets. **Disjoint sets** have no elements in common.

Example

Student Activities Of 100 students who play sports or take music lessons, 70 students play a sport and 50 students play a sport and take music lessons. How many students *only* take music lessons?

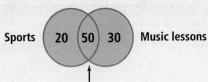

Sports   20   50   30   Music lessons

↑
Both sports and music lessons

So, 30 students take only music lessons.

Exercises

24. Given $A = \{1, 2, 3, 4, 5, 6, 7, 8, 9\}$ and $B = \{2, 4, 6, 8\}$, what is $A \cup B$?

25. Let $P = \{1, 5, 7, 9, 13\}$, $R = \{1, 2, 3, 4, 5, 6, 8\}$, and $Q = \{1, 3, 5\}$. Draw a Venn diagram that represents the intersection and union of the sets.

26. Let $N = \{x \mid x$ is a multiple of 2$\}$ and $P = \{x \mid x$ is a multiple of 6$\}$. Describe the intersection of N and P.

27. Cats There are 15 cats. Ten are striped and 7 are striped and have green eyes. The rest of the cats have green eyes but are not striped. How many cats have green eyes but are not striped?

Do you know HOW?

Write an inequality for each graph.

1. A number line from -12 to 4 with an open circle at -7 and shading to the left.

2. A number line from -2 to 6 with a closed circle at 4 and shading to the left.

3. A number line from -6 to 2 with an open circle at -5 and shading to the right.

4. A number line from -3 to 5 with an open circle at 2 and shading to the right.

Solve each inequality. Graph the solutions.

5. $z + 7 \le 9$

6. $-\frac{1}{3}x < 2$

7. $5w \ge -6w + 11$

8. $-\frac{7}{2}(m - 2) < 21$

9. $|x - 5| \ge 3$

10. $9 \le 6 - b < 12$

11. $4 + 3n \ge 1$ or $-5n > 25$

12. $10k < 75$ and $4 - k \le 0$

List the subsets of each set.

13. $\{1, 3, 5, 7\}$ **14.** $\{red, blue, yellow\}$

15. Quality Control A manufacturer is cutting fabric into rectangles that are 18.55 in. long by 36.75 in. wide. Each rectangle's length and width must be within 0.05 in. of the desired size. Write and solve inequalities to find the acceptable range for the length ℓ and the width w.

Write a compound inequality that each graph could represent.

16. A number line from -10 to 6 with a closed circle at -6 and an open circle at 2, shaded between.

17. A number line from -4 to 4 with open circles at -3 and 2, shaded between.

18. Multiple Choice Suppose $A = \{x \,|\, x > -1\}$ and $B = \{x \,|\, -3 \le x \le 2\}$. Which statement is true?

Ⓐ $A \cup B = \{\ \}$

Ⓑ $A' = \{x \,|\, x < -1\}$

Ⓒ $A \cap B = \{x \,|\, -1 < x \le 2\}$

Ⓓ $B \subseteq \{x \,|\, x < 2\}$

Solve each equation. Check your solution.

19. $|4k - 2| = 11$ **20.** $23 = |n + 10|$

21. $|3c + 1| - 4 = 13$ **22.** $4|5 - t| = 20$

23. Fundraising A drama club wants to raise at least $500 in ticket sales for its annual show. The members of the club sold 50 tickets at a special $5 rate. The usual ticket price the day of the show is $7.50. At least how many tickets do they have to sell the day of the show to meet the goal?

24. Of 145 runners, 72 run only on weekends and 63 run on both weekends and during the week. How many of the runners run only during the week?

Do you UNDERSTAND?

25. Open-Ended Write an absolute value inequality that has 3 and -5 as two of its solutions.

26. Writing Compare and contrast the Multiplication Property of Equality and the Multiplication Property of Inequality.

27. Describe the region labeled C in terms of set A and set B.

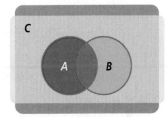

28. Suppose set A has 9 elements. What is the greatest number of elements a subset of A can have?

Cumulative Test Prep

Some questions on tests ask you to write an extended response. In this textbook, an extended response question is usually worth a maximum of 4 points. Sometimes these questions have multiple parts. To get full credit, you need to answer each part and show all your work or justify your reasoning.

TIP 1

A 1-point response might show an incorrect equation without giving the number of children who must attend to cover costs.

The Theatre Club needs to raise $440 to cover the cost of its children's play. The ticket prices are $14 for an adult and $2 for a child. The club expects that three times as many children as adults will attend the play. Write and solve an equation to find how many adult and child tickets the club needs to sell to cover the cost.

Solution

x = number of adults

$3x$ = number of children

$$14(x) + 2(3x) = 440$$
$$14x + 6x = 440$$
$$20x = 440$$
$$x = 22$$
$$3x = 66$$

So, 22 adults and 66 children must attend.

TIP 2

A 3-point response might approach the problem correctly, but have an error.

Think It Through

A 4–point response defines variables, shows the work, and gives a written answer to the problem. So relate what is given to what has been asked. Identify the variables and make a model that you can use to write an equation. Then show your work as you use this equation to find the solution.

Vocabulary Builder

As you solve test items, you must understand the meanings of mathematical terms. Choose the correct term to complete each sentence.

A. Two inequalities that are joined by the word *and* or the word *or* form a (*compound, connected*) inequality.

B. (*Equivalent, Similar*) inequalities are inequalities with the same solutions.

C. Any number that makes an inequality true is a (*union, solution*) of the inequality.

D. A (*proportion, conversion factor*) is an equation that states that two ratios are equal.

E. A(n) (*open, closed*) dot on the graph of an inequality shows that the point is a solution of the inequality.

Multiple Choice

Read each question. Then write the letter of the correct answer on your paper.

1. You are making bracelets to sell at a fair. The table shows the total cost c of making b bracelets. Which equation represents the relationship between the number of bracelets you make and the total cost?

Bracelets, b	Cost, c
10	$9.00
15	$13.50
20	$18.00
25	$22.50

   Ⓐ $c = 9b$ Ⓒ $9c = b$

   Ⓑ $c = 0.9b$ Ⓓ $0.9c = b$

2. What are the solutions of $2u + 5.2 \le 9.4 + u$?

   Ⓕ $u \ge 4.2$ Ⓗ $u \le 14.6$

   Ⓖ $u \le 48.9$ Ⓘ $u \le 4.2$

3. A baseball team can spend up to $1500 on bats. Bats cost $32 each. Which inequality represents the number of bats b they can buy?

Ⓐ $32b \le 1500$

Ⓑ $32b \ge 1500$

Ⓒ $32b + b \le 1500$

Ⓓ $32b + b \ge 1500$

4. What is the solution of $w - 4 = 18 + 3w$?

Ⓕ -11 Ⓗ 3.5

Ⓖ -3.5 Ⓘ 11

5. Which graph represents the solutions to the inequality $3n \le -6$?

Ⓐ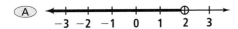

Ⓑ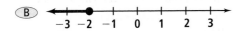

Ⓒ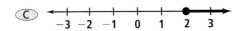

Ⓓ

6. In the spring, you could serve a tennis ball at a rate of 43 mi/h. The speed of your serve increased 12% after practicing all summer. About how fast is your serve after practicing?

Ⓕ 38 mi/h   Ⓗ 51 mi/h

Ⓖ 48 mi/h   Ⓘ 55 mi/h

7. The cost of a hardcover book x is at least $3 more than twice the cost of the paperback book y. Which inequality represents this situation?

Ⓐ $2y + 3 \ge x$ Ⓒ $2y + 3 \le x$

Ⓑ $x + 3 \le 2y$ Ⓓ $x + 2y \le 3$

8. What is the solution of $\frac{18}{x} = \frac{5}{7}$?

Ⓕ 12.9 Ⓖ 20 Ⓗ 25.2 Ⓘ 35

9. A fox runs at a rate of 42 mi/h and a cat runs at a rate of 44 ft/s. What is the difference in their speeds? (*Hint:* 1 mi = 5280 ft)

Ⓐ 12 ft/s   Ⓒ 17.6 mi/h

Ⓑ 17.6 ft/s   Ⓓ 30 mi/h

10. When simplifying the expression $206 - 4(17 - 3^2)$, which part of the expression do you simplify first?

Ⓕ $206 - 4$ Ⓗ $17 - 3$

Ⓖ 3^2 Ⓘ $4(17)$

11. Which expression is equivalent to $8y - (6y - 5)$?

Ⓐ $2y - 5$

Ⓑ $14y - 5$

Ⓒ $2y + 5$

Ⓓ $14y + 5$

12. Max saved $16,000 and bought a car that costs $10,500. He will pay $1200 each year for car insurance. Which inequality can you use to find the maximum number of years he can pay for insurance with his remaining savings?

Ⓕ $10{,}500 + 1200x \le 16{,}000$

Ⓖ $10{,}500 - 1200x \le 16{,}000$

Ⓗ $16{,}000 + 1200x \le 10{,}500$

Ⓘ $16{,}000 - 1200x \le 10{,}500$

13. Let $L = \{3, 4, 5\}$, $M = \{x \mid x$ is a negative integer greater than $-5\}$, and $N = \{-1, 0, 1\}$. What is $L \cap M$?

Ⓐ $\{3, 4, 5\}$ Ⓒ $\{-4, -3, -2, -1, 3, 4, 5\}$

Ⓑ $\{-5, -4, -3\}$ Ⓓ $\{\,\}$

14. What are the solutions of $-\frac{1}{9}a + 1 < 8$?

Ⓕ $a > 7$ Ⓗ $a > -63$

Ⓖ $a < 7$ Ⓘ $a < -63$

15. Which choice best describes the following statement?
If $x < 0$ and $y \ge 0$, then $xy < 0$.

Ⓐ always true

Ⓑ sometimes true, when $y < 0$

Ⓒ sometimes true, when $y > 0$

Ⓓ never true

16. What are the solutions of $4 < 6b - 2 \le 28$?

Ⓕ $\frac{1}{3} < b \le \frac{13}{3}$

Ⓖ $6 < b \le 30$

Ⓗ $\frac{2}{3} < b \le \frac{14}{3}$

Ⓘ $1 < b \le 5$

17. You count the number of melons you use based on the number of bowls of fruit salad made, as shown in the table at the right. Which equation describes the relationship between the number of bowls of fruit salad f and the number of melons used m?

Fruit salad, f	Melons, m
2	1
4	2
6	3
8	4
10	5

Ⓐ $f = 0.5m$ Ⓒ $m = 0.5f$

Ⓑ $2f = m$ Ⓓ $2m = 0.5f$

18. Which graph represents the solutions to the inequality $3(f + 2) > 2f + 4$?

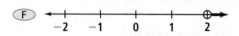

Ⓕ

Ⓖ

Ⓗ

Ⓘ

GRIDDED RESPONSE

Record your answers in a grid.

19. You can mow 400 ft² of grass if you work for 5 min, 800 ft² if you work for 10 min, 1200 ft² of grass if you work for 15 min, and so on. How many square feet can you mow in 45 min?

20. An insect flies 20 ft in 1 s. How fast does the insect fly in miles per hour? Round to the nearest hundredth if necessary.

21. Isabella is covering a square tabletop with square mosaic tiles. The tabletop is 2 ft long and 2 ft wide. Each tile is $\frac{1}{4}$ in. long and $\frac{1}{4}$ in. wide. What is the minimum number of tiles needed to cover the tabletop?

22. What is the solution of $\frac{7}{5} = \frac{9}{x}$? Round your answer to the nearest thousandth if necessary.

23. Suppose $P = \{-2, 6, 7, 9\}$ and $Q = \{0, 2, 4, 6\}$. How many elements are in the set $P \cup Q$?

24. A family visited an amusement park. A person must be 3 ft tall to ride the roller coaster. One child is 4 in. short of the height regulation. By what percent must the child's height increase so that the whole family can ride the roller coaster?

25. What is the value of d when $11(d + 1) = 4(d + 8)$?

26. You are making a scale model of a sports field. The actual field is a rectangle with a length of 315 ft and a width of 300 ft. Your scale model is 15 in. wide. What is its length in inches?

Short Response

27. You have a wireless phone plan that costs $25 per month. You must also pay $.10 per minute for each minute over 500 min. Your phone bill was more than $30 last month. Write an inequality to represent the number of minutes m you spent on the phone last month. Suppose you use 525 min next month. How much will your bill be?

28. An electric company charges a monthly fee of $30.60 plus $.0176 for each kilowatt-hour (kWh) of energy used. Write an equation to represent the cost of the family's electric bill each month. Suppose the family used 1327 kWh of energy. How much was their bill?

29. A vending machine starts with 360 snacks. After 1 day it has 327 snacks, after 2 days it has 294 snacks, after 3 days it has 261 snacks, and so on. Describe the pattern of the number of snacks n based on the number of days d.

Extended Response

30. A company has $1500 in its budget for paper this year. The regular price of paper is $32 per box, with a 10% discount for bulk orders. If the company spends at least $1400 on paper, the shipping is free. Write a compound inequality to represent the number of boxes the company can buy with the discount and receive free shipping. What are the possible numbers of boxes the company can buy with the discount and free shipping?

Get Ready!

Lesson 1-2

Evaluating Expressions

Evaluate each expression for the given value(s) of the variable(s).

1. $3x - 2y; x = -1, y = 2$

2. $-w^2 + 3w; w = -3$

3. $\frac{3 + k}{k}; k = 3$

4. $h - (h^2 - 1) \div 2; h = -1$

Lesson 1-9

Using Tables, Equations, and Graphs

Use a table, an equation, and a graph to represent each relationship.

5. Bob is 9 years older than his dog.

6. Sue swims 1.5 laps per minute.

7. Each carton of eggs costs \$3.

Review, page 68

Graphing in the Coordinate Plane

Graph the ordered pairs in the same coordinate plane.

8. $(3, -3)$

9. $(0, -5)$

10. $(-2, 2)$

11. $(-2, 0)$

Lesson 2-2

Solving Two-Step Equations

Solve each equation. Check your answer.

12. $5x + 3 = -12$

13. $\frac{n}{6} - 1 = 10$

14. $7 = \frac{x + 8}{2}$

15. $\frac{x - 1}{4} = \frac{3}{4}$

Lesson 3-7

Solving Absolute Value Equations

Solve each equation. If there is no solution, write *no solution*.

16. $|r + 2| = 2$

17. $-3|d - 5| = -6$

18. $-3.2 = |8p|$

19. $5|2x - 7| = 20$

Looking Ahead Vocabulary

20. The amount of money you earn from a summer job is *dependent* upon the number of hours you work. What do you think it means when a variable is *dependent* upon another variable?

21. A *relation* is a person to whom you are related. If $(1, 2)$, $(3, 4)$, and $(5, 6)$ form a mathematical *relation*, to which number is 3 related?

22. When a furnace runs *continuously*, there are no breaks or interruptions in its operation. What do you think a *continuous* graph looks like?

CHAPTER 4

An Introduction to Functions

PowerAlgebra.com

Your place to get all things digital

VIDEO
Download videos connecting math to your world.

VOCABULARY
Math definitions in English and Spanish

SOLVE IT!
The online Solve It will get you in gear for each lesson.

DYNAMIC ACTIVITIES
Interactive! Vary numbers, graphs, and figures to explore math concepts.

ONLINE PROBLEMS
Download Step-by-Step Problems with Instant Replay.

ONLINE HOMEWORK
Get and view your assignments online.

MathXL FOR SCHOOL
Extra practice and review online

This double-dutch team has some pretty amazing moves! Did you know that there's math involved in jump-rope? An equation relates the number of jumps a person makes to the speed the rope is moving. This chapter will teach you about a special kind of math relationship called a function.

Vocabulary

English/Spanish Vocabulary Audio Online:

English	Spanish
continuous graph, p. 272	gráfica continua
dependent variable, p. 255	variable dependiente
discrete graph, p. 272	gráfica discreta
domain, p. 286	dominio
function, p. 257	función
function notation, p. 286	notación de una función
independent variable, p. 255	variable independiente
linear function, p. 257	función lineal
nonlinear function, p. 262	función no lineal
range, p. 286	rango
relation, p. 286	relación
sequence, p. 295	progresión

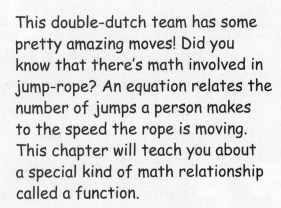

My Math Video

00:04:04

VIDEO

BIGideas

1 Functions

Essential Question How can you represent and describe functions?

2 Modeling

Essential Question Can functions describe real-world situations?

Chapter Preview

4-1 Using Graphs to Relate Two Quantities

Objective To represent mathematical relationships using graphs

Graphs help you to <u>see</u> relationships that have been described in other ways.

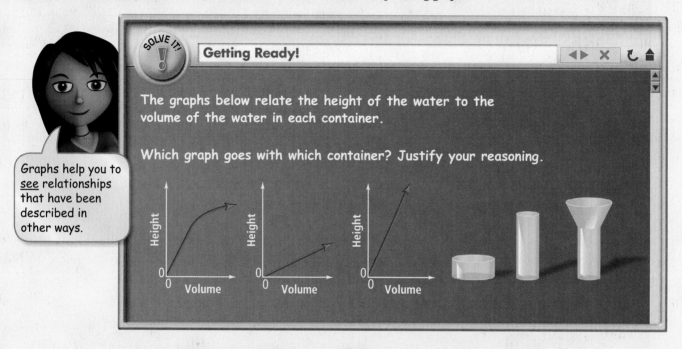

Getting Ready!

The graphs below relate the height of the water to the volume of the water in each container.

Which graph goes with which container? Justify your reasoning.

As you may have noticed in the Solve It, the change in the height of the water as the volume increases is related to the shape of the container.

Focus Question How can you represent a mathematical relationship using graphs?

The table below lists some key phrases that can help you analyze a situation and sketch a graph that relates two variable quantities as they change.

Key Phrase	Graph Meaning
rise, speed up, increase	line or curve that goes up from left to right
fall, slow down, decrease	line or curve that goes down from left to right
constant	horizontal line
sudden decrease to 0	vertical line

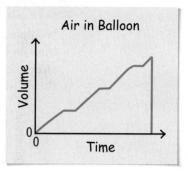

Think

The graph shows the volume of air in a balloon as you blow it up, until it pops. What are the variables? Describe how the variables are related at various points on the graph.

Examine each section of the graph separately. It begins with an increasing section, then a constant section. The increasing and constant sections alternate three times. Finally, the last section shows an instant drop to a volume of 0.

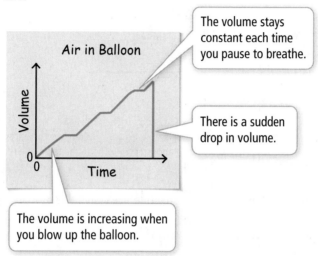

The volume stays constant each time you pause to breathe.

There is a sudden drop in volume.

The volume is increasing when you blow up the balloon.

The variables are volume and time. The volume increases each time you blow, and it stays constant each time you pause to breathe. When the balloon pops in the middle of the fourth blow, the volume decreases to 0.

 Got It? **1.** What are the variables in each graph? Describe how the variables are related at various points on the graph.

a.
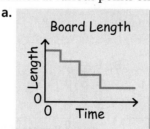

b.
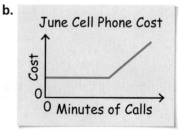

Tables and graphs can both show relationships between variables. Data from a table are often displayed using a graph to visually represent the relationship.

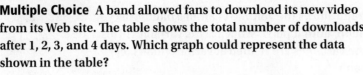 **Problem 2** Matching a Table and a Graph

Multiple Choice A band allowed fans to download its new video from its Web site. The table shows the total number of downloads after 1, 2, 3, and 4 days. Which graph could represent the data shown in the table?

Video Downloads

Day	Total Downloads
1	346
2	1011
3	3455
4	10,426

A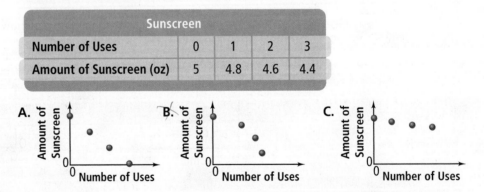

Know	**Need**	**Plan**
The relationship represented by a table	A graph that could represent the relationship	Compare the pattern of changes in the table to each graph.

In the table, the total number of downloads increases each day, and each increase is noticeably greater than the previous increase. So the graph should rise from left to right, and each rise should be steeper than the previous rise. The correct answer is B.

 Got It? **2.** The table shows the amount of sunscreen left in a can based on the number of times the sunscreen has been used. Which graph could represent the data shown in the table?

Sunscreen				
Number of Uses	0	1	2	3
Amount of Sunscreen (oz)	5	4.8	4.6	4.4

In Problem 2, the number of downloads, which is on the vertical axis of each graph, depends on the day, which is on the horizontal axis. When one quantity depends on another, show the independent quantity on the horizontal axis and the dependent quantity on the vertical axis.

Problem 3 Sketching a Graph

Rocketry A model rocket rises quickly, and then slows to a stop as its fuel burns out. It begins to fall quickly until the parachute opens, after which it falls slowly back to Earth. What sketch of a graph could represent the height of the rocket during its flight? Label each section.

Think

How can you get started?
Identify the two variables that are being related, such as *height* and *time*. Then look for key words that describe the relationship, such as *rises quickly* or *falls slowly*.

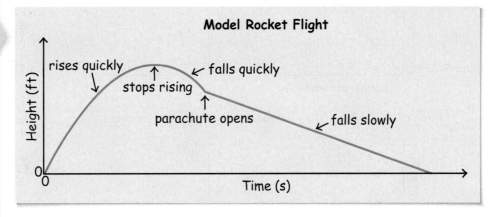

Got It? **3.** Suppose you start to swing yourself on a playground swing. You move back and forth and swing higher in the air. Then you slowly swing to a stop. What sketch of a graph could represent how your height from the ground might change over time? Label each section.

Focus Question How can you represent mathematical relationships using graphs?

Answer You can use graphs to represent visually the relationship between two variable quantities as they both change

Lesson Check

Do you know HOW?

1. What are the variables in the graph at the right? Use the graph to describe how the variables are related.

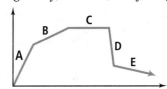

2. Describe the relationship between time and temperature in the table below.

Time (number of hours after noon)	1	3	5	7
Temperature (°F)	61	62	58	51

Do you UNDERSTAND?

3. Match one of the labeled segments in the graph below with each of the following verbal descriptions: *rising slowly*, *constant*, and *falling quickly*.

4. **Reasoning** Describe a real-world relationship that could be represented by the graph sketched above.

Practice and Problem-Solving Exercises

 Practice

What are the variables in each graph? Describe how the variables are related at various points on the graph.

 **See Problem 1.**

5.
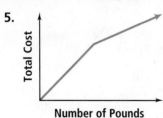

6.
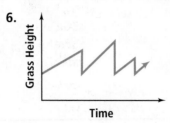

7.
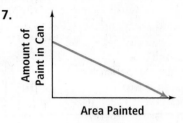

Match each graph with its related table. Explain your answers.

See Problem 2.

8.
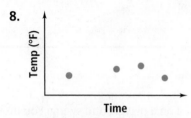

9.
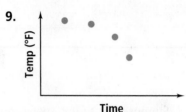

10.
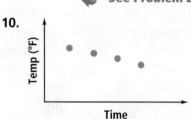

A.

Time	Temperature (°F)
1 P.M.	91°
3 P.M.	89°
5 P.M.	81°
7 P.M.	64°

B.

Time	Temperature (°F)
1 P.M.	61°
3 P.M.	60°
5 P.M.	59°
7 P.M.	58°

C.

Time	Temperature (°F)
1 P.M.	24°
3 P.M.	26°
5 P.M.	27°
7 P.M.	21°

Sketch a graph to represent each situation. Label each section.

See Problem 3.

Guided Practice

To start, identify the two related variables.

11. hours of daylight each day over the course of one year

The number of daylight hours depends on the number of days since the start of the year. So, the number of daylight hours is on the vertical axis, and number of days is on the horizontal axis.

12. your distance from the ground as you ride a Ferris wheel

13. your pulse rate as you watch a scary movie

14. Think About a Plan The *shishi-odoshi*, a popular Japanese garden ornament, was originally designed to frighten away deer. Using water, it makes a sharp rap each time a bamboo tube rises. Sketch a graph that could represent the volume of water in the bamboo tube as it operates.

Tube begins filling.

Full tube begins falling.

Tube falls and empties water.

Tube rises and hits rock, making noise.

- What quantities vary in this situation?
- How are these quantities related?

15. Error Analysis T-shirts cost $12.99 each for the first 5 shirts purchased. Each additional T-shirt costs $4.99 each. Describe and correct the error in the graph below that represents the relationship between total cost and number of shirts purchased.

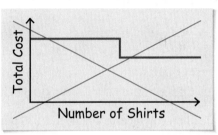

16. Open-Ended Describe a real-world relationship between the area of a rectangle and its width, as the width varies and the length stays the same. Sketch a graph to show this relationship.

17. Skiing Sketch a graph of each situation. Are the graphs the same? Explain.
 a. your speed as you travel on a ski lift from the bottom of a ski slope to the top
 b. your speed as you ski from the top of a ski slope to the bottom

18. Reasoning The diagram at the left below shows a portion of a bike trail.

  a. Explain whether the graph below is a reasonable representation of how the speed might change for the rider of the blue bike.

Blue Bike's Speed

Speed

Time

  b. Sketch two graphs that could represent a bike's speed over time. Sketch one graph for the blue bike, and the other for the red bike.

Standardized Test Prep

SAT/ACT

19. The graph at the right shows your distance from home as you walk to the bus stop, wait for the bus, and then ride the bus to school. Which point represents a time that you are waiting for the bus?

  Ⓐ A   Ⓒ C

  Ⓑ B   Ⓓ D

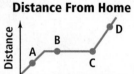

Distance From Home

Distance

Time

20. What is the solution of $-2x < 4$?

  Ⓕ $x < 2$ Ⓖ $x > 2$ Ⓗ $x < -2$ Ⓘ $x > -2$

Short Response

21. You earn $8.50 per hour. Then you receive a raise to $9.35 per hour. Find the percent increase. Then find your pay per hour if you receive the same percent increase two more times. Show your work.

Mixed Review

Let $A = \{-3, 1, 4\}$, $B = \{x \mid x$ is an odd number greater than -2 and less than 10$\}$, and $C = \{1, 4, 7, 12\}$. Find each union or intersection.

◀ **See Lesson 3-8.**

22. $A \cup B$ **23.** $A \cap B$ **24.** $B \cup C$ **25.** $A \cap C$

Get Ready!   **To prepare for Lesson 4-2, do Exercises 26 and 27.**

Use a table, an equation, and a graph to represent each relationship.

◀ **See Lesson 1-9.**

26. Donald is 4 years older than Connie.   **27.** You make 3 cards per hour.

4-2 Patterns and Linear Functions

Objective To identify and represent patterns that describe linear functions

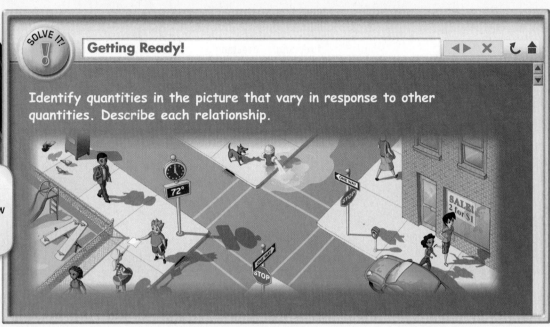

Getting Ready!

Identify quantities in the picture that vary in response to other quantities. Describe each relationship.

One relationship is between the length of a shadow and the time of day.

Lesson Vocabulary
- dependent variable
- independent variable
- input
- output
- function
- linear function

In the Solve It, you identified variables whose value *depends* on the value of another variable. In a relationship between variables, the **dependent variable** changes in response to another variable, the **independent variable.** Values of the independent variable are called **inputs.** Values of the dependent variable are called **outputs.**

Focus Question What are several ways to identify and represent patterns that describe linear functions?

The value of one variable may be uniquely determined by the value of another variable.

For example, in a regular polygon, the length of a side determines its perimeter. In a number pattern, you may add, subtract, multiply, or divide by a number to find the next number in the pattern. For example, in the number pattern 2, 4, 6, 8, . . . , adding 2 determines the next term is $8 + 2 = 10$.

Problem 1 **Representing a Geometric Relationship**

In the diagram below, what is the relationship between the number of rectangles and the perimeter of the figure they form? Represent this relationship using a table, words, an equation, and a graph.

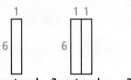

1 rectangle   2 rectangles   3 rectangles   4 rectangles

Step 1 Make a table. Use x as the independent variable and y as the dependent variable.

Let $x =$ the number of rectangles.
Let $y =$ the perimeter of the figure.

Write each pair of input and output values x and y as an ordered pair (x, y).

Number of Rectangles, x	Perimeter, y	Ordered Pair (x, y)
1	$2(1) + 2(6) = 14$	$(1, 14)$
2	$2(2) + 2(6) = 16$	$(2, 16)$
3	$2(3) + 2(6) = 18$	$(3, 18)$
4	$2(4) + 2(6) = 20$	$(4, 20)$

Think

Which variable is the dependent variable?
The perimeter *depends* on the number of rectangles, so perimeter is the dependent variable.

Step 2 Look for a pattern in the table. Describe the pattern in words so you can write an equation to represent the relationship.

Words Multiply the number of rectangles in each figure by 2 to get the total length of the top and bottom sides of the combined figure. Then add 2(6), or 12, for the total length of the left and right sides of the combined figure to get the entire perimeter.

Equation $y = 2x + 12$

Step 3 Use the table to make a graph.

With a graph, you can see a pattern formed by the relationship between the number of rectangles and the perimeter of the combined figure.

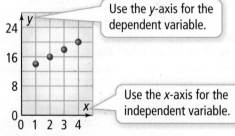

Use the y-axis for the dependent variable.

Use the x-axis for the independent variable.

Got It? **1.** In the diagram below, what is the relationship between the number of triangles and the perimeter of the figure they form? Represent this relationship using a table, words, an equation, and a graph.

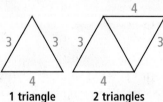
1 triangle

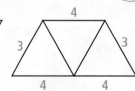
2 triangles

3 triangles

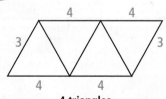
4 triangles

You can describe the relationship in Problem 1 by saying that the perimeter is a function of the number of rectangles. A **function** is a relationship that pairs each input value with exactly one output value.

You have seen that one way to represent a function is with a graph. A **linear function** is a function whose graph is a nonvertical line or part of a nonvertical line.

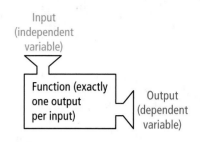

Input (independent variable)

Function (exactly one output per input)

Output (dependent variable)

Problem 2 Representing a Linear Function

Photography The table shows the relationship between the number of photos *x* you take and the amount of memory *y* in megabytes (MB) left on your camera's memory chip. Is the relationship a linear function? Describe the relationship using words, an equation, and a graph.

Camera Memory

Number of Photos, *x*	Memory (MB), *y*
0	512
1	509
2	506
3	503

Know
The amount of memory left given the number of pictures taken, as shown in the table

Need
Other representations that describe the relationship

Plan
Look for a pattern that you can describe in words to write an equation. Make a graph to show the pattern.

Think

How can you tell whether a relationship in a table is a function?
If each input is paired with *exactly* one output, then the relationship is a function.

The amount *y* of memory left is uniquely determined by the number *x* of photos you take. You can see this in the table above, where each input value of *x* corresponds to exactly one output value of *y*. So *y* is a function of *x*. To describe the relationship, look at how *y* changes for each change in *x* in the table below.

Camera Memory

Memory is 512 MB before any photos are taken.

The independent variable *x* increases by 1 each time.

Number of Photos, *x*	Memory (MB), *y*
0	512
1	509
2	506
3	503

+ 1   − 3
+ 1   − 3
+ 1   − 3

The dependent variable *y* decreases by 3 each time *x* increases by 1.

Words The amount of memory left on the chip is 512 minus the quantity 3 times the number of photos taken.

Equation $y = 512 - 3x$

Graph You can use the table to make a graph. The points lie on a line, so the relationship between the number of photos taken and the amount of memory remaining is a linear function.

Got It? **2. a.** Is the relationship in the table below a linear function? Describe the relationship using words, an equation, and a graph.

Input, x	0	1	2	3
Output, y	8	10	12	14

b. Reasoning Does the set of ordered pairs (0, 2), (1, 4), (3, 5), and (1, 8) represent a linear function? Explain.

Focus Question What are several ways to identify and represent patterns that describe linear functions?

Answer You can represent relationships or patterns using tables, words, equations, sets of ordered pairs, and graphs.

 ## Lesson Check

Do you know HOW?

1. Graph each set of ordered pairs. Use words to describe the pattern shown in the graph.
   a. (0, 0), (1, 1), (2, 2), (3, 3), (4, 4)
   b. (0, 8), (1, 6), (2, 4), (3, 2), (4, 0)
   c. (3, 0), (3, 1), (3, 2), (3, 3), (3, 4)

2. Use the diagram below. Copy and complete the table showing the relationship between the number of squares and the perimeter of the figure they form.

1 square   2 squares   3 squares

Number of Squares	Perimeter
1	4
2	6
3	■
4	■
10	■
■	62
n	■

Do you UNDERSTAND?

3. **Vocabulary** The amount of toothpaste in a tube decreases each time you brush your teeth. Identify the independent and dependent variables in this relationship.

4. **Reasoning** Tell whether each set of ordered pairs in Exercise 1 represents a function. Justify your answers.

5. **Reasoning** Does the graph below represent a linear function? Explain.

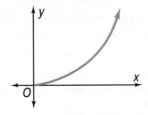

Practice and Problem-Solving Exercises

 Practice

For each diagram, find the relationship between the number of shapes and the perimeter of the figure they form. Represent this relationship using a table, words, an equation, and a graph.

◀ **See Problem 1.**

6.

1 pentagon   2 pentagons   3 pentagons

Guided Practice

To start, make a table.

Let *x* = the number of pentagons.

Let *y* = the perimeter of the figure.

Pentagons, *x*	Perimeter, *y*	Ordered Pair (*x*, *y*)
1	5	(1, 5)
2	8	(2, 8)
3	11	(3, 11)

7.

1 hexagon   2 hexagons   3 hexagons

For each table, determine whether the relationship is a linear function. Then represent the relationship using words, an equation, and a graph.

◀ **See Problem 2.**

8.

x	*y*
0	5
1	8
2	11
3	14

Guided Practice

To start, identify the change in the variables *x* and *y*.

The variable *x* increases by 1.
The variable *y* increases by 3.

9.

x	*y*
0	−3
1	2
2	7
3	12

10.

x	*y*
0	43
1	32
2	21
3	10

For each table, determine whether the relationship is a linear function. Then represent the relationship using words, an equation, and a graph.

11. **Mountain Climbing**

Number of Hours Climbing, x	Elevation (ft), y
0	1127
1	1219
2	1311
3	1403

12. **Grocery Bill**

Number of Soup Cans, x	Total Bill, y
0	$52.07
1	$53.36
2	$54.65
3	$55.94

13. **Gas in Tank**

Miles Traveled, x	Gallons of Gas, y
0	11.2
17	10.2
34	9.2
51	8.2

Ⓑ Apply

14. Error Analysis A bakery makes bread in batches. Several loaves per batch are rejected for sale due to defects. Your friend says that the total number of defective loaves is the independent variable. Explain and correct the error.

15. Gardening You can make 5 gal of liquid fertilizer by mixing 8 tsp of powdered fertilizer with water. Represent the relationship between the teaspoons of powder used and the gallons of fertilizer made using a table, an equation, and a graph. Is the amount of fertilizer made a function of the amount of powder used? Explain.

16. Reasoning Graph the set of ordered pairs $(-2, -3)$, $(0, -1)$, $(1, 0)$, $(3, 2)$, and $(4, 4)$. Determine whether the relationship is a linear function. Explain how you know.

17. Think About a Plan Gears are common parts in many types of machinery. In the diagram below, Gear A turns in response to the cranking of Gear B. Describe the relationship between the number of turns of Gear B and the number of turns of Gear A. Use words, an equation, and a graph.

- What are the independent and dependent variables?
- How much must you turn Gear B to get Gear A to go around once?

18. Electric Car An automaker produces a car that can travel 40 mi on its charged battery before it begins to use gas. Then the car travels 50 mi for each gallon of gas used. Represent the relationship between the amount of gas used and the distance traveled using a table, an equation, and a graph. Is total distance traveled a function of the amount of gas used? What are the independent and dependent variables? Explain.

Standardized Test Prep

SAT/ACT

19. A 3-ft fire hydrant is next to a road sign. The shadow of the fire hydrant is 4.5 ft long. The shadow of the road sign is 12 ft long. The shadows form similar triangles. What is the height in feet of the sign?

   Ⓐ 1.6875   Ⓑ 8

   Ⓒ 12   Ⓓ 16.5

20. What is the solution of $5d + 6 - 3d = 12$?

   Ⓕ 2.25   Ⓖ 3

   Ⓗ 9   Ⓘ 18

21. What are the solutions of $4x - 11 = 13$?

   Ⓐ −6   Ⓑ 0.5

   Ⓒ 6   Ⓓ no solution

Short Response

22. The table below shows the relationship between the number of sprays x a bottle of throat spray delivers and the amount of spray y (in milligrams) left in the bottle. Describe the relationship using words, an equation, and a graph.

Throat Spray					
Number of Sprays, x	0	1	2	3	4
Spray Left (mg), y	62,250	62,200	62,150	62,100	62,050

Mixed Review

23. A spring day begins cool and warms up as noon approaches. The temperature levels off just after noon. It drops more and more rapidly as sunset approaches. Draw a sketch of a graph that shows the possible temperature during the course of the day. Label each section.

See Lesson 4-1.

Get Ready! **To prepare for Lesson 4-3, do Exercises 24 and 25.**

Use a table, an equation, and a graph to represent each relationship.

See Lesson 1-9.

24. The number of mustard packets used is two times the number of hot dogs sold.

25. You are three places ahead of your friend while waiting in a long line.

4-3

Patterns and Nonlinear Functions

Objective To identify and represent patterns that describe nonlinear functions

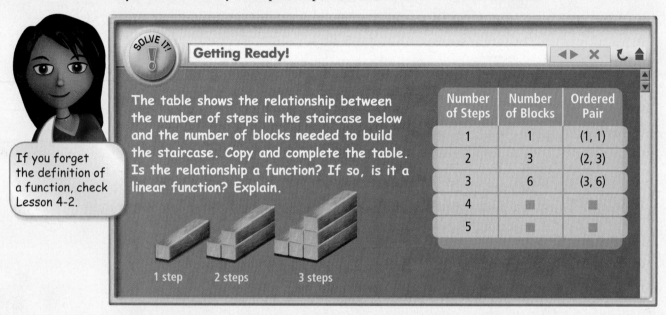

Getting Ready!

The table shows the relationship between the number of steps in the staircase below and the number of blocks needed to build the staircase. Copy and complete the table. Is the relationship a function? If so, is it a linear function? Explain.

Number of Steps	Number of Blocks	Ordered Pair
1	1	(1, 1)
2	3	(2, 3)
3	6	(3, 6)
4	■	■
5	■	■

If you forget the definition of a function, check Lesson 4-2.

1 step   2 steps   3 steps

Lesson Vocabulary
• nonlinear function

The relationship in the Solve It is an example of a nonlinear function. A **nonlinear function** is a function whose graph is not a line or part of a line.

Focus Question Can you identify and represent patterns for nonlinear and linear functions in the same way?

take note

Concept Summary   Linear and Nonlinear Functions

Linear Function
A linear function is a function whose graph is a nonvertical line or part of a nonvertical line.

Nonlinear Function
A nonlinear function is a function whose graph is not a line or part of a line.

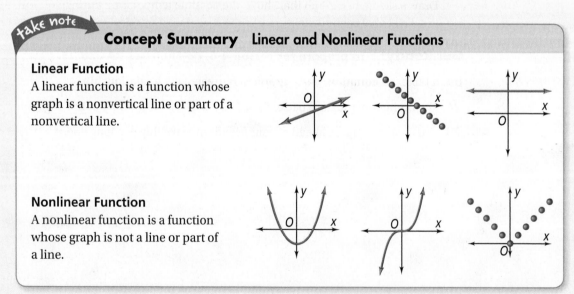

Problem 1 **Classifying Functions as Linear or Nonlinear**

Pizza The area A, in square inches, of a pizza is a function of its radius r, in inches. The cost C, in dollars, of the sauce for a pizza is a function of the weight w, in ounces, of sauce used. Graph these functions shown by the tables below. Is each function *linear* or *nonlinear*?

Pizza Area

Radius (in.), r	Area (in.^{2}), A
2	12.57
4	50.27
6	113.10
8	201.06
10	314.16

Sauce Cost

Weight (oz), w	Cost, C
2	$.80
4	$1.60
6	$2.40
8	$3.20
10	$4.00

Know

The relationships shown in the tables are functions.

Need

To classify the functions as *linear* or *nonlinear*

Plan

Use the tables to make graphs.

Think

How can a graph tell you if a function is linear or nonlinear?
The graph of a linear function is a nonvertical line or part of a line, but the graph of a nonlinear function is not.

Graph A as a function of r.

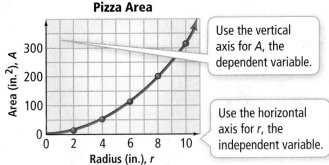

Use the vertical axis for A, the dependent variable.

Use the horizontal axis for r, the independent variable.

The graph is a curve, not a line, so the function is nonlinear.

Graph C as a function of w.

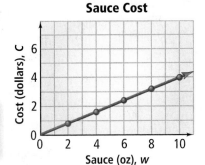

The graph is a line, so the function is linear.

 Got It? **1. a.** The table below shows the fraction A of the original area of a piece of paper that remains after the paper has been cut in half n times. Graph the function represented by the table. Is the function *linear* or *nonlinear*?

Cutting Paper				
Number of Cuts, n	1	2	3	4
Fraction of Original Area Remaining, A	$\frac{1}{2}$	$\frac{1}{4}$	$\frac{1}{8}$	$\frac{1}{16}$

b. Reasoning Will the area A in part (a) ever reach zero? Explain.

The table shows the total number of blocks in each figure below as a function of the number of blocks on one edge.

1   2   3

Number of Blocks on Edge, x	Total Number of Blocks, y	Ordered Pair (x, y)
1	1	(1, 1)
2	8	(2, 8)
3	27	(3, 27)
4	◼	◼
5	◼	◼

What is a pattern you can use to complete the table? Represent the relationship using words, an equation, and a graph.

Draw the next two figures to complete the table.

Think

How can you use a pattern to complete the table?
You can draw figures with 4 and 5 blocks on an edge. Then analyze the figures to determine the total number of blocks they contain.

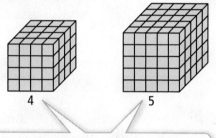

4   5

A cube with 4 blocks on an edge contains $4 \cdot 4 \cdot 4 = 64$ blocks. A cube with 5 blocks on an edge contains $5 \cdot 5 \cdot 5 = 125$ blocks.

Number of Blocks on Edge, x	Total Number of Blocks, y	Ordered Pair (x, y)
1	1	(1, 1)
2	8	(2, 8)
3	27	(3, 27)
4	64	(4, 64)
5	125	(5, 125)

Words   The total number of blocks y is the cube of the number of blocks on one edge x.

Equation $y = x^3$

You can use the table to make a graph. The points do not lie on a line. So the relationship between the number of blocks on one edge and the total number of blocks is a nonlinear function.

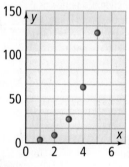

Got It? **2.** The table shows the number of new branches in each figure of the pattern below. What is a pattern you can use to complete the table? Represent the relationship using words, an equation, and a graph.

1   2   3

Number of Figure, x	1	2	3	4	5
Number of New Branches, y	3	9	27	◼	◼

A function can be thought of as a rule that you apply to the input in order to get the output. You can describe a nonlinear function with words or with an equation, just as you did with linear functions.

 Problem 3 **Writing a Rule to Describe a Nonlinear Function**

The ordered pairs (1, 2), (2, 4), (3, 8), (4, 16), and (5, 32) represent a function. What is a rule that represents this function?

Make a table to organize the x- and y-values. For each row, identify rules that produce the given y-value when you substitute the x-value. Look for a pattern in the y-values.

x	y
1	2
2	4
3	8
4	16
5	32

Think
How can you use reasoning to write a rule?
You can *solve a simpler problem* by writing a rule based on the first one or two rows of the table. Then see if the rule works for the other rows.

Step 1 Find a rule that produces 2, when $x = 1$.

The rules $y = 2x$, $y = x + 1$, and $y = 2^x$ work for (1, 2).

Step 2 Check each rule by substituting the values of the ordered pairs in the equations.

In Step 1, there are 3 rules that work for (1, 2), so check the ordered pair (2, 4).

$y = 2x$ $\qquad$ $y = x + 1$ $\qquad$ $y = 2^x$

$4 \stackrel{?}{=} 2(2)$ $\qquad$ $4 \stackrel{?}{=} 2 + 1$ $\qquad$ $4 \stackrel{?}{=} 2^2$

$4 = 4$ ✔ $\qquad$ $4 \neq 3$ ✗ $\qquad$ $4 = 4$ ✔

The ordered pair (2, 4) does not work for $y = x + 1$, so eliminate this rule. Check the ordered pair (3, 8).

$y = 2x$ $\qquad$ $y = 2^x$

$8 \stackrel{?}{=} 2(3)$ $\qquad$ $8 \stackrel{?}{=} 2^3$

$8 = 6$ ✗ $\qquad$ $8 = 8$ ✔

The ordered pair (3, 8) does not work for $y = 2x$, so eliminate this rule.

Step 3 Verify that all of the ordered pairs work for $y = 2^x$.

$2 = 2^1$ $\qquad$ $4 = 2^2$ $\qquad$ $8 = 2^3$ $\qquad$ $16 = 2^4$ $\qquad$ $32 = 2^5$

The function can be represented by the rule $y = 2^x$.

 Got It? **3.** What is a rule for the function represented by the ordered pairs (1, 1), (2, 4), (3, 9), (4, 16), and (5, 25)?

Focus Question Can you identify and represent patterns for nonlinear and linear functions in the same way?

Answer Yes, you can use words, tables, equations, sets of ordered pairs, and graphs.

Lesson Check

Do you know HOW?

1. Graph the function represented by the table below. Is the function *linear* or *nonlinear*?

x	0	1	2	3	4
y	12	13	14	15	16

2. The ordered pairs $(0, -2)$, $(1, 1)$, $(2, 4)$, $(3, 7)$, and $(4, 10)$ represent a function. What is a rule that represents this function?

3. Which rule could represent the function shown by the table below?

x	0	1	2	3	4
y	0	-1	-4	-9	-16

A. $y = x^2$ **B.** $y = -x^3$ **C.** $y = -x^2$

Do you UNDERSTAND?

4. Vocabulary Does the graph represent a *linear function* or a *nonlinear function*? Explain.

a.   b.

5. Error Analysis A classmate says that the function shown by the table at the right can be represented by the rule $y = x + 1$. Describe and correct your classmate's error.

x	y
0	1
1	2
2	5
3	10
4	17

Practice and Problem-Solving Exercises

 Practice

The cost C, in dollars, for pencils is a function of the number n of pencils purchased. The length L of a pencil, in inches, is a function of the time t, in seconds, it has been sharpened. Graph the function shown by each table below. Tell whether the function is *linear* or *nonlinear*.

 See Problem 1.

Guided Practice

To start, identify the dependent and independent variables. Label the axes.

6.

Pencil Cost					
Number of Pencils, n	6	12	18	24	30
Cost, C	$1	$2	$3	$4	$5

The cost C depends on the number of pencils n. Label the vertical axis C, the dependent variable. Label the horizontal axis n, the independent variable.

7.

Pencil Sharpening						
Time (s), t	0	3	6	9	12	15
Length (in.), L	7.5	7.5	7.5	7.5	7.4	7.3

Graph the function shown by each table. Tell whether the function is *linear* or *nonlinear*.

8.

x	y
0	5
1	5
2	5
3	5

9.

x	y
0	−4
1	−3
2	0
3	5

10.

x	y
0	0
1	1
2	−5
3	8

11.

x	y
0	0
1	3
2	6
3	9

12. For the diagram below, the table gives the total number of small triangles *y* in figure number *x*. What pattern can you use to complete the table? Represent the relationship using words, an equation, and a graph.

See Problem 2.

Figure 1

Figure 2

Figure 3

Figure Number, x	Total Small Triangles, y	Ordered Pair (x, y)
1	3	(1, 3)
2	12	(2, 12)
3	27	(3, 27)
4	■	■
5	■	■

Each set of ordered pairs represents a function. Write a rule that represents the function.

See Problem 3.

Guided Practice

To start, make a table of *x*- and *y*-values.

13. $(0, 0), (1, 4), (2, 16), (3, 36), (4, 64)$

x	0	1	2	3	4
y	0	4	16	36	64

14. $\left(1, \frac{2}{3}\right), \left(2, \frac{4}{9}\right), \left(3, \frac{8}{27}\right), \left(4, \frac{16}{81}\right), \left(5, \frac{32}{243}\right)$

15. $(1, 2), (2, 16), (3, 54), (4, 128), (5, 250)$

B Apply

16. Writing The rule $V = \frac{4}{3}\pi r^3$ gives the volume *V* of a sphere as a function of its radius *r*. Identify the independent and dependent variables in this relationship. Explain your reasoning.

17. Open-Ended Write a rule for a nonlinear function such that *y* is negative when *x* = 1, positive when *x* = 2, negative when *x* = 3, positive when *x* = 4, and so on.

18. **Think About a Plan** Concrete forming tubes are used as molds for cylindrical concrete supports. The volume V of a tube is the product of its length ℓ and the area A of its circular base. You can make $\frac{2}{3}$ ft^3 of cement per bag. Write a rule to find the number of bags of cement needed to fill a tube 4 ft long as a function of its radius r. How many bags are needed to fill a tube with a 4-in. radius? A 5-in. radius? A 6-in. radius?

4 ft

- What is a rule for the volume V of any tube?
- What operation do you use to find the number of bags needed for a given volume?

19. **Fountain** A designer wants to make a circular fountain inside a square of grass as shown at the right. What is a rule for the area A of the grass as a function of r?

$2r$

Standardized Test Prep

SAT/ACT

20. The ordered pairs $(-2, 1)$, $(-1, -2)$, $(0, -3)$, $(1, -2)$, and $(2, 1)$ represent a function. Which rule could represent the function?

   Ⓐ $y = -3x - 5$ Ⓑ $y = x^2 - 3$ Ⓒ $y = x + 3$ Ⓓ $y = x^2 + 5$

21. You are making a model of the library. The floor plans for the library and the plans for your model are shown. What is the value of x?

   Ⓕ 1.4 in.   Ⓗ 23.2 in.

   Ⓖ 2.8 in.   Ⓘ 437.5 in.

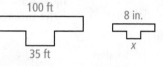

100 ft   8 in.   35 ft x

Short Response

22. A 15-oz can of tomatoes costs $.89, and a 29-oz can costs $1.69. Which can has the lower cost per ounce? Justify your answer.

Mixed Review

23. Determine whether the relationship in the table is a function. Then describe the relationship using words, an equation, and a graph.

x	0	1	2	3
y	3	5	7	9

◀ **See Lesson 4-2.**

Get Ready! To prepare for Lesson 4-4, do Exercises 24–26.

Evaluate each expression for $x = -3$, $x = 0$, and $x = 2.5$.

◀ **See Lesson 1-2.**

24. $7x - 3$ 25. $1 + 4x$ 26. $-2x^2$

Do you know HOW?

1. **Buffet** The graph shows the number of slices of French toast in a serving dish at a breakfast buffet as time passes. What are the variables? Describe how the variables are related at various points on the graph.

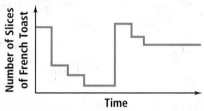

Sketch a graph of the height of each object over time. Label each section.

2. **Recreation** You throw a flying disc into the air. It hits a tree branch on its way up and comes to rest on a roof. It stays on the roof for a minute before the wind blows it back to the ground.

3. **Elevator** An elevator fills with people on the ground floor. Most get off at the seventh floor, and the remainder get off at the ninth floor. Then two people get on at the tenth floor and are carried back to the ground floor without any more stops.

For each table, identify the independent and dependent variables. Then describe the relationship using words, an equation, and a graph.

4. **Ounces of Soda**

Number of Cans	Soda (oz)
1	12
2	24
3	36
4	48

5. **Dog Biscuits Left**

Number of Tricks	Number of Biscuits
1	20
2	17
3	14
4	11

Tell whether the function shown by each table is *linear* or *nonlinear*.

6.

x	1	2	3	4
y	6	8	10	12

7.

x	0	2	4	6
y	5	5	5	5

8.

x	0	1	2	3
y	−3	−4	−5	6

Do you UNDERSTAND?

9. **Vocabulary** Does each graph represent a *linear function* or a *nonlinear function*? Explain.

a.

b.

c.

d.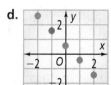

10. **Writing** The size of a bees' nest increases as time passes. Your friend says that time is the dependent variable because size depends on time. Is your friend correct? Explain.

11. **Open-Ended** With some functions, the value of the dependent variable decreases as the value of the independent variable increases. What is a real-world example of this?

4-4 Graphing a Function Rule

Objective To graph equations that represent functions

You connect the dots in certain real-world graphs.

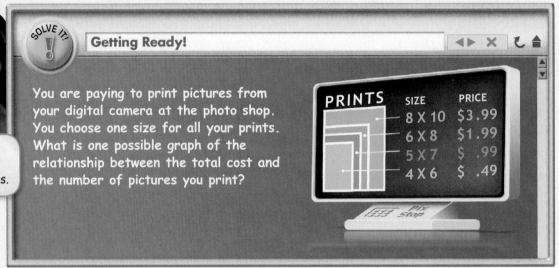

Getting Ready!

You are paying to print pictures from your digital camera at the photo shop. You choose one size for all your prints. What is one possible graph of the relationship between the total cost and the number of pictures you print?

PRINTS

SIZE	PRICE
8 X 10	$3.99
6 X 8	$1.99
5 X 7	$ .99
4 X 6	$ .49

You can use a table of values to help you make a graph in the Solve It.

Lesson Vocabulary
- continuous graph
- discrete graph

Focus Question How are the graph of an equation and the set of all solutions of an equation related?

A graph may include solutions that do not appear in a table.
A real-world graph should only show points that make sense in the given situation.

Problem 1 Graphing a Function Rule

What is the graph of the function rule $y = -2x + 1$?

Step 1   Make a table of values.

x	$y = -2x + 1$	(x, y)
-1	$y = -2(-1) + 1 = 3$	$(-1, 3)$
0	$y = -2(0) + 1 = 1$	$(0, 1)$
1	$y = -2(1) + 1 = -1$	$(1, -1)$
2	$y = -2(2) + 1 = -3$	$(2, -3)$

Step 2   Graph the ordered pairs.

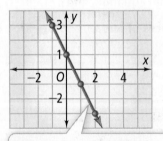

Connect the points with a line to represent *all* solutions.

Hint

What input values make sense here? It is possible to use any input x in the equation and get an output y. Choose integer values of x to produce integer values of y, which are easier to graph.

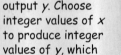 **Got It?** **1.** What is the graph of the function rule $y = \frac{1}{2}x - 1$?

When you graph a real-world function rule, choose appropriate intervals for the units on the axes. Every interval on an axis should represent the same change in value. If all the data are nonnegative, show only the first quadrant.

Problem 2 Graphing a Real-World Function Rule

Trucking The function rule $W = 146c + 30,000$ represents the total weight W, in pounds, of a concrete mixer truck that carries c cubic feet of concrete. What is a reasonable graph of the function rule given that the capacity of the truck is about 200 ft^3?

Plan

How do you choose values for a real-world independent variable?
Look for information about what the values can be. The independent variable c in this problem is limited by the capacity of the truck, 200 ft^3.

Step 1
Make a table to find ordered pairs (c, W).

c	$W = 146c + 30,000$	(c, W)
0	$W = 146(0) + 30,000 = 30,000$	(0, 30,000)
50	$W = 146(50) + 30,000 = 37,300$	(50, 37,300)
100	$W = 146(100) + 30,000 = 44,600$	(100, 44,600)
150	$W = 146(150) + 30,000 = 51,900$	(150, 51,900)
200	$W = 146(200) + 30,000 = 59,200$	(200, 59,200)

The truck can hold 0 to 200 ft^3 of concrete. So only c-values from 0 to 200 are reasonable.

Step 2
Graph the ordered pairs from the table.

W reaches almost 60,000 lb. So W-values from 0 to 60,000 in grid increments of 10,000 make sense.

Truck Weight

All c-values from 0 to 200 make sense, so connect the points. Stop at 200 ft^3, the capacity of the truck.

The c-values go from 0 to 200. 200 is evenly divisible by 25, so use grid increments of 25.

Got It? **2. a.** The function rule $W = 8g + 700$ represents the total weight W, in pounds, of a spa that contains g gallons of water. What is a reasonable graph of the function rule, given that the capacity of the spa is 250 gal?

b. Reasoning What is the weight of the spa when empty? Explain.

In Problem 2, the truck could contain any amount of concrete from 0 to 200 ft^3, such as 27.3 ft^3 or $105\frac{2}{3}$ ft^3. You can connect the data points from the table because any point between the data points has meaning.

Some graphs may be composed of isolated points. For example, in the Solve It you graphed only points that represent printing whole numbers of photos.

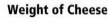

Key Concept Continuous and Discrete Graphs

Continuous Graph
A **continuous graph** is a graph that is unbroken.

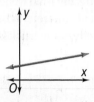

Discrete Graph
A **discrete graph** is composed of distinct, isolated points.

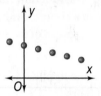

Problem 3 Identifying Continuous and Discrete Graphs

Farmer's Market A local cheese maker is making cheddar cheese to sell at a farmer's market. The amount of milk used to make the cheese and the price at which he sells the cheese are shown. Write a function for each situation. Graph each function. Is the graph *continuous* or *discrete*?

1 gal of milk makes 16 oz of cheddar cheese.

Each wheel of cheddar cheese costs $9.

Think

How can you decide if a graph is continuous or discrete?
Decide what values are reasonable for the independent variable. For example, even if 3 and 4 make sense, 3.3 and 3.7 may not make sense.

The weight w of cheese, in ounces, depends on the number of gallons m of milk used. So $w = 16m$. Make a table of values.

m	0	1	2	3	4
w	0	16	32	48	64

Graph each ordered pair (m, w).

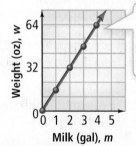

Any amount of milk makes sense, so connect the points. The graph is continuous.

The amount a of money made from selling cheese depends on the number n of wheels sold. So $a = 9n$. Make a table of values.

n	0	1	2	3	4
a	0	9	18	27	36

Graph each ordered pair (n, a)

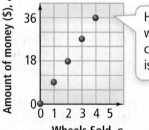

He can only sell whole wheels of cheese. The graph is discrete.

Got It? **3.** Graph each function rule. Is the graph *continuous or discrete*? Justify your answer.

    a. The amount of water w in a wading pool, in gallons, depends on the amount of time t, in minutes, the wading pool has been filling, as related by the function rule $w = 3t$.

    b. The cost C for baseball tickets, in dollars, depends on the number n of tickets bought, as related by the function rule $C = 16n$.

The function rules graphed in Problems 1–3 represent linear functions. You can also graph a nonlinear function rule. When a function rule does not represent a real-world situation, graph it as a continuous function.

 Problem 4 **Graphing Nonlinear Function Rules**

What is the graph of each function rule?

A $y = |x| - 4$

Step 1
Make a table of values.

Step 2
Graph the ordered pairs.
Connect the points.

Think

What input values make sense for these nonlinear functions?
Include 0 as well as negative and positive values so that you can see how the graphs change.

x	$y = |x| - 4$	(x, y)
-4	$y = |-4| - 4 = 0$	$(-4, 0)$
-2	$y = |-2| - 4 = -2$	$(-2, -2)$
0	$y = |0| - 4 = -4$	$(0, -4)$
2	$y = |2| - 4 = -2$	$(2, -2)$
4	$y = |4| - 4 = 0$	$(4, 0)$

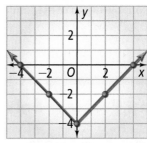

B $y = x^2 + 1$

Step 1
Make a table of values.

Step 2
Graph the ordered pairs.
Connect the points.

x	$y = x^2 + 1$	(x, y)
-2	$y = (-2)^2 + 1 = 5$	$(-2, 5)$
-1	$y = (-1)^2 + 1 = 2$	$(-1, 2)$
0	$y = 0^2 + 1 = 1$	$(0, 1)$
1	$y = 1^2 + 1 = 2$	$(1, 2)$
2	$y = 2^2 + 1 = 5$	$(2, 5)$

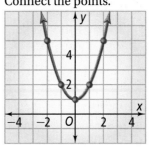

 Got It? **4.** What is the graph of the function rule $y = x^3 + 1$?

Focus Question How are the graph of an equation and the set of all solutions of an equation related?

Answer The graph visually shows the set of all solutions of an equation.

Lesson Check

Do you know HOW?

Graph each function rule.

1. $y = 2x + 4$

2. $y = \frac{1}{2}x - 7$

3. $y = 9 - x$

4. $y = -x^2 + 2$

5. The function rule $h = 18 + 1.5n$ represents the height h, in inches, of a stack of traffic cones.

   a. Make a table for the function rule.

   b. Suppose the stack of cones can be no taller than 30 in. What is a reasonable graph of the function rule?

Do you UNDERSTAND?

Vocabulary Tell whether each relationship should be represented by a *continuous* or a *discrete* graph.

6. The number of bagels b remaining in a dozen depends on the number s that have been sold.

7. The amount of gas g remaining in the tank of a gas grill depends on the amount of time t the grill has been used.

8. **Error Analysis** Your friend graphs $y = x + 3$ at the right. Describe and correct your friend's error.

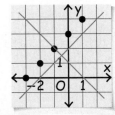

Practice and Problem-Solving Exercises

A Practice   Graph each function rule.   ◀ See Problem 1.

> **Guided Practice**

9. $y = x - 3$

To start, make a table of values.

x	$y = x - 3$	(x, y)
-2	$y = -2 - 3 = -5$	$(-2, -5)$
0	$y = 0 - 3 = -3$	$(0, -3)$
2	$y = 2 - 3 = -1$	$(2, -1)$
4	$y = 4 - 3 = 1$	$(4, 1)$

10. $y = 2x + 5$ **11.** $y = 3x - 2$ **12.** $y = 5 + 2x$

13. $y = 3 - x$ **14.** $y = -5x + 12$ **15.** $y = 10x$

16. $y = 4x - 5$ **17.** $y = 2x - 1$ **18.** $y = \frac{3}{4}x + 2$

Graph each function rule. Explain your choice of intervals on the axes of the graph. Tell whether the graph is *continuous* or *discrete*.

See Problems 2 and 3.

19. Beverages The height h, in inches, of the juice in a 20-oz bottle depends on the amount of juice j, in ounces, you drink. This situation is represented by the function rule $h = 6 - 0.3j$.

Guided Practice

To start, make a table. Find ordered pairs (j, h).

j	$h = 6 - 0.3j$	(j, h)
2	$y = 6 - 0.3(2) = 5.4$	$(2, 5.4)$
4	$y = 6 - 0.3(4) = 4.8$	$(4, 4.8)$
6	$y = 6 - 0.3(6) = 4.2$	$(6, 4.2)$
8	$y = 6 - 0.3(8) = 3.6$	$(8, 3.6)$

20. Trucking The total weight w, in pounds, of a tractor-trailer capable of carrying 8 cars depends on the number of cars c on the trailer. This situation is represented by the function rule $w = 37,000 + 4200c$.

21. Food Delivery The cost C, in dollars, for delivered pizza depends on the number p of pizzas ordered. This situation is represented by the function rule $C = 5 + 9p$.

Graph each function rule.

See Problem 4.

22. $y = |x| - 7$

23. $y = |x| + 2$

24. $y = 2|x|$

25. $y = x^3 - 1$

26. $y = 3x^3$

27. $y = -2x^2$

28. $y = |-2x| - 1$

29. $y = -x^3$

30. $y = |x - 3| - 1$

 Apply

31. Error Analysis The graph at the right shows the distance d you run, in miles, as a function of time t, in minutes, during a 5-mi run. Your friend says that the graph is not continuous because it stops at $d = 5$, so the graph is discrete. Do you agree? Explain.

32. Writing Is the point $\left(2, 2\frac{1}{2}\right)$ on the graph of $y = x + 2$? How do you know?

33. Geometry The area A of an isosceles right triangle depends on the length ℓ of each leg of the triangle. This is represented by the rule $A = \frac{1}{2}\ell^2$. Graph the function rule. Is the graph *continuous* or *discrete*? How do you know?

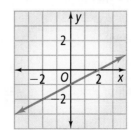

5-Mile Run

34. Which function rule is graphed below?

Ⓐ $y = -\frac{1}{2}x + 1$

Ⓑ $y = \frac{1}{2}x - 1$

Ⓒ $y = \left|\frac{1}{2}x\right| - 1$

Ⓓ $y = \frac{1}{2}x + 1$

35. **Sporting Goods** The amount a basketball coach spends at a sporting goods store depends on the number of basketballs the coach buys. The situation is represented by the function rule $a = 15b$.
   a. Make a table of values and graph the function rule. Is the graph *continuous* or *discrete*? Explain.
   b. Suppose the coach spent $120 before tax. How many basketballs did she buy?

36. **Think About a Plan** The height h, in inches, of the vinegar in the jars of pickle chips shown below depends on the number of chips p you eat. About how many chips must you eat to lower the level of the vinegar in the jar on the left to the level of the jar on the right? Use a graph to find the answer.

$$h = 4.75 - 0.22p$$

4 in.

   • What should the maximum value of p be on the horizontal axis?
   • What are reasonable values of p in this situation?

37. **Falling Objects** The height h, in feet, of an acorn that falls from a branch 100 ft above the ground depends on the time t, in seconds, since it has fallen. This is represented by the rule $h = 100 - 16t^2$. About how much time does it take for the acorn to hit the ground? Use a graph and give an answer between two consecutive whole-number values of t.

Standardized Test Prep

GRIDDED RESPONSE

SAT/ACT

38. A plumber's bill b is based on $125 for materials and $50 per hour for t hours of labor. This situation can be represented by the function rule $b = 50t + 125$. Suppose the plumber works for $3\frac{1}{4}$h. How much is the bill?

39. No more than $\frac{1}{10}$ of the people attending an auto race will be given a free hat. If maximum attendance is 3510 people, what is the greatest number of free hats that can be given away?

40. What is the solution of $\frac{12}{b} = \frac{36}{51}$?

41. What is the solution of $2(x - 5) = 2 - x$?

Mixed Review

See Lesson 4-3.

Tell whether the function shown in each table is *linear* or *nonlinear*.

42.

x	0	1	2	3	4
y	0	−1	−1	−3	−2

43.

x	0	1	2	3	4
y	−7	−6	−5	−4	−3

See Lesson 3-7.

Solve each equation. If there is no solution, write *no solution*.

44. $|x - 5| = 7$

45. $|x + 3| = 4$

46. $6 = |a - 7|$

47. $20 = |n + 11|$

48. $-3|4q| = 10$

49. $-2|5y| = -40$

50. $8|z - 1| = 24$

51. $|b + 2| + 5 = 1$

52. $3|t + 1| + 1 = 7$

Get Ready!   To prepare for Lesson 4-5, do Exercises 53 and 54.

See Lesson 2-2.

Define a variable and write an equation for each situation. Then solve the problem.

53. Shopping You have $14. Ice-cream cones cost $4, and the store offers $2 off the price of the first ice-cream cone. How many ice-cream cones can you buy?

54. Gardening You order 5 yd of mulch and pay a delivery fee of $35. The total cost including the delivery fee is $200. What is the cost of each yard of mulch?

Graphing Functions and Solving Equations

You have learned to graph function rules by making a table of values. You can also use a graphing calculator to graph function rules.

Example 1

Graph $y = \frac{1}{2}x - 4$ using a graphing calculator.

Step 1 Press the **y=** key. To the right of Y_1 =, enter $\frac{1}{2}x - 4$ by pressing **(** 1 **÷** 2 **)** **x,t,θ,n** **−** 4.

Step 2 The screen on the graphing calculator is a "window" that lets you look at only part of the graph. Press the **window** key to set the borders of the graph. A good window for this function rule is the standard viewing window, $-10 \le x \le 10$ and $-10 \le y \le 10$.

You can have the axes show 1 unit between tick marks by setting **Xscl** and **Yscl** to 1, as shown.

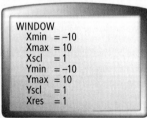

Step 3 Press the **graph** key. The graph of the function rule is shown.

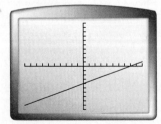

In Chapter 2 you learned how to solve equations in one variable. You can also solve equations by using a graphing calculator to graph each side of the equation as a function rule. The x-coordinate of the point where the graphs intersect is the solution of the equation.

Example 2

Solve $7 = -\frac{3}{4}k + 3$ **using a graphing calculator.**

Step 1 Press (**y=**). Clear any equations. Then enter each side of the given equation. For $Y_1=$, enter 7. For $Y_2=$, enter $-\frac{3}{4}x + 3$ by pressing (((-) 3 ÷ 4) (x,t,θ,n) + 3. Notice that you must replace the variable k with x.

Step 2 Graph the function rules. Use a standard graphing window by pressing (**zoom**) 6. This gives a window defined by $-10 \le x \le 10$ and $-10 \le y \le 10$.

Step 3 Use the **CALC** feature. Select **INTERSECT** and press (**enter**) 3 times to find the point where the graphs intersect.

The calculator's value for the x-coordinate of the point of intersection is -5.333333. The actual x-coordinate is $-5\frac{1}{3}$.

The solution of the equation $7 = -\frac{3}{4}k + 3$ is $-5\frac{1}{3}$.

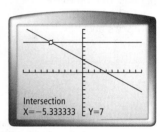

Exercises

Graph each function rule using a graphing calculator.

1. $y = 6x + 3$

2. $y = -3x + 8$

3. $y = 0.2x - 7$

4. $y = -1.8x - 6$

5. $y = -\frac{1}{3}x + 5$

6. $y = \frac{8}{3}x - 5$

7. Open-Ended Graph $y = -0.4x + 8$. Using the (**window**) screen, experiment with values for **Xmin**, **Xmax**, **Ymin**, and **Ymax** until you can see the graph crossing both axes. What values did you use for **Xmin**, **Xmax**, **Ymin**, and **Ymax**?

8. Reasoning How can you graph the equation $2x + 3y = 6$ on a graphing calculator?

Use a graphing calculator to solve each equation.

9. $8a - 12 = 6$

10. $-4 = -3t + 2$

11. $-5 = -0.5x - 2$

12. $4 + \frac{3}{2}n = -7$

13. $\frac{5}{4}d - \frac{1}{2} = 6$

14. $-3y - 1 = 3.5$

4-5 Writing a Function Rule

Objective To write equations that represent functions

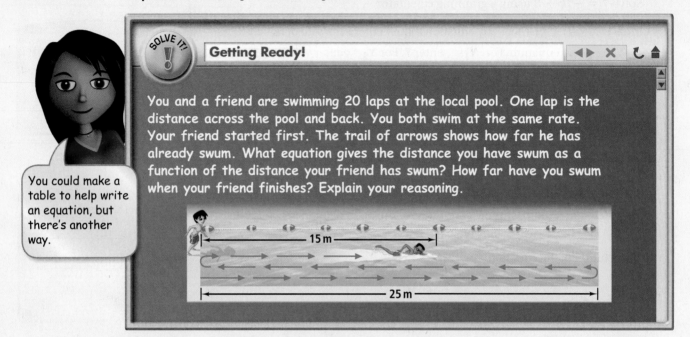

SOLVE IT!

Getting Ready!

You and a friend are swimming 20 laps at the local pool. One lap is the distance across the pool and back. You both swim at the same rate. Your friend started first. The trail of arrows shows how far he has already swum. What equation gives the distance you have swum as a function of the distance your friend has swum? How far have you swum when your friend finishes? Explain your reasoning.

You could make a table to help write an equation, but there's another way.

—15 m—

—25 m—

In the Solve It, you can see how the value of one variable depends on another. Once you see a pattern in a relationship, you can write a rule.

Focus Question Why is it useful to write and solve equations that represent functions?

Many real-world functional relationships can be represented by equations. You can use an equation to find the solution of a given real-world problem.

Think

How can a model help you visualize a real-world situation?
Use a model like the one below to represent the relationship that is described.

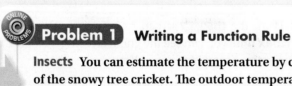

| T |
| $\frac{1}{4}n$ ----40---- |

Problem 1 Writing a Function Rule

Insects You can estimate the temperature by counting the number of chirps of the snowy tree cricket. The outdoor temperature is about 40°F more than one fourth the number of chirps the cricket makes in one minute. What is a function rule that represents this situation?

Relate   temperature is 40°F more than $\frac{1}{4}$ of chirps in 1 min

Define   Let T = the temperature. Let n = the number of chirps in 1 min.

Write T =   40   + $\frac{1}{4}$ · n

A function rule that represents this situation is $T = 40 + \frac{1}{4}n$.

Got It? **1.** A landfill has 50,000 tons of waste in it. Each month it accumulates an average of 420 more tons of waste. What is a function rule that represents the total amount of waste after *m* months?

Problem 2 **Writing and Evaluating a Function Rule**

Concert Revenue A concert seating plan is shown below. Reserved seating is sold out. Total revenue from ticket sales will depend on the number of general-seating tickets sold. Write a function rule to represent this situation. What is the maximum possible total revenue?

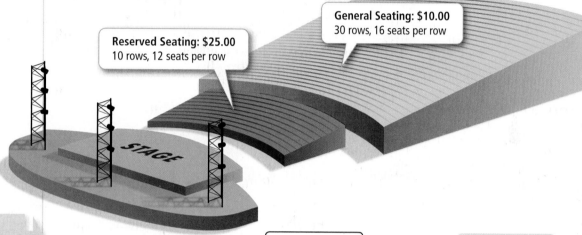

General Seating: $10.00
30 rows, 16 seats per row

Reserved Seating: $25.00
10 rows, 12 seats per row

STAGE

Plan

How can a model help you write an equation?
A model like the one below can help you write an expression for the general-seating revenue.

|◄——— Gen. seating ———►|
| 10 |- - - - - - - - - - - - ►|
        n tickets

Add the reserved-seating revenue to get the total revenue.

Relate

| total revenue | is | general seating revenue | plus | reserved seating revenue |

price per ticket · number of tickets sold

Define Let R = the total revenue.

Let n = the number of general-seating tickets sold.

Write R = 10 · n + (25 · 10 · 12)

$$R = 10n + 3000$$

The function rule $R = 10n + 3000$ represents this situation. There are $30 \cdot 16 = 480$ general-seating tickets. Substitute 480 for *n* to find the maximum possible revenue.

$$R = 10(480) + 3000 = 7800$$

The maximum possible revenue from ticket sales is $7800.

Got It? **2. a.** A kennel charges $15 per day to board dogs. Upon arrival, each dog must have a flea bath that costs $12. Write a function rule for the total cost for *n* days of boarding plus a bath. How much does a 10-day stay cost?

b. Reasoning Does a 5-day stay cost half as much as a 10-day stay? Explain.

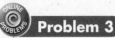 **Problem 3** Writing a Nonlinear Function Rule GRIDDED RESPONSE

Geometry Write a function rule for the area of a rectangle whose length is 5 ft more than its width. What is the area of the rectangle when its width is 9 ft?

Think

How can *drawing a diagram* help you to write a rule?
A diagram visually represents information in the problem. It can give you a clearer understanding of how variables are related.

Step 1 Represent the general relationship first. The area A of a rectangle is the product of its length ℓ and its width w.

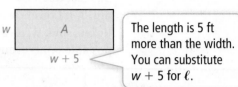

$A = \ell \cdot w$

Step 2 Revise the model to show that the length is 5 ft more than the width.

The length is 5 ft more than the width. You can substitute $w + 5$ for ℓ.

Step 3 Use the diagram in Step 2 to write the function rule. The function rule $A = (w + 5)w$, or $A = w^2 + 5w$, represents the rectangle's area. Substitute 9 for w to find the area when the width is 9 ft.

$$A = 9^2 + 5(9)$$
$$= 81 + 45$$
$$= 126$$

When the width of the rectangle is 9 ft, its area is 126 ft^2.

 Got It? 3. Write a function rule for the area of a triangle whose height is 4 in. more than twice the length of its base. What is the area of the triangle when the length of its base is 16 in.?

Focus Question Why is it useful to write and solve equations that represent functions?

Answer You can find the solutions to real-world problems that are represented by linear and nonlinear functions.

 Lesson Check

Do you know HOW?

Write a function rule to represent each situation.

1. the total cost C for p pounds of copper if each pound costs \$3.57

2. the height f, in feet, of an object when you know the object's height h in inches

3. the amount y of your friend's allowance if the amount she receives is \$2 more than the amount x you receive

4. the volume V of a cube-shaped box whose edge lengths are 1 in. greater than the diameter d of the ball that the box will hold

Do you UNDERSTAND?

5. Vocabulary Suppose you write an equation that gives a as a function of b. Which is the dependent variable and which is the independent variable?

6. Error Analysis A worker has dug 3 holes for fence posts. It will take 15 min to dig each additional hole. Your friend writes the rule $t = 15n + 3$ for the time t, in minutes, required to dig n additional holes. Describe and correct your friend's error.

7. Reasoning Is the graph of a function rule that relates a square's area to its side length *continuous* or *discrete*? Explain.

Practice and Problem-Solving Exercises

 Practice   Write a function rule that represents each sentence.   ◀ See Problem 1.

8. y is 5 less than the product of 4 and x.

9. C is 8 more than half of n.

10. 7 less than three fifths of b is a.

11. 2.5 more than the quotient of h and 3 is w.

Write a function rule that represents each situation.

Guided Practice

12. Wages A worker's earnings e are a function of the number of hours n worked at a rate of $8.75 per hour.

To start, use a model to represent the relationship that has been described.

e
$8.75n$

13. Pizza The price p of a pizza is $6.95 plus $.95 for each topping t on the pizza.

14. Weight Loads The load L, in pounds, of a wheelbarrow is the sum of its own 42-lb weight and the weight of the bricks that it carries, as shown at the right.

The wheelbarrow holds n 4-lb bricks.

15. Baking The almond extract a remaining in an 8-oz bottle decreases by $\frac{1}{6}$ oz for each batch b of waffle cookies made.

Guided Practice

16. Aviation A helicopter hovers 40 ft above the ground. Then the helicopter climbs at a rate of 21ft/s. Write a rule that represents the helicopter's height h above the ground as a function of time t. What is the helicopter's height after 45 s?   ◀ See Problem 2.

To start, describe what you know.   height is 40 ft above the ground plus the helicopter climbs at 21 ft/s

17. Scuba Diving A team of divers assembles at an elevation of -10 ft relative to the surface of the water. Then the team dives at a rate of -50 ft/min. Write a rule that represents the team's depth d as a function of time t. What is the team's depth after 3 min?

18. Publishing A new book is being planned. It will have 24 pages of introduction. Then it will have c 12-page chapters and 48 more pages at the end. Write a rule that represents the total number of pages p in the book as a function of the number of chapters. Suppose the book has 25 chapters. How many pages will it have?

19. Write a function rule for the area of a triangle with a base 3 cm greater than 5 times its height. What is the area of the triangle when its height is 6 cm?

See Problem 3.

20. Write a function rule for the volume of the cylinder shown at the right with a height 3 in. more than 4 times the radius of the cylinder's base. What is the volume of the cylinder when it has a radius of 2 in.?

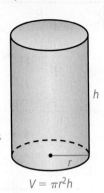

$V = \pi r^2 h$

21. Write a function rule for the area of a rectangle with a length 2 ft less than three times its width. What is the area of the rectangle when its width is 2 ft?

B Apply

22. History of Math The golden ratio has been studied and used by mathematicians and artists for more than 2000 years. A golden rectangle, constructed using the golden ratio, has a length about 1.6 times its width. Write a rule for the area of a golden rectangle as a function of its width.

23. Whales From an elevation of 3.5 m below the surface of the water, a northern bottlenose whale dives at a rate of 1.8 m/s. Write a rule that gives the whale's depth d as a function of time in minutes. What is the whale's depth after 4 min?

24. Think About a Plan The height h, in inches, of the juice j in the pitcher shown at the right is a function of the amount of juice j, in ounces, that has been poured out of the pitcher. Write a function rule that represents this situation. What is the height of the juice after 47 oz have been poured out?
 • What is the height of the juice when half of it has been poured out?
 • What fraction of the juice would you pour out to make the height decrease by 1 in.?

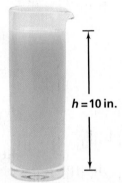

$h = 10$ in.

volume = 64 oz

25. Tips You go to dinner and decide to leave a 15% tip for the server. You had $55 when you entered the restaurant.
 a. Make a table showing how much money you would have left after buying a meal that costs $15, $21, $24, or $30.
 b. Write a function rule for the amount of money m you would have left if the meal costs c dollars before the tip.
 c. Graph the function rule.

26. Projectors You consult your new projector's instruction manual before mounting it on the wall. The manual says to multiply the desired image width by 1.8 to find the correct distance of the projector lens from the wall.
 a. Write a rule to describe the distance of the lens from the wall as a function of desired image width.
 b. The diagram shows the room in which the projector will be installed. Will you be able to project an image 7 ft wide? Explain.
 c. What is the maximum image width you can project in the room?

— 12 ft — | ? ft

27. Car Rental A car rental agency charges $29 per day to rent a car and $13.95 per day for a global positioning system (GPS). Customers are charged for their full tank of gas at $3.80 per gallon.
 a. A car has a 12-gal tank and a GPS. Write a rule for the total bill b as a function of the number of days d the car is rented.
 b. What is the bill for a 9-day rental?

Standardized Test Prep

SAT/ACT

28. You buy x pounds of cherries for \$2.99/lb. What is a function rule for the amount of change C you receive from a \$50 bill?

    Ⓐ $C = 2.99x - 50$ Ⓒ $C = 50x - 2.99$

    Ⓑ $C = 50 - 2.99x$ Ⓓ $C = 2.99 - 50x$

29. What is the solution of $-5 < h + 2 < 11$?

    Ⓕ $-3 < h < 11$ Ⓖ $-7 < h < 9$ Ⓗ $-7 > h > 9$ Ⓘ $h < -7$ or $h > 9$

30. Which equation do you get when you solve $-ax + by^2 = c$ for b?

    Ⓐ $b = \dfrac{c - ax}{y^2}$ Ⓑ $b = y^2(c + ax)$ Ⓒ $b = \dfrac{c + ax}{y^2}$ Ⓓ $b = \dfrac{c}{y^2} + ax$

Extended Response

31. The recommended dosage D, in milligrams, of a certain medicine depends on a person's body mass m, in kilograms. The function rule $D = 0.1m^2 + 5m$ represents this relationship.

    a. What is the recommended dosage for a person whose mass is 60 kg? Show your work.

    b. One pound is equivalent to approximately 0.45 kg. Explain how to find the recommended dosage for a 200-lb person. What is this dosage?

Mixed Review

Graph each function rule.   ◀ See Lesson 4-4.

32. $y = 9 - x$ **33.** $y = 4 + 3x$ **34.** $y = x + 1.5$

35. $y = 4x - 1$ **36.** $y = 6x$ **37.** $y = 12 - 3x$

Convert the given amount to the given unit.   ◀ See Lesson 2-6.

38. 8.25 lb; ounces   **39.** 450 cm; meters   **40.** 17 yd; feet

41. 90 s; minutes   **42.** 216 h; days   **43.** 9.5 km; meters

Get Ready!   **To prepare for Lesson 4-6, do Exercises 44–51.**

Find each product. Simplify if necessary.   ◀ See Lesson 1-6.

44. $-4(9)$ **45.** $-3(-7)$ **46.** $-7.2(-15.5)$ **47.** $-6(1.5)$

48. $-4\left(-\dfrac{7}{2}\right)$ **49.** $-\dfrac{4}{9}\left(-\dfrac{9}{4}\right)$ **50.** $\dfrac{25}{9}\left(\dfrac{3}{5}\right)$ **51.** $\dfrac{7}{10}\left(\dfrac{15}{8}\right)$

4-6
PART 1

Formalizing Relations and Functions

Objective To determine whether a relation is a function

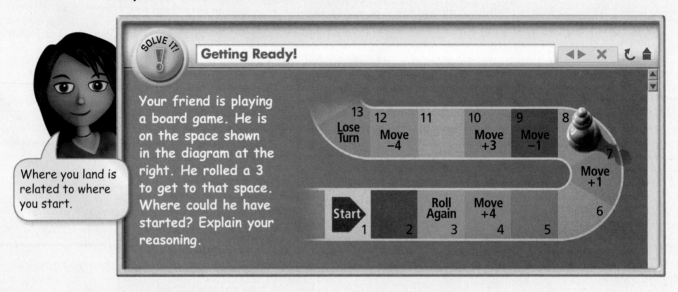

Getting Ready!

Your friend is playing a board game. He is on the space shown in the diagram at the right. He rolled a 3 to get to that space. Where could he have started? Explain your reasoning.

Where you land is related to where you start.

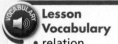

Lesson Vocabulary
- relation
- domain
- range
- vertical line test
- function notation

Focus Question How can you determine whether a relation is a function?

A **relation** is a pairing of numbers in one set, called the **domain,** with numbers in another set, called the **range.** A relation is often represented as a set of ordered pairs (x, y). In this case, the domain is the set of x-values and the range is the set of y-values.

A function is a special type of relation in which each value in the domain is paired with exactly one value in the range.

take note

Key Concept   Domain and Range in an Ordered Pair

The set of ordered pairs $(1, 2)$, $(3, 4)$, $(5, 6)$, $(7, 8)$ is a relation. Each ordered pair in the relation is made up of an x-coordinate and a y-coordinate. The set of x-coordinates is the domain of the relation. The set of y-coordinates is the range of the relation.

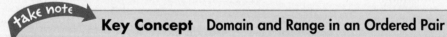

$$(1, 2), (3, 4), (5, 6), (7, 8)$$

The domain is {1, 3, 5, 7}.
The range is {2, 4, 6, 8}.

Problem 1 **Identifying Functions Using Mapping Diagrams**

Think

When is a relation *not* a function?
A function maps each domain value to exactly one range value. So a relation that maps a domain value to more than one range value cannot be a function.

Identify the domain and range of each relation. Represent the relation with a mapping diagram. Is the relation a function?

Ⓐ {(−2, 0.5), (0, 2.5), (4, 6.5), (5, 2.5)}

Step 1 Identify the domain and range.
The domain is {−2, 0, 4, 5}.
The range is {0.5, 2.5, 6.5}.

Step 2 Write the domain and range in a mapping diagram.

Domain	Range
−2	0.5
0	2.5
4	6.5
5	

Step 3 Draw arrows from the domain to the range to show the ordered pairs.

Each domain value is mapped to only one range value. The relation is a function.

Ⓑ {(6, 5), (4, 3), (6, 4), (5, 8)}

Step 1 Identify the domain and range.
The domain is {4, 5, 6}.
The range is {3, 4, 5, 8}.

Step 2 Write the domain and range in a mapping diagram.

Domain	Range
4	3
5	4
6	5
	8

Step 3 Draw arrows from the domain to the range to show the ordered pairs.

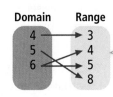

The domain value 6 is mapped to two range values. The relation is not a function.

Dynamic Activity
Function Explorer

 Got It? **1.** Identify the domain and range of each relation. Represent the relation with a mapping diagram. Is the relation a function?
    a. {(4.2, 1.5), (5, 2.2), (7, 4.8), (4.2, 0)}   **b.** {(−1, 1), (−2, 2), (4, −4), (7, −7)}

Another way to decide if a relation is a function is to analyze the graph of the relation using the **vertical line test.** If any vertical line passes through more than one point of the graph, then for some domain value there is more than one range value. So the relation is not a function.

 Problem 2 **Identifying Functions Using the Vertical Line Test**

Is the relation a function? Use the vertical line test.

A $\{(-4, 2), (-3, 1), (0, -2), (-4, -1), (1, 2)\}$

Think

Use a pencil as a vertical line. Place the pencil parallel to the *y*-axis and slide it across the graph. See if the pencil intersects more than one point at any time.

The domain value -4 corresponds to two range values, 2 and -1.

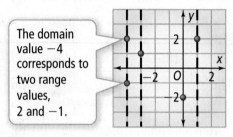

The relation is not a function.

B $y = -x^2 + 3$

There is no vertical line that passes through more than one point of the graph.

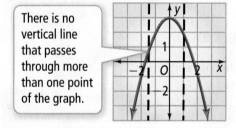

The relation is a function.

 Got It? **2.** Is the relation a function? Use the vertical line test.

     a. $\{(4, 2), (1, 2), (0, 1), (-2, 2), (3, 3)\}$ **b.** $\{(0, 2), (1 -1), (-1, 4), (0, -3), (2, 1)\}$

You have seen functions represented as equations involving *x* and *y*, such as $y = -3x + 1$. Below is the same equation written using **function notation.**

$$f(x) = -3x + 1$$

Notice that $f(x)$ replaces *y*. It is read "*f* of *x*." The letter *f* is the name of the function, not a variable. Function notation is used to emphasize that the function value $f(x)$ depends on the independent variable *x*. Other letters besides *f* can also be used, such as *g* and *h*.

Think

How is this function like ones you've seen before?

The function $w(x) = 250x$ can be written as $y = 250x$. Remember that $w(x)$ does not mean w times x.

 Problem 3 Evaluating a Function

Reading The function $w(x) = 250x$ represents the number of words $w(x)$ you can read in x minutes. How many words can you read in 8 min?

Write the original function.	$w(x) = 250x$
Substitute 8 for x.	$w(8) = 250(8)$
Simplify.	$w(8) = 2000$

You can read 2000 words in 8 min.

✔ **Got It?** **3.** Use the function in Problem 3. How many words can you read in 6 min?

Focus Question How can you determine whether a relation is a function?

Answer In a function, you can pair each value in the domain with exactly one value in the range. Use a mapping or a vertical line test to tell whether a relation is a function.

Lesson Check

Do you know HOW?

1. Identify the domain and range of the relation $\{(-2, 3), (-1, 4), (0, 5), (1, 6)\}$. Represent the relation with a mapping diagram. Is the relation a function?

2. Is the relation in the graph shown below a function? Use the vertical line test.

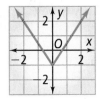

3. What is $f(2)$ for the function $f(x) = 4x + 1$?

Do you UNDERSTAND?

4. **Vocabulary** Write $y = 2x + 7$ using function notation.

5. **Compare and Contrast** You can use a mapping diagram or the vertical line test to tell if a relation is a function. Which method do you prefer? Explain.

6. **Error Analysis** A student drew the dashed line on the graph shown and concluded that the graph represented a function. Is the student correct? Explain.

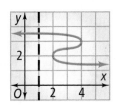

Practice and Problem-Solving Exercises

A **Practice**

Identify the domain and range of each relation. Use a mapping diagram to determine whether the relation is a function.

◆ **See Problem 1.**

Guided Practice

To start, identify the domain and range.

7. $\{(3, 7), (3, 8), (3, -2), (3, 4), (3, 1)\}$

The domain is $\{3\}$.

The range is $\{-2, 1, 4, 7, 8\}$.

8. $\{(6, -7), (5, -8), (1, 4), (7, 5)\}$

9. $\{(4, 2), (1, 1), (0, 0), (1, -1), (4, -2)\}$

Use the vertical line test to determine whether the relation is a function.

◆ **See Problem 2.**

10.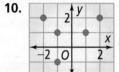

11.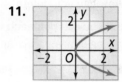

12.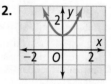

13. Physics Light travels about 186,000 mi/s. The function $d(t) = 186{,}000t$ gives the distance $d(t)$, in miles, that light travels in t seconds. How far does light travel in 30 s?

◆ **See Problem 3.**

Guided Practice

To start, write the given function. $d(t) = 186{,}000t$

Substitute 30 for t. $d(30) = 186{,}000(30)$

14. Shopping You are buying orange juice for $4.50 per container and have a gift card worth $7. The function $f(x) = 4.50x - 7$ represents your total cost $f(x)$ if you buy x containers of orange juice and use the gift card. How much do you pay to buy 4 containers of orange juice?

B **Apply**

Determine whether the relation represented by each table is a function. If the relation is a function, state the domain and range.

15.

x	0	3	3	5
y	2	1	-1	3

16.

x	-4	-1	0	3
y	-4	-4	-4	-4

Hint Do any of the x-values correspond to more than one y-value?

17. Open-Ended Make a table that represents a relation that is not a function. Explain why the relation is not a function.

18. Reasoning If $f(x) = 6x - 4$ and $f(a) = 26$, what is the value of a? Explain.

19. Open-Ended What value of x make the relation $\{(1, 5), (x, 8), (-7, 9)\}$ a function?

20. Reasoning Can the graph of a function be a horizontal line? A vertical line? Explain why or why not.

Objectives To determine whether a relation is a function
To find domain and range and use function notation

In Part 1 of the lesson, you learned how to find the domain and range of a relation and tell if it is a function.

Connect to What You Know

Here, you will learn how to find the range of a function given the domain.

Focus Question How do you find the range of a function given the domain?

Problem 4 Finding the Range of a Function

Multiple Choice The domain of $f(x) = -1.5x + 4$ is $\{1, 2, 3, 4\}$. What is the range?

(A) $\{-2, -0.5, 1, 2.5\}$

(C) $\{-2.5, -1, -0.5, 2\}$

(B) $\{-2.5, -1, 0.5, 2\}$

(D) $\{-2.5, -0.5, 1, 2\}$

Step 1 Make a table. List the domain values as the x-values.

x	$-1.5x + 4$	$f(x)$
1	$-1.5(1) + 4$	2.5
2	$-1.5(2) + 4$	1
3	$-1.5(3) + 4$	-0.5
4	$-1.5(4) + 4$	-2

Step 2 Evaluate $f(x)$ for each domain value. The values of $f(x)$ form the range.

The range is $\{-2, -0.5, 1, 2.5\}$. The correct answer is A.

Got It? **4.** The domain of $g(x) = 4x - 12$ is $\{1, 3, 5, 7\}$. What is the range?

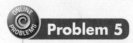 **Problem 5** Identifying a Reasonable Domain and Range

Painting You have 3 qt of paint to paint the trim in your house. A quart of paint covers 100 ft^2. The function $A(q) = 100q$ represents the area $A(q)$, in square feet, that q quarts of paint cover. What domain and range are reasonable for the function? What is the graph of the function?

Know	Need	Plan
• One quart of paint covers 100 ft^2. • You have 3 qt of paint.	Reasonable domain and range values in order to graph the function	Find the least and greatest amounts of paint you can use and areas of trim you can cover. Use these values to make a graph.

The least amount of paint you can use is none. So the least domain value is 0. You have only 3 qt of paint, so the most paint you can use is 3 qt. The greatest domain value is 3. The domain is $0 \le q \le 3$.

To find the range, evaluate the function using the least and greatest domain values.

$$A(0) = 100(0) = 0 \qquad A(3) = 100(3) = 300$$

The range is $0 \le A(q) \le 300$.

To graph the function, make a table of values. Choose values of q that are in the domain. The graph is a line segment that extends from (0, 0) to (3, 300).

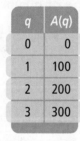

q	A(q)
0	0
1	100
2	200
3	300

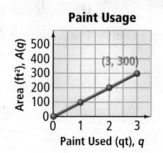

Paint Usage

 Got It? **5. a.** If you have 7 qt of paint, what domain and range are reasonable for Problem 5?

b. Reasoning Why does it *not* make sense to have domain values less than 0 or greater than 3 in Problem 5?

Focus Question How do you find the range of a function given certain domain values?

Answer You evaluate $f(x)$ for each domain value to find the range values.

Lesson Check

Do you know HOW?

1. The domain of $f(x) = \frac{1}{2}x$ is $\{-4, -2, 0, 2, 4\}$. What is the range?

Do you UNDERSTAND?

2. **Writing** Write a real-world problem that includes a function. What are a reasonable domain and range of the function?

Practice and Problem-Solving Exercises

 Practice

Find the range of each function for the given domain.

See Problem 4.

Guided Practice

To start, make a table. List the domain values as the x-values.

3. $f(x) = 2x - 7; \{-2, -1, 0, 1, 2\}$

x	2x − 7	f(x)
−2	2(−2) − 7	−11
−1	2(−1) − 7	−9
0	2(0) − 7	−7
1	2(1) − 7	−5
2	2(2) − 7	−3

4. $g(x) = -4x + 1; \{-5, -1, 0, 2, 10\}$

5. $h(x) = x^2; \{-1.2, 0, 0.2, 1.2, 4\}$

Find a reasonable domain and range for each function. Then graph the function.

See Problem 5.

6. **Fuel** A car can travel 32 mi for each gallon of gasoline. The function $d(x) = 32x$ represents the distance $d(x)$, in miles, that the car can travel with x gallons of gasoline. The car's fuel tank holds 17 gal.

Guided Practice

To start, write what you know.
The least amount of gasoline you can use is none. So, the least domain value is 0.

The fuel tank can only hold 17 gal of gasoline, so the most gasoline you can use is 17 gal. The greatest domain value is 17.

7. **Nutrition** There are 98 International Units (IUs) of vitamin D in 1 cup of milk. The function $V(c) = 98c$ represents the amount $V(c)$ of vitamin D, in IUs, you get from c cups of milk. You have a 16-cup jug of milk.

 Apply

8. **Think About a Plan** In a factory, a certain machine needs 10 min to warm up. It takes 15 min for the machine to run a cycle. The machine can operate for as long as 6 h per day including warm-up time. Draw a graph showing the total time the machine operates during 1 day as a function of the number of cycles it runs.
   • What domain and range are reasonable?
   • Is the function a linear function?

9. **Carwash** A theater group is having a carwash fundraiser. The group can only spend $34 on soap, which is enough to wash 40 cars. Each car is charged $5.
   a. If c is the total number of cars washed and p is the profit, which is the independent variable and which is the dependent variable?
   b. Is the relationship between c and p a function? Explain.
   c. Write an equation that shows this relationship.
   d. Find a reasonable domain and range for the situation.

Standardized Test Prep

GRIDDED RESPONSE

SAT/ACT

10. What is the value of the function $f(x) = 7x$ when $x = 0.75$?

11. Andrew needs x dollars for a snack. Scott needs 2 more dollars than Andrew, but Nick only needs half as many dollars as Andrew. Altogether they need $17 to pay for their snacks. How many dollars does Nick need?

12. What is the greatest number of $.43 stamps you can buy for $5?

13. What is the greatest possible width of the rectangle, to the nearest inch?

$\ell = 35$ in.

$A < 184$ in.^{2}

Mixed Review

Write a function rule to represent each situation.

See Lesson 4-5.

14. You baby-sit for $5 per hour and get a $7 tip. Your earnings E are a function of the number of hours h you work.

15. You buy several pairs of socks for $4.50 per pair, plus a shirt for $10. The total amount a you spend is a function of the number of pairs of socks s you buy.

16. The graph shows a family's distance from home as they drive to the mountains for a vacation.
    a. What are the variables in the graph?
    b. Copy the graph. Describe how the variables are related at various points in the graph.

See Lesson 4-1.

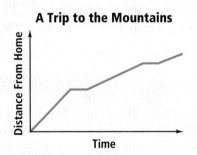

A Trip to the Mountains

Distance From Home

Time

Get Ready! To prepare for Lesson 4-7, do Exercises 17–19.

Evaluate each expression for $x = 1, 2, 3,$ and 4.

See Lesson 1-2.

17. $9 + 3(x - 1)$

18. $8 + 7(x - 1)$

19. $0.4 - 3(x - 1)$

4-7

Sequences and Functions

Objectives To identify and extend patterns in sequences
To represent arithmetic sequences using function notation

Identify the pattern so you can extend it.

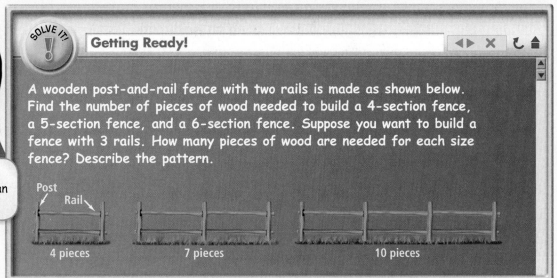

Getting Ready!

A wooden post-and-rail fence with two rails is made as shown below. Find the number of pieces of wood needed to build a 4-section fence, a 5-section fence, and a 6-section fence. Suppose you want to build a fence with 3 rails. How many pieces of wood are needed for each size fence? Describe the pattern.

Post
Rail

4 pieces   7 pieces   10 pieces

Lesson Vocabulary

• sequence
• term of a sequence
• arithmetic sequence
• common difference

In the Solve It, the numbers of pieces of wood used for 1 section of fence, 2 sections of fence, and so on, form a pattern, or a sequence. A **sequence** is an ordered list of numbers that often form a pattern. Each number in the list is called a **term of a sequence.**

Focus Question How can you use function notation to represent the patterns in arithmetic sequences?

Problem 1 Extending Sequences

Describe the pattern in each sequence. What are the next two terms of each sequence?

Plan

How can you identify a pattern?
Look at how each term of the sequence is related to the previous term. Your goal is to identify a single rule that you can apply to every term to produce the next term.

A 5,   8,   11,   14, . . .
      +3   +3   +3

A pattern is "add 3 to the previous term." So the next two terms are 14 + 3 = 17 and 17 + 3 = 20.

B 2.5,   5,   10,   20, . . .
          ×2   ×2   ×2

A pattern is "multiply the previous term by 2." So the next two terms are 2(20) = 40 and 2(40) = 80.

Got It? 1. Describe a pattern in each sequence. What are the next two terms of each sequence?

    a. 5, 11, 17, 23, . . .   **b.** 400, 200, 100, 50, . . .

    c. 2, −4, 8, −16, . . .   **d.** −15, −11, −7, −3, . . .

In an **arithmetic sequence,** the difference between consecutive terms is constant. This difference is called the **common difference.**

 Problem 2   **Identifying an Arithmetic Sequence**

Plan

How can you identify an arithmetic sequence?
The difference between every pair of consecutive terms must be the same.

Tell whether the sequence is arithmetic. If it is, what is the common difference?

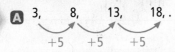

Ⓐ   3,   8,   13,   18, . . .
        +5   +5   +5

Ⓑ   6,   9,   13,   17, . . .
        +3   +4   +4

The sequence has a common difference of 5, so it is arithmetic.

The sequence does not have a common difference, so it is not arithmetic.

 Got It? 2. Tell whether the sequence is arithmetic. If it is, what is the common difference?

    a. 8, 15, 22, 30, . . .   **b.** 7, 9, 11, 13, . . .

    c. 10, 4, −2, −8, . . .   **d.** 2, −2, 2, −2, . . .

A sequence is a function that relates the term number to the value of the term. Consider the sequence 7, 11, 15, 19, . . . Think of each term as the output of a function. Think of the term number as the input.

term number	1	2	3	4	← input
term	7	11	15	19	← output

You can use the common difference of the terms of an arithmetic sequence to write a function rule for the sequence. For the sequence 7, 11, 15, 19, . . . , the common difference is 4.

    Let n = the term number in the sequence.

    Let $A(n)$ = the value of the nth term of the sequence.

      value of term 1 = $A(1) = 7$ The common difference is 4.

      value of term 2 = $A(2) = 7 + 4$

      value of term 3 = $A(3) = 7 + 4 + 4$ The number of 4's added is *1 less than* the term number.

      value of term 4 = $A(4) = 7 + 4 + 4 + 4$

      value of term n = $A(n) = 7 + 4 + 4 + \ldots + 4 = 7 + (n - 1)4$

The function rule for the sequence above is $A(n) = 7 + (n - 1)4$.
You can find the tenth term by finding $A(10)$. So the tenth term is
$A(10) = 7 + (10 - 1)4 = 7 + 36 = 43$.

You can find any term of an arithmetic sequence if you know the first term and the common difference.

Key Concept Rule For an Arithmetic Sequence

The nth term of an arithmetic sequence with first term $A(1)$ and common difference d is given by

$$A(n) = A(1) + (n - 1)d$$

nth term   first term   term number   common difference

Problem 3 Writing a Rule for an Arithmetic Sequence

Online Auction An online auction works as shown below. Write a rule to represent the bids as an arithmetic sequence. What is the twelfth bid?

Bass Guitar   **Minimum Price: $200**

Bid 1: $200
Bid 2: $210
Bid 3: $220
Bid 4: $230

First Bid: The seller sets a minimum price, which must be met by the first bid.

Following Bids: Bids increase in regular increments.

Make a table of the bids. Identify the first term and common difference.

Term Number, n	1	2	3	4
Value of Term, $A(n)$	200	210	220	230

The first term $A(1)$ is 200.

+10   +10   +10

The common difference d is 10.

Plan

What information do you need to write a rule for an arithmetic sequence?
You need the first term of the sequence and the common difference.

Substitute $A(1) = 200$ and $d = 10$ into the formula $A(n) = A(1) + (n - 1)d$. The rule $A(n) = 200 + (n - 1)10$ represents the sequence of the auction bids. To find the twelfth bid, evaluate $A(n)$ for $n = 12$.

$$A(12) = 200 + (12 - 1)10 = 310$$

The twelfth bid is $310.

Got It? 3. a. A subway pass has a starting value of $100. After one ride, the value of the pass is $98.25. After two rides, its value is $96.50. After three rides, its value is $94.75. Write a rule to represent the remaining value on the card as an arithmetic sequence. What is the value of the pass after 15 rides?

 b. Reasoning How many rides can be taken with the $100 pass?

Focus Question How can you use function notation to represent the patterns in arithmetic sequences?

Answer When you can identify a pattern in a sequence, you can use it to extend the sequence. For some sequences, you can write a function rule to find any term of the sequence.

Lesson Check

Do you know HOW?

Describe a pattern in each sequence. Then find the next two terms of the sequence.

1. 3, 11, 19, 27, . . .

2. 3, −6, 12, −24, . . .

Tell whether the sequence is arithmetic. If it is, identify the common difference.

3. 1, −7, −14, −21, . . .

4. 11, 20, 29, 38, . . .

5. Write a rule for an arithmetic sequence with a first term of 9 and a common difference of −2. What is the seventh term of the sequence?

Do you UNDERSTAND?

6. Vocabulary Consider the following arithmetic sequence: 25, 19, 13, 7, . . . Is the common difference 6 or −6? Explain.

7. Error Analysis Describe and correct the error below in finding the tenth term of the arithmetic sequence 4, 12, 20, 28, . . .

> first term = 4
> common difference = 8
> tenth term = 4 + 10(8) = 84

8. Reasoning Can you use the rule below to find the nth term of an arithmetic sequence with a first term $A(1)$ and a common difference d? Explain.

$$A(n) = A(1) + nd - d$$

Practice and Problem-Solving Exercises

A Practice Describe a pattern in each sequence. Then find the next two terms of the sequence.

◀ See Problem 1.

9. 6, 13, 20, 27, . . .

Guided Practice To start, find how each term is related to the previous term.

10. 8, 4, 2, 1, . . .

11. 2, 6, 10, 14, . . .

12. 10, 4, −2, −8, . . .

13. 13, 11, 9, 7, . . .

14. 2, 20, 200, 2000, . . .

15. 1.1, 2.2, 3.3, 4.4, . . .

16. 99, 88, 77, 66, . . .

17. 4.5, 9, 18, 36, . . .

Hint Determine how each term in the sequence relates to the term before it. Start by checking the operations +, −, ×, ÷.

Tell whether the sequence is arithmetic. If it is, identify the common difference. See Problem 2.

18. $-7, -3, 1, 5, \ldots$

19. $-9, -17, -26, -33, \ldots$

20. $19, 8, -3, -14, \ldots$

21. $2, 11, 21, 32, \ldots$

22. $\frac{1}{2}, \frac{1}{3}, \frac{1}{6}, 0, \ldots$

23. $0.2, 1.5, 2.8, 4.1, \ldots$

24. $10, 8, 6, 4, \ldots$

25. $10, 24, 36, 52, \ldots$

26. $3, 6, 12, 24, \ldots$

27. $15, 14.5, 14, 13.5, 13, \ldots$

28. $4, 4.4, 4.44, 4.444, \ldots$

29. $-3, -7, -10, -14, \ldots$

Guided Practice

30. **Garage** After one customer buys 4 new tires, a garage recycling bin has 20 tires in it. After another customer buys 4 new tires, the bin has 24 tires in it. Write a rule to represent the number of tires in the bin as an arithmetic sequence. How many tires are in the bin after 9 customers each buy 4 new tires? See Problem 3.

To start, identify the first term and the common difference. The recycling bin has 20 tires in it, so the first term is 20.

When a customer buys 4 new tires, 4 old tires are added to the bin, so the common difference is 4.

31. **Cafeteria** You have a cafeteria card worth $50. After you buy lunch on Monday, its value is $46.75. After you buy lunch on Tuesday, its value is $43.50. Write a rule to represent the value of the card as an arithmetic sequence. What is the value of the card after you buy 12 lunches?

Find the second, fourth, and eleventh terms of the sequence described by each rule.

32. $A(n) = 5 + (n - 1)(-3)$

33. $A(n) = -3 + (n - 1)(5)$

34. $A(n) = -11 + (n - 1)(2)$

35. $A(n) = 9 + (n - 1)(8)$

36. $A(n) = 0.5 + (n - 1)(3.5)$

37. $A(n) = -7 + (n - 1)(5)$

38. $A(n) = 1 + (n - 1)(-6)$

39. $A(n) = -2.1 + (n - 1)(-1.1)$

 Apply

Tell whether each sequence is arithmetic. Justify your answer. If the sequence is arithmetic, write a function rule to represent it.

40. $0.3, 0.9, 1.5, 2.1, \ldots$

41. $-3, -7, -11, -15, \ldots$

42. $1, 8, 27, 64, \ldots$

43. $-5, 5, -5, 5, \ldots$

44. $46, 31, 16, 2, \ldots$

45. $0.2, -0.6, -1.4, -2.2, \ldots$

46. **Reasoning** An arithmetic sequence has a common difference of zero. The thirty-eighth term of the sequence is 2.1. What is the eighty-fifth term of the sequence? Explain.

47. **Open-Ended** Write a function rule for a sequence that has 25 as the sixth term.

Write the first six terms in each sequence. Explain what the sixth term means in the context of the situation.

48. A cane of bamboo is 30 in. tall the first week and grows 6 in. per week thereafter.

49. You borrow $350 from a friend the first week and pay the friend back $25 each week thereafter.

50. Think About a Plan Suppose the first Friday of a new year is the fourth day of that year. Will the year have 53 Fridays regardless of whether or not it is a leap year?
- What is a rule that represents the sequence of the days in the year that are Fridays?
- How many full weeks are in a 365-day year?

51. Look For a Pattern The first five rows of Pascal's Triangle are shown below.

```
          1
        1   1
      1   2   1
    1   3   3   1
  1   4   6   4   1
```

> **Hint** Determine how the numbers in each row are generated from the numbers in the previous row.

    a. Predict the numbers in the seventh row.
    b. Find the sum of the numbers in each of the first five rows. Predict the sum of the numbers in the seventh row.

52. Transportation Buses run every 9 min starting at 6:00 A.M. You get to the bus stop at 7:16 A.M. How long will you wait for a bus?

53. Multiple Representations Use the table at the right that shows an arithmetic sequence.
    a. Copy and complete the table.
    b. Graph the ordered pairs (x, y) on a coordinate plane.
    c. What do you notice about the points on your graph?

x	y
1	5
2	8
3	■
4	■

54. Number Theory The Fibonacci sequence is 1, 1, 2, 3, 5, 8, 13, . . . After the first two numbers, each number is the sum of the two previous numbers.
    a. What is the next term of the sequence? The eleventh term of the sequence?
    b. Open-Ended Choose two other numbers to start a Fibonacci-like sequence. Write the first seven terms of your sequence.

Standardized Test Prep

SAT/ACT

55. What is the seventh term of the arithmetic sequence represented by the rule
$A(n) = -9 + (n-1)(0.5)$?

Ⓐ -7 Ⓑ -6.5 Ⓒ -6 Ⓓ -5.5

56. What is the solution of $-24 + s > 38$?

Ⓕ $s < 14$ Ⓖ $s > 14$ Ⓗ $s < 62$ Ⓘ $s > 62$

Short
Response

57. Marta's starting annual salary is $26,500. At the beginning of each new year, she receives a $2880 raise. Write a function rule to find Marta's salary $f(n)$ after n years. What will Marta's salary be after 6 yr?

Mixed Review

Find the range of each function for the domain $\{-3, -1.2, 0, 1, 10\}$.

See Lesson 4-6.

58. $f(x) = -4x$

59. $g(x) = 1 - 4x$

60. $h(x) = 3x^2$

61. $g(x) = 11 - 1.5x^2$

62. $h(x) = 9x + 8$

63. $f(x) = \frac{3}{4}x - 5$

Get Ready! To prepare for Lesson 5-1, do Exercises 64–66.

See Lesson 2-6.

64. A pool fills at a rate of 8 gal/min. What is this rate in gallons per hour?

65. A ball is thrown at a speed of 90 mi/h. What is this speed in feet per second?

66. You buy bottled water in 12-packs that cost $3 each. If you drink 3 bottles per day, what is your cost per week?

Pull It All Together

To solve these problems, you will pull together many concepts and skills that you have studied about functions.

BIG idea Functions

A function is a relationship that pairs one input value with exactly one output value. You can use words, tables, equations, sets of ordered pairs, and graphs to represent functions.

Task 1

Solve. Show your work and explain your steps.

You are riding your bike at a constant speed of 30 ft/s. A friend uses a stopwatch to time you as you ride along a city block that is 264 ft long.

   a. Make a graph to represent the situation, where the independent variable is time and the dependent variable is distance traveled.
   b. Make a second graph to represent the situation, where the independent variable is time and the dependent variable is speed.
   c. Do both graphs represent functions? If so, are they linear or nonlinear? Explain.
   d. Find a reasonable domain and range for each graph.
   e. Write a function rule for each graph.

Task 2

Solve. Show your work and explain your steps.

A shop manager is ordering shopping bags. The price per bag is determined by how many bags the manager buys. The graph at the right shows the price per bag based on the number of bags that are bought.

   a. Does the graph represent a function? If so, is it *linear* or *nonlinear*? Explain.
   b. Find a reasonable domain and range for the graph.
   c. How much would it cost to buy 1500 bags?

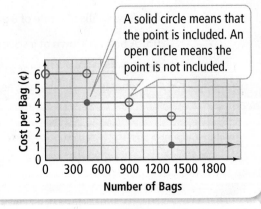

A solid circle means that the point is included. An open circle means the point is not included.

BIG idea Modeling

You can use functions to model real-world situations that pair one input value with a unique output value.

Task 3

Solve. Show your work and explain your steps.

You are making a knotted necklace. The table at the right shows the amount of string you need for different necklace lengths.

   a. Identify the independent and dependent variables.
   b. Write and graph a function rule that represents the situation.
   c. Is the graph *continuous* or *discrete*? Explain your reasoning.
   d. How much string do you need to make a 15-in. necklace?

Length of Necklace (in.)	Amount of String (in.)
10	200
11	202
12	204
13	206

Chapter Review

Connecting BIG ideas and Answering the Essential Questions

1 Functions

A function is a relationship that pairs one input value with exactly one output value. You can use words, tables, equations, sets of ordered pairs, and graphs to represent functions.

Patterns and Functions (Lessons 4-2 and 4-3)

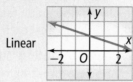

Linear

Nonlinear

Function Notation and Sequences (Lessons 4-6 and 4-7)

n	$A(n) = 3 + (n - 1)\,(2)$	$A(n)$
1	$3 + (1 - 1)\,(2)$	3
2	$3 + (2 - 1)\,(2)$	5
3	$3 + (3 - 1)\,(2)$	7

2 Modeling

You can use functions to model real-world situations that pair one input value with a unique output value.

Using Graphs to Relate Two Quantities (Lesson 4-1)

Bus Trip

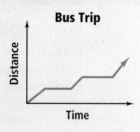

Graphing a Function Rule (Lesson 4-4)

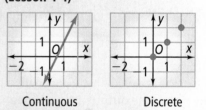

Continuous   Discrete

Writing a Function Rule (Lesson 4-5)

$$C = \frac{1}{4}n + 6 \qquad A = s^2$$

Chapter Vocabulary

- arithmetic sequence, p. 296
- common difference, p. 296
- continuous graph, p. 272
- dependent variable, p. 255
- discrete graph, p. 272
- domain, p. 286

- function, p. 257
- function notation, p. 288
- inputs, p. 255
- independent variable, p. 255
- linear function, p. 257
- nonlinear function, p. 262

- outputs, p. 255
- range, p. 286
- relation, p. 286
- sequence, p. 295
- term of a sequence, p. 295
- vertical line test, p. 288

Choose the correct term to complete each sentence.

1. If the value of a changes in response to the value of b, then b is the ? .

2. The graph of a(n) ? function is a nonvertical line or part of a nonvertical line.

3. A(n) ? graph consists of distinct, isolated points.

4. The ? of a function consists of the set of all output values.

4-1 Using Graphs to Relate Two Quantities

Quick Review

You can use graphs to represent the relationship between two variables.

Example

A dog owner plays fetch with her dog. Sketch a graph to represent the distance between them and the time.

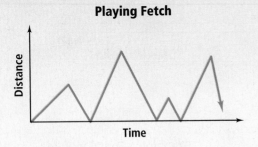

Playing Fetch

Exercises

5. Travel A car's speed increases as it merges onto a highway. The car travels at 65 mi/h on the highway until it slows to exit. The car then stops at three traffic lights before reaching its destination. Draw a sketch of a graph that shows the car's possible speed over time. Label each section.

6. Surfing A professional surfer paddles out past breaking waves, rides a wave, paddles back out past the breaking waves, rides another wave, and paddles back to the beach. Draw a sketch of a graph that shows the surfer's possible distance from the beach over time.

4-2 Patterns and Linear Functions

Quick Review

A **function** is a relationship that pairs each **input** value with exactly one **output** value. A **linear function** is a function whose graph is a line or part of a line.

Example

The number y of eggs left in a dozen depends on the number x of 2-egg omelets you make, as shown in the table. Represent this relationship using words, an equation, and a graph.

Number of Omelets Made, x	0	1	2	3
Number of Eggs Left, y	12	10	8	6

Look for a pattern in the table. Each time x increases by 1, y decreases by 2. The number y of eggs left is 12 minus the quantity 2 times the number x of omelets made: $y = 12 - 2x$.

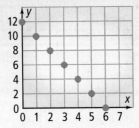

Exercises

For each table, identify the independent and dependent variables. Represent the relationship using words, an equation, and a graph.

7.

Paint in Can

Number of Chairs Painted, p	Paint Left (oz), L
0	128
1	98
2	68
3	38

8.

Game Cost

Number of Snacks Purchased, s	Total Cost, C
0	$18
1	$21
2	$24
3	$27

9.

Elevation

Number of Flights of Stairs Climbed, n	0	1	2	3
Elevation (ft above sea level), E	311	326	341	356

4-3 Patterns and Nonlinear Functions

Quick Review

A **nonlinear function** is a function whose graph is *not* a line or part of a line.

Example

The area A of a square field is a function of the side length s of the field. Is the function *linear* or *nonlinear*?

Side Length (ft), s	10	15	20	25
Area (ft²), A	100	225	400	625

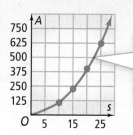

Graph the ordered pairs and connect the points. The graph is not a line, so the function is nonlinear.

Exercises

Graph the function shown by each table. Tell whether the function is *linear* or *nonlinear*.

10.

x	y
1	0
2	1
3	8
4	20

11.

x	y
1	0
2	4.5
3	9
4	13.5

12.

x	y
1	2
2	6
3	12
4	72

13.

x	y
1	−2
2	−9
3	−16
4	−23

4-4 Graphing a Function Rule

Quick Review

A **continuous graph** is a graph that is unbroken. A **discrete graph** is composed of distinct, isolated points. In a real-world graph, show only points that make sense.

Example

The total height h of a stack of cans is a function of the number n of layers of 4.5-in. cans used. This situation is represented by $h = 4.5n$. Graph the function.

n	h
0	0
1	4.5
2	9
3	13.5
4	18

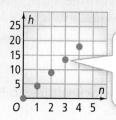

The graph is discrete because only whole numbers of layers make sense.

Exercises

Graph the function rule. Explain why the graph is *continuous* or *discrete*.

14. **Walnuts** Your cost c to buy w pounds of walnuts at $6/lb is represented by $c = 6w$.

15. **Moving** A truck originally held 24 chairs. You remove 2 chairs at a time. The number of chairs n remaining after you make t trips is represented by $n = 24 - 2t$.

16. **Flood** A burst pipe fills a basement with 37 in. of water. A pump empties the water at a rate of 1.5 in./h. The water level ℓ, in inches, after t hours is represented by $\ell = 37 - 1.5t$.

17. Graph $y = -|x| + 2$.

4-5 Writing a Function Rule

Quick Review

To write a function rule describing a real-world situation, it is often helpful to start with a verbal model of the situation.

Example

At a bicycle motocross (BMX) track, you pay $40 for a racing license plus $15 per race. What is a function rule that represents your total cost?

total cost = license fee + fee per race · number of races

$$C = 40 + 15 \cdot r$$

A function rule is $C = 40 + 15 \cdot r$.

Exercises

Write a function rule to represent each situation.

18. **Landscaping** The volume V remaining in a 243-ft^3 pile of gravel decreases by 0.2 ft^3 with each shovelful s of gravel spread in a walkway.

19. **Design** Your total cost C for hiring a garden designer is $200 for an initial consultation plus $45 for each hour h the designer spends drawing plans.

4-6 Formalizing Relations and Functions

Quick Review

A **relation** pairs numbers in the **domain** with numbers in the **range.** A relation may or may not be a function.

Example

Is the relation {(0, 1), (3, 3), (4, 4), (0, 0)} a function?

The x-values of the ordered pairs form the domain, and the y-values form the range. The domain value 0 is paired with two range values, 1 and 0. So the relation is not a function.

Exercises

Tell whether each relation is a function.

20. $\{(-1, 7), (9, 4), (3, -2), (5, 3), (9, 1)\}$

21. $\{(2, 5), (3, 5), (4, -4), (5, -4), (6, 8)\}$

Evaluate each function for $x = 2$ and $x = 7$.

22. $f(x) = 2x - 8$ 23. $h(x) = -4x + 61$

24. The domain of $t(x) = -3.8x - 4.2$ is $\{-3, -1.4, 0, 8\}$. What is the range?

4-7 Sequences and Functions

Quick Review

A **sequence** is an ordered list of numbers, called terms, that often forms a pattern. In an **arithmetic sequence,** there is a **common difference** between consecutive terms.

Example

Tell whether the sequence is arithmetic.

5,   2,   −1,   −4, . . .

−3   −3   −3

The sequence has a common difference of −3, so it is arithmetic.

Exercises

Describe a pattern in each sequence. Then find the next two terms of the difference.

25. 1, 5, 25, 125, . . .   26. −2, −5, −8, −11, . . .

27. 4, 6.5, 9, 11.5, . . .   28. 2, −4, 8, −16, . . .

Tell whether the sequence is arithmetic. If it is, identify the common difference.

29. 2.9, 4.1, 5.3, 6.5, . . .   30. −15, −5, 5, 15, . . .

31. −7, −13, −20, −26, . . .   32. 3, 6, 12, 24, . . .

4 Chapter Test

Do you know HOW?

1. **Recreation** You ride your bike to the park, sit to read for a while, and then ride your bike home. It takes you less time to ride from the park to your house than it took to ride from your house to the park. Draw a sketch of a graph that shows your possible distance traveled over time. Label each section.

2. Identify the independent and dependent variables in the table below. Then describe the relationship using words, an equation, and a graph.

Speed of Sound in Air				
Temperature (°C)	10	15	20	25
Velocity (m/s)	337	340	343	346

Graph the function shown by each table. Tell whether the function is *linear* or *nonlinear*.

3.

x	y
−3	−5
−1	−1
1	3
3	7

4.

x	y
0	1
1	2
2	5
3	10

Make a table of values for each function rule. Then graph the function.

5. $y = 1.5x - 3$

6. $y = -x^2 + 4$

Identify the domain and range of each relation. Use a mapping diagram to determine whether the relation is a function.

7. $\{(-2, 5), (8, 6), (3, 12), (5, 6)\}$

8. $\{(9, 6), (3, 8), (4, 9.5), (9, 2)\}$

9. **Baking** A bottle holds 48 tsp of vanilla. The amount A of vanilla remaining in the bottle decreases by 2 tsp per batch b of cookies. Write a function rule to represent this situation. How much vanilla remains after 12 batches of cookies?

10. **Party Favors** You are buying party favors that cost $2.47 each. You can spend no more than $30 on the party favors. What domain and range are reasonable for this situation?

Find the range of each function for the domain $\{-4, -2, 0, 1.5, 4\}$.

11. $f(x) = -2x - 3$

12. $f(x) = 5x^2 + 4$

Find the second, fourth, and eleventh terms of the sequence described by each rule.

13. $A(n) = 2 + (n - 1)(-2.5)$

14. $A(n) = -9 + (n - 1)(3)$

Tell whether each sequence is arithmetic. Justify your answer. If the sequence is arithmetic, write a function rule to represent it.

15. 128, 64, 32, 16, . . .

16. 3, 3.25, 3.5, 3.75, . . .

Do you UNDERSTAND?

Vocabulary Tell whether each relationship should be represented by a *continuous* or *discrete* graph.

17. the price of turkey that sells for $.89 per pound

18. the profit you make selling flowers at $1.50 each when each flower costs you $.80

19. **Reasoning** Can a function have an infinite number of values in its domain and only a finite number of values in its range? If so, describe a real-world situation that can be modeled by such a function.

20. **Writing** What is the difference between a relation and a function? Is every relation a function? Is every function a relation? Explain.

4 · Cumulative Test Prep

TIPS FOR SUCCESS

Some questions on standardized tests ask you to choose a graph that best represents a real-world situation. Read the question at the right. Then follow the tips to answer it.

Aiko ran at a constant speed for most of a race. Toward the end of the race, she increased her speed until she reached the finish line. Which graph best represents Aiko's distance traveled over time?

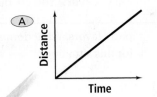

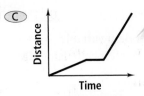

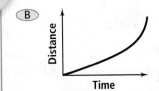

TIP 2

Aiko's speed increases toward the end of the race, so the graph should rise more quickly at the end.

Think It Through

Choice A shows a *constant* speed during the *entire* race.

Choice B shows an *increasing* speed near the race's *end*.

Choice C shows a *complete stop* in the *middle* of the race.

Choice D shows a *decreasing* speed near the race's *end*.

The correct answer is B.

TIP 1

Aiko's speed is constant for most of the race, so the graph should be a straight line most of the time.

Vocabulary Builder

As you solve test items, you must understand the meanings of mathematical terms. Match each term with its mathematical meaning.

A. dependent variable

B. equation

C. numerical expression

D. function

E. domain

I. a math sentence stating two quantities have the same value

II. a relation where each input value corresponds to exactly one output value

III. a math phrase that contains operations and numbers but no variables

IV. a variable whose value changes in response to another variable

V. the possible values for the input of a function or relation

Multiple Choice

Read each question. Then write the letter of the correct answer on your paper.

1. Which values of x and y will make the expression $5(x - y)^2$ equal to 20?

   Ⓐ $x = 0, y = 3$　　Ⓒ $x = 3, y = 5$

   Ⓑ $x = 1, y = 1$　　Ⓓ $x = 5, y = 1$

2. Angie uses the equation $E = 0.03s + 25,000$ to find her yearly earnings E based on her total sales s. What is the independent variable?

   Ⓕ E　　　　　　Ⓗ s

   Ⓖ 0.03　　　　　Ⓘ $25,000$

3. Which expression is equivalent to $6b - 3a + b + 2a$?

   Ⓐ $5b - a$　　　Ⓒ $7b - a$

   Ⓑ $5b - 5a$　　　Ⓓ $7b - 5a$

4. A point is missing from the graph of the relationship at the right. The relation is *not* a function. Which point is missing?

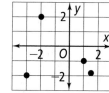

- (F) $(0, 0)$
- (H) $(-1, 2)$
- (G) $(1, 1)$
- (I) $(2, -2)$

5. Lindsey is using a map to find the distance between her house and Juanita's house. On the map, the distance is 2.5 in. If the map scale is $\frac{1}{8}$ in. : 1.5 mi, how far from Juanita does Lindsey live?

- (A) 0.5 mi
- (C) 4.8 mi
- (B) 3.75 mi
- (D) 30 mi

6. Pedro ran 2 more than $\frac{3}{4}$ the number of miles that Cierra ran. Which equation represents the relationship between the number of miles p that Pedro ran and the number of miles c that Cierra ran?

- (F) $c = \frac{3}{4}p + 2$
- (H) $c = \frac{3}{4}p - 2$
- (G) $p = \frac{3}{4}c + 2$
- (I) $p = \frac{3}{4}c - 2$

7. The relationship between degrees Fahrenheit F and degrees Celsius C is given by $C = \frac{5}{9}(F - 32)$. Manuel's pen pal from Europe said that the temperature last week was 25°C. What was the temperature in degrees Fahrenheit?

- (A) $-18°F$
- (C) $77°F$
- (B) $-4°F$
- (D) $102°F$

8. Which graph could represent the circumference of a balloon as the air is being let out?

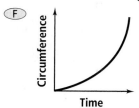
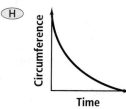
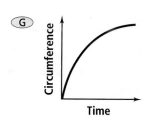
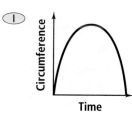

9. Mr. Washington is buying a gallon of milk for $3.99 and some boxes of cereal for $4.39 each. If Mr. Washington has $20, how many boxes of cereal can he buy?

- (A) 3
- (C) 5
- (B) 4
- (D) 6

10. During a clinical study, a medical company found that 3 out of 70 people experienced a side effect when using a certain medicine. The company predicts 63,000 people will use the medicine next year. How many people are expected to experience a side effect?

- (F) 300
- (H) 2700
- (G) 900
- (I) 21,000

11. Which equation can be used to generate the table of values at the right?

- (A) $y = x + 9$
- (B) $y = 2x + 4$
- (C) $y = x + 3$
- (D) $y = 3x - 2$

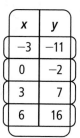

x	y
-3	-11
0	-2
3	7
6	16

12. Which number line displays the solution of the compound inequality $-5 < -2x + 7 < 15$?

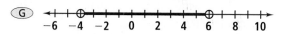
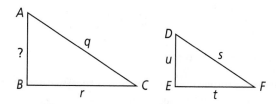

13. In the diagram below, $\triangle ABC$ and $\triangle DEF$ are similar.

Which expression represents AB?

- (A) $\frac{qu}{s}$
- (C) $\frac{qr}{u}$
- (B) $\frac{ru}{s}$
- (D) $\frac{rs}{t}$

14. The sum of two consecutive odd integers is 24. Which equation can be used to find the first integer n?

    F $n + 1 = 24$ **H** $2n + 1 = 24$

    G $n + 2 = 24$ **I** $2n + 2 = 24$

15. The table below shows the relationship between how long an ice cube is in the sun and its weight.

Time (min)	0	1	2	3	4
Weight (g)	9	8	5	2	0

Which graph best represents the data in the table?

A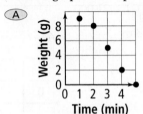

C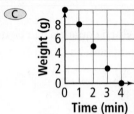

B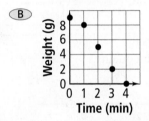

D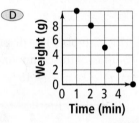

16. Which of the following situations can be represented by a linear function?

    F the height of a person, given the person's age

    G the weight of a bag of pennies, given the number of pennies

    H the length of a day, given the day of the year

    I the test grade, given the hours the student studied

GRIDDED RESPONSE

Record your answers in a grid.

17. Sasha is framing a 5 in.-by-7 in. picture with a frame that is 3 in. wide, as shown at the right. What is the frame's area, in square inches?

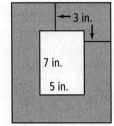

18. The sum of two consecutive integers is −15. What is the product of the two integers?

19. Max writes a number pattern in which each number in the pattern is 1 less than twice the previous number. If the first number is 2, what is the fifth number?

20. The rectangles shown below are similar.

Rectangle A

20 ft

Rectangle B

The area of rectangle A is 180 ft². The area of rectangle B is 45 ft². What is rectangle B's perimeter in feet?

21. One lap of a swimming pool is 50 m from one end of the pool to the other. Tamara swims 25 laps in a swim meet. How many kilometers does she swim?

22. An Internet company charges $8.95 per month for the first 3 months that it hosts your Web site. Then the company charges $11.95 per month for Web hosting. How much money, in dollars, will the company charge for 8 months of Web hosting?

Short Response

23. You are taking a plane trip that begins in Seattle and ends in Boston, with a layover in Dallas. The flight from Seattle to Dallas is 2 h 55 min. The layover in Dallas is 1 h 25 min. The flight from Dallas to Boston is 3 h 40 min. How long in hours is the entire trip?

24. What values of x make both inequalities true?

    $3x < 4x + 6$

    $2x + 1 < 15$

Extended Response

25. A particular washing machine uses an average of 41 gallons of water for every load of laundry.

    a. Identify the independent and dependent variables in this situation.

    b. Write a function rule to represent the situation.

    c. Suppose you used 533 gallons of water for laundry in one month. How many loads of laundry did you wash?

Get Ready!

Lesson 1-9 ◀ **Solutions of a Two-Variable Equation**

Tell whether the given ordered pair is a solution of the equation.

1. $4y + 2x = 3; (1.5, 0)$ **2.** $y = 7x - 5; (0, 5)$ **3.** $y = -2x + 5; (2, 1)$

Lesson 2-5 ◀ **Transforming Equations**

Solve each equation for y.

4. $2y - x = 4$ **5.** $3x = y + 2$ **6.** $-2y - 2x = 4$

Lesson 2-6 ◀ **Comparing Unit Rates**

7. Transportation A car traveled 360 km in 6 h. A train traveled 400 km in 8 h. A boat traveled 375 km in 5 h. Which had the fastest average speed?

8. Plants A birch tree grew 2.5 in. in 5 months. A bean plant grew 8 in. in 10 months. A rose bush grew 5 in. in 8 months. Which grew the fastest?

Lesson 4-4 ◀ **Graphing a Function Rule**

Make a table of values for each function rule. Then graph each function.

9. $f(x) = x + 3$ **10.** $f(x) = -2x$ **11.** $f(x) = x - 4$

Lesson 4-7 ◀ **Arithmetic Sequences**

Write a rule for each arithmetic sequence.

12. $2, 5, 8, 11, \ldots$ **13.** $13, 10, 7, 4, \ldots$ **14.** $-3, -0.5, 2, 4.5, \ldots$

 Looking Ahead Vocabulary

15. A steep hill has a greater *slope* than a flat plain. What does the *slope* of a line on a graph describe?

16. Two streets are *parallel* when they go the same way and do not cross. What does it mean in math to call two lines *parallel*?

17. John was bringing a message to the principal's office when the principal *intercepted* him and took the message. When a graph passes through the y-axis, it has a *y-intercept*. What do you think a y-intercept of a graph represents?

Linear Functions

PowerAlgebra.com

Your place to get
all things digital

ownload videos
onnecting math
 your world.

ath definitions
 English and
panish

he online
olve It will get
ou in gear for
ach lesson.

Interactive!
ary numbers,
raphs, and figures
o explore math
oncepts.

Download
Step-by-Step
Problems with
Instant Replay.

Get and view your
assignments online.

Extra practice and
review online

These performers are arranged in
parallel lines. How do you think they
decided where to stand to make the
lines?

Did you know that there are lots
of ways to describe lines? They're
not just straight or slanted. In this
chapter, you'll learn to use algebra
to describe lines.

Vocabulary for Part A

English/Spanish Vocabulary Audio Online:

English	Spanish
direct variation, *p. 321*	variación directa
linear equation, *p. 329*	ecuación lineal
parent function, *p. 329*	función elemental
point-slope form, *p. 338*	forma punto-pendiente
rate of change, *p. 314*	tasa de cambio
slope, *p. 315*	pendiente
slope-intercept form, *p. 329*	forma pendiente-intercepto
y-intercept, *p. 329*	intercepto en *y*

00:04:04

BIG ideas

1 Proportionality

Essential Question: What does the slope of a line indicate about the line?

2 Functions

Essential Question: What information does the equation of a line give you?

3 Modeling

Essential Question: How can you make predictions based on a scatter plot?

Chapter Preview for Part A

5-1 Rate of Change and Slope

Objectives To find rates of change from tables
To find slope

Before you hit the slopes, better check the steepness of the trail!

The table shows the horizontal and vertical distances from the base of the mountain at several poles along the path of a ski lift. The poles are connected by cable. Between which two poles is the cable's path the steepest? How do you know?

Pole	Horizontal Distance	Vertical Distance
A	20	30
B	40	35
C	60	60
D	100	70

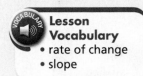

Lesson Vocabulary
• rate of change
• slope

Rate of change shows the relationship between two changing quantities. When one quantity depends on the other, the following is true.

$$\text{rate of change} = \frac{\text{change in the dependent variable}}{\text{change in the independent variable}}$$

Focus Question What is the relationship between rate of change and slope?

Problem 1 Finding Rate of Change Using a Table

Think

Does this problem look like one you've seen before?
Yes. In Lesson 2-6, you wrote rates and unit rates. The rate of change in Problem 1 is an example of a unit rate.

Marching Band The table shows the distance a band marches over time. Is the rate of change in distance with respect to time constant? What does the rate of change represent?

$$\text{rate of change} = \frac{\text{change in distance}}{\text{change in time}}$$

Calculate the rate of change from one row of the table to the next.

$$\frac{520 - 260}{2 - 1} = \frac{260}{1} \qquad \frac{780 - 520}{3 - 2} = \frac{260}{1} \qquad \frac{1040 - 780}{4 - 3} = \frac{260}{1}$$

The rate of change is constant and equals $\frac{260 \text{ ft}}{1 \text{ min}}$. It represents the distance the band marches per minute.

Distance Marched

Time (min)	Distance (ft)
1	260
2	520
3	780
4	1040

 Got It? 1. In Problem 1, do you get the same rate of change if you use nonconsecutive rows of the table? Explain.

The graphs of the ordered pairs (time, distance) in Problem 1 lie on a line, as shown at the right. The relationship between time and distance is linear. When data are linear, the rate of change is constant.

Notice also that the rate of change found in Problem 1 is just the ratio of the vertical change (or *rise*) to the horizontal change (or *run*) between two points on the line. The rate of change is called the *slope* of the line.

Distance Marched

$$\textbf{slope} = \frac{\text{vertical change}}{\text{horizontal change}} = \frac{\text{rise}}{\text{run}}$$

Problem 2 **Finding Slope Using a Graph**

ONLINE PROBLEMS

What is the slope of each line?

Plan

What do you need to find the slope?
You need to find the rise and run. You can use the graph to count units of rise and units of run.

Ⓐ

right 3 units

up 2 units

(1, 1)

(−2, −1)

$$\text{slope} = \frac{\text{rise}}{\text{run}}$$

$$= \frac{2}{3}$$

The slope of the line is $\frac{2}{3}$.

Ⓑ

down 4 units

(−3, 2)

right 5 units

(2, −2)

$$\text{slope} = \frac{\text{rise}}{\text{run}}$$

$$= \frac{-4}{5} = -\frac{4}{5}$$

The slope of the line is $-\frac{4}{5}$.

Got It? **2.** What is the slope of each line in parts (a) and (b)?

a.

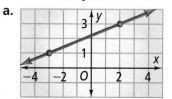

b.

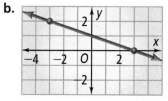

c. Reasoning In part (A) of Problem 2, pick two new points on the line to find the slope. Do you get the same slope?

Notice that the line in part (A) of Problem 2 has a positive slope and slants upward from left to right. The line in part (B) of Problem 2 has a negative slope and slopes downward from left to right.

You can use any two points on a line to find its slope. Use subscripts to distinguish between the two points. In the diagram, (x_1, y_1) are the coordinates of point A, and (x_2, y_2) are the coordinates of point B. To find the slope of $\overleftrightarrow{AB}$, you can use the *slope formula*.

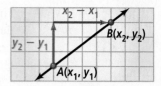

take note

Key Concept   The Slope Formula

$$\text{slope} = \frac{\text{rise}}{\text{run}} = \frac{y_2 - y_1}{x_2 - x_1}, \text{ where } x_2 - x_1 \neq 0$$

The x-coordinate you use first in the denominator must belong to the same ordered pair as the y-coordinate you use first in the numerator.

Problem 3   Finding Slope Using Points

GRIDDED RESPONSE

What is the slope of the line through $(-1, 0)$ and $(3, -2)$?

Plan

Does it matter which point is (x_1, y_1) and which is (x_2, y_2)?
No. You can pick either point for (x_1, y_1) in the slope formula. The other point is then (x_2, y_2).

Think

You need the slope, so start with the slope formula.

Substitute $(-1, 0)$ for (x_1, y_1) and $(3, -2)$ for (x_2, y_2).

Simplify to find the answer to place on the grid.

Write

$$\text{slope} = \frac{y_2 - y_1}{x_2 - x_1}$$

$$= \frac{-2 - 0}{3 - (-1)}$$

$$= \frac{-2}{4} = -\frac{1}{2}$$

 Got It?   3. What is the slope of the line through $(1, 3)$ and $(4, -1)$?

Problem 4   Finding Slopes of Horizontal and Vertical Lines

What is the slope of each line?

Think

Can you generalize these results?
Yes. All points on a horizontal line have the same y-value, so the slope is always zero. Finding the slope of a vertical line always leads to division by zero. The slope is always undefined.

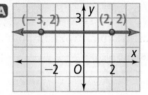
A

Let $(x_1, y_1) = (-3, 2)$ and $(x_2, y_2) = (2, 2)$.

$$\text{slope} = \frac{y_2 - y_1}{x_2 - x_1} = \frac{2 - 2}{2 - (-3)} = \frac{0}{5} = 0$$

The slope of the horizontal line is 0.

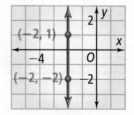
B

Let $(x_1, y_1) = (-2, -2)$ and $(x_2, y_2) = (-2, 1)$.

$$\text{slope} = \frac{y_2 - y_1}{x_2 - x_1} = \frac{1 - (-2)}{-2 - (-2)} = \frac{3}{0}$$

Division by zero is undefined. The slope of the vertical line is undefined.

Got It? 4. What is the slope of the line through the given points?

        a. $(4, -3), (4, 2)$ **b.** $(-1, -3), (5, -3)$

The following summarizes what you have learned about slope.

take note

Concept Summary   Slopes of Lines

A line with positive slope slants upward from left to right.		A line with negative slope slants downward from left to right.	
A line with a slope of 0 is horizontal.		A line with an undefined slope is vertical.	

Focus Question What is the relationship between rate of change and slope?

Answer They have the same value. Rate of change is the ratio of change in the dependent variable to the change in the independent variable. The slope is the ratio of the vertical change (or rise) to the horizontal change (or run). The dependent variable is on the vertical axis and the independent variable is on the horizontal axis.

 ## Lesson Check

Do you know HOW?

1. Is the rate of change in cost constant with respect to the number of pencils bought? Explain.

Cost of Pencils				
Number of Pencils	1	4	7	12
Cost ($)	0.25	1	1.75	3

2. What is the slope of the line through $(-1, 2)$ and $(2, -3)$?

Do you UNDERSTAND?

3. **Vocabulary** What characteristic of a graph represents the rate of change? Explain.

4. **Open-Ended** Give an example of a real-world situation that you can model with a horizontal line. What is the rate of change for the situation? Explain.

5. **Compare and Contrast** How does finding a line's slope by counting units of vertical and horizontal change on a graph compare with finding it using the slope formula?

Practice and Problem-Solving Exercises

A Practice

Determine whether each rate of change is constant. If it is, find the rate of change and explain what it represents.

See Problem 1.

6. **Turtle Walking**

Time (min)	Distance (m)
1	6
2	12
3	15
4	21

7. **Airplane Descent**

Time (min)	Elevation (ft)
0	30,000
2	29,000
5	27,500
12	24,000

Find the slope of each line.

See Problem 2.

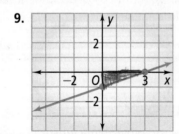

Guided Practice

To start, find the rise and run. Start at point (0, 2).

8.

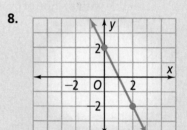

rise = −2, run = 1

9.

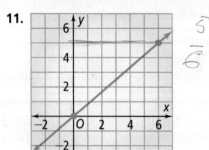

10.

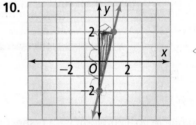

11.

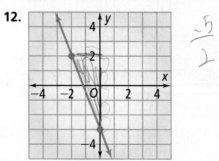

12.

Find the slope of the line that passes through each pair of points.

See Problem 3.

Guided Practice

To start, substitute (1, 3) for (x_1, y_1) and (5, 5) for (x_2, y_2) in the slope formula.

13. $(1, 3), (5, 5)$

$$\text{slope} = \frac{y_2 - y_1}{x_2 - x_1} = \frac{5 - 3}{5 - 1}$$

14. $(0, 0), (3, 3)$ **15.** $(4, -5), (2, 7)$ **16.** $(4, 4), (5, 3)$

17. $(0, -1), (2, 3)$ **18.** $(-6, 1), (4, 8)$ **19.** $(2, -3), (5, -4)$

Find the slope of each line.

See Problem 4.

20.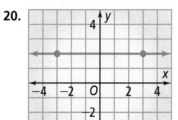

21.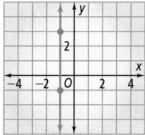

B Apply

Without graphing, tell whether the slope of a line that models each linear relationship is *positive*, *negative*, *zero*, or *undefined*. Then find the slope.

22. The length of a bus route is 4 mi long on the sixth day and 4 mi long on the seventeenth day.

23. A baby-sitter earns $9 for 1 h and $36 for 4 h.

24. A student earns a 98 on a test for answering one question incorrectly and earns a 90 for answering five questions incorrectly.

25. The total cost, including shipping, for ordering five uniforms is $66. The total cost, including shipping, for ordering nine uniforms is $114.

State the independent variable and the dependent variable in each linear relationship. Then find the rate of change for each situation.

26. Snow is 0.02 m deep after 1 h and 0.06 m deep after 3 h.

27. The cost of tickets is $36 for three people and $84 for seven people.

28. A car is 200 km from its destination after 1 h and 80 km from its destination after 3 h.

Find the slope of the line that passes through each pair of points.

29. $(-2, 1), (7, 1)$ **30.** $(4.25, 0), (3.5, 3)$

31. $\left(-\frac{1}{2}, \frac{4}{7}\right), \left(8, \frac{4}{7}\right)$ **32.** $(-42.25, 5.2), (3.25, 3)$

33. Reasoning Is it true that a line with slope 1 always passes through the origin? Explain your reasoning.

34. Think About a Plan The graph shows the average growth rates for three different animals. Which animal's growth shows the fastest rate of change? The slowest rate of change?
  • How can you use the graph to find the rates of change?
  • Are your answers reasonable?

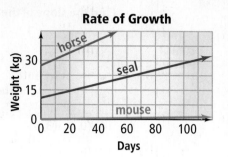

Rate of Growth

35. Open-Ended Find two points that lie on a line with slope −9.

36. Profit John's business made $4500 in January and $8600 in March. What is the rate of change in his profit for this time period?

Each pair of points lies on a line with the given slope. Find x or y.

37. $(2, 4)$, $(x, 8)$; slope $= -2$

38. $(4, 3)$, $(x, 7)$; slope $= 2$

39. $(2, 4)$, $(x, 8)$; slope $= -\frac{1}{2}$

40. $(3, 5)$, $(x, 2)$; undefined slope

Standardized Test Prep

SAT/ACT

41. A line has slope $\frac{4}{3}$. Through which two points could this line pass?

  Ⓐ $(24, 19)$, $(8, 10)$ Ⓑ $(10, 8)$, $(16, 0)$ Ⓒ $(28, 10)$, $(22, 2)$ Ⓓ $(4, 20)$, $(0, 17)$

42. Let the domain of the function $f(x) = \frac{1}{5}x - 12$ be $\{-5, 0, 10\}$. What is the range?

  Ⓕ $\{-5, 0, 10\}$ Ⓖ $\{0, 12, 13\}$ Ⓗ $\{-13, -12, -11\}$ Ⓘ $\{-13, -12, -10\}$

Extended Response

43. The perimeter of the rectangle at the right is less than 30 in. and less than 20 in.
  a. What is an inequality that represents the situation?
  b. What is a graph that shows all the possible values of x?
  c. What is a graph that shows all the possible perimeters of the triangle?

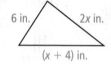

6 in.

$(x + 2)$ in.

6 in.   2x in.

$(x + 4)$ in.

Mixed Review

Find the second, fourth, and tenth terms of each sequence.   See Lesson 4-7.

44. $A(n) = 3 + (n - 1)(2)$ **45.** $A(n) = -5 + (n - 1)(6)$ **46.** $A(n) = 12 + (n - 1)(3)$

Find each union or intersection. Let $A = \{1, 2, 3, 4\}$, $B = \{2, 4, 6, 8, 10\}$, and $C = \{3, 5, 7, 8\}$.   See Lesson 3-8.

47. $A \cap B$ **48.** $A \cap C$ **49.** $B \cap C$ **50.** $B \cup C$ **51.** $A \cup C$

Get Ready!   **To prepare for Lesson 5-2, do Exercises 52–56.**

Solve each proportion.   See Lesson 2-7.

52. $\frac{5}{8} = \frac{x}{12}$ **53.** $\frac{-4}{9} = \frac{n}{-45}$ **54.** $\frac{y}{3} = \frac{25}{15}$ **55.** $\frac{7}{n} = \frac{-35}{50}$ **56.** $\frac{14}{18} = \frac{63}{n}$

Direct Variation

Objective To write and graph an equation of a direct variation

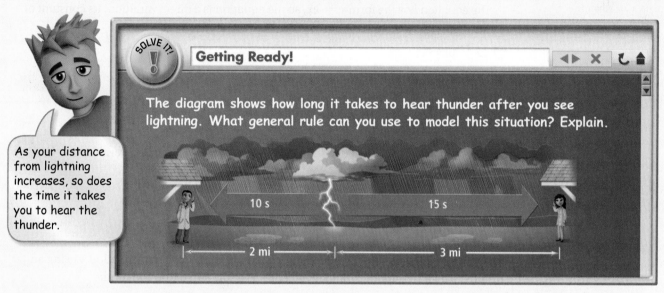

SOLVE IT!

Getting Ready!

The diagram shows how long it takes to hear thunder after you see lightning. What general rule can you use to model this situation? Explain.

10 s   15 s

2 mi   3 mi

As your distance from lightning increases, so does the time it takes you to hear the thunder.

Dynamic Activity
Direct Variation

Lesson Vocabulary
• direct variation
• constant of variation for a direct variation

The time it takes to hear thunder *varies directly with* the distance from lightning.

If the ratio of two variables is constant, then the variables have a special relationship, known as a *direct variation.*

A **direct variation** is a relationship that can be represented by a function in the form $y = kx$, where $k \neq 0$.

The **constant of variation for a direct variation** k is the coefficient of x. By dividing each side of $y = kx$ by x, you can see that the ratio of the variables is constant: $\frac{y}{x} = k$.

To determine whether an equation represents a direct variation, solve it for y. If you can write the equation in the form $y = kx$, where $k \neq 0$, it represents a direct variation.

Focus Question When do you use direct variation?

take note

Key Concept	**Direct Variation**
y varies directly as x	when x increases, y increases by the same factor when x decreases, y decreases by the same factor
k is constant of variation	same for every point (x, y)

Think

Do these equations look like ones you've seen before?
Yes. They contain two variables, so they're literal equations. To determine whether they're direct variation equations, solve for y.

 Problem 1 Identifying a Direct Variation

Does the equation represent a direct variation? If so, find the constant of variation.

A $7y = 2x$

Write the original equation.	$7y = 2x$
Divide both sides by 7.	$y = \frac{2}{7}x$

The equation has the form $y = kx$, so the equation is a direct variation. Its constant of variation is $\frac{2}{7}$.

B $3y + 4x = 8$

Write the original equation.	$3y + 4x = 8$
Subtract $4x$ from both sides.	$3y = 8 - 4x$
Divide both sides by 3.	$y = \frac{8}{3} - \frac{4}{3}x$

You cannot write the equation in the form $y = kx$. It is not a direct variation.

 Got It? 1. Does the equation represent a direct variation? If so, find the constant of variation.
    a. $4x + 5y = 0$ **b.** $-3y = 6x - 9$

To write an equation for a direct variation, first find the constant of variation k using an ordered pair, other than $(0, 0)$, that you know is a solution of the equation.

 Problem 2 Writing a Direct Variation Equation

Suppose y varies directly with x, and $y = 35$ when $x = 5$. What direct variation equation relates x and y? What is the value of y when $x = 9$?

Think

Make sure you don't stop at $7 = k$. To write the direct variation equation, you have to substitute 7 for k in $y = kx$.

Start with the function form of a direct variation.	$y = kx$
Substitute 5 for x and 35 for y.	$35 = k(5)$
Divide each side by 5 to solve for k.	$7 = k$
Write an equation. Substitute 7 for k in $y = kx$.	$y = 7x$

The equation $y = 7x$ relates x and y. When $x = 9$, $y = 7(9)$, or 63.

 Got It? 2. Suppose y varies directly with x, and $y = 10$ when $x = -2$. What direct variation equation relates x and y? What is the value of y when $x = -15$?

Problem 3 Graphing a Direct Variation

Space Exploration Weight on Mars y varies directly with weight on Earth x. The weights of the science instruments onboard the Phoenix Mars Lander on Earth and Mars are shown.

Weight on Mars
50 lb

Weight on Earth
130 lb

A What is an equation that relates weight, in pounds, on Earth x and on Mars y?

Start with the function form of a direct variation. $y = kx$

Substitute 130 for x and 50 for y. $50 = k(130)$

Divide each side by 130 to solve for k. $0.38 \approx k$

Write an equation. Substitute 0.38 for k in $y = kx$. $y = 0.38x$

The equation $y = 0.38x$ gives the weight y on Mars, in pounds, of an object that weighs x pounds on Earth.

Think

Have you graphed equations like $y = 0.38x$ before?
Yes. In Chapter 4, you graphed linear functions by making a table of values and plotting points.

B What is the graph of the equation in part (A)?

Make a table of values. Then draw the graph.

x	y
0	$0.38(0) = 0$
50	$0.38(50) = 19$
100	$0.38(100) = 38$
150	$0.38(150) = 57$

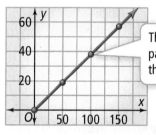

The points form a linear pattern. Draw a line through them.

Got It? **3. a.** Weight on the moon y varies directly with weight on Earth x. A person who weighs 100 lb on Earth weighs 16.6 lb on the moon. What is an equation that relates weight on Earth x and weight on the moon y? What is the graph of this equation?

  b. Reasoning What is the slope of the graph of $y = 0.38x$ in Problem 3? How is the slope related to the equation?

take note

Concept Summary   Graphs of Direct Variations

The graph of a direct variation equation $y = kx$ is a line with the following properties.
• The line passes through $(0, 0)$.
• The slope of the line is k.

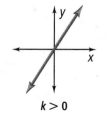

$k > 0$

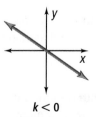

$k < 0$

You can rewrite a direct variation equation $y = kx$ as $\frac{y}{x} = k$. When a set of data pairs (x, y) vary directly, $\frac{y}{x}$ is the constant of variation. It is the same for each data pair.

 Problem 4 **Writing a Direct Variation From a Table**

For the data in the table, does y vary directly with x? If it does, write an equation for the direct variation.

A

x	y
4	6
8	12
10	15

B

x	y
−2	3.2
1	2.4
4	1.6

Find $\frac{y}{x}$ for each ordered pair.

$\frac{6}{4} = 1.5 \quad \frac{12}{8} = 1.5 \quad \frac{15}{10} = 1.5$

The ratio $\frac{y}{x} = 1.5$ for each data pair. So y varies directly with x. The direct variation equation is $y = 1.5x$.

Find $\frac{y}{x}$ for each ordered pair.

$\frac{3.2}{-2} = -1.6 \quad \frac{2.4}{1} = 2.4 \quad \frac{1.6}{4} = 0.4$

The ratio $\frac{y}{x}$ is not the same for all data pairs. So y does not vary directly with x.

Plan

How can you check your answer?
Graph the ordered pairs in the coordinate plane. If you can connect them with a line that passes through (0, 0), then y varies directly with x.

✓ **Got It?** **4.** For the data in the table at the right, does y vary directly with x? If it does, write an equation for the direct variation.

x	y
−3	2.25
1	−0.75
4	−3

Focus Question When do you use direct variation?

Answer Direct variation relates quantities where the ratio of corresponding values is constant. To write a direct variation equation, substitute the known values for x and y into the function form of a direct variation. Solve for k. Then substitute the value of k into $y = kx$.

✓ **Lesson Check**

Do you know HOW?

1. Does the equation $6y = 18x$ represent a direct variation? If it does, what is its constant of variation?

2. Suppose y varies directly with x, and $y = 30$ when $x = 3$. What direct variation equation relates x and y?

3. A recipe for 12 corn muffins calls for 1 cup of flour. The number of muffins you can make varies directly with the amount of flour you use. You have $2\frac{1}{2}$ cups of flour. How many muffins can you make?

Do you UNDERSTAND?

Vocabulary Determine whether each statement is *always*, *sometimes*, or *never* true.

4. The ordered pair (0, 0) is a solution of the direct variation equation $y = kx$.

5. You can write a direct variation in the form $y = k + x$, where $k \neq 0$.

6. The constant of variation for a direct variation represented by $y = kx$ is $\frac{y}{x}$.

Practice and Problem-Solving Exercises

A Practice

Determine whether each equation represents a direct variation. If it does, find the constant of variation.

See Problem 1.

7. $2y = 5x + 1$

8. $8x + 9y = 10$

9. $-12x = 6y$

10. $y + 8 = -x$

11. $-4 + 7x + 4 = 3y$

12. $0.7x - 1.4y = 0$

Suppose y varies directly with x. Write a direct variation equation that relates x and y. Then find the value of y when $x = 12$.

See Problem 2.

Guided Practice

13. $y = 7\frac{1}{2}$ when $x = 3$

To start, write the function form of a direct variation.

$y = kx$

Substitute 3 for x and $7\frac{1}{2}$ for y.

$7\frac{1}{2} = k(3)$

14. $y = -10$ when $x = 2$.

15. $y = 5$ when $x = 2$.

16. $y = 125$ when $x = -5$.

17. $y = 9\frac{1}{3}$ when $x = -\frac{1}{2}$.

Graph each direct variation equation.

See Problem 3.

18. $y = 2x$

19. $y = \frac{1}{3}x$

20. $y = -x$

21. $y = -\frac{1}{2}x$

22. Travel Time The distance d you bike varies directly with the amount of time t you bike. Suppose you bike 13.2 mi in 1.25 h. What is an equation that relates d and t? What is the graph of the equation?

23. Geometry The perimeter p of a regular hexagon varies directly with the length ℓ of one side of the hexagon. What is an equation that relates p and ℓ? What is the graph of the equation?

For the data in each table, tell whether y varies directly with x. If it does, write an equation for the direct variation.

◄ See Problem 4.

24.

x	y
−6	9
1	−1.5
8	−12

Guided Practice

To start, find the ratio of each ordered pair in the table.

$\frac{9}{-6} = -1.5 \quad \frac{-1.5}{1} = -1.5 \quad \frac{-12}{8} = -1.5$

25.

x	y
3	5.4
7	12.6
12	21.6

26.

x	y
−2	1
3	6
8	11

Ⓑ Apply

Suppose y varies directly with x. Write a direct variation equation that relates x and y. Then graph the equation.

27. $y = \frac{1}{2}$ when $x = 3$.

28. $y = -5$ when $x = \frac{1}{4}$.

29. $y = \frac{6}{5}$ when $x = -\frac{5}{6}$.

30. $y = 7.2$ when $x = 1.2$.

31. Think About a Plan The amount of blood in a person's body varies directly with body weight. A person who weighs 160 lb has about 4.6 qt of blood. About how many quarts of blood are in the body of a 175-lb person?
  - How can you find the constant of variation?
  - Can you write an equation that relates quarts of blood to weight?
  - How can you use the equation to determine the solution?

32. Electricity Ohm's Law $V = I \times R$ relates the voltage, current, and resistance of a circuit. V is the voltage measured in volts. I is the current measured in amperes. R is the resistance measured in ohms.
  a. Find the voltage of a circuit with a current of 24 amperes and a resistance of 2 ohms.
  b. Find the resistance of a circuit with a current of 24 amperes and a voltage of 18 volts.

Reasoning Tell whether the two quantities vary directly. Explain your reasoning.

33. the number of ounces of cereal and the number of Calories the cereal contains

34. the time it takes to travel a certain distance and the rate at which you travel

35. the perimeter of a square and the side length of the square

36. the amount of money you have left and the number of items you purchase

37. a. Graph the following direct variation equations in the same coordinate plane:
$y = x$, $y = 2x$, $y = 3x$, and $y = 4x$.

  b. Look for a Pattern Describe how the graphs change as the constant of variation increases.

  c. Predict how the graph of $y = \frac{1}{2}x$ would appear.

38. Error Analysis Use the table at the right. A student says that y varies directly with x because as x increases by 1, y also increases by 1. Explain the student's error.

39. Writing Suppose y varies directly with x. Explain how the value of y changes in each situation.

  a. The value of x is doubled. **b.** The value of x is halved.

x	y
0	3
1	4
2	5

40. Physics The force you need to apply to a lever varies directly with the weight you want to lift. Suppose you can lift a 50-lb weight by applying 20 lb of force to a certain lever.

  a. What is the ratio of force to weight for the lever?

  b. Write an equation relating force and weight. What is the force you need to lift a friend who weighs 130 lb?

Standardized Test Prep

SAT/ACT

41. The price p you pay varies directly with the number of pencils you buy. Suppose you buy 3 pencils for $.51. How much is each pencil, in dollars?

42. A scooter can travel 72 mi per gallon of gasoline and holds 2.3 gal. The function $d(x) = 72x$ represents the distance $d(x)$, in miles, that the scooter can travel with x gallons of gasoline. How many miles can the scooter go with a full tank of gas?

43. The table at the right shows the number of hours a clerk works per week and the amount of money she earns before taxes. If she worked 34 h per week, how much money would she earn, in dollars?

44. What is the greatest value in the range of $y = x^2 - 3$ for the domain $\{-3, 0, 1\}$?

Weekly Wages

Time (h)	Wages ($)
12	99.00
17	140.25
21	173.25
32	264.00

Mixed Review

Find the slope of the line that passes through each pair of points.   ◀ See Lesson 5-1.

45. $(2, 4), (0, 2)$ **46.** $(5, 8), (-5, 8)$ **47.** $(0, 0), (3, 18)$ **48.** $(1, -2), (-2, 3)$

Get Ready! **To prepare for Lesson 5-3, do Exercises 49–52.**

Evaluate each expression.   ◀ See Lesson 1-2.

49. $6a + 3$ for $a = 2$ **50.** $-2x - 5$ for $x = 3$ **51.** $\frac{1}{4}x + 2$ for $x = 16$ **52.** $8 - 5n$ for $n = 3$

Concept Byte

Use With Lesson 5-3

TECHNOLOGY

Investigating
$y = mx + b$

You can use a graphing calculator to explore the graph of an equation in the form $y = mx + b$. For this activity, choose a standard screen by pressing (zoom) 6.

1. Graph these equations on the same screen. Then complete each statement.

$$y = x + 3 \qquad\qquad y = 2x + 3 \qquad\qquad y = \tfrac{1}{2}x + 3$$

a. The graph of _?_ is steepest.
b. The graph of _?_ is the least steep.

2. Match each equation with the best choice for its graph.

A. $y = \tfrac{1}{4}x - 2$ **B.** $y = 4x - 2$ **C.** $y = x - 2$

I. 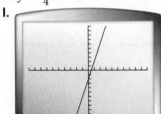   **II.** 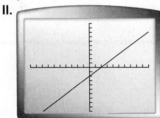   **III.**

3. Graph these equations on the same screen.

$$y = 2x + 3 \qquad\qquad y = -2x + 3$$

How does the sign of m affect the graph of the equation?

4. Reasoning How does changing the value of m affect the graph of an equation in the form $y = mx + b$?

5. Graph these equations on the same screen.

$$y = 2x + 3 \qquad\qquad y = 2x - 3 \qquad\qquad y = 2x + 2$$

Where does the graph of each equation cross the y-axis? (*Hint:* Use the **ZOOM** feature to better see the points of intersection.)

6. Match each equation with the best choice for its graph.

A. $y = \tfrac{1}{3}x - 3$ **B.** $y = \tfrac{1}{3}x + 1$ **C.** $y = \tfrac{1}{3}x$

I. 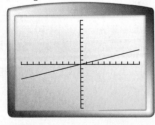   **II.** 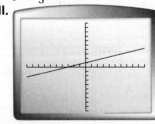   **III.**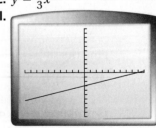

7. Reasoning How does changing the value of b affect the graph of an equation in the form $y = mx + b$?

Slope-Intercept Form

Objective To write linear equations using slope-intercept form

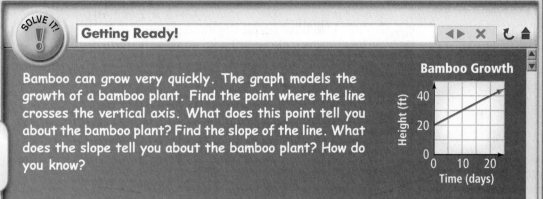

Getting Ready!

Bamboo can grow very quickly. The graph models the growth of a bamboo plant. Find the point where the line crosses the vertical axis. What does this point tell you about the bamboo plant? Find the slope of the line. What does the slope tell you about the bamboo plant? How do you know?

Bamboo Growth

Here is a linear function that is <u>not</u> a direct variation.

Dynamic Activity
Slope-Intercept Form of a Line

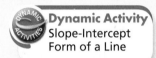

Lesson Vocabulary
• parent function
• linear parent function
• linear equation
• *y*-intercept
• slope-intercept form

The function in the Solve It is a linear function, but it is not a direct variation. Direct variations are only part of the family of linear functions.

A family of functions is a group of functions with common characteristics. A **parent function** is the simplest function with these characteristics. The **linear parent function** is $y = x$ or $f(x) = x$. The graphs of three linear functions are shown at the right.

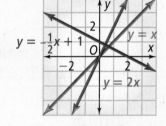

$y = -\frac{1}{2}x + 1$

$y = x$

$y = 2x$

A **linear equation** is an equation that models a linear function. In a linear equation, the variables cannot be raised to a power other than 1. So $y = 2x$ is a linear equation, but $y = x^2$ and $y = 2^x$ are not. The graph of a linear equation contains all the ordered pairs that are solutions of the equation.

Graphs of linear functions may cross the *y*-axis at any point. A **y-intercept** of a graph is the *y*-coordinate of a point where the graph crosses the *y*-axis.

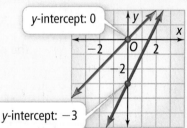

y-intercept: 0

y-intercept: −3

Focus Question How do you write linear equations using the slope and the *y*-intercept?

 take note

Key Concept Slope-Intercept Form of a Linear Equation

The **slope-intercept form** of a linear equation of a nonvertical line is $y = mx + b$.

↑ ↑
slope *y*-intercept

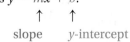

Problem 1 Identifying Slope and *y*-Intercept

Think

Why isn't the *y*-intercept 2?
In slope-intercept form, the *y*-intercept *b* is added to the term *mx*. Instead of subtracting 2, you add the opposite, −2.

What are the slope and *y*-intercept of the graph of $y = 5x - 2$?

Use slope-intercept form.

$$y = mx + b$$

slope   *y*-intercept

Think of $y = 5x - 2$ as $y = 5x + (-2)$. $y = 5x + (-2)$

The slope is 5; the *y*–intercept is −2.

 Got It? **1. a.** What are the slope and *y*–intercept of the graph of $y = -\frac{1}{2}x + \frac{2}{3}$?

b. **Reasoning** How do the graph of the line and the equation in part (a) change if the *y*-intercept is moved down 3 units?

Problem 2 Writing an Equation in Slope-Intercept Form

Plan

When can you use slope-intercept form?
You can write an equation of a nonvertical line in slope-intercept form if you know its slope and *y*-intercept.

What is an equation of the line with slope $-\frac{4}{5}$ and *y*-intercept 7?

Use slope-intercept form. $y = mx + b$

Substitute $-\frac{4}{5}$ for *m* and 7 for *b*. $y = -\frac{4}{5}x + 7$

An equation for the line is $y = -\frac{4}{5}x + 7$.

 Got It? **2.** What is an equation of the line with slope $\frac{3}{2}$ and *y*-intercept −1?

Problem 3 Writing an Equation From a Graph

Plan

How can you use a graph to write an equation of a line?
You can use points on the graph to find the slope and the *y*-intercept of the line. Then use slope-intercept form.

Multiple Choice Which equation represents the line shown?

Ⓐ $y = -2x + 1$ Ⓒ $y = \frac{1}{2}x - 2$

Ⓑ $y = 2x + 1$ Ⓓ $y = 2x - 2$

Find the slope. Two points on the line are $(0, -2)$ and $(2, 2)$.

$$\text{slope} = \frac{2 - (-2)}{2 - 0} = \frac{4}{2} = 2$$

The *y*-intercept is −2. Write an equation in slope-intercept form.

Use slope-intercept form. $y = mx + b$

Substitute 2 for *m* and −2 for *b*. $y = 2x + (-2)$

An equation for the line is $y = 2x - 2$. The correct answer is D.

 Got It? **3. a.** What is an equation of the line shown at the right?

b. **Reasoning** If you use two different points to find the slope of the line, will the equation of the line change? Explain.

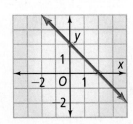

Problem 4 **Writing an Equation From Two Points**

What equation in slope-intercept form represents the line that passes through the points $(2, 1)$ and $(5, -8)$?

Know	Need	Plan
The line passes through $(2, 1)$ and $(5, -8)$.	An equation of the line	Use the two points to find the slope. Then use the slope and one point to solve for the y-intercept.

Step 1 Use the two points to find the slope.

$$\text{slope} = \frac{-8 - 1}{5 - 2} = \frac{-9}{3} = -3$$

Think

Can you use either point to find the *y*-intercept?
Yes. You can substitute the slope and the coordinates of any point on the line into the form $y = mx + b$ and solve for *b*.

Step 2 Use the slope and the coordinates of one of the points to find b.

Use slope-intercept form. $\qquad\qquad y = mx + b$

Substitute -3 for m, 2 for x, and 1 for y. $\quad 1 = -3(2) + b$

Solve for *b*. $\qquad\qquad\qquad\qquad 7 = b$

Step 3 Substitute the slope and y-intercept into the slope-intercept form.

Use slope-intercept form. $\qquad y = mx + b$

Substitute -3 for *m* and 7 for *b*. $\quad y = -3x + 7$

An equation of the line is $y = -3x + 7$.

 Got It? **4.** What equation in slope-intercept form represents the line that passes through the points $(3, -2)$ and $(1, -3)$?

Focus Question How do you write linear equations using the slope and the y-intercept?

Answer You can use the slope and the y-intercept of a line to write an equation of a line. In the equation $y = mx + b$, substitute the slope for *m* and the y-intercept for *b*.

✓ Lesson Check

Do you know HOW?

1. What is an equation of the line with slope 6 and y-intercept -4?

2. What equation in slope-intercept form represents the line that passes through the points $(-3, 4)$ and $(2, -1)$?

Do you UNDERSTAND?

3. Vocabulary Is $y = 5$ a linear equation? Explain.

4. Reasoning Is it *always, sometimes,* or *never* true that an equation in slope-intercept form represents a direct variation? Support your answer with examples.

Practice and Problem-Solving Exercises

 Practice Find the slope and *y*-intercept of the graph of each equation. ◀ **See Problem 1.**

5. $y = 3x + 1$ **6.** $y = -x + 4$ **7.** $y = 2x - 5$

8. $y = -3x + 2$ **9.** $y = 5x - 3$ **10.** $y = -6x$

11. $y = 4$ **12.** $y = -0.2x + 3$ **13.** $y = \frac{1}{4}x - \frac{1}{3}$

Write an equation in slope-intercept form of the line with the given slope *m* and *y*-intercept *b*. ◀ **See Problem 2.**

14. $m = 1, b = -1$ **15.** $m = 3, b = 2$

16. $m = \frac{1}{2}, b = -\frac{1}{2}$ **17.** $m = 0.7, b = -2$

18. $m = -0.5, b = 1.5$ **19.** $m = -2, b = \frac{8}{5}$

Write an equation in slope-intercept form of each line. ◀ **See Problem 3.**

20.
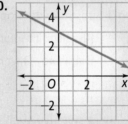

Guided Practice

To start, find the slope. Two points on the line are (0, 3) and (2, 2).

$\text{slope} = \dfrac{2 - 3}{2 - 0} = -\dfrac{1}{2}$

21.
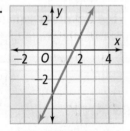

22.
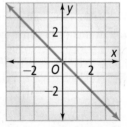

23.
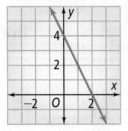

24.
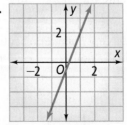

Chapter Vocabulary

- direct variation (p. 321)
- linear equation (p. 329)
- point-slope form (p. 338)
- rate of change (p. 314)
- slope (p. 315)
- slope-intercept form (p. 329)
- *y*-intercept (p. 329)

Choose the vocabulary term that correctly completes the sentence.

1. The slope of a line models the __?__ of a function.

2. The form of a linear equation that shows the slope and one point is the __?__.

5-1 Rate of Change and Slope

Quick Review

Rate of change shows the relationship between two changing quantities. The **slope** of a line is the ratio of the vertical change (the rise) to the horizontal change (the run).

$$\text{slope} = \frac{\text{rise}}{\text{run}} = \frac{y_2 - y_1}{x_2 - x_1}$$

The slope of a horizontal line is 0, and the slope of a vertical line is undefined.

Example

What is the slope of the line that passes through the points (1, 12) and (6, 22)?

$$\text{slope} = \frac{y_2 - y_1}{x_2 - x_1} = \frac{22 - 12}{6 - 1} = \frac{10}{5} = 2$$

Exercises

Find the slope of the line that passes through each pair of points.

3. (2, 2), (3, 1)

4. (4, 2), (0, 2)

5. (−1, 2), (0, 5)

6. (−3, −2), (−3, 2)

Find the slope of each line.

7.

8.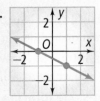

5-2 Direct Variation

Quick Review

A function represents a **direct variation** if it has the form $y = kx$, where $k \neq 0$. The coefficient k is the **constant of variation**.

Example

Suppose y varies directly with x, and $y = 15$ when $x = 5$. Write a direct variation equation that relates x and y. What is the value of y when $x = 9$?

Start with the general form of a direct variation.	$y = kx$
Substitute 5 for x and 15 for y.	$15 = k(5)$
Divide each side by 5 to solve for k.	$3 = k$
Write an equation. Substitute 3 for k in $y = kx$.	$y = 3x$

The equation $y = 3x$ relates x and y. When $x = 9$, $y = 3(9)$, or 27.

Exercises

Suppose y varies directly with x. Write a direct variation equation that relates x and y. Then find the value of y when $x = 7$.

9. $y = 8$ when $x = -4$.   **10.** $y = 15$ when $x = 6$.

11. $y = 3$ when $x = 9$.   **12.** $y = -4$ when $x = 4$.

For the data in each table, tell whether y varies directly with x. If it does, write an equation for the direct variation.

13.

x	y
−1	−6
2	3
5	12
9	24

14.

x	y
−3	7.5
−1	2.5
2	−5
5	−12.5

5-3 and 5-4 Forms of Linear Equations

Quick Review

The graph of a linear equation is a line. You can write a linear equation in different forms.

The **slope-intercept form** of a linear equation is $y = mx + b$, where m is the slope and b is the **y-intercept**.

The **point-slope form** of a linear equation is $y - y_1 = m(x - x_1)$, where m is the slope and (x_1, y_1) is a point on the line.

Example

What is an equation of the line that has slope -4 and passes through the point $(-1, 7)$?

Use point-slope form.	$y - y_1 = m(x - x_1)$
Substitute $(-1, 7)$ for (x_1, y_1) and -4 for m.	$y - 7 = -4(x - (-1))$
Simplify inside grouping symbols.	$y - 7 = -4(x + 1)$

An equation of the line is $y - 7 = -4(x + 1)$.

Exercises

Write an equation in slope-intercept form of the line that passes through the given points.

15. $(-3, 4), (1, 4)$ **16.** $(3, -2), (6, 1)$

Write an equation of each line.

17.

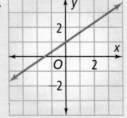

18.

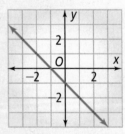

Graph each equation.

19. $y = 4x - 3$ **20.** $y = 2$

21. $y + 3 = 2(x - 1)$ **22.** $x + 4y = 10$

Do you know HOW?

Each rate of change is constant. Find the rate of change and explain what it means.

1. Studying for a Test

Study Time (h)	Grade
5	85
6	87
7	89
8	91

2. Distance a Car Travels

Time (s)	Distance (m)
3	75
6	150
9	225
12	300

Find the slope of the line that passes through each pair of points.

3. $(7, 3), (5, 1)$

4. $(-2, 1), (3, 6)$

5. $(6, -4), (6, 6)$

6. $(2, 5), (-8, 5)$

Tell whether each equation is a direct variation. If it is, find the constant of variation.

7. $y = 3x$

8. $5x + 3 = 8y + 3$

9. $-3x - 35y = 14$

Find the slope and y-intercept of the graph of each equation.

10. $y = \frac{1}{5}x + 3$

11. $3x + 4y = 12$

12. $6y = -8x - 18$

13. Credit Cards In 2000, people charged $1,243 billion on the four most-used types of credit cards. In 2005, people charged $1,838 billion on these same four types of credit cards. What was the rate of change?

14. Bicycling The distance a wheel moves forward varies directly with the number of rotations. Suppose the wheel moves 56 ft in 8 rotations. What distance does the wheel move in 20 rotations?

Write an equation in slope-intercept form of each line.

15.

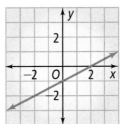

16.

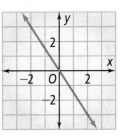

Graph each equation.

17. $y = 4x - 3$

18. $y + 3 = \frac{1}{2}(x + 2)$

Write an equation in point-slope form for the line through the given point and with the given slope m.

19. $(2, -2); m = -\frac{1}{2}$

20. $(4, 0); m = 4$

Write an equation of the line that passes through each pair of points.

21. $(4, -2)$ and $(8, -6)$

22. $(-1, -5)$ and $(2, 10)$

Do you UNDERSTAND?

23. Writing Describe two methods you can use to write an equation of a line given its graph.

24. Vocabulary How can you find the y-intercept of the graph of a linear equation?

25. Reasoning Can you graph a line if its slope is undefined? Explain.

26. Business A salesperson earns $18 per hour plus a $75 bonus for meeting her sales quota. Write and graph an equation that represents her total earnings, including her bonus. What does the independent variable represent? What does the dependent variable represent?

Linear Functions

In Part A, you learned about slope and different forms of a line. Now you will learn about relationships between lines and how to use lines to discover trends in data.

Vocabulary for Part B

English/Spanish Vocabulary Audio Online:

English	Spanish
correlation coefficient, *p. 366*	coeficiente de correlación
line of best fit, *p. 366*	recta de mayor aproximación
parallel lines, *p. 357* ✓	rectas paralelas
perpendicular lines, *p. 358* ✓	rectas perpendiculares
scatter plot, *p. 363* ✓	diagrama de puntos
standard form, *p. 349* ✓	forma normal
trend line, *p. 364* ✓	línea de tendencia
x-intercept, *p. 349* ✓	intercepto en *x*

BIGideas

1 Proportionality

Essential Question: What does the slope of a line indicate about the line?

2 Functions

Essential Question: What information does the equation of a line give you?

3 Modeling

Essential Question: How can you make predictions based on a scatter plot?

Chapter Preview for Part B

5-5 Standard Form
5-6 Parallel and Perpendicular Lines
5-7 Scatter Plots and Trend Lines

5-5 Standard Form

Objectives To graph linear equations using intercepts
To write linear equations in standard form

Getting Ready! ◄► ✕ ↺ ⬆

An athlete wants to make a snack mix of peanuts and cashews that will contain a certain amount of protein. Cashews have 4 g of protein per ounce, and peanuts have 7 g of protein per ounce. How many grams of protein will the athlete's mix contain? What do the points (7, 0) and (0, 4) represent? Explain.

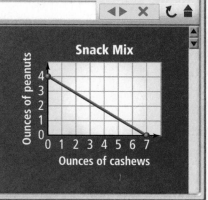

Have you ever made a snack mix? How did you decide how much of each ingredient to use?

Lesson Vocabulary
• *x*-intercept
• standard form of a linear equation

In this lesson, you will learn to use intercepts to graph a line. Recall that a *y*-intercept is the *y*-coordinate of a point where a graph crosses the *y*-axis. The **x-intercept** is the *x*-coordinate of a point where a graph crosses the *x*-axis.

Focus Question When should you graph a line using intercepts?

One form of a linear equation, called *standard form*, allows you to find intercepts quickly. You can use the intercepts to draw the graph.

take note

Key Concept Standard Form of a Linear Equation

The **standard form of a linear equation** is $Ax + By = C$, where A, B, and C are real numbers, and A and B are not both zero.

Problem 1 Finding x- and y-Intercepts

What are the x- and y-intercepts of the graph of $3x + 4y = 24$?

Step 1 To find the x-intercept, substitute 0 for y. Solve for x.

$$3x + 4y = 24$$
$$3x + 4(0) = 24$$
$$3x = 24$$
$$x = 8$$

The x-intercept is 8.

Step 2 To find the y-intercept, substitute 0 for x. Solve for y.

$$3x + 4y = 24$$
$$3(0) + 4y = 24$$
$$4y = 24$$
$$y = 6$$

The y-intercept is 6.

 Got It? 1. What are the x- and y-intercepts of the graph of each equation?
a. $5x - 6y = 60$ **b.** $3x + 4y = 12$

 Problem 2 Graphing a Line Using Intercepts

What is the graph of $x - 2y = -2$?

Know	Need	Plan
An equation of the line	The coordinates of at least two points on the line	Find and plot the x- and y-intercepts. Draw a line through the points.

Step 1 Find the intercepts.

$$x - 2y = -2$$
$$x - 2(0) = -2$$
$$x = -2$$

$$x - 2y = -2$$
$$0 - 2y = -2$$
$$-2y = -2$$
$$y = 1$$

Step 2 Plot (−2, 0) and (0, 1). Draw a line through the points.

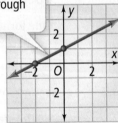

 Got It? 2. What is the graph of $2x + 5y = 20$?

If $A = 0$ in the standard form $Ax + By = C$, then you can write the equation in the form $y = b$, where b is a constant. If $B = 0$, you can write the equation in the form $x = a$, where a is a constant. The graph of $y = b$ is a horizontal line, and the graph of $x = a$ is a vertical line.

Problem 3 Graphing Horizontal and Vertical Lines

What is the graph of each equation?

Think

Why write x = 3 in standard form?
When you write $x = 3$ in standard form, you can see that, for any value of y, $x = 3$. This form of the equation makes graphing the line easier.

A $x = 3$

Write in standard form. $1x + 0y = 3$

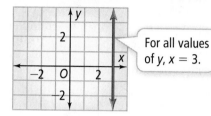

For all values of y, $x = 3$.

B $y = 3$

Write in standard form. $0x + 1y = 3$

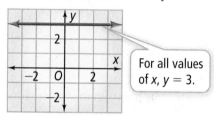

For all values of x, $y = 3$.

 Got It? **3.** What is the graph of each equation?

　　a. $x = 4$　　　　　　　　　　**c.** $y = 0$
　　b. $x = -1$　　　　　　　　　**d.** $y = 1$

Focus Question How do you write linear equations in standard form using only integers?

Given an equation in slope-intercept form or point-slope form, you can rewrite the equation in standard form using only integers.

Problem 4 Transforming to Standard Form

Plan

How can you get started?
You need to clear the fraction. So, multiply each side of the equation by the denominator of the fraction.

What is $y = -\frac{3}{7}x + 5$ written in standard form using integers?

Write the original equation.	$y = -\frac{3}{7}x + 5$
Multiply each side by 7.	$7y = 7\left(-\frac{3}{7}x + 5\right)$
Use the Distributive Property.	$7y = -3x + 35$
Add $3x$ to each side.	$3x + 7y = 35$

 Got It? **4.** Write $y - 2 = -\frac{1}{3}(x + 6)$ in standard form using integers.

Online Shopping A media download store sells songs for $1 each and movies for $12 each. You have $60 to spend. Write and graph an equation that describes the items you can purchase. What are three combinations of numbers of songs and movies you can purchase?

Relate | cost of a song | times | number of songs | plus | cost of a movie | times | number of movies | equals | $60 |

Define   Let x = the number of songs purchased.

Let y = the number of movies purchased.

Write | 1 | · | x | + | 12 | · | y | = | 60 |

An equation for this situation is $x + 12y = 60$.
Find the intercepts.

$$x + 12y = 60 \qquad\qquad x + 12y = 60$$
$$x + 12(0) = 60 \qquad\qquad 0 + 12y = 60$$
$$x = 60 \qquad\qquad\qquad y = 5$$

Use the intercepts to draw the graph. Only points in the first quadrant make sense.

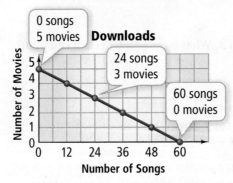

The intercepts give you two combinations of songs and movies. Use the graph to identify a third combination. Each of the red points is a possible solution.

Check for Reasonableness You cannot buy a fraction of a song or movie. The graph is a line, but only points with integer coordinates are solutions.

Got It? **5. a.** In Problem 5, suppose the store charged $15 for each movie. What equation describes the numbers of songs and movies you can purchase for $60?

   b. **Reasoning** What domain and range are reasonable for the equation in part (a)? Explain.

Think

Is there another way to find solutions?
You can *guess and check* by substituting values for one variable and solving for the other. Then check if your solution makes sense in the context of the problem. Graphing is the quickest way to see *all* the solutions.

Concept Summary   Linear Equations

You can describe any line using one or more of these forms of a linear equation. Any two equations for the same line are equivalent.

Graph

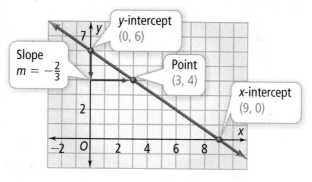

Forms

Slope-Intercept Form
$y = mx + b$
$y = -\frac{2}{3}x + 6$

Point-Slope Form
$y - y_1 = m(x - x_1)$
$y - 4 = -\frac{2}{3}(x - 3)$

Standard Form
$Ax + By = C$
$2x + 3y = 18$

Focus Question When should you graph a line using intercepts?

Answer Graph a line using intercepts when the equation is in standard form. First substitute 0 for y and solve for the x-intercept. Then substitute 0 for x and solve for the y-intercept. Plot the x- and y-intercepts and then draw a line through the points.

Focus Question How do you write linear equations in standard form using only integers?

Answer First, clear any fraction by multiplying each side of the equation by the denominator of the fraction. Use properties of equality to rewrite the equation in $Ax + By = C$ form.

Lesson Check

Do you know HOW?

1. What are the x- and y-intercepts of the graph of $3x - 4y = 9$?

2. What is the graph of $5x + 4y = 20$?

3. Is the graph of $y = -0.5$ a *horizontal line*, a *vertical line*, or *neither*?

4. What is $y = \frac{1}{2}x + 3$ written in standard form using integers?

5. A store sells gift cards in preset amounts. You can purchase gift cards for $10 or $25. You have spent $285 on gift cards. Write an equation in standard form to represent this situation. What are three combinations of gift cards you could have purchased?

Do you UNDERSTAND?

6. **Vocabulary** Tell whether each linear equation is in *slope-intercept form*, *point-slope form*, or *standard form*.
   a. $y + 5 = -(x - 2)$
   b. $y = -2x + 5$
   c. $y - 10 = -2(x - 1)$
   d. $2x + 4y = 12$

7. **Reasoning** Which form would you use to write an equation of the line at the right: *slope-intercept form*, *point-slope form*, or *standard form*? Explain.

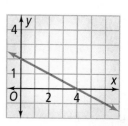

Practice and Problem-Solving Exercises

 Practice

Find the *x*- and *y*-intercepts of the graph of each equation.

See Problem 1.

Guided Practice

To start, substitute 0 for *y* to find the *x*-intercept.

8. $-3x + 3y = 9$
$-3x + 3(0) = 9$

9. $x + y = 9$

10. $x - 2y = 2$

11. $4x - 5y = -20$

12. $7x - y = 21$

Draw a line with the given intercepts.

See Problem 2.

13. *x*-intercept: 3
      y-intercept: 5

14. *x*-intercept: -1
      y-intercept: -4

15. *x*-intercept: 4
      y-intercept: -3

Graph each equation using *x*- and *y*-intercepts.

16. $x + y = 4$

17. $x + y = -3$

18. $x - y = -8$

19. $-2x + y = 8$

20. $-4x + y = -12$

21. $6x - 2y = 18$

For each equation, tell whether its graph is a *horizontal* or a *vertical* line.

See Problem 3.

22. $y = -4$

23. $x = 3$

24. $y = \frac{7}{4}$

25. $x = -1.8$

Graph each equation.

26. $y = 6$

27. $x = -3$

28. $y = -2$

29. $x = 7$

Write each equation in standard form using integers.

See Problem 4.

Guided Practice

To start, multiply each side by 4.

30. $y = \frac{1}{4}x - 2$

$4y = 4\left(\frac{1}{4}x - 2\right)$

31. $y = 2x + 5$

32. $y + 3 = 4(x - 1)$

33. $y - 4 = -2(x - 3)$

34. $y = -\frac{2}{3}x - 1$

Hint To remove the fraction, multiply each side by the reciprocal of $-\frac{2}{3}$.

35. **Video Games** In a video game, you earn 5 points for each jewel you find. You earn 2 points for each star you find. Write and graph an equation that represents the numbers of jewels and stars you must find to earn 250 points. What are three combinations of jewels and stars you can find that will earn you 250 points?

See Problem 5.

36. **Clothing** A store sells T-shirts for $12 each and sweatshirts for $15 each. You plan to spend $120 on T-shirts and sweatshirts. Write and graph an equation that represents this situation. What are three combinations of T-shirts and sweatshirts you can buy for $120?

Apply

37. **Writing** The three forms of linear equations you have studied are slope-intercept form, point-slope form, and standard form. Explain when each form is most useful.

38. **Think About a Plan** You are preparing a fruit salad. You want the total carbohydrates from pineapple and watermelon to equal 24 g. Pineapple has 3 g of carbohydrates per ounce and watermelon has 2 g of carbohydrates per ounce. What is a graph that shows all possible combinations of ounces of pineapple and ounces of watermelon?
   • Can you write an equation to model the situation?
   • What domain and range are reasonable for the graph?

39. **Compare and Contrast** Graph $3x + y = 6$, $3x - y = 6$, and $-3x + y = 6$. How are the graphs similar? How are they different?

40. **Reasoning** What are the slope and y-intercept of the graph of $Ax + By = C$?

41. **Error Analysis** A student says the equation $y = 4x + 1$ can be written in standard form as $4x - y = 1$. Describe and correct the student's error.

42. **Reasoning** The coefficients of x and y in the standard form of a linear equation cannot both be zero. Explain why.

Graphing Calculator Use a graphing calculator to graph each equation. Make a sketch of the graph. Include the x- and y-intercepts.

43. $2x - 8y = -16$

44. $-3x - 4y = 0$

45. $x + 3.5y = 7$

46. $-x + 2y = -8$

47. $3x + 3y = -15$

48. $4x - 6y = 9$

For each graph, find the x- and y-intercepts. Then write an equation in standard form using integers.

49.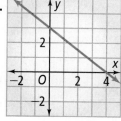

50.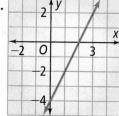

51.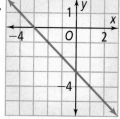

Find the *x*- and *y*-intercepts of the line that passes through the given points.

52. $(-6, 4), (3, -5)$

53. $(-5, -5), (4, -2)$

54. $(-7, 6), (-4, 11)$

55. $(-2, 8), (4, 2)$

56. $(3, -8), (-4, 13)$

57. $(5, 0.4), (-1, -2)$

58. Sports The scoreboard for a football game is shown at the right. All of the points the home team scored came from field goals worth 3 points and touchdowns with successful extra-point attempts worth 7 points. Write and graph a linear equation that represents this situation. List every possible combination of field goals and touchdowns the team could have scored.

SAT/ACT

59. What is $y = -\frac{3}{4}x + 2$ written in standard form using integers?

Ⓐ $\frac{3}{4}x + y = 2$ Ⓑ $3x + 4y = 2$ Ⓒ $3x + 4y = 8$ Ⓓ $-3x - 4y = 8$

60. Which of the following is an equation of a horizontal line?

Ⓕ $3x + 6y = 0$ Ⓖ $2x + 7 = 0$ Ⓗ $-3y = 29$ Ⓘ $x - 2y = 4$

61. Which equation models a line with the same *y*-intercept but half the slope of the line $y = 6 - 8x$?

Ⓐ $y = -4x + 3$ Ⓑ $y = 6 - 4x$ Ⓒ $y = 3 - 8x$ Ⓓ $y = -16x + 6$

62. What is the solution of $\frac{7}{2}x - 19 = -13 + 2x$?

Ⓕ -9 Ⓖ -4 Ⓗ 4 Ⓘ 9

Short Response

63. The drama club plans to attend a professional production. Between 10 and 15 students will go. Each ticket costs $25 plus a $2 surcharge. There is a one-time handling fee of $3 for the entire order. What is a linear function that models this situation? What domain and range are reasonable for the function?

Mixed Review

Write an equation in point-slope form of the line that passes through the given points. Then write the equation in slope-intercept form.

See Lesson 5-4.

64. $(5, -1), (-3, 4)$

65. $(0, -2), (3, 2)$

66. $(-2, -1), (1, 2)$

Solve each compound inequality. Graph your solution.

See Lesson 3-6.

67. $-6 < 3t \le 9$

68. $-9.5 < 3 - y \le 1.3$

69. $3x + 1 > 10$ or $5x + 3 \le -2$

Get Ready! To prepare for Lesson 5-6, do Exercises 70–72.

Find the slope of the line that passes through each pair of points.

See Lesson 5-1.

70. $(0, -4), (2, 0)$

71. $(5, 5), (3, -1)$

72. $(-4, 2), (5, 2)$

Parallel and Perpendicular Lines

Objectives To determine whether lines are parallel, perpendicular, or neither
To write equations of parallel lines and perpendicular lines

Lines that never intersect have a special relationship.

Getting Ready!

Copy the graph shown at the right. Can you draw a line that will not intersect either of the lines in the graph? If so, draw the line. If not, why not?
Can you draw a line that will intersect one of the lines in such a way that the intersection forms four congruent angles? If so, draw the line. If not, why not?

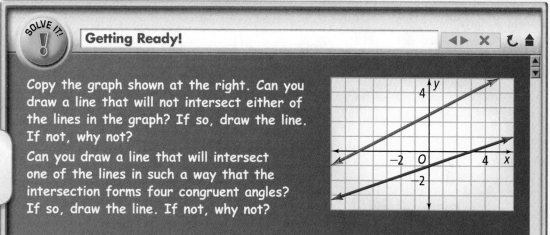

Lesson Vocabulary
• parallel lines
• perpendicular lines
• opposite reciprocals

Two distinct lines in a coordinate plane either intersect or are *parallel*. **Parallel lines** are lines in the same plane that never intersect.

Focus Question How do you use slope to find the relationship between two lines?

take note

Key Concept   Slopes of Parallel Lines

Words
Nonvertical lines are parallel if they have the same slope and different y-intercepts. Vertical lines are parallel if they have different x-intercepts.

Graph

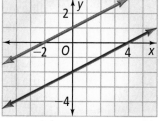

Example
The graphs of $y = \frac{1}{2}x + 1$ and $y = \frac{1}{2}x - 2$ are lines that have the same slope, $\frac{1}{2}$, and different y-intercepts. The lines are parallel.

You can use the fact that the slopes of parallel lines are the same to write the equation of a line parallel to a given line.

Problem 1 **Writing an Equation of a Parallel Line**

A line passes through $(-3, -1)$ and is parallel to the graph of $y = 2x + 3$. What equation represents the line in slope-intercept form?

Step 1 Identify the slope of the given line. The slope of the graph of $y = 2x + 3$ is 2. The parallel line has the same slope.

Step 2 Write an equation in slope-intercept form of the line through $(-3, -1)$ with slope 2.

Think

Why start with point-slope form?
You know a point on the line. You can use what you know about parallel lines to find the slope. So, point-slope form is convenient to use.

Start with point-slope form.	$y - y_1 = m(x - x_1)$
Substitute $(-3, -1)$ for (x_1, y_1) and 2 for m.	$y - (-1) = 2[x - (-3)]$
Use the Distributive Property.	$y + 1 = 2x + 2(3)$
Simplify.	$y + 1 = 2x + 6$
Subtract 1 from each side.	$y = 2x + 5$

The graph of $y = 2x + 5$ passes through $(-3, -1)$ and is parallel to the graph of $y = 2x + 3$.

Got It? 1. A line passes through $(12, 5)$ and is parallel to the graph of $y = \frac{2}{3}x - 1$. What equation represents the line in slope-intercept form?

You can also use slope to determine whether two lines are *perpendicular*. **Perpendicular lines** are lines that intersect to form right angles.

 Key Concept **Slopes of Perpendicular Lines**

Words

Two nonvertical lines are perpendicular if the product of their slopes is -1. A vertical line and a horizontal line are also perpendicular.

Graph

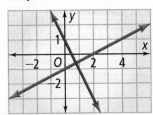

Example
The graph of $y = \frac{1}{2}x - 1$ has a slope of $\frac{1}{2}$.
The graph of $y = -2x + 1$ has a slope of -2.
Since $\frac{1}{2}(-2) = -1$, the lines are perpendicular.

Two numbers whose product is -1 are **opposite reciprocals.** So, the slopes of perpendicular lines are opposite reciprocals. To find the opposite reciprocal of $-\frac{3}{4}$, for example, first find the reciprocal, $-\frac{4}{3}$. Then write its opposite, $\frac{4}{3}$. Since $-\frac{3}{4} \cdot \frac{4}{3} = -1$, $\frac{4}{3}$ is the opposite reciprocal of $-\frac{3}{4}$.

Problem 2 · Classifying Lines

ONLINE PROBLEMS

Think

Why write each equation in slope-intercept form?
You can easily identify the slope of an equation in slope-intercept form. Just look at the coefficient of *x*.

Are the graphs of $4y = -5x + 12$ and $y = \frac{4}{5}x - 8$ *parallel*, *perpendicular*, or *neither*? Explain.

Step 1 Find the slope of each line by writing its equation in slope-intercept form, if necessary. Only the first equation needs to be rewritten.

Write the first equation. $\qquad 4y = -5x + 12$

Divide each side by 4. $\qquad \dfrac{4y}{4} = \dfrac{-5x + 12}{4}$

Simplify. $\qquad\qquad y = -\dfrac{5}{4}x + 3$

The slope of the graph of $y = -\frac{5}{4}x + 3$ is $-\frac{5}{4}$.

The slope of the graph of $y = \frac{4}{5}x - 8$ is $\frac{4}{5}$.

Step 2 The slopes are not the same, so the lines cannot be parallel. Multiply the slopes to see if they are opposite reciprocals.

$$-\frac{5}{4} \cdot \frac{4}{5} = -1$$

The slopes are opposite reciprocals, so the lines are perpendicular.

 Got It? **2.** Are the graphs of the equations *parallel*, *perpendicular*, or *neither*? Explain.

a. $y = \frac{3}{4}x + 7$ and $4x - 3y = 9$ **b.** $6y = -x + 6$ and $y = -\frac{1}{6}x + 6$

Problem 3 · Writing an Equation of a Perpendicular Line

ONLINE PROBLEMS

Multiple Choice Which equation represents the line that passes through (2, 4) and is perpendicular to the graph of $y = \frac{1}{3}x - 1$?

Ⓐ $y = \frac{1}{3}x + 10$ Ⓑ $y = 3x + 10$ Ⓒ $y = -3x - 2$ Ⓓ $y = -3x + 10$

Think

How do you know you have found the opposite reciprocal?
Multiply the two numbers together as a check. If the product is -1, the numbers are opposite reciprocals:
$\frac{1}{3}(-3) = -1$.

Step 1 Identify the slope of the graph of the given equation. The slope is $\frac{1}{3}$.

Step 2 Find the opposite reciprocal of the slope from Step 1. The opposite reciprocal of $\frac{1}{3}$ is -3. So, the perpendicular line has a slope of -3.

Step 3 Use point-slope form to write an equation of the perpendicular line.

Write point-slope form. $\qquad\qquad y - y_1 = m(x - x_1)$

Substitute (2, 4) for (x_1, y_1) and -3 for m. $\quad y - 4 = -3(x - 2)$

Use the Distributive Property. $\qquad\qquad y - 4 = -3x + 6$

Add 4 to each side. $\qquad\qquad\qquad\qquad y = -3x + 10$

The equation is $y = -3x + 10$. The correct answer is D.

 Got It? **3.** A line passes through (1, 8) and is perpendicular to the graph of $y = 2x + 1$. What equation represents the line in slope-intercept form?

Problem 4 **Solving a Real-World Problem**

Architecture An architect uses software to design the ceiling of a room. The architect needs to enter an equation that represents a new beam. The new beam will be perpendicular to the existing beam, which is represented by the red line. The new beam will pass through the corner represented by the blue point. What is an equation that represents the new beam?

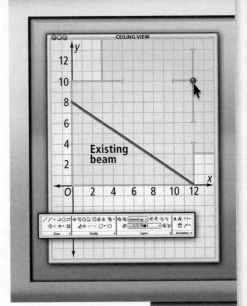

Plan

Have you seen a problem like this before?
Yes. You wrote the equation of a perpendicular line in Problem 3. Follow the same steps here after you calculate the slope of the line from the graph.

Step 1 Use the slope formula to find the slope of the red line that represents the existing beam.

Points (3, 6) and (6, 4) are on the red line. $m = \dfrac{4 - 6}{6 - 3}$

Simplify. $= -\dfrac{2}{3}$

The slope of the line that represents the existing beam is $-\dfrac{2}{3}$.

Step 2 Find the opposite reciprocal of the slope from Step 1. The opposite reciprocal of $-\dfrac{2}{3}$ is $\dfrac{3}{2}$.

Step 3 Use point-slope form to write an equation. The slope of the line that represents the new beam is $\dfrac{3}{2}$. It will pass through (12, 10). An equation that represents the new beam is $y - 10 = \dfrac{3}{2}(x - 12)$ or, in slope-intercept form, $y = \dfrac{3}{2}x - 8$.

 Got It? **4.** What equation could the architect enter to represent a second beam whose graph will pass through the corner at (0, 10) and be parallel to the existing beam? Give your answer in slope-intercept form.

Focus Question How do you use slope to find the relationship between two lines?

Answer You can find a relationship between two lines by comparing their slopes. Parallel lines have the same slope. Perpendicular lines have slopes that are opposite reciprocals.

 Lesson Check

Do you know HOW?

1. Which equations below have graphs that are parallel to one another? Which have graphs that are perpendicular to one another?

$y = -\dfrac{1}{6}x$ $y = 6x$ $y = 6x - 2$

2. What is an equation of the line that passes through $(3, -1)$ and is parallel to $y = -4x + 1$? Give your answer in slope-intercept form.

Do you UNDERSTAND?

3. Vocabulary Tell whether the two numbers in each pair are opposite reciprocals.

a. $-2, \dfrac{1}{2}$ **b.** $\dfrac{1}{4}, 4$ **c.** $5, -5$

4. Open-Ended Write equations of two parallel lines.

5. Compare and Contrast How is determining if two lines are parallel similar to determining if they are perpendicular? How are the processes different?

Practice and Problem-Solving Exercises

 Practice

Write an equation in slope-intercept form of the line that passes through the given point and is parallel to the graph of the given equation.

🔵 **See Problem 1.**

Guided Practice

6. $(2, -2); y = -x - 2$

To start, identify the slope of the line parallel to the given line.

The slope of $y = -x - 2$ is -1. The parallel line has the same slope.

7. $(1, 3); y = 3x + 2$

8. $(1, -3); y + 2 = 4(x - 1)$

9. $(0, 0); y = \frac{2}{3}x + 1$

10. $(4, 2); x = -3$

Determine whether the graphs of the given equations are *parallel*, *perpendicular*, or *neither*. Explain.

🔵 **See Problem 2.**

11. $y = x + 11$
$y = -x + 2$

12. $y = \frac{3}{4}x - 1$
$y = \frac{3}{4}x + 29$

13. $y = -2x + 3$
$2x + y = 7$

> **Hint** Don't forget that all vertical lines are parallel.

14. $y - 4 = 3(x + 2)$
$2x + 6y = 10$

15. $y = -7$
$x = 2$

16. $y = 4x - 2$
$-x + 4y = 0$

Write an equation in slope-intercept form of the line that passes through the given point and is perpendicular to the graph of the given equation.

🔵 **See Problem 3.**

Guided Practice

17. $(-2, 3); y = \frac{1}{2}x - 1$

To start, identify the slope of the line perpendicular to the given line.

The slope of $y = \frac{1}{2}x - 1$ is $\frac{1}{2}$. The slope of the perpendicular line is the opposite reciprocal of $\frac{1}{2}$, which is -2.

18. $(0, 0); y = -3x + 2$

19. $(1, -2); y = 5x + 4$

20. $(-3, 2); x - 2y = 7$

21. $(5, 0); y + 1 = 2(x - 3)$

22. Urban Planning A path for a new city park will connect the park entrance to Main Street. The path should be perpendicular to Main Street. What is an equation that represents the path?

🔵 **See Problem 4.**

23. Bike Path A bike path is being planned for the park in Exercise 22. The bike path will be parallel to Main Street and will pass through the park entrance. What is an equation of the line that represents the bike path?

 Apply

24. Identify each pair of parallel lines. Then identify each pair of perpendicular lines.

line a: $y = 3x + 3$

line b: $x = -1$

line c: $y - 5 = \frac{1}{2}(x - 2)$

line d: $y = 3$

line e: $y + 4 = -2(x + 6)$

line f: $9x - 3y = 5$

Determine whether each statement is *always*, *sometimes*, or *never* true. Explain.

25. A horizontal line is parallel to the *x*-axis.

26. Two lines with positive slopes are parallel.

27. Two lines with the same slope and different *y*-intercepts are perpendicular.

28. Open-Ended What is an equation of a line that is parallel to the *x*-axis? What is an equation of a line that is parallel to the *y*-axis?

29. Think About a Plan A designer is creating a new logo, as shown at the right. The designer wants to add a line to the logo that will be perpendicular to the blue line and pass through the red point. What equation represents the new line?
  • What is the slope of the blue line?
  • What is the slope of the new line?

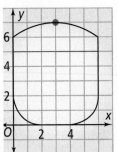

30. Reasoning For what value of *k* are the graphs of $12y = -3x + 8$ and $6y = kx - 5$ parallel? For what value of *k* are they perpendicular?

31. Agriculture Two farmers use combines to harvest corn from their fields. One farmer has 600 acres of corn, and the other has 1000 acres of corn. Each farmer's combine can harvest 100 acres per day. Write two equations for the number of acres *y* of corn *not* harvested after *x* days. Are the graphs of the equations *parallel*, *perpendicular*, or *neither*? How do you know?

Standardized Test Prep

SAT/ACT

32. Which equation represents the graph of a line parallel to the line at the right?

  Ⓐ $y = \frac{1}{2}x + 5$ Ⓒ $y = -2x + 4$

  Ⓑ $y = 2x - 6$ Ⓓ $y = -\frac{1}{2}x - 2$

33. What is the solution of $(5x - 1) + (-2x + 7) = 9$?

  Ⓕ $\frac{3}{7}$ Ⓖ 1   Ⓗ 3   Ⓘ 5

Short Response

34. Sal's Supermarket sells cases of twenty-four 12-oz bottles of water for $15.50. Shopper's World sells 12-packs of 12-oz bottles of water for $8.15. Which store has the better price per bottle? Explain.

Mixed Review

Graph each equation using *x*- and *y*-intercepts.   ◀ **See Lesson 5-5.**

35. $x + y = 8$ **36.** $2x + y = -3$ **37.** $x - 3y = -6$

Get Ready! **To prepare for Lesson 5-7, do Exercises 38–41.**

Write an equation in slope-intercept form of the line that passes through the given points.   ◀ **See Lesson 5-3.**

38. (1, 1), (3, 7)   **39.** (2, 5), (12, 1)   **40.** (0.5, 2), (4.5, 3)   **41.** (13, 20), (6, 60)

5-7 Scatter Plots and Trend Lines

Objectives To write an equation of a trend line and of a line of best fit
To use a trend line and a line of best fit to make predictions

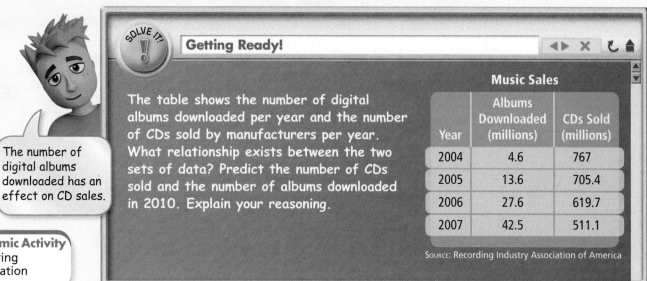

SOLVE IT!

Getting Ready!

The table shows the number of digital albums downloaded per year and the number of CDs sold by manufacturers per year. What relationship exists between the two sets of data? Predict the number of CDs sold and the number of albums downloaded in 2010. Explain your reasoning.

The number of digital albums downloaded has an effect on CD sales.

Music Sales

Year	Albums Downloaded (millions)	CDs Sold (millions)
2004	4.6	767
2005	13.6	705.4
2006	27.6	619.7
2007	42.5	511.1

SOURCE: Recording Industry Association of America

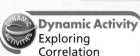

Lesson Vocabulary

• scatter plot
• positive correlation
• negative correlation
• no correlation
• trend line
• interpolation
• extrapolation
• line of best fit
• correlation coefficient
• causation

In the Solve It, the number of albums downloaded per year and the number of CDs sold per year are related.

A **scatter plot** is a graph that relates two different sets of data by displaying them as ordered pairs. Most scatter plots are in the first quadrant of the coordinate plane because the data are usually positive numbers.

You can use scatter plots to find trends in data. The scatter plots below show the three types of relationships that two sets of data may have.

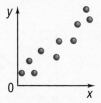

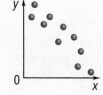

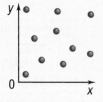

When *y* tends to increase as *x* increases, the two sets of data have a **positive correlation.**

When *y* tends to decrease as *x* increases, the two sets of data have a **negative correlation.**

When *x* and *y* are not related, the two sets of data have **no correlation.**

Focus Question How do you write an equation to show trends in data?

 **Problem 1** **Making a Scatter Plot and Describing Its Correlation**

Temperature The table shows the altitude of an airplane and the temperature outside the plane.

Plane Altitude and Outside Temperature											
Altitude (m)	0	500	1000	1500	2000	2500	3000	3500	4000	4500	5000
Temperature (°F)	59.0	59.2	61.3	55.5	41.6	29.8	29.9	18.1	26.2	12.4	0.6

Think

The highest altitude is 5000 m. So a reasonable scale on the altitude axis is 0 to 5500 with every 1000 m labeled. You can use similar reasoning to label the temperature axis.

A **Make a scatter plot of the data.**

Treat the data as ordered pairs. For the altitude of 1500 m and the temperature of 55.5°F, plot (1500, 55.5).

B **What type of relationship does the scatter plot show?**

The temperature outside the plane tends to decrease as the altitude of the plane increases. So the data have a negative correlation.

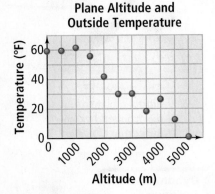

Plane Altitude and Outside Temperature

 Got It? **1. a.** Make a scatter plot of the data in the table below. What type of relationship does the scatter plot show?

Gasoline Purchases							
Dollars Spent	10	11	9	10	13	5	8	4
Gallons Bought	2.5	2.8	2.3	2.6	3.3	1.3	2.2	1.1

b. **Reasoning** Consider the population of a city and the number of letters in the name of the city. Would you expect a *positive correlation*, a *negative correlation*, or *no correlation* between the two sets of data? Explain your reasoning.

When two sets of data have a positive or negative correlation, you can use a trend line to show the correlation more clearly. A **trend line** is a line on a scatter plot, drawn near the points, that shows a correlation.

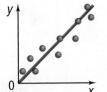

You can use a trend line to estimate a value between two known data values or to predict a value outside the range of known data values. **Interpolation** is estimating a value between two known values. **Extrapolation** is predicting a value outside the range of known values.

Problem 2 **Writing an Equation of a Trend Line**

Biology Make a scatter plot of the data at the right. What is the approximate weight of a 7-month-old panda?

Weight of a Panda

Age (months)	Weight (lb)
1	2.5
2	7.6
3	12.5
4	17.1
6	24.3
8	37.9
10	49.2
12	54.9

Step 1 Make a scatter plot and draw a trend line. Estimate the coordinates of two points on the line.

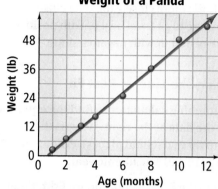

Weight of a Panda

Plan

How do you draw an accurate trend line?
An accurate trend line should fit the data closely. There should be about the same number of points above the line as below it.

Two points on the trend line are (4, 17.1) and (8, 37.9).

Step 2 Write an equation of the trend line.

Find the slope of the trend line.
$$m = \frac{y_2 - y_1}{x_2 - x_1} = \frac{37.9 - 17.1}{8 - 4} = \frac{20.8}{4} = 5.2$$

Use point-slope form.
$$y - y_1 = m(x - x_1)$$

Substitute 5.2 for m and (4, 17.1) for (x_1, y_1).
$$y - 17.1 = 5.2(x - 4)$$

Use the Distributive Property.
$$y - 17.1 = 5.2x - 20.8$$

Add 17.1 to each side.
$$y = 5.2x - 3.7$$

Step 3 Estimate the weight of a 7-month-old panda.

Substitute 7 for x.
$$y = 5.2(7) - 3.7$$

Simplify.
$$y = 32.7$$

Think

How can you check the reasonableness of your answer?
Since $x = 7$ is visible on the graph, find its corresponding y-value. When $x = 7$, $y \approx 32.7$. So the estimate is reasonable.

The weight of a 7-month-old panda is about 32.7 lb.

Got It? **2. a.** Make a scatter plot of the data below. Draw a trend line and write its equation. What is the approximate body length of a 7-month-old panda?

Body Length of a Panda								
Age (month)	1	2	3	4	5	6	8	9
Body Length (in.)	8.0	11.75	15.5	16.7	20.1	22.2	26.5	29.0

b. Reasoning Do you think you can use your model to extrapolate the body length of a 3-year-old panda? Explain.

The trend line that shows the relationship between two sets of data most accurately is called the **line of best fit.** A graphing calculator computes the equation of the line of best fit using a method called linear regression.

The graphing calculator gives the **correlation coefficient** r, a number from -1 to 1, that tells you how closely the equation models the data.

$r = -1$ $r = 0$ $r = 1$

strong negative   no   strong positive
correlation   correlation   correlation

The nearer r is to 1 or -1, the more closely the data cluster around the line of best fit. If r is near 1, the data lie close to a line of best fit with positive slope. If r is near -1, the data lie close to a line of best fit with negative slope.

Problem 3   **Finding the Line of Best Fit**

College Tuition Use a graphing calculator to find the equation of the line of best fit for the data at the right. What is the correlation coefficient to three decimal places? Predict the cost of attending in the 2012–2013 academic year.

Average Tuition and Fees at Public 4-Year Colleges

Academic Year	Cost ($)
2000–2001	3508
2001–2002	3766
2002–2003	4098
2003–2004	4645
2004–2005	5126
2005–2006	5492
2006–2007	5836

SOURCE: The College Board

Step 1   Press **stat**. From the **EDIT** menu, choose **Edit**. Enter the years into L_1. Let $x = 2000$ represent academic year 2000–2001, $x = 2001$ represent 2001–2002, and so on. Enter the costs into L_2.

Step 2   Press **stat**. Choose **LinReg(ax + b)** from the **CALC** menu. Press **enter** to find the equation of the line of best fit and the correlation coefficient. The calculator uses the form $y = ax + b$ for the equation.

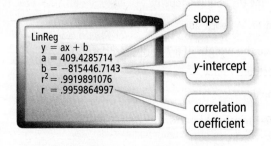

LinReg
  y = ax + b
  a = 409.4285714 → slope
  b = -815446.7143 → y-intercept
  r^2 = .9919891076
  r = .9959864997 → correlation coefficient

Think

What does the value of the correlation coefficient mean?
The correlation coefficient of 0.996 is close to 1. So there is a strong positive correlation between the academic year and the cost of attending college.

Round to the nearest hundredth. The equation of the line of best fit is $y = 409.43x - 815{,}446.71$. The correlation coefficient is about 0.996.

Step 3   Predict the cost of attending in the 2012–2013 academic year.

Use the equation of the line of best fit. $y = 409.43x - 815{,}446.71$

Substitute 2012 for x. $y = 409.43(2012) - 815{,}446.71$

Simplify. Round to the nearest whole number. $y \approx 8326$

The cost of attending a four-year public college in the 2012–2013 academic year is predicted to be about $8326.

 Got It? 3. Predict the cost of attending in the 2016–2017 academic year.

Causation is when a change in one quantity causes a change in a second quantity. A correlation between quantities does not always imply causation.

 Problem 4 Identifying Whether Relationships Are Causal

In the following situations, is there likely to be a correlation? If so, does the correlation reflect a causal relationship? Explain.

A the number of loaves of bread baked and the amount of flour used

There is a positive correlation and also a causal relationship. As the number of loaves of bread baked increases, the amount of flour used increases.

B the number of mailboxes and the number of firefighters in a city

There is likely to be a positive correlation because both the number of mailboxes and the number of firefighters tend to increase as the population of a city increases. However, installing more mailboxes will not *cause* the number of firefighters to increase, so there is no causal relationship.

Think

Causal relationships always have a correlation. However, two data sets that have a correlation may not have a causal relationship.

 Got It? **4.** In the following situations, is there likely to be a correlation? If so, does the correlation reflect a causal relationship? Explain.
   a. the cost of a family's vacation and the size of their house
   b. the time spent exercising and the number of Calories burned

Focus Question How do you write an equation to show trends in data?

Answer Make a scatter plot. If there is a correlation, draw the best possible trend line. Use any two points on the trend line to determine the equation of the line. Check your equation with the equation of the line of best fit.

 Lesson Check

Do you know HOW?

Use the table.

Average Maximum Daily Temperature in January for Northern Latitudes							
Latitude (° N)	35	33	30	25	43	40	39
Temperature (°F)	46	52	67	76	32	37	44

SOURCE: U.S. Department of Commerce

1. Make a scatter plot of the data. What type of relationship does the scatter plot show?

2. Draw a trend line and write its equation.

3. Predict the average maximum daily temperature in January at a latitude of 50° N.

Do you UNDERSTAND?

4. **Vocabulary** Given a set of data pairs, how would you decide whether to use interpolation or extrapolation to find a certain value?

5. **Compare and Contrast** How are a trend line and the line of best fit for a set of data pairs similar? How are they different?

6. **Error Analysis** Refer to the table below. A student says that the data have a negative correlation because as x decreases, y also decreases. What is the student's error?

x	10	7	5	4	1	0
y	1	0	−2	−4	−7	−9

Practice and Problem-Solving Exercises

See Problem 1.

A Practice

For each table, make a scatter plot of the data. Describe the type of correlation the scatter plot shows.

7.

Jeans Sales				
Average Price ($)	21	28	36	40
Number Sold	130	112	82	65

Guided Practice

To start, think about the labels for the *x*- and *y*-axes.

Write the ordered pairs from the table.

The *x*-axis represents the average price and the *y*-axis represents the number sold.

(21, 130), (28, 112), (36, 82), (40, 65)

8.

Gasoline Purchases					
Dollars Spent	10	11	9	8	13
Gallons Bought	2.6	3	2.4	2.2	3.5

Theme Parks Use the table below for Exercises 9 and 10.

See Problem 2.

Attendance and Revenue at U.S. Theme Parks									
Year	1990	1992	1994	1996	1998	2000	2002	2004	2006
Attendance (millions)	253	267	267	290	300	317	324	328	335
Revenue (billions of dollars)	5.7	6.5	7.0	7.9	8.7	9.6	9.9	10.8	11.5

SOURCE: International Association of Amusement Parks and Attractions

9. Make a scatter plot of the data pairs (year, attendance). Draw a trend line and write its equation. Estimate the attendance at U.S. theme parks in 2005.

10. Make a scatter plot of the data pairs (year, revenue). Draw a trend line and write its equation. Predict the revenue at U.S. theme parks in 2012.

11. Entertainment Use a graphing calculator to find the equation of the line of best fit for the data in the table. Find the value of the correlation coefficient *r* to three decimal places. Then predict the number of movie tickets sold in the U.S. in 2014.

See Problem 3.

Movie Tickets Sold in U.S. by Year										
Year	1998	1999	2000	2001	2002	2003	2004	2005	2006	2007
Tickets Sold (millions)	1289	1311	1340	1339	1406	1421	1470	1415	1472	1470

SOURCE: Motion Picture Association of America

In each situation, tell whether a correlation is likely. If it is, tell whether the correlation reflects a causal relationship. Explain your reasoning.

◀ See Problem 4.

12. the amount of time you study for a test and the score you receive

To start, look for a relationship. The more time you study for a test, the more likely you are to receive a better score.

13. a person's height and the number of letters in the person's name

14. the shoe size and the salary of a teacher

15. the price of hamburger at a grocery store and the amount of hamburger sold

B **Apply**

16. Open-Ended Describe three real-world situations: one with a positive correlation, one with a negative correlation, and one with no correlation.

17. Writing Give two data sets that are correlated but do *not* have a causal relationship.

18. Business During one month at a local deli, the amount of ham sold decreased as the amount of turkey sold increased. Is this an example of *positive correlation*, *negative correlation*, or *no correlation*?

19. Think About a Plan Students measured the diameters and circumferences of the tops of a variety of cylinders. Below are the data that they collected. Estimate the diameter of a cylinder with circumference 22 cm.

Cylinder Tops									
Diameter (cm)	3	3	5	6	8	8	9.5	10	10	12
Circumference (cm)	9.3	9.5	16	18.8	25	25.6	29.5	31.5	30.9	39.5

• How can you use a scatter plot to find an equation of a trend line?
• How can you use the equation of the trend line to make an estimate?

20. U.S. Population Use the data below.

Estimated Population of the United States (thousands)							
Year	2000	2001	2002	2003	2004	2005	2006
Male	138,482	140,079	141,592	142,937	144,467	145,973	147,512
Female	143,734	145,147	146,533	147,858	149,170	150,533	151,886

Source: U.S. Census Bureau

a. Make a scatter plot of the data pairs (male population, female population).
b. Draw a trend line and write its equation.
c. Use your equation to predict the U.S. female population if the U.S. male population increases to 150,000,000.
d. Reasoning Consider a scatter plot of the data pairs (year, male population). Would it be reasonable to use this scatter plot to predict the U.S. male population in 2035? Explain your reasoning.

21. a. Graphing Calculator Use a graphing calculator to find the equation of the line of best fit for the data below. Let $x = 8$ represent 1998, $x = 9$ represent 1999, and so on.

U.S. Computer and Video Game Unit Sales										
Year	1998	1999	2000	2001	2002	2003	2004	2005	2006	2007
Unit Sales (in millions)	152.4	184.5	196.3	210.3	225.8	240.9	249.5	229.5	241.6	267.9

SOURCE: The NPD Group/Retail Tracking Service

b. What is the slope of the line of best fit? What does the slope mean in terms of the number of computer and video game units sold?

c. What is the y-intercept of the line of best fit? What does the y-intercept mean in terms of the number of computer and video game units sold?

Standardized Test Prep

SAT/ACT

22. Suppose you survey each school in your state. What relationship would you expect between the number of students and the number of teachers in each school?

(A) positive correlation

(B) negative correlation

(C) no correlation

(D) none of the above

23. A horizontal line passes through $(5, -2)$. Which other point is also on the line?

(F) $(5, 2)$ (G) $(-5, -2)$ (H) $(-5, 2)$ (I) $(5, 0)$

24. When 18 gal of water are pumped into an empty tank, the tank is filled to three fourths of its capacity. How many gallons of water does the tank hold?

(A) 12   (B) 13.5   (C) 18.5   (D) 24

Short Response

25. The table shows the balance of a student's bank account at various times. Estimate how much money is in the student's bank account in Week 6. Justify your answer.

Weekly Account Balance					
Week	1	3	4	7	9
Account Balance	\$35	\$68	\$85	\$105	\$136

Mixed Review

Write an equation of the line in slope-intercept form that passes through the given point and is parallel to the graph of the given equation.

See Lesson 5-6.

26. $y = 5x + 1; (2, -3)$ **27.** $y = -x - 9; (0, 5)$ **28.** $2x + 3y = 9; (-1, 4)$

Get Ready! **To prepare for Lesson 6-1, do Exercises 29–32.**

Graph each equation.

See Lesson 5-3.

29. $y = 2x - 1$ **30.** $y = -3x + 5$ **31.** $y = \frac{1}{3}x + 2$ **32.** $y = -\frac{5}{2}x - 7$

In this activity, you will release a ball from different heights and record the maximum height after its first bounce. Complete this activity over a hard surface. Measure all heights from the bottom of the ball.

Activity

Place one end of a meter stick on the floor and tape it to the wall. Tape a second meter stick to the wall starting at the top of the first meter stick.

1. **Data Collection** Drop the ball from 50 cm. Carefully record its maximum height after the first bounce. Repeat.

2. Copy and complete the table at the right. You may make additional measurements using different starting heights.

3. Graph the data from both trials on the same coordinate plane.

4. **Reasoning** Why is it reasonable to use $(0, 0)$ as a data point?

5. Draw a trend line that includes $(0, 0)$.

6. **a. Predict** Use your line to predict the maximum height of the first bounce after the ball is dropped from 175 cm.

   b. From what height would you have to drop the ball for it to reach 2 m after the first bounce?

7. **a.** Use a graphing calculator to find the equation of the line of best fit for the data in the table.

   b. Predict Use your equation to predict the maximum height of the first bounce after the ball is dropped from 175 cm.

   c. How do your predictions from part (a) of Step 6 and part (b) of Step 7 compare?

Bounce Height Data

Initial Height (cm)	Maximum Height After First Bounce	
	Trial 1	Trial 2
50	■	■
100	■	■
150	■	■
200	■	■

Exercises

8. **Multiple Choice** The graph at the right shows the bounce data for a ball. Let x = the initial height in centimeters. Let y = the maximum height in centimeters. Which equation best models the data?

   Ⓐ $y = 0.3x$ Ⓒ $y = 0.5x$

   Ⓑ $y = 0.4x$ Ⓓ $y = 0.6x$

9. Suppose students used several different types of balls and found that the slopes of the trend lines were not the same. What is the significance of the slope?

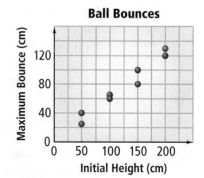

Ball Bounces

Pull It **All Together**

To solve these problems you will pull together many concepts and skills that you have studied about linear functions.

BIG idea Proportionality

In the graph of a line, the ratio for the slope indicates the rate of change.

Task 1

Find the rate of change for each table, equation, or graph. How did you find the rate of change?

a.

x	2	4	6
y	10	20	30

b. $5x + 3y = -2$

c.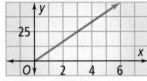

BIG idea Functions

There are several forms for the equation of a line. Each form communicates different information. For instance, from the point-slope form, you can determine a point and the slope of a line.

Task 2

Write an equation in slope-intercept, point-slope, or standard form for the line with the given information. Explain why you chose the form you used.

a. passes through $(-1, 4)$ and $(-5, 2)$

b. slope 2, y-intercept -4

c. has an x-intercept of 6 and a y-intercept of 3

d. passes through $(1, 2)$ with slope $-\frac{5}{3}$

BIG idea Modeling

You can model the trend of the real-world data in a scatter plot with an equation of a line. You can use the equation to estimate or to make predictions.

Task 3

At the beginning of a 20-month period, Stacie owns one clothing store. During that period, she opens a second clothing store in a different location. The table shows the total monthly sales of Stacie's clothing stores for the 20-month period.

Monthly Sales (in thousands of dollars)										
Month	2	4	6	8	10	12	14	16	18	20
Sales	3	5	4	6	5	12	16	22	26	32

a. Make a scatter plot of the data in the table.

b. What are two equations that model the data? What are the domain and range of each equation? Explain your process.

c. About how much money did Stacie's stores earn in the fifth month? How much money do you expect the stores to earn in the twenty-fourth month? Explain.

5 Chapter Review for Part B

Connecting BIG ideas and Answering the Essential Questions

1 Proportionality
In the graph of a line, the ratio for the slope indicates the rate of change.

→ **Rate of Change and Slope (Lesson 5-1)**
$$\text{slope} = \frac{\text{rise}}{\text{run}} = \frac{y_2 - y_1}{x_2 - x_1}$$

→ **Parallel and Perpendicular Lines (Lesson 5-6)**
Parallel lines have the same slope. The product of the slopes of perpendicular lines is -1.

2 Functions
There are several forms for the equation of a line. Each form communicates different information. For instance, from the point-slope form, you can determine a point and the slope of a line.

→ **Slope-Intercept Form (Lesson 5-3)**
$$y = mx + b$$

→ **Point-Slope Form (Lesson 5-4)**
$$y - y_1 = m(x - x_1)$$

→ **Standard Form (Lesson 5-5)**
$$Ax + By = C$$

3 Modeling
You can model the trend of the real-world data in a scatter plot with the equation of a line. You can use the equation to estimate or to make predictions.

→ **Scatter Plots and Trend Lines (Lesson 5-7)**
The trend line that shows the relationship between two sets of data most accurately is called the line of best fit.

Chapter Vocabulary

- causation (p. 367)
- correlation coefficient (p. 366)
- extrapolation (p. 364)
- interpolation (p. 364)
- line of best fit (p. 366)
- negative correlation (p. 363)
- no correlation (p. 363)
- opposite reciprocals (p. 358)
- parallel lines (p. 357)
- perpendicular lines (p. 358)
- positive correlation (p. 363)
- scatter plot (p. 363)
- standard form of a linear equation (p. 349)
- trend line (p. 364)
- x-intercept (p. 349)

Choose the vocabulary term that correctly completes the sentence.

1. Estimating a value between two known values in a data set is called __?__.

2. Two lines are perpendicular when their slopes are __?__.

3. The line that most accurately models data in a scatter plot is the __?__.

5-5 and 5-6 Standard Form and Parallel and Perpendicular Lines

Quick Review

The **standard form** of a linear equation is $Ax + By = C$, where A, B, and C are real numbers, and A and B are not both zero.

Parallel lines are lines in the same plane that never intersect. Two lines are **perpendicular** if they intersect to form right angles.

Example

Are the graphs of $y = \frac{4}{3}x + 5$ and $y = -\frac{3}{4}x + 2$ *parallel, perpendicular,* or *neither*? Explain.

The slope of the graph of $y = \frac{4}{3}x + 5$ is $\frac{4}{3}$.

The slope of the graph of $y = -\frac{3}{4}x + 2$ is $-\frac{3}{4}$.

$$\frac{4}{3}\left(-\frac{3}{4}\right) = -1$$

The slopes are opposite reciprocals, so the graphs are perpendicular.

Exercises

Write an equation of the line that passes through the given point and is parallel to the graph of the given equation.

4. $(2, -1); y = 5x - 2$ **5.** $(0, -5); y = 9x$

Determine whether the graphs of the two equations are *parallel, perpendicular,* or *neither.* Explain.

6. $y = 6x + 2$ **7.** $2x - 5y = 0$

     $18x - 3y = 15$ $y + 3 = \frac{5}{2}x$

Write an equation of the line that passes through the given point and is perpendicular to the graph of the given equation.

8. $(3, 5); y = -3x + 7$ **9.** $(4, 10); y = 8x - 1$

5-7 Scatter Plots and Trend Lines

Quick Review

A **scatter plot** displays two sets of data as ordered pairs. A **trend line** for a scatter plot shows the correlation between the two sets of data. The most accurate trend line is the **line of best fit**. To estimate or predict values on a scatter plot, you can use **interpolation** or **extrapolation**.

Example

Estimate the length of the kudzu vine in Week 3.

When $w = 3$, $\ell \approx 10$. So in Week 3, the length of the kudzu vine was about 10 ft.

Predict the length of the kudzu vine in Week 11.

    Use the equation of the trend line. $\ell = 3.5w$

    Substitute 11 for w. $\ell = 3.5(11)$

    Simplify. $\ell = 38.5$

The length of the vine in Week 11 will be about 38.5 ft.

Kudzu Vine Growth

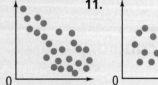

Exercises

Describe the type of correlation the scatter plot shows.

10.   **11.**   **12.**

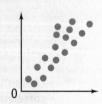

13. a. Make a scatter plot of the data below.

Heights and Arm Spans					
Height (m)	1.5	1.8	1.7	2.0	1.7	2.1
Arm Span (m)	1.4	1.7	1.7	1.9	1.6	2.0

    b. Write an equation of a reasonable trend line or use a graphing calculator to find the equation of the line of best fit.

    c. Estimate the arm span of someone who is 1.6 m tall.

    d. Predict the arm span of someone who is 2.2 m tall.

Do you know HOW?

Write an equation in slope-intercept form of each line.

1.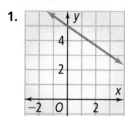

2.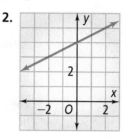

Write an equation in point-slope form of the line through the given point and with the given slope.

3. $(5, 1); m = \frac{1}{3}$

4. $(-2, 3); m = -2$

Write each equation in standard form using integers.

5. $y = \frac{3}{4}x + 5$

6. $y + 4 = \frac{1}{3}(x + 6)$

Graph each equation.

7. $y = 4x - 3$

8. $y = 7$

9. $y + 3 = \frac{1}{2}(x + 2)$

10. $-3x + 5y = 15$

Determine whether each equation represents a direct variation. If it does, find the constant of variation.

11. $2x + 3y = 0$

12. $4x + 6y = 3$

Write an equation in slope-intercept form of the line passing through each pair of points.

13. $(6, 0)$ and $(3, -1)$

14. $(-7, 2)$ and $(1, -2)$

15. Pet Grooming You start a pet grooming service. You spend $30 on supplies. You plan to charge $5 to groom each pet.
   a. Write an equation to relate your profit y to the number of pets x you groom.
   b. Graph the equation. What are the x- and y-intercepts?

16. Make a scatter plot and draw a trend line for the data in the table. Interpolate or extrapolate to estimate the number of inventors applying for patents in 2006 and in 2015.

17. What is an equation of the line parallel to $y = -x + 1$ and through $(4, 4)$?

18. What is an equation of the line perpendicular to $y = -x - 2$ and through $(-2, 4)$?

Number of Inventors Applying for Patents

Year	Inventors
1999	22,052
2001	20,588
2003	18,462
2005	14,039
2007	13,748

SOURCE: U.S. Patent Office

Do you UNDERSTAND?

19. Writing How are lines of best fit and other trend lines used with scatter plots?

20. Open-Ended Write an equation whose graph is parallel to the graph of $y = 0.5x - 10$.

21. Compare and Contrast Is an equation that represents a direct variation a type of linear equation? Explain.

22. Vocabulary What does it mean when a line of best fit has a correlation coefficient close to 1?

23. Reasoning How many lines can you draw that are parallel to the line and through the point shown at the right? Explain.

5 Cumulative Test Prep

Some questions on standardized tests ask you to use a graph. Read the sample question at the right. Then follow the tips to answer it.

TIP 1

Identifying the *y*-intercept may help eliminate some possibilities.

What is an equation of the line shown below?

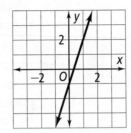

Ⓐ $y = \frac{1}{3}x - 1$ Ⓒ $y = 3x - 1$

Ⓑ $y = \frac{1}{3}x + \frac{1}{2}$ Ⓓ $y = 3x + \frac{1}{2}$

TIP 2

Find the slope by using the point that represents the *y*-intercept and another point on the line.

Think It Through

You can see from the graph that the *y*-intercept is -1. So you can eliminate choices B and D. To get from $(0, -1)$ to $(1, 2)$, move 3 units up and 1 unit to the right. The slope is $\frac{3}{1} = 3$. So an equation is $y = 3x - 1$. The correct answer is C.

Vocabulary Builder

As you solve test items, you must understand the meanings of mathematical terms. Choose the correct term to complete each sentence.

A. The (*dependent, independent*) variable provides the output values of a function.

B. The set of all possible values for the dependent variable is called the (*domain, range*).

C. The (*slope, y-intercept*) of a line is determined by the ratio $\frac{\text{rise}}{\text{run}}$.

D. An (*equation, inequality*) is a math sentence that shows the relationship between two quantities that may not have the same value.

E. (*Parallel, Perpendicular*) lines are lines in the same plane that never intersect.

Multiple Choice

Read each question. Then write the letter of the correct answer on your paper.

1. Which is an equation of a line with slope 3?

Ⓐ $y = 3x - 4$ Ⓒ $y = 4x - 3$

Ⓑ $y = -3x + 3$ Ⓓ $y = -3x - 5$

2. Ben has a cell phone plan where he pays $12 per month plus $.10 per minute of talk time. The equation $y = 0.10x + 12$ can be used to find his monthly phone bill *y* given the number of minutes *x* he spends talking. Which set or inequality represents a reasonable range of the function?

Ⓕ $\{0, 12\}$ Ⓗ $12 \leq y$

Ⓖ $0 \leq y \leq 12$ Ⓘ $0 \leq y$

3. Which expression is equivalent to
$3(12x + 2) - 2(10x + 3)$?

Ⓐ $16x$ Ⓒ $16x + 9$

Ⓑ $16x + 5$ Ⓓ $16x + 12$

4. What is the slope of the line at the right?

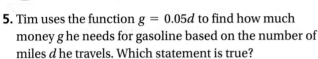

Ⓕ -2

Ⓖ $\frac{2}{3}$

Ⓗ $\frac{3}{2}$

Ⓘ 3

5. Tim uses the function $g = 0.05d$ to find how much money g he needs for gasoline based on the number of miles d he travels. Which statement is true?

Ⓐ The number of miles Tim travels depends on how much money he needs for gasoline.

Ⓑ The number of miles Tim travels depends on the price of a gallon of gasoline.

Ⓒ The amount of money Tim needs for gasoline depends on the number of miles he travels.

Ⓓ The amount of money Tim needs for gasoline is constant.

6. Which equation is *not* a function?

Ⓕ $y = 0$ Ⓗ $x = -3$

Ⓖ $y = 2x - 4$ Ⓘ $y = -x$

7. The perimeter P of a rectangle can be found using the formula $P = 2(\ell + w)$, where ℓ represents the length and w represents the width. Which equation represents the width in terms of P and ℓ?

Ⓐ $w = 2(P - \ell)$ Ⓒ $w = 2P - \ell$

Ⓑ $w = \frac{P - \ell}{2}$ Ⓓ $w = \frac{P}{2} - \ell$

8. Use the graph at the right. If the y-intercept increases by 2 and the slope remains the same, what will the x-intercept be?

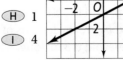

Ⓕ -3 Ⓗ 1

Ⓖ -2 Ⓘ 4

9. The U.S. Mint charges $25 for a limited edition coin, plus a $6 shipping charge. The cost c of purchasing n coins can be found using the function $c = 25n + 6$. There is a limit of 5 coins per purchase. What is a reasonable domain of the function?

Ⓐ $\{5\}$

Ⓑ $\{1, 2, 3, 4, 5\}$

Ⓒ $\{25, 50, 75, 100, 125\}$

Ⓓ $\{31, 56, 81, 106, 131\}$

10. A financial advisor collected data on the amount of money earned and saved each year by people ages 20–29. The results are shown in the scatter plot. Which best describes the slope of the line of best fit?

Ⓕ positive Ⓗ zero

Ⓖ negative Ⓘ undefined

11. Which graph shows a line with slope $\frac{1}{3}$ and y-intercept -1?

Ⓐ 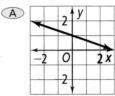 Ⓒ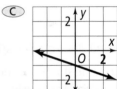

Ⓑ 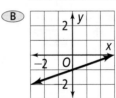 Ⓓ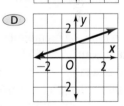

12. Which set is the intersection of $X = \{3, 4, 5, 6, 7, 8\}$ and $Y = \{1, 2, 5, 6, 7, 8, 11\}$?

Ⓕ $\varnothing$ Ⓗ $\{3, 4, 5, 6, 7\}$

Ⓖ $\{5, 6, 7, 8\}$ Ⓘ $\{5, 6, 7, 8, 11\}$

13. If a, b, and c are real numbers where $b > c$, for which values of a is the expression $\frac{b}{a} < \frac{c}{a}$ always true?

Ⓐ $a > 0$ Ⓒ $a < 0$

Ⓑ $a \geq 0$ Ⓓ $a \leq 0$

14. The graph shows the relationship between the total price of tomatoes and the number of pounds of tomatoes purchased. Which statement is true?

Price of Tomatoes

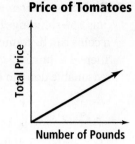

- **F** The number of pounds depends on the total price.
- **G** The number of tomatoes depends on the total price.
- **H** The total price depends on the number of pounds.
- **I** The number of tomatoes depends on the number of pounds.

15. A line passes through the point $(2, 1)$ and has a slope of $-\frac{3}{5}$. What is an equation of the line?

- **A** $y - 1 = -\frac{3}{5}(x - 2)$
- **B** $y - 1 = -\frac{5}{3}(x - 2)$
- **C** $y - 2 = -\frac{3}{5}(x - 1)$
- **D** $y - 2 = -\frac{5}{3}(x - 1)$

GRIDDED RESPONSE

Record your answers in a grid.

16. What is the slope of a line that is perpendicular to the line shown at the right?

17. Fran makes a rectangular tablecloth that has an area of 5 ft². Her mother makes a tablecloth that is three times the length and three times the width of Fran's. What is the area, in square feet, of her mother's tablecloth?

18. In a gymnastics competition, a floor routine must last no longer than 90 s. For every second over 90 s, 0.05 point is deducted from an athlete's score. Suppose Jenny would have earned 9.865 points for her routine, but it lasted 93 s. What was the actual number of points that she earned?

19. The points $(-2, 11)$ and $(6, 3)$ lie on the same line. What is the x-intercept of the line?

20. Hannah took a survey of 500 students at her school to find out whether they liked baseball or football. The results are shown in the Venn diagram below. How many of the students surveyed liked football?

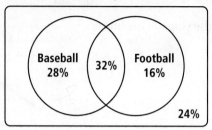

21. What is the volume, in cubic inches, of the rectangular prism at the right?

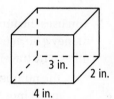

22. What is the solution of the equation $4x + 7 = 9x + 2$?

23. Corporate bond prices are quoted in fourths of a point. The price of a bond increases from $84\frac{1}{2}$ to $86\frac{1}{4}$. By how many points did the price increase?

24. An online bookseller charges $3 per order plus $1 per book for shipping. John places an order for four books that have the same price. The total cost of his order is $30. What is the price, in dollars, of each book?

Short Response

25. Determine whether the following statement is *always*, *sometimes*, or *never* true: If $x + y > 0$, then $xy > 0$. Justify your answer.

26. Line p passes through the point $(5, -2)$ and has a slope of 0. Line q passes through the point $(-13, -9)$ and is parallel to line p. What is an equation of line q? Show your work.

Extended Response

27. The perimeter of a square is 16 in. A trapezoid has the same area and height as the square. The area of a trapezoid is $\frac{1}{2}h(b_1 + b_2)$, where h is the height and b_1 and b_2 are the lengths of the bases. If one base of the trapezoid is 3 in. long, what is the length of the other base? Show your work.

Get Ready!

Lesson 2-4

Solving Equations

Solve each equation. If the equation is an identity, write *identity*. If it has no solution, write *no solution*.

1. $3(2 - 2x) = -6(x - 1)$

2. $3p + 1 = -p + 5$

3. $4x - 1 = 3(x + 1) + x$

4. $\frac{1}{2}(6c - 4) = 4 + c$

5. $5x = 2 - (x - 7)$

6. $v + 5 = v - 5$

Lesson 3-4

Solving Inequalities

Solve each inequality.

7. $5x + 3 < 18$

8. $-\frac{r}{5} + 1 \geq -6$

9. $-3t - 5 < 34$

10. $-(7f + 18) - 2f \leq 0$

11. $8s + 7 > -3(5s - 4)$

12. $\frac{1}{2}(x + 6) + 1 \geq -5$

Lesson 4-5

Writing Functions

13. The height of a triangle is 1 cm less than twice the length of the base. Let $x =$ the length of the base.

    a. Write an expression for the height of the triangle.

    b. Write a function rule for the area of the triangle.

    c. What is the area of such a triangle if the length of its base is 16 cm?

Lessons 5-3, 5-4, and 5-5

Graphing Linear Equations

Graph each equation.

14. $2x + 4y = -8$

15. $y = -\frac{2}{3}x + 3$

16. $y + 5 = -2(x - 2)$

Looking Ahead Vocabulary

17. After a team loses a game, they're *eliminated* from a tournament. The *elimination method* is a way to solve a system of equations. Do you think using the elimination method adds or deletes a variable from a system of equations?

Systems of Equations and Inequalities

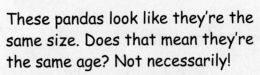

These pandas look like they're the same size. Does that mean they're the same age? Not necessarily!

Individuals grow at different rates.

In this chapter, you'll learn how to solve problems involving more than one equation, like finding out when two animals that grow at different rates will be the same size.

Vocabulary for Part A

English/Spanish Vocabulary Audio Online:

English	Spanish
elimination method, *p. 396*	eliminación
solution of a system of linear equations, *p. 382*	solución de un sistema de ecuaciones lineales
substitution method, *p. 390*	método de sustitución
system of linear equations, *p. 382*	sistema de ecuaciones lineales

My Math Video

00:04:04

BIG ideas

1 **Solving Equations and Inequalities**
Essential Question: How can you solve a system of equations or inequalities?

2 **Modeling**
Essential Question: Can systems of equations model real-world situations?

Chapter Preview for Part A

6-1 **Solving Systems by Graphing**
6-2 **Solving Systems Using Substitution**
6-3 PART 1 **Solving Systems Using Elimination**
    PART 2 **Solving Systems Using Elimination**
6-4 **Applications of Linear Systems**

Solving Systems by Graphing

Objectives To solve systems of equations by graphing
To analyze special systems

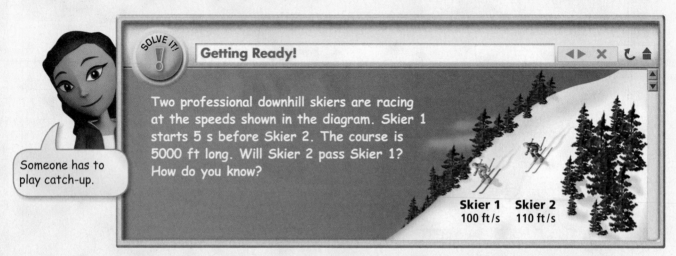

SOLVE IT!

Getting Ready!

Two professional downhill skiers are racing at the speeds shown in the diagram. Skier 1 starts 5 s before Skier 2. The course is 5000 ft long. Will Skier 2 pass Skier 1? How do you know?

Someone has to play catch-up.

	Skier 1	Skier 2
	100 ft/s	110 ft/s

Lesson Vocabulary
- system of linear equations
- solution of a system of linear equations

You can model the problem in the Solve It with two linear equations. Two or more linear equations form a **system of linear equations.** Any ordered pair that makes *all* of the equations in a system true is a **solution of a system of linear equations.**

Systems of equations can be solved in more than one way. One method is to graph each equation and find the intersection point, if one exists.

Focus Question How can a graph help you find the solution of a system of equations?

Problem 1 Solving a System of Equations by Graphing

What is the solution of the system? Use a graph. $\quad y = x + 2$
$\qquad\qquad\qquad\qquad\qquad\qquad\qquad\qquad\qquad\quad y = 3x - 2$

Think

How does graphing each equation help you find the solution?
A line represents the solutions of *one* linear equation. The intersection point is a solution of *both* equations.

Graph both equations in the same coordinate plane.

$y = x + 2$ The slope is 1. The y-intercept is 2.

$y = 3x - 2$ The slope is 3. The y-intercept is -2.

Find the point of intersection. The lines appear to intersect at (2, 4). Check to see if (2, 4) makes both equations true.

$y = x + 2$
$4 \stackrel{?}{=} 2 + 2$
$4 = 4 \ ✔$

Substitute (2, 4) for (x, y) in both equations.

$y = 3x - 2$
$4 \stackrel{?}{=} 3(2) - 2$
$4 = 4 \ ✔$

The solution of the system is (2, 4).

Got It? 1. What is the solution of the system? Use a graph.
Check your answer.

$y = 2x + 4$
$y = x + 2$

 Problem 2 Writing a System of Equations

Biology Scientists studied the weights of two alligators over a period of 12 months. The initial weight and growth rate of each alligator are shown below. After how many months did the alligators weigh the same amount?

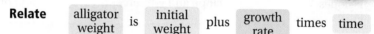

ALLIGATOR 1	ALLIGATOR 2
Initial Weight: 4 lb	Initial Weight: 6 lb
Rate of Growth: 1.5 lb per month	Rate of Growth: 1 lb per month

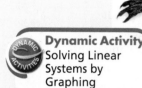
Dynamic Activity
Solving Linear Systems by Graphing

Relate | alligator weight | is | initial weight | plus | growth rate | times | time

Define Let w = alligator weight.
Let t = time in months.

Write Alligator 1: w = 4 + 1.5 · t

Alligator 2: w = 6 + 1 · t

Graph both equations in the same coordinate plane.

Think

Is there another way to solve this problem?
Yes. You can *make a table*. Show the weight of each alligator after 1 month, 2 months, and so on.

$w = 4 + 1.5t$ The slope is 1.5. The w-intercept is 4.

$w = 6 + t$ The slope is 1. The w-intercept is 6.

The lines intersect at (4, 10).

After 4 months, both alligators weighed 10 lb.

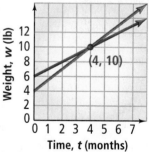
Alligator Weights

Weight, w (lb) / Time, t (months)

(4, 10)

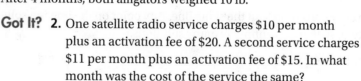
 **Got It?** 2. One satellite radio service charges $10 per month plus an activation fee of $20. A second service charges $11 per month plus an activation fee of $15. In what month was the cost of the service the same?

If the lines representing a system of equations intersect, the equations have one point in common so the system has one solution. If the lines are parallel, the equations have no points in common so the system has no solution. If the lines representing the equations are the same line, the system has an infinite number of points in common, so it has an infinite number of solutions.

take note

Concept Summary   Systems of Linear Equations

One solution

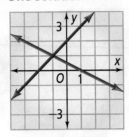

The lines intersect at one point. The lines have different slopes.

Infinitely many solutions

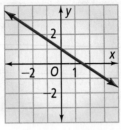

The lines are the same. The lines have the same slope and *y*-intercept.

No solution

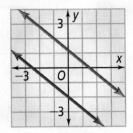

The lines are parallel. The lines have the same slope and different *y*-intercepts.

Problem 3   Systems With Infinitely Many Solutions or No Solution

Think

If two equations have the same slope and *y*-intercept, their graphs will be the same line. If two equations have the same slope but different *y*-intercepts, their graphs will be parallel lines.

What is the solution of each system? Use a graph.

A $2y - x = 2$

$y = \frac{1}{2}x + 1$

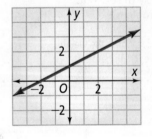

Graph the equations $2y - x = 2$ and $y = \frac{1}{2}x + 1$ in the same coordinate plane.

To graph $2y - x = 2$, you can find the *x*- and *y*-intercepts as you did in Problem 2 of Lesson 5-5. Then you can plot the points $(0, 1)$ and $(-2, 0)$.

The equations represent the same line. Any point on the line is a solution of the system, so there are infinitely many solutions.

B $y = 2x + 2$

$y = 2x - 1$

Graph the equations $y = 2x + 2$ and $y = 2x - 1$ in the same coordinate plane.

The lines have the same slope, so they are parallel and there is no solution.

 Got It? **3.** What is the solution of each system in parts (a) and (b)? Use a graph. Describe the number of solutions.

    a. $y = -x - 3$

        $y = -x + 5$

    b. $y = 3x - 3$

        $3y = 9x - 9$

Focus Question How can a graph help you find the solution of a system of equations?

Answer You can graph both equations in the system on the same coordinate plane. If the lines intersect, the intersection point is the solution of the system. If the lines are the same line, there are an infinite number of solutions. If the lines are parallel, there are no solutions.

Lesson Check

Do you know HOW?

Solve each system by graphing.

1. $y = x + 7$
$y = 2x + 1$

2. $y = \frac{1}{2}x + 6$
$y = x - 2$

3. $y = -3x - 3$
$y = 2x + 2$

4. $y = -x - 4$
$4x - y = -1$

5. Concert Tickets Tickets for a concert cost $10 each if you order them online, but you must pay a service charge of $8 per order. The tickets are $12 each if you buy them at the door on the night of the concert.

a. Write a system of equations to model the situation. Let c be the total cost. Let t be the number of tickets.

b. Graph the equations and find the intersection point. What does this point represent?

Do you UNDERSTAND?

6. Vocabulary Match each description of the graph of a system with the number of solutions the system has.

A. parallel lines   **I.** exactly one
B. lines that are the same   **II.** infinitely many
C. lines that intersect   **III.** no solution

7. Writing Suppose you graph a system of linear equations. If a point is on only one of the lines, is it a solution of the system? Explain.

8. Reasoning Can a system of two linear equations have exactly two solutions? Explain.

9. Reasoning Suppose you find that two linear equations are true when $x = -2$ and $y = 3$. What can you conclude about the graphs of the equations? Explain.

Practice and Problem-Solving Exercises

A Practice

Solve each system by graphing. Check your solution.

See Problem 1.

Guided Practice

To start, find the slope and y-intercept of each line.

10. $y = 2x$
$y = -2x + 8$

$y = 2x$ The slope is 2.
                The y-intercept is 0.

$y = -2x + 8$ The slope is -2.
                The y-intercept is 8.

11. $y = \frac{1}{3}x + 1$
$y = -3x + 11$

12. $y = x - 4$
$y = -x$

13. $y = -x + 3$
$y = x + 1$

14. $4x - y = -1$
$-x + y = x - 5$

15. $2x - y = -5$
$-2x - y = -1$

16. $x = -3$
$y = 5$

17. Student Statistics The number of right-handed students in a mathematics class is nine times the number of left-handed students. The total number of students in the class is 30. How many right-handed students are in the class? How many left-handed students are in the class?

See Problem 2.

To start, define variables and write a system.

Let $r =$ the number of right-handed students.

Let $\ell =$ the number of left-handed students.

$r = 9\ell$

$r + \ell = 30$

18. Plants A plant nursery is growing a tree that is 3 ft tall and grows at an average rate of 1 ft per year. Another tree at the nursery is 4 ft tall and grows at an average rate of 0.5 ft per year. After how many years will the trees be the same height?

19. Fitness At a local fitness center, members pay a $20 membership fee and $3 for each aerobics class. Nonmembers pay $5 for each aerobics class. For what number of aerobics classes will the cost for members and nonmembers be the same?

Solve each system by graphing. Tell whether the system has *one solution, infinitely many solutions,* or *no solution.*

See Problem 3.

20. $y = x + 3$
$y = x - 1$

21. $y = 2x - 1$
$3y = 6x - 5$

22. $3x + y = 2$
$4y = 12 - 12x$

23. $2x - 2y = 5$
$y = x - 4$

24. $y = 2x - 2$
$2y = 4x - 4$

25. $y - x = 5$
$3y = 3x + 15$

Ⓑ Apply

26. Think About a Plan You are looking for an after-school job. One job pays $9 per hour. Another pays $12 per hour, but you must buy a uniform that costs $39. After how many hours of work would your net earnings from either job be the same?
- What equations can you write to model the situation?
- How will graphing the equations help you solve the problem?

27. Error Analysis A student graphs the system $y = -x + 3$ and $y = -2x - 1$ as shown at the right. The student concludes there is no solution. Describe and correct the student's error.

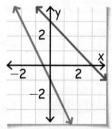

28. Reasoning Suppose you graph a system of linear equations and the intersection point appears to be (3, 7). Can you be sure that the ordered pair (3, 7) is the solution? What must you do to be sure?

29. Cell Phone Plans A cell phone provider offers a plan that costs $40 per month plus $.20 per text message sent or received. A comparable plan costs $60 per month but offers unlimited text messaging.
- **a.** How many text messages would you have to send or receive in order for the plans to cost the same each month?
- **b.** If you send or receive an average of 50 text messages each month, which plan would you choose? Why?

Without graphing, decide whether each system has *one solution, infinitely many solutions,* or *no solution.* Justify your answer.

30. $y = x - 4$
$y = x - 3$

31. $x - y = -\frac{1}{2}$
$2x - 2y = -1$

32. $y = 5x - 1$
$10x = 2y + 2$

33. Banking The graph at the right shows the balances in two bank accounts over time. Use the graph to write a system of equations giving the amount in each account over time. Let $t =$ the time in weeks and let $b =$ the balance in dollars. If the accounts continue to grow as shown, when will they have the same balance?

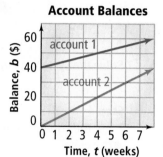

Account Balances

Standardized Test Prep

SAT/ACT

34. Which ordered pair is the solution of the system?
$2x + 3y = -17$
$3x + 2y = -8$

Ⓐ $(2, -7)$ 　　 Ⓑ $(-4, 2)$ 　　 Ⓒ $(-2, -1)$ 　　 Ⓓ $\left(-\frac{4}{3}, -2\right)$

35. Which expression is equivalent to $5(m - 12) + 8$?

Ⓕ $5m - 68$ 　　 Ⓖ $5m - 20$ 　　 Ⓗ $5m - 4$ 　　 Ⓘ $5m - 52$

Extended Response

36. The costs for parking in two different parking garages are given in the table at the right.

a. What is a system of equations that models the situation?
b. How many hours of parking would cost the same parking in either garage?
c. If you needed to park a car for 3 hours, which garage would you choose? Why?

Garage Parking Fees

Garage	Flat Fee	Hourly Fee
A	$5	$2.50
B	$20	$0

Mixed Review

Find the slope of a line that is parallel to the graph of the equation.

See Lesson 5-6.

37. $y = x + 3$ 　　 **38.** $y = -\frac{1}{2}x - 4$ 　　 **39.** $3x = 5y + 10$

Get Ready! To prepare for Lesson 6-2, do Exercises 40–42.

Solve each equation for y.

See Lesson 2-5.

40. $4x + 2y = 38$ 　　 **41.** $2x + \frac{1}{3}y = 5$ 　　 **42.** $1.5x - 4.5y = 21$

Concept Byte

Use With Lesson 6-1

TECHNOLOGY

Solving Systems Using Tables and Graphs

Activity 1

Solve the system using a table.
$y = 3x - 7$
$y = -0.5x + 7$

Step 1
Enter the equations in the **y=** screen.

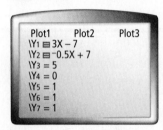

```
Plot1    Plot2    Plot3
\Y1 ◼ 3X − 7
\Y2 ◼ −0.5X + 7
\Y3 = 5
\Y4 = 0
\Y5 = 1
\Y6 = 1
\Y7 = 1
```

Step 2
Use the **tblset** function. Set TblStart to 0 and △Tbl to 1.

```
TABLE SETUP
 TblStart = 0
 △ Tbl = 1
Indpnt  : Auto Ask
Depend : Auto Ask
```

Step 3
Press **table** to show the table on the screen.

X	Y₁	Y₂
0	−7	7
1	−4	6.5
2	−1	6
3	2	5.5
4	5	5
5	8	4.5
6	11	4

X=0

1. Which x-value gives the same value for Y_1 and Y_2?

2. What ordered pair is the solution of the system?

Activity 2

Solve the system using a graph.
$y = -5x + 6$
$y = -x - 2$

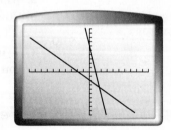

Step 1 Enter the equations in the **y=** screen.

Step 2 Graph the equations. Use a standard graphing window.

Step 3 Use the **calc** feature. Choose **INTERSECT** to find the point where the lines intersect.

3. Copy and complete: The lines intersect at (__?__ , __?__), so this point is the solution of the system.

Exercises

Use a table and a graph to solve each system. Sketch your graph.

4. $y = 5x - 3$
$y = 3x + 1$

5. $y = 2x - 13$
$y = x - 9$

6. $2x - y = 1.5$
$y = -\frac{1}{2}x - 1.5$

Concept Byte

Use With Lesson 6-2

ACTIVITY

Solving Systems Using Algebra Tiles

Just as algebra tiles can help you solve linear equations in one variable, they can also help you solve systems of linear equations in two variables.

Activity

Model and solve the system.

$$-x + 2y = 4$$
$$y = x + 1$$

> Since $y = x + 1$, use tiles for $x + 1$ to model y.

Steps	Equation	Algebra Tiles
Substitute $x + 1$ for y in the first equation.	$-x + 2y = 4$ $-x + 2(x + 1) = 4$ $-x + 2x + 2 = 4$	
Remove the zero pair x and $-x$.	$(-x + x) + x + 2 = 4$ $x + 2 = 4$	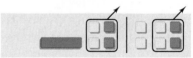
Subtract 2 from each side. Remove zero pairs.	$x + 2 - 2 = 4 - 2$	
Solve for x.	$x = 2$	
Model the second equation.	$y = x + 1$	y 
Substitute 2 for x and simplify.	$y = 2 + 1$ $y = 3$	y

The solution of the system is (2, 3).

Exercises

Model and solve each system.

1. $y = x + 1$
$2x + y = 10$

2. $x + 4y = 1$
$x + 4 = y$

3. $y = 2x - 1$
$y = x + 2$

6-2

Solving Systems Using Substitution

Objective To solve systems of equations using substitution

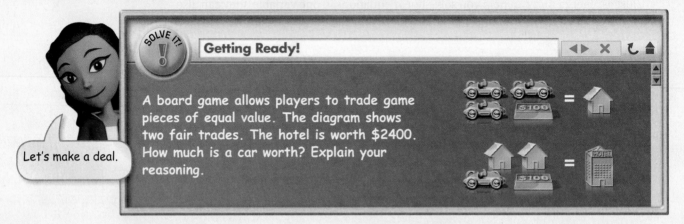

SOLVE IT!

Getting Ready!

A board game allows players to trade game pieces of equal value. The diagram shows two fair trades. The hotel is worth $2400. How much is a car worth? Explain your reasoning.

Let's make a deal.

Lesson Vocabulary
• substitution method

You can model fair trades with a linear system. You can solve linear systems by solving one of the equations for one of the variables. Then substitute the expression for the variable into the other equation. This is called the **substitution method.**

When a system has at least one equation that can be solved quickly for a variable, the system can be solved efficiently using substitution.

Focus Question How do you use substitution to solve a system of equations?

ONLINE PROBLEMS

Problem 1 Using Substitution

What is the solution of the system? Use substitution. $\quad y = 3x$
$\qquad\qquad\qquad\qquad\qquad\qquad\qquad\qquad\qquad\qquad\quad x + y = -32$

Plan

How can you get started?
If one equation is already solved for one variable, use it for the substitution. If both equations are solved for a variable, you can use either one.

Step 1 Because $y = 3x$, you can substitute $3x$ for y in $x + y = -32$.

Write the second equation.	$x + y = -32$
Substitute $3x$ for y.	$x + 3x = -32$
Simplify.	$4x = -32$
Divide each side by 4.	$x = -8$

Step 2 Substitute -8 for x in either equation and solve for y.

Write either equation.	$y = 3x$
Substitute -8 for x and solve.	$y = 3(-8) = -24$

The solution is $(-8, -24)$. Check by substituting $(-8, -24)$ into each equation.

Check $\quad y = 3x$ $\qquad\qquad\qquad x + y = -32$

$\qquad\qquad -24 \stackrel{?}{=} 3(-8)$ $\qquad -8 + (-24) \stackrel{?}{=} -32$

$\qquad\qquad -24 = -24 \; ✔$ $\qquad\qquad -32 = -32 \; ✔$

 Got It? 1. What is the solution of the system? Use substitution. $\quad y = 2x + 7$
Check your answer. $\qquad\qquad\qquad\qquad\qquad\qquad y = x - 1$

To use substitution to solve a system of equations, one of the equations must be solved for a variable.

 Problem 2 Solving for a Variable and Using Substitution

What is the solution of the system? Use substitution. $\quad 3y + 4x = 16$
$\qquad\qquad\qquad\qquad\qquad\qquad\qquad\qquad\qquad\qquad\qquad\qquad -2x + y = 2$

Know	Need	Plan
Neither equation is solved for one of the variables.	The solution of the system	Solve one of the equations for one of the variables. Then use the substitution method to find the solution of the system.

Think

Which variable should you solve for? If one equation has a variable with a coefficient of 1 or −1, solve for that variable. It is generally easier to solve for a variable with a coefficient of 1 or −1.

Step 1 Solve one of the equations for one of the variables.

Write the second equation. $\qquad\qquad -2x + y = 2$

Add $2x$ to each side. $\qquad\qquad -2x + y + 2x = 2 + 2x$

Simplify. $\qquad\qquad\qquad\qquad\qquad y = 2x + 2$

Step 2 Substitute $2x + 2$ for y in the other equation and solve for x.

Write the first equation. $\qquad\qquad 3y + 4x = 16$

Substitute $2x + 2$ for y. Use parentheses. $\quad 3(2x + 2) + 4x = 16$

Use the Distributive Property. $\qquad\quad 6x + 6 + 4x = 16$

Subtract 6 from each side. Simplify. $\qquad\qquad 10x = 10$

Divide each side by 10. $\qquad\qquad\qquad\qquad x = 1$

Step 3 Substitute 1 for x in either equation and solve for y.

Write either equation. $\qquad\qquad -2x + y = 2$

Substitute 1 for x. $\qquad\qquad -2(1) + y = 2$

Simplify. $\qquad\qquad\qquad\qquad -2 + y = 2$

Add 2 to each side. $\qquad\qquad\qquad y = 4$

Hint

Solve for a variable that is almost isolated. Here, the x in the second equation has a coefficient of 1.

The solution is $(1, 4)$.

 Got It? 2. a. What is the solution of the system? Use substitution. $\quad 4y - 2x = 10$
$\qquad\qquad\qquad\qquad\qquad\qquad\qquad\qquad\qquad\qquad\qquad\qquad 3y + x = 15$

b. Reasoning In your first step in part (a), which variable did you solve for? Which equation did you use to solve for the variable?

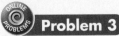 **Problem 3** Using Systems of Equations `GRIDDED RESPONSE`

Snack Bar A snack bar sells two sizes of snack packs. A large snack pack is $5, and a small snack pack is $3. In one day, the snack bar sold 60 snack packs for a total of $220. How many small snack packs did the snack bar sell?

Think

If one large snack pack costs $5 · 1, then two large packs cost $5 · 2. So x large packs cost $5 · x$. Small snack packs cost $3, so y small packs cost $3 · y$. The total that the snack bar earns from snack packs is $5x + 3y$.

Step 1 Write the system of equations. Let $x =$ the number of large $5 snack packs, and let $y =$ the number of small $3 snack packs.

Represent the total number of snack packs. $x + y = 60$

Represent the amount earned from 60 snack packs. $5x + 3y = 220$

Step 2 Use the first equation to solve for y. $x + y = 60$

Subtract x from each side. $y = 60 - x$

Step 3 Substitute $60 - x$ for y in the second equation. $5x + 3(60 - x) = 220$

Use the Distributive Property. $5x + 180 - 3x = 220$

Simplify. $2x = 40$

Divide each side by 2. $x = 20$

Step 4 Substitute 20 for x in the first equation. $20 + y = 60$

Subtract 20 from each side. $y = 40$

The system's solution is $(20, 40)$. The snack bar sold 40 small snack packs.

Think

What does the solution represent in the real world?

Check what the assigned variables represent. Here, $(20, 40)$ represents 20 large snack packs and 40 small snack packs.

 Got It? **3.** You pay $22 to rent 6 video games. The store charges $4 for new games and $2 for older games. How many new games did you rent?

If you get an identity, like $2 = 2$, when you solve a system of equations, then the system has infinitely many solutions. If you get a false statement, like $8 = 2$, then the system has no solution.

 Problem 4 Systems With Infinitely Many Solutions or No Solution

How many solutions does each system have?

A $x = -2y + 4$

$2x + 4y = 8$

Think

How many solutions can a system of linear equations have?

A system can have exactly one solution, infinitely many solutions, or no solution.

Write the second equation. $2x + 4y = 8$

Substitute $-2y + 4$ for x. Use parentheses. $2(-2y + 4) + 4y = 8$

Use the Distributive Property. $-4y + 8 + 4y = 8$

Simplify. $8 = 8$

$8 = 8$ is an identity, so the system has infinitely many solutions.

B $y = 3x - 11$

  $y - 3x = -13$

Write the second equation.	$y - 3x = -13$
Substitute $3x - 11$ for y.	$3x - 11 - 3x = -13$
Simplify.	$-11 = -13$ ✗

$-11 = -13$ is a false statement, so the system has no solution.

 Got It? **4.** How many solutions does the system have? $\quad x + 3y = 10$

$\qquad\qquad\qquad\qquad\qquad\qquad\qquad\qquad\qquad\qquad\quad 9y + 3x = 30$

Focus Question How do you use substitution to solve a system of equations?

Answer Solve one equation for a variable. Substitute the expression equal to the variable into the other equation and solve.

 Lesson Check

Do you know HOW?

Solve each system using substitution. Check your solution.

1. $4y = x$

  $3x - y = 70$

2. $-2x + 5y = 19$

  $3x - 4 = y$

Tell whether the system has *one solution*, *infinitely many solutions*, or *no solution*.

3. $y = 2x + 1$

  $4x - 2y = 6$

4. $-x + \frac{1}{2}y = 13$

  $x + 15 = \frac{1}{2}y$

5. **Talent Show** In a talent show of singing and comedy acts, singing acts are 5 min long and comedy acts are 3 min long. The show has 12 acts and lasts 50 min. How many singing acts and how many comedy acts are in the show?

Do you UNDERSTAND?

6. Vocabulary When is the substitution method a better method than graphing for solving a system of linear equations?

For each system, tell which equation you would first use to solve for a variable in the first step of the substitution method. Explain your choice.

7. $-2x + y = -1$

  $4x + 2y = 12$

8. $2.5x - 7y = 7.5$

  $6x - y = 1$

Tell whether each statement is *true* or *false*. Explain.

9. When solving a system using substitution, if you obtain an identity, then the system has no solution.

10. You cannot use substitution to solve a system that does not have a variable with a coefficient of 1 or -1.

Practice and Problem-Solving Exercises

A Practice

Solve each system using substitution. Check your answer.

See Problems 1 and 2.

Guided Practice

To start, substitute 3x for y in x + y = 8.

11. $x + y = 8$
$y = 3x$
$x + y = 8$
$x + 3x = 8$

12. $2x + 2y = 38$
$y = x + 3$

13. $x + 3 = y$
$3x + 4y = 7$

14. $y = 8 - x$
$7 = 2 - y$

15. $y - 2x = 3$
$3x - 2y = 5$

16. $4x = 3y - 2$
$18 = 3x + y$

17. $2 = 2y - x$
$23 = 5y - 4x$

18. Theater Tickets Adult tickets to a play cost $22. Tickets for children cost $15. Tickets for a group of 11 people cost a total of $228. Write and solve a system of equations to find how many children and how many adults were in the group.

See Problem 3.

19. Transportation A school is planning a field trip for 142 people. The trip will use six drivers and two types of vehicles: buses and vans. A bus can seat 51 passengers. A van can seat 10 passengers. Write and solve a system of equations to find how many buses and how many vans will be needed.

Tell whether the system has *one solution, infinitely many solutions,* or *no solution.*

See Problem 4.

Guided Practice

To start, substitute $\frac{1}{2}x + 3$ for y in $2y - x = 6$.

20. $y = \frac{1}{2}x + 3$
$2y - x = 6$
$2y - x = 6$
$2\left(\frac{1}{2}x + 3\right) - x = 6$

21. $y = -x + 4$
$3x + 3y = 12$

22. $x = -7y + 34$
$x + 7y = 32$

23. $1.5x + 2y = 11$
$3x + 6y = 22$

B Apply

24. Geometry The rectangle shown has a perimeter of 34 cm and the given area. Its length is 5 more than twice its width. Write and solve a system of equations to find the dimensions of the rectangle.

ℓ

w | $A = 52$ cm²

25. Writing What would your first step be in solving the system below? Explain.

$1.2x + y = 2$
$1.4y = 2.8x + 1$

26. Error Analysis Describe and correct the error at the right in finding the solution of the following system:

$7x + 5y = 14$
$x + 8y = 21$

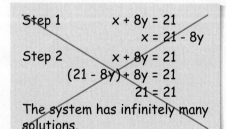

Step 1   x + 8y = 21
                 x = 21 - 8y
Step 2   x + 8y = 21
      (21 - 8y) + 8y = 21
               21 = 21
The system has infinitely many solutions.

27. Art An artist is going to sell two sizes of prints at an art fair. The artist will charge $20 for a small print and $45 for a large print. The artist would like to sell twice as many small prints as large prints. The booth the artist is renting for the day costs $510. How many of each size print must the artist sell in order to break even at the fair?

28. Think About a Plan At a certain high school, 350 students are taking an algebra course. The ratio of boys to girls taking algebra is 33 : 37. How many more girls are taking algebra than boys?
- How can you write a system of equations to model the situation?
- Which equation will you solve for a variable in the first step of solving the system? Why?
- How can you interpret the solution in the context of the problem?

Standardized Test Prep

GRIDDED RESPONSE

SAT/ACT

29. What is the value of the x-coordinate of the solution of the given system?
$$2x + 3y = 144$$
$$y - x = 24$$

30. You are making blueberry muffins and need to buy a muffin tin and baking cups. Each package of baking cups has 50 baking cups and costs $1.25. The muffin tin costs $15. If you have $22 to spend, at most how many baking cups can you buy?

31. What is the x-intercept of $2y - 3x = 24$?

32. An online store charges 4% of the cost of an order to cover shipping costs. How much would you pay in dollars for shipping on an order that costs $146?

33. What is the solution of the equation $2x - 3 = 8$?

Mixed Review

Solve each system by graphing. Tell whether the system has *one solution, infinitely many solutions,* or *no solution.*

◀ See Lesson 6-1.

34. $y = 3x + 3$
  $y = x - 3$

35. $y = x + 1$
  $2x + y = 10$

36. $y = -x + 2$
  $x + y = 3$

Find the slope of a line perpendicular to the graph of each equation.

◀ See Lesson 5-6.

37. $y = 3x$

38. $y = -\frac{1}{4}x$

39. $\frac{1}{3}x - y = 2$

Get Ready! **To prepare for Lesson 6-3, do Exercises 40–42.**

Solve each equation. Check your answer.

◀ See Lesson 2-4.

40. $5x + 1 = 3x - 5$

41. $4c - 7 = -c + 3$

42. $5k + 7 = 3k + 10$

6-3
PART 1

Solving Systems Using Elimination

Objective   To solve systems by adding or subtracting to eliminate a variable

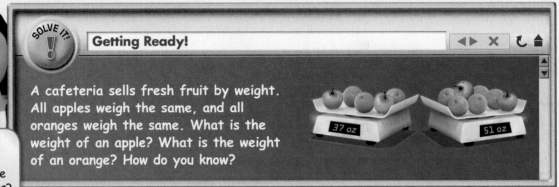

Getting Ready!

A cafeteria sells fresh fruit by weight. All apples weigh the same, and all oranges weigh the same. What is the weight of an apple? What is the weight of an orange? How do you know?

37 oz   51 oz

Hmm... Can the methods from earlier lessons be used to solve this?

In the **elimination method,** you use the Addition or Subtraction Properties of Equality to add or subtract equations in order to eliminate a variable in a system.

Focus Question How do you use elimination to solve a system of equations?

 Problem 1   **Solving a System by Adding Equations**

Plan

Which variable should you eliminate?
You can eliminate either variable. Since the coefficients of y are opposites, you can add the equations to eliminate y in one step.

What is the solution of the system? Use elimination. $2x + 5y = 17$
$6x - 5y = -9$

Step 1 Eliminate one variable. Because the sum of the coefficients of y is 0, add the equations to eliminate y.

Write the original equations.

$$2x + 5y = 17$$
$$6x - 5y = -9$$

Add the two equations. $8x + 0 = 8$

Solve for x. $x = 1$

Step 2 Substitute 1 for x to solve for the eliminated variable.

You can use the first equation. $2x + 5y = 17$

Substitute 1 for x. $2(1) + 5y = 17$

Simplify. $2 + 5y = 17$

Solve for y. $y = 3$

Because $x = 1$ and $y = 3$, the solution is $(1, 3)$.

 Got It? 1. What is the solution of the system? Use elimination. $5x - 6y = -32$
$3x + 6y = 48$

 **Problem 2** **Solving a System by Subtracting Equations**

Multiple Choice The theater club sells a total of 101 tickets for $164. A student ticket costs $1. An adult ticket costs $2.50. How many student tickets were sold?

  (A) 25   (B) 42   (C) 59   (D) 76

Define Let a = the number of adult tickets sold. Let s = the number of student tickets sold.

Relate total number of tickets   total ticket sales

Write $a + s = 101$ $2.5a + s = 164$

Step 1 Eliminate one variable. Because the difference of the coefficients of s is 0, eliminate s.

Write the original equations.

$$a + s = 101$$
$$\underline{2.5a + s = 164}$$

Subtract the equations. $-1.5a + 0 = -63$

Solve for a. $a = 42$

Step 2 Solve for the eliminated variable. Use either equation.

You can use the first equation. $a + s = 101$

Substitute 42 for a. $42 + s = 101$

Solve for s. $s = 59$

There were 59 student tickets sold. The correct answer is C.

 Got It? **2.** Washing 2 cars and 3 trucks takes 130 min. Washing 2 cars and 5 trucks takes 190 min. How long does it take to wash each type of vehicle?

Think

How is this problem similar to Problem 1?
In each problem, you are looking for coefficients of one variable that are either the same or opposites. Here, the coefficients of s are the same, so eliminate s.

Focus Question How do you use elimination to solve a system of equations?

Answer Use the Addition or Subtraction Properties of Equality to eliminate a variable and solve a system of equations.

 Lesson Check

Do you know HOW?

Solve each system using elimination.

1. $3x - 2y = 0$
     $4x + 2y = 14$

2. $2x + 2y = 10$
     $3x + 2y = 14$

Do you UNDERSTAND?

3. Vocabulary If you add two equations in two variables and the sum is an equation in one variable, what method are you using to solve the system? Explain.

4. Reasoning Explain how the Addition Property of Equality allows you to add equations.

Practice and Problem-Solving Exercises

A **Practice**   Solve each system using elimination.   ◀ **See Problem 1.**

Guided
Practice

To start, add the two equations to
eliminate y.

5. $3x + 3y = 27$
$x - 3y = -11$

$3x + 3y = 27$
$\underline{x - 3y = -11}$
$4x + 0 = 16$

6. $-x + 5y = 13$
$x - y = 15$

7. $2x + 4y = 22$
$2x - 2y = -8$

8. $5x - y = 0$
$3x + y = 24$

Solve each system using elimination.   ◀ **See Problem 2.**

9. $3x + 7y = 44$
$3x + 4y = 29$

10. $4x - 7y = 3$
$x - 7y = -15$

11. $6x + 5y = 39$
$3x + 5y = 27$

12. Talent Show A talent show will feature 12 solo acts and 2 ensemble acts. The
show will last 90 min. The 6 best solo performers and the 2 ensemble acts will give
a repeat performance at a second show that will last 60 min. Each solo act lasts x
minutes, and each ensemble act lasts y minutes.
  a. Write a system of equations to model the situation.
  b. Solve the system. How long is each solo act? How long is each ensemble act?

Guided
Practice

To start, write the system.

$12x + 2y = 90$
$6x + 2y = 60$

> **Hint** After you
> write the system of
> equations, decide
> whether you want
> to add or subtract
> the two equations.
> Remember that
> $x + (-x) = 0$, but
> $x - (-x) = 2x$.

13. Furniture A carpenter is designing a drop-leaf table with two drop leaves of
equal size. The lengths of the table when one leaf is folded up and when both leaves
are folded up are shown. How long is the table when no leaves are folded up?

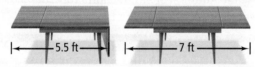

B **Apply**   Solve each system using elimination with addition, elimination with subtraction,
or the substitution method. Explain why you chose the method you used.

14. $3x + 2y = -15$
$x - 2y = 19$

15. $5x + 3y = -19$
$5x - y = -7$

16. $x = -4y - 4$
$5x + 4y = 12$

17. $y = 3x + 14$
$2y - 3x = 10$

18. $-7x + y = -18$
$-7x + 2y = -15$

19. $6x - 2y = 22$
$-6x + 5y = -37$

20. The sum of two numbers is 20. When the larger number is subtracted from twice
the smaller number, the difference is 4. What are the numbers?

21. The cost to rent a chain saw for two days and a brush chipper for two days is $272.
The cost to rent a chain saw for two days and a brush chipper for one day is $195.
How much does it cost to rent a chain saw for one day?

6-3 PART 2 Solving Systems Using Elimination

Objective To solve systems by adding or subtracting to eliminate a variable

In Part 1 of the lesson, you learned how to add or subtract equations to eliminate a variable.

Connect to What You Know

Here you will learn how to multiply by a constant in systems that don't have opposite coefficients.

Lesson Vocabulary
• elimination method

In Part 1 of this lesson, you saw that to eliminate a variable, its coefficients must have a sum or difference of zero. Sometimes you have to multiply one or both of the equations by a constant so that adding or subtracting the equations will eliminate one variable.

Focus Question When should you multiply by a constant to solve a system of equations?

Problem 3 Solving a System by Multiplying One Equation

What is the solution of the system? Use elimination. $-2x + 15y = -32$
$7x - 5y = 17$

Know

A system of equations that can't quickly be solved by graphing or substitution

Need

The solution of the system

Plan

Multiply one or both equations by a constant so that the coefficients of one variable are the same or opposites. Then eliminate the variable.

Think

You can eliminate either variable. You can eliminate y in fewer steps than x because you only need to multiply one equation.

Step 1 To eliminate one variable, you can multiply $7x - 5y = 17$ by 3 and then add.

$-2x + 15y = -32$ $-2x + 15y = -32$
$7x - 5y = 17$ Multiply by 3. $\underline{21x - 15y = 51}$

Add the equations. $19x + 0 = 19$
Solve for x. $x = 1$

Step 2 Solve for the eliminated variable. Use either of the original equations.

You can use the second equation. $7x - 5y = 17$
Substitute 1 for x. $7(1) - 5y = 17$
Solve for y. $y = -2$

The solution is $(1, -2)$.

Got It? **3. a.** What is the solution of the system? Use elimination. $-6x - 6y = -30$
$-4x + 3y = -34$

      b. **Reasoning** Describe another way to solve the system in part (a).

Problem 4   **Solving a System by Multiplying Both Equations**

What is the solution of the system? Use elimination. $3x + 2y = 1$
$4x + 3y = -2$

Plan

How can you get started?
Find the LCM of the coefficients of the variable that you want to eliminate. Multiply to make the coefficients equal to the LCM.

Step 1   Multiply each equation so you can eliminate one variable.

To eliminate y, multiply both equations so the y–term coefficients are 6.

Write the first equation.	$3x + 2y = 1$
Multiply both sides of the first equation by 3.	$3 \cdot (3x + 2y) = 3 \cdot 1$
Use the Distributive Property and simplify.	$9x + 6y = 3$
Write the second equation.	$4x + 3y = -2$
Multiply both sides of the second equation by 2.	$2 \cdot (4x + 3y) = 2 \cdot (-2)$
Use the Distributive Property and simplify.	$8x + 6y = -4$

Step 2   Subtract the new equations.

This eliminates the y-variable.

$$9x + 6y = 3$$
$$8x + 6y = -4$$

Subtract the equations.	$x + 0 = 7$
Simplify.	$x = 7$

> Don't forget that $3 - (-4)$ is equal to $3 + 4$.

Step 3   Solve for the eliminated variable.

Use either of the original equations.

You can use the first equation.	$3x + 2y = 1$
Substitute 7 for x.	$3(7) + 2y = 1$
Multiply.	$21 + 2y = 1$
Subtract 21 from each side.	$2y = 1 - 21$
Simplify.	$2y = -20$
Divide both sides by 2.	$\dfrac{2y}{2} = \dfrac{-20}{2}$
Simplify.	$y = -10$

The solution is $(7, -10)$.

Got It? **4.** What is the solution of the system? Use elimination. $5x + 3y = 26$
$-2x + 7y = 6$

Recall that if you get a false statement as you solve a system, then the system has no solution. If you get an identity, then the system has infinitely many solutions.

Here's Why It Works If both variable terms are eliminated as you solve a system of equations, your answer is either no solution or infinitely many solutions.

No Solution

In a system of equations with no solution, you will arrive at a false statement such as $0 = 3$ or $5 = -8$.

The graph of the system $4x - 2y = -8$ and $4x - 2y = -2$ shows that the lines are parallel. If you solve the system, you get $0 = -6$.

Since $0 = -6$ is a false statement, you can conclude that the lines are parallel and the system has no solution. No point is a solution of both equations in the system.

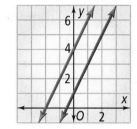

Infinitely Many Solutions

In a system of equations with infinitely many solutions, you will arrive at an identity such as $0 = 0$ or $3 = 3$.

The graph of the system $x + 2y = 4$ and $3x + 6y = 12$ shows that the lines are the same. If you solve the system, you get $0 = 0$.

Since $0 = 0$ is an identity, you can conclude the equations are the same line and the system has infinitely many solutions. Any point that is a solution of one of the equations is also a solution of the other equation.

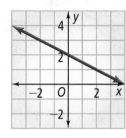

Problem 5 **Finding the Number of Solutions**

Think

Could you have solved this problem another way?
Yes. For example, you could have multiplied the second equation by 2 and subtracted.

How many solutions does the system have?
$$2x + 6y = 18$$
$$x + 3y = 9$$

Multiply the second equation by -2.

$$2x + 6y = 18 \qquad\qquad 2x + 6y = 18$$
$$x + 3y = 9 \quad \text{Multiply by } -2. \quad \underline{-2x - 6y = -18}$$
$$\text{Add the equations.} \qquad 0 = 0$$

Because $0 = 0$ is an identity, there are infinitely many solutions.

 Got It? **5.** How many solutions does the system have?
$$-2x + 5y = 7$$
$$-2x + 5y = 12$$

The flowchart below can help you decide which steps to take when solving a system of equations using elimination.

Can I eliminate a variable by adding or subtracting the given equations? — *yes* → Do so.

no →

Can I multiply one of the equations by a number, and then add or subtract the equations? — *yes* → Do so.

no →

Multiply both equations by different numbers. Then add or subtract the equations.

Focus Question When should you multiply by a constant to solve a system of equations?

Answer Multiply one or both equations by a constant to make the coefficients of one variable the same or opposite. Then you will eliminate that variable when you add or subtract the equations.

Lesson Check

Do you know HOW?

Solve each system using elimination.

1. $3p + q = 7$
$2p - 2q = -6$

2. $3x - 2y = 1$
$8x + 3y = 2$

Do you UNDERSTAND?

3. Reasoning Describe two ways you can use elimination to solve the system of equations below.

$$2x - y = 21$$
$$3x + 4y = 16$$

4. Writing Explain how you would solve a system of equations using elimination.

Practice and Problem-Solving Exercises

A Practice Solve each system using elimination.

◆ See Problems 3 and 4.

5. $2x + 3y = 9$
$x + 5y = 8$
$-2 \cdot (x + 5y) = -2 \cdot 8$
$-2x - 10y = -16$

Guided Practice
To start, multiply the second equation by -2 so that the x-terms will be opposites.

6. $3x + y = 5$
$2x - 2y = -2$

7. $3x + 2y = 17$
$2x + 5y = 26$

8. $6x - 3y = 15$
$7x + 4y = 10$

9. $5x - 9y = -43$
$3x + 8y = 68$

Tell whether the system has *one solution, infinitely many solutions,* or *no solution.*

See Problem 5.

Guided Practice

To start, multiply the second equation by −1 so that the *x*-terms will be opposites.

10. $9x + 8y = 15$
$9x + 8y = 30$

$-1 \cdot (9x + 8y) = -1 \cdot 30$
$-9x - 8y = -30$

11. $3x + 4y = 24$
$6x + 8y = 24$

12. $5x - 3y = 10$
$10x + 6y = 20$

13. $2x - 5y = 17$
$6x - 15y = 51$

14. $4x - 8y = 15$
$-5x + 10y = -30$

B Apply

15. Think About a Plan A photo studio offers portraits in 8 × 10 and wallet-sized formats. One customer bought two 8 × 10 portraits and four wallet-sized portraits and paid $52. Another customer bought three 8 × 10 portraits and two wallet-sized portraits and paid $50. What is the cost of an 8 × 10 portrait? What is the cost of a wallet-sized portrait?
- Can you eliminate a variable simply by adding or subtracting?
- If not, how many of the equations do you need to multiply by a constant?

16. Error Analysis A student solved a system of equations by elimination. Describe and correct the error made in the part of the solution shown.

$$5x + 4y = 2 \quad — \times 3 \rightarrow \quad 15x + 12y = 6$$
$$3x + 3y = -3 \quad — \times 4 \rightarrow \quad 12x + 12y = -3$$
$$\underline{}$$
$$3x + 0 = 9$$
$$x = 3$$

17. Nutrition Half a pepperoni pizza plus three fourths of a ham-and-pineapple pizza contains 765 Calories. One fourth of a pepperoni pizza plus a whole ham-and-pineapple pizza contains 745 Calories. How many Calories are in a whole pepperoni pizza? How many Calories are in a whole ham-and-pineapple pizza?

Hint After you write two equations, multiply each equation by a constant to eliminate the fractions.

Solve each system using any method. Explain why you chose the method you used.

18. $y = 2.5x$
$2y + 3x = 32$

19. $2x + y = 4$
$6x + 7y = 12$

20. $3x + 2y = 5$
$4x + 5y = 16$

21. Compare and Contrast What do the substitution method and the elimination method have in common? Explain. Give an example of a system that you would prefer to solve using one method instead of the other. Justify your choice.

22. Vacations A hotel offers two activity packages. One costs $192 and includes 3 h of horseback riding and 2 h of parasailing. The second costs $213 and includes 2 h of horseback riding and 3 h of parasailing. What is the cost for 1 h of each activity?

23. **Geometry** Each of the squares in the figures shown at the right has the same area, and each of the triangles has the same area. The total area of Figure A is 141 cm². The total area of Figure B is 192 cm². What is the area of each square and each triangle?

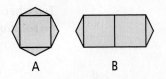

A   B

SAT/ACT

24. What is the value of the y-coordinate of the solution of the given system?

$$4x + 3y = 33$$
$$3x + 2y = 23$$

25. What is the y-intercept of $2x + 5y = 15$?

26. You buy a toothbrush for $2.83 and a tube of toothpaste for $2.37. There is a 5% sales tax. Including tax, what is the total cost in dollars of your purchases?

27. Three fire trucks and 4 ambulances can fit into a parking lane 152 ft long. Two fire trucks and 5 ambulances can fit into a lane 136 ft long. How many feet long must a parking lane be for 1 fire truck and 5 ambulances? Assume there is 1 ft of space in between each vehicle.

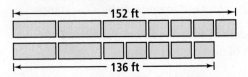

28. You are competing in a mountain bike race. Your average speed is 10 mi/h. If the racecourse is 65 mi long, how many minutes will it take you to finish the race?

Mixed Review

Solve each system using substitution.

See Lesson 6-2.

29. $y = \frac{1}{2}x$
$2y + 3x = 28$

30. $x - 7 = y$
$2x - y = 41$

31. $x + 2y = -1$
$3x - 5y = 30$

Solve each inequality.

See Lesson 3-4.

32. $4 - 2a < 3a - 1$

33. $3(2x - 1) \geq 5x + 4$

34. $2.7 + 2b > 3.4 - 1.5b$

Get Ready! **To prepare for Lesson 6-4, do Exercise 35.**

35. Two trains run on two sets of parallel tracks. The first train leaves a city $\frac{1}{2}$ h before the second train. The first train travels at 55 mi/h. The second train travels at 65 mi/h. How long does it take for the second train to pass the first train?

See Lesson 2-4.

Matrices and Solving Systems

A *matrix* is a rectangular arrangement of numbers in rows and columns. The plural of *matrix* is *matrices*. You will learn more about matrix operations, including adding and subtracting matrices, in Chapter 12.

You can use a special type of matrix, called an *augmented matrix*, to solve a system of linear equations. An augmented matrix is formed using the coefficients and constants in the equations in a system. The equations must be written in standard form.

System of Equations

$$7x + 6y = 10$$
$$4x + 5y = -5$$

Augmented Matrix

$$\begin{bmatrix} 7 & 6 & | & 10 \\ 4 & 5 & | & -5 \end{bmatrix}$$

Recall the operations you performed when you solved systems using elimination. You can perform similar operations on the rows of an augmented matrix.

You can perform any of the following row operations on an augmented matrix to produce an equivalent augmented matrix.

Interchange two rows. $\begin{bmatrix} 7 & 6 & | & 10 \\ 4 & 5 & | & -5 \end{bmatrix} \rightarrow \begin{bmatrix} 4 & 5 & | & -5 \\ 7 & 6 & | & 10 \end{bmatrix}$

Multiply a row by any constant except 0. $\begin{bmatrix} 7 & 6 & | & 10 \\ 4 & 5 & | & -5 \end{bmatrix} \rightarrow \begin{bmatrix} 7 & 6 & | & 10 \\ 2(4) & 2(5) & | & 2(-5) \end{bmatrix} \rightarrow \begin{bmatrix} 7 & 6 & | & 10 \\ 8 & 10 & | & -10 \end{bmatrix}$

Add a multiple of one row to another row.

$\begin{bmatrix} 7 & 6 & | & 10 \\ 4 & 5 & | & -5 \end{bmatrix} \rightarrow \begin{bmatrix} 7 + 2(4) & 6 + 2(5) & | & 10 + 2(-5) \\ 4 & 5 & | & -5 \end{bmatrix} \rightarrow \begin{bmatrix} 15 & 16 & | & 0 \\ 4 & 5 & | & -5 \end{bmatrix}$

To solve a system using an augmented matrix, choose row operations that will transform the augmented matrix into a matrix with 1's along the main diagonal (top left to lower right) and 0's above and below the main diagonal, as shown below.

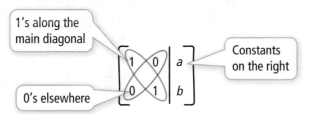

1's along the main diagonal

Constants on the right

0's elsewhere

$$\begin{bmatrix} 1 & 0 & | & a \\ 0 & 1 & | & b \end{bmatrix}$$

Example

Solve the system using an augmented matrix. $3x + 2y = 11$
$$4x + 1y = 18$$

$$\begin{bmatrix} 3 & 2 & | & 11 \\ 4 & 1 & | & 18 \end{bmatrix}$$

Write the system as an augmented matrix.

$$\begin{bmatrix} 3 + (-2)(4) & 2 + (-2)(1) & | & 11 + (-2)(18) \\ 4 & 1 & | & 18 \end{bmatrix} \rightarrow \begin{bmatrix} -5 & 0 & | & -25 \\ 4 & 1 & | & 18 \end{bmatrix}$$

Multiply row 2 by -2 and add to row 1.

$$\begin{bmatrix} -\frac{1}{5}(-5) & -\frac{1}{5}(0) & | & -\frac{1}{5}(-25) \\ 4 & 1 & | & 18 \end{bmatrix} \rightarrow \begin{bmatrix} 1 & 0 & | & 5 \\ 4 & 1 & | & 18 \end{bmatrix}$$

Multiply row 1 by $-\frac{1}{5}$.

$$\begin{bmatrix} 1 & 0 & | & 5 \\ 4 + (-4)(1) & 1 + (-4)(0) & | & 18 + (-4)(5) \end{bmatrix} \rightarrow \begin{bmatrix} 1 & 0 & | & 5 \\ 0 & 1 & | & -2 \end{bmatrix}$$

Multiply row 1 by -4 and add to row 2.

$$x = 5$$
$$y = -2$$

Write each row of the matrix as an equation.

The solution of the system is $(5, -2)$.

Exercises

Solve each system using an augmented matrix.

1. $3x + 2y = 26$
   $x + y = 7$

2. $-4x - 4y = 16$
   $4x + 5y = 14$

3. $2x + 2y = 14$
   $-x - 2y = -13$

4. Compare and Contrast Solve the system of equations in the example above using the elimination method. How are the row operations you have used in this activity like the operations you performed using the elimination method? How are they different?

5. Writing Are the row operations more like the substitution method or the elimination method? Explain.

6. Cosmetology A hairdresser finds that he can give 3 haircuts and 2 hair dyes in 315 min. Giving 2 haircuts and 4 hair dyes takes 450 min. How long does it take him to give a haircut? How long does it take him to dye a customer's hair? Write a system of equations and solve it using an augmented matrix.

7. Error Analysis A student says the augmented matrix at the right shows that the solution of the system is $(5, 3)$. What is the student's error? What is the correct solution of the system?

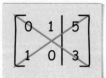

6-4

Applications of Linear Systems

Objective   To choose the best method for solving a system of linear equations

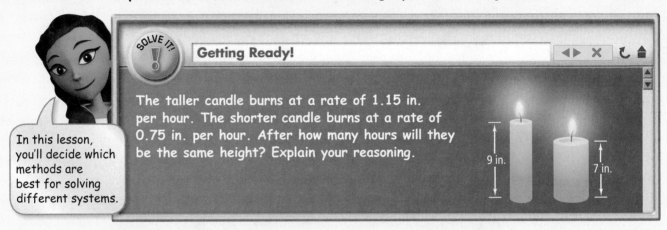

In this lesson, you'll decide which methods are best for solving different systems.

SOLVE IT!

Getting Ready!

The taller candle burns at a rate of 1.15 in. per hour. The shorter candle burns at a rate of 0.75 in. per hour. After how many hours will they be the same height? Explain your reasoning.

9 in.   7 in.

You can solve systems of linear equations using a graph, the substitution method, or the elimination method.

Dynamic Activity
Modeling Linear Systems

Focus Question   How do you choose the best method for solving a system of linear equations?

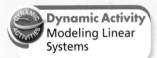

Concept Summary Choosing a Method for Solving Linear Systems	
Method	**When to Use**
Graphing	When you want a visual display of the equations, or when you want to estimate a solution
Substitution	When one equation is already solved for one of the variables, or when it is easy to solve for one of the variables
Elimination	When the coefficients of one variable are the same or opposites, or when it is not convenient to use graphing or substitution

Systems of equations are useful for modeling problems involving mixtures, rates, and break-even points.

The break-even point for a business is the point at which income equals expenses. The graph shows the break-even point for one business.

Notice that the values of y on the red line represent dollars spent on expenses. The values of y on the blue line represent dollars received as income. So y is used to represent both expenses and income.

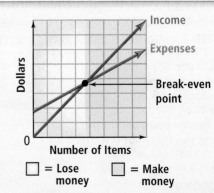

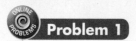 **Problem 1** Finding a Break-Even Point

Business A fashion designer makes and sells hats. The material for each hat costs $5.50. The hats sell for $12.50 each. The designer spends $1400 on advertising. How many hats must the designer sell to break even?

Plan

The break-even point is when income equals expense. To find this point, write an income equation and an expense equation and solve the system.

Think

Define variables and write an expense equation and an income equation.

Use the substitution method because both equations are solved for *y*. Substitute 12.5*x* for *y* in the expense equation and solve for *x*.

Interpret your answer in the context of the problem. Remember *x* = the number of hats sold.

Graph the system to check your answer. Enter the expense and income equations in your calculator. Check that the lines intersect at *x* = 200.

Write

Let *x* = the number of hats sold.

Let *y* = the number of dollars of expense or income.

Expense: $y = 5.5x + 1400$

Income: $y = 12.5x$

$$y = 5.5x + 1400$$
$$12.5x = 5.5x + 1400$$
$$7x = 1400$$
$$x = 200$$

The designer must sell 200 hats to break even.

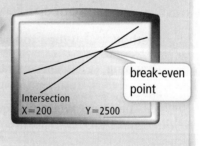

break-even point

Intersection
X=200   Y=2500

Hint

Write an expense equation using the fact that initial costs are $864 and binding and packaging is $.80 per book. Write an income equation using the fact that each book will sell for $2.

 Got It? 1. A puzzle expert wrote a new sudoku puzzle book. His initial costs are $864. Binding and packaging each book costs $.80. The price of the book is $2. How many copies must be sold to break even?

Problem 2 Solving a Mixture Problem

Dairy A dairy owner produces low-fat milk containing 1% fat and whole milk containing 3.5% fat. How many gallons of each type should be combined to make 100 gal of milk that is 2% fat?

Think

What do the percents mean when used as coefficients?
The percents describe the fat concentration in each type of milk. If you multiply the percents by some number of gallons, you'll get the amount of fat in that number of gallons. Remember that 1% = 0.01 and 3.5% = 0.035.

Step 1 Write a system of equations. Let $x =$ the number of gallons of low-fat milk, and let $y =$ the number of gallons of whole milk.

Total gallons: $x + y = 100$ Fat content: $0.01x + 0.035y = 0.02(100)$

Step 2 The first equation is easy to solve for either x or y, so use substitution.

Write the first equation. $x + y = 100$

Subtract y from each side. $x = 100 - y$

Step 3 Substitute $100 - y$ for x in the second equation and solve for y.

Write the second equation. $0.01x + 0.035y = 0.02(100)$

Substitute $100 - y$ for x. $0.01(100 - y) + 0.035y = 0.02(100)$

Distributive Property $1 - 0.01y + 0.035y = 2$

Subtract 1 from each side. Then simplify. $0.025y = 1$

Divide each side by 0.025. $y = 40$

Step 4 Substitute 40 for y in either equation and solve for x.

Substitute 40 for y in the first equation. $x + 40 = 100$

Solve for x. $x = 60$

The owner should mix 60 gal of low-fat milk with 40 gal of whole milk.

Hint

Write one equation that shows the total amount of antifreeze is 15 L. Write another equation that shows $0.2x$ mixed with $0.12y$ makes $0.18(15)$.

Got It? **2.** One antifreeze solution is 20% alcohol. Another antifreeze solution is 12% alcohol. How many liters of each solution should be combined to make 15 L of antifreeze solution that is 18% alcohol?

Focus Question How do you choose the best method for solving a system of linear equations?

Answer The best method to use depends on the forms of the given equations and how precise the solution should be. Use graphing when you want a visual display of the equations, or when you want to estimate a solution. Use substitution when it is easy to solve for one of the variables. Use elimination all other times.

Lesson Check

Do you know HOW?

1. **Newsletters** Printing a newsletter costs $1.50 per copy plus $450 in printer's fees. The copies are sold for $3 each. How many copies of the newsletter must be sold to break even?

2. **Jewelry** A metal alloy is a metal made by blending 2 or more types of metal. A jeweler has supplies of two metal alloys. One alloy is 30% gold and the other is 10% gold. How much of each alloy should the jeweler combine to create 4 kg of an alloy containing 15% gold?

Do you UNDERSTAND?

3. **Vocabulary** What is the relationship between income and expenses before a break-even point is reached? What is the relationship between income and expenses after a break-even point is reached?

4. **Reasoning** Which method would you use to solve the following system? Explain.
$$3x + 2y = 9$$
$$-2x + 3y = 5$$

Practice and Problem-Solving Exercises

A Practice

Guided Practice

5. **Business** A bicycle store costs $2400 per month to operate. The store pays an average of $60 per bicycle. The average selling price of each bicycle is $120. How many bicycles must the store sell each month to break even?

See Problem 1.

To start, define variables and write a system.

Let x = the number of bikes sold.
Let y = the number of dollars of expense or income.

Expense: $y = 60x + 2400$
Income: $y = 120x$

6. **Theater** Producing a musical costs $88,000 plus $5900 per performance. One sold-out performance earns $7500 in revenue. If every performance sells out, how many performances are needed to break even?

Guided Practice

7. **Metalwork** A metalworker has a metal alloy that is 20% copper and another alloy that is 60% copper. How many kilograms of each alloy should the metalworker combine to create 80 kg of a 52% copper alloy?

See Problem 2.

To start, define variables and write a system.

Let x = the number of kilograms of 20% copper alloy.
Let y = the number of kilograms of 60% copper alloy.

Total kilograms: $x + y = 80$
Copper content: $0.2x + 0.6y = 0.52(80)$

8. **Investment** You split $1500 between two savings accounts. Account A pays annual 5% interest and Account B pays 4% annual interest. After one year, you have earned a total of $69.50 in interest. How much money did you invest in each account?

Hint Write an equation that shows the total amount of money you deposit is $1500. Write another equation that shows 0.05x plus 0.04y equals the amount of interest earned.

Solve each system. Explain why you chose the method you used.

9. $4x + 5y = 3$
$3x - 2y = 8$

10. $2x + 7y = -20$
$y = 3x + 7$

11. $5x + 2y = 17$
$x - 2y = 8$

12. Think About a Plan You have a jar of pennies and quarters. You want to choose 15 coins that are worth exactly $4.35.

- What equations can you write to model the situation?
- Is your solution reasonable in terms of the original problem?

Open-Ended Without solving, decide what method you would use to solve each system: *graphing*, *substitution*, or *elimination*. Explain.

13. $y = 3x - 1$
$y = 4x$

14. $3m - 4n = 1$
$3m - 2n = -1$

15. $4s - 3t = 8$
$t = -2s - 1$

16. Chemistry In a chemistry lab, you have two vinegars. One is 5% acetic acid, and one is 6.5% acetic acid. You want to make 200 mL of a vinegar with 6% acetic acid. How many milliliters of each vinegar do you need to mix together?

17. Entertainment A contestant on a quiz show gets 150 points for every correct answer and loses 250 points for each incorrect answer. After answering 20 questions, the contestant has 200 points. How many questions has the contestant answered correctly? Incorrectly?

> **Hint** The contestant *loses* 250 points for each incorrect answer, which you should represent with subtraction.

Standardized Test Prep

SAT/ACT

18. Last year, one fourth of the students in your class played an instrument. This year, 6 students joined the class. Four of the new students play an instrument. Now, one third of the students play an instrument. How many students are in your class now?

Ⓐ 18   Ⓑ 24   Ⓒ 30   Ⓓ 48

19. Which answer choice shows $2x - y = z$ correctly solved for y?

Ⓕ $y = 2x + z$ Ⓖ $y = 2x - z$ Ⓗ $y = -2x + z$ Ⓘ $y = -2x - z$

Short Response

20. What is an equation of a line passing through the points $(3, 1)$ and $(4, 3)$ written in slope-intercept form?

Mixed Review

Solve each system using elimination.

◀ See Lesson 6-3.

21. $x + 3y = 11$
$2x + 3y = 4$

22. $2x + 4y = -12$
$-6x + 5y = 2$

23. $5x + 8y = 40$
$3x - 10y = -13$

Get Ready! To prepare for Lesson 6-5, do Exercises 24–26.

Solve each inequality. Check your solution.

◀ See Lesson 3-4.

24. $3a + 5 > 20$ **25.** $2d - 3 \geq 4d + 2$ **26.** $3(q + 4) \leq -2q - 8$

Chapter Review for Part A

- elimination method (p. 396)
- solution of a system of linear equations (p. 382)
- substitution method (p. 390)
- system of linear equations (p. 382)

Choose the correct term to complete each sentence.

1. You can solve a system of equations by replacing a variable with an equivalent expression. This is called the __?__ method.

2. You can solve a system of equations by adding or subtracting the equations in such a way that one variable drops out. This is called the __?__ method.

3. Two or more linear equations together form a(n) __?__.

6-1 Solving Systems by Graphing

Quick Review

One way to solve a system of linear equations is by graphing each equation and finding the intersection point of the graph, if one exists.

Example

What is the solution of the system? $y = -2x + 2$
$y = 0.5x - 3$

$y = -2x + 2$ Slope is -2; y-intercept is 2.

$y = 0.5x - 3$ Slope is 0.5; y-intercept is -3.

Graph the equations on the same coordinate plane.

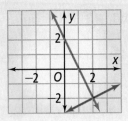

The lines appear to intersect at $(2, -2)$. Check if $(2, -2)$ makes both equations true.

$-2 = -2(2) + 2$ ✔

$-2 = 0.5(2) - 3$ ✔

So, the solution is $(2, -2)$.

Exercises

Solve each system by graphing. Check your answer.

4. $y = 3x + 13$
   $y = x - 3$

5. $y = -x + 4$
   $y = 3x + 12$

6. $y = 2x + 3$
   $y = \frac{1}{3}x - 2$

7. $y = 1.5x + 2$
   $4.5x - 3y = -9$

8. $y = -2x - 21$
   $y = x - 7$

9. $y = x + 1$
   $2x - 2y = -2$

10. **Songwriting** Jay has written 24 songs to date. He writes an average of 6 songs per year. Jenna started writing songs this year and expects to write about 12 songs per year. How many years from now will Jenna have written as many songs as Jay? Write and graph a system of equations to find your answer.

11. **Reasoning** Describe the graph of a system of equations that has no solution.

6-2 Solving Systems Using Substitution

Quick Review

You can solve a system of equations by solving one equation for one variable and then substituting the expression for that variable into the other equation.

Example

What is the solution of the system?
$$y = -\frac{1}{3}x$$
$$3x + 3y = -18$$

Write the second equation.	$3x + 3y = -18$
Substitute $-\frac{1}{3}x$ for y.	$3x + 3(-\frac{1}{3}x) = -18$
Simplify.	$2x = -18$
Solve for x.	$x = -9$
Substitute -9 for x in the first equation.	$y = -\frac{1}{3}(-9)$
	$y = 3$

The solution is $(-9, 3)$.

Exercises

Solve each system using substitution. Tell whether the system has *one solution, infinitely many solutions*, or *no solution*.

12. $y = 2x - 1$
$2x + 2y = 22$

13. $-x + y = -13$
$3x - y = 19$

14. $2x + y = -12$
$-4x - 2y = 30$

15. $\frac{1}{3}y = \frac{7}{3}x + \frac{5}{3}$
$x - 3y = 5$

16. $y = x - 7$
$3x - 3y = 21$

17. $3x + y = -13$
$-2x + 5y = -54$

18. Business The owner of a hair salon charges $20 more per haircut than the assistant. Yesterday the assistant gave 12 haircuts. The owner gave 6 haircuts. The total earnings from haircuts were $750. How much does the owner charge for a haircut? Solve by writing and solving a system of equations.

6-3 and 6-4 Solving Systems Using Elimination; Applications of Systems

Quick Review

You can add or subtract equations in a system to eliminate a variable. Before you add or subtract, you may have to multiply one or both equations by a constant to make eliminating a variable possible.

Example

What is the solution of the system?
$$3x + 2y = 41$$
$$5x - 3y = 24$$

$3x + 2y = 41$	Multiply by 3.	$9x + 6y = 123$
$5x - 3y = 24$	Multiply by 2.	$10x - 6y = 48$
		$19x + 0 = 171$
		$x = 9$

Write the first equation.	$3x + 2y = 41$
Substitute 9 for x.	$3(9) + 2y = 41$
Solve for y.	$y = 7$

The solution is $(9, 7)$.

Exercises

Solve each system using elimination. Tell whether the system has *one solution, infinitely many solutions*, or *no solution*.

19. $x + 2y = 23$
$5x + 10y = 55$

20. $7x + y = 6$
$5x + 3y = 34$

21. $5x + 4y = -83$
$3x - 3y = -12$

22. $9x + \frac{1}{2}y = 51$
$7x + \frac{1}{3}y = 39$

23. $4x + y = 21$
$-2x + 6y = 9$

24. $y = 3x - 27$
$x - \frac{1}{3}y = 9$

25. Flower Arranging It takes a florist 3 h 15 min to make 3 small centerpieces and 3 large centerpieces. It takes 6 h 20 min to make 4 small centerpieces and 7 large centerpieces. How long does it take to make each small centerpiece and each large centerpiece? Write and solve a system of equations to find your answer.

MathXL® for School
Go to PowerAlgebra.com

Do you know HOW?

Solve each system by graphing. Tell whether the system has *one solution*, *infinitely many solutions*, or *no solution*.

1. $y = x - 1$
   $y = -3x - 5$

2. $y = \frac{4}{3}x - 2$
   $3y - 4x = -6$

3. $y = 3x - 4$
   $y - 3x = 1$

4. $y = 3x - 14$
   $y - x = 10$

Solve each system using substitution.

5. $y = 2x + 5$
   $y = 6x + 1$

6. $x = y + 7$
   $y - 8 = 2x$

7. $4x + y = 2$
   $3y + 2x = -1$

8. $4x + 9y = 24$
   $y = -\frac{1}{3}x + 2$

Solve each system using elimination.

9. $2x + 5y = 2$
   $3x - 5y = 53$

10. $4x + 2y = 34$
    $10x - 4y = -5$

11. $11x - 13y = 89$
    $-11x + 13y = 107$

12. $3x + 6y = 42$
    $-7x + 8y = -109$

Write and solve a system of equations to solve each problem. Explain why you chose the method you used.

13. **Geometry** The length of a rectangle is 3 times the width. The perimeter is 44 cm. What are the dimensions of the rectangle?

14. **Farming** A farmer grows only pumpkins and corn on her 420-acre farm. This year she wants to plant 250 more acres of corn than pumpkins. How many acres of each crop should the farmer plant?

15. **Coins** You have a total of 21 coins, all nickels and dimes. The total value is $1.70. How many nickels and how many dimes do you have?

16. **Business** Suppose you start an ice cream business. You buy a freezer for $200. It costs you $.45 to make each single-scoop ice cream cone. You sell each cone for $1.25. How many cones do you need to sell to break even?

Do you UNDERSTAND?

Reasoning Without solving, tell which method you would choose to solve each system: *graphing*, *substitution*, or *elimination*. Explain your answer.

17. $y = 2x - 5$
    $4y + 8x = 15$

18. $2y + 7x = 3$
    $y - 7x = 9$

19. **Reasoning** If a system of linear equations has infinitely many solutions, what do you know about the slopes and *y*-intercepts of the graphs of the equations?

20. **Open-Ended** Write a system of equations that you would solve using substitution.

21. **Reasoning** Suppose you write a system of equations to find a break-even point for a business. You solve the system and find that it has no solution. What would that mean in terms of the business?

Systems of Equations and Inequalities

In Part A, you learned how to solve
systems of linear equations. Now
you will apply what you have learned
to systems of linear inequalities.

 Vocabulary for Part B

English/Spanish Vocabulary Audio Online:

English	Spanish
linear inequality, *p. 416*	desigualdad lineal
solution of an inequality, *p. 416*	solución de una desigualdad
solution of a system of linear inequalities, *p. 425*	solución de un sistema de desigualdades lineales
system of linear inequalities, *p. 425*	sistema de desigualdades lineales

BIG ideas

1 **Solving Equations and Inequalities**
Essential Question: How can you solve
a system of equations or inequalities?

2 **Modeling**
Essential Question: Can systems of
equations model real-world situations?

Chapter Preview for Part B

6-5

PART 1

Linear Inequalities

Objective To graph linear inequalities in two variables

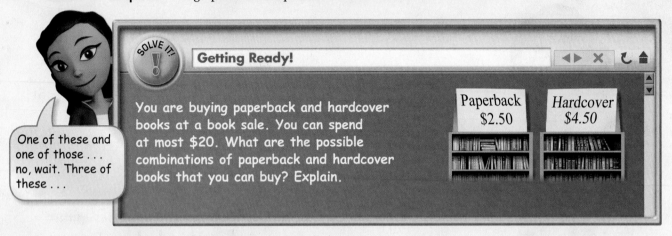

Getting Ready!

You are buying paperback and hardcover books at a book sale. You can spend at most $20. What are the possible combinations of paperback and hardcover books that you can buy? Explain.

Paperback $2.50

Hardcover $4.50

One of these and one of those . . . no, wait. Three of these . . .

Lesson Vocabulary
- linear inequality
- solution of an inequality

A **linear inequality** in two variables, such as $y \geq x - 2$, can be formed by replacing the equals sign in a linear equation with an inequality symbol.

Focus Question How is graphing a linear inequality similar to graphing a linear equation?

A linear inequality in two variables has an infinite number of solutions. These solutions can be represented in the coordinate plane as the set of all points on one side of a boundary line.

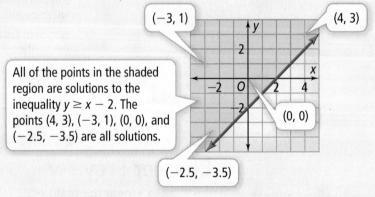

(−3, 1) (4, 3)

All of the points in the shaded region are solutions to the inequality $y \geq x - 2$. The points (4, 3), (−3, 1), (0, 0), and (−2.5, −3.5) are all solutions.

(0, 0)

(−2.5, −3.5)

A **solution of an inequality** in two variables is an ordered pair that makes the inequality true. To determine whether an ordered pair is a solution to a linear inequality, substitute the values for x and y into the linear inequality. Then simplify. If the resulting statement is true, the ordered pair is a solution. If the resulting ordered pair is false, the ordered pair is *not* a solution.

416 **Chapter 6** Systems of Equations and Inequalities

Problem 1 Identifying Solutions of a Linear Inequality

Is the ordered pair a solution of $y > x - 3$?

A $(1, 2)$

Write the inequality.	$y > x - 3$
Substitute 1 for x and 2 for y.	$2 \overset{?}{>} 1 - 3$
Simplify.	$2 > -2$ ✔

$2 > -2$ is a true statement, so $(1, 2)$ is a solution.

B $(-3, -7)$

Write the inequality.	$y > x - 3$
Substitute -3 for x and -7 for y.	$-7 \overset{?}{>} -3 - 3$
Simplify.	$-7 > -6$ ✘

$-7 > -6$ is a false statement, so $(-3, -7)$ is not a solution.

Got It? 1. Is $(3, 6)$ a solution of $y \le \frac{2}{3}x + 4$?

Dynamic Activity
Linear Inequalities

The graph of a linear inequality in two variables consists of all points in the coordinate plane that represent solutions. The graph is a region called a *half-plane* that is bounded by a line. All points on one side of the boundary line are solutions, while all points on the other side are not solutions.

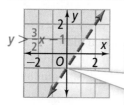

$y > \frac{3}{2}x - 1$

Each point on a *dashed* line is not a solution. A dashed line is used for inequalities with $>$ or $<$.

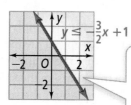

$y \le -\frac{3}{2}x + 1$

Each point on a *solid* line is a solution. A solid line is used for inequalities with $\ge$ or $\le$.

Problem 2 Graphing an Inequality in Two Variables

Think

Why does $y = x - 2$ represent the boundary line?
For any value of x, the corresponding value of y is the boundary between values of y that are greater than $x - 2$ and values of y that are less than $x - 2$.

What is the graph of $y > x - 2$?

First, graph the boundary line $y = x - 2$. Since the inequality symbol is $>$, the points on the boundary line are *not* solutions. Use a dashed line to indicate that the points are not included in the solution.

To determine which side of the boundary line to shade, test a point that is not on the line. For example, test the point $(0, 0)$.

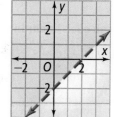

Write the inequality.	$y > x - 2$
Substitute $(0, 0)$ for (x, y).	$0 \overset{?}{>} 0 - 2$
$(0, 0)$ is a solution.	$0 > -2$ ✔

Because the point $(0, 0)$ is a solution of the inequality, so are all the points on the same side of the boundary line as $(0, 0)$. Shade the area above the boundary line.

Got It? 2. What is the graph of $y \le \frac{1}{2}x + 1$?

An inequality in one variable can be graphed on a number line or in the coordinate plane. The boundary line will be a horizontal or vertical line.

 ONLINE PROBLEMS

Problem 3 Graphing a Linear Inequality in One Variable

Think

Have you graphed inequalities like these before?
Yes. In Lesson 3-1, you graphed inequalities in one variable on a number line. Here you graph them in the coordinate plane.

What is the graph of each inequality in the coordinate plane?

A $x > -1$

Graph $x = -1$ using a dashed line. Use $(0, 0)$ as a test point.

$$x > -1$$
$$0 > -1 \; ✔$$

Shade on the side of the line that contains $(0, 0)$.

B $y \geq 2$

Graph $y = 2$ using a solid line. Use $(0, 0)$ as a test point.

$$y \geq 2$$
$$0 \geq 2 \; ✗$$

Shade on the side of the line that does *not* contain $(0, 0)$.

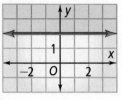

 Got It? **3.** What is the graph of each inequality?

a. $x < -5$ 　　　　　　　　　 **b.** $y \leq 2$

Focus Question How is graphing a linear inequality similar to graphing a linear equation?

Answer To graph a linear inequality, graph the equation related to the inequality. For example, if the inequality is $y \geq x + 3$, graph the equation $y = x + 3$. This becomes the boundary line. Make the line dashed if the inequality is $<$ or $>$. Shade all of the points on the side of the boundary line that make the inequality true. The shaded side represents the solutions of the inequality.

 Lesson Check

Do you know HOW?

1. Is $(-1, 4)$ a solution of the inequality $y < 2x + 5$?

Graph each linear inequality.

2. $y \leq -2x + 3$ 　　　　　**3.** $x < -1$

Do you UNDERSTAND?

4. Vocabulary How is a linear inequality in two variables like a linear equation in two variables? How are they different?

5. Writing To graph the inequality $y < \frac{3}{2}x + 3$, do you shade above or below the boundary line? Explain.

Practice and Problem-Solving Exercises

A Practice Determine whether the ordered pair is a solution of the linear inequality.   ◀ **See Problem 1.**

Guided Practice

6. $y \le -2x + 1;\ (2, 2)$

To start, substitute 2 for x and 2 for y. $2 \overset{?}{\le} -2(2) + 1$

7. $x < 2;\ (-1, 0)$

8. $y \ge 3x - 2;\ (0, 0)$

9. $y > x - 1;\ (0, 1)$

10. $y \ge -\frac{2}{5}x + 4;\ (0, 0)$

11. $y > 5x - 12;\ (-6, 1)$

12. $y < 3x - 5;\ (2, 1)$

Graph each linear inequality.   ◀ **See Problem 2.**

Guided Practice

13. $y \le x - 1$

To start, graph the boundary line $y = x - 1$.

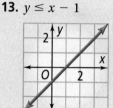

14. $y \ge 3x - 2$

15. $y < -4x - 1$

16. $y > 2x - 6$

17. $y < 5x - 5$

18. $y \le \frac{1}{2}x - 3$

19. $y > -3x$

Graph each inequality in the coordinate plane.   ◀ **See Problem 3.**

20. $x \le 4$

21. $y \ge -1$

22. $x > -2$

23. $y < -4$

B Apply **24. Error Analysis** A student graphed $y \ge 2x + 3$ as shown below. Describe and correct the student's error.

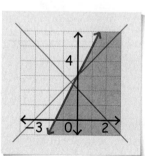

25. Writing When graphing an inequality, can you always use $(0, 0)$ as a test point to determine where to shade? If not, how would you choose a test point?

Linear Inequalities

Objective   To use linear inequalities when modeling real-world situations

In Part 1 of the lesson, you learned how to graph inequalities on the coordinate plane.

Connect to What You Know

Here you will learn how to use inequalities when modeling real-world situations.

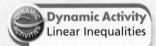

Dynamic Activity
Linear Inequalities

Focus Question   Can a linear inequality model a real-world situation?

When a linear inequality is solved for y, the direction of the inequality symbol determines which side of the boundary line to shade. If the symbol is $<$ or $\leq$, shade below the boundary line. If the symbol is $>$ or $\geq$, shade above it.

take note

Concept Summary   Shading the Graph of an Inequality

When a line is in slope-intercept form, you can quickly determine whether to shade above or below the line.

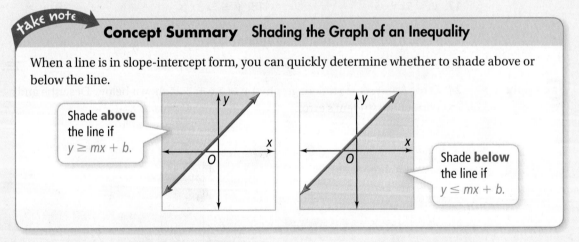

Shade **above** the line if $y \geq mx + b$.

Shade **below** the line if $y \leq mx + b$.

Sometimes you must first solve an inequality for y before using the method described above to determine where to shade.

Problem 4   Rewriting to Graph an Inequality

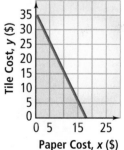

Think

Which inequality symbol should you use?
You must read the problem statement carefully. Here "$420 or less" means that the solution includes, but cannot exceed, $420, so use ≤.

Interior Design An interior decorator is going to remodel a kitchen. The wall above the stove and the counter is going to be redone as shown. The owners can spend $420 or less. Write a linear inequality and graph the solutions. What are three possible prices for the wallpaper and tiles?

Tiled Area
3 ft • 4 ft = 12 ft²

Papered Area
3 ft • 8 ft = 24 ft²

Let $x =$ the cost per square foot of the paper.

Let $y =$ the cost per square foot of the tiles.

Write an inequality and solve it for y.

Total cost is $420 or less.	$24x + 12y \leq 420$
Subtract $24x$ from each side.	$12y \leq -24x + 420$
Divide each side by 12.	$y \leq -2x + 35$

Hint

From the diagram, you know there are 24 ft² of papered area. If x is the cost per square foot, then the total cost for the papered area is $24x$.

Graph $y \leq -2x + 35$. The inequality symbol is ≤, so the boundary line is solid and you shade below it. The graph only makes sense in the first quadrant. Three possible prices per square foot for wallpaper and tile are $5 and $25, $5 and $15, and $10 and $10.

Paper and Tile Costs

Got It? **4.** For a party, you can spend no more than $12 on nuts. Peanuts cost $2/lb. Cashews cost $4/lb. What are three possible combinations of peanuts and cashews you can buy?

Think

Can you eliminate choices?

Yes. The boundary line is solid and the region below it is shaded, so you know the inequality symbol must be ≤. You can eliminate choices C and D.

 **Problem 5** **Writing an Inequality From a Graph**

Multiple Choice Which inequality represents the graph at the right?

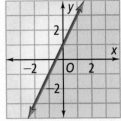

Ⓐ $y \leq 2x + 1$

Ⓑ $y \leq x + 1$

Ⓒ $y \geq 2x + 1$

Ⓓ $y < 2x + 1$

The slope of the line is 2 and the y-intercept is 1, so the equation of the boundary line is $y = 2x + 1$. The boundary line is solid, so the inequality symbol is either ≤ or ≥. The symbol must be ≤, because the region below the boundary line is shaded. The inequality is $y \leq 2x + 1$.

The correct answer is A.

 Got It? **5.** You are writing an inequality from a graph. The boundary line is dashed and has slope $\frac{1}{3}$ and y-intercept -2. The area above the line is shaded. What inequality should you write?

Focus Question Can a linear inequality model a real-world situation?

Answer Yes. When a problem describes a situation using terms such as no more than, at least, and at most, you can write an inequality. First define variables. Then write an inequality modeling the situation and carefully choose ≤, ≥, <, or >. Graph the boundary line and determine possible solutions from the graph.

 Lesson Check

Do you know HOW?

1. What is an inequality that represents the graph at the right?

Do you UNDERSTAND?

2. Reasoning Write an inequality that describes the region of the coordinate plane *not* included in the graph of $y < 5x + 1$.

Practice and Problem-Solving Exercises

A Practice

Graph each inequality in the coordinate plane.

See Problem 4.

3. $-2x + y \geq 3$ 4. $x + 3y < 15$ 5. $4x - y > 2$ 6. $-x + 0.25y \leq -1.75$

Guided Practice

7. **Carpentry** You budget $200 for wooden planks for outdoor furniture. Cedar costs $2.50 per foot and pine costs $1.75 per foot. Let $x =$ the number of feet of cedar and let $y =$ the number of feet of pine. What is an inequality that shows how much of each type of wood can be bought? Graph the inequality. What are three possible amounts of each type of wood that can be bought within your budget?

   To start, write an inequality. If your budget is $200, you can spend $200 or less. $2.5x + 1.75y \leq 200$

8. **Business** A fish market charges $9 per pound for cod and $12 per pound for flounder. Let $x =$ the number of pounds of cod. Let $y =$ the number of pounds of flounder. What is an inequality that shows how much of each type of fish the store must sell today to reach a daily quota of at least $120? Graph the inequality. What are three possible amounts of each fish that would satisfy the quota?

Write a linear inequality that represents each graph.

See Problem 5.

9.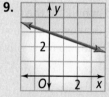

Guided Practice

To start, find the y-intercept and slope of the boundary line.

The y-intercept is 3. The slope is $-\frac{1}{3}$.

10.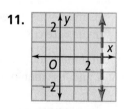

11.

B Apply

12. **Think About a Plan** A truck that can carry no more than 6400 lb is being used to transport refrigerators and upright pianos. Each refrigerator weighs 250 lb and each piano weighs 475 lb. Write and graph an inequality to show how many refrigerators and how many pianos the truck could carry. Will 12 refrigerators and 8 pianos overload the truck? Explain.
    - What inequality symbol should you use?
    - Which side of the boundary line should you shade?

13. **Employment** A student with two summer jobs earns $10 per hour at a cafe and $8 per hour at a market. The student would like to earn at least $800 per month.
   a. Write and graph an inequality to represent the situation.
   b. The student works at the market for 60 h per month and can work at most 90 h per month. Can the student earn at least $800 each month? Explain how you can you use your graph to determine this.

Standardized Test Prep

SAT/ACT

14. What is the equation of the graph shown?

   Ⓐ $y + x \geq -3$ Ⓒ $x - y > -3$

   Ⓑ $y - x \geq 3$ Ⓓ $y > -x + 3$

15. You secure pictures to your scrapbook using 3 stickers. You started with 24 stickers. There are now 2 pictures in your scrapbook. You write the equation $3(x + 2) = 24$ to find the number x of additional pictures you can put in your scrapbook. How many more pictures can you add?

   Ⓕ 4   Ⓗ 8

   Ⓖ 6   Ⓘ 12

Short Response

16. At Market A, 1-lb packages of rice are sold for the price shown. At Market B, rice is sold in bulk for the price shown. For each market, write a function describing the cost of buying rice in terms of the weight. How are the domains of the two functions different?

$2.00 $2.00/lb

Mixed Review

17. **Small Business** An electrician spends $12,000 on initial costs to start a new business. He estimates his expenses at $25 per day. He expects to earn $150 per day. If his estimates are correct, after how many working days will he break even?

   ◀ See Lesson 6-4.

18. What compound inequality represents the phrase "all real numbers that are greater than 2 and less than or equal to 7"? Graph the solutions.

   ◀ See Lesson 3-6.

Get Ready! To prepare for Lesson 6-6, do Exercises 19–21.

Solve each system by graphing. Tell whether the system has *one solution*, *infinitely many solutions*, or *no solution*.

   ◀ See Lesson 6-1.

19. $y = \frac{3}{2}x$
    $-2x + y = 3$

20. $3x + y = 6$
    $2x - y = 4$

21. $x + y = 11$
    $x + y = 16$

Systems of Linear Inequalities

Objectives To solve systems of linear inequalities by graphing

To model real-world situations using systems of linear inequalities

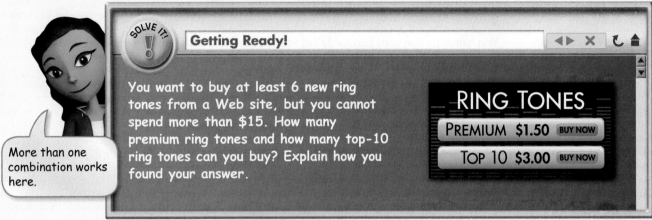

A **system of linear inequalities** is made up of two or more linear inequalities. A **solution of a system of linear inequalities** is an ordered pair that makes *all* the inequalities in the system true. The graph of a system of linear inequalities is the set of points that represent all of the solutions of the system.

Focus Question Which method used to solve systems of linear equations can you use to solve systems of linear inequalities?

Lesson Vocabulary

- system of linear inequalities
- solution of a system of linear inequalities

Problem 1 Graphing a System of Inequalities

What is the graph of the system? $y < 2x - 3$
$2x + y > 2$

Graph $y < 2x - 3$ and $2x + y > 2$.

> To graph $2x + y = 2$, find x- and y-intercepts like you did in Problem 2 of Lesson 5–5.

Think

Have you seen a problem like this before?
Yes. The solution of a system of equations is shown by the intersection of two lines. The solutions of a system of inequalities are shown by the intersection of two shaded areas.

> The blue region represents solutions of $2x + y > 2$.

> The yellow region represents solutions of $y < 2x - 3$.

> The green region represents solutions of *both* inequalities.

The system's solutions lie in the green region where the graphs overlap.

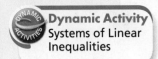
Check   (3, 0) is in the green region. See if (3, 0) satisfies both inequalities.

$y \overset{?}{\leq} 2x - 3$ ← Write both inequalities. → $2x + y \overset{?}{\geq} 2$

$0 \overset{?}{\leq} 2(3) - 3$ ← Substitute (3, 0) for (x, y). → $2(3) + 0 \overset{?}{\geq} 2$

$0 < 3$ ✔   ← Simplify. The solution checks. → $6 > 2$ ✔

 Got It?   **1.** What is the graph of the system? $y \geq -x + 5$
$-3x + y \leq -4$

You can combine your knowledge of linear equations with your knowledge of inequalities to describe a graph using a system of inequalities.

Problem 2   **Writing a System of Inequalities From a Graph**

What system of inequalities is represented by the graph below?

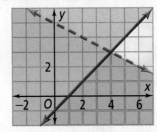

To write a system that is represented by the graph, write an inequality that represents the yellow region and an inequality that represents the blue region.

The red boundary line is $y = -\frac{1}{2}x + 5$. The region does not include the line, only points below. The inequality is $y < -\frac{1}{2}x + 5$.

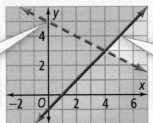

The blue boundary line is $y = x - 1$. The region includes the boundary line and points above. The inequality is $y \geq x - 1$.

The graph shows the intersection of the system $y < -\frac{1}{2}x + 5$ and $y \geq x - 1$.

 Got It?   **2. a.** What system of inequalities is represented by the graph?
  b. Reasoning In part (a), is the point where the boundary lines intersect a solution of the system? Explain.

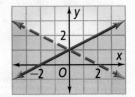

You can model many real-world situations by writing and graphing systems of linear inequalities. Some real-world situations involve three or more restrictions, so you must write a system of at least three inequalities.

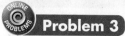 **Problem 3** Using a System of Inequalities

Time Management You are planning what to do after school. You can spend at most 6 h daily playing basketball and doing homework. You want to spend less than 2 h playing basketball. You must spend at least 2 h on homework. What is a graph showing how you can spend your time?

Know	Need	Plan
• At most 6 h playing basketball and doing homework • Less than 2 h playing basketball • At least 2 h doing homework	To find different ways you can spend your time	Write and graph an inequality for each restriction. Find the region where all three restrictions are met.

Let x = the number of hours playing basketball.

Let y = the number of hours doing homework.

Write a system of inequalities.

$x + y \le 6$ At most 6 h of basketball and homework

$x < 2$ Less than 2 h of basketball

$y \ge 2$ At least 2 h of homework

Graph the system. Because time cannot be negative, the graph makes sense only in the first quadrant. The solutions of the system are all of the points in the shaded region, including the points on the solid boundary lines.

After-School Activities

 Got It? 3. You want to build a fence for a rectangular dog run. You want the run to be at least 10 feet wide. The run can be at most 50 ft long. You have 126 ft of fencing. What is a graph showing the possible dimensions of the dog run?

Focus Question Which method used to solve systems of linear equations can you use to solve systems of linear inequalities?

Answer You can graph the inequalities on the same coordinate plane. The solution of the system is the region where the graphs of the individual inequalities overlap.

Lesson Check

Do you know HOW?

1. What is the graph of the system?

$$y > 3x - 2$$
$$2y - x \leq 6$$

2. What system of inequalities is represented by the graph at the right?

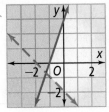

3. Cherries cost \$4/lb. Grapes cost \$2.50/lb. You can spend no more than \$15 on fruit, and you need at least 4 lb in all. What is a graph showing the amount of each fruit you can buy?

Do you UNDERSTAND?

4. **Vocabulary** How can you determine whether an ordered pair is a solution of a system of linear inequalities?

5. **Reasoning** Suppose you are graphing a system of two linear inequalities, and the boundary lines for the inequalities are parallel. Does that mean that the system has no solution? Explain.

6. **Writing** How is finding the solution of a system of inequalities different from finding the solution of a system of equations? How is it the same? Explain.

Practice and Problem-Solving Exercises

 Practice

Determine whether the ordered pair is a solution of the given system.

See Problem 1.

7. $(2, 12)$; $\quad y > 2x + 4$
$\qquad\qquad y < 3x + 7$

8. $(8, 2)$; $\quad 3x - 2y \leq 17$
$\qquad\qquad 0.3x + 4y > 9$

9. $(-3, 17)$; $\quad y > -5x + 2$
$\qquad\qquad\quad y \geq -3x + 7$

Solve each system of inequalities by graphing.

Guided Practice

	10. $y < 2x + 4$
	$-3x - 2y \geq 6$
To start, solve the inequality $-3x - 2y \geq 6$ for y.	$-3x - 2y \geq 6$
Add $3x$ to each side.	$-3x + 3x - 2y \geq 6 + 3x$
Simplify.	$-2y \geq 3x + 6$
Divide both sides by -2.	$\dfrac{-2y}{-2} \leq \dfrac{3x + 6}{-2}$
Simplify.	$y \leq -\dfrac{3}{2}x - 3$

11. $y < 2x + 4$
$\quad 2x - y \leq 4$

12. $y > 2x + 4$
$\quad 2x - y \leq 4$

13. $y > \dfrac{1}{4}x$
$\quad y \leq -x + 4$

14. $y < 2x - 3$
$\quad y > 5$

15. $x + 2y \leq 10$
$\quad x + 2y \geq 9$

16. $y \geq -x + 5$
$\quad y \leq 3x - 4$

Write a system of inequalities for each graph.

See Problem 2.

17.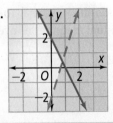

18.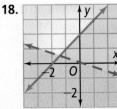

19.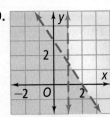

20.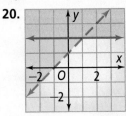

21. Earnings Suppose you have a job mowing lawns that pays $12 per hour. You also have a job at a clothing store that pays $10 per hour. You need to earn at least $350 per week, but you can work no more than 35 h per week. You must work a minimum of 10 h per week at the clothing store. What is a graph showing how many hours per week you can work at each job?

◀ **See Problem 3.**

To start, define variables and write a system of inequalities.	Let x = the number of hours mowing lawns. Let y = the number of hours at a clothing store.
You must earn at least $350.	$12x + 10y \geq 350$
You can work no more than 35 h per week.	$x + y \leq 35$
You must work a minimum of 10 h per week at the clothing store.	$y \geq 10$

22. Driving Two friends agree to split the driving on a road trip from Philadelphia, Pennsylvania, to Denver, Colorado. One friend drives at an average speed of 60 mi/h. The other friend drives at an average speed of 55 mi/h. They want to drive at least 500 mi per day. They plan to spend no more than 10 h driving each day. The friend who drives slower wants to drive fewer hours. What is a graph showing how they can split the driving each day?

Apply

23. Error Analysis A student graphs the system as shown below. Describe and correct the student's error.

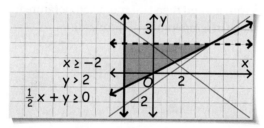

24. a. Graph the system $y > 3x + 3$ and $y \leq 3x - 5$.
  b. Writing Will the boundary lines $y = 3x + 3$ and $y = 3x - 5$ ever intersect? How do you know?
  c. Do the shaded regions in the graph from part (a) overlap?
  d. Does the system of inequalities have any solutions? Explain.

25. Think About a Plan You are fencing in a rectangular area for a garden. You have only 150 ft of fence. You want the length of the garden to be at least 40 ft. You want the width of the garden to be at least 5 ft. What is a graph showing the possible dimensions your garden could have?
  • What variables will you use? What will they represent?
  • How many inequalities do you need to write?

26. Gift Certificates You received a $100 gift certificate to a clothing store. The store sells T-shirts for $15 and dress shirts for $22. You want to spend no more than the amount of the gift certificate. You want to leave at most $10 of the gift certificate unspent. You need at least one dress shirt. What are all of the possible combinations of T-shirts and dress shirts you could buy?

27. a. Geometry Graph the system of linear inequalities.
   b. Describe the shape of the solution region.
   c. Find the vertices of the solution region.
   d. Find the area of the solution region.

$x \geq 2$
$y \geq -3$
$x + y \leq 4$

28. Which region represents the solution of the system?

$y \leq -\frac{3}{2}x - 2$
$3y - 9x \geq 6$

(A) I
(C) III
(B) II
(D) IV

Standardized Test Prep

SAT/ACT

29. The point $(-3, 11)$ is a solution of which of the following systems?

(A) $y \geq x - 2$
  $2x + y \leq 5$

(B) $y > x + 8$
  $3x + y > 2$

(C) $y > -x + 8$
  $2x + 3y \geq 7$

(D) $y \leq -3x + 1$
  $x - y \geq -15$

30. A plane has 18 passengers. Some have 1 bag and others have 2 bags. There are a total of 27 bags. Let $b =$ the number of passengers with 1 bag and $t =$ the number of passengers with 2 bags. Which system describes this situation?

(F) $b + t = 27$
  $b + 2t = 18$

(G) $t = 18 - b$
  $b + 2t = 27$

(H) $b + t = 18$
  $b = 27 + 2t$

(I) $b = 18 - t$
  $b + 2t = 18$

31. You fill your glass with ice and then add room-temperature water. Which graph best represents the change in temperature of the glass?

(A)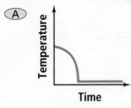
(B)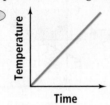
(C)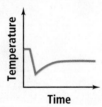
(D)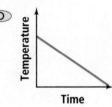

Extended Response

32. Suppose the line through points $(-1, 6)$ and $(x, 2)$ is perpendicular to the graph of $2x + y = 3$.

   a. Find the value of x. Show your work.
   b. What is an equation of the line perpendicular to the graph of $2x + y = 3$ and through the given points?
   c. What ordered pair is a solution of both equations? Explain.

Mixed Review

Graph each linear inequality.

◀ **See Lesson 6-5.**

33. $y - x \leq 3$
34. $3y + x > 4$
35. $y \leq 5$

Get Ready! To prepare for Lesson 7-1, do Exercises 36–38.

Simplify each expression.

◀ **See Lesson 1-2.**

36. $(1 + 3)^2 - (1 + 3)$
37. $4^3 + 5^2 + (4 - 3)^1$
38. $7^2 + 2(3^3 + 5)$

Graphing Linear Inequalities

A graphing calculator can show the solutions of an inequality or a system of inequalities. To enter an inequality, press **apps** and scroll down to select **INEQUAL**. Move the cursor over the = symbol for one of the equations. Notice the inequality symbols at the bottom of the screen, above the keys labeled **F2–F5**. Change the = symbol to an inequality symbol by pressing **alpha** followed by one of **F2–F5**.

Activity 1

Graph the inequality $y < 3x - 7$.

1. Move the cursor over the = symbol for **Y₁**. Press **alpha** and **F2** to select the < symbol.

2. Enter the given inequality as **Y₁**.

3. Press **graph** to graph the inequality.

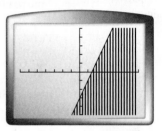

Activity 2

Graph the system. $y < -2x - 3$
$$y \geq x + 4$$

4. Move the cursor over the = symbol for **Y₁**. Press **alpha** and **F2** to select the < symbol. Enter the first inequality as **Y₁**.

5. Then move the cursor over the = symbol for **Y₂**, and press **alpha** and **F5** to select the ≥ symbol. Enter the second inequality as **Y₂**.

6. Press **graph** to graph the system of inequalities.

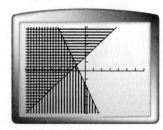

Exercises

Use a graphing calculator to graph each inequality. Sketch your graph.

7. $y \leq x$

8. $y > 5x - 9$

9. $y \geq -1$

10. $y < -x + 8$

Use a graphing calculator to graph each system of inequalities. Sketch your graph.

11. $y \geq -x + 3$
$y \leq x + 2$

12. $y > x$
$y \geq -2x + 5$

13. $y \geq -1$
$y < 0.5x - 2$

14. $y \geq 2x - 2$
$y \leq 2x - 4$

Pull It **All Together**

To solve these problems you will pull together many concepts and skills that you have studied about systems of equations and inequalities.

BIG idea Solving Equations and Inequalities

There are several ways to solve systems of equations and inequalities, including graphing and using equivalent forms of equations and inequalities within the system. The number of solutions depends on the type of system.

Task 1

Solve using two different methods. Explain which method you found to be more efficient.

a. $3x - 9y = 3$
$6x - 3y = -24$

b. $7x - 3y = 20$
$5x + 3y = 16$

c. $y = \frac{1}{2}x - 6$
$2x + 6y = 19$

Task 2

Solve. Show all your work and explain your steps.

The triangle on the left has a perimeter of 14. The triangle on the right has a perimeter of 21. What are x and y?

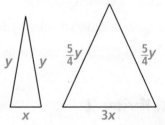

BIG idea Modeling

You can represent many real-world mathematical problems algebraically. When you need to find two unknowns, you may be able to write and solve a system of equations or inequalities.

Task 3

Solve the problem. Show all of your work and explain your steps.

A town is organizing a Fourth of July parade. There will be two sizes of floats in the parade, as shown below. A space of 10 ft will be left after each float.

a. The parade must be at least 150 ft long, but less than 200 ft long. What combinations of large and small floats are possible?

b. Large floats cost $600 to operate. Small floats cost $300 to operate. The town has a budget of $2500 to operate the floats. How does this change your answer to part (a)? What combinations of large and small floats are possible?

Hint Let s = the number of small floats. Let ℓ = the number of large floats. After you write and graph two inequalities, find the points with integer coordinates that fall where the shaded regions overlap.

Connecting **BIG** ideas and Answering the Essential Questions

1 Solving Equations and Inequalities
There are several ways to solve systems of equations and inequalities, including graphing and using equivalent forms of equations and inequalities within the system. The number of solutions depends on the type of system.

Solving Systems of Equations (Lessons 6-1, 6-2, and 6-3)

$y = x$
$y = -3x - 4$

The solution is $(-1, -1)$.

Linear Inequalities (Lessons 6-5 and 6-6)

2 Modeling
You can represent many real-world mathematical problems algebraically. When you need to find two unknowns, you may be able to write and solve a system of equations.

Applying Linear Systems (Lesson 6-4)

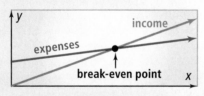

Chapter Vocabulary

- linear inequality (p. 416)
- solution of an inequality (p. 416)
- solution of a system of linear inequalities (p. 425)
- system of linear inequalities (p. 425)

Choose the correct term to complete each sentence.

1. A __?__ is an ordered pair that makes all the inequalities in the system true.

2. The inequality $y < 3x + 5$ is a __?__.

6-5 and 6-6 Linear Inequalities and Systems of Inequalities

Quick Review

A **linear inequality** describes a region of the coordinate plane with a boundary line. Two or more inequalities form a **system of inequalities.** The system's solutions lie where the graphs of the inequalities overlap.

Example

What is the graph of the system? $y > 2x - 4$
$$y \le -x + 2$$

Graph the boundary lines
$y = 2x - 4$ and $y = -x + 2$.
For $y > 2x - 4$, use a dashed
boundary line and shade above
it. For $y \le -x + 2$, use a solid
boundary line and shade below. The
green region of overlap contains the
system's solutions.

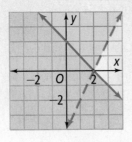

Exercises

Solve each system of inequalities by graphing.

3. $y \ge x + 4$
$y < 2x - 1$

4. $4y < -3x$
$y < -\dfrac{3}{4}x$

5. $2x - y > 0$
$3x + 2y \le -14$

6. $y < \dfrac{3}{4}x + 5$
$y < -\dfrac{1}{2}x + 1$

7. $y < 10x$
$y > x - 5$

8. $4x + 4 > 2y$
$3x - 4y \ge 1$

9. Downloads You have 60 megabytes (MB) of space left on your portable media player. You can choose to download song files that use 3.5 MB or video files that use 8 MB. You want to download at least 12 files. What is a graph showing the numbers of song and video files you can download?

Do you know HOW?

Solve each system by graphing. Tell whether the system has *one solution, infinitely many solutions,* or *no solution.*

1. $y = 3x - 7$
  $y = -x + 1$

2. $x + 3y = 12$
  $x = y - 8$

3. $x + y = 5$
  $x + y = -2$

Solve each system using substitution.

4. $y = 4x - 7$
  $y = 2x + 9$

5. $8x + 2y = -2$
  $y = -5x + 1$

6. $y + 2x = -1$
  $y - 3x = -16$

Solve each system using elimination.

7. $4x + y = 8$
  $-3x - y = 0$

8. $2x + 5y = 20$
  $3x - 10y = 37$

9. $3x + 2y = -10$
  $2x - 5y = 3$

Solve each system of inequalities by graphing.

10. $y > 4x - 1$
  $y \leq -x + 4$

11. $x > -3$
  $-3x + y \geq 6$

12. Garage Sale You go to a garage sale. All the items cost $1 or $5. You spend less than $45. Write and graph a linear inequality that models the situation.

13. Gardening A farmer plans to create a rectangular garden that he will enclose with chicken wire. The garden can be no more than 30 ft wide. The farmer would like to use at most 180 ft of chicken wire.
  a. Write a system of linear inequalities that models this situation.
  b. Graph the system to show all possible solutions.

Write a system of equations to model each situation. Solve by any method.

14. Education A writing workshop enrolls novelists and poets in a ratio of 5 : 3. There are 24 people at the workshop. How many novelists are there? How many poets are there?

15. Chemistry A chemist has one solution containing 30% insecticide and another solution containing 50% insecticide. How much of each solution should the chemist mix to get 200 L of a 42% insecticide?

Do you UNDERSTAND?

16. Open-Ended Write a system of two linear equations that has no solution.

17. Error Analysis A student concluded that $(-2, -1)$ is a solution of the inequality $y < 3x + 2$, as shown below. Describe and correct the student's error.

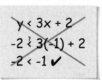

18. Reasoning Consider a system of two linear equations in two variables. If the graphs of the equations are not the same line, is it possible for the system to have infinitely many solutions? Explain.

Reasoning **Suppose you add two linear equations that form a system, and you get the result shown below. How many solutions does the system have?**

19. $x = 8$ **20.** $0 = 4$ **21.** $0 = 0$

Cumulative Test Prep

Some questions on tests ask you to solve a problem that involves a system of equations. Read the sample question at the right. Then follow the tips to answer the question.

TIP 1

When writing an equation, try to use variables that make sense for the problem. Instead of using x and y, use q for quarters and n for nickels.

Melissa keeps a jar for holding change. The jar holds 21 coins. All of the coins are quarters and nickels. The total amount in the jar is $3.85. How many quarters are in the jar?

- (A) 3
- (B) 7
- (C) 14
- (D) 21

TIP 2

Make sure to answer the question asked. Here you only need to find the number of quarters.

Think It Through

Write a system of equations.
$$q + n = 21$$
$$0.25q + 0.05n = 3.85$$

Solve the first equation for n and substitute to find q.
$$0.25q + 0.05n = 3.85$$
$$0.25q + 0.05(21 - q) = 3.85$$
$$0.2q + 1.05 = 3.85$$
$$q = 14$$

The correct answer is C.

Vocabulary Builder

As you solve test items, you must understand the meanings of mathematical terms. Choose the correct term to complete each sentence.

A. The (*substitution*, *elimination*) method is a way to solve a system of equations in which you replace one variable with an equivalent expression containing the other variable.

B. A linear (*equation*, *inequality*) is a mathematical sentence that describes a region of the coordinate plane having a boundary line.

C. A(n) (*x-intercept*, *y-intercept*) is the coordinate of a point where a graph intersects the *y*-axis.

D. The (*area*, *perimeter*) of a figure is the distance around the outside of the figure.

E. A (*function rule*, *relation*) is an equation that can be used to find a unique range value given a domain value.

Multiple Choice

Read each question. Then write the letter of the correct answer on your paper.

1. A group of students are going on a field trip. If the group takes 3 vans and 1 car, 22 students can be transported. If the group takes 2 vans and 4 cars, 28 students can be transported. How many students can fit in each van?

- (A) 2
- (B) 4
- (C) 6
- (D) 10

2. Greg's school paid $1012.50 for 135 homecoming T-shirts. How much would it cost the school to purchase 235 T-shirts?

- (F) $750.00
- (G) $1762.50
- (H) $2025.00
- (I) $2775.00

3. Which expression is equivalent to $64s - (8s - 4)$?

  (A) $52s$ (C) $56s + 4$

  (B) $60s$ (D) $56s - 4$

4. Which equation describes a line with slope 12 and y-intercept 4?

  (F) $y = 12x + 4$ (H) $y = 4x + 12$

  (G) $y = 12(x + 4)$ (I) $y = x + 3$

5. What is the solution of the system of equations shown at the right?

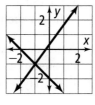

  (A) $(1, -1)$

  (B) $(-1, 1)$

  (C) $(-1, -1)$

  (D) $(1, 1)$

6. The width of Ben's rectangular family room is 3 ft less than the length. The perimeter is 70 ft. Which equation can be used to find the length ℓ of the room?

  (F) $70 = \ell - 3$ (H) $70 = 2(\ell - 3)$

  (G) $70 = 2\ell - 3$ (I) $70 = 2(2\ell - 3)$

7. Marisa's Flower Shop charges $3 per rose plus $16 for a delivery. Chris wants to have a bouquet of roses delivered to his mother. Which value is in the range of the function that gives the bouquet's cost in terms of the number of roses?

  (A) $16   (C) $34

  (B) $27   (D) $48

8. Which number is a solution of $8 > 3x - 1$?

  (F) 0   (H) 4

  (G) 3   (I) 6

9. The formula for the area A of a trapezoid is $A = \frac{1}{2}(b_1 + b_2)h$, where b_1 and b_2 represent the lengths of the bases and h represents the height. Which equation can be used to find the height of a trapezoid?

  (A) $h = 2A - b_1 - b_2$

  (B) $h = \dfrac{2A}{b_1 + b_2}$

  (C) $h = \dfrac{A(b_1 + b_2)}{2}$

  (D) $h = \dfrac{A - 2}{b_1 + b_2}$

10. Martin used 400 ft of fencing to enclose a rectangular area in his backyard. Isabella wants to enclose a similar area that is twice as long and twice as wide as the one in Martin's backyard. How much fencing does Isabella need?

  (F) 800 ft   (H) 1600 ft

  (G) 1200 ft   (I) 2000 ft

11. At the Conic Company, a new employee's earnings E, in dollars, can be calculated using the function $E = 0.05s + 30,000$, where s represents the employee's total sales, in dollars. All of the new employees earned between $50,000 and $60,000 last year. Which value is in the domain of the function?

  (A) $34,000   (C) $430,000

  (B) $300,000   (D) $3,400,000

12. Hilo's class fund has $65. The class is having a car wash to raise more money for a trip. The graph below models the amount of money the class will have if it charges $4 for each car washed.

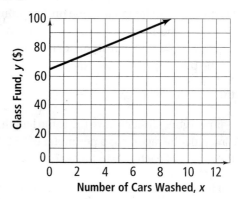

How would the graph change if the class charged $5 per car washed?

  (F) The y-intercept would increase.

  (G) The slope would increase.

  (H) The y-intercept would decrease.

  (I) The slope would decrease.

13. A system has two linear equations in two variables. The graphs of the equations have the same slope but different y-intercepts. How many solutions does the system have?

  (A) 0   (C) 2

  (B) 1   (D) infinitely many

14. Rhonda has 25 coins in her pocket. All of the coins are either dimes or nickels. If Rhonda has a total of $2.30, how many dimes does she have?

- F 4
- G 15
- H 18
- I 21

15. Which problem can be represented by the equation $19.2 = 3.2x$?

- A Elizabeth had $3.20, and she then received her paycheck. How much was her paycheck?
- B Jack bought some boxes of cereal at the store for $3.20 each. How much did he spend on cereal?
- C Mia spent $19.20 on socks. If each pair of socks cost $3.20, how many pairs did she buy?
- D Amos had $19.20 and spent $3.20 on lunch. How much money did Amos have after lunch?

GRIDDED RESPONSE

Record your answers in a grid.

16. An artist is putting a rectangular frame on a painting that is 12 in. wide and 19 in. long. The frame is 3 in. wide on each side. To the nearest square inch, what is the area of the painting with the frame?

17. What is the solution of $4(-3x + 6) - 1 = -13$?

18. In a regular polygon, all sides have the same length. Suppose a regular hexagon has a perimeter of 25.2 in. What is the length of each side in inches?

19. The sum of four consecutive integers is 250. What is the greatest of these integers?

20. What is the slope of a line that is perpendicular to the line with equation $y = -5x + 8$?

21. On a map, Julia's home is 8.5 in. from the library. If the map scale is 1 in. : 0.25 mi, how many miles from the library does Julia live?

22. The graph shows Jillian's distance from her house as she walks home from school. How many blocks per minute does Jillian walk?

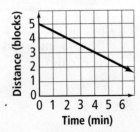

23. Sam is ordering pizza. Tony's Pizza charges $7 for a large cheese pizza plus $.75 for each additional topping. Maria's Pizza charges $8 for a large cheese pizza plus $.50 for each additional topping. For what number of toppings will the cost of a large pizza be the same at either restaurant?

24. Pam paid $9500 in college expenses this year. The college projects a 6% increase in expenses next year. What dollar amount should Pam expect to pay for college expenses next year?

25. A museum exhibit is showing various pieces of artwork created by an artist. The table below shows the number of each type of artwork shown.

Artwork	Number
Photographs	37
Paintings	43
Sculptures	10

What is the ratio of sculptures to all artwork? Give your answer as a fraction in lowest terms.

Short Response

26. The volume V of a cube is given by the formula $V = s^3$, where s represents the length of an edge of the cube. Suppose the edge length is 24 in. What is the volume of the cube in cubic feet?

27. You plan to mail surveys to different households. A box of 50 envelopes costs $3.50, and a postage stamp costs $.42. How much will it cost you to mail 400 surveys?

Extended Response

28. The vertices of quadrilateral $ABCD$ are $A(1, 1)$, $B(1, 5)$, $C(5, 5)$, and $D(7, 1)$.

- **a.** A trapezoid is a four-sided figure with exactly one pair of parallel sides. Is $ABCD$ a trapezoid? Explain your answer.
- **b.** You want to transform $ABCD$ into a parallelogram by only moving point B. A parallelogram is a four-sided figure with both pairs of opposite sides parallel. What should be the new coordinates of point B? Explain.

Get Ready!

Skills Handbook Page 787

Converting Fractions to Decimals

Write as a decimal.

1. $\frac{7}{10}$ **2.** $6\frac{2}{5}$ **3.** $\frac{8}{1000}$ **4.** $\frac{7}{2}$ **5.** $\frac{3}{11}$

Lesson 1-2

Using Order of Operations

Simplify each expression.

6. $(9 \div 3 + 4)^2$ **7.** $5 + (0.3)^2$ **8.** $3 - (1.5)^2$ **9.** $64 \div 2^4$

10. $4 \div (0.5)^2$ **11.** $(0.25)4^2$ **12.** $2(3 + 7)^3$ **13.** $-3(4 + 6 \div 2)^2$

Lesson 1-2

Evaluating Expressions

Evaluate each expression for $a = -2$ and $b = 5$.

14. $(ab)^2$ **15.** $(a - b)^2$ **16.** $a^3 + b^3$ **17.** $b - (3a)^2$

Lesson 2-10

Finding Percent Change

Tell whether each percent change is an increase or decrease. Then find the percent change. Round to the nearest percent.

18. $15 to $20   **19.** $20 to $15

20. $600 to $500   **21.** $2000 to $2100

Looking Ahead Vocabulary

22. If you say that a plant has new growth, has the size of the plant changed? What do you think the *growth factor* of the plant describes?

23. In a mathematical expression, an exponent indicates repeated multiplication by the same number. How would you expect a quantity to change when it experiences *exponential growth*?

24. Tooth decay occurs when tooth enamel wears away over time. If *exponential decay* models the change in the number of dentists in the United States over time, do you think the number of dentists in the United States is increasing or decreasing?

Exponents and Exponential Functions

Check out this photo! The bacteria population in the Grand Prismatic Spring in Yellowstone National Park causes the different colors you see around the spring.

Did you know you can use exponents to describe the growth of a population? You'll learn how in this chapter.

Vocabulary

English/Spanish Vocabulary Audio Online:

English	Spanish
compound interest, p. 484	interés compuesto
decay factor, p. 485	factor de decremento
exponential decay, p. 485	decremento exponencial
exponential function, p. 475	función exponencial
exponential growth, p. 483	incremento exponencial
growth factor, p. 483	factor incremental
scientific notation, p. 449	notación científica

My Math Video

00:04:04

BIG ideas

1 Equivalence

Essential Question: How can you represent very large and very small numbers?

2 Properties

Essential Question: How can you simplify expressions involving exponents?

3 Functions

Essential Question: What are the characteristics of exponential functions?

Chapter Preview

7-1 Zero and Negative Exponents

Objective To simplify expressions involving zero and negative exponents

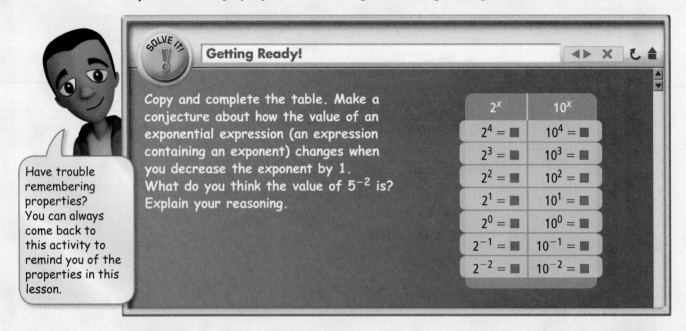

SOLVE IT!

Getting Ready!

Copy and complete the table. Make a conjecture about how the value of an exponential expression (an expression containing an exponent) changes when you decrease the exponent by 1. What do you think the value of 5^{-2} is? Explain your reasoning.

Have trouble remembering properties? You can always come back to this activity to remind you of the properties in this lesson.

2^x	10^x
$2^4 = \blacksquare$	$10^4 = \blacksquare$
$2^3 = \blacksquare$	$10^3 = \blacksquare$
$2^2 = \blacksquare$	$10^2 = \blacksquare$
$2^1 = \blacksquare$	$10^1 = \blacksquare$
$2^0 = \blacksquare$	$10^0 = \blacksquare$
$2^{-1} = \blacksquare$	$10^{-1} = \blacksquare$
$2^{-2} = \blacksquare$	$10^{-2} = \blacksquare$

The patterns you found in the Solve It illustrate the properties of zero and negative exponents.

Focus Question How can patterns help you simplify expressions involving zero and negative exponents?

Suppose you add two columns to the table in the Solve It. What pattern do you find in the table below?

3^x	4^x
$3^3 = 27$	$4^3 = 64$
$3^2 = 9$	$4^2 = 16$
$3^1 = 3$	$4^1 = 4$
$3^0 = 1$	$4^0 = 1$
$3^{-1} = \frac{1}{3}$	$4^{-1} = \frac{1}{4}$

Decreasing the exponent by 1 is the same as dividing by the base value.

Properties   Zero and Negative Exponents

Zero as an Exponent For every nonzero number a, $a^0 = 1$.

Examples $4^0 = 1$ $\qquad\qquad$ $(-3)^0 = 1$ $\qquad\qquad$ $(5.14)^0 = 1$

Negative Exponent For every nonzero number a and integer n, $a^{-n} = \frac{1}{a^n}$.

Examples $7^{-3} = \frac{1}{7^3}$ $\qquad\qquad$ $(-5)^{-2} = \frac{1}{(-5)^2}$

Why is 0^0 undefined? The property of zero as an exponent implies the following pattern.

$3^0 = 1$ $\qquad$ $2^0 = 1$ $\qquad$ $1^0 = 1$ $\qquad$ $0^0 \overset{?}{=} 1$

However, switching the exponent and the base implies the following pattern.

$0^3 = 0$ $\qquad$ $0^2 = 0$ $\qquad$ $0^1 = 0$ $\qquad$ $0^0 \overset{?}{=} 0$

It is not possible for 0^0 to equal both 1 and 0. So, 0^0 is undefined.

Why is an expression with a base of 0 and a negative exponent undefined? Using 0 as a base with a negative exponent will result in division by zero, which is undefined.

Problem 1   Simplifying Powers

What is the simplified form of each expression?

A 9^{-2}

Use the definition of negative exponent. $\qquad$ $9^{-2} = \frac{1}{9^2}$

Simplify. $\qquad\qquad\qquad\qquad\qquad\qquad = \frac{1}{9 \cdot 9}$

Multiply. $\qquad\qquad\qquad\qquad\qquad\qquad = \frac{1}{81}$

B $(-3.6)^0$

Use the definition of zero as an exponent. $\quad (-3.6)^0 = 1$

Got It? **1.** What is the simplified form of each expression?

$\qquad$ **a.** 4^{-3} $\qquad$ **b.** $(-5)^0$ $\qquad$ **c.** 3^{-2} $\qquad$ **d.** 6^{-1} $\qquad$ **e.** $(-4)^{-2}$

An algebraic expression is in simplest form when powers with a variable base are written with only positive exponents.

 Problem 2 **Simplifying Exponential Expressions**

Think

Which part of the expression do you need to rewrite?
The base b has a negative exponent, so you need to rewrite it with a positive exponent.

What is the simplified form of each expression?

Ⓐ $5a^3b^{-2}$

Use the definition of negative exponent.　$5a^3b^{-2} = 5a^3\left(\dfrac{1}{b^2}\right)$

Simplify.　　　　　　　　　　　　　　　$= \dfrac{5a^3}{b^2}$

Ⓑ $\dfrac{1}{x^{-5}}$

Rewrite the fraction using a division symbol.　$\dfrac{1}{x^{-5}} = 1 \div x^{-5}$

Use the definition of negative exponent.　　　　$= 1 \div \dfrac{1}{x^5}$

Multiply by the reciprocal of $\dfrac{1}{x^5}$, which is $\dfrac{x^5}{1}$.　$= 1 \cdot \dfrac{x^5}{1}$
Use the Identity Property of Multiplication.　　$= x^5$

Got It? **2.** What is the simplified form of each expression?

    a. x^{-9}　　　　**b.** $\dfrac{1}{n^{-3}}$　　　　**c.** $4c^{-3}b$　　　　**d.** $\dfrac{2}{a^{-3}}$　　　　**e.** $\dfrac{n^{-5}}{m^2}$

When you evaluate an exponential expression, you can simplify the expression before substituting values for the variables.

 Problem 3 **Evaluating an Exponential Expression**

Plan

How do you simplify the expression?
Use the definition of negative exponent to rewrite the expression with only positive exponents.

What is the value of $3s^3t^{-2}$ for $s = 2$ and $t = -3$?

Use the definition of negative exponent.　　　　$3s^3t^{-2} = \dfrac{3s^3}{t^2}$

Substitute the values for s and t into the expression.　$= \dfrac{3(2)^3}{(-3)^2}$

Simplify exponents.　　　　　　　　　　　　$= \dfrac{3(8)}{9}$

Multiply.　　　　　　　　　　　　　　　$= \dfrac{24}{9}$

Simplify.　　　　　　　　　　　　　　　$= 2\dfrac{2}{3}$

Got It? **3.** What is the value of each expression in parts (a)–(d) for $n = -2$ and $w = 5$?

    a. $n^{-4}w^0$　　　　　　　　　　　　**b.** $\dfrac{n^{-1}}{w^2}$

    c. $\dfrac{n^0}{w^6}$　　　　　　　　　　　　**d.** $\dfrac{1}{nw^{-1}}$

    e. Reasoning In Problem 3, you rewrote the expression and then substituted 2 for s and -3 for t. Instead, you could substitute before you simplify. Which method would you prefer to use to evaluate n^0w^0 for $n = -2$ and $w = 3$? Explain.

Problem 4 **Using an Exponential Expression**

Population Growth A population of marine bacteria doubles every hour under controlled laboratory conditions. The number of bacteria is modeled by the expression $1000 \cdot 2^h$, where h is the number of hours after a scientist measures the population size. Evaluate the expression for $h = 0$ and $h = -3$. What does each value of the expression represent in the situation?

Know	Need	Plan
$1000 \cdot 2^h$ models the population.	Values of the expression for $h = 0$ and $h = -3$	Substitute each value of h into the expression and simplify.

Substitute 0 for h. $1000 \cdot 2^h = 1000 \cdot 2^0$

Simplify. $= 1000 \cdot 1$

Multiply. $= 1000$

The value of the expression for $h = 0$ is 1000. There were 1000 bacteria at the time the scientist measured the population.

Substitute -3 for h. $1000 \cdot 2^h = 1000 \cdot 2^{-3}$

Simplify. $= 1000 \cdot \frac{1}{8}$

Multiply. $= 125$

The value of the expression for $h = -3$ is 125. There were 125 bacteria 3 h before the scientist measured the population.

Hint
Make sure your answer is reasonable. Does your answer make sense compared to the population at $h = 0$?

 Got It? **4.** A population of insects triples every week. The number of insects is modeled by the expression $5400 \cdot 3^w$, where w is the number of weeks after the population was measured. Evaluate the expression for $w = -2$, $w = 0$, and $w = 1$. What does each value of the expression represent in the situation?

Focus Question How can patterns help you simplify expressions involving zero and negative exponents?

Answer Any number raised to the zero power, except 0, is 1. Any number raised to a negative power is first changed to the reciprocal of that number raised to a positive power, and then simplified.

Lesson Check

Do you know HOW?

Simplify each expression.

1. 2^{-5}

2. m^0

3. $5s^2t^{-1}$

4. $\frac{4}{x^{-3}}$

Evaluate each expression for $a = 2$ and $b = -4$.

5. a^3b^{-1}

6. $2a^{-4}b^0$

Do you UNDERSTAND?

7. **Vocabulary** A positive exponent shows repeated multiplication. What repeated operation does a negative exponent show?

8. **Error Analysis** A student incorrectly simplified $\frac{x^n}{a^{-n}b^0}$ as shown below. Find and correct the student's error.

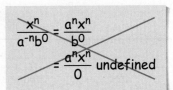

Practice and Problem-Solving Exercises

A Practice

Simplify each expression.

◀ **See Problem 1.**

Guided Practice

To start, use the definition of negative exponent.

9. 3^{-2}

$3^{-2} = \frac{1}{3^2}$

10. $(-4.25)^0$

11. $(-6)^{-2}$

12. -5^{-2}

13. $(-4)^{-2}$

14. 2^{-6}

15. -3^0

16. -12^{-1}

17. $\frac{1}{2^0}$

18. $(-5)^{-3}$

Simplify each expression.

◀ **See Problem 2.**

19. $4ab^0$

20. $\frac{1}{x^{-7}}$

21. $\frac{3^{-2}}{n}$

22. $k^{-4}j^0$

23. $\frac{3x^{-2}}{y}$

24. $c^{-5}d^{-7}$

25. $c^{-5}d^7$

26. $\frac{7s}{5t^{-3}}$

27. $\frac{6a^{-1}c^{-3}}{d^0}$

Evaluate each expression for $r = -3$ and $s = 5$.

See Problem 3.

Guided Practice

To start, substitute -3 for r.
Use the definition of negative exponent.

28. r^{-3}

$r^{-3} = (-3)^{-3}$

$= \dfrac{1}{(-3)^3}$

29. s^{-3}

30. $\dfrac{3r}{s^{-2}}$

31. $\dfrac{s^0}{r^{-2}}$

32. $4s^{-1}$

33. $r^0 s^{-2}$

34. $r^{-4} s^2$

35. Internet Traffic The number of visitors to a certain Web site triples every month. The number of visitors is modeled by the expression $8100 \cdot 3^m$, where m is the number of months after the number of visitors was measured. Evaluate the expression $m = -4$. What does the value of the expression represent in the situation?

See Problem 4.

36. Population Growth A Galápagos cactus finch population increases by half every decade. The number of finches is modeled by the expression $45 \cdot 1.5^d$, where d is the number of decades after the population was measured. Evaluate the expression for $d = -2$, $d = 0$, and $d = 1$. What does each value of the expression represent in the situation?

Galápagos cactus finch

 Apply

Mental Math Is the value of each expression *positive* or *negative*?

37. -2^2

38. $(-2)^3$

39. $(-2)^{-3}$

Write each number as a power of 10 using negative exponents.

40. $\dfrac{1}{10}$

41. $\dfrac{1}{100}$

42. $\dfrac{1}{10,000}$

Rewrite each fraction with all the variables in the numerator.

43. $\dfrac{a}{b^{-2}}$

44. $\dfrac{4g}{h^3}$

45. $\dfrac{8c^5}{11d^4 e^{-2}}$

46. Think About a Plan Suppose your drama club's budget doubles every year. This year the budget is $500. How much was the club's budget 2 yr ago?
- What expression models what the budget of the club will be in 1 yr? In 2 yr? In y years?
- What value of y can you substitute into your expression to find the budget of the club 2 yr ago?

47. Copy and complete the table at the right.

48. a. Simplify $a^n \cdot a^{-n}$.
  b. Reasoning What is the mathematical relationship between a^n and a^{-n}? Explain.

n	3	▪	▪	$\frac{5}{8}$	▪
n^{-1}	▪	6	$\frac{1}{7}$	▪	0.5

49. **Open-Ended** Choose a fraction to use as a value for the variable a. Find the values of a^{-1}, a^2, and a^{-2}.

50. **Manufacturing** A company is making metal rods with a target diameter of 1.5 mm. A rod is acceptable when its diameter is within 10^{-3} mm of the target diameter. Write an inequality for the acceptable range of diameters.

SAT/ACT

51. What is the simplified form of $-6(-6)^{-1}$?

52. Segment CD represents the flight of a bird that passes through the points $(1, 2)$ and $(5, 4)$. What is the slope of a line that represents the flight of a second bird that flew perpendicular to the first bird?

53. What is the solution of the equation $1.5(x - 2.5) = 3$?

54. What is the simplified form of $|3.5 - 4.7| + 5.6$?

55. What is the y-intercept of the graph of $3x - 2y = -8$?

Mixed Review

Solve each system by graphing.   See Lesson 6-6.

56. $y > 3x + 4$
    $y \le -3x + 1$

57. $y \le -2x + 1$
    $y < 2x - 1$

58. $y \ge 0.5x$
    $y \le x + 2$

Write an equation in slope-intercept form for the line with the given slope m and y-intercept b.   See Lesson 5-3.

59. $m = -1, b = 4$

60. $m = 5, b = -2$

61. $m = \frac{2}{5}, b = -3$

Get Ready!   To prepare for Lesson 7-2, do Exercises 62–66.

Simplify each expression.   See Lesson 7-1.

62. $6 \cdot 10^4$

63. $7 \cdot 10^{-2}$

64. $8.2 \cdot 10^5$

65. $3 \cdot 10^{-3}$

66. $3.4 \cdot 10^5$

7-2 Scientific Notation

Objectives To write numbers in scientific and standard notation
To compare and order numbers using scientific notation

That's an awful lot of digits for such small numbers.

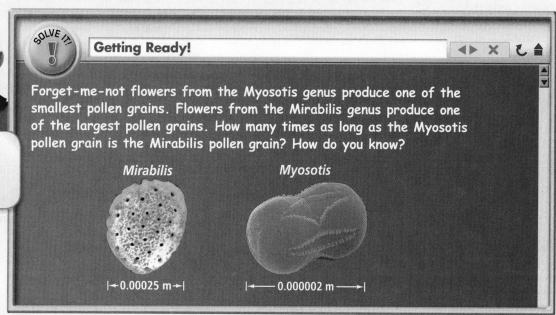

Getting Ready!

Forget-me-not flowers from the Myosotis genus produce one of the smallest pollen grains. Flowers from the Mirabilis genus produce one of the largest pollen grains. How many times as long as the Myosotis pollen grain is the Mirabilis pollen grain? How do you know?

Mirabilis

|← 0.00025 m →|

Myosotis

|← 0.000002 m →|

Lesson Vocabulary
• scientific notation

In the Solve It, you worked with very small numbers. Scientists and mathematicians write very small or very large numbers, such as the masses of subatomic particles or the diameters of planets, using powers of 10.

Focus Question Why would you use powers of 10 to write and compare numbers? *Scientific notation* is a shorthand way to write numbers using powers of 10.

take note

Key Concept Scientific Notation

A number in **scientific notation** is written as the product of two factors in the form $a \times 10^n$, where n is an integer and $1 \le |a| < 10$.

Examples 8.3×10^5 4.12×10^{22} 7.1×10^{-5}

Hint

Not all calculators are the same. Check the manual for your calculator to see how it displays scientific notation.

You can use a scientific calculator to work with numbers in scientific notation. The E on a calculator readout stands for exponentiation. The readout 1.35E8 means 1.35×10^8, or 135,000,000. The ⓔ key lets you input an exponent for a power of 10. So to enter 4×10^6, you can enter 4 ⓔ 6.

Problem 1 Recognizing Scientific Notation

Is the number written in scientific notation? If not, explain.

A 0.23×10^{-3}

No. 0.23 is less than 1.

B 2.3×10^7

Yes

C 9.3×100^9

No. 100^9 is not in the form 10^n.

 Got It? **1.** Is the number written in scientific notation? If not, explain.

a. 53×10^4

b. 3.42×10^{-7}

c. 0.35×100

With scientific notation, you use negative exponents to write numbers between 0 and 1. You use nonnegative exponents to write numbers greater than 1. Notice that $1{,}430{,}000{,}000 = 1.43 \times 1{,}000{,}000{,}000 = 1.43 \times 10^9$. Problem 2 shows you a shortcut.

 Problem 2 Writing a Number in Scientific Notation

Physical Science What is each number written in scientific notation?

A approximate distance between the sun and Saturn: 1,430,000,000 km

$$1{,}430{,}000{,}000 = 1.43 \times 10^9$$

Use 9 as the exponent.

Move the decimal point 9 places to the left.

Remove the zeros after the 3.

B the radius of an atom: 0.0000000001 m

Move the decimal point 10 places to the right.
Use −10 as the exponent. Remove the zeros before the 1.

$$0.0000000001 = 1 \times 10^{-10}$$

Got It? **2.** What is each number written in scientific notation?

a. 678,000

b. 0.000032

c. 51,400,000

d. 0.0000007

Notice that $5.5 \times 10^6 = 5.5 \times 1{,}000{,}000 = 5{,}500{,}000$. Problem 3 shows you a shortcut.

Problem 3 Writing a Number in Standard Notation

Biology What is each number written in standard notation?

A weight of an Asian elephant: 5.5×10^6 g

Move the decimal point 6 places to the right. $5.5 \times 10^6 = 5{,}500{,}000$

$$= 5{,}500{,}000$$

B weight of an ant: 3.1×10^{-3} g

Move the decimal point 3 places to the left. $3.1 \times 10^{-3} = 0.0031$

$$= 0.0031$$

 Got It? **3.** What is each number in parts (a)–(d) written in standard notation?

a. 5.23×10^7 **b.** 4.6×10^{-5} **c.** 2.09×10^{-4} **d.** 3.8×10^{12}

e. Reasoning How do you write a number of the form $a \times 10^0$ in standard notation?

Think

What does the exponent tell you about the number?
If the exponent of 10 is positive, the number is greater than or equal to 1. If the exponent of 10 is negative, the number is less than 1.

You can compare and order numbers in scientific notation. First compare the powers of 10. If numbers have the same power of 10 then compare the decimals.

Problem 4 Comparing Numbers in Scientific Notation

Geography The map below shows four major world oceans and their surface areas. What is the order of the oceans from least to greatest surface area?

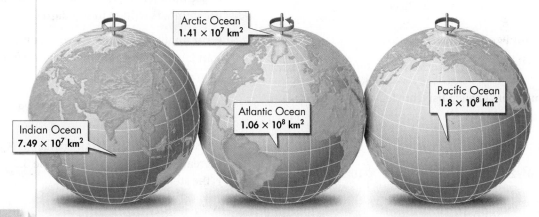

Arctic Ocean 1.41×10^7 km²

Pacific Ocean 1.8×10^8 km²

Atlantic Ocean 1.06×10^8 km²

Indian Ocean 7.49×10^7 km²

Think

Why do you arrange the numbers by the powers of 10 first?
If two numbers written in scientific notation have different powers of 10, then the number with the greater power of 10 is greater.

Order the numbers by the powers of 10. Arrange the numbers with the same power of 10 in order by their decimal parts.

1.41×10^7 km²	7.49×10^7 km²	1.06×10^8 km²	1.8×10^8 km²
Arctic	Indian	Atlantic	Pacific

From least to greatest surface area, the order of the oceans is the Arctic, the Indian, the Atlantic, and the Pacific.

Got It? **4.** What is the order of the following parts of an atom from least to greatest mass?

neutron: 1.675×10^{-24} g, electron: 9.109×10^{-28} g,
proton: 1.673×10^{-24} g

You can write numbers like 815×10^5 and 0.078×10^{-2} in scientific notation.

$$815 \times 10^5 = 81,500,000 = 8.15 \times 10^7$$

$$0.078 \times 10^{-2} = 0.00078 = 7.8 \times 10^{-4}$$

The problems above show a pattern. When you move a decimal point n places to the left, the exponent of 10 increases by n. When you move a decimal point n places to the right, the exponent of 10 decreases by n.

Focus Question Why would you use powers of 10 to write and compare numbers?

Answer Powers of 10 make very large and small numbers easier to work with. Write the product of two factors in the form $a \times 10^n$, where a is greater than or equal to 1 and less than 10 and n is an integer.

 ## Lesson Check

Do you know HOW?

Write each number in scientific notation.

1. 0.0007

2. 32,000,000

Write each number in standard notation.

3. 3.5×10^6

4. 1.27×10^{-4}

Order the numbers in each list from least to greatest.

5. $10^5, 10^{-3}, 10^0, 10^{-1}, 10^1$

6. $5 \times 10^{-3}, 2 \times 10^4, 3 \times 10^0, 7 \times 10^{-1}$

7. $2.5 \times 10^7, 2.1 \times 10^7, 3.5 \times 10^6, 3.6 \times 10^6$

Do you UNDERSTAND?

8. Open-Ended Describe a situation in which it is easier to use numbers written in scientific notation than to use numbers written in standard form.

9. Error Analysis A student wrote 1.88×10^{-5} in standard notation as shown below. Describe and correct the student's mistake.

$$1.88 \times 10^{-5} = 0.00188$$

10. Reasoning A student claims that 3.5×10^{11} is greater than 1.4×10^{13} because $3.5 > 1.4$. Is the student correct? Explain.

 ## Practice and Problem-Solving Exercises

 Practice Is the number written in scientific notation? If not, explain.

 **See Problem 1.**

11. 44×10^8

12. 3.2×10^6

13. 0.9×10^{-2}

14. 6.7×1000^9

15. 7.3×10^{-5}

16. 1.12×10^1

Write each number in scientific notation.

See Problem 2.

Guided Practice

17. 9,040,000,000

To start, move the decimal point 9 places to the left.

9,040,000,000

18. 0.02 **19.** 9.3 million **20.** 21,700

21. 0.00325 **22.** 8,003,000 **23.** 0.0156

Write each number in standard notation.

See Problem 3.

24. 5×10^2 **25.** 7.45×10^2 **26.** 8.97×10^{-1}

27. 1.3×10^0 **28.** 2.74×10^5 **29.** 4.8×10^{-3}

Order the numbers in each list from least to greatest.

See Problem 4.

Guided Practice

30. $9 \times 10^{-7}, 8 \times 10^{-8}, 7 \times 10^{-6}, 6 \times 10^{-10}$

To start, compare the powers of 10.

$10^{-10} < 10^{-8} < 10^{-7} < 10^{-6}$

31. $8.2 \times 10^5, 7.9 \times 10^5, 2.7 \times 10^5, 8.1 \times 10^5$

32. $50.1 \times 10^{-3}, 4.8 \times 10^{-3}, 0.52 \times 10^{-3}, 56 \times 10^{-3}$

33. $0.53 \times 10^7, 5300 \times 10^{-1}, 5.3 \times 10^5, 530 \times 10^8$

34. Physics The half-life of a radioactive isotope is the amount of time it takes one half of a sample of the isotope to decay. What is the order of the following radioactive isotopes of uranium from shortest to longest half-life?

Isotope	^{232}U	^{234}U	^{235}U	^{236}U
Half-life (years)	68.9	2.45×10^5	7.04×10^8	2.34×10^7

Apply

Simplify. Write each answer using scientific notation.

35. $4(2 \times 10^{-3})$ **36.** $8(3 \times 10^{14})$ **37.** $0.2(3 \times 10^2)$

38. Writing You write 1 billion in scientific notation as 10^9. Explain why you write 436 billion in scientific notation as 4.36×10^{11} rather than as 436×10^9.

39. Think About a Plan A light-year is the distance light travels in one year. One light-year is about 5,878,000,000,000 mi. The table shows the estimated distance, in light-years, of several stars from Earth. How many miles is each star from Earth?
- How do you convert from light-years to miles?
- What notation is easier to use for writing long distances?

40. Physics The radius of a water molecule is about 1.4 angstroms. One angstrom is 0.00000001 cm. What is the diameter of a water molecule in centimeters? Use scientific notation.

Distance From Earth

Star	Distance (light-years)
Proxima Centauri	4.2
Sirius	8.7
Vega	27
Polaris	431

SOURCE: NASA

Standardized Test Prep

SAT/ACT

41. A lab sample has a mass of 0.000345 g. What is this amount written in scientific notation?

(A) 0.345×10^3 (B) 0.345×10^{-3} (C) 3.45×10^{-4} (D) 3.45×10^4

42. What is the union of $\{1, 3, 5, 7\}$ and $\{3, 4, 5\}$?

(F) $\{\,\}$ (G) $\{1, 7\}$ (H) $\{3, 5\}$ (I) $\{1, 3, 4, 5, 7\}$

43. What is the equation of the graph at the right?

(A) $y = 2x - \frac{1}{2}$ (C) $y = \frac{1}{2}x - \frac{1}{2}$

(B) $y = -2x - \frac{1}{2}$ (D) $y = -\frac{1}{2}x + 2$

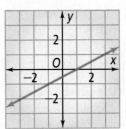

Short Response

44. A student is collecting cans to raise money for a class trip. Each week the student collects 150 cans. Make a graph of the situation. How many weeks will it take the student to collect 1200 cans?

Mixed Review

Simplify each expression.

◀ See Lesson 7-1.

45. cd^{-6} **46.** $a^0 b^3$ **47.** $9w^{-3}$ **48.** $\frac{4m}{n^{-5}}$ **49.** $\frac{3^{-2}}{k^{-5}}$

Graph each linear inequality.

◀ See Lesson 6-5.

50. $y < -\frac{1}{4}x + 2$ **51.** $y \geq \frac{2}{3}x$ **52.** $y < 3x - 4$ **53.** $y > -3x + \frac{1}{2}$

Get Ready!   To prepare for Lesson 7-3, do Exercises 54–59.

Rewrite each expression using exponents.

◀ See p. 791.

54. $t \cdot t \cdot t \cdot t \cdot t \cdot t \cdot t$ **55.** $(6 - m)(6 - m)(6 - m)$ **56.** $(r + 2)(r + 2)(r + 2)(r + 2)$

57. $5 \cdot 5 \cdot 5 \cdot s \cdot s \cdot s$ **58.** $2 \cdot 2 \cdot 2 \cdot 2 \cdot 2 \cdot x \cdot x \cdot x$ **59.** $8 \cdot 8 \cdot (x - 1)(x - 1)(x - 1)$

Multiplying Powers With the Same Base

Objective To multiply powers with the same base

I wonder if they counted all the stars.

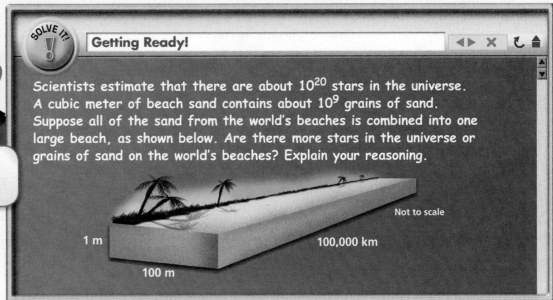

Getting Ready!

Scientists estimate that there are about 10^{20} stars in the universe. A cubic meter of beach sand contains about 10^9 grains of sand. Suppose all of the sand from the world's beaches is combined into one large beach, as shown below. Are there more stars in the universe or grains of sand on the world's beaches? Explain your reasoning.

Not to scale

1 m

100,000 km

100 m

All of the numbers in the Solve It are powers of 10. In this lesson, you will learn a method for multiplying powers that have the same base.

Focus Question How do properties of exponents make problem solving easier?

You can write a product of powers with the same base, such as $3^4 \cdot 3^2$, using one exponent.

$$3^4 \cdot 3^2 = (3 \cdot 3 \cdot 3 \cdot 3) \cdot (3 \cdot 3) = 3^6$$

Notice that the sum of the exponents in the expression $3^4 \cdot 3^2$ equals the exponent of 3^6.

take note

Property Multiplying Powers With the Same Base

Words To multiply powers with the same base, add the exponents.

Algebra $a^m \cdot a^n = a^{m+n}$, where $a \neq 0$ and m and n are integers

Examples $4^3 \cdot 4^5 = 4^{3+5} = 4^8$ $b^7 \cdot b^{-4} = b^{7+(-4)} = b^3$

Problem 1 **Multiplying Powers**

What is each expression written using each base only once?

A $12^4 \cdot 12^3$

Add the exponents of the powers with the same base. $\quad 12^4 \cdot 12^3 = 12^{4+3}$

Simplify the exponent. $\qquad\qquad\qquad = 12^7$

B $(-5)^{-2}(-5)^7$

Add the exponents of the powers with the same base. $\quad (-5)^{-2}(-5)^7 = (-5)^{-2+7}$

Simplify the exponent. $\qquad\qquad\qquad = (-5)^5$

Got It? **1.** What is each expression written using each base only once?

a. $8^3 \cdot 8^6$ **b.** $(0.5)^{-3}(0.5)^{-8}$ **c.** $9^{-3} \cdot 9^2 \cdot 9^6$

Remember that you can combine only those powers with the same base.

Problem 2 **Multiplying Powers in Algebraic Expressions**

What is the simplified form of each expression?

A $n^{-4} \cdot n^7$

Add the exponents of the powers with the same base. $\quad n^{-4} \cdot n^7 = n^{(-4+7)}$

Simplify the exponent. $\qquad\qquad\qquad = n^3$

B $4z^5 \cdot 9z^{-12}$

Use the commutative and associative properties of multiplication. $\quad 4z^5 \cdot 9z^{-12} = (4 \cdot 9)(z^5 \cdot z^{-12})$

Multiply the coefficients. Add the exponents of the powers with the same base. $\qquad\qquad\qquad = 36(z^{5+(-12)})$

Simplify the exponent. $\qquad\qquad\qquad = 36z^{-7}$

Rewrite using a positive exponent. $\qquad\qquad\qquad = \dfrac{36}{z^7}$

Hint

Start by separating the coefficients from the powers. Then group powers with the same base.

C $2a \cdot 9b^4 \cdot 3a^2$

Use the commutative and associative properties of multiplication. $\quad 2a \cdot 9b^4 \cdot 3a^2 = (2 \cdot 9 \cdot 3)(a \cdot a^2)(b^4)$

$\boxed{a = a^1}$

Multiply the coefficients. Write a as a^1. $\qquad\qquad = 54(a^1 \cdot a^2)(b^4)$

Add exponents of powers with the same base. $\qquad\qquad = 54(a^{1+2})(b^4)$

Simplify. $\qquad\qquad = 54a^3b^4$

Got It? **2.** What is the simplified form of each expression in parts (a)-(c)?

a. $x^4 \cdot x^9$ **b.** $-4c^3 \cdot 7d^2 \cdot 2c^{-2}$ **c.** $j^2 \cdot k^{-2} \cdot 12j$

d. **Reasoning** Explain how to simplify the expression $x^a \cdot x^b \cdot x^c$.

You can use the property for multiplying powers with the same base to multiply two numbers written in scientific notation.

 Problem 3 Multiplying Numbers in Scientific Notation

What is the simplified form of $(3 \times 10^5)(5 \times 10^{-12})$? Write your answer in scientific notation.

 Plan

Which numbers can you group to make the calculation easier?
Group 3 and 5. Group the powers of 10.

Use the commutative and associative properties of multiplication.

$$(3 \times 10^5)(5 \times 10^{-12}) = (3 \cdot 5)(10^5 \cdot 10^{-12})$$

When multiplying powers with the same base, add exponents.

$$= 15 \cdot 10^{(5+(-12))}$$

Add exponents.

$$= 15 \cdot 10^{-7}$$

Write 15 in scientific notation.

$$= 1.5 \times 10^1 \cdot 10^{-7}$$

Add exponents.

$$= 1.5 \times 10^{-6}$$

Got It? 3. What is the simplified form of $(7 \times 10^8)(4 \times 10^5)$? Write your answer in scientific notation.

Problem 4 Multiplying Numbers in Scientific Notation

Chemistry At 20°C, one cubic meter of water has a mass of about 9.98×10^5 g. Each gram of water contains about 3.34×10^{22} molecules of water. About how many molecules of water does the droplet of water shown below contain?

$V = 1.13 \times 10^{-7} \, m^3$

1 m³

Plan

How do you find the number of molecules?
Use unit analysis. Divide out the common units.

Use unit analysis.   number of water molecules $= \cancel{\text{cubic meters}} \cdot \dfrac{\text{grams}}{\cancel{\text{cubic meters}}} \cdot \dfrac{\text{molecules}}{\cancel{\text{grams}}}$

Substitute.

$$= (1.13 \times 10^{-7}) \cdot (9.98 \times 10^5) \cdot (3.34 \times 10^{22})$$

Use the commutative and associative properties of multiplication.

$$= (1.13 \cdot 9.98 \cdot 3.34) \times (10^{-7} \cdot 10^5 \cdot 10^{22})$$

Multiply. Add the exponents.

$$\approx 37.7 \times 10^{-7+5+22}$$

Simplify.

$$= 37.7 \times 10^{20}$$

Write in scientific notation.

$$= 3.77 \times 10^{21}$$

The droplet contains about 3.77×10^{21} molecules of water.

Got It? **4.** About how many molecules of water are in a swimming pool that holds 200 m^3 of water? Write your answer in scientific notation.

Focus Question How do properties of exponents make problem solving easier?

Answer After learning the properties of exponents, you can quickly simplify expressions. Use the properties of exponents to multiply powers with the same base by adding the exponents.

 ## Lesson Check

Do you know HOW?

1. What is $8^4 \cdot 8^8$ written using each base only once?

2. What is the simplified form of $2n^3 \cdot 3n^{-2}$?

3. What is $(3 \times 10^5)(8 \times 10^4)$ written in scientific notation?

4. Measurement The diameter of a penny is about 1.9×10^{-5} km. It would take about 2.1×10^9 pennies placed end to end to circle the equator once. What is the approximate length of the equator?

Do you UNDERSTAND?

5. Writing Can $x^8 \cdot y^3$ be written using only one base? Explain your reasoning.

6. Reasoning Suppose $a \times 10^m$ and $b \times 10^n$ are two numbers in scientific notation. Is their product $ab \times 10^{m+n}$ always, *sometimes*, or *never* a number in scientific notation? Justify your answer.

7. Error Analysis Your friend says $4a^2 \cdot 3a^5 = 7a^7$. Do you agree with your friend? Explain.

  ## Practice and Problem-Solving Exercises

A Practice Rewrite each expression using each base only once. ◀ **See Problem 1.**

> **Guided Practice**
>
> To start, add the exponents of powers with the same base.

8. $7^3 \cdot 7^4$

$7^3 \cdot 7^4 = 7^{3+4}$

9. $(-6)^{12} \cdot (-6)^5 \cdot (-6)^2$

10. $9^6 \cdot 9^{-4} \cdot 9^{-2}$

11. $2^2 \cdot 2^7 \cdot 2^0$

12. $(-8)^5 \cdot (-8)^{-5}$

Simplify each expression. ◀ **See Problem 2.**

13. $m^3 m^4$

14. $5c^4 \cdot c^6$

15. $4t^{-5} \cdot 2t^{-3}$

16. $(7x^5)(8x)$

17. $3x^2 \cdot x^2$

18. $(-2.4n^4)(2n^{-1})$

19. $b^{-2} \cdot b^4 \cdot b$

20. $(-2m^3)(3.5m^{-3})$

21. $(15a^3)(-3a)$

22. $(x^5y^2)(x^{-6}y)$

23. $(5x^5)(3y^6)(3x^2)$

24. $(4c^4)(ac^3)(-3a^5c)$

Simplify each expression. Write each answer in scientific notation.

See Problem 3.

Guided Practice

To start, use the commutative and associative properties of multiplication.

25. $(2 \times 10^3) \cdot (3 \times 10^2)$

$(2 \times 10^3) \cdot (3 \times 10^2) = (2 \cdot 3)(10^3 \cdot 10^2)$

26. $(2 \times 10^6)(3 \times 10^3)$

27. $(1 \times 10^3)(3.4 \times 10^{-8})$

28. $(8 \times 10^{-5})(7 \times 10^{-3})$

29. $(5 \times 10^7)(3 \times 10^{14})$

Write each answer in scientific notation.

See Problem 4.

30. Astronomy The distance light travels in one second (one light-second) is about 1.86×10^5 mi. Saturn is about 475 light-seconds from the sun. About how many miles from the sun is Saturn?

31. Biology A human body contains about 2.7×10^4 microliters (μL) of blood for each pound of body weight. Each microliter of blood contains about 7×10^4 white blood cells. About how many white blood cells are in the body of a 140-lb person?

B Apply

Complete each equation.

32. $5^2 \cdot 5^{\blacksquare} = 5^{11}$

33. $5^7 \cdot 5^{\blacksquare} = 5^3$

34. $2^{\blacksquare} \cdot 2^4 = 2^1$

35. $c^{-5} \cdot c^{\blacksquare} = c^6$

36. $m^{\blacksquare} \cdot m^{-4} = m^{-9}$

37. $a \cdot a \cdot a^3 = a^{\blacksquare}$

38. $a^{\blacksquare} \cdot a^4 = 1$

39. $a^{12} \cdot a^{\blacksquare} = a^{12}$

40. $x^3 y^{\blacksquare} \cdot x^{\blacksquare} = y^2$

41. Think About a Plan A liter of water contains about 3.35×10^{25} molecules. The Mississippi River discharges about 1.7×10^7 L of water every second. About how many molecules does the Mississippi River discharge every minute? Write your answer in scientific notation.
• How can you use unit analysis to help you find the answer?
• What properties can you use to make the calculation easier?

Geometry Find the area of each figure.

42.

$2x$

$3x^2 + x$

43.

$2x^2$

44.

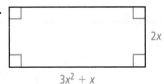

$4y^2$

$y^3 + 2$

45.

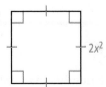

$4c$

$2c^3$

Simplify each expression. Write each answer in scientific notation.

46. $(9 \times 10^7)(3 \times 10^{-16})$

47. $(8 \times 10^{-3})(0.1 \times 10^9)$

48. $(0.7 \times 10^{-12})(0.3 \times 10^8)$

49. $(0.4 \times 10^0)(3 \times 10^{-4})$

50. $(0.2 \times 10^5)(4 \times 10^{-12})$

51. $(0.5 \times 10^{13})(0.3 \times 10^{-4})$

PowerAlgebra.com | Lesson 7-3 Multiplying Powers With the Same Base | 459

52. Chemistry In chemistry, a *mole* is a unit of measure equal to 6.02×10^{23} atoms of a substance. The mass of a single neon atom is about 3.35×10^{-23} g. What is the mass of 2 moles of neon atoms? Write your answer in scientific notation.

53. a. Open-Ended Write y^6 as a product of two powers with the same base in four different ways. Use only positive exponents.

    b. Write y^6 as a product of two powers with the same base in four different ways, using negative or exponents of zero in each product.

    c. Reasoning How many ways can you write y^6 as the product of two powers? Explain your reasoning.

> **Hint** Find the possible values of *a* and *b* in the equation $y^a \cdot y^b = y^6$.

Standardized Test Prep

SAT/ACT

54. What is the simplified form of $(2x^2y^3)(4xy^{-2})$?

   Ⓐ $6x^3y^5$ Ⓑ $6x^2y^6$ Ⓒ $8x^2y$ Ⓓ $8x^3y$

55. What is the *x*-intercept of the graph of $5x - 3y = 30$?

   Ⓕ -10 Ⓖ -6 Ⓗ 6 Ⓘ 10

56. At the Athens Olympics, the winning time for the women's 100-m hurdles was 2.06×10^{-1} min. Which number is another way to express this time in minutes?

   Ⓐ 0.206 Ⓑ 20.6 Ⓒ 206×10^1 Ⓓ 206×10^{-2}

57. What is the solution of $4x - 5 = 2x + 13$?

   Ⓕ 3 Ⓖ 4 Ⓗ 9 Ⓘ 32

Extended Response

58. Bill's company packages its circular mirrors in boxes with square bottoms, as shown at the right. Show your work for each answer.

    a. What is an expression for the area of the bottom of the box?

    b. If the mirror has a radius of 4 in., what is the area of the bottom of the box?

    c. The area of the bottom of a second box is 196 in.^{2}. What is the diameter of the largest mirror the box can hold?

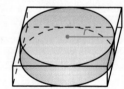

Mixed Review

Write each number in scientific notation.   ◀ See Lesson 7-2.

59. 2,358,000   **60.** 0.00465   **61.** 0.00007   **62.** 5.1 billion

Find the third, seventh, and tenth terms of the sequence described by each rule.   ◀ See Lesson 4-7.

63. $A(n) = 10 + (n - 1)(4)$ **64.** $A(n) = -5 + (n - 1)(2)$ **65.** $A(n) = 1.2 + (n - 1)(-4)$

Get Ready!   **To prepare for Lesson 7-4, do Exercises 66–69.**

Simplify each expression.   ◀ See Lesson 7-1.

66. $(-2)^{-4}$ **67.** $5xy^0$ **68.** $4m^{-1}n^2$ **69.** $-3x^3y^{-2}z^6$

More Multiplication Properties of Exponents

Objectives To raise a power to a power
To raise a product to a power

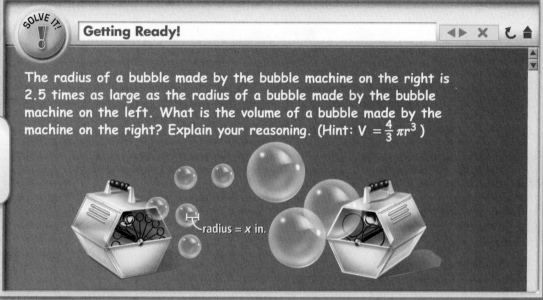

Getting Ready!

The radius of a bubble made by the bubble machine on the right is 2.5 times as large as the radius of a bubble made by the bubble machine on the left. What is the volume of a bubble made by the machine on the right? Explain your reasoning. (Hint: $V = \frac{4}{3}\pi r^3$)

radius = x in.

Be careful! Multiplying r by 2.5 doesn't multiply the volume by 2.5.

Dynamic Activity
Multiplying Exponential Expressions

In the Solve It, the expression for the volume of the larger bubble involves a product raised to a power. In this lesson, you will use properties of exponents to simplify similar expressions.

Focus Question Why should you use properties of exponents to simplify a power raised to a power or a product raised to a power?

You can use repeated multiplication to simplify a power raised to a power.

$$(x^5)^2 = x^5 \cdot x^5 = x^{5+5} = x^{5 \cdot 2} = x^{10}$$

Notice that $(x^5)^2 = x^{5 \cdot 2}$. Raising a power to a power is the same as raising the base to the product of the exponents.

take note

Property Raising a Power to a Power

Words To raise a power to a power, multiply the exponents.

Algebra $(a^m)^n = a^{mn}$, where $a \neq 0$ and m and n are integers

Examples $(5^4)^2 = 5^{4 \cdot 2} = 5^8$ $(m^3)^5 = m^{3 \cdot 5} = m^{15}$

Problem 1 Simplifying a Power Raised to a Power

What is the simplified form of $(n^4)^7$?

Multiply exponents when raising a power to a power. $\qquad (n^4)^7 = n^{4 \cdot 7}$

Simplify. $\qquad\qquad\qquad\qquad\qquad\qquad\qquad = n^{28}$

Think

Should you add or multiply the exponents to simplify the expression?
You multiply the exponents when raising a power to a power.

 Got It? 1. What is the simplified form of each expression in parts (a)–(c)?

    a. $(p^5)^4$ **b.** $(p^4)^5$ **c.** $(p^{-5})^4$

    d. Reasoning Is $(a^m)^n = (a^n)^m$ true for all integers m and n? Explain.

Use the order of operations when you simplify an exponential expression.

Problem 2 Simplifying an Expression With Powers

What is the simplified form of $y^3(y^5)^{-2}$?

Plan

What is the first step in simplifying the expression?
By the order of operations, you simplify powers before you multiply.

Think	Write
You multiply exponents when raising a power to a power.	$y^3(y^5)^{-2} = y^3 y^{5 \cdot (-2)}$ $= y^3 y^{-10}$
You add exponents when multiplying powers with the same base.	$= y^{3+(-10)}$ $= y^{-7}$
Write the expression using only positive exponents.	$= \dfrac{1}{y^7}$

 Got It? 2. What is the simplified form of each expression?

    a. $x^2(x^6)^{-4}$ **b.** $w^{-2}(w^7)^3$ **c.** $(r^{-5})^{-2}r^3$

You can use repeated multiplication to simplify an expression like $(4m)^3$.

$$(4m)^3 = 4m \cdot 4m \cdot 4m$$
$$= 4 \cdot 4 \cdot 4 \cdot m \cdot m \cdot m$$
$$= 4^3 m^3$$
$$= 64m^3$$

Notice that $(4m)^3 = 4^3 m^3$. This example illustrates another property of exponents.

462 Chapter 7 Exponents and Exponential Functions

Property Raising a Product to a Power

Words To raise a product to a power, raise each factor to the power and multiply.

Algebra $(ab)^n = a^n b^n$, where $a \neq 0$, $b \neq 0$, and n is an integer

Example $(3x)^4 = 3^4 x^4 = 81x^4$

 Problem 3 Simplifying a Product Raised to a Power

Multiple Choice Which expression represents the area of the square?

Ⓐ $10x^3$ Ⓑ $5x^6$ Ⓒ $25x^5$ Ⓓ $25x^6$

Plan

How do you find the area of the square?
The area of a square with side length s is s^2. Square the side length of the square to find the area.

Write the area formula.	$A = s^2$
Use the side length $5x^3$ to write the area of the square.	$= (5x^3)^2$
Raise each factor to the second power.	$= 5^2(x^3)^2$
Multiply the exponents of a power raised to a power.	$= 5^2 x^{3 \cdot 2}$
Simplify the exponent.	$= 5^2 x^6$
Simplify.	$= 25x^6$

The correct answer is D.

5x³

Got It? 3. What is the simplified form of each expression?
a. $(7m^9)^3$ **b.** $(2z)^{-4}$ **c.** $(3g^4)^{-2}$

 Problem 4 Simplifying Products With Multiple Variables

What is the simplified form of $(4mn^{-2})^3$?

Think

What is the exponent of m?
It has an implied exponent of 1. Similar to coefficients, exponents of 1 don't need to be written.

Raise each factor of $4mn^{-2}$ to the third power.	$(4mn^{-2})^3 = 4^3 m^3 (n^{-2})^3$
Multiply the exponents of a power raised to a power.	$= 4^3 m^3 n^{-2 \cdot 3}$
Simplify the exponent.	$= 4^3 m^3 n^{-6}$
Simplify.	$= 64 m^3 n^{-6}$
Rewrite using a positive exponent.	$= \dfrac{64m^3}{n^6}$

Got It? 4. What is the simplified form of each expression?
a. $(3xy^5)^4$ **b.** $(3bc^5)^{-4}$ **c.** $(6ab)^3$

Focus Question Why should you use properties of exponents to simplify a power raised to a power or a product raised to a power?

Answer To solve for an unknown variable or simplify an expression, it is necessary to multiply exponents when raising a power to a power. To raise a product to a power, you should raise each factor to the power and multiply.

Lesson Check

Do you know HOW?

Simplify each expression.

1. $(n^3)^6$

2. $(b^{-7})^3$

3. $(3a)^4$

4. $(9x^5)^2(x^2)^5$

5. $(3ab)^2$

6. $(-2a)^{-4}$

Do you UNDERSTAND?

7. **Vocabulary** Compare and contrast the property for raising a power to a power and the property for multiplying powers with the same base.

8. **Error Analysis** One student simplified $(x^5)^2$ to x^{10}. A second student simplified $(x^5)^2$ to x^7. Which student is correct? Explain.

9. **Open-Ended** Write four different expressions that are equivalent to $(x^4)^3$.

Practice and Problem–Solving Exercises

A Practice

Simplify each expression.

See Problems 1 and 2.

Guided Practice

To start, multiply exponents when raising a power to a power.

10. $(n^8)^4$

$(n^8)^4 = n^{8 \cdot 4}$

11. $(c^2)^5$

12. $(q^{10})^{10}$

13. $(w^7)^{-1}$

14. $(x^3)^{-5}$

15. $d(d^{-2})^{-9}$

16. $(z^8)^0 z^5$

17. $(c^3)^5(d^3)^0$

18. $(t^2)^{-2}(t^2)^{-5}$

19. $(m^3)^{-1}(x^2)^5$

Simplify each expression.

See Problems 3 and 4.

Guided Practice

To start, raise each factor in the parentheses to the fifth power.

20. $(4m)^5$

$(4m)^5 = 4^5 m^5$

21. $(7a)^{-2}$

22. $(5y)^4$

23. $(12g^4)^{-1}$

24. $(3n^{-6})^{-4}$

25. $(2y^4)^{-3}$

26. $(xy)^0$

27. $(r^2s)^5$

28. $(2x)^3 x^2$

29. $(y^2z^{-3})^5(y^3)^2$

Complete each equation.

30. $(b^2)^{\blacksquare} = b^8$

31. $(m^{\blacksquare})^3 = m^{-12}$

32. $(x^{\blacksquare})^7 = x^6$

33. $(n^9)^{\blacksquare} = 1$

34. $(y^{-4})^{\blacksquare} = y^{12}$

35. $7(c^1)^{\blacksquare} = 7c^8$

36. $(5x^{\blacksquare})^2 = 25x^{-4}$

37. $(3x^3y^{\blacksquare})^3 = 27x^9$

38. $(m^2n^3)^{\blacksquare} = \dfrac{1}{m^6n^9}$

39. Think About a Plan How many times the volume of the small cube is the volume of the large cube?
- What expression can you write for the volume of the small cube? For the volume of the large cube?
- What property of exponents can you use to simplify the volume expressions?

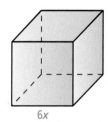

$3x$

$6x$

Simplify each expression.

40. $3^2(3x)^3$

41. $(4.1)^5(4.1)^{-5}$

42. $(b^5)^3b^2$

43. $(-5x)^2 + 5x^2$

44. $(-2a^2b)^3(ab)^3$

45. $4xy^20^4(-y)^{-3}$

46. Reasoning Simplify $(x^2)^3$ and x^{2^3}. Are the expressions equivalent? Explain.

47. Measurement How many cubic millimeters are in a cubic meter? Write your answer as a power of 10.

> **Hint** A cubic meter is a cube with side lengths of 1 meter.

48. Wind Energy The power generated by a wind turbine depends on the wind speed. The expression $800v^3$ gives the power in watts for a certain wind turbine at wind speed v in meters per second. If the wind speed triples, by what factor does the power generated by the wind turbine increase?

49. Can you write the expression $49x^2y^2z^2$ using only one exponent? Show how or explain why not.

50. a. Geography Earth has a radius of about 6.4×10^6 m. What is the approximate surface area of Earth? Use the formula for the surface area of a sphere, $S = 4\pi r^2$. Write your answer in scientific notation.
   b. Oceans cover about 70% of the surface of the Earth. About how many square meters of Earth's surface are covered by ocean water?
   c. The oceans have an average depth of 3790 m. Estimate the volume of water in Earth's oceans.

> **Hint** The formula for volume of a sphere is $V = \frac{4}{3}\pi r^3$.

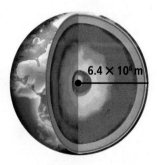

6.4×10^6 m

Standardized Test Prep

SAT/ACT

51. Which expression does NOT equal $25n^{12}$?

(A) $(5n^6)^2$ (B) $(5n^3)(5n^9)$ (C) $25(n^3)^9$ (D) $5^2(n^2)^6$

52. One morning an employee washed 4 cars and 2 vans in less than 115 min. That afternoon it took the employee more than 150 min to wash 3 cars and 5 vans. The information can be represented by the inequalities $4x + 2y < 115$ and $3x + 5y > 150$, where x is the time it takes to wash one car and y is the time it takes to wash one van. Which region of the graph at the right represents the possible number of minutes it takes to wash a car and a van?

(F) A   (G) B   (H) C   (I) D

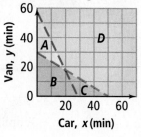

Washing Times

Short Response

53. A snail travels at a speed of 3×10^{-2} mi/h. What is the snail's speed in inches per minute? Show your work.

Mixed Review

Simplify each expression.

◀ See Lesson 7-3.

54. $bc^{-6}b^3$

55. $(a^2b^3)(a^6)$

56. $9m^3(6m^2n^4)$

57. $2t(-2t^4)$

Find the slope of the line that passes through each pair of points.

◀ See Lesson 5-1.

58. $(0, 3), (4, 0)$

59. $(2, -5), (3, 1)$

60. $(-3, 6), (1, 0)$

61. $(0, 0), (1, -9)$

Get Ready!   To prepare for Lesson 7-5, do Exercises 62–66.

Write each fraction in simplest form.

◀ See p. 786.

62. $\dfrac{5}{20}$ **63.** $\dfrac{124}{4}$ **64.** $\dfrac{6}{15}$ **65.** $\dfrac{5xy}{15x}$ **66.** $\dfrac{3ac}{12a}$

Do you know HOW?

Simplify each expression.

1. $5^{-1}(3^{-2})$

2. $(r^{-5})^{-4}$

3. $(2x^5)(3x^{12})$

4. $\dfrac{mn^{-4}}{p^0 q^{-2}}$

5. $a^2 b^0 (a^{-3})$

6. $(4m^2)^3$

7. $(2m^3)^0 (3m^6)^{-1}$

8. $(3t^2)^3 (t^0)^3$

Write each number in scientific notation.

9. 48,030,000,000

10. 0.0042

11. 0.0000312

12. 76 million

Write each number in standard notation.

13. 8.3×10^9

14. 6.12×10^3

15. 1.2×10^{-4}

16. 4.326×10^{-1}

Simplify. Write each answer in scientific notation.

17. $0.5(8 \times 10^5)$

18. $(4 \times 10^7)(3 \times 10^{-1})$

19. $(6 \times 10^5)(1.2 \times 10^8)$

20. $(9 \times 10^{-3})(9 \times 10^{-3})$

21. **Astronomy** The radius of Mars is about 3.4×10^3 km.

   a. What is the approximate diameter of Mars? Write your answer in scientific notation.

   b. Write your answer from part (a) in standard form.

22. **Geometry** A box has a square bottom with sides of length $3x^2$ cm. The height of the box is $4xy$ cm. What is the volume of the box?

23. Evaluate $\frac{1}{2}a^{-4}b^2$ for $a = -2$ and $b = 4$.

Do you UNDERSTAND?

24. **Reasoning** A population of bacteria triples every week in a laboratory. The number of bacteria is modeled by the expression $900 \cdot 3^x$, where x is the number of weeks after a scientist measures the population size. When $x = -2$, what does the value of the expression represent?

25. Use the properties of exponents to explain whether each of the following expressions is equal to 64.

   a. $2^5 \cdot 2$ b. $2^2 \cdot 2^3$ c. $(2^2)(2^2)^2$

26. **Reasoning** Is the number 10^5 written in scientific notation? Explain.

27. **Writing** Decide whether the following statement is *always, sometimes,* or *never* true. Explain your choice.

   A number raised to a negative exponent is negative.

28. **Error Analysis** Identify and correct the error in the student's work below.

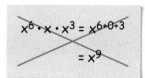

$$x^6 \cdot x \cdot x^3 = x^{6+0+3}$$
$$= x^9$$

Division Properties of Exponents

Objectives To divide powers with the same base
To raise a quotient to a power

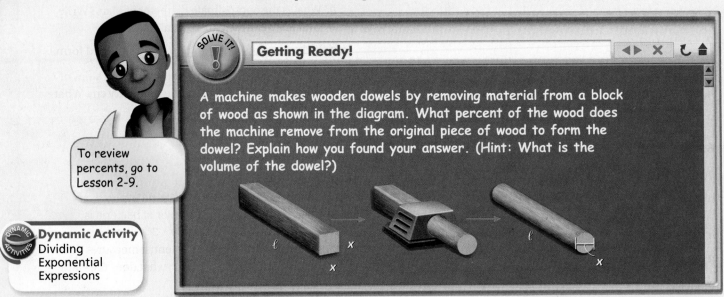

SOLVE IT!

Getting Ready!

A machine makes wooden dowels by removing material from a block of wood as shown in the diagram. What percent of the wood does the machine remove from the original piece of wood to form the dowel? Explain how you found your answer. (Hint: What is the volume of the dowel?)

To review percents, go to Lesson 2-9.

Dynamic Activity
Dividing Exponential Expressions

In the Solve It, the expression for the volume of the dowel involves a quotient raised to a power.

Focus Question How are the properties of dividing powers and multiplying powers similar?

You can use repeated multiplication to simplify quotients of powers with the same base. Expand the numerator and the denominator. Then divide out the common factors.

$$\frac{4^5}{4^3} = \frac{4 \cdot 4 \cdot 4 \cdot 4 \cdot 4}{4 \cdot 4 \cdot 4} = 4^2$$

This example illustrates the following property of exponents.

take note

Property   Dividing Powers With the Same Base

Words	To divide powers with the same base, subtract the exponents.
Algebra	$\frac{a^m}{a^n} = a^{m-n}$, where $a \neq 0$ and m and n are integers
Examples	$\frac{2^6}{2^2} = 2^{6-2} = 2^4$ $\frac{x^4}{x^7} = x^{4-7} = x^{-3} = \frac{1}{x^3}$

Problem 1 Dividing Algebraic Expressions

How are the properties for dividing powers and multiplying powers similar?
For both properties, the bases of the powers must be the same. Dividing a power is the same as multiplying by a negative exponent.

What is the simplified form of each expression?

A $\dfrac{x^8}{x^3}$

Subtract exponents when dividing powers with the same base. $\qquad \dfrac{x^8}{x^3} = x^{8-3}$

Simplify. $\qquad\qquad = x^5$

B $\dfrac{m^2 n^4}{m^5 n^3}$

Subtract exponents when dividing powers with the same base. $\qquad \dfrac{m^2 n^4}{m^5 n^3} = m^{2-5} n^{4-3}$

Simplify the exponents. $\qquad\qquad = m^{-3} n^1$

Rewrite using positive exponents. $\qquad\qquad = \dfrac{n}{m^3}$

 Got It? **1.** What is the simplified form of each expression?

a. $\dfrac{y^5}{y^4}$ b. $\dfrac{d^3}{d^9}$ c. $\dfrac{k^6 j^2}{kj^5}$ d. $\dfrac{a^{-3} b^7}{a^5 b^2}$ e. $\dfrac{x^4 y^{-1} z^8}{x^4 y^{-5} z}$

You can use the property of dividing powers with the same base to divide numbers in scientific notation.

Problem 2 Dividing Numbers in Scientific Notation

Demographics Population density describes the number of people per unit area. During one year, the population of Angola was 1.21×10^7 people. The area of Angola is 4.81×10^5 mi^2. What was the population density of Angola that year?

Know	Need	Plan
• The population • The area	The population density	Write the ratio of population to area.

Rewrite multiplication with two factors. $\qquad \dfrac{1.21 \times 10^7}{4.81 \times 10^5} = \dfrac{1.21}{4.81} \times \dfrac{10^7}{10^5}$

Subtract exponents when dividing powers with the same base. $\qquad = \dfrac{1.21}{4.81} \times 10^{7-5}$

Simplify the exponent. $\qquad = \dfrac{1.21}{4.81} \times 10^2$

Divide. Round to the nearest thousandth. $\qquad \approx 0.252 \times 10^2$

Write in standard notation. $\qquad = 25.2$

The population density of Angola was about 25 people per square mile in 2006.

 Got It? **2.** During one year, Honduras had a population of 7.33×10^6 people. The area of Honduras is 4.33×10^4 mi^2. What was the population density of Honduras that year?

You can use repeated multiplication to simplify a quotient raised to a power.

$$\left(\frac{x}{y}\right)^3 = \frac{x}{y} \cdot \frac{x}{y} \cdot \frac{x}{y} = \frac{x \cdot x \cdot x}{y \cdot y \cdot y} = \frac{x^3}{y^3}$$

This illustrates another property of exponents.

take note

Property   Raising a Quotient to a Power

Words   To raise a quotient to a power, raise the numerator and the denominator to the power and simplify.

Algebra $\left(\frac{a}{b}\right)^n = \frac{a^n}{b^n}$, where $a \neq 0$, $b \neq 0$, and n is an integer

Examples $\left(\frac{3}{5}\right)^3 = \frac{3^3}{5^3} = \frac{27}{125}$ $\left(\frac{x}{y}\right)^5 = \frac{x^5}{y^5}$

ONLINE PROBLEMS

Problem 3   Raising a Quotient to a Power

Multiple Choice What is the simplified form of $\left(\frac{z^4}{5}\right)^3$?

A $\dfrac{z^7}{15}$ B $\dfrac{z^{12}}{15}$ C $\dfrac{z^7}{125}$ D $\dfrac{z^{12}}{125}$

Think

How can you check your answer?
Substitute the same number for the variable in the original expression and the simplified expression. The expressions should be equal.

Raise the numerator and the denominator to the third power. $\left(\frac{z^4}{5}\right)^3 = \frac{(z^4)^3}{5^3}$

Multiply the exponents in the numerator. $= \frac{z^{4 \cdot 3}}{5^3}$

Simplify. $= \frac{z^{12}}{125}$

The correct answer is D.

 Got It? 3. a. What is the simplified form of $\left(\frac{4}{x^3}\right)^2$?

b. Reasoning Describe two different ways to simplify the expression $\left(\frac{a^7}{a^5}\right)^3$. Which method do you prefer? Explain.

You can write an expression of the form $\left(\frac{a}{b}\right)^{-n}$ using positive exponents.

Use the definition of negative exponent. $\left(\frac{2}{3}\right)^{-4} = \frac{1}{\left(\frac{2}{3}\right)^4}$

Raise the quotient to a power. $= \frac{1}{\left(\frac{2^4}{3^4}\right)}$

Hint

Notice that a fraction to a negative power is equal to the reciprocal of the fraction raised to a positive power.

Multiply by the reciprocal of $\frac{2^4}{3^4}$ which is $\frac{3^4}{2^4}$. $= 1 \cdot \frac{3^4}{2^4}$

Simplify. Write the quotient using one exponent. $= \frac{3^4}{2^4} = \left(\frac{3}{2}\right)^4$

So, $\left(\frac{a}{b}\right)^{-n} = \left(\frac{b}{a}\right)^n$ for all nonzero numbers a and b and positive integers n.

Problem 4 **Simplifying an Exponential Expression**

What is the simplified form of $\left(\frac{2}{y^4}\right)^{-3}$?

Plan

How do you write an expression in simplified form?
Use the properties of exponents to write each variable with a single positive exponent.

Rewrite using the reciprocal of $\frac{2}{y^4}$.

$$\left(\frac{2}{y^4}\right)^{-3} = \left(\frac{y^4}{2}\right)^3$$

Raise the numerator and denominator to the third power.

$$= \frac{(y^4)^3}{2^3}$$

Simplify.

$$= \frac{y^{12}}{8}$$

 Got It? **4.** What is the simplified form of $\left(\frac{a}{b}\right)^{-2}$?

Focus Question How are the properties of dividing powers and multiplying powers similar?

Answer When you divide powers, you subtract exponents. When you multiply powers, you add exponents.

Lesson Check

Do you know HOW?

Simplify each expression.

1. $\frac{y^3}{y^{10}}$

2. $\left(\frac{x^4}{3}\right)^3$

3. $\left(\frac{m}{n}\right)^{-3}$

4. $\left(\frac{x^2}{y^4}\right)^{-4}$

5. A large cube is made up of many small cubes. The volume of the large cube is 7.506×10^5 mm^3. The volume of each small cube is 2.78×10^4 mm^3. How many small cubes make up the large cube?

Do you UNDERSTAND?

6. Vocabulary How is the property for raising a quotient to a power similar to the property for raising a product to a power?

7. a. Reasoning Ross simplifies $\frac{a^3}{a^7}$ as shown at the right. Explain why Ross's method works.

$$\frac{a^3}{a^7} = \frac{1}{a^{7-3}} = \frac{1}{a^4}$$

b. Open-Ended Write a quotient of powers and use Ross's method to simplify it.

Practice and Problem-Solving Exercises

 Practice Copy and complete each equation.

◀ **See Problem 1.**

8. $\frac{5^9}{5^2} = 5^{\blacksquare}$

9. $\frac{2^4}{2^3} = 2^{\blacksquare}$

10. $\frac{3^2}{3^5} = 3^{\blacksquare}$

11. $\frac{5^2 5^3}{5^3 5^2} = 5^{\blacksquare}$

Simplify each expression.

Guided Practice

To start, subtract exponents when dividing powers with the same base.

12. $\dfrac{3^8}{3^6}$

$\dfrac{3^8}{3^6} = 3^{8-6}$

13. $\dfrac{3^6}{3^8}$

14. $\dfrac{d^{14}}{d^{17}}$

15. $\dfrac{n^{-1}}{n^{-4}}$

16. $\dfrac{5s^{-7}}{10s^{-9}}$

17. $\dfrac{x^{11}y^3}{x^{11}y}$

18. $\dfrac{c^3d^{-5}}{c^4d^{-1}}$

19. $\dfrac{10m^6n^3}{5m^2n^7}$

20. $\dfrac{m^3n^2}{m^{-1}n^3}$

21. $\dfrac{3^2m^5t^6}{3^5m^7t^{-5}}$

Simplify each quotient. Write each answer in scientific notation. ◀ **See Problem 2.**

Guided Practice

To start, rewrite using two factors.

22. $\dfrac{5.2 \times 10^{13}}{1.3 \times 10^7}$

$\dfrac{5.2 \times 10^{13}}{1.3 \times 10^7} = \dfrac{5.2}{1.3} \times \dfrac{10^{13}}{10^7}$

23. $\dfrac{3.6 \times 10^{-10}}{9 \times 10^{-6}}$

24. $\dfrac{6.5 \times 10^4}{5 \times 10^6}$

25. $\dfrac{4.65 \times 10^{-4}}{3.1 \times 10^2}$

26. $\dfrac{3.5 \times 10^6}{5 \times 10^8}$

27. Computers The average time it takes a computer to execute one instruction is measured in picoseconds. There are 3.6×10^{15} picoseconds per hour. What fraction of a second is a picosecond?

28. Wildlife Data from a deer count in a forested area show that an estimated 3.16×10^3 deer inhabit 7.228×10^4 acres of land. What is the density of the deer population?

29. Astronomy The sun's mass is 1.998×10^{30} kg. Saturn's mass is 5.69×10^{26} kg. How many times as great as the mass of Saturn is the mass of the sun?

Simplify each expression. ◀ **See Problems 3 and 4.**

30. $\left(\dfrac{3}{8}\right)^2$

31. $\left(\dfrac{1}{a}\right)^3$

32. $\left(\dfrac{3x}{y}\right)^4$

33. $\left(\dfrac{2x}{3y}\right)^5$

34. $\left(\dfrac{6}{5^2}\right)^3$

35. $\left(\dfrac{2^2}{2^3}\right)^5$

36. $\left(\dfrac{8}{n^5}\right)^6$

37. $\left(\dfrac{2}{5}\right)^{-1}$

38. $\left(\dfrac{5}{4}\right)^{-4}$

39. $\left(-\dfrac{x^5}{5^4}\right)^{-2}$

40. $\left(\dfrac{b^4}{b^7}\right)^{-5}$

41. $\left(\dfrac{3}{5c^2}\right)^0$

Apply

Explain why each expression is *not* in simplest form.

42. 5^3m^3

43. x^5y^{-2}

44. $(2c)^4$

45. x^0y

46. $\dfrac{d^7}{d}$

47. **Think About a Plan** During one year, about 163 million adults over 18 years old in the United States spent a total of about 93 billion hours online at home. On average, how many hours per day did each adult spend online at home?
   - How do you write each number in scientific notation?
   - How do you convert the units to hours per day?

48. **Television** During one year, people in the United States older than 18 years old watched a total of 342 billion hours of television. The population of the United States older than 18 years old was about 209 million people.
   a. On average, how many hours of television did each person older than 18 years old watch that year? Round to the nearest hour.
   b. On average, how many hours per week did each person older than 18 years old watch that year? Round to the nearest hour.

Which property or properties of exponents would you use to simplify each expression?

49. 2^{-3}
50. $\dfrac{2^2}{2^5}$
51. $\dfrac{1}{2^{-4}2^7}$
52. $\dfrac{(2^4)^3}{2^{15}}$

Simplify each expression.

53. $\dfrac{3n^2(5^0)}{2n^3}$
54. $\left(\dfrac{2m^4}{m^2}\right)^{-4}$
55. $\dfrac{3x^3}{(3x)^3}$
56. $\left(\dfrac{9t^2}{36t}\right)^3$
57. $\left(\dfrac{a^4a}{a^2}\right)^{-3}$
58. $\left(\dfrac{2x^2}{5x^3}\right)^{-2}$

59. a. **Error Analysis** What mistake did the student make in simplifying the expression at the right?
   b. What is the correct simplified form of the expression?

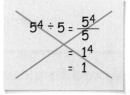

60. **Writing** Suppose $\dfrac{a^x}{a^y} = a^3$ and $\dfrac{a^x}{a^{3y}} = a^{-5}$. Find the values of x and y. Explain how you found your answer.

61. **Geometry** The area of the rectangle is $72a^3b^4$. What is the length of the rectangle?

   Ⓐ $\dfrac{a^3b^4}{12}$
   Ⓒ $\dfrac{12}{a^3b^4}$
   Ⓑ $12a^2b^3$
   Ⓓ $12a^3b^4$

62. **Physics** The wavelength of a radio wave is defined as speed divided by frequency. An FM radio station has a frequency of 9×10^7 waves per second. The speed of the waves is about 3×10^8 meters per second. What is the wavelength of the station?

63. Simplify the expression $\left(\dfrac{3}{x^2}\right)^{-3}$ in three different ways. Justify each step.

64. a. **Finance** In 2000, the United States government owed about $5.63 trillion to its creditors. The population of the United States was 282.4 million people. How much did the government owe per person in 2000? Round to the nearest dollar.
   b. In 2005, the debt had grown to $7.91 trillion, with a population of 296.9 million. How much did the government owe per person? Round to the nearest dollar.
   c. What was the percent increase in the average amount owed per person from 2000 to 2005?

Write each expression with only one exponent. You may need to use parentheses.

65. $\dfrac{m^7}{n^7}$ 　　　　**66.** $\dfrac{10^7 \cdot 10^0}{10^{-3}}$ 　　　　**67.** $\dfrac{27x^3}{8y^3}$ 　　　　**68.** $\dfrac{4m^2}{169m^4}$

69. a. Use the property for dividing powers with the same base to write $\dfrac{a^0}{a^n}$ as a power of a.

　　b. Use the definition of a zero exponent to simplify $\dfrac{a^0}{a^n}$.

　　c. Reasoning Explain how your results from parts (a) and (b) justify the definition of a negative exponent.

Standardized Test Prep

 SAT/ACT

70. Which expression is equivalent to $\dfrac{(2x)^5}{x^3}$?

　　Ⓐ $2x^2$ 　　　　Ⓑ $32x^2$ 　　　　Ⓒ $2x^8$ 　　　　Ⓓ $32x^{-2}$

71. What is the solution of $\frac{1}{3}(x - 2) = 4$?

　　Ⓕ 10 　　　　Ⓖ 12 　　　　Ⓗ 14 　　　　Ⓘ 18

72. What is the solution of the system of equations $y = -3x + 5$ and $y = -4x - 1$?

　　Ⓐ $(23, 6)$ 　　　　Ⓑ $(6, 23)$ 　　　　Ⓒ $(-6, 23)$ 　　　　Ⓓ $(-6, -23)$

Short Response

73. You have 8 bags of grass seed. Each bag of seed covers 1200 ft^2 of ground. The function $A(b) = 1200b$ represents the area $A(b)$, in square feet, that b bags of seed cover. What are a reasonable domain and range for the function? Explain.

Mixed Review

Simplify each expression. 　　　　　　　　　　　　　　　　　　◀ See Lesson 7-4.

74. $(2m^{-7})^3$ 　　**75.** $2(3s^{-2})^{-3}$ 　　**76.** $(4^3c^2)^{-1}$ 　　**77.** $(-3)^2(r^5)^2$ 　　**78.** $(7^0n^{-3})^2(n^7)^3$

Solve each system by graphing. 　　　　　　　　　　　　　　　　◀ See Lesson 6-1.

79. $y = 3x$ 　　**80.** $y = 2x + 1$ 　　**81.** $y = 5$ 　　**82.** $y = 7$
　　　$y = -2x$ 　　　　　$y = x - 3$ 　　　　　$x = 3$ 　　　　　$y = 8$

Get Ready! To prepare for Lesson 7-6, do Exercises 83–86.

Graph each function. 　　　　　　　　　　　　　　　　　　　　　◀ See Lesson 4-4.

83. $y = 4x$ 　　**84.** $y = 5x$ 　　**85.** $y = -3x$ 　　**86.** $y = 1.5x$

Exponential Functions

Objective To evaluate and graph exponential functions

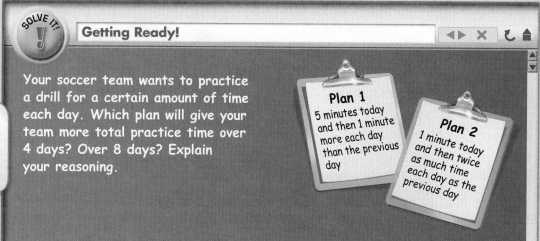

Getting Ready!

Your soccer team wants to practice a drill for a certain amount of time each day. Which plan will give your team more total practice time over 4 days? Over 8 days? Explain your reasoning.

Plan 1
5 minutes today and then 1 minute more each day than the previous day

Plan 2
1 minute today and then twice as much time each day as the previous day

Family feud! These functions don't belong in the same family of functions.

Dynamic Activity
Exponential Functions

Lesson Vocabulary
• exponential function

The two plans in the Solve It have different patterns of growth. You can model each type of growth with a different type of function.

Focus Question Why should you graph exponential functions?

Key Concept Exponential Function

Definition

An **exponential function** is a function of the form $y = a \cdot b^x$, where $a \neq 0$, $b > 0$, $b \neq 1$, and x is a real number.

Examples

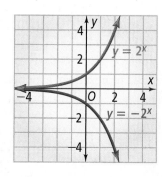

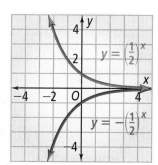

If all of the x-values in a table of values have a constant difference and all of the y-values have a constant ratio, then the table represents an exponential function.

Here's Why It Works From the first graph shown in the Take Note on the previous page, you can generate the following table of values.

Note that the x-values have a constant difference. The y-values have a constant ratio.

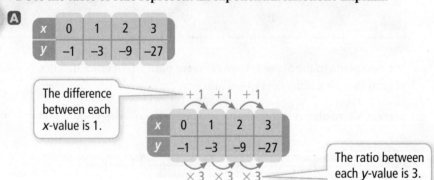

The difference between each pair of x-values is 1.

Upper branch of the graph on the left:
$y = 2^x$

x	-1	0	1	2
y	$\frac{1}{2}$	1	2	4

The ratio of each pair of y-values is 2.

 Problem 1 **Identifying an Exponential Function**

ONLINE PROBLEMS

Think

How can you identify a constant ratio between y-values?
When you multiply each y-value by the same constant and get the next y-value, there is a constant ratio between the values.

Does the table or rule represent an exponential function? Explain.

A

x	0	1	2	3
y	-1	-3	-9	-27

The difference between each x-value is 1.

$+1$ $+1$ $+1$

x	0	1	2	3
y	-1	-3	-9	-27

$\times 3$ $\times 3$ $\times 3$

The ratio between each y-value is 3.

Yes, the table represents an exponential function. There is a constant difference between x-values and a constant ratio between y-values.

B $y = 3x^2$

No, the function is not in the form $y = a \cdot b^x$. In $y = 3x^2$, the independent variable x is not an exponent.

Got It? **1.** Does the table or rule represent an exponential function? Explain.

a.

x	1	2	3	4
y	-1	1	3	5

b. $y = 3 \cdot 6^x$

Problem 2 **Evaluating an Exponential Function**   `GRIDDED RESPONSE`

Population Growth Suppose 30 flour beetles are left undisturbed in a warehouse bin. The beetle population doubles each week. The function $f(x) = 30 \cdot 2^x$ gives the population after x weeks. How many beetles will there be after 56 days?

Step 1 Convert 56 days to weeks.

Write a proportion relating days to weeks.

$$\frac{56\ \text{days}}{x} = \frac{7\ \text{days}}{1\ \text{week}}$$

Write the proportion without units. $\frac{56}{x} = \frac{7}{1}$

Use the Cross Products Property. $7x = 56$

Divide each side of the equation by 7. $x = 8$

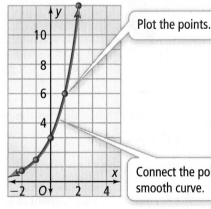

Step 2 Evaluate $f(x) = 30 \cdot 2^x$ for $x = 8$.

$$f(x) = 30 \cdot 2^x$$

Substitute 8 for x. $= 30 \cdot 2^8$

Simplify the power. $= 30 \cdot 256$

Simplify. $= 7680$

After 56 days, there will be 7680 beetles.

 Got It? **2.** An initial population of 20 rabbits triples every half year. The function $f(x) = 20 \cdot 3^x$ gives the population after x half-year periods. How many rabbits will there be after 3 years?

Problem 3 **Graphing an Exponential Function**

What is the graph of $y = 3 \cdot 2^x$?

Make a table of x- and y-values.

x	$y = 3 \cdot 2^x$	(x, y)
−2	$3 \cdot 2^{-2} = \frac{3}{2^2} = \frac{3}{4}$	$\left(-2, \frac{3}{4}\right)$
−1	$3 \cdot 2^{-1} = \frac{3}{2^1} = 1\frac{1}{2}$	$\left(-1, 1\frac{1}{2}\right)$
0	$3 \cdot 2^0 = 3 \cdot 1 = 3$	$(0, 3)$
1	$3 \cdot 2^1 = 3 \cdot 2 = 6$	$(1, 6)$
2	$3 \cdot 2^2 = 3 \cdot 4 = 12$	$(2, 12)$

Plot the points.

Connect the points with a smooth curve.

 Got It? **3.** What is the graph of each function?

a. $y = 0.5 \cdot 3^x$ **b.** $y = -0.5 \cdot 3^x$

Focus Question Why should you graph exponential functions?

Answer If you graph an exponential growth function you will see that it grows very quickly. To see this, make a table of values, plot the points, and connect the points with a smooth curve.

Lesson Check

Do you know HOW?

Evaluate each function for the given value.

1. $f(x) = 6 \cdot 2^x$ for $x = 3$

2. $g(w) = 45 \cdot 3^w$ for $w = -2$

Graph each function.

3. $y = 3^x$

4. $f(x) = 4\left(\frac{1}{2}\right)^x$

Do you UNDERSTAND?

5. Vocabulary Describe the differences between a linear function and an exponential function.

6. Reasoning Is $y = (-2)^x$ an exponential function? Justify your answer.

7. Error Analysis A student evaluated the function $f(x) = 3 \cdot 4^x$ for $x = -1$ as shown at the right. Describe and correct the student's mistake.

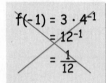

$f(-1) = 3 \cdot 4^{-1}$
$= 12^{-1}$
$= \frac{1}{12}$

Practice and Problem-Solving Exercises

A Practice Determine whether each table or rule represents an exponential function. Explain why or why not.

◀ **See Problem 1.**

Guided Practice →

To start, determine if the difference between x-values is constant.

8.

x	1	2	3	4
y	2	8	32	128

The difference between each pair of x-values is 1.

9.

x	0	1	2	3
y	6	9	18	33

10. $y = 4 \cdot 5^x$

11. $y = 12 \cdot x^2$

12. $y = -5 \cdot 0.25^x$

Evaluate each function for the given value.

◀ **See Problem 2.**

13. $f(x) = 6^x$ for $x = 2$

14. $g(t) = 2 \cdot 0.4^t$ for $t = -2$

15. $y = 20 \cdot 0.5^x$ for $x = 3$

16. $h(w) = -0.5 \cdot 4^w$ for $w = 18$

17. Finance An investment of $5000 doubles in value every decade. The function $f(x) = 5000 \cdot 2^x$, where x is the number of decades, models the growth of the value of the investment. How much is the investment worth after 30 yr?

18. Wildlife Management A population of 75 foxes in a wildlife preserve quadruples in size every 15 yr. The function $y = 75 \cdot 4^x$, where x is the number of 15-yr periods, models the population growth. How many foxes will there be after 45 yr?

Graph each exponential function.

◀ **See Problem 3.**

19. $y = 4^x$

Guided Practice →

To start, make a table of values.

x	$y = 4^x$	(x, y)
−2	$4^{-2} = \frac{1}{4^2} = \frac{1}{16}$	$\left(-2, \frac{1}{16}\right)$
−1	$4^{-1} = \frac{1}{4^1} = \frac{1}{4}$	$\left(-1, \frac{1}{4}\right)$
0	$4^0 = \blacksquare$	$\blacksquare$
1	$4^1 = \blacksquare$	$\blacksquare$

20. $y = -4^x$

21. $y = \left(\frac{1}{3}\right)^x$

22. $y = -\left(\frac{1}{3}\right)^x$

23. $y = 0.1 \cdot 2^x$

24. $y = \frac{1}{4} \cdot 2^x$

25. $y = 1.25^x$

Ⓑ Apply

Evaluate each function over the domain $\{-2, -1, 0, 1, 2, 3\}$. As the values of the domain increase, do the values of the range *increase* or *decrease*?

26. $f(x) = 5^x$

27. $y = 2.5^x$

28. $h(x) = 0.1^x$

29. $f(x) = 5 \cdot 4^x$

30. $y = 8^x$

31. $g(x) = 4 \cdot 10^x$

32. Think About a Plan Hydra are small freshwater animals. They can double in number every two days in a laboratory tank. Suppose one tank has an initial population of 60 hydra. When will there be more than 5000 hydra?
- How can a table help you identify a pattern?
- What function models the situation? (*Hint:* Remember that in the function $y = a \cdot b^x$, a is the starting population and b is the rate of change.)

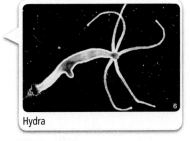

Hydra

33. a. Graph $y = 2^x$, $y = 4^x$, and $y = 0.25^x$ on the same axes.
   b. What point is on all three graphs?
   c. Does the graph of an exponential function intersect the *x*-axis? Explain.
   d. Reasoning How does the graph of $y = b^x$ change as the base b increases or decreases?

Which function has the greater value for the given value of *x*?

34. $y = 4^x$ or $y = x^4$ for $x = 2$

35. $f(x) = 10 \cdot 2^x$ or $f(x) = 200 \cdot x^2$ for $x = 7$

36. $y = 3^x$ or $y = x^3$ for $x = 5$

37. $f(x) = 2^x$ or $f(x) = 100x^2$ for $x = 10$

38. Computers A computer valued at $1500 loses 20% of its value each year.

    a. Write a function rule that models the value of the computer.

    b. Find the value of the computer after 3 yr.

    c. In how many years will the value of the computer be less than $500?

39. Writing Find the range of the function $f(x) = 500 \cdot 1^x$ using the domain $\{1, 2, 3, 4, 5\}$. Explain why the definition of *exponential function* states that $b \neq 1$.

Standardized Test Prep

SAT/ACT

40. A population of 30 swans doubles every 10 yr. Which graph represents the population growth?

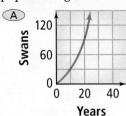 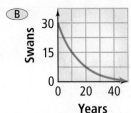 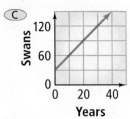 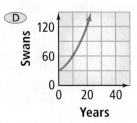

41. Which equation do you get when you solve $y = 2x - 12$ for x?

    Ⓕ $x = y - 6$ Ⓖ $x = y + 6$ Ⓗ $x = 0.5y - 6$ Ⓘ $x = 0.5y + 6$

Short Response

42. What are the solutions of the inequality $11 \leq |x - 2| + 4$? Graph the solutions on a number line. Show your work.

Mixed Review

Simplify each expression.

See Lesson 7-5.

43. $\left(\dfrac{a^2}{a^3}\right)^{-4}$ **44.** $\left(\dfrac{m^4}{n^2}\right)^{-7}$ **45.** $\left(\dfrac{pq^0}{p^4}\right)^5$

Write an equation for the line that is parallel to the given line and passes through the given point.

See Lesson 5-6.

46. $y = 5x + 1; (0, 0)$ **47.** $y = 3x - 2; (0, 1)$ **48.** $y = 0.4x + 5; (2, -3)$

Get Ready! **To prepare for Lesson 7-7, do Exercises 49–52.**

Tell whether each percent change is an increase or decrease. Then find the percent change. If necessary, round to the nearest percent.

See Lesson 2-10.

49. original price: $25; sale price: $22   **50.** height last week: 15 cm; height this week: 18 cm

51. price this year: $999; price last year: $1450   **52.** birth weight: 220 lb; weight at 1 month: 300 lb

Geometric Sequences

Recall that a sequence is a list of numbers that often forms a pattern. Each number in a sequence is a term of the sequence.

In Chapter 4 you studied arithmetic sequences, where you found each new term by adding the same number to the previous term. Another kind of sequence is a *geometric sequence*. In a geometric sequence, the ratio between consecutive terms is constant. This ratio is called the *common ratio*.

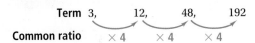

Activity 1

1. **a.** What is the common ratio of the sequence 2, 4, 8, 16, . . . ?
   b. What are the next three terms in the sequence?

2. **a.** What is the common ratio of the sequence 80, 20, 5, $\frac{5}{4}$, . . . ?
   b. What are the next three terms in the sequence?

3. **a.** What is the common ratio of the sequence 2, −6, 18, −54, . . . ?
   b. What are the next three terms in the sequence?

You can use the common ratio of a geometric sequence to write a function rule for the sequence.

Activity 2

Consider the sequence 2, 6, 18, 54, . . .
Let $n =$ the term number in the sequence.
Let $A(n) =$ the value of the nth term of the sequence.

4. What is the common ratio of the sequence?

5. Complete each statement.
   a. $A(1) = 2 = 2 \cdot 3^{\blacksquare}$
   b. $A(2) = 6 = 2 \cdot 3 = 2 \cdot 3^{\blacksquare}$
   c. $A(3) = 18 = 2 \cdot 3 \cdot 3 = 2 \cdot 3^{\blacksquare}$
   d. $A(4) = 54 = 2 \cdot 3 \cdot 3 \cdot 3 = 2 \cdot 3^{\blacksquare}$

6. What is the relationship between the exponent of the base 3 and the value of n?

7. Complete the statement: $A(n) = 2 \cdot 3^{\blacksquare}$.

In general, you can write a function rule for a geometric sequence using the first term, the term number, and the common ratio.

Geometric Sequence Rule

$$\underbrace{A(n)}_{\substack{n\text{th} \\ \text{term}}} = \underset{\substack{\text{first} \\ \text{term}}}{a} \cdot \underset{\substack{\text{common} \\ \text{ratio}}}{r}^{\overset{\substack{\text{term} \\ \text{number}}}{n-1}}$$

For example, the rule for the sequence 5, 15, 45, 135, . . . is $A(n) = 5 \cdot 3^{n-1}$.

Activity 3

8. a. Fold a piece of paper in half. How many layers are there?
   b. Continue folding the paper in half. Copy and complete the table.
   c. Rewrite each entry in the Number of Layers column from the table in the form $2^{\blacksquare}$.
   d. Write a rule for the geometric sequence. (*Hint:* The first term is 2, not 1.)
   e. Use the rule to find the number of layers after 12 folds.
   f. If there were 256 layers, how many folds would there be?
   g. **Reasoning** Is it possible to fold a piece of paper in halves and get 144 layers? Explain.

Number of Folds	Number of Layers
1	2
2	■
3	■
4	■
5	■

Exercises

Find the common ratio of each sequence. Then find the next three terms of the sequence.

9. 1, 3, 9, 27, . . .

10. 256, 64, 16, 4, . . .

11. −3, −6, −12, −24, . . .

12. 70, 7, 0.7, 0.07, . . .

13. 8, −20, 50, −125, . . .

14. 0.45, 0.9, 1.8, 3.6, . . .

Determine whether each sequence is *arithmetic* or *geometric*.

15. 2, 4, 6, 8, . . .

16. 6, 1, −4, −9, . . .

17. 0.04, 0.12, 0.36, 1.08, . . .

18. 14, 21, 28, 35, . . .

19. 7, −21, 63, −189, . . .

20. 18, 9, 4.5, 2.25, . . .

Find the first, fourth, and eighth terms of each sequence.

21. $A(n) = 4 \cdot 2^{n-1}$

22. $A(n) = -2 \cdot 5^{n-1}$

23. $A(n) = 5(-0.8)^{n-1}$

24. Reasoning Can zero be a term of a geometric sequence where the first three terms are not zero? Explain.

25. Compare and Contrast How are an exponential function and a geometric sequence rule alike? How are they different? Can you use an exponential function to describe a geometric sequence? Explain.

7-7 Exponential Growth and Decay

Objective To model exponential growth and decay

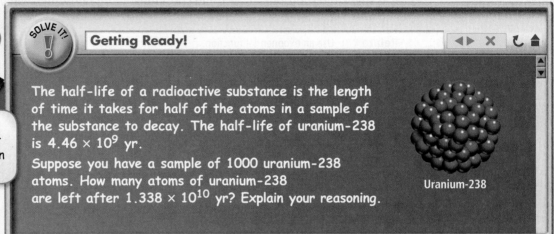

Getting Ready!

The half-life of a radioactive substance is the length of time it takes for half of the atoms in a sample of the substance to decay. The half-life of uranium-238 is 4.46×10^9 yr.

Suppose you have a sample of 1000 uranium-238 atoms. How many atoms of uranium-238 are left after 1.338×10^{10} yr? Explain your reasoning.

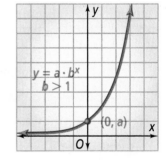

Uranium-238

Many things decay—some just decay faster than others.

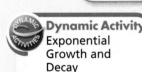

Dynamic Activity
Exponential Growth and Decay

Lesson Vocabulary
• exponential growth
• growth factor
• compound interest
• exponential decay
• decay factor

In the Solve It, the number of uranium-238 atoms decreases exponentially. In this lesson, you will use exponential functions to model similar situations.

Focus Question What is a model for exponential growth or decay?

Key Concept Exponential Growth

Definitions
Exponential growth can be modeled by the function $y = a \cdot b^x$, where $a > 0$ and $b > 1$. The base b is the **growth factor,** which equals 1 plus the percent rate of change expressed as a decimal.

Graph

initial amount (when $x = 0$)
$$y = a \cdot b^x \leftarrow \text{exponent}$$
The base, which is greater than 1, is the growth factor.

$y = a \cdot b^x$
$b > 1$

$(0, a)$

You can use an exponential growth function when an initial amount increases by a fixed percent each time period.

Problem 1 Modeling Exponential Growth

Economics Since 2005, the amount of money spent at restaurants in the United States has increased about 7% each yr. In 2005, about $360 billion was spent at restaurants. If the trend continues, about how much will be spent at restaurants in 2015?

Think

Write a statement defining each variable in the exponential growth function using information that is given in the problem.

Relate   Use an exponential function. $y = a \cdot b^x$

Define   Let $x =$ the number of years since 2005.
         Let $y =$ the annual amount spent at restaurants (in billions of dollars).
         Let $a =$ the initial amount spent (in billions of dollars) 360.
         Let $b =$ the growth factor, which is $1 + 0.07 = 1.07$.

Write $y = 360 \cdot 1.07^x$

Use the equation to predict the annual spending in 2015.

$$y = 360 \cdot 1.07^x$$

2015 is 10 yr after 2005, so substitute 10 for x. $= 360 \cdot 1.07^{10}$

Round to the nearest billion dollars. ≈ 708

About $708 billion will be spent at restaurants in the United States in 2015 if the trend continues.

 Got It? **1.** Suppose the population of a town was 25,000 people in 2000. If the population grows about 1.5% each year, what will the approximate population be in 2025?

When a bank pays interest on both the principal *and* the interest an account has already earned, the bank is paying **compound interest.** Compound interest is an example of exponential growth.

You can use the following formula to find the balance of an account that earns compound interest.

$$A = P\left(1 + \frac{r}{n}\right)^{nt}$$

$A =$ the balance
$P =$ the principal (the initial deposit)
$r =$ the annual interest rate (expressed as a decimal)
$n =$ the number of times interest is compounded per year
$t =$ the time in years

 **Problem 2** **Compound Interest**

Finance Suppose that when your friend was born, your friend's parents deposited $2000 in an account paying 4.5% interest compounded quarterly. What will the account balance be after 18 yr?

Know
- $2000 principal
- 4.5% interest
- interest compounded quarterly, 4 times per yr

Need
Account balance in 18 yr

Plan
Use the compound interest formula.

Think

Is the formula an exponential growth function?
Yes. You can rewrite the formula as
$A = P\left[\left(1 + \frac{r}{n}\right)^n\right]^t$.
So it is an exponential function with initial amount P and growth factor $\left(1 + \frac{r}{n}\right)^n$.

Use the compound interest formula.

$A = P\left(1 + \frac{r}{n}\right)^{nt}$

Substitute the values for P, r, n, and t.

$= 2000\left(1 + \frac{0.045}{4}\right)^{4 \cdot 18}$

Simplify.

$= 2000(1.01125)^{72}$

Use a calculator. Round to the nearest cent.

≈ 4475.53

The balance will be $4475.53 after 18 yr.

 Got It? **2.** Suppose the account in Problem 2 pays interest compounded monthly. What will the account balance be after 18 yr?

The function $y = a \cdot b^x$ can model *exponential decay* as well as exponential growth. In both cases, b is determined by the percent rate of change. The value of b tells if the equation models exponential growth or decay.

take note

Key Concept Exponential Decay

Definitions
Exponential decay can be modeled by the function $y = a \cdot b^x$, where $a > 0$ and $0 < b < 1$. The base b is the **decay factor,** which equals 1 minus the percent rate of change expressed as a decimal.

Graph

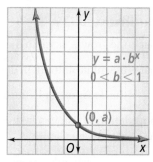

Algebra

initial amount (when $x = 0$)
$\downarrow$
$y = a \cdot b^x \leftarrow$ exponent
$\uparrow$
The base, which is between 0 and 1, is the decay factor.

Problem 3 Modeling Exponential Decay

Physics The kilopascal is a unit of measure for atmospheric pressure. The atmospheric pressure at sea level is about 101 kilopascals. For every 1000–m increase in altitude, the pressure decreases about 11.5%. What is the approximate pressure at an altitude of 3000 m?

Think

Will the pressure ever be negative?
No. The range of an exponential decay function is all positive real numbers. The graph of an exponential decay function approaches but does not cross the *x*-axis.

Relate $y = a \cdot b^x$ Use an exponential function.

Define   Let $x =$ the altitude (in thousands of meters).
Let $y =$ the atmospheric pressure (in kilopascals).
Let $a =$ the initial pressure (in kilopascals), 101.
Let $b =$ the decay factor, which is $1 - 0.115 = 0.885$.

Write $y = 101 \cdot 0.885^x$

Use the equation to estimate the pressure at an altitude of 3000 m.

$$y = 101 \cdot 0.885^x$$

Substitute 3 for *x*. $= 101 \cdot 0.885^3$

Round to the nearest kilopascal. ≈ 70

The pressure at an altitude of 3000 m is about 70 kilopascals.

Got It? 3. a. What is the atmospheric pressure at an altitude of 5000 m?
 b. **Reasoning** Why do you subtract the percent decrease from 1 to find the decay factor?

Focus Question What is a model for exponential growth or decay?

Answer A model for exponential growth is a function that shows the growth of a population or an amount over a period of time. Decay shows a declining population.

Lesson Check

Do you know HOW?

1. What is the growth factor in the equation $y = 34 \cdot 4^x$?

2. What is the initial amount in the function $y = 15 \cdot 3^x$?

3. What is the decay factor in the function $y = 17 \cdot 0.2^x$?

4. A population of fish in a lake decreases 6% annually. What is the decay factor?

5. Suppose your friend's parents invest $20,000 in an account paying 5% interest compounded annually. What will the balance be after 10 yr?

Do you UNDERSTAND?

6. Vocabulary How can you tell if an exponential function models growth or decay?

7. Reasoning How can you simplify the compound interest formula when the interest is compounded annually? Explain.

8. Error Analysis A student deposits $500 into an account that earns 3.5% interest compounded quarterly. Describe and correct the student's error in calculating the account balance after 2 yr.

$$A = 500 \left(1 + \frac{3.5}{4}\right)^{4 \cdot 2}$$
$$= 500 \,(1.875)^8$$
$$\approx 76,380.09$$

Practice and Problem-Solving Exercises

 Practice Identify the initial amount a and the growth factor b in each exponential function.

See Problem 1.

9. $g(x) = 14 \cdot 2^x$

10. $y = 150 \cdot 1.0894^x$

11. $y = 25{,}600 \cdot 1.01^x$

12. $f(t) = 1.4^t$

Guided Practice

13. Employment Suppose a town has 10 acres of conservation land. The town plans to increase the amount of conservation land about 5% every 10 yr. If the town continues to follow their plan, how much conservation land will there be after 50 yr?

To start, define the variables.

Let x = the number of 10 year periods in 50 yr.
Let y = the amount of conservation land (in acres) after x yr.
Let a = the initial amount (in acres) of conservation land.
Let b = the growth factor, which is $1 + 0.05 = 1.05$.

Write an exponential function.

$y = a \cdot b^x$
$y = 10 \cdot 1.05^5$

14. College Enrollment The number of students enrolled at a college is 15,000 and grows 4% each yr.

 a. The initial amount a is ■.
 b. The percent rate of change is 4%, so the growth factor b is $1 + ■ = ■$.
 c. To find the number of students enrolled after one yr, you calculate $15{,}000 \cdot ■$.
 d. Complete the equation $y = ■ \cdot ■^{■}$ to find the number of students enrolled after x yr.
 e. Use your equation to predict the number of students enrolled after 25 yr.

Find the balance in each account after the given period.

See Problem 2.

Guided Practice

15. $4000 principal earning 6% compounded annually, after 5 yr

To start, substitute the values for *P, r, n,* and *t* in the compound interest formula.

$A = P\left(1 + \dfrac{r}{n}\right)^{nt}$

$A = 4000\left(1 + \dfrac{0.06}{1}\right)^{1 \cdot 5}$

16. $12,000 principal earning 4.8% compounded annually, after 7 yr

17. $500 principal earning 4% compounded quarterly, after 6 yr

18. $5000 deposit earning 1.5% compounded quarterly, after 3 yr

19. $13,500 deposit earning 3.3% compounded monthly, after 1 yr

Identify the initial amount a and the decay factor b in each exponential function.

◀ See Problem 3.

20. $y = 5 \cdot 0.5^x$ **21.** $f(x) = 10 \cdot 0.1^x$ **22.** $g(x) = 100\left(\frac{2}{3}\right)^x$ **23.** $y = 0.1 \cdot 0.9^x$

24. Population The population of a city is 45,000 and decreases 2% each yr. If the trend continues, what will be the population be after 15 yr?

 Apply State whether the equation represents *exponential growth*, *exponential decay*, or *neither*.

25. $y = 0.93 \cdot 2^x$ **26.** $y = 2 \cdot 0.68^x$ **27.** $y = 68 \cdot x^2$ **28.** $y = 68 \cdot 0.2^x$

29. Think About a Plan You invest $100 and expect your money to grow 8% each yr. About how many yr will it take for your investment to double?
- What function models the growth of your investment?
- How can you use a table to find the approximate amount of time it takes for your investment to double?

30. Reasoning Give an example of an exponential function in the form $y = a \cdot b^x$ that is neither an exponential growth function nor an exponential decay function. Explain your reasoning.

State whether each graph shows an *exponential growth function*, an *exponential decay function*, or *neither*.

31.
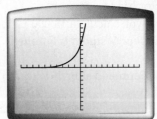

32.
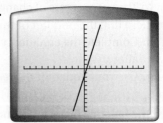

33.
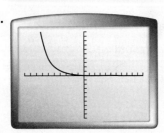

34.
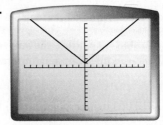

35. Writing Would you rather have $500 in an account paying 6% interest compounded quarterly or $600 in an account paying 5% interest compounded annually? Explain your reasoning.

36. Medicine Doctors can use radioactive iodine to treat some forms of cancer. The half-life of iodine-131 is 8 days. A patient receives a treatment of 12 millicuries of iodine-131. (A millicurie is a unit of radioactivity.) How much iodine-131 remains in the patient 16 days later?

37. Business Suppose you start a lawn-mowing business and make a profit of $400 in the first year. Each year, your profit increases 5%.
   a. Write a function that models your annual profit.
   b. If you continue your business for 10 yr, what will your *total* profit be?

Standardized Test Prep

SAT/ACT

38. A new fitness center opens with 120 members. Each month the fitness center increases the number of members by 40 members. How many members will the fitness center have after being open for 3 months?

39. What is the slope of the line at the right?

40. What is the simplified form of 8^0?

41. What is the simplified form of 5^{-2}?

42. A manufacturing company is making metal sheets with a thickness of 5.4×10^{-2} mm. What is 5.4×10^{-2} written in standard form?

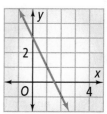

Mixed Review

Graph each function.   ◀ See Lesson 7-6.

43. $y = 2 \cdot 10^x$ **44.** $f(x) = 100 \cdot 0.9^x$ **45.** $g(x) = \frac{1}{10} \cdot 2^x$

Solve each inequality.   ◀ See Lesson 3-4.

46. $7x + 2 < 16$ **47.** $\frac{3}{4}t - 4 \geq 5$ **48.** $-0.08 > 0.35k - 0.15$

Get Ready!   **To prepare for Lesson 8-1, do Exercises 49–52.**

Simplify each expression.   ◀ See Lesson 1-7.

49. $6t + 13t$ **50.** $7k - 15k$ **51.** $2b - 6 + 9b$ **52.** $8x^2 + x^2$

Pull It **All Together**

BIG idea Equivalence

One way to represent numbers is in scientific notation. This form uses powers of ten to write very large or very small numbers.

Task 1

Medical X-rays, with a wavelength of about 10^{-10} m, can penetrate completely through your skin.

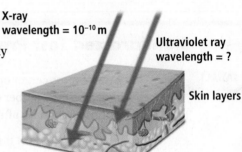

X-ray wavelength = 10^{-10} m

Ultraviolet ray wavelength = ?

Skin layers

a. Ultraviolet rays, which cause sun burn by penetrating only the top level of skin, have a wavelength about 1000 times the wavelength of an X-ray. Find the wavelength of ultraviolet rays. Show your work.

b. The wavelengths of visible light are between 3.8×10^{-7} m and 7.6×10^{-7} m. Are these wavelengths longer or shorter than those of ultraviolet rays? Explain.

BIG idea Properties

Just as there are properties that describe how to rewrite expressions involving addition and multiplication, there are properties that describe how to rewrite and simplify exponential expressions.

Task 2

Write each answer as a power of 2. Show your work and explain your steps.

Hint

a. Computer capacity is often measured in bits and bytes. A bit is the smallest unit, which is a 1 or 0, in the computer's memory. A byte is 2^3 bits. A megabyte (MB) is 2^{20} bytes. How many bits are in a megabyte?

b. A gigabyte (GB) is 2^{30} bytes. How many megabytes are in a gigabyte? How many bits are in a gigabyte?

BIG idea Functions

The family of exponential functions has equations of the form $y = a \cdot b^x$. They can be used to model exponential growth or decay.

Task 3

On January 1, 2010, Chessville has a population of 50,000 people. Chessville then enters a period of population growth. Its population increases 7% each year. On the same day, Checkersville has a population of 70,000 people. Checkersville starts to experience a population decline. Its population decreases 4% each year. During what year will the population of Chessville first exceed that of Checkersville? Show all of your work and explain your steps.

7 Chapter Review

Connecting **BIG** ideas and Answering the Essential Questions

1 Equivalence
One way to represent numbers is in scientific notation. This form uses powers of ten to write very large or very small numbers.

→

Zero and Negative Exponents (Lesson 7-1)
$$10^0 = 1$$
$$10^{-3} = \frac{1}{10^3}$$

→

Scientific Notation (Lesson 7-2)
175,000,000,000,000
$$= 1.75 \times 10^{14}$$
$$0.0000568 = 5.68 \times 10^{-5}$$

2 Properties
Just as there are properties that describe how to rewrite expressions involving addition and multiplication, there are properties that describe how to rewrite and simplify exponential expressions.

→

Properties of Exponents (Lessons 7-3, 7-4, and 7-5)
$$5^2 \cdot 5^4 = 5^{2+4} = 5^6$$
$$(3^7)^4 = 3^{7 \cdot 4} = 3^{28}$$
$$(6x)^4 = 6^4 x^4$$
$$\frac{7^8}{7^5} = 7^{8-5} = 7^3$$
$$\left(\frac{y}{2}\right)^5 = \frac{y^5}{2^5}$$

3 Function
The family of exponential functions has equations of the form $y = a \cdot b^x$. They can be used to model exponential growth or decay.

→

Exponential Functions (Lesson 7-6)
$$y = 2 \cdot \left(\frac{5}{4}\right)^x$$
$$y = 3 \cdot \left(\frac{1}{4}\right)^x$$

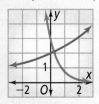

→

Exponential Growth and Decay (Lesson 7-7)
Exponential growth is modeled by the function $y = a \cdot b^x$, where $a > 0$ and $b > 1$. Exponential decay is modeled by the function $y = a \cdot b^x$, where $a > 0$ and $0 < b < 1$.

Chapter Vocabulary

- compound interest (p. 484)
- decay factor (p. 485)
- exponential decay (p. 485)
- exponential function (p. 475)
- exponential growth (p. 483)
- growth factor (p. 483)
- scientific notation (p. 449)

Choose the correct term to complete each sentence.

1. __?__ is a shorthand way to write very large and very small numbers.

2. For a function $y = a \cdot b^x$, where $a > 0$ and $b > 1$, b is the __?__.

3. For a function $y = a \cdot b^x$, where $a > 0$ and $0 < b < 1$, b is the __?__.

4. The function $y = a \cdot b^x$ models __?__ for $a > 0$ and $b > 1$.

5. The function $y = a \cdot b^x$ models __?__ for $a > 0$ and $0 < b < 1$.

7-1 Zero and Negative Exponents

Quick Review

You can use zero and negative integers as exponents. For every nonzero number a, $a^0 = 1$. For every nonzero number a and any integer n, $a^{-n} = \frac{1}{a^n}$. When you evaluate an exponential expression, you can simplify the expression before substituting values for the variables.

Example

What is the value of $a^2 b^{-4} c^0$ for $a = 3$, $b = 2$, and $c = -5$?

Use the definition of negative exponents. $a^2 b^{-4} c^0 = \dfrac{a^2 c^0}{b^4}$

Use the definition of zero exponent. $= \dfrac{a^2(1)}{b^4}$

Substitute. $= \dfrac{3^2}{2^4}$

Simplify. $= \dfrac{9}{16}$

Exercises

Simplify each expression.

6. 5^0

7. 7^{-2}

8. $\dfrac{4x^{-2}}{y^{-8}}$

9. $\dfrac{1}{p^2 q^{-4} r^0}$

Evaluate each expression for $x = 2$, $y = -3$, and $z = -5$.

10. $x^0 y^2$

11. $(-x)^{-4} y^2$

12. $x^0 z^0$

13. $\dfrac{5x^0}{y^{-2}}$

14. $y^{-2} z^2$

15. $\dfrac{2x}{y^2 z^{-1}}$

16. **Reasoning** Is it true that $(-3b)^4 = -12b^4$? Explain why or why not.

7-2 Scientific Notation

Quick Review

You can use **scientific notation** to write very large or very small numbers. A number is written in scientific notation if it has the form $a \times 10^n$, where $1 \le |a| < 10$ and n is an integer.

Example

What is each number written in scientific notation?

a. 510,000,000,000

   Move the decimal point $510{,}000{,}000{,}000 = 5.1 \times 10^{11}$
   11 places to the left.

b. 0.0000087

   Move the decimal point $0.0000087 = 8.7 \times 10^{-6}$
   6 places to the right.

Exercises

Is the number written in scientific notation? If not, explain why not.

17. 950×10^5

18. 7.23×100^8

19. 1.6×10^{-6}

20. 0.84×10^{-5}

Write each number in scientific notation.

21. 2,793,000

22. 189,000,000

23. 0.000043

24. 0.0000000027

25. 3,860,000,000,000

26. 0.00000478

7-3 and 7-4 Multiplication Properties of Exponents

Quick Review

To multiply powers with the same base, add the exponents.

$a^m \cdot a^n = a^{m+n}$, where $a \neq 0$ and m and n are integers

To raise a power to a power, multiply the exponents.

$(a^m)^n = a^{mn}$, where $a \neq 0$ and m and n are integers

To raise a product to a power, raise each factor in the product to the power.

$(ab)^n = a^n b^n$, where $a \neq 0$, $b \neq 0$, and n is an integer

Example

What is the simplified form of each expression?

a. $3^{10} \cdot 3^4 = 3^{10+4} = 3^{14}$

b. $(x^5)^7 = x^{5 \cdot 7} = x^{35}$

c. $(pq)^8 = p^8 q^8$

Exercises

Complete each equation.

27. $3^2 \cdot 3^{\blacksquare} = 3^{10}$

28. $a^6 \cdot a^{\blacksquare} = a^8$

29. $x^2 y^5 \cdot x^{\blacksquare} y^{\blacksquare} = x^5 y^{11}$

30. $(5^5)^{\blacksquare} = 5^{15}$

31. $(b^{-4})^{\blacksquare} = b^{20}$

32. $(4x^3 y^5)^{\blacksquare} = 16 x^6 y^{10}$

Simplify each expression.

33. $2d^2 \cdot d^3$

34. $(q^3 r)^4$

35. $(5c^{-4})(-4m^2 c^8)$

36. $(1.34^2)^5 (1.34)^{-8}$

37. Estimation Each square inch of your body has about 6.5×10^2 pores. Suppose the back of your hand has an area of about 0.12×10^2 in.^{2}. About how many pores are on the back of your hand? Write your answer in scientific notation.

7-5 Division Properties of Exponents

Quick Review

To divide powers with the same base, subtract the exponents.

$\dfrac{a^m}{a^n} = a^{m-n}$, where $a \neq 0$ and m and n are integers

To raise a quotient to a power, raise the numerator and the denominator to the power.

$\left(\dfrac{a}{b}\right)^n = \dfrac{a^n}{b^n}$, where $a \neq 0$, $b \neq 0$, and n is an integer

Example

What is the simplified form of $\left(\dfrac{5x^4}{z^2}\right)^3$**?**

$$\left(\frac{5x^4}{z^2}\right)^3 = \frac{(5x^4)^3}{(z^2)^3} = \frac{5^3 x^{4 \cdot 3}}{z^{2 \cdot 3}} = \frac{125 x^{12}}{z^6}$$

Exercises

Simplify each expression.

38. $\dfrac{w^2}{w^5}$

39. $\dfrac{21x^3}{3x^{-1}}$

40. $\left(\dfrac{n^5}{v^3}\right)^7$

41. $\left(\dfrac{c^3}{e^5}\right)^{-4}$

Simplify each quotient. Write your answer in scientific notation.

42. $\dfrac{4.2 \times 10^8}{2.1 \times 10^{11}}$

43. $\dfrac{3.1 \times 10^4}{1.24 \times 10^2}$

44. $\dfrac{4.5 \times 10^3}{9 \times 10^7}$

45. $\dfrac{5.1 \times 10^5}{1.7 \times 10^2}$

46. Writing List the steps that you would use to simplify $\left(\dfrac{5a}{a^6}\right)^{-3}$.

7-6 Exponential Functions

Quick Review

An **exponential function** involves repeated multiplication of an initial amount a by the same positive number b. The general form of an exponential function is $y = a \cdot b^x$, where $a \neq 0$, $b > 0$, and $b \neq 1$.

Example

What is the graph of $y = \frac{1}{2} \cdot 5^x$?

Make a table of values. Graph the ordered pairs.

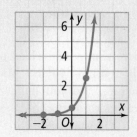

x	y
−2	$\frac{1}{50}$
−1	$\frac{1}{10}$
0	$\frac{1}{2}$
1	$\frac{5}{2}$
2	$\frac{25}{2}$

Exercises

Evaluate each function for the domain {1, 2, 3}.

47. $f(x) = 4^x$

48. $y = 0.01^x$

49. $y = 40\left(\frac{1}{2}\right)^x$

50. $f(x) = 3 \cdot 2^x$

Graph each function.

51. $f(x) = 2.5^x$

52. $f(x) = \frac{1}{2} \cdot 3^x$

53. Biology A population of 50 bacteria in a laboratory culture doubles every 30 min. The function $p(x) = 50 \cdot 2^x$ models the population, where x is the number of 30-min periods.

   a. How many bacteria will there be after 2 h?

   b. How many bacteria will there be after 1 day?

7-7 Exponential Growth and Decay

Quick Review

When $a > 0$ and $b > 1$, the function $y = a \cdot b^x$ models **exponential growth**. The base b is called the **growth factor**. When $a > 0$ and $0 < b < 1$, the function $y = a \cdot b^x$ models **exponential decay**. In this case the base b is called the **decay factor**.

Example

The population of a city is 25,000 and decreases 1% each year. Predict the population after 6 yr.

Use the exponential decay function.	$y = 25{,}000 \cdot 0.99^x$
Substitute 6 for x.	$= 25{,}000 \cdot 0.99^6$
Simplify.	$\approx 23{,}537$

The population will be about 23,537 after 6 yr.

Exercises

Tell whether the function represents *exponential growth* or *exponential decay*. Identify the growth or decay factor.

54. $y = 5.2 \cdot 3^x$

55. $f(x) = 7 \cdot 0.32^x$

56. $y = 0.15\left(\frac{3}{2}\right)^x$

57. $g(x) = 1.3\left(\frac{1}{4}\right)^x$

58. Finance Suppose $2000 is deposited in an account paying 2.5% interest compounded quarterly. What will the account balance be after 12 yr?

59. Music A band performs a free concert in a local park. There are 200 people in the crowd at the start of the concert. The number of people in the crowd grows 15% every half hour. How many people are in the crowd after 3 h? Round to the nearest person.

Do you know HOW?

Simplify each expression.

1. $\dfrac{r^3 t^{-7}}{t^5}$

2. $\left(\dfrac{a^3}{5m}\right)^{-4}$

3. $c^3 v^9 c^{-1} c^0$

4. $(-3q^{-1})^3 q^2$

Write each number in scientific notation.

5. 79,500,000,000

6. 0.0000000405

Write each number in standard notation.

7. 8.4×10^{-6}

8. 9.52×10^{11}

Simplify each expression. Write each answer in scientific notation.

9. $(6 \times 10^4)(4.8 \times 10^2)$

10. $\dfrac{1.5 \times 10^7}{5 \times 10^{-2}}$

11. **Medicine** The human body normally produces about 2×10^6 red blood cells per second.

    a. Use scientific notation to express how many red blood cells your body produces in one day.

    b. One pint of blood contains about 2.4×10^{12} red blood cells. How many seconds will it take your body to replace the red blood cells lost by donating one pint of blood? How many days?

Evaluate each function for $x = -1$, 2, and 3.

12. $y = 3 \cdot 5^x$

13. $f(x) = \dfrac{1}{2} \cdot 4^x$

Graph each function.

14. $y = \dfrac{1}{2} \cdot 2^x$

15. $y = 2 \cdot \left(\dfrac{1}{2}\right)^x$

16. **Banking** A customer deposits $2000 in a savings account that pays 5.2% interest compounded quarterly. How much money will the customer have in the account after 2 yr? After 5 yr?

17. **Automobiles** Suppose a new car is worth $30,000. You can use the function $y = 30,000(0.85)^x$ to estimate the car's value after x years.

    a. What is the decay factor? What does it mean?

    b. Estimate the car's value after 1 yr.

    c. Estimate the car's value after 4 yr.

Do you UNDERSTAND?

18. **Error Analysis** Find and correct the error in the work shown below.

$$3^4 \cdot 3^3 = 9^7$$

19. **Open-Ended** Write two equivalent expressions. Use a negative exponent in one of the expressions.

20. **Writing** Explain when a function in the form $y = a \cdot b^x$ models exponential growth and when it models exponential decay.

21. Simplify the expression $\left(\dfrac{a^6}{a^4}\right)^2$ in two different ways. Justify each step.

22. **Reasoning** Explain how you can use the property for dividing powers with the same base to justify the definition of a zero exponent.

7 Cumulative Test Prep

Some questions on tests ask you to solve problems involving exponents. Read the sample question at the right. Then follow the tips to answer it.

If the side length of a square can be represented by the expression $4x^2y^6$, which expression could represent the area of the square?

- (A) $2xy^3$
- (B) $8x^4y^{12}$
- (C) $16x^4y^{12}$
- (D) $16x^4y^{36}$

TIP 1

Look to eliminate answer choices. You need to square 4, so you can eliminate A and B.

TIP 2

Use properties of exponents to help you solve the problem.

Think It Through

The side length of the square is $4x^2y^6$, so the area is $(4x^2y^6)^2$. Multiply the exponents when you are raising a power to a power.

$$(4x^2y^6)^2 = 4^2x^{2 \cdot 2}y^{6 \cdot 2}$$
$$= 16x^4y^{12}$$

The correct answer is C.

Vocabulary Builder

As you solve test items, you must understand the meanings of mathematical terms. Choose the correct term to complete each sentence.

A. The values of the (*independent*, *dependent*) variable are the output values of the function.

B. The (*base*, *exponent*) of a power is the number that is multiplied repeatedly.

C. A number in (*scientific*, *standard*) notation is a shorthand way to write numbers using powers of 10.

D. The (*slope*, *y-intercept*) of a line is the ratio of the vertical change to the horizontal change.

E. A system of two equations has exactly one solution if the lines are (*parallel*, *intersecting*) lines.

Multiple Choice

Read each question. Then write the letter of the correct answer on your paper.

1. Which expression is equivalent to $(j^2k^3)(jk^2)$?
- (A) j^2k^2
- (B) j^3k^5
- (C) j^2k^6
- (D) j^3k^6

2. Which equation has $(2, -6)$ and $(-3, 4)$ as solutions?
- (F) $y = \frac{1}{2}x - 7$
- (G) $y = 2x - 10$
- (H) $y = -\frac{1}{2}x - 5$
- (I) $y = -2x - 2$

3. Which equation best represents the statement *two more than twice a number is the number tripled*?
- (A) $2 + n = 3n$
- (B) $2n + 2 = 3n$
- (C) $2(2 + n) = 3n$
- (D) $2n + 2 = 3 + n$

4. The graph at the right shows how Manuel's height changed during the past year. Which conclusion can you make from the graph?

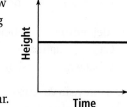

Height / Time

- **F** His height is average.
- **G** He will grow more next year.
- **H** His height did not change during the year.
- **I** His height steadily increased during the year.

5. All of the students in Haley's class received between 36 and 48 points on the last quiz. Each question was worth 2 points. There was no partial credit. How many questions could Haley have answered correctly?

- **A** 12
- **B** 21
- **C** 44
- **D** 72

6. Which *cannot* be represented by a linear function?

- **F** the area of a square, given its side length
- **G** the price of fruit, given the weight of the fruit
- **H** the number of steps on a ladder, given the height
- **I** the number of inches, given the number of yards

7. A light-year is the distance light travels in one year. One light-year is about 5.9×10^{12} mi. If it takes light 3 months to travel from one star to another, about how far apart are the stars?

- **A** 2×10^3 mi
- **B** 1.5×10^4 mi
- **C** 1.5×10^{12} mi
- **D** 2×10^{12} mi

8. Use the graph at the right. Suppose the y-intercept increases by 2 and the slope stays the same. What will the x-intercept be?

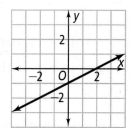

- **F** -3
- **G** -2
- **H** 1
- **I** 4

9. At lunchtime, Mitchell makes his own salad. The salad bar costs $1.25 per pound. Suppose Mitchell's salad weighs 1.8 lb, what is the cost of his salad?

- **A** $1.44
- **B** $2.25
- **C** $2.50
- **D** $22.50

10. The dimensions of a rectangular prism are shown in the diagram at the right. Which expression represents the volume of the rectangular prism?

a^2b, ab^3, ab^2

- **F** a^2b^5
- **G** a^2b^6
- **H** a^4b^5
- **I** a^4b^6

11. Suppose you are buying apples and bananas. The price of apples is $.40 each and the price of bananas is $.25 each. Which equation models the number of apples and bananas you can buy for $2?

- **A** $40x + 25y = 200$
- **B** $40x - 25y = 2$
- **C** $5x + 8y = 200$
- **D** $5x + 8y = 2$

12. At lunchtime, Mitchell cast a shadow 0.5 ft long while a nearby flagpole cast a shadow 2.5 ft long. If Mitchell is 5 ft 3 in. tall, how tall is the flagpole?

- **F** 26 ft 3 in.
- **G** 26 ft 4 in.
- **H** 26 ft 5 in.
- **I** 26 ft 6 in.

13. Laura rented a car that cost $20 for the day plus $.12 for each mile driven. She returned the car later that day. Laura gave the salesperson $50 and received change. Which inequality represents the possible numbers of miles m that she could have driven?

- **A** $50 > 0.12m + 20$
- **B** $50 < 0.12m + 20$
- **C** $50 > 0.12m - 20$
- **D** $50 < 0.12m - 20$

14. A doctor did a 6-month study on resting heart rate and exercise in healthy adults. The doctor found that for every 20 min of exercise added to a daily routine, the resting heart rate decreased by 1 beat per minute. According to the doctor's study, what does the resting heart rate depend on?

- **F** the 6-month study
- **G** minutes of exercise
- **H** a daily routine
- **I** diet

15. Which linear function has a graph that never intersects the *x*-axis?

   Ⓐ $y = x$ Ⓒ $y = x + 1$

   Ⓑ $y = -1$ Ⓓ $y = -x - 1$

16. What is the *y*-intercept of the graph at the right?

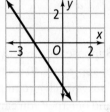

   Ⓕ -3

   Ⓖ -2

   Ⓗ $-\dfrac{3}{2}$

   Ⓘ 0

17. What is the value of $|(-3) + 7(-2)|$?

   Ⓐ -17 Ⓒ 8

   Ⓑ -8 Ⓓ 17

 GRIDDED RESPONSE

Record your answers in a grid.

18. What is the area, in square units, of the triangle below?

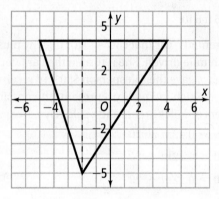

19. Charles purchased 50 shares of a stock at $23 per share. He paid a $15 commission to his broker for the purchase. How much money, in dollars, did he spend for the purchase and commission combined?

20. What is the value of the expression $9x - (4x - 1)$ when $x = 7$?

21. A designer tested 50 jackets in a clothing warehouse and found that 4% of the jackets were labeled with the wrong size. How many jackets did the designer find that were labeled the wrong size?

22. If $b = 2a - 16$ and $b = a + 2$, what is $a + b$?

23. Alejandro bought 6 notebooks and 2 binders for $23.52. Cassie bought 3 notebooks and 4 binders for $25.53. What was the cost, in dollars, of 1 notebook?

24. Ashley surveyed 200 students in her school to find out whether they liked mustard or mayo on a turkey sandwich. Her results are shown in the diagram below.

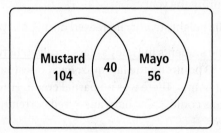

What fraction of the students surveyed liked mustard but not mayo? Write your answer in lowest terms.

25. The area of a parallelogram is $A = bh$. What is the area, in square units, of a parallelogram with vertices $(-3, 2)$, $(0, 7)$, $(7, 7)$, and $(4, 2)$?

Short Response

26. The sum of six consecutive integers is 165. What are the six integers? Show your work.

27. On April 1, 2000, the day of the 2000 national census, the population of the United States was 281,421,906 people. This was a 13.2% increase from the 1990 census. What was the 1990 population of the United States?

Extended Response

28. A triangle is enclosed by the following lines:

$$x - y = -1$$
$$y = 2$$
$$-0.4x - y = -5.2$$

  a. What are the coordinates of the vertices of the triangle? Use algebraic methods to justify your answers.

  b. Draw the triangle using your answers in part (a). What is the area, in square units, of the triangle?

Get Ready!

Skills
Handbook,
page 783

Finding Factors of Composite Numbers

List all the factors of each number.

1. 12   **2.** 18   **3.** 100   **4.** 81

5. 72   **6.** 300   **7.** 250   **8.** 207

Lesson 1-7

Simplifying Expressions

Simplify each expression.

9. $3x^2 - 4x - 2x^2 - 5x$

10. $-2d + 7 + 5d + 8$

11. $3(2r + 4r^2 - 7r + 4r^2)$

12. $-2(m + 1) + 9(4m - 3)$

13. $6(a - 3a^2 - 2a - 3a^2)$

14. $s - 4 - (s^2 - 2) - 8s$

Lessons 7-3
and 7-4

Multiplying Expressions With Exponents

Simplify each expression.

15. $(5x)^2$ **16.** $(-3v^2)(-3v)$ **17.** $(4c^2)^3$ **18.** $(8m^2)(7m^5)$

19. $(9b^3)^2$ **20.** $(-6pq)^2$ **21.** $7(n^2)^2$ **22.** $(-5t^4)^3$

Lesson 7-5

Dividing Expressions With Exponents

Simplify each expression.

23. $\dfrac{p^4 q^9}{p^2 q^6}$ **24.** $\dfrac{(5x)^2}{5x}$ **25.** $\dfrac{-3n}{(6n^4)(4n^2)}$ **26.** $\dfrac{(2y)(9y^4)}{6y^3}$

Looking Ahead Vocabulary

27. Both of the words *tricycle* and *triangle* begin with the prefix *tri-*. A *trinomial* is a type of mathematical expression. How many terms do you think a trinomial has?

28. Use your knowledge of the meaning of the words *binocular* and *bicycle* to guess at the meaning of the word *binomial*.

29. Which of the following products do you think is a *perfect-square trinomial* when multiplied? Explain your reasoning.

  a. $(x + 4)(x + 7)$ **b.** $(x + 4)(x + 4)$

Polynomials and Factoring

I bet this girl has practiced skating the half-pipe for a while! The skate park she's in has to have enough area for all the half-pipes, boxes, and rails she'll use in her tricks.

In this chapter, you'll use polynomials to describe the areas of geometric figures.

 Vocabulary

My Math Video

00:04:04

VIDEO

BIG ideas

1 Equivalence

Essential Question Can two algebraic expressions that appear to be different be equivalent?

2 Properties

Essential Question How are the properties of real numbers related to polynomials?

Chapter Preview for Part A

8-1 Adding and Subtracting Polynomials

Objective To classify, add, and subtract polynomials

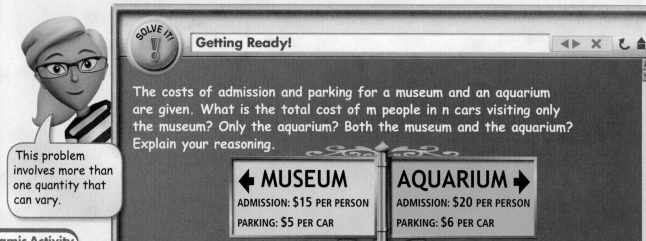

SOLVE IT!

Getting Ready!

The costs of admission and parking for a museum and an aquarium are given. What is the total cost of m people in n cars visiting only the museum? Only the aquarium? Both the museum and the aquarium? Explain your reasoning.

This problem involves more than one quantity that can vary.

← MUSEUM
ADMISSION: $15 PER PERSON
PARKING: $5 PER CAR

AQUARIUM →
ADMISSION: $20 PER PERSON
PARKING: $6 PER CAR

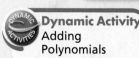
Dynamic Activity
Adding Polynomials

Lesson Vocabulary
- monomial
- degree of a monomial
- polynomial
- standard form of a polynomial
- degree of a polynomial
- binomial
- trinomial

In some cases, you can model a situation with an expression composed of *monomials*. A **monomial** is a real number, a variable, or a product of a real number and one or more variables with whole-number exponents. Here are some examples of monomials.

$$18 \qquad z \qquad -4x^2 \qquad 2.5xy^3 \qquad \frac{a}{3}$$

Focus Question How are monomials and polynomials related?

The **degree of a monomial** is the sum of the exponents of its variables. The degree of a nonzero constant is 0. Zero has no degree.

Think

Why is the degree of a nonzero constant 0?
You can write a nonzero constant c as cx^0. The exponent is 0, so the degree is 0 also.

Problem 1 **Finding the Degree of a Monomial**

What is the degree of each monomial?

A $5x$

$5x = 5x^1$ The exponent is 1.   Degree: 1

B $6x^3y^2$ The exponents are 3 and 2. Their sum is 5.   Degree: 5

C 4

$4 = 4x^0$ The degree of a nonzero constant is 0.   Degree: 0

Got It? **1.** What is the degree of each monomial?
     a. $8xy$ **b.** $-7y^4z$ **c.** 11

You can add or subtract monomials by adding or subtracting like terms.

 Problem 2 Adding and Subtracting Monomials

Think

Will the sum of two monomials always be a monomial?
No. The monomials must be like terms.

What is the sum or difference?

Ⓐ $3x^2 + 5x^2$

Combine like terms. $3x^2 + 5x^2 = 8x^2$

Ⓑ $4x^3y - x^3y$

Combine like terms. $4x^3y - x^3y = 3x^3y$

Got It? **2. a.** What is the sum $-6x^4 + 11x^4$?
b. What is the difference $2x^2y^4 - 7x^2y^4$?

A **polynomial** is a monomial or a sum of monomials. The following polynomial is the sum of the monomials $3x^4$, $5x^2$, $-7x$, and 1.

$$3x^4 + 5x^2 - 7x + 1$$
$$\uparrow \qquad \uparrow \qquad \uparrow \qquad \uparrow$$

Degree of each monomial ⟩ 4   2   1   0

The polynomial shown above is in *standard form*. **Standard form of a polynomial** means that the degrees of its monomial terms decrease from left to right. The **degree of a polynomial** in one variable is the same as the degree of the monomial with the greatest exponent. The degree of $3x^4 + 5x^2 - 7x + 1$ is 4.

You can name a polynomial based on its degree or the number of monomials it contains.

Polynomial	Degree	Name Using Degree	Number of Terms	Name Using Number of Terms
6	0	Constant	1	Monomial
$5x + 9$	1	Linear	2	**Binomial**
$4x^2 + 7x + 3$	2	Quadratic	3	**Trinomial**
$2x^3$	3	Cubic	1	Monomial
$8x^4 - 2x^3 + 3x$	4	Fourth degree	3	Trinomial

Problem 3 Classifying Polynomials

Think

Why do you need to combine like terms in part (B)?
To name a polynomial correctly based on its number of terms, you must first combine all like terms.

Write each polynomial in standard form. What is the name of the polynomial based on its degree and number of terms?

Ⓐ $3x + 4x^3$

Place terms in order from $4x^3 + 3x$
greatest to least exponent.

The degree is 3 and there are 2 terms.
The polynomial is a cubic binomial.

Ⓑ $4x - 1 + 5x^2 + 7x$

Place terms in order from $5x^2 + 4x + 7x - 1$
greatest to least exponent.

Combine like terms. $5x^2 + 11x - 1$

The degree is 2 and there are three terms.
The polynomial is a quadratic trinomial.

Got It? 3. Write $2x - 3 + 8x^3$ in standard form. What is the name of the polynomial based on its degree and number of terms?

You can add polynomials by adding like terms.

 Problem 4 Adding Polynomials

Travel A researcher studied the number of overnight stays in U.S. National Park Service campgrounds and in the backcountry of the national park system over a 5-yr period. The researcher modeled the results, in thousands, with the following polynomials.

Campgrounds: $-7.1x^2 - 180x + 5800$ Backcountry: $21x^2 - 140x + 1900$

In each polynomial, $x = 0$ corresponds to the first year in the 5-yr period. What polynomial models the total number of overnight stays in both campgrounds and backcountry?

Know	Need	Plan
• Overnight stays in campgrounds: $-7.1x^2 - 180x + 5800$ • Overnight stays in backcountry: $21x^2 - 140x + 1900$	A polynomial for the total number of overnight stays in campgrounds and backcountry	The word *both* implies addition, so add the two polynomials to find the total.

Method 1 Add vertically.

$$-7.1x^2 - 180x + 5800$$

Line up like terms. $\underline{+\ 21x^2 - 140x + 1900}$

Add the coefficients. $13.9x^2 - 320x + 7700$

Method 2 Add horizontally.

Write the original expression. $\left(-7.1x^2 - 180x + 5800\right) + \left(21x^2 - 140x + 1900\right)$

Group like terms. $= \left(-7.1x^2 + 21x^2\right) + \left(-180x - 140x\right) + \left(5800 + 1900\right)$

Add the coefficients. $= 13.9x^2 - 320x + 7700$

A polynomial that models the number of stays (in thousands) in campgrounds and backcountry over the 5-yr period is $13.9x^2 - 320x + 7700$.

 Got It? 4. A nutritionist studied the U.S. consumption of carrots and celery and of broccoli over a 6-yr period. The nutritionist modeled the results, in millions of pounds, with the following polynomials.

Carrots and celery: $-12x^3 + 106x^2 - 241x + 4477$

Broccoli: $14x^2 - 14x + 1545$

In each polynomial, $x = 0$ corresponds to the first year in the 6-yr period. What polynomial models the total number of pounds, in millions, of carrots, celery, and broccoli consumed during the 6-yr period?

Recall that subtraction means to add the opposite. So when you subtract a polynomial, change each of the terms to its opposite. Then add the coefficients.

Problem 5 Subtracting Polynomials

What is a simpler form of $(x^3 - 3x^2 + 5x) - (7x^3 + 5x^2 - 12)$?

Method 1 Subtract vertically.

Line up like terms.

$$x^3 - 3x^2 + 5x$$
$$- (7x^3 + 5x^2 \qquad - 12)$$

Then add the opposite of each term in the polynomial being subtracted.

$$x^3 - 3x^2 + 5x$$
$$-7x^3 - 5x^2 \qquad + 12$$
$$\overline{-6x^3 - 8x^2 + 5x + 12}$$

Method 2 Subtract horizontally.

Write the original expression.

$$(x^3 - 3x^2 + 5x) - (7x^3 + 5x^2 - 12)$$

Write the opposite of each term in the polynomial being subtracted.

$$= x^3 - 3x^2 + 5x - 7x^3 - 5x^2 + 12$$

Group like terms.

$$= (x^3 - 7x^3) + (-3x^2 - 5x^2) + 5x + 12$$

Simplify.

$$= -6x^3 - 8x^2 + 5x + 12$$

Got It? 5. What is a simpler form of $(-4m^3 - m + 9) - (4m^2 + m - 12)$?

Plan

How can Problem 4 help you solve this problem?
Change the subtraction to addition by adding the opposite. Then use the vertical or horizontal method from Problem 4 to add the polynomials.

Focus Question How are monomials and polynomials related?

Answer Polynomials are formed by adding and subtracting monomials. You can add and subtract two polynomials by combining like terms.

Lesson Check

Do you know HOW?

Find the degree of each monomial.

1. $-7x^4$ **2.** $8y^2z^3$

Simplify each sum or difference.

3. $(5r^3 + 8) + (6r^3 + 3)$

4. $(x^2 - 2) - (3x + 5)$

Do you UNDERSTAND?

Vocabulary Name each polynomial based on its degree and number of terms.

5. $5x^2 + 2x + 1$ **6.** $3z - 2$

7. Compare and Contrast How are the processes of adding monomials and adding polynomials alike? How are the processes different?

Practice and Problem-Solving Exercises

 Practice

Find the degree of each monomial.

 See Problem 1.

8. $8a^3$

9. $2b^8c^2$

10. $-7y^3z$

11. -3

12. $12w^4$

13. 0

Simplify.

See Problem 2.

14. $2m^3n^3 + 9m^3n^3$

15. $8w^2x + w^2x$

16. $3t^4 + 11t^4$

17. $30v^4w^3 - 12v^4w^3$

18. $7x^2 - 2x^2$

19. $5bc^4 - 13bc^4$

Write each polynomial in standard form. Then name each polynomial based on its degree and number of terms.

See Problem 3.

Guided Practice

To start, write terms in decreasing order of degree.

20. $5y - 2y^2$

$-2y^2 + 5y$

21. $-2q + 7$

22. $x^2 + 4 - 3x$

23. $c + 8c^3 - 3c^7$

24. $3z^4 - 5z - 2z^2$

Simplify.

See Problem 4.

Guided Practice

To start, line up like terms. Here, the w terms are lined up and the constants are lined up.

25. $\quad 4w - 5$

$\underline{+\ 9w + 2}$

26. $\quad 6x^2 + 7$

$\underline{+\ 3x^2 + 1}$

27. $\quad 2k^2 - \ k + 3$

$\underline{+\ 5k^2 + 3k - 7}$

28. $\left(5x^2 + 3\right) + \left(15x^2 + 2\right)$

29. $\left(2g^4 - 3g + 9\right) + \left(-g^3 + 12g\right)$

30. Education The number of students at East High School and the number of students at Central High School over a ten-year period can be modeled by the following polynomials.

    East High School: $-11x^2 + 133x + 1200$
    Central High School: $-7x^2 + 95x + 1100$

In each polynomial, $x = 0$ corresponds to the first year in the 10-year period. What polynomial models the total number of students at both high schools?

Simplify.

See Problem 5.

31. $\quad 5n - 2$

$\underline{-\left(3n + 8\right)}$

32. $\quad 6x^3 + 17$

$\underline{-\left(4x^3 + \ 9\right)}$

33. $\left(14h^4 + 3h^3\right) - \left(9h^4 + 2h^3\right)$

34. $\left(-6w^4 + w^2\right) - \left(-2w^3 + 4w^2 - w\right)$

35. Think About a Plan The perimeter of a triangular park is $16x + 3$. What is the missing length?

- What is the sum of the two given side lengths?
- What operation should you use to find the remaining side length?

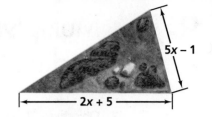

36. Geometry The perimeter of a trapezoid is $39a - 7$. Three sides have the following lengths: $9a$, $5a + 1$, and $17a - 6$. What is the length of the fourth side?

37. Error Analysis Describe and correct the error in finding the difference of the polynomials.

$$\overline{(4x^2 - x + 3)} - (3x^2 - 5x - 6) = 4x^2 - x + 3 - 3x^2 - 5x - 6$$
$$= 4x^2 - 3x^2 - x - 5x + 3 - 6$$
$$= x^2 - 6x - 3$$

38. Writing Is the sum of two trinomials always a trinomial? Explain.

39. Reasoning Is it possible to write a trinomial with degree 0? Explain.

Standardized Test Prep

40. What is a simpler form of $(3x^2 + 6x - 1) + (4x^2 + 5x + 9)$?

- Ⓐ $-x^2 + x - 10$
- Ⓑ $x^2 - x + 10$
- Ⓒ $7x^2 + 11x + 8$
- Ⓓ $7x^2 + 11x + 10$

41. The price of a gift basket of food can be modeled by a linear equation. You can use the graph at the right to find the price of the basket y, based on pounds of food x. What is the equation of the line?

- Ⓕ $y = 5x + 10$
- Ⓗ $y = 10x + 5$
- Ⓖ $y = x + 10$
- Ⓘ $y = 10x + 10$

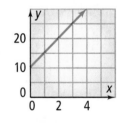

42. Simplify $(8x^3 - 5x + 1) - (x^2 + 4)$. Show your work.

Mixed Review

Find the slope of the line that passes through each pair of points.　　　　◀ **See Lesson 5-1.**

43. $(0, 2), (5, 0)$　　　　**44.** $(3, -7), (4, 1)$　　　　**45.** $(9, -6), (0, 0)$

Get Ready!　To prepare for Lesson 8-2, do Exercises 46–48.

Simplify each expression.　　　　◀ **See Lesson 7-3.**

46. $a^{-3}a^8$　　　　**47.** $(4x^5)(7x^3)$　　　　**48.** $(2t^4)(-5t^2)$

Multiplying and Factoring

Objectives To multiply a monomial by a polynomial
To factor a monomial from a polynomial

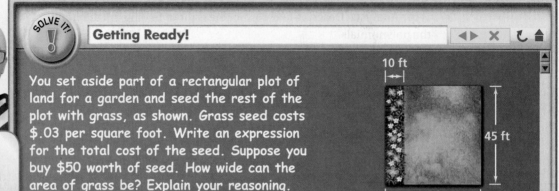

SOLVE IT!

Getting Ready!

You set aside part of a rectangular plot of land for a garden and seed the rest of the plot with grass, as shown. Grass seed costs $.03 per square foot. Write an expression for the total cost of the seed. Suppose you buy $50 worth of seed. How wide can the area of grass be? Explain your reasoning.

10 ft

45 ft

x ft

Remember the Distributive Property? It can help you here.

Focus Question How can you use the Distributive Property to multiply a monomial and a polynomial?

Consider the product $2x(3x + 1)$.

$$2x(3x + 1) = 2x(3x) + 2x(1)$$
$$= 6x^2 + 2x$$

You can show why the multiplication makes sense using the area model at the right.

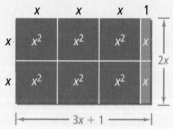

The Distributive Property was used to multiply the monomial by the polynomial.

Problem 1 **Multiplying a Monomial and a Trinomial**

Multiple Choice What is a simpler form of $-x^3(9x^4 - 2x^3 + 7)$?

Ⓐ $-9x^{12} + 2x^9 - 7x^3$

Ⓒ $-9x^7 - 2x^3 + 7$

Ⓑ $9x^7 - 2x^6 + 7x^3$

Ⓓ $-9x^7 + 2x^6 - 7x^3$

Plan

What should I keep in mind when multiplying?
Remember to distribute $-x^3$ to *all* of the terms. Also remember to add the exponents instead of multiplying them.

Use the Distributive Property. $-x^3(9x^4 - 2x^3 + 7) = -x^3(9x^4) - x^3(-2x^3) - x^3(7)$

Multiply coefficients and add exponents.

$$= -9x^{3+4} + 2x^{3+3} - 7x^3$$

Simplify.

$$= -9x^7 + 2x^6 - 7x^3$$

The correct answer is D.

 Got It? **1.** What is a simpler form of $5n(3n^3 - n^2 + 8)$?

Focus Question How do you factor a monomial from a polynomial?

Factoring a polynomial reverses the multiplication process. When factoring a monomial from a polynomial, the first step is to find the greatest common factor (GCF) of the polynomial's terms.

 Problem 2 **Finding the Greatest Common Factor**

What is the GCF of the terms of $5x^3 + 25x^2 + 45x$?

List the prime factors of each term. Identify the factors common to all terms.

$$5x^3 = 5 \cdot x \cdot x \cdot x$$

$$25x^2 = 5 \cdot 5 \cdot x \cdot x$$

$$45x = 3 \cdot 3 \cdot 5 \cdot x$$

> Remember to list only the prime factors of the variables.

The GCF is $5 \cdot x$, or $5x$.

 Got It? **2.** What is the GCF of the terms of $3x^4 - 9x^2 - 12x$?

Think

Why use the factors 5 and x to form the GCF, but not 3?

Both 5 and x are factors of *every* term of the polynomial, but 3 is only a factor of the last term.

Once you find the GCF of a polynomial's terms, you can factor it out of the polynomial.

 Problem 3 **Factoring Out a Monomial**

What is the factored form of $4x^5 - 24x^3 + 8x$?

Think

To factor the polynomial, first factor each term.

Find the GCF of the three terms.

Factor out the GCF from each term. Then factor it out of the polynomial.

Write

$$4x^5 = 2 \cdot 2 \cdot x \cdot x \cdot x \cdot x \cdot x$$

$$24x^3 = 2 \cdot 2 \cdot 2 \cdot 3 \cdot x \cdot x \cdot x$$

$$8x = 2 \cdot 2 \cdot 2 \cdot x$$

The GCF is $2 \cdot 2 \cdot x$, or $4x$.

$$4x^5 - 24x^3 + 8x = 4x(x^4) + 4x(-6x^2) + 4x(2)$$
$$= 4x(x^4 - 6x^2 + 2)$$

The factored form of the polynomial is $4x(x^4 - 6x^2 + 2)$.

Got It? **3. a.** What is the factored form of $9x^6 + 15x^4 + 12x^2$?

    b. Reasoning What is $-6x^4 - 18x^3 - 12x^2$ written as the product of a polynomial with positive coefficients and a monomial?

Problem 4 Factoring a Polynomial Model

How can you find the shaded region's area?
The shaded region is the entire square except for the circular portion. So, subtract the area of the circle from the area of the square.

Helipads A helicopter landing pad, or helipad, is sometimes marked with a circle inside a square so that it is visible from the air. What is the area of the shaded region of the helipad at the right? Write your answer in factored form.

Step 1 Find the area of the shaded region.

Use the formula for the area of a square.	$A_1 = s^2$
Substitute $2x$ for s.	$= (2x)^2$
Simplify.	$= 4x^2$
Use the formula for the area of a circle.	$A_2 = \pi r^2$
Substitute x for r.	$= \pi x^2$

The area of the shaded region is
$A_1 - A_2$, or $4x^2 - \pi x^2$.

Step 2 Factor the expression.

First find the GCF.

$4x^2 = 2 \cdot 2 \cdot x \cdot x$

$\pi x^2 = \pi \cdot x \cdot x$

The GCF is $x \cdot x$, or x^2.

Step 3 Factor out the GCF.

$4x^2 - \pi x^2 = x^2(4) + x^2(-\pi)$

$\qquad\qquad = x^2(4 - \pi)$

The factored form of the area of the shaded region is $x^2(4 - \pi)$.

2x

x

 Got It? **4.** In Problem 4, suppose the side length of the square is $6x$ and the radius of the circle is $3x$. What is the factored form of the area of the shaded region?

Focus Question How can you use the Distributive Property to multiply a monomial and a polynomial?

Answer You use the Distributive Property when you multiply each term of the polynomial by the monomial.

Focus Question How do you factor a monomial from a polynomial?

Answer Find the GCF of each term in the polynomial. Then factor out the GCF from each term of the polynomial.

Lesson Check

Do you know HOW?

1. What is a simpler form of $6x(2x^3 + 7x)$?

2. What is the GCF of the terms in $4a^4 + 6a^2$?

Factor each polynomial.

3. $6m^2 - 15m$

4. $4x^3 + 8x^2 + 12x$

Do you UNDERSTAND?

Match each pair of monomials with its GCF.

5. $14n^2, 35n^4$ **A.** 1

6. $21n^3, 18n^2$ **B.** $7n^2$

7. $7n^2, 9$ **C.** $3n^2$

8. Reasoning Write a binomial with $9x^2$ as the GCF of its terms.

Practice and Problem-Solving Exercises

Ⓐ Practice   **Simplify each product.**   ◀ See Problem 1.

Guided Practice

To start, use the Distributive Property.

9. $7x(x + 4)$
$$7x(x) + 7x(4)$$

10. $(b + 11)2b$ **11.** $3m^2(10 + m)$ **12.** $-w^2(w - 15)$

13. $4x(2x^3 - 7x^2 + x)$ **14.** $-8y^3(7y^2 - 4y - 1)$ **15.** $5b^2(6b + 7)$

Find the GCF of the terms of each polynomial.   ◀ See Problem 2.

16. $12x + 20$ **17.** $8w^2 - 18w$ **18.** $45b + 27$

19. $a^3 + 6a^2 - 11a$ **20.** $4x^3 + 12x - 28$ **21.** $14z^4 - 42z^3 + 21z^2$

Factor each polynomial.   ◀ See Problem 3.

Guided Practice

To start, factor each term.

22. $t^2 + 8t$
$$t^2 = t \cdot t$$
$$8t = 8 \cdot t$$

23. $9x - 6$ **24.** $14n^3 - 35n^2 + 28$ **25.** $5k^3 + 20k^2 - 15$

26. $14x^3 - 2x^2 + 8x$ **27.** $g^4 + 12g^2$ **28.** $24h^3 - 4h$

29. Art A circular mirror is surrounded by a square metal frame. The radius of the   ◀ See Problem 4.
mirror is $5x$. The side length of the metal frame is $15x$. What is the area of the metal
frame? Write your answer in factored form.

30. Design A circular table is painted yellow with a red square in the middle. The
radius of the tabletop is $6x$. The side length of the red square is $3x$. What is the
area of the yellow part of the tabletop? Write your answer in factored form.

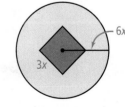

Ⓑ Apply   **Simplify. Write in standard form.**

31. $-2x(5x^2 - 4x + 13)$ **32.** $-5y^2(-3y^3 + 8y)$ **33.** $10a(-6a^2 + 2a - 7)$

34. $p(p + 2) - 3p(p - 5)$ **35.** $t^2(t + 1) - t(2t^2 - 1)$ **36.** $3c(4c^2 - 5) - c(9c)$

37. Think About a Plan A rectangular wooden frame has side lengths $5x$ and $7x + 1$. The rectangular opening for a picture has side lengths $3x$ and $5x$. What is the area of the wooden part of the frame? Write your answer in factored form.
- How can drawing a diagram help you solve the problem?
- How can you express the area of the wooden part of the frame as a difference of areas?

38. Error Analysis Describe and correct the error made in multiplying.

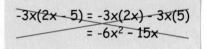

Factor each polynomial.

39. $17xy^4 + 51x^2y^3$

40. $9m^4n^5 - 27m^2n^3$

41. $31a^6b^3 + 63a^5$

42. Reasoning The GCF of two numbers p and q is 7. What is the GCF of p^2 and q^2? Justify your answer.

43. a. Factor $n^2 + n$.
 b. Writing Suppose n is an integer. Is $n^2 + n$ *always*, *sometimes*, or *never* an even integer? Justify your answer.

Standardized Test Prep

SAT/ACT

44. Simplify the product $4x(5x^2 + 3x + 7)$. What is the coefficient of the x^2-term?

45. What is the slope of the line that passes through $\overline{CD}$?

46. What is the solution of the equation $7x - 11 = 3$?

47. Simplify the product $8x^3(2x^2)$. What is the exponent?

48. The expression $9x^3 - 15x$ can be factored as $ax(3x^2 - 5)$. What is the value of a?

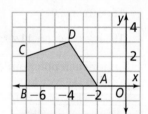

Mixed Review

Simplify each sum or difference.

See Lesson 8-1.

49. $(5x^2 + 4x - 2) + (3x^2 + 7)$

50. $(3x^3 - 2x) - (8x^3 + 4x)$

Solve each inequality for y. Then graph the inequality.

See Lesson 6-5.

51. $4x - 5y \geq 10$

52. $7x - 2y \leq 8$

53. $-3y - x > 9$

Get Ready! To prepare for Lesson 8-3, do Exercises 54–56.

Use the Distributive Property to simplify each expression.

See Lesson 1-7.

54. $8(x - 5)$

55. $-3(w + 4)$

56. $0.25(6c + 16)$

Using Models to Multiply

You can use algebra tiles to model the multiplication of two binomials.

Activity

Find the product $(x + 4)(2x + 3)$.

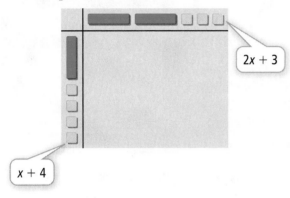

The product is $2x^2 + 11x + 12$.

$2x^2 + 3x + 8x + 12$

$2x^2 + 11x + 12$ Add coefficients of like terms.

You can also model products that involve subtraction. Red tiles indicate negative variables and negative numbers.

Activity

Find the product $(x - 1)(2x + 1)$.

The product is $2x^2 - x - 1$.

$2x^2 + x - 2x - 1$

$2x^2 - x - 1$ Add coefficients of like terms.

Exercises

Use algebra tiles to find each product.

1. $(x + 4)(x + 2)$ **2.** $(x + 2)(x - 3)$ **3.** $(x + 1)(3x - 2)$ **4.** $(3x + 2)(2x + 1)$

8-3
PART 1

Multiplying Binomials

Objective To multiply two binomials or a binomial by a trinomial

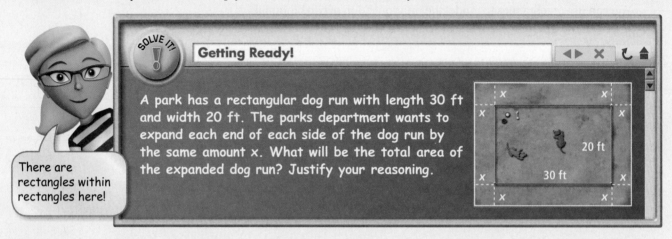

SOLVE IT!

Getting Ready!

A park has a rectangular dog run with length 30 ft and width 20 ft. The parks department wants to expand each end of each side of the dog run by the same amount x. What will be the total area of the expanded dog run? Justify your reasoning.

20 ft

30 ft

There are rectangles within rectangles here!

Dynamic Activity
Multiplying Binomials

Focus Question How is the Distributive Property used to multiply binomials?

One way to find the product of two binomials is to use an area model, as shown below.

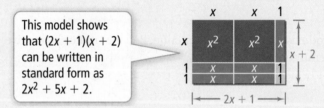

This model shows that $(2x + 1)(x + 2)$ can be written in standard form as $2x^2 + 5x + 2$.

You can also use the Distributive Property to find the product of two binomials.

Plan

How can you use the Distributive Property with two binomials?
Consider the second binomial as a single variable, and distribute it to each term of the first binomial.

Problem 1 Using the Distributive Property

What is a simpler form of $(2x + 4)(3x - 7)$?

Distribute the second factor, $3x - 7$. 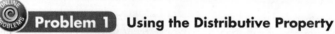 $(2x + 4)(3x - 7) = 2x(3x - 7) + 4(3x - 7)$

Distribute $2x$. $= 6x^2 - 14x + 4(3x - 7)$

Distribute 4. $= 6x^2 - 14x + 12x - 28$

Combine like terms. 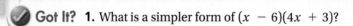 $= 6x^2 - 2x - 28$

Got It? **1.** What is a simpler form of $(x - 6)(4x + 3)$?

When you use the Distributive Property to multiply binomials, notice that you multiply each term of the first binomial by each term of the second binomial. A table can help you organize your work.

 Problem 2 Using a Table

What is a simpler form of $(x - 3)(4x - 5)$?

Know → Need → Plan

Know	Need	Plan
Binomial factors	Product of binomials written in standard form	Use a table.

Make a table of products.

Think

Is this the only table you can make?
No. You can write the terms of $x - 3$ in a row and the terms of $4x - 5$ in a column. You will get the same answer.

	$4x$	-5
x	$4x^2$	$-5x$
-3	$-12x$	15

When labeling the rows and columns, think of $x - 3$ as $x + (-3)$. Think of $4x - 5$ as $4x + (-5)$.

The product is $4x^2 - 5x - 12x + 15$, or $4x^2 - 17x + 15$.

 Got It? **2.** What is a simpler form of $(3x + 1)(x + 4)$? Use a table.

Focus Question How is the Distributive Property used to multiply binomials?

Answer Distribute one binomial to each term of the other binomial.

 Lesson Check

Do you know HOW?

Simplify each product.

1. $(x + 3)(x + 6)$

2. $(2x - 5)(x + 3)$

Do you UNDERSTAND?

3. Compare and Contrast The product $(x + 2)(x - 5)$ is similar to the product $(x - 2)(x + 5)$. Simplify the products and determine how the resulting trinomials are similar and how they are different.

Practice and Problem-Solving Exercises

 Simplify each product using the Distributive Property.

See Problem 1.

Guided Practice

To start, distribute the seond factor, $x + 4$.

4. $(x + 7)(x + 4)$

$x(x + 4) + 7(x + 4)$

5. $(y - 3)(y + 8)$

6. $(m + 6)(m - 7)$

7. $(c - 10)(c - 5)$

8. $(2r - 3)(r + 1)$

9. $(2x + 7)(3x - 4)$

10. $(p + 9)(2p - 1)$

Simplify each product using a table.

See Problem 2.

Guided Practice

To start, make a table of products.

11. $(x + 5)(x - 4)$

	x	-4
x	x^2	$-4x$
$+5$	$5x$	-20

12. $(a - 1)(a - 11)$

13. $(w - 2)(w + 6)$

14. $(2h - 7)(h + 9)$

15. $(3p + 4)(2p + 5)$

 Simplify each product. Write in standard form.

16. $(x^2 + 1)(x - 3)$

17. $(-n^2 - 1)(n + 3)$

18. $(b^2 - 1)(b^2 + 3)$

19. $(2m^2 + 1)(m + 5)$

20. $(c^2 - 4)(2c + 3)$

21. $(4z^2 + 1)(z + 3z^2)$

22. Error Analysis Describe and correct the error made in finding the product.

$$(x - 2)(3x + 4) = x(3x) + x(4) - 2(4)$$
$$= 3x^2 + 4x - 8$$

23. a. Simplify each pair of products.

    i. $(x + 1)(x + 1)$ **ii.** $(x + 1)(x + 2)$ **iii.** $(x + 1)(x + 3)$

       $11 \cdot 11$ $11 \cdot 12$ $11 \cdot 13$

   b. Reasoning What are the similarities between your two answers in each pair of products?

Multiplying Binomials

Objective   To multiply two binomials or a binomial by a trinomial

In Part 1, you learned how to multiply two binomials using an area model or the Distributive Property.

Connect to What You Know

Here you will learn how to multiply using the FOIL method and multiply a binomial by a trinomial.

Focus Question   How is multiplying a binomial and a trinomial similar to multiplying two binomials?

There is a shortcut you can use to multiply two binomials. Consider the product of $2x + 2$ and $x + 3$. The large rectangle below models this product. You can divide the large rectangle into four smaller rectangles.

The area of the large rectangle is the sum of the areas of the four smaller rectangles.

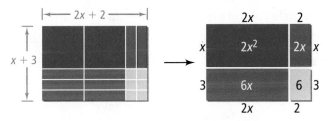

$$(2x + 2)(x + 3) = (2x)(x) + (2x)(3) + (2)(x) + (2)(3)$$
$$= 2x^2 + 6x + 2x + 6$$
$$= 2x^2 + 8x + 6$$

The area of each rectangle is the product of one term of $2x + 2$ and one term of $x + 3$.

This model illustrates another way to find the product of two binomials. You find the sum of the products of the First terms, the Outer terms, the Inner terms, and the Last terms of the binomials. The acronym FOIL may help you remember this method.

Problem 3 Using FOIL

What is a simpler form of $(5x - 3)(2x + 1)$?

	First	Outer	Inner	Last
$(5x - 3)(2x + 1) =$	$(5x)(2x)$ +	$(5x)(1)$ +	$(-3)(2x)$ +	$(-3)(1)$
	$= 10x^2$ +	$5x$ −	$6x$ −	3
	$= 10x^2$ −	x −	3	

The product is $10x^2 - x - 3$.

Got It? 3. What is a simpler form of each product? Use the FOIL method.

a. $(3x - 4)(x + 2)$ **b.** $(n - 6)(4n - 7)$ **c.** $(2p^2 + 3)(2p - 5)$

Problem 4 Applying Multiplication of Binomials

Multiple Choice A cylinder has the dimensions shown in the diagram. Which polynomial in standard form best describes the total surface area of the cylinder?

Ⓐ $2\pi x^2 + 4\pi x + 2\pi$ Ⓒ $4\pi x^2 + 14\pi x + 10\pi$

Ⓑ $2\pi x^2 + 10\pi x + 8\pi$ Ⓓ $2\pi x^2 + 2\pi x + 10\pi$

The total surface area S.A. of a cylinder is given by the formula
S.A. $= 2\pi r^2 + 2\pi rh$, where r is the radius of the cylinder and h is the height.

Use the formula for surface area of a cylinder.	S.A. $= 2\pi r^2 + 2\pi rh$
Substitute $x + 1$ for r and $x + 4$ for h.	$= 2\pi(x + 1)^2 + 2\pi(x + 1)(x + 4)$
Write $(x + 1)^2$ as $(x + 1)(x + 1)$.	$= 2\pi(x + 1)(x + 1) + 2\pi(x + 1)(x + 4)$
Multiply binomials.	$= 2\pi(x^2 + x + x + 1) + 2\pi(x^2 + 4x + x + 4)$
Combine like terms.	$= 2\pi(x^2 + 2x + 1) + 2\pi(x^2 + 5x + 4)$
Factor out 2π.	$= 2\pi(x^2 + 2x + 1 + x^2 + 5x + 4)$
Combine like terms.	$= 2\pi(2x^2 + 7x + 5)$
Write in standard form.	$= 4\pi x^2 + 14\pi x + 10\pi$

The correct answer is C.

 Got It? 4. What is the total surface area of a cylinder with radius $x + 2$ and height $x + 4$? Write your answer as a polynomial in standard form.

You can use the FOIL method when you multiply two binomials, but it is not helpful when multiplying a trinomial and a binomial. In this case, you can use a vertical method to distribute each term.

 Problem 5 **Multiplying a Trinomial and a Binomial**

What is a simpler form of $(3x^2 + x - 5)(2x - 7)$?

Multiply by arranging the polynomials vertically as shown.

Plan

How should you align the polynomials?
Write the polynomials so that like terms are vertically aligned.

$$3x^2 + x - 5$$
$$\underline{\hspace{3cm} 2x - 7}$$

Multiply the top expression by -7. $\quad -21x^2 - 7x + 35$

Multiply the top expression by $2x$. $\quad \underline{6x^3 + 2x^2 - 10x}$

Add like terms. $\quad 6x^3 - 19x^2 - 17x + 35$

The product is $6x^3 - 19x^2 - 17x + 35$.

 Got It? **5. a.** What is a simpler form of $(2x^2 - 3x + 1)(x - 3)$?
      b. Reasoning How can you use the Distributive Property to find the product of a trinomial and a binomial?

Focus Question How is multiplying a binomial and a trinomial similar to multiplying two binomials?

Answer Use the Distributive Property, a table, or FOIL to multiply two binomials. These methods help you to multiply each term of one binomial by each term of the other. Similarly, when you multiply a binomial and a trinomial, you must multiply each term of the binomial by each term of the trinomial.

 Lesson Check

Do you know HOW?

1. Simplify $(x + 2)(x^2 + 3x - 4)$.

2. A rectangle has length $x + 5$ and width $x - 3$. What is the area of the rectangle? Write your answer as a polynomial in standard form.

Do you UNDERSTAND?

3. **Compare and Contrast** Simplify $(3x + 8)(x + 1)$ using a table, the Distributive Property, and the FOIL method. Which method is most efficient? Explain.

4. **Writing** How is the degree of the product of two polynomials $p(x)$ and $q(x)$ related to the degrees of $p(x)$ and $q(x)$?

Practice and Problem-Solving Exercises

A Practice

Simplify each product using the FOIL method.

See Problem 3.

5. $(a + 8)(a - 2)$ **6.** $(x + 4)(4x - 5)$ **7.** $(k - 6)(k + 8)$

8. $(b - 3)(b - 9)$ **9.** $(5m - 2)(m + 3)$ **10.** $(9z + 4)(5z - 3)$

11. $(3h + 2)(6h - 5)$ **12.** $(4w + 13)(w + 2)$ **13.** $(8c - 1)(6c - 7)$

14. Design The radius of a cylindrical gift box is $(2x + 3)$ in. The height of the gift box is twice the radius. What is the surface area of the cylinder? Write your answer as a polynomial in standard form.

See Problem 4.

Guided Practice

To start, write the formula for surface area of a cylinder.	S.A. $= 2\pi r^2 + 2\pi rh$
Substitute $2x + 3$ for *r*.	S.A. $= 2\pi(2x + 3)^2 + 2\pi(2x + 3)h$
Since $h = 2r = 2(2x + 3)$, substitute $2(2x + 3)$ for *h*.	S.A. $= 2\pi(2x + 3)^2 + 2\pi(2x + 3)(2)(2x + 3)$

15. Geometry What is the total surface area of the cylinder below? Write your answer as a polynomial in standard form.

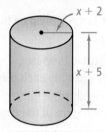

Simplify each product.

See Problem 5.

Guided Practice

16. $(x + 5)(x^2 - 3x + 1)$

To start, arrange the polynomials vertically.	$x^2 - 3x + 1$
	$x + 5$
Multiply the top expression by 5.	$5x^2 - 15x + 5$

17. $(k^2 - 4k + 3)(k - 2)$ **18.** $(2a^2 + 4a + 5)(5a - 4)$ **19.** $(2g + 7)(3g^2 - 5g + 2)$

20. Sports A school's rectangular athletic fields currently have a length of 125 yd and a width of 75 yd. The school plans to expand both the length and the width of the fields by *x* yards. What polynomial in standard form represents the area of the expanded athletic field?

B **Apply**

21. Open-Ended Write a binomial and a trinomial. Find their product.

22. Geometry The dimensions of a rectangular prism are n, $n + 7$, and $n + 8$. Use the formula $V = \ell wh$ to write a polynomial in standard form for the volume of the prism.

23. Think About a Plan You are planning a rectangular dining pavilion. Its length is three times its width x. You want a stone walkway that is 3 ft wide around the pavilion. You have enough stones to cover 396 ft^2 and want to use them all in the walkway. What should the dimensions of the pavilion be?
- Can you draw a diagram that represents this situation?
- How can you write a variable expression for the area of the walkway?

Standardized Test Prep

SAT/ACT

24. Which expression is equivalent to $(x + 4)(x - 9)$?

Ⓐ $x^2 + 5x - 36$　　　Ⓑ $x^2 - 5x - 36$　　　Ⓒ $x^2 - 13x - 36$　　　Ⓓ $x^2 - 13x - 5$

25. Malia is making a landscape drawing for her backyard. She is drawing a sidewalk. She uses the graph of the equation $y = 3x + 2$ to represent one edge of the sidewalk. She wants the other edge of the sidewalk to be parallel to the first edge through the point $(3, 4)$. The graph of which of the following lines represents the other edge of the sidewalk?

Ⓕ $y = x + 2$　　　Ⓖ $y = 4x + 2$　　　Ⓗ $y = 3x - 9$　　　Ⓘ $y = 3x - 5$

26. What is (are) the solution(s) of the equation $|x + 3| = 7$?

Ⓐ 4 and -10　　　Ⓑ 4 and -4　　　Ⓒ 4　　　Ⓓ 10

Extended Response

27. A trapezoid is determined by the following system of inequalities.

$y \geq 3$　　　　　$y \leq 9$　　　　　$x \leq 8$　　　　　$y \leq 2x + 3$

a. Graph the trapezoid in the coordinate plane.

b. The formula for the area A of a trapezoid is $A = \frac{1}{2}(b_1 + b_2)h$, where b_1 and b_2 are the bases of the trapezoid and h is its height. What is the area of the trapezoid you graphed in part (a)? Show your work.

Mixed Review

Factor each polynomial.　　　　　　　　　　　　　　◀ **See Lesson 8-2.**

28. $6x - 4$　　　　　　**29.** $b^2 + 8b$　　　　　　**30.** $10t^3 - 25t^2 + 20t$

Get Ready!　**To prepare for Lesson 8-4, do Exercises 31–34.**

Simplify each expression.　　　　　　　　　　　　　◀ **See Lesson 7-4.**

31. $(6x)^2$　　　　**32.** $(2y)^2$　　　　**33.** $(-3m)^2$　　　　**34.** $(-5n)^2$

8-4 Multiplying Special Cases

Objective To find the square of a binomial and to find the product of a sum and difference

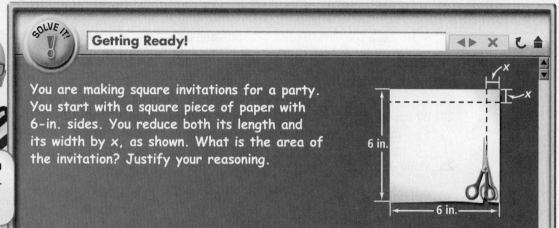

In Lesson 8-3 you expanded an area. Now you want to reduce an area.

SOLVE IT!

Getting Ready!

You are making square invitations for a party. You start with a square piece of paper with 6-in. sides. You reduce both its length and its width by x, as shown. What is the area of the invitation? Justify your reasoning.

6 in.

6 in.

Focus Question How do you simplify the square of a binomial?

Squares of binomials have the form $(a + b)^2$ or $(a - b)^2$. You can algebraically simplify the product or you can use an area model to discover the rule for simplifying $(a + b)^2$, as shown below.

Simplify the product.

Write the polynomial in expanded form. $(a + b)^2 = (a + b)(a + b)$

Multiply the binomials. $= a^2 + ab + ba + b^2$

Simplify. $= a^2 + 2ab + b^2$

Area Model

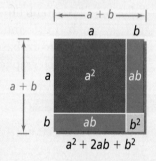

$$a^2 + 2ab + b^2$$

take note

Key Concept The Square of a Binomial

Words The square of a binomial is the square of the first term plus twice the product of the two terms plus the square of the last term.

Algebra

$(a + b)^2 = a^2 + 2ab + b^2$

$(a - b)^2 = a^2 - 2ab + b^2$

Examples

$(x + 4)^2 = x^2 + 8x + 16$

$(x - 3)^2 = x^2 - 6x + 9$

Problem 1 **Squaring a Binomial**

What is a simpler form of each product?

Plan

What rule can you use to simplify this product?
$(2m - 3)^2$ may not look like $(a - b)^2$, but it has the same form. Use the rule for $(a - b)^2$ and let $a = 2m$ and $b = 3$.

Ⓐ $(x + 8)^2$

Square the binomial. $(x + 8)^2 = x^2 + 2x(8) + 8^2$

Simplify. $= x^2 + 16x + 64$

Ⓑ $(2m - 3)^2$

Square the binomial. $(2m - 3)^2 = (2m)^2 - 2(2m)(3) + 3^2$

Simplify. $= 4m^2 - 12m + 9$

 Got It? **1.** What is a simpler form of each product?

         a. $(n - 7)^2$ **b.** $(2x + 9)^2$

 Problem 2 **Applying Squares of Binomials**

Plan

How do you find the area of the walkway?
The area of the walkway is the difference of the total area and the area of the patio.

Exterior Design A square outdoor patio is surrounded by a brick walkway as shown. What is the area of the walkway?

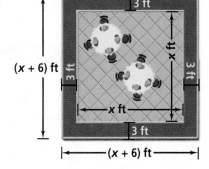

Step 1 Find the total area of the patio and walkway.

Square the binomial. $(x + 6)^2 = x^2 + 2(x)(6) + 6^2$

Simplify. $= x^2 + 12x + 36$

Step 2 Find the area of the patio.

The area of the patio is $x \cdot x$, or x^2.

Step 3 Find the area of the walkway.

  Area of walkway $=$ Total area $-$ Area of patio

Substitute. $= (x^2 + 12x + 36) - x^2$

Group like terms. $= (x^2 - x^2) + 12x + 36$

Simplify. $= 12x + 36$

The area of the walkway is $(12x + 36)$ ft^2.

 Got It? **2.** In Problem 2, suppose the brick walkway is 4 ft wide. What is its area?

Using mental math, you can square a binomial to find the square of a number.

 Problem 3 Using Mental Math

Think

What number close to 39 can you square mentally?
The nearest multiple of 10 to 39 is 40, which is a number you should be able to square mentally.

What is 39^2? Use mental math.

Write 39^2 as the square of a binomial.	$39^2 = (40 - 1)^2$
Square the binomial.	$= 40^2 - 2(40)(1) + 1^2$
Simplify.	$= 1600 - 80 + 1$
Simplify.	$= 1521$

 Got It? 3. What is 85^2? Use mental math.

Focus Question How do you simplify the product of a sum and difference?

The product of the sum and difference of the same two terms also produces a pattern.

$$(a + b)(a - b) = a^2 - ab + ba - b^2$$

> Notice that the sum of $-ab$ and ba is 0, leaving $a^2 - b^2$.

$$= a^2 - b^2$$

take note

Key Concept The Product of a Sum and Difference

Words The product of the sum and difference of the same two terms is the difference of their squares.

Algebra	**Examples**
$(a + b)(a - b) = a^2 - b^2$	$(x + 2)(x - 2) = x^2 - 2^2 = x^2 - 4$

 Problem 4 Finding the Product of a Sum and Difference

What is a simpler form of $(x^3 + 8)(x^3 - 8)$?

Plan

How do you choose which rule to use?
The first factor in the product is the sum of x^3 and 8. The second factor is the difference of x^3 and 8. So, use the rule for the product of a sum and difference.

Think	**Write**
Write the original product.	$(x^3 + 8)(x^3 - 8)$
Identify which terms correspond to a and b in the rule for the product of a sum and difference.	$a = x^3;\ b = 8$
Substitute for a and b in the rule.	$(x^3 + 8)(x^3 - 8) = (x^3)^2 - (8)^2$
Simplify.	$= x^6 - 64$

Got It? **4.** What is a simpler form of each product?

   a. $(x + 9)(x - 9)$ **b.** $(6 + m^2)(6 - m^2)$ **c.** $(3c - 4)(3c + 4)$

You can use the rule for the product of a sum and difference to calculate products using mental math.

Think

How can you write 64 · 56 as the product of a sum and difference?
Find the number halfway between the factors. 60 is 4 units from each factor. Write the factors in terms of 60 and 4.

 Problem 5 **Using Mental Math**

What is 64 · 56?

Write as a product of a sum and a difference.	$64 \cdot 56 = (60 + 4)(60 - 4)$
Use $(a + b)(a - b) = a^2 - b^2$.	$= 60^2 - 4^2$
Simplify powers.	$= 3600 - 16$
Simplify.	$= 3584$

GRIDDED RESPONSE

 Got It? **5.** What is 52 · 48? Use mental math.

Focus Question How do you simplify the square of a binomial?

Answer The square of a binomial is the square of the first term plus twice the product of the two terms plus the square of the last term.

Focus Question How do you simplify the product of a sum and difference?

Answer The product of a sum and difference of the same two terms is the difference of their squares.

 ## Lesson Check

Do you know HOW?

Simplify each product.

1. $(c + 3)(c + 3)$

2. $(g - 4)^2$

3. $(2r - 3)(2r + 3)$

4. A square has side length $(2x + 3)$ in. What is the area of the square?

Do you UNDERSTAND?

What rule would you use to find each product? Why?

5. $(3x - 1)^2$

6. $(4x - 9)(4x + 9)$

7. $(7x + 2)(7x + 2)$

8. **Reasoning** How do you know whether it is convenient to use the rule for the product of a sum and difference to mentally multiply two numbers?

 ## Practice and Problem-Solving Exercises

A Practice   Simplify each expression.   ◀ See Problem 1.

9. $(w + 5)^2$ **10.** $(3s + 9)^2$ **11.** $(2n + 7)^2$

12. $(a - 8)^2$ **13.** $(k - 11)^2$ **14.** $(4x - 6)^2$

Geometry The figures below are squares. Find an expression for the area of each shaded region. Write your answers in standard form.

See Problem 2.

15.

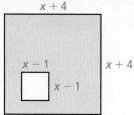

16.

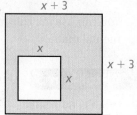

17. Interior Design A square green rug has a blue square in the center. The side length of the blue square is x inches. The width of the green band that surrounds the blue square is 6 in. What is the area of the green band?

Mental Math Simplify each product.

See Problem 3.

Guided Practice

To start, write 61^2 as the square of a binomial.

18. 61^2

$61^2 = (60 + 1)^2$

19. 79^2 **20.** 48^2 **21.** 403^2

Simplify each product.

See Problem 4.

22. $(v + 6)(v - 6)$ **23.** $(b + 1)(b - 1)$ **24.** $(z - 5)(z + 5)$

25. $(x - 3)(x + 3)$ **26.** $(10 + y)(10 - y)$ **27.** $(t - 13)(t + 13)$

Mental Math Simplify each product.

See Problem 5.

Guided Practice

To start, write $42 \cdot 38$ as a product of a sum and a difference.

28. $42 \cdot 38$

$42 \cdot 38 = (40 + 2)(40 - 2)$

29. $79 \cdot 81$ **30.** $63 \cdot 57$ **31.** $399 \cdot 401$

 Apply   **Simplify each product.**

32. $(m + 3n)^2$ **33.** $(2a + b)^2$ **34.** $(4s - t)^2$

35. $(g - 7h)^2$ **36.** $(9k + 2q)^2$ **37.** $(8r - 5s)^2$

38. $(r^2 + 3s)(r^2 - 3s)$ **39.** $(2p^2 + 7q)(2p^2 - 7q)$ **40.** $(3w^3 - z^2)(3w^3 + z^2)$

41. Error Analysis Describe and correct the error made in simplifying the product.

$$(3a - 7)^2 = 9a^2 - 21a + 49$$

42. **Think About a Plan** A company logo is a white square inside a red square. The side length of the white square is $x + 2$. The side length of the red square is three times the side length of the white square. What is the area of the red part of the logo? Write your answer in standard form.
   - How can drawing a diagram help you solve the problem?
   - How can you express the area of the red part of the logo as a difference of areas?

43. **Construction** A square deck has a side length of $x + 5$. You are expanding the deck so that each side is four times as long as the side length of the original deck. What is the area of the new deck? Write your answer in standard form.

Standardized Test Prep

SAT/ACT

44. What is a simpler form of $(2x + 5)(2x - 5)$?

   Ⓐ $4x^2 - 20x - 25$ Ⓑ $4x^2 + 20x + 25$ Ⓒ $4x^2 - 25$ Ⓓ $2x^2 - 5$

45. Sara and Nick sold tickets to a play. Sara sold 20 student tickets and 3 adult tickets for more than \$60. Nick sold 15 student tickets and 5 adult tickets for less than \$75. This information can be represented by $20x + 3y > 60$ and $15x + 5y < 75$, where x is the price of a student ticket and y is the price of an adult ticket. The inequalities are graphed at the right. Which could be the price of a student ticket?

Ticket Sales

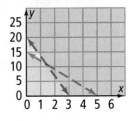

   Ⓕ \$1   Ⓗ \$5.50

   Ⓖ \$2.75   Ⓘ \$6

Short Response

46. Graph the solutions of the system. $5x + 4y \geq 20$
                                             $5x + 4y \leq 20$

Mixed Review

Simplify each product.   ◀ **See Lesson 8-3.**

47. $(3x + 2)(2x - 5)$ 48. $(4m - 1)(6m - 7)$ 49. $(x + 9)(5x + 8)$

Find each percent change. Describe the percent change as an *increase* or   ◀ **See Lesson 2-10.**
decrease. If necessary, round to the nearest tenth.

50. 4 ft to 5 ft   51. 12 lb to 15 lb   52. \$40 to \$35

Get Ready!   **To prepare for Lesson 8-5, do Exercises 53–55.**

Factor each polynomial.   ◀ **See Lesson 8-2.**

53. $12x^4 + 30x^3 + 42x$ 54. $72x^3 + 54x^2 + 27$ 55. $35x^3 + 7x^2 + 63x$

8 Chapter Review for Part A

Chapter Vocabulary

- binomial (p. 503)
- degree of a monomial (p. 502)
- degree of a polynomial (p. 503)
- monomial (p. 502)
- polynomial (p. 503)
- standard form of a polynomial (p. 503)
- trinomial (p. 503)

Choose the correct term to complete each sentence.

1. A polynomial that has two terms is a(n) __?__ .

2. A monomial or the sum of two or more monomials is a(n) __?__ .

3. A(n) __?__ is an expression that is a number, a variable, or a product of a number and one or more variables.

4. The sum of the exponents of the variables in a monomial is the __?__ .

8-1 Adding and Subtracting Polynomials

Quick Review

A **monomial** is a number, a variable, or a product of a number and one or more variables. A **polynomial** is a monomial or the sum of two or more monomials. The **degree of a polynomial** in one variable is the same as the degree of the monomial with the greatest exponent. To add two polynomials, add the like terms of the polynomials. To subtract a polynomial, add the opposite of the polynomial.

Example

What is the difference of $3x^3 - 7x^2 + 5$ and $2x^2 - 9x - 1$?

$$(3x^3 - 7x^2 + 5) - (2x^2 - 9x - 1)$$
$$= 3x^3 - 7x^2 + 5 - 2x^2 + 9x + 1$$
$$= 3x^3 + (-7x^2 - 2x^2) + 9x + (1 + 5)$$
$$= 3x^3 - 9x^2 + 9x + 6$$

Exercises

Write each polynomial in standard form. Then name each polynomial based on its degree and number of terms.

5. $4r + 3 - 9r^2 + 7r$

6. $3 + b^3 + b^2$

7. $3 + 8t^2$

8. $n^3 + 4n^5 + n - n^3$

9. $7x^2 + 8 + 6x - 7x^2$

10. p^3q^3

Simplify. Write each answer in standard form.

11. $(2v^3 - v + 8) + (-v^3 + v - 3)$

12. $(6s^4 + 7s^2 + 7) + (8s^4 - 11s^2 + 9s)$

13. $(4h^3 + 3h + 1) - (-5h^3 + 6h - 2)$

14. $(8z^3 - 3z^2 - 7) - (z^3 - z^2 + 9)$

8-2 Multiplying and Factoring

Quick Review

You can multiply a monomial and a polynomial using the Distributive Property. You can factor a polynomial by finding the greatest common factor (GCF) of the terms of the polynomial.

Example

What is the factored form of $10y^4 - 12y^3 + 4y^2$?

First find the GCF of the terms of the polynomial.

$10y^4 = 2 \cdot 5 \cdot y \cdot y \cdot y \cdot y$

$12y^3 = 2 \cdot 2 \cdot 3 \cdot y \cdot y \cdot y$

$4y^2 = 2 \cdot 2 \cdot y \cdot y$

The GCF is $2 \cdot y \cdot y$ or $2y^2$.

Then factor out the GCF.

$10y^4 - 12y^3 + 4y^2 = 2y^2(5y^2) + 2y^2(-6y) + 2y^2(2)$

$= 2y^2(5y^2 - 6y + 2)$

Exercises

Simplify each product. Write in standard form.

15. $5k(3 - 4k)$ **16.** $4m(2m + 9m^2 - 6)$

17. $6g^2(g - 8)$ **18.** $3d(6d + d^2)$

19. $-2n^2(5n - 9 + 4n^2)$ **20.** $q(11 + 8q - 2q^2)$

Find the GCF of the terms of each polynomial. Then factor the polynomial.

21. $12p^4 + 16p^3 + 8p$ **22.** $3b^4 - 9b^2 + 6b$

23. $45c^5 - 63c^3 + 27c$ **24.** $4g^2 + 8g$

25. $3t^4 - 6t^3 - 9t + 12$ **26.** $30h^5 - 6h^4 - 15h^3$

27. Reasoning The GCF of two numbers p and q is 5. Can you find the GCF of $6p$ and $6q$? Explain your answer.

8-3 and 8-4 Multiplying Binomials

Quick Review

You can use algebra tiles, tables, or the Distributive Property to multiply polynomials. The FOIL method (First, Outer, Inner, Last) can be used to multiply two binomials. You can also use rules to multiply special case binomials.

Example

What is the simplified form of $(4x + 3)(3x + 2)$?

Use FOIL to multiply the binomials. Find the product of the first terms, the outer terms, the inner terms, and the last terms. Then add.

$(4x + 3)(3x + 2) = (4x)(3x) + (4x)(2) + (3)(3x) + (3)(2)$

$= 12x^2 + 8x + 9x + 6$

$= 12x^2 + 17x + 6$

Exercises

Simplify each product. Write in standard form.

28. $(w + 1)(w + 12)$ **29.** $(2s - 3)(5s + 4)$

30. $(3r - 2)^2$ **31.** $(6g + 7)(g - 8)$

32. $(7q + 2)(3q + 8)$ **33.** $(4n^3 + 5)(3n + 5)$

34. $(t + 9)(t - 3)$ **35.** $(6c + 5)^2$

36. $(7h - 3)(7h + 3)$ **37.** $(y - 6)(3y + 7)$

38. $(4a - 7)(8a + 3)$ **39.** $(4b - 3)(4b + 3)$

40. Geometry A rectangle has dimensions $3x + 5$ and $x + 7$. Write an expression for the area of the rectangle as a product and as a polynomial in standard form.

Do you know HOW?

Find the degree of each monomial.

1. $-5a^8$

2. $4x^2y^3$

Write each polynomial in standard form. Then name each polynomial based on its degree and number of terms.

3. $4x + 3x^2$

4. $7p^2 - 3p + 2p^3$

Simplify each sum or difference.

5. $(x^2 + 6x + 11) + (3x^2 + 7x + 4)$

6. $(5w^3 + 3w^2 + 8w + 2) + (7w^2 + 3w + 1)$

7. $(4q^2 + 10q + 7) - (2q^2 + 7q + 5)$

8. $(9t^4 + 5t + 8) - (3t^2 - 6t - 4)$

Simplify each product.

9. $6x^2(4x^2 + 3)$

10. $-8c^3(3c^2 + 2c - 9)$

Factor each polynomial.

11. $16b^4 + 8b^2 + 20b$

12. $77x^3 + 22x^2 - 33x - 88$

Simplify each product.

13. $(x + 2)(x + 9)$

14. $(4b - 1)(b - 8)$

15. $(h + 2)(3h^2 + h - 7)$

16. $(z - 1)(z^2 - 4z + 9)$

17. **Design** You are designing a rectangular rubber stamp. The length of the stamp is $2r + 3$. The width of the stamp is $r - 4$. What polynomial in standard form represents the area of the stamp?

Simplify each product.

18. $(r + 3)^2$

19. $(k - 3)(k + 3)$

20. $(3d + 10)^2$

21. $(g + 10)(g - 10)$

22. $(2m - 7)^2$

23. $(7h - 2)(7h + 2)$

24. **Woodworking** A birdhouse has a square base with side length $3x - 4$. What polynomial in standard form represents the area of the base?

Do you UNDERSTAND?

25. **Writing** Can the degree of a monomial ever be negative? Explain.

26. **Geometry** The figures below are rectangles. What polynomial in standard form represents the area of the shaded region?

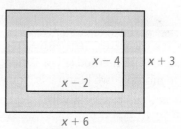

27. **Open-Ended** Write a trinomial that has $9x^2$ as the GCF of its terms.

28. **Open-Ended** Write a trinomial of degree 4 such that the GCF of its terms is 1.

29. **Reasoning** Suppose n represents an even number. Write a simplified expression that represents the product of the next two even numbers.

30. **Writing** Describe how to simplify $(8k^2 + k - 1) - (k^3 - 4k^2 - 7k + 15)$. Write your answer as a polynomial in standard form.

Polynomials and Factoring

In Part A, you learned how to add, subtract, and multiply polynomials. Now you will learn how to factor polynomials.

Vocabulary for Part B

English/Spanish Vocabulary Audio Online:

English	Spanish
difference of two squares, *p. 547*	diferencia de dos cuadrados
factoring by grouping, *p. 551*	factor común por agrupación de términos
perfect-square trinomial, *p. 545*	trinomio cuadrado perfecto

BIG ideas

1 Equivalence
Essential Question Can two algebraic expressions that appear to be different be equivalent?

2 Properties
Essential Question How are the properties of real numbers related to polynomials?

Chapter Preview for Part B

Concept Byte

Use With Lesson 8-5

ACTIVITY

Using Models to Factor

You can sometimes write a trinomial as the product of two binomial factors. You can use algebra tiles to find the factors by arranging all of the tiles to form a rectangle. The lengths of the sides of the rectangle are the factors of the trinomial.

Activity

Write $x^2 + 7x + 12$ as the product of two binomial factors.

Model of polynomial

Use the tiles to form a rectangle.

First try:

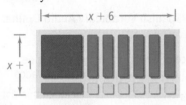

There are six ☐ tiles left over.

Second try:

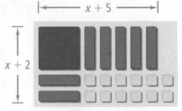

There is one ▮ tile too few.

Third try:

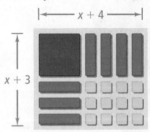

Correct! There is the exact number of tiles needed.

$x^2 + 7x + 12 = (x + 3)(x + 4)$

Exercises

Use algebra tiles to find binomial factors of each trinomial.

1. $x^2 + 4x + 4$ **2.** $x^2 + 5x + 6$ **3.** $x^2 + 10x + 9$

4. $x^2 + 7x + 10$ **5.** $x^2 + 9x + 14$ **6.** $x^2 + 8x + 16$

7. Reasoning Explain why you cannot use algebra tiles to represent the trinomial $x^2 + 2x + 3$ as a rectangle.

Factoring $x^2 + bx + c$

Objective To factor trinomials of the form $x^2 + bx + c$

Getting Ready!

The area of the rectangular solar panel is given by the trinomial $x^2 + 7x + 12$. The height of the solar panel is $x + 3$. What is an expression for the length of the panel? Explain your reasoning.

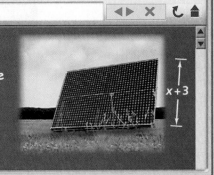

$x + 3$

You can use what you know about factors to help you solve this problem.

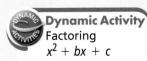

Dynamic Activity
Factoring
$x^2 + bx + c$

Focus Question How do you factor trinomials of the form $x^2 + bx + c$?

To understand how to write a trinomial as a product of two binomials, consider the product of binomials below.

$$(x + 3)(x + 7) = x^2 + (7 + 3)x + 3 \cdot 7 = x^2 + 10x + 21$$

The coefficient of the trinomial's x^2-term is 1. The coefficient of the trinomial's x-term, 10, is the *sum* of the numbers 3 and 7 in the binomials. The trinomial's constant term, 21, is the *product* of the same numbers, 3 and 7. To factor a trinomial of the form $x^2 + bx + c$ as the product of binomials, you must find two numbers that have a sum of b and a product of c.

Plan

What is an easy way to organize your factoring?
Use a table to list the pairs of factors of the constant term c and the sums of those pairs of factors.

Problem 1 Factoring $x^2 + bx + c$ Where $b > 0$, $c > 0$

What is the factored form of $x^2 + 8x + 15$?

List the pairs of factors of 15. Identify the pair that has a sum of 8.

Factors of 15	Sum of Factors
1 and 15	16
3 and 5	8 ✔

$x^2 + 8x + 15 = (x + 3)(x + 5)$

Check $(x + 3)(x + 5) = x^2 + 5x + 3x + 15$

$= x^2 + 8x + 15$ ✔

Got It? **1.** What is the factored form of $r^2 + 11r + 24$?

Some factorable trinomials have a negative coefficient of x and a positive constant term. In this case, you need to inspect the negative factors of c to find the factors of the trinomial.

 Problem 2 Factoring $x^2 + bx + c$ Where $b < 0$, $c > 0$

What is the factored form of $x^2 - 11x + 24$?

List the pairs of negative factors of 24. Identify the pair that has a sum of -11.

Factors of 24	Sum of Factors
-1 and -24	-25
-2 and -12	-14
-3 and -8	-11 ✔
-4 and -6	-10

$x^2 - 11x + 24 = (x - 3)(x - 8)$

Check $(x - 3)(x - 8) = x^2 - 8x - 3x + 24$
$= x^2 - 11x + 24$ ✔

Think

Why look at pairs of *negative* factors of 24?
You want the factors of 24 with a sum of -11. Only two negative numbers have a positive product *and* a negative sum.

Hint

Find two numbers that have a product of $+8$ and a sum of -6.

Got It? **2. a.** What is the factored form of $y^2 - 6y + 8$?
     b. Reasoning Can you factor $x^2 - x + 2$? Explain.

When you factor trinomials with a negative constant term, you need to inspect pairs of positive and negative factors of c.

 Problem 3 Factoring $x^2 + bx + c$ Where $c < 0$

What is the factored form of $x^2 + 2x - 15$?

Identify the pair of factors of -15 that has a sum of 2.

Factors of -15	Sum of Factors
1 and -15	-14
-1 and 15	14
3 and -5	-2
-3 and 5	2 ✔

$x^2 + 2x - 15 = (x - 3)(x + 5)$

Think

What's another way to do this problem?
Find two positive factors of 15 that *differ* by 2. The factors are 3 and 5. Then attach a negative sign to one of the factors so that their sum is positive. You get -3 and 5.

Got It? **3.** What is the factored form of each polynomial?
     a. $n^2 + 9n - 36$ **b.** $c^2 - 4c - 21$

Geometry The area of a rectangle is given by the trinomial $x^2 - 2x - 35$. What are the possible dimensions of the rectangle? Use factoring.

Know	Need	Plan
The area of the rectangle	Possible dimensions of the rectangle	Area = length × width, so factor the trinomial for area as the product of binomials that represent the length and width.

To factor $x^2 - 2x - 35$, identify the pair of factors of -35 that has a sum of -2.

Factors of −35	Sum of Factors
1 and −35	−34
−1 and 35	34
5 and −7	−2 ✔
−5 and 7	2

$x^2 - 2x - 35 = (x + 5)(x - 7)$

So the possible dimensions of the rectangle are $x + 5$ and $x - 7$.

 Got It? **4.** A rectangle's area is $x^2 - x - 72$. What are possible dimensions of the rectangle? Use factoring.

Focus Question How do you factor trinomials of the form $x^2 + bx + c$?

Answer To factor trinomials of the form $x^2 + bx + c$, list the pairs of factors of c. Then identify the pair of factors that has a sum of b.

 ## Lesson Check

Do you know HOW?

Factor each expression. Check your answer.

1. $x^2 + 7x + 12$

2. $r^2 - 13r + 42$

3. $p^2 + 3p - 40$

4. $m^2 + 12m + 32$

5. The area of a rectangle is given by the trinomial $n^2 - 3n - 28$. What are the possible dimensions of the rectangle? Use factoring.

Do you UNDERSTAND?

Tell whether the sum of the factors of the constant term should be *positive* or *negative* when you factor the trinomial.

6. $s^2 + s - 30$

7. $w^2 + 11w + 18$

8. $x^2 - x - 20$

9. **Reasoning** Under what circumstances should you look at pairs of negative factors of the constant term when factoring a trinomial of the form $x^2 + bx + c$?

Practice and Problem-Solving Exercises

A **Practice**

Complete.

⬤ See Problems 1 and 2.

10. $k^2 + 5k + 6 = (k + 2)(k + \blacksquare)$

11. $x^2 - 7x + 10 = (x - 5)(x - \blacksquare)$

12. $t^2 - 10t + 24 = (t - 4)(t - \blacksquare)$

13. $v^2 + 12v + 20 = (v + 10)(v + \blacksquare)$

Factor each expression. Check your answer.

Guided Practice

To start, list the factor pairs of 16 and their sums.

14. $t^2 + 10t + 16$

Factors of 16	Sum of Factors
1 and 16	17
2 and 8	10
4 and 4	8

15. $y^2 + 6y + 5$

16. $x^2 + 15x + 56$

17. $n^2 - 15n + 56$

18. $q^2 - 8q + 12$

Complete.

⬤ See Problem 3.

19. $q^2 + 3q - 54 = (q - 6)(q + \blacksquare)$

20. $z^2 - 2z - 48 = (z - 8)(z + \blacksquare)$

21. $n^2 - 5n - 50 = (n + 5)(n - \blacksquare)$

22. $y^2 + 8y - 9 = (y + 9)(y - \blacksquare)$

Factor each expression. Check your answer.

Guided Practice

To start, list the factor pairs of −8 and their sums.

23. $w^2 - 7w - 8$

Factors of −8	Sum of Factors
1 and −8	−7
−1 and 8	7
2 and −4	−2
−2 and 4	2

24. $r^2 + 6r - 27$

25. $z^2 + 2z - 8$

26. $v^2 + 5v - 36$

27. $n^2 - 3n - 10$

28. Carpentry The area of a rectangular desk is given by the trinomial $d^2 - 7d - 18$. ⬤ See Problem 4. What are the possible dimensions of the desk? Use factoring.

29. Design The area of a rectangular rug is given by the trinomial $r^2 - 3r - 4$. What are the possible dimensions of the rug? Use factoring.

30. Writing Suppose you can factor $x^2 + bx + c$ as $(x + p)(x + q)$.
 a. Explain what you know about p and q when $c > 0$.
 b. Explain what you know about p and q when $c < 0$.

31. Error Analysis Describe and correct the error made in factoring the trinomial.

$$x^2 - 10x - 24 = (x - 6)(x - 4)$$

32. Think About a Plan The area of a parallelogram is given by the trinomial $x^2 - 14x + 24$. The base of the parallelogram is $x - 2$. What is an expression for the height of the parallelogram?
 • What is the formula for the area of a parallelogram?
 • How can you tell whether the binomial that represents the height has a positive or negative constant term?

33. Recreation A rectangular skateboard park has an area of $x^2 + 15x + 54$. What are the possible dimensions of the park? Use factoring.

34. Your classmate is factoring $x^2 - 3x - 10$ and makes the following table. Describe your classmate's error.

Factors of -10	Sum of Factors
1 and -10	-9
-10 and 1	-9
2 and -5	-3
-5 and 2	-3

Write the standard form of each polynomial modeled below. Then factor each expression.

35.

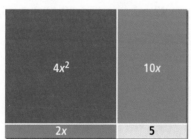

36.

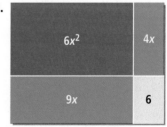

SAT/ACT

37. What is the factored form of $x^2 + x - 42$?

   Ⓐ $(x - 7)(x - 6)$ Ⓑ $(x - 7)(x + 6)$ Ⓒ $(x + 7)(x - 6)$ Ⓓ $(x + 7)(x + 6)$

38. What is the solution of the equation $6x + 7 = 25$?

   Ⓕ 2   Ⓖ 3   Ⓗ $5\frac{1}{3}$ Ⓘ 8

39. A museum charges an admission price of $12 per person when you buy tickets online. There is also a $5 charge per order. You spend $65 purchasing p tickets online. Which equation best represents this situation?

   Ⓐ $12p + 5 = 65$ Ⓑ $5p + 12 = 65$ Ⓒ $12p - 5 = 65$ Ⓓ $65p + 12 = 5$

Short Response

40. You and your friend bike to school at the rates shown. Who is faster? Show your work.

You: 7 mi/h   Your friend: 11 ft/s

Mixed Review

Simplify each product.   ◀ See Lesson 8-4.

41. $(c + 4)^2$ **42.** $(2v - 9)^2$ **43.** $(3w + 7)(3w - 7)$

Solve each equation for x.   ◀ See Lesson 2-5.

44. $\frac{a}{b} = \frac{x}{d}$ **45.** $8(x - d) = x$ **46.** $m = \frac{(c + x)}{n}$

Get Ready!   **To prepare for Lesson 8-6, do Exercises 47–49.**

Find the GCF of the terms of each polynomial.   ◀ See Lesson 8-2.

47. $14x^2 + 7x$ **48.** $24x^2 - 30x + 12$ **49.** $6x^3 + 45x^2 + 15$

8-6 Factoring $ax^2 + bx + c$

Objective To factor trinomials of the form $ax^2 + bx + c$

You did this for one panel in Lesson 8-5—now there are more.

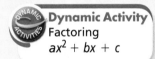

Dynamic Activity
Factoring
$ax^2 + bx + c$

Focus Question How do you factor trinomials of the form $ax^2 + bx + c$?

You can write some trinomials of the form $ax^2 + bx + c$ as the product of two binomials.

Consider the trinomial $6x^2 + 23x + 7$. To factor it, think of $23x$ as $2x + 21x$.

Rewrite $23x$ as $2x + 21x$.	$6x^2 + 23x + 7 = 6x^2 + 2x + 21x + 7$
Factor out the GCF of each pair of terms.	$= 2x(3x + 1) + 7(3x + 1)$
Use the Distributive Property.	$= (2x + 7)(3x + 1)$

To factor a trinomial of the form $ax^2 + bx + c$, you should look for factors of the product ac that have a sum of b.

Problem 1 Factoring When *ac* Is Positive

What is the factored form of $5x^2 + 11x + 2$?

Step 1 Find factors of ac that have sum b.
Since $ac = 10$ and $b = 11$, find positive factors of 10 that have sum 11.

Factors of 10	1, 10	2, 5
Sum of Factors	11 ✔	7

Step 2 To factor the trinomial, use the factors you found to rewrite bx.

Rewrite bx: $11x = 1x + 10x$.	$5x^2 + 11x + 2 = 5x^2 + 1x + 10x + 2$
Factor out the GCF of each pair of terms.	$= x(5x + 1) + 2(5x + 1)$
Use the Distributive Property.	$= (x + 2)(5x + 1)$

Think

Will the process still work if you write $5x^2 + 10x + x + 2$?
Yes. You can rewrite this alternate expression as $5x(x + 2) + (x + 2)$, which equals $(5x + 1)(x + 2)$.

Got It? **1. a.** What is the factored form of $3x^2 + 5x + 2$?

             b. What is the factored form of $6x^2 + 13x + 5$?

 Problem 2   **Factoring When ac Is Negative**

Plan

Can you apply the steps for Problem 1 to this problem?
Yes. Your goal is still to find factors of ac that have sum b. Because $ac < 0$, the factors must have different signs.

What is the factored form of $3x^2 + 4x - 15$?

Step 1   Find factors of ac that have sum b. Since $ac = -45$ and $b = 4$, find factors of -45 that have sum 4.

Factors of -45	1, -45	-1, 45	3, -15	-3, 15	5, -9	-5, 9
Sum of Factors	-44	44	-12	12	-4	4 ✔

Step 2   To factor the trinomial, use the factors you found to rewrite bx.

Rewrite bx: $4x = -5x + 9x$. $3x^2 + 4x - 15 = 3x^2 - 5x + 9x - 15$

Factor out the GCF of each pair of terms. $= x(3x - 5) + 3(3x - 5)$

Use the Distributive Property. $= (3x - 5)(x + 3)$

 Got It? **2.** What is the factored form of $10x^2 + 31x - 14$?

Problem 3   **Applying Trinomial Factoring**

Plan

How can you find the dimensions of the rectangle?
Factor the rectangle's area as the product of two binomials, one of which is the width. The other must be the length since area = length · width.

Geometry The area of a rectangle is $2x^2 - 13x - 7$. What are the possible dimensions of the rectangle? Use factoring.

Step 1   Find factors of ac that have sum b. Since $ac = -14$ and $b = -13$, find factors of -14 that have sum -13.

Factors of -14	1, -14	-1, 14	2, -7	-2, 7
Sum of Factors	-13 ✔	13	-5	5

Step 2   To factor the trinomial, use the factors you found to rewrite bx.

Rewrite bx: $-13x = x - 14x$. $2x^2 - 13x - 7 = 2x^2 + x - 14x - 7$

Factor out the GCF of each pair of terms. $= x(2x + 1) - 7(2x + 1)$

Use the Distributive Property. $= (2x + 1)(x - 7)$

The possible dimensions of the rectangle are $2x + 1$ and $x - 7$.

Got It? **3.** The area of a rectangle is $8x^2 + 22x + 15$. What are the possible dimensions of the rectangle? Use factoring.

To factor a polynomial completely, first factor out the GCF of the polynomial's terms. Then factor the remaining polynomial until it is written as the product of polynomials that cannot be factored further.

 Problem 4 **Factoring Out a Monomial First**

What is the factored form of $18x^2 - 33x + 12$?

Plan

How can you simplify this problem?
Factor out the GCF of the trinomial's terms. The trinomial that remains is similar to those in Problems 1–3.

Think

Factor out the GCF.

Write

$18x^2 - 33x + 12 = 3(6x^2 - 11x + 4)$

Factor $6x^2 - 11x + 4$. Since $ac = 24$ and $b = -11$, find negative factors of 24 that have sum -11.

Factors of 24	−1, −24	−2, −12	−3, −8	−4, −6
Sum of Factors	−25	−14	−11 ✔	−10

Rewrite the term bx. Then use the Distributive Property to finish factoring.

$3(6x^2 - 3x - 8x + 4)$
$3[3x(2x - 1) - 4(2x - 1)]$
$3(3x - 4)(2x - 1)$

 Got It? **4.** What is the factored form of $8x^2 - 36x - 20$?

Focus Question How do you factor trinomials of the form $ax^2 + bx + c$?

Answer To factor trinomials of the form $ax^2 + bx + c$, find the factors of ac that have a sum of b.

 Lesson Check

Do you know HOW?

Factor each expression.

1. $3x^2 + 16x + 5$

2. $10q^2 + 9q + 2$

3. $4w^2 + 4w - 3$

4. The area of a rectangle is $6x^2 - 11x - 72$. What are the possible dimensions of the rectangle? Use factoring.

Do you UNDERSTAND?

5. Reasoning Explain why you cannot factor the trinomial $2x^2 + 7x + 10$.

6. Reasoning To factor $8x^2 + bx + 3$, a student correctly rewrites the trinomial as $8x^2 + px + qx + 3$. What is the value of pq?

7. Compare and Contrast How is factoring a trinomial $ax^2 + bx + c$ when $a \neq 1$ different from factoring a trinomial when $a = 1$? How is it similar?

Practice and Problem-Solving Exercises

A Practice

Factor each expression.

● **See Problem 1.**

Guided Practice

To start, find the factors of ac that have sum b. Since $ac = 12$ and $b = 13$, find positive factors of 12 that have sum 13.

8. $2x^2 + 13x + 6$

Factors of 12	Sum of Factors
1 and 12	13
2 and 6	8
3 and 4	7

9. $3d^2 + 23d + 14$

10. $4n^2 - 8n + 3$

11. $4p^2 + 7p + 3$

12. $6r^2 - 23r + 20$

Factor each expression.

● **See Problem 2.**

13. $5z^2 + 19z - 4$

14. $2k^2 - 13k - 24$

15. $6t^2 + 7t - 5$

16. $3x^2 + 23x - 36$

17. $4w^2 - 5w - 6$

18. $4d^2 - 4d - 35$

19. Interior Design The area of a rectangular kitchen tile is $8x^2 + 30x + 7$. What are the possible dimensions of the tile? Use factoring.

● **See Problem 3.**

20. Crafts The area of a rectangular knitted blanket is $15x^2 - 14x - 8$. What are the possible dimensions of the blanket? Use factoring.

Factor each expression completely.

● **See Problem 4.**

Guided Practice

To start, factor out the GCF, 4.

21. $12p^2 + 20p - 8$

$4(3p^2 + 5p - 2)$

22. $8v^2 + 34v - 30$

23. $6s^2 + 57s + 72$

24. $20w^2 - 45w + 10$

25. $12x^2 - 46x - 8$

26. $9r^2 + 3r - 30$

27. $12d^2 - 2d - 4$

B Apply

Open-Ended Find two different values that complete each expression so that the trinomial can be factored into the product of two binomials. Factor your trinomials.

28. $4s^2 + \blacksquare s + 10$

29. $15v^2 + \blacksquare v - 24$

30. $35m^2 + \blacksquare m - 16$

31. $9g^2 + \blacksquare g + 4$

32. $6n^2 + \blacksquare n + 28$

33. $8r^2 + \blacksquare r - 42$

34. a. Write each area as a product of two binomials.

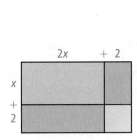

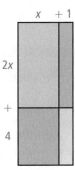

b. Are the products equal?

c. Writing Explain how the two products you found in part (a) can equal the same trinomial.

35. Error Analysis. Describe and correct the error made in factoring the expression below.

$$3x^2 - 16x - 12 = 3x^2 + 4x - 20x - 12$$
$$= x(3x + 4) - 4(5x + 3)$$
$$= (x - 4)(3x + 4)(5x + 3)$$

36. Think About a Plan A triangle has area $9x^2 - 9x - 10$. The base of the triangle is $3x - 5$. What is the height of the triangle?
  • What is the formula for the area of a triangle?
  • How does factoring the given trinomial help you solve the problem?

37. Carpentry The top of a rectangular table has an area of $18x^2 + 69x + 60$. The width of the table is $3x + 4$. What is the length of the table?

Factor each expression.

38. $54x^2 + 87x + 28$

39. $66k^2 + 57k + 12$

40. $14z^2 - 53z + 14$

41. $28h^2 + 28h - 56$

42. $21y^2 + 72y - 48$

43. $55n^2 - 52n + 12$

44. $36p^2 + 114p - 20$

45. $63g^2 - 89g + 30$

46. Reasoning If a and c in $ax^2 + bx + c$ are prime numbers and the trinomial is factorable, how many positive values are possible for b? Explain your reasoning.

Standardized Test Prep

SAT/ACT

47. What is the missing value in the statement $7x^2 - 61x - 18 = (7x + 2)(x - \blacksquare)$?

48. What is the y-intercept of the graph of $-3x + y = 1$?

49. A book has a spine 4.3×10^{-2} m thick. What is 4.3×10^{-2} written in standard form?

50. The number of tourists who visit a certain country is expected to be 440% greater in the year 2020 than in the year 2000. What is 440% written as a decimal?

51. What is the slope of the line shown in the graph?

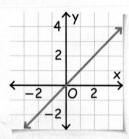

Mixed Review

Factor each expression. Check your answer. ◀ See Lesson 8-5.

52. $w^2 + 15w + 44$　　　　**53.** $t^2 - 3t - 28$　　　　**54.** $x^2 - 17x + 60$

Solve each proportion. ◀ See Lesson 2-7.

55. $\frac{5}{6} = \frac{x}{15}$　　**56.** $\frac{2}{3} = \frac{d}{18}$　　**57.** $\frac{5}{8} = \frac{a}{60}$　　**58.** $\frac{6}{10} = \frac{z}{35}$

Get Ready!　**To prepare for Lesson 8-7, do Exercises 59–62.**

Simplify each product. ◀ See Lesson 8-4.

59. $(a + 9)^2$　　**60.** $(q - 15)^2$　　**61.** $(h - 10)(h + 10)$　　**62.** $(2x - 7)(2x + 7)$

8-7 Factoring Special Cases

Objective To factor perfect-square trinomials and the differences of two squares

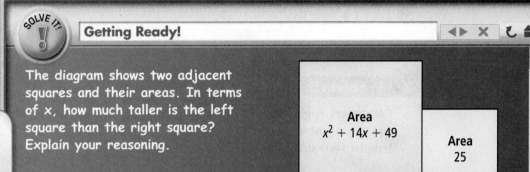

SOLVE IT!

Getting Ready!

The diagram shows two adjacent squares and their areas. In terms of x, how much taller is the left square than the right square? Explain your reasoning.

Area
$x^2 + 14x + 49$

Area
25

This problem is about the difference of squares!

Dynamic Activity
Factoring Special Products

Lesson Vocabulary
• perfect-square trinomial
• difference of two squares

Focus Question How do you factor perfect square trinomials?

You can factor some trinomials by "reversing" the rules for multiplying special case binomials that you learned in Lesson 8-4.

For example, recall the rules for finding squares of binomials.

$$(a + b)^2 = (a + b)(a + b) = a^2 + 2ab + b^2$$
$$(a - b)^2 = (a - b)(a - b) = a^2 - 2ab + b^2$$

Any trinomial of the form $a^2 + 2ab + b^2$ or $a^2 - 2ab + b^2$ is a **perfect-square trinomial** because it is the result of squaring a binomial. Reading the equations above from right to left gives you rules for factoring perfect-square trinomials.

take note

Key Concept Factoring Perfect-Square Trinomials

Algebra For every real number a and b:
$$a^2 + 2ab + b^2 = (a + b)(a + b) = (a + b)^2$$
$$a^2 - 2ab + b^2 = (a - b)(a - b) = (a - b)^2$$

Examples $x^2 + 8x + 16 = (x + 4)(x + 4) = (x + 4)^2$
$4n^2 - 12n + 9 = (2n - 3)(2n - 3) = (2n - 3)^2$

Here is how to recognize a perfect-square trinomial:

• The first and the last terms are perfect squares.
• The middle term is twice the product of one factor from the first term and one factor from the last term.

Problem 1 Factoring a Perfect-Square Trinomial

Think

Will the answer have the form $(a + b)^2$ or $(a - b)^2$?
The middle term $-12x$ has a negative coefficient, so the factored expression will have the form $(a - b)^2$.

What is the factored form of $x^2 - 12x + 36$?

Write the last term as a square.	$x^2 - 12x + 36 = x^2 - 12x + 6^2$
Does middle term equal $-2ab$? $-12x = -2(x)(6)$ ✔	$= x^2 - 2(x)(6) + 6^2$
Write as the square of a binomial.	$= (x - 6)^2$

Got It? **1.** What is the factored form of each expression?

    a. $x^2 + 6x + 9$ **b.** $x^2 - 14x + 49$

Problem 2 Factoring to Find a Length

Computers Digital images are composed of thousands of tiny pixels rendered as squares, as shown below. Suppose the area of a pixel is $4x^2 + 20x + 25$. What is the length of one side of the pixel?

One Pixel
$A = 4x^2 + 20x + 25$

Plan

How can you find the side length?
Since the pixel's area is its side length squared, factor the expression for area as the square of a binomial. The binomial is the side length.

Write first and last terms as squares.	$4x^2 + 20x + 25 = (2x)^2 + 20x + 5^2$
Does middle term equal $2ab$? $20x = 2(2x)(5)$ ✔	$= (2x)^2 + 2(2x)(5) + 5^2$
Write as the square of a binomial.	$= (2x + 5)^2$

The length of one side of the pixel is $2x + 5$.

 Got It? **2.** You are building a square patio. The area of the patio is $16m^2 - 72m + 81$. What is the length of one side of the patio?

Focus Question How do you factor the difference of two squares?

Recall from Lesson 8-4 that $(a + b)(a - b) = a^2 - b^2$. So you can factor a **difference of two squares**, $a^2 - b^2$, as $(a + b)(a - b)$.

---

take note

Key Concept   Factoring a Difference of Two Squares

Algebra   For all real numbers a and b:
$$a^2 - b^2 = (a + b)(a - b)$$

Examples $x^2 - 64 = (x + 8)(x - 8)$
$$25x^2 - 36 = (5x + 6)(5x - 6)$$

 Problem 3   **Factoring a Difference of Two Squares**

What is the factored form of $z^2 - 9$?

Plan

Can you use the rule for the difference of two squares?
Yes. The binomial is a difference *and* both its terms are perfect squares.

Think

Rewrite 9 as a square.

Factor using the rule for a difference of two squares.

Check your answer by multiplying the factored form.

Write

$$z^2 - 9 = z^2 - 3^2$$

$$= (z + 3)(z - 3)$$

$$(z + 3)(z - 3) = z^2 - 3z + 3z - 9$$
$$= z^2 - 9 ✔$$

 Got It? **3.** What is the factored form of each expression?
a. $v^2 - 100$ **b.** $s^2 - 16$

 Problem 4   **Factoring a Difference of Two Squares**

Think

When is a term of the form ax^2 a perfect square?
ax^2 is a perfect square when a is a perfect square. For example, $16x^2$ is a perfect square but $17x^2$ is not.

What is the factored form of $16x^2 - 81$?

Write each term as a square. $16x^2 - 81 = (4x)^2 - 9^2$

Use the rule for the difference of squares. $= (4x + 9)(4x - 9)$

Got It? **4. a.** What is the factored form of $25d^2 - 64$?
b. **Reasoning** The expression $25d^2 + 64$ contains two perfect squares. Can you use the method in Problem 4 to factor it? Explain your reasoning.

When you factor out the GCF of a polynomial, sometimes the expression that remains is a perfect-square trinomial or the difference of two squares. You can then factor this expression further using the rules from this lesson.

 Problem 5 **Factoring Out a Common Factor**

Think

Is $24g^2 - 6$ a difference of two squares?
No. $24g^2$ and 6 are not perfect squares. To get a difference of squares, you must first factor out the GCF.

What is the factored form of $24g^2 - 6$?

Factor out the GCF, 6.	$24g^2 - 6 = 6(4g^2 - 1)$
Write the difference as $a^2 - b^2$.	$= 6[(2g)^2 - 1^2]$
Use the rule for the difference of squares.	$= 6(2g + 1)(2g - 1)$

 Got It? **5.** What is the factored form of each expression?

     a. $12t^2 - 48$ **b.** $12x^2 + 12x + 3$

Focus Question How do you factor perfect square trinomials?

Answer To factor a perfect square trinomial, write the first and last terms as squares. Then verify that the middle term equals $2ab$. Finally, write as the square of a binomial.

Focus Question How do you factor the difference of two squares?

Answer To factor a difference of two squares, write each term as a square. Then use the difference of two squares rule.

Lesson Check

Do you know HOW?

Factor each expression.

1. $y^2 - 16y + 64$

2. $9q^2 + 12q + 4$

3. $p^2 - 36$

4. The area of a square is $36w^2 + 60w + 25$. What is the side length of the square?

Do you UNDERSTAND?

Identify the rule you would use to factor each expression.

5. $81r^2 - 90r + 25$

6. $k^2 + 12k + 36$

7. $9h^2 - 64$

8. **Reasoning** Explain how to determine whether a binomial is a difference of two squares.

Practice and Problem-Solving Exercises

 Practice

Factor each expression.

 See Problems 1 and 2.

Guided Practice

To start, write the last term as a square.

9. $v^2 - 10v + 25$

$v^2 - 10v + 25 = v^2 - 10v + 5^2$

10. $h^2 + 8h + 16$ **11.** $d^2 - 20d + 100$ **12.** $m^2 + 18m + 81$

13. $q^2 + 2q + 1$ **14.** $p^2 - 4p + 4$ **15.** $4r^2 + 36r + 81$

16. $9n^2 - 42n + 49$ **17.** $36s^2 - 60s + 25$ **18.** $25z^2 + 40z + 16$

The given expression represents the area. Find the side length of the square.

19.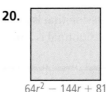

$100r^2 - 220r + 121$

20.

$64r^2 - 144r + 81$

21.

$25r^2 + 30r + 9$

Factor each expression.

See Problems 3–5.

Guided Practice

To start, write 144 as a square.

22. $w^2 - 144$

$w^2 - 144 = w^2 - 12^2$

23. $a^2 - 49$ **24.** $y^2 - 121$ **25.** $t^2 - 25$

26. $k^2 - 64$ **27.** $4p^2 - 49$ **28.** $81r^2 - 1$

29. $36v^2 - 25$ **30.** $64q^2 - 81$ **31.** $16x^2 - 121$

32. $9n^2 - 400$ **33.** $2h^2 - 2$ **34.** $27w^2 - 12$

35. $80g^2 - 45$ **36.** $8p^2 + 56p + 98$ **37.** $8s^2 - 64s + 128$

B **Apply**

38. **Error Analysis** Describe and correct the error made in factoring.

$9x^2 - 49 = (9x + 7)(9x - 7)$

39. **Writing** Summarize the procedure for factoring a difference of two squares. Give at least two examples.

40. **Think About a Plan** Two square windows and their areas are shown at the right. What is an expression that represents the difference of the areas of the windows? Show two different ways to find the solution.
- How can you solve the problem without factoring?
- How can you use the factored forms of the areas to find the difference of the areas of the windows?

$25x^2 + 40x + 16$

$x^2 - 18x + 81$

41. Interior Design A square rug has an area of $49x^2 - 56x + 16$. A second square rug has an area of $16x^2 + 24x + 9$. What is an expression that represents the difference of the areas of the rugs? Show two different ways to find the solution.

Mental Math For Exercises 42–45, find a pair of factors for each number by using the difference of two squares.

Sample Write 117 as the difference of two squares. $117 = 121 - 4$

Write each term as a square. $= 11^2 - 2^2$

Use the rule for the difference of squares. $= (11 + 2)(11 - 2)$

Simplify. $= (13)(9)$

42. 143   **43.** 99   **44.** 224   **45.** 84

46. a. Open-Ended Write an expression that is a perfect-square trinomial.
   b. Explain how you know your trinomial is a perfect-square trinomial.

Standardized Test Prep

SAT/ACT

47. What is the factored form of $4x^2 - 20x + 25$?

Ⓐ $(2x + 5)(2x - 5)$ Ⓑ $(2x - 5)(2x - 5)$ Ⓒ $(4x - 5)(4x - 5)$ Ⓓ $(4x + 5)(4x - 5)$

48. Which equation has -2 as its solution?

Ⓕ $x + 3 = 2x + 1$ Ⓖ $x - 5 = 2x - 7$ Ⓗ $2x + 5 = 5x + 11$ Ⓘ $3x + 1 = x - 5$

49. Which equation illustrates the Commutative Property of Multiplication?

Ⓐ $ab = ba$ Ⓑ $a(bc) = (ab)c$ Ⓒ $ab = ab$ Ⓓ $a(b + c) = ab + ac$

Short Response

50. A film club sponsors a film fest at a local movie theater. Renting the theater costs $190. The admission is $2 per person.

   a. Write an equation that relates the film club's total cost c and the number of people p who attend the film fest.
   b. Graph the equation you wrote in part (a).

Mixed Review

Factor each expression.   ◀ **See Lesson 8-6.**

51. $18x^2 + 9x - 14$ **52.** $8x^2 + 18x + 9$ **53.** $12x^2 - 41x + 35$

Get Ready!   To prepare for Lesson 8-8, do Exercises 54–56.

Find the GCF of the terms of each polynomial.   ◀ **See Lesson 8-2.**

54. $6t^2 + 12t - 4$ **55.** $9m^3 + 15m^2 - 21m$ **56.** $16h^4 - 12h^3 - 36h^2$

Factoring by Grouping

Objective To factor higher-degree polynomials by grouping

Hmm . . . you know one dimension, so factoring might help.

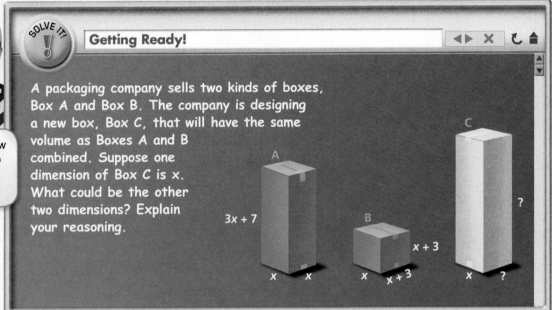

SOLVE IT!

Getting Ready!

A packaging company sells two kinds of boxes, Box A and Box B. The company is designing a new box, Box C, that will have the same volume as Boxes A and B combined. Suppose one dimension of Box C is x. What could be the other two dimensions? Explain your reasoning.

3x + 7

A

B

x + 3

C

?

x   x   x   x + 3   x   ?

Lesson Vocabulary
• factoring by grouping

Focus Question How do you factor higher-degree polynomials by grouping?

In Lesson 8-6, you factored trinomials of the form $ax^2 + bx + c$ by rewriting bx as a sum of two monomials. You then grouped the terms in pairs, factored the GCF from each pair, and looked for a common binomial factor. This process is called **factoring by grouping.** You can extend this technique to higher-degree polynomials.

Plan

How should you group the terms of the polynomial?
First group the two terms with the highest degrees. If that doesn't work, try another grouping. Your goal is to find a common binomial factor.

Problem 1 Factoring a Cubic Polynomial

What is the factored form of $3n^3 - 12n^2 + 2n - 8$?

Factor out the GCF of each group of two terms.
$$3n^3 - 12n^2 + 2n - 8 = 3n^2(n - 4) + 2(n - 4)$$

Factor out the common factor $n - 4$.
$$= (3n^2 + 2)(n - 4)$$

Check $(3n^2 + 2)(n - 4) = 3n^3 - 12n^2 + 2n - 8$ ✔

Got It? 1. a. What is the factored form of $8t^3 + 16t^2 + 5t + 10$?

b. Reasoning How is the factoring method used in Problem 1 like the method used in Lesson 8-6? How is it different?

Before factoring by grouping, you may need to factor out the GCF of all the terms.

Problem 2 Factoring a Polynomial Completely

ONLINE PROBLEMS

Think

Do the terms share any numerical or variable factors?
Yes. The terms have a common numerical factor of 2 and a common variable factor of q. The GCF is $2q$.

What is the factored form of $4q^4 - 10q^3 + 16q^2 - 40q$? Factor completely.

Factor out the GCF. $4q^4 - 10q^3 + 16q^2 - 40q = 2q(2q^3 - 5q^2 + 8q - 20)$

Factor by grouping. $= 2q[q^2(2q - 5) + 4(2q - 5)]$

Factor again. $= 2q(q^2 + 4)(2q - 5)$

Got It? 2. What is the factored form of $6h^4 + 9h^3 + 12h^2 + 18h$? Factor completely.

You can sometimes factor to find possible expressions for the length, width, and height of a rectangular prism.

Problem 3 Finding the Dimensions of a Rectangular Prism

Entertainment The toy shown below is made of several bars that can fold together to form a rectangular prism or unfold to form a "ladder." What expressions can represent the dimensions of the toy when it is folded up? Use factoring.

$$V = 6x^3 + 19x^2 + 15x$$

Plan

How can you find the prism's dimensions?
Factor the cubic expression for the volume of the prism as the product of three linear expressions. Each linear expression is a dimension.

Step 1 Factor out the GCF.
$$6x^3 + 19x^2 + 15x = x(6x^2 + 19x + 15)$$

Step 2 To factor the trinomial, find factors of ac that have sum b.
Since $ac = 90$ and $b = 19$, find factors of 90 that have sum 19.

Factors of 90	1, 90	2, 45	3, 30	5, 18	6, 15	9, 10
Sum of Factors	91	47	33	23	21	19 ✔

Step 3 To factor the trinomial, use the factors you found to rewrite bx.

Rewrite bx: $19x = 9x + 10x$. $x(6x^2 + 19x + 15) = x(6x^2 + 9x + 10x + 15)$

Factor by grouping. $= x[3x(2x + 3) + 5(2x + 3)]$

Use the Distributive Property. $= x(3x + 5)(2x + 3)$

The possible dimensions are x, $3x + 5$, and $2x + 3$.

Got It? 3. Geometry A rectangular prism has volume $60x^3 + 34x^2 + 4x$. What expressions can represent the dimensions of the prism? Use factoring.

Here is a summary of what to remember as you factor polynomials.

take note

Summary Factoring Polynomials

1. Factor out the greatest common factor (GCF).

2. If the polynomial has two terms or three terms, look for a difference of two squares, a perfect-square trinomial, or a pair of binomial factors.

3. If the polynomial has four or more terms, group terms and factor to find common binomial factors.

4. As a final check, make sure there are no common factors other than 1.

Focus Question How do you factor higher-degree polynomials by grouping?

Answer To factor higher-degree polynomials by grouping, group terms and factor to find common binomial factors.

Lesson Check

Do you know HOW?

Factor each expression.

1. $20r^3 + 8r^2 + 15r + 6$

2. $6d^3 + 3d^2 - 10d - 5$

3. $24x^3 + 60x^2 + 36x + 90$

4. A rectangular prism has a volume of $36x^3 + 36x^2 + 8x$. What expressions can represent the dimensions of the prism? Use factoring.

Do you UNDERSTAND?

Vocabulary Tell whether you would factor the polynomial by grouping. Explain your answer.

5. $x^2 - 6x + 9$

6. $4w^2 + 23w + 15$

7. $24t^3 - 42t^2 - 28t + 49$

8. Reasoning Can you factor the polynomial $6q^3 + 2q^2 + 12q - 3$ by grouping? Explain.

Practice and Problem-Solving Exercises

A Practice Find the GCF of the first two terms and the GCF of the last two terms for each polynomial.   ◆ **See Problem 1.**

9. $2z^3 + 6z^2 + 3z + 9$

10. $10g^3 - 25g^2 + 4g - 10$

11. $2r^3 + 12r^2 - 5r - 30$

12. $6p^3 + 3p^2 + 2p + 1$

Factor each expression.

Guided Practice

To start, factor out the GCF from each group of two terms.

13. $15q^3 + 40q^2 + 3q + 8$

$15q^3 + 40q^2 + 3q + 8$

$= (15q^3 + 40q^2) + (3q + 8)$

$= 5q^2(3q + 8) + 1(3q + 8)$

14. $14y^3 + 8y^2 + 7y + 4$ **15.** $14z^3 - 35z^2 + 16z - 40$

16. $11w^3 - 9w^2 + 11w - 9$ **17.** $8m^3 + 12m^2 - 2m - 3$

18. $12k^3 - 27k^2 - 40k + 90$ **19.** $20v^3 + 24v^2 - 25v - 30$

20. $18h^3 + 45h^2 - 8h - 20$ **21.** $12y^3 + 4y^2 - 9y - 3$

Factor completely.

◀ See Problem 2.

Practice

To start, factor out the GCF.

22. $8p^3 - 32p^2 + 28p - 112$

$8p^3 - 32p^2 + 28p - 112$

$= 4(2p^3 - 8p^2 + 7p - 28)$

23. $3w^4 - 2w^3 + 18w^2 - 12w$ **24.** $5g^4 - 5g^3 + 20g^2 - 20g$

25. $6q^4 + 3q^3 - 24q^2 - 12q$ **26.** $4d^3 - 6d^2 + 16d - 24$

Find expressions for the possible dimensions of each rectangular prism.

◀ See Problem 3.

27.

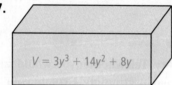

$V = 3y^3 + 14y^2 + 8y$

28.

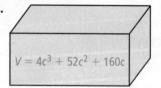

$V = 4c^3 + 52c^2 + 160c$

29. Carpentry A trunk in the shape of a rectangular prism has a volume of $6x^3 + 38x^2 - 28x$. What expressions can represent the dimensions of the trunk?

 Apply

Factor completely.

30. $9t^3 - 90t^2 + 144t$ **31.** $60y^4 - 300y^3 - 42y^2 + 210y$

32. $8m^3 + 32m^2 + 40m + 160$ **33.** $10p^2 - 5pq - 180q^2$

34. Error Analysis Describe and correct the error made in factoring completely.

$$4x^4 + 12x^3 + 8x^2 + 24x = 4(x^4 + 3x^3 + 2x^2 + 6x)$$
$$= 4[x^3(x + 3) + 2x(x + 3)]$$
$$= 4(x^3 + 2x)(x + 3)$$

35. a. Factor $(20x^3 - 5x^2) + (44x - 11)$.

     b. Factor $(20x^3 + 44x) + (-5x^2 - 11)$.

     c. Reasoning Why can you factor the same polynomial using different pairs of terms?

36. Writing Describe how to factor the expression $6x^5 + 4x^4 + 12x^3 + 8x^2 + 9x + 6$.

37. Think About a Plan Bat houses, such as the one at the right, are large wooden structures that people mount on buildings to attract bats. What expressions can represent the dimensions of the bat house?
- Into how many factors should you factor the expression for the volume?
- What is the first step in factoring this expression?

$V = 4x^3 + 22x^2 + 24x$

38. Open-Ended Write a four-term polynomial that you can factor by grouping. Factor your polynomial.

39. Art The pedestal of a sculpture is a rectangular prism with a volume of $63x^3 - 28x$. What expressions can represent the dimensions of the pedestal? Use factoring.

Standardized Test Prep

SAT/ACT

40. What is $30z^3 - 12z^2 + 120z - 48$ factored completely?

Ⓐ $2(15z^3 - 6z^2 + 60z - 24)$ Ⓒ $6(5z^3 - 2z^2 + 20z - 8)$

Ⓑ $(6z^2 + 24)(5z - 2)$ Ⓓ $6(z^2 + 4)(5z - 2)$

41. What is the simplified form of $2x^3 \cdot x^8$?

Ⓕ $2x^{11}$ Ⓖ $8x^{11}$ Ⓗ $2x^{24}$ Ⓘ $8x^{24}$

42. Which equation represents the line with slope -3 that passes through $(2, 5)$?

Ⓐ $y = -3x + 17$ Ⓑ $y = -3x + 11$ Ⓒ $y = 4x - 3$ Ⓓ $y = x - 3$

43. What is the solution of the inequality $7 < -2x + 5$?

Ⓕ $x > -1$ Ⓖ $x < -1$ Ⓗ $x > 1$ Ⓘ $x < 1$

Short Response

44. Factor $10r^4 + 30r^3 + 5r^2 + 15r$ completely. Show your work.

Mixed Review

Factor each expression.

See Lesson 8-7.

45. $m^2 + 12m + 36$ **46.** $64x^2 - 144x + 81$ **47.** $49p^2 - 4$

Use a mapping diagram to determine whether each relation is a function.

See Lesson 4-6.

48. $\{(4, 3), (3, 4), (4, 7), (7, 4)\}$ **49.** $\{(-1, 8), (1, 8), (3, 8), (5, 8)\}$ **50.** $\{(2, 7), (4, -7), (6, 7), (8, -7)\}$

Get Ready! **To prepare for Lesson 9-1, do Exercises 51–54.**

Use the slope and y-intercept to graph each equation.

See Lesson 5-3.

51. $y = \frac{1}{2}x + 3$ **52.** $y = -4x - 1$ **53.** $y = 2x - 3$ **54.** $y = -\frac{5}{3}x + 2$

Pull It **All Together**

To solve these problems you will pull together many concepts and skills that you have studied about polynomials and factoring.

BIG idea Equivalence

You can represent algebraic expressions in many ways. When you add, subtract, multiply, divide, and factor polynomials, you replace one expression with an equivalent expression.

BIG idea Properties

The properties of real numbers are the basis of the laws of algebra. You can apply properties of real numbers, such as the Distributive Property, to polynomials.

Task 1

Solve. Show all of your work and explain your steps.

An archery target consists of a circular bull's-eye with radius x, surrounded by four rings with width y. What is the area of the outermost ring in terms of x and y?

Task 2

Solve. Show all of your work and explain your steps.

You are painting the outside of a jewelry box, including the bottom. To find the surface area (S.A.) of the jewelry box, you can use the formula S.A. $= 2w\ell + 2\ell h + 2wh$, where ℓ is the length, w is the width, and h is the height. What is the surface area of the jewelry box in terms of x?

Hint

Start by factoring the polynomial. If two of the prism's faces are square, what must be true of two of the polynomial's factors?

Task 3

Solve. Show all of your work and explain your steps.

The volume of a square prism is $144x^3 + 216x^2 + 81x$. What is an expression that could describe the perimeter of one of the prism's square faces?

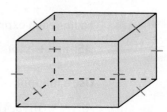

Connecting BIG ideas and Answering the Essential Questions

1 Equivalence
You can represent algebraic expressions in many ways. When you add, subtract, multiply, divide, and factor polynomials, you replace one expression with an equivalent expression.

Adding and Subtracting Polynomials (Lesson 8-1)
$$(3x^2 + 4x + 1) + (2x^2 + 5x + 8)$$
$$= (3x^2 + 2x^2) + (4x + 5x) + (1 + 8)$$
$$= 5x^2 + 9x + 9$$

Multiplying Binomials (Lesson 8-3)
$$(m + 4)(2m - 5) = 2m^2 - 5m + 8m - 20$$
$$= 2m^2 + 3m - 20$$

Multiplying Special Cases (Lesson 8-4)
$$(2x + 3)(2x - 3) = 4x^2 - 9$$

2 Properties
The properties of real numbers are the basis of the laws of algebra. You can apply properties of real numbers, such as the Distributive Property, to polynomials.

Factoring Trinomials (Lessons 8-5 and 8-6)
$$x^2 - 6x + 8 = (x - 2)(x - 4)$$

Factoring Special Cases (Lesson 8-7)
$$49p^2 - 16 = (7p + 4)(7p - 4)$$

Factoring by Grouping (Lesson 8-8)
$$3x^2 - 10x - 8 = 3x^2 - 12x + 2x - 8$$
$$= (3x^2 - 12x) + (2x - 8)$$
$$= 3x(x - 4) + 2(x - 4)$$
$$= (3x + 2)(x - 4)$$

Chapter Vocabulary

- difference of two squares (p. 547)
- factoring by grouping (p. 551)
- perfect-square trinomial (p. 545)

Choose the correct term to complete each sentence.

1. A polynomial that is the product of two identical binomial factors is a(n) __?__.

2. A binomial in the form $a^2 - b^2$ is a(n) __?__.

3. To factor a polynomial that has four or more terms, try __?__, where you group terms and factor to find a common binomial factor.

8-5, 8-6, and 8-7 Factoring Quadratic Trinomials and Special Cases

Quick Review

You can write some quadratic trinomials as the product of two binomial factors. When you factor a polynomial, be sure to factor out the GCF first.

When you factor a perfect-square trinomial, the two binomial factors are the same.

$$a^2 + 2ab + b^2 = (a + b)(a + b) = (a + b)^2$$
$$a^2 - 2ab + b^2 = (a - b)(a - b) = (a - b)^2$$

When you factor a difference of squares of two terms, the two binomial factors are the sum and the difference of the two terms.

$$a^2 - b^2 = (a + b)(a - b)$$

Example

What is the factored form of $81t^2 - 90t + 25$?

First rewrite the first and last terms as squares. Then determine if the middle term equals $-2ab$.

$$81t^2 - 90t + 25 = (9t)^2 - 90t + 5^2$$
$$= (9t)^2 - 2(9t)(5) + 5^2$$
$$= (9t - 5)^2$$

Exercises

Factor each expression.

4. $r^2 + 6r - 40$ **5.** $p^2 + 8p + 12$

6. $t^2 - 13t - 30$ **7.** $2g^2 - 35g + 17$

8. $s^2 - 20s + 100$ **9.** $16q^2 + 56q + 49$

10. $r^2 - 64$ **11.** $9z^2 - 16$

12. $25m^2 + 80m + 64$ **13.** $49n^2 - 4$

14. $g^2 - 225$ **15.** $9p^2 - 42p + 49$

16. $36h^2 - 12h + 1$ **17.** $w^2 + 24w + 144$

18. $32v^2 - 8$ **19.** $25x^2 - 36$

20. Reasoning Can you factor the expression $2x^2 + 15x + 9$? Explain why or why not.

21. Geometry Find an expression for the length of a side of a square with an area of $9n^2 + 54n + 81$.

22. Reasoning Suppose you are using algebra tiles to factor a quadratic trinomial. What do you know about the factors of the trinomial when the tiles form a square?

8-8 Factoring by Grouping

Quick Review

When a polynomial has four or more terms, you may be able to group the terms and find a common binomial factor. Then you can use the Distributive Property to factor the polynomial.

Example

What is the factored form of $2r^3 - 12r^2 + 5r - 30$?

First factor out the GCF from each group of two terms. Then factor out a common binomial factor.

$$2r^3 - 12r^2 + 5r - 30 = 2r^2(r - 6) + 5(r - 6)$$
$$= (2r^2 + 5)(r - 6)$$

Exercises

Find the GCF of the first two terms and the GCF of the last two terms for each polynomial.

23. $6y^3 - 3y^2 + 2y - 1$

24. $8m^3 + 40m^2 + 6m + 15$

Factor completely.

25. $6d^4 + 4d^3 - 6d^2 - 4d$

26. $11b^3 - 6b^2 + 11b - 6$

27. $45z^3 + 20z^2 + 9z + 4$

28. $9a^3 - 12a^2 + 18a - 24$

Do you know HOW?

Write each polynomial in standard form.

1. $2x - 3x^2 + 6 + 5x^3$

2. $7 + 9x + 2x^2 + 8x^5$

Simplify. Write each answer in standard form.

3. $(4x^2 + 9x + 1) + (2x^2 + 7x + 13)$

4. $(8x^2 + 5x + 7) - (5x^2 + 8x - 6)$

5. $(5x^4 + 7x + 2) - (3x^2 - 2x + 9)$

6. $(-7x^3 + 4x - 6) + (6x^3 + 10x^2 + 3)$

Simplify each product. Write in standard form.

7. $-p(8p^2 + 3p)$

8. $(r + 8)(r + 6)$

9. $(5w - 6)(2w + 7)$

10. $(4s + 5)(7s^2 - 4s + 3)$

11. $(q - 1)^2$

12. $(3g - 5)(3g + 5)$

13. **Camping** A rectangular campground has length $4x + 7$ and width $3x - 2$. What is the area of the campground?

Find the GCF of the terms of each polynomial.

14. $16x^6 + 22x^2 + 30x^5$

15. $7v^3 - 10v^2 + 9v^4$

Factor each expression.

16. $x^2 + 17x + 72$

17. $4v^2 - 16v + 7$

18. $n^2 - 16n + 64$

19. $6t^2 - 54$

20. $y^2 - 121$

Factor completely.

21. $7h^4 - 4h^3 + 28h^2 - 16h$

22. $15t^3 + 2t^2 - 45t - 6$

23. $6n^4 + 15n^3 - 9n^2$

24. $9v^4 + 12v^3 - 18v^2 - 24v$

25. **Art** The area of a square painting is $81p^2 + 90p + 25$. What is the side length of the painting?

Do you UNDERSTAND?

26. **Open-Ended** Write a trinomial with degree 5.

27. **Writing** Explain how to use the Distributive Property to multiply two binomials. Include an example.

28. **Geometry** What is an expression for the area of the figure? Write your answer as a polynomial in standard form.

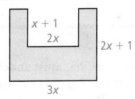

29. **Open-Ended** What are three different values that complete the expression $x^2 + \blacksquare x + 24$ so that you can factor it into the product of two binomials? Show each factorization.

Write the missing value in each perfect-square trinomial.

30. $n^2 + \blacksquare n + 81$

31. $16y^2 - 56y + \blacksquare$

32. $\blacksquare p^2 + 30p + 25$

33. **Reasoning** The expression $(x - 2)^2 - 9$ has the form $a^2 - b^2$.

   a. Identify a and b.

   b. Factor $(x - 2)^2 - 9$. Then simplify.

8 Cumulative Test Prep

TIPS FOR SUCCESS

Some questions on tests ask you to use polynomials to represent perimeter, area, and volume. Read the sample question at the right. Then follow the tips to answer it.

TIP 1

Make sure you look at the figure and understand it. This figure is a rectangular prism. The expressions $x + 1$, $x + 2$, and $x + 3$ represent the lengths of its edges.

The figure below is a rectangular prism.

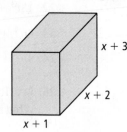

$x + 3$

$x + 2$

$x + 1$

Which expression represents the volume of the prism?

- (A) $x^3 + 6$
- (B) $x^2 + 2x + 2$
- (C) $x^3 + x^2 + 10x + 6$
- (D) $x^3 + 6x^2 + 11x + 6$

TIP 2

Be sure to answer the question being asked. In this problem, you need to find the volume of the prism.

Think It Through

The volume of a rectangular prism is given by $V = \ell wh$. Substitute the edge lengths into the formula. Then simplify the product.

$$V = \ell wh$$
$$= (x + 1)(x + 2)(x + 3)$$
$$= (x^2 + 3x + 2)(x + 3)$$
$$= x^3 + 6x^2 + 11x + 6$$

The correct answer is D.

Vocabulary Builder

As you solve test items, you must understand the meanings of mathematical terms. Match each term with its mathematical meaning.

A. polynomial

B. power

C. area

D. volume

E. scale

I. an expression of the form a^n, where a is the base and n is the exponent

II. the ratio of a distance in a drawing and the actual distance

III. the number of cubic units contained in a space figure

IV. a monomial or the sum of two or more monomials

V. the number of square units contained in a planar figure

Multiple Choice

Read each question. Then write the letter of the correct answer on your paper.

1. What is $y = \frac{2}{7}x - 4$ written in standard form?
- (A) $2x + 7y = -28$
- (C) $-2x - 7y = -28$
- (B) $2x - 7y = 28$
- (D) $-2x + 7y = 28$

2. Suppose $b = 2a - 16$ and $b = a + 2$. What is the value of a?
- (F) 5
- (H) 14
- (G) 6
- (I) 18

3. Which expression is equivalent to $10x - (5x - 1)$?
- (A) $2x - 1$
- (C) $5x - 1$
- (B) $2x + 1$
- (D) $5x + 1$

4. A student's score on a history test varies directly with the number of questions the student correctly answers. A student who correctly answers 14 questions receives a score of 70. What score would a student receive for correctly answering 15 questions?

(F) 72 (H) 85

(G) 75 (I) 90

5. The areas of three squares are shown in the figure at the right. What is the area of the triangle?

(A) $6\,\text{m}^2$

(B) $8\,\text{m}^2$

(C) $12\,\text{m}^2$

(D) $72\,\text{m}^2$

6. You bought a candlestick holder for $11.78 and several candles for $.62 each. You spent a total of $18.60. How many candles did you buy?

(F) 11 (H) 25

(G) 19 (I) 30

7. You are using a map to find the distance between your house and a friend's house. On the map, the distance is 2.5 in. Suppose the map's scale is $\frac{1}{8}$ in. $= 1.5$ mi. How far do you live from your friend?

(A) 0.08 mi (C) 3.75 mi

(B) 0.2 mi (D) 30 mi

8. Which expression represents the volume of the prism at the right?

(F) $x^3 + 4$

(G) $x^3 + 6x^2 + 9x + 4$

(H) $x^3 + 9x^2 + 6x + 4$

(I) $x^3 + 4x^2 + x + 4$

$x + 4$

$x + 1$

$x + 1$

9. Which equation models a line with positive slope and a positive x-intercept?

(A) $5x - 2y = 14$

(B) $-5x - 2y = 14$

(C) $-5x + 2y = 14$

(D) $5x + 2y = -14$

10. You can represent the width of a certain rectangle with the expression $x + 2$. The length of the rectangle is twice the width. What is the area of the rectangle?

(F) $2x + 4$

(G) $2x^2 + 8$

(H) $2x^2 + 8x + 8$

(I) $4x^2 + 16x + 16$

11. Which equation represents a line with slope that is greater than the slope of the line with equation $y = \frac{3}{4}x - 1$?

(A) $y = -\frac{3}{4}x - 2$

(B) $y = \frac{4}{3}x - 2$

(C) $y = \frac{2}{3}x - 1$

(D) $y = \frac{3}{4}x + 2$

12. What is the x-intercept of the line that passes through $(0, -4)$ and $(1, 4)$?

(F) -4

(G) $\frac{1}{4}$

(H) $\frac{1}{2}$

(I) 2

13. Megan earns $20,000 per year plus 5% commission on her sales. Laurie earns $32,000 per year plus 1% commission on her sales. Which system of equations can you use to determine the amounts that Megan and Laurie must sell s to receive equal pay p?

(A) $p = 5s + 20,000$
$p = s + 32,000$

(B) $p + 5s = 20,000$
$p + s = 32,000$

(C) $p + 0.5s = 20,000$
$p + 0.1s = 32,000$

(D) $p = 0.05s + 20,000$
$p = 0.01s + 32,000$

14. A family is driving to the beach. The graph at the right relates the distance from the beach to the amount of time they spend driving.

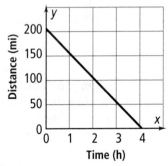

What does the y-intercept of the graph represent?

(F) a stop on the way to the beach

(G) the average speed in miles per hour

(H) the distance from the beach before they started driving

(I) the amount of time it takes to get to the beach

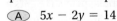

15. The area of a rectangle is $6n^2 + n - 2$. Which expression could represent the perimeter of the rectangle?

Ⓐ $2n - 1$ Ⓒ $5n + 1$

Ⓑ $3n + 2$ Ⓓ $10n + 2$

16. A company sells calculators for $35 each. Businesses must order a minimum of 100 calculators, and they must pay a shipping cost of $50. Which amount of money represents a reasonable sum that a business might spend to purchase calculators?

Ⓕ $750   Ⓗ $2990

Ⓖ $1070   Ⓘ $3585

17. Which expression is equivalent to $\frac{3x^3 y}{(3y)^{-2}}$?

Ⓐ $9x^3 y^3$ Ⓒ $27x^3 y^3$

Ⓑ $\frac{x^3}{y}$ Ⓓ $\frac{x^3 y^3}{3}$

18. The formula for the volume V of a pyramid is $V = \frac{1}{3}Bh$, where B is the area of the base of the pyramid and h is the height of the pyramid. Which equation represents the height of the pyramid in terms of V and B?

Ⓕ $h = \frac{3V}{B}$ Ⓗ $h = 3VB$

Ⓖ $h = \frac{V}{3B}$ Ⓘ $h = \frac{B}{3V}$

GRIDDED RESPONSE

19. An artist is making a scale model of a ladybug for an insect museum. What is the length in millimeters of the actual ladybug that the artist is using to make this model?

|← 180 cm →|
Scale: 15 cm = 1 mm

20. A flagpole casts a shadow that is 9.1 m long. At the same time, a meter stick casts a shadow that is 1.4 m long. How tall is the flagpole in meters?

21. What is the seventh term in the following sequence?

$$81, 27, 9, 3, 1, \ldots$$

22. Suppose you have $200. Sweaters cost $45 each. What is the greatest number of sweaters you can buy?

23. How many whole-number solutions does the inequality $|x - 5| \le 8$ have?

24. Line m passes through $(-9, 4)$ and $(9, 6)$. What is the y-intercept of line m?

25. You made a graph to model the height of a tree each year since you planted it.

Suppose the tree had been 5 ft. tall when you planted it. How tall would the tree be in 6 yr? Assume its growth rate did not change.

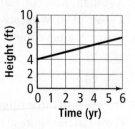

26. A laundromat charges $2.25 to wash one load of clothes and $1.75 to dry one load. The machines accept only quarters. To wash and dry one load of clothes, how many quarters would you need?

27. Suppose that $xy = 0$ and $y = 3\frac{1}{2}$. What is the value of $x + 3y$?

Short Response

28. The formula for the area A of a trapezoid is $A = \frac{1}{2}h(b_1 + b_2)$, where h is the height of the trapezoid and b_1 and b_2 are the lengths of its two bases.

Suppose the height of a trapezoid is $x - 2$. The lengths of the bases are $x + 2$ and $3x - 2$. What polynomial in standard form represents the area of the trapezoid? Show your work.

29. A monthly subway pass costs $60. A one-ride ticket costs $1.80. You plan to ride the subway to school and back for 21 days this month. How much more money would you spend to buy one-way tickets than to buy a monthly pass? Show your work.

Extended Response

30. Jeremy purchases a home for $200,000. He pays a down payment equal to 20% of the purchase price. He gets a home loan for the remainder of the purchase price.

   a. What is the amount of Jeremy's home loan?

   b. In addition, Jeremy pays closing costs that equal 3% of the amount of the home loan. How much does Jeremy pay altogether for the down payment and the closing costs?

Get Ready!

Lesson 1-2 ◆ **Evaluating Expressions**

Evaluate each expression for $a = -1$, $b = 3$, and $c = -2$.

1. $2a - b^2 + c$

2. $\dfrac{c^2 - ab}{2a}$

3. $bc - 3a^2$

4. $\dfrac{b^2 - 4ac}{2a}$

5. $5a + 2b(c - 1)$

6. $c^2 + 2ab - 1$

Lesson 4-4 ◆ **Graphing Functions**

Graph each function.

7. $y = x$

8. $y = -x^2$

9. $y = |x|$

10. $y = 2x - 5$

11. $y = 2|x|$

12. $y = -4x + 3$

Lesson 4-6 ◆ **Evaluating Function Rules**

Evaluate each function rule for $x = -6$.

13. $f(x) = -3x^2$

14. $h(x) = x^2 + 6x$

15. $g(x) = (x - 1)^2$

16. $f(x) = (1 + x)^2$

17. $g(x) = \frac{2}{3}x^2$

18. $h(x) = (2x)^2$

Lessons 8-5 and 8-6 ◆ **Factoring**

Factor each expression.

19. $4x^2 + 4x + 1$

20. $5x^2 + 32x - 21$

21. $8x^2 - 10x + 3$

22. $x^2 - 18x + 81$

23. $12y^2 + 8y - 15$

24. $m^2 - 7m - 18$

 ## Looking Ahead Vocabulary

25. Use your knowledge of the definition of a quadratic polynomial to make a conjecture about the definition of a *quadratic function*.

26. The graph of a quadratic function is a U-shaped curve that has an *axis of symmetry*. What do you think this means?

27. The following is an example of the *Zero-Product Property*:
$(x + 3)(x - 4) = 0$, so $x + 3 = 0$ or $x - 4 = 0$.
What do you think this means?

Quadratic Functions and Equations

This photo makes it look easy, but it takes quite a bit of practice to get good at basketball! How hard you throw the ball can mean the difference between making a basket and missing it. The player might not think about it, but there's an equation that relates the height of the ball or other object over time and the speed it's thrown. You'll use this model and other quadratic equations in this chapter.

Vocabulary for Part A

English/Spanish Vocabulary Audio Online:

English	Spanish
axis of symmetry, *p. 566*	eje de simetría
maximum, *p. 567*	valor máximo
minimum, *p. 567*	valor mínimo
parabola, *p. 566*	parábola
quadratic equation, *p. 580*	ecuación cuadrática
quadratic function, *p. 566*	función cuadrática
root of an equation, *p. 580*	raíz de una ecuación
vertex, *p. 567*	vértice

BIGideas

1 Functions

Essential Question What are the characteristics of quadratic functions?

2 Solving Equations and Inequalities

Essential Question How can you solve a quadratic equation?

Chapter Preview for Part A

Quadratic Graphs and Their Properties

Objective To graph quadratic functions of the form $y = ax^2$ and $y = ax^2 + c$

A certain type of function models the motion of a falling object.

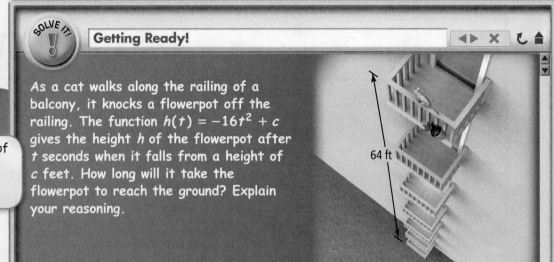

SOLVE IT!

Getting Ready!

As a cat walks along the railing of a balcony, it knocks a flowerpot off the railing. The function $h(t) = -16t^2 + c$ gives the height h of the flowerpot after t seconds when it falls from a height of c feet. How long will it take the flowerpot to reach the ground? Explain your reasoning.

64 ft

Lesson Vocabulary

- quadratic function
- standard form of a quadratic function
- quadratic parent function
- parabola
- axis of symmetry
- vertex
- minimum
- maximum

Recall that a polynomial of degree 2, such as $-16x^2 + 64$, is a quadratic polynomial. You can use a quadratic polynomial to define a *quadratic function* like the one in the Solve It.

Focus Question What is the shape of the graph of a quadratic function?

A quadratic function is a type of nonlinear function that models certain situations. In a quadratic function, the rate of change is not constant. The graph of a quadratic function is a symmetric curve with a highest or lowest point corresponding to a maximum or minimum value.

take note

Key Concept Standard Form of a Quadratic Function

A **quadratic function** is a function that can be written in the form $y = ax^2 + bx + c$, where $a \neq 0$. This form is called the **standard form of a quadratic function.**

Examples $y = 3x^2$ $y = x^2 + 9$ $y = x^2 - x - 2$

The simplest quadratic function $f(x) = x^2$ or $y = x^2$ is the **quadratic parent function.**

The graph of a quadratic function is a U-shaped curve called a **parabola.** The parabola with equation $y = x^2$ is shown at the right.

You can fold a parabola so that the two sides match exactly. This property is called *symmetry*. The fold or line that divides the parabola into two matching halves is called the **axis of symmetry.**

The highest or lowest point of a parabola is its **vertex,** which is on the axis of symmetry.

If $a > 0$ in $y = ax^2 + bx + c$, the parabola opens upward.

↓

The vertex is the **minimum** point, or lowest point, of the parabola.

If $a < 0$ in $y = ax^2 + bx + c$, the parabola opens downward.

↓

The vertex is the **maximum** point, or highest point, of the parabola.

 Problem 1 Identifying a Vertex

What are the coordinates of the vertex of each graph? Is it a minimum or a maximum?

A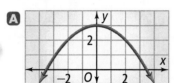

B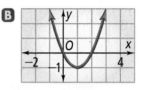

The vertex is $(0, 3)$. It is a maximum.

The vertex is $(1, -1)$. It is a minimum.

Got It? 1. What is the vertex of the graph at the right? Is it a minimum or a maximum?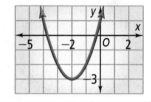

You can use the fact that a parabola is symmetric to graph it quickly. First, find the coordinates of the vertex and several points on one side of the vertex. Then reflect the points across the axis of symmetry. For graphs of functions of the form $y = ax^2$, the vertex is at the origin. The axis of symmetry is the y-axis, or $x = 0$.

 Problem 2 Graphing $y = ax^2$

Graph the function $y = \frac{1}{3}x^2$. Make a table of values. What are the domain and range?

x	$y = \frac{1}{3}x^2$	(x, y)
0	$\frac{1}{3}(0)^2 = 0$	$(0, 0)$
3	$\frac{1}{3}(3)^2 = 3$	$(3, 3)$
6	$\frac{1}{3}(6)^2 = 12$	$(6, 12)$

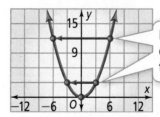

Reflect the points from the table over the axis of symmetry, $x = 0$, to find more points on the graph.

The domain is all real numbers. The range is $y \geq 0$.

Got It? 2. Graph the function $y = -3x^2$. What are the domain and range?

The coefficient of the x^2-term in a quadratic function affects the width of a parabola. It also tells the direction it opens. When $|m| < |n|$, the graph of $y = mx^2$ is wider than the graph of $y = nx^2$.

Problem 3 Comparing Widths of Parabolas

Think

Does the sign of the x^2-term affect the parabola's width?
No. The sign of the x^2-term affects only whether the parabola opens upward or downward.

Use the graphs below. What is the order, from widest to narrowest, of the graphs of the quadratic functions $f(x) = -4x^2$, $f(x) = \frac{1}{4}x^2$, and $f(x) = x^2$?

$$f(x) = -4x^2 \qquad\qquad f(x) = \frac{1}{4}x^2 \qquad\qquad f(x) = x^2$$

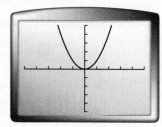

Of the three graphs, $f(x) = \frac{1}{4}x^2$ is the widest and $f(x) = -4x^2$ is the narrowest. So, the order from widest to narrowest is $f(x) = \frac{1}{4}x^2$, $f(x) = x^2$, and $f(x) = -4x^2$.

Got It? **3.** What is the order, from widest to narrowest, of the graphs of the functions $f(x) = -x^2$, $f(x) = 3x^2$, and $f(x) = -\frac{1}{3}x^2$?

The y-axis is the axis of symmetry for graphs of functions of the form $y = ax^2 + c$. The value of c translates the graph up or down. When c is positive the curve shifts up. When c is negative the curve shifts down.

Problem 4 Graphing $y = ax^2 + c$

Multiple Choice How is the graph of $y = 2x^2 + 3$ different from the graph of $y = 2x^2$?

  Ⓐ It is shifted 3 units up.
  Ⓒ It is shifted 3 units to the right.
  Ⓑ It is shifted 3 units down.
  Ⓓ It is shifted 3 units to the left.

Plan

What values should you choose for x?
Use the same values of x for graphing both functions so that you can see the relationship between corresponding y-coordinates.

x	$y = 2x^2$	$y = 2x^2 + 3$
-2	8	11
-1	2	5
0	0	3
1	2	5
2	8	11

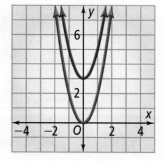

The graph of $y = 2x^2 + 3$ has the same shape as the graph of $y = 2x^2$ but is shifted up 3 units. The correct answer is A.

Got It? **4.** Graph $y = x^2$ and $y = x^2 - 3$. How are the graphs related?

As an object falls, its speed continues to increase, so its height above the ground decreases at a faster and faster rate. Ignoring air resistance, you can model the object's height with the function $h = -16t^2 + c$. The height h is in feet, the time t is in seconds, and the object's initial height c is in feet.

 Problem 5 **Using the Falling Object Model**

Nature An acorn drops from a tree branch 20 ft above the ground. The function $h = -16t^2 + 20$ gives the height h of the acorn (in feet) after t seconds. What is the graph of this quadratic function? At about what time does the acorn hit the ground?

Know	Need	Plan
• The function for the acorn's height • The initial height is 20 ft	The function's graph and the time the acorn hits the ground	Use a table of values to graph the function. Use the graph to estimate when the acorn hits the ground.

Think

Can you choose negative values for t?
No. t represents time, so it cannot be negative.

t	$h = -16t^2 + 20$
0	20
0.5	16
1	4
1.5	-16

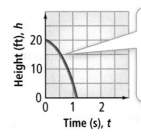

Graph the function using the first three ordered pairs from the table. Do not plot $(1.5, -16)$ because height cannot be negative.

The acorn hits the ground when its height above the ground is 0 ft. From the graph, you can see that the acorn hits the ground after slightly more than 1 s.

 Got It? **5. a.** In Problem 5, suppose the acorn drops from a tree branch 70 ft above the ground. The function $h = -16t^2 + 70$ gives the height h of the acorn (in feet) after t seconds. What is the graph of this function? At about what time does the acorn hit the ground?

   b. Reasoning What are a reasonable domain and range for the original function in Problem 5 above? Explain your reasoning.

Focus Question What is the shape of the graph of a quadratic function?

Answer The shape is a symmetric curve with a highest or lowest point that corresponds to a maximum or minimum value.

 ## Lesson Check

Do you know HOW?

Graph the parabola. Identify the vertex.

1. $y = -3x^2$

2. $y = 4x^2$

3. $y = \frac{1}{2}x^2 + 2$

4. $y = -2x^2 - 1$

Do you UNDERSTAND?

5. Vocabulary When is the vertex of a parabola the minimum point? When is it the maximum point?

6. Compare and Contrast How are the graphs of $y = -\frac{1}{2}x^2$ and $y = -\frac{1}{2}x^2 + 1$ similar? How are they different?

Practice and Problem-Solving Exercises

 Practice   Identify the vertex of each graph. Tell whether it is a minimum or a maximum.   ◀ **See Problem 1.**

7.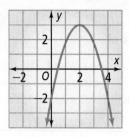

8.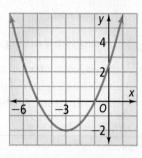

9.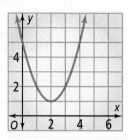

Graph each function. Then identify the domain and range of the function.   ◀ **See Problem 2.**

10. $y = -4x^2$ **11.** $f(x) = 1.5x^2$ **12.** $f(x) = 3x^2$

13. $f(x) = \frac{2}{3}x^2$ **14.** $y = -\frac{1}{2}x^2$ **15.** $y = -\frac{1}{3}x^2$

Order each group of quadratic functions from widest to narrowest graph.   ◀ **See Problem 3.**

Guided Practice

To start, identify the coefficients of the x^2 terms.	**16.** $y = 3x^2, y = 2x^2, y = 4x^2$ The coefficients are 3, 2, and 4.

17. $f(x) = 5x^2, f(x) = -3x^2, f(x) = x^2$ **18.** $y = -\frac{1}{2}x^2, y = 5x^2, y = -\frac{1}{4}x^2$

Graph each function.   ◀ **See Problem 4.**

Guided Practice

To start, make a table.

19. $f(x) = x^2 + 4$

x	$y = x^2 + 4$	(x, y)
−1	$y = (-1)^2 + 4$	$(-1, 5)$
0	■	■
1	■	■

20. $y = x^2 - 7$ **21.** $y = \frac{1}{2}x^2 + 2$

22. $f(x) = -x^2 - 3$ **23.** $y = -2x^2 + 4$

24. Dropped Object A person walking across a bridge accidentally drops an orange into the river below from a height of 40 ft. The function $h = -16t^2 + 40$ gives the orange's approximate height h above the water, in feet, after t seconds. Graph the function. In how many seconds will the orange hit the water?   ◀ **See Problem 5.**

25. Nature A bird drops a stick to the ground from a height of 80 ft. The function $h = -16t^2 + 80$ gives the stick's approximate height h above the ground, in feet, after t seconds. Graph the function. At about what time does the stick hit the ground?

26. Error Analysis Describe and correct the error made in graphing the function $y = -2x^2 + 1$.

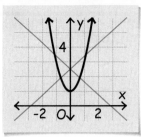

Identify the domain and range of each function.

27. $f(x) = 3x^2 + 6$

28. $y = -2x^2 - 1$

29. $y = -\frac{3}{4}x^2 - 9$

30. $y = \frac{2}{3}x^2 + 12$

31. Writing What information do the numbers a and c give you about the graph of $y = ax^2 + c$?

Match each function with its graph.

32. $f(x) = x^2 - 1$

33. $f(x) = x^2 + 4$

34. $f(x) = -x^2 + 2$

35. $f(x) = 3x^2 - 5$

36. $f(x) = -3x^2 + 8$

37. $f(x) = -0.2x^2 + 5$

A.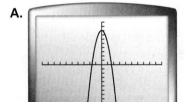

B.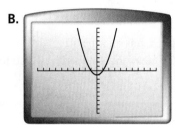

C.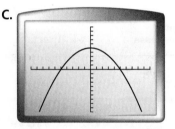

D.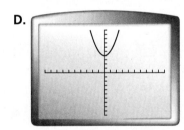

E.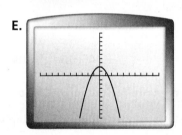

F.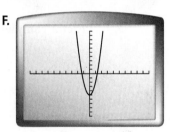

38. Think About a Plan Suppose a person is riding in a hot-air balloon, 154 ft above the ground. He drops an apple. The height h, in feet, of the apple above the ground is given by the formula $h = -16t^2 + 154$, where t is the time in seconds. To the nearest tenth of a second, at what time does the apple hit the ground?
* How can you use a table to approximate the answer between two consecutive whole numbers of seconds?
* How can you use a second table to make your approximation more accurate?

39. Physics In a physics class demonstration, a ball is dropped from the roof of a building, 72 ft above the ground. The height h, in feet, of the ball above the ground is given by the function $h = -16t^2 + 72$, where t is the time in seconds.
a. Graph the function.
b. How far has the ball fallen from time $t = 0$ to $t = 1$?
c. Reasoning Does the ball fall the same distance from time $t = 1$ to $t = 2$ as it does from $t = 0$ to $t = 1$? Explain.

Standardized Test Prep

SAT/ACT

40. Which equation has a graph that is narrower than the graph of $y = 4x^2 + 5$?

    Ⓐ $y = 4x^2 - 5$ Ⓒ $y = 0.75x^2 + 5$

    Ⓑ $y = -5x^2 + 4$ Ⓓ $y = -0.75x^2 - 4$

41. Kristina is evaluating some formulas as part of a science experiment. One of the formulas involves the expression $24 - (-17)$. What is the value of this expression?

    Ⓕ -41 Ⓖ -7 Ⓗ 7   Ⓘ 41

42. Which expression is equivalent to $8(x + 9)$?

    Ⓐ $x + 72$ Ⓑ $8x + 72$ Ⓒ $8x + 17$ Ⓓ $8x + 9$

43. What is the solution of the equation $2(x + 3) + 7 = -11$?

    Ⓕ -12 Ⓖ -1 Ⓗ 1   Ⓘ 12

Short Response

44. A rectangular dog run has an area of $x^2 - 22x - 48$. What are possible dimensions of the dog run? Use factoring. Explain how you found the dimensions.

Mixed Review

Factor completely.   ◀ See Lesson 8-8.

45. $30r^3 + 51r^2 + 9r$ **46.** $15q^3 - 18q^2 - 10q + 12$ **47.** $7b^4 + 14b^3 + b + 2$

Get Ready!   **To prepare for Lesson 9-2, do Exercises 48–53.**

Evaluate the expression $\frac{-b}{2a}$ for the following values of a and b.   ◀ See Lesson 1-6.

48. $a = -2, b = 3$ **49.** $a = -5, b = -4$ **50.** $a = 8, b = 6$

51. $a = 10, b = -7$ **52.** $a = -4, b = 1$ **53.** $a = -12, b = -48$

Objective To graph quadratic functions of the form $y = ax^2 + bx + c$

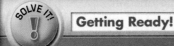

Getting Ready!

You throw a ball straight up into the air and catch it at the same height you released it. The parabola at the right shows the height h of the ball in feet after t seconds. What is the total distance the ball travels? For how long does the ball travel up? Explain your reasoning.

Be careful! The graph shows the height of the ball, not the path of the ball.

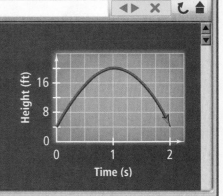

Dynamic Activity
Quadratic Equations in Polynomial Form

The parabola in the Solve It has the equation $h = -16t^2 + 32t + 4$. Unlike the quadratic functions you saw in previous lessons, this function has a linear term, $32t$.

Focus Question How do the graphs of $y = ax^2 + c$ and $y = ax^2 + bx + c$ differ?

In the quadratic function $y = ax^2 + bx + c$, the value of b affects the position of the axis of symmetry.

Consider the graphs of the following functions.

$y = 2x^2 + 2x$ $\qquad\qquad$ $y = 2x^2 + 4x$ $\qquad\qquad$ $y = 2x^2 + 6x$

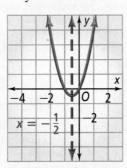 $\qquad$ 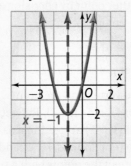 $\qquad$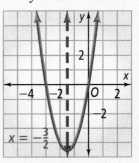

Notice that the axis of symmetry changes with each change in the b-value. The equation of the axis of symmetry is related to the ratio $\frac{b}{a}$.

equation:	$y = 2x^2 + 2x$	$y = 2x^2 + 4x$	$y = 2x^2 + 6x$
$\frac{b}{a}$:	$\frac{2}{2} = 1$	$\frac{4}{2} = 2$	$\frac{6}{2} = 3$
axis of symmetry:	$x = -\frac{1}{2}$	$x = -1$, or $-\frac{2}{2}$	$x = -\frac{3}{2}$

The equation of the axis of symmetry is $x = -\frac{1}{2}\left(\frac{b}{a}\right)$, or $x = \frac{-b}{2a}$.

Key Concept   Graph of a Quadratic Function

The graph of $y = ax^2 + bx + c$, where $a \neq 0$, has the line $x = \frac{-b}{2a}$ as its axis of symmetry. The x-coordinate of the vertex is $\frac{-b}{2a}$.

When you substitute $x = 0$ into the equation $y = ax^2 + bx + c$, you get $y = c$. So the y-intercept of a quadratic function is c. You can use the axis of symmetry and the y-intercept to help you graph a quadratic function.

Problem 1   Graphing $y = ax^2 + bx + c$

What is the graph of the function $y = x^2 - 6x + 4$?

Step 1 Find the axis of symmetry and the coordinates of the vertex.

<table>
<tr><td>Identify a, b, and c.</td><td>$a = 1, b = -6, c = 4$</td></tr>
<tr><td>Find the equation of the axis of symmetry.</td><td>$x = \dfrac{-b}{2a} = \dfrac{-(-6)}{2(1)} = 3$</td></tr>
</table>

Think

How are the vertex and the axis of symmetry related?
The vertex is on the axis of symmetry. You can use the equation for the axis of symmetry to find the x-coordinate of the vertex.

The axis of symmetry is $x = 3$. So, the x-coordinate of the vertex is 3.

<table>
<tr><td>Write the original function.</td><td>$y = x^2 - 6x + 4$</td></tr>
<tr><td>Substitute 3 for x to find the y-coordinate of the vertex.</td><td>$= 3^2 - 6(3) + 4$</td></tr>
<tr><td>Simplify.</td><td>$= -5$</td></tr>
</table>

The vertex is $(3, -5)$.

Step 2 Find two other points on the graph.

Find the y-intercept. Let $x = 0$.

Substitute 0 for x. $\quad y = x^2 - 6x + 4 = 0^2 - 6(0) + 4 = 4$

So one point is $(0, 4)$.

Find another point by choosing a value for x on the same side of the vertex as the y-intercept. Let $x = 1$.

Substitute 1 for x. $\quad y = x^2 - 6x + 4 = 1^2 - 6(1) + 4 = -1$

So another point is $(1, -1)$.

Hint

The reflected points on the graph are the same distance from the axis of symmetry as the original points.

Step 3 Graph the vertex and the points you found in Step 2, $(0, 4)$ and $(1, -1)$. Reflect the points $(0, 4)$ and $(1, -1)$ across the axis of symmetry to get two more points, $(6, 4)$ and $(5, -1)$. Then connect the points with a parabola.

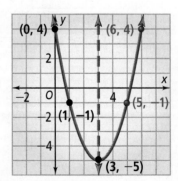

 Got It? 1. What is the graph of the function $y = x^2 + 4x - 2$?

In lesson 9-1, you used $h = -16t^2 + c$ to find the height h above the ground of an object falling from an initial height c at time t. If an object projected into the air given an initial upward velocity v continues with no additional force of its own, the formula $h = -16t^2 + vt + c$ gives its approximate height above the ground.

 ONLINE PROBLEMS

Problem 2 Using the Vertical Motion Model

Entertainment During halftime of a basketball game, a sling shot launches T-shirts at the crowd. A T-shirt is launched with an initial upward velocity of 72 ft/s. The T-shirt is caught 35 ft above the court. How long will it take the T-shirt to reach its maximum height? What is the maximum height? What is the range of the function that models the height of the T-shirt over time?

5 ft

Plan

What are the values of v and c?
The T-shirt is launched from a height of 5 ft, so $c = 5$. The T-shirt has an initial upward velocity of 72 ft/s, so $v = 72$.

The function $h = -16t^2 + 72t + 5$ gives the T-shirt's height h, in feet, after t seconds. Since the coefficient of t^2 is negative, the parabola opens downward, and the vertex is the maximum point.

Method 1 Use the equation for the axis of symmetry.

Substitute -16 for a and 72 for b to find the t-coordinate.

$$t = \frac{-b}{2(a)} = \frac{-72}{2(-16)} = 2.25$$

Substitute 2.25 for t in the original equation to find the h-coordinate.

$$h = -16(2.25)^2 + 72(2.25) + 5 = 86$$

The T-shirt will reach its maximum height of 86 ft after 2.25 s. The range describes the height of the T-shirt during its flight. The T-shirt starts at 5 ft, peaks at 86 ft, and then is caught at 35 ft. The height of the T-shirt at any time is between 5 ft and 86 ft inclusive, so the range is $5 \le h \le 86$.

Method 2 Use a graphing calculator.

Enter the function $h = -16t^2 + 72t + 5$ as $y = -16x^2 + 72x + 5$ on the **Y =** screen, and graph the function.

Use the **CALC** feature and select **MAXIMUM**. Set left and right bounds on the maximum point. The coordinates of the maximum point are (2.25, 86).

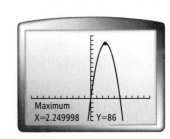

Maximum
X=2.249998 Y=86

The T-shirt will reach its maximum height of 86 ft after 2.25 s. The range of the function is $5 \le h \le 86$.

Got It? **2.** In Problem 2, suppose a T-shirt is launched with an initial upward velocity of 64 ft/s and is caught 35 ft above the court. How long will it take the T-shirt to reach its maximum height? How far above court level will it be? What is the range of the function that models the height of the T-shirt over time?

Focus Question How do the graphs of $y = ax^2 + c$ and $y = ax^2 + bx + c$ differ?

Answer The axis of symmetry in the graph of $y = ax^2 + c$ is zero. The value b affects the position of the axis of symmetry in the graph of $y = ax^2 + bx + c$.

 ## Lesson Check

Do you know HOW?

Graph each function.

1. $y = x^2 - 4x + 1$

2. $y = -2x^2 - 8x - 3$

3. $y = 3x^2 + 6x + 2$

4. $f(x) = -x^2 + 2x - 5$

Do you UNDERSTAND?

5. Reasoning How does each of the numbers a, b, and c affect the graph of a quadratic function $y = ax^2 + bx + c$?

6. Writing Explain how you can use the y-intercept, vertex, and axis of symmetry to graph a quadratic function. Assume the vertex is not on the y axis.

 ## Practice and Problem-Solving Exercises

 Practice Find the equation of the axis of symmetry and the coordinates of the vertex of the graph of each function.

 See Problem 1.

Guided Practice

To start, write the given equation in quadratic form $y = ax^2 + bx + c$. Find a, b, and c.

7. $y = 2x^2 + 3$

$y = 2x^2 + 0x + 3$

$a = 2, b = 0, c = 3$

8. $y = -3x^2 + 12x + 1$

9. $f(x) = 2x^2 + 4x - 1$

10. $y = x^2 - 8x - 7$

11. $f(x) = 3x^2 - 9x + 2$

12. $y = -4x^2 + 11$

13. $f(x) = -5x^2 + 3x + 2$

14. $y = -4x^2 - 16x - 3$

15. $f(x) = 6x^2 + 6x - 5$

Match each function with its graph.

16. $y = -x^2 - 6x$ **17.** $y = -x^2 + 6$ **18.** $y = x^2 - 6$ **19.** $y = x^2 + 6x$

A.
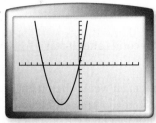

B.
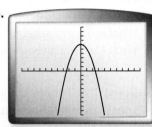

C.
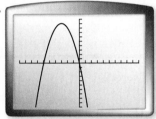

D.
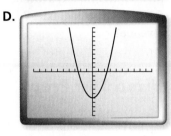

Graph each function. Label the axis of symmetry and the vertex.

20. $f(x) = x^2 + 4x - 5$ **21.** $y = 3x^2 - 20x$

22. $y = -2x^2 + 8x + 9$ **23.** $y = -2x^2 - 10x$

Guided Practice

24. Sports A baseball is thrown into the air with an upward velocity of 30 ft/s. Its height h, in feet, after t seconds is given by the function $h = -16t^2 + 30t + 6$. How long will it take the ball to reach its maximum height? What is the ball's maximum height? What is the range of the function?

◀ **See Problem 2.**

To start, find a, b, and c. Find the t-coordinate of the vertex of the function using a ratio.

$a = -16, b = 30, c = 6$

$t = -\dfrac{b}{2a} = -\dfrac{30}{2(-16)} = \dfrac{15}{16}$

25. School Fair Suppose you have 100 ft of string to rope off a rectangular section for a bake sale at a school fair. The function $A = -x^2 + 50x$ gives the area of the section in square feet, where x is the width in feet. What width gives you the maximum area you can rope off? What is the maximum area? What is the range of the function?

B Apply

Graph each function. Label the axis of symmetry and the vertex.

26. $y = \frac{1}{2}x^2 + 2x + 1$ **27.** $y = \frac{1}{4}x^2 - 2x - 1$

28. $y = \frac{3}{2}x^2 - 3x + 2$ **29.** $f(x) = -\frac{5}{2}x^2 - x + 3$

30. Error Analysis Describe and correct the error made in finding the axis of symmetry for the graph $y = -x^2 - 6x + 2$.

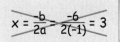

$x = \dfrac{-b}{2a} = \dfrac{-6}{2(-1)} = 3$

31. Reasoning What do you know about the value of b in the function $y = ax^2 + bx + c$ when the x-coordinate of the vertex is an integer?

32. Think About a Plan The Riverside Geyser in Yellowstone National Park erupts about every 6.25 h. When the geyser erupts, the water has an initial upward velocity of 69 ft/s. What is the maximum height of the geyser? Round your answer to the nearest foot.
- What is the initial height of the geyser?
- What function gives the geyser's height h (in feet) t seconds after it starts erupting?

33. Business A cell phone company sells about 500 phones each week when it charges $75 per phone. It sells about 20 more phones per week for each $1 decrease in price. The company's revenue is the product of the number of phones sold and the price of each phone. What price should the company charge to maximize its revenue?

Standardized Test Prep

SAT/ACT

34. What is the simplified form of the product $4(-8)(5)(-1)$?

   (F) -160 (G) -80 (H) 80 (I) 160

35. Which of the following is equivalent to $(-4)^3$?

   (A) -64 (B) -12 (C) 12 (D) 64

36. Toby needs to write an example of the Commutative Property of Multiplication for his homework. Which of the following expressions could he use?

   (F) $ab = ba$ (G) $a = a$ (H) $ab = ab$ (I) $a(bc) = (ab)c$

Short Response

37. Simplify the product $(3r - 1)(4r^2 + r + 2)$. Justify each step.

Mixed Review

Graph each function.   ◀ **See Lesson 9-1.**

38. $y = -x^2 - 2$ **39.** $y = -\frac{1}{2}x^2 + 1$ **40.** $y = 2x^2 + 7$

Get Ready!   **To prepare for Lesson 9-3, do Exercises 41–44.**

                                      ◀ **See Lessons 1-3 and 1–6.**

Simplify each expression.

41. $\sqrt{25}$ **42.** $-\sqrt{64}$ **43.** $\pm\sqrt{144}$ **44.** $\sqrt{1.21}$

Collecting Quadratic Data

In this activity, you will use a loop of string to make rectangles, record their dimensions, and explore the graph of length versus area.

Activity

Take a piece of string, no more than 40 cm long, and tie the ends to form a loop. Use your thumbs and fingers to make a rectangle with the string. Hold it over a piece of graph paper to make right angles.

Step 1 Copy the table at the right. Use the units on your graph paper to measure the length ℓ and width w of the rectangle. Record the measurements to the nearest tenth of a centimeter.

Step 2 Repeat Step 1 four more times, and complete the first two columns.

Step 3 Record the area of each rectangle in the third column of the table.

Step 4 Graph ordered pairs (length, area). Connect the points with a smooth curve.

Length (ℓ)	Width (w)	Area (A)
■	■	■
■	■	■
■	■	■
■	■	■
■	■	■

Exercises

1. **Writing** Based on your graph from Step 4, explain why the data you collected in the activity cannot be modeled by a linear or exponential function.

2. **a.** Find the length of your loop of string.
   b. Write an expression for the width of any rectangle made with your loop of string in terms of the rectangle's length ℓ.
   c. Write a function for the area A of any rectangle made with your loop of string in terms of the rectangle's length ℓ.
   d. Graph the function.
   e. Find the vertex of the graph. What is the meaning of the vertex?

3. Does your graph from part (d) of Exercise 2 exactly match the graph from Step 4 of the activity? If not, explain why not.

4. Suppose you repeated the activity with a loop of string that was 140 cm long. Write a function for the area A of any rectangle made with your loop of string in terms of the rectangle's length ℓ.

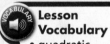

9-3 Solving Quadratic Equations

Objective To solve quadratic equations by graphing and using square roots

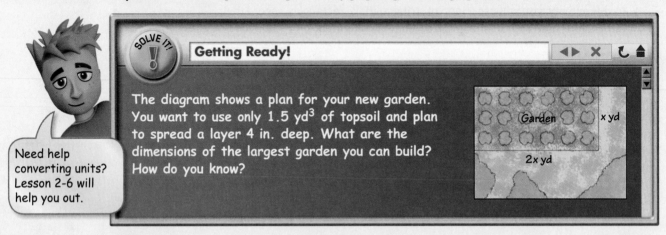

Getting Ready!

The diagram shows a plan for your new garden. You want to use only 1.5 yd³ of topsoil and plan to spread a layer 4 in. deep. What are the dimensions of the largest garden you can build? How do you know?

Need help converting units? Lesson 2-6 will help you out.

Garden   x yd

2x yd

Lesson Vocabulary
- quadratic equation
- standard form of a quadratic equation
- root of an equation
- zero of a function

The situation in the Solve It can be modeled by a *quadratic equation*.

take note

Key Concept **Standard Form of a Quadratic Equation**

A **quadratic equation** is an equation that can be written in the form $ax^2 + bx + c = 0$, where $a \neq 0$. This form is called the **standard form of a quadratic equation.**

Focus Question How do you find the solution to a quadratic equation in standard form by looking at its graph?

One way to solve a quadratic equation $ax^2 + bx + c = 0$ is to graph the related quadratic function $y = ax^2 + bx + c$. The solutions of the equation are the x-intercepts of the related function.

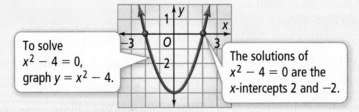

To solve $x^2 - 4 = 0$, graph $y = x^2 - 4$.

The solutions of $x^2 - 4 = 0$ are the x-intercepts 2 and −2.

Hint

Zeros of the function $y = f(x)$ are called zeros because they are the values of x that make the value of y zero.

A quadratic equation can have two, one, or no real-number solutions. In a future course you will learn about solutions of quadratic equations that are not real numbers. In this course, *solutions* refers to real-number solutions.

The solutions of a quadratic equation in standard form and the x-intercepts of the graph of the related function are often called **roots of the equation** or **zeros of the function.**

 **Problem 1** Solving by Graphing

What are the solutions of each equation? Use a graph of the related function.

A $x^2 - 1 = 0$

Graph $y = x^2 - 1$.

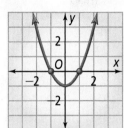

There are two solutions, ± 1.

B $x^2 = 0$

Graph $y = x^2$.

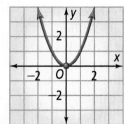

There is one solution, 0.

C $x^2 + 1 = 0$

Graph $y = x^2 + 1$.

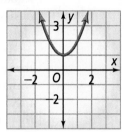

There is no real-number solution.

Think

What feature of the graph shows the solutions of a quadratic equation in standard form?
The *x*-intercepts show the solutions of the equation.

 Got It? 1. What are the solutions of each equation? Use a graph of the related function.

a. $x^2 - 16 = 0$ **b.** $3x^2 + 6 = 0$ **c.** $x^2 - 25 = -25$

Focus Question Why is it useful to solve a quadratic equation using square roots?

You can solve equations of the form $x^2 = k$ by finding the square roots of each side. For example, the solutions of $x^2 = 81$ are $\pm\sqrt{81}$, or ± 9.

Problem 2 Solving Using Square Roots

What are the solutions of $3x^2 - 75 = 0$?

Think

Write the original equation.

Isolate x^2 on one side of the equation.

Find the square roots of each side and simplify.

Write

$3x^2 - 75 = 0$

$3x^2 = 75$
$x^2 = 25$

$x = \pm\sqrt{25}$
$x = \pm 5$

Plan

How do you know you can solve using square roots?
The equation has an x^2-term and a constant term, but no *x*-term. So, you can write the equation in the form $x^2 = k$ and then find the square roots of each side.

 Got It? 2. What are the solutions of each equation?

a. $m^2 - 36 = 0$ **b.** $3x^2 + 15 = 0$ **c.** $4d^2 + 16 = 16$

You can solve some quadratic equations that model real-world problems by finding square roots. In many cases, the negative square root may not be a reasonable solution.

 Problem 3 **Choosing a Reasonable Solution** GRIDDED RESPONSE

Aquarium An aquarium is designing a new exhibit to showcase tropical fish. The exhibit will include a tank that is a rectangular prism with a length ℓ that is twice the width w. The volume of the tank is 420 ft^3. What is the width of the tank to the nearest tenth of a foot?

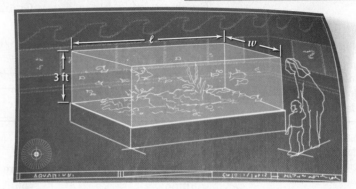

Plan

How can you write the length of the tank?
The length ℓ is twice the width w, so write the length as $2w$.

Use the formula for volume of a rectangular prism.	$V = \ell w h$
Substitute 420 for V, $2w$ for ℓ, and 3 for h.	$420 = (2w)w(3)$
Simplify.	$420 = 6w^2$
Divide each side by 6.	$70 = w^2$
Find the square roots of each side.	$\pm\sqrt{70} = w$
Use a calculator.	$\pm 8.366600265 \approx w$

A tank cannot have a negative width, so only the positive square root makes sense. The tank will have a width of about 8.4 ft.

 Got It? **3.** Suppose the tank in Problem 3 will have a height of 4 ft and a volume of 500 ft^3. What is the width of the tank to the nearest tenth of a foot?

Focus Question How do you find the solution to a quadratic equation in standard form by looking at its graph?

Answer You find the coordinates of the points on the graph that are on the x-axis.

Focus Question Why is it useful to solve a quadratic equation using square roots?

Answer Equations of the form $x^2 = k$ may be easier to solve using square roots than by graphing. Isolate the squared term and find the square root of each side.

 Lesson Check

Do you know HOW?

Solve each equation by graphing the related function or by finding square roots.

1. $x^2 - 25 = 0$ **2.** $2x^2 - 8 = 0$

3. $t^2 - 144 = 0$ **4.** $y^2 - 225 = 0$

Do you UNDERSTAND?

5. Vocabulary What are the zeros of a function? Give an example of a quadratic function and its zeros.

6. Reasoning Consider the equation $ax^2 + c = 0$, where $a \neq 0$. What is true of a and c if the equation has two solutions? Only one solution? No solutions?

Practice and Problem-Solving Exercises

 Practice

Solve each equation by graphing the related function. If the equation has no real-number solution, write *no solution*.

◀ **See Problem 1.**

> **Guided Practice**
>
> To start, identify the related function.
>
> **7.** $x^2 - 9 = 0$
> $y = x^2 - 9$

8. $3x^2 = 0$ **9.** $3x^2 - 12 = 0$ **10.** $x^2 + 4 = 0$

11. $\frac{1}{3}x^2 - 3 = 0$ **12.** $\frac{1}{2}x^2 + 1 = 0$ **13.** $x^2 + 5 = 5$

14. $\frac{1}{4}x^2 - 1 = 0$ **15.** $x^2 + 25 = 0$ **16.** $2x^2 - 18 = 0$

Solve each equation by finding square roots. If the equation has no real-number solution, write *no solution*.

◀ **See Problem 2.**

> **Guided Practice**
>
> To start, take the square root of each side of the equation.
>
> **17.** $n^2 = 81$
> $\sqrt{n^2} = \sqrt{81}$

18. $a^2 = 324$ **19.** $k^2 - 196 = 0$ **20.** $r^2 + 49 = 49$

21. $w^2 - 36 = -64$ **22.** $64b^2 = 16$ **23.** $5q^2 - 20 = 0$

24. $144 - p^2 = 0$ **25.** $3a^2 + 12 = 0$ **26.** $5z^2 - 45 = 0$

Model each problem with a quadratic equation. Then solve. If necessary, round to the nearest tenth.

◀ **See Problem 3.**

27. Find the length of a side of a square with an area of 169 m^2.

28. Find the length of a side of a square with an area of 75 ft^2.

29. Find the radius of a circle with an area of 90 cm^2.

30. **Painting** You have enough paint to cover an area of 50 ft^2. What is the side length of the largest square that you could paint? Round your answer to the nearest tenth of a foot.

31. **Gardening** You have enough shrubs to cover an area of 100 ft^2. What is the radius of the largest circular region you can plant with these shrubs? Round your answer to the nearest tenth of a foot.

 Apply

32. **Compare and Contrast** When is it easier to solve a quadratic equation of the form $ax^2 + c = 0$ using square roots than to solve it using a graph?

Mental Math Tell how many solutions each equation has.

33. $h^2 = -49$

34. $c^2 - 18 = 9$

35. $s^2 - 35 = -35$

36. Think About a Plan A circular above-ground pool has a height of 52 in. and a volume of 1100 ft³. What is the radius of the pool to the nearest tenth of a foot? Use the equation $V = \pi r^2 h$, where V is the volume, r is the radius, and h is the height.
- How can drawing a diagram help you solve this problem?
- Do you need to convert any of the given measurements to different units?

37. Reasoning For what values of n will the equation $x^2 = n$ have two solutions? Exactly one solution? No solution?

38. Quilting You are making a square quilt with the design shown at the right. Find the side length of the inner square that would make its area equal to 50% of the total area of the quilt. Round to the nearest tenth of a foot.

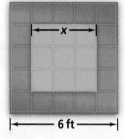

Solve each equation by finding square roots. If the equation has no real-number solution, write *no solution*. If a solution is irrational, round to the nearest tenth.

39. $49p^2 - 16 = -7$

40. $3m^2 - \frac{1}{12} = 0$

41. $\frac{1}{2}t^2 - 4 = 0$

42. $-\frac{1}{4}x^2 + 3 = 0$

43. Find the value of c such that the equation $x^2 - c = 0$ has 12 and -12 as solutions.

44. Physics The equation $d = \frac{1}{2}at^2$ gives the distance d that an object starting at rest travels given acceleration a and time t. Suppose a ball rolls down the ramp shown below with acceleration $a = 2$ ft/s². Find the time it will take the ball to roll from the top of the ramp to the bottom. Round to the nearest tenth of a second.

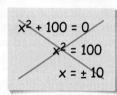

12 ft

45. Error Analysis Describe and correct the error made in solving the equation.

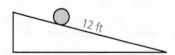

$$x^2 + 100 = 0$$
$$x^2 = 100$$
$$x = \pm 10$$

46. Open-Ended Write and solve an equation in the form $ax^2 + c = 0$, where $a \neq 0$, that satisfies the given condition.
- **a.** The equation has no solution.
- **b.** The equation has exactly one solution.
- **c.** The equation has two solutions.

Geometry Find the value of h for each triangle. If necessary, round to the nearest tenth.

47.

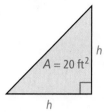

$A = 20 \text{ ft}^2$

h

h

48.

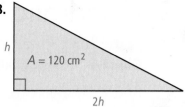

h

$A = 120 \text{ cm}^2$

$2h$

SAT/ACT

49. A package is shaped like a rectangular prism. The length and the width are equal. The volume of the package is 32 ft^3. The height is 2 ft. What is its length?

　Ⓐ -4 ft 　　　　Ⓑ 4 ft 　　　　Ⓒ 8 ft 　　　　Ⓓ 16 ft

50. What is the y-intercept of the line with equation $y = 3x - 4$?

　Ⓕ -4 　　　　Ⓖ -3 　　　　Ⓗ 3 　　　　Ⓘ 4

51. What is the domain of the relation $\{(3, -1), (4, 2), (-2, 5), (1, 0)\}$?

　Ⓐ $\{-1, 0, 2, 5\}$ 　Ⓑ $\{0, 2, 5\}$ 　Ⓒ $\{-2, 1, 3, 4\}$ 　Ⓓ $\{1, 3, 4\}$

52. What is the solution of the inequality $-3x + 2 \leq 14$?

　Ⓕ $x \leq -4$ 　　Ⓖ $x \geq -4$ 　　Ⓗ $x \leq 4$ 　　Ⓘ $x \geq 4$

Extended Response

53. The surface area of a cube is 96 ft^2.
   a. What is the length of each edge? Show your work.
   b. Suppose you double the length of each edge. What happens to the surface area of the cube? Show your work.

Mixed Review

Graph each function. Label the axis of symmetry and the vertex.　　　　⬤ **See Lesson 9-2.**

54. $y = x^2 + 4x + 3$　　　　**55.** $y = x^2 + 5x + 4$　　　　**56.** $y = 2x^2 - 8x - 5$

57. $y = -x^2 + 6x - 1$　　　　**58.** $y = 6x^2 - 12x + 1$　　　**59.** $y = -3x^2 + 18x$

Get Ready!　**To prepare for Lesson 9-4, do Exercises 60–65.**

Factor each expression.　　　　　　　　　　　　　　　　　⬤ **See Lesson 8-6.**

60. $2c^2 + 29c + 14$　　　**61.** $3w^2 + 32w + 20$　　　**62.** $4g^2 - 21g - 18$

63. $2r^2 - 13r - 24$　　　**64.** $3w^2 + 16w - 12$　　　**65.** $5p^2 - 34p + 24$

9-4 Factoring to Solve Quadratic Equations

Objective To solve quadratic equations by factoring

Getting Ready!

You are finishing a stained glass hanging that your friend has started. You have enough supplies to add 6 ft² to the hanging. You are planning to add the same amount to the length and width. What will be the dimensions of the hanging when you are finished? How do you know?

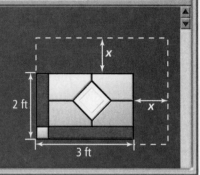

This problem is like the one in Lesson 8-3, but here you need to find numerical values.

In the previous lesson, you solved quadratic equations $ax^2 + bx + c = 0$ by finding square roots. This method works if $b = 0$.

Focus Question How is the Zero-Product Property helpful in solving a quadratic equation?

The Multiplication Property of Zero states that for any real number a, $a \cdot 0 = 0$. This is equivalent to the following statement: For any real numbers a and b, if $a = 0$ or $b = 0$, then $ab = 0$. The Zero-Product Property reverses this statement.

Lesson Vocabulary
• Zero-Product Property

 take note

Property Zero-Product Property

For any real numbers a and b, if $ab = 0$, then $a = 0$ or $b = 0$.

Example If $(x + 3)(x + 2) = 0$, then $x + 3 = 0$ or $x + 2 = 0$.

Problem 1 Using the Zero-Product Property

What are the solutions of the equation $(4t + 1)(t - 2) = 0$?

Write the original equation.	$(4t + 1)(t - 2) = 0$
Use the Zero-Product Property.	$4t + 1 = 0$ or $t - 2 = 0$
Solve for t.	$4t = -1$ or $t = 2$
Use inverse operations, if needed.	$t = -\dfrac{1}{4}$ or $t = 2$

Think

How else can you write the solutions?
You can write the solutions as a set in roster form: $\{-\frac{1}{4}, 2\}$.

Got It? **1.** What are the solutions of each equation?

    a. $(x + 1)(x - 5) = 0$ **b.** $(2x + 3)(x - 4) = 0$

    c. $(2y + 1)(y + 14) = 0$ **d.** $(7n - 2)(5n - 4) = 0$

You can also use the Zero-Product Property to solve equations of the form $ax^2 + bx + c = 0$ if the quadratic expression $ax^2 + bx + c$ can be factored.

 Problem 2   **Solving by Factoring**

Multiple Choice What are the solutions of the equation $x^2 + 8x + 15 = 0$?

    Ⓐ $-5, -3$ Ⓒ $-3, 5$

    Ⓑ $-5, 3$ Ⓓ $3, 5$

Write the original equation.	$x^2 + 8x + 15 = 0$
Factor $x^2 + 8x + 15$.	$(x + 3)(x + 5) = 0$
Use the Zero-Product Property.	$x + 3 = 0$ or $x + 5 = 0$
Solve for x.	$x = -3$ or $x = -5$

The solutions are -3 and -5. The correct answer is A.

Plan

How can you factor $x^2 + 8x + 15$?
Find two integers with a product of 15 and a sum of 8.

 Got It? **2.** What are the solutions of each equation?

    a. $m^2 - 5m - 14 = 0$ **b.** $p^2 + p - 20 = 0$ **c.** $2a^2 - 15a + 18 = 0$

Before solving a quadratic equation, you may need to add or subtract terms from each side in order to write the equation in standard form. Then factor the quadratic expression.

 Problem 3   **Writing in Standard Form First**

What are the solutions of $4x^2 - 21x = 18$?

Think

Why do you need to subtract 18 from each side before you factor?
To use the Zero-Product Property, one side of the equation must be zero.

Write the original equation.	$4x^2 - 21x = 18$
Subtract 18 from each side.	$4x^2 - 21x - 18 = 0$
Factor $4x^2 - 21x - 18$.	$(4x + 3)(x - 6) = 0$
Use the Zero-Product Property.	$4x + 3 = 0$ or $x - 6 = 0$
Solve for x.	$4x = -3$ or $x = 6$
Use inverse operations, if needed.	$x = -\dfrac{3}{4}$ or $x = 6$

The solutions are $-\frac{3}{4}$ and 6.

 Got It? **3. a.** What are the solutions of $x^2 + 14x = -49$?

    b. Reasoning Why do quadratic equations of the form $x^2 + 2ax + a^2 = 0$ or $x^2 - 2ax + a^2 = 0$ have only one real-number solution?

Problem 4 **Using Factoring to Solve a Real-World Problem**

Hint

The frame is wider and longer than the picture by the same amount on all four sides.

Photography You are constructing a frame for the rectangular photo shown. You want the frame to be the same width all the way around and the total area of the frame and photo to be 315 in.². What should the outer dimensions of the frame be?

Know

The size of the photo is 11 in. by 17 in. The total area is 315 in.².

Need

The outer dimensions of the frame

Plan

Write the frame's outer dimensions in terms of its width x. Use these dimensions to write an equation for the area of the frame and photo.

Width × Length = Area	$(2x + 11)(2x + 17) = 315$
Find the product $(2x + 11)(2x + 17)$.	$4x^2 + 56x + 187 = 315$
Subtract 315 from each side.	$4x^2 + 56x - 128 = 0$
Factor out 4.	$4(x^2 + 14x - 32) = 0$
Factor $x^2 + 14x - 32$.	$4(x + 16)(x - 2) = 0$
Use the Zero-Product Property.	$x + 16 = 0$ or $x - 2 = 0$
Solve for x.	$x = -16$ or $x = 2$

Think

Why can you ignore the factor of 4?
By the Zero Product Property, one of the factors, 4, $x + 16$, or $x - 2$ must equal 0. Since $4 \neq 0$, either $x + 16$ or $x - 2$ equals 0.

The only reasonable solution is 2. So the outer dimensions of the frame are $2(2) + 11$ in. by $2(2) + 17$ in., or 15 in. by 21 in.

Got It? **4.** In Problem 4, suppose the total area of the frame and photo were 391 in.². What would the outer dimensions of the frame be?

Focus Question How is the Zero-Product Property helpful in solving a quadratic equation?

Answer The Zero-Product Property tells you that one factor in an equation equals zero. You can set each factor to zero and solve for the variable.

Lesson Check

Do you know HOW?

Solve each equation.

1. $(v - 4)(v - 7) = 0$

2. $t^2 + 3t - 54 = 0$

3. $3y^2 - 17y + 24 = 0$

4. Carpentry You are making a rectangular table. The area of the table should be 10 ft². You want the length of the table to be 1 ft shorter than twice its width. What should the dimensions of the table be?

Do you UNDERSTAND?

5. Vocabulary Give an example of how the Zero-Product Property can be used to solve a quadratic equation.

6. Compare and Contrast How is factoring the expression $x^2 - 6x + 8$ similar to solving the equation $x^2 - 6x + 8 = 0$? How is it different?

7. Reasoning Can you extend the Zero-Product Property to nonzero products of numbers? For example, if $ab = 8$, is it always true that $a = 8$ or $b = 8$? Explain.

Practice and Problem-Solving Exercises

 Practice

Use the Zero-Product Property to solve each equation.

◀ See Problem 1.

Guided Practice

To start, use the Zero-Product Property.

8. $(x - 9)(x - 8) = 0$

$x - 9 = 0$ or $x - 8 = 0$

9. $(4k + 5)(k + 7) = 0$

10. $n(n + 2) = 0$

11. $-3n(2n - 5) = 0$

12. $(7x + 2)(5x - 4) = 0$

Solve by factoring.

◀ See Problems 2 and 3.

Guided Practice

To start, find two factors of 10 that add to 11.

13. $x^2 + 11x + 10 = 0$

The factors of 10 are 2 and 5, 1 and 10.

$1 + 10 = 11$

14. $g^2 + 4g - 32 = 0$

15. $s^2 - 14s + 45 = 0$

16. $2z^2 - 21z - 36 = 0$

17. $3q^2 + q - 14 = 0$

18. $4m^2 - 27m - 40 = 0$

19. $x^2 + 13x = -42$

20. $c^2 = 5c$

21. $3h^2 + 17h = -10$

22. $9b^2 = 16$

23. Geometry A box shaped like a rectangular prism has a volume of 280 in.^{3}. Its dimensions are 4 in. by $(n + 2)$ in. by $(n + 5)$ in. Find n.

◀ See Problem 4.

24. Knitting You are knitting a blanket. You want the area of the blanket to be 24 ft^2. You want the length of the blanket to be 2 ft longer than its width. What should the dimensions of the blanket be?

25. Construction You are building a rectangular deck. The area of the deck should be 250 ft^2. You want the length of the deck to be 5 ft longer than twice its width. What should the dimensions of the deck be?

 Apply

Use the Zero-Product Property to solve each equation. Write your solutions as a set in roster form.

26. $x^2 + 6x + 8 = 0$

27. $a^2 + 8a + 12 = 0$

28. $k^2 + 7k + 10 = 0$

29. Think About a Plan You have a rectangular koi pond that measures 6 ft by 8 ft. You have enough concrete to cover 72 ft^2 for a walkway, as shown in the diagram. What should the width of the walkway be?
- How can you write the outer dimensions of the walkway?
- How can you represent the total area of the walkway and pond in two ways?

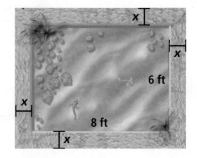

30. Open-Ended Write a quadratic equation in standard form $ax^2 + bx + c = 0$ such that a, b, and c are integers, but the solutions are rational numbers that are not integers.

31. Reasoning How many solutions does an equation of the form $x^2 - k^2 = 0$ have? Explain.

32. Sports You throw a softball into the air with an initial upward velocity of 38 ft/s and an initial height of 5 ft.
    a. Use the vertical motion model to write an equation that gives the ball's height h, in feet, at time t, in seconds.
    b. The ball's height is 0 ft when it is on the ground. Solve the equation you wrote in part (a) for $h = 0$ to find when the ball lands.

Solve each cubic equation by factoring out the GCF first.

33. $x^3 - 10x^2 + 24x = 0$ **34.** $x^3 - 5x^2 + 4x = 0$ **35.** $3x^3 - 9x^2 = 0$

Standardized Test Prep

GRIDDED RESPONSE

SAT/ACT

36. What is the negative solution of the equation $2x^2 - 13x - 7 = 0$? Round to the nearest thousandth.

37. Phil, Toby, and Sam bowled four games last weekend. Their scores are shown in the Venn diagram at the right. What is the highest score that only Toby and Sam have in common?

38. What is the y-intercept of the line with equation $3y - 4x = 9$?

39. How many elements are in the union of the two sets $M = \{1, 2, -3, 4\}$ and $N = \{1, -2, 3, 5\}$?

40. Nina makes a rectangular card. The length is 1 in. longer than twice the width. The card has an area of 15 in.^{2}. What is the width of the card, in inches?

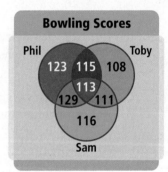

Bowling Scores

Phil   Toby
123   115   108
113
129   111
116
Sam

Mixed Review

Solve each equation by finding square roots. If the equation has no real-number solution, write *no solution*.

◆ **See Lesson 9-3.**

41. $t^2 = 144$ **42.** $w^2 - 8 = -17$ **43.** $b^2 + 100 = 100$

44. $5h^2 - 80 = 0$ **45.** $49 - m^2 = 0$ **46.** $3q^2 = 27$

Get Ready!   **To prepare for Lesson 9-5, do Exercises 47–49.**

Factor each expression.

◆ **See Lesson 8-7.**

47. $y^2 - 10y + 25$ **48.** $g^2 - 14g + 49$ **49.** $m^2 + 18m + 81$

Chapter Review for Part A

Chapter Vocabulary

- axis of symmetry (p. 566)
- maximum (p. 567)
- minimum (p. 567)

- parabola (p. 566)
- quadratic equation (p. 580)
- quadratic function (p. 566)

- root of an equation (p. 580)
- vertex (p. 567)
- zero of a function (p. 580)

Choose the correct term to complete each sentence.

1. The U-shaped graph of a quadratic function is a(n) _?_ .

2. The line that divides a parabola in half is the _?_ .

3. The _?_ of a parabola is the point at which the parabola intersects the axis of symmetry.

9-1 and 9-2 Graphing Quadratic Functions

Quick Review

A function of the form $y = ax^2 + bx + c$, where $a \neq 0$, is a **quadratic function.** Its graph is a **parabola.** The **axis of symmetry** of a parabola divides it into two matching halves. The **vertex** of a parabola is the point at which the parabola intersects the axis of symmetry.

Example

What is the vertex of the graph of $y = x^2 + 6x - 2$?

The x-coordinate of the vertex is given by $x = \frac{-b}{2a}$.

$$x = \frac{-b}{2a} = \frac{-6}{2(1)} = -3$$

Find the y-coordinate of the vertex.

Substitute -3 for x. $y = (-3)^2 + 6(-3) - 2$

Simplify. $y = -11$

The vertex is $(-3, -11)$.

Exercises

Graph each function. Label the axis of symmetry and the vertex.

4. $y = \frac{2}{3}x^2$

5. $y = -x^2 + 1$

6. $y = x^2 - 4$

7. $y = 5x^2 + 8$

8. $y = -\frac{1}{2}x^2 + 4x + 1$

9. $y = -2x^2 - 3x + 10$

10. $y = \frac{1}{2}x^2 + 2x - 3$

11. $y = 3x^2 + x - 5$

Open-Ended **Give an example of a quadratic function that matches each description.**

12. Its graph opens downward.

13. The vertex of its graph is at the origin.

14. Its graph opens upward.

15. Its graph is wider than the graph of $y = x^2$.

9-3 Solving Quadratic Equations

Quick Review

The **standard form of a quadratic equation** is $ax^2 + bx + c = 0$, where $a \neq 0$. Quadratic equations can have two, one, or no real-number solutions. You can solve a quadratic equation by graphing the related function and finding the x-intercepts. Some quadratic equations can also be solved using square roots.

Example

What are the solutions of $2x^2 - 72 = 0$?

Write the original equation.	$2x^2 - 72 = 0$
Add 72 to each side.	$2x^2 = 72$
Divide each side by 2.	$x^2 = 36$
Find the square roots of each side.	$x = \pm\sqrt{36}$
Simplify.	$x = \pm 6$

Exercises

Solve each equation by finding square roots. If the equation has no real-number solution, write *no solution*.

16. $6(x^2 - 2) = 12$

17. $-5m^2 = -125$

18. $9(w^2 + 1) = 9$

19. $3r^2 + 27 = 0$

20. $4 = 9k^2$

21. $4n^2 = 64$

22. Geometry The area of a circle A is given by the formula $A = \pi r^2$, where r is the radius of the circle. Find the radius of a circle with area 16 in.^{2}. Round to the nearest tenth of an inch.

9-4 Factoring to Solve Quadratic Equations

Quick Review

If you can factor the left side of $ax^2 + bx + c = 0$, you can use the **Zero-Product Property** to solve the equation. To use the Zero-Product Property, set each factor equal to zero and solve for the variable.

Example

What are the solutions of the equation $(3x - 6)(x + 4) = 0$?

Write the original equation.	$(3x - 6)(x + 4) = 0$
Use the Zero-Product Property.	$3x - 6 = 0$ or $x + 4 = 0$
Solve for x.	$3x = 6$ or $x = -4$
Isolate x, if necessary.	$x = 2$ or $x = -4$

Exercises

Solve by factoring.

23. $x^2 + 7x + 12 = 0$ **24.** $5x^2 - 10x = 0$

25. $2x^2 - 9x = x^2 - 20$ **26.** $2x^2 + 5x = 3$

27. $3x^2 - 5x = -3x^2 + 6$ **28.** $x^2 - 5x + 4 = 0$

29. Construction You are building a rectangular flower garden. You want the area of the garden to be 39 ft^2. You want the length of the garden to be 10 ft longer than its width. What dimensions of the garden should you use?

Do you know HOW?

Order each group of quadratic functions from widest to narrowest graph.

1. $y = 2x^2, y = 0.5x^2, y = -x^2$

2. $f(x) = 4x^2, f(x) = \frac{2}{3}x^2, f(x) = 3x^2$

3. $f(x) = 0.6x^2, f(x) = 0.3x^2, f(x) = 0.2x^2$

4. $y = -2x^2, y = x^2, y = -0.25x^2$

Graph each function. Label the axis of symmetry and the vertex.

5. $y = \frac{1}{2}x^2$

6. $y = -2x^2 - 1$

7. $y = 3x^2 - 6x$

8. $y = x^2 + 2x + 4$

9. $y = -0.5x^2 + 2x + 1$

Solve each equation by graphing the related function. If the equation has no real-number solution, write _no solution_.

10. $x^2 - 16 = 0$

11. $x^2 + 9 = 0$

12. $0.25x^2 = 0$

Solve each equation by finding square roots. If the equation has no real-number solution, write _no solution_.

13. $m^2 = 81$

14. $t^2 - 7 = -18$

15. $5r^2 - 180 = 0$

16. $36n^2 = 9$

17. **Sewing** You have 324 ft² of fabric to make a circular play parachute for kids. What is the radius of the largest parachute you could make? Round to the nearest tenth of a foot.

Solve by factoring.

18. $b^2 + 3b - 4 = 0$

19. $n^2 + n - 12 = 0$

20. $2x^2 - 5x - 3 = 0$

21. $t^2 - 3t = 28$

22. $3n^2 = 6n$

23. **Construction** You are building a rectangular planter for your school garden. You want the area of the bottom to be 90 ft². You want the length of the planter to be 3 ft longer than twice its width. What should the dimensions of the bottom of the planter be?

Do you UNDERSTAND?

24. **Writing** Describe the steps you would use to graph the function $y = 2x^2 + 5$.

25. **Reasoning** Does the value of c in the quadratic function $y = ax^2 + bx + c$ affect the horizontal position of the vertex of the graph? Explain why or why not.

26. **Writing** Describe how the graph of $y = 3x^2$ differs from the graph of $y = x^2$.

Open-Ended Give an example of a quadratic function that matches each description.

27. The axis of symmetry is to the left of the y-axis.

28. Its graph lies entirely below the x-axis.

29. Its graph opens upward and has its vertex at $(0, 0)$.

30. **a.** Solve $x^2 - 4 = 0$ and $2x^2 - 8 = 0$ by graphing their related functions.
    b. **Reasoning** Why does it make sense that the graphs have the same x-intercepts?

Quadratic Functions and Equations

In Part A, you learned about quadratic functions and their graphs, and how to solve some quadratic equations. Now you will learn how to solve quadratic equations that can't be factored.

Vocabulary for Part B

English/Spanish Vocabulary Audio Online:

English	Spanish
completing the square, p. 595	completar el cuadrado
discriminant, p. 604	discriminante
quadratic formula, p. 601	fórmula cuadrática

BIGideas

1 Functions
Essential Question What are the characteristics of quadratic functions?

2 Solving Equations and Inequalities
Essential Question How can you solve a quadratic equation?

Chapter Preview for Part B

Objective To solve quadratic equations by completing the square

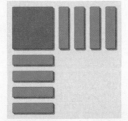

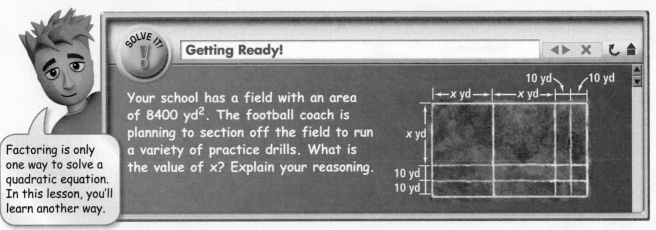

SOLVE IT!

Getting Ready!

Your school has a field with an area of 8400 yd². The football coach is planning to section off the field to run a variety of practice drills. What is the value of x? Explain your reasoning.

Factoring is only one way to solve a quadratic equation. In this lesson, you'll learn another way.

Lesson Vocabulary
• completing the square

In previous lessons, you solved quadratic equations by finding square roots and by factoring. These methods work in some cases, but not all.

Focus Question How is solving a quadratic equation using square roots similar to solving a quadratic equation by completing the square?

You can solve any quadratic equation by first writing it in the form $m^2 = n$.

You can model this process using algebra tiles. The algebra tiles at the right represent the expression $x^2 + 8x$.

Here is the same expression rearranged to form part of a square. Notice that the x-tiles have been split evenly into two groups of four.

You can complete the square by adding 4^2, or 16, 1-tiles. The completed square is $x^2 + 8x + 16$, or $(x + 4)^2$.

In general, you can change the expression $x^2 + bx$ into a perfect-square trinomial by adding $\left(\frac{b}{2}\right)^2$ to $x^2 + bx$. This gives you $x^2 + bx + \left(\frac{b}{2}\right)^2$, which is equal to $\left(x + \frac{b}{2}\right)^2$. This process is called **completing the square.** The process is the same whether b is positive or negative.

Problem 1 Finding *c* to Complete the Square

What is the value of *c* such that $x^2 - 16x + c$ is a perfect-square trinomial?

The value of *b* is -16. The term to add to $x^2 - 16x$ is $\left(\frac{-16}{2}\right)^2 = (-8)^2 = 64$. So $c = 64$.

 Got It? 1. What is the value of *c* such that $x^2 + 20x + c$ is a perfect-square trinomial?

Problem 2 Solving $x^2 + bx = c$

What are the solutions of the equation $x^2 + 6x = 216$?

Write the original equation.	$x^2 + 6x = 216$
Add $\left(\frac{6}{2}\right)^2$, or 9, to each side.	$x^2 + 6x + 9 = 216 + 9$
Write $x^2 + 6x + 9$ as a square.	$(x + 3)^2 = 216 + 9$
Simplify the right side.	$(x + 3)^2 = 225$
Find square roots of each side.	$x + 3 = \pm\sqrt{225}$
Simplify.	$x + 3 = \pm15$
Write as two equations.	$x + 3 = 15$ or $x + 3 = -15$
Subtract 3 from each side.	$x = 12$ or $x = -18$

 Got It? 2. What are the solutions of the equation $t^2 - 6t = 247$?

To solve an equation in the form $x^2 + bx + c = 0$, first subtract the constant term *c* from each side of the equation.

Problem 3 Solving $x^2 + bx + c = 0$

What are the solutions of the equation $x^2 - 14x + 16 = 0$?

Write the original equation.	$x^2 - 14x + 16 = 0$
Subtract 16 from each side.	$x^2 - 14x = -16$
Add $\left(\frac{-14}{2}\right)^2$, or 49, to each side.	$x^2 - 14x + 49 = -16 + 49$
Write $x^2 - 14x + 49$ as a square.	$(x - 7)^2 = 33$
Find square roots of each side.	$x - 7 = \pm\sqrt{33}$
Use a calculator to approximate $\sqrt{33}$.	$x - 7 \approx \pm5.74$
Write as two equations.	$x - 7 \approx 5.74$ or $x - 7 \approx -5.74$
Add 7 to each side.	$x \approx 5.74 + 7$ or $x \approx -5.74 + 7$
Simplify.	$x \approx 12.74$ or $x \approx 1.26$

Got It? 3. a. What are the solutions of the equation $x^2 + 9x + 15 = 0$?

b. Reasoning Could you use factoring to solve part (a)? Explain.

The method of completing the square works when $a = 1$ in $ax^2 + bx + c = 0$. To solve an equation when $a \neq 1$, divide each side by a before completing the square.

Problem 4 Completing the Square When $a \neq 1$

Gardening You are planning a flower garden consisting of three square plots surrounded by a 1-ft border. The total area of the garden and the border is 100 ft². What is the side length x of each square plot?

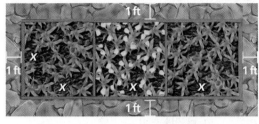

🌷 **Red tulips**   🌷 **Yellow tulips**

Know

• Area of garden and border
• Expressions for the dimensions of the garden and border

Need

The side length x of each square plot

Plan

Write and solve an equation that relates the dimensions and area of the garden and border.

Step 1 Write an equation that you can use to solve the problem.

Length × Width = Area	$(3x + 2)(x + 2) = 100$
Find the product $(3x + 2)(x + 2)$.	$3x^2 + 8x + 4 = 100$
Subtract 4 from each side.	$3x^2 + 8x = 96$
Divide each side by 3.	$x^2 + \frac{8}{3}x = 32$

Step 2 Complete the square.

Add $\left(\frac{4}{3}\right)^2$, or $\frac{16}{9}$, to each side. $x^2 + \frac{8}{3}x + \frac{16}{9} = 32 + \frac{16}{9}$

Write left side as a square and right side as a fraction. $\left(x + \frac{4}{3}\right)^2 = \frac{304}{9}$

Step 3 Solve the equation.

Find square roots of each side.	$x + \frac{4}{3} = \pm\sqrt{\frac{304}{9}}$	
Use a calculator to approximate $\sqrt{\frac{304}{9}}$.	$x + \frac{4}{3} \approx \pm 5.81$	
Write as two equations.	$x + \frac{4}{3} \approx 5.81$ or	$x + \frac{4}{3} \approx -5.81$
Solve for x.	$x \approx 4.48$ or	$x \approx -7.14$

The negative answer does not make sense in this problem. So the side length of each square plot is about 4.48 ft.

Think

Why do you need to find $\frac{1}{2}\left(\frac{8}{3}\right)$?
To make $x^2 + \frac{8}{3}x = 32$ have a perfect-square trinomial on the left side, find $\frac{1}{2}\left(\frac{8}{3}\right)$. Then square the result and add to each side of the equation.

Got It? 4. Suppose the total area of the garden and border in Problem 4 is 150 ft². What is the side length x of each square plot? Round to the nearest hundredth.

Focus Question How is solving a quadratic equation using square roots similar to solving a quadratic equation by completing the square?

Answer You take the square root of each side of the equation and isolate the variable.

 ## Lesson Check

Do you know HOW?

Solve each equation by completing the square.

1. $x^2 + 8x = 180$

2. $t^2 - 4t - 165 = 0$

3. $m^2 + 7m - 294 = 0$

4. $2z^2 + 3z = 135$

Do you UNDERSTAND?

5. Vocabulary Tell whether you would use square roots, factoring, or completing the square to solve each equation. Explain your choice of method.

    a. $k^2 - 3k = 304$ **b.** $t^2 - 6t + 16 = 0$

6. Compare and Contrast How is solving a quadratic equation using square roots like completing the square? How is it different?

 ## Practice and Problem-Solving Exercises

 Practice   Find the value of c such that each expression is a perfect-square trinomial.    **See Problem 1.**

    7. $x^2 + 18x + c$ **8.** $z^2 + 22z + c$ **9.** $p^2 - 30p + c$

    10. $k^2 - 5k + c$ **11.** $g^2 + 17g + c$ **12.** $q^2 - 4q + c$

Solve each equation by completing the square. If necessary, round to the nearest hundredth.   **See Problems 2 and 3.**

Guided Practice

13. $g^2 + 7g = 144$

To start, identify the form of the equation given. Find $\left(\dfrac{b}{2}\right)^2$.

$$x^2 + bx = c$$

$$\left(\dfrac{b}{2}\right)^2 = \left(\dfrac{7}{2}\right)^2 = \dfrac{49}{4}$$

    14. $r^2 - 4r = 30$ **15.** $m^2 + 16m = -59$ **16.** $q^2 + 4q = 16$

    17. $z^2 - 2z = 323$ **18.** $a^2 - 2a - 35 = 0$ **19.** $m^2 + 12m + 19 = 0$

    20. $w^2 - 14w + 13 = 0$ **21.** $p^2 + 5p - 7 = 0$ **22.** $t^2 + t - 28 = 0$

Solve each equation by completing the square. If necessary, round to the nearest hundredth.

◀ See Problem 4.

Guided Practice

23. $4a^2 - 8a = 24$

To start, divide each side by 4, which holds the position of *a* in the equation $ax^2 + bx = c$.

$$\frac{4a^2}{4} - \frac{8a}{4} = \frac{24}{4}$$

$$a^2 - 2a = 6$$

24. $2y^2 - 8y - 10 = 0$

25. $5n^2 - 3n - 15 = 10$

26. $4w^2 + 12w - 44 = 0$

27. $3r^2 + 18r = 21$

28. Art The painting shown at the right has an area of 420 in.². What is the value of *x*?

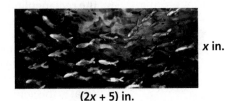

x in.

(2*x* + 5) in.

B Apply

29. Think About a Plan A park is installing a rectangular reflecting pool surrounded by a concrete walkway of uniform width. The reflecting pool will measure 42 ft by 26 ft. There is enough concrete to cover 460 ft² for the walkway. What is the maximum width *x* of the walkway?
- How can drawing a diagram help you solve this problem?
- How can you write an expression in terms of *x* for the area of the walkway?

30. Landscaping A school is fencing in a rectangular area for a playground. It plans to enclose the playground using fencing on three sides, as shown at the right. The school has budgeted enough money for 75 ft of fencing material and would like to make a playground with an area of 600 ft².
a. Let *w* represent the width of the playground. Write an expression in terms of *w* for the length of the playground.
b. Write and solve an equation to find the width *w*. Round to the nearest tenth of a foot.
c. What should the length of the playground be?

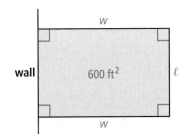

Use each graph to estimate the values of *x* for which $f(x) = 5$. Then write and solve an equation to find the values of *x* such that $f(x) = 5$. Round to the nearest hundredth.

31. $f(x) = x^2 - 2x - 1$

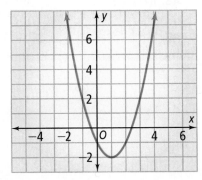

32. $f(x) = -\frac{1}{2}x^2 + 2x + 6$

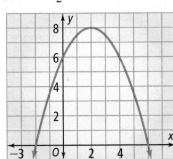

33. Error Analysis A classmate was completing the square to solve $4x^2 + 10x = 8$. For her first step she wrote $4x^2 + 10x + 25 = 8 + 25$. What was her error?

34. Reasoning Explain why completing the square is a better strategy for solving $x^2 - 7x - 9 = 0$ than graphing or factoring.

35. Open-Ended Write a quadratic equation and solve it by completing the square. Show your work.

Standardized Test Prep

GRIDDED RESPONSE

SAT/ACT

36. The rectangular poster has an area 40 ft^2. What is the value of x to the nearest tenth of a foot?

37. The width of a notebook is 2.15×10^{-2} m. In decimal form, how many meters wide is the notebook?

$(x+1)$ ft

$(x+2)$ ft

38. What is the solution of the equation $19 + x = 35$?

39. How many elements are in the intersection of the two sets $M = \{2, 3, 4, 5\}$ and $N = \{1, 3, 5, 9\}$?

40. A ribbon with straight edges has an area of 24 in.^{2}. Its width is x and its length is $2x + 13$. What is the width of the ribbon in inches?

41. What is the x-intercept of the graph of $2x + 3y = 9$?

42. The sum of two numbers is 20. The difference between three times the larger number and twice the smaller number is 40. What is the larger number?

Mixed Review

Solve by factoring.   ◀ See Lesson 9-4.

43. $n^2 + 11n + 30 = 0$ **44.** $9v^2 - 64 = 0$ **45.** $12w^2 = 28w + 5$

Simplify.   ◀ See Lesson 7-4.

46. $(m^3)^4$ **47.** $-b^7(b^8)^{-1}$ **48.** $t(t^2)^6$ **49.** $y^8(y^{-7})^{-3}$

Get Ready! **To prepare for Lesson 9-6, do Exercises 50–52.**

Evaluate $b^2 - 4ac$ for the given values of a, b, and c.   ◀ See Lesson 1-2.

50. $a = 2, b = 5, c = -7$ **51.** $a = 2, b = 4, c = 2$ **52.** $a = 1, b = 3, c = 6$

9-6 The Quadratic Formula and the Discriminant

Objectives To solve quadratic equations using the quadratic formula
To find the number of solutions of a quadratic equation

Ever wonder how to tell if an equation has no solution?

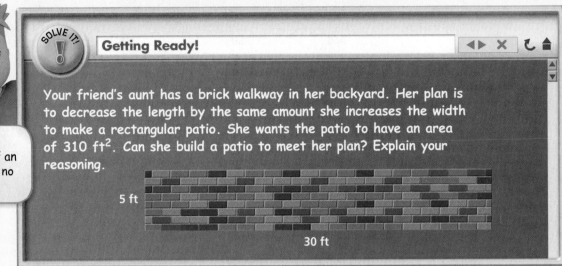

SOLVE IT!

Getting Ready!

Your friend's aunt has a brick walkway in her backyard. Her plan is to decrease the length by the same amount she increases the width to make a rectangular patio. She wants the patio to have an area of 310 ft². Can she build a patio to meet her plan? Explain your reasoning.

5 ft

30 ft

Lesson Vocabulary
• quadratic formula
• discriminant

Recall that quadratic equations can have two, one, or no real-number solutions. A quadratic equation can never have more than two solutions.

Focus Question Why is the quadratic formula useful in solving a quadratic equation?

You can find the solution(s) of *any* quadratic equation using the **quadratic formula.**

---

take note

Key Concept Quadratic Formula

Algebra

If $ax^2 + bx + c = 0$, and $a \neq 0$, then

$$x = \frac{-b \pm \sqrt{b^2 - 4ac}}{2a}$$

Example

Suppose $2x^2 + 3x - 5 = 0$. Then $a = 2$, $b = 3$, and $c = -5$. Therefore

$$x = \frac{-(3) \pm \sqrt{(3)^2 - 4(2)(-5)}}{2(2)}$$

Here's Why It Works If you complete the square for the general equation $ax^2 + bx + c = 0$, you can derive the quadratic formula.

Step 1 Write $ax^2 + bx + c = 0$ so the coefficient of x^2 is 1.

Write the general equation. $\qquad ax^2 + bx + c = 0$

Divide each side by a. $\qquad x^2 + \frac{b}{a}x + \frac{c}{a} = 0$

Step 2 Complete the square.

Subtract $\frac{c}{a}$ from each side. $\qquad\qquad\qquad x^2 + \frac{b}{a}x = -\frac{c}{a}$

Add $\left(\frac{b}{2a}\right)^2$ to each side. $\qquad\qquad\quad x^2 + \frac{b}{a}x + \left(\frac{b}{2a}\right)^2 = -\frac{c}{a} + \left(\frac{b}{2a}\right)^2$

Write the left side as a square. $\qquad\qquad \left(x + \frac{b}{2a}\right)^2 = -\frac{c}{a} + \frac{b^2}{4a^2}$

Multiply $-\frac{c}{a}$ by $\frac{4a}{4a}$ to get like denominators. $\qquad \left(x + \frac{b}{2a}\right)^2 = -\frac{4ac}{4a^2} + \frac{b^2}{4a^2}$

Simplify the right side. $\qquad\qquad\qquad \left(x + \frac{b}{2a}\right)^2 = \frac{b^2 - 4ac}{4a^2}$

Step 3 Solve the equation for x.

Take square roots of each side. $\qquad \sqrt{\left(x + \frac{b}{2a}\right)^2} = \pm\sqrt{\frac{b^2 - 4ac}{4a^2}}$

Simplify the right side. $\qquad\qquad\qquad x + \frac{b}{2a} = \pm\frac{\sqrt{b^2 - 4ac}}{2a}$

> This step uses the property $\sqrt{\frac{m}{n}} = \frac{\sqrt{m}}{\sqrt{n}}$, which you will study in Lesson 10-2.

Subtract $\frac{b}{2a}$ from each side. $\qquad\qquad x = -\frac{b}{2a} \pm \frac{\sqrt{b^2 - 4ac}}{2a}$

Simplify. $\qquad\qquad\qquad\qquad\qquad\quad x = \frac{-b \pm \sqrt{b^2 - 4ac}}{2a}$

Be sure to write a quadratic equation in standard form before using the quadratic formula.

Problem 1 Using the Quadratic Formula

Think

Why do you need to write the equation in standard form?
You can only use the quadratic formula with equations in the form $ax^2 + bx + c = 0$.

What are the solutions of $x^2 - 8 = 2x$? Use the quadratic formula.

Write the original equation. $\qquad\qquad\qquad x^2 - 8 = 2x$

Write the equation in standard form. $\qquad\quad x^2 - 2x - 8 = 0$

Use the quadratic formula. $\qquad\qquad\qquad x = \frac{-b \pm \sqrt{b^2 - 4ac}}{2a}$

Substitute 1 for a, -2 for b, and -8 for c. $\qquad x = \frac{-(-2) \pm \sqrt{(-2)^2 - 4(1)(-8)}}{2(1)}$

Simplify. $\qquad\qquad\qquad\qquad\qquad\qquad x = \frac{2 \pm \sqrt{36}}{2}$

Write as two equations. $\qquad\qquad x = \frac{2 + 6}{2} \quad$ or $\quad x = \frac{2 - 6}{2}$

Simplify. $\qquad\qquad\qquad\qquad\quad x = 4 \qquad$ or $\qquad x = -2$

 Got It? 1. What are the solutions of $x^2 - 4x = 21$? Use the quadratic formula.

When the radicand in the quadratic formula is not a perfect square, you can use a calculator to approximate the solutions of an equation.

Problem 2 **Finding Approximate Solutions**

Sports In the shot put, an athlete throws a heavy metal ball through the air. The arc of the ball can be modeled by the equation $y = -0.04x^2 + 0.84x + 2$, where x is the horizontal distance, in meters, from the athlete and y is the height, in meters, of the ball. How far from the athlete will the ball land?

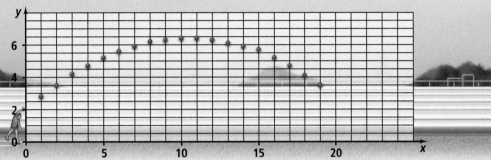

Think

Why do you substitute 0 for *y*?
When the ball hits the ground, its height will be 0.

Write the original equation.	$y = -0.04x^2 + 0.84x + 2$
Substitute 0 for y in the given equation.	$0 = -0.04x^2 + 0.84x + 2$
Use the quadratic formula.	$x = \dfrac{-b \pm \sqrt{b^2 - 4ac}}{2a}$
Substitute -0.04 for a, 0.84 for b, and 2 for c.	$x = \dfrac{-0.84 \pm \sqrt{0.84^2 - 4(-0.04)(2)}}{2(-0.04)}$
Simplify.	$x = \dfrac{-0.84 \pm \sqrt{1.0256}}{-0.08}$

Write as two equations.	$x = \dfrac{-0.84 + \sqrt{1.0256}}{-0.08}$	or	$x = \dfrac{-0.84 - \sqrt{1.0256}}{-0.08}$
Simplify.	$x \approx -2.16$	or	$x \approx 23.16$

Only the positive answer makes sense in this situation. The ball will land about 23.16 m from the athlete.

 Got It? **2.** A batter strikes a baseball. The equation $y = -0.005x^2 + 0.7x + 3.5$ models its path, where x is the horizontal distance, in feet, the ball travels and y is the height, in feet, of the ball. How far from the batter will the ball land? Round to the nearest tenth of a foot.

There are many methods for solving a quadratic equation.

Method	When to Use
Graphing	Use if you have a graphing calculator handy.
Square roots	Use if the equation has no x-term.
Factoring	Use if you can factor the equation easily.
Completing the square	Use if the coefficient of x^2 is 1, but you cannot easily factor the equation.
Quadratic formula	Use if the equation cannot be factored easily or at all.

Think

Can you use the quadratic formula to solve part (A)?
Yes, the quadratic formula with $a = 3$, $b = 0$, and $c = -9$. However, it is faster to use square roots.

Which method(s) would you choose to solve each equation? Explain your reasoning.

A $3x^2 - 9 = 0$ Square roots; there is no x-term

B $x^2 - x - 30 = 0$ Factoring; the equation is easily factorable

C $6x^2 + 13x - 17$ Quadratic formula, graphing; the equation cannot be factored

D $x^2 - 5x + 3 = 0$ Quadratic formula, completing the square, or graphing; the coefficient of the x^2-term is 1, but the equation cannot be factored

E $-16x^2 - 50x + 21 = 0$ Quadratic formula, graphing; the equation cannot be factored easily since the numbers are large

Got It? 3. Which method(s) would you choose to solve each equation? Justify your reasoning.

    a. $x^2 - 8x + 12 = 0$ **b.** $169x^2 = 36$ **c.** $5x^2 + 13x - 1 = 0$

Quadratic equations can have two, one, or no real-number solutions. Before you solve a quadratic equation, you can determine how many real-number solutions it has by using the discriminant. The **discriminant** is the expression under the radical sign in the quadratic formula.

$$x = \frac{-b \pm \sqrt{b^2 - 4ac}}{2a} \longleftarrow \text{the discriminant}$$

The discriminant of a quadratic equation can be positive, zero, or negative.

 take note

Key Concept   Using the Discriminant

Discriminant	$b^2 - 4ac > 0$	$b^2 - 4ac = 0$	$b^2 - 4ac < 0$
Example	$x^2 - 6x + 7 = 0$ The discriminant is $(-6)^2 - 4(1)(7) = 8$, which is positive.	$x^2 - 6x + 9 = 0$ The discriminant is $(-6)^2 - 4(1)(9) = 0$.	$x^2 - 6x + 11 = 0$ The discriminant is $(-6)^2 - 4(1)(11) = -8$, which is negative.
	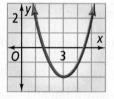	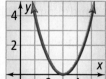	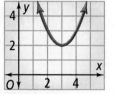
Number of Solutions	There are two real-number solutions.	There is one real-number solution.	There are no real-number solutions.

Hint

The solutions of a quadratic equation are the x-values where the graph crosses the x-axis.

How many real-number solutions does $2x^2 - 3x = -5$ have?

Think

Write

Plan

Can you solve this problem another way?
Yes. You could actually solve the equation to find any solutions. However, you only need to know the number of solutions, so use the discriminant.

Write the equation in standard form.

$2x^2 - 3x + 5 = 0$

Evaluate the discriminant by substituting 2 for a, -3 for b, and 5 for c.

$b^2 - 4ac = (-3)^2 - 4(2)(5)$
$= -31$

Draw a conclusion.

Because the discriminant is negative, the equation has no real-number solutions.

 Got It? **4. a.** How many real-number solutions does $6x^2 - 5x = 7$ have?

b. **Reasoning** If a is positive and c is negative, how many real-number solutions will the equation $ax^2 + bx + c = 0$ have? Explain.

Focus Question Why is the quadratic formula useful in solving a quadratic equation?

Answer You can find the number of solutions and the exact solutions of a quadratic equation for any quadratic equation.

 Lesson Check

Do you know HOW?

Use the quadratic formula to solve each equation. If necessary, round answers to the nearest hundredth.

1. $-3x^2 - 11x + 4 = 0$

2. $7x^2 - 2x = 8$

3. How many real-number solutions does the equation $-2x^2 + 8x - 5 = 0$ have?

Do you UNDERSTAND?

4. **Vocabulary** Explain how the discriminant of the equation $ax^2 + bx + c = 0$ is related to the number of x-intercepts of the graph of $y = ax^2 + bx + c$.

5. **Reasoning** What method would you use to solve the equation $x^2 + 9x + c = 0$ if $c = 14$? If $c = 7$? Explain.

6. **Writing** Explain how completing the square is used to derive the quadratic formula.

Practice and Problem-Solving Exercises

 Practice

Use the quadratic formula to solve each equation.

See Problem 1.

Guided Practice

To start, identify the values of *a*, *b*, and *c*.

7. $2x^2 + 5x + 3 = 0$

$ax^2 + bx + c = 0$

$2x^2 + 5x + 3 = 0$

$a = 2, b = 5, c = 3$

8. $5x^2 + 16x - 84 = 0$ **9.** $4x^2 + 7x - 15 = 0$ **10.** $3x^2 - 41x = -110$

11. $3x^2 + 19x = 154$ **12.** $2x^2 - x - 120 = 0$ **13.** $5x^2 - 47x = 156$

Use the quadratic formula to solve each equation. Round your answer to the nearest hundredth.

See Problem 2.

14. $x^2 + 8x + 11 = 0$ **15.** $5x^2 + 12x - 2 = 0$

16. $8x^2 - 7x - 5 = 0$ **17.** $6x^2 + 9x = 32$

18. Football A football player punts a ball. The path of the ball can be modeled by the equation $y = -0.004x^2 + x + 2.5$, where *x* is the horizontal distance, in feet, the ball travels and *y* is the height, in feet, of the ball. How far from the football player will the ball land? Round to the nearest tenth of a foot.

Which method(s) would you choose to solve each equation? Justify your reasoning.

See Problem 3.

19. $x^2 + 4x - 15 = 0$ **20.** $9x^2 - 49 = 0$

21. $3x^2 - 7x + 3 = 0$ **22.** $x^2 + 4x - 60 = 0$

Find the number of real-number solutions of each equation.

See Problem 4.

Guided Practice

To start, identify the values of *a*, *b*, and *c* and evaluate the discriminant.

23. $x^2 - 2x + 3 = 0$

$a = 1, b = -2, c = 3$

$b^2 - 4ac = (-2)^2 - 4(1)(3)$

24. $x^2 + 7x - 5 = 0$ **25.** $x^2 + 3x + 11 = 0$

26. $x^2 - 15 = 0$ **27.** $x^2 + 2x = 0$

 Apply

28. Think About a Plan You operate a dog-walking service. You have 50 customers per week when you charge $14 per walk. For each $1 decrease in your fee for walking a dog, you get 5 more customers per week. Can you ever earn $750 in a week? Explain.
  - What quadratic equation in standard form can you use to model this situation?
  - How can the discriminant of the equation help you solve the problem?

29. Sports Your school wants to take out an ad in the paper congratulating the basketball team on a successful season, as shown at the right. The area of the photo will be half the area of the entire ad. What is the value of x?

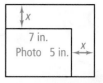

30. Writing How can you use the discriminant to write a quadratic equation that has two solutions?

31. Error Analysis Describe and correct the error at the right that a student made in finding the discriminant of $2x^2 + 5x - 6 = 0$.

$a = 2, b = 5, c = -6$
$b^2 - 4ac = 5^2 - 4(2)(-6)$
$= 25 - 48$
$= -23$

32. Find the discriminant and the solution of each equation in parts (a)-(c). If necessary, round to the nearest hundredth.

  a. $x^2 - 6x + 5 = 0$ **b.** $x^2 + x - 20 = 0$
  c. $2x^2 - 7x - 3 = 0$
  d. Reasoning When the discriminant is a perfect square, are the solutions rational or irrational? Explain.

Standardized Test Prep

SAT/ACT

33. What are the approximate solutions of the equation $x^2 - 7x + 3 = 0$?

  Ⓐ $-6.54, 0.46$ Ⓑ $-6.54, -0.46$ Ⓒ $-0.46, 6.54$ Ⓓ $0.46, 6.54$

34. Which of the following relations is a function?

  Ⓕ $\{(1, 2), (3, 5), (1, 4), (2, 3)\}$ Ⓗ $\{(8, 2), (6, 3), (6, 11), (-8, 2)\}$
  Ⓖ $\{(-5, 6), (0, 9), (-1, 2), (0, 6)\}$ Ⓘ $\{(-1, 3), (7, 3), (-7, 2), (4, 5)\}$

35. What equation do you get when you solve $3a - b = 2c$ for b?

  Ⓐ $b = -3a + 2c$ Ⓑ $b = 3a - 2c$ Ⓒ $b = 3a + 2c$ Ⓓ $b = -3a - 2c$

36. What are the approximate solutions of the equation $\frac{1}{3}x^2 - \frac{5}{4}x + 1 = 0$? Use a graphing calculator.

  Ⓕ $1.07, 2.77$ Ⓖ $1.16, 2.59$ Ⓗ $0.87, 10.38$ Ⓘ $0.19, 16.01$

Short Response

37. Suppose the line through points $(n, 6)$ and $(1, 2)$ is parallel to the graph of $2x + y = 3$. Find the value of n. Show your work.

Mixed Review

Solve each equation by completing the square.   ◀ **See Lesson 9-5.**

38. $s^2 - 10s + 13 = 0$ **39.** $m^2 + 3m = -2$ **40.** $3w^2 + 18w - 1 = 0$

Get Ready! **To prepare for Lesson 9-7, do Exercises 41–44.**

Graph each function.   ◀ **See Lesson 7-6.**

41. $y = 2^x$ **42.** $y = 3^x$ **43.** $y = \left(\frac{1}{3}\right)^x$ **44.** $y = \left(\frac{1}{2}\right)^x$

9-7 Linear, Quadratic, and Exponential Models

Objective To choose a linear, quadratic, or exponential model for data

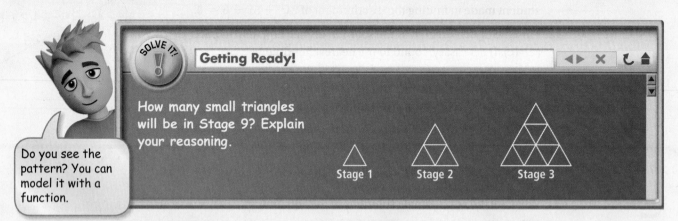

Getting Ready!

How many small triangles will be in Stage 9? Explain your reasoning.

Stage 1   Stage 2   Stage 3

Do you see the pattern? You can model it with a function.

Focus Question When should you use a quadratic function instead of an exponential or linear function to model a data set?

take note

Concept Summary   Linear, Quadratic, and Exponential Functions

Linear: $y = mx + b$ Quadratic: $y = ax^2 + bx + c$ Exponential: $y = a \cdot b^x$

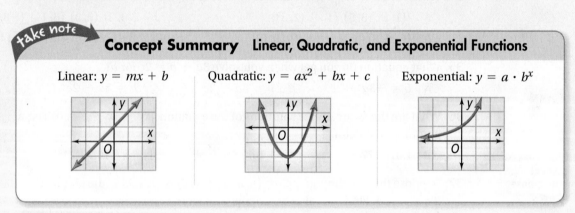

Problem 1   Choosing a Model by Graphing

Graph each set of points. Which model is most appropriate for each set?

Think

Can you eliminate possibilities?
Yes. For example, you know that a linear model isn't appropriate in parts (A) and (B) because the slope between any two points is not constant.

A (1, 3), (0, 0), (−3, 3), (−1, −1), (−2, 0)

B (0, 2), (−1, 4), (1, 1), (2, 0.5)

C (−1, −2), (0, −1), (1, 0), (3, 2)

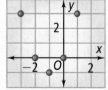

Quadratic model

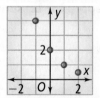

Exponential model

Linear model

a. $(0, 0), (1, 1), (-1, -0.5), (2, 3)$ **b.** $(-2, 11), (-1, 5), (0, 3), (1, 5)$

You can use a linear function to model data pairs with y-values that have a common difference. You can use an exponential function to model data pairs with y-values that have a common ratio.

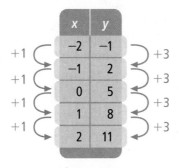

x	y
−2	−1
−1	2
0	5
1	8
2	11

+1 / +3 (left side +1's, right side +3's)

x	y
−2	0.25
−1	0.5
0	1
1	2
2	4

+1 / ×2

The y-values have a common difference of 3. A linear model fits the data.

The y-values have a common ratio of 2. An exponential model fits the data.

Hint

In quadratic functions, the y-values increase and then decrease, or decrease and then increase.

For quadratic functions, the second differences are constant.

In the table at the right, the second differences of the y-values are all 4, so a quadratic model fits the data.

First differences

Second differences

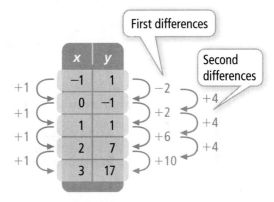

x	y
−1	1
0	−1
1	1
2	7
3	17

+1 | −2 +4
+1 | +2 +4
+1 | +6 +4
+1 | +10

Problem 2 **Choosing a Model Using Differences or Ratios**

Which type of function best models the data? Use differences or ratios.

Plan

How can you get started?
Begin by checking the first differences of the y-values. Then check the second differences and ratios, if necessary.

A

x	y
−3	9
−2	5
−1	1
0	−3
1	−7

+1 | −4
+1 | −4
+1 | −4
+1 | −4

The first differences are constant, so a linear function models the data.

B

x	y
0	0
1	−0.25
2	−1
3	−2.25
4	−4

+1 | −0.25 −0.5
+1 | −0.75 −0.5
+1 | −1.25 −0.5
+1 | −1.75

The second differences are constant, so a quadratic function models the data.

Got It? **2.** Which type of function best models the ordered pairs
$(-1, 0.5)$, $(0, 1)$, $(1, 2)$, $(2, 4)$, and $(3, 8)$? Use differences or ratios.

Problem 3 **Modeling Data**

Which type of function best models the data in the table at the right? Write an
equation to model the data.

x	y
0	0
1	0.5
2	2
3	4.5
4	8

Plan

**How can a graph help
you get started?**
A graph may suggest
the type of function that
models the data. You can
then use differences or
ratios to confirm the type
of function.

Step 1
Graph the data.

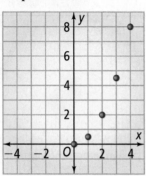

Step 2
The data appear quadratic. Test
for a common second difference.

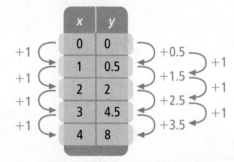

There is a common second difference, 1.

Step 3
The graph appears to be a parabola
with vertex at $(0, 0)$, so use $y = ax^2$.

Write the quadratic model.	$y = ax^2$
Use a point other than $(0, 0)$ to find a.	$2 = a(2)^2$
Simplify.	$2 = 4a$
Divide each side by 4.	$0.5 = a$
Write a quadratic function.	$y = 0.5x^2$

Step 4
Test two points in the data set other than
$(2, 2)$ and $(0, 0)$.

Test $(3, 4.5)$:   Test $(4, 8)$:
$y = 0.5x^2$ $y = 0.5x^2$
$y = 0.5(3)^2$ $y = 0.5(4)^2$
$y = 4.5$ ✔ $y = 8$ ✔

The points $(3, 4.5)$ and $(4, 8)$ both satisfy $y = 0.5x^2$.
The equation $y = 0.5x^2$ models the data.

Got It? **3.** Which type of function best
models the data in the table at
the right? Write an equation to
model the data.

x	−1	0	1	2	3
y	30	6	1.2	0.24	0.048

Focus Question When should you use a quadratic function instead of an exponential or
linear function to model a data set?

Answer When the x-values in a data set have a common difference but the y-values have a
common second difference, you should use a quadratic function as a model.

Lesson Check

Do you know HOW?

Which type of function best models each set of data points?

1. $(0, 11), (1, 5), (2, 3), (3, 5), (4, 11)$

2. $(-4, -10), (-2, -7), (0, -4), (2, -1), (4, 2)$

3. $(-1, 8), (0, 4), (2, 1), (3, 0.5)$

Do you UNDERSTAND?

4. Reasoning Can the y-values in a set of data pairs have both a common ratio and a common difference? Explain why or why not.

5. Writing Explain how to decide whether a linear, exponential, or quadratic function is the most appropriate model for a set of data.

Practice and Problem-Solving Exercises

 Practice

Graph each set of points. Which model is most appropriate for each set?

◀ **See Problem 1.**

Guided Practice

To start, graph the data set.

6. $(-2, -3), (-1, 0), (0, 1), (1, 0), (2, -3)$

7. $(-2, -8), (0, -4), (3, 2), (5, 6)$

8. $(-3, 6), (-1, 0), (0, -1), (1, -1.5)$

9. $(-2, 5), (-1, -1), (0, -3), (1, -1), (2, 5)$

10. $(-1, -5\frac{2}{3}), (0, -5), (2, 3), (3, 27)$

Which type of function best models the data in each table? Use differences or ratios.

◀ **See Problem 2.**

11.

x	y
0	0
1	1.5
2	6
3	13.5
4	24

12.

x	y
0	−5
1	−3
2	−1
3	1
4	3

13.

x	y
0	1
1	1.2
2	1.44
3	1.728
4	2.0736

Which type of function best models the data in each table? Write an equation to model the data.

See Problem 3.

14.

x	y
0	0
1	2.8
2	11.2
3	25.2
4	44.8

15.

x	y
0	5
1	2
2	0.8
3	0.32
4	0.128

16.

x	y
0	2
1	1.5
2	1
3	0.5
4	0

B Apply

17. Sports The number of people attending a school's first five football games is shown in the table below. Which type of function best models the data? Write an equation to model the data.

Game	1	2	3	4	5
Attendance	248	307	366	425	484

Hint

Real-world data seldom fall exactly into linear, exponential, or quadratic patterns. Look for which type of pattern best fits the data.

18. Error Analysis Tom claims that, because the data pairs $(1, 4)$, $(2, 6)$, $(3, 9)$, and $(4, 13.5)$ have y-values with a common ratio, they are best modeled by a quadratic function. What is his error?

19. Think About a Plan The number of visitors at a Web site over several days is shown in the table at the right. What is an equation that models the data?

- Does the graph of the data suggest a type of function to use?
- Will your equation fit the data exactly? How do you know?

Day	Visitors
1	52
2	197
3	447
4	805
5	1270

20. Open-Ended Write a set of data pairs that you could model with a quadratic function.

21. The table below shows the projected population of a small town. Let $t = 0$ correspond to the year 2020.
  a. Graph the data. Does the graph suggest a linear, exponential, or quadratic model?
  b. Find the rate of change in population with respect to time from one data pair to the next. How do the results support your answer to part (a)?
  c. Write a function that models the data shown in the table.
  d. Use the function from part (c) to predict the town's population in 2050.

Year, t	0	5	10	15
Population, p	5100	5700	6300	6900

22. Zoology A conservation organization collected the data on the number of frogs in a local wetland, shown in the table at the right. Which type of function best models the data? Write an equation to model the data.

23. a. Make a table of five ordered pairs for each function using consecutive x-values. Find the common second difference.

  i. $f(x) = x^2 - 3$　　**ii.** $f(x) = 3x^2$　　**iii.** $f(x) = 4x^2 - 5x$

  b. What is the relationship between the common second difference and the coefficient of the x^2-term?

  c. Reasoning Explain how you could use this relationship to model data.

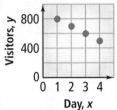

Year	Number of Frogs
0	120
1	101
2	86
3	72
4	60

Standardized Test Prep

SAT/ACT

24. The graph at the right shows the number y of visitors to a museum over x days. Which function models the number of visitors?

　Ⓐ $y = -100x + 900$　　　　　Ⓒ $y = -100x + 800$

　Ⓑ $y = 900(0.875)^x$　　　　　Ⓓ $y = -50x^2 - 400x + 1300$

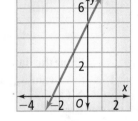

25. Which expression is equivalent to $(4x^3 + 2x^2 + 1) + (3x^2 + 8x + 2)$?

　Ⓕ $7x^2 + 10x + 3$　　Ⓖ $7x^3 + 10x^2 + 3x$　　Ⓗ $4x^3 + 5x^2 + 3$　　Ⓘ $4x^3 + 5x^2 + 8x + 3$

26. Which line passes through the point $(1, 3)$ and is parallel to the line graphed at the right?

　Ⓐ $y = 2x + 1$　　　　　Ⓒ $y = 2x - 5$

　Ⓑ $y = 2x + 3$　　　　　Ⓓ $y = -5x + 8$

Short Response

27. What are the factors of $10x^2 - x - 2$? Show your work.

Mixed Review

Use the quadratic formula to solve each equation. If necessary, round to the nearest hundredth.
◀ See Lesson 9-6.

28. $4x^2 + 4x - 3 = 0$　　　**29.** $x^2 + 2x - 7 = 0$　　　**30.** $3x^2 - 8x = -1$

Get Ready!　To prepare for Lesson 10-1, do Exercises 31–36.

Simplify each expression.
◀ See Lesson 1-3.

31. $\sqrt{196}$　　　　　**32.** $\sqrt{\dfrac{25}{49}}$　　　　　**33.** $\sqrt{1.44}$

34. $\sqrt{81}$　　　　　**35.** $\sqrt{0.36}$　　　　　**36.** $\sqrt{400}$

Performing Regressions

You can use a graphing calculator to perform quadratic regressions and exponential regressions.

Activity

Use a graphing calculator to find a model for the given data.

x	0	1	2	3	4	5
y	4	1	2	5	8	19

Step 1

Enter the data into two lists. Enter the x-values in **L1** and the y-values in **L2**.

Step 2

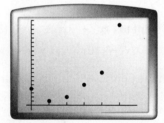

Make a scatter plot of the data. Press (zoom) 9 to graph. The graph appears to be quadratic.

Step 3

Perform the regression. Press (stat). Select **CALC** and **QUADREG** to find the model.

The equation $y = 1.39x^2 - 4.14x + 4.07$ models the data. Check the equation by graphing it and the ordered pairs from the table in the same coordinate plane. To perform an exponential regression, press (stat). Select **CALC** and **EXPREG** to find the model.

Exercises

Use a graphing calculator to find a model for each set of data.

1.

x	y
−1	4.3
0	5.1
1	4.3
2	2.2
3	1.3

2.

x	y
−1	12.75
0	2.83
1	0.64
2	0.12
3	0.04

3.

x	y
−1	0.1
0	1.2
1	11.8
2	115.3
3	1129.4

Pull It All Together

To solve these problems you will pull together many concepts and skills that you have studied about quadratic functions and equations.

BIG idea Functions

The family of quadratic functions has equations of the form $y = ax^2 + bx + c$, where $a \neq 0$. The graph of a quadratic function is a parabola.

Task 1

Solve. Show your work and explain your steps.

Suppose you have a quadratic function $y = ax^2 + bx + c$, where $a < -1$, $b = 2a$, and $c = -b$. What do you know about the graph of this function? Justify each detail.

BIG idea Solving Equations and Inequalities

You can solve quadratic equations by several methods, including graphing, finding square roots, factoring, completing the square, and using the quadratic formula. Sometimes the characteristics of the equation make one method more efficient than the others.

Task 2

Solve. Show your work and explain your steps.

A manufacturer makes 50-cm lengths of steel pipe. A pipe uses 400 cm^3 of steel and has an inner radius of 2 cm. What is the thickness x of the pipe?

BIG idea Modeling

To model a data set, choose a function that most closely matches the pattern in the data or graph.

Task 3

Solve. Show your work and explain your steps.

Suppose you draw chords to divide a circle into as many regions as possible. The maximum number of regions R you can make is a quadratic function of the number of chords x you draw. The values of R for $x = 0$, $x = 1$, and $x = 2$ are shown. What function models this situation? How many regions can you make with 10 chords?

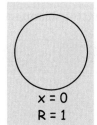

x = 0
R = 1

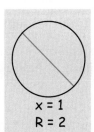

x = 1
R = 2

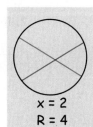

x = 2
R = 4

Connecting BIG ideas and Answering the Essential Questions

1 Function
The family of quadratic functions has equations of the form $y = ax^2 + bx + c$, where $a \neq 0$. The graph of a quadratic function is a parabola.

Graphing Quadratic Functions (Lessons 9-1 and 9-2)

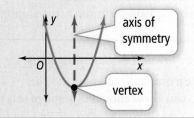

axis of symmetry

vertex

2 Solving Equations and Inequalities
You can solve quadratic equations using several methods.

Solving Quadratic Equations (Lessons 9-3, 9-4, 9-5, and 9-6)
$$ax^2 + bx + c = 0$$
$$x = \frac{-b \pm \sqrt{b^2 - 4ac}}{2a}$$

3 Modeling
To model a data set, choose a function that most closely matches the pattern in the data or graph.

Choosing a Model (Lesson 9-7)

$y = mx + b$ $y = ax^2 + bx + c$ $y = a \cdot b^x$

Chapter Vocabulary

- completing the square (p. 595)
- discriminant (p. 604)
- quadratic formula (p. 601)

Choose the correct term to complete each sentence.

1. The ___?___ can be used to determine the number of real-number solutions of a quadratic equation.

2. The ___?___ can be used to find the solutions of any quadratic equation.

3. ___?___ is a process used to change the expression $x^2 + bx$ into a perfect-square trinomial.

9-5 Completing the Square

Quick Review

You can solve any quadratic equation by writing it in the form $x^2 + bx = c$, **completing the square,** and finding the square roots of each side of the equation.

Example

What are the solutions of $x^2 + 8x = 513$?

Add $\left(\frac{8}{2}\right)^2$, or 16, to each side.
$$x^2 + 8x + 16 = 513 + 16$$

Write $x^2 + 8x + 16$ as a square.
$$(x + 4)^2 = 529$$

Find the square roots.
$$x + 4 = \pm\sqrt{529}$$

Simplify.
$$x + 4 = \pm 23$$

Write as two equations. $\quad x + 4 = 23 \quad$ or $\quad x + 4 = -23$

Solve for x. $\qquad x = 19 \quad$ or $\qquad x = -27$

Exercises

Solve each equation by completing the square. If necessary, round to the nearest hundredth.

4. $x^2 + 6x - 5 = 0$ **5.** $x^2 = 3x - 1$

6. $2x^2 + 7x = -6$ **7.** $x^2 + 10x = -8$

8. $4x^2 - 8x = 24$ **9.** $x^2 - 14x + 16 = 0$

10. Construction You are planning a rectangular patio with length that is 7 ft less than three times its width. The area of the patio is 120 ft². What are the dimensions of the patio?

11. Design You are designing a rectangular birthday card for a friend. You want the card's length to be 1 in. more than twice the card's width. The area of the card is 88 in.². What are the dimensions of the card?

9-6 The Quadratic Formula and the Discriminant

Quick Review

You can solve the quadratic equation $ax^2 + bx + c = 0$, where $a \neq 0$, by using the **quadratic formula**
$$x = \frac{-b \pm \sqrt{b^2 - 4ac}}{2a}.$$
The **discriminant** is $b^2 - 4ac$. The discriminant tells you how many real-number solutions the equation has.

Example

How many real-number solutions does the equation $x^2 + 3 = 2x$ have?

Write in standard form. $\quad x^2 - 2x + 3 = 0$

Evaluate discriminant. $\quad b^2 - 4ac = (-2)^2 - 4(1)(3)$

Simplify. $\qquad\qquad\qquad = -8$

Because the discriminant is negative, the equation has no real-number solutions.

Exercises

Find the number of real-number solutions of each equation.

12. $x^2 + 7x - 10 = 3$ **13.** $3x^2 - 2 = 5x$

Solve each equation using the quadratic formula. Round to the nearest hundredth.

14. $4x^2 + 3x - 8 = 0$ **15.** $2x^2 - 3x = 20$

16. $-x^2 + 8x + 4 = 5$ **17.** $64x^2 + 12x - 1 = 0$

Solve each equation using any method. Explain why you chose the method you used.

18. $5x^2 - 10 = x^2 + 90$ **19.** $x^2 - 6x + 9 = 0$

20. Vertical Motion A ball is thrown into the air. The height h, in feet, of the ball can be modeled by the equation $h = -16t^2 + 20t + 6$, where t is the time, in seconds, the ball is in the air. When will the ball hit the ground?

9-7 Linear, Quadratic, and Exponential Models

Quick Review

Graphing data points or analyzing data numerically can help you find the best model. Linear data have a common first difference. Exponential data have a common ratio. Quadratic data have a common second difference.

Example

Graph the points (1, 4), (4, 2), (2, 3), (5, 3.5), and (6, 5). Which model is most appropriate?

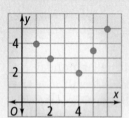

A quadratic model is most appropriate.

Exercises

Graph each set of points. Which model is most appropriate for each data set?

21. $(-3, 0), (1, 4), (-1, 6), (2, 0)$

22. $(0, 6), (5, 2), (1, 4), (8, 1.5), (2, 3)$

Write an equation to model the data.

23.

x	y
−1	−5
0	−2
1	1
2	4
3	7

24.

x	y
−1	2.5
0	5
1	10
2	20
3	40

Do you know HOW?

Graph each function.

1. $y = 3x^2 - 7$

2. $y = -x^2 - 2$

3. $y = -2x^2 + 10x - 1$

Solve each equation.

4. $x^2 + 11x - 26 = 0$

5. $x^2 - 25 = 0$

6. $x^2 - 19x + 80 = -8$

7. $x^2 - 5x = -4x$

8. $4x^2 - 100 = 0$

9. Design You are creating a rectangular banner for a school pep rally. You have 100 ft² of paper, and you want the length to be 15 ft longer than the width. What should be the dimensions of the banner?

Find the number of real-number solutions of each equation.

10. $x^2 + 4x = -4$

11. $x^2 + 8 = 0$

12. $3x^2 - 9x = -5$

Solve each equation. If necessary, round to the nearest hundredth.

13. $-3x^2 + 7x = -10$

14. $x^2 + 4x = 1$

15. $12x^2 + 16x - 28 = 0$

16. Vertical Motion You throw a ball upward. Its height h, in feet, after t seconds can be modeled by the function $h = -16t^2 + 30t + 6$. After how many seconds will it hit the ground?

17. Identify the graph at the right as *linear*, *quadratic*, or *exponential*. Write an equation that models the data points shown.

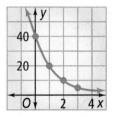

Do you UNDERSTAND?

18. Writing Explain what you can determine about the shape of a parabola from its equation alone.

19. Open-Ended Write an equation of a parabola that has two x-intercepts and a maximum value. Include a graph of your parabola.

20. Reasoning The graph of a quadratic function $y = ax^2 + bx + c$ is shown. What do you know about the values of a, b, and c just by looking at the graph?

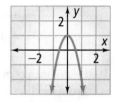

21. Geometry Suppose a rectangle has an area of 60 ft² and dimensions, in feet, of x and $x + 1$.
  a. Estimate each dimension of the rectangle to the nearest foot.
  b. Write a quadratic equation and use the quadratic formula to find each dimension to the nearest hundredth of a foot.

9 Cumulative Test Prep

Some questions on standardized tests ask you to describe how changing an equation affects its graph. Read the sample question at the right. Then follow the tips to answer it.

TIP 1

You may want to sketch the graphs of both equations and compare the graphs.

How would the graph of $y = x^2 - 1$ change if the equation became $y = x^2 + 2$?

Ⓐ The graph would shift 3 units down.

Ⓑ The graph would shift 3 units up.

Ⓒ The graph would shift 2 units down.

Ⓓ The graph would shift 2 units up.

TIP 2

Think about what operation you would use to change $y = x^2 - 1$ to $y = x^2 + 2$.

Think It Through

To change the equation $y = x^2 - 1$ to $y = x^2 + 2$, you add 3 to the expression $x^2 - 1$:

$$y = x^2 - 1 + 3 = x^2 + 2$$

Adding 3 to the constant term of a quadratic function causes the graph to shift 3 units up.

The correct answer is B.

Vocabulary Builder

As you solve test items, you must understand the meanings of mathematical terms. Choose the correct term to complete each sentence.

A. The (*vertex, axis of symmetry*) is the highest or lowest point of a parabola.

B. Two distinct lines are (*parallel, perpendicular*) if they have the same slope.

C. The (*domain, range*) of a function is the set of all possible values for the input, or independent variable, of the function.

D. A (*proportion, rate*) is an equation that states that two ratios are equal.

E. A(n) (*quadratic, exponential*) function is a function of the form $y = ax^2 + bx + c$.

Multiple Choice

Read each question. Then write the letter of the correct answer on your paper.

1. The maximum distance from the sun to Mars is about 155 million miles. What is the round-trip distance in scientific notation?

Ⓐ 3.1×10^{-8} mi   Ⓒ 3.1×10^8 mi

Ⓑ 3.1×10^7 mi   Ⓓ 3.1×10^9 mi

2. A copy center charges $.09 per copy for the first 100 copies and $.07 per copy for the next 100 copies. There is also a sales tax of 5% of the total order. How much will an order of 150 copies cost?

Ⓕ $13.13   Ⓗ $14.70

Ⓖ $14.18   Ⓘ $18.19

3. Manuela can type about 150 words in 4 minutes. At this rate, about how long will she take to type 2000 words?

Ⓐ 10 minutes   Ⓒ 75 minutes

Ⓑ 50 minutes   Ⓓ 750 minutes

4. Which inequality represents the graph at the right?

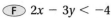

- (F) $2x - 3y < -4$
- (G) $2x - 3y > -4$
- (H) $3x - 2y < 4$
- (I) $3x - 2y > 4$

5. What is an equation of the line at the right?

- (A) $2x - y = 6$
- (B) $x - 2y = 12$
- (C) $2x + y = 3$
- (D) $x + 2y = 6$

6. Which expression is equivalent to $(m^4 n^{-1})(mp^2)(np^{-6})$?

- (F) $m^5 p^{-4}$
- (H) $m^3 np^4$
- (G) $m^5 np^{-4}$
- (I) $m^4 np^{-12}$

7. How would the graph of the function $y = x^2 - 5$ change if the function became $y = x^2 + 2$?

- (A) The graph would shift 2 units down.
- (B) The graph would shift 3 units up.
- (C) The graph would shift 7 units up.
- (D) The graph would shift 10 units down.

8. Let set A be the set containing 0 and all positive numbers. Let the universe U be the set of all real numbers. What is A'?

- (F) {all real numbers}
- (H) {all positive numbers}
- (G) {0}
- (I) {all negative numbers}

9. What are the solutions of $2x^2 - 11x + 5 = 0$?

- (A) 2, 5
- (C) 0.5, 5
- (B) −5, −0.5
- (D) −5, −2

10. What is the range of the function $y = |x|$?

- (F) $y \geq 0$
- (H) all real numbers
- (G) $y \leq 0$
- (I) $y = 0$

11. The area of a rectangle is $3n^2 + 10n + 3$. If the expression $n + 3$ represents the width, which expression represents the length?

- (A) $3n + 1$
- (C) $3n^2 + 10$
- (B) $3n + 10$
- (D) $3n^2 + 9$

12. Keisha's grandmother gave her a doll that she paid $6 for 60 years ago. The doll's current value is $96. Its value doubles every 15 years. What will the doll be worth in 60 years?

- (F) $570
- (H) $1536
- (G) $768
- (I) $3072

13. Rick's car holds 16 gal of gasoline. When he pulled into the gas station, he had less than half of a tank of gasoline. Gasoline costs $3.85 per gallon. Which is a reasonable amount that Rick paid to fill his tank?

- (A) $19.25
- (C) $33.89
- (B) $27.38
- (D) $69.30

14. Which expression is equivalent to $\left(\dfrac{x^4 y^{-2}}{z^3}\right)^{-3}$?

- (F) $\dfrac{y^6 z^3}{x^{12}}$
- (H) $\dfrac{y^6 z^9}{x^{12}}$
- (G) $\dfrac{y^6}{x^{12} z^9}$
- (I) $\dfrac{y^6}{x^{12} z^3}$

15. The table shows the number of volunteers v needed based on the number of children c who will go on a field trip. Which equation best represents the relationship between the number of volunteers and the number of children?

c	v
20	6
25	7
30	8
35	9

- (A) $v = 0.25c + 10$
- (C) $v = 0.2c + 2$
- (B) $v = 5c - 10$
- (D) $v = 4c + 2$

16. Which graph shows a line that is parallel to the line with equation $4x - 8y = 10$?

- (F)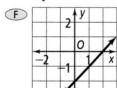
- (H)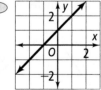
- (G)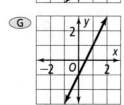
- (I)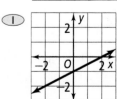

17. The difference of Ann's and Jay's heights is half of Jay's height. Which equation represents Ann's height a in terms of Jay's height j?

(A) $a = \frac{1}{2}j - j$

(C) $a = \frac{1}{2}j + j$

(B) $a = j - \frac{1}{2}j$

(D) $a = 2j - j$

18. The graphs of
$y = -7x + 12$ and
$y = -\frac{2}{3}x - \frac{2}{3}$ are shown.
Which region describes
the solutions of the
system of inequalities
$y \leq -7x + 12$ and
$y \leq -\frac{2}{3}x - \frac{2}{3}$?

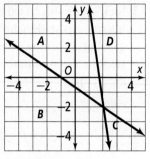

(F) Region A

(H) Region C

(G) Region B

(I) Region D

GRIDDED RESPONSE

Record your answers in a grid.

19. Alan is tiling a 6 ft-by-8 ft rectangular floor with square tiles that measure 4 in. on each side. How many tiles does Alan need to cover the floor?

20. A library is having a used book sale. All hardcover books have the same price and all softcover books have the same price. You buy 4 hardcover books and 2 softcover books for $24. Your friend buys 3 hardcover books and 3 softcover books for $21. What is the cost in dollars of a hardcover book?

21. The two triangles below are similar.

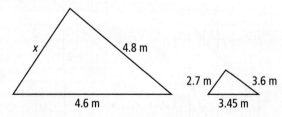

What is the length, in meters, of the side labeled x?

22. A soup company sells chicken broth in a container shaped like a rectangular prism. The container is 3.5 in. long, 2.5 in. wide, and 6.5 in. high. One cubic inch of broth weighs about 0.56 oz. To the nearest whole number, how many ounces does the container hold?

23. Anne surveyed 50 people at a movie theater to see whether they liked action or drama films. Her results are shown in the Venn diagram below.

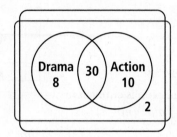

What fraction of the people surveyed liked both action and drama films? Write your answer in lowest terms.

24. How many real-number solutions does the quadratic equation $2x^2 + 7x + 9 = 0$ have?

25. A right circular cylinder has a diameter of 6 in. You pour water into the cylinder until the water level reaches 3 in. What is the volume, in cubic inches, of the water? Use 3.14 for π. Round your answer to the nearest cubic inch.

Short Response

26. Terry says that a quadratic equation has two solutions. Is this statement *always*, *sometimes*, or *never* true? Give two examples to support your answer.

27. An equation of line p is $y = 4x - 3$. Line n is perpendicular to line p and contains the point $(8, -1)$. What is an equation of line n? Show your work.

Extended Response

28. A system of equations is shown below.

$$y = 2x + 5$$
$$y = -x + 11$$

a. Graph the equations in the same coordinate plane.

b. What is the point of intersection of the two graphs?

CHAPTER 10

Get Ready!

Lesson 2-7 ◀ ## Solving Proportions

Solve each proportion.

1. $\frac{2}{3} = \frac{x}{15}$ **2.** $\frac{3}{a} = \frac{1}{6}$ **3.** $\frac{4}{3} = \frac{6}{m}$

Lesson 1-3 ◀ ## Estimating Square Roots

Estimate the square root. Round to the nearest integer.

4. $\sqrt{61}$ **5.** $\sqrt{94}$ **6.** $\sqrt{15}$ **7.** $\sqrt{148}$ **8.** $\sqrt{197}$

Lesson 8-3 ◀ ## Multiplying Binomials

Simplify each product.

9. $(2h + 3)(4 - h)$ **10.** $(3b^2 + 7)(3b^2 - 7)$ **11.** $(5x + 2)(-3x - 1)$

Lesson 9-1 ◀ ## Quadratic Graphs

Graph each function.

12. $y = 3x^2$ **13.** $y = x^2 + 4$ **14.** $y = 2x^2 + 3$

Lesson 9-6 ◀ ## The Quadratic Formula and the Discriminant

Find the number of real-number solutions of each equation.

15. $x^2 + 6x + 1 = 0$ **16.** $x^2 - 5x - 6 = 0$ **17.** $x^2 - 2x + 9 = 0$

18. $4x^2 - 4x = -1$ **19.** $6x^2 + 5x - 2 = -3$ **20.** $(2x - 5)^2 = 121$

 ## Looking Ahead Vocabulary

21. Things are *alike* if part of them is the same. Why would $2\sqrt{3}$ and $6\sqrt{3}$ be *like radicals*?

22. The *conclusion* is the end of a book. Which part is the *conclusion* of the statement, "If I had a lot of money, I would be rich"?

Radical Expressions and Equations

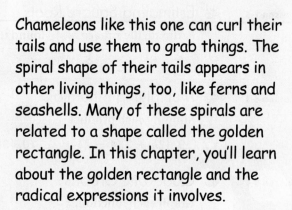

Chameleons like this one can curl their tails and use them to grab things. The spiral shape of their tails appears in other living things, too, like ferns and seashells. Many of these spirals are related to a shape called the golden rectangle. In this chapter, you'll learn about the golden rectangle and the radical expressions it involves.

Vocabulary

English/Spanish Vocabulary Audio Online:

English	Spanish
conclusion, *p. 627*	conclusión
conditional, *p. 627*	condicional
conjugates, *p. 642*	valores conjugados
hypotenuse, *p. 626*	hipotenusa
hypothesis, *p. 627*	hipótesis
like radicals, *p. 640*	radicales semejantes
Pythagorean Theorem, *p. 626*	Teorema de Pitágoras
radical expression, *p. 632*	expresión radical

My Math Video

00:04:04

BIGideas

1 **Equivalence**
Essential Question How are radical expressions represented?

2 **Solving Equations and Inequalities**
Essential Question How can you solve a radical equation?

Chapter Preview

10-1 | The Pythagorean Theorem

Objectives To solve problems using the Pythagorean Theorem
To identify right triangles

Getting Ready!

The diagram shows three square house lots that border a pond shaped like a right triangle. What is the area of each house lot? Can you write an equation to relate all three areas? Explain.

This is almost like an optical illusion. What do you see, three squares or three sides of a triangle?

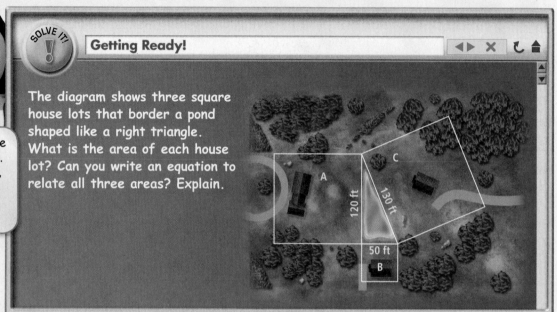

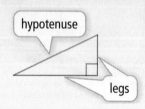

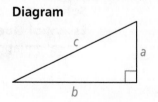

There are special names for the sides of a right triangle like the one in the Solve It. The side opposite the right angle is the **hypotenuse.** It is the longest side. Each of the sides forming the right angle is a **leg.** The **Pythagorean Theorem,** named after the Greek mathematician Pythagoras, relates the lengths of the legs and the length of the hypotenuse.

hypotenuse

legs

Focus Question Why is the Pythagorean Theorem useful?

take note

Theorem   The Pythagorean Theorem

Words
In any right triangle, the sum of the squares of the lengths of the legs is equal to the square of the length of the hypotenuse.

Diagram

c

a

b

Algebra
$a^2 + b^2 = c^2$

You can use the Pythagorean Theorem to find the length of a right triangle's hypotenuse given the lengths of its legs. Using the Pythagorean Theorem to solve for a side length involves finding a principal square root because side lengths are always positive.

 Problem 1 Finding the Length of a Hypotenuse

The tiles at the right are squares with 6-in. sides. What is the length of the hypotenuse of the right triangle shown?

Plan

What do you know? What do you need?
You know the lengths a and b of the two legs. You need to find the length c of the hypotenuse. Substitute for a and b in $a^2 + b^2 = c^2$, and then solve for c.

Use the Pythagorean Theorem.	$a^2 + b^2 = c^2$
Substitute 6 for a and b.	$6^2 + 6^2 = c^2$
Simplify.	$36 + 36 = c^2$
Simplify.	$72 = c^2$
Find the principal square root.	$\sqrt{72} = c$
Use a calculator.	$8.5 \approx c$

The length of the hypotenuse is about 8.5 in.

 Got It? 1. What is the length of the hypotenuse of a right triangle with leg lengths 9 cm and 12 cm?

You can also use the Pythagorean Theorem to find the length of a leg of a right triangle.

 Problem 2 Finding the Length of a Leg

What is the side length b in the triangle at the right?

Think

How is this problem different from Problem 1?
In Problem 1, the length of the hypotenuse was unknown. In this problem, the length of a leg is unknown.

Use the Pythagorean Theorem.	$a^2 + b^2 = c^2$
Substitute 5 for a and 13 for c.	$5^2 + b^2 = 13^2$
Simplify.	$25 + b^2 = 169$
Subtract 25 from each side.	$b^2 = 144$
Find the principal square root of each side.	$b = 12$

The side length b is 12 cm.

 Got It? 2. What is the side length a in the triangle at the right?

An *if-then* statement such as "If an animal is a horse, then it has four legs" is called a **conditional.** Conditionals have two parts. The part following *if* is the **hypothesis.** The part following *then* is the **conclusion.** The **converse** of a conditional switches the hypothesis and the conclusion.

You can write the Pythagorean Theorem as a conditional: "If a triangle is a right triangle with legs of lengths a and b and hypotenuse of length c, then $a^2 + b^2 = c^2$." The converse of the Pythagorean Theorem is always true.

> **take note**
>
> **Property** **The Converse of the Pythagorean Theorem**
>
> If a triangle has sides of lengths a, b, and c, and $a^2 + b^2 = c^2$, then the triangle is a right triangle with hypotenuse of length c.

You can use the Pythagorean Theorem and its converse to determine whether a triangle is a right triangle. If the side lengths make the equation $a^2 + b^2 = c^2$ true, then the triangle is a right triangle. If they do not, then it is not a right triangle.

 Problem 3 **Identifying Right Triangles**

Multiple Choice Which set of lengths could be the side lengths of a right triangle?

   Ⓐ 6 in., 24 in., 25 in.   Ⓑ 4 m, 8 m, 10 m   Ⓒ 10 in., 24 in., 26 in.   Ⓓ 8 ft, 15 ft, 16 ft

Determine whether the lengths make the equation $a^2 + b^2 = c^2$ true. The greatest length is c.

$6^2 + 24^2 \overset{?}{=} 25^2$	$4^2 + 8^2 \overset{?}{=} 10^2$	$10^2 + 24^2 \overset{?}{=} 26^2$	$8^2 + 15^2 \overset{?}{=} 16^2$
$36 + 576 \overset{?}{=} 625$	$16 + 64 \overset{?}{=} 100$	$100 + 576 \overset{?}{=} 676$	$64 + 225 \overset{?}{=} 256$
$612 \neq 625$	$80 \neq 100$	$676 = 676$ ✔	$289 \neq 256$

By the Converse of the Pythagorean Theorem, the lengths 10 in., 24 in., and 26 in. could be the side lengths of a right triangle. The correct answer is C.

Got It? **3.** Could the lengths 20 mm, 47 mm, and 52 mm be the side lengths of a right triangle? Explain.

Plan

Why should you check each answer choice?
If you find two answer choices that appear to be correct, then you know you have made a mistake.

Focus Question Why is the Pythagorean Theorem useful?

Answer You can use the Pythagorean Theorem to find the length of the third side of a right triangle if you know the length of any two sides.

✔ **Lesson Check**

Do you know HOW?

Find each missing side length.

1.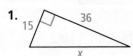

2.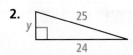

3. Could the lengths 12 cm, 35 cm, and 37 cm be the side lengths of a right triangle? Explain.

Do you UNDERSTAND?

4. Vocabulary What is the converse of the conditional, "If you study math, then you are a student"?

5. Error Analysis A student found the length x in the triangle at the right by solving the equation $12^2 + 13^2 = x^2$. Describe and correct the error.

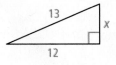

Practice and Problem-Solving Exercises

See Problems 1 and 2.

(A) Practice

Use the triangle at the right. Find the missing side length. If necessary, round to the nearest tenth.

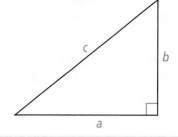

Guided Practice

To start, write the Pythagorean Theorem.

Then substitute 3 for *a* and 4 for *b*.

6. $a = 3, b = 4$

$a^2 + b^2 = c^2$

$3^2 + 4^2 = c^2$

7. $a = 6, c = 10$

8. $b = 1, c = \frac{5}{4}$

9. $a = 5, c = 13$

10. $a = 0.3, b = 0.4$

11. $a = 8, c = 17$

12. $a = 9, b = 40$

13. Fitness A jogger goes half a mile north and then turns west. If the jogger finishes 1.3 mi from the starting point, how far west did the jogger go?

14. Construction A construction worker is cutting along the diagonal of a rectangular board 15 ft long and 8 ft wide. What will be the length of the cut?

Determine whether the given lengths can be side lengths of a right triangle.

See Problem 3.

Guided Practice

To start, write the Pythagorean Theorem.

Find the greatest length *c*.

15. 15 ft, 36 ft, 39 ft

$a^2 + b^2 = c^2$

39 is the greatest length, so $c = 39$.

16. 12 m, 60 m, 61 m

17. 13 in., 35 in., 38 in.

18. 16 cm, 63 cm, 65 cm

19. 14 in., 48 in., 50 in.

(B) Apply

20. Swimming A swimmer asks a question to a lifeguard sitting on a tall chair, as shown in the diagram. The swimmer needs to be close to the lifeguard to hear the answer. What is the distance between the swimmer's head and the lifeguard's head?

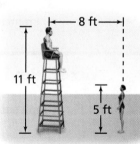

Any set of three positive integers that satisfies the equation $a^2 + b^2 = c^2$ is a *Pythagorean triple*. Determine whether each set of numbers is a Pythagorean triple.

21. 11, 60, 61

22. 13, 84, 85

23. 40, 41, 58

24. Think About a Plan A banner shaped like a right triangle has a hypotenuse of length 26 ft and a leg of length 10 ft. What is the area of the banner?
- What information do you need to find the area of a triangle?
- How can you find the length of the other leg?

25. History Originally, each face of the Great Pyramid of Giza was a triangle with the dimensions shown. How far was a corner of the base from the pyramid's top? Round to the nearest foot.

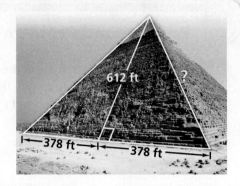
612 ft ?
378 ft 378 ft

26. Writing Two sides of a right triangle measure 10 in. and 8 in. Explain why this is not enough information to be sure of the length of the third side.

27. Physics If two forces pull at right angles to each other, the resultant force can be represented by the diagonal of a rectangle, as shown at the right. This diagonal is a hypotenuse of a right triangle. A 50-lb force and a 120-lb force combine for a resultant force of 130 lb. Are the forces pulling at right angles to each other? Explain.

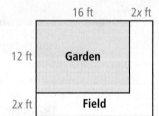
Force A
Resultant Force C
Force B

28. A rectangular box is 4 cm wide, 4 cm tall, and 10 cm long. What is the diameter of the smallest circular opening through which the box will fit? Round to the nearest tenth of a centimeter.

Standardized Test Prep

GRIDDED RESPONSE

SAT/ACT

29. A park has two walking paths shaped like right triangles. The first path has legs 75 yd and 100 yd long. The second path has legs 50 yd and 240 yd long. What is the total length of the shorter path, in yards?

30. Joe plants a rectangular garden in the corner of his field, as shown. The area of the garden is 60% of the area of the field. What is the longest side length of Joe's field, in feet?

31. What is the slope of the graph of the equation $y = \frac{1}{2}x + 7$?

32. What is the solution of the equation $-3.2t = -17.28$?

16 ft   2x ft
12 ft   Garden
2x ft   Field

33. A candidate in an election received 72.5% of the vote. What decimal represents the portion of the voters who did NOT vote for the candidate?

Mixed Review

Graph each function.
◀ See Lesson 9-1.

34. $y = x^2 - 1$
35. $y = 2x^2 - 8$
36. $y = -x^2 + 13$

Get Ready! To prepare for Lesson 10-2, do Exercises 37–40.

Simplify each product.
◀ See Lesson 8-2.

37. $9a(5a - 3)$
38. $4x(3x^2 - 6x)$
39. $4d(4d^2 + 7d^3)$
40. $(6m + 3m^3)(-2m)$

Distance and Midpoint Formulas

The diagram at the right shows that you can use the Pythagorean Theorem to find the distance d between two points, (x_1, y_1) and (x_2, y_2).

$$d^2 = (x_2 - x_1)^2 + (y_2 - y_1)^2$$
$$d = \sqrt{(x_2 - x_1)^2 + (y_2 - y_1)^2}$$

The second equation above is the *Distance Formula*.

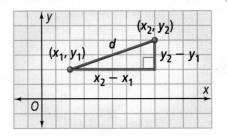

Example 1

What is the distance between points $(1, 1)$ and $(7, 9)$?

Let $(x_1, y_1) = (1, 1)$ and $(x_2, y_2) = (7, 9)$.

Use the Distance Formula.	$d = \sqrt{(x_2 - x_1)^2 + (y_2 - y_1)^2}$
Substitute for (x_1, y_1) and (x_2, y_2).	$= \sqrt{(7 - 1)^2 + (9 - 1)^2}$
Simplify.	$= \sqrt{(6)^2 + (8)^2} = 10$

The *midpoint* of a line segment is the point M on the segment that is the same distance from each endpoint, (x_1, y_1) and (x_2, y_2). The coordinates of M are given by the *midpoint formula*:

$$M\left(\frac{x_1 + x_2}{2}, \frac{y_1 + y_2}{2}\right)$$

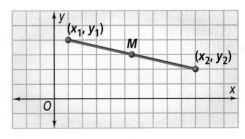

Example 2

What is the midpoint of the line segment with endpoints $(3, 6)$ and $(-5, 1)$?

Let $(x_1, y_1) = (3, 6)$ and $(x_2, y_2) = (-5, 1)$.

Substitute for (x_1, y_1) and (x_2, y_2).	$\left(\frac{x_1 + x_2}{2}, \frac{y_1 + y_2}{2}\right) = \left(\frac{3 + (-5)}{2}, \frac{6 + 1}{2}\right)$
Simplify.	$= \left(-1, 3\frac{1}{2}\right)$

Exercises

Find the distance between the two points. Then find the midpoint of the line segment joining the two points.

1. $(-1, 3), (11, -2)$ **2.** $(2, 1), (6, 4)$ **3.** $(-4, 1), (11, 9)$

4. $(-4, -3), (2, 5)$ **5.** $\left(\frac{1}{2}, 5\right), (3, -1)$ **6.** $(-6, 3), \left(6, -\frac{1}{2}\right)$

Simplifying Radicals

Objective To simplify radicals involving products

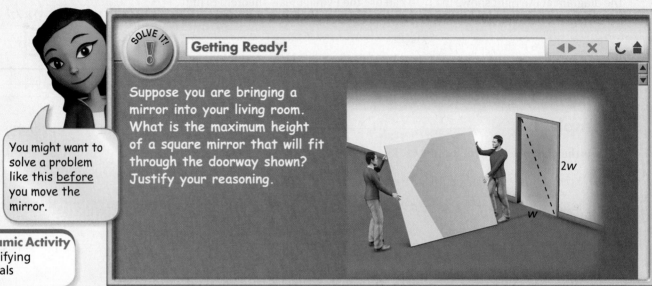

You might want to solve a problem like this *before* you move the mirror.

Dynamic Activity
Simplifying Radicals

Lesson Vocabulary
• radical expression

In the Solve It, the maximum height of the mirror is a *radical expression*. A **radical expression,** such as $2\sqrt{3}$ or $\sqrt{x + 3}$, is an expression that contains a radical. A radical expression is simplified if the following statements are true.

• The radicand has no perfect-square factors other than 1.
• The radicand contains no fractions.
• No radicals appear in the denominator of a fraction.

Simplified

$3\sqrt{5}$ $9\sqrt{x}$ $\dfrac{\sqrt{2}}{4}$

Not Simplified

$3\sqrt{12}$ $\sqrt{\dfrac{x}{2}}$ $\dfrac{5}{\sqrt{7}}$

Focus Question How can you simplify radicals using the Multiplication Property of Square Roots?

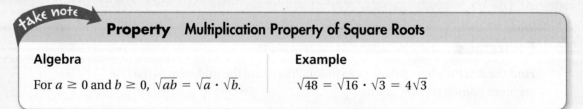

Property Multiplication Property of Square Roots

Algebra	Example
For $a \geq 0$ and $b \geq 0$, $\sqrt{ab} = \sqrt{a} \cdot \sqrt{b}$.	$\sqrt{48} = \sqrt{16} \cdot \sqrt{3} = 4\sqrt{3}$

You can use the Multiplication Property of Square Roots to simplify radicals by removing perfect-square factors from the radicand.

Problem 1 Removing Perfect-Square Factors

What is the simplified form of $\sqrt{160}$?

Write the original radical.	$\sqrt{160}$
16 is the greatest perfect-square factor of 160.	$= \sqrt{16 \cdot 10}$
Use the Multiplication Property of Square Roots.	$= \sqrt{16} \cdot \sqrt{10}$
Simplify $\sqrt{16}$.	$= 4\sqrt{10}$

> **Hint** When simplifying radicals, choose the greatest perfect-square factor.

 Got It? 1. What is the simplified form of $\sqrt{72}$?

Sometimes you can simplify radical expressions that contain variables. A variable with an even exponent is a perfect square. A variable with an odd exponent is the product of a perfect square and the variable. For example, $n^3 = n^2 \cdot n$, so $\sqrt{n^3} = \sqrt{n^2 \cdot n}$. In this lesson, assume that all variables in radicands represent nonnegative numbers.

Problem 2 Removing Variable Factors

Think

How is this problem similar to Problem 1?
In both problems, you need to remove a perfect-square factor from the radicand. In this problem, however, the factor you remove contains a variable.

Multiple Choice What is the simplified form of $\sqrt{54n^7}$?

$\quad$ Ⓐ $n^3\sqrt{54n}$ $\qquad$ Ⓑ $9n^6\sqrt{6n}$ $\qquad$ Ⓒ $3n^3\sqrt{6n}$ $\qquad$ Ⓓ $3n\sqrt{27n}$

Write the original radical.	$\sqrt{54n^7}$
$9n^6$, or $(3n^3)^2$, is a perfect-square factor of $54n^7$.	$= \sqrt{9n^6 \cdot 6n}$
Use the Multiplication Property of Square Roots.	$= \sqrt{9n^6} \cdot \sqrt{6n}$
Simplify $\sqrt{9n^6}$.	$= 3n^3\sqrt{6n}$

The correct answer is C.

 Got It? 2. What is the simplified form of $-m\sqrt{80m^9}$?

You can use the Multiplication Property of Square Roots to write $\sqrt{a} \cdot \sqrt{b} = \sqrt{ab}$.

Problem 3 Multiplying Two Radical Expressions

Think

What property allows you to multiply the whole numbers first?
The Commutative Property of Multiplication allows you to change the order of the factors.

What is the simplified form of $2\sqrt{7t} \cdot 3\sqrt{14t^2}$?

Write the original expression.	$2\sqrt{7t} \cdot 3\sqrt{14t^2}$
Multiply the whole numbers and use the Multiplication Property of Square Roots.	$= 6\sqrt{7t \cdot 14t^2}$
Simplify under the radical symbol.	$= 6\sqrt{98t^3}$
$49t^2$, or $(7t)^2$, is a perfect-square factor of $98t^3$.	$= 6\sqrt{49t^2 \cdot 2t}$
Use the Multiplication Property of Square Roots.	$= 6\sqrt{49t^2} \cdot \sqrt{2t}$
Simplify $\sqrt{49t^2}$.	$= 6 \cdot 7t\sqrt{2t}$
Simplify.	$= 42t\sqrt{2t}$

Got It? **3.** What is the simplified form of each expression in parts (a)–(c)?

    a. $3\sqrt{6} \cdot \sqrt{18}$ **b.** $\sqrt{2a} \cdot \sqrt{9a^3}$ **c.** $7\sqrt{5x} \cdot 3\sqrt{20x^5}$

    d. Reasoning In Problem 3, can you simplify the given product by first simplifying $\sqrt{14t^2}$? Explain.

 Problem 4 **Writing a Radical Expression**

Art A rectangular door in a museum is three times as tall as it is wide. What is a simplified expression for the maximum length of a painting that fits through the door?

 Know

The door is w units wide and $3w$ units high.

Need

The diagonal length d of the doorway

Plan

Use the Pythagorean Theorem.

Think

How is this like problems you have done before?
The width and height of the door are two legs of a right triangle. This is an example of finding the hypotenuse of a right triangle using the Pythagorean Theorem.

Use the Pythagorean Theorem.	$d^2 = w^2 + (3w)^2$
Simplify $(3w)^2$.	$d^2 = w^2 + 9w^2$
Combine like terms.	$d^2 = 10w^2$
Find the principal square root of each side.	$d = \sqrt{10w^2}$
Use the Multiplication Property of Square Roots.	$d = \sqrt{w^2} \cdot \sqrt{10}$
Simplify $\sqrt{w^2}$.	$d = w\sqrt{10}$

An expression for the maximum length of the painting is $w\sqrt{10}$, or about $3.16w$.

 Got It? **4.** A door's height is four times its width w. What is the maximum length of a painting that fits through the door?

Focus Question How can you simplify radicals using the Multiplication Property of Square Roots?

Answer You can use the Multiplication Property of Square Roots to remove perfect-square factors and variable factors from the radicand.

 Lesson Check

Do you know HOW?

Simplify each radical expression.

1. $\sqrt{98}$

2. $\sqrt{16b^5}$

Do you UNDERSTAND?

3. Vocabulary Is the radical expression $-5\sqrt{175}$ in simplified form? Explain.

4. Writing Explain how you can tell whether a radical expression is in simplified form.

Practice and Problem-Solving Exercises

A Practice

Simplify each radical expression.

See Problems 1 and 2.

Guided Practice

To start, write the radicand as a product with a perfect square factor.

5. $\sqrt{99}$

$\sqrt{99} = \sqrt{9 \cdot 11}$

> **Hint** The radicand is the expression under the radical sign.

6. $\sqrt{225}$ **7.** $\sqrt{128}$ **8.** $-\sqrt{60}$

9. $-4\sqrt{117}$ **10.** $5\sqrt{700}$ **11.** $\sqrt{50t^5}$

12. $3\sqrt{18a^2}$ **13.** $-21\sqrt{27x^9}$ **14.** $3\sqrt{150b^8}$

Simplify each product.

See Problem 3.

Guided Practice

To start, multiply the radicands.

15. $\sqrt{8} \cdot \sqrt{32}$

$\sqrt{8} \cdot \sqrt{32} = \sqrt{256}$

16. $\frac{1}{3}\sqrt{6} \cdot \sqrt{24}$ **17.** $4\sqrt{10} \cdot 2\sqrt{90}$ **18.** $5\sqrt{6} \cdot \frac{1}{6}\sqrt{216}$

19. $-5\sqrt{21} \cdot (-3\sqrt{42})$ **20.** $\sqrt{18n} \cdot \sqrt{98n^3}$ **21.** $\sqrt{2y} \cdot \sqrt{128y^5}$

22. $-6\sqrt{15s^3} \cdot 2\sqrt{75}$ **23.** $-9\sqrt{28a^2} \cdot \frac{1}{3}\sqrt{63a}$ **24.** $10\sqrt{12x^3} \cdot 2\sqrt{6x^3}$

25. Construction Students are building rectangular wooden frames for the set of a school play. The height of a frame is 6 times the width w. Each frame has a brace that connects two opposite corners of the frame. What is a simplified expression for the length of a brace?

See Problem 4.

26. Park A park is shaped like a rectangle with a length 5 times its width w. What is a simplified expression for the distance between opposite corners of the park?

B Apply

27. Suppose a and b are positive integers.

     a. Verify that if $a = 18$ and $b = 10$, then $\sqrt{a} \cdot \sqrt{b} = 6\sqrt{5}$.

     b. Open-Ended Find two other pairs of positive integers a and b such that $\sqrt{a} \cdot \sqrt{b} = 6\sqrt{5}$.

Simplify each radical expression.

28. $\sqrt{12} \cdot \sqrt{75}$ **29.** $\sqrt{26 \cdot 2}$

30. $\sqrt{20a^2b^3}$ **31.** $\sqrt{a^3b^5c^3}$

32. Open-Ended What are three numbers whose square roots can be written in the form $a\sqrt{3}$ for some integer value of a?

10-2 Simplifying Radicals

PART 2

Objective To simplify radicals involving quotients

In Part 1 of the lesson, you learned how to simplify radicals using the Multiplication Property of Square Roots.

Connect to What You Know

Here you will learn how to simplify radicals using the Division Property of Square Roots.

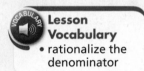

Lesson Vocabulary
• rationalize the denominator

Focus Question How can you simplify radicals using the Division Property of Square Roots?

You can simplify some radical expressions using the following property.

take note

Property **Division Property of Square Roots**

Algebra	**Example**
For $a \geq 0$ and $b > 0$, $\sqrt{\dfrac{a}{b}} = \dfrac{\sqrt{a}}{\sqrt{b}}$.	$\sqrt{\dfrac{36}{49}} = \dfrac{\sqrt{36}}{\sqrt{49}} = \dfrac{6}{7}$

When a radicand has a denominator that is a perfect square, it is easier to apply the Division Property of Square Roots first and then simplify the numerator and denominator of the result. When the denominator of a radicand is not a perfect square, it may be easier to simplify the fraction first.

Problem 5 **Simplifying Fractions Within Radicals**

What is the simplified form of each radical expression?

Think

Which method should you use?
If the denominator is a perfect square, apply the Division Property of Square Roots first. If not, simplify the fraction first.

A $\sqrt{\dfrac{64}{49}}$

Use the Division Property of Square Roots. $\sqrt{\dfrac{64}{49}} = \dfrac{\sqrt{64}}{\sqrt{49}}$

Simplify $\sqrt{64}$ and $\sqrt{49}$. $= \dfrac{8}{7}$

B $\sqrt{\dfrac{8x^3}{50x}}$

Divide the numerator and denominator by $2x$. $\sqrt{\dfrac{8x^3}{50x}} = \sqrt{\dfrac{4x^2}{25}}$

Use the Division Property of Square Roots. $= \dfrac{\sqrt{4x^2}}{\sqrt{25}}$

Use the Multiplication Property of Square Roots. $= \dfrac{\sqrt{4} \cdot \sqrt{x^2}}{\sqrt{25}}$

Simplify $\sqrt{4}$, $\sqrt{x^2}$, and $\sqrt{25}$. $= \dfrac{2x}{5}$

 Got It? **5.** What is the simplified form of each radical expression?

    a. $\sqrt{\dfrac{144}{9}}$ **b.** $\sqrt{\dfrac{36a}{4a^3}}$ **c.** $\sqrt{\dfrac{25y^3}{z^2}}$

When a radicand in a denominator is not a perfect square, you may need to **rationalize the denominator** to remove the radical. To do this, multiply the numerator and denominator by the same radical expression. Choose an expression that makes the radicand in the denominator a perfect square. It may be helpful to start by simplifying the original radical in the denominator.

 Problem 6 **Rationalizing Denominators**

What is the simplified form of each expression?

A $\dfrac{\sqrt{3}}{\sqrt{7}}$ **B** $\dfrac{\sqrt{7}}{\sqrt{8n}}$

Think

Does multiplying an expression by $\dfrac{\sqrt{7}}{\sqrt{7}}$ change its value?
No. The fraction $\dfrac{\sqrt{7}}{\sqrt{7}}$ is equal to 1. Multiplying an expression by 1 won't change its value.

$\dfrac{\sqrt{3}}{\sqrt{7}} = \dfrac{\sqrt{3}}{\sqrt{7}} \cdot \dfrac{\sqrt{7}}{\sqrt{7}}$ Multiply by $\dfrac{\sqrt{7}}{\sqrt{7}}$.

$= \dfrac{\sqrt{21}}{\sqrt{49}}$

$= \dfrac{\sqrt{21}}{7}$

$\dfrac{\sqrt{7}}{\sqrt{8n}} = \dfrac{\sqrt{7}}{\sqrt{4 \cdot 2n}} = \dfrac{\sqrt{7}}{2\sqrt{2n}}$

$= \dfrac{\sqrt{7}}{2\sqrt{2n}} \cdot \dfrac{\sqrt{2n}}{\sqrt{2n}}$ Multiply by $\dfrac{\sqrt{2n}}{\sqrt{2n}}$.

$= \dfrac{\sqrt{14n}}{2\sqrt{4n^2}}$

$= \dfrac{\sqrt{14n}}{2 \cdot 2n}$

$= \dfrac{\sqrt{14n}}{4n}$

 Got It? **6.** What is the simplified form of each radical expression?

    a. $\dfrac{\sqrt{2}}{\sqrt{3}}$ **b.** $\dfrac{\sqrt{5}}{\sqrt{18m}}$ **c.** $\sqrt{\dfrac{7s}{3}}$

Focus Question How can you simplify radicals using the Division Property of Square Roots?

Answer You can use the Division Property of Square Roots to remove a perfect square from either the numerator or the denominator, or both.

Lesson Check

Do you KNOW HOW?

Simplify each radical expression.

1. $3\sqrt{5m} \cdot 4\sqrt{\frac{1}{5}m^3}$

2. $\sqrt{\frac{15x}{x^3}}$

3. $\frac{\sqrt{5}}{\sqrt{3}}$

4. $\frac{\sqrt{6}}{\sqrt{2n}}$

Do you UNDERSTAND?

5. **Vocabulary** Is the radical expression in simplified form? Explain.

   a. $\frac{\sqrt{31}}{3}$

   b. $7\sqrt{\frac{6}{11}}$

6. **Compare and Contrast** Simplify $\frac{3}{\sqrt{12}}$ two different ways. Which way do you prefer? Explain.

Practice and Problem-Solving Exercises

A Practice   Simplify each radical expression.   ◀ **See Problems 5 and 6.**

> **Guided Practice**
>
> To start, simplify the fraction.
>
> 7. $7\sqrt{\frac{6}{32}}$
>
> $7\sqrt{\frac{6}{32}} = 7\sqrt{\frac{6 \div 2}{32 \div 2}}$
>
> $= 7\sqrt{\frac{3}{16}}$

8. $\sqrt{\frac{16}{25}}$

9. $-4\sqrt{\frac{100}{729}}$

10. $\sqrt{\frac{3x^3}{64x^2}}$

11. $11\sqrt{\frac{49a^5}{4a^3}}$

12. $\frac{1}{\sqrt{11}}$

13. $\frac{\sqrt{5}}{\sqrt{8x}}$

14. $\frac{3\sqrt{6}}{\sqrt{15}}$

15. $\frac{22}{\sqrt{11}}$

16. $\frac{2\sqrt{24}}{\sqrt{48t^4}}$

B Apply

17. **Look for a Pattern** From a viewing height of h feet, the approximate distance d to the horizon, in miles, is given by the equation $d = \sqrt{\frac{3h}{2}}$.

   a. To the nearest mile, what is the distance to the horizon from a height of 150 ft? 225 ft? 300 ft?

   b. How does the distance to the horizon increase as the height increases?

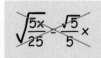

Explain why each radical expression is or is not in simplified form.

18. $\frac{13x}{\sqrt{4}}$

19. $\frac{3}{\sqrt{3}}$

20. **Error Analysis** A student simplified the radical expression at the right. What mistake did the student make? What is the correct answer?

21. Sports The bases in a softball diamond are located at the corners of a 3600-ft^2 square. How far is a throw from second base to home plate?

Simplify each radical expression.

22. $\dfrac{\sqrt{72}}{\sqrt{64}}$

23. $\dfrac{\sqrt{180}}{\sqrt{3}}$

24. $\dfrac{\sqrt{x^2}}{\sqrt{y^3}}$

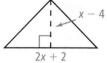

Second base

Third base

First base

Home plate

25. Think About a Plan A square picture on the front page of a newspaper occupies an area of 24 in.^{2}. What is the length of each side of the picture? Write your answer as a radical in simplified form.
  • How can you find the side length of a square if you know the area?
  • What property can you use to write your answer in simplified form?

Standardized Test Prep

SAT/ACT

26. What is the simplified form of $\sqrt{12y^5}$?

Ⓐ $2\sqrt{3y^5}$ Ⓑ $4y^4\sqrt{3y}$ Ⓒ $2y^2\sqrt{3y}$ Ⓓ $3y^3$

27. In the proportion $\dfrac{3}{b} = \dfrac{7}{8-b}$, what is the value of b?

Ⓕ 6   Ⓖ $\dfrac{21}{8}$ Ⓗ $\dfrac{12}{5}$ Ⓘ $\dfrac{5}{12}$

28. The area of the triangle at the right is 24 in.^{2}. What is the height of the triangle?

Ⓐ 1.8 in.   Ⓒ 7 in.

Ⓑ 3 in.   Ⓓ 16 in.

$x - 4$

$2x + 2$

Short Response

29. An architect is sketching a line on a coordinate grid showing the location of a pipe. The line has an x-intercept of -2 and a y-intercept of 3. What is an equation of the architect's line?

Mixed Review

Determine whether the given lengths can be side lengths of a right triangle.   ◀ See Lesson 10-1.

30. 7, 24, 25

31. $1, \dfrac{4}{3}, \dfrac{5}{3}$

32. 5, 13, 14

Factor each expression.   ◀ See Lesson 8-7.

33. $64y^2 - 9$

34. $a^2 - 81$

35. $25 - 16b^2$

Get Ready!   To prepare for Lesson 10-3, do Exercises 36–38.

Simplify each product.   ◀ See Lesson 8-3.

36. $(3a - 4)(2a + 1)$

37. $(2m - 3n)(4n - 2m)$

38. $(5 + 2x)(2x + 3)$

10-3 Operations With Radical Expressions

Objectives To simplify sums and differences of radical expressions
To simplify products and quotients of radical expressions

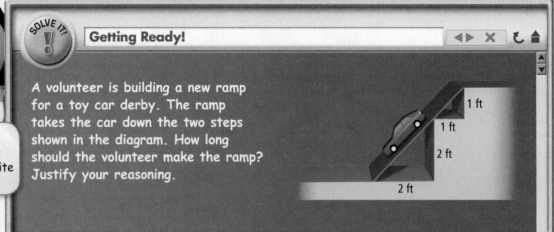

Getting Ready!

A volunteer is building a new ramp for a toy car derby. The ramp takes the car down the two steps shown in the diagram. How long should the volunteer make the ramp? Justify your reasoning.

1 ft
1 ft
2 ft
2 ft

This answer could be messy. Learn a simpler way to write it in the lesson.

Dynamic Activity
Operations With Radical Expressions

Lesson Vocabulary
• like radicals
• unlike radicals
• conjugates

Focus Question What properties of real numbers can you use to perform operations with radical expressions?

For example, you can use the Distributive Property to simplify sums or differences of radical expressions by combining *like radicals*. **Like radicals,** such as $3\sqrt{5}$ and $7\sqrt{5}$, have the same radicand. **Unlike radicals,** such as $4\sqrt{3}$ and $-2\sqrt{2}$, have different radicands.

Think

Have you seen a problem like this before?
Yes. Combining like radicals is similar to combining like terms. For example, simplifying the expression in part (A) is similar to simplifying $6x + 9x$.

Problem 1   Combining Like Radicals

What is the simplified form of each expression?

Ⓐ $6\sqrt{11} + 9\sqrt{11}$

Write the original expression.	$6\sqrt{11} + 9\sqrt{11}$
Use the Distributive Property to combine like radicals.	$= (6 + 9)\sqrt{11}$
Simplify.	$= 15\sqrt{11}$

Ⓑ $\sqrt{3} - 5\sqrt{3}$

Write the original expression.	$\sqrt{3} - 5\sqrt{3}$
Write $\sqrt{3}$ as $1\sqrt{3}$.	$= 1\sqrt{3} - 5\sqrt{3}$
Use the Distributive Property to combine like radicals.	$= (1 - 5)\sqrt{3}$
Simplify.	$= -4\sqrt{3}$

Hint
$\sqrt{3}$ has a coefficient of 1.

Got It? **1.** What is the simplified form of $5\sqrt{5} + 2\sqrt{5}$?

You may need to simplify radical expressions first to determine if they can be added or subtracted by combining like radicals.

Problem 2 **Simplifying to Combine Like Radicals**

Think

How do you know if radical expressions can be combined?
Simplify all radicals. Although $\sqrt{3}$ and $\sqrt{12}$ are unlike radicals, they can be combined after $\sqrt{12}$ is simplified.

What is the simplified form of $5\sqrt{3} - \sqrt{12}$?

Write the original expression.	$5\sqrt{3} - \sqrt{12}$
4 is a perfect-square factor of 12.	$= 5\sqrt{3} - \sqrt{4 \cdot 3}$
Multiplication Property of Square Roots	$= 5\sqrt{3} - \sqrt{4} \cdot \sqrt{3}$
Simplify $\sqrt{4}$.	$= 5\sqrt{3} - 2\sqrt{3}$
Use the Distributive Property to combine like radicals.	$= (5 - 2)\sqrt{3}$
Simplify.	$= 3\sqrt{3}$

 Got It? **2.** What is the simplified form of each expression in parts (a) and (b)?
  a. $4\sqrt{7} + 2\sqrt{28}$ **b.** $5\sqrt{32} - 4\sqrt{18}$
  c. Reasoning Can you combine two unlike radicals when the radicands have no common factors other than 1? Explain.

When simplifying a product like $\sqrt{10}(\sqrt{6} + 3)$, you can use the Distributive Property to multiply $\sqrt{10}$ times $\sqrt{6}$ and $\sqrt{10}$ times 3. If both factors in the product have two terms, as in $(\sqrt{6} - 2\sqrt{3})(\sqrt{6} + \sqrt{3})$, you can use FOIL to multiply just as you do when multiplying binomials.

Problem 3 **Multiplying Radical Expressions**

Think

Have you seen a problem like this before?
Yes. Parts (A) and (B) are similar to simplifying products like $3(x + 2)$ and $(2x + 1)(x - 5)$.

What is the simplified form of each expression?

A $\sqrt{10}(\sqrt{6} + 3)$

Write the original expression.	$\sqrt{10}(\sqrt{6} + 3)$
Use the Distributive Property.	$= (\sqrt{10} \cdot \sqrt{6}) + (\sqrt{10} \cdot 3)$
Use the Multiplication Property of Square Roots.	$= \sqrt{60} + 3\sqrt{10}$
4 is a perfect-square factor of 60.	$= \sqrt{4} \cdot \sqrt{15} + 3\sqrt{10}$
Simplify $\sqrt{4}$.	$= 2\sqrt{15} + 3\sqrt{10}$

B $(\sqrt{6} - 2\sqrt{3})(\sqrt{6} + \sqrt{3})$

Write the original expression.	$(\sqrt{6} - 2\sqrt{3})(\sqrt{6} + \sqrt{3})$
Use FOIL.	$= \sqrt{36} + \sqrt{18} - 2\sqrt{18} - 2\sqrt{9}$
Combine like radicals and simplify.	$= 6 - \sqrt{18} - 2(3)$
9 is a perfect-square factor of 18.	$= 6 - \sqrt{9} \cdot \sqrt{2} - 6$
Simplify.	$= -3\sqrt{2}$

 Got It? **3.** What is the simplified form of each expression?
  a. $\sqrt{2}(\sqrt{6} + 5)$ **b.** $(\sqrt{11} - 2)^2$ **c.** $(\sqrt{6} - 2\sqrt{3})(4\sqrt{3} + 3\sqrt{6})$

Conjugates are the sum and difference of the same two terms. For example, $\sqrt{7} + \sqrt{3}$ and $\sqrt{7} - \sqrt{3}$ are conjugates. The product of conjugates is a difference of squares.

$$(\sqrt{7} + \sqrt{3})(\sqrt{7} - \sqrt{3}) = (\sqrt{7})^2 - (\sqrt{3})^2$$

$$= 7 - 3 = 4 \quad \text{The product of the conjugates has no radicals.}$$

You can use conjugates to simplify a quotient whose denominator is a sum or difference of radicals.

Problem 4 Rationalizing a Denominator Using Conjugates

Plan

How do you rationalize the denominator?
Multiply by the conjugate of the denominator. If the denominator has the form $a - b$, the conjugate is $a + b$.

What is the simplified form of $\dfrac{10}{\sqrt{7} - \sqrt{2}}$?

Write the original expression.	$\dfrac{10}{\sqrt{7} - \sqrt{2}}$
Multiply the numerator and denominator by the conjugate of the denominator.	$= \dfrac{10}{\sqrt{7} - \sqrt{2}} \cdot \dfrac{\sqrt{7} + \sqrt{2}}{\sqrt{7} + \sqrt{2}}$
Multiply in the denominator.	$= \dfrac{10(\sqrt{7} + \sqrt{2})}{7 - 2}$
Simplify the denominator.	$= \dfrac{10(\sqrt{7} + \sqrt{2})}{5}$
Divide 10 and 5 by the common factor 5.	$= 2(\sqrt{7} + \sqrt{2})$
Simplify the expression.	$= 2\sqrt{7} + 2\sqrt{2}$

 Got It? 4. What is the simplified form of $\dfrac{-3}{\sqrt{10} + \sqrt{5}}$?

Golden rectangles appear frequently in nature and art. The ratio of the length to the width of a golden rectangle is $(1 + \sqrt{5}) : 2$.

Problem 5 Solving a Proportion Involving Radicals

Think

How do you begin this problem?
Since the rectangle is a golden rectangle, the length divided by the width has to equal $\dfrac{1 + \sqrt{5}}{2}$.

Biology Fiddlehead ferns naturally grow in spirals that fit into golden rectangles. What is the width w of the fern shown?

Write a proportion.	$\dfrac{1 + \sqrt{5}}{2} = \dfrac{4}{w}$
Use the Cross Products Property.	$w(1 + \sqrt{5}) = 8$
Divide each side by $1 + \sqrt{5}$.	$w = \dfrac{8}{1 + \sqrt{5}}$
Multiply the numerator and denominator by the conjugate of the denominator.	$w = \dfrac{8}{1 + \sqrt{5}} \cdot \dfrac{1 - \sqrt{5}}{1 - \sqrt{5}}$
Multiply.	$w = \dfrac{8 - 8\sqrt{5}}{1 - 5}$
Simplify the denominator.	$w = \dfrac{8 - 8\sqrt{5}}{-4}$
Simplify. Use a calculator.	$w = -2 + 2\sqrt{5} \approx 2.5$

The width of the fern is about 2.5 cm.

w

4 cm

Got It? **5.** A golden rectangle is 12 in. long. What is the width of the rectangle? Write your answer in simplified radical form. Round to the nearest tenth of an inch.

Focus Question What properties of real numbers can you use to perform operations with radical expressions?

Answer You can use the Distributive Property and the Multiplication Property of Square Roots.

Lesson Check

Do you know HOW?

Simplify each radical expression.

1. $4\sqrt{3} + \sqrt{3}$ **2.** $3\sqrt{6} - \sqrt{24}$

3. $\sqrt{7}(\sqrt{3} - 2)$ **4.** $(\sqrt{5} - 6)^2$

5. $\dfrac{7\sqrt{5}}{3 + \sqrt{2}}$ **6.** $\dfrac{6}{\sqrt{7} + 2}$

Do you UNDERSTAND?

7. Vocabulary What is the conjugate of each expression?

   a. $\sqrt{13} - 2$ **b.** $\sqrt{6} + \sqrt{3}$ **c.** $\sqrt{5} - \sqrt{10}$

8. Error Analysis A student simplified an expression, as shown below. Describe and correct the error.

$$\frac{1}{\sqrt{3}-1} = \frac{1}{\sqrt{3}-1} \cdot \frac{\sqrt{3}+1}{\sqrt{3}+1} = \frac{\sqrt{3}+1}{9-1} = \frac{\sqrt{3}+1}{8}$$

Practice and Problem-Solving Exercises

 Practice   Simplify each sum or difference.   ◀ **See Problems 1 and 2.**

Guided Practice

To start, rewrite the expression using the Distributive Property.

9. $\sqrt{5} + 6\sqrt{5}$

$\sqrt{5} + 6\sqrt{5} = (1 + 6)\sqrt{5}$

10. $12\sqrt{5} - 3\sqrt{5}$ **11.** $7\sqrt{3} + \sqrt{3}$ **12.** $4\sqrt{2} - 7\sqrt{2}$

13. $3\sqrt{7} - \sqrt{63}$ **14.** $4\sqrt{128} + 5\sqrt{18}$ **15.** $3\sqrt{45} - 8\sqrt{20}$

16. $-6\sqrt{10} + 5\sqrt{90}$ **17.** $3\sqrt{3} - 2\sqrt{12}$ **18.** $-\frac{1}{2}\sqrt{5} + 2\sqrt{125}$

Simplify each product.   ◀ **See Problem 3.**

Guided Practice

To start, rewrite the expression using the Distributive Property.

19. $\sqrt{6}(\sqrt{2} + \sqrt{3})$

$(\sqrt{6} \cdot \sqrt{2}) + (\sqrt{6} \cdot \sqrt{3})$

20. $\sqrt{5}(\sqrt{15} - 3)$ **21.** $3\sqrt{7}(1 - \sqrt{7})$ **22.** $-\sqrt{12}(4 - 2\sqrt{3})$

23. $(2 + \sqrt{10})(2 - \sqrt{10})$ **24.** $(\sqrt{6} + \sqrt{3})(\sqrt{2} - 2)$ **25.** $(5\sqrt{2} - 2\sqrt{3})^2$

Simplify each quotient.

See Problem 4.

26. $\dfrac{5}{\sqrt{2} - 1}$

27. $\dfrac{3}{\sqrt{7} - \sqrt{3}}$

28. $\dfrac{-2}{\sqrt{6} + \sqrt{11}}$

29. $\dfrac{\sqrt{5}}{2 - \sqrt{5}}$

30. $\dfrac{-1}{2 - 2\sqrt{3}}$

31. $\dfrac{7}{\sqrt{5} + \sqrt{13}}$

32. **Biology** A shell fits into a golden rectangle with a length of 8 in. What is the shell's width? Write your answer in simplified radical form and rounded to the nearest tenth of an inch.

See Problem 5.

33. **Architecture** A room is approximately shaped like a golden rectangle. Its length is 23 ft. What is the room's width? Write your answer in simplified radical form and rounded to the nearest tenth of a foot.

 Apply

Find the exact solution for each equation. Find the approximate solution to the nearest tenth.

34. $\dfrac{5\sqrt{2}}{\sqrt{2} - 1} = \dfrac{x}{\sqrt{2}}$

35. $\dfrac{3}{1 + \sqrt{5}} = \dfrac{1 - \sqrt{5}}{x}$

36. $\dfrac{\sqrt{2} - 1}{\sqrt{2} + 1} = \dfrac{x}{2}$

37. $\dfrac{x}{2 + \sqrt{7}} = \dfrac{3 - \sqrt{7}}{4}$

38. **History** The floor plan of the Parthenon in Athens, Greece, is shown below. The marked room approximates a golden rectangle. What is the width of the room? Write your answer in simplified radical form. Round to the nearest tenth of a meter.

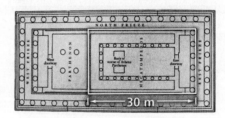

30 m

39. **Error Analysis** A student added two radical expressions as shown at the right. Describe and correct the student's mistake.

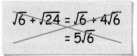

$$\sqrt{6} + \sqrt{24} = \sqrt{6} + 4\sqrt{6}$$
$$= 5\sqrt{6}$$

Simplify each expression.

40. $\sqrt{40} + \sqrt{90}$

41. $3\sqrt{2}(2 + \sqrt{6})$

42. $\sqrt{12} + 4\sqrt{75} - \sqrt{36}$

43. $(\sqrt{3} + \sqrt{5})^2$

44. $\dfrac{\sqrt{13} + \sqrt{10}}{\sqrt{13} - \sqrt{5}}$

45. $4\sqrt{50} - 7\sqrt{18}$

46. **Chemistry** The ratio of the diffusion rates of two gases is given by the formula $\dfrac{r_1}{r_2} = \dfrac{\sqrt{m_2}}{\sqrt{m_1}}$, where m_1 and m_2 are the masses of the molecules of the gases. Find $\dfrac{r_1}{r_2}$ if $m_1 = 12$ units and $m_2 = 30$ units. Write your answer in simplified radical form.

47. **Reasoning** The diagram at the right shows the dimensions of a kite. The length of the vertical blue crosspiece is s. What is the length of the horizontal red crosspiece in terms of s?

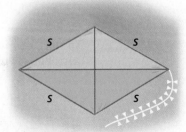

48. Think About a Plan The formula $r = \sqrt{\dfrac{A}{P}} - 1$ gives the interest rate r, expressed as a decimal, that will allow principal P to grow into amount A in 2 yr, if the interest is compounded annually. If you invest \$10,000 and want to make \$2000 in interest over 2 yr, what interest rate do you need?

- What amount do you want in the account after 2 yr?
- What radical expression gives the interest rate you need?

49. a. Suppose n is an even number. Simplify $\sqrt{x^n}$.
　　b. Suppose n is an odd number greater than 1. Simplify $\sqrt{x^n}$.

Standardized Test Prep

SAT/ACT

50. What is the simplified form of $2\sqrt{18} - \sqrt{32} + 4\sqrt{8}$?

　Ⓐ $8\sqrt{3}$　　　Ⓑ $10\sqrt{2}$　　　Ⓒ $18\sqrt{2}$　　　Ⓓ $10\sqrt{18}$

51. A surveyor is calculating the areas of lots that are going to be sold. The dimensions of one lot are shown at the right. What is the area of the lot shown?

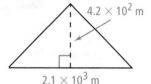

　Ⓕ $8.82 \times 10^6 \, m^2$　　　　　Ⓗ $4.41 \times 10^5 \, m^2$

　Ⓖ $8.82 \times 10^5 \, m^2$　　　　　Ⓘ $4.41 \times 10^6 \, m^2$

52. What are the approximate solutions of the equation $\dfrac{5}{2}x^2 + \dfrac{3}{4}x - 5 = 0$? Use a graphing calculator.

　Ⓐ $-5, 0$　　　Ⓑ $-1.57, 1.27$　　　Ⓒ $-1.36, 0.71$　　　Ⓓ $-0.96, 0.84$

Short Response

53. What are the domain and range of the function $y = |x|$? Show how you find your answer.

Mixed Review

Simplify each radical expression.　　　　　　　　　　　　See Lesson 10-2.

54. $\sqrt{108}$　　　**55.** $3\sqrt{150}$　　　**56.** $\dfrac{4}{\sqrt{18c^2}}$　　　**57.** $\sqrt{5} \cdot \sqrt{45}$

Rewrite each expression using each base only once.　　　　See Lesson 7-3.

58. $8^5 \cdot 8^{11}$　　　**59.** $2^{24} \cdot 2^{-13}$　　　**60.** $5^{11} \cdot 5^{16}$　　　**61.** $3^7 \cdot 3^{-4}$

Get Ready! To prepare for Lesson 10-4, do Exercises 62–67.

Solve by factoring.　　　　　　　　　　　　　　　　　See Lesson 9-4.

62. $x^2 + 2x + 1 = 0$　　　**63.** $x^2 + x - 12 = 0$　　　**64.** $x^2 + 2x - 15 = 0$

65. $3x^2 + 7x - 6 = 0$　　　**66.** $2x^2 + 3x - 2 = 0$　　　**67.** $x^2 + 14x + 49 = 0$

10-4 Solving Radical Equations

Objectives To solve equations containing radicals
To identify extraneous solutions

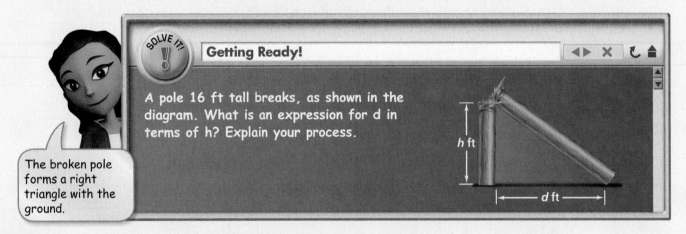

SOLVE IT! Getting Ready!

A pole 16 ft tall breaks, as shown in the diagram. What is an expression for d in terms of h? Explain your process.

h ft
d ft

The broken pole forms a right triangle with the ground.

Lesson Vocabulary
- radical equation
- extraneous solution

The expression for d in the Solve It has a variable in a radicand. A **radical equation** is an equation that has a variable in a radicand. Examples include $\sqrt{x} - 5 = 3$ and $\sqrt{x - 2} = 1$. To solve a radical equation, get the radical by itself on one side of the equation. Then square both sides. The expression under the radical must be nonnegative.

Focus Question How can you solve an equation that contains a radical?

Problem 1 Solving by Isolating the Radical

Plan
How do you start when solving a radical equation? Use the properties of equality to get the radical by itself on one side of the equation.

What is the solution of $\sqrt{x} + 7 = 16$?

Write the original equation.	$\sqrt{x} + 7 = 16$
Get the radical by itself on one side of the equation.	$\sqrt{x} = 9$
Square each side to remove the radical.	$(\sqrt{x})^2 = 9^2$
Simplify.	$x = 81$

Check

Write the original equation.	$\sqrt{x} + 7 = 16$
Substitute 81 for x.	$\sqrt{81} + 7 \stackrel{?}{=} 16$
Yes, 81 is the solution.	$9 + 7 = 16$ ✔

Got It? **1.** What is the solution of $\sqrt{x} - 5 = -2$?

Sometimes there is an operation in the expression under the radical. In this case, you still isolate the radical and square each side. Then you have to perform further operations to isolate the variable.

Problem 2 Using a Radical Equation

Clocks The time t in seconds it takes for a pendulum of a clock to complete a full swing is approximated by the equation $t = 2\sqrt{\frac{\ell}{3.3}}$, where ℓ is the length of the pendulum, in feet. If the pendulum of a clock completes a full swing in 3 s, what is the length of the pendulum? Round to the nearest tenth of a foot.

Think

Have you solved problems like this before?
Yes. You have substituted a value for one variable in a function and then solved for the other variable.

Know	Need	Plan
• A function relating t and ℓ • The value of t	The value for ℓ, the length of the pendulum	Substitute for t in the function and solve for ℓ.

Write the original equation. $\qquad\qquad t = 2\sqrt{\frac{\ell}{3.3}}$

Substitute 3 for t. $\qquad\qquad\qquad\quad 3 = 2\sqrt{\frac{\ell}{3.3}}$

Divide each side by 2 to isolate the radical. $\quad 1.5 = \sqrt{\frac{\ell}{3.3}}$

Square each side. $\qquad\qquad\qquad (1.5)^2 = \left(\sqrt{\frac{\ell}{3.3}}\right)^2$

Simplify. $\qquad\qquad\qquad\qquad\quad 2.25 = \frac{\ell}{3.3}$

Multiply each side by 3.3. $\qquad\quad 7.425 = \ell$

Check Write the original equation. $\qquad t = 2\sqrt{\frac{1}{3.3}}$

Substitute 7.425 for ℓ and 3 for t. $\quad 3 \stackrel{?}{=} 2\sqrt{\frac{7.425}{3.3}}$

Simplify. $\qquad\qquad\qquad\qquad\qquad 3 \stackrel{?}{=} 2\sqrt{2.25}$

Yes, 7.425 is the solution. $\qquad\qquad 3 = 3$ ✔

The pendulum is about 7.4 ft long.

Got It? **2. a.** How long is a pendulum if each swing takes 1 s?

b. Reasoning Without doing any calculations, do you think a pendulum that completes a full swing in 5 s is longer or shorter than 7 feet? Explain your reasoning.

Problem 3 Solving With Radical Expressions on Both Sides

Think

How can you make the equation simpler to solve?
You can *solve a simpler problem* by squaring each side of the equation. You know how to solve equations like $5t - 11 = t + 5$.

What is the solution of $\sqrt{5t - 11} = \sqrt{t + 5}$?

Write the original equation.	$\sqrt{5t - 11} = \sqrt{t + 5}$
Square each side.	$(\sqrt{5t - 11})^2 = (\sqrt{t + 5})^2$
Simplify.	$5t - 11 = t + 5$
Subtract t from each side.	$4t - 11 = 5$
Add 11 to each side.	$4t = 16$
Divide each side by 4.	$t = 4$

Check Substitute 4 for t in the original equation. $\quad \sqrt{5(4) - 11} \stackrel{?}{=} \sqrt{4 + 5}$

Yes, 4 is the solution. $\qquad\qquad\qquad\qquad\qquad \sqrt{9} = \sqrt{9}$ ✔

Got It? **3.** What is the solution of $\sqrt{7x - 4} = \sqrt{5x + 10}$?

When you solve an equation by squaring each side, you create a new equation. The new equation may have solutions that do not satisfy the original equation.

Original Equation	Square each side.	New Equation	Apparent Solutions
$x = 3$	$x^2 = 3^2$	$x^2 = 9$	$3, -3$

Hint

-3 does not satisfy the original equation $x = 3$ because $-3 \neq 3$.

In the example above, -3 does not satisfy the original equation. It is an *extraneous* solution. An **extraneous solution** is an apparent solution that does not satisfy the original equation. Always substitute each apparent solution into the original equation to check for extraneous solutions.

 Problem 4 Identifying Extraneous Solutions

What is the solution of $n = \sqrt{n + 12}$?

Write the original equation.	$n = \sqrt{n + 12}$
Square each side.	$n^2 = (\sqrt{n + 12})^2$
Simplify.	$n^2 = n + 12$
Subtract $n + 12$ from each side.	$n^2 - n - 12 = 0$
Factor the quadratic equation.	$(n - 4)(n + 3) = 0$
Use the Zero-Product Property.	$n - 4 = 0 \quad$ or $\quad n + 3 = 0$
Solve for n.	$n = 4 \quad$ or $\qquad n = -3$

Think

Does an extraneous solution solve the problem?
No. An extraneous solution solves only the new equation formed after squaring both sides. It is not a solution to the problem.

Check $\quad 4 \stackrel{?}{=} \sqrt{4 + 12} \quad$ Substitute 4 and -3 for n. $\quad -3 \stackrel{?}{=} \sqrt{-3 + 12}$

$\qquad\quad 4 = 4$ ✔ $\qquad\qquad\qquad\qquad\qquad\qquad -3 \neq 3$ ✔

The solution of the original equation is 4. The value -3 is an extraneous solution.

Got It? **4.** What is the solution of $-y = \sqrt{y + 6}$?

Sometimes you get only extraneous solutions after squaring each side of an equation. In that case, the original equation has no solution.

 Problem 5 Identifying Equations With No Solution

What is the solution of $\sqrt{3y} + 8 = 2$?

Write the original equation.	$\sqrt{3y} + 8 = 2$
Subtract 8 from each side.	$\sqrt{3y} = -6$
Square each side.	$3y = 36$
Divide each side by 3.	$y = 12$

Check Substitute 12 for y in the original equation. $\sqrt{3(12)} + 8 \overset{?}{=} 2$

$y = 12$ does not satisfy the original equation. $14 \neq 2$ ✗

The apparent solution 12 is extraneous. The original equation has no solution.

Think

Have you seen other equations with no solutions?
Yes. You learned that equations such as $x + 1 = x$ have no solution.

 Got It? 5. a. What is the solution of $6 - \sqrt{2x} = 10$?
   b. Reasoning How can you determine that the equation $\sqrt{x} = -5$ does not have a solution without going through all the steps of solving the equation?

Focus Question How can you solve an equation that contains a radical?

Answer Isolate the radical on one side of the equation. Then square each side of the equation to eliminate the radical.

 Lesson Check

Do you know HOW?

Solve each radical equation. Check your solution. If there is no solution, write *no solution*.

1. $\sqrt{3x} + 10 = 16$

2. $\sqrt{r + 5} = 2\sqrt{r - 1}$

3. $\sqrt{2x - 1} = x$

4. $\sqrt{x - 3} = \sqrt{x + 5}$

Do you UNDERSTAND?

5. Vocabulary Which is an extraneous solution of $s = \sqrt{s + 2}$?

   Ⓐ 2   Ⓒ −1

   Ⓑ 0   Ⓓ −2

6. Reasoning What is the converse of the conditional statement "If $x = y$, then $x^2 = y^2$"? Is the converse of this statement always true? Explain.

PowerAlgebra.com   Lesson 10-4   Solving Radical Equations   649

Practice and Problem-Solving Exercises

 Practice

Solve each radical equation. Check your solution.

See Problem 1.

7. $\sqrt{x} + 3 = 5$

8. $\sqrt{t} + 2 = 9$

9. $\sqrt{z} - 1 = 5$

10. $\sqrt{n} - 3 = 6$

11. $\sqrt{2b} + 4 = 8$

12. $3 - \sqrt{t} = -2$

13. $\sqrt{3a + 1} = 7$

14. $\sqrt{10b + 6} = 6$

15. $1 = \sqrt{-2v - 3}$

16. $\sqrt{x - 3} = 4$

17. Recreation You are making a tire swing for a playground. The time t in seconds for the tire to make one swing is given by $t = 2\sqrt{\frac{\ell}{3.3}}$, where ℓ is the length of the swing in feet. You want one swing to take 2.5 s. How many feet long should the swing be?

See Problem 2.

18. Geometry The length s of one edge of a cube is given by $s = \sqrt{\frac{A}{6}}$, where A represents the cube's surface area. Suppose a cube has an edge length of 9 cm. What is its surface area? Round to the nearest hundredth.

Solve each radical equation. Check your solution.

See Problem 3.

Guided Practice

To start, square each side of the equation.

Simplify.

19. $\sqrt{3x + 1} = \sqrt{5x - 8}$

$(\sqrt{3x + 1})^2 = (\sqrt{5x - 8})^2$

$3x + 1 = 5x - 8$

20. $\sqrt{2y} = \sqrt{9 - y}$

21. $\sqrt{7v - 4} = \sqrt{5v + 10}$

22. $\sqrt{s + 10} = \sqrt{6 - s}$

23. $\sqrt{n + 5} = \sqrt{5n - 11}$

Tell which solutions, if any, are extraneous for each equation.   See Problems 4 and 5.

Guided Practice

To start, substitute -3 for z.

Simplify.

24. $-z = \sqrt{-z + 6}; z = -3, z = 2$
$-(-3x) = \sqrt{-(-3 + 6}$
$3 = \sqrt{9}$

25. $\sqrt{12 - n} = n; n = -4, n = 3$

26. $y = \sqrt{2y}; y = 0, y = 2$

27. $2a = \sqrt{4a + 3}; a = \frac{3}{2}, a = -\frac{1}{2}$

28. $x = \sqrt{28 - 3x}; x = 4, x = -7$

Solve each radical equation. Check your solution. If there is no solution, write *no solution*.

29. $x = \sqrt{2x + 3}$

30. $n = \sqrt{4n + 5}$

31. $\sqrt{3b} = -3$

32. $2y = \sqrt{5y + 6}$

33. $-2\sqrt{2r + 5} = 6$

34. $\sqrt{d + 12} = d$

B Apply

35. Error Analysis A student solved the equation $r = \sqrt{-6r - 5}$ and found the solutions -1 and -5. Describe and correct the student's error.

Hint
Did the student check the solutions in the original equation?

36. Think About a Plan The total surface area A of Earth, in square kilometers, is related to Earth's radius r, in kilometers, by $r = \sqrt{\frac{A}{4\pi}}$. Earth's radius is about 6378 km. What is its surface area? Round to the nearest square kilometer.
- What equation in one variable can you solve to find Earth's surface area?
- How can you check the reasonableness of your solution?

37. Geometry In the right triangle $\triangle ABC$, the altitude $\overline{CD}$ is at a right angle to the hypotenuse. You can use $CD = \sqrt{(AD)(DB)}$ to find missing lengths.
  a. Find AD if $CD = 10$ and $DB = 4$.
  b. Find DB if $AD = 20$ and $CD = 15$.

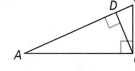

38. Packaging The radius r of a cylindrical can with volume V and height h is given by $r = \sqrt{\frac{V}{\pi h}}$. What is the height of a can with a radius of 2 in. and a volume of 75 in.³?

39. Writing Explain how you would solve the equation $\sqrt{2y} - \sqrt{y + 2} = 0$.

40. Open-Ended Write two radical equations that have 3 for a solution.

Solve each radical equation. Check your solution. If there is no solution, write *no solution*.

41. $\sqrt{5x + 10} = 5$

42. $-6 - \sqrt{3y} = -3$

43. $\sqrt{7p + 5} = \sqrt{p - 3}$

44. $\sqrt{y + 12} = 3\sqrt{y}$

45. Packaging The diagram at the right shows a piece of cardboard that makes a box when sections of it are folded and taped. The ends of the box are x inches by x inches, and the body of the box is 10 in. long.
  a. Write an equation for the volume V of the box.
  b. Solve the equation in part (a) for x.
  c. Find the integer values of x that would give the box a volume between 40 in.³ and 490 in.³, inclusive.

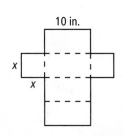
10 in.

Standardized Test Prep

46. What are the solutions of $\sqrt{c^2 - 17} = 8$?

   (A) $6, 9$　　　　(B) $8, -8$　　　　(C) $8, 0$　　　　(D) $9, -9$

47. Sam is building a fence around a triangular flower garden. What is the perimeter of the garden? Round your answer to the nearest tenth of a meter.

   (F) 14.1 m　　　　(H) 24.1 m

   (G) 20.0 m　　　　(I) 50.0 m

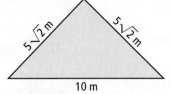

48. What is the slope-intercept form of the equation $2x + 5y = 40$?

   (A) $y = -2x + 8$　　(B) $y = -\frac{2}{5}x + 8$　　(C) $y = \frac{2}{5}x + 8$　　(D) $y = 2x + 8$

49. Write the equation of the line passing through $(1, -1)$ with a slope of $\frac{1}{2}$ in three different forms. When would each of the forms be useful?

Mixed Review

Simplify each expression.

◀ See Lesson 10-3.

50. $\sqrt{8} + 3\sqrt{2}$　　　　**51.** $(2\sqrt{5} - 6)(9 + 3\sqrt{5})$　　　　**52.** $\dfrac{2}{\sqrt{3} + \sqrt{8}}$

Use the quadratic formula to solve each equation.

◀ See Lesson 9-6.

53. $3a^2 + 4a + 3 = 0$　　　　**54.** $2f^2 - 8 = 0$　　　　**55.** $6m^2 + 13m + 6 = 0$

Get Ready!　To prepare for Lesson 11-1, do Exercises 56–59.

Factor each expression.

◀ See Lesson 8-5.

56. $x^2 + x - 12$　　**57.** $x^2 + 6x + 8$　　**58.** $x^2 - 2x - 15$　　**59.** $x^2 + 9x + 18$

Pull It **All** Together

To solve these problems you will pull together many concepts and skills that you have studied about radical expressions and equations.

BIG idea Equivalence

Radical expressions can be represented many ways. To simplify a square root, factor out perfect squares from the radicand.

Task 1

Use the isosceles right triangle shown to answer the following questions.

    a. What is an expression for c in terms of x? Write your answer as a radical in simplified form.

    b. How can you use your result from part (a) to find the length of the hypotenuse of an isosceles right triangle if you know the length of each leg?

BIG idea Solving Equations and Inequalities

To isolate the variable in a radical equation, first isolate the radical, and then square both sides.

Task 2

Solve. Show all your work and explain your steps.

The distance d in feet of a certain projector from a screen is given by $d = 1.2\sqrt{A}$, where A is the area of the projector's image in square feet. Suppose you move the projector from its current position 8 ft from the screen to a new position 12 ft from the screen. By how much does the area of the image increase?

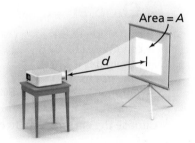

Area = A

Connecting BIG ideas and Answering the Essential Questions

1 Equivalence
Radical expressions can be represented in many ways. To simplify a square root, factor out perfect squares from the radicand.

Simplifying Radicals
(Lesson 10-2)
$$\sqrt{12} = \sqrt{4} \cdot \sqrt{3} = 2\sqrt{3}$$

Operations With Radical Expressions
(Lesson 10-3)
$$\sqrt{5} \cdot \sqrt{10} = \sqrt{50} = 5\sqrt{2}$$

3 Solving Equations and Inequalities
To isolate the variable in a radical equation, first isolate the radical and then square both sides.

Solving Radical Equations
(Lesson 10-4)
$$2x = \sqrt{4x + 3}$$

 ## Chapter Vocabulary

- conclusion (p. 627)
- conditional (p. 627)
- conjugates (p. 642)
- converse (p. 627)
- extraneous solution (p. 648)
- hypotenuse (p. 626)
- hypothesis (p. 627)
- leg (p. 626)
- like radicals (p. 640)
- Pythagorean Theorem (p. 626)
- radical equation (p. 646)
- radical expression (p. 632)
- rationalize the denominator (p. 637)
- unlike radicals (p. 640)

Choose the correct term to complete each sentence.

1. A(n) __?__ is an apparent solution that does not make the original equation true.

2. The radical expressions $2\sqrt{3}$ and $3\sqrt{2}$ contain __?__.

3. You __?__ of a radical expression by rewriting it without radicals in the denominator.

4. The radical expressions $5 + \sqrt{5}$ and $5 - \sqrt{5}$ are __?__.

10-1 The Pythagorean Theorem

Quick Review

Given the lengths of two sides of a right triangle, you can use the **Pythagorean Theorem** to find the length of the third side. Given the lengths of all three sides of a triangle, you can determine whether it is a right triangle.

Example

What is the side length x in the triangle at the right?

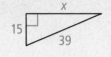

Pythagorean Theorem	$a^2 + b^2 = c^2$
Substitute 15 for a, x for b, and 39 for c.	$15^2 + x^2 = 39^2$
Simplify.	$225 + x^2 = 1521$
Subtract 225 from each side.	$x^2 = 1296$
Find the principal square root of each side.	$x = 36$

Exercises

Use the triangle at the right. Find the missing side length. If necessary, round to the nearest tenth.

5. $a = 2.5, b = 6$ **6.** $a = 3.5, b = 12$

7. $a = 1.1, b = 6$ **8.** $a = 13, c = 85$

9. $a = 6, c = 18.5$ **10.** $b = 2.4, c = 2.5$

11. $b = 8.8, c = 11$ **12.** $a = 1, c = 2.6$

Determine whether the given lengths can be side lengths of a right triangle.

13. 4, 7.5, 8.5   **14.** 22, 120, 122   **15.** 8, 40, 41

16. 1.6, 3, 3.4   **17.** 6, 24, 25   **18.** 18, 52.5, 55.5

19. 1.2, 6, 6.1   **20.** 0.7, 2.3, 2.5   **21.** 1.3, 8.4, 8.5

10-2 Simplifying Radicals

Quick Review

A **radical expression** is simplified if the following statements are true.
- The radicand has no perfect-square factors other than 1.
- The radicand contains no fractions.
- No radicals appear in the denominator of a fraction.

Example

What is the simplified form of $\dfrac{\sqrt{3x}}{\sqrt{2}}$?

Multiply by $\dfrac{\sqrt{2}}{\sqrt{2}}$.	$\dfrac{\sqrt{3x}}{\sqrt{2}} = \dfrac{\sqrt{3x}}{\sqrt{2}} \cdot \dfrac{\sqrt{2}}{\sqrt{2}}$
Multiply numerators and denominators.	$= \dfrac{\sqrt{6x}}{\sqrt{4}}$
Simplify.	$= \dfrac{\sqrt{6x}}{2}$

Exercises

Simplify each radical expression.

22. $3\sqrt{14} \cdot (-2\sqrt{21})$ **23.** $\sqrt{8} \cdot \frac{1}{4}\sqrt{6}$

24. $\sqrt{\dfrac{25a^3}{4a}}$ **25.** $\dfrac{\sqrt{8s}}{\sqrt{18s^3}}$

26. $-2\sqrt{7x^2} \cdot \frac{1}{3}\sqrt{28x^3}$ **27.** $6\sqrt{5t^3} \cdot \sqrt{15t^5}$

28. Open-Ended Write three radical expressions that have $4\sqrt{2s}$ as their simplified form. What do the three expressions have in common? Explain.

29. Geometry The width of a rectangle is s. Its length is $3s$. How long is a diagonal of the rectangle? Express your answer in simplified radical form.

10-3 Operations With Radical Expressions

Quick Review

You can use the properties of real numbers to combine radical expressions. To simplify radical expressions such as $\frac{2}{\sqrt{5} + 3}$, multiply the numerator and denominator by the **conjugate** of the denominator, $\sqrt{5} - 3$.

Example

What is the simplified form of $\frac{2\sqrt{5}}{\sqrt{5} + 2}$**?**

Multiply by $\frac{\sqrt{5} - 2}{\sqrt{5} - 2}$. $\frac{2\sqrt{5}}{\sqrt{5} + 2} = \frac{2\sqrt{5}}{\sqrt{5} + 2} \cdot \frac{\sqrt{5} - 2}{\sqrt{5} - 2}$

Multiply fractions. $= \frac{2\sqrt{5}(\sqrt{5} - 2)}{(\sqrt{5} + 2)(\sqrt{5} - 2)}$

Simplify the numerator and denominator. $= \frac{10 - 4\sqrt{5}}{1}$

Simplify the fraction. $= 10 - 4\sqrt{5}$

Exercises

Simplify each radical expression.

30. $5\sqrt{6} - 3\sqrt{6}$

31. $\sqrt{2}(\sqrt{8} + \sqrt{6})$

32. $(3\sqrt{2} - 2\sqrt{5})(4\sqrt{2} + 2\sqrt{5})$

33. $\frac{3}{\sqrt{2} - 3}$

34. $\frac{\sqrt{3} - 3}{\sqrt{3} + 3}$

35. Geometry A golden rectangle is 3 in. long. The ratio of its length to its width is $(1 + \sqrt{5}) : 2$. What is the width of the rectangle? Write your answer in simplified radical form.

10-4 Solving Radical Equations

Quick Review

You can solve some **radical equations** by isolating the radicals, squaring both sides of the equation, and then testing the solutions.

Some solutions may be extraneous. Some equations may have no solution.

Example

What is the solution of $\sqrt{x + 16} = \sqrt{9x}$**?**

Write the original equation. $\sqrt{x + 16} = \sqrt{9x}$

Square each side. $(\sqrt{x + 16})^2 = (\sqrt{9x})^2$

Simplify. $x + 16 = 9x$

Subtract x from each side. $16 = 8x$

Divide each side by 8. $2 = x$

Check   Substitute 2 for x. $\sqrt{2 + 16} \stackrel{?}{=} \sqrt{9(2)}$

Simplify. $\sqrt{18} = \sqrt{18}$ ✔

The solution is 2.

Exercises

Solve each radical equation. Check your solution. If there is no solution, write *no solution*.

36. $\sqrt{x} - 5 = 8$

37. $4 + \sqrt{y} = 7$

38. $\sqrt{w - 2} = 4$

39. $\sqrt{f + 4} = 5$

40. $\sqrt{2 + d} = d$

41. $2\sqrt{r} = \sqrt{3r + 1}$

42. $n\sqrt{2} = \sqrt{9 - 3n}$

43. $2x = \sqrt{2 - 2x}$

44. Geometry The radius r of a cylinder is given by the equation $r = \sqrt{\frac{V}{\pi h}}$, where V is the volume and h is the height. If the radius of a cylinder is 3 cm and the height is 2 cm, what is the volume of the cylinder? Round to the nearest tenth of a cubic centimeter.

Do you know HOW?

Use the triangle below. Find the missing side length. If necessary, round to the nearest tenth.

1. $a = 28, b = 35$

2. $a = 12, b = 35$

3. $b = 4.0, c = 4.1$

4. $a = 10, c = 26$

State whether segments of the given lengths can be sides of a right triangle.

5. $7, 24, 25$

6. $0.9, 1.2, 1.5$

7. $8, 16, 17$

Simplify each radical expression.

8. $\sqrt{3} + \sqrt{12}$

9. $\sqrt{300}$

10. $4\sqrt{10} - \sqrt{10}$

11. $\dfrac{-\sqrt{18}}{\sqrt{12}}$

12. $\dfrac{1}{\sqrt{3} + 4}$

13. $\dfrac{\sqrt{6}}{4 - \sqrt{6}}$

14. $\dfrac{\sqrt{2}}{\sqrt{2} + 3}$

15. $-3\sqrt{5x^3} \cdot \sqrt{10x^3}$

Solve the following radical equations. Check your solutions.

16. $\sqrt{2x} + 4 = 7$

17. $\sqrt{k} - 8 = 28$

18. $\sqrt{3m + 2} = 3$

19. $\sqrt{2x + 4} = \sqrt{3x}$

20. $\sqrt{2 - x} = x$

21. $\sqrt{-5a + 6} = -a$

Simplify each radical expression.

22. $5\sqrt{5} + 3\sqrt{5}$

23. $2\sqrt{28} - 3\sqrt{7}$

24. $\sqrt{3}(\sqrt{6} - 4)$

25. $(2\sqrt{21} + 4\sqrt{3})(5\sqrt{21} - \sqrt{3})$

26. $\dfrac{1}{\sqrt{3} - 2}$

27. $\dfrac{3 + \sqrt{2}}{4\sqrt{2} + 2}$

Find the exact solution for each equation. Find the approximate solution to the nearest tenth.

28. $\dfrac{5}{\sqrt{8} - 2} = \dfrac{\sqrt{8} + 2}{x}$

29. $\dfrac{x}{\sqrt{10}} = \dfrac{3\sqrt{2}}{\sqrt{2} + 1}$

30. **Transportation** A bus leaves the bus station and drives 3.75 mi east. The bus then turns and drives 5 mi south. How far is the bus from the bus station?

Do you UNDERSTAND?

31. What type of angle is formed by the two legs of a right triangle?

32. **Writing** How do you use a conjugate to simplify a fraction with a radical expression in its denominator?

33. **Reasoning** Is the equation $\sqrt{a} + \sqrt{b} = \sqrt{a + b}$ *always, sometimes,* or *never* true? Justify your answer.

34. **Error Analysis** Describe and correct the error shown below in simplifying the radical expression.

35. **Open-Ended** Give the side lengths of a triangle that is not a right triangle. Explain why these lengths cannot be the side lengths of a right triangle.

Cumulative Test Prep

TIPS FOR SUCCESS

Some questions on tests ask you to perform operations on radicals. Read the sample question at the right. Then follow the tips to answer it.

> Which expression is equivalent to $\sqrt{180} - \sqrt{80}$?
>
> (A) 10   (C) $10\sqrt{5}$
>
> (B) $2\sqrt{5}$ (D) $5\sqrt{10}$

TIP 2

For any number $a \geq 0$, $\sqrt{a^2} = a$. So look for perfect-square factors when trying to simplify a radical.

TIP 1

Simplify each radical expression to see if you can obtain like radicals.

Think It Through

Simplify the expression.

$$\sqrt{180} - \sqrt{80}$$
$$= \sqrt{36 \cdot 5} - \sqrt{16 \cdot 5}$$
$$= \sqrt{36} \cdot \sqrt{5} - \sqrt{16} \cdot \sqrt{5}$$
$$= 6\sqrt{5} - 4\sqrt{5}$$
$$= 2\sqrt{5}$$

The correct answer is B.

Vocabulary Builder

As you solve test items, you must understand the meanings of mathematical terms. Match each term with its mathematical meaning.

A. square root

B. arithmetic sequence

C. function

D. literal equation

I. a number pattern formed by adding a fixed number to each previous term

II. a relation that pairs each input value with exactly one output value

III. an equation involving two or more variables

IV. a number a such that $a^2 = b$

Multiple Choice

Read each question. Then write the letter of the correct answer on your paper.

1. If the graph of the function $y = x^2 - 6$ were shifted 3 units down, which equation could represent the shifted graph?

(A) $y = 3x^2 - 6$ (C) $y = x^2 - 9$

(B) $y = x^2 - 3$ (D) $y = 3x^2 - 3$

2. Which ordered pair is a solution of $3x - y < 20$?

(F) $(7, 1)$ (H) $(8, 0)$

(G) $(5, -6)$ (I) $(-1, -4)$

3. Brianna has a cylindrical glass that is 15 cm tall. The diameter of the base is 5 cm. About how much water can the glass hold?

(A) 75 cm^3 (C) 295 cm^3

(B) 118 cm^3 (D) 1178 cm^3

4. Marco is laying a 15-ft² brick walkway. He used 18 bricks for the first 3 ft². Which is a reasonable number of bricks Marco should buy to finish the walkway?

(F) 50   (H) 200

(G) 100   (I) 300

5. Jeremiah made the graph at the right to show how much money he saved after working for a few months. Which of the following represents the amount of money Jeremiah had when he started working?

Savings

(A) x-intercept

(B) y-intercept

(C) slope

(D) domain

6. Which expression is equivalent to $\sqrt{18} + \sqrt{72}$?

(F) $30\sqrt{3}$ (H) $3\sqrt{10}$

(G) $18\sqrt{2}$ (I) $9\sqrt{2}$

7. Kieko took an inventory of the T-shirts she has in her store and displayed her data in the diagram below.

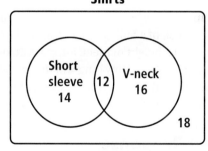

Shirts

How many short-sleeve shirts does she have?

(A) 12   (C) 26

(B) 14   (D) 42

8. What is the simplified form of $\sqrt{75x^3}$?

(F) $5x\sqrt{3x}$ (H) $5\sqrt{3x}$

(G) $25x\sqrt{x}$ (I) $25\sqrt{3x}$

9. Eduardo is drawing the graph of a function. Each time the x-value increases by 3, the y-value decreases by 4. The function includes the point (1, 3). Which could be Eduardo's graph?

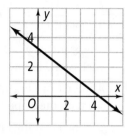
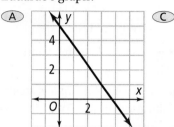

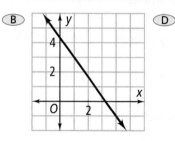
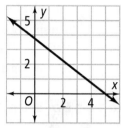

10. The data shown in the table at the right represent points on a line. What is the y-intercept of the line?

(F) -5

(G) -3

(H) 0

(I) 2.5

x	y
2	-1
3	1
4	3
5	5

11. What is the factored form of $3x^2 + 2x - 8$?

(A) $(x + 1)(3x - 8)$ (C) $(x + 2)(3x - 4)$

(B) $(x + 4)(3x - 2)$ (D) $(3x + 2)(x - 4)$

12. The formula for the area A of a circle is $A = \pi r^2$, where r is the radius of the circle. Which equation can be used to find the radius?

(F) $r = \dfrac{\sqrt{A\pi}}{\pi}$ (H) $r = \dfrac{A^2}{\pi}$

(G) $r = \dfrac{A}{\pi}$ (I) $r = \sqrt{A\pi}$

13. Which function has y-values that always increase when the corresponding x-values increase?

(A) $y = |x| + 2$ (C) $y = x + 2$

(B) $y = x^2 + 2$ (D) $y = -x - 1$

14. What is the solution of this system of equations?

$$x + 2y = 23$$
$$4x - y = -7$$

- F (1, 11)
- G (−11, 1)
- H (−1, −11)
- I (11, 1)

15. If the graph of $y = 5x - 4$ is translated up 3 units, which of the following is true?

- A The resulting line will have a slope that is greater than the slope of the graph of $y = 5x - 4$.
- B The resulting line will have the same x-intercept as the graph of $y = 5x - 4$.
- C The resulting line will be parallel to the graph of $y = 5x - 4$.
- D The resulting line will have a slope of −1.

GRIDDED RESPONSE

Record your answers in a grid.

16. What is the solution of the following proportion?
$$\frac{-a}{4} = \frac{-3(a - 2)}{6}$$

17. Mariah made a model of a square pyramid. The height h of the pyramid is 6 in. The area of the base B is 36 in.^{2}. What is the volume V, in cubic inches, of the pyramid? Use the formula $V = \frac{1}{3}Bh$.

18. The list below shows the heights, in inches, of the students in Corey's class.

60, 64, 58, 57, 60, 65, 51, 53, 57, 56

How many students are more than 5 ft tall?

19. What is the fifth term in the sequence below?

3.25, 4, 4.75, 5.5, . . .

20. Mr. Wong drove to the grocery store. The graph at the right shows his distance from home during the drive. How many times did Mr. Wong stop the car before reaching the grocery store?

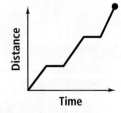

21. The volume of a rectangular prism is 720 in.^{3}. The height of the prism is 10 in. The width is 4 in. What is the length, in inches?

22. The freshman reading list contains 90 books, categorized as shown in the table below.

Freshman Reading List

Author	Mystery	Biography	Classic
Male	14	14	16
Female	10	16	20

What fraction of the books are classics?

23. Your cell phone plan costs $39.99 per month plus $.10 for every text message that you receive or send. This month, you receive 7 text messages and send 10 text messages. What is your bill, in dollars, for this month?

Short Response

24. Rosita states that the solutions of the equation $x = \sqrt{x + 12}$ are −3 and 4. Is Rosita's statement correct? Explain your answer by solving the equation and checking the possible solutions.

25. The formula $h = -16t^2 + c$ can be used to find the height h, in feet, of a falling object t seconds after it is dropped from a height of c feet. Suppose an object falls from a height of 40 ft. How long will the object take to reach the ground? Round your answer to the nearest tenth of a second.

Extended Response

26. What is the area, in square units, of quadrilateral $MPQR$ shown below? Show your work.

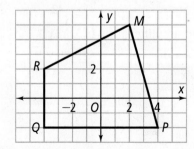

Get Ready!

Lesson 1-5 ◆ Adding and Subtracting Fractions

Find each sum or difference.

1. $\frac{6}{5} + \frac{5}{6}$ **2.** $\frac{5}{2} + \frac{3}{4}$ **3.** $\frac{7}{24} - \frac{9}{10}$ **4.** $\frac{3}{5} - \frac{2}{7}$

Lesson 7-5 ◆ Simplifying Expressions

Simplify each expression.

5. $\frac{m^2 p^{-3} q^4}{m^2 p^2 q^{-2}}$ **6.** $\frac{(3a^2)^3(2b^{-1})^2}{(7a^3)^2(3b^2)^{-1}}$ **7.** $\frac{\left(\frac{2}{3}\right)^4}{\left(\frac{3}{2}\right)^2}$ **8.** $\frac{8x^{-3} y^2 z^4}{5x^3 y z^{-2}}$

Lesson 9-4 ◆ Factoring to Solve Quadratic Equations

Solve each equation by factoring.

9. $x^2 - 2x - 63 = 0$ **10.** $12y^2 - y = 35$ **11.** $z^2 + 26z + 169 = 0$

12. $w^2 - 3w = 0$ **13.** $11p + 20 = 3p^2$ **14.** $6r^2 + 20 = -34r$

15. $3m^2 + 33m + 30 = 0$ **16.** $5d^2 - 20d = 105$ **17.** $6g^2 - 7g = 5$

Lesson 10-4 ◆ Solving Radical Equations

Solve each equation. If there is no solution, write *no solution*.

18. $\sqrt{x + 1} = \sqrt{x - 2}$ **19.** $2b = \sqrt{b + 3}$ **20.** $\sqrt{x} + 2 = x$

 Looking Ahead Vocabulary

21. If tickets are required for admission to a show, anyone without a ticket will be *excluded*. What do you think it means when some input values of a function are allowed but other input values are *excluded*?

22. When people are *rational*, they make sense. When a number is *rational*, it can be written as the ratio of two integers. Do you think that the term *rational expression* refers to an expression that makes sense or to an expression that involves a ratio?

CHAPTER 11

Rational Expressions

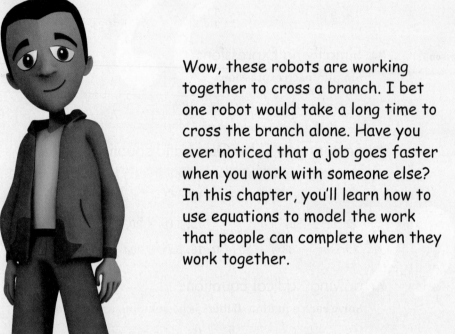

PowerAlgebra.com

Your place to get all things digital

Download videos connecting math to your world.

Math definitions in English and Spanish

The online Solve It will get you in gear for each lesson.

Interactive! Vary numbers, graphs, and figures to explore math concepts.

Download Step-by-Step Problems with Instant Replay.

Get and view your assignments online.

Extra practice and review online

Wow, these robots are working together to cross a branch. I bet one robot would take a long time to cross the branch alone. Have you ever noticed that a job goes faster when you work with someone else? In this chapter, you'll learn how to use equations to model the work that people can complete when they work together.

Vocabulary

English/Spanish Vocabulary Audio Online:

English	Spanish
complex fraction, *p. 674*	fracción compleja
excluded value, *p. 664*	valor excluido
rational equation, *p. 692*	ecuación racional
rational expression, *p. 664*	expresión racional

My Math Video

00:04:04

BIGideas

1 **Equivalence**
   Essential Question How are rational expressions represented?

2 **Solving Equations and Inequalities**
   Essential Question How can you solve a rational equation?

Chapter Preview

11-1 Simplifying Rational Expressions

Objective To simplify rational expressions

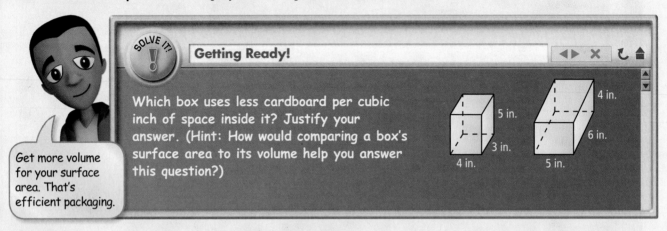

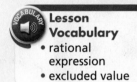

Lesson Vocabulary
- rational expression
- excluded value

An expression of the form $\frac{\text{polynomial}}{\text{polynomial}}$ is a **rational expression.**

Focus Question How is the simplified form of a rational expression like the simplified form of a numerical fraction?

To simplify a rational expression, divide out common factors from the numerator and denominator. Like a numerical fraction, a rational expression is undefined when the denominator is 0.

---

take note

Key Concept Excluded Value

A value of a variable for which a rational expression is undefined is an **excluded value.**

Example

$\frac{3}{x}$

A denominator cannot equal 0, so $x = 0$ is undefined. 0 is an excluded value.

Example

$\frac{3}{x + 2}$

A denominator cannot equal 0, so $x + 2$ cannot equal 0. Set $x + 2$ equal to 0 and solve for x.

$$x + 2 = 0$$
$$x = -2$$

-2 is an excluded value.

Problem 1 **Simplifying a Rational Expression**

What is the simplified form of the expression? State any excluded values.

A $\dfrac{10n^2}{5n^4}$

Factor the denominators and numerators. $\quad \dfrac{10n^2}{5n^4} = \dfrac{2 \cdot 5 \cdot n \cdot n}{5 \cdot n \cdot n \cdot n \cdot n}$

Cancel out common factors. $\qquad\qquad\qquad = \dfrac{2 \cdot \cancel{5}^1 \cdot \cancel{n}^1 \cdot \cancel{n}^1}{\cancel{5}_1 \cdot \cancel{n}_1 \cdot \cancel{n}_1 \cdot n \cdot n}$

Simplify. $\qquad\qquad\qquad\qquad\qquad = \dfrac{2}{n^2}$

The denominator of the original expression is 0 when $n = 0$. The simplified form is $\dfrac{2}{n^2}$, where $n \neq 0$.

B $\dfrac{x-1}{5x-5}$

Think

Should you use the simplified form to find excluded values?
No. You must check the original expression to see which values of *x* make the denominator 0.

Factor the denominator. The numerator cannot be factored. $\quad \dfrac{x-1}{5x-5} = \dfrac{x-1}{5(x-1)}$

Divide out the common factor $x - 1$. $\qquad\qquad = \dfrac{\cancel{x-1}^1}{5_1\cancel{(x-1)}}$

Simplify. $\qquad\qquad\qquad\qquad\qquad\qquad = \dfrac{1}{5}$

The denominator of the original expression is 0 when $x = 1$. The simplified form is $\dfrac{1}{5}$, where $x \neq 1$.

Hint

To find the excluded values, set the denominator equal to zero and solve the equation.

 Got It? **1.** What is the simplified form of the expression? State any excluded values.

a. $\dfrac{21a^2}{7a^3}$ **b.** $\dfrac{18d^2}{4d+8}$ **c.** $\dfrac{2n-3}{6n-9}$ **d.** $\dfrac{26c^3+91c}{2c^2+7}$

Problem 2 **Simplifying a Rational Expression Containing a Trinomial**

What is the simplified form of $\dfrac{3x-6}{x^2+x-6}$? State any excluded values.

Think

To see if there are any common factors, factor the numerator and the denominator.

Write

$$\dfrac{3x-6}{x^2+x-6} = \dfrac{3(x-2)}{(x+3)(x-2)}$$

Think

Could you also find the restricted values *before* simplifying?
Yes. You use the original expression to find the restrictions on *x*, so you don't need to simplify first.

Divide out the common factor $x - 2$. Simplify.

$$= \dfrac{3\cancel{(x-2)}^1}{(x+3)_1\cancel{(x-2)}}$$

$$= \dfrac{3}{(x+3)}$$

State the simplified form with any restrictions on the variable.

The denominator of the original expression is 0 when $x = -3$ or $x = 2$. So the simplified form is $\dfrac{3}{x+3}$, where $x \neq -3$ and $x \neq 2$.

Got It? 2. What is the simplified form of the expression? State any excluded values.

a. $\dfrac{2x - 8}{x^2 - 2x - 8}$ b. $\dfrac{a^2 - 3a + 2}{3a - 3}$ c. $\dfrac{6z + 12}{2z^2 + 7z + 6}$ d. $\dfrac{c^2 - c - 6}{c^2 + 5c + 6}$

The numerator and denominator of $\dfrac{x - 3}{3 - x}$ are opposites. To simplify the expression, you can factor -1 from $3 - x$ to get $-1(-3 + x)$, which you can rewrite as $-1(x - 3)$. Then simplify $\dfrac{x - 3}{-1(x - 3)}$.

 Problem 3 **Recognizing Opposite Factors**

What is the simplified form of the expression? State any excluded values.

Ⓐ $\dfrac{3 - x}{2x - 6}$

Plan

When should you factor -1 from an expression?
You should factor -1 from $a - x$ when factoring -1 results in a common factor.

Factor the denominator. $\dfrac{3 - x}{2x - 6} = \dfrac{3 - x}{2(x - 3)}$

Factor -1 from $3 - x$. $= \dfrac{-1(x - 3)}{2(x - 3)}$

Divide out the common factor $x - 3$. $= \dfrac{-1\cancel{(x - 3)}^{1}}{2\,\cancel{(x - 3)}}$

Simplify. $= -\dfrac{1}{2}$

The denominator of the original expression is 0 when $x = 3$. The simplified form is $-\dfrac{1}{2}$, where $x \neq 3$.

Ⓑ $\dfrac{4 - x^2}{7x - 14}$

Factor the numerator and the denominator. $\dfrac{4 - x^2}{7x - 14} = \dfrac{(2 - x)(2 + x)}{7(x - 2)}$

Hint

When you factor -1 from $(2 - x)(2 + x)$, you get $-1(x - 2)(2 + x)$ or $-1(2 - x)(-x - 2)$.

Factor -1 from $2 - x$. $= \dfrac{-1(x - 2)(2 + x)}{7(x - 2)}$

Divide out the common factor $x - 2$. $= \dfrac{-1\cancel{(x - 2)}^{1}(2 + x)}{7\,\cancel{(x - 2)}}$

Simplify. $= -\dfrac{x + 2}{7}$

The denominator of the original expression is 0 when $x = 2$. The simplified form is $-\dfrac{x + 2}{7}$, where $x \neq 2$.

 Got It? 3. What is the simplified form of the expression? State any excluded values.

a. $\dfrac{2x - 5}{5 - 2x}$ b. $\dfrac{y^2 - 16}{4 - y}$ c. $\dfrac{3 - 9d}{6d^2 + d - 1}$ d. $\dfrac{3 - 3z}{2z^2 - 2}$

You can use rational expressions to model some real-world situations.

 Problem 4 Using a Rational Expression

Shopping You are choosing between the two wastebaskets that have the shape of the figures at the right. They both have the same volume. What is the height h of the rectangular wastebasket? Give your answer in terms of a.

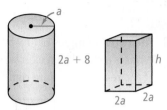

Step 1 Find the volume of the cylinder.

Formula for volume of a cylinder $V = \pi r^2 h$

Substitute a for r and $2a + 8$ for h. $= \pi a^2 (2a + 8)$

Step 2 Find the height of a rectangular prism with volume $\pi a^2(2a + 8)$ and base area $B = (2a)^2 = 4a^2$.

Write the formula for the volume of a prism. $V = Bh$

Solve for h. $h = \dfrac{V}{B}$

Substitute the volume of the cylinder for the volume of the rectangular prism and $4a^2$ for B. $= \dfrac{\pi a^2(2a + 8)}{4a^2}$

Factor out 2 from $(2a + 8)$. $= \dfrac{\pi a^2(2)(a + 4)}{4a^2}$

Divide out common factors 2 and a^2. $= \dfrac{\pi a^{2^1}(2)^1(a + 4)}{{}_2 4_1 a^2}$

Simplify. $= \dfrac{\pi(a + 4)}{2}$

The height of the rectangular prism is $\dfrac{\pi(a + 4)}{2}$.

 Got It? **4. a.** A square has side length $6x + 2$. A rectangle with width $3x + 1$ has the same area as the square. What is the length of the rectangle?

b. Reasoning Suppose the dimensions of the wastebaskets in Problem 4 are measured in feet. Is it possible for the height of the rectangular wastebasket to be 1 ft? What are the possible heights? Explain.

Plan

Is there another way to solve the problem?
Yes. You can set the volumes equal to each other and then solve for h.

Hint

The height of the rectangular prism is $\dfrac{\pi(a + 4)}{2}$. Solve $\dfrac{\pi(a + 4)}{2} = 1$.

Focus Question How is the simplified form of a rational expression like the simplified form of a numerical fraction?

Answer The numerator and denominator have no common factor other than 1.

Lesson Check

Do you know HOW?

Simplify each expression. State any excluded values.

1. $\dfrac{3x + 9}{x + 3}$

2. $\dfrac{5 - x}{x^2 - 2x - 15}$

3. The two rectangles below have the same area. What is a simplified expression for the length ℓ of the rectangle on the right?

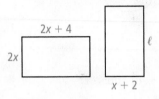

Do you UNDERSTAND?

4. Vocabulary Is each expression a rational expression? Explain your reasoning.

a. $\dfrac{\sqrt{x} + 2}{x^2 + 4}$

b. $\dfrac{y}{y - 1}$

5. Writing When simplifying a rational expression, why may it be necessary to exclude values? Explain.

6. Reasoning Suppose neither the numerator nor the denominator of a rational expression can be factored. Is the expression necessarily in simplified form? Explain.

7. Are the given factors opposites? Explain.

a. $3 - x;\ x - 3$

b. $2 - y;\ -y + 2$

Practice and Problem-Solving Exercises

 Practice   Simplify each expression. State any excluded values.   ◀ See Problems 1, 2, and 3.

Guided Practice

To start, factor the numerator.

8. $\dfrac{6a + 9}{12}$

$\dfrac{6a + 9}{12} = \dfrac{3(2a + 3)}{12}$

9. $\dfrac{4x^3}{28x^4}$

10. $\dfrac{2m - 5}{6m - 15}$

11. $\dfrac{2p - 24}{4p - 48}$

12. $\dfrac{3x^2 - 9x}{x - 3}$

13. $\dfrac{3x + 6}{3x^2}$

14. $\dfrac{2x^2 + 2x}{3x^2 + 3x}$

15. $\dfrac{2b - 8}{b^2 - 16}$

16. $\dfrac{m + 6}{m^2 - m - 42}$

17. $\dfrac{w^2 + 7w}{w^2 - 49}$

18. $\dfrac{a^2 + 2a + 1}{5a + 5}$

19. $\dfrac{m^2 + 7m + 12}{m^2 + 6m + 8}$

20. $\dfrac{c^2 - 6c + 8}{c^2 + c - 6}$

21. $\dfrac{b^2 + 8b + 15}{b + 5}$

22. $\dfrac{m + 4}{m^2 + 2m - 8}$

23. $\dfrac{5 - 4n}{4n - 5}$

24. $\dfrac{12 - 4t}{t^2 - 2t - 3}$

25. $\dfrac{m - 2}{4 - 2m}$

26. $\dfrac{v - 5}{25 - v^2}$

27. Geometry The length of a rectangular prism is 5 more than twice the width w. ◀ **See Problem 4.** The volume of the prism is $2w^3 + 7w^2 + 5w$. What is a simplified expression for the height of the prism?

28. Geometry Rectangle A has length $2x + 6$ and width $3x$. Rectangle B has length $x + 2$ and an area 12 square units greater than Rectangle A's area. What is a simplified expression for the width of Rectangle B?

 Apply

Simplify each expression. State any excluded values.

29. $\dfrac{2r^2 + 9r - 5}{r^2 + 10r + 25}$

30. $\dfrac{7z^2 + 23z + 6}{z^2 + 2z - 3}$

31. $\dfrac{32a^3}{16a^2 - 8a}$

32. $\dfrac{3z^2 + 12z}{z^4}$

33. $\dfrac{4a^2 - 8a - 5}{15 - a - 2a^2}$

34. $\dfrac{16 + 16m + 3m^2}{m^2 - 3m - 28}$

35. Think About a Plan In the figure at the right, what is the ratio of the area of the shaded triangle to the area of the rectangle? Write your answer in simplified form.
- What is an expression for the length of the rectangle?
- How do you find the area of a triangle?

36. Writing Is $\dfrac{x^2 - 9}{x + 3}$ the same as $x - 3$? Explain.

37. a. Construction To keep heating costs down for a building, architects want the ratio of surface area to volume to be as small as possible. What is an expression for the ratio of surface area to volume for each figure?

    i. square prism   **ii.** cylinder

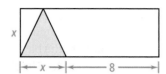

> **Hint** The formula for the volume of a cylinder is $V = \pi r^2 h$ and the formula for the surface area of a cylinder is $S.A. = 2\pi r^2 + 2\pi rh$.

    b. For each figure, what is the ratio of surface area to volume when $b = 12$ ft, $h = 18$ ft, and $r = 6$ ft?

38. Error Analysis A student simplified a rational expression as shown at the right. Describe and correct the error.

39. Banking A bank account with principal P earns interest at rate r (expressed as a decimal), compounded annually. What is the ratio of the balance after 3 yr to the balance after 1 yr?

40. Open-Ended Write a rational expression that has 4 and -3 as excluded values.

Write a ratio in simplified form of the area of the shaded figure to the area of the figure that encloses it.

41.

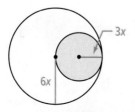

42.

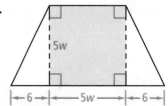

Standardized Test Prep

SAT/ACT

43. Which expression simplifies to -1?

Ⓐ $\frac{x+1}{x-1}, x \neq 1$ Ⓑ $\frac{r+3}{3-r}, r \neq 3$ Ⓒ $\frac{n-2}{2-n}, n \neq 2$ Ⓓ $\frac{4-p}{4+p}, p \neq -4$

44. Which inequality represents the graph at the right?

Ⓕ $y > \frac{1}{3}x + 1$ Ⓗ $y \geq \frac{1}{3}x + 1$

Ⓖ $y < \frac{1}{3}x + 1$ Ⓘ $y \leq \frac{1}{3}x + 1$

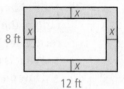

45. What is $\frac{\sqrt{6}}{\sqrt{96}}$ in simplified form?

Ⓐ 16 Ⓒ $\frac{1}{4}$

Ⓑ 4 Ⓓ $\frac{1}{16}$

Short Response

46. You are painting a wall for a display. You want to have a blue border of uniform width around a white rectangle, as shown. The areas of the blue border and the white rectangle should be the same. What should be the approximate width x of the blue border? Show your work.

Mixed Review

Simplify each radical expression.   ◀ **See Lesson 10-2.**

47. $\sqrt{20} \cdot \sqrt{10}$ **48.** $\sqrt{a^4 b^7 c^8}$ **49.** $\sqrt{9x} \cdot \sqrt{11x}$

50. $\sqrt{\dfrac{2m}{25m^5}}$ **51.** $\dfrac{\sqrt{80}}{\sqrt{10}}$ **52.** $\sqrt{\dfrac{28y^5}{7y^2}}$

Get Ready!   To prepare for Lesson 11-2, do Exercises 53–58.

Factor each expression.   ◀ **See Lesson 8-6.**

53. $2c^2 + 15c + 7$ **54.** $15t^2 - 26t + 11$ **55.** $9q^2 + 12q + 4$

56. $4c^2 - 12c + 5$ **57.** $24t^2 - 14t - 3$ **58.** $3q^2 - q - 14$

11-2 Multiplying and Dividing Rational Expressions

Objectives To multiply and divide rational expressions
To simplify complex fractions

SOLVE IT!

Getting Ready!

In the figure at the right, the diameter of the sphere is equal to the edge length x of the cube. What percent of the cube's volume is taken up by the sphere? Justify your reasoning.

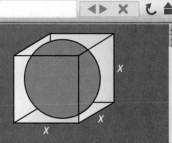

Sometimes you need to divide things that are already divided.

Many problems require finding products and quotients of rational expressions.

Lesson Vocabulary
• complex fraction

Focus Question How is multiplying and dividing rational expressions similar to multiplying and dividing numerical fractions?

If a, b, c, and d represent polynomials (where $b \neq 0$ and $d \neq 0$), then $\frac{a}{b} \cdot \frac{c}{d} = \frac{ac}{bd}$.

Problem 1 Multiplying Rational Expressions

What is the product? State any excluded values.

A $\frac{6}{a^2} \cdot \frac{-2}{a^3}$

Multiply numerators and multiply denominators. $\frac{6}{a^2} \cdot \frac{-2}{a^3} = \frac{6(-2)}{a^2(a^3)}$

Simplify. $= \frac{-12}{a^5}$

The product is $\frac{-12}{a^5}$, where $a \neq 0$.

B $\frac{x-7}{x} \cdot \frac{x-5}{x+3}$

Multiply numerators and multiply denominators. Leave the product in factored form. $\frac{x-7}{x} \cdot \frac{x-5}{x+3} = \frac{(x-7)(x-5)}{x(x+3)}$

The product is $\frac{(x-7)(x-5)}{x(x+3)}$, where $x \neq 0$ and $x \neq -3$.

> The excluded values are the excluded values of each factor.

Think
Are products of rational expressions defined for all real numbers?
No. The products may have excluded values. In part (A), the excluded value is 0. In part (B), the excluded values are 0 and −3.

 Got It?

1. What is the product? State any excluded values.

a. $\frac{5}{y} \cdot \frac{3}{y^3}$

b. $\frac{x}{x-2} \cdot \frac{x+1}{x-3}$

As Problem 1 indicates, products of rational expressions may have excluded values. For the rest of this chapter, it is not necessary to state excluded values unless you are asked.

Sometimes the product $\frac{ac}{bd}$ of two rational expressions may not be in simplified form. You may need to divide out common factors.

Problem 2 Using Factoring

What is the product $\frac{x + 5}{7x - 21} \cdot \frac{14x}{x^2 + 3x - 10}$?

Plan

What is a reasonable first step?
When you multiply rational expressions, a reasonable first step is to factor. Look for GCFs to factor out. Then look for quadratic expressions that you can factor.

Factor denominators.

$$\frac{x + 5}{7x - 21} \cdot \frac{14x}{x^2 + 3x - 10} = \frac{x + 5}{7(x - 3)} \cdot \frac{14x}{(x + 5)(x - 2)}$$

Divide out the common factors 7 and $x + 5$.

$$= \frac{\overset{1}{\cancel{x + 5}}}{\underset{1}{\cancel{7}}(x - 3)} \cdot \frac{\overset{2}{\cancel{14}}x}{\underset{1}{\cancel{(x + 5)}}(x - 2)}$$

Simplify.

$$= \frac{1}{x - 3} \cdot \frac{2x}{x - 2}$$

Multiply numerators and multiply denominators. Leave the product in factored form.

$$= \frac{2x}{(x - 3)(x - 2)}$$

Got It? **2. a.** What is the product $\frac{3x^2}{x + 2} \cdot \frac{x^2 + 3x + 2}{x}$?

b. Reasoning In Problem 2, suppose you multiply the numerators and denominators *before* you factor. Will you still get the same product? Explain.

You can also multiply a rational expression by a polynomial. Leave the product in factored form.

Problem 3 Multiplying a Rational Expression by a Polynomial

What is the product $\frac{2m + 5}{3m - 6} \cdot (m^2 + m - 6)$?

Plan

How do you get started?
Write the polynomial as a rational expression with denominator 1. Then multiply the two rational expressions.

Factor.

$$\frac{2m + 5}{3m - 6} \cdot (m^2 + m - 6) = \frac{2m + 5}{3(m - 2)} \cdot \frac{(m - 2)(m + 3)}{1}$$

Divide out the common factor $m - 2$.

$$= \frac{(2m + 5)}{3\underset{1}{\cancel{(m - 2)}}} \cdot \frac{\overset{1}{\cancel{(m - 2)}}(m + 3)}{1}$$

Multiply. Leave the product in factored form.

$$= \frac{(2m + 5)(m + 3)}{3}$$

Got It? **3.** What is the product?

a. $\frac{2x - 14}{4x - 6} \cdot (6x^2 - 13x + 6)$

b. $\frac{x^2 + 2x + 1}{x^2 - 1} \cdot (x^2 + 2x - 3)$

Recall that $\frac{a}{b} \div \frac{c}{d} = \frac{a}{b} \cdot \frac{d}{c}$, where $b \neq 0$, $c \neq 0$, and $d \neq 0$. When you divide rational expressions, first rewrite the quotient as a product using the reciprocal before dividing out common factors.

Problem 4 Dividing Rational Expressions

What is the quotient $\dfrac{x^2 - 25}{4x + 28} \div \dfrac{x - 5}{x^2 + 9x + 14}$?

Think

To divide by a rational expression, multiply by its reciprocal.

Write

$$\dfrac{x^2 - 25}{4x + 28} \div \dfrac{x - 5}{x^2 + 9x + 14}$$

$$= \dfrac{x^2 - 25}{4x + 28} \cdot \dfrac{x^2 + 9x + 14}{x - 5}$$

Hint

$x^2 - 25$ is a difference of squares.

Before multiplying, factor.

$$= \dfrac{(x + 5)(x - 5)}{4(x + 7)} \cdot \dfrac{(x + 7)(x + 2)}{x - 5}$$

Divide out the common factors $x - 5$ and $x + 7$.

$$= \dfrac{(x + 5)\cancel{(x - 5)}^1}{4_1\cancel{(x + 7)}} \cdot \dfrac{\cancel{(x + 7)}^1(x + 2)}{_1\cancel{x - 5}}$$

Multiply numerators and multiply denominators. Leave the quotient in factored form.

$$= \dfrac{(x + 5)(x + 2)}{4}$$

 Got It? **4.** What is the quotient?

a. $\dfrac{x}{x + y} \div \dfrac{xy}{x + y}$

b. $\dfrac{4k + 8}{6k - 10} \div \dfrac{k^2 + 6k + 8}{9k - 15}$

The reciprocal of a polynomial such as $x^2 + 3x + 2$ is $\dfrac{1}{x^2 + 3x + 2}$.

Problem 5 Dividing a Rational Expression by a Polynomial

Multiple Choice What is the quotient $\dfrac{3x^2 - 12x}{5x} \div (x^2 - 3x - 4)$?

Ⓐ $\dfrac{3x}{(x - 4)(x + 1)}$ Ⓑ $\dfrac{3x}{5x^2 + 5}$ Ⓒ $\dfrac{3(x - 4)^2(x + 1)}{5x}$ Ⓓ $\dfrac{3}{5(x + 1)}$

Plan

Why write the polynomial as a rational expression?
To divide a rational expression by a polynomial, you have to multiply by the reciprocal of the polynomial. Writing the polynomial over 1 may help you find its reciprocal.

Multiply by the reciprocal.

$$\dfrac{3x^2 - 12x}{5x} \div \dfrac{x^2 - 3x - 4}{1} = \dfrac{3x^2 - 12x}{5x} \cdot \dfrac{1}{x^2 - 3x - 4}$$

Factor.

$$= \dfrac{3x(x - 4)}{5x} \cdot \dfrac{1}{(x - 4)(x + 1)}$$

Divide out the common factors x and $x - 4$.

$$= \dfrac{3\cancel{x}^1\cancel{(x - 4)}^1}{5_1\cancel{x}} \cdot \dfrac{1}{_1\cancel{(x - 4)}(x + 1)}$$

Simplify.

$$= \dfrac{3}{5(x + 1)}$$

The correct answer is D.

 Got It? **5.** What is the quotient $\dfrac{z^2 - 2z + 1}{z^2 + 2} \div (z - 1)$?

A **complex fraction** is a fraction that contains one or more fractions in its numerator, in its denominator, or in both. You can simplify a complex fraction by dividing its numerator by its denominator.

Any complex fraction of the form $\dfrac{\frac{a}{b}}{\frac{c}{d}}$ (where $b \neq 0$, $c \neq 0$, and $d \neq 0$) can be expressed as $\dfrac{a}{b} \div \dfrac{c}{d}$.

 Problem 6 **Simplifying a Complex Fraction**

What is the simplified form of $\dfrac{\frac{1}{x-2}}{\frac{x+3}{x^2-4}}$?

Think

Have you solved a similar problem before?
Yes. In Problem 4, you found the quotient of two rational expressions. You simplify this complex fraction in the same way, but first write it as a quotient.

Write as a quotient.
$$\frac{\frac{1}{x-2}}{\frac{x+3}{x^2-4}} = \frac{1}{x-2} \div \frac{x+3}{x^2-4}$$

Multiply by the reciprocal.
$$= \frac{1}{x-2} \cdot \frac{x^2-4}{x+3}$$

Factor.
$$= \frac{1}{x-2} \cdot \frac{(x+2)(x-2)}{x+3}$$

Divide out the common factor $x-2$.
$$= \frac{1}{\cancel{x-2}} \cdot \frac{(x+2)\cancel{(x-2)}^{1}}{x+3}$$

Simplify.
$$= \frac{x+2}{x+3}$$

 Got It? **6.** What is the simplified form of $\dfrac{\frac{1}{q+4}}{\frac{2q^2}{2q+8}}$?

Focus Question How is multiplying and dividing rational expressions similar to multiplying and dividing numerical fractions?

Answer You can multiply and divide rational expressions using the same properties you use to multiply and divide numerical fractions.

 Lesson Check

Do you know HOW?

Multiply.

1. $\dfrac{2}{5t} \cdot \dfrac{3}{t^5}$

2. $\dfrac{2x+5}{4x-12} \cdot (x^2 - 8x + 15)$

Divide.

3. $\dfrac{k^2 + k}{5k} \div \dfrac{1}{15k^2}$

4. $\dfrac{8x^2 - 12x}{x+7} \div (4x^2 - 9)$

Simplify each complex fraction.

5. $\dfrac{\frac{a^2 + 2a - 8}{3a}}{\frac{a+4}{a-2}}$

6. $\dfrac{\frac{x^2 + 6x}{x+6}}{x}$

Do you UNDERSTAND?

7. Reasoning Are the complex fractions $\dfrac{\frac{a}{b}}{c}$ and $\dfrac{a}{\frac{b}{c}}$ equivalent? Explain.

> **Hint** Write the c in the first complex fraction and the a in the second complex fraction as fractions with denominators of 1.

8. Compare and Contrast How are multiplying rational expressions and multiplying numerical fractions similar? How are they different?

9. Reasoning Consider that $\dfrac{a}{b} \div \dfrac{c}{d} = \dfrac{a}{b} \cdot \dfrac{d}{c}$. Why must it be true that $b \neq 0$, $c \neq 0$, and $d \neq 0$?

10. a. Writing Explain how to multiply a rational expression by a polynomial.
b. Explain how to divide a rational expression by a polynomial.

Practice and Problem-Solving Exercises

 Practice   **Multiply.**   ◀ **See Problems 1, 2, and 3.**

11. $\frac{7}{3} \cdot \frac{5x}{12}$

12. $\frac{3}{t} \cdot \frac{4}{t}$

13. $\frac{5}{3a^2} \cdot \frac{8}{a^3}$

14. $\frac{m-2}{m+2} \cdot \frac{m}{m-1}$

15. $\frac{2x}{x+1} \cdot \frac{x-1}{3}$

16. $\frac{6x^2}{5} \cdot \frac{2}{x+1}$

17. $\frac{4c}{2c+2} \cdot \frac{c^2+3c+2}{c-1}$

18. $\frac{r^2+5r+6}{2r} \cdot \frac{r-2}{r+3}$

19. $\frac{m-2}{3m+9} \cdot \frac{2m+6}{2m-4}$

20. $\frac{t^2-t-12}{t+1} \cdot \frac{t+1}{t+3}$

21. $\frac{4x+1}{5x+10} \cdot \frac{30x+60}{2x-2}$

22. $\frac{4t+4}{t-3} \cdot (t^2-t-6)$

23. $\frac{2m+1}{3m-6} \cdot (9m^2-36)$

24. $(x^2-1) \cdot \frac{x-2}{3x+3}$

25. $\frac{2y+9}{4y+12} \cdot (y^2+y-6)$

Find the reciprocal of each expression.   ◀ **See Problems 4 and 5.**

26. $\frac{2}{x+1}$

27. $\frac{-6d^2}{2d-5}$

28. c^2-1

Divide.

Guided Practice

29. $\frac{x-1}{x+4} \div \frac{x+3}{x+4}$

To start, multiply by the reciprocal of $\frac{x+3}{x+4}$.

$$\frac{x-1}{x+4} \div \frac{x+3}{x+4} = \frac{x-1}{x+4} \cdot \frac{x+4}{x+3}$$

30. $\frac{3t+12}{5t} \div \frac{t+4}{10t}$

31. $\frac{x-3}{6} \div \frac{3-x}{2}$

32. $\frac{y-4}{10} \div \frac{4-y}{5}$

33. $\frac{x^2+6x+8}{x^2+x-2} \div \frac{x+4}{2x+4}$

34. $\frac{2n^2-5n-3}{4n^2-12n-7} \div \frac{4n+5}{2n-7}$

35. $\frac{3x+9}{x} \div (x+3)$

Simplify each complex fraction.   ◀ **See Problem 6.**

Guided Practice

36. $\dfrac{\dfrac{4b-1}{b^2+2b+1}}{\dfrac{12b-3}{b^2-1}}$

To start, write the compound fraction as a quotient.

$$\dfrac{\dfrac{4b-1}{b^2+2b+1}}{\dfrac{12b-3}{b^2-1}} = \frac{4b-1}{b^2+2b+1} \div \frac{12b-3}{b^2-1}$$

37. $\dfrac{\dfrac{3x^2+2x+1}{8x}}{12x^2+8x+4}$

38. $\dfrac{6s+12}{\dfrac{s+2}{3}}$

39. $\dfrac{t^2-t-6}{\dfrac{t-3}{t+2}}$

40. $\dfrac{\dfrac{x^2-25}{x^2+6x+5}}{2x-10}$

41. $\dfrac{\dfrac{g+2}{3g-1}}{\dfrac{g^2+2g}{6g+2}}$

42. $\dfrac{\dfrac{z-10}{z+10}}{3z^2-30z}$

Multiply or divide.

43. $\dfrac{t^2 + 5t + 6}{t - 3} \cdot \dfrac{t^2 - 2t - 3}{t^2 + 3t + 2}$

44. $\dfrac{c^2 + 3c + 2}{c^2 - 4c + 3} \div \dfrac{c + 2}{c - 3}$

45. $\dfrac{7t^2 - 28t}{2t^2 - 5t - 12} \cdot \dfrac{6t^2 - t - 15}{49t^3}$

46. $\left(\dfrac{x^2 - 25}{x^2 - 4x}\right)\left(\dfrac{x^2 + x - 20}{x^2 + 10x + 25}\right)$

Loan Payments The formula below gives the monthly payment m on a loan as a function of the amount borrowed A, the annual rate of interest r (expressed as a decimal), and the number of months n of the loan. Use this formula and a calculator for Exercises 47–50.

$$m = \dfrac{A\left(\frac{r}{12}\right)\left(1 + \frac{r}{12}\right)^n}{\left(1 + \frac{r}{12}\right)^n - 1}$$

> **Hint** If time is given in years, multiply by 12 to find the number of months.

47. What is the monthly payment on a loan of $1500 at 8% annual interest paid over 18 months?

48. What is the monthly payment on a loan of $3000 at 6% annual interest paid over 24 months?

49. Think About a Plan Suppose a family wants to buy the house advertised at the right. They have $60,000 for a down payment. Their mortgage will have an annual interest rate of 6%. The loan is to be repaid over a 30-yr period. How much will it cost the family to repay this mortgage over the 30 yr?
- What information can you obtain from the formula above?
- How can you use the information given by the formula to solve the problem?

50. Auto Loans You want to purchase a car that costs $18,000. The car dealership offers two different 48-month financing plans. The first plan offers 0% interest for 4 yr. The second plan offers a $2000 discount, but you must finance the rest of the purchase price at an interest rate of 7.9% for 4 yr. For which financing plan will your total cost be less? How much less will it be?

51. Error Analysis In the work shown at the right, what error did the student make in dividing the rational expressions?

52. Open-Ended Write two rational expressions. Find their product.

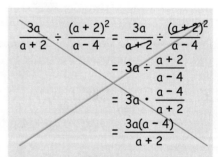

53. Reasoning For what values of x is the expression $\frac{2x^2 - 5x - 12}{6x} \div \frac{-3x - 12}{x^2 - 16}$ undefined? Explain your reasoning.

> **Hint** Denominators can never equal zero.

Geometry Find the volume of each rectangular prism.

54.

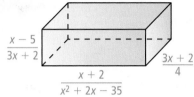

$\frac{x - 5}{3x + 2}$ $\frac{3x + 2}{4}$ $\frac{x + 2}{x^2 + 2x - 35}$

55.

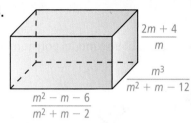

$\frac{2m + 4}{m}$ $\frac{m^3}{m^2 + m - 12}$ $\frac{m^2 - m - 6}{m^2 + m - 2}$

Standardized Test Prep

SAT/ACT

56. What is the simplified form of $(2x - 5) \cdot \frac{2x}{2x^2 - 9x + 10}$?

Ⓐ 1   Ⓑ $\frac{2x}{x - 2}$ Ⓒ $\frac{x - 5}{-4x + 5}$ Ⓓ $\frac{2x - 5}{-8x - 10}$

57. The volume of the rectangular prism is $4x^3 + 6x^2$. What is the width w of the prism?

Ⓕ $4x^3 + 6x^2 - 2x$ Ⓗ $2x + 4$

Ⓖ $2x + 3$ Ⓘ $2x + 6$

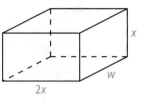

58. What is the vertex of the parabola with the equation $y = 2x^2 + 3x - 1$?

Ⓐ $(-0.75, -2.125)$ Ⓒ $(-2.125, -0.75)$

Ⓑ $(0.75, 2.125)$ Ⓓ $(-0.75, 2.125)$

Short Response

59. A soccer ball is kicked with an initial upward velocity of 35 ft/s from a starting height of 2.5 ft. If no one touches the ball, how long will it be in the air? Use the formula $h = -16t^2 + vt + c$, where h is the ball's height at time t, v is the initial upward velocity, and c is the starting height. Show your work.

Mixed Review

Simplify each expression. State any excluded values.   ◀ **See Lesson 11-1.**

60. $\frac{7m - 14}{3m - 6}$ **61.** $\frac{5a^2}{10a^4 - 15a^2}$ **62.** $\frac{4c^2 - 36c + 81}{4c^2 - 2c - 72}$

Get Ready! To prepare for Lesson 11-3, do Exercises 63–65.

Find each product.   ◀ **See Lesson 8-3.**

63. $(2x + 4)(x + 3)$ **64.** $(-3n - 4)(n - 5)$ **65.** $(3a^2 + 1)(2a - 7)$

Dividing Polynomials Using Algebra Tiles

You can use algebra tiles to model polynomial division.

Activity

What is $(x^2 + 4x + 3) \div (x + 3)$? Use algebra tiles.

Step 1 Use algebra tiles to model the dividend, $x^2 + 4x + 3$.

Step 2 Use the x^2-tile and the 1-tiles to form a figure with length $x + 3$, the divisor.

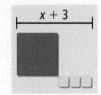

Step 3 Use the remaining tiles to fill in the rectangle.

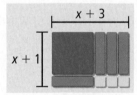

Since $(x + 1)(x + 3) = x^2 + 4x + 3$, you can write $(x^2 + 4x + 3) \div (x + 3) = x + 1$.

Check Check your result by multiplying $x + 1$ and $x + 3$. The product should be the dividend, $x^2 + 4x + 3$.

$$(x + 1)(x + 3) = (x)(x) + (x)(3) + (1)(x) + (1)(3)$$
$$= x^2 + 3x + x + 3$$
$$= x^2 + 4x + 3 \ ✔$$

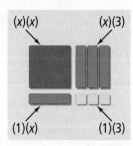

Exercises

Use algebra tiles to find each quotient. Check your result.

1. $(x^2 + 6x + 8) \div (x + 4)$

2. $(x^2 + 5x + 6) \div (x + 2)$

3. $(x^2 + 8x + 12) \div (x + 6)$

4. $(x^2 + 8x + 7) \div (x + 1)$

5. Reasoning In Exercises 1–4, the divisor is a factor of the dividend. How do you know? Can you use algebra tiles to represent polynomial division when the divisor is *not* a factor of the dividend? Explain.

11-3 Dividing Polynomials

Objective To divide polynomials

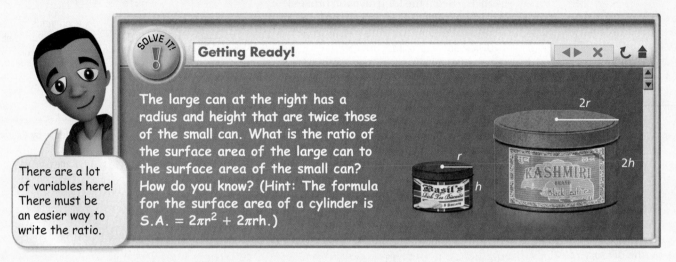

There are a lot of variables here! There must be an easier way to write the ratio.

SOLVE IT!

Getting Ready!

The large can at the right has a radius and height that are twice those of the small can. What is the ratio of the surface area of the large can to the surface area of the small can? How do you know? (Hint: The formula for the surface area of a cylinder is S.A. = $2\pi r^2 + 2\pi rh$.)

2r

r

h

KASHMIRI

2h

In the Solve It, finding the ratio of the cans' surface areas involves dividing one polynomial by another.

Focus Question What techniques can you use to divide polynomials?

Problem 1 Dividing by a Monomial

Plan

Is there another way to solve this problem?
Yes. You can cancel out common factors to reduce each term.

What is $(9x^3 - 6x^2 + 15x) \div 3x^2$?

Multiply by $\frac{1}{3x^2}$, the reciprocal of $3x^2$. $(9x^3 - 6x^2 + 15x) \div 3x^2 = (9x^3 - 6x^2 + 15x) \cdot \frac{1}{3x^2}$

Use the Distributive Property. $= \frac{9x^3}{3x^2} - \frac{6x^2}{3x^2} + \frac{15x}{3x^2}$

Divide. Subtract exponents when dividing powers with the same base. $= 3x^1 - 2x^0 + 5x^{-1}$

Simplify. $= 3x - 2 + \frac{5}{x}$

The answer is $3x - 2 + \frac{5}{x}$.

Got It? 1. Divide.

     a. $(4a^3 + 10a^2 + 3a) \div 2a^2$
     b. $(5b^4 - 15b^2 + 1) \div 5b^3$
     c. $(12c^4 + 18c^2 + 9c) \div 6c$

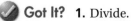

The process of dividing a polynomial by a binomial is similar to long division of real numbers. You write the answer as quotient $+ \frac{\text{remainder}}{\text{divisor}}$.

 Problem 2 **Dividing by a Binomial**

What is $(3d^2 - 4d + 13) \div (d + 3)$?

Step 1 Begin the long division process.

Plan

How do you get started?
Divide the first term in the dividend by the first term in the divisor. Here, you divide $3d^2$ by d.

Divide: $3d^2 \div d = 3d$.
Multiply: $3d(d + 3) = 3d^2 + 9d$. Then subtract.
Bring down 13.

$$
\begin{array}{r}
3d \\
d + 3 \overline{)3d^2 - 4d + 13} \\
\underline{3d^2 + 9d} \\
-13d + 13
\end{array}
$$

Align terms by their degrees. Put $3d$ above $-4d$ of the dividend.

Step 2 Repeat the process: divide, multiply, subtract, and bring down.

$$
\begin{array}{r}
3d - 13 \\
d + 3 \overline{)3d^2 - 4d + 13} \\
\underline{3d^2 + 9d} \\
-13d + 13 \\
\underline{-13d - 39} \\
52
\end{array}
$$

Align terms by their degrees. Put -13 above 13 of the dividend.

Hint

To check your answer, multiply by the divisor. You should get the dividend.

Divide: $-13d \div d = -13$.
Multiply: $-13(d + 3) = -13d - 39$.
Then subtract. The remainder is 52.

The answer is $3d - 13 + \frac{52}{d + 3}$.

Got It? **2.** What is $(2m^2 - m - 3) \div (m + 1)$?

If a polynomial does not have a term for one of the exponents, add a term with a coefficient of zero. For example, rewrite $6x^2 + 7$ as $6x^2 + 0x + 7$.

Problem 3 **Dividing Polynomials With a Zero Coefficient**

Geometry The width w of a rectangle is $3z - 1$. The area A of the rectangle is $18z^3 - 8z + 2$. What is an expression for the length of the rectangle?

Know	Need	Plan
Area: $18z^3 - 8z + 2$ Width: $3z - 1$	The length of the rectangle	Use the formula for the area of a rectangle, $A = \ell w$. Divide A by w to solve for ℓ.

Think

Why add a term with a coefficient of 0?
If the dividend is missing a term when written in standard form, you must add the term with a coefficient of 0 to act as a placeholder.

$$
\begin{array}{r}
6z^2 + 2z - 2 \\
3z - 1 \overline{)18z^3 + 0z^2 - 8z + 2} \\
\underline{18z^3 - 6z^2} \\
6z^2 - 8z \\
\underline{6z^2 - 2z} \\
-6z + 2 \\
\underline{-6z + 2} \\
0
\end{array}
$$

The dividend has no z^2-term. So rewrite the dividend to include a z^2-term with coefficient 0.

An expression for the length of the rectangle is $6z^2 + 2z - 2$.

Got It? 3. Divide.

$$\textbf{a. } (q^4 + q^2 + q - 3) \div (q - 1) \qquad \textbf{b. } (h^3 - 4h + 12) \div (h + 3)$$

To divide polynomials using long division, you should write the divisor and the dividend in standard form before you divide.

Problem 4   Reordering Terms and Dividing Polynomials

ONLINE PROBLEMS

Multiple Choice What is $(-10x - 1 + 4x^2) \div (-3 + 2x)$?

Ⓐ $2x - 2$

Ⓒ $2x - 2 + \dfrac{7}{2x - 3}$

Ⓑ $2x - 2 - \dfrac{7}{2x - 3}$

Ⓓ $2x - 2 + \dfrac{7}{2x + 2}$

Think

How can you eliminate choices?
If the product of the divisor and choice A equals the dividend, then choice A is correct. Here, the product does not equal the dividend, so eliminate choice A.

$$
\begin{array}{r}
2x - 2 \\
2x - 3 \overline{)\,4x^2 - 10x - 1} \\
\underline{4x^2 - 6x} \\
-4x - 1 \\
\underline{-4x + 6} \\
-7
\end{array}
$$

> You must rewrite $-10x - 1 + 4x^2$ and $-3 + 2x$ in standard form before you divide.

The answer is $2x - 2 - \dfrac{7}{2x - 3}$. The correct answer is B.

 Got It? 4. In parts (a) and (b), divide.

$$\textbf{a. } (-7 - 10y + 6y^2) \div (4 + 3y) \qquad \textbf{b. } (21a + 2 + 18a^2) \div (5 + 6a)$$

c. Reasoning How can you check the answer to Problem 4? Show your work.

---

take note

Concept Summary   Dividing a Polynomial by a Polynomial

Step 1   Arrange the terms of the dividend and divisor in standard form. If a term is absent from the dividend, add the term with a coefficient of 0.

Step 2   Divide the first term of the dividend by the first term of the divisor. This is the first term of the quotient.

Step 3   Multiply the first term of the quotient by the whole divisor and place the product under the dividend.

Step 4   Subtract this product from the dividend.

Step 5   Bring down the next term with its sign.

Repeat Steps 2–5 as necessary until the degree of the remainder is less than the degree of the divisor.

Hint

When a polynomial is in standard form, the degrees of its terms will decrease from left to right.

Focus Question What techniques can you use to divide polynomials?

Answer You can divide polynomials using techniques similar to the techniques used for dividing real numbers, including long division.

Lesson Check

Do you know HOW?

Divide.

1. $(20m^3 + 10m^2 - 5m - 3) \div 5m^2$

2. $(20c^2 + 23c - 7) \div (c - 1)$

3. $(25n^3 - 11n + 4) \div (5n + 4)$

4. $(-16a - 15 + 15a^2) \div (3 + 5a)$

Do you UNDERSTAND?

5. **Vocabulary** How is dividing polynomials like dividing real numbers? How is it different?

6. **Writing** What are the steps that you repeat when performing polynomial long division?

7. **Reasoning** How would you rewrite $1 - x^4$ before dividing it by $x - 1$?

Practice and Problem-Solving Exercises

 Practice   Divide.   ◀ **See Problems 1, 2, and 3.**

Guided Practice →

To start, multiply $(x^6 - x^5 + x^4)$ by the reciprocal of x^2.

8. $(x^6 - x^5 + x^4) \div x^2$

$(x^6 - x^5 + x^4) \div x^2 = (x^6 - x^5 + x^4) \cdot \dfrac{1}{x^2}$

9. $(12x^8 - 8x^3) \div 4x^4$

10. $(9c^4 + 6c^3 - c^2) \div 3c^2$

11. $(n^5 - 18n^4 + 3n^3) \div n^3$

12. $(8q^2 - 32q) \div 2q^2$

13. $(7t^5 + 14t^4 - 28t^3 + 35t^2) \div 7t^2$

14. $(6x^4 - 5x^3 + 6x^2) \div 2x^2$

15. $(y^2 - y + 2) \div (y + 2)$

16. $(3x^2 - 10x + 3) \div (x - 3)$

Write an expression for the missing dimension in each figure.

17.

$\ell = \blacksquare$

$A = r^3 - 24r - 5$ $w = r - 5$

18.

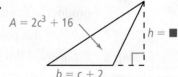

$A = 2c^3 + 16$

$h = \blacksquare$

$b = c + 2$

Divide.

◀ See Problem 4.

Guided Practice

To start, write the expressions in standard form.

19. $(49 + 16b + 2b^2) \div (2b + 4)$

$(2b^2 + 16b + 49) \div (2b + 4)$

20. $(39w + 14 + 3w^2) \div (9 + 3w)$ **21.** $(-13x + 6x^3 - 6 - x^2) \div (3x - 5)$

22. $(6x^4 + 4x^3 - x^2) \div (6 + 2x)$ **23.** $(7b + 16b^3) \div (-1 + 8b)$

Ⓑ Apply

24. Open-Ended Write a binomial and a trinomial using the same variable. Divide the trinomial by the binomial.

25. Think About a Plan The area A of a trapezoid is $x^3 + 2x^2 - 2x - 3$. The lengths of its two bases b_1 and b_2 are x and $x^2 - 3$, respectively. What is an expression for the height h of the trapezoid? Write your answer in the form quotient $+ \frac{\text{remainder}}{\text{divisor}}$.
- What formula can you use to find the area of a trapezoid?
- How can you use the formula to write an expression for h?

Hint Use the formula for the area of a trapezoid $A = \frac{1}{2}h(b_1 + b_2)$. Solve for h.

Divide.

26. $(56a^2 + 4a - 12) \div (2a + 1)$ **27.** $(5t^4 - 10t^2 + 6) \div (t + 5)$

28. $(3k^3 - 0.9k^2 - 1.2k) \div 3k$ **29.** $(-7s + 6s^2 + 5) \div (2s + 3)$

30. Writing Suppose you divide a polynomial by a binomial. How do you know if the binomial is a factor of the polynomial?

31. Geometry The volume of the rectangular prism shown at the right is $m^3 + 8m^2 + 19m + 12$. What is the area of the shaded base of the prism?

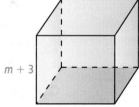
$m + 3$

32. Business One way to measure a business's efficiency is by dividing the business's revenue by its expenses. The annual revenue, in millions of dollars, of a certain airline can be modeled by $200s^3 - s^2 + 400s + 1500$, where s is the number of passengers, in hundreds of thousands. The expenses, in millions of dollars, of the airline can be modeled by $200s + 300$. What is the airline's revenue divided by its expenses? Write your answer in the form quotient $+ \frac{\text{remainder}}{\text{divisor}}$.

33. Reasoning If $x + 3$ is a factor of $x^2 - x - k$, what is the value of k?

34. Physics Consider the formula for distance traveled, $d = rt$.
  a. Solve the formula for t.
  b. Use your answer from part (a). What is an expression for the time it takes to travel $t^3 - 6t^2 + 5t + 12$ miles at a rate of $t + 1$ miles per hour?

35. Packaging Three tennis balls with radius r are packed into a cylindrical can with radius r and height $6r + 1$. What fraction of the can is empty? Write your answer in the form quotient $+ \frac{\text{remainder}}{\text{divisor}}$.

Hint The volume of a sphere is $V = \frac{4}{3}\pi r^3$. The volume of a cylinder is $V = \pi r^2 h$.

Standardized Test Prep

SAT/ACT

36. Which of the following is true for $(2x^2 + 4x + 2) \div 2x$?

　I. The remainder is negative.

　II. The dividend is in standard form.

　III. The quotient is greater than the divisor for positive values of x.

　Ⓐ I only　　　　Ⓑ II only　　　　Ⓒ I and II　　　　Ⓓ II and III

37. Which equation represents the line that passes through $(5, -8)$ and is parallel to the line at the right?

　Ⓕ $y = 2x + 2$　　　　　　　Ⓗ $y = -2x$

　Ⓖ $y + 2x = 2$　　　　　　　Ⓘ $y - 2x = 2$

38. What are the factors of the expression $x^3 - 4x$?

　Ⓐ $x^3, -4x$　　　Ⓑ $x, x^2 - 4$　　　Ⓒ $x - 2, x + 2$　　　Ⓓ $x, x - 2, x + 2$

Short Response

39. A theater has 18 rows of seats. Each row has 28 seats. Tickets cost $4 for adults and $2.50 for children. The Friday night show was sold out and the revenue from ticket sales was $1935. Barbara says that 445 adults were at the show. Is her statement reasonable? Explain your answer.

Mixed Review

Multiply or divide.　　　　　　　　　　　　　　　　　　　◀ See Lesson 11-2.

40. $\dfrac{n^2 + 7n - 8}{n - 1} \cdot \dfrac{n^2 - 4}{n^2 + 6n - 16}$

41. $\dfrac{6t^2 - 30t}{2t^2 - 53t - 55} \cdot \dfrac{6t^2 + 35t + 11}{18t^2}$

42. $\dfrac{3c^2 - 4c - 32}{2c^2 + 17c + 35} \div \dfrac{c - 4}{c + 5}$

43. $\dfrac{x^2 + 9x + 20}{x^2 + 5x - 24} \div \dfrac{x^2 + 15x + 56}{x^2 + x - 12}$

Get Ready!　**To prepare for Lesson 11-4, do Exercises 44–47.**

Simplify each expression.　　　　　　　　　　　　　　　　◀ See Lesson 1-5.

44. $\dfrac{4}{9} + \dfrac{2}{9}$ 　　　　**45.** $\dfrac{1}{4} - \dfrac{1}{3}$ 　　　　**46.** $\dfrac{7x}{8} + \dfrac{x}{8}$ 　　　　**47.** $\dfrac{7}{12y} - \dfrac{1}{12y}$

Adding and Subtracting Rational Expressions

Objective To add and subtract rational expressions

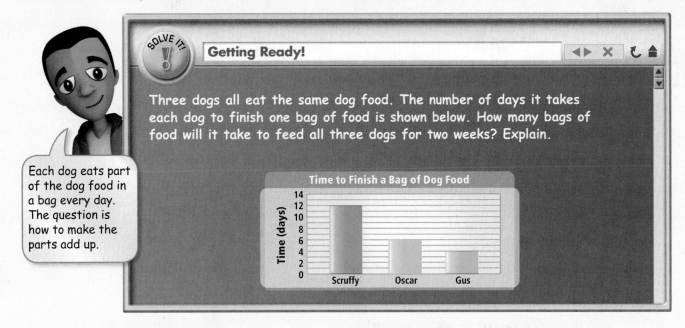

Each dog eats part of the dog food in a bag every day. The question is how to make the parts add up.

Getting Ready!

Three dogs all eat the same dog food. The number of days it takes each dog to finish one bag of food is shown below. How many bags of food will it take to feed all three dogs for two weeks? Explain.

Time to Finish a Bag of Dog Food

Time (days): Scruffy, Oscar, Gus

Focus Question How is adding and subtracting rational expressions similar to adding and subtracting numerical fractions?

You can add the numerators of rational expressions with like denominators. If a, b, and c represent polynomials (with $c \neq 0$), then $\frac{a}{c} + \frac{b}{c} = \frac{a + b}{c}$.

Problem 1 Adding Expressions With Like Denominators

What is the sum?

Think

Once you are comfortable adding rational expressions with like denominators, you can add the numerators and simplify all in one step.

A $\frac{4}{3y} + \frac{7}{3y}$

Add the numerators. $\frac{4}{3y} + \frac{7}{3y} = \frac{4 + 7}{3y}$

Simplify the numerator. $= \frac{11}{3y}$

B $\frac{3x}{x - 2} + \frac{x}{x - 2}$

Add the numerators. $\frac{3x}{x - 2} + \frac{x}{x - 2} = \frac{3x + x}{x - 2}$

Simplify the numerator. $= \frac{4x}{x - 2}$

Got It? **1.** What is the sum $\frac{2a}{3a - 4} + \frac{3a}{3a - 4}$?

Similarly, you can subtract rational expressions with like denominators.

 Problem 2 **Subtracting Expressions With Like Denominators**

What is the difference?

A $\dfrac{9}{m-3} - \dfrac{4}{m-3}$

Subtract the numerators. $\quad \dfrac{9}{m-3} - \dfrac{4}{m-3} = \dfrac{9-4}{m-3}$

Simplify. $\qquad\qquad\qquad\qquad\qquad = \dfrac{5}{m-3}$

B $\dfrac{7x+5}{3x^2-x-2} - \dfrac{4x+3}{3x^2-x-2}$

> **Think**
>
> **Why put parentheses around $4x+3$?**
> You want to subtract the entire numerator $4x+3$, and parentheses are needed to indicate that. Without the parentheses, you would only be subtracting $4x$.

Subtract the numerators. $\quad \dfrac{7x+5}{3x^2-x-2} - \dfrac{4x+3}{3x^2-x-2} = \dfrac{7x+5-(4x+3)}{3x^2-x-2}$

Distributive Property $\qquad\qquad\qquad\qquad\qquad = \dfrac{7x+5-4x-3}{3x^2-x-2}$

Simplify the numerator. $\qquad\qquad\qquad\qquad = \dfrac{3x+2}{3x^2-x-2}$

Factor the denominator. $\qquad\qquad\qquad\qquad = \dfrac{3x+2}{(3x+2)(x-1)}$

Divide out the common factor $3x+2$. $\qquad = \dfrac{\overset{1}{\cancel{3x+2}}}{\underset{1}{\cancel{(3x+2)}}(x-1)}$

Simplify. $\qquad\qquad\qquad\qquad\qquad\qquad = \dfrac{1}{x-1}$

 Got It? 2. What is the difference?

a. $\dfrac{2}{z+3} - \dfrac{7}{z+3}$

b. $\dfrac{9n-3}{10n-4} - \dfrac{3n+5}{10n-4}$

c. $\dfrac{7q-3}{q^2-4} - \dfrac{6q-5}{q^2-4}$

To add or subtract rational expressions with different denominators, you can write the expressions with the least common denominator (LCD).

 Problem 3 **Adding Expressions With Different Denominators**

What is the sum $\frac{5}{6x} + \frac{3}{2x^2}$?

Step 1 Find the LCD of $\frac{5}{6x}$ and $\frac{3}{2x^2}$. First write the denominators $6x$ and $2x^2$ as products of prime factors. To form the LCD, list each factor the greatest number of times it appears in a denominator.

Think

Why is the LCD $6x^2$ instead of $6x$?
One of the denominators has two factors of x. So the LCD must also have two factors of x.

Factor each denominator. $6x = 2 \cdot 3 \cdot x$
$$2x^2 = 2 \cdot x \cdot x$$

The LCD is the LCM of $6x$ and $2x^2$. $\text{LCD} = 2 \cdot 3 \cdot x \cdot x = 6x^2$

Step 2 Rewrite each rational expression using the LCD and then add.

Rewrite each fraction using the LCD. $\dfrac{5}{6x} + \dfrac{3}{2x^2} = \dfrac{5 \cdot x}{6x \cdot x} + \dfrac{3 \cdot 3}{2x^2 \cdot 3}$

Simplify numerators and denominators. $= \dfrac{5x}{6x^2} + \dfrac{9}{6x^2}$

Add the numerators. $= \dfrac{5x + 9}{6x^2}$

Got It? **3.** What is the sum $\frac{3}{7y^4} + \frac{2}{3y^2}$?

 Problem 4 **Subtracting Expressions With Different Denominators**

What is the difference $\frac{3}{d - 1} - \frac{2}{d + 2}$?

Step 1 Find the LCD of $\frac{3}{d - 1}$ and $\frac{2}{d + 2}$.

Since there are no common factors, the LCD is $(d - 1)(d + 2)$.

Step 2 Rewrite each rational expression using the LCD and then subtract.

Hint

Sometimes two denominators won't have a common factor. In that case, multiply to get the LCD.

Rewrite each fraction using the LCD. $\dfrac{3}{d - 1} - \dfrac{2}{d + 2} = \dfrac{3(d + 2)}{(d - 1)(d + 2)} - \dfrac{2(d - 1)}{(d - 1)(d + 2)}$

Think

Should you multiply the denominator or leave it in factored form?
There might be common factors to divide out later. So leave the denominator in factored form.

Simplify each numerator. $= \dfrac{3d + 6}{(d - 1)(d + 2)} - \dfrac{2d - 2}{(d - 1)(d + 2)}$

Subtract the numerators. $= \dfrac{3d + 6 - (2d - 2)}{(d - 1)(d + 2)}$

Use the Distributive Property. $= \dfrac{3d + 6 - 2d + 2}{(d - 1)(d + 2)}$

Simplify the numerator. $= \dfrac{d + 8}{(d - 1)(d + 2)}$

Got It? **4.** What is the difference $\frac{c}{3c - 1} - \frac{4}{c - 2}$?

Problem 5 Using Rational Expressions

Gas Mileage A certain truck gets 25% better gas mileage when it holds no cargo than when it is fully loaded. Let m be the number of miles per gallon of gasoline the truck gets when it is fully loaded. The truck drops off a full load and returns empty. What is an expression for the number of gallons of gasoline the truck uses?

Gas mileage = m

Gas mileage = $1.25m$

Think

How can unit analysis help you?
You can use unit analysis to verify that gallons of gasoline used equals distance traveled divided by miles per gallon.
$$\frac{mi}{mi/gal} = mi \cdot \frac{gal}{mi} = gal$$

Step 1 Write expressions for the amount of gasoline used on the outward trip and on the return trip.

Outward trip: gasoline used $= \dfrac{\text{distance traveled}}{\text{miles per gallon}} = \dfrac{80}{m}$

Return trip: gasoline used $= \dfrac{\text{distance traveled}}{\text{miles per gallon}} = \dfrac{80}{1.25m}$

80-mi trip outward

80-mi return trip

Step 2 Add the expressions to find the total amount of gasoline the truck uses.

total gasoline used $= \dfrac{80}{m} + \dfrac{80}{1.25m}$

Rewrite using the LCD, 1.25m. $= \dfrac{80(1.25)}{1.25m} + \dfrac{80}{1.25m}$

Simplify the first numerator. $= \dfrac{100}{1.25m} + \dfrac{80}{1.25m}$

Add the numerators. $= \dfrac{180}{1.25m}$

Simplify. $= \dfrac{144}{m}$

Got It? **5. a.** A bicyclist rides 5 mi out and then rides back. His speed returning is reduced 20% because it is raining. Let r be his speed in miles per hour riding out. What is an expression that represents his total time in hours riding out and back?

b. **Reasoning** In Problem 5, suppose m represents the number of miles per gallon of gasoline the truck gets when it holds no cargo. What expression represents the number of miles per gallon of gasoline the truck gets when fully loaded? Explain.

Focus Question How is adding and subtracting rational expressions similar to adding and subtracting numerical fractions?

Answer You can use the same rules to add and subtract rational expressions that you use to add and subtract numerical fractions. In both cases, you must have like denominators.

Lesson Check

Do you know HOW?

Add or subtract.

1. $\dfrac{4}{x-7} + \dfrac{7}{x-7}$

2. $\dfrac{9}{2y+4} - \dfrac{5}{2y+4}$

3. $\dfrac{4}{6b^2} + \dfrac{5}{8b^3}$

4. A runner practices running 2 mi up a slope and 2 mi down. She runs down the slope 50% faster than she runs up it. Let r be the runner's speed, in miles per hour, when running up the slope. What expression represents the time she spends running?

Do you UNDERSTAND?

5. **Writing** Suppose your friend was absent today. How would you explain to your friend how to add and subtract rational expressions?

6. **Compare and Contrast** How is finding the LCD of two rational expressions similar to finding the LCD of two numerical fractions? How is it different?

7. **Reasoning** Your friend says she can always find a common denominator for two rational expressions by finding the product of the denominators.
   a. Is your friend correct? Explain.
   b. Will your friend's method always give you the LCD? Explain.

Practice and Problem-Solving Exercises

 Practice

Add or subtract.

See Problems 1 and 2.

8. $\dfrac{5}{2m} + \dfrac{4}{2m}$

9. $\dfrac{5}{c-5} + \dfrac{9}{c-5}$

10. $\dfrac{3}{b-3} - \dfrac{b}{b-3}$

11. $\dfrac{5c}{2c+7} + \dfrac{c-28}{2c+7}$

12. $\dfrac{1}{2-b} - \dfrac{4}{2-b}$

13. $\dfrac{n}{n^2+4n+4} + \dfrac{2}{n^2+4n+4}$

14. $\dfrac{2y+1}{y-1} - \dfrac{y+2}{y-1}$

15. $\dfrac{3n+2}{n+4} - \dfrac{n-6}{n+4}$

16. $\dfrac{2t}{2t^2-t-3} - \dfrac{3}{2t^2-t-3}$

Find the LCD of each pair of expressions.

See Problems 3 and 4.

Guided Practice

To start, factor each denominator.

17. $\dfrac{1}{2}; \dfrac{4}{x^2}$

$2 = 2 \qquad x^2 = x \cdot x$

18. $\dfrac{b}{6}; \dfrac{2b}{9}$

19. $\dfrac{1}{z}; \dfrac{3}{7z}$

20. $\dfrac{8}{5b}; \dfrac{12}{7b^3c}$

21. $\dfrac{3m}{m+n}; \dfrac{3n}{m-n}$

Add or subtract.

Guided Practice

To start, find the LCD of $3a$ and 5.

22. $\dfrac{7}{3a} + \dfrac{2}{5}$

$3a$ and 5 have no common factors, so the LCD is $3a \cdot 5 = 15a$.

23. $\dfrac{4}{x} - \dfrac{2}{3}$

24. $\dfrac{27}{n^3} - \dfrac{9}{7n^2}$

25. $\dfrac{a}{a+3} - \dfrac{4}{a+5}$

26. $\dfrac{5}{t^2} - \dfrac{4}{t+1}$

27. Exercise Jane walks one mile from her house to her grandparents' house. Then she returns home, walking with her grandfather. Her return rate is 70% of her rate walking alone. Let r represent her rate walking alone.

See Problem 5.

   a. Write an expression for the amount of time Jane spends walking.

   b. Simplify your expression.

   c. Suppose Jane's rate walking alone is 3 mi/h. About how much time does she spend walking?

 Apply

28. Error Analysis A student added two rational expressions as shown. What error did the student make?

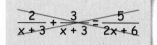

$$\frac{2}{x+3} + \frac{3}{x+3} = \frac{5}{2x+6}$$

29. Writing When you use the LCD to add or subtract rational expressions, will the answer always be in simplest form if you use the LCD? Explain.

30. Open-Ended Write two rational expressions with different denominators. Find the LCD and add the two expressions.

Add or subtract.

31. $\dfrac{y^2 + 2y - 1}{3y + 1} - \dfrac{2y^2 - 3}{3y + 1}$

32. $\dfrac{h^2 + 1}{2t^2 - 7} + \dfrac{h}{2t^2 - 7}$

33. $\dfrac{r - 5}{9 + p^3} - \dfrac{2k + 1}{9 + p^3}$

34. $\dfrac{2 - x}{xy^2z} - \dfrac{5 + z}{xy^2z}$

35. $9 + \dfrac{x - 3}{x + 2}$

36. $\dfrac{t}{2t - 3} - 11$

37. Think About a Plan The groundspeed for jet traffic from Los Angeles to New York City can be about 100 mi/h faster than the groundspeed from New York City to Los Angeles. This difference is due to a strong westerly wind at high altitudes. If r is a jet's groundspeed from New York City to Los Angeles, write and simplify an expression for the round-trip air time. The two cities are about 2500 mi apart.

- Can you write an expression for the air time from New York City to Los Angeles?

- In terms of r, what is the jet's groundspeed from Los Angeles to New York City? Can you use this speed to write an expression for the air time from Los Angeles to New York City?

> **Hint** Remember $d = rt$. To find the distance the jet travels, multiply speed by time.

38. Rowing A rowing team practices rowing 2 mi upstream and 2 mi downstream. The team can row downstream 25% faster than they can row upstream.

   a. Let u represent the team's rate rowing upstream. Write and simplify an expression involving u for the total amount of time they spend rowing.

   b. Let d represent the team's rate rowing downstream. Write and simplify an expression involving d for the total amount of time they spend rowing.

   c. Reasoning Do the expressions you wrote in parts (a) and (b) represent the same time? Explain.

For $f(x) = 8x, g(x) = \frac{1}{x}$, and $h(x) = \frac{4}{x - 5}$, perform the indicated operation.

Example $f(x) \div g(x) = 8x \div \dfrac{1}{x} = 8x \cdot \dfrac{x}{1} = 8x^2$

39. $f(x) + g(x)$ **40.** $f(x) \cdot g(x)$ **41.** $g(x) - h(x)$ **42.** $h(x) \div f(x)$

SAT/ACT

43. What is the difference $\frac{3x}{3x-2} - \frac{2}{3x-2}$ when $x \neq \frac{2}{3}$?

44. The area of the figure shown at the right is 200 cm². What is the value of x to the nearest hundredth of a centimeter?

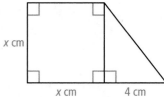

45. A band director can line up the band members in equal rows of 4, 5, or 8. What is the least number of band members?

46. The members of a bicycle club rode a 20-mi round-trip route. On the way back, they had a tailwind and averaged 3 mi/h faster than on the first half of the trip. Suppose the bicyclists averaged a rate of 12 mi/h for the first half of the trip. How many hours did the round trip take?

Mixed Review

Divide.

◀ **See Lesson 11-3.**

47. $(2x^4 + 8x^3 - 4x^2) \div 4x^2$ **48.** $(10b + 5b^2) \div (b + 2)$ **49.** $(y^4 - y^2) \div (y^2 - 2y - 3)$

Solve each radical equation. Check your answers. If there is no solution, write *no solution*.

◀ **See Lesson 10-4.**

50. $x = \sqrt{5x + 6}$ **51.** $n = \sqrt{24 - 5n}$ **52.** $\sqrt{16y} = -8$

Get Ready!   **To prepare for Lesson 11-5, do Exercises 53–55.**

Solve each proportion.

◀ **See Lesson 2-7.**

53. $\frac{1}{x} = \frac{3}{5}$ **54.** $\frac{3}{t} = \frac{5}{2}$ **55.** $\frac{m}{3} = \frac{17}{51}$

11-5 Solving Rational Equations

Objective   To solve rational equations and proportions

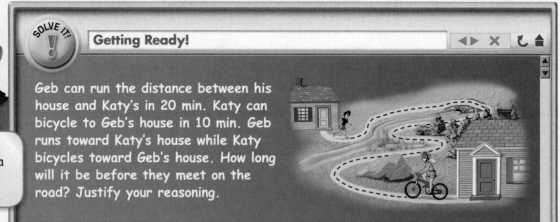

SOLVE IT!

Getting Ready!

Geb can run the distance between his house and Katy's in 20 min. Katy can bicycle to Geb's house in 10 min. Geb runs toward Katy's house while Katy bicycles toward Geb's house. How long will it be before they meet on the road? Justify your reasoning.

I bet each of them only goes a fraction of the distance!

A **rational equation** is an equation that contains one or more rational expressions.

Focus Question   How can you solve a rational equation?

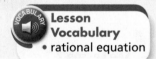

Lesson Vocabulary
• rational equation

Problem 1   Solving Equations With Rational Expressions

What is the solution of $\frac{5}{12} - \frac{4}{x} = \frac{1}{x}$? Check the solution.

The denominators are 12, x, and x. The LCD is $12x$.

$$\frac{5}{12} - \frac{4}{x} = \frac{1}{x}$$

Multiply each side by $12x$.

$$12x\left(\frac{5}{12} - \frac{4}{x}\right) = 12x\left(\frac{1}{x}\right)$$

Use the Distributive Property.

$$12x\left(\frac{5}{12}\right) - 12x\left(\frac{4}{x}\right) = 12x\left(\frac{1}{x}\right)$$

Cancel out the common factors 12 and x.

$$\cancel{12}^{1}x\left(\frac{5}{\cancel{12}_{1}}\right) - 12\cancel{x}^{1}\left(\frac{4}{\cancel{x}_{1}}\right) = 12\cancel{x}^{1}\left(\frac{1}{\cancel{x}_{1}}\right)$$

Simplify.

$$5x - 48 = 12$$

Add 48 to each side.

$$5x = 60$$

Divide each side by 5.

$$x = 12$$

Check   See if $x = 12$ makes $\frac{5}{12} - \frac{4}{x} = \frac{1}{x}$ true.

$$\frac{5}{12} - \frac{4}{12} \stackrel{?}{=} \frac{1}{12}$$

$$\frac{1}{12} = \frac{1}{12} \checkmark$$

Plan

Have you seen an equation like this before?
Yes. In Lesson 2-3, you solved equations that contained fractions. As you did there, you can clear the fractions from the equation by multiplying by a common denominator.

Got It? **1.** What is the solution of each equation? Check your solution.

      a. $\dfrac{1}{3} + \dfrac{3}{x} = \dfrac{2}{x}$ **b.** $\dfrac{4}{7x} + \dfrac{1}{3} = \dfrac{7}{3x}$

To solve some rational equations, you need to factor a quadratic expression.

Problem 2   Solving by Factoring

Multiple Choice What are the solutions of $1 - \dfrac{1}{x} = \dfrac{12}{x^2}$?

  Ⓐ $-11, 12$ Ⓑ $-4, 3$ Ⓒ $-3, 4$ Ⓓ $12, 13$

The denominators are x and x^2. The LCD is x^2.	$1 - \dfrac{1}{x} = \dfrac{12}{x^2}$
Multiply each side by x^2.	$x^2\left(1 - \dfrac{1}{x}\right) = x^2\left(\dfrac{12}{x^2}\right)$
Use the Distributive Property.	$x^2(1) - x^2\left(\dfrac{1}{x}\right) = x^2\left(\dfrac{12}{x^2}\right)$
Cancel out common factors.	$x^2(1) - {}^x\!x^2\left(\dfrac{1}{\not{x}_1}\right) = {}^1\!x^2\left(\dfrac{12}{x^2{}_1}\right)$
Simplify.	$x^2 - x = 12$
Collect terms on one side.	$x^2 - x - 12 = 0$
Factor the quadratic expression.	$(x - 4)(x + 3) = 0$
Zero-Product Property	$x - 4 = 0$ or $x + 3 = 0$
Solve for x.	$x = 4$ or $\quad x = -3$

Think

Is there a different way to solve this equation?
Yes. Because it's a quadratic equation, you can also solve it by using the quadratic formula, by completing the square, or by graphing.

Check   Determine whether 4 and -3 both make $1 - \dfrac{1}{x} = \dfrac{12}{x^2}$ a true statement.

When $x = 4$:   When $x = -3$:

$$1 - \frac{1}{x} = \frac{12}{x^2} \qquad\qquad 1 - \frac{1}{x} = \frac{12}{x^2}$$

$$1 - \frac{1}{4} \stackrel{?}{=} \frac{12}{(4)^2} \qquad\qquad 1 - \frac{1}{(-3)} \stackrel{?}{=} \frac{12}{(-3)^2}$$

$$1 - \frac{1}{4} \stackrel{?}{=} \frac{12}{16} \qquad\qquad\qquad 1 + \frac{1}{3} \stackrel{?}{=} \frac{12}{9}$$

$$\frac{3}{4} = \frac{3}{4} \; ✔ \qquad\qquad\qquad\qquad \frac{4}{3} = \frac{4}{3} \; ✔$$

The solutions are 4 and -3. The correct answer is C.

Got It? **2.** What are the solutions of each equation in parts (a) and (b)?
      Check your solutions.

      a. $\dfrac{5}{y} = \dfrac{6}{y^2} - 6$ **b.** $d + 6 = \dfrac{d + 11}{d + 3}$

      c. Reasoning How can you tell that the rational equation $\dfrac{2}{x^2} = -1$
      has no solutions just by looking at the equation?

Hint

What do you know about the sign of a square number?

To solve a work problem, find the fraction of the job each person does in one unit of time (for example, in 1 h or 1 min). The sum of the fractions for everyone working is the fraction of the job completed in one unit of time.

 Problem 3 Solving a Work Problem

Painting Amy can paint a loft apartment in 7 h. Jeremy can paint a loft apartment of the same size in 9 h. If they work together, how long will it take them to paint a third loft apartment of the same size?

Know
- Amy's painting time is 7 h.
- Jeremy's painting time is 9 h.

Need
Amy and Jeremy's combined painting time

Plan
Find what fraction of a loft each person can paint in 1 h. Then write and solve a rational equation.

Relate
| fraction of loft Amy can paint in 1 h | + | fraction of loft Jeremy can paint in 1 h | = | fraction of loft painted in 1 h |

Define Let t = the painting time, in hours, if Amy and Jeremy work together.

Think

Where have you seen a problem like this before?
In Problem 1 of this lesson, you solved a similar equation containing rational expressions.

Write

$$\frac{1}{7} \quad + \quad \frac{1}{9} \quad = \quad \frac{1}{t}$$

Multiply each side by the LCD, 63t. $63t\left(\frac{1}{7} + \frac{1}{9}\right) = 63t\left(\frac{1}{t}\right)$

Distributive Property $9t + 7t = 63$

Simplify. $16t = 63$

Divide each side by 16. $t = \frac{63}{16}$, or $3\frac{15}{16}$

It will take Amy and Jeremy about 4 h to paint the loft apartment together.

 Got It? 3. One hose can fill a pool in 12 h. Another hose can fill the same pool in 8 h. How long will it take for both hoses to fill the pool together?

Some rational equations are proportions. You can solve them by using the Cross Products Property.

 Problem 4 **Solving a Rational Proportion**

What is the solution of $\frac{4}{x+2} = \frac{3}{x+1}$?

Think

Can you use the LCD to solve this equation?
Yes, but when each side of a rational equation is a single rational expression, using cross products is often easier. Otherwise, you have to multiply each side of the equation by the LCD, $(x+2)(x+1)$.

Write the original equation.	$\frac{4}{x+2} = \frac{3}{x+1}$
Cross Products Property	$4(x+1) = 3(x+2)$
Distributive Property	$4x + 4 = 3x + 6$
Solve for x.	$x = 2$

Check $\frac{4}{2+2} \stackrel{?}{=} \frac{3}{2+1}$

$1 = 1$ ✔

 Got It? **4.** Find the solution(s) of each equation. Check your solutions.

a. $\frac{3}{b+2} = \frac{5}{b-2}$ **b.** $\frac{3}{c} = \frac{7}{c-4}$

The process of solving a rational equation may give a solution that is extraneous because it makes a denominator in the original equation equal 0. An extraneous solution is a solution of an equation that is derived from the original equation, but is not a solution of the original equation itself. So you must check your solutions.

 Problem 5 **Checking to Find an Extraneous Solution**

What is the solution of $\frac{6}{x+5} = \frac{x+3}{x+5}$?

Think

What extraneous solutions are possible?
Since $\frac{6}{x+5}$ and $\frac{x+3}{x+5}$ are undefined when $x = -5$, a possible extraneous solution is -5.

Write the original equation.	$\frac{6}{x+5} = \frac{x+3}{x+5}$
Cross Products Property	$6(x+5) = (x+3)(x+5)$
Simplify each side of the equation.	$6x + 30 = x^2 + 8x + 15$
Collect terms on one side.	$0 = x^2 + 2x - 15$
Factor.	$0 = (x-3)(x+5)$
Zero-Product Property	$x - 3 = 0$ or $x + 5 = 0$
Solve for x.	$x = 3$ or $x = -5$

Check $\frac{6}{3+5} \stackrel{?}{=} \frac{3+3}{3+5}$ $\frac{6}{-5+5} \stackrel{?}{=} \frac{-5+3}{-5+5}$

$\frac{6}{8} = \frac{6}{8}$ ✔ $\frac{6}{0} = \frac{-2}{0}$ ✗ Undefined!

The equation has one solution, 3.

 Got It? **5.** What is the solution of $\frac{x-4}{x^2-4} = \frac{-2}{x-2}$? Check your solution.

Focus Question How can you solve a rational equation?

Answer You can solve a rational equation by first multiplying each side by the LCD. When each side of a rational equation is a single rational expression, you can solve the equation using the Cross Products Property.

Lesson Check

Do you know HOW?

Solve each equation. Check your solutions.

1. $\frac{1}{2x} + \frac{3}{10} = \frac{1}{5x}$

2. $\frac{5}{x^2} = \frac{6}{x} - 1$

3. $\frac{-2}{x+2} = \frac{x+4}{x^2-4}$

4. Sarah picks a bushel of apples in 45 min. Andy picks a bushel of apples in 75 min. How long will it take them to pick a bushel together?

Do you UNDERSTAND?

5. Vocabulary How is an extraneous solution of a rational equation similar to an excluded value of a rational expression? How is it different?

6. Open-Ended Write a rational equation that has one solution and one extraneous solution.

7. Error Analysis In the work shown at the right, what error did the student make in solving the rational equation?

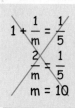

Practice and Problem-Solving Exercises

Ⓐ Practice Solve each equation. Check your solutions.

◀ See Problems 1 and 2.

8. $\frac{1}{2} + \frac{2}{x} = \frac{1}{x}$

To start, multiply each side of the equation by the LCD, 2x.

$2x\left(\frac{1}{2} + \frac{2}{x}\right) = 2x\left(\frac{1}{x}\right)$

9. $5 + \frac{2}{p} = \frac{17}{p}$

10. $y - \frac{6}{y} = 5$

11. $\frac{5}{2s} + \frac{3}{4} = \frac{9}{4s}$

12. $\frac{2}{c-2} = 2 - \frac{4}{c}$

13. $\frac{5}{3p} + \frac{2}{3} = \frac{5+p}{2p}$

14. $\frac{1}{t-2} = \frac{t}{8}$

15. $\frac{v+2}{v} + \frac{4}{3v} = 11$

16. $\frac{3+a}{2a} = \frac{1}{3} + \frac{5}{6a}$

17. $\frac{a}{a+3} = \frac{2a}{a-3} - 1$

18. Gardening Marian can weed a garden in 3 h. Robin can weed the same garden in 4 h. If they work together, how long will the weeding take them?

◀ See Problem 3.

19. Trucking David can unload a delivery truck in 20 min. Allie can unload the same delivery truck in 35 min. If they work together, how long will the unloading take?

Solve each equation. Check your solutions. If there is no solution, write *no solution*.

◀ See Problems 4 and 5.

Guided Practice

20. $\dfrac{5}{x+1} = \dfrac{x+2}{x+1}$

To start, use the Cross Products Property.

$5(x+1) = (x+1)(x+2)$

21. $\dfrac{4}{c+4} = \dfrac{c}{c+25}$

22. $\dfrac{3}{m-1} = \dfrac{2m}{m+4}$

23. $\dfrac{2x+4}{x-3} = \dfrac{3x}{x-3}$

B Apply

24. Writing How could you use cross products to solve $\dfrac{1}{x-2} = \dfrac{2x-6}{x+6} + 1$?

25. Open-Ended Write a rational equation that has 5 as a solution.

Solve each equation. Check your solutions.

26. $\dfrac{2r}{r-4} - 2 = \dfrac{4}{r+5}$

27. $\dfrac{r+1}{r-1} = \dfrac{r}{3} + \dfrac{2}{r-1}$

28. $\dfrac{s}{3s+2} + \dfrac{s+3}{2s-4} = \dfrac{-2s}{3s^2-4s-4}$

29. $\dfrac{u+1}{u+2} = \dfrac{-1}{u-3} + \dfrac{u-1}{u^2-u-6}$

30. Think About a Plan Two pipes fill a storage tank with water in 9 h. The smaller pipe takes three times as long to fill the tank as the larger pipe. How long would it take the larger pipe to fill the tank alone?
- What variable should you define for this situation?
- In terms of your variable, what fraction of the tank is filled in 1 h by the larger pipe alone? By the smaller pipe alone?

31. Running You take 94 min to complete a 10-mi race. Your average speed during the first half of the race is 2 mi/h greater than your average speed during the second half. What is your average speed during the first half of the race?

Hint You run 5 miles during each half of the race.

Electricity Two lamps can be connected to a battery in a circuit in series or in parallel. You can calculate the total resistance R_T in a circuit if you know the resistance in each lamp. Resistance is measured in ohms (Ω). For a circuit connected in series, $R_T = R_1 + R_2$. For a circuit connected in parallel, $\dfrac{1}{R_T} = \dfrac{1}{R_1} + \dfrac{1}{R_2}$.

32. The lamps are connected in series. $R_T = 20\ \Omega$. Find R_2.

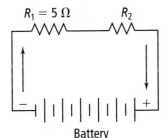

$R_1 = 5\ \Omega$ R_2

Battery

33. The lamps are connected in parallel. $R_T = 12\ \Omega$. Find R_2.

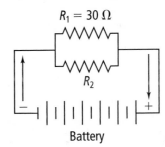

$R_1 = 30\ \Omega$

R_2

Battery

34. Travel A plane flies 450 mi/h. It can travel 980 mi with a tailwind in the same amount of time as it travels 820 mi against the wind. Solve the equation $\dfrac{980}{450+s} = \dfrac{820}{450-s}$ to find the speed s of the wind.

Standardized Test Prep

SAT/ACT

35. Which inequality contains both solutions of $x = \frac{1}{2} + \frac{3}{x}$?

    (A) $-1 < x < 3$ (B) $-2 < x \le 2$ (C) $-2 \le x < 0$ (D) $-3 \le x \le -1$

36. Which expression is equivalent to $\dfrac{\frac{4}{x+3}}{\frac{2x-6}{x^2-9}}$?

    (F) 2 (G) -2 (H) $\dfrac{8}{x^2+6x+9}$ (I) $\dfrac{2x+6}{x-3}$

37. Which is the least common denominator of $\frac{1}{x}$, $\frac{x}{3}$, and $\frac{3}{2x}$?

    (A) $2x$ (B) $3x$ (C) $6x$ (D) $6x^2$

Short Response

38. A grizzly bear can run as fast as 30 mi/h. At that rate, how many feet would a grizzly bear travel in 1 s? Explain your answer.

Mixed Review

Add or subtract.

See Lesson 11-4.

39. $\dfrac{5}{x^2y^2z} - \dfrac{8}{x^2y^2z}$ **40.** $\dfrac{3h^2}{2t^2-8} + \dfrac{h}{t-2}$ **41.** $\dfrac{k-11}{k^2+6k-40} - \dfrac{5}{k-4}$

Get Ready!   **To prepare for Lesson 12-1, do Exercises 42–45.**

Find each sum or difference.

See Lesson 1-5.

42. $-7.2 + 8.9$ **43.** $8.7 - (-4.4)$ **44.** $16.2 + 4.95$ **45.** $-10.25 - (-5.35)$

Pull It **All Together**

BIG idea Equivalence

Rational expressions can be represented in many ways. When a rational expression is simplified, the numerator and denominator have no common factors except 1.

Task 1

A cylinder with radius r and height $2r + 4$ contains a cube with edge length $r\sqrt{2}$, as shown. What fraction of the cylinder's volume is taken up by the cube? Write your answer in simplified form.

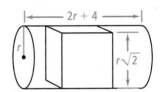

BIG idea Solving Equations and Inequalities

To isolate the variable in a rational equation, multiply each side by the LCD and then solve the resulting equation. Check for extraneous solutions.

Task 2

A restaurant has 45 tables. Each table seats 4 people. The manager has 4 employees to prepare the tables. The chart shows how fast each employee works. Use this information to answer the following questions.

a. In order to get the tables ready in the least amount of time, which two employees should the manager ask to fold napkins? Which two employees should the manager ask to set the tables?

b. If everyone starts working at the same time, how quickly can the employees get the tables ready for dinner? The first pair of employees to finish their job should help the other pair to finish the tables. Explain your answer.

Employee	Time to Fold 4 Napkins (min)	Time to Set 4 Places (min)
Stacie	3	5
Jeff	4	3
Tiffany	5	2
Nick	3.5	4

Connecting **BIG** ideas and Answering the Essential Questions

1 Equivalence
Rational expressions can be represented many ways. When a rational expression is simplified, the numerator and denominator have no common factors except 1.

Simplifying Rational Expressions (Lesson 11-1)

$$\frac{7y + 21}{y + 3} = \frac{7(y + 3)^1}{_1 y + 3}$$

$$= 7$$

Multiplying, Dividing, Adding, and Subtracting Rational Expressions (Lessons 11-2, 11-3, and 11-4)

$$\frac{7}{3x} - \frac{5}{3x} = \frac{7 - 5}{3x}$$

$$= \frac{2}{3x}$$

2 Solving Equations and Inequalities
To isolate the variable in a rational equation, multiply by the LCD and then solve the resulting equation. Check for extraneous solutions.

Solving Rational Equations (Lesson 11-5)

$$\frac{1}{2} + \frac{3}{t} = \frac{5}{8}$$

$$8t\left(\frac{1}{2} + \frac{3}{t}\right) = 8t\left(\frac{5}{8}\right)$$

$$4t + 24 = 5t$$

$$24 = t$$

Chapter Vocabulary

- complex fraction (p. 674)
- excluded value (p. 664)
- rational equation (p. 692)
- rational expression (p. 664)

Choose the correct term to complete each sentence.

1. A value of x for which a rational function $f(x)$ is undefined is a(n) _?_ .

2. A(n) _?_ contains one or more fractions in its numerator, in its denominator, or in both.

3. A(n) _?_ is a ratio of two polynomial expressions.

11-1 Simplifying Rational Expressions

Quick Review

A **rational expression** is an expression that can be written in the form $\frac{polynomial}{polynomial}$. A rational expression is in simplified form when the numerator and denominator have no common factors other than 1.

Example

What is the simplified form of $\frac{x^2 - 9}{x^2 - 2x - 15}$?

Factor the numerator and denominator.
$$\frac{x^2 - 9}{x^2 - 2x - 15} = \frac{(x + 3)(x - 3)}{(x + 3)(x - 5)}$$

Divide out the common factor.
$$= \frac{\cancel{(x + 3)}^1(x - 3)}{{}_1\cancel{(x + 3)}(x - 5)}$$

Simplify.
$$= \frac{x - 3}{x - 5}$$

Exercises

Simplify each expression. State any excluded values.

4. $\dfrac{2x^2 + 6x}{10x^3}$

5. $\dfrac{m - 3}{3m - 9}$

6. $\dfrac{x^2 + 6x + 9}{5x + 15}$

7. $\dfrac{2a^2 - 4a + 2}{3a^2 - 3}$

8. $\dfrac{2s^2 - 5s - 12}{2s^2 - 9s + 4}$

9. $\dfrac{4 - c}{2c - 8}$

10. **Geometry** What fraction of the rectangle is shaded? Write your answer as a rational expression in simplified form.

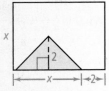

11-2 and 11-3 Multiplying and Dividing Rational Expressions and Dividing Polynomials

Quick Review

You can multiply and divide rational expressions using the same properties you use to multiply and divide numerical fractions.

$\dfrac{a}{b} \cdot \dfrac{c}{d} = \dfrac{ac}{bd}$, where $b \neq 0$ and $d \neq 0$.

$\dfrac{a}{b} \div \dfrac{c}{d} = \dfrac{a}{b} \cdot \dfrac{d}{c} = \dfrac{ad}{bc}$, where $b \neq 0$, $c \neq 0$, and $d \neq 0$.

To divide a polynomial by a monomial, divide each term of the polynomial by the monomial. To divide a polynomial by another polynomial, use long division. When dividing polynomials, write the answer as quotient $+ \dfrac{remainder}{divisor}$.

Example

What is the quotient $\dfrac{y}{y + 3} \div \dfrac{y - 3}{y - 2}$?

$$\frac{y}{y + 3} \div \frac{y - 3}{y - 2} = \frac{y}{y + 3} \cdot \frac{y - 2}{y - 3}$$

$$= \frac{y(y - 2)}{(y + 3)(y - 3)}$$

Exercises

Multiply or divide.

11. $\dfrac{4x + 12}{x^2 - 2x} \cdot \dfrac{x}{6x + 18}$

12. $\dfrac{a^2 + 5a + 4}{a^3} \div \dfrac{a^2 + 3a + 2}{a^2 - 2a}$

13. $\dfrac{x^2 + 13x + 40}{x - 7} \div \dfrac{x + 8}{x^2 - 49}$

14. $(12x^2 + 9x - 7) \div 3x$

15. $(3d^2 + 2d - 29) \div (d + 3)$

16. **Geometry** The width and area of a rectangle are shown in the figure at the right. What is the length of the rectangle?

$(2b - 1)$ in.

$A = (4b^3 + 5b - 3)$ in.^{2}

11-4 Adding and Subtracting Rational Expressions

Quick Review

You can add and subtract rational expressions. To add or subtract expressions with like denominators, add or subtract the numerators and write the result over the common denominator. To add or subtract expressions with different denominators, write the expressions with the LCD and then add or subtract the numerators.

Example

What is $\dfrac{1}{a+7} + \dfrac{a}{a-5}$?

$$\dfrac{1}{a+7} + \dfrac{a}{a-5} = \dfrac{1(a-5)}{(a+7)(a-5)} + \dfrac{a(a+7)}{(a+7)(a-5)}$$

$$= \dfrac{a-5}{(a+7)(a-5)} + \dfrac{a^2+7a}{(a+7)(a-5)}$$

$$= \dfrac{a-5+a^2+7a}{(a+7)(a-5)}$$

$$= \dfrac{a^2+8a-5}{(a+7)(a-5)}$$

Exercises

Add or subtract.

17. $\dfrac{8x}{x+1} - \dfrac{3}{x+1}$

18. $\dfrac{6}{7x} + \dfrac{1}{4}$

19. $\dfrac{5}{2+x} + \dfrac{x}{x-4}$

20. $\dfrac{9}{3x-1} - \dfrac{5x}{2x+3}$

21. Air Travel The distance between Atlanta, Georgia, and Albuquerque, New Mexico, is about 1270 mi. The groundspeed for jet traffic from Albuquerque to Atlanta can be about 18% faster than the groundspeed from Atlanta to Albuquerque. Let r be the speed from Atlanta to Albuquerque in miles per hour. What is a simplified expression for the round-trip flying time?

11-5 Solving Rational Equations

Quick Review

You can solve a **rational equation** by multiplying each side by the LCD. Check possible solutions to make sure each satisfies the original equation.

Example

What is the solution of $\dfrac{3}{8} + \dfrac{4}{x} = \dfrac{7}{x}$?

$$\dfrac{3}{8} + \dfrac{4}{x} = \dfrac{7}{x}$$

$$8x\left(\dfrac{3}{8} + \dfrac{4}{x}\right) = 8x\left(\dfrac{7}{x}\right)$$

$$8^1x\left(\dfrac{3}{\cancel{8}_1}\right) + 8x^1\left(\dfrac{4}{\cancel{x}_1}\right) = 8x^1\left(\dfrac{7}{\cancel{x}_1}\right)$$

$$3x + 32 = 56$$

$$3x = 24$$

$$x = 8$$

Check $\quad \dfrac{3}{8} + \dfrac{4}{8} \stackrel{?}{=} \dfrac{7}{8}$

$$\dfrac{7}{8} = \dfrac{7}{8} \quad ✔$$

Exercises

Solve each equation. Check your solutions.

22. $\dfrac{1}{2} + \dfrac{3}{t} = \dfrac{5}{8}$

23. $\dfrac{3}{m-4} + \dfrac{1}{3(m-4)} = \dfrac{6}{m}$

24. $\dfrac{2c}{c-4} - 2 = \dfrac{4}{c+5}$

25. $\dfrac{5}{2x-3} = \dfrac{7}{3x}$

26. Business A new photocopier can make 72 copies in 2 min. When an older photocopier is operational, the two photocopiers together can make 72 copies in 1.5 min. How long would it take the older photocopier to make 72 copies working alone?

Do you know HOW?

Identify the excluded value for each rational expression.

1. $\dfrac{19 + x}{x - 5}$

2. $\dfrac{2x}{8x - 12}$

Simplify each expression. State any excluded values.

3. $\dfrac{6p - 30}{3p - 15}$

4. $\dfrac{n^2 + 4n - 5}{n + 5}$

Multiply or divide.

5. $\dfrac{3}{x - 2} \cdot \dfrac{x^2 - 4}{12}$

6. $\dfrac{5x}{x^2 + 2x} \div \dfrac{30x^2}{x + 2}$

Divide.

7. $(12x^4 + 9x^3 - 10x^2) \div 3x^3$

8. $(4x^4 - 6x^3 - 2x^2 - 2x) \div (2x - 1)$

Find the LCD of each pair of expressions.

9. $\dfrac{5}{h}, \dfrac{6}{3h}$

10. $\dfrac{4}{a^2 b^3}, \dfrac{3}{9ab^4}$

Add or subtract.

11. $\dfrac{4b - 2}{3b} + \dfrac{b}{b + 2}$

12. $\dfrac{9}{n} - \dfrac{8}{n + 1}$

Solve each equation. Check your solutions.

13. $\dfrac{v}{3} + \dfrac{v}{v + 5} = \dfrac{-4}{v + 5}$

14. $\dfrac{16}{x + 10} = \dfrac{8}{2x - 1}$

15. Cleaning Mark can clean his father's office in 30 min. His younger sister Lynn can clean the office in 40 min. How long will it take the two of them together to clean the office?

Do you UNDERSTAND?

16. Open-Ended Write a rational expression for which 6 and 3 are excluded values.

17. Geometry The height of a square prism is $3n + 1$. The volume of the prism is $3n^3 + 13n^2 + 16n + 4$. What is the area of the square base of the prism?

18 Reasoning Rosa divided a polynomial $p(x)$ by $x - 4$ and obtained this result: $2x + 13 + \dfrac{59}{x - 4}$. What is $p(x)$?

19. Error Analysis Your friend says the solution of the rational equation $\dfrac{m}{m - 3} + \dfrac{1}{4} = \dfrac{3}{m - 3}$ is 3. Explain the error that your friend may have made.

20. Reasoning Consider the equation $\dfrac{3}{x - a} = \dfrac{x}{x - a}$. For what value(s) of a does the equation have exactly one solution? No solution? Explain.

Cumulative Test Prep

11

TIPS FOR SUCCESS

Some questions on tests ask you to simplify an expression. Read the question at the right. Then follow the tips to answer it.

Which expression is equivalent to
$$\frac{20x^3y^5 - 30x^6y^4}{5x^3y^3}?$$

(A) $4x^6y^8 - 6x^9y^7$

(B) $4y^2 - 6x^3y$

(C) $-2x^6y^6$

(D) $15y^2 - 25x^3y$

TIP 2

When you divide powers that have the same base, you subtract the exponents.

Think It Through

Write the expression as a difference of two fractions. Then simplify each fraction using the laws of exponents.

$$\frac{20x^3y^5 - 30x^6y^4}{5x^3y^3}$$

$$= \frac{20x^3y^5}{5x^3y^3} - \frac{30x^6y^4}{5x^3y^3}$$

$$= 4x^{3-3}y^{5-3} - 6x^{6-3}y^{4-3}$$

$$= 4x^0y^2 - 6x^3y^1$$

$$= 4y^2 - 6x^3y$$

TIP 1

Use the fact that a fraction $\frac{a+b}{c}$ can be written in the form $\frac{a}{c} + \frac{b}{c}$.

Vocabulary Builder

As you solve test items, you must understand the meanings of mathematical terms. Choose the correct term to complete each sentence.

A. The quantity $b^2 - 4ac$ is the (*vertex, discriminant*) of the equation $ax^2 + bx + c = 0$.

B. Two lines are (*parallel, perpendicular*) if their slopes are negative reciprocals of each other.

C. A (*linear, quadratic*) equation is an equation that can be written in the form $Ax + By = C$, where A, B, and C are real numbers, and A and B are not both 0.

D. A(n) (*rational, exponential*) expression is a ratio of two polynomials.

E. When you (*solve, evaluate*) an equation, you are finding the value or values that make the equation true.

Multiple Choice

Read each question. Then write the letter of the correct answer on your paper.

1. Which function describes the tables of values?

x	−2	−1	0	1
f(x)	−3	−1	1	3

(A) $f(x) = x - 1$ (C) $f(x) = x + 1$

(B) $f(x) = 2x$ (D) $f(x) = 2x + 1$

2. A rectangle has an area of $8x^2 + 16x + 6$. Which of the following could be the length and width of the rectangle?

(F) $4x + 1, 2x + 6$ (H) $4x + 6, 2x + 1$

(G) $4x + 3, 2x + 2$ (I) $8x + 1, x + 6$

3. Which expression is equivalent to $\frac{x+2}{x+4} - \frac{x+1}{x-3}$?

  Ⓐ $\dfrac{-2(3x-5)}{(x+4)(x-3)}$

  Ⓑ $\dfrac{-2(3x+5)}{(x+4)(x-3)}$

  Ⓒ $\dfrac{-2(3x+5)}{(x-4)(x+3)}$

  Ⓓ $\dfrac{2(3x-5)}{(x+4)(x-3)}$

4. Which is equivalent to $\dfrac{18x^2y + 24x^3y^4 - 12x^7y^2}{6x^2y}$?

  Ⓕ $12 + 18xy^3 - 6x^5y$

  Ⓖ $4xy^3 - 2x^5y$

  Ⓗ $3 + 4xy^3 - 2x^5y$

  Ⓘ $3x^2y + 4x^3y^4 - 2x^7y^2$

5. Which expression is equivalent to $\dfrac{x-4}{\frac{x+3}{x-1}}$?

  Ⓐ $\dfrac{x^2 + 5x - 4}{x+3}$

  Ⓑ $\dfrac{x+4}{x^2 + 2x - 3}$

  Ⓒ $\dfrac{x^2 + 7x + 12}{x-1}$

  Ⓓ $\dfrac{x^2 - 5x + 4}{x+3}$

6. Which of the following points are on the graph of $y = -2x + 3$?

  Ⓕ $(0, -2)$ and $(1, 1)$

  Ⓖ $(0, 3)$ and $(1, -1)$

  Ⓗ $(1, 1)$ and $(0, 3)$

  Ⓘ $(-1, 1)$ and $(0, -2)$

7. Which real-number property is illustrated below?

$$2x^2 + 3x^2 = (2+3)x^2 = 5x^2$$

  Ⓐ Associative Property of Addition

  Ⓑ Commutative Property of Addition

  Ⓒ Distributive Property

  Ⓓ Identity Property of Addition

8. What is (are) the solution(s) of the equation $\dfrac{2x+1}{5x} = \dfrac{4x-5}{3x}$?

  Ⓕ 0

  Ⓖ 2

  Ⓗ 0 and 2

  Ⓘ no solution

9. About 8 babies are born in the United States each minute. Using this estimate, about how many babies are born each year?

  Ⓐ 70,000

  Ⓑ 200,000

  Ⓒ 4,000,000

  Ⓓ 300,000,000

10. Which expression is equivalent to $(3m^2n^4)^3$?

  Ⓕ $27m^6n^{12}$

  Ⓖ $27m^5n^7$

  Ⓗ $9m^6n^{12}$

  Ⓘ $9m^5n^7$

11. Which statement below about the function $y = 2x^2 - 3$ is correct?

  Ⓐ The value of y is never less than -3.

  Ⓑ The value of y is never greater than 2.

  Ⓒ The value of x is always greater than the value of y.

  Ⓓ The value of y is always greater than the value of x.

12. Each day Michael goes for a run through a rectangular park. The diagonal of the park is $\sqrt{80,000}$ m long. Which of the following is equivalent to $\sqrt{80,000}$?

  Ⓕ $100\sqrt{2}$

  Ⓖ $200\sqrt{2}$

  Ⓗ $800\sqrt{2}$

  Ⓘ $8000\sqrt{10}$

13. What is the x-intercept of the graph of $-5x + y = -20$?

  Ⓐ -20

  Ⓑ -4

  Ⓒ 4

  Ⓓ 20

14. Davis bought 2 candy bars and 3 bags of chips for $5.45. Reese bought 5 bags of chips for $6.25. How much did each candy bar cost?

  Ⓕ $.85

  Ⓖ $.95

  Ⓗ $1.25

  Ⓘ $1.70

15. What is the simplified form of $\sqrt{5}(2 + \sqrt{10})$?

(A) $2\sqrt{10}$

(B) $2\sqrt{5} + \sqrt{50}$

(C) $2\sqrt{5} + 5\sqrt{2}$

(D) $2\sqrt{5} + \sqrt{10}$

16. What is the factored form of $6w^4 + 15w^2$?

(F) $w^2(6w^2 + 15)$

(G) $3w^2(2w^2 + 5)$

(H) $3w(2w^3 + 5w)$

(I) $3w^2(2w^2 + 5w)$

17. Which of the following is equivalent to $(3\sqrt{2})^2$?

(A) 6

(C) 18

(B) $9\sqrt{2}$

(D) 36

18. What is the simplified form of $\dfrac{x^2 - 81}{2x^2 + 23x + 45}$?

(F) $\dfrac{x + 9}{2x + 5}$

(G) $\dfrac{x - 9}{x + 9}$

(H) $\dfrac{x - 9}{2x - 5}$

(I) $\dfrac{x - 9}{2x + 5}$

GRIDDED RESPONSE

Record your answers in a grid.

19. A dinner party at a restaurant had 37 people. Each person ordered one of two entrées. One entrée cost $15, and the other entrée cost $18. The total cost of all the entrées was $606. How many $15 entrées were ordered?

20. Sandra takes 6 h to drive 300 mi. If she increases her speed by 5 mi/h, how many hours will she take to drive 440 mi?

21. Suzanne rolled a number cube 200 times and recorded her results in the table below. What percent of the time did she roll an even number? Write the percent in decimal form.

Numbers	1	2	3	4	5	6
Rolls	56	30	20	36	44	14

22. A roof on a house has a triangular cross section with at least two angles of equal measure. One angle of the triangle measures 120°. What is the measure, in degrees, of one of the other two angles?

23. Line p passes through points $(5, -4)$ and $(2, 7)$. What is the slope of a line that is perpendicular to line p?

24. A cylinder has a height of 20 cm and a diameter of 6 cm. What is the volume, in cubic centimeters, of the cylinder? Use 3.14 for π.

Short Response

25. Phillip works at a grocery store after school and on weekends. He earns $8.50 per hour. What is a function rule for his total earnings $f(h)$ for working h hours?

26. What is the simplified form of $\dfrac{x^2 + 3x - 18}{6x + 36}$? Show your work.

Extended Response

27. The formula $C = \dfrac{5}{9}(F - 32)$ can be used to find the Celsius temperature C if you know the Fahrenheit temperature F.

a. Transform the equation to find the Fahrenheit temperature F in terms of the Celsius temperature C.

b. Use the formula in part (a) to find the Fahrenheit temperature equivalent to 35°C.

Skills Handbook, p. 788

Adding and Subtracting Fractions

Add or subtract. Write each answer in simplest form.

1. $\frac{2}{3} + \frac{1}{2}$ 2. $\frac{7}{12} - \frac{5}{8}$ 3. $\frac{16}{25} + \frac{3}{10}$ 4. $\frac{5}{9} - \frac{5}{36}$

Lesson 1-6

Multiplying and Dividing Real Numbers

Simplify each fraction.

5. $\frac{6 + 4 + 7 + 9}{4}$ 6. $\frac{1.7 + 4.2 + 3.1}{3}$ 7. $\frac{11 + 16 + 9 + 12 + 7}{5}$

Lesson 1-7

Distributive Property

Simplify each expression.

8. $6(x - 7)$ 9. $\frac{1}{2}(4x + 6)$ 10. $-2(5 - x)$ 11. $0.5(5 + 4x)$

Lesson 3-8

Unions and Intersections of Sets

Let $X = \{x \mid x$ is an odd whole number less than 16$\}$, $Y = \{2, 6, 9, 10, 16\}$, and $Z = \{z \mid z$ is an even whole number less than 19$\}$. Find each union or intersection.

12. $X \cup Y$ 13. $X \cap Y$ 14. $Y \cap Z$ 15. $X \cup Y \cup Z$

Lesson 5-7

Scatter Plots

For each table, make a scatter plot of the data. Describe the type of correlation that the scatter plot shows.

16.

Messenger Bag Sales				
Price ($)	30	45	60	75
Number Sold	150	123	85	50

17.

Driving Distances and Times				
Distance (mi)	5	38	15	8
Time (min)	15	56	28	22

Looking Ahead Vocabulary

18. There are three *outcomes* for a hockey team during a game: win, lose, or tie. What are the possible *outcomes* for flipping a coin?

19. On a highway, the *median* is the strip of land that divides the two sides of opposing traffic. How would you expect a *median* to divide a data set?

20. The color purple is a *combination* of the colors red and blue. Does the order in which the colors are combined change the result of the *combination*?

Data Analysis and Probability

One of these ducks is different from the others! If I close my eyes and grab one, do you think I'll get a pink one or a yellow one? You'll learn how to use probability to decide whether an event is likely or not in this chapter.

Vocabulary for Part A

English/Spanish Vocabulary Audio Online:

English	Spanish
bias, *p. 739*	parcialidad
bivariate, *p. 738*	bivariado
box-and-whisker plot, *p. 731*	gráfica de cajas
element, *p. 710*	elemento
frequency, *p. 716*	frecuencia
matrix, *p. 710*	matriz
measure of central tendency, *p. 722*	medida de tendencia central
outlier, *p. 722*	valor extremo
percentile, *p. 733*	percentil
quartile, *p. 730*	cuartiles

My Math Video

00:04:04

BIG ideas

1 Data Collection and Analysis
Essential Question How can collecting and analyzing data help you make decisions or predictions?

2 Data Representation
Essential Question How can you make and interpret different representations of data?

3 Probability
Essential Question How is probability related to real-world events?

Chapter Preview for Part A

12-1 Organizing Data Using Matrices
12-2 Frequency and Histograms
12-3 Measures of Central Tendency and Dispersion
12-4 Box-and-Whisker Plots
12-5 Samples and Surveys

12-1 Organizing Data Using Matrices

Objectives To organize data in a matrix

To add and subtract matrices and multiply a matrix by a scalar

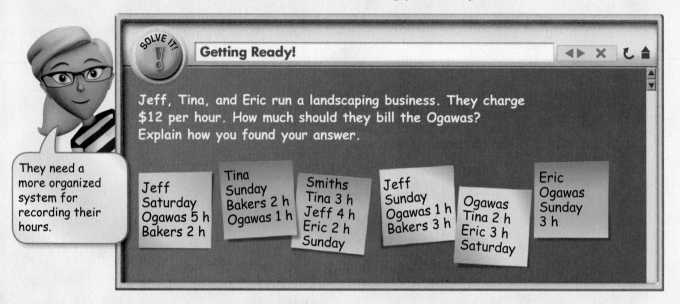

SOLVE IT!

Getting Ready!

Jeff, Tina, and Eric run a landscaping business. They charge $12 per hour. How much should they bill the Ogawas? Explain how you found your answer.

They need a more organized system for recording their hours.

Jeff
Saturday
Ogawas 5 h
Bakers 2 h

Tina
Sunday
Bakers 2 h
Ogawas 1 h

Smiths
Tina 3 h
Jeff 4 h
Eric 2 h
Sunday

Jeff
Sunday
Ogawas 1 h
Bakers 3 h

Ogawas
Tina 2 h
Eric 3 h
Saturday

Eric
Ogawas
Sunday
3 h

Lesson Vocabulary
- matrix
- element
- scalar
- scalar multiplication

A **matrix** is a rectangular arrangement of numbers in rows and columns. The plural of *matrix* is *matrices* (pronounced MAY truh seez). The matrix on the right shows the hours Jeff, Tina, and Eric worked on Saturday.

To identify the size of a matrix, look at the number of rows and the number of columns. The matrix on the right has 3 rows and 2 columns, so it is a 3 × 2 matrix.

$$\begin{array}{c} \text{Ogawas} \quad \text{Bakers} \\ \begin{array}{c} \text{Jeff} \\ \text{Tina} \\ \text{Eric} \end{array} \begin{bmatrix} 5 & 2 \\ 2 & 0 \\ 3 & 0 \end{bmatrix} \begin{array}{l} \leftarrow \text{Row 1} \\ \leftarrow \text{Row 2} \\ \leftarrow \text{Row 3} \end{array} \\ \uparrow \qquad \uparrow \\ \text{Column 1} \quad \text{Column 2} \end{array}$$

Each number in a matrix is an **element**. Matrices are equal if they are the same size and the elements in corresponding positions are equal.

2 and $\frac{4}{2}$ are corresponding elements.

$$\begin{bmatrix} -1 & 2 \\ 4 & 0 \end{bmatrix} = \begin{bmatrix} -1 & \frac{4}{2} \\ (5-1) & 0 \end{bmatrix}$$

Focus Question Why is it helpful to use matrices to organize data?

You add or subtract matrices by adding or subtracting the corresponding elements. You can only add or subtract matrices that are the same size.

 Problem 1 Adding and Subtracting Matrices

What is each sum or difference?

Think

Can you add the matrices?
Yes, you can add the matrices because they are the same size. Each matrix has 2 rows and 2 columns.

A $\begin{bmatrix} -5 & 2.7 \\ 7 & -3 \end{bmatrix} + \begin{bmatrix} -3 & -3.9 \\ -4 & 2 \end{bmatrix}$

Add corresponding elements.
$$\begin{bmatrix} -5 & 2.7 \\ 7 & -3 \end{bmatrix} + \begin{bmatrix} -3 & -3.9 \\ -4 & 2 \end{bmatrix} = \begin{bmatrix} -5 + (-3) & 2.7 + (-3.9) \\ 7 + (-4) & -3 + 2 \end{bmatrix}$$

Simplify.
$$= \begin{bmatrix} -8 & -1.2 \\ 3 & -1 \end{bmatrix}$$

B $\begin{bmatrix} 2 & 11 \\ -4 & 3.2 \\ 1.5 & -5 \end{bmatrix} - \begin{bmatrix} -1 & 8 \\ -6.5 & 4 \\ 0 & -3 \end{bmatrix}$

Subtract corresponding elements.
$$\begin{bmatrix} 2 & 11 \\ -4 & 3.2 \\ 1.5 & -5 \end{bmatrix} - \begin{bmatrix} -1 & 8 \\ -6.5 & 4 \\ 0 & -3 \end{bmatrix} = \begin{bmatrix} 2 - (-1) & 11 - 8 \\ -4 - (-6.5) & 3.2 - 4 \\ 1.5 - 0 & -5 - (-3) \end{bmatrix}$$

Simplify.
$$= \begin{bmatrix} 3 & 3 \\ 2.5 & -0.8 \\ 1.5 & -2 \end{bmatrix}$$

 Got It?

1. What is each sum or difference in parts (a) and (b)?

   a. $\begin{bmatrix} 5 \\ 3.2 \\ -4.9 \end{bmatrix} + \begin{bmatrix} -9 \\ -1.7 \\ -11.1 \end{bmatrix}$

   b. $\begin{bmatrix} -4 & 0 \\ 3 & 7 \end{bmatrix} - \begin{bmatrix} -5 & -1 \\ 0.5 & -3 \end{bmatrix}$

   c. Reasoning Explain why you cannot add or subtract matrices that are not the same size.

You may also need to multiply a matrix by a real number. The real-number factor is called a **scalar.** Multiplying a matrix by a scalar is called **scalar multiplication.** To use scalar multiplication, multiply each element in the matrix by the scalar.

 Problem 2 Multiplying a Matrix by a Scalar

Think

Which factor is the scalar?
The scalar is the real-number factor, 3.

What is the product $3\begin{bmatrix} 4 & -1.5 \\ 1 & -6 \end{bmatrix}$**?**

Multiply each element by the scalar, 3.
$$3\begin{bmatrix} 4 & -1.5 \\ 1 & -6 \end{bmatrix} = \begin{bmatrix} 3(4) & 3(-1.5) \\ 3(1) & 3(-6) \end{bmatrix}$$

Simplify.
$$= \begin{bmatrix} 12 & -4.5 \\ 3 & -18 \end{bmatrix}$$

Got It? **2.** What is each product?

a. $-2\begin{bmatrix} -3 & 7.1 & 5 \end{bmatrix}$

b. $1.5\begin{bmatrix} -11 & 3 \\ 0 & -1.5 \end{bmatrix}$

You can use matrices to organize real-world data.

 Problem 3 **Using Matrices**

Weather Use the weather chart below. Which city has the greatest average number of clear days in a full year?

Average Number of Clear and Cloudy Days

September – February
Phoenix: 102 clear, 41 cloudy
Miami: 43 clear, 58 cloudy
Portland: 55 clear, 82 cloudy

March – August
Phoenix: 110 clear, 27 cloudy
Miami: 31 clear, 59 cloudy
Portland: 45 clear, 83 cloudy

Phoenix, AZ
Portland, ME
Miami, FL

Plan

What size matrices should you use?
There are three cities and two types of weather represented by the data. So you can use 3 × 2 matrices or 2 × 3 matrices.

Step 1 Use matrices to organize the information.

September–February

	Clear	Cloudy
Phoenix	102	41
Miami	43	58
Portland	55	82

March–August

	Clear	Cloudy
Phoenix	110	27
Miami	31	59
Portland	45	83

Step 2 Add the matrices to find the average numbers of clear and cloudy days in a full year for each city. The matrices are the same size, so you can add them.

Add corresponding elements.
$$\begin{bmatrix} 102 & 41 \\ 43 & 58 \\ 55 & 82 \end{bmatrix} + \begin{bmatrix} 110 & 27 \\ 31 & 59 \\ 45 & 83 \end{bmatrix} = \begin{bmatrix} 212 & 68 \\ 74 & 117 \\ 100 & 165 \end{bmatrix}$$

Step 3 Find the greatest average number of clear days in a full year. The first column of the matrix represents the average number of clear days in a full year for each city. The greatest number in that column is 212, which corresponds to Phoenix. So Phoenix has the greatest average number of clear days in a full year.

$$\begin{bmatrix} 212 & 68 \\ 74 & 117 \\ 100 & 165 \end{bmatrix}$$

 Got It? **3.** Which city in Problem 3 has the greatest average number of cloudy days in a full year?

Focus Question Why is it helpful to use matrices to organize data?

Answer Matrices make it easier to perform calculations on data.

Lesson Check

Do you know HOW?

Find each sum or difference.

1. $\begin{bmatrix} 0 & 7 \\ -4 & 5 \end{bmatrix} + \begin{bmatrix} -3 & 2 \\ 4 & -1 \end{bmatrix}$ 2. $\begin{bmatrix} 5 & 4 \\ -1 & 0 \end{bmatrix} - \begin{bmatrix} 3 & 1 \\ -3 & 3 \end{bmatrix}$

Find each product.

3. $2 \begin{bmatrix} 4 & 0 & 5 \\ -2 & 1 & 2 \end{bmatrix}$ 4. $-6 \begin{bmatrix} 5 & 0 \\ 2 & -3 \end{bmatrix}$

Do you UNDERSTAND?

5. **Vocabulary** How many elements are there in a 3×3 matrix?

6. **Error Analysis** A student added two matrices as shown at the right. Describe and correct the mistake.

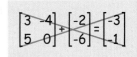

7. **Open-Ended** Write two different 3×3 matrices. Then add your matrices.

Practice and Problem-Solving Exercises

A Practice

Find each sum or difference.

➤ See Problem 1.

Guided Practice

To start, add the corresponding elements.

8. $\begin{bmatrix} 1 & -1 \\ 0 & 1 \end{bmatrix} + \begin{bmatrix} 0 & 1 \\ 1 & -1 \end{bmatrix}$

$\begin{bmatrix} 1+0 & -1+1 \\ 0+1 & 1+(-1) \end{bmatrix}$

9. $\begin{bmatrix} -3 & 6 \\ 2 & 0 \end{bmatrix} - \begin{bmatrix} -2 & 5 \\ 2 & 0 \end{bmatrix}$ 10. $\begin{bmatrix} 5 & 2 \\ -1 & 8 \end{bmatrix} - \begin{bmatrix} 7 & -4 \\ 0 & 2 \end{bmatrix}$

11. $\begin{bmatrix} 4 & -1 \\ 2 & 0 \\ 3 & 5 \end{bmatrix} + \begin{bmatrix} -2 & 0 \\ 3 & -1 \\ -3 & 5 \end{bmatrix}$ 12. $\begin{bmatrix} 0 & 0.4 \\ -2 & 5.3 \\ 1.2 & 3.7 \end{bmatrix} + \begin{bmatrix} 1.8 & -5 \\ 7.1 & 0 \\ 0.3 & 2.3 \end{bmatrix}$

Find each product.

➤ See Problem 2.

Guided Practice

To start, multiply each element by the scalar 4.

13. $4 \begin{bmatrix} 6 & -3 \\ 0 & 5 \end{bmatrix}$

$\begin{bmatrix} 4(6) & 4(-3) \\ 4(0) & 4(5) \end{bmatrix}$

14. $-2 \begin{bmatrix} 3 & -1 \\ 7 & -2 \end{bmatrix}$ 15. $0 \begin{bmatrix} 5.3 & -7.2 \\ -1.8 & 0.6 \end{bmatrix}$ 16. $-5 \begin{bmatrix} 3.8 & 2.1 & 7 \\ 9.4 & -6 & 0 \end{bmatrix}$ 17. $2.7 \begin{bmatrix} 3 & 4.7 \\ 0 & -3 \\ 5.7 & 2.7 \end{bmatrix}$

18. Sports For a certain city, the tables below show the numbers of participants in various sports in 2005 and 2010. Which sport had the greatest numerical increase in student participation between 2005 and 2010? Find your answer using matrices.

◀ See Problem 3.

Sports Participation, 2005

Sport	Students	Adults
Baseball	739	215
Basketball	1023	437
Football	690	58
Soccer	1546	42

Sports Participation, 2010

Sport	Students	Adults
Baseball	892	351
Basketball	1114	483
Football	653	64
Soccer	1712	37

19. Manufacturing A furniture company has two factories. During the first shift, Factory A made 250 chairs and 145 tables, and Factory B made 300 chairs and 75 tables. During the second shift, Factory A made 275 chairs and 90 tables, and Factory B made 240 chairs and 120 tables. Which factory made more chairs during the two shifts? Find your answer using matrices.

20. Sales The weekly sales records below show the numbers of different colors and models of shoes sold in two weeks. Which is the color and model shoe with the highest sales between February 2 and 15? Find your answer using matrices.

Shoe Sales, Feb. 2–8

Color	Model 73	Model 84
Black	153	79
White	241	116
Blue	58	32
Brown	95	47

Shoe Sales, Feb. 9–15

Color	Model 73	Model 84
Black	172	82
White	278	130
Blue	65	29
Brown	103	54

 Apply

Simplify each expression. (*Hint:* Multiply before adding or subtracting.)

21. $2\begin{bmatrix} 6 & 0 & -2 \\ -5 & 3 & 1 \end{bmatrix} - \begin{bmatrix} 3 & -1 & -6 \\ 0 & 4 & 2 \end{bmatrix}$

22. $-3\begin{bmatrix} 4.2 & -7.3 & 0.7 \\ 2.7 & -9.3 & 11.8 \\ 3.6 & 8.2 & -4.8 \end{bmatrix} - 2\begin{bmatrix} 7.8 & -4.1 & 9.4 \\ -8 & 0 & 0.8 \\ -1.4 & 5.9 & 3.3 \end{bmatrix}$

23. Think About a Plan Use the table at the right that shows nutrition information for 1 serving of each type of food. For which item(s) do 6 servings have less than 1000 Calories?

- What matrix represents the nutrition information for 1 serving?
- How can you find the nutrition information for 6 servings?

FOOD ITEM		Serving	Calories	Protein (g)	Fat (g)
	Chicken	1	148	29	3.5
	Fruit salad	1	221	1	0
	Spaghetti & meatballs	1	273	11	13

Source: U.S. Department of Agriculture

24. Politics The results of an election for mayor are shown on the right. The town will hold a runoff election between the top two candidates if no one received more than 50% of the votes. Should the town hold a runoff? If so, which candidates should be in the runoff? Explain your reasoning.

Votes by Precinct

Candidate	Precinct			
	1	2	3	4
Greene	373	285	479	415
Jackson	941	871	114	97
Voigt	146	183	728	682

Standardized Test Prep

SAT/ACT

25. Which matrix is equal to $-3\begin{bmatrix} 5.5 & -1 \\ -3 & 2 \end{bmatrix}$?

Ⓐ $\begin{bmatrix} 8.5 & 2 \\ 0 & 5 \end{bmatrix}$ Ⓑ $\begin{bmatrix} 2.5 & -4 \\ -6 & -1 \end{bmatrix}$ Ⓒ $\begin{bmatrix} 16.5 & -3 \\ -9 & 6 \end{bmatrix}$ Ⓓ $\begin{bmatrix} -16.5 & 3 \\ 9 & -6 \end{bmatrix}$

26. What is the simplified form of $2\sqrt{108}$?

Ⓐ $12\sqrt{3}$ Ⓑ $6\sqrt{12}$ Ⓒ $3\sqrt{26}$ Ⓓ $2\sqrt{6}$

Short Response

27. Carlos does his homework at a rate of 25 problems per hour. Cecelia does her homework at a rate of 30 problems per hour. Carlos started his homework 12 min before Cecelia. How many hours after Carlos started his homework will they have done the same number of problems? Show your work.

Mixed Review

 See Lesson 11-5.

Solve each equation. If there is no solution, write *no solution*.

28. $\dfrac{2}{a+5} = \dfrac{3}{a-5}$ **29.** $\dfrac{-1}{y} + \dfrac{1}{y} = 1$ **30.** $\dfrac{3}{m-1} + 2 = \dfrac{5m}{m-1}$

Get Ready! To prepare for Lesson 12-2, do Exercises 31 and 32.

For each table, make a scatter plot of the data. Tell whether a correlation exists. If so, tell whether the correlation reflects a causal relationship. Explain your reasoning.

See Lesson 5-7.

31. **Shoe Sizes and Test Scores**

Name	Shoe Size	Test Score
Baker	9	87
Johns	11	94
Rivera	8	96
Samuels	7	75

32. **Sales Commissions**

Employee	Products Sold	Commission Earned ($)
Andrews	38	310
Garcia	24	250
Jordan	47	448
Walker	53	495

12-2 Frequency and Histograms

Objective To make and interpret frequency tables and histograms

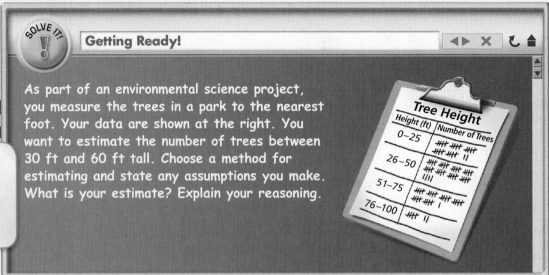

If you don't have the exact information you need, sometimes you have to estimate.

Getting Ready!

As part of an environmental science project, you measure the trees in a park to the nearest foot. Your data are shown at the right. You want to estimate the number of trees between 30 ft and 60 ft tall. Choose a method for estimating and state any assumptions you make. What is your estimate? Explain your reasoning.

Tree Height

Height (ft)	Number of Trees
0–25	卌 卌 卌 卌 ll
26–50	卌 卌 卌 卌 卌 卌 卌 llll
51–75	卌 卌 卌 卌 卌 卌
76–100	卌 ll

Sometimes it is helpful to organize numerical data into intervals.

The **frequency** of an interval is the number of data values in that interval. A **frequency table** groups a set of data values into intervals and shows the frequency for each interval. Intervals in frequency tables do not overlap, do not have any gaps, and are usually of equal size.

Focus Question What are two ways to organize and visually display data?

Lesson Vocabulary
- frequency
- frequency table
- histogram
- cumulative frequency table

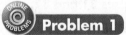

Problem 1 Making a Frequency Table

Baseball The numbers of home runs by the batters in a local home run derby are listed below. What is a frequency table that represents the data?

7 17 14 2 7 9 5 12 3 10 4 12 7 15

The minimum data value is 2 and the maximum is 17. Intervals of 4 seem reasonable. In the first column of the table, list the intervals. Count the number of data values in each interval and list the number in the second column.

Plan

How do you choose intervals?
The data values range from 2 to 17, so there are a total of 16 possible values. You can divide these 16 values into 4 intervals of size 4.

Home Run Results

Home Runs	Frequency
2–5	4
6–9	4
10–13	3
14–17	3

 Got It? **1.** What is a frequency table for the data in Problem 1 that uses intervals of 5?

A **histogram** is a graph that can display data from a frequency table. A histogram has one bar for each interval. The height of each bar shows the frequency of data in the interval it represents. There are no gaps between bars. The bars are usually of equal width.

 Problem 2 Making a Histogram

Television The data below are the numbers of hours per week a group of students spent watching television. What is a histogram that represents the data?

7 10 1 5 14 22 6 8 0 11 13 3 4 14 5

Know	Need	Plan
A set of data values	A histogram of the data values	Make a frequency table. This will help you construct the histogram.

Use the intervals from the frequency table for the histogram. Draw a bar for each interval. Make the height of each bar equal to the frequency of its interval. The bars should touch but not overlap. Label each axis.

Hint

The data values range from 0 to 22. This is a range of 23 possible values, which is a prime number. Make the last interval extend to 23, and then have 4 intervals of 6.

Watching Television

Hours	Frequency
0–5	6
6–11	5
12–17	3
18–23	1

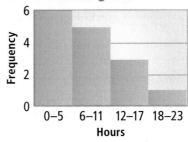

Watching Television

 Got It? **2.** The finishing times, in seconds, for a race are shown below. What is a histogram that represents the data?

95 105 83 80 93 98 102 99 82 89 90 82 89

You can describe histograms in terms of their shape. Three types are shown below.

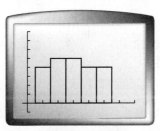

If the bars are roughly the same height, the histogram is *uniform*.

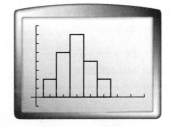

If a vertical line can divide the histogram into two parts that are close to mirror images, then the histogram is *symmetric*.

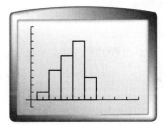

If the histogram has one peak that is not in the center, the histogram is *skewed*.

Problem 3 Interpreting Histograms

Is each histogram *uniform, symmetric,* or *skewed*?

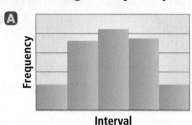

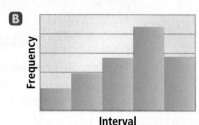

This histogram is symmetric because the halves are close to mirror images.

This histogram is skewed because the peak is not in the center.

Got It? **3. a.** The following set of data shows the numbers of dollars Jay spent on lunch over the last two weeks. Make a histogram of the data. Is the histogram *uniform, symmetric,* or *skewed*?

17 1 4 11 14 14 5 16 6 5 9 10 13 9

b. **Reasoning** How much money should Jay plan to bring for lunch next week? Explain your reasoning.

A **cumulative frequency table** shows the number of data values that lie in or below a given interval. For example, if the cumulative frequency for the interval 70–79 is 20, then there are 20 data values less than or equal to 79.

Problem 4 Making a Cumulative Frequency Table

Text Messaging The numbers of text messages sent on one day by different students are shown below. What is a cumulative frequency table that represents the data?

17 3 1 30 11 7 1 5 2 39 22 13 2 0 21 1 49 41 27 2 0

Step 1 Divide the data into intervals. The minimum is 0 and the maximum is 49. You can divide the data into 5 intervals.

Step 2 Write the intervals in the first column. Record the frequency of each interval in the second column.

Daily Text Messaging

Number of Text Messages	Frequency	Cumulative Frequency
0–9	11	11
10–19	3	14
20–29	3	17
30–39	2	19
40–49	2	21

$11 + 3 = 14$

$14 + 3 = 17$

$17 + 2 = 19$

$19 + 2 = 21$

Step 3 For the third column, add the frequency of each interval to the frequencies of all the previous intervals.

Got It? **4.** What is a cumulative frequency table that represents the data below?

12 13 15 1 5 7 10 9 2 2 7 11 2 1 0 15

Focus Question What are two ways to organize and visually display data?

Answer A frequency table organizes data into uniform intervals. A histogram displays data by assigning a bar to each interval. The number of values in an interval determines the height of the bar.

Lesson Check

Do you know HOW?

The data below show battery life, in hours, for different brands of batteries.

12 9 10 14 10 11 10 18 21 10 14 22

1. Make a frequency table of the data.

2. Make a histogram of the data.

3. Make a cumulative frequency table of the data.

Do you UNDERSTAND?

4. **Vocabulary** How might a frequency table help a store owner determine the busiest business hours?

5. **Compare and Contrast** What is the difference between a symmetric histogram and a skewed histogram?

6. **Writing** How can you use a frequency table of a data set to construct a cumulative frequency table?

Practice and Problem-Solving Exercises

A Practice

Use the data to make a frequency table.

See Problem 1.

Guided Practice

7. wing spans (cm): 150 126 139 144 125 149 133 140 142 149 150 127 130

To start, find the minimum and maximum data values. Determine a reasonable interval.

minimum: 125
maximum: 150

Make 3 intervals of 10:
125 to 134, 135 to 144, and 145 to 154.

8. marathon times (min): 135 211 220 180 175 161 246 201 192 167 235 208

9. top speeds (mi/h): 108 90 96 150 120 115 135 126 165 155 130 125 100

Use the data to make a histogram.

See Problem 2.

Guided Practice

10. costs of items: $11 $30 $22 $8 $15 $28 $17 $17 $1 $19 $29 $21 $12 $25

To start, choose an interval.
minimum: $1
maximum: $30
intervals: 6 intervals of 5

1–5; 6–10; 11–15; 16–20; 21–25; 26–30

11. ages of relatives: 18 5 27 34 56 54 9 14 35 22 78 94 47 52 2 16 17 10

12. restaurant waiting times (min): 20 35 15 25 5 10 40 30 10 50 20 60 10 8

Tell whether each histogram is *uniform*, *symmetric*, or *skewed*.

See Problem 3.

13.

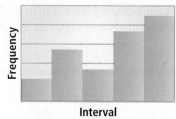

14.

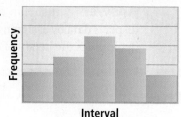

15.

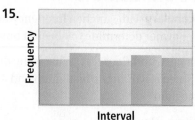

16.

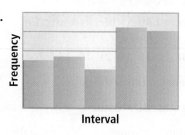

Use the data to make a cumulative frequency table.

See Problem 4.

17. trail lengths (mi): 4 1 5 2 1 3 7 12 6 3 11 9 2 1 3 4 1 2 5 3 1 1

18. heights of buildings (ft): 105 245 300 234 225 156 180 308 250 114 150 285

B **Apply**

19. Think About a Plan A travel agent conducted a survey to find out how many times people go to the beach each year. The results of the survey are shown in the histogram at the right. About how many people were surveyed?

- What does the height of each bar represent?
- How can you use the bar heights to find the number of people surveyed?

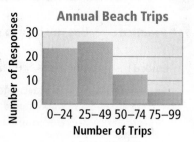

Use the test scores below.

81 70 73 89 68 79 91 59 77 73 80 75 88 65 82 94 77 67 82

20. What is a histogram of the data that uses intervals of 5?

21. What is a histogram of the data that uses intervals of 10?

22. What is a histogram of the data that uses intervals of 20?

23. Reasoning Which interval size would you use—5, 10, or 20—to make it seem as though there were little variation in the test scores?

24. Music The Perpendicular Bisectors' new CD is shown at the right.
  a. Make a cumulative frequency table that represents the lengths of the songs in seconds.
  b. About what percent of the songs are under 4 min? How do you know?

Add It (intro)	1:25
A Fraction of My Love	3:30
Common Denominator	4:14
Always, Sometimes, Never	2:56
Factorial	3:15
Transitive Property	4:20
All You Need Is Math	4:58
SAS	3:51
Frequency	3:32
Subtract It (outro)	1:56

25. Error Analysis A student made the frequency table at the right using the data below. Describe and correct the error.

40 21 28 53 24 48 50 55 42 29 22 52 43 26 44

Interval	Frequency
20-29	6
40-49	5
50-59	4

The histogram at the right shows the amounts of money that 50 customers spent in a supermarket.

26. What is the upper limit on the amount of money that any customer spent?

27. Which interval represents the greatest number of customers?

28. How many customers spent less than $20?

29. Writing Summarize the spending of the 50 customers represented in the histogram.

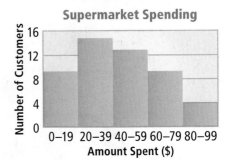

Supermarket Spending

Standardized Test Prep

SAT/ACT

30. What is the shape of the histogram at the right?

Ⓐ symmetric   Ⓒ skewed

Ⓑ proportional   Ⓓ uniform

31. What is the solution of $(-4x - 6) + (6x + 1) = -13$?

Ⓕ -4 Ⓗ 6

Ⓖ 5 Ⓘ 9

32. What is the factored form of $x^2 - 6x - 16$?

Ⓐ $(x + 2)(x + 8)$ Ⓑ $(x - 2)(x + 8)$ Ⓒ $(x + 2)(x - 8)$ Ⓓ $(x - 2)(x - 8)$

Short Response

33. Between what two integer values of x do the graphs of $y = 20(0.5)^x$ and $y = 0.5 \cdot 4^x$ intersect? Show your work.

Mixed Review

Find each sum or difference.

See Lesson 12-1.

34. $\begin{bmatrix} 4 & 6 \\ 5 & 7 \end{bmatrix} + \begin{bmatrix} 8 & 10 \\ 9 & 11 \end{bmatrix}$

35. $\begin{bmatrix} 0.2 & 0.6 \\ 0.8 & 0.5 \end{bmatrix} - \begin{bmatrix} 2.3 & 5.9 \\ 7.5 & 1.0 \end{bmatrix}$

Get Ready! **To prepare for Lesson 12-3, do Exercises 36 and 37.**

Order the numbers in each exercise from least to greatest.

See Lesson 1-3.

36. $13, \frac{5}{4}, -4, -16, 0, 2, 16, \frac{1}{2}$

37. $0.9, -0.2, 1.2, 5, -1, 0, 0.1, 2$

Measures of Central Tendency and Dispersion

Objective To find mean, median, mode, and range

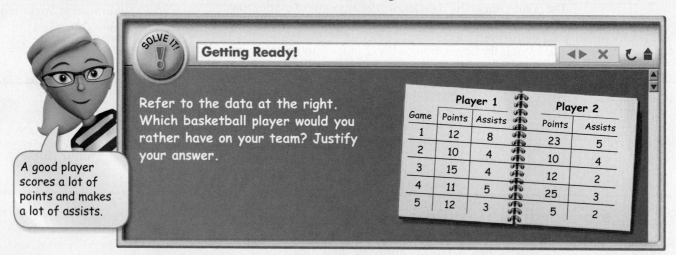

A good player scores a lot of points and makes a lot of assists.

Focus Question When would you use a measure of central tendency and when would you use a measure of dispersion to describe a data set?

One way to summarize a set of data is to use a *measure of central tendency*. Mean, median, and mode are all **measures of central tendency.**

The measure of central tendency that best describes a data set may depend on whether the data set has an *outlier*. An **outlier** is a data value that is much greater or less than the other values in the set. Below is a review of mean, median, and mode, and when to use each as the measure of central tendency.

Lesson Vocabulary

- measure of central tendency
- outlier
- mean
- median
- mode
- measure of dispersion
- range of a set of data

Hint

To distinguish between median and mode, think of mode as *most* and of median as *middle*.

Key Concept Mean, Median, and Mode

Measure	When to Use
The **mean** equals $\frac{\text{sum of the data values}}{\text{total number of data values}}$. The mean is often referred to as the *average*.	Use mean to describe the middle of a set of data that *does not* have an outlier.
The **median** is the middle value in a data set when the values are arranged in order. For a set containing an even number of data values, the median is the mean of the two middle data values.	Use median to describe the middle of a set of data that *does* have an outlier.
The **mode** is the data item that occurs the most times. A data set can have no mode, one mode, or more than one mode.	Use mode when the data are nonnumeric or when choosing the most popular item.

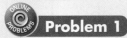 **Problem 1** **Finding Measures of Central Tendency**

Bowling What are the mean, median, and mode of the bowling scores below? Which measure of central tendency best describes the scores?

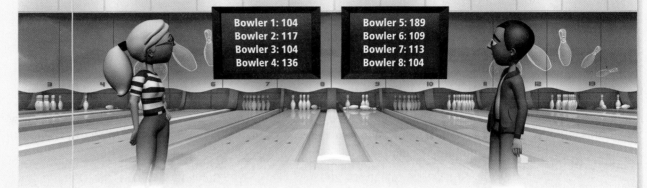

Bowler 1: 104
Bowler 2: 117
Bowler 3: 104
Bowler 4: 136

Bowler 5: 189
Bowler 6: 109
Bowler 7: 113
Bowler 8: 104

Think

Is there an outlier in the data set?
Yes, the score 189 is much higher than the other scores.

The mean is the sum of the scores divided by the number of scores.

Mean: $\dfrac{104 + 117 + 104 + 136 + 189 + 109 + 113 + 104}{8} = 122$

List the data in order.

Median: 104 104 104 109 113 117 136 189

The median of an even number of data values is the mean of the two middle data values.

$\dfrac{109 + 113}{2} = 111$

The mode is the data item that occurs the most times.

Mode: 104

Because there is an outlier, 189, the median is the best measure to describe the scores. The mean, 122, is greater than most of the scores. The mode, 104, is the lowest score. Neither the mean nor the mode describes the data well. The median best describes the data.

Hint

The best measure is the one that most fairly and accurately describes all of the bowling scores.

 Got It? 1. Consider the scores from Problem 1 that do not include the outlier, 189. What are the mean, median, and mode of the scores? Which measure of central tendency best describes the data?

You can use an equation to find a value needed to achieve a given average.

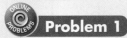 **Problem 2** **Finding a Data Value**

Grades Your grades on three exams are 80, 93, and 91. What grade do you need on the next exam to have an average of 90 on the four exams?

Plan

What information is unknown?
The grade on the fourth exam is unknown. Use a variable to represent this grade.

Use the formula for the mean. Let $x =$ the grade on the fourth exam.

$\dfrac{80 + 93 + 91 + x}{4} = 90$

Simplify the numerator.

$\dfrac{264 + x}{4} = 90$

Multiply each side by 4.

$264 + x = 360$

Subtract 264 from each side.

$x = 96$

Your grade on the next exam must be 96 for you to have an average of 90.

Got It? 2. a. The grades in Problem 2 were 80, 93, and 91. What grade would you need on your next exam to have an average of 88 on the four exams?

A **measure of dispersion** describes how *dispersed*, or spread out, the values in a data set are. One measure of dispersion is *range*. The **range of a set of data** is the difference between the greatest and least data values.

Problem 3 Finding the Range

Finance The closing prices, in dollars, of two stocks for the first five days in February are shown below. **What are the range and mean of each set of data? Use the results to compare the data sets.**

Think

How do the purposes of the range and the mean differ?
The range helps you find how spread out the data values are. The mean helps you find a typical data value.

Stock A: 25 30 30 47 28

range: $47 - 25 = 22$

mean: $\dfrac{25 + 30 + 30 + 47 + 28}{5}$

$= \dfrac{160}{5} = 32$

Stock B: 34 28 31 36 31

range: $36 - 28 = 8$

mean: $\dfrac{34 + 28 + 31 + 36 + 31}{5}$

$= \dfrac{160}{5} = 32$

Both sets of stock prices have a mean of 32. The range of the prices for Stock A is 22, and the range of the prices for Stock B is 8. Both stocks had the same average price during the 5-day period, but the prices for Stock A were more spread out.

 Got It? 3. For the same days, the closing prices, in dollars, of Stock C were 7, 4, 3, 6, and 1. The closing prices, in dollars, of Stock D were 24, 15, 2, 10, and 5. What are the range and mean of each set of data? Use your results to compare Stock C with Stock D.

Adding the same amount to each value in a set of data has special consequences for the mean, median, mode, and range.

Consider the data set 5, 16, 3, 5, 11.

If you add 5 to each data value, you get the data set 10, 21, 8, 10, 16.

mean: $\dfrac{5 + 16 + 3 + 5 + 11}{5} = 8$

median: 3, 5, (5), 11, 16

mode: 5

range: $16 - 3 = 13$

mean: $\dfrac{10 + 21 + 8 + 10 + 16}{5} = 13$

median: 8, 10, (10), 16, 21

mode: 10

range: $21 - 8 = 13$

Notice that the mean, median, and mode all increased by 5. The range did not change. For any data set, if you add the same amount k to each item, the mean, median, and mode of the new data set also increase by k. The range does not change.

Problem 4 Adding a Constant to Data Values

Athletics The table shows the times several athletes spend on a treadmill each day during the first week of training. The athletes add 5 min to their training times during the second week. What are the mean, median, mode, and range of the times for the second week?

Time on Treadmill	
Athlete	Time (min)
Bob	50
Carlota	20
Juan	41
Manuel	20
Rosita	30
Sonia	20
Xavier	50

Step 1 Find the mean, median, mode, and range for the first week.

$$\text{mean: } \frac{20 + 20 + 20 + 30 + 41 + 50 + 50}{7} = 33$$

median: 30   mode: 20   range: $50 - 20 = 30$

Step 2 Find the mean, median, mode, and range for the second week.

mean: $33 + 5 = 38$
median: $30 + 5 = 35$ ⎫ Add 5 to each measure of central tendency.
mode: $20 + 5 = 25$ ⎭
range: 30   The range does not change.

Think

How can you check your results?
Add 5 to each time in the first week to find the times for the second week. Then calculate the mean, median, mode, and range of the new data set directly.

Got It? **4.** In the third week of training, the athletes add 10 min to their training times from the second week. What are the mean, median, mode, and range of the athletes' training times for the third week?

Suppose you multiply each value in a data set by the same amount k. You can find the mean, median, mode, and range of the new data set by multiplying the mean, median, mode, and range of the original data set by k.

Problem 5 Multiplying Data Values by a Constant

Shopping A store sells seven models of televisions. The regular prices are $144, $479, $379, $1299, $171, $479, and $269. This week the store offers a 30% discount on all televisions. What are the mean, median, mode, and range of the discounted prices?

Step 1 Find the mean, median, mode, and range of the regular prices.

$$\text{mean: } \frac{144 + 171 + 269 + 379 + 479 + 479 + 1299}{7} = 460$$

median: 379   mode: 479   range: $1299 - 144 = 1155$

Step 2 Multiply the mean, median, mode, and range in Step 1 by 0.7 to find the mean, median, mode, and range of the discounted prices.

mean: $460(0.7) = 322$ mode: $479(0.7) = 335.30$
median: $379(0.7) = 265.30$ range: $1155(0.7) = 808.50$

Think

How do you calculate a discounted price?
To calculate a price discounted by 30%, multiply the original amount by $(1 - 0.3)$, or 0.7.

Hint

To find the discounted price of a model, you can find 75% of the original price.

Got It? **5.** The following week the store offers a 25% discount off the regular prices. What are the mean, median, mode, and range of the discounted prices?

Focus Question When would you use a measure of central tendency and when would you use a measure of dispersion to describe a data set?

Answer Use mean to describe the middle of a set of data that does not have an outlier. Use median if there is an outlier. Use mode when the data are nonnumeric. Use range, a measure of dispersion, when you want to determine the difference between the greatest and least data values.

Lesson Check

Do you know HOW?

Find the mean, median, and mode of each data set. Explain which measure best describes the data.

1. 1 29 33 31 30 33   **2.** 8.2 9.3 8.5 8.8 9.0

3. If you multiply each value in the data set below by 3, what are the mean, median, mode, and range of the resulting data set?

$$8\ 2\ 5\ 7\ 0\ 6\ 5$$

Do you UNDERSTAND?

4. Vocabulary How do mean, median, and mode describe the central tendency of a data set? Why are three different measures needed?

5. Error Analysis One student said 10 was the range of the data set 2, 10, 8, and 3. Another student said the range was 8. Which student is correct? Explain.

6. Reasoning How is the range of a data set affected by an outlier?

Practice and Problem-Solving Exercises

 Practice   Find the mean, median, and mode of each data set. Tell which measure of central tendency best describes the data.

◀ **See Problem 1.**

7. weights of books (oz): 12 10 9 15 16 10

8. golf scores: 98 96 98 134 99

9. time spent on Internet (min/day): 75 38 43 120 65 48 52

Find the value of x such that the data set has the given mean.

◀ **See Problem 2.**

Guided Practice →   To start, use the formula for the mean to write an equation.

10. 17, 10, 5, x; mean 11

$$\frac{17 + 10 + 5 + x}{4} = 11$$

11. 3.8, 4.2, 5.3, x; mean 4.8   **12.** 99, 86, 76, 95, x; mean 91

13. Sales The line plot at the right shows the numbers of weekly sales a salesperson made in the first nine weeks of a ten-week sales period. The salesperson's target is an average of 14 sales each week. How many sales does the salesperson need in the tenth week to meet the target average?

Number of Weekly Sales

```
                  X    X
            X     X    X
      X     X     X    X
     _____
      12    13    14   15
```

Find the range and mean of each data set. Use your results to compare the two data sets.

See Problem 3.

Guided Practice

To start, use the maximum and minimum of each set to find the range of each set.

14. Set A: 0 12 7 19 21
Set B: 13 16 15 17 12

Set A: $21 - 0 = 21$
Set B: $17 - 12 = 5$

15. Set C: 4.5 7.1 8.3 6.9

Set D: 2.1 29.5 1.2 3.3

16. Set E: 113 183 479 120 117

Set F: 145 129 153 135 142

17. Sports Over the past 6 seasons, one baseball player's batting averages were .265, .327, .294, .316, .281, and .318. A second player's batting averages were .304, .285, .312, .291, .303, and .314. What are the range and mean of each player's batting averages? Use your results to compare the players' batting skills.

Find the mean, median, mode, and range of each data set after you perform the given operation on each data value.

See Problems 4 and 5.

18. 9, 7, 12, 13, 9, 3; add 5

19. 10.6, 9.5, 0, 9.4, 10.3, 10.6; add 15

20. 13.2, 12.4, 15.1, 14.7, 14.2; multiply by 3

21. 23, 53, 37, 64, 53, 70, 20; multiply by 0.1

22. 169, 54, 92, 107, 92; divide by 5

23. 5.8, 2.3, 6.4, 6.1, 6.4; subtract 2.1

24. Shopping The costs of 6 different belts available from an online store are $6.95, $15.99, $5.25, $7.45, $5.25, and $8.85. A shipping charge of $.50 is added to each price. Including the shipping charge, what are the mean, median, mode, and range of the prices of the belts?

25. Workshop The lengths of the electrical extension cords in a workshop are 6 ft, 8 ft, 25 ft, 8 ft, 12 ft, 50 ft, and 25 ft. What are the mean, median, mode, and range of the lengths of the cords *in inches*?

> **Hint**
> 1 foot = 12 inches.

 Apply

26. Manufacturing Two manufacturing plants make sheets of steel for medical instruments. The back-to-back stem-and-leaf plot at the right shows data collected from the two plants.
  a. What is the mean, median, mode, and range of each data set?
  b. Which measure of central tendency best describes each data set? Explain.
  c. Which plant has better quality control? Explain.

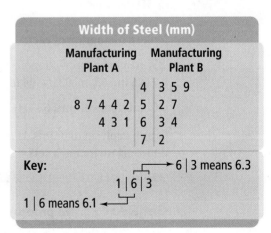

Width of Steel (mm)	
Manufacturing Plant A	Manufacturing Plant B
	4 | 3 5 9
8 7 4 4 2 | 5 | 2 7
4 3 1 | 6 | 3 4
	7 | 2

Key: 6 \| 3 means 6.3
1 \| 6 \| 3
1 \| 6 means 6.1

27. Think About a Plan The diameters of 5 circles are given below. What are the mean, median, mode, and range of the circumferences of the circles?

　　6.5 in.　3.2 in.　7.4 in.　6.5 in.　5.8 in.

- What are the mean, median, mode, and range of the diameters?
- How do the mean, median, mode, and range change when the data change from diameters to circumferences?

28. Reasoning How does subtracting the same amount from each value in a data set affect the mean, median, mode, and range? Explain.

29. Reasoning How does dividing each value in a data set by the same nonzero amount affect the mean, median, mode, and range? Explain.

30. Wildlife Management A wildlife manager measured and tagged twelve adult male crocodiles. The data he collected are at the right. He estimates the crocodiles will grow 0.1 m each year. What will be the mean, median, mode, and range of the crocodiles' lengths after 4 yr?

Crocodile Lengths (m)			
2.4	2.5	2.5	2.3
2.8	2.4	2.3	2.4
2.1	2.2	2.5	2.7

Standardized Test Prep

SAT/ACT

31. What is the mean of the data set 9, 16, 13, 20, and 17?

　Ⓐ 13　　　　　　Ⓑ 15　　　　　　Ⓒ 16　　　　　　Ⓓ 17

32. What is the slope of a line perpendicular to the graph of $y = -\frac{1}{2}x + 3$?

　Ⓕ −2　　　　　　Ⓖ $-\frac{1}{2}$　　　　　　Ⓗ $\frac{1}{2}$　　　　　　Ⓘ 2

33. What are the solutions of the equation $x^2 + 4x = 5$?

　Ⓐ −5 and 0　　　Ⓑ −5 and −1　　　Ⓒ −5 and 1　　　Ⓓ 1 and 5

Short Response

34. Two points are 2.5 in. apart on a map with a scale of 1 in. : 100 m. How far apart are the actual locations represented by the points on the map? Show your work.

Mixed Review

Make a histogram of each data set.　　　　　　　　　　　◀ **See Lesson 12-2.**

35. heights of professional basketball players:
　　85 in.　82 in.　83 in.　84 in.　80 in.　82 in.　86 in.　85 in.　83 in.　84 in.　81 in.　82 in.

36. numbers of cars: 53　84　22　38　41　27　25　12　17　27　33　41　60　73　62　59　43

Graph each set of points. Is a *linear*, *quadratic*, or *exponential* model most appropriate for each set?　　　　　　　　　◀ **See Lesson 9-7.**

37. (0, 1), (1, 3), (2, 9), (3, 27), (4, 81)　　　　**38.** (6, 5), (7, 2), (8, −1), (9, −4), (10, −7)

Get Ready!　**To prepare for Lesson 12-4, do Exercises 39–41.**

Find the range and median of each data set.　　　　　◀ **See Lesson 12-3.**

39. 0　2　7　10 −1　−4　−11　　　**40.** 64　16　23　57　14　22　　　**41.** 2.1　3.3　−5.4　0.8　3.5

Standard Deviation

You have learned about one measure of dispersion, range. Another measure of dispersion is *standard deviation*. **Standard deviation** is a measure of how the values in a data set vary, or deviate, from the mean.

Statisticians use several special symbols in the formula for standard deviation.

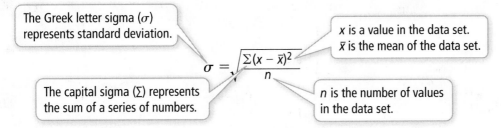

The Greek letter sigma (σ) represents standard deviation.

x is a value in the data set.
$\bar{x}$ is the mean of the data set.

$$\sigma = \sqrt{\frac{\Sigma(x - \bar{x})^2}{n}}$$

The capital sigma (Σ) represents the sum of a series of numbers.

n is the number of values in the data set.

Example

Find the mean and standard deviation of the data set 12.6, 15.1, 11.2, 17.9, and 18.2. Use a table to help organize your work.

Step 1 Find the mean: $\bar{x} = \frac{12.6 + 15.1 + 11.2 + 17.9 + 18.2}{5} = 15$.

Step 2 Find the difference between each data value and the mean: $x - \bar{x}$.

Step 3 Square each difference: $(x - \bar{x})^2$.

Step 4 Find the average (mean) of these squares: $\frac{\Sigma(x - \bar{x})^2}{n}$.

$\frac{5.76 + 0.01 + 14.44 + 8.41 + 10.24}{5} = 7.772$

Step 5 Take the square root to find the standard deviation:

$$\sqrt{\frac{\Sigma(x - \bar{x})^2}{n}} = \sqrt{7.772} \approx 2.79.$$

x	$\bar{x}$	$x - \bar{x}$	$(x - \bar{x})^2$
12.6	15	−2.4	5.76
15.1	15	0.1	0.01
11.2	15	−3.8	14.44
17.9	15	2.9	8.41
18.2	15	3.2	10.24

The mean is 15 and the standard deviation is about 2.79.

A small standard deviation (compared to the data values) means that the data are clustered tightly around the mean. As the data become more widely distributed, the standard deviation increases.

Exercises

Find the mean and standard deviation of each data set. Round to the nearest hundredth.

1. 4 8 5 12 3 9 5 2

2. 102 98 103 86 101 110

3. 8.2 11.6 8.7 10.6 9.4 10.1 9.3

12-4 Box-and-Whisker Plots

Objectives To make and interpret box-and-whisker plots
To find quartiles and percentiles

Suppose you are moving to a new town and are looking for a warm climate. You can choose between Morrell or Glenville. Based on the average monthly temperatures below, which town would you choose? How did you decide?

Both towns seem pretty warm. What makes them different?

Average Monthly Temperatures												
Month	Jan	Feb	Mar	Apr	May	Jun	Jul	Aug	Sept	Oct	Nov	Dec
Morrell	56	57	60	68	74	82	83	85	79	70	62	55
Glenville	58	62	66	70	76	78	81	84	77	73	68	63

Lesson Vocabulary
- quartile
- interquartile range
- box-and-whisker plot
- percentile
- percentile rank

In the Solve It, you may have looked at different parts of each data set in order to compare the two data sets. Separating data into subsets is a useful way to summarize and compare data sets.

Focus Question What information about a data set is displayed in a box-and-whisker plot?

Quartiles are values that divide a data set into four equal parts. When a data set is ordered from least to greatest, the first quartile (Q_1) is the median of the lower half of the data. The third quartile (Q_3) is the median of the upper half. The median of the entire data set is the second quartile (Q_2). The **interquartile range** is the difference between the third and first quartiles.

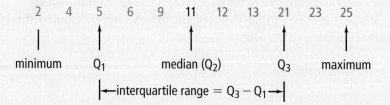

For a set of data that has an odd number of values like the one above you do not include the median in either half when finding the first and third quartiles.

 **Problem 1** **Summarizing a Data Set**

What are the minimum, first quartile, median, third quartile, and maximum of the data set below?

125 80 140 135 126 140 350 75

Step 1 Arrange the data in order from least to greatest.

75 80 125 126 135 140 140 350

Step 2 Find the minimum, maximum, and median.

75 80 125 126 135 140 140 350

$$\text{median } (Q_2) = \frac{126 + 135}{2} = 130.5$$

The minimum is 75. The maximum is 350. The median is 130.5.

Step 3 Find the first quartile and the third quartile.

75 80 125 126 135 140 140 350

$$\text{first quartile } (Q_1) = \frac{80 + 125}{2} = 102.5$$

$$\text{third quartile } (Q_3) = \frac{140 + 140}{2} = 140$$

The first quartile is 102.5. The third quartile is 140.

Think

How do you find the first quartile for an even number of values?
You find the mean of the middle two values in the lower half.

 Got It? **1.** What are the minimum, first quartile, median, third quartile, and maximum of each data set?

a. 95 85 75 85 65 60 100 105 75 85 75

b. 11 19 7 5 21 53

 **Dynamic Activity**
Box-and-Whisker Plots

A **box-and-whisker plot** is a graph that summarizes a set of data by displaying it along a number line. It consists of three parts: a box and two whiskers.

Box-and-Whisker Plot

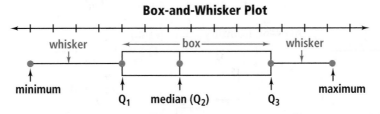

- The left whisker extends from the minimum to the first quartile. It represents about 25% of the data.

- The box extends from the first quartile to the third quartile and has a vertical line through the median. The length of the box represents the interquartile range. It contains about 50% of the data.

- The right whisker extends from the third quartile to the maximum. It represents about 25% of the data.

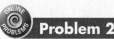

Problem 2 Making a Box-and-Whisker Plot

Agriculture What box-and-whisker plot represents the data at the right?

Step 1 Order the data to find the minimum, maximum, and quartiles.

303 307 311 312 314 314 314 315 316 316 321

minimum Q_1 median (Q_2) Q_3 maximum

Step 2 Draw the box-and-whisker plot.

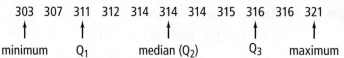

Crops Harvested in the United States	
Year	Acres (millions)
0	314
1	321
2	315
3	316
4	314
5	311
6	307
7	316
8	312
9	314
10	303

SOURCE: U.S. Department of Agriculture

Hint

To make a box-and-whisker plot, start by summarizing the data set like in Problem 1. Find the minimum, maximum, and quartiles.

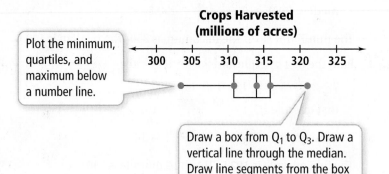

Plot the minimum, quartiles, and maximum below a number line.

Crops Harvested (millions of acres)

Draw a box from Q_1 to Q_3. Draw a vertical line through the median. Draw line segments from the box to the minimum and maximum.

Got It? **2.** What box-and-whisker plot represents the following monthly sales, in millions of dollars, of audio devices: 15 4 9 16 10 16 8 14 25 34?

Problem 3 Interpreting Box-and-Whisker Plots

Weather Use the box-and-whisker plots below. What do the interquartile ranges tell you about the average monthly rainfall for each city?

Think

Why is the interquartile range useful?
It represents the middle of the data set, so it is not affected by the minimum, maximum, or any outliers.

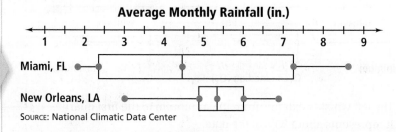

Average Monthly Rainfall (in.)

Miami, FL

New Orleans, LA

SOURCE: National Climatic Data Center

The box for Miami is longer, so Miami has the greater interquartile range.
This greater range means the middle 50% of Miami's monthly rainfalls vary more widely than those of New Orleans.

Got It? **3.** What do the medians tell you about the average monthly rainfalls for Miami and New Orleans?

Percentiles separate data sets into 100 equal parts. The **percentile rank** of a data value is the percentage of data values that are less than or equal to that value.

 Problem 4 Finding a Percentile Rank

Multiple Choice Of 25 test scores, eight are less than or equal to 75. What is the percentile rank of a test score of 75?

      Ⓐ 8   Ⓑ 17   Ⓒ 32   Ⓓ 75

Think

How else could you find the percentile rank?
You could solve the proportion $\frac{8}{25} = \frac{p}{100}$ for p.

Write the ratio of the number of test scores less than or equal to 75 compared to the total number of test scores. $\frac{8}{25}$

Rewrite the fraction as a percent. $\frac{8}{25} = 0.32$

                                             $= 32\%$

The percentile rank of 75 is 32. The correct answer is C.

Got It? **4. a.** Of the 25 scores in Problem 4, there are 15 scores less than or equal to 85. What is the percentile rank of 85?

          b. Reasoning Is it possible to have a percentile rank of 0? Explain.

Focus Question What information about a data set is displayed in a box-and-whisker plot?

Answer A box-and-whisker plot displays the minimum, maximum, and quartiles of a data set.

 Lesson Check

Do you know HOW?

Identify the minimum, first quartile, median, third quartile, and maximum of each data set. Then make a box-and-whisker plot of each data set.

1. file sizes (megabytes): 54 100 84 124 188 48 256

2. daily attendance: 29 24 28 32 30 31 26 33

3. In the box-and-whisker plots below, which class has the greater interquartile range of arm spans?

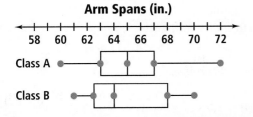

Arm Spans (in.)

58 60 62 64 66 68 70 72

Class A

Class B

Do you UNDERSTAND?

4. Vocabulary Which portion of a box-and-whisker plot represents the interquartile range?

5. Students taking a make-up test receive the following grades: 77, 89, 88, 67, 91, 95, 83, 79, 81, and 65. Which grade has a percentile rank of 70?

6. Reasoning About what percent of the data in a data set falls between the minimum value and the third quartile? Explain.

7. Error Analysis A test is graded on a scale from 0 to 100. Your friend says that if you score a 78, your percentile rank must be 78. Is your friend correct? Explain.

Practice and Problem-Solving Exercises

 Practice

Find the minimum, first quartile, median, third quartile, and maximum of each data set.

See Problem 1.

8. 12 10 11 7 9 10 5

9. 4.5 3.2 6.3 5.2 5 4.8 6 3.9 12

10. 55 53 67 52 50 49 51 52 52

11. 101 100 100 105 101 102 104

Make a box-and-whisker plot to represent each set of data.

See Problem 2.

Guided Practice

12. song lengths (s): 227 221 347 173 344 438 171 129 165 333

To start, rewrite the data from least to greatest.   129 165 171 173 221 227 333 344 347 438

13. movie ratings: 1 5 1 2.5 3 2 3.5 2 3 1.5 4 2 4 1 3 4.5

14. camera prices: $280 $220 $224 $70 $410 $90 $30 $120

15. Fuel Use Use the box-and-whisker plots below. What do they tell you about the fuel efficiencies for each type of vehicle? Explain.

See Problem 3.

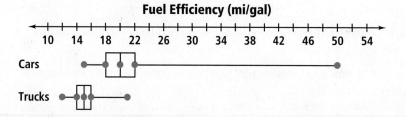

16. Of 10 test scores, six are less than or equal to 80. What is the percentile rank of a test score of 80?

See Problem 4.

Guided Practice

To start, write the ratio of the number of test scores less than or equal to 80 compared to the total number of test scores.

$$\frac{\text{test scores} \le 80}{\text{total number of test scores}} = \frac{6}{10}$$

17. Of 35 judges' scores awarded during a gymnastics event, 28 are less than or equal to 7.5. What is the percentile rank of a score of 7.5?

 Apply

18. Think About a Plan You are one of the finalists at a science fair. The scores of the other finalists are 87, 89, 81, 85, 87, 83, 86, 94, 90, 97, 80, 89, 85, and 88. Write an inequality that represents your possible scores if your percentile rank is 80.
- What percent of the scores must be less than or equal to your score?
- What is the total number of finalists' scores?

19. Writing Explain the difference between *range* and *interquartile range*.

20. Open-Ended Make a data set of 10 numbers that has a median of 22, an interquartile range of 10, and a minimum less than 4.

Hint To start, think about what it means if a data set with an even number of values has a median of 22.

21. Basketball The heights of the players on a basketball team are 74 in., 79 in., 71.5 in., 81 in., 73 in., 76 in., 78 in., 71 in., 72 in., and 73.5 in. When the 76-in.-tall player is replaced, the percentile rank of the 73.5-in.-tall player becomes 60. Write an inequality that represents the possible heights of the replacement player.

22. Packaging A cereal company is choosing between two devices to package their cereal into bags. The box-and-whisker plots at the right show the weights of the bags packed by each device.

    a. Which device produces packages with a more consistent weight? Explain.

    b. Which device should be chosen if the manufacturer wants to minimize the number of packages with weights less than 17 oz? More than 17.2 oz? Explain.

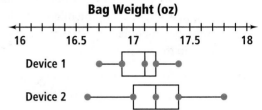

Standardized Test Prep

GRIDDED RESPONSE

SAT/ACT

23. During one week, the employees of a small business work 17, 21, 42, 29, 12, 17, 18, 19, 27, and 36 h. What is the third quartile of this data set?

24. What is the range of the data set 100, 32, 101, 96, 89, 120, and 40?

25. Jared can clear his driveway of snow in 36 min. It takes his brother 48 min. To the nearest minute, how long does it take to clear the driveway if they work together?

26. To the nearest hundredth, what is the value of $\sqrt{15} \cdot \frac{7}{\sqrt{3}}$?

Mixed Review

Find the mean, median, and mode of each data set.

◀ See Lesson 12-3.

27. prize pumpkin weights (lb): 948 627 731 697 988 643 719 627

28. daily customers: 47 41 22 17 55 34 71 46 39 41 38 60 52

Get Ready! To prepare for Lesson 12-5, do Exercise 29.

29. Bowling Make a scatter plot of the data below. Draw a trend line and write its equation. Predict the number of tenpin bowling establishments in 2015.

◀ See Lesson 5-7.

Tenpin Bowling					
Year	2002	2003	2004	2005	2006
Bowling Establishments	5973	5811	5761	5818	5566

Source: United States Bowling Congress

Designing Your Own Survey

You have learned how to organize, display, and summarize data. In this activity you will explore methods of collecting data.

Suppose a statistician is trying to predict how a town will vote in an upcoming election. She could ask every person in the town, but this method takes too much time and work. Instead, she might rely on an information-gathering survey that is sent to only some people in the town. She can then use the results to predict how other people in the town might vote.

When you design a survey, you need to make sure that the people you survey are representative of the group you want to study.

Activity 1

Suppose you want to find out how many hours of exercise the students at your school get each week. At the school gym you ask everybody you see, "How many hours of exercise do you get every week?"

1. Will the results of your survey be representative of your entire school? Explain.

2. Is there a better location to conduct your survey?

3. Suppose you asked, "Do you work out every day like a healthy person, or are you a lazy couch potato who only works out once in a while?" Do you think the results of your survey would change? Explain your reasoning.

Activity 2

In this activity, you will design and conduct a survey.

4. Select a topic for your survey. You could ask about favorite sporting events, snacks, musical instruments, or another topic of your choice.

5. Writing What question will you ask? Will your question influence the opinion of the people you are surveying?

6. What group of people do you want to study? Are you going to ask the entire group, or just a portion of the whole group?

7. Data Collection Complete your survey.

8. Writing Summarize your results with a graph and a brief description.

9. Reasoning Are the people you surveyed representative of the group you want to study? Explain.

12-5 | Samples and Surveys

Objective To classify data and analyze samples and surveys

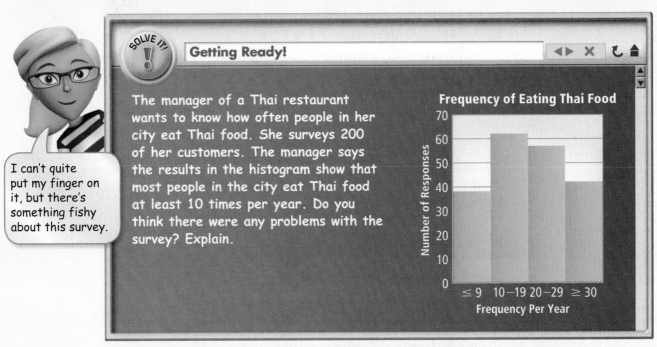

Getting Ready!

The manager of a Thai restaurant wants to know how often people in her city eat Thai food. She surveys 200 of her customers. The manager says the results in the histogram show that most people in the city eat Thai food at least 10 times per year. Do you think there were any problems with the survey? Explain.

I can't quite put my finger on it, but there's something fishy about this survey.

Frequency of Eating Thai Food

(histogram: x-axis "Frequency Per Year" with categories ≤ 9, 10–19, 20–29, ≥ 30; y-axis "Number of Responses" from 0 to 70)

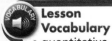
Lesson Vocabulary
- quantitative
- qualitative
- univariate
- bivariate
- population
- sample
- bias

In the Solve It, the restaurant manager collected data from the customers of the restaurant. In this lesson, you will learn about ways to collect data.

Focus Question How do you make sure the data you collect is representative of the group you are studying?

You can collect data using measurements or categories. **Quantitative** data measure quantities and can be described numerically, such as test scores and ages. **Qualitative** data name qualities and can be words or numbers, such as sports or ZIP codes.

Types of Data	Description	Examples
Quantitative	Has units and can be measured and numerically compared	**Age:** 13 yr **Weight:** 214 g **Time:** 23 min
Qualitative	Describes a category and cannot be measured or numerically compared	**Hair color:** brown **Attitude:** optimistic **ZIP code:** 02125

Think

Are the data numerical measurements?
Movie titles and jersey numbers are not numerical measurements, but a number of students is.

 Problem 1 Classifying Data

Is each data set *qualitative* or *quantitative*?

Ⓐ favorite movies

The data are not numerical quantities. These are qualitative data.

Ⓑ numbers of students in different schools who take Spanish

The data are numerical quantities. These are quantitative data.

Ⓒ football jersey numbers

The data are numerical but not measurements. They are qualitative data.

Got It? **1.** Is each data set *qualitative* or *quantitative*? Explain.
    a. costs of CDs   **b.** eye colors

The kind of data you are working with determines the type of graph you use to display the data. A set of data that uses only one variable is **univariate.** A set of data that uses two variables is **bivariate.**

Think

Does the data set involve one or two variables?
One variable means the data set is univariate. Two variables means the data set is bivariate.

 Problem 2 Identifying Types of Data

Is each data set *univariate* or *bivariate*?

Ⓐ the atomic weights of the elements in the periodic table

There is only one variable, atomic weight. The data set is univariate.

Ⓑ the edge lengths and volumes of cubes

There are two variables, edge length and volume. The data set is bivariate.

Got It? **2.** Is each data set *univariate* or *bivariate*? Explain.
    a. heights and weights of mammals
    b. the cost of Internet service from several different providers

---

Statisticians collect information about specific groups of objects or people. The entire group that you want information about is called a **population.** When a population is too large to survey, statisticians survey a part of it to find characteristics of the whole. The part that is surveyed is called a **sample.**

Three sampling methods are shown on the next page. When designing a survey, you should choose a sample that reflects the population.

Name	Sampling Method	Example
Random	Survey a population at random.	Survey people whose names are drawn out of a hat.
Systematic	Select a number *n* at random. Then survey every *n*th person.	Select the number 5 at random. Survey every fifth person.
Stratified	Separate a population into smaller groups, each with a certain characteristic. Then survey at random within each group.	Separate a high school into four groups by grade level. Survey a random sample of students from each grade.

 Problem 3 Choosing a Sample

DVD Rentals You want to find out how many DVDs students at your school rent in a month. You interview every tenth teenager you see at a mall. What sampling method are you using? Is this a good sample?

Think

What population are you trying to represent with this sample?
You want to collect information about the students at your school.

Since you are interviewing every tenth teenager, this method is systematic. This is not a good sample because it will likely include teenagers who do not attend your school.

 Got It? **3.** You revise your plan and interview all students leaving a school assembly who are wearing the school colors. Will this plan give a good sample? Explain.

A survey question has **bias** when it contains assumptions that may or may not be true. Bias can influence opinion and can make one answer seem better than another. Survey questions must be carefully worded to avoid bias.

 Problem 4 Determining Bias in a Survey Question

Movies A reporter wants to find out what kinds of movies are most popular with local residents. The reporter asks, "Do you prefer exciting action movies or boring documentaries?" Is the question biased? Explain.

Know	Need	Plan
The survey question	To determine whether the question is biased	Check the question for adjectives or phrases that make one category seem more appealing.

The question is biased because the words *exciting* and *boring* make action films sound more interesting than documentaries.

Hint

Avoid words that reflect your opinion about a subject.

 Got It? **4. Reasoning** How can the question in Problem 4 be reworded so that it is not biased?

Samples can also be biased. For example, all voluntary-response samples are biased because you cannot be sure that the people who choose to respond are representative of the population. The location where a survey is conducted can also cause a sample to be biased.

 Problem 5 Determining Bias in a Sample

Think

Ask yourself whether the sample and the population have similar characteristics. If not, the sample is biased.

Sports You want to determine what percent of teens ages 14 to 18 watch wrestling on TV. At a high school wrestling match, you ask every third teenager whether he or she watches wrestling on TV. How might this cause bias in the results of your survey?

The sample chosen is not representative of the population. People who attend a high school wrestling match may be more likely to watch wrestling on TV.

 Got It? **5.** You want to know how many of your classmates have cell phones. To determine this, you send every classmate an e-mail asking, "Do you own a cell phone?" How might this method of gathering data affect the results of your survey?

Focus Question How do you make sure the data you collect is representative of the group you are studying?

Answer Avoid bias in your survey and samples. Choose appropriate sampling methods.

 Lesson Check

Do you know HOW?

Determine whether each sampling method is *random*, *systematic*, or *stratified*.

1. You survey every tenth student who enters the cafeteria.

2. You draw student ID numbers out of a hat and survey those students.

3. You survey two students at random from each class.

Do you UNDERSTAND?

4. Vocabulary Is a data set of your class's test scores *qualitative* or *quantitative* data?

5. Writing Explain why "Do you prefer delicious fruit or plain vegetables for a snack food?" is a biased survey question.

6. Compare and Contrast What is the difference between univariate data and bivariate data? Give an example of each type of data.

 Practice and Problem-Solving Exercises

 Practice Determine whether each data set is *qualitative* or *quantitative*.

 See Problem 1.

7. favorite recording stars

8. best-selling DVDs

9. numbers of gigabytes in memory cards

10. prices of TVs

Determine whether each data set is *univariate* or *bivariate*.

See Problem 2.

Guided Practice →

To start, identify the variable(s).

11. number of classes your friends take and the number of sports they play

number of classes

number of sports

12. numbers of CDs your classmates own

13. ages and heights of your friends

14. Zip codes of your relatives

15. circumferences and radii of circles

Determine whether the sampling method is *random*, *systematic*, or *stratified*. Tell whether the method will produce a good sample.

See Problem 3.

16. A pollster randomly selects 100 people from each town in a certain candidate's district to see if they support the candidate.

17. A factory tests the quality of every thirtieth shirt made.

18. A printing company randomly selects 10 of 450 books it printed to see if all the books were printed properly.

Determine whether each question is biased. Explain your answer.

See Problem 4.

Guided Practice →

19. Since global warming is a big problem, do you support government funding of studies on global warming?

To start, identify adjectives or phrases that make one category seem more appealing.

big problem

20. Where would you most like to go on vacation?

21. Do you prefer shopping online or the excitement of going to stores with friends?

22. You want to find out how much time people in your town spend doing volunteer work. You call 100 homes in the community during the day. Of those surveyed, 85% are over the age of 60. How might this create bias in your survey results?

See Problem 5.

23. You want to find out how many people in your neighborhood have pets in their homes. You ask every fourth person at the local dog park. How might this create bias in your survey results?

B Apply

24. Think About a Plan You want to find out what types of music students would like to listen to at the next school dance. How would you conduct a survey to find the music preferences of your entire school?
- What sampling method can you use to choose an unbiased sample?
- How can you write survey questions that are not biased?

25. Travel A travel agent wants to determine whether a trip to France is a popular vacation for young adults. How could each factor described below create bias in the survey results?
 a. The agent interviews people at an international airport.
 b. The agent asks, "Would you prefer to vacation in France or in Italy?"
 c. Of the people interviewed, 86% took a French class in high school.

In each situation, identify the population and sample. Tell whether each sample is a *random*, *systematic*, or *stratified* sample.

26. For one month, the owner of a sporting goods store asks every fifteenth customer which sport he or she most enjoys watching on TV.

27. At a high school football game, every spectator places his or her ticket stub in a bowl. After the game, the coach chooses ten people to march in the victory parade.

28. A restaurant asks every third customer to complete an evaluation form.

Classify the data as *qualitative* or *quantitative* and as *univariate* or *bivariate*.

29. average number of visitors per day at each of six different theme parks

30. monthly low temperatures in Rochester, New York

31. names of U.S. presidents and the states they were born in

32. **Sports** A student posts a survey on a Web site asking readers to choose their favorite sport to play from a list of five sports. The results are shown below.

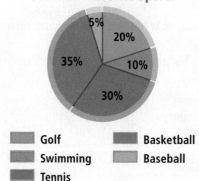

Students' Favorite Sports

5%
20%
35%
10%
30%

Golf Basketball
Swimming Baseball
Tennis

a. What biases might exist as a result of the design of this survey?
b. Do you believe the results of this survey are valid? Explain your answer.

33. **Writing** You are writing an article for the school newspaper about support for the mayor's proposal for bike paths. For each situation below, determine whether the data collection method will result in an unbiased sample of town residents. Explain your answer.
a. You survey every tenth person leaving a bicycle repair store.
b. You call homes in your neighborhood every morning Monday through Friday for one week.
c. You send an e-mail to 100 classmates chosen at random.
d. You poll every fifth person at a popular local sandwich shop.

34. Elections A radio station asks its listeners to call and tell who their favorite candidate is in an upcoming election. Sixty-eight percent of the callers prefer a certain candidate, so the radio station announces that the candidate will win the election. Is the conclusion valid? Explain.

> **Hint** Do all radio stations cater to the same population?

Standardized Test Prep

SAT/ACT

35. What is the solution of the equation $\frac{x}{2} - 11 = 19$?

  Ⓐ 8   Ⓑ 16   Ⓒ 30   Ⓓ 60

36. What is 0.0000212 written in scientific notation?

  Ⓕ 2.12×10^5 Ⓖ 2.12×10^{-5} Ⓗ 21.2×10^{-6} Ⓘ 2.12×10^{-6}

37. 40% of what number is 50?

  Ⓐ 155   Ⓑ 125   Ⓒ 20   Ⓓ 2

Short Response

38. A reporter is trying to predict who will win an open seat on the city council. Her plan is to ask 20 coworkers who they think will win. Will this plan give a good sample? Explain.

Mixed Review

39. Of 30 test scores, 12 are less than or equal to 85. What is the percentile rank of a test score of 85?

> ◀ **See Lesson 12-4.**

40. There are 15 bands in a competition. The judges give 9 bands a score of 7.5 or lower. What is the percentile rank of 7.5?

Solve each inequality.

> ◀ **See Lesson 3-4.**

41. $4 - 3a < 3a - 2$ **42.** $3(x - 2) \le 6x + 3$ **43.** $2.7 + 2b > 3.4 - 1.5b$

Get Ready! **To prepare for Lesson 12-6, do Exercises 44–46.**

Write each fraction in simplest form.

> ◀ **See p. 786.**

44. $\dfrac{5 \cdot 4 \cdot 3 \cdot 2 \cdot 1}{3 \cdot 2 \cdot 1}$ **45.** $\dfrac{7 \cdot 6 \cdot 5 \cdot 4 \cdot 3 \cdot 2 \cdot 1}{5 \cdot 4 \cdot 3 \cdot 2 \cdot 1}$ **46.** $\dfrac{6 \cdot 5 \cdot 4 \cdot 3 \cdot 2 \cdot 1}{5 \cdot 4 \cdot 3 \cdot 2 \cdot 1}$

Concept Byte

Use With Lesson 12-5

ACTIVITY

Misleading Graphs and Statistics

There are many ways to graph data that show the data accurately. There are also ways to graph data that are misleading.

Activity 1

A company uses the two graphs below to display its monthly profits.

1. How are the scales of the axes different in the two graphs?

2. An investor looks at the graph on the left and concludes that the company's profits doubled from January to June. Is the investor correct? Explain.

3. Another investor looks at the graph on the right and concludes that the company's profits increased about 25% from January to June. Is the investor correct? Explain.

4. Reasoning Which graph most accurately displays the data? Explain.

Activity 2

A local newpaper conducts a survey about where people in your town go on vacation. The paper uses the graph at the right to display the results.

5. A columnist writes that many more people vacation in the United States than outside the United States. Do you think the graph supports the columnist's statement? Explain.

6. According to the graph, how many people vacation in the United States? How many people vacation outside the United States?

7. How do the areas of the bars in the graph compare?

8. Why is the graph misleading?

9. Reasoning How could you redraw the graph so that it is not misleading? Explain your answer.

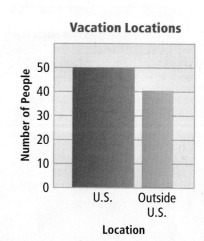

Chapter Vocabulary

- bias (p. 739)
- bivariate (p. 738)
- box-and-whisker plot (p. 731)
- cumulative frequency table (p. 718)
- element (p. 710)
- frequency (p. 716)
- histogram (p. 717)
- interquartile range (p. 730)
- matrix (p. 710)
- mean (p. 722)
- measure of central tendency (p. 722)
- measure of dispersion (p. 724)
- median (p. 722)
- mode (p. 722)
- outlier (p. 722)
- percentile (p. 733)
- population (p. 738)
- qualitative (p. 737)
- quantitative (p. 737)
- quartile (p. 730)
- range of a set of data (p. 724)
- sample (p. 738)
- scalar (p. 711)
- scalar multiplication (p. 711)
- univariate (p. 738)

Choose the correct term to complete each sentence.

1. Each numerical item of data in a matrix is called a(n) __?__.

2. The number of data values in an interval is the __?__ of the interval.

3. A(n) __?__ is a data value much greater or less than the other values in a data set.

4. The median of the lower half of an ordered data set is the first __?__.

12-1 Organizing Data Using Matrices

Quick Review

You can use **matrices** to organize data. To add or subtract matrices that are the same size, add or subtract the corresponding **elements**. To multiply a matrix by a **scalar**, multiply each element by the scalar.

Example

What is the difference?

$$\begin{bmatrix} 3 & 2 \\ -1 & 5 \\ 2 & -2 \end{bmatrix} - \begin{bmatrix} 2 & 4 \\ 4 & -3 \\ 1 & 0 \end{bmatrix} = \begin{bmatrix} 3-2 & 2-4 \\ -1-4 & 5-(-3) \\ 2-1 & -2-0 \end{bmatrix}$$

$$= \begin{bmatrix} 1 & -2 \\ -5 & 8 \\ 1 & -2 \end{bmatrix}$$

Exercises

Find each sum, difference, or product.

5. $\begin{bmatrix} -5 & 1 \\ 0 & 8 \end{bmatrix} - \begin{bmatrix} 7 & -6 \\ -4 & 2 \end{bmatrix}$

6. $\begin{bmatrix} 0.4 & 1.5 \\ 3.2 & -3 \\ 1.5 & -2.1 \end{bmatrix} + \begin{bmatrix} 4 & 3 \\ 6.3 & -7.2 \\ 1.9 & -0.5 \end{bmatrix}$

7. $-4.2 \begin{bmatrix} 3 & 1.1 \\ 3 & -2 \\ -1 & 2.9 \end{bmatrix}$

12-2 Frequency and Histograms

Quick Review

The **frequency** of an interval is the number of data values in that interval. A **histogram** is a graph that groups data into intervals and shows the frequency of values in each interval.

Example

Below are the prices of the television models sold at an electronics store. What is a histogram of the data?

$1399 $1349 $999 $2149 $149 $279 $449 $379 $1379
$799 $3199 $1099 $499 $899 $949 $1799 $1699 $3499

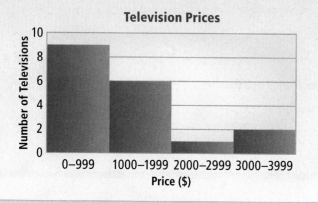

Exercises

Use the data to make a histogram.

8. customers: 141 128 132 141 152 169 121 133 131 156 142 136 135 144 135 153

9. workout times (min): 41 29 46 39 37 44 33 51 42 30

Tell whether each histogram is *uniform*, *symmetric*, or *skewed*.

10.

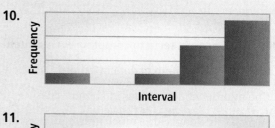

11.

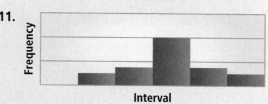

12-3 Measures of Central Tendency and Dispersion

Quick Review

The **mean** of a data set equals $\frac{\text{sum of the data values}}{\text{total number of data values}}$. The **median** is the middle value in the data set when the values are arranged in order. The **mode** is the data item that occurs the most times.

Example

The quality ratings of 9 movies showing at a movie theater near you are 5.6, 7.9, 7.0, 5.9, 7.8, 6.2, 6.4, 5.2, and 5.6. What are the mean, median and mode of the data?

mean:

$$\frac{5.6 + 7.9 + 7.0 + 5.9 + 7.8 + 6.2 + 6.4 + 5.2 + 5.6}{9} = 6.4$$

Order the data.   5.2 5.6 5.6 5.9 6.2 6.4 7.0 7.8 7.9

6.2 is the middle value.   median: 6.2

5.6 occurs most often.   mode: 5.6

Exercises

Find the mean, median, mode, and range of each data set.

12. points scored by a football team: 23 31 26 27 25 28 23 23 25 29 29 29 25 22 30

13. clips per package: 12 12 13 12 12 12 12 12 12 13 12 11 12 12 12 12 12

14. Cats A veterinarian examines 9 cats. The weights of the cats are 13.4 lb, 13.1 lb, 10.4 lb, 6.8 lb, 11.4 lb, 10.8 lb, 13.4 lb, 11.3 lb, and 9.3 lb. Find the mean, median, and mode of the data. Which measure of central tendency best describes the data?

15. Basketball A basketball player scores 22, 19, 25, and 17 points in four games. How many points does the basketball player need to score in the fifth game to average 22 points scored per game?

12-4 Box-and-Whisker Plots

Quick Review

A **box-and-whisker plot** organizes data values into four groups using the minimum value, the first quartile, the median, the third quartile, and the maximum value.

Example

What box-and-whisker plot represents the test scores below?

62 57 78 69 85 43 94 82 61 90 83 51 67 88 55

Arrange the data in order from least to greatest.

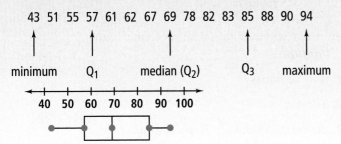

43 51 55 57 61 62 67 69 78 82 83 85 88 90 94

minimum Q_1 median (Q_2) Q_3 maximum

Exercises

Make a box-and-whisker plot of each data set.

16. movie lengths (min):
125 117 174 131 142 108 188 162 155 167 129 133 147 175 150

17. dog weights (lb):
23 15 88 34 33 49 52 67 42 71 28

18. book lengths (pages):
178 223 198 376 284 156 245 202 315 266

19. Which box-and-whisker plot represents the data set with the greater interquartile range? Explain.

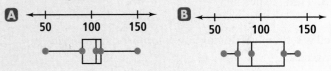

12-5 Samples and Surveys

Quick Review

You can obtain information about a **population** of people by surveying a smaller part of it, called a **sample**. The sample should be representative of the population. An unrepresentative sample or a poorly worded question can result in **bias**.

Example

A survey asks, "Should Plainville make itself proud by building a beautiful new library?" Is the question biased?

The question is biased. The words *proud* and *beautiful* make it clear that the answer is expected to be yes.

Exercises

Determine whether the sampling method is *random*, *systematic*, or *stratified*. Tell whether the method will give a good sample. Then write an unbiased survey question for the situation.

20. Movies An interviewer outside a movie theater asks every third person in line whether he or she will see more or fewer movies in the coming year.

21. Student Government Ten randomly chosen students in each class (freshman, sophomore, junior, and senior) are asked whom they support for student council president.

Do you know HOW?

Find each sum or difference.

1. $\begin{bmatrix} -2 & 3 \\ 0 & 4 \\ -1 & 1 \end{bmatrix} + \begin{bmatrix} 4 & -1 \\ 3 & 0 \\ -3 & 2 \end{bmatrix}$

2. $\begin{bmatrix} 0 & -2 \\ 3 & 1 \\ -4 & 3 \end{bmatrix} - \begin{bmatrix} -1 & 0 \\ 2 & 5 \\ -4 & 3 \end{bmatrix}$

3. Find the product. $-2\begin{bmatrix} 3 & 0 \\ -2 & 1 \end{bmatrix}$

Tell whether each histogram is *uniform*, *symmetric*, or *skewed*.

4.

5.

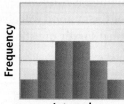

6. **Gymnastics** A gymnast's scores from his tryouts are listed below. Make a frequency table and a histogram that represent the data.
8.8 9.1 3.5 6.9 7.3 9.6 9.0 5.7 7.2 4.3 8.9 9.5

7. **Music** The hours per week that a school band practiced are listed below. What are the mean, median, mode, and range of their practice times? Which measure of central tendency best describes their practice times?
7 5 9 7 4 6 10 8 5 7 8 7 3 12 15 13 8

Identify the minimum, first quartile, median, third quartile, and maximum of each data set. Then make a box-and-whisker plot of each data set.

8. daily visitors: 34 29 32 25 97 93 112 108 90

9. commute (mi): 8 33 28 7 42 9 30 38 22 6 37

10. **Movies** Of the ratings for ten movies, eight ratings are less than or equal to 7. What is the percentile rank of a rating of 7?

Determine whether each data set is *qualitative* or *quantitative*.

11. favorite books

12. prices of DVDs

13. **Business** A software business e-mails every thousandth name on an e-mail list to find out what software the people are using. Is the survey plan *random*, *systematic*, or *stratified*? Will it give a good sample? Explain.

Do you UNDERSTAND?

14. **Reasoning** When you compare two sets of data, will the set with the greater interquartile range always have the greater range? Explain and give an example.

15. **Writing** When is each measure of central tendency most useful?

16. **Open-Ended** Describe a problem that you could solve by conducting a survey. Write an unbiased survey question, and explain how to choose a good sample for your survey.

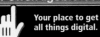

Data Analysis and Probability

In Part A, you learned about collecting and organizing data. Now you will learn about permutations, combinations, and probability.

Vocabulary for Part B

English/Spanish Vocabulary Audio Online:

English	Spanish
combination, *p. 753*	combinación
compound event, *p. 765*	suceso compuesto
dependent events, *p. 768*	sucesos dependientes
event, *p. 757*	suceso
independent events, *p. 766*	sucesos independientes
odds, *p. 759*	probabilidad a favor
outcome, *p. 757*	resultado
permutation, *p. 752*	permutación
probability, *p. 757*	probabilidad

BIGideas

1 Data Collection and Analysis
Essential Question How can collecting and analyzing data help you make decisions or predictions?

2 Data Representation
Essential Question How can you make and interpret different representations of data?

3 Probability
Essential Question How is probability related to real-world events?

Chapter Preview for Part B

12-6 Permutations and Combinations
12-7 Theoretical and Experimental Probability
12-8 Probability of Compound Events

12-6 Permutations and Combinations

Objective To find permutations and combinations

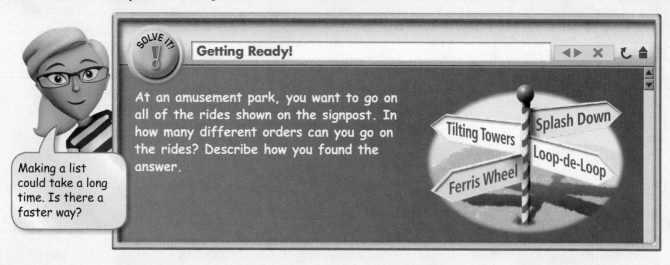

SOLVE IT!

Getting Ready!

At an amusement park, you want to go on all of the rides shown on the signpost. In how many different orders can you go on the rides? Describe how you found the answer.

Tilting Towers · Splash Down · Loop-de-Loop · Ferris Wheel

Making a list could take a long time. Is there a faster way?

Lesson Vocabulary
- Multiplication Counting Principle
- permutation
- *n* factorial
- combination

You can use counting methods to find the number of possible ways to choose objects with and without regard to order.

Focus Question What is the difference between a permutation and a combination?

One way to find the possible orders of objects is to make an organized list. Another way is to make a tree diagram. Both methods help you see if you have thought of all the possibilities.

The tree diagram below shows all the possible orders for watching three movies (a comedy, a drama, and an action film).

First Movie	Second Movie	Third Movie	Order of Movies
comedy	drama	action	comedy, drama, action
	action	drama	comedy, action, drama
drama	comedy	action	drama, comedy, action
	action	comedy	drama, action, comedy
action	comedy	drama	action, comedy, drama
	drama	comedy	action, drama, comedy

There are six possible orders for watching the three movies.

When one event does not affect the result of a second event, the events are *independent*. When events are independent, you can find the number of outcomes using the Multiplication Counting Principle.

 take note

Key Concept Multiplication Counting Principle

If there are m ways to make a first selection and n ways to make a second selection, then there are $m \cdot n$ ways to make the two selections.

Example
For 5 shirts and 8 pairs of shorts, the number of possible outfits is $5 \cdot 8 = 40$.

Problem 1 Using the Multiplication Counting Principle

Shopping Use the diagram below. How many ways are there to get from the first floor to the third floor using only escalators?

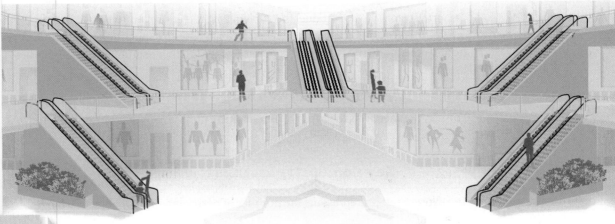

Think

What is another way to solve this problem?
You can draw a diagram like the tree diagram on the previous page to show all of the possible escalator routes.

$2 \cdot 3 = 6$

Routes by escalator from first floor to second floor

Routes by escalator from second floor to third floor

Routes by escalator from first floor to third floor

There are 6 possible ways to get from the first floor to the third floor using only escalators.

 Got It? **1. a.** A pizza shop offers 8 vegetable toppings and 6 meat toppings. How many different pizzas can you order with one meat topping and one vegetable topping?
b. Reasoning Is a tree diagram a convenient way to find the answer to part (a)? Explain.

A **permutation** is an arrangement of objects in a specific order. Here are the possible permutations of the letters A, B, and C without repeating any letters.

ABC   ACB   BAC   BCA   CAB   CBA

 Problem 2   **Finding Permutations**

Concert A band has 7 new songs to perform in a concert. In how many different orders can they perform the new songs?

Plan

How do you use the Multiplication Counting Principle to find the number of permutations?
Multiply the number of ways to make each selection.

There are 7 choices for the first song, 6 for the second, and so on.

    Use a calculator. $7 \cdot 6 \cdot 5 \cdot 4 \cdot 3 \cdot 2 \cdot 1 = 5040$

There are 5040 possible orders for the 7 songs.

 Got It?   **2.** A swimming pool has 8 lanes. In how many ways can 8 swimmers be assigned lanes for a race?

A short way to write the product in Problem 2 is 7!, read "seven factorial." For any positive integer n, the expression ***n* factorial** is written as $n!$ and is the product of the integers from n down to 1. The value of 0! is defined to be 1. Other examples of factorials are listed below.

     $4! = 4 \cdot 3 \cdot 2 \cdot 1 = 24$ $8! = 8 \cdot 7 \cdot 6 \cdot 5 \cdot 4 \cdot 3 \cdot 2 \cdot 1 = 40,320$

You can use factorials to write a formula for the number of permutations of n objects arranged r at a time.

Key Concept   Permutation Notation

The expression $_nP_r$ represents the number of permutations of n objects arranged r at a time.

$$_nP_r = \frac{n!}{(n - r)!}$$

Example $_8P_2 = \frac{8!}{(8 - 2)!} = \frac{8!}{6!} = \frac{8 \cdot 7 \cdot 6 \cdot 5 \cdot 4 \cdot 3 \cdot 2 \cdot 1}{6 \cdot 5 \cdot 4 \cdot 3 \cdot 2 \cdot 1} = 56$

 Problem 3   **Using Permutation Notation**

Demo CD A band has 7 new songs and wants to put 5 of them on a demo CD. How many arrangements of 5 songs are possible?

Think

How can you think about this problem in a different way?
You can use the Multiplication Counting Principle. There are 7 choices for the first song, 6 for the second, 5 for the third, 4 for the fourth, and 3 for the fifth.

Method 1   Use the formula for permutations.

     Write using factorials and cross out factors that are in the numerator and denominator. $_7P_5 = \frac{7!}{(7 - 5)!} = \frac{7!}{2!} = \frac{7 \cdot 6 \cdot 5 \cdot 4 \cdot 3 \cdot \cancel{2} \cdot \cancel{1}}{\cancel{2} \cdot \cancel{1}}$

     Simplify. $= 2520$

Hint

n represents the number of objects arranged r at a time. If there are only 6 students, then only 6 desks are used at a time.

Method 2 Use a graphing calculator.

Press 7 math ◄ 2 5 enter.

$$_7P_5 = 2520$$

There are 2520 possible arrangements of 5 songs.

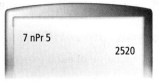

7 nPr 5
2520

Got It? **3.** There are 6 students in a classroom with 8 desks. How many possible seating arrangements are there?

A **combination** is a selection of objects without regard to order. For example, if you are selecting two side dishes from a list of five, the order in which you choose the side dishes does not matter.

take note

Key Concept Combination Notation

The expression $_nC_r$ represents the number of combinations of n objects chosen r at a time.

$$_nC_r = \frac{n!}{r!(n-r)!}$$

Example $_8C_2 = \frac{8!}{2!(8-2)!} = \frac{8!}{2!6!} = \frac{8 \cdot 7 \cdot 6 \cdot 5 \cdot 4 \cdot 3 \cdot 2 \cdot 1}{(2 \cdot 1)(6 \cdot 5 \cdot 4 \cdot 3 \cdot 2 \cdot 1)} = 28$

 Problem 4 **Using Combination Notation**

Multiple Choice There are 15 toddlers in a preschool class. How many different 8 student groups can be chosen to play outside?

Ⓐ 15   Ⓑ 120   Ⓒ 6435   Ⓓ 32,432,400

Plan

Do you use a permutation or a combination?
The order of the people on the jury does not matter, so use a combination.

You need the number of combinations of 15 toddlers chosen 8 at a time. Find $_{15}C_8$.

Write using factorials. $_{15}C_8 = \frac{15!}{8!(15-8)!} = \frac{15!}{8!7!}$

Simplify using a calculator. $= 6435$

There are 6435 different groups of 8 toddlers. The correct answer is C.

Got It? **4.** In how many different ways can you choose 3 types of flowers for a bouquet from a selection of 15 types of flowers?

Focus Question What is the difference between a permutation and a combination?

Answer Permutations are used to count selections of objects when order is important. Combinations are used to count selections of objects when order is not important.

Lesson Check

Do you know HOW?

Find the value of each expression.

1. $7!$ **2.** $13!$ **3.** $_6P_3$

4. $_{10}P_4$ **5.** $_5C_3$ **6.** $_7C_3$

7. How many outfits can you make with 6 shirts and 4 pairs of pants?

Do you UNDERSTAND?

8. Vocabulary Would you use permutations or combinations to find the number of possible arrangements of 10 students in a line? Why?

9. Compare and Contrast How are permutations and combinations similar? How are they different?

10. Reasoning Explain why $_nC_n$ is equal to 1.

Practice and Problem-Solving Exercises

Practice

11. Telephones A seven-digit telephone number can begin with any digit except 0 or 1. There are no restrictions on digits after the first digit.
   a. How many possible choices are there for the first digit? For each digit after the first digit?
   b. How many different seven-digit telephone numbers are possible?

    See Problem 1.

12. Use the diagram and the Multiplication Counting Principle to find each of the following:
   a. the number of routes from A to C
   b. the number of routes from A to D

$$A \quad B \rightarrow C \quad D$$

13. Sports In an ice-skating competition, the order in which competitors skate is determined by a drawing. Suppose there are 10 skaters in the finals. How many different orders are possible for the final program?

    See Problem 2.

14. Photography Suppose you are lining up with 4 cousins for a photo. How many different arrangements are possible?

Find the value of each expression.

    See Problem 3.

Guided Practice →

To start, substitute 8 for n and 4 for r in the Permutation formula.

15. $_8P_4$

$$_8P_4 = \frac{8!}{(8-4)!} = \frac{8!}{4!}$$

16. $_9P_3$ **17.** $_7P_6$ **18.** $_7P_2$ **19.** $_5P_5$

20. $_6P_1$ **21.** $_{11}P_0$ **22.** $_{10}P_2$ **23.** $_{12}P_9$

24. Reading You have 10 books on your bookshelf. In how many orders can you read 4 of the books on a summer vacation?

25. **Student Government** A student council has 24 members. The council is selecting a 3-person committee to plan a car wash. Each person on the committee will have one task: one person will find a location, another person will organize publicity, and the third person will schedule volunteers. In how many different ways can 3 students be chosen and given a task?

Find the value of each expression.

◀ See Problem 4.

26. $_6C_6$

To start, substitute 6 for n and 6 for r in the Combination formula.

$$_6C_6 = \frac{6!}{6!(6-6)!} = \frac{6!}{6!0!} = \frac{6!}{6!}$$

27. $_5C_4$ 28. $_9C_1$ 29. $_7C_2$ 30. $_3C_0$

31. $_8C_6$ 32. $_7C_5$ 33. $_{10}C_9$ 34. $_{15}C_4$

35. **Law** For some civil cases, at least 9 of 12 jurors must agree on a verdict. How many combinations of 9 jurors are possible on a 12-person jury?

36. **Gift Certificates** For your birthday you received a gift certificate from a music store for 3 CDs. There are 8 CDs you would like to have. How many different groups of 3 CDs can you select from the 8 you want?

37. **Quilting** There are 30 fabrics available at a quilt store. How many different groups of 5 fabrics can you choose for a quilt?

B Apply

38. **Think About a Plan** Draw four points like those in Figure 1. Draw line segments so that every point is joined to every other point. How many line segments did you draw? How many segments would you need to join each point to all the others in Figure 2?
   • How many points are there in Figure 2?
   • Should you use combinations or permutations to find the number of segments that join pairs of points?

Figure 1   Figure 2

39. **License Plates** In one state, a regular license plate has a two-digit number that is fixed by county, then one letter, and then four one-digit numbers.
   a. How many different license plates are possible in each county?
   b. Suppose there are 92 counties in the state. How many license plates are possible in the entire state?

Find the number of arrangements of letters taken three at a time that can be formed from each set of cards.

40. A B C D E

41. P Q R

42. E F G H I J K

43. M N O P

Reasoning Explain whether each situation is a permutation problem or a combination problem.

44. A locker contains 8 books. You select 3 books at random. How many different sets of books can you select?

45. You take 4 books out of the school library to read during spring vacation. In how many different orders can you read the 4 books?

46. Media The call signs of radio and television stations in the United States generally begin with the letter W east of the Mississippi River and the letter K west of the Mississippi. Repetition of letters is allowed.

a. How many different call signs are possible if each station uses a W or K followed by 3 letters?

b. How many different call signs are possible if each station uses a W or K followed by 4 letters?

Standardized Test Prep

GRIDDED RESPONSE

SAT/ACT

47. The school cafeteria serves lunches consisting of 1 main dish, 1 vegetable, 1 salad, and 1 dessert. The menu has choices of 2 main dishes, 3 vegetables, 3 salads, and 4 desserts. How many different lunches are possible?

48. What is 7.3×10^{-2} written in standard form?

49. How many elements are in the union of the two sets $M = \{4, 5, -6, 7, 8\}$ and $N = \{-4, 5, 6, 7, -8\}$?

50. You deposit $500 in an account earning 5.25% annual interest. You make no further deposits to the account and the interest is compounded annually. What is the balance in dollars after 10 yr? Round to the nearest dollar.

Mixed Review

Determine whether each data set is *qualitative* or *quantitative*. ◀ See Lesson 12-5.

51. ZIP codes   **52.** race times   **53.** heights of people   **54.** emotions

Use the quadratic formula to solve each equation. If necessary, round answers to the nearest hundredth. ◀ See Lesson 9-6.

55. $2x^2 + 12x - 11 = 0$ **56.** $x^2 - 7x + 2 = 0$ **57.** $x^2 + 4x - 8 = 0$ **58.** $3x^2 + 8x + 5 = 0$

Get Ready! **To prepare for Lesson 12-7, do Exercises 59–62.**

Rewrite each decimal or fraction as a percent. ◀ See p. 790

59. 0.32   **60.** 0.09   **61.** $\frac{45}{200}$ **62.** $\frac{9}{50}$

12-7 Theoretical and Experimental Probability

Objective To find theoretical and experimental probabilities

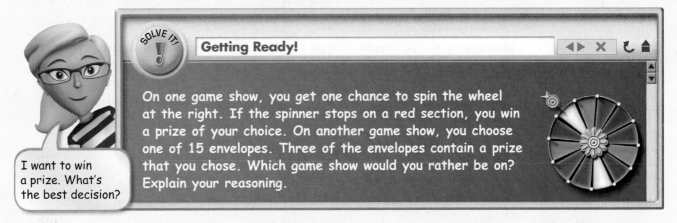

I want to win a prize. What's the best decision?

Getting Ready!

On one game show, you get one chance to spin the wheel at the right. If the spinner stops on a red section, you win a prize of your choice. On another game show, you choose one of 15 envelopes. Three of the envelopes contain a prize that you chose. Which game show would you rather be on? Explain your reasoning.

Lesson Vocabulary
- outcome
- sample space
- event
- probability
- theoretical probability
- complement of an event
- odds
- experimental probability

In the Solve It, spinning red and choosing the right envelope are desired outcomes. An **outcome** is the result of a single trial, such as spinning a wheel. The **sample space** is all the possible outcomes. An **event** is any outcome or group of outcomes. The outcomes that match a given event are favorable outcomes.

Here is how these terms apply to rolling an even number on a number cube.

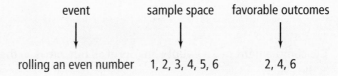

event	sample space	favorable outcomes
↓	↓	↓
rolling an even number	1, 2, 3, 4, 5, 6	2, 4, 6

Focus Question What is the difference between theoretical and experimental probability?

The **probability** of an event, or *P*(event), tells you how likely it is that the event will occur. You can find probabilities by reasoning mathematically or by using data collected from an experiment.

You can write the probability of an event as a fraction, a decimal, or a percent. The probability of an event ranges from 0 to 1.

The probability of rolling 7 is 0 since 7 does not appear on any of the sides of the number cube. It is impossible to roll 7.

```
                    equally likely to occur
impossible            or not occur              certain
    0   ←── less likely   0.5   more likely ──→   1
```

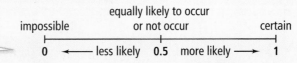

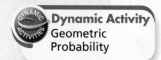 **Dynamic Activity**
Geometric
Probability

In the number-cube example, the outcomes in the sample space are equally likely to occur. When all possible outcomes are equally likely, you can find the *theoretical probability* of an event using the following formula.

theoretical probability $P(\text{event}) = \dfrac{\text{number of favorable outcomes}}{\text{number of possible outcomes}}$

$$P(\text{rolling an even number}) = \dfrac{3}{6} = \dfrac{1}{2}$$

 Problem 1 **Finding Theoretical Probability**

Astronomy Our solar system's 8 planets, in order of least to greatest distance from the sun, are Mercury, Venus, Earth, Mars, Jupiter, Saturn, Uranus, and Neptune. You will randomly draw one of the names of the planets and write a report on that planet. What is the theoretical probability that you will select a planet whose distance from the sun is less than Earth's?

Think

Does a "favorable outcome" always mean that something good happens?
No. For example, if you are determining the probability of losing a game, the "favorable" outcomes are the outcomes where you lose.

$$P(\text{event}) = \dfrac{\text{number of favorable outcomes}}{\text{number of possible outcomes}}$$

Two planets out of 8 are nearer to the sun than Earth: Mercury and Venus. $= \dfrac{2}{8}$

Simplify. $= \dfrac{1}{4}$

The probability of selecting a planet whose distance from the sun is less than Earth's is $\frac{1}{4}$.

 Got It? **1.** In Problem 1, what is the theoretical probability that you will select a planet whose distance from the sun is greater than Earth's?

The **complement of an event** consists of all outcomes in the sample space that are not in the event.

The sum of the probabilities of an event and its complement is 1.

$P(\text{event}) + P(\text{not event}) = 1$ or $P(\text{not event}) = 1 - P(\text{event})$

The possible outcomes for rolling a number cube are 1, 2, 3, 4, 5, and 6. The outcomes for rolling an even number are 2, 4, and 6. The outcomes for the complement of rolling an even number are 1, 3, and 5.

$P(\text{even}) + P(\text{not even}) = 1$ or $P(\text{not even}) = 1 - P(\text{even})$

Problem 2 Finding the Probability of the Complement of an Event

Consumer Research In a taste test, 50 participants are randomly given a beverage to sample. There are 20 samples of Drink A, 10 samples of Drink B, 10 samples of Drink C, and 10 samples of Drink D. What is the probability of a participant not getting Drink A?

Think

How else can you find _P_(not Drink A)?
You can divide the number of other drink samples by the total number of samples.
$P(\text{not Drink A})$
$= \dfrac{10 + 10 + 10}{50}$
$= \dfrac{30}{50} = \dfrac{3}{5}$

Find $P(\text{Drink A})$.

$P(\text{Drink A}) = \dfrac{\text{number of samples of Drink A}}{\text{total number of samples}} = \dfrac{20}{50} = \dfrac{2}{5}$

Use the complement formula.

$P(\text{not Drink A}) = 1 - P(\text{Drink A})$

Substitute and simplify.

$= 1 - \dfrac{2}{5} = \dfrac{3}{5}$

The probability of not getting Drink A is $\frac{3}{5}$.

✓ **Got It?** 2. **Reasoning** Suppose a taste test is repeated with the same number of samples of Drink A, but more samples of other drinks. What happens to $P(\text{not Drink A})$?

Odds describe the likelihood of an event as a ratio comparing the number of favorable and unfavorable outcomes.

$$\text{odds in favor of an event} = \dfrac{\text{number of favorable outcomes}}{\text{number of unfavorable outcomes}}$$

$$\text{odds against an event} = \dfrac{\text{number of unfavorable outcomes}}{\text{number of favorable outcomes}}$$

Problem 3 Finding Odds

Think

How is finding odds different from finding probability?
To find odds, you compare favorable and unfavorable outcomes. To find probability, you compare favorable outcomes and all possible outcomes.

What are the odds in favor of the spinner landing on a number greater than or equal to 6?

Favorable outcomes: 6, 7, 8   Total: 3
Unfavorable outcomes: 1, 2, 3, 4, 5   Total: 5

The odds in favor of the event are $\frac{3}{5}$, or 3 : 5.

✓ **Got It?** 3. What are the odds against the spinner landing on a number less than 3?

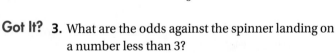

Experimental probability is based on data collected from repeated trials.

experimental probability $P(\text{event}) = \dfrac{\text{number of times the event occurs}}{\text{number of times the experiment is done}}$

 Problem 4 **Finding Experimental Probability**

Quality Control After receiving complaints, a skateboard manufacturer inspects 1000 skateboards at random. The manufacturer finds no defects in 992 skateboards. What is the probability that a skateboard selected at random has no defects? Write the probability as a percent.

Think

How is the formula for experimental probability similar to the formula for theoretical probability?
In each formula, you divide a number of items corresponding to an event by a total number of items.

$$P(\text{no defects}) = \dfrac{\text{number of skateboards with no defects}}{\text{number of skateboards examined}}$$

Substitute.	$= \dfrac{992}{1000}$
Write as a decimal.	$= 0.992$
Change to percent.	$= 99.2\%$

The probability that a skateboard selected at random has no defects is 99.2%.

 Got It? **4.** Suppose the manufacturer in Problem 4 inspects 2500 skateboards. There are 2450 skateboards with no defects. What is the probability that a skateboard selected at random has no defects? Write the probability as a percent.

You can use experimental probability to make a prediction. Predictions are not exact, so round your results.

 Problem 5 **Using Experimental Probability**

Pets You ask 500 randomly selected households in your town if they have a dog. Of the 500 households, 197 respond that they do have a dog. If your town has 24,800 households, about how many households are likely to have a dog?

Know	Need	Plan
• 197 of 500 respondents own a dog • Your town has 24,800 households	Likely number of households that own a dog	Find the experimental probability that a household owns a dog. Then multiply it by the total number of households.

$$P(\text{own dog}) = \dfrac{\text{number of respondents that own a dog}}{\text{number of households surveyed}} = \dfrac{197}{500} = 0.394$$

$$\text{households with dog} = P(\text{own dog}) \cdot \text{total number of households}$$

Substitute.	$= 0.394 \cdot 24{,}800$
Simplify.	$= 9771.2$

It is likely that approximately 9770 households in your town own a dog.

Got It? **5.** A manufacturer inspects 700 light bulbs and finds that 692 of the light bulbs work. There are about 35,400 light bulbs in the manufacturer's warehouse. About how many of the light bulbs in the warehouse are likely to work?

Focus Question What is the difference between theoretical and experimental probability?

Answer Theoretical probability is when all possible outcomes are equally likely. Experimental probability is based on the results of an experiment.

Lesson Check

Do you know HOW?

Find the theoretical probability of each event when rolling a number cube.

1. $P(4)$ **2.** P(less than 3)

3. P(not 3)   **4.** P(not greater than 4)

5. What are the odds in favor of rolling a 4 on a number cube?

6. You toss a dart at a dartboard 500 times. You hit the bull's-eye 80 times. What is the experimental probability that you hit the bull's-eye?

Do you UNDERSTAND?

7. Error Analysis Eric calculated the probability of getting a number less than 3 when randomly choosing an integer from 1 to 10. Describe and correct his error.

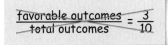

8. Open-Ended Describe a real-world situation in which one event is nearly certain to occur and another event is highly unlikely.

Practice and Problem-Solving Exercises

A Practice The spinner is divided into six equal parts. Find the theoretical probability of landing on the given section(s) of the spinner.

◀ See Problems 1 and 2.

Guided Practice

To start, identify the information needed to find the theoretical probability.

9. P(blue)

$$P(\text{blue}) = \frac{\text{number of blue sections}}{\text{total number of sections}}$$

10. P(white)   **11.** $P(5)$ **12.** $P(8)$

13. P(even)   **14.** P(not 2)   **15.** P(less than 5)

16. P(not green)   **17.** P(even or odd)   **18.** P(greater than 4)

Use the spinner on page 761. Find the odds.

See Problem 3.

19. odds in favor of even number **20.** odds against 2   **21.** odds against a factor of 6

22. odds against green   **23.** odds in favor of blue   **24.** odds in favor of a multiple of 5

The results of a survey of 100 randomly selected students at a
2000-student high school are shown below. Find the experimental
probability that a student selected at random has the given plans after
graduation.

See Problem 4.

Plans for After Graduation

Response	Number of Responses
Go to community college	24
Go to 4-year college	43
Take a year off before college	12
Go to trade school	15
Do not plan to go to college	6

Guided Practice

To start, identify the information needed
to find the experimental probability.

25. P(community college)

$P(\text{community college}) = \dfrac{\text{number going to community college}}{\text{number of students surveyed}}$

26. P(4-year college)   **27.** P(trade school)

28. P(not trade school)   **29.** P(trade school or community college)

30. A park has about 500 trees. You find that 27 of 67 randomly chosen trees are oak
trees. About how many trees in the entire park are likely to be oak trees?

See Problem 5.

 Apply

31. Think About a Plan The United States has a land area of about 3,536,278 mi².
Illinois has a land area of about 57,918 mi². What is the probability that a location
in the United States chosen at random is not in Illinois? Give your answer to the
nearest tenth of a percent.
- How can you solve this problem using the complement of an event?
- How do you write a fraction as a percent?

32. Transportation Out of 80 workers surveyed at a company, 17 walk to work.
- **a.** What is the experimental probability that a randomly selected worker at that
company walks to work?
- **b.** Predict about how many of the 3600 workers at the company walk to work.

33. Open-Ended Suppose your teacher chooses a student at random from your
algebra class. What is the probability that a boy is not selected?

Football The stem-and-leaf plot at the right shows the difference between the points scored by the winning and losing teams in the Super Bowl during one 20-yr period.

34. Find the probability that the winning team won by less than 10 points.

35. Find the odds that the winning team won by 10 to 15 points.

36. Find the probability that the winning team won by more than 20 points.

Difference Between Winning and Losing Super Bowl Scores

0	1 3 3 3 3 4 7 7
1	0 1 2 3 4 5 7
2	3 7 7
3	5
4	5

Key: 1 | 0 means 10 points

Standardized Test Prep

SAT/ACT

37. What is the median of the following class sizes: 29, 31, 28, 25, 27, 33, 33, 26?

   Ⓐ 28   Ⓑ 28.5   Ⓒ 29   Ⓓ 33

38. If $y = 10$ and $x = 5$, and y varies directly with x, which equation relates x and y?

   Ⓕ $y = 5x$ Ⓖ $y = 2x$ Ⓗ $y = 2x + 10$ Ⓘ $y = 50x$

Short Response

39. A basketball team has 11 players. How many different 5-player groups can the coach choose to play during a game? Show your work.

Mixed Review

Find the number of permutations or combinations.

See Lesson 12-6.

40. $_7P_4$ **41.** $_3P_3$ **42.** $_6P_2$ **43.** $_9C_1$ **44.** $_5C_4$

Get Ready! **To prepare for Lesson 12-8, do Exercises 45–49.**

Find each union or intersection. Let $J = \{4, 5, 6, 7\}$, $K = \{1, 4, 7, 10\}$, and $L = \{x \mid x \text{ is an even whole number less than } 12\}$.

See Lesson 3-8.

45. $J \cup K$ **46.** $J \cap L$ **47.** $J \cup L$ **48.** $L \cap K$ **49.** $K \cup L$

Concept Byte

Conducting Simulations

Use With Lesson 12-7

ACTIVITY

A *simulation* is a model of a real-life situation. One way to do a simulation is to use random numbers generated by a graphing calculator or computer program.

On a graphing calculator, the command **RANDINT** generates random integers. To create a list of random integers, press (math) ◄ (5). The calculator will display **RANDINT(**. After the parenthesis, type (0) (,) (9) (9), and press (enter) repeatedly to create random 1- and 2-digit numbers from 0 to 99.

Activity 1

About 40% of people in the United States have type A blood. Estimate the probability that the next two people who donate blood in a blood drive have type A blood.

Step 1   To simulate this situation, let a 2-digit number represent 2 people. Use a calculator to generate 40 random 2-digit numbers, like the example at the right.

Step 2   Since about 40% of people in the United States have type A blood, 40% of the digits 0–9 can be used to represent these people. Let 0, 1, 2, and 3 represent people with type A blood, and let 4, 5, 6, 7, 8, and 9 represent people without type A blood. So, the 2-digit number 53 represents one person without type A blood (the digit 5) and one person with type A blood (the digit 3).

Step 3   In the example at the right, the six numbers in red represent two consecutive people who have type A blood. The other 2-digit numbers have at least one digit that represents a person of a blood type other than type A.

$$P(\text{two consecutive people of blood type A}) = \frac{\text{number of times the event occurs}}{\text{number of times the experiment is done}}$$

$$= \frac{6}{40} = 0.15$$

53	18	33	75
93	34	36	45
25	71	47	46
66	13	63	36
21	59	27	07
83	25	72	24
73	52	59	81
14	09	40	64
81	72	02	38
21	09	92	10

Convert 1-digit numbers like 9 into 2-digit numbers by adding a leading zero.

You can also simulate situations using other methods, such as rolling number cubes, spinning spinners, or flipping coins.

Activity 2

A cereal company has a promotion in which 1 in every 6 boxes contains a movie ticket.

Step 1   Roll two number cubes to represent two boxes of the cereal. Let 1 represent a winning box and let 2, 3, 4, 5, and 6 represent a nonwinning box.

Step 2   Record the result. Repeat this process 30 times. Use your results to estimate the probability that both boxes contain a movie ticket.

12-8 Probability of Compound Events

Objectives To find probabilities of mutually exclusive and overlapping events
To find probabilities of independent and dependent events

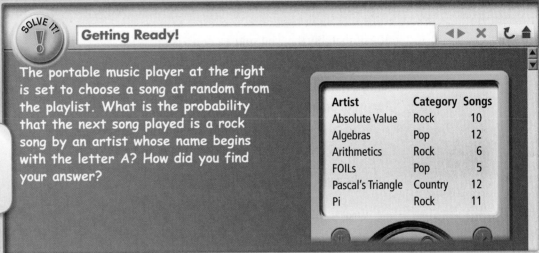

Getting Ready!

The portable music player at the right is set to choose a song at random from the playlist. What is the probability that the next song played is a rock song by an artist whose name begins with the letter A? How did you find your answer?

Hmm, this problem involves two events occurring at the same time.

Artist	Category	Songs
Absolute Value	Rock	10
Algebras	Pop	12
Arithmetics	Rock	6
FOILs	Pop	5
Pascal's Triangle	Country	12
Pi	Rock	11

Dynamic Activity
Independent and Dependent Events

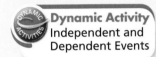

Lesson Vocabulary
• compound event
• mutually exclusive events
• overlapping events
• independent events
• dependent events

In the Solve It, you found the probability that the next song is both a rock song and also a song by an artist whose name begins with the letter A. This is an example of a **compound event,** which consists of two or more events linked by the word *and* or the word *or*.

Focus Question How can you write the probability of a compound event as an expression involving probabilities of simpler events?

When two events have no outcomes in common, the events are **mutually exclusive events.** If A and B are mutually exclusive events, then $P(A \text{ and } B) = 0$. When events have at least one outcome in common, they are **overlapping events.**

You need to determine whether two events A and B are mutually exclusive before you can find $P(A \text{ or } B)$.

take note

Key Concept Probability of A or B

Probability of Mutually Exclusive Events
If A and B are mutually exclusive events, $P(A \text{ or } B) = P(A) + P(B)$.

Probability of Overlapping Events
If A and B are overlapping events, $P(A \text{ or } B) = P(A) + P(B) - P(A \text{ and } B)$.

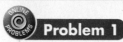 **Problem 1** **Mutually Exclusive and Overlapping Events**

Suppose you spin a spinner that has 20 equal-sized sections numbered from 1 to 20.

A **What is the probability that you spin a 2 or a 5?**

Because the spinner cannot land on both 2 and 5, the events are mutually exclusive.

$$P(2 \text{ or } 5) = P(2) + P(5)$$

Hint

The probability the spinner will land on a 2 is 1 out of 20.

Substitute. $\quad= \frac{1}{20} + \frac{1}{20}$

Simplify. $\quad= \frac{2}{20} = \frac{1}{10}$

The probability that you spin a 2 or a 5 is $\frac{1}{10}$.

B **What is the probability that you spin a number that is a multiple of 2 or 5?**

Since a number can be a multiple of 2 and a multiple of 5, such as 10, the events are overlapping.

$$P(\text{multiple of 2 or multiple of 5})$$
$$= P(\text{multiple of 2}) + P(\text{multiple of 5}) - P(\text{multiple of 2 and 5})$$

Think

How many multiples are there?
There are 10 multiples of 2: 2, 4, 6, 8, 10, 12, 14, 16, 18, and 20. There are 4 multiples of 5: 5, 10, 15, and 20. There are 2 multiples of 2 and 5: 10 and 20.

Substitute. $\quad= \frac{10}{20} + \frac{4}{20} - \frac{2}{20}$

Simplify. $\quad= \frac{12}{20} = \frac{3}{5}$

The probability that you spin a number that is a multiple of 2 or a multiple of 5 is $\frac{3}{5}$.

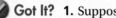 **Got It?** **1.** Suppose you roll a standard number cube.
  a. What is the probability that you roll an even number or a number less than 4?
  b. What is the probability that you roll a 2 or an odd number?

A standard set of checkers has an equal number of red and black checkers. The diagram at the right shows the possible outcomes when randomly choosing a checker, putting it back, and choosing again. The probability of getting a red on either choice is $\frac{1}{2}$. The first choice, or event, does not affect the second event because you put the first checker back. The events are *independent*.

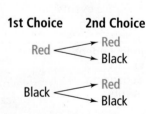

Two events are **independent events** if the occurrence of one event does not affect the probability of the second event.

Key Concept **Probability of Two Independent Events**

If A and B are independent events, $P(A \text{ and } B) = P(A) \cdot P(B)$.

Problem 2 Finding the Probability of Independent Events

Suppose you roll a red number cube and a blue number cube. What is the probability that you will roll a 3 on the red cube and an even number on the blue cube?

Find the probability of rolling a 3 on the red cube. Only one of the six numbers is a 3.

$$P(\text{red } 3) = \frac{1}{6}$$

Find the probability of rolling an even number on the blue cube. Three of the six numbers are even.

$$P(\text{blue even}) = \frac{3}{6} = \frac{1}{2}$$

$$P(\text{red 3 and blue even}) = P(\text{red 3}) \cdot P(\text{blue even})$$

Substitute and then simplify.

$$= \frac{1}{6} \cdot \frac{1}{2} = \frac{1}{12}$$

The probability is $\frac{1}{12}$.

Think

Are the events independent?
Yes. The outcome of rolling one number cube does not affect the outcome of rolling another number cube.

 Got It? **2.** You roll a red number cube and a blue number cube. What is the probability that you roll a 5 on the red cube and a 1 or 2 on the blue cube?

 Problem 3 Selecting With Replacement

Games You choose a tile at random from the game tiles shown. You replace the first tile and then choose again. What is the probability that you choose a dotted tile and then a dragon tile?

Because you replace the first tile, the events are independent. Start by finding the probability of choosing a dotted tile. Then find the probability of choosing a dragon tile.

4 of the 15 tiles are dotted. $P(\text{dotted}) = \frac{4}{15}$

3 of the 15 tiles are dragons. $P(\text{dragon}) = \frac{3}{15} = \frac{1}{5}$

$$P(\text{dotted and dragon}) = P(\text{dotted}) \cdot P(\text{dragon})$$

Substitute. $= \frac{4}{15} \cdot \frac{1}{5}$

Simplify. $= \frac{4}{75}$

The probability that you will choose a dotted tile and then a dragon tile is $\frac{4}{75}$.

Plan

Why are the events independent when you select with replacement?
When you replace the tile, the conditions for the second selection are exactly the same as for the first selection.

 Got It? **3.** In Problem 3, what is the probability that you randomly choose a bird and then, after replacing the first tile, a flower?

Two events are **dependent events** if the occurrence of one event affects the probability of the second event. For example, suppose in Problem 3 that you do *not* replace the first tile before choosing another. This changes the set of possible outcomes for your second selection.

> ### Key Concept Probability of Two Dependent Events
>
> If A and B are dependent events, $P(A$ then $B) = P(A) \cdot P(B$ after $A)$.

Problem 4 Selecting Without Replacement

GRIDDED RESPONSE

Games Suppose you choose a tile at random from the tiles shown in Problem 3. Without replacing the first tile, you select a second tile. What is the probability that you choose a dotted tile and then a dragon tile?

Because you do not replace the first tile, the events are dependent.

Step 1 Find $P(A)$, where A is the event you choose a dotted tile.

Think

How is *P*(dragon after dotted) different from *P*(dragon)?
After selecting the first tile without replacement, there is one less tile to choose from for the second choice.

4 of the 15 tiles are dotted. $P(\text{dotted}) = \frac{4}{15}$

Step 2 Find $P(B$ after $A)$, where B is the event you choose a dragon tile.

3 of the 14 remaining tiles are dragons. $P(\text{dragon after dotted}) = \frac{3}{14}$

Step 3 Find $P(A$ then $B)$, which equals $P(A) \cdot P(B$ after $A)$.

$$P(\text{dotted then dragon}) = P(\text{dotted}) \cdot P(\text{dragon after dotted})$$

Substitute and then simplify. $= \frac{4}{15} \cdot \frac{3}{14} = \frac{2}{35}$

The probability that you will choose a dotted tile and then a dragon tile is $\frac{2}{35}$.

 Got It? **4.** In Problem 4, what is the probability that you will randomly choose a flower and then, without replacing the first tile, a bird?

 **Problem 5** **Finding the Probability of a Compound Event**

Essay Contest One freshman, 2 sophomores, 4 juniors, and 5 seniors receive top scores in a school essay contest. To choose which 2 students will read their essays at the town fair, 2 names are chosen at random from a hat. What is the probability that a junior and then a senior are chosen?

Know	**Need**	**Plan**
Grade levels of the 12 students	P(junior then senior)	Determine whether the events are dependent or independent and use the formula that applies.

The first outcome affects the probability of the second. So the events are dependent.

Step 1 Find $P(A)$, where A is the event they choose a junior.

4 of the 12 students are juniors. $P(\text{junior}) = \frac{4}{12} = \frac{1}{3}$

Step 2 Find $P(B \text{ after } A)$, where B is the event they choose a senior.

5 of the 11 remaining students are seniors. $P(\text{senior after junior}) = \frac{5}{11}$

Step 3 Find $P(A \text{ then } B)$, which equals $P(A) \cdot P(B \text{ after } A)$.

$$P(\text{junior then senior}) = P(\text{junior}) \cdot P(\text{senior after junior})$$

Substitute and then simplify. $= \frac{1}{3} \cdot \frac{5}{11} = \frac{5}{33}$

The probability that a junior and then a senior are chosen is $\frac{5}{33}$.

 Got It? **5.** In Problem 5, what is the probability that a senior and then a junior are chosen?

Focus Question How can you write the probability of a compound event as an expression involving probabilities of simpler events?

Answer Decide if the events are mutually exclusive or overlapping, or independent or dependent.

 Lesson Check

Do you know HOW?

Use the cards at the right.   **B** **1** **5** **D** **10**

1. You choose a card at random. What is $P(B \text{ or number})$?

2. You choose a card at random. What is $P(\text{yellow or letter})$?

3. What is the probability of choosing a yellow card and then a D if the first card *is not* replaced before the second card is drawn?

Do you UNDERSTAND?

4. Reasoning Are an event and its complement mutually exclusive or overlapping? Use an example to explain.

5. Error Analysis Describe and correct the error below in calculating $P(\text{yellow or letter})$ from Exercise 2.

$$P(\text{yellow or letter}) = P(\text{yellow}) \text{ or } P(\text{letter})$$
$$= \frac{3}{5} + \frac{2}{5}$$
$$= 1$$

Practice and Problem-Solving Exercises

A **Practice**

You spin the spinner, which is divided into equal sections. Find each probability.

See Problem 1.

Guided Practice

To start, separate *P*(red or more than 8) into two events.

6. *P*(red or more than 8)

P(red): spinner lands on 3, 4, 5, 6, or 7

P(more than 8): spinner lands on 9 or 10

Determine if the events are mutually exclusive or overlapping.

The spinner cannot land on a red section that is more than 8, so the events are mutually exclusive.

7. *P*(4 or 7) **8.** *P*(even or red) **9.** *P*(odd or 10)

10. *P*(red or less than 3) **11.** *P*(odd or multiple of 3) **12.** *P*(greater than 6 or blue)

You roll a blue number cube and a green number cube. Find each probability.

See Problem 2.

13. *P*(blue even and green even) **14.** *P*(blue and green both less than 6)

15. *P*(green less than 7 and blue 4) **16.** *P*(blue 1 or 2 and green 1)

You choose a tile at random from a bag containing 2 A's, 3 B's, and 4 C's. You replace the first tile in the bag and then choose again. Find each probability.

See Problem 3.

17. *P*(A and A) **18.** *P*(A and B) **19.** *P*(B and B) **20.** *P*(C and C)

You pick a coin at random from the set shown at the right and then pick a second coin without replacing the first. Find each probability.

See Problem 4.

21. *P*(dime then nickel) **22.** *P*(quarter then penny)

23. *P*(penny then dime) **24.** *P*(penny then quarter)

25. *P*(dime then dime) **26.** *P*(quarter then quarter)

27. Cafeteria Each day, you, Terry, and 3 other friends randomly choose one of 5 names from a hat to decide who throws away everyone's lunch trash. What is the probability that you are chosen on Monday and Terry is chosen on Tuesday?

See Problem 5.

28. Free Samples Samples of a new drink are handed out at random from a cooler holding 5 citrus drinks, 3 apple drinks, and 3 raspberry drinks. What is the probability that an apple drink and then a citrus drink are handed out?

Apply

Are the two events *dependent* or *independent*? Explain.

29. Toss a penny. Then toss a nickel.

30. Pick a ball from a basket of yellow and pink balls. Return the ball and pick again.

31. Think About a Plan An acre of land is chosen at random from each of the three states listed in the table at the right. What is the probability that all three acres will be farmland?
  - Does the choice of an acre from one state affect the choice from the other states?
  - How must you rewrite the percents to use a formula from this lesson?

Percent of State that is Farmland	
Alabama	27%
Florida	27%
Indiana	65%

32. Phone Poll A pollster conducts a survey by phone. The probability that a call does not result in a person taking this survey is 85%. What is the probability that the pollster makes 4 calls and none result in a person taking the survey?

33. Open-Ended Find the number of left-handed students and the number of right-handed students in your class. Suppose your teacher randomly selects one student to take attendance and then a different student to work on a problem on the board.
  a. What is the probability that both students are left-handed?
  b. What is the probability that both students are right-handed?
  c. What is the probability that the first student is right-handed and the second student is left-handed?

Standardized Test Prep

SAT/ACT

34. You take a three-question true-or-false quiz. You guess on all the questions. What is the probability that you will get a perfect score?

  Ⓐ 1　　　　Ⓑ $\frac{1}{2}$　　　　Ⓒ $\frac{1}{4}$　　　　Ⓓ $\frac{1}{8}$

Extended Response

35. A survey at your school is being taken to gather student input on the items offered by the cafeteria.
  a. Possible sampling methods are asking the nutrition club, asking the boys' wrestling team, and asking 5 students from each homeroom. Explain whether or not each sample could lead to biased results.
  b. Write a question designed to encourage respondents to favor more pizza. Then write another question about menu choices that is unbiased.

Mixed Review

You select a number at random from the integers 10 through 30, inclusive. Find each probability.

◀ See Lesson 12-7.

36. $P(\text{number is even})$

37. $P(\text{number is a multiple of 6})$

Simplify each complex fraction.

◀ See Lesson 11-2.

38. $\dfrac{12q + 10}{\dfrac{6q + 5}{11}}$

39. $\dfrac{\dfrac{3a + 2}{a^2 - 10a + 25}}{\dfrac{15a + 10}{a^2 - 25}}$

Pull It **All Together**

> To solve these problems you will pull together many concepts and skills that you have studied about data analysis and probability.

BIG idea Data Collection and Analysis

When you collect data, you should use a sampling technique free of bias. You can use standard measures to describe data sets and make estimates, decisions, or predictions.

BIG idea Data Representation

You can use matrices, frequency tables, histograms, box-and-whisker plots, tree diagrams, and other representations to describe different types of data sets.

Task 1

You are writing an article on gaming systems for your school newspaper. You take a survey of 250 people ages 13 to 18 and ask whether they have a home gaming system, a portable gaming system, or no gaming system. The results of your survey are shown in the matrix at the right.

	Age					
	13	14	15	16	17	18
Home gaming	12	22	26	32	24	26
Portable gaming	5	5	4	9	7	6
No gaming	18	12	8	6	12	16

a. Make a histogram that represents the number of students who have gaming systems, either home or portable. Is the histogram *uniform, symmetric,* or *skewed*?

b. What is another way you could have drawn the histogram in part (a)? Explain.

c. Display some or all of the data using a different representation. Explain your choice.

d. If a person needed to know as much specific data as possible, what kind of data display would you show the person? Why?

e. What is the experimental probability that the next person you survey does *not* have a gaming system?

BIG idea Probability

You can find theoretical and experimental probabilities to make decisions or predictions about future events.

Task 2

The Web site at the right shows the results of an online survey that asks, "Would you rather go on a beach vacation, a city vacation, or stay at home?"

a. Is the survey question biased? Why or why not?

b. Based on the survey, what are the odds that a person will want to stay at home for vacation?

c. Based on the survey, what is the probability that a person will travel for vacation?

Would you rather go on a beach vacation, a city vacation, or stay home?

☐ Beach ▸ 212

☐ City ▸ 120

☐ Home ▸ 113

Total Number of Votes **445**

CLOSE ✕

Connecting BIG ideas and Answering the Essential Questions

1. Data Collection and Analysis

When you collect data, you should use a sampling technique free of bias. You can use standard measures to describe data sets and make estimates, decisions, or predictions.

Data Analysis (Lessons 12-3 and 12-4)

11 12 14 16 11 10 13 7

Mean: 11.75   Median: 11.5

Mode: 11   Range: 9

Samples and Surveys (Lesson 12-5)

Data Types: qualitative, quantitative, univariate, bivariate

Sample Types: random, systematic, stratified

2. Data Representation

You can use matrices, frequency tables, histograms, box-and-whisker plots, tree diagrams, and other representations to describe different types of data sets.

Data Displays (Lessons 12-1, 12-2, 12-4, and 12-6)

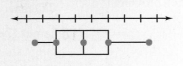

3. Probability

You can find theoretical and experimental probabilities to make decisions or predictions about future events.

Theoretical and Experimental Probability (Lesson 12-7)

Theoretical: $\dfrac{\text{number of favorable outcomes}}{\text{number of possible outcomes}}$

Experimental: $\dfrac{\text{number of times event occurs}}{\text{number of times experiment is done}}$

Probability of Compound Events (Lesson 12-8)

Independent:

$P(A \text{ and } B) = P(A) \cdot P(B)$

Dependent:

$P(A \text{ then } B) = P(A) \cdot P(B \text{ after } A)$

Chapter Vocabulary

- combination (p. 753)
- complement of an event (p. 758)
- compound event (p. 765)
- dependent events (p. 768)
- event (p. 757)
- experimental probability (p. 760)
- independent events (p. 766)
- mutually exclusive event (p. 765)
- *n* factorial (p. 752)
- odds (p. 759)
- outcome (p. 757)
- overlapping events (p. 765)
- permutation (p. 752)
- probability (p. 757)
- sample space (p.757)
- theoretical probability (p. 758)

Choose the correct term to complete each sentence.

1. A ? is a selection of objects without regard to order.

2. Two events are ? if the occurrence of one event does not affect the probability of the second event.

3. The ? of an event tells you how likely it is that the event will occur.

12-6 Permutations and Combinations

Quick Review

If there are m ways to make a first selection and n ways to make a second selection, then there are $m \cdot n$ ways to make the two selections.

A **permutation** is an arrangement of objects in a specific order. The number of permutations of n objects arranged r at a time, $_nP_r$, equals $\frac{n!}{(n-r)!}$.

A **combination** is a selection of objects without regard to order. The number of combinations of n objects chosen r at a time, $_nC_r$, equals $\frac{n!}{r!(n-r)!}$.

Example

In how many ways can you choose 3 people to serve on a committee out of a group of 7 volunteers?

The order does not matter, so this is a combination problem.

Write using factorials. $\quad _7C_3 = \dfrac{7!}{3!(7-3)!} = \dfrac{7!}{3!4!}$

Write the factorials as products. $\quad = \dfrac{7 \cdot 6 \cdot 5 \cdot 4 \cdot 3 \cdot 2 \cdot 1}{(3 \cdot 2 \cdot 1)(4 \cdot 3 \cdot 2 \cdot 1)}$

Simplify. $\quad\quad\quad\quad\quad\quad = 35$

There are 35 ways to choose 3 people out of a group of 7.

Exercises

Find the number of permutations.

4. $_9P_5$ 5. $_3P_2$

6. $_8P_3$ 7. $_5P_2$

8. $_6P_4$ 9. $_7P_2$

Find the number of combinations.

10. $_8C_2$ 11. $_9C_4$

12. $_5C_3$ 13. $_6C_3$

14. $_7C_3$ 15. $_5C_4$

16. **Side Dishes** You can choose any 2 of the following side dishes with your dinner: mashed potatoes, cole slaw, french fries, applesauce, or rice. How many different combinations of side dishes can you choose?

17. **Talent Show** There are 8 groups participating in a talent show. In how many different orders can the groups perform?

18. **Clothing** You have 6 shirts, 7 pairs of pants, and 3 pairs of shoes. How many different outfits can you wear?

12-7 Theoretical and Experimental Probability

Quick Review

An **event** is an **outcome** or group of outcomes. The **probability** of an event, which indicates how likely it is to occur, is written $P(\text{event})$. When all possible outcomes are equally likely, the **theoretical probability** of an event is given by $P(\text{event}) = \frac{\text{number of favorable outcomes}}{\text{number of possible outcomes}}$.

Example

What is the theoretical probability that a randomly chosen date is a day beginning with a T?

There are 2 favorable outcomes, Tuesday and Thursday.

There are 7 possible outcomes, the 7 days of the week.

$$P(\text{day beginning with a T}) = \frac{\text{number of favorable outcomes}}{\text{number of possible outcomes}}$$
$$= \frac{2}{7}$$

The probability of a day beginning with a T is $\frac{2}{7}$.

Exercises

The spinner at the right is divided into six equal sections. Find the theoretical probability of landing on the given sections of the spinner.

19. $P(\text{even})$

20. $P(\text{odd})$

21. $P(5)$

22. $P(\text{not } 3)$

23. $P(7)$

24. $P(\text{more than } 4)$

25. Apples An apple farmer finds that he has to throw out 15 bad apples from the 225 he has picked. What is the experimental probability that the next apple he picks will be good?

12-8 Probability of Compound Events

Quick Review

You can use a formula to find the probability of a **compound event** involving two events A and B.

Mutually exclusive events: $P(A \text{ or } B) = P(A) + P(B)$

Overlapping events:
$P(A \text{ or } B) = P(A) + P(B) - P(A \text{ and } B)$

Independent events: $P(A \text{ and } B) = P(A) \cdot P(B)$

Dependent events: $P(A \text{ then } B) = P(A) \cdot P(B \text{ after } A)$

Example

You roll a number cube and flip a coin. What is the probability that you roll a 5 and the coin comes up heads?

Rolling a 5 and flipping heads are independent events.

$P(5 \text{ and heads}) = P(5) \cdot P(\text{heads}) = \frac{1}{6} \cdot \frac{1}{2} = \frac{1}{12}$

The probability of rolling a 5 and flipping heads is $\frac{1}{12}$.

Exercises

You randomly pick two marbles from a bag containing 3 yellow marbles and 4 red marbles. You pick the second marble without replacing the first marble. Find each probability.

26. $P(\text{red then red})$

27. $P(\text{yellow then red})$

You roll a number cube twice. Find each probability.

28. $P(6 \text{ then } 3)$

29. $P(\text{odd then even})$

Are the two events *dependent* or *independent*? Explain.

30. You pick one of 7 names from a hat and then pick a second name without replacing the first one.

31. You spin a spinner with 5 equal sections and pick a marble from a bag containing 2 green marbles and 4 blue marbles.

Do you know HOW?

Simplify.

1. $\begin{bmatrix} 0 & -3 \\ 2 & 0 \\ 1 & -1 \end{bmatrix} - \begin{bmatrix} 2 & 0 \\ -1 & 1 \\ -2 & 3 \end{bmatrix}$

2. $-3\begin{bmatrix} 1 & 2 & -1 \\ 0 & -2 & 3 \\ -3 & 1 & 0 \end{bmatrix}$

Tell whether each histogram is *uniform*, *symmetric*, or *skewed*.

3.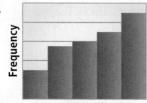
Frequency
Interval

4.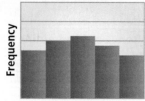
Frequency
Interval

5. **Landscaping** The hours a gardener worked over the past 14 weeks are listed below. What are the mean, median, mode, and range of the hours the gardener worked? Which measure of central tendency best describes the data?

   39 52 41 44 47 36 51 44 50 40 53 46 44 35

6. Identify the minimum, first quartile, median, third quartile, and maximum of the data set. Then make a box-and-whisker plot of the data set.

   Test scores: 87 52 91 66 79 56 73 90 78 51 83

7. Out of 10 dogs, 4 weigh no more than 12.5 kg. What is the percentile rank of the weight 12.5 kg?

8. **Cafeteria** A teacher asks a student chosen at random from each table in the cafeteria for his or her opinion of school food. Will this survey method give a good sample? Explain.

9. **Security** Suppose a password contains 4 lowercase letters. How many permutations are possible if no letters are repeated?

The spinner at the right is divided into four equal sections. Find the theoretical probability of landing on the given section(s) of the spinner.

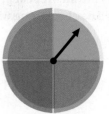

10. $P(\text{red})$

11. $P(\text{not green})$

12. Suppose you choose a marble at random from a bag containing 3 blue, 5 yellow, and 7 red marbles. You choose a second marble without replacing the first. What is the probability of choosing 2 blue marbles?

Do you UNDERSTAND?

13. **Reasoning** Could a student use the formula $P(A \text{ or } B) = P(A) + P(B) - P(A \text{ and } B)$ to solve a problem about mutually exclusive events and get the correct answer? Explain.

14. **Open-Ended** Give examples of univariate and bivariate data. How do these types of data differ?

15. **Reasoning** Is it possible for r to be greater than n in $_nC_r$? Explain.

End-of-Course Assessment
to Prepare for the Algebra I ADP End-of-Course Exam

The following items should be completed *without* a calculator. For multiple choice questions, write the letter of the correct answer on your paper. For all other questions, show your work and clearly explain your answer.

1. Which equation represents a line with a greater slope and lesser y-intercept than the line shown?

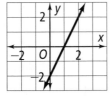

- Ⓐ $y = x - 1$
- Ⓑ $y = -x - 1$
- Ⓒ $y = -2x - 2$
- Ⓓ $y = 3x - 3$

2. Which expression is equivalent to $3(x^2 + 1) - 5x(x^2 + x + 1)$?

- Ⓐ $-5x^3 + 8x^2 + 5x + 3$
- Ⓑ $-5x^3 - 2x^2 - 5x + 3$
- Ⓒ $-10x^3 + x^2 - 7x + 6$
- Ⓓ $5x^3 - 2x^2 - 5x + 3$

3. You roll a pair of number cubes. What is the probability of rolling odd numbers on both cubes?

- Ⓐ $\frac{1}{12}$
- Ⓑ $\frac{1}{6}$
- Ⓒ $\frac{1}{4}$
- Ⓓ $\frac{2}{3}$

4. What is the greatest value in the range of $f(x) = x^2 - 3$ for the domain $\{-3, 0, 1, 2\}$?

- Ⓐ -3
- Ⓒ 2
- Ⓑ 0
- Ⓓ 6

5. Which equation best represents the graph at the right?

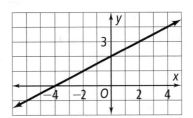

- Ⓐ $y = x^2$
- Ⓑ $y = -x^2$
- Ⓒ $y = x^2 - 2$
- Ⓓ $y = x^2 + 2$

6. Which table models the graph shown below?

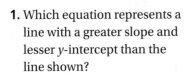

Ⓐ

x	−2	0	1	4
y	1	2	3	4

Ⓑ

x	−6	−3	0	6
y	−1	0.5	2	5

Ⓒ

x	−1	0	3	4
y	−6	−4	2	4

Ⓓ

x	0	0.5	1	2
y	−4	−3	−2	0

7. Which of the graphs below represents the solution set of $-3 < x + 3 \le 7$?

Ⓐ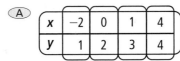

Ⓑ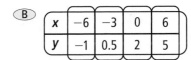

Ⓒ

Ⓓ

8. Consider the graph shown below. Which statement is always a correct conclusion about the coordinates of the points on the graph?

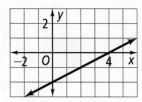

- Ⓐ The x-values are always 2 less than the y-values.
- Ⓑ The y-values are always 4 more than the x-values.
- Ⓒ For positive values of x, the x-values are always greater than the y-values.
- Ⓓ For positive values of x, the y-values are always greater than the x-values.

9. Which expression is equivalent to $\frac{4x^2 - 9}{6x^2 + 9x}$?

- Ⓐ $\frac{2x - 3}{x + 3}$
- Ⓑ $\frac{2}{3 + x}$
- Ⓒ $\frac{2x + 3}{3x}$
- Ⓓ $\frac{2x - 3}{3x}$

10. Which ordered pair is a solution of the given system?

$$2x + 5y = -11$$
$$10x + 3y = 11$$

- Ⓐ $(3, -2)$
- Ⓒ $(-2, 3)$
- Ⓑ $(-3, 2)$
- Ⓓ $(2, -3)$

11. What is the slope-intercept form of the equation $-3x + 4y = 8$?

- Ⓐ $y = 3x + 2$
- Ⓑ $y = 3x + 8$
- Ⓒ $y = \frac{3}{4}x + 2$
- Ⓓ $y = -\frac{3}{4}x + 2$

12. What is the y-coordinate of the vertex of the function $y = 2x^2 + 5x - 8$?

13. Lisa is driving a car at an average speed of 55 mi/h.
- **a.** What is Lisa's average speed in feet per second?
- **b.** How many feet will Lisa travel in 40 min?

14. What is a linear inequality that describes the graph below?

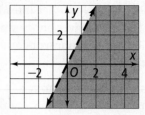

- Ⓐ $y \leq 2x$
- Ⓒ $y > 2x$
- Ⓑ $y < 2x$
- Ⓓ $y \geq 2x$

15. What equation do you get when you solve $2x^2y - 4y = -24$ for y?

- Ⓐ $y = -\frac{12}{x^2 - 2}$
- Ⓑ $y = \frac{12}{x^2 + 2}$
- Ⓒ $y = \frac{12}{x^2 - 2}$
- Ⓓ $y = -x^2 - 22$

16. What is the minimum point of the parabola graphed below?

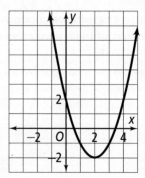

- Ⓐ $(-2, 2)$
- Ⓑ $(2, -2)$
- Ⓒ $(0, 2)$
- Ⓓ There is no minimum.

17. What is the graph of the given system of equations?

$2x + y = -3$
$-x + y = -1$

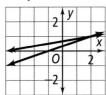 **A**

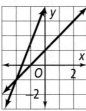 **C**

 B

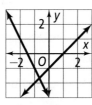 **D**

18. What is the simplified form of $\sqrt{27n^3}$?

- **A** $3n\sqrt{3n^2}$
- **B** $3n\sqrt{3n}$
- **C** $3n^2\sqrt{3n}$
- **D** $3n^2\sqrt{3}$

19. What is the vertex of the parabola graphed below?

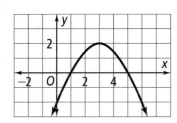

- **A** $(0, -1)$
- **C** $(3, 2)$
- **B** $(1, 0)$
- **D** $(5, 0)$

20. A line passes through the point $(-3, -2)$ and has slope 2. What is an equation of the line?

- **A** $y = 2x - 0.5$
- **B** $y = 2x + 0.5$
- **C** $y = 2x + 1$
- **D** $y = 2x + 4$

21. What equation describes a line that is parallel to the line below and passes through the point $(-2, 1)$?

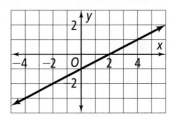

- **A** $y = 2x + 2$
- **B** $y = \frac{1}{2}x + 2$
- **C** $y = \frac{1}{2}x + 1$
- **D** $y = 2x + 3$

22. What is an equation of the axis of symmetry for the graph of the function $f(x) = 2x^2 + 4x - 5$?

- **A** $x = -1$
- **B** $x = 1$
- **C** $x = -2$
- **D** $x = 2$

23. The box-and-whisker plots below show the points scored by two college football teams in games over the course of one season. What do the medians tell you about each team's points per game?

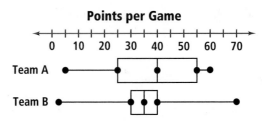

24. What is the solution of the equation
$\frac{4x + 3}{3} - \frac{2x - 1}{2} = 3$?

- **A** 0
- **B** 4.5
- **C** 7
- **D** 8

A calculator may be used for the following questions. For multiple choice questions, write the letter of the correct answer on your paper. For all other questions, show your work and clearly explain your answer.

25. The width of a rectangle is 10 in. less than its length. If the perimeter of the rectangle is 36 in., what is its width in inches?

26. Erin surveyed 256 people to find out what type of bread they prefer. Her results are shown in the table below. Based on her data, which statement is true?

Bread Preference

Type of Bread	Percent
Wheat	32
Whole grain	26
White	20
Rye	22

Ⓐ Exactly 26 people prefer whole grain.

Ⓑ More than half of the people prefer white or rye.

Ⓒ About 80 people prefer wheat.

Ⓓ About $\frac{1}{20}$ of the people prefer white.

27. Is the question "Do you prefer delicious steak or ordinary meatloaf for dinner?" biased? Explain.

28. What are the solutions of the equation $3x^2 + 11x - 4 = 0$?

Ⓐ $\frac{1}{3}, 4$

Ⓑ $\frac{1}{3}, -4$

Ⓒ $-\frac{1}{3}, 4$

Ⓓ $3, -4$

29. Which is NOT a rational number?

Ⓐ 4

Ⓑ $\sqrt{25}$

Ⓒ $6.\overline{3}$

Ⓓ $\sqrt{35}$

30. How does the mean of the data set below change if each value is increased by 8?
105 110 104 107 102 106 133 81

Ⓐ The mean increases by 1.

Ⓑ The mean increases by 8.

Ⓒ The mean decreases by 8.

Ⓓ The mean does not change.

31. What is $(2x^2 - 4x + 8) - (3x^2 + 10x + 2)$?

Ⓐ $-x^2 - 14x - 6$

Ⓑ $-x^2 + 6x + 6$

Ⓒ $-x^2 - 14x + 6$

Ⓓ $5x^2 + 6x + 10$

32. What is the simplified form of $\sqrt{32} + \sqrt{50}$?

Ⓐ $\sqrt{82}$

Ⓑ $9\sqrt{2}$

Ⓒ $8\sqrt{4} + 10\sqrt{5}$

Ⓓ $2\sqrt{8} + 5\sqrt{2}$

33. An airplane flies 500 mi/h in still air. Flying with the jet stream, the plane travels 1200 mi from City A to City B. The plane then returns to City A, flying against the jet stream. The round-trip flight time is 5 h. What is the speed of the jet stream in miles per hour?

Ⓐ 25 mi/h

Ⓑ 100 mi/h

Ⓒ 150 mi/h

Ⓓ 223 mi/h

34. A new toy store is opening next week, and the owner is deciding how to price one of the toys. The equation $S = -32p^2 + 960p$ predicts the totals sales S as a function of the toy's price p, where S and p are in dollars. What price will produce the highest total sales?

Ⓐ $12

Ⓑ $15

Ⓒ $30

Ⓓ $32

35. Which of the following is the solution set for the equation $|p - 2| = 7$?

A $\{-5, 9\}$

B $\{-9, 9\}$

C $\{-5\}$

D $\{9\}$

36. Natalia spent $153 of her savings at the mall. She bought clothes, a few paperback novels, and an $18 DVD. She spent 4 times as much on clothes as she did on the paperbacks.

  a. Write an equation that can be used to determine how much money Natalia spent on the paperback novels.

  b. Use the equation to determine how much Natalia spent on paperbacks.

37. Keysha randomly surveyed 150 people at a football game last weekend to find out whether they like hot dogs, hamburgers, or nachos. She recorded her results in the Venn diagram below. Of the 850 people at the game, how many should she expect to like both hot dogs and hamburgers?

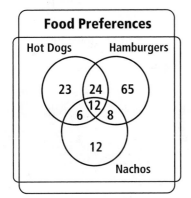

Food Preferences

Hot Dogs   Hamburgers

23   24   65

12

6   8

12

Nachos

A 204

B 281

C 306

D 782

38. What is the simplified form of $\dfrac{5x^2y^3}{3x^3y^4}$?

A $\dfrac{5x^5y^7}{3}$

B $\dfrac{5}{3xy}$

C $\dfrac{5x^2y^3}{3x^3y^4}$

D $\dfrac{5y^7}{3x^5}$

39. Line p passes through points $(5, -4)$ and $(2, 7)$. What is the slope of a line that is perpendicular to line p?

A $-\dfrac{11}{3}$

B $-\dfrac{3}{11}$

C $\dfrac{3}{11}$

D $\dfrac{11}{3}$

40. Which of the following is an equation of a reasonable trend line for the scatter plot shown?

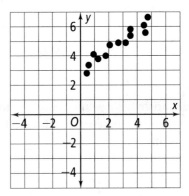

A $y = \dfrac{1}{3}x + 8$

B $y = \dfrac{2}{3}x + 3$

C $y = \dfrac{1}{2}x - 3$

D $y = 3x + 3$

41. The sides of a square are all increased by 2 in. The area of the new square is 49 in.^{2}. What is the length of a side of the original square?

- Ⓐ 2 in.
- Ⓑ 4.5 in.
- Ⓒ 5 in.
- Ⓓ 9 in.

42. Which of the following sets of points does NOT represent a function?

- Ⓐ $\{(-2, 0), (-1, 1), (0, 4), (1, -2), (2, -6)\}$
- Ⓑ $\{(-5, 0), (-4, 0), (-3, 0), (-2, 0), (-1, 0)\}$
- Ⓒ $\{(0, 1), (1, 10), (1, 100), (10, 100), (100, 1000)\}$
- Ⓓ $\{(2, 4), (3, 9), (4, 16), (5, 25), (6, 36)\}$

43. How do you write $\dfrac{8x^2y^{-3}z^2}{10x^{-1}y^2z}$ using only positive exponents?

- Ⓐ $\dfrac{4xyz}{5}$

- Ⓑ $\dfrac{4x^3}{5yz}$

- Ⓒ $\dfrac{4x^3z}{5y^5}$

- Ⓓ $\dfrac{4xz}{5y}$

44. A rectangular prism has a volume of $6x^4 - 13x^3 - 5x^2$. What expressions can represent the dimensions of the prism? Use factoring.

45. Lucia has 8 shirts, 4 sweaters, and 5 jackets. How many different outfits can she make using one item from each category?

- Ⓐ 17
- Ⓑ 40
- Ⓒ 160
- Ⓓ 185

46. Ricardo's art class is making a tile mosaic using similar right triangles.

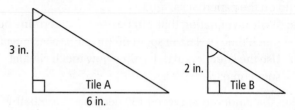

Tile A and Tile B are similar. What is the area of Tile B?

- Ⓐ 4 in.^{2}
- Ⓑ 5 in.^{2}
- Ⓒ 6 in.^{2}
- Ⓓ 12 in.^{2}

47. What type of histogram is shown below?

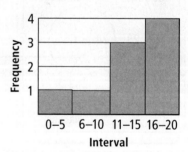

- Ⓐ skewed
- Ⓑ uniform
- Ⓒ symmetric
- Ⓓ none of these

Skills **Handbook**

Prime Numbers and Composite Numbers

A prime number is a whole number greater than 1 that has exactly two factors, the number 1 and itself.

Prime number	2	5	17	29
Factors	1, 2	1, 5	1, 17	1, 29

A composite number is a number that has more than two factors. The number 1 is neither prime nor composite.

Composite number	6	15	48
Factors	1, 2, 3, 6	1, 3, 5, 15	1, 2, 3, 4, 6, 8, 12, 16, 24, 48

Example 1

Is 51 prime or composite?

$51 = 3 \cdot 17$ Try to find factors other than 1 and 51.

51 is a composite number.

You can use a factor tree to find the prime factors of a number. When all the factors are prime numbers, it is called the prime factorization of the number.

Example 2

Use a factor tree to write the prime factorization of 28.

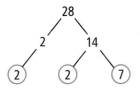 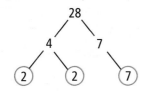

The order of listing the factors may be different, but the prime factorization is the same.

The prime factorization of 28 is $2 \cdot 2 \cdot 7$.

Exercises

Is each number prime or composite?

1. 9	**2.** 16	**3.** 34	**4.** 61	**5.** 7	**6.** 13
7. 12	**8.** 40	**9.** 57	**10.** 64	**11.** 120	**12.** 700

List all the factors of each number.

13. 46	**14.** 32	**15.** 11	**16.** 65	**17.** 27	**18.** 29

Use a factor tree to write the prime factorization of each number.

19. 18	**20.** 20	**21.** 27	**22.** 54	**23.** 64	**24.** 96

Factors and Multiples

Skills Handbook

A common factor is a number that is a factor of two or more numbers. The greatest common factor (GCF) is the greatest number that is a common factor of two or more numbers.

Example 1

Find the GCF of 24 and 64.

Method 1 List all the factors of each number.

Factors of 24   1, 2, 3, 4, 6, 8, 12, 24   Find the common factors: 1, 2, 4, 8.

Factors of 64   1, 2, 4, 8, 16, 32, 64   The greatest common factor is 8.

The GCF of 24 and 64 is 8.

Method 2 Use the prime factorization of each number.

$24 = 2 \cdot 2 \cdot 2 \cdot 3$ Find the prime factorization of each number.

$64 = 2 \cdot 2 \cdot 2 \cdot 2 \cdot 2 \cdot 2$

$GCF = 2 \cdot 2 \cdot 2 = 8$ The product of the common prime factors is the GCF.

A common multiple is a number that is a multiple of two or more numbers. The least common multiple (LCM) is the least number that is a common multiple of two or more numbers.

Example 2

Find the LCM of 12 and 18.

Method 1 List the multiples of each number.

Multiples of 12   12, 24, 36, . . .   List the multiples of each number until you find

Multiples of 18   18, 36, . . .   the first common multiple.

The LCM of 12 and 18 is 36.

Method 2 Use the prime factorization of each number.

$12 = 2 \cdot 2 \cdot 3$

$18 = 2 \cdot 3 \cdot 3$

$LCM = 2 \cdot 2 \cdot 3 \cdot 3 = 36$ Use each prime factor the greatest number of times it appears in either number.

Exercises

Find the GCF of each set of numbers.

1. 12 and 22   **2.** 7 and 21   **3.** 24 and 48   **4.** 42, 63, and 105

Find the LCM of each set of numbers.

5. 16 and 20   **6.** 14 and 21   **7.** 11 and 33   **8.** 6, 7, and 12

Using Estimation

To make sure the answer to a problem is reasonable, you can estimate before you calculate. If the answer is close to your estimate, the answer is probably correct.

Example 1

Estimate to find whether each calculation is correct.

a. Calculation   **Estimate**

$126.91	≈	$130
$14.05	≈	$10
+$25.14	≈	+$30
$266.10		$170

The answer is not close to the estimate. It is not reasonable. The calculation is incorrect.

b. Calculation   **Estimate**

372.85	≈	370
−227.31	≈	−230
145.54		140

The answer is close to the estimate. It is reasonable. The calculation is correct.

For some situations, like estimating a grocery bill, you may not need an exact answer. A *front-end estimate* will give you a good estimate that is usually closer to the exact answer than an estimate you would get by rounding alone. Add the front-end digits, estimate the sum of the remaining digits by rounding, and then combine sums.

Example 2

Tomatoes cost $3.54, squash costs $2.75, and lemons cost $1.20. Estimate the total cost of the produce.

Add the	3.54	→	0.50	Estimate by rounding. Then add.
front-end digits.	2.75	→	0.80	
	+1.20	→	+0.20	
	6		1.50	

Since 6 + 1.50 = 7.50, the total cost is about $7.50.

Exercises

Estimate by rounding.

1. the sum of $15.70, $49.62, and $278.01

2. 563 − 125

3. the sum of $163.90, $107.21, and $33.56

4. 824 − 467

Use front-end estimation to find each sum or difference.

5. $1.65 + $5.42 + $9.89

6. 1.369 + 7.421 + 2.700

7. 9.563 − 2.480

8. 1.17 + 3.92 + 2.26

9. 8.611 − 1.584

10. $2.52 + $3.04 + $5.25

11. Ticket prices at an amusement park cost $11.25 for adults and $6.50 for children under 12. Estimate the cost for three children and one adult.

Simplifying Fractions

Skills Handbook

A fraction can name a part of a group or region. The region below is divided into 10 equal parts and 6 of the equal parts are shaded.

$$\frac{6}{10} \begin{array}{l} \leftarrow \text{Numerator} \\ \leftarrow \text{Denominator} \end{array} \quad \text{Read as "six tenths."}$$

Two fractions that represent the same value are called equivalent fractions. You can find a fraction that is equivalent to a given fraction by multiplying the numerator and the denominator of the given fraction by the same nonzero number.

Example 1

Write five fractions that are equivalent to $\frac{3}{5}$.

$$\frac{3}{5} = \frac{3 \cdot 2}{5 \cdot 2} = \frac{6}{10} \qquad \frac{3}{5} = \frac{3 \cdot 3}{5 \cdot 3} = \frac{9}{15} \qquad \frac{3}{5} = \frac{3 \cdot 4}{5 \cdot 4} = \frac{12}{20} \qquad \frac{3}{5} = \frac{3 \cdot 5}{5 \cdot 5} = \frac{15}{25} \qquad \frac{3}{5} = \frac{3 \cdot 6}{5 \cdot 6} = \frac{18}{30}$$

The fraction $\frac{3}{5}$ is in simplest form because its numerator and denominator are relatively prime, which means their only common factor is 1. To write a fraction in simplest form, divide its numerator and its denominator by their greatest common factor (GCF).

Example 2

Write $\frac{6}{24}$ in simplest form.

Step 1 Find the GCF of 6 and 24.

$$6 = 2 \cdot 3 \qquad\qquad \text{Multiply the common prime factors, 2 and 3.}$$
$$24 = 2 \cdot 2 \cdot 2 \cdot 3 \qquad \text{GCF} = 2 \cdot 3 = 6.$$

Step 2 Divide the numerator and the denominator of $\frac{6}{24}$ by the GCF, 6.

$$\frac{6}{24} = \frac{6 \div 6}{24 \div 6} = \frac{1}{4} \qquad \text{Simplify.}$$

Exercises

Write five fractions that are equivalent to each fraction.

1. $\frac{4}{7}$ **2.** $\frac{9}{16}$ **3.** $\frac{3}{8}$ **4.** $\frac{8}{17}$ **5.** $\frac{5}{6}$ **6.** $\frac{7}{10}$

Complete each statement.

7. $\frac{3}{7} = \frac{\blacksquare}{21}$ **8.** $\frac{5}{8} = \frac{20}{\blacksquare}$ **9.** $\frac{11}{12} = \frac{44}{\blacksquare}$ **10.** $\frac{12}{16} = \frac{\blacksquare}{4}$ **11.** $\frac{50}{100} = \frac{1}{\blacksquare}$

Is each fraction in simplest form? If not, write the fraction in simplest form.

12. $\frac{4}{12}$ **13.** $\frac{3}{16}$ **14.** $\frac{5}{30}$ **15.** $\frac{9}{72}$ **16.** $\frac{11}{22}$ **17.** $\frac{24}{25}$

Write each fraction in simplest form.

18. $\frac{8}{16}$ **19.** $\frac{7}{14}$ **20.** $\frac{6}{9}$ **21.** $\frac{20}{30}$ **22.** $\frac{8}{20}$ **23.** $\frac{12}{40}$

Fractions and Decimals

You can write a fraction as a decimal.

Example 1

Write $\frac{3}{5}$ as a decimal.

$$5\overline{)3.0}^{\,0.6}$$ Divide the numerator by the denominator.

So $\frac{3}{5} = 0.6$.

You can write a decimal as a fraction.

Example 2

Write 0.38 as a fraction.

$0.38 = 38$ hundredths $= \frac{38}{100} = \frac{19}{50}$

Some fractions can be written as decimals that repeat, but do not end.

Example 3

Write $\frac{3}{11}$ as a decimal.

Divide the numerator by the denominator, as shown at the right. The remainders 8 and 3 keep repeating. Therefore 2 and 7 will keep repeating in the quotient.

$\frac{3}{11} = 0.2727\ldots = 0.\overline{27}$

$$
\begin{array}{r}
0.2727\ldots \\
11\overline{)3.0000\ldots} \\
2.2 \\
\hline
80 \\
77 \\
\hline
30 \\
22 \\
\hline
80 \\
77 \\
\hline
3
\end{array}
$$

You can write a repeating decimal as a fraction.

Example 4

Write 0.363636 . . . as a fraction.

Let $x = 0.363636\ldots$

$\qquad 100x = 36.36363636\ldots$ When 2 digits repeat, multiply by 100.

$\qquad 99x = 36$ Subtract $x = 0.363636$.

$\qquad x = \frac{36}{99}$, or $\frac{4}{11}$ Divide each side by 99.

Exercises

Write each fraction or mixed number as a decimal.

1. $\frac{3}{10}$ **2.** $\frac{13}{12}$ **3.** $\frac{4}{20}$ **4.** $\frac{25}{75}$ **5.** $\frac{5}{7}$ **6.** $4\frac{3}{25}$

Write each decimal as a fraction in simplest form.

7. 0.07   **8.** 0.25   **9.** 0.875   **10.** 0.4545   **11.** 6.333   **12.** 7.2626

Adding and Subtracting Fractions

You can add and subtract fractions when they have the same denominator. Fractions with the same denominator are called like fractions.

Example 1

a. Add $\frac{4}{5} + \frac{3}{5}$.

$$\frac{4}{5} + \frac{3}{5} = \frac{4 + 3}{5} = \frac{7}{5} = 1\frac{2}{5} \quad \leftarrow \quad \text{Add or subtract the numerators and keep the same denominator.}$$

b. Subtract $\frac{5}{9} - \frac{2}{9}$.

$$\rightarrow \quad \frac{5}{9} - \frac{2}{9} = \frac{5 - 2}{9} = \frac{3}{9} = \frac{1}{3}$$

Fractions with unlike denominators are called unlike fractions. To add or subtract unlike fractions, find the least common denominator (LCD) and write equivalent fractions with the same denominator. Then add or subtract the like fractions.

Example 2

Add $\frac{3}{4} + \frac{5}{6}$.

$$\frac{3}{4} + \frac{5}{6} = \frac{9}{12} + \frac{10}{12}$$

Find the LCD. The LCD is the least common multiple (LCM) of the denominators. The LCD of 4 and 6 is 12. Write equivalent fractions.

$$= \frac{9 + 10}{12} = \frac{19}{12}, \text{ or } 1\frac{7}{12}$$

Add like fractions and simplify.

To add or subtract mixed numbers, add or subtract the fractions. Then add or subtract the whole numbers. Sometimes when subtracting mixed numbers you have to regroup so that you can subtract the fractions.

Example 3

Subtract $5\frac{1}{4} - 3\frac{2}{3}$.

$$5\frac{1}{4} - 3\frac{2}{3} = 5\frac{3}{12} - 3\frac{8}{12}$$

Write equivalent fractions with the same denominator.

$$= 4\frac{15}{12} - 3\frac{8}{12}$$

Write $5\frac{3}{12}$ as $4\frac{15}{12}$ so you can subtract the fractions.

$$= 1\frac{7}{12}$$

Subtract the fractions. Then subtract the whole numbers.

Exercises

Add or subtract. Write each answer in simplest form.

1. $\frac{2}{7} + \frac{3}{7}$

2. $\frac{3}{8} + \frac{7}{8}$

3. $\frac{6}{5} + \frac{9}{5}$

4. $\frac{4}{9} + \frac{8}{9}$

5. $6\frac{2}{3} + 3\frac{4}{5}$

6. $1\frac{4}{7} + 2\frac{3}{14}$

7. $4\frac{5}{6} + 1\frac{7}{18}$

8. $2\frac{4}{5} + 3\frac{6}{7}$

9. $4\frac{2}{3} + 1\frac{6}{11}$

10. $3\frac{7}{9} + 5\frac{4}{11}$

11. $8 + 1\frac{2}{3}$

12. $8\frac{1}{5} + 3\frac{3}{4}$

13. $11\frac{3}{8} + 2\frac{1}{16}$

14. $\frac{7}{8} - \frac{3}{8}$

15. $\frac{9}{10} - \frac{3}{10}$

16. $\frac{17}{5} - \frac{2}{5}$

17. $\frac{11}{7} - \frac{2}{7}$

18. $\frac{5}{11} - \frac{4}{11}$

19. $8\frac{5}{8} - 6\frac{1}{4}$

20. $3\frac{2}{3} - 1\frac{8}{9}$

21. $8\frac{5}{6} - 5\frac{1}{2}$

22. $12\frac{3}{4} - 4\frac{5}{6}$

23. $17\frac{2}{7} - 8\frac{2}{9}$

24. $7\frac{3}{4} - 3\frac{3}{8}$

25. $4\frac{1}{12} - 1\frac{11}{12}$

Multiplying and Dividing Fractions

To multiply two or more fractions, multiply the numerators, multiply the denominators, and simplify the product, if necessary.

Example 1

Multiply $\frac{3}{7} \cdot \frac{5}{6}$.

Method 1 Multiply the numerators and the denominators. Then simplify.

$$\frac{3}{7} \cdot \frac{5}{6} = \frac{3 \cdot 5}{7 \cdot 6} = \frac{15}{42} = \frac{15 \div 3}{42 \div 3} = \frac{5}{14}$$

Method 2 Simplify before multiplying.

$$\frac{{}^{1}3}{7} \cdot \frac{5}{6\,{}_{2}} = \frac{1 \cdot 5}{7 \cdot 2} = \frac{5}{14}$$

To multiply mixed numbers, change the mixed numbers to improper fractions and multiply the fractions. Write the product as a mixed number.

Example 2

Multiply $2\frac{4}{5} \cdot 1\frac{2}{3}$.

$$2\frac{4}{5} \cdot 1\frac{2}{3} = \frac{14}{5} \cdot \frac{5\,{}^{1}}{3} = \frac{14}{3} = 4\frac{2}{3}$$

To divide fractions, change the division problem to a multiplication problem. Remember that $8 \div \frac{1}{4}$ is the same as $8 \cdot 4$. To divide mixed numbers, change the mixed numbers to improper fractions and divide the fractions.

Example 3

a. Divide $\frac{4}{5} \div \frac{3}{7}$.

$$\frac{4}{5} \div \frac{3}{7} = \frac{4}{5} \cdot \frac{7}{3}$$ Multiply by the reciprocal of the divisor.

$$= \frac{28}{15}$$ Simplify.

$$= 1\frac{13}{15}$$ Write as a mixed number.

b. Divide $4\frac{2}{3} \div 7\frac{3}{5}$.

$$4\frac{2}{3} \div 7\frac{3}{5} = \frac{14}{3} \div \frac{38}{5}$$ Change to improper fractions.

$$= \frac{14\,{}^{7}}{3} \cdot \frac{5}{38\,{}_{19}}$$ Simplify.

$$= \frac{35}{57}$$ Multiply.

Exercises

Multiply or divide. Write your answers in simplest form.

1. $\frac{2}{5} \cdot \frac{3}{4}$ **2.** $\frac{3}{7} \cdot \frac{4}{3}$ **3.** $1\frac{1}{2} \cdot 5\frac{3}{4}$ **4.** $3\frac{4}{5} \cdot 10$ **5.** $5\frac{1}{4} \cdot \frac{2}{3}$

6. $4\frac{1}{2} \cdot 7\frac{1}{2}$ **7.** $3\frac{2}{3} \cdot 6\frac{9}{10}$ **8.** $6\frac{1}{2} \cdot 7\frac{2}{3}$ **9.** $2\frac{2}{5} \cdot 1\frac{1}{6}$ **10.** $4\frac{1}{9} \cdot 3\frac{3}{8}$

11. $\frac{3}{5} \div \frac{1}{2}$ **12.** $\frac{4}{5} \div \frac{9}{10}$ **13.** $2\frac{1}{2} \div 3\frac{1}{2}$ **14.** $1\frac{4}{5} \div 2\frac{1}{2}$ **15.** $3\frac{1}{6} \div 1\frac{3}{4}$

16. $5 \div \frac{3}{8}$ **17.** $\frac{4}{9} \div \frac{3}{5}$ **18.** $\frac{5}{8} \div \frac{3}{4}$ **19.** $2\frac{1}{5} \div 2\frac{1}{2}$ **20.** $6\frac{1}{2} \div \frac{1}{4}$

Fractions, Decimals, and Percents

Percent means per hundred. 50% means 50 per hundred. $50\% = \frac{50}{100} = 0.50$.

You can write a fraction as a percent by writing the fraction as a decimal first. Then move the decimal point two places to the right and write a percent sign.

Example 1

Write each number as a percent.

a. $\frac{3}{5}$

$\frac{3}{5} = 0.6$

$0.6 = 60\%$

b. $\frac{7}{20}$

$\frac{7}{20} = 0.35$

$0.35 = 35\%$

c. $\frac{2}{3}$

$\frac{2}{3} = 0.66\overline{6}$

$0.66\overline{6} = 66.\overline{6}\% \approx 66.7\%$

You can write a percent as a decimal by moving the decimal point two places to the left and removing the percent sign. You can write a percent as a fraction with a denominator of 100. Then simplify the fraction, if possible.

Example 2

Write each percent as a decimal and as a fraction or mixed number.

a. 25%

$25\% = 0.25$

$25\% = \frac{25}{100} = \frac{1}{4}$

b. $\frac{1}{2}\%$

$\frac{1}{2}\% = 0.5\% = 0.005$

$\frac{1}{2}\% = \frac{\frac{1}{2}}{100} = \frac{1}{2} \div 100$

$= \frac{1}{2} \cdot \frac{1}{100} = \frac{1}{200}$

c. 360%

$360\% = 3.6$

$360\% = \frac{360}{100} = \frac{18}{5} = 3\frac{3}{5}$

Exercises

Write each number as a percent. If necessary, round to the nearest tenth.

1. 0.56   **2.** 0.09   **3.** 6.02   **4.** 5.245   **5.** 8.2   **6.** 0.14

7. $\frac{1}{7}$ **8.** $\frac{9}{20}$ **9.** $\frac{1}{9}$ **10.** $\frac{5}{6}$ **11.** $\frac{3}{4}$ **12.** $\frac{7}{8}$

Write each percent as a decimal.

13. 7%   **14.** 8.5%   **15.** 0.9%   **16.** 250%   **17.** 83%   **18.** 110%

19. 15%   **20.** 72%   **21.** 0.03%   **22.** 36.2%   **23.** 365%   **24.** 101%

Write each percent as a fraction or mixed number in simplest form.

25. 19%   **26.** $\frac{3}{4}\%$ **27.** 450%   **28.** $\frac{4}{5}\%$ **29.** 64%   **30.** $\frac{2}{3}\%$

31. 24%   **32.** 845%   **33.** $\frac{3}{8}\%$ **34.** 480%   **35.** 60%   **36.** 350%

Exponents

You can express $2 \cdot 2 \cdot 2 \cdot 2 \cdot 2$ as 2^5. The raised number 5 shows the number of times 2 is used as a factor. The number 2 is the base. The number 5 is the exponent.

$2^5 \leftarrow$ **exponent**

$\uparrow$

base

Factored Form: $2 \cdot 2 \cdot 2 \cdot 2 \cdot 2$ Exponential Form: 2^5 Standard Form: 32

A number with an exponent of 1 is the number itself: $8^1 = 8$.
Any number, except 0, with an exponent of 0 is 1: $5^0 = 1$.

Example 1

Write each expression using exponents.

a. $8 \cdot 8 \cdot 8 \cdot 8 \cdot 8$ **b.** $2 \cdot 9 \cdot 9 \cdot 9 \cdot 9 \cdot 9 \cdot 9$ **c.** $6 \cdot 6 \cdot 10 \cdot 10 \cdot 10 \cdot 6 \cdot 6$

Count the number of times each number is used as a factor.

$= 8^5$ $= 2 \cdot 9^6$ $= 6^4 \cdot 10^3$

Example 2

Write each expression in standard form.

a. 2^3 **b.** $8^2 \cdot 3^4$ **c.** $10^3 \cdot 15^2$

Write each expression in factored form and multiply.

$2 \cdot 2 \cdot 2 = 8$ $8 \cdot 8 \cdot 3 \cdot 3 \cdot 3 \cdot 3 = 5184$ $10 \cdot 10 \cdot 10 \cdot 15 \cdot 15 = 225{,}000$

For powers of 10, the exponent tells how many zeros are in the number in standard form.

$10^1 = 10$ $10^3 = 10 \cdot 10 \cdot 10 = 1000$ $10^5 = 10 \cdot 10 \cdot 10 \cdot 10 \cdot 10 = 100{,}000$

You can use powers of 10 to write numbers in expanded form.

Example 3

Write 739 in expanded form using powers of 10.

$739 = 700 + 30 + 9 = (7 \cdot 100) + (3 \cdot 10) + (9 \cdot 1) = (7 \cdot 10^2) + (3 \cdot 10^1) + (9 \cdot 10^0)$

Exercises

Write each expression using exponents.

1. $6 \cdot 6 \cdot 6 \cdot 6$ **2.** $7 \cdot 7 \cdot 7 \cdot 7 \cdot 7$ **3.** $5 \cdot 2 \cdot 2 \cdot 2 \cdot 2$

4. $3 \cdot 3 \cdot 3 \cdot 3 \cdot 3 \cdot 14 \cdot 14$ **5.** $4 \cdot 4 \cdot 3 \cdot 3 \cdot 2$ **6.** $3 \cdot 5 \cdot 5 \cdot 7 \cdot 7 \cdot 7$

Write each number in standard form.

7. 4^3 **8.** 9^4 **9.** 12^2 **10.** $6^2 \cdot 7^1$ **11.** $11^2 \cdot 3^3$

Write each number in expanded form using powers of 10.

12. 658   **13.** 1254   **14.** 7125   **15.** 83,401   **16.** 294,863

Perimeter, Area, and Volume

The perimeter of a figure is the distance around the figure. The area of a figure is the number of square units contained in the figure. The volume of a three-dimensional figure is the number of cubic units contained in the figure.

Example 1

Find the perimeter of each figure.

a.

Add the measures of the sides.

$3 + 4 + 5 = 12$

The perimeter is 12 in.

b.

Use the formula $P = 2\ell + 2w$.

$P = 2(3) + 2(4)$

$= 6 + 8 = 14$

The perimeter is 14 cm.

Example 2

Find the area of each figure.

a.

Use the formula $A = bh$.

$A = 6 \cdot 5 = 30$

The area is 30 in.^{2}.

b.

Use the formula $A = \frac{1}{2}(bh)$.

$A = \frac{1}{2}(7 \cdot 6) = 21$

The area is 21 in.^{2}.

Example 3

Find the volume of each figure.

a.

Use the formula $V = Bh$.

$B = $ area of the base

$= 3 \cdot 5 = 15$

$V = 15 \cdot 6 = 90$ in.^{3}

The volume is 90 in.^{3}.

b.

Use the formula $V = \pi r^2 h$.

$V = 3.14 \cdot 2^2 \cdot 5$

$= 3.14 \cdot 4 \cdot 5 = 62.8$ in.^{3}

The volume is 62.8 in.^{3}.

Exercises

For Exercises 1–2, find the perimeter of each figure. For Exercises 3–4, find the area of each figure. For Exercises 5–7, find the volume of each figure.

1.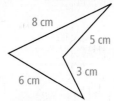

2.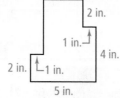

3.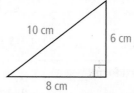

4.

5.

6.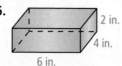

7.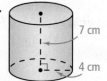

Line Plots

A line plot is created by placing a mark above a number line corresponding to each data value. Line plots have two main advantages:

- You can see the frequency of data values.

- You can see how the data values compare.

Example

The table at the right gives the heights, in inches, of a group of 25 adults. Display the data in a line plot. Describe the data shown in the line plot.

Heights of Adults (in.)				
59	60	63	63	64
64	64	65	65	65
67	67	67	67	68
68	68	69	70	70
71	72	73	73	77

The data are graphed on a number line.

The title describes the data.

An **X** represents one element of the data set.

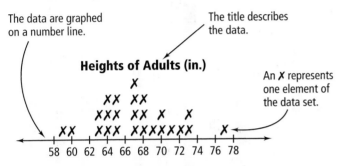

Heights of Adults (in.)

The line plot shows that most of the heights are concentrated around 67 in., the maximum value is 77 in., and the minimum value is 59 in.

Exercises

Display each set of data in a line plot.

1. 3, 6, 4, 3, 6, 0, 4, 5, 0, 4, 6, 1, 5, 1, 0, 5, 5, 6, 5, 3

2. 19, 18, 18, 18, 19, 20, 19, 18, 18, 17, 18, 20, 19, 17

Draw a line plot for each frequency table.

3.

Number	1	2	3	4	5	6
Frequency	4	1	0	5	7	2

4.

Number	12	13	15	16	18	19
Frequency	2	5	1	3	6	3

5. Olympics The numbers of gold medals won by different countries during the 2002 Winter Olympics are listed below.

   1, 1, 1, 2, 2, 2, 3, 3, 3, 3, 4, 4, 4, 5, 7, 10, 12, 13

Display the data in a line plot. Describe the data shown in the line plot.

Bar Graphs

Bar graphs are used to display and compare data. The horizontal axis shows categories and the vertical axis shows amounts. A multiple bar graph includes a key.

Example

Draw a bar graph for the data in the table below.

Median Household Income

Town	2 person	3 person	4 person
Mason	$62,690	$68,070	$77,014
Barstow	$68,208	$82,160	$99,584
York	$51,203	$58,902	$67,911
Rexford	$52,878	$54,943	$63,945
Onham	$54,715	$61,437	$69,260

The highest median income is $99,584. A reasonable range for the vertical scale is $0 to $108,000.

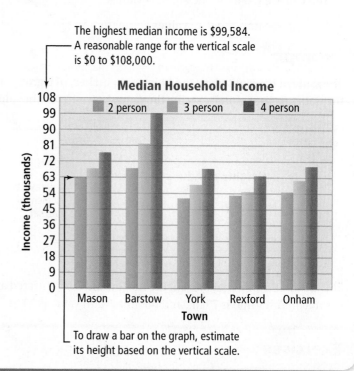

The categories (in the first column) are placed on the horizontal scale. The amounts (in the second, third, and fourth columns) are used to create the scale on the vertical scale and to draw each bar.

Graph the data for each town. Use the values in the top row to create the key.

To draw a bar on the graph, estimate its height based on the vertical scale.

Exercises

1. Draw a bar graph for the data in the table below.

Highest Temperatures (°F)

Town	March	June	August
Mason	61	86	83
Barstow	84	104	101
York	89	101	102
Rexford	88	92	93
Onham	81	104	100

2. a. Reasoning If one more column of data were added to the table in the example, how would the bar graph be different?

   b. If one more row of data were added to the table in the example, how would the bar graph be different?

Line Graphs

Line graphs are used to display the change in a set of data over a period of time. A multiple-line graph shows change in more than one category of data over time. You can use a line graph to look for trends and make predictions.

Example

The data in the table below show the number of households, in thousands, that have cable TV and the number of households that subscribe to newspapers in a certain city. Graph the data.

Households With Cable TV and Newspapers (thousands)

Year	1980	1990	1995	2000	2005
Cable TV	15.2	51.9	60.5	68.6	73.9
Newspapers	62.2	62.3	58.2	55.8	53.3

Since the data show changes over time for two sets of data, use a double line graph. The horizontal scale displays years. The vertical axis shows the number of households for each category.

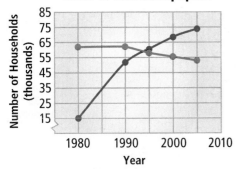

Notice that there is a *break* in the vertical axis. You can use a zigzag line to indicate a break from 0 to 15 since there is no data less than 15 to graph.

Exercises

Graph the data in each table.

1. **Market Share (percent)**

Year	2004	2005	2006	2007
Rap/Hip Hop	12.1	13.3	11.4	10.8
Pop	10.0	8.1	7.1	10.7

SOURCE: Recording Industry of America

2. **Percent of Schools With Internet Access**

Year	1997	1999	2001	2003
Elementary	75	94	99	100
Secondary	89	98	100	100

SOURCE: National Center for Education Statistics

Circle Graphs

A circle graph is an efficient way to present certain types of data. The entire circle represents all of the data. Each section of the circle represents a part of the whole and can be labeled with the actual data or the data expressed as a fraction, decimal, or percent. The angles at the center are central angles, and each angle is proportional to the percent or fraction of the total.

Example

Students at a high school were asked to pick their favorite instrument. The table at the right shows the number of students who chose each instrument. Draw a circle graph for the data.

Favorite Musical Instruments

Instrument	Number of Students
Bass	35
Drums	103
Piano	150
Guitar	182

Step 1 Add to find the total number.

$$35 + 103 + 150 + 182 = 470$$

Step 2 For each central angle, set up a proportion to find the measure. Use a calculator to solve each proportion.

$$\frac{35}{470} = \frac{a}{360°} \qquad \frac{103}{470} = \frac{b}{360°} \qquad \frac{150}{470} = \frac{c}{360°} \qquad \frac{182}{470} = \frac{d}{360°}$$

$$a \approx 27° \qquad b \approx 79° \qquad c \approx 115° \qquad d \approx 139°$$

Step 3 Use a compass to draw a circle. Draw the approximate central angles using a protractor.

Step 4 Label each sector.

Favorite Musical Instruments

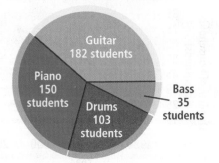

Exercises

1. **a.** Use the data in the table to draw a circle graph.
   b. Approximately what percent of students ride the bus?
   c. Approximately how many times more students walk than ride in a car?

Methods of Transportation

Transportation Method	Walk	Bicycle	Bus	Car
Number of Students	252	135	432	81

2. **Data Collection** Survey your class to find out how they get to school. Use the data to draw a circle graph.

Stem-and-Leaf Plots

A stem-and-leaf plot is a display of data that uses the digits of the data values. To make a stem-and-leaf plot, separate each number into a stem and a leaf. A stem and leaf for the number 2.39 is shown at the right.

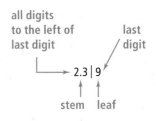

all digits to the left of last digit

last digit

2.3 | 9

stem   leaf

You can use a stem-and-leaf plot to organize data. The data below describe the price for the same notebook at several stores.

Notebook Prices: $2.39 $2.47 $2.43 $2.21 $2.33 $2.28 $2.26

Use the first two digits for the "stems."

2.2	1 6 8
2.3	3 9
2.4	3 7

Key: 2.4 | 3 means 2.43

Use the corresponding last digits for the "leaves." Arrange the numbers in order.

You can use a back-to-back stem-and-leaf plot to display two related data sets. The stems are between two vertical bars, and the leaves are on each side. Leaves are in increasing order from the stems. In the back-to-back stem-and-leaf plot below, 3|4|1 represents a commute time of 43 min in Town A and a commute time of 41 min in Town B.

Daily Commute (min)

Town A		Town B
6 6 4 3	4	1 1 4 5 7
9 8 6 4 4 4	5	0 2 2 2 4
5 2 1 0	6	4 5 8 9
8 7 6 6 4 2	7	3 6 7 9 9 9

Key: → 7 | 3 means 73

2 | 7 | 3

2 | 7 means 72 ←

Exercises

Make a stem-and-leaf plot for each set of data.

1. 18 35 28 15 36 10 25 22 15

2. 18.6 18.4 17.6 15.7 15.3 17.5

3. 785 776 788 761 768 768 785

4. 0.8 0.2 1.4 3.5 4.3 4.5 2.6 2.2

5. Make a back-to-back stem-and-leaf plot of the test scores of the two classes below.
Class A: 98 78 85 72 94 81 68 83
Class B: 87 91 79 75 90 81 82 100

Skills Handbook

Reference

Table 1 Measures

	United States Customary	Metric
Length	12 inches (in.) = 1 foot (ft) 36 in. = 1 yard (yd) 3 ft = 1 yard 5280 ft = 1 mile (mi) 1760 yd = 1 mile	10 millimeters (mm) = 1 centimeter (cm) 100 cm = 1 meter (m) 1000 mm = 1 meter 1000 m = 1 kilometer (km)
Area	144 square inches (in.^{2}) = 1 square foot (ft^2) 9 ft^2 = 1 square yard (yd^2) 43,560 ft^2 = 1 acre (a) 4840 yd^2 = 1 acre	100 square millimeters (mm^2) = 1 square centimeter (cm^2) 10,000 cm^2 = 1 square meter (m^2) 10,000 m^2 = 1 hectare (ha)
Volume	1728 cubic inches (in.^{3}) = 1 cubic foot (ft^3) 27 ft^3 = 1 cubic yard (yd^3)	1000 cubic millimeters (mm^3) = 1 cubic centimeter (cm^3) 1,000,000 cm^3 = 1 cubic meter (m^3)
Liquid Capacity	8 fluid ounces (fl oz) = 1 cup (c) 2 c = 1 pint (pt) 2 pt = 1 quart (qt) 4 qt = 1 gallon (gal)	1000 milliliters (mL) = 1 liter (L) 1000 L = 1 kiloliter (kL)
Weight or Mass	16 ounces (oz) = 1 pound (lb) 2000 pounds = 1 ton (t)	1000 milligrams (mg) = 1 gram (g) 1000 g = 1 kilogram (kg) 1000 kg = 1 metric ton
Temperature	32°F = freezing point of water 98.6°F = normal human body temperature 212°F = boiling point of water	0°C = freezing point of water 37°C = normal human body temperature 100°C = boiling point of water

Customary Units and Metric Units	
Length	1 in. = 2.54 cm 1 mi ≈ 1.61 km 1 ft ≈ 0.305 m
Capacity	1 qt ≈ 0.946 L
Weight and Mass	1 oz ≈ 28.4 g 1 lb ≈ 0.454 kg

Time		
60 seconds (s) = 1 minute (min) 60 minutes = 1 hour (h) 24 hours = 1 day (d) 7 days = 1 week (wk)	4 weeks (approx.) = 1 month (mo) 365 days = 1 year (yr) 52 weeks (approx.) = 1 year	12 months = 1 year 10 years = 1 decade 100 years = 1 century

Table 2 **Reading Math Symbols**

Symbols	Words
·	multiplication sign, times ($\times$)
=	equals
$\stackrel{?}{=}$	Are the statements equal?
$\approx$	is approximately equal to
$\neq$	is not equal to
$<$	is less than
$>$	is greater than
$\leq$	is less than or equal to
$\geq$	is greater than or equal to
$\cong$	is congruent to
$\pm$	plus or minus
( )	parentheses for grouping
[ ]	brackets for grouping
{ }	set braces
%	percent
$\lvert a \rvert$	absolute value of a
...	and so on
$-a$	opposite of a
π	pi, an irrational number, approximately equal to 3.14
$°$	degree(s)
a^n	nth power of a
$\sqrt{x}$	nonnegative square root of x
$\frac{1}{a}, a \neq 0$	reciprocal of a
a^{-n}	$\frac{1}{a^n}, a \neq 0$
$\overleftrightarrow{AB}$	line through points A and B
$\overline{AB}$	segment with endpoints A and B
AB	length of $\overline{AB}$; distance between points A and B

Symbols	Words
$\angle A$	angle A
$m\angle A$	measure of angle A
$\triangle ABC$	triangle ABC
(x, y)	ordered pair
$x_1, x_2, \ldots$	specific values of the variable x
$y_1, y_2, \ldots$	specific values of the variable y
$\bar{x}$	mean of data values of x
σ	standard deviation
$f(x)$	f of x; the function value at x
m	slope of a line
b	y-intercept of a line
$a{:}b$	ratio of a to b
$\begin{bmatrix} 1 & 3 \\ 2 & 4 \end{bmatrix}$	matrix
$\sin A$	sine of $\angle A$
$\cos A$	cosine of $\angle A$
$\tan A$	tangent of $\angle A$
$n!$	n factorial
$_nP_r$	permutations of n objects arranged r at a time
$_nC_r$	combinations of n objects chosen r at a time
$P(\text{event})$	probability of an event
$\wedge$	raised to a power (in a spreadsheet formula)
$*$	multiply (in a spreadsheet formula)
$/$	divide (in a spreadsheet formula)

Properties and Formulas

Chapter 1 Foundations for Algebra

Order of Operations
1. Perform an operation(s) inside grouping symbols.
2. Simplify powers.
3. Multiply and divide from left to right.
4. Add and subtract from left to right.

Commutative Property of Addition
For every real number a and b, $a + b = b + a$.

Commutative Property of Multiplication
For every real number a and b, $a \cdot b = b \cdot a$.

Associative Property of Addition
For every real number a, b, and c,
$(a + b) + c = a + (b + c)$.

Associative Property of Multiplication
For every real number a, b, and c,
$(a \cdot b) \cdot c = a \cdot (b \cdot c)$.

Identity Property of Addition
For every real number a, $a + 0 = a$.

Identity Property of Multiplication
For every real number a, $1 \cdot a = a$.

Multiplication Property of −1
For every real number a, $-1 \cdot a = -a$.

Zero Property of Multiplication
For every real number a, $a \cdot 0 = 0$.

Inverse Property of Addition
For every real number a, there is an additive inverse
$-a$ such that $a + (-a) = 0$.

Inverse Property of Multiplication
For every nonzero number a, there is a multiplicative inverse
such that $a \cdot \frac{1}{a} = 1$.

Distributive Property
For every real number a, b, and c:
$a(b + c) = ab + ac$
$(b + c)a = ba + ca$
$a(b - c) = ab - ac$
$(b - c)a = ba - ca$

Chapter 2 Solving Equations

Addition Property of Equality
For every real number a, b, and c, if $a = b$, then
$a + c = b + c$.

Subtraction Property of Equality
For every real number a, b, and c, if $a = b$, then
$a - c = b - c$.

Multiplication Property of Equality
For every real number a, b, and c, if $a = b$, then $a \cdot c = b \cdot c$.

Division Property of Equality
For every real number a, b, and c, where $c \neq 0$, if $a = b$,
then $\frac{a}{c} = \frac{b}{c}$.

Cross Products of a Proportion
If $\frac{a}{b} = \frac{c}{d}$, then $ad = bc$.

Percent Proportion
$\frac{a}{b} = \frac{p}{100}$, where $b \neq 0$.

Percent Equation
$a = p\% \cdot b$, where $b \neq 0$.

Simple Interest Formula
$I = prt$

Percent of Change
$p\% = \frac{\text{amount of increase or decrease}}{\text{original amount}}$
amount of increase = new amount − original amount
amount of decrease = original amount − new amount

Relative Error
relative error $= \frac{|\text{measured or estimated value} - \text{actual value}|}{\text{actual value}}$

Chapter 3 Solving Inequalities

The following properties of inequality are also true for
$\geq$ and $\leq$.

Addition Property of Inequality
For every real number a, b, and c,
if $a > b$, then $a + c > b + c$;
if $a < b$, then $a + c < b + c$.

Subtraction Property of Inequality
For every real number a, b, and c,
if $a > b$, then $a - c > b - c$;
if $a < b$, then $a - c < b - c$.

Multiplication Property of Inequality
For every real number a, b, and c, where $c > 0$,
if $a > b$, then $ac > bc$;
if $a < b$, then $ac < bc$.
For every real number a, b, and c, where $c < 0$,
if $a > b$, then $ac < bc$;
if $a < b$, then $ac > bc$.

Division Property of Inequality
For every real number a, b, and c, where $c > 0$,
if $a > b$, then $\frac{a}{c} > \frac{b}{c}$;
if $a < b$, then $\frac{a}{c} < \frac{b}{c}$.
For every real number a, b, and c, where $c < 0$,
if $a > b$, then $\frac{a}{c} < \frac{b}{c}$;
if $a < b$, then $\frac{a}{c} > \frac{b}{c}$.

Reflexive Property of Equality
For every real number a, $a = a$.

Symmetric Property of Equality
For every real number a and b,
if $a = b$, then $b = a$.

Transitive Property of Equality
For every real number a, b, and c,
if $a = b$ and $b = c$, then $a = c$.

Transitive Property of Inequality
For every real number a, b, and c,
if $a < b$ and $b < c$, then $a < c$.

Chapter 4 An Introduction to Functions

Arithmetic Sequence
The form for the rule of an arithmetic sequence is
$A(n) = A(1) + (n - 1)d$, where $A(n)$ is the nth term,
$A(1)$ is the first term, n is the term number, and
d is the common difference.

Chapter 5 Linear Functions

Slope
$$\text{slope} = \frac{\text{vertical change}}{\text{horizontal change}} = \frac{\text{rise}}{\text{run}}$$

Direct Variation
A direct variation is a relationship that can be represented by
a function of the form $y = kx$, where $k \neq 0$.

Slope-Intercept Form of a Linear Equation
The slope-intercept form of a linear equation is
$y = mx + b$, where m is the slope and b is the
y-intercept.

Point-Slope Form of a Linear Equation
The point-slope form of the equation of a nonvertical line
that passes through the point (x_1, y_1) with slope m is
$y - y_1 = m(x - x_1)$.

Standard Form of a Linear Equation
The standard form of a linear equation is $Ax + By = C$,
where A, B, and C are real numbers and A and B are not
both zero.

Slopes of Parallel Lines
Nonvertical lines are parallel if they have the same slope and
different y-intercepts. Any two vertical lines are parallel.

Slopes of Perpendicular Lines
Two lines are perpendicular if the product of their slopes is
-1. A vertical line and horizontal line are perpendicular.

Chapter 6 Systems of Equations and Inequalities

Solutions of Systems of Linear Equations
A system of linear equations can have one solution, no
solution, or infinitely many solutions:
- If the lines have different slopes, the lines intersect, so
  there is one solution.
- If the lines have the same slopes and different
  y-intercepts, the lines are parallel, so there are no
  solutions.
- If the lines have the same slopes and the same
  y-intercepts, the lines are the same, so there are infinitely
  many solutions.

Chapter 7 Exponents and Exponential Functions

Zero as an Exponent
For every nonzero number a, $a^0 = 1$.

Negative Exponent
For every nonzero number a and integer n, $a^{-n} = \frac{1}{a^n}$.

Scientific Notation
A number in scientific notation is written as the product of two factors in the form $a \times 10^n$, where n is an integer and $1 \leq a < 10$.

Multiplying Powers With the Same Base
For every nonzero number a and integers m and n, $a^m \cdot a^n = a^{m+n}$.

Dividing Powers With the Same Base
For every nonzero number a and integers m and n, $\frac{a^m}{a^n} = a^{m-n}$.

Raising a Power to a Power
For every nonzero number a and integers m and n, $(a^m)^n = a^{mn}$.

Raising a Product to a Power
For every nonzero number a and b and integer n, $(ab)^n = a^n b^n$.

Raising a Quotient to a Power
For every nonzero number a and b and integer n, $\left(\frac{a}{b}\right)^n = \frac{a^n}{b^n}$.

Geometric Sequence
The form for the rule of a geometric sequence is $A(n) = a \cdot r^{n-1}$, where $A(n)$ is the nth term, a is the first term, n is the term number, and r is the common ratio.

Exponential Growth and Decay
An exponential function has the form $y = a \cdot b^x$, where a is a nonzero constant, b is greater than 0 and not equal to 1, and x is a real number.

- The function $y = a \cdot b^x$, where b is the growth factor, models exponential growth for $a > 0$ and $b > 1$.
- The function $y = a \cdot b^x$, where b is the decay factor, models exponential decay for $a > 0$ and $0 < b < 1$.

Chapter 8 Polynomials and Factoring

Factoring Special Cases
For every nonzero number a and b:
$$a^2 - b^2 = (a + b)(a - b)$$
$$a^2 + 2ab + b^2 = (a + b)(a + b) = (a + b)^2$$
$$a^2 - 2ab + b^2 = (a - b)(a - b) = (a - b)^2$$

Chapter 9 Quadratic Functions and Equations

Graph of a Quadratic Function
The graph of $y = ax^2 + bx + c$, where $a \neq 0$, has the line $x = \frac{-b}{2a}$ as its axis of symmetry. The x-coordinate of the vertex is $\frac{-b}{2a}$.

Zero-Product Property
For every real number a and b, if $ab = 0$, then $a = 0$ or $b = 0$.

Quadratic Formula
If $ax^2 + bx + c = 0$, where $a \neq 0$, then
$$x = \frac{-b \pm \sqrt{b^2 - 4ac}}{2a}.$$

Property of the Discriminant
For the quadratic equation $ax^2 + bx + c = 0$, where $a \neq 0$, the value of the discriminant $b^2 - 4ac$ tells you the number of solutions.

- If $b^2 - 4ac > 0$, there are two real solutions.
- If $b^2 - 4ac = 0$, there is one real solution.
- If $b^2 - 4ac < 0$, there are no real solutions.

Chapter 10 Radical Expressions and Equations

The Pythagorean Theorem
In a right triangle, the sum of the squares of the lengths of the legs is equal to the square of the length of the hypotenuse: $a^2 + b^2 = c^2$.

The Converse of the Pythagorean Theorem
If a triangle has sides of lengths a, b, and c, and $a^2 + b^2 = c^2$, then the triangle is a right triangle with hypotenuse of length c.

Multiplication Property of Square Roots
For every number $a \geq 0$ and $b \geq 0$, $\sqrt{ab} = \sqrt{a} \cdot \sqrt{b}$.

Division Property of Square Roots

For every number $a \geq 0$ and $b > 0$, $\sqrt{\dfrac{a}{b}} = \dfrac{\sqrt{a}}{\sqrt{b}}$.

Chapter 12 Data Analysis and Probability

Mean

The mean of a set of data values $= \dfrac{\text{sum of the data values}}{\text{total number of data values}}$.

Standard Deviation

Standard deviation is a measure of how the values in a data set vary, or deviate from the mean.

$$\sigma = \sqrt{\dfrac{\Sigma(x - \bar{x})^2}{n}}$$

Multiplication Counting Principle

If there are m ways to make a first selection and n ways to make a second selection, there are $m \cdot n$ ways to make the two selections.

Permutation Notation

The expression $_nP_r$ represents the number of permutations of n objects arranged r at a time.

$$_nP_r = \dfrac{n!}{(n - r)!}$$

Combination Notation

The expression $_nC_r$ represents the number of combinations of n objects chosen r at a time.

$$_nC_r = \dfrac{n!}{r!(n - r)!}$$

Theoretical Probability

$P(\text{event}) = \dfrac{\text{number of favorable outcomes}}{\text{number of possible outcomes}}$

Probability of an Event and Its Complement

$P(\text{event}) + P(\text{not event}) = 1$, or
$P(\text{not event}) = 1 - P(\text{event})$

Odds

Odds in favor of an event $= \dfrac{\text{number of favorable outcomes}}{\text{number of unfavorable outcomes}}$

Odds against an event $= \dfrac{\text{number of unfavorable outcomes}}{\text{number of favorable outcomes}}$

Experimental Probability

$P(\text{event}) = \dfrac{\text{number of times the event occurs}}{\text{number of times the experiment is done}}$

Probability of Mutually Exclusive Events

If A and B are mutually exclusive events, then
$P(A \text{ or } B) = P(A) + P(B)$.

Probability of Overlapping Events

If A and B are overlapping events, then
$P(A \text{ or } B) = P(A) + P(B) - P(A \text{ and } B)$.

Probability of Two Independent Events

If A and B are independent events, then
$P(A \text{ and } B) = P(A) \cdot P(B)$.

Probability of Two Dependent Events

If A and B are independent events, then
$P(A \text{ then } B) = P(A) \cdot P(B \text{ after } A)$.

Formulas of **Geometry**

You will use a number of geometric formulas as you work through your algebra book. Here are some perimeter, area, and volume formulas.

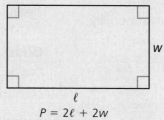

$P = 2\ell + 2w$
$A = \ell w$

Rectangle

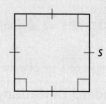

$P = 4s$
$A = s^2$

Square

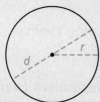

$C = 2\pi r$ or $C = \pi d$
$A = \pi r^2$

Circle

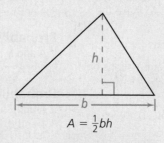

$A = \frac{1}{2}bh$

Triangle

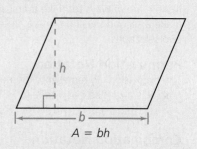

$A = bh$

Parallelogram

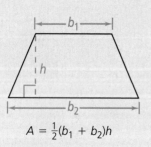

$A = \frac{1}{2}(b_1 + b_2)h$

Trapezoid

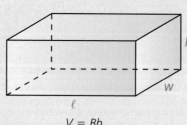

$V = Bh$
$V = \ell wh$

Right Prism

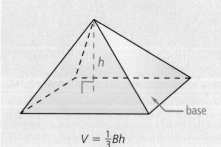

$V = \frac{1}{3}Bh$

Pyramid

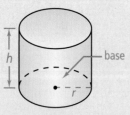

$V = Bh$
$V = \pi r^2 h$

Right Cylinder

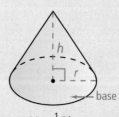

$V = \frac{1}{3}Bh$
$V = \frac{1}{3}\pi r^2 h$

Right Cone

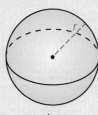

$V = \frac{4}{3}\pi r^3$

Sphere

Visual **Glossary**

English   Spanish

A

Absolute value (p. 38) The distance that a number is from zero on a number line.

Valor absoluto (p. 38) La distancia a la que un número está del cero en una recta numérica.

Example -7 is 7 units from 0, so $|-7| = 7$.

Additive inverse (p. 39) The opposite or additive inverse of any number a is $-a$. The sum of opposites is 0.

Inverso aditivo (p. 39) El opuesto o inverso aditivo de cualquier número a es $-a$. La suma de los opuestos es 0.

Example -5 and 5 are additive inverses because $-5 + 5 = 0$.

Algebraic expression (p. 4) A mathematical phrase that includes one or more variables.

Expresión algebraica (p. 4) Frase matemática que contiene una o más variables.

Example $7 + x$ is an algebraic expression.

Arithmetic sequence (p. 296) A number sequence formed by adding a fixed number to each previous term to find the next term. The fixed number is called the common difference.

Progresión aritmética (p. 296) En una progresión aritmética la diferencia entre términos consecutivos es un número constante. El número constante se llama la diferencia común.

Example 4, 7, 10, 13, . . . is an arithmetic sequence.

Axis of symmetry (p. 566) The line that divides a parabola into two matching halves.

Eje de simetría (p. 566) El eje de simetría es la línea que divide una parábola en dos mitades exactamente iguales.

Example

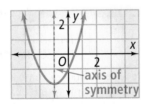

B

Base (p. 11) A number that is multiplied repeatedly.

Base (p. 11) El número que se multiplica repetidas veces.

Example $4^5 = 4 \cdot 4 \cdot 4 \cdot 4 \cdot 4$. The base 4 is used as a factor 5 times.

Bias (p. 739) A sampling error that causes one option to seem better than another. Survey questions or samples can be biased.

Parcialidad (p. 739) Error de muestreo que hace que una opción parezca mejor que otra. Preguntas en una encuesta o muestras pueden ser parciales.

Binomial (p. 503) A polynomial of two terms.

Binomio (p. 503) Polinomio compuesto de dos términos.

Example $3x + 7$ is a binomial.

English

Spanish

Bivariate (p. 742)   A set of data that uses two variables is bivariate.

Bivariado (p. 742)   Un conjunto de datos que usa dos variables es bivariado.

Box-and-whisker plot (p. 731)   A graph that summarizes data along a number line. The left whisker extends from the minimum to the first quartile. The box extends from the first quartile to the third quartile and has a vertical line through the median. The right whisker extends from the third quartile to the maximum.

Gráfica de cajas (p. 731)   Gráfica que resume los datos a lo largo de una recta numérica. El brazo izquierdo se extiende desde el valor mínimo del primer cuartil. La caja se extiende desde el primer cuartil hasta el tercer cuartil y tiene una línea vertical que atraviesa la mediana. El brazo derecho se extiende desde el tercer cuartil hasta el valor máximo.

Example

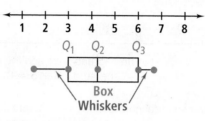

Causation (p. 367)   When a change in one quantity causes a change in a second quantity. A correlation between quantities does not always imply causation.

Causalidad (p. 367)   Cuando un cambio en una cantidad causa un cambio en una segunda cantidad. Una correlación entre las cantidades no implica siempre la causalidad.

Coefficient (p. 57)   The numerical factor when a term has a variable.

Coeficiente (p. 57)   Factor numérico de un término que contiene una variable.

Example   In the expression $2x + 3y + 16$, 2 and 3 are coefficients.

Combination (p. 753)   Any unordered selection of r objects from a set of n objects is a combination. The number of combinations of n objects taken r at a time is $_nC_r = \frac{n!}{r!(n-r)!}$ for $0 \le r \le n$.

Combinación (p. 753)   Cualquier selección no ordenada de r objetos tomados de un conjunto de n objetos es una combinación. El número de combinaciones de n objetos, cuando se toman r objetos cada vez, es $_nC_r = \frac{n!}{r!(n-r)!}$ para $0 \le r \le n$.

Example   The number of combinations of seven items taken four at a time is $_7C_4 = \frac{7!}{4!(7-4)!} = 35$. There are 35 ways to choose four items from seven items without regard to order.

Common difference (p. 296)   The difference between consecutive terms of an arithmetic sequence.

Diferencia común (p. 296)   La diferencia común es la diferencia entre los términos consecutivos de una progresión aritmética.

Example   The common difference is 3 in the arithmetic sequence 4, 7, 10, 13, . . .

English

Spanish

Common ratio (p. 481) The fixed number used to find terms in a geometric sequence.

Razón común (p. 481) Número constante que se usa para hallar los términos en una progresión geométrica.

Example The common ratio is $\frac{1}{3}$ in the geometric sequence $9, 3, 1, \frac{1}{3}, \ldots$

Complement of an event (p. 758) All possible outcomes that are not in the event.
$P(\text{complement of event}) = 1 - P(\text{event})$

Complemento de un suceso (p. 758) Todos los resultados posibles que no se dan en el suceso.
$P(\text{complemento de un suceso}) = 1 - P(\text{suceso})$

Example The complement of rolling a 1 or a 2 on a number cube is rolling a 3, 4, 5, or 6.

Complement of a set (p. 212) The set of all elements in the universal set that are not in a given set.

Complemento de un conjunto (p. 212) Conjunto de todos los elementos en el conjunto universal que no se incluyen en el conjunto dado.

Example If $U = \{\ldots, -3, -2, -1, 0, 1, 2, 3, \ldots\}$ and $A = \{0, 1, 2, 3, \ldots\}$, then the complement of A is $A' = \{\ldots, -3, -2, -1\}$.

Completing the square (p. 595) A method of solving quadratic equations. Completing the square turns every quadratic equation into the form $x^2 = c$.

Completar el cuadrado (p. 595) Método para solucionar ecuaciones cuadráticas. Cuando se completa el cuadrado se transforma la ecuación cuadrática a la fórmula $x^2 = c$.

Example $x^2 + 6x - 7 = 9$ is rewritten as $(x + 3)^2 = 25$ by completing the square.

Complex fraction (p. 674) A fraction that has a fraction in its numerator or denominator or in both its numerator and denominator.

Fracción compleja (p. 674) Una fracción compleja es una fracción que contiene otra fracción en el numerador o en el denominador, o en ambos.

Example $\dfrac{\frac{2}{7}}{\frac{3}{2}}$

Compound event (p. 765) An event that consists of two or more events linked by the word *and* or the word *or*.

Suceso compuesto (p. 765) Suceso que consiste en dos o más sucesos unidos por medio de la palabra *y* o la palabra *o*.

Examples Rolling a 5 on a number cube and then rolling a 4 is a compound event.

Compound inequalities (p. 216) Two inequalities that are joined by *and* or *or*.

Desigualdades compuestas (p. 216) Dos desigualdades que están enlazadas por medio de una *y* o una *o*.

Examples $5 < x$ and $x < 10$
$14 < x$ or $x \leq -3$

Compound interest (p. 484) Interest paid on both the principal and the interest that has already been paid.

Interés compuesto (p. 484) Interés calculado tanto sobre el capital como sobre los intereses ya pagados.

Example For an initial deposit of $1000 at a 6% interest rate with interest compounded quarterly, the function $y = 1000\left(\frac{0.06}{4}\right)x$ gives the account balance y after x years.

Conclusion (p. 627) The part of an *if-then* statement (conditional) that follows *then*.

Conclusión (p. 627) La conclusión es lo que sigue a la palabra *entonces* en un enunciado condicional.

Example In the conditional "If an animal has four legs, then it is a horse," the conclusion is "it is a horse."

Conditional (p. 627) An *if-then* statement.

Condicional (p. 627) Un enunciado condicional es del tipo *si..., entonces...*

Example If an animal has four legs, then it is a horse.

Conjugates (p. 642) The sum and the difference of the same two terms.

Valores conjugados (p. 642) La suma y resta de los mismos dos términos.

Example $(\sqrt{3} + 2)$ and $(\sqrt{3} - 2)$ are conjugates.

Constant (p. 57) A term that has no variable factor.

Constante (p. 57) Término que tiene un valor fijo.

Example In the expression $4x + 13y + 17$, 17 is a constant term.

Constant of variation for direct variation (p. 321) The nonzero constant k in the function $y = kx$.

Constante de variación en variaciones directas (p. 321) La constante k cuyo valor no es cero en la función $y = kx$.

Example For the direct variation $y = 24x$, 24 is the constant of variation.

Continuous graph (p. 272) A graph that is unbroken.

Gráfica continua (p. 272) Una gráfica continua es una gráfica ininterrumpida.

Example

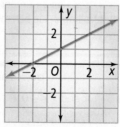

English

Spanish

Converse (p. 627)   The statement obtained by reversing the hypothesis and conclusion of a conditional.

Expresión recíproca (p. 627)   Enunciado que se obtiene al intercambiar la hipótesis y la conclusión de un enunciado condicional.

Example The converse of "If I was born in Houston, then I am a Texan" is "If I am a Texan, then I was born in Houston."

Conversion factor (p. 131)   A ratio of two equivalent measures in different units.

Factor de conversion (p. 131)   Razón de dos medidas equivalentes en unidades diferentes.

Example The ratio $\frac{1 \text{ ft}}{12 \text{ in.}}$ is a conversion factor.

Coordinate plane (p. 68)   A plane formed by two number lines that intersect at right angles.

Plano de coordenadas (p. 68)   Se forma cuando dos rectas numéricas se cortan formando ángulos rectos.

Example

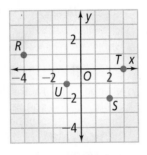

Coordinates (p. 68)   The numbers that make an ordered pair and identify the location of a point.

Coordenadas (p. 68)   Números ordenados por pares que determinan la posición de un punto sobre un plano.

Example

The coordinates of R are $(-4, 1)$.

Correlation coefficient (p. 366)   A number from -1 to 1 that tells you how closely the equation of the line of best fit models the data.

Coeficiente de correlación (p. 366)   Número de -1 a 1 que indica con cuánta exactitud la línea de mejor encaje representa los datos.

Example

```
LinReg
  y  = ax+b
  a  = .0134039132
  b  = −.3622031627
  r² = .886327776
  r  = .9414498267

■
```

The correlation coefficient is approximately 0.94.

Counterexample (p. 28)   An example showing that a statement is false.

Contraejemplo (p. 28)   Ejemplo que demuestra que un enunciado es falso.

Example Statement   All apples are red.
Counterexample   A Granny Smith apple is green.

Cross product (of sets) (p. 236)   The cross product of two sets A and B, denoted by $A \times B$, is the set of all ordered pairs with the first element in A and with the second element in B.

Producto cruzado (de dos conjuntos) (p. 236)   El producto cruzado de dos conjuntos A y B, definido por $A \times B$, es el conjunto de todos los pares ordenados cuyo primer elemento está en A y cuyo segundo elemento está en B.

Cross products (of a proportion) (p. 137)   In a proportion $\frac{a}{b} = \frac{c}{d}$, the products ad and bc. These products are equal.

Productos cruzados (de una proporción) (p. 137)   En una proporción $\frac{a}{b} = \frac{c}{d}$, los productos ad y bc. Estos productos son iguales.

Example   The cross products for $\frac{3}{4} = \frac{6}{8}$ are $3 \cdot 8$ and $4 \cdot 6$.

Cumulative frequency table (p. 718)   A table that shows the number of data values that lie in or below the given intervals.

Tabla de frecuencia cumulativa (p. 718)   Tabla que muestra el número de valores de datos que están dentro o por debajo de los intervalos dados.

Example

Interval	Frequency	Cumulative Frequency
0–9	5	5
10–19	8	13
20–29	4	17

D

Decay factor (p. 485)   1 minus the percent rate of change, expressed as a decimal, for an exponential decay situation.

Factor de decremento (p. 485)   1 menos la tasa porcentual de cambio, expresada como decimal, en una situación de reducción exponencial.

Example   The decay factor of the function $y = 5(0.3)^x$ is 0.3.

Deductive reasoning (p. 26)   A process of reasoning logically from given facts to a conclusion.

Razonamiento deductivo (p. 26)   El razonamiento deductivo es un proceso de razonamiento lógico que parte de hechos dados hasta llegar a una conclusión.

Example   Based on the fact that the sum of any two even numbers is even, you can deduce that the product of any whole number and any even number is even.

English

Spanish

Degree of a monomial (p. 502) The sum of the exponents of the variables of a monomial.

Grado de un monomio (p. 502) La suma de los exponentes de las variables de un monomio.

Example $-4x^3y^2$ is a monomial of degree 5.

Degree of a polynomial (p. 503) The highest degree of any term of the polynomial.

Grado de un polinomio (p. 503) El grado de un polinomio es el grado mayor de cualquier término del polinomio.

Example The polynomial $P(x) = x^6 + 2x^3 - 3$ has degree 6.

Dependent events (p. 768) When the outcome of one event affects the probability of a second event, the events are dependent events.

Sucesos dependientes (p. 768) Dos sucesos son dependientes si el resultado de un suceso afecta la probabilidad del otro.

Example You have a bag with marbles of different colors. If you pick a marble from the bag and pick another without replacing the first, the events are dependent events.

Dependent variable (p. 255) A variable that provides the output values of a function.

Variable dependiente (p. 255) Variable de la que dependen los valores de salida de una función.

Example In the equation $y = 3x$, y is the dependent variable.

Difference of squares (p. 547) A difference of two squares is an expression of the form $a^2 - b^2$. It can be factored as $(a + b)(a - b)$.

Diferencia de dos cuadrados (p. 547) La diferencia de dos cuadrados es una expresión de la forma $a^2 - b^2$. Se puede factorizar como $(a + b)(a - b)$.

Examples $25a^2 - 4 = (5a + 2)(5a - 2)$
$m^6 - 1 = (m^3 + 1)(m^3 - 1)$

Direct variation (p. 321) A linear function defined by an equation of the form $y = kx$, where $k \neq 0$.

Variación directa (p. 321) Una función lineal definida por una ecuación de la forma $y = kx$, donde $k \neq 0$, representa una variación directa.

Example $y = 18x$ is a direct variation.

Discrete graph (p. 272) A graph composed of isolated points.

Gráfica discreta (p. 272) Una gráfica discreta es compuesta de puntos aislados.

Example

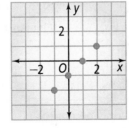

Discriminant (p. 604) The discriminant of a quadratic equation of the form $ax^2 + bx + c = 0$ is $b^2 - 4ac$. The value of the discriminant determines the number of solutions of the equation.

Discriminante (p. 604) El discriminante de una ecuación cuadrática $ax^2 + bx + c = 0$ es $b^2 - 4ac$. El valor del discriminante determina el número de soluciones de la ecuación.

Example The discriminant of
$$2x^2 + 9x - 2 = 0 \text{ is } 97.$$

Disjoint sets (p. 231) Sets that do not have any elements in common.

Conjuntos ajenos (p. 231) Conjuntos que no tienen elementos en común.

Example The set of positive integers and the set of negative integers are disjoint sets.

Distance Formula (p. 609) The distance d between any two points (x_1, y_1) and (x_2, y_2) is

$$d = \sqrt{(x_2 - x_1)^2 + (y_2 - y_1)^2}.$$

Fórmula de distancia (p. 609) La distancia d entre dos puntos cualesquiera (x_1, y_1) y (x_2, y_2) es

$$d = \sqrt{(x_2 - x_1)^2 + (y_2 - y_1)^2}.$$

Example The distance between $(-2, 4)$ and $(4, 5)$ is

$$d = \sqrt{(4 - (-2))^2 + (5 - 4)^2}$$
$$= \sqrt{(6)^2 + (1)^2}$$
$$= \sqrt{37}$$

Distributive Property (p. 52) For every real number a, b, and c:

$a(b + c) = ab + ac$ $\quad (b + c)a = ba + ca$
$a(b - c) = ab - ac$ $\quad (b - c)a = ba - ca$

Propiedad Distributiva (p. 52) Para cada número real a, b y c:

$a(b + c) = ab + ac$ $\quad (b + c)a = ba + ca$
$a(b - c) = ab - ac$ $\quad (b - c)a = ba - ca$

Examples $3(19 + 4) = 3(19) + 3(4)$
$(19 + 4)3 = 19(3) + 4(3)$
$7(11 - 2) = 7(11) - 7(2)$
$(11 - 2)7 = 11(7) - 2(7)$

Domain (of a relation or function) (p. 286) The possible values for the input of a relation or function.

Dominio (de una relación o función) (p. 286) Posibles valores de entrada de una relación o función.

Example In the function $f(x) = x + 22$, the domain is all real numbers.

E

Element (of a matrix) (p. 710) An item in a matrix.

Elemento (de una matriz) (p. 710) Componente de una matriz.

Example
$$\begin{bmatrix} 5 & -2 \\ 7 & 3 \end{bmatrix}$$

5, 7, -2, and 3 are the four elements of the matrix.

Elements (of a set) (p. 20) Members of a set.

Elementos (p. 20) Partes integrantes de un conjunto.

Example Cats and dogs are elements of the set of mammals.

Elimination method (p. 396) A method for solving a system of linear equations. You add or subtract the equations to eliminate a variable.

Eliminación (p. 396) Método para resolver un sistema de ecuaciones lineales. Se suman o se restan las ecuaciones para eliminar una variable.

Example
$$3x + y = 19$$
$$\underline{2x - y = 1}$$
$$5x + 0 = 20 \quad \text{Add the equations to get } x = 4.$$
$$2(4) - y = 1 \rightarrow \begin{array}{l}\text{Substitute 4 for } x \text{ in} \\ \text{the second equation.}\end{array}$$
$$8 - y = 1$$
$$y = 7 \rightarrow \text{Solve for } y.$$

Empty set (p. 211) A set that does not contain any elements.

Conjunto vacío (p. 211) Conjunto que no contiene elementos.

Example The intersection of the set of positive integers and the set of negative integers is the empty set.

Equation (p. 61) A mathematical sentence that uses an equal sign.

Ecuación (p. 61) Enunciado matemático que tiene el signo de igual.

Example $x + 5 = 3x - 7$

Equivalent equations (p. 87) Equations that have the same solution.

Ecuaciones equivalentes (p. 87) Ecuaciones que tienen la misma solución.

Example $\frac{9}{3} = 3$ and $\frac{9}{3} + a = 3 + a$ are equivalent equations.

Equivalent expressions (p. 26) Algebraic expressions that have the same value for all values of the variable(s).

Ecuaciones equivalentes (p. 26) Expresiones algebraicas que tienen el mismo valor para todos los valores de la(s) variable(s).

Example $3a + 2a$ and $5a$ are equivalent expressions.

Equivalent inequalities (p. 184) Inequalities that have the same set of solutions.

Desigualdades equivalentes (p. 184) Las desigualdades equivalentes tienen el mismo conjunto de soluciones.

Example $x + 4 < 7$ and $x < 3$ are equivalent inequalities.

Evaluate (p. 15) To substitute a given number for each variable, and then simplify.

Evaluar (p. 15) Método de sustituir cada variable por un número dado para luego simplificar la expresión.

Example To evaluate $3x + 4$ for $x = 2$, substitute 2 for x and simplify.
$$3(2) + 4 = 6 + 4 = 10$$

English

Event (p. 757)   Any group of outcomes in a situation involving probability.

Example   When rolling a number cube, there are six possible outcomes. Rolling an even number is an event with three possible outcomes, 2, 4, and 6.

Excluded value (p. 664)   A value of x for which a rational expression $f(x)$ is undefined.

Experimental probability (p. 760)   The ratio of the number of times an event actually happens to the number of times the experiment is done.

$$P(\text{event}) = \frac{\text{number of times an event happens}}{\text{number of times the experiment is done}}$$

Example   A baseball player's batting average shows how likely it is that a player will get a hit, based on previous times at bat.

Exponent (p. 11)   A number that shows repeated multiplication.

Example $3^4 = 3 \cdot 3 \cdot 3 \cdot 3$
The exponent 4 indicates that 3 is used as a factor four times.

Exponential decay (p. 485)   A situation modeled with a function of the form $y = ab^x$, where $a > 0$ and $0 < b < 1$.

Example $y = 5(0.1)^x$

Exponential function (p. 475)   A function that repeatedly multiplies an initial amount by the same positive number. You can model all exponential functions using $y = ab^x$, where a is a nonzero constant, $b > 0$, and $b \neq 1$.

Spanish

Suceso (p. 757)   En la probabilidad, cualquier grupo de resultados.

Valor excluido (p. 664)   Valor de x para el cual una expresión racional es indefinida.

Probabilidad experimental (p. 760)   La razón entre el número de veces que un suceso sucede en la realidad y el número de veces que se hace el experimento.

$$P(\text{suceso}) = \frac{\text{número de veces que sucede un suceso}}{\text{número de veces que se hace el experimento}}$$

Exponente (p. 11)   Denota el número de veces que debe multiplicarse.

Decremento exponencial (p. 485)   Para $a > 0$ y $0 < b < 1$, la función $y = ab^x$ representa el decremento exponencial.

Función exponencial (p. 475)   Función que multiplica repetidas veces una cantidad inicial por el mismo número positivo. Todas las funciones exponenciales se pueden representar mediante $y = ab^x$, donde a es una constante con valor distinto de cero, $b > 0$ y $b \neq 1$.

Example

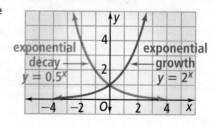

English

Spanish

Exponential growth (p. 483)   A situation modeled with a function of the form $y = ab^x$, where $a > 0$ and $b > 1$.

Example $y = 100(2)^x$

Incremento exponencial (p. 483)   Para $a > 0$ y $b > 1$, la función $y = ab^x$ representa el incremento exponencial.

Extraneous solution (p. 648)   A solution of an equation derived from an original equation that is not a solution of the original equation.

Solución extraña (p. 648)   Una solución extraña es una solución de una ecuación derivada que no es una solución de la ecuación original.

Example $\dfrac{b}{b + 4} = 3 - \dfrac{4}{b + 4}$

$b = 3(b + 4) - 4$ Multiply by $(b + 4)$.

$b = 3b + 12 - 4$

$-2b = 8$

$b = -4$

Replace b with -4 in the original equation. The denominator is 0, so -4 is an extraneous solution.

Extrapolation (p. 364)   The process of predicting a value outside the range of known values.

Extrapolación (p. 364)   Proceso que se usa para predecir un valor por fuera del ámbito de los valores dados.

F

Factor by grouping (p. 551)   A method of factoring that uses the Distributive Property to remove a common binomial factor of two pairs of terms.

Factor común por agrupación de términos (p. 551)   Método de factorización que aplica la propiedad distributiva para sacar un factor común de dos pares de términos en un binomio.

Example The expression $7x(x - 1) + 4(x - 1)$ can be factored as $(7x + 4)(x - 1)$.

Formula (p. 118)   An equation that states a relationship among quantities.

Fórmula (p. 118)   Ecuación que establece una relación entre cantidades.

Example The formula for the volume V of a cylinder is $V = \pi r^2 h$, where r is the radius of the cylinder and h is its height.

Frequency (p. 716)   The number of data items in an interval.

Frecuencia (p. 716)   Número de datos de un intervalo.

Example In the data set 4, 7, 12, 4, 5, 8, 11, 2, the frequency of the interval 5–9 is 3.

Visual **Glossary**

English

Frequency table (p. 716)   A table that groups a set of data values into intervals and shows the frequency for each interval.

Example

Interval	Frequency
0–9	5
10–19	8
20–29	4

Function (p. 257)   A relation that assigns exactly one value in the range to each value of the domain.

Example   Earned income is a function of the number of hours worked. If you earn $4.50/h, then your income is expressed by the function $f(h) = 4.5h$.

Function notation (p. 286)   To write a rule in function notation, you use the symbol $f(x)$ in place of y.

Example $f(x) = 3x - 8$ is in function notation.

Function rule (p. 265)   An equation that describes a function.

Example $y = 4x + 1$ is a function rule.

Geometric sequence (p. 481)   A number sequence formed by multiplying a term in a sequence by a fixed number to find the next term.

Example $9, 3, 1, \frac{1}{3}, \ldots$ is an example of a geometric sequence.

Growth factor (p. 483)   1 plus the percent rate of change for an exponential growth situation.

Example   The growth factor of $y = 7(1.3)^x$ is 1.3.

Spanish

Tabla de frecuencias (p. 716)   Tabla que agrupa un conjunto de datos en intervalos y muestra la frecuencia de cada intervalo.

Función (p. 257)   La relación que asigna exactamente un valor del rango a cada valor del dominio.

Notación de una función (p. 286)   Para expresar una regla en notación de función se usa el símbolo $f(x)$ en lugar de y.

Regla de una función (p. 265)   Ecuación que describe una función.

Progresión geométrica (p. 481)   Tipo de sucesión numérica formada al multiplicar un término de la secuencia por un número constante, para hallar el siguiente término.

Factor incremental (p. 483)   1 más la tasa porcentual de cambio en una situación de incremento exponencial.

H

Histogram (p. 717) A special type of bar graph that can display data from a frequency table. Each bar represents an interval. The height of each bar shows the frequency of the interval it represents.

Histograma (p. 717) Tipo de gráfica de barras que muestra los datos de una tabla de frecuencia. Cada barra representa un intervalo. La altura de cada barra muestra la frecuencia del intervalo al que representa.

Example

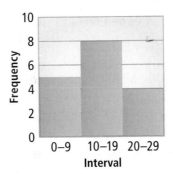

Hypotenuse (p. 626) The side opposite the right angle in a right triangle. It is the longest side in the triangle.

Hipotenusa (p. 626) En un triángulo rectángulo, el lado opuesto al ángulo recto. Es el lado más largo del triángulo.

Example

c **is the hypotenuse.**

Hypothesis (p. 627) In an *if-then* statement (conditional), the hypothesis is the part that follows *if*.

Hipótesis (p. 627) En un enunciado *si. . . entonces. . .* (condicional), la hipótesis es la parte del enunciado que sigue el *si*.

Example In the conditional "If an animal has four legs, then it is a horse," the hypothesis is "an animal has four legs."

I

Identity (p. 112) An equation that is true for every value.

Identidad (p. 112) Una ecuación que es verdadera para todos los valores.

Example $5 - 14x = 5\left(1 - \frac{14}{5}x\right)$ is an identity because it is true for any value of x.

Independent events (p. 766) When the outcome of one event does not affect the probability of a second event, the two events are independent.

Sucesos independientes (p. 766) Cuando el resultado de un suceso no altera la probabilidad de otro, los dos sucesos son independientes.

Example The results of two rolls of a number cube are independent. Getting a 5 on the first roll does not change the probability of getting a 5 on the second roll.

Visual **Glossary**

Independent variable (p. 255) A variable that provides the input values of a function.

Variable independiente (p. 255) Variable de la que dependen los valores de entrada de una función.

Example In the equation $y = 3x$, x is the independent variable.

Inductive reasoning (p. 71) Making conclusions based on observed patterns.

Razonamiento inductivo (p. 71) Sacar conclusiones a partir de patrones observados.

Inequality (p. 22) A mathematical sentence that compares the values of two expressions using an inequality symbol.

Desigualdad (p. 22) Expresión matemática que compara el valor de dos expresiones con el símbolo de desigualdad.

Example $3 < 7$

Input (p. 255) A value of the independent variable.

Entrada (p. 255) Valor de una variable independiente.

Example The input is any value of x you substitute into a function.

Integers (p. 21) Whole numbers and their opposites.

Números enteros (p. 21) Números que constan exclusivamente de una o más unidades, y sus opuestos.

Example $\ldots -3, -2, -1, 0, 1, 2, 3, \ldots$

Interpolation (p. 364) The process of estimating a value between two known quantities.

Interpolación (p. 364) Proceso que se usa para estimar el valor entre dos cantidades dadas.

Interquartile range (p. 730) The interquartile range of a set of data is the difference between the third and first quartiles.

Intervalo intercuartil (p. 730) El rango intercuartil de un conjunto de datos es la diferencia entre el tercero y el primer cuartiles.

Example The first and third quartiles of the data set 2, 3, 4, 5, 5, 6, 7, and 7 are 3.5 and 6.5. The interquartile range is $6.5 - 3.5 = 3$.

Intersection (p. 231) The set of elements that are common to two or more sets.

Intersección (p. 231) El conjunto de elementos que son comunes a dos o más conjuntos.

Example If $C = \{1, 2, 3, 4\}$ and $D = \{2, 4, 6, 8\}$, then the intersection of C and D, or $C \cap D$, is $\{2, 4\}$.

Inverse operations (p. 88) Operations that undo one another.

Operaciones inversas (p. 88) Las operaciones que se cancelan una a la otra.

Example Addition and subtraction are inverse operations. Multiplication and division are inverse operations.

English

Irrational number (p. 21) A number that cannot be written as a ratio of two integers. Irrational numbers in decimal form are nonterminating and nonrepeating.

Example $\sqrt{11}$ and π are irrational numbers.

Isolate (p. 88) Using properties of equality and inverse operations to get a variable with a coefficient of 1 alone on one side of the equation.

Example
$$x + 3 = 7$$
$$x + 3 - 3 = 7 - 3$$
$$x = 4$$

L

Leg (p. 626) Each of the sides that form the right angle of a right triangle.

Example  a and b are legs.

Like radicals (p. 640) Radical expressions with the same radicands.

Example $3\sqrt{7}$ and $25\sqrt{7}$ are like radicals.

Like terms (p. 57) Terms with exactly the same variable factors in a variable expression.

Example $4y$ and $16y$ are like terms.

Linear equation (p. 329) An equation whose graph forms a straight line.

Example

Linear function (p. 257) A function whose graph is a line is a linear function. You can represent a linear function with a linear equation.

Example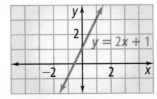

Spanish

Número irracional (p. 21) Número que no puede expresarse como razón de dos números enteros. Los números irracionales en forma decimal no tienen término y no se repiten.

Aislar (p. 88) Usar propiedades de igualdad y operaciones inversas para poner una variable con un coeficiente de 1 sola a un lado de la ecuación.

Cateto (p. 626) Cada uno de los dos lados que forman el ángulo recto en un triángulo rectángulo.

Radicales semejantes (p. 640) Expresiones radicales con los mismos radicandos.

Términos semejantes (p. 57) Términos con los mismos factores variables en una expresión variable.

Ecuación lineal (p. 329) Ecuación cuya gráfica es una línea recta.

Función lineal (p. 257) Una función cuya gráfica es una recta es una función lineal. La función lineal se representa con una ecuación lineal.

English

Spanish

Linear inequality (p. 414)   An inequality in two variables whose graph is a region of the coordinate plane that is bounded by a line. Each point in the region is a solution of the inequality.

Desigualdad lineal (p. 414)   Una desigualdad lineal es una desigualdad de dos variables cuya gráfica es una región del plano de coordenadas delimitado por una recta. Cada punto de la región es una solución de la desigualdad.

Example

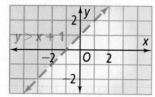

Linear parent function (p. 329)   The simplest form of a linear function.

Función lineal elemental (p. 329)   La forma más simple de una función lineal.

Example $y = x$

Line of best fit (p. 366)   The most accurate trend line on a scatter plot showing the relationship between two sets of data.

Recta de mayor aproximación (p. 366)   La línea de tendencia en un diagrama de puntos que más se acerca a los puntos que representan la relación entre dos conjuntos de datos.

Example

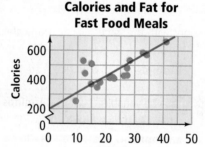

Calories and Fat for Fast Food Meals

Literal equation (p. 117)   An equation involving two or more variables.

Ecuación literal (p. 117)   Ecuación que incluye dos o más variables.

Example $4x + 2y = 18$ is a literal equation.

Matrix (p. 710)   A matrix is a rectangular array of numbers written within brackets. A matrix with m horizontal rows and n vertical columns is an $m \times n$ matrix.

Matriz (p. 710)   Una matriz es un conjunto de números encerrados en corchetes y dispuestos en forma de rectángulo. Una matriz que contenga m filas y n columnas es una matriz $m \times n$.

Example $\begin{bmatrix} 2 & 5 & 6.3 \\ -8 & 0 & -1 \end{bmatrix}$ is a 2 × 3 matrix.

English

Maximum (p. 553) The y-coordinate of the vertex of a parabola that opens downward.

Example

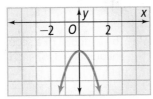

Since the parabola opens downward, the y-coordinate of the vertex is the function's maximum value.

Mean (p. 722) To find the mean of a set of data values, find the sum of the data values and divide the sum by the number of data values. The mean is $\frac{\text{sum of the data values}}{\text{total number of data values}}$.

Example In the data set 12, 11, 12, 10, 13, 12, and 7, the mean is
$$\frac{12 + 11 + 12 + 10 + 13 + 12 + 7}{7} = 11.$$

Measure of central tendency (p. 722) Mean, median, and mode. They are used to organize and summarize a set of data.

Example For examples, see *mean*, *median*, and *mode*.

Measure of dispersion (p. 724) A measure that describes how dispersed, or spread out, the values in a data set are. Range is a measure of dispersion.

Example For an example, see *range*.

Median (p. 722) The middle value in an ordered set of numbers.

Example In the data set 7, 10, 11, 12, 12, 12, and 13, the median is 12.

Midpoint (p. 609) The point M that divides a segment $\overline{AB}$ into two equal segments, $\overline{AM}$ and $\overline{MB}$.

Example M is the midpoint of $\overline{XY}$.

X — M — Y

Spanish

Valor máximo (p. 553) La coordenada y del vértice en una parábola que se abre hacia abajo.

Media (p. 722) Para hallar la media de un conjunto de datos, halla la suma de los valores de los datos y divide la suma por el total del valor de los datos. La media es $\frac{\text{la suma de los datos}}{\text{el número total de valores de datos}}$.

Medida de tendencia central (p. 722) La media, la mediana y la moda. Se usan para organizar y resumir un conjunto de datos.

Medida de dispersión (p. 724) Medida que describe cómo se dispersan, o esparcen, los valores de un conjunto de datos. La amplitud es una medida de dispersión.

Mediana (p. 722) El valor del medio en un conjunto ordenado de números.

Punto medio (p. 609) El punto M que divide un segmento $\overline{AB}$ en dos segmentos iguales, $\overline{AM}$ y $\overline{MB}$.

English

Spanish

Midpoint Formula (p. 609)   The midpoint M of a line segment with endpoints $A(x_1, y_1)$ and $B(x_2, y_2)$ is $\left(\dfrac{x_1 + x_2}{2}, \dfrac{y_1 + y_2}{2}\right)$.

Fórmula del punto medio (p. 609)   El punto medio M de un segmento con puntos extremos $A(x_1, y_1)$ y $B(x_2, y_2)$ es $\left(\dfrac{x_1 + x_2}{2}, \dfrac{y_1 + y_2}{2}\right)$.

Example   The midpoint of a segment with endpoints $A(3, 5)$ and $B(7, 1)$ is $(5, 3)$.

Minimum (p. 553)   The y-coordinate of the vertex of a parabola that opens upward.

Valor mínimo (p. 553)   La coordenada y del vértice en una parábola que se abre hacia arriba.

Example

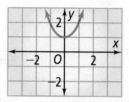

Since the parabola opens upward, the y-coordinate of the vertex is the function's minimum value.

Mode (p. 722)   The mode is the most frequently occurring value (or values) in a set of data. A data set may have no mode, one mode, or more than one mode.

Moda (p. 722)   La moda es el valor o valores que ocurren con mayor frequencia en un conjunto de datos. El conjunto de datos puede no tener moda, o tener una o más modas.

Example   In the data set 7, 7, 9, 10, 11, and 13, the mode is 7.

Monomial (p. 502)   A real number, a variable, or a product of a real number and one or more variables with whole-number exponents.

Monomio (p. 502)   Número real, variable o el producto de un número real y una o más variables con números enteros como exponentes.

Example   9, n, and $-5xy^2$ are examples of monomials.

Multiplication Counting Principle (p. 751)   If there are m ways to make the first selection and n ways to make the second selection, then there are $m \cdot n$ ways to make the two selections.

Principio de Conteo en la Multiplicación (p. 751)   Si hay m maneras de hacer la primera selección y n maneras de hacer la segunda selección, quiere decir que hay $m \cdot n$ maneras de hacer las dos selecciones.

Example   For 5 shirts and 8 pairs of shorts, the number of possible outfits is $5 \cdot 8 = 40$.

Multiplicative inverse (p. 47)   Given a nonzero rational number $\dfrac{a}{b}$, the multiplicative inverse, or reciprocal, is $\dfrac{b}{a}$. The product of a nonzero number and its multiplicative inverse is 1.

Inverso multiplicativo (p. 47)   Dado un número racional $\dfrac{a}{b}$ distinto de cero, el inverso multiplicativo, o recíproco, es $\dfrac{b}{a}$. El producto de un número distinto de cero y su inverso multiplicativo es 1.

Example $\dfrac{4}{3}$ is the multiplicative inverse of $\dfrac{3}{4}$ because $\dfrac{3}{4} \times \dfrac{4}{3} = 1$.

English

Mutually exclusive events (p. 765) When two events cannot happen at the same time, the events are mutually exclusive. If A and B are mutually exclusive events, then $P(A \text{ or } B) = P(A) + P(B)$.

Example Rolling an even number E and rolling a multiple of five M on a standard number cube are mutually exclusive events.

$$P(E \text{ or } M) = P(E) + P(M)$$
$$= \frac{3}{6} + \frac{1}{6}$$
$$= \frac{4}{6}$$
$$= \frac{2}{3}$$

Spanish

Sucesos mutuamente excluyentes (p. 765) Cuando dos sucesos no pueden ocurrir al mismo tiempo, son mutuamente excluyentes. Si A y B son sucesos mutuamente excluyentes, entonces $P(A \text{ o } B) = P(A) + P(B)$.

N

Natural numbers (p. 21) The counting numbers.

Example 1, 2, 3, . . .

Números naturales (p. 21) Los números que se emplean para contar.

Negative correlation (p. 363) The relationship between two sets of data, in which one set of data decreases as the other set of data increases.

Example

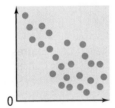

Correlación negativa (p. 363) Relación entre dos conjuntos de datos en la que uno de los conjuntos disminuye a medida que el otro aumenta.

Negative square root (p. 46) A number of the form $-\sqrt{b}$, which is the negative square root of b.

Example -7 is the negative square root of $\sqrt{49}$.

Raíz cuadrada negativa (p. 46) $-\sqrt{b}$ es la raíz cuadrada negativa de b.

---

n factorial (p. 752) The product of the integers from n down to 1, for any positive integer n. You write n factorial as $n!$. The value of $0!$ is defined to be 1.

Example $4! = 4 \times 3 \times 2 \times 1 = 24$

n factorial (p. 752) Producto de todos los enteros desde n hasta 1, de cualquier entero positivo n. El factorial de n se escribe $n!$. El valor de $0!$ se define como 1.

English

Spanish

No correlation (p. 363)   There does not appear to be a relationship between two sets of data.

Sin correlación (p. 363)   No hay relación entre dos conjuntos de datos.

Example

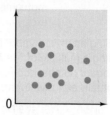

Nonlinear function (p. 262)   A function whose graph is not a line or part of a line.

Función no lineal (p. 262)   Función cuya gráfica no es una línea o parte de una línea.

Example

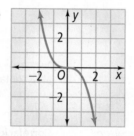

Null set (p. 211)   A set that has no elements.

Conjunto vacío (p. 211)   Conjunto que no tiene elementos.

Example $\{\}$ or $\varnothing$

Numerical expression (p. 4)   A mathematical phrase involving numbers and operation symbols, but no variables.

Expresión numérica (p. 4)   Frase matemática que contiene números y operaciones con símbolos, pero no variables.

Example $2 + 4$

Odds (p. 759)   A ratio that compares the number of favorable and unfavorable outcomes. Odds in favor are number of favorable outcomes : number of unfavorable outcomes. Odds against are number of unfavorable outcomes : number of favorable outcomes.

Probabilidad a favor (p. 759)   Razón que compara el número de resultados favorables y no favorables. Las posibilidades a favor son el número de resultados favorables : número de resultados no favorables. Las posibilidades en contra son el número de resultados no favorables : número de resultados favorables.

Example You have 3 red marbles and 5 blue marbles. The odds in favor of selecting red are 3 : 5.

Open sentence (p. 61)   An equation that contains one or more variables and may be true or false depending on the value of its variables.

Enunciado abierto (p. 61)   Una ecuación es un enunciado abierto si contiene una o más variables y puede ser verdadera o falsa dependiendo del valor de sus variables.

Example $5 + x = 12$ is an open sentence.

Opposite (p. 39)   A number that is the same distance from zero on the number line as a given number, but lies in the opposite direction.

Opuestos (p. 39)   Dos números son opuestos si están a la misma distancia del cero en la recta numérica, pero en sentido opuesto.

Example -3 and 3 are opposites.

English

Spanish

Opposite reciprocals (p. 358) A number of the form $-\frac{b}{a}$, where $\frac{a}{b}$ is a nonzero rational number. The product of a number and its opposite reciprocal is -1.

Recíproco inverso (p. 358) Número en la forma $-\frac{b}{a}$, donde $\frac{a}{b}$ es un número racional diferente de cero. El producto de un número y su recíproco inverso es -1.

Example $\frac{2}{5}$ and $-\frac{5}{2}$ are opposite reciprocals because $\left(\frac{2}{5}\right)\left(-\frac{5}{2}\right) = -1$.

Ordered pair (p. 68) Two numbers that identify the location of a point.

Par ordenado (p. 68) Un par ordenado de números que denota la ubicación de un punto.

Example The ordered pair $(4, -1)$ identifies the point 4 units to the right on the x-axis and 1 unit down on the y-axis.

Order of operations (p. 12)
1. Perform any operation(s) inside grouping symbols.
2. Simplify powers.
3. Multiply and divide in order from left to right.
4. Add and subtract in order from left to right.

Orden de las operaciones (p. 12)
1. Se hacen las operaciones que están dentro de símbolos de agrupación.
2. Se simplifican todos los términos que tengan exponentes.
3. Se hacen las multiplicaciones y divisiones en orden de izquierda a derecha.
4. Se hacen las sumas y restas en orden de izquierda a derecha.

Example
$$6 - (4^2 - [2 \cdot 5]) \div 3$$
$$= 6 - (16 - 10) \div 3$$
$$= 6 - 6 \div 3$$
$$= 6 - 2$$
$$= 4$$

Origin (p. 68) The point at which the axes of the coordinate plane intersect.

Origen (p. 68) Punto de intersección de los ejes del plano de coordenadas.

Example

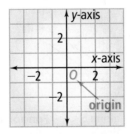

Outcome (p. 757) The result of a single trial in a probability experiment.

Resultado (p. 757) Lo que se obtiene al hacer una sola prueba en un experimento de probabilidad.

Example The outcomes of rolling a number cube are 1, 2, 3, 4, 5, and 6.

Visual Glossary

Outlier (p. 722) An outlier is a data value that is much higher or lower than the other data values in the set.

Valor extremo (p. 722) Un valor extremo es el valor de un dato que es mucho más alto o mucho más bajo que los otros valores del conjunto de datos.

Example For the set of values 2, 5, 3, 7, 12, the data value 12 is an outlier.

Output (p. 255) A value of the dependent variable.

Salida (p. 255) Valor de una variable dependiente.

Example The output of the function $f(x) = x^2$ when $x = 3$ is 9.

Overlapping events (p. 765) Events that have at least one common outcome. If A and B are overlapping events, then $P(A$ or $B) = P(A) + P(B) - P(A$ and $B)$.

Sucesos traslapados (p. 765) Sucesos que tienen por lo menos un resultado en común. Si A y B son sucesos traslapados, entonces $P(A$ ó $B) = P(A) + P(B) - P(A$ y $B)$.

Example Rolling a multiple of 3 and rolling an odd number on a number cube are overlapping events.

$$P(\text{multiple of 3 or odd}) = P(\text{multiple of 3}) + P(\text{odd}) - P(\text{multiple of 3 and odd})$$
$$= \frac{1}{3} + \frac{1}{2} - \frac{1}{6}$$
$$= \frac{2}{3}$$

Parabola (p. 552) The graph of a quadratic function.

Parábola (p. 552) La gráfica de una función cuadrática.

Example

Parallel lines (p. 357) Two lines in the same plane that never intersect. Parallel lines have the same slope.

Rectas paralelas (p. 357) Dos rectas situadas en el mismo plano que nunca se cortan. Las rectas paralelas tienen la misma pendiente.

Example

Parent function (p. 329) A family of functions is a group of functions with common characteristics. A parent function is the simplest function with these characteristics.

Función elemental (p. 329) Una familia de funciones es un grupo de funciones con características en común. La función elemental es la función más simple que reúne esas características.

Example $y = x$ is the parent function for the family of linear equations of the form $y = mx + b$.

English

Percent change (p. 157) The ratio of the amount of change to the original amount expressed as a percent.

Example The price of a sweater was $20. The price increases $2. The percent change is $\frac{2}{20} = 10\%$.

Percent decrease (p. 157) The percent change found when the original amount decreases.

Example The price of a sweater was $22. The price decreases $2. The percent change is $\frac{2}{22} \approx 9\%$.

Percent error (p. 159) The ratio of the absolute value of the difference of the measured (or estimated) value and an actual value compared to the actual value, expressed as a percent.

Example The diameter of a CD is measured as 12.1 cm. The greatest possible error is 0.05 cm. The percent error is $\frac{0.05}{12.1} \approx 0.4\%$.

Percentile (p. 733) A value that separates a data set into 100 equal parts.

Percentile rank (p. 733) The percentage of data values that are less than or equal to a given value.

Percent increase (p. 157) The percent change found when the original amount increases.

Example See example for *percent change* above.

Perfect squares (p. 20) Numbers whose square roots are integers.

Example The numbers 1, 4, 9, 16, 25, 36, . . . are perfect squares because they are the squares of integers.

Perfect square trinomial (p. 545) Any trinomial of the form $a^2 + 2ab + b^2$ or $a^2 - 2ab + b^2$.

Example $(x + 3)^2 = x^2 + 6x + 9$

Spanish

Cambio porcentual (p. 157) La razón de la cantidad de cambio y la cantidad original, expresada como un porcentaje.

Disminución porcentual (p. 157) Cambio porcentual que se encuentra cuando la cantidad original disminuye.

Error porcentual (p. 159) Razón del valor absoluto de la diferencia de un valor medido (o estimado) y un valor actual en comparación con el valor actual, expresada como un porcentaje.

Percentil (p. 733) Valor que separa el conjunto de datos en 100 partes iguales.

Rango percentil (p. 733) Porcentaje de valores de datos que es menos o igual a un valor dado.

Aumento porcentual (p. 157) Cambio porcentual que se encuentra cuando la cantidad original aumenta.

Cuadrado perfecto (p. 20) Número cuya raíz cuadrada es un número entero.

Trinomio cuadrado perfecto (p. 545) Todo trinomio de la forma $a^2 + 2ab + b^2$ ó $a^2 - 2ab + b^2$.

Visual **Glossary**

English

Spanish

Permutation (p. 752)   An arrangement of some or all of a set of objects in a specific order. You can use the notation $_nP_r$ to express the number of permutations, where n equals the number of objects available and r equals the number of selections to make.

Permutación (p. 752)   Disposición de algunos o de todos los objetos de un conjunto en un orden determinado. El número de permutaciones se puede expresar con la notación $_nP_r$, donde n es igual al número total de objetos y r es igual al número de selecciones que han de hacerse.

Example   How many ways can you arrange 5 objects 3 at a time?

$$_5P_3 = \frac{5!}{(5-3)!} = \frac{5!}{2!} = \frac{5 \cdot 4 \cdot 3 \cdot 2 \cdot 1}{2 \cdot 1} = 60$$

There are 60 ways to arrange 5 objects 3 at a time.

Perpendicular lines (p. 358)   Lines that intersect to form right angles. Two lines are perpendicular if the product of their slopes is -1.

Rectas perpendiculares (p. 358)   Rectas que forman ángulos rectos en su intersección. Dos rectas son perpendiculares si el producto de sus pendientes es -1.

Example

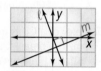

Point-slope form (p. 338)   A linear equation of a nonvertical line written as $y - y_1 = m(x - x_1)$. The line passes through the point (x_1, y_1) with slope m.

Forma punto-pendiente (p. 338)   La ecuación lineal de una recta no vertical que pasa por el punto (x_1, y_1) con pendiente m está dada por $y - y_1 = m(x - x_1)$.

Example   An equation with a slope of $-\frac{1}{2}$ passing through $(2, -1)$ would be written $y + 1 = -\frac{1}{2}(x - 2)$ in point-slope form.

Polynomial (p. 503)   A monomial or the sum or difference of two or more monomials. A quotient with a variable in the denominator is not a polynomial.

Polinomio (p. 503)   Un monomio o la suma o diferencia de dos o más monomios. Un cociente con una variable en el denominador no es un polinomio.

Example $2x^2$, $3x + 7$, 28, and $-7x^3 - 2x^2 + 9$ are all polynomials.

Population (p. 738)   The entire group that you are collecting information about.

Población (p. 738)   El grupo entero del cual juntas información.

Positive correlation (p. 363)   The relationship between two sets of data in which both sets of data increase together.

Correlación positiva (p. 363)   La relación entre dos conjuntos de datos en la que ambos conjuntos incrementan a la vez.

Example

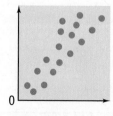

English

Spanish

Power (p. 11)   The base and the exponent of an expression of the form a^n.

Potencia (p. 11)   La base y el exponente de una expresión de la forma a^n.

Example 5^4

Principal square root (p. 19)   A number of the form $\sqrt{b}$. The expression $\sqrt{b}$ is called the principal (or positive) square root of b.

Raíz cuadrada principal (p. 19)   La expresión $\sqrt{b}$ se llama raíz cuadrada principal (o positiva) de b.

Example   5 is the principal square root of $\sqrt{25}$.

Probability (p. 757)   How likely it is that an event will occur (written formally as P(event)).

Probabilidad (p. 757)   La posibilidad de que un suceso ocurra, escrita formalmente P(suceso).

Example   You have 4 red marbles and 3 white marbles. The probability that you select one red marble, and then, without replacing it, randomly select another red marble is $P(\text{red}) = \frac{4}{7} \cdot \frac{3}{6} = \frac{2}{7}$.

Properties of equality (p. 87, 89)   For all real numbers a, b, and c:
  Addition: If $a = b$, then $a + c = b + c$.
  Subtraction: If $a = b$, then $a - c = b - c$.
  Multiplication: If $a = b$, then $a \cdot c = b \cdot c$.
  Division: If $a = b$, and $c \neq 0$, then $\frac{a}{c} = \frac{b}{c}$.

Propiedades de la igualdad (p. 87, 89)   Para todos los números reales a, b y c:
  Suma: Si $a = b$, entonces $a + c = b + c$.
  Resta: Si $a = b$, entonces $a - c = b - c$.
  Multiplicación: Si $a = b$, entonces $a \cdot c = b \cdot c$.
  División: Si $a = b$, y $c \neq 0$, entonces $\frac{a}{c} = \frac{b}{c}$.

Example   Since $\frac{2}{4} = \frac{1}{2}, \frac{2}{4} + 5 = \frac{1}{2} + 5$.

Since $\frac{9}{3} = 3, \frac{9}{3} - 6 = 3 - 6$.

Proportion (p. 136)   An equation that states that two ratios are equal.

Proporción (p. 136)   Es una ecuación que establece que dos razones son iguales.

Example $\frac{7.5}{9} = \frac{5}{6}$

Pythagorean Theorem (p. 626)   In any right triangle, the sum of the squares of the lengths of the legs is equal to the square of the length of the hypotenuse: $a^2 + b^2 = c^2$.

Teorema de Pitágoras (p. 626)   En un triángulo rectángulo, la suma de los cuadrados de los catetos es igual al cuadrado de la hipotenusa: $a^2 + b^2 = c^2$.

Example $3^2 + 4^2 = 5^2$

Quadrants (p. 68) The four parts into which the coordinate plane is divided by its axes.

Cuadrantes (p. 68) El plano de coordenadas está dividido por sus ejes en cuatro regiones llamadas cuadrantes.

Example

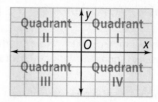

Quadratic equation (p. 566) A quadratic equation is one that can be written in the standard form $ax^2 + bx + c = 0$, where $a \neq 0$.

Ecuación cuadrática (p. 566) Ecuación que puede expresarse de la forma normal como $ax^2 + bx + c = 0$, en la que $a \neq 0$.

Example $4x^2 + 9x - 5 = 0$

Quadratic formula (p. 601) If $ax^2 + bx + c = 0$ and $a \neq 0$, then $x = \dfrac{-b \pm \sqrt{b^2 - 4ac}}{2a}$.

Fórmula cuadrática (p. 601) Si $ax^2 + bx + c = 0$ y $a \neq 0$, entonces $x = \dfrac{-b \pm \sqrt{b^2 - 4ac}}{2a}$.

Example $2x^2 + 10x + 12 = 0$

$$x = \frac{-b \pm \sqrt{b^2 - 4ac}}{2a}$$

$$x = \frac{-10 \pm \sqrt{10^2 - 4(2)(12)}}{2(2)}$$

$$x = \frac{-10 \pm \sqrt{4}}{4}$$

$$x = \frac{-10 + 2}{4} \text{ or } \frac{-10 - 2}{4}$$

$$x = -2 \text{ or } -3$$

Quadratic function (p. 552) A function of the form $y = ax^2 + bx + c$, where $a \neq 0$. The graph of a quadratic function is a parabola, a U-shaped curve that opens up or down.

Función cuadrática (p. 552) La función $y = ax^2 + bx + c$, en la que $a \neq 0$. La gráfica de una función cuadrática es una parábola, o curva en forma de U que se abre hacia arriba o hacia abajo.

Example $y = 5x^2 - 2x + 1$ is a quadratic function.

Quadratic parent function (p. 552) The simplest quadratic function $f(x) = x^2$ or $y = x^2$.

Función cuadrática madre (p. 552) La función cuadrática más simple $f(x) = x^2$ ó $y = x^2$.

Example $y = x^2$ is the parent function for the family of quadratic equations of the form $y = ax^2 + bx + c$.

Qualitative (p. 737) Data that name qualities are qualitative.

Cualitativo (p. 737) Los datos que indican cualidades son cualitativos.

Example The data red, blue, red, green, blue, and blue are qualitative data.

English

Spanish

Quantitative (p. 737) Data that measure quantity and can be described numerically are quantitative.

    Example The data 5 ft, 4 ft, 7 ft, 4 ft, 8 ft, and 10 ft are quantitative.

Cuantitativo (p. 737) Los datos que miden cantidades y pueden ser descritos numéricamente son cuantitativos.

Quantity (p. 4) Anything that can be measured or counted.

    Example A dozen is another way to describe a quantity of 12 eggs.

Cantidad (p. 4) Cualquier cosa que se puede medir o contar.

Quartile (p. 730) A quartile is a value that separates a finite data set into four equal parts. The second quartile (Q_2) is the median of the data set. The first and third quartiles (Q_1 and Q_3) are the medians of the lower half and upper half of the data, respectively.

    Example For the data set 2, 3, 4, 5, 5, 6, 7, 7, the first quartile is 3.5, the second quartile (or median) is 5, and the third quartile is 6.5.

Cuartil (p. 730) Un cuartil es el valor que separa un conjunto de datos finitos en cuatro partes iguales. El segundo cuartil (Q_2) es la mediana del conjunto de datos. El primer cuartil y el tercer cuartil (Q_1 y Q_3) son medianas de la mitad inferior y de la mitad superior de los datos, respectivamente.

Radical (p. 19) An expression made up of a radical symbol and a radicand.

    Example $\sqrt{a}$

Radical (p. 19) Expresión compuesta por un símbolo radical y un radicando.

Radical equation (p. 646) An equation that has a variable in a radicand.

    Example
$$\sqrt{x} - 2 = 12$$
$$\sqrt{x} = 14$$
$$(\sqrt{x})^2 = 14^2$$
$$x = 196$$

Ecuación radical (p. 646) Ecuación que tiene una variable en un radicando.

Radical expression (p. 632) Expression that contains a radical.

    Example $\sqrt{3}$, $\sqrt{5x}$, and $\sqrt{x - 10}$ are examples of radical expressions.

Expresión radical (p. 632) Expresiones que contienen radicales.

Radicand (p. 19) The expression under the radical sign is the radicand.

    Example The radicand of the radical expression $\sqrt{x + 2}$ is $x + 2$.

Radicando (p. 19) La expresión que aparece debajo del signo radical es el radicando.

Range (of a relation or function) (p. 286) The possible values of the output, or dependent variable, of a relation or function.

    Example In the function $y = |x|$, the range is the set of all nonnegative numbers.

Rango (de una relación o función) (p. 286) El conjunto de todos los valores posibles de la salida, o variable dependiente, de una relación o función.

English	Spanish

Range of a set of data (p. 724) The difference between the greatest and the least data values for a set of data.

Rango de un conjunto de datos (p. 724) Diferencia entre el valor mayor y el menor en un conjunto de datos.

Example For the set 2, 5, 8, 12, the range is
$12 - 2 = 10$.

Rate (p. 130) A ratio of a to b where a and b represent quantities measured in different units.

Tasa (p. 130) La relación que existe entre a y b cuando a y b son cantidades medidas con distintas unidades.

Example Traveling 125 miles in 2 hours

results in the rate $\frac{125 \text{ miles}}{2 \text{ hours}}$
or 62.5 mi/h.

Rate of change (p. 314) The relationship between two quantities that are changing. The rate of change is also called slope.

rate of change $= \dfrac{\text{change in the dependent variable}}{\text{change in the independent variable}}$

Tasa de cambio (p. 314) La relación entre dos cantidades que cambian. La tasa de cambio se llama también pendiente.

tasa de cambio $= \dfrac{\text{cambio en la variable dependiente}}{\text{cambio en la variable independiente}}$

Example Video rental for 1 day is $1.99.
Video rental for 2 days is $2.99.

rate of change $= \dfrac{2.99 - 1.99}{2 - 1}$

$= \dfrac{1.00}{1}$

$= 1$

Ratio (p. 130) A ratio is the comparison of two quantities by division.

Razón (p. 130) Una razón es la comparación de dos cantidades por medio de una división.

Example $\frac{5}{7}$ and $7 : 3$ are ratios.

Rational equation (p. 692) An equation containing rational expressions.

Ecuación racional (p. 692) Ecuación que contiene expresiones racionales.

Example $\frac{1}{x} = \frac{3}{2x - 1}$ is a rational equation.

Rational expression (p. 664) A ratio of two polynomials. The value of the variable cannot make the denominator equal to 0.

Expresión racional (p. 664) Una razón de dos polinomios. El valor de la variable no puede hacer el denominador igual a 0.

Example $\frac{3}{x^3 + x}$, where $x \neq 0$

Rationalize the denominator (p. 637) To rationalize the denominator of an expression, rewrite it so there are no radicals in any denominator and no denominators in any radical.

Racionalizar el denominador (p. 637) Para racionalizar el denominador de una expresión, ésta se escribe de modo que no haya radicales en ningún denominador y no haya denominadores en ningún radical.

Example $\dfrac{2}{\sqrt{5}} = \dfrac{2}{\sqrt{5}} \cdot \dfrac{\sqrt{5}}{\sqrt{5}} = \dfrac{2\sqrt{5}}{\sqrt{25}} = \dfrac{2\sqrt{5}}{5}$

English

Spanish

Rational number (p. 21) A real number that can be written as a ratio of two integers. Rational numbers in decimal form are terminating or repeating.

Número racional (p. 21) Número real que puede expresarse como la razón de dos números enteros. Los números racionales en forma decimal son exactos o periódicos.

Example $\frac{2}{3}$, 1.548, and 2.292929 . . . are all rational numbers.

Real number (p. 21) A number that is either rational or irrational.

Número real (p. 21) Un número que es o racional o irracional.

Example 5, −3, $\sqrt{11}$, 0.666 . . . , $5\frac{4}{11}$, 0, and π are all real numbers.

Reciprocal (p. 48) Given a nonzero rational number $\frac{a}{b}$, the reciprocal, or multiplicative inverse, is $\frac{b}{a}$. The product of a nonzero number and its reciprocal is 1.

Recíproco (p. 48) El recíproco, o inverso multiplicativo, de un número racional $\frac{a}{b}$ cuyo valor no es cero es $\frac{b}{a}$. El producto de un número que no es cero y su valor recíproco es 1.

Example $\frac{2}{5}$ and $\frac{5}{2}$ are reciprocals because $\frac{2}{5} \times \frac{5}{2} = 1$.

Relation (p. 286) Any set of ordered pairs.

Relación (p. 286) Cualquier conjunto de pares ordenados.

Example {(0, 0), (2, 3), (2, −7)} is a relation.

Relative error (p. 159) The ratio of the absolute value of the difference of a measured (or estimated) value and an actual value compared to the actual value.

Error relativo (p. 159) Razón del valor absoluto de la diferencia de un valor medido (o estimado) y un valor actual en comparación con el valor actual.

Example You estimated that a plant would be 5 in. tall 3 months after it was planted. The plant was actually 5.5 in. tall 3 months after it was planted. The relative error is $\frac{|5-5.5|}{5.5} = \frac{|-0.5|}{5.5} = \frac{0.5}{5.5} = \frac{1}{11}$, or about 9%.

Root of the equation (p. 566) A solution of an equation.

Ráiz de la ecuación (p. 566) Solucion de una ecuacion.

Roster form (p. 210) A notation for listing all of the elements in a set using set braces and commas.

Lísta (p. 210) Una notación en la que se enlistan todos los elementos en un conjunto usando llaves y commas.

Example The set of prime numbers less than 10, expressed in roster form, is {2, 3, 5, 7}.

Visual **Glossary**

English

Spanish

Sample (p. 738) The part of a population that is surveyed.

Example Let the set of all males between the ages of 19 and 34 be the population. A random selection of 900 males between those ages would be a sample of the population.

Muestra (p. 738) Porción que se estudia de una población.

Sample space (p. 757) All possible outcomes in a situation.

Example When you roll a number cube, the sample space is {1, 2, 3, 4, 5, 6}.

Espacio muestral (p. 757) Todos los resultados posibles de un experimento.

Scalar (p. 711) A real number is called a scalar for certain special uses, such as multiplying a matrix. See *Scalar multiplication*.

Example $2.5\begin{bmatrix} 1 & 0 \\ -2 & 3 \end{bmatrix} = \begin{bmatrix} 2.5(1) & 2.5(0) \\ 2.5(-2) & 2.5(3) \end{bmatrix}$

$= \begin{bmatrix} 2.5 & 0 \\ -5 & 7.5 \end{bmatrix}$

Escalar (p. 711) Un número real se llama escalar en ciertos casos especiales, como en la multiplicación de una matriz. Ver *Scalar multiplication*.

Scalar multiplication (p. 711) Scalar multiplication is an operation that multiplies a matrix A by a scalar c. To find the resulting matrix cA, multiply each element of A by c.

Example $2.5\begin{bmatrix} 1 & 0 \\ -2 & 3 \end{bmatrix} = \begin{bmatrix} 2.5(1) & 2.5(0) \\ 2.5(-2) & 2.5(3) \end{bmatrix}$

$= \begin{bmatrix} 2.5 & 0 \\ -5 & 7.5 \end{bmatrix}$

Multiplicación escalar (p. 711) La multiplicación escalar es la que multiplica una matriz A por un número escalar c. Para hallar la matriz cA resultante, multiplica cada elemento de A por c.

Scale (p. 145) The ratio of any length in a scale drawing to the corresponding actual length. The lengths may be in different units.

Example For a drawing in which a 2-in. length represents an actual length of 18 ft, the scale is 1 in. : 9 ft.

Escala (p. 145) Razón de cualquier longitud de un dibujo a escala a la longitud real correspondiente. Las longitudes pueden tener diferentes unidades.

English

Spanish

Scale drawing (p. 145)   An enlarged or reduced drawing similar to an actual object or place.

Dibujo a escala (p. 145)   Dibujo que muestra de mayor o menor tamaño un objeto o lugar dado.

Example

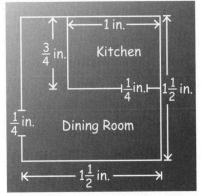

Scale model (p. 146)   A three-dimensional model that is similar to a three-dimensional object.

Modelo de escala (p. 146)   Modelo tridimensional que es similar a un objeto tridimensional.

Example   A ship in a bottle is a scale model of a real ship.

Scatter plot (p. 363)   A graph that relates two different sets of data by displaying them as ordered pairs.

Diagrama de puntos (p. 363)   Gráfica que muestra la relación entre dos conjuntos. Los datos de ambos conjuntos se presentan como pares ordenados.

Example

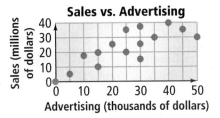

The scatter plot displays the amount spent on advertising (in thousands of dollars) versus product sales (in millions of dollars).

Scientific notation (p. 449)   A number expressed in the form $a \times 10^n$, where n is an integer and $1 < |a| < 10$.

Notación científica (p. 449)   Un número expresado en forma de $a \times 10^n$, donde n es un número entero y $1 < |a| < 10$.

Example 3.4×10^6

Sequence (p. 295)   An ordered list of numbers that often forms a pattern.

Progresión (p. 295)   Lista ordenada de números que muchas veces forma un patrón.

Example   −4, 5, 14, 23 is a sequence.

English

Set (p. 20) A well-defined collection of elements.

Example The set of integers:
$$Z = \{\ldots, -3, -2, -1, 0, 1, 2, 3, \ldots\}$$

Set-builder notation (p. 210) A notation used to describe the elements of a set.

Example The set of all positive real numbers in set-builder notation is $\{x \mid x \in \mathbb{R} \text{ and } x > 0\}$. This is read as "the set of all values of x such that x is a real number and x is greater than 0."

Similar figures (p. 143) Similar figures are two figures that have the same shape, but not necessarily the same size.

Example

$\triangle DEF$ and $\triangle GHI$ are similar.

Simple interest (p. 153) Interest paid only on the principal.

Example The interest on $1000 at 6% for 5 years is $1000(0.06)5 = $300.

Simplify (p. 11) To replace an expression with its simplest name or form.

Example $\dfrac{3 + 5}{8}$

Slope (p. 315) The ratio of the vertical change to the horizontal change.

$\text{slope} = \dfrac{\text{vertical change}}{\text{horizontal change}} = \dfrac{y_2 - y_1}{x_2 - x_1}$, where $x_2 - x_1 \neq 0$

Example

The slope of the line above is $\dfrac{2}{4} = \dfrac{1}{2}$.

Spanish

Conjunto (p. 20) Un grupo bien definido de elementos.

Notación conjuntista (p. 210) Notación que se usa para describir los elementos de un conjunto.

Figuras semejantes (p. 143) Dos figuras semejantes son dos figuras que tienen la misma forma pero no son necesariamente del mismo tamaño.

Interés simple (p. 153) Interés basado en el capital solamente.

Simplificar (p. 11) Reemplazar una expresión por su versión o forma más simple.

Pendiente (p. 315) La razón del cambio vertical al cambio horizontal.

$\text{pendiente} = \dfrac{\text{cambio vertical}}{\text{cambio horizontal}} = \dfrac{y_2 - y_1}{x_2 - x_1}$, donde $x_2 - x_1 \neq 0$

Visual **Glossary**

English

Slope-intercept form (p. 329) The slope-intercept form of a linear equation is $y = mx + b$, where m is the slope of the line and b is the y-intercept.

Example $y = 8x - 2$

Solution of an equation (one variable) (p. 62) Any value or values that make an equation true.

Example 3 is the solution of the equation $4x - 1 = 11$.

Solution of an equation (two variables) (p. 69) A solution of a two-variable equation with the variables x and y is any ordered pair (x, y) that makes the equation true.

Example $(4, 1)$ is one solution of the equation $x = 4y$.

Solution of an inequality (one variable) (p.175) Any value or values of a variable in the inequality that makes an inequality true.

Example The solution of the inequality $x < 9$ is all numbers less than 9.

Solution of an inequality (two variables) (p. 414) Any ordered pair that makes the inequality true.

Example Each ordered pair in the yellow area and on the solid red line is a solution of $3x - 5y \le 10$.

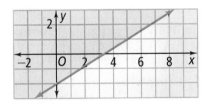

Solution of a system of linear equations (p. 382) Any ordered pair in a system that makes all the equations of that system true.

Example $(2, 1)$ is a solution of the system

$y = 2x - 3$

$y = x - 1$

because the ordered pair makes both equations true.

Spanish

Forma pendiente-intercepto (p. 329) La forma pendiente-intercepto es la ecuación lineal $y = mx + b$, en la que m es la pendiente de la recta y b es el punto de intersección de esa recta con el eje y.

Solución de una ecuación (una variable) (p. 62) Cualquier valor o valores que hagan verdadera una ecuación.

Solución de una ecuación (dos variables) (p. 69) La solución de una ecuación con dos variables que tiene las variables x e y es cualquier par ordenado que hace que la ecuación sea verdadera.

Solución de una desigualdad (una variable) (p. 175) Cualquier valor o valores de una variable de la desigualdad que hagan verdadera la desigualdad.

Solución de una desigualdad (dos variables) (p. 414) Cualquier par ordenado que haga verdadera la desigualdad.

Solución de un sistema de ecuaciones lineales (p. 382) Todo par ordenado de un sistema que hace verdaderas todas las ecuaciones de ese sistema.

Solution of a system of linear inequalities (p. 423)
Any ordered pair that makes all of the inequalities in the system true.

Solución de un sistema de desigualdades lineales (p. 423)
Todo par ordenado que hace verdaderas todas las desigualdades del sistema.

Example

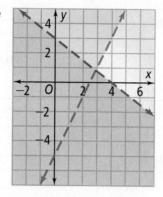

The shaded green area shows the solution of the system $\begin{array}{l} y > 2x - 5 \\ 3x + 4y < 12 \end{array}$.

Square root (p. 19) A number a such that $a^2 = b$. $\sqrt{b}$ is the principal square root. $-\sqrt{b}$ is the negative square root.

Raíz cuadrada (p. 19) Si $a^2 = b$, entonces a es la raíz cuadrada de b. $\sqrt{b}$ es la raíz cuadrada principal. $-\sqrt{b}$ es la raíz cuadrada negativa.

Example -3 and 3 are square roots of 9.

Standard deviation (p. 729) A measure of how data varies, or deviates, from the mean.

Desviación típica (p. 729) Medida de cómo los datos varían, o se desvían, de la media.

Example Use the following formula to find the standard deviation.

$$\sigma = \sqrt{\frac{\sum (x - \bar{x})^2}{n}}$$

Standard form of a linear equation (p. 349) The standard form of a linear equation is $Ax + By = C$, where A, B, and C are real numbers and A and B are not both zero.

Forma normal de una ecuación lineal (p. 349) La forma normal de una ecuación lineal es $Ax + By = C$, donde A, B y C son números reales, y donde A y B no son iguales a cero.

Example $6x - y = 12$

Standard form of a polynomial (p. 503) The form of a polynomial that places the terms in descending order by degree.

Forma normal de un polinomio (p. 503) Cuando el grado de los términos de un polinomio disminuye de izquierda a derecha, está en forma normal, o en orden descendente.

Example $15x^3 + x^2 + 3x + 9$

Standard form of a quadratic equation (p. 566) The standard form of a quadratic equation is $ax^2 + bx + c = 0$, where $a \neq 0$.

Forma normal de una ecuación cuadrática (p. 566) Cuando una ecuación cuadrática se expresa de forma $ax^2 + bx + c = 0$.

Example $-x^2 + 2x - 9 = 0$

English

Spanish

Standard form of a quadratic function (p. 552)   The standard form of a quadratic function is $f(x) = ax^2 + bx + c$, where $a \neq 0$.

Forma normal de una función cuadrática (p. 552)
La forma normal de una función cuadrática es
$f(x) = ax^2 + bx + c$, donde $a \neq 0$.

Example $f(x) = 2x^2 - 5x + 2$

Stem-and-leaf plot (p. 648)   A display of data made by using the digits of the values.

Diagrama de tallo y hojas (p. 648)   Un arreglo de los datos que usa los dígitos de los valores.

Example

Number of Points				
0	1	7		
1	0	0	2	
2	3	3	7	8
3	2	1	5	9	9

Key: 2 | 3 means 23

Subset (p. 20)   A subset of a set consists of elements from the given set.

Subconjunto (p. 20)   Un subconjunto de un conjunto consiste en elementos del conjunto dado.

Example If $B = \{1, 2, 3, 4, 5, 6, 7\}$
and $A = \{1, 2, 5\}$, then A is a
subset of B.

Substitution method (p. 390)   A method of solving a system of equations by replacing one variable with an equivalent expression containing the other variable.

Método de sustitución (p. 390)   Método para resolver un sistema de ecuaciones en el que se reemplaza una variable por una expresión equivalente que contenga la otra variable.

Example If $y = 2x + 5$ and
$x + 3y = 7$, then
$x + 3(2x + 5) = 7$.

System of linear equations (p. 382)   Two or more linear equations using the same variables.

Sistema de ecuaciones lineales (p. 382)   Dos o más ecuaciones lineales que usen las mismas variables.

Example $y = 5x + 7$
$y = \frac{1}{2}x - 3$

System of linear inequalities (p. 423)   Two or more linear inequalities using the same variables.

Sistema de desigualdades lineales (p. 423)   Dos o más desigualdades lineales que usen las mismas variables.

Example $y \leq x + 11$
$y < 5x$

T

Term (p. 57)   A number, variable, or the product or quotient of a number and one or more variables.

Término (p. 57)   Un número, una variable o el producto o cociente de un número y una o más variables.

Example The expression $5x + \frac{y}{2} - 8$ has
three terms: $5x$, $\frac{y}{2}$, and -8.

Term of a sequence (p. 295) A term of a sequence is any number in a sequence.

> **Example** -4 is the first term of the sequence $-4, 5, 14, 23$.

Término de una progresión (p. 295) Un término de una secuencia es cualquier número de una secuencia.

Theoretical probability (p. 758) The ratio of the number of favorable outcomes to the number of possible outcomes if all outcomes have the same chance of happening.

$$P(\text{event}) = \frac{\text{number of favorable outcomes}}{\text{number of possible outcomes}}$$

> **Example** In tossing a coin, the events of getting heads or tails are equally likely. The likelihood of getting heads is $P(\text{heads}) = \frac{1}{2}$.

Probabilidad teórica (p. 758) Si cada resultado tiene la misma probabilidad de darse, la probabilidad teórica de un suceso se calcula como la razón del número de resultados favorables al número de resultados posibles.

$$P(\text{suceso}) = \frac{\text{numero de resultados favorables}}{\text{numero de resultados posibles}}$$

Trend line (p. 364) A line on a scatter plot drawn near the points. It shows a correlation.

Línea de tendencia (p. 364) Línea de un diagrama de puntos que se traza cerca de los puntos para mostrar una correlación.

> **Example**

Positive　**Negative**

Trinomial (p. 503) A polynomial of three terms.

> **Example** $3x^2 + 2x - 5$

Trinomio (p. 503) Polinomio compuesto de tres términos.

Union (p. 230) The set that contains all of the elements of two or more sets.

> **Example** If $A = \{1, 3, 6, 9\}$ and $B = \{1, 5, 10\}$, then the union of A and B, or $A \cup B$, is $\{1, 3, 5, 6, 9, 10\}$.

Unión (p. 230) El conjunto que contiene todos los elementos de dos o más conjuntos.

Unit analysis (p. 132) Including units for each quantity in a calculation to determine the unit of the answer.

> **Example** To change 10 ft to yards, multiply by the conversion factor $\frac{1\ \text{yd}}{3\ \text{ft}}$.
>
> $10\ \text{ft}\left(\frac{1\ \text{yd}}{3\ \text{ft}}\right) = 3\frac{1}{3}\ \text{yd}$

Análisis de unidades (p. 132) Incluir unidades para cada cantidad de un cálculo como ayuda para determinar la unidad que se debe usar para la respuesta.

English

Spanish

Unit rate (p. 130) A rate with a denominator of 1.

Razón en unidades (p. 130) Razón cuyo denominador es 1.

Example The unit rate for 120 miles driven in 2 hours is 60 mi/h.

Univariate (p. 738) A set of data that uses only one variable is univariate.

Univariado (p. 738) Un conjunto de datos que tiene sólo una variable es univariado.

Universal set (p. 212) The set of all possible elements from which subsets are formed.

Conjunto universal (p. 212) Conjunto de todos los posibles elementos específicos del cual se forma un subconjunto.

Unlike radicals (p. 640) Radical expressions that do not have the same radicands.

Radicales no semejantes (p. 640) Expresiones radicales que no tienen radicandos semejantes.

Example $\sqrt{2}$ and $\sqrt{3}$ are unlike radicals.

 V

Variable (p. 4) A symbol, usually a letter, that represents one or more numbers.

Variable (p. 4) Símbolo, generalmente una letra, que representa uno o más valores de una cantidad.

Example x is the variable in the equation $9 - x = 3$.

Vertex (p. 553) The highest or lowest point on a parabola. The axis of symmetry intersects the parabola at the vertex.

Vértice (p. 553) El punto más alto o más bajo de una parábola. El punto de intersección del eje de simetría y la parábola.

Example

Vertical-line test (p. 286) The vertical-line test is a method used to determine if a relation is a function or not. If a vertical line passes through a graph more than once, the graph is not the graph of a function.

Prueba de la recta vertical (p. 286) La prueba de recta vertical es un método que se usa para determinar si una relación es una función o no. Si una recta vertical pasa por el medio de una gráfica más de una vez, la gráfica no es una gráfica de una función.

Example

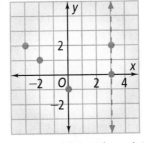

A line would pass through (3, 0) and (3, 2), so the relation is not a function.

English

Whole numbers (p. 21)   The nonnegative integers.

Números enteros positivos (p. 21)   Todos los números enteros que no son negativos.

Example 0, 1, 2, 3, . . .

x-axis (p. 68)   The horizontal axis of the coordinate plane.

Eje x (p. 68)   El eje horizontal del plano de coordenadas.

Example

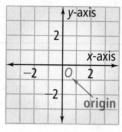

x-coordinate (p. 68)   The first number in an ordered pair, specifying the distance left or right of the y-axis of a point in the coordinate plane.

Coordenada x (p. 68)   El primer número de un par ordenado, que indica la distancia a la izquierda o a la derecha del eje y de un punto en el plano de coordenadas.

Example In the ordered pair $(4, -1)$, 4 is the x-coordinate.

x-intercept (p. 349)   The x-coordinate of a point where a graph crosses the x-axis.

Intercepto en x (p. 349)   Coordenada x por donde la gráfica cruza el eje de las x.

Example The x-intercept of $3x + 4y = 12$ is 4.

Y

y-axis (p. 68)   The vertical axis of the coordinate plane.

Eje y (p. 68)   El eje vertical del plano de coordenadas.

Example

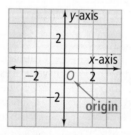

y-coordinate (p. 68)   The second number in an ordered pair, specifying the distance above or below the x-axis of a point in the coordinate plane.

Coordenada y (p. 68)   El segundo número de un par ordenado, que indica la distancia arriba o abajo del eje x de un punto en el plano de coordenadas.

Example In the ordered pair $(4, -1)$, -1 is the y-coordinate.

y-intercept (p. 329)   The y-coordinate of a point where a graph crosses the y-axis.

Intercepto en y (p. 329)   Coordenada y por donde la gráfica cruza el eje de las y.

Example The y-intercept of $y = 5x + 2$ is 2.

Zero-Product Property (p. 572)   For all real numbers a and b, if $ab = 0$, then $a = 0$ or $b = 0$.

Propiedad del producto cero (p. 572)   Para todos los números reales a y b, si $ab = 0$, entonces $a = 0$ ó $b = 0$.

Example $x(x + 3) = 0$
$x = 0$ or $x + 3 = 0$
$x = 0$ or $\qquad x = -3$

Zero of a function (p. 566)   An x-intercept of the graph of a function.

Cero de una función (p. 566)   Intercepto x de la gráfica de una función.

Example   The zeros of $y = x^2 - 4$ are ± 2.

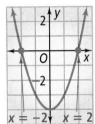

Selected Answers

Chapter 1

Get Ready! p. 1

1. 6 **2.** 5 **3.** 1 **4.** 20 **5.** 15 **6.** 44 **7.** 72 **8.** 150 **9.** 400
10. 8 **11.** $294 **12.** $\frac{4}{5}$ **13.** $\frac{5}{7}$ **14.** $\frac{1}{7}$ **15.** $\frac{12}{13}$ **16.** 0.79
or $\frac{11}{14}$ **17.** 10.47 or $10\frac{7}{15}$ **18.** 0.10 or $\frac{1}{10}$ **19.** 3.92 or
$3\frac{11}{12}$ **20.** 0.70 **21.** 0.60 **22.** 0.65 **23.** 0.93 **24.** 0.47
25. Answers may vary. Sample: 20 + 15 **26.** Answers
may vary. Sample: A simplified expression is one that is
briefer or easier to work with than the original
expression. **27.** Answers may vary. Sample: To evaluate
an expression means to find its numeric value for given
values of the variables.

Lesson 1-1 pp. 4–10

Got It? 1. $n + 18$ **2a.** 6n **b.** $\frac{18}{n}$ **3a.** $4x - 8$
b. $2(x + 8)$ **4.** Answers may vary. Samples are given.
a. the sum of a number x and 8.1 **b.** the sum of ten
times a number x and 9 **c.** the quotient of a number n
and 3 **d.** five times a number x less 1 **5.** Subtract 2 from
the number of sides in the polygon; $n - 2$.
Lesson Check 1a. numerical **b.** algebraic **c.** numerical
2a. 9t **b.** $x - \frac{1}{2}$ **c.** $m + 7.1$ **d.** $\frac{207}{n}$ **3–6.** Answers may
vary. Samples are given. **3.** six times a number c **4.** one
less than a number x **5.** the quotient of a number t and 2
6. 4 less than the product of 3 and number t **7.** An
algebraic expression includes at least one variable.
A numerical expression does not include any variables.
8. $49 + 0.75n$
Exercises 9. $n - 12$ **11.** $p + 4$ **13.** $\frac{n}{8}$ **15.** $x - 23$
17. $\frac{1}{3}n$ **19.** $2w + 2$ **21.** $(17 - k) + 9$ **23.** $37t - 9.85$
25. $15 + \frac{60}{w}$ **27–37.** Answers may vary. Samples are
given. **27.** 3 less a number t **29.** the product of 12 and x
31. the sum of 49 and m **33.** the sum of 62 and the
product of 7 and a number h **35.** the sum of 13 times a
number p and 0.1 **37.** twice the difference of 5 and a
number n **39.** the sum of 150 and 2 times a number n;
$150 + 2n$ **41.** $(15 + x) + 7$ **43.** $\frac{12}{5t}$ **45.** 13b **47.** A
51. $\frac{3}{4}$ **52.** $\frac{5}{14}$ **53.** $\frac{7}{10}$ **54.** $\frac{1}{6}$ **55.** 3 **56.** 3 **57.** 1 **58.** 4

Lesson 1-2 Part 1 pp. 11–14

Got It? 1a. 81 **b.** $\frac{8}{27}$ **c.** 0.125 **2a.** 27 **b.** 7 **c.** 9
Lesson Check 1. 25 **2.** 8 **3.** $\frac{9}{16}$ **4.** 0.001 **5.** 4 **6.** 3
7. exponent 3; base 4 **8.** The student subtracted before
multiplying; $23 - 8 \cdot 2 + 3^2 = 23 - 8 \cdot 2 + 9 =$
$23 - 16 + 9 = 7 + 9 = 16$.

Exercises 9. 243 **11.** 16 **13.** $\frac{8}{27}$ **15.** 0.004096
17. 0.125 **19.** 2 **21.** 11 **23.** 18 **25.** 92 **27.** 6 **29.** 36
31. −1.125 **33.** $\frac{-38}{9}$ **35.** 20; $14 - 5 \cdot 3 + 3^2$

Lesson 1-2 Part 2 pp. 15–18

Got It? 3a. 3 **b.** 11 **c.** 20; $(xy)^2 \neq xy^2$
4. $c + \frac{1}{10}c$; $47.30, $86.90, $104.50, $113.30
Lesson Check 1. 23 **2.** 1728 **3.** 0 **4.** Replace each
variable with the number given for it. Then use the order
of operations to simplify the expression.
5. $2xy^2$ $\qquad$ $x^5 + 8y$
$\quad 2(2)(4)^2$ $\qquad (2)^5 + 8(4)$
$\quad 2(2)(16)$ $\qquad 32 + 32$
$\qquad 64 = 64$
Exercises 7. 322 **9.** 30 **11.** 512 **13.** 0 **15.** $20 - p$;
$8.41, $2.50, $1.00, $0.00 **17a.** 24.0 in.^{3} **b.** 2.0 in.^{3}
19. 10h; $100, $200, $300, $400 **21.** 1.75 **23.** 196
25. 33 **27.** $\frac{5}{9}$ **33.** $p + 4$ **34.** $5 - 3y$ **35.** $\frac{m}{10}$
36. $3(7 - d)$ **37.** prime **38.** composite **39.** prime
40. composite **41.** 0.6 **42.** 0.875 **43.** $0.\overline{6}$
44. $0.\overline{571428}$ **45.** $\frac{7}{10}$ **46.** $\frac{7}{100}$ **47.** $4\frac{1}{4}$ **48.** $\frac{17}{40}$

Lesson 1-3 pp. 19–25

Got It? 1a. 8 **b.** 5 **c.** $\frac{1}{6}$ **d.** $\frac{9}{11}$ **2.** about 6 **3a.** natural
numbers, whole numbers, integers, rational numbers
b. rational numbers **c.** rational numbers **d.** irrational
numbers **4a.** $\sqrt{129} < 11.52$ **b.** Yes $4\frac{1}{3} > \sqrt{17}$ also
compares the two numbers.
5.

$-\frac{7}{2}, -2.1, \sqrt{5}, \sqrt{9}, 3.5$

Lesson Check 1. irrational numbers **2.** rational
numbers, integers **3.** $-5, \sqrt{16}, 4.1, \frac{47}{10}$ **4.** about 4 in.
5. rational numbers and irrational numbers **6.** Answers
may vary. Sample: 0.5 **7.** Rational; its value is 10 which
can be written as a ratio of two integers, $\frac{10}{1}$. **8.** Irrational;
$\sqrt{0.29}$ is a non-repeating, non-terminating number.
Exercises 9. 6 **11.** 4 **13.** $\frac{6}{7}$ **15.** $\frac{1}{3}$ **17.** 0.5
19. about 6 **21.** about 8 **23.** about 4 m **25.** about 55 ft
27. rational numbers, whole numbers, natural numbers,
integers **29.** rational numbers **31.** rational numbers
33. irrational numbers **35.** $5\frac{2}{3} > \sqrt{29}$ **37.** $\frac{4}{3} < \sqrt{2}$
39. $-\frac{7}{11} < -0.63$ **41.** $-\frac{22}{25} < -0.\overline{8}$ **43.** $-\frac{60}{11}, -3,$
$\sqrt{11}, 5.5, \sqrt{31}$ **45.** $\sqrt{7}, \sqrt{8}, 2.9, 3, \frac{10}{3}$ **47.** $-0.3, -\frac{1}{6},$
$-\frac{2}{13}, \frac{7}{8}, \sqrt{1}$ **49.** False; explanations may vary. Sample: A

counterexample is $-\frac{1}{2}$. **51.** False, explanations may vary. Sample: a counterexample is $\sqrt{49}$. **53.** Find the square root of 185. **55.** $\frac{37}{100}$ **57.** $\frac{21}{10}$ **59.** No; a rational number must be written as the ratio of two integers and $\sqrt{7}$ is not an integer. **61.** Check students' work. **63.** 20.6 ft **65.** Yes; check students' work. **69.** 16 **70.** 78 **71.** 512 **72.** $14 + x$ **73.** $4(y + 1)$ **74.** $\frac{3880}{z}$ **75.** $\frac{19}{3}t$ **76.** 18 **77.** 72 **78.** 442 **79.** 9

Lesson 1-4   pp. 26–31

Got It? 1a. Identity Prop. of Mult. **b.** Commutative Prop. of Add. **2.** 720 tennis balls **3a.** $9.45x$ **b.** $9 + 4h$ **c.** $\frac{2}{3n}$ **4a.** True; Commutative Prop. of Mult. and Identity Prop. of Add. **b.** False; answers may vary. Sample: $4(2 + 1) \neq 4(2) + 1$ **c.** No; it is true when a and b are both either 0 or 2.
Lesson Check 1. Comm. Prop. of Add. **2.** Assoc. Prop. of Mult. **3.** $4.45 **4.** $24d$ **5a.** no **b.** yes **6.** Comm. Prop. of Mult.; Assoc. Prop. of Mult.; multiply; multiply
Exercises 7. Comm. Prop. of Add. **9.** Ident. Prop. of Add. **11.** Comm. Prop. of Mult. **13.** 36 **15.** 9.7 **17.** 80 **19.** $110 **21–29.** Steps may vary. Answers given. **21.** $18x$ **23.** $110p$ **25.** $11 + 3x$ **27.** $1.2 + 7d$ **29.** $\frac{13}{q}$ **31.** False; answers may vary. Sample: $8 \div 4 \neq 4 \div 8$ **33.** True; Mult. Prop. of -1 **35a.** 497 mi **b.** 497 mi **c.** Check students work. The commutative property of addition applies to this situation. **37.** no **39.** yes **41.** yes **43.** no **45.** Hannah can only afford to give her friends all the same gift. **50.** -6, 1.6, $\sqrt{6}$, 6^3 **51.** -17, 1.4, $\frac{8}{5}$, 10^2 **52.** -4.5, 1.75, $\sqrt{4}$, 14^1 **53.** 14 **54.** 1 **55.** 1.1 **56.** $\frac{1}{18}$

Chapter Review for Part A   pp. 32–34

1. irrational **2.** simplify **3.** power **4.** evaluate **5.** inequality **6.** radicand **7.** perfect square **8.** set **9.** counterexample **10.** variable **11.** $737w$ **12.** $q - 8$ **13.** $x + 84$ **14.** $51t + 9$ **15.** $\frac{63}{h} - 14$ **16.** $b - \frac{k}{5}$ **17.** the sum of 12 and a number a **18.** 31 less than a number r **19.** the product of 19 and a number t **20.** the quotient of b and 3 **21.** the difference between the product of 7 and c, and 3 **22.** the sum of 2 and the quotient of x and 8 **23.** 6 less than the quotient of y and 11 **24.** 13 more than the product of 21 and d **25.** 81 **26.** 125 **27.** $\frac{1}{36}$ **28.** 9.8 **29.** 100 **30.** 48 **31.** $8\frac{1}{3}$ **32.** 40 **33.** 79 **34.** 123 **35a.** 216 **b.** The surface area is reduced to a fourth of its previous value. **36.** 615 mi **37.** irrational **38.** rational **39.** irrational **40.** rational **41.** 10 **42.** 7 **43.** 5 **44.** rational numbers, integers **45.** rational numbers **46.** irrational numbers **47.** rational numbers, whole numbers, natural numbers,

integers **48.** rational numbers **49.** rational numbers **50.** $-1\frac{4}{5}$, $-1\frac{2}{3}$, 1.6 **51.** -0.8, $\frac{7}{9}$, $\sqrt{3}$ **52.** $9w - 31$, Comm. Prop. of Add. **53.** -96, Assoc. Prop. of Mult. **54.** 0, Zero. Prop. of Mult. **55.** $41 - 4t$, addition **56.** 1, addition **57.** yes **58.** no **59.** no **60.** no

Lesson 1-5   pp. 37–43

Got It? 1a. 12 **b.** 4 **c.** -4 **d.** -12 **2a.** -24 **b.** -2 **c.** -2.1 **d.** $-\frac{11}{12}$ **3a.** 13.5 **b.** any value where $a = b$ **4.** -2473 ft, or 2473 feet below sea level
Lesson Check 1. -3 **2.** -3 **3.** -3 **4.** -7 **5.** 2 **6.** -7 **7.** 0 **8.** Subtracting is the same as adding the opposite. **9.** The opposite of a number is the number that is added to it to equal 0. If a number is positive, its opposite is negative. However, if a number is negative, its opposite is positive.
Exercises
11. 3;

```
  ┣━━━━━━━━▶
-5-4-3-2-1 0 1 2 3 4 5
```

13. -5;

```
  ◀━━━━┫
-7-6-5-4-3-2-1 0 1 2
```

15. -14;

```
  ◀━━━┫
-15  -13  -11  -9  -7  -5
```

17. 20 **19.** 3 **21.** -24 **23.** 4.6 **25.** -6 **27.** $-\frac{19}{15}$ **29.** -10 **31.** 48 **33.** -2 **35.** -20.3 **37.** $-\frac{5}{8}$ **39.** $42 + 144 - 126 + 25 - 65$; 20 ft **41.** 7.1 **43.** -3 **45.** the sum of -135 and 257; the absolute value of the positive number is greater so the answer will be positive. **47.** 6 **49.** 34 strokes **51.** negative **53a.** 251 K **b.** 273 K **c.** 241 K **55.** False; the sign of the number with the larger absolute value will be the sign of the sum. **57.** true **59.** C **66.** yes **67.** no **68.** yes **69.** rational numbers **70.** rational numbers **71.** rational numbers, whole numbers, natural numbers, and integers **72.** rational numbers **73.** irrational numbers **74.** 18.75 **75.** 17 **76.** 318

Lesson 1-6   pp. 45–51

Got It? 1a. -90 **b.** 2.4 **c.** $-\frac{21}{50}$ **d.** 16 **2a.** 8 **b.** ± 4 **c.** -11 **d.** $\pm\frac{1}{6}$ **3.** $-$72 **4a.** $-\frac{3}{10}$ **b.** yes; a positive divided by a negative is negative and the opposite of a positive divided by a positive is also negative.
Lesson Check 1. 36 **2.** $-\frac{5}{32}$ **3.** -16 **4.** $\frac{9}{8}$ **5.** -5 **6.**

```
  -5    -5    -5
◀━━┫━━━━┫━━━━┫
-15  -10   -5    0
```

7a. 2; a positive number has a positive and negative square root **b.** 1; $\sqrt{0} = 0$, so there is one square root
Exercises 9. 96 **11.** 20.5 **13.** -25 **15.** $\frac{1}{12}$ **17.** 1 **19.** 1.44 **21.** 13 **23.** -30 **25.** $-\frac{5}{9}$ **27.** $-\frac{11}{4}$

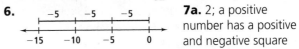

Selected Answers

53. Check students' work. **55.** 20 **57.** $\frac{1}{4}$
59. $-2(-2)(-2)(-2)(-2) = -32;$
$-2(-2)(-2)(-2)(-2)(-2) = 64;$
If the number of negative factors is odd, the product is negative and if the number of negative factors is even, the product is positive.
61a. when the signs of a and b are the same **b.** when the signs of a and b are different **c.** when $a = 0$
d. when $b = 0$ **63.** positive because an even number of negative factors has a positive product **65a.** If $0 \div x = y$, then $xy = 0$. Since $x \neq 0$, then $y = 0$ by the Zero Property of Multiplication. **b.** Suppose there is a value of y such that $x \div 0 = y$. Then $x = 0y$, so $x = 0$. But this is a contradiction, since $x \neq 0$. So there is no value of y such that $x \div 0 = y$. **69.** 30 **70.** -10 **71.** -10 **72.** Ident. Prop. of Add. **73.** Comm. Prop. of Mult. **74.** Assoc. Prop. of Mult.

Lesson 1-7 Part 1   pp. 52–55

Got It? 1a. $5x + 35$ **b.** $-2y^2 + y$ **2.** $\frac{1}{2} - \frac{1}{4}x$
3. $-6m + 9n$
Lesson Check 1a. $7j + 14$ **b.** $-8x + 24$ **c.** $-4 + c$
d. $-11 - 2b$ **2a.** yes **b.** no; commutative prop. of mult.
c. yes
Exercises 3. $6a + 60$ **5.** $25 + 5w$ **7.** $90 - 10t$
9. $112b + 96$ **11.** $4.5 - 12c$ **13.** $f - 2$ **15.** $12z + 15$
17. $\frac{3}{11} - \frac{7d}{17}$ **19.** $\frac{2}{5}x + \frac{7}{5}$ **21.** $\frac{8}{3} - 3x$ **23.** $5 - \frac{8}{5}t$
25. $11 - n$ **27.** $\frac{16}{9} + 4b$ **29.** $\frac{19}{8} - 3h$ **31.** the product of 4 and the sum of d and 7; $4d + 28$ **33.** the product of 5 and the sum of 2 times m and 1; $10m + 5$ **35.** the product of negative 12 and the difference of k and one fourth; $-12k + 3$ **37.** The 4 was not distributed to both terms inside parentheses; $8b - 20$.

Lesson 1-7 Part 2   pp. 56–60

Got It? 4. $29 **5a.** $-12mn^4$ **b.** $-16n + 8$
Lesson Check 1. $-8x^2 + 3xy + (-9x) + (-3)$
2. $2ab + (-5ab^2) + (-9a^2b)$ **3.** yes **4.** no **5.** $500 - 1$; Answers may vary. Sample: These numbers are easily multiplied by 5, making it possible to use the Distr. Prop. to solve this using mental math. **6a.** yes; no like terms **b.** This expression can be simplified by using the Distr. Prop. **c.** No; $12xy$ and $3yx$ are like terms.
Exercises 7. $-20 - d$ **9.** $-9 + 7c$ **11.** $-18a + 17b$
13. $m - n - 1$ **15.** 40.8 **17.** 897 **19.** 23.4 **21.** 54.6
23. 4320 ft **25.** 985 mi **27.** $20x$ **29.** $3n$ **31.** $5y^2$
33. $-3x + y + 11$ **35.** $ab + 2ab^2$ **37.** $33x + 22$
39. $35n - 63$ **41.** 0 **43.** $-5m^3n + 5mn$
45. $23x^2y - 8x^2y^2 - 4x^3y^2 - 9xy^2$ **52.** -25
53. $\frac{9}{16}$ **54.** 1.44 **55.** 10 less than a number x
56. 18 less than the product of 5 and x **57.** 12 more than the quotient of 7 and y

Lesson 1-8   pp. 61–66

Got It? 1a. open **b.** true **c.** false **2.** yes **3.** $49 = 14h$
4. 9 **5a.** -10 **b.** Answers may vary. Sample: -5.
6. The solution is between -8 and -9.
Lesson Check 1. no **2.** 15 **3.** $p = 1.5n$ **5.** Answers may vary. Sample: $\frac{x}{3} = 15$ **6.** 9

Exercises 7. false **9.** true **11.** false **13.** open
15. open **17.** no **19.** yes **21.** yes **23.** $4x + (-3) = 8$
25. $115d = 690$ **27.** 13 **29.** 6 **31.** 5 **33.** 6 **35.** -2
37. -2 **39.** 8 **41.** between -5 and -4 **43.** 2004
45. An expression describes the relationship between numbers and variables. An equation shows that two expressions are equal. An expression has no solution since it is not equal to any value in particular. **47.** -6 **49.** 22
51. -5 **53.** between 3 and 4 hours **59.** $28 + 14y$
60. $-18b - 66$ **61.** $-16.8 - 4.2t$ **62.** $-5 + 25x$
63. 10 **64.** -1 **65.** -12 **66.** 7 **67.** -9 **68.** -7 **69.** 2
70. $-7\frac{1}{2}$ **71.** 2 **72.** -1 **73.** 3 **74.** 0

Review   p. 68

Exercises 1. Answers may vary. Sample: For the sum -3 for the x-coordinate, you could roll a 4 on the negative cube and a 1 on the positive cube. For the sum 4 for the y-coordinate, you could roll a 1 on the negative cube and a 5 on the positive cube. **3.** Answers may vary. The number on the negative cube must be greater than the number on the positive cube.

Lesson 1-9   pp. 69–74

Got It? 1a. yes **b.** no
2a.

Megan's and Will's Laps

Megan's laps	1	2	3	4	5
Will's laps	7	8	9	10	11

$y = x + 6$;

Megan's and Will's Laps

b. The graph would start at (0, 5) instead of (0, 2). The y would always be 5 greater than x.
3a.

Orange tiles	4	8	12	16
Total tiles	9	18	27	36

54 tiles

b.

Blue tiles	1	2	3	4
Yellow tiles	2	4	6	8

48 yellow tiles

Lesson Check 1. no **2.** yes

3.

Drink Cost				
Drinks bought	1	2	3	4
Cost ($)	2.50	5	7.50	10

$y = 2.50x$;

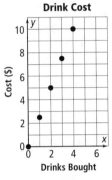

Drink Cost

4. 110 Calories **5.** With inductive reasoning, conclusions are reached by observing patterns. With deductive reasoning, conclusions are reached by reasoning logically from given facts. **6.** Answers may vary. Sample: Both equations contain unknown values. An equation in one-variable represents a situation with one unknown quantity. An equation in 2 variable represents a situation where two variables quantities have a relationship.
7. All; y is 2 more than x.

Exercises 9. yes **11.** no **13.** yes

15.

Bea's and Ty's Ages				
Bea's age	4	5	6	7
Ty's age	1	2	3	4

$y = x - 3$;

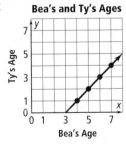

Bea's and Ty's Ages

17.

Sides and Triangles				
Number of sides	3	6	9	12
Number of triangles	1	2	3	4

$y = \frac{1}{3}x$;

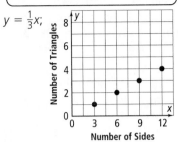

19. 56 in. **21.** 52 in. **23.** yes **25.** no **27.** no
29. yes **31.** no **33.** coordinates are reversed; the student should write (1, 4). **34.** They are both correct because subtracting 6 from x is the same as adding the opposite of 6 to x. **41.** no **42.** yes **43.** yes **48.** 9 **49.** -3
50. -14 **51.** -27 **52.** 40 **53.** -30 **54.** -1 **55.** -81

Chapter Review for Part B   pp. 76–78

1. opposite **2.** like terms **3.** absolute value **4.** inductive reasoning **5.** additive inverses **6.** like terms **7.** open sentence **8.** coefficient **9.** 5 **10.** -5 **11.** -9 **12.** 1.8
13. -144 **14.** 40 **15.** -3 **16.** -19 **17.** 3 **18.** -8
19. 60 **20.** 16 **21.** 12 **22.** -11 **23.** 19 **24.** -100
25. 2 **26.** -56 **27.** 225 **28.** $-\frac{3}{10}$ **29.** $-14 + 2a$
30. $-\frac{1}{2}j + 4$ **31.** v^2 **32.** $6y - 6$ **33.** $\frac{3}{2}y - \frac{1}{4}$
34. $6 - 6y$ **35.** $y - 3$ **36.** $-\frac{1}{3}y + 6$ **37.** $-2ab^2$
38. $2850 **39.** Yes; the variable parts of the terms are the same. **40.** yes **41.** no **42.** no **43.** yes **44.** 10
45. between 12 and 13 **46.** between 2 and 3
47. between 3 and 4 **48.** yes **49.** no **50.** no **51.** no
52. y is 5 more than the product of 10 and x;
$y = 10x + 5$;

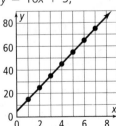

55, 65, 75

Chapter 2

Get Ready! p. 83

1. Answers may vary. Sample: For each lawn mowed, $7.50 is earned; $y = 7.50x$. **2.** Answers may vary. Sample: 30 pages are read each hour; $y = 30x$. **3.** 3 **4.** −10 **5.** 8 **6.** −8 **7.** 7.14 **8.** 16.4 **9.** $-\frac{9}{20}$ **10.** $-\frac{7}{15}$ **11.** 17 **12.** −3 **13.** 576 **14.** −2.75 **15.** $16k^2$ **16.** $13xy$ **17.** $2t + 2$ **18.** $12x - 4$ **19.** Answers may vary. Sample: The shirts might look the same but be different sizes or different colors; the triangles will be the same shape but different sizes. **20.** Answers may vary. Sample: The model ship is the same shape but just a smaller size than the actual ship.

Lesson 2-1 pp. 87–93

Got It? 1. −8 **2a.** −6 **b.** 2 **3a.** $\frac{2}{3}$ **b.** −4.375 **4a.** 57 **b.** −72 **5a.** 16 **b.** Yes; multiplying each side of the first equation by the $\frac{2}{3}$ produces the second equation. **6.** 6 months

Lesson Check 1. −4 **2.** 13 **3.** $4\frac{4}{5}$ **4.** $\frac{1}{3}b = 117$; 351 pages **5.** Subtr. Prop. of Eq. **6.** Div. Prop. of Eq. **7.** Add. Prop. of Eq. **8.** Mult. Prop. of Eq.

Exercises 11. 19 **13.** 11 **15.** 7.5 **17.** 132 **19.** 13.5 **21.** −9.6 **23.** 8 **25.** 29 **27.** −24 **29.** $-\frac{1}{2}$ **31.** 175 **33.** 28 **35.** −34 **37.** 12 **39.** $-1\frac{3}{7}$ **41.** −14 **43.** p = city's population at start of three-year period; $p - 7525 = 581,600$; 589,125 **45.** $4500 **47a.** $17p = 102$; 6 **b.** $102p = 17$; 0.17 **49.** $7\frac{1}{3}$ **51.** −6.5 **53.** −18 **55.** 14.2 **57.** The number 9 should multiply each side of the equation; $(9)(-36) = (9)\left(\frac{x}{9}\right)$, so $x = -324$. **59.** 21 aces **63.** 10,000 **64.** $52x$ **65.** $6 - x$ **66.** $m + 4$ **67.** 2 **68.** $\frac{25}{36}$ **69.** 1

Lesson 2-2 pp. 94–100

Got It? 1a. 5 **b.** 5 **c.** 16 **2.** 56 ads **3.** 26 **4.**

$$\frac{x}{3} - 5 + 5 = 4 + 5 \quad \text{Add. Prop. of Eq.}$$
$$\frac{x}{3} = 9 \quad \text{Use addition to simplify.}$$
$$\frac{x}{3} \cdot 3 = 9 \cdot 3 \quad \text{Mult. Prop. of Eq.}$$
$$x = 27 \quad \text{Use multiplication to simplify.}$$

Lesson Check 1. −5 **2.** 63 **3.** −7 **4.** −13 **5.** $.62 **6.** Subtr. Prop. of Eq. and Mult. Prop. of Eq.; subtr. **7.** Add. Prop. of Eq. and Div. Prop. of Eq.; add. **8.** Add. Prop. of Eq. and Mult. Prop. of Eq.; add. **9.** Subtr. Prop. of Eq. and Div. Prop. of Eq.; subtr. **10.** Answers may vary. Sample: no, you must either multiply both sides by 5 first or write the left side as the difference of two fractions and then add $\frac{3}{5}$ to both sides.

Exercises 11. −12 **13.** −1 **15.** −2 **17.** −27

19. 126 **21.** 16 boxes **23.** $1150 **25.** 29 **27.** 12 **29.** −7 **31.** 6 **33.** −15 **35.** 2.7 **37.** −3.8 **39.** 100 **41.** Negative; x must be negative in order for $-3x + 5$ to equal 44. **43.** 500 times **45.** 2 km **47.** 13 h **51.** 5 **52.** 3.8 **53.** 144 **54.** 6.5 **55.** false; sample: $|-5| - |2| \neq -5 - 2$ **56.** false; sample: $-4 + 1 = -3$, $|-4| = 4$ and $|-3| = 3$ **57.** $35 - 7t$ **58.** $4x - 10$ **59.** $-6 + 3b$ **60.** $10 - 25n$

Lesson 2-3 Part 1 pp. 101–104

Got It? 1a. 6 **b.** 3 **2.** $14 **3a.** 6 **b.** Yes; divide both sides of the equation by 3 first.

Lesson Check 1. 1.5 **2.** −7 **3.** 2 **4.** 2 **5.** Answers may vary. Sample: Apply the Distr. Prop., and then add 28 to each side and divide each side by 21. **6.** Answers may vary. Sample: Add 8 to both sides and then divide both sides by −4, solution: $-\frac{11}{2}$. **7.** Answers may vary. Sample: Amelia's method does not involve working with fractions until the end.

Exercises 9. 7 **11.** 10 **13.** −10 **15.** $3x + 6x + 20 = 92$; $8 per h **17.** 6 **19.** 3.75 or $3\frac{3}{4}$ **21.** −3.25 or $-3\frac{1}{4}$ **23.** 2 **25.** 9 **27.** −5 **29.** 4 wks **31.** 26

Lesson 2-3 Part 2 pp. 105–108

Got It? 4a. $2\frac{14}{23}$; check students' work. **b.** $2\frac{1}{6}$; check students' work. **5.** 12.55

Lesson Check 1. 6 **2.** 2 **3.** 16 ft **4.** Answers may vary. Sample: Subtract 1.3 from each side, and then divide each side by 0.5 to find the solution −9.42. **5.** Answers may vary. Sample: Add 4 to both sides. Then multiply both sides by $-\frac{9}{2}$ which is the reciprocal of $-\frac{2}{9}$. Simplify the mixed number to find the solution $-19\frac{4}{9}$. **6.** Answers may vary. Sample: Combine like terms or multiply both sides by 12.

Exercises 7. 11 **9.** 46 **11.** $2\frac{1}{3}$ **13.** $-\frac{9}{5}$ **15.** 9 **17.** 6 **19.** $28\frac{1}{2}$ **21.** $56\frac{5}{8}$ **23.** $15 **25.** 60 mi **29.** −5 **30.** 7 **31.** 4 **32.** Inv. Prop. of Add. **33.** Assoc. Prop. of Mult. **34.** Mult. Prop. of Zero **35.** $3y$ **36.** $-3y$ **37.** 0

Lesson 2-4 pp. 110–116

Got It? 1a. −4 **b.** The answer is the same, 4. **2.** about 27 months **3a.** −5 **b.** 4 **4a.** infinitely many solutions **b.** no solution

Lesson Check 1. 7 **2.** −3 **3.** infinitely many solutions **4.** no solution **5.** 100 business cards **6.** C **7.** A **8.** B **9.** If the numeric values are the same, it is an identity. If they are different, there is no solution.

Exercises 11. −9 **13.** 2 **15.** $-1\frac{3}{4}$ **17.** 22 ft **19.** 7 **21.** 1 **23.** no solution **25.** no solution **27.** identity **29.** $\frac{2}{63}$ **31.** $\frac{13}{33}$ **33.** −9 **35a.** $\frac{d}{60}$ **b.** $\frac{d}{40}$ **c.** $\frac{d}{60} + 1 = \frac{d}{40}$;

120 mi; 48 mi/h **37.** Subtraction should be used to isolate the variable, not division by the variable. $2x = 6x$, so $0 = 4x$, and $x = 0$. **39.** 2 months **43.** 5 **44.** −6 **45.** 1 **46.** 0.9 m **47.** 22 **48.** 9 **49.** 11.2

Lesson 2-5 pp. 117–122

Got It? 1a. $\frac{4 + 5n}{2}$; −3; 2, 7 **b.** $y = 10$; $y = 4$
2a. $x = \frac{-t - r}{p}$ **b.** $d = m - ge$ **3.** 6 in.
4. about 55 days
Lesson Check 1. $y = \frac{2x + 12}{5}$ **2.** $b = \frac{a + 10}{2}$
3. $x = \frac{p}{m + 2n}$ **4.** $F = \frac{9}{5}C + 32$ **5.** 40 yd **6.** literal equation **7.** literal equation **8.** both **9.** both
10. Answers may vary. Sample: They are the same in each case since you are isolating a variable by using inverse operations. They are different because, in an equation in one variable, to isolate the variable, inverse operations are used on numbers only. In a literal equation, inverse operations are used on variables as well as numbers.
Exercises 11. $y = -2x + 5$; 7; 5; −1 **13.** $y = \frac{3x - 9}{5}$;
$-\frac{12}{5}$; $-\frac{9}{5}$; $-\frac{6}{5}$ **15.** $y = -\frac{5x - 4}{4}$; $-\frac{1}{4}$; $-\frac{3}{2}$; $-\frac{11}{4}$
17. $y = \frac{x + 4}{4}$; $\frac{1}{2}$; 2; $\frac{5}{2}$ **19.** $x = \frac{p}{m + n}$ **21.** $x = \frac{ay}{b}$
23. $x = \frac{4b}{3}$ **25.** 3.5 m **27.** 16 ft **29.** 75 yd **31.** $h = an$;
87 hits **33.** $x = \frac{2m - n}{3}$ **35.** $y = \frac{14 - a}{2x}$
37. $g = \frac{2A}{h} - f$ **39.** 9 sides **41.** −108.4°F **43.** 5 cm³
48. 5 **49.** 3 **50.** −4 **51.** 3 **52.** identity **53.** no solution **54.** 147 **55.** −40 **56.** 567 **57.** 100 **58.** 3
59. $\frac{8}{5}$ **60.** $\frac{7}{45}$

Chapter Review for Part A pp. 125–127

1. inverse operations **2.** identity **3.** literal equation
4. equivalent equations **5.** isolate **6.** −7 **7.** 7 **8.** 14
9. 65 **10.** 17.7 **11.** −18 **12.** $6.50 **13.** −5
14. −6 **15.** 3.5 **16.** −4 **17.** −5 **18.** −8 **19.** 4.47 h
20. Add. Prop. of Eq.; Simplify.; Div. Prop. of Eq.;
Simplify. **21.** 11 **22.** 8 **23.** −7.5 **24.** $3\frac{18}{85}$ **25.** 28
26. 14.7 **27.** $4h + 8h + 50 = 164$; $9.50
28. $37t + 8.50t + 14.99 = 242.49$; 5 tickets
29. −90 **30.** 7.2 **31.** identity **32.** no solution
33. $8h = 16 + 6h$; 8 ft **34.** $65t = 130(t - 3)$;
390 mi **35.** $x = \frac{-c}{a + b}$ **36.** $x = -t - r$ **37.** $x = \frac{m - p}{5}$
38. $x = \frac{pqs}{p + q}$ **39.** 40 cm **40.** 15 mm **41.** 16 in.

Lesson 2-6 pp. 130–135

Got It? 1. No; Store C is still the lowest. **2a.** 12.5 m
b. 176 oz **c.** 6.75 h **3a.** about 442 m **b.** about 205
euros **4.** about 22 mi/h
Lesson Check 1. 8 bagels for $4.15 **2.** 116 oz
3. 12 m **4.** $80\frac{2}{3}$ ft/s **5.** not a unit rate **6.** unit rate

7. No; a conversion factor is a ratio of two equivalent measures in different units and is always equal to 1.
8. Greater; to convert you multiply by 16.
Exercises 9. $57 for 4 DVDs **11.** Olga **13.** 189 ft
15. 40 oz **17.** 240 s **19.** about 8.2 m **21.** 7900 cents
23. $.09 a day **25.** about 4.8 **27.** $\frac{1}{120}$ **29.** about
65.8 **31.** 63 in. **33.** $317.55 per year **35.** The numbers are correct but the units are reversed in the conversion factor; 9 yd $\cdot \frac{3 \text{ ft}}{1 \text{ yd}} = 27$ ft. **37.** 48 km **39.** No; exchange rates vary from day to day. **43.** 5 cm **44.** 15 in.
45. 5 **46.** 6 **47.** 0.5 **48.** 3 **49.** 27 **50.** $\frac{1}{112}$ **51.** 20m

Lesson 2-7 pp. 136–142

Got It? 1. 5.6 **2a.** 1.8 **3.** −5 **4.** 145.5 mg
Lesson Check 1. 4.8 **2.** 27 **3.** 3 **4.** 5 **5.** 6.75 h
6. m and q **7.** n and p **8.** mq and np **9.** Yes; sample: One method creates an equation using the fact that the cross products are equal, and the other method creates an equivalent equation using the Mult. Prop. of Eq. to clear the denominators.
Exercises 11. −19.5 **13.** 4.2 **15.** 5 **17.** 4.875
19. 14 **21.** $26\frac{2}{3}$ **23.** −15 **25.** 11 **27.** $-6\frac{2}{3}$ **29.** −5
31. 8 dozen **33.** 3.5 **35.** $4\frac{2}{3}$ **37.** −3 **39.** about 17
people **41.** $\frac{\$.07}{1 \text{ kw-h}} = \frac{\$143.32}{x \text{ kw-h}}$; 2047.4 kw-h **43.** 3 is not fully distributed when multiplying 3 and $x + 3$;
$16 = 3x + 9$, $7 = 3x$, $x = \frac{7}{3}$. **50.** 1.5 **51.** 7 **52.** 90 **53.**
190 **54.** no solution **55.** $\frac{1}{5}$ **56.** identity **57.** $2\frac{4}{5}$ or 2.8
58. $2\frac{2}{15}$ or 2.1$\overline{3}$ **59.** $6\frac{2}{3}$ or 6.$\overline{6}$ **60.** $\frac{3}{5}$ or 0.6

Lesson 2-8 pp. 143–149

Got It? 1. 24 **2.** 30 ft **3a.** about 66 mi **b.** Write and
solve the proportion $\frac{2}{250} = \frac{1}{x}$; 1 in. represents 125 mi.
4. 300 ft
Lesson Check 1a. 32.5 cm **b.** 1 : 2.5 **2.** 225 km
3. The order of the letters in each triangle tells which parts are corresponding. **4a.** yes **b.** no **c.** yes
5. Answers may vary. Sample: No, it is greater than 100 times since 100 mi is more than 100 times greater than 1 in.
Exercises 7. $\angle F \cong \angle K$, $\angle G \cong \angle L$, $\angle H \cong \angle M$,
$\angle I \cong \angle N$, $\frac{FG}{KL} = \frac{GH}{LM} = \frac{HI}{MN} = \frac{FI}{KN}$ **9.** 52.5 **11.** 48 yd
13. 3 km **15.** 69 km **17.** 1 in. : 70 mi **19.** 20 ft × 10 ft
21a. The student used CJ instead of AJ. **b.** $\frac{BC}{AJ} = \frac{GH}{FN}$
23. 39,304 times **25.** B **30.** 34 **31.** 4.5 **32.** −8
33. $-\frac{3}{5}$ **34.** 1.5 **35.** 8 **36.** 0.04 **37.** 0.25 **38.** 2.9

Lesson 2-9 pp. 150–156

Got It? 1. 60% **2.** 75%; the answers are the same.
3. $3600 **4.** $41\frac{2}{3}$ **5.** 4 yr

Lesson Check 1. 30% **2.** 120% **3.** 28 **4.** 48
5. $180 **6.** 100 **7.** $75 **8.** Answers may vary. Sample: 12 is what percent of 10?
Exercises 9. 20% **11.** 62.5% **13.** 100% **15.** 94.5
17. 1.536 **19.** $52 **21.** 400 **23.** 22.5 **25.** $108
27. part; 142.5 **29.** base; 24 **31.** 60 **33.** B **35.** A
37. The values for a and b are reversed; $\frac{3}{1.5} = \frac{p}{100}$, 1.5p = 300, p = 200%. **39.** $181 **44.** 14.4 cm
45. 18 cans **46.** $c = 1.75 + 2.4\left(m - \frac{1}{8}\right)$; about 3 mi **47.** 1250% **48.** 0.6 **49.** 175%

Lesson 2-10   pp. 157–162

Got It? 1. about 32% **2.** about 17% **3.** about 16%
Lesson Check 1. about 2% **2.** 25% **3a.** percent decrease **b.** percent decrease **c.** percent increase
4. A percent increase involves an increase of the original amount and a percent decrease involves a decrease of the original amount.
Exercises 5. increase; 50% **7.** decrease; 7%
9. decrease; 4% **11.** increase; 54% **13.** about 55%
15. about 13% **17.** 175% increase **19.** 78% increase
21. $12.63 **23.** 7280 fans **25.** The original amount should be 12, not 18; $\frac{18 - 12}{12} = \frac{6}{12} = 0.5 = 50\%$.
30. $66\frac{2}{3}$% **31.** 64.75 **32.** 21
33–36.

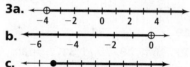

$-3, -2.8, \frac{1}{2}, 2$

Chapter Review for Part B pp. 164–166

1. rate **2.** scale **3.** cross products **4.** percent change
5. percent difference **6.** 78 in. **7.** 71 oz **8.** 2.25 min
9. 3960 yd **10.** 240 loaves **11.** about 6 lb **12.** $\frac{5}{11}$ s or about 0.45 s **13.** 21 **14.** −4 **15.** 1.6 **16.** 21 **17.** 39
18. −1 **19.** 12 in. **20.** 42 in. **21.** 300% **22.** 108
23. 170 **24.** 60 seeds **25.** 30% **26.** 72 students
27. increase; 11% **28.** decrease; 20% **29.** decrease; 11% **30.** increase; 32% **31.** about 47% **32.** about 39%

Chapter 3

Get Ready!   p. 171

1. > **2.** = **3.** > **4.** < **5.** 7 **6.** −4 **7.** 1 **8.** 2
9. 3 **10.** −12 **11.** 32.4 **12.** 23 **13.** 29.5 **14.** 48 **15.** 5
16. −24 **17.** −10 **18.** 1.85 **19.** −24 **20.** −4 **21.** 3
22. 2.5 **23.** 4.1 **24.** Answers may vary. Sample: Two inequalities are joined together. **25.** Answers may vary. Sample: the part that the two groups of objects have in common

Lesson 3-1 Part 1   pp. 174–177

Got It? 1a. $p \geq 1.5$ **b.** $t + 7 < -3$ **2a.** 1 and 3
b. The solution of the equation is −2. The solution of the inequality is all real numbers greater than −2.
Lesson Check 1. $y \geq 12$ **2a.** no **b.** no **c.** yes **d.** yes
3. Substitute the number for the variable and simplify. If the number makes the inequality true, then it is a solution of the inequality. **4.** Both inequalities have solutions greater than 5. The inequality $x > 5$ does not include the solution of 5. The inequality $x \geq 5$ does include the solution of 5. **5.** Answers will vary. Sample: −4, −5, −6
Exercises 7. $6t > 12$ **9.** $g - 3 \leq 17$ **11a.** yes **b.** no
c. yes **13a.** no **b.** no **c.** no **15a.** no **b.** yes **c.** no
17. Answers may vary. Sample: $x \leq 12$ **19.** b is greater than 0. **21.** 21 is greater than or equal to m.
23. a is less than or equal to 3. **25.** 1.2 is greater than k. **27a.** yes **b.** yes **c.** yes

Lesson 3-1 Part 2   pp. 178–183

Got It?
3a.

b.

c.

4a. $x < -3$ **b.** $x \geq 0$ **5.** No; the speed limit can only be positive real numbers.
Lesson Check
1.

2. $x \leq -3$ **3.** Answers may vary. Sample: $x \geq 0$, whole numbers, a baseball team's score during an inning, amount in cubic centimeters of liquid in a chemistry beaker; $x > 0$, counting numbers, length of a poster, distance in blocks between your house and a park
Exercises 5. D **7.** A
9.

11.

13.

15.

17. $x \leq 8$ **19.** $x < -7$ **21.** $x < 2$ **23.** Let a = age of person being elected; $a \geq 35$. **25.** Let s = number of students at concert; $s \geq 475$. **27.** D **29.** $x \leq 186{,}000$
31. $m \leq 108$ **33.** $x \geq 973$ mi **39.** increase; 20%
40. decrease; 10% **41.** decrease; 67% **42.** 44 **43.** $-\frac{5}{24}$
44. −3 **45.** $-1\frac{3}{7}$ **46.** 11 **47.** −2 **48.** −11 **49.** $-\frac{1}{9}$

Lesson 3-2 pp. 184–190

Got It?

1. $n < 2$

2. $m \geq 9$

3. $y \leq -13$

4a. $p \geq 8$ **b.** Yes. The $\geq$ symbol can be used to represent all 3 phrases.

Lesson Check

1. $p < 5$

2. $d \leq 10$

3. $y < -12$

4. $c > 3$

5. $w \leq 524$ **6.** Add or subtract the same number from each side of the inequality. **7a.** Subtract 4 from each side. **b.** Add 2 to each side. **8.** They are similar in that 4 is being added to or subtracted from each side of the inequalities. They are different in that one inequality adds 4 and the other subtracts 4.

Exercises 9. 6 **11.** 18

13. $v < 1$

15. $f \geq 12$

17. $s \leq 11$

19. $z \leq 8$

21. $y \geq 2.5$

23. 4.2

25. $x \leq 5$

27. $c > -7$

29. $a \geq -1$

31. $b \leq -0.2$

33. $3 + 4 + g \geq 10$; $g \geq 3$ **35.** Add 4 to each side.

37.

51	
17	x

39. $z < 5.3$ **41.** $a < -9.8$ **43.** $v > -\frac{3}{16}$ **45.** $m \leq \frac{1}{7}$

47. $5\frac{7}{16} \geq m$ **49.** any number greater than 8.3 and less than or equal to 10; sample: 8.4, 8.5, 8.6

51. 3 should be added to both sides of the inequality; $-3 + x + 3 > 1 + 3$, $x > 4$.

55. at least $88.74 **60.** Let h = distance in miles the hummingbird migrates; $h > 1850$. **61.** Let o = length of octopus in feet; $o \leq 18$. **62.** 72 **63.** -1 **64.** 0.56 **65.** 20 **66.** $-\frac{15}{22}$ **67.** -24

Lesson 3-3 pp. 191–196

Got It?

1a. $x < 20$

b. $c > 2$

2a. $x \geq -10$

b. $n > 3$

3a. 1, 2, 3, or 4 cases **b.** $\frac{75}{4.50} = 16\frac{2}{3}$, but you cannot walk $\frac{2}{3}$ of a dog. If you round down to 16, you will only make $72. So round up to 17.

4. $x < 2$

Lesson Check 1. D **2.** B **3.** A **4.** C **5a.** Multiplication by -2; it is the inverse of division by -2. **b.** Addition of 4; it is the inverse of subtraction of 4. **c.** Division by -6; it is the inverse of multiplication by -6. **6.** The inequality symbol was not reversed when multiplying by a negative. $-5\left(-\frac{n}{5}\right) < -5(2)$, $n < -10$

Exercises

7. $x \geq -10$

9. $p < 32$

11. $v \leq -3$

13. $x \geq -3$

15. $b > -4$

17. $c > 6$

19. $t < -3$

21. $z > -3$

23. $b \leq -\frac{1}{6}$

25. $t \leq 8$

27–29. Answers may vary. Samples are given.

27. −5, −4, −3, −2 **29.** −6, −5, −4, −3 **31.** Divide each side by 5. **33.** −2 **35.** 18 **37.** Always true; the product of two negative numbers is always greater than 0. **39.** Sometimes true; sample: It is true when $x = 4$ and $y = 2$ but false when $x = 4$ and $y = 0$.
41. at most 6 tetras

43. $\dfrac{-4.5}{9} > \dfrac{9p}{9}$ Div. Prop. of Ineq.
    $-0.5 > p$ Simplify.
45. $\dfrac{4}{3}\left(\dfrac{3}{4}n\right) < \dfrac{4}{3}(4)$ Mult. Prop. of Ineq.
    $n < \dfrac{16}{3}$ Simplify.
47. $5\left(\dfrac{n}{5}\right) \le 5(-2)$ Mult. Prop. of Ineq.
    $n \le -10$ Simplify.

49. at least $7\frac{3}{11}$ h **55.** $x \le -11$ **57.** $q < 5$
58. $-\frac{1}{4} > c$ **59.** $-1 < b$ **60.** $y \le 75$ **61.** 2
62. −2 **63.** 1

Lesson 3-4 pp. 199–205

Got It? 1a. $a \ge -4$ **b.** $n < 3$ **c.** $x < 25$ **2.** any width greater than 0 ft and less than or equal to 6 ft **3.** $m \ge 3$
4a. $b > 3$ **b.** Answers may vary. Sample: adding 1 to each side. This would gather the constant terms onto one side of the inequality. **5a.** no solution **b.** all real numbers
Lesson Check 1. $a > 2$ **2.** $t \ge -5$ **3.** $z < 13$ **4.** no solution; $0 < -1$ is never true. **5.** greater than 0 cm and less than or equal to 8 cm **6.** The variable terms cancel each other out and a false inequality results. **7.** Yes; each side can be divided by 2 first. **8.** No; there is no solution, since −6 is not greater than itself. If the inequality symbol were ≥, your friend would be correct.
Exercises 9. $f \le 3$ **11.** $y > -2$ **13.** $r \ge 3.5$
15. $5s \ge 250$; $s \ge 50$ mph **17.** $k \ge 4$ **19.** $j > 2$
21. $x < 3$ **23.** $f \le 6$ **25.** $m \ge -5$ **27.** all real numbers
29. all real numbers **31.** all real numbers **33.** $x \ge -4$
35. $n \ge -2$ **37.** 5.5 h **39.** D **41a.** always true
b. always true **c.** never true **43.** $3y$ was subtracted from left side and added to right side instead of being added to both sides; $7y \le 2$, $y \le \frac{2}{7}$. **49.** $m \le -4$ **50.** $y \ge -8$
51. $y > -20$ **52.** $t \ge -3$ **53.** whole numbers
54. natural numbers **55.** integers

Chapter Review for Part A pp. 206–207

1. solution of an inequality **2.** equivalent inequalities

3.

4.

5.

6.

7. $x \le -2$ **8.** $x > -5.5$
9. $w > 6$

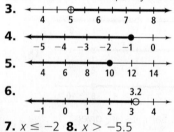

10. $v < 10$

11. $-12 < t$

12. $n \ge \frac{5}{4}$

13. $8.6 \le h$

14. $q > -2.5$

15. $4.25 + x \le 15.00$; $x \le 10.75$
16. $x < 3$

17. $t < -3$

18. $y \le 6$

19. $h > -24$

20. $g > 4$

21. $n \le 15$

22. $d \ge 22$

23. $m > -\frac{3}{2}$

24. $7.25h \ge 200$; at least 28 full hours **25.** $k \ge -0.5$
26. $c < -2$ **27.** $t < -6$ **28.** $y \le -56$ **29.** $x < 2\frac{2}{3}$
30. $x \le -13$ **31.** $a \le 5.8$ **32.** $w > 0.35$
33. $200 + 0.04s \ge 450$; $s \ge 6250$

Lesson 3-5 pp. 210–215

Got It? 1a. $N = \{2, 4, 6, 8, 10, 12\}$ **b.** $N = \{x \mid x$ is an even natural number, $x \le 12\}$ **2.** $\{n \mid n < -3\}$
3a. $\{\ \}$ or $\varnothing$, $\{a\}$, $\{b\}$, $\{a, b\}$ **b.** $\{\ \}$ or $\varnothing$, $\{a\}$, $\{b\}$, $\{c\}$, $\{a, b\}$, $\{a, c\}$, $\{b, c\}$, $\{a, b, c\}$ **c.** Yes; every element of set A is part of set B, since $-3 < 0$. **4.** $A' = \{$February, April, June, September, November$\}$
Lesson Check 1. $G = \{1, 3, 5, 7, 9, 11, 13, 15, 17\}$; $G = \{x \mid x$ is an odd natural number, $x < 18\}$
2. $\{d \mid d \le 3\}$ **3.** $\{\ \}$ or $\varnothing$, $\{4\}$, $\{8\}$, $\{12\}$, $\{4, 8\}$, $\{4, 12\}$, $\{8, 12\}$, $\{4, 8, 12\}$ **4.** $W' = \{$spring, summer, fall$\}$ **5.** A; Its complement is the set of all elements in the universal set that are not in A'. **6a.** Yes; the empty set is a subset of every set. **b.** No; the number 5 in the first set is not an element of the second set. **c.** Yes; the element in the first set is also an element of the second set. **7.** sometimes
8. The student forgot that 0 is also a whole number.
Exercises 9. $\{0, 1, 2, 3\}$; $\{m \mid m$ is an integer, $-1 < m < 4\}$ **11.** $\{1, 2, 3, 4, 5, 6, 7, 8, 9, 10\}$;

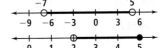

{$p \mid p$ is a natural number, $p < 11$} **13.** {$y \mid y \geq 4$}
15. {$m \mid m > -5$} **17.** { } or Ø, {a}, {e}, {i}, {o}, {a, e},
{a, i}, {a, o}, {e, i}, {e, o}, {i, o}, {a, e, i}, {a, e, o}, {a, i, o},
{e, i, o}, {a, e, i, o} **19.** { } or Ø, {1} **21.** {1, 4, 5}
23. {. . . , −4, −2, 0, 2, 4, . . .} **25.** $A' =$ {Tuesday,
Thursday, Friday, Saturday} **27.** False; some elements of U
are not elements of B. **29.** True; the empty set is a subset
of every set. **31.** $M =$ {$m \mid m$ is odd integer,
$1 \leq m \leq 19$} **33.** $G =$ {$g \mid g$ is an integer}
35. {Mercury, Venus, Earth} **37.** {$y \mid y < 5$} **39.** { } or Ø
41. $T' =$ {$x \mid x$ is an integer, $x \leq 0$} **43.** 1 **49.** $b > 8$
50. $t \leq 5$ **51.** $z < 13$ **52.** 6 **53.** −3 **54.** 3
55.

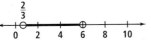

56.

57.

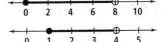

Lesson 3-6   pp. 216–221

Got It?
1a. $-4 \leq x < 6$

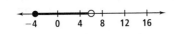

b. $x \leq 2\frac{1}{2}$ or $x > 6$

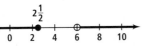

c. x is between −5 and 7 does not include −5 or 7.
Inclusive means that −5 and 7 are included.
2. $\frac{2}{3} < y < 6$

3. Answers may vary. Sample: No, to get a B, the average
of the 4 tests must be at least 84. If x is the 4th test score,
$\frac{78 + 78 + 79 + x}{4} \geq 84$, $235 + x \geq 336$, and $x \geq 101$,
which is impossible.
4. $y > 3$ or $y \leq -2$

Lesson Check
1. $0 \leq x < 8$

2. $1 \leq r < 4$

3. $85 \leq x \leq 100$ **4.** A, C, and D **5.** $x \leq 7$ or
$x > 7$; $(-\infty, \infty)$ **6.** The graph of a compound inequality
with the word *and* contains the overlap of the graphs that
form the inequality. The graph of a compound inequality
with the word *or* contains both of the graphs that form
the inequality.
Exercises
7. $-5 < x < 7$

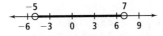

9. $-7 < k < 5$

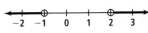

11. $2 < p \leq 5$

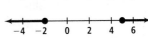

13. $b < -1$ or $b > 2$

15. $y \leq -2$ or $y \geq 5$

17. $1 < x \leq 6$ **19.** $f < -5$ or $f \geq 5$ **21.** $-3 < x < 4$
23. $3 \leq x < 6$ **25.** $2\frac{2}{3} \leq v \leq 6$ **27.** $-7 \leq w < 21$
29. $4 < x < 14$ **34.** { } or Ø, {1}, {3}, {5}, {7}, {1, 3}, {1, 5},
{1, 7}, {3, 5}, {3, 7}, {5, 7}, {1, 3, 5}, {1, 3, 7}, {1, 5, 7},
{3, 5, 7}, {1, 3, 5, 7} **35.** $B' =$ {1, 2, 3, 5, 7, 15} **36.** no
37. $\frac{1}{3} < b$ **38.** $n \leq 3$ **39.** $7 \geq r$ **40.** = **41.** > **42.** >

Lesson 3-7 Part 1   pp. 222–225

Got It?
1. $n = 3$ and $n = -3$

2. $x = 3$ or $x = -\frac{7}{3}$ **3.** no solution
Lesson Check
1. $x = 5$ or $x = -5$

2. $n = 7$ or $n = -7$

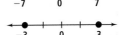

3. $t = 3$ or $t = -3$

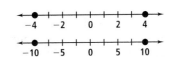

4. 2; there are two values on a number line that are the
same distance from 0. **5.** The absolute value cannot be
equal to a negative number since distance from 0 on a
number line must be nonnegative.
Exercises
7. $y = 4$ or $y = -4$

9. $s = 10$ or $s = -10$

11. $d = 4$ or $d = -4$

13. $r = 13$ or $r = 3$ **15.** $g = -1$ or $g = -5$
17. no solution **19.** $d = 0$ or $d = -8$ **21.** $n = 2$ or
$n = -2$ **23.** $d = 9$ or $d = -9$ **25.** no solution
26. $f = 1\frac{1}{2}$ or $f = -1\frac{1}{2}$ **27.** $y = 3.4$ or $y = -0.6$
28. $t = 1.8$ or $t = -1.8$ **29.** $t = 4\frac{4}{9}$ s and $17\frac{7}{9}$ s
30. There is no solution since the absolute value cannot
be a negative number. **31.** Answers may vary. Sample:
$|x - 4| = 2$ **32.** $|v - 0.4| \leq 0.03$;
$0.37 \leq v \leq 0.43$ **33.** minimum 850,000 barrels,
maximum 950,000 barrels **34.** $|x - 5| \leq 0.25$;
minimum 4.75 ft, maximum 5.25 ft

Lesson 3-7 Part 2   pp. 226–229

Got It?

4. $x \geq 0.5$ or $x \leq -4.5$

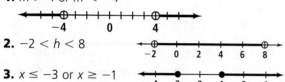

5a. $|w - 32| \leq 0.05$; $31.95 \leq w \leq 32.05$ **b.** No; 213 is part of the absolute value expression. You cannot add 213 until after you write the absolute value inequality as a compound inequality.

Lesson Check

1. $m > 4$ or $m < -4$

2. $-2 < h < 8$

3. $x \leq -3$ or $x \geq -1$

4. Answers may vary. Sample: The equation is set equal to 2 and -2. The first inequality is set to be ≤ 2 and ≥ -2. The second inequality is set to be ≥ 2 or ≤ -2. **5.** An absolute value inequality has no solution when the absolute value expression isolated must be less than a negative value.

Exercises

7. $-5 < x < 5$

9. $y \leq -11$ or $y \geq -5$

11. $4 \leq p \leq 10$

13. $t \leq -2.4$ or $t \geq 4$

15. $d < -7$ or $d > 11\frac{2}{3}$

17. any length between 28.5 in. and 29 in., inclusive
19. $c < -7\frac{7}{8}$ or $c > -6\frac{1}{8}$ **21.** $49°F \leq T \leq 64°F$
23. $-1 \leq y + 7 \leq 1$, $-8 \leq y \leq -6$ **25.** $|x| < 4$
27. $|x - 6| > 2$ **33.** $-282 \leq e \leq 20{,}320$
34. $36.9 \leq T \leq 37.5$ **35.** $2x + 10$ **36.** $-3y + 21$
37. $4\ell + 5$ **38.** $-m + 12$ **39.** $A = \{x \mid x$ is a whole number, $x < 10\}$ **40.** $B = \{x \mid x$ is an odd integer, $1 \leq x \leq 7\}$ **41.** $C = \{-14, -12, -10, -8, -6\}$
42. $D = \{8, 9, 10, 12, 14, 15, 16\}$

Lesson 3-8   pp. 230–236

Got It? 1a. $P = \{0, 1, 2, 3, 4\}$; $Q = \{2, 4\}$; $P \cup Q = \{0, 1, 2, 3, 4\}$ **b.** Answers may vary. Sample: If $B \subseteq A$, then $A \cup B$ will contain the same elements as A.
2a. $A \cap B = \{2, 8\}$ **b.** $A \cap C = \varnothing$ **c.** $C \cap B = \{5, 7\}$
3. A and E **4.** 10
Lesson Check 1. $X \cup Y = \{1, 2, 3, 4, 5, 6, 7, 8, 9, 10\}$

2. $X \cap Y = \{2, 4, 6, 8, 10\}$ **3.** $X \cap Z = \varnothing$ **4.** $Y \cup Z = \{1, 2, 3, 4, 5, 6, 7, 8, 9, 10\}$ **5.** 31 people **6.** $A \cup B$ contains more elements because it contains all the elements in both sets. **7.** The union of sets is the set that contains all elements of each set. The intersection of sets is the set of elements that are common to each set.
8. true **9.** false
Exercises 11. $B \cup C = \{0, 2, 4, 5, 6, 7, 8, 10\}$
13. $C \cup D = \{1, 2, 3, 5, 7, 9, 10\}$ **15.** $A \cap C = \varnothing$
17. $B \cap C = \{2\}$ **19.** $C \cap D = \{5, 7\}$
21.

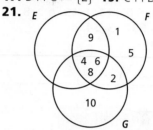

23. 10 girls **25.** $W \cup Y \cup Z = \{0, 2, 3, 4, 5, 6, 7, 8\}$
27. $W \cap X \cap Z = \{6\}$ **29.** 62 patients **31.** $\{(1, -3),$ $(1, -2), (1, -1), (1, 0), (2, -3), (2, -2), (2, -1), (2, 0),$ $(3, -3), (3, -2), (3, -1), (3, 0)\}$ **33.** $\{$(grape, jam), (grape, juice), (apple, jam), (apple, juice), (orange, jam), (orange, juice)$\}$ **35.** $A \cap B = A$ **39.** $x = 4$ or $x = -4$
40. $n = 2$ or $n = -2$ **41.** $f = 2$ or $f = 8$ **42.** $y = \frac{4}{3}$ or $y = -\frac{8}{3}$ **43.** $-5 \leq d \leq 5$ **44.** $x \leq -4$ or $x \geq 10$
45. $w < -15$ or $w > 9$ **46.** $x = \frac{4}{3}$ or $x = -\frac{4}{3}$
47. yes **48.** no **49.** yes
50–53.

Chapter Review for Part B   pp. 238–240

1. roster form **2.** union **3.** empty set **4.** { } or $\varnothing$, $\{s\}$, $\{t\}$, $\{s, t\}$ **5.** { } or $\varnothing$, $\{5\}$, $\{10\}$, $\{15\}$, $\{5, 10\}$, $\{5, 15\}$, $\{10, 15\}$, $\{5, 10, 15\}$ **6.** $A = \{0, 2, 4, 6, 8, 10, 12, 14, 16\}$; $A = \{x \mid x$ is an even whole number less than 18$\}$
7. $B' = \{1, 3, 5, 7\}$ **8.** $-2\frac{1}{2} \leq d < 4$ **9.** $-1.5 \leq b < 0$
10. $t \leq -2$ or $t \geq 7$ **11.** $m < -2$ or $m > 3$
12. $2 \leq a \leq 5$ **13.** $6.5 > p \geq -4.5$ **14.** $65 \leq t \leq 88$
15. $y = 3$ or $y = -3$ **16.** $n = 2$ or $n = -6$
17. $r = 1$ or $r = -5$ **18.** no solution **19.** $-3 \leq x \leq 3$
20. no solution **21.** $x < 3$ or $x > 4$ **22.** $k < -7$ or $k > -3$ **23.** any length between 19.6 mm and 20.4 mm, inclusive **24.** $A \cup B = A$

25.

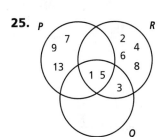

26. $N \cap P = \{x \mid x \text{ is a multiple of 6}\}$ **27.** 5 cats

Chapter 4

Get Ready!   p. 245

1. −7 **2.** −18 **3.** 2 **4.** −1

5.

Bob's and His Dog's Ages (years)										
Dog's Age	0	1	2	3	4	5	6	7	8	9
Bob's Age	9	10	11	12	13	14	15	16	17	18

$B = 9 + d$, where B is Bob's age and d is his dog's age.

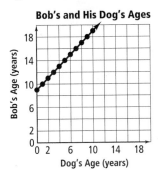

6.

Sue's Number of Laps Over Time										
Number of Minutes	0	1	2	3	4	5	6	7	8	9
Number of Laps	0	1.5	3	4.5	6	7.5	9	10.5	12	13.5

$\ell = 1.5m$, where m is the number of minutes and ℓ is the number of laps.

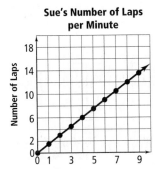

7.

Total Cost for Cartons of Eggs										
Number of Cartons	0	1	2	3	4	5	6	7	8	9
Total Cost (dollars)	0	3	6	9	12	15	18	21	24	27

$C = 3n$, where C is the cost and n is the number of cartons.

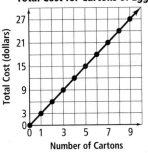

8–11.

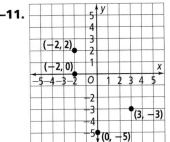

12. −3 **13.** 66 **14.** 6 **15.** 4 **16.** 0, −4 **17.** 3, 7 **18.** no solution **19.** $\frac{11}{2}, \frac{3}{2}$ **20.** Its value is based on the value of the other variable. **21.** 4 **22.** There are no breaks in the graph.

Lesson 4-1   pp. 248–254

Got It? 1a. Time, length; the length of the board remains constant (stays the same) for a time before another piece is cut off. **b.** Time, cost; the cost remains constant (stays the same) for a certain number of minutes. **2.** C
3. Answers may vary. Sample:

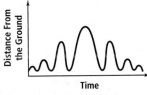

Lesson Check 1. Car weight, fuel used; the heavier the car, the more the fuel used. **2.** The temperature rises slightly in the first 2 h and then falls over the next 4 h.
3. rising slowly: B; constant: C; falling quickly: D
4. Answers may vary. Sample: the depth of water in a stream bed over time

Exercises 5. Number of pounds, total cost; as the number of pounds increases, the total cost goes up, at first quickly and then more slowly. **7.** Area painted, paint in can; the more you paint, the less paint left in the can. You are using the paint at a constant rate. **9.** A
11. Answers may vary. Sample:

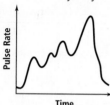

13. Answers may vary. Sample:

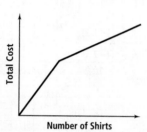

15. The graph shown represents the relationship between the number of shirts and the cost per shirt, not the total cost.

17. No, they are not the same. Your speed on the ski lift is constant. Your speed going downhill is not.

a. 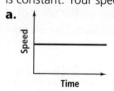 **b.**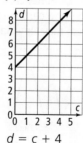

22. $\{-3, -1, 1, 3, 4, 5, 7, 9\}$ **23.** $\{1\}$
24. $\{-1, 1, 3, 4, 5, 7, 9, 12\}$ **25.** $\{1, 4\}$

26.

Connie's Age	Donald's Age
0	4
1	5
2	6
3	7

$d = c + 4$

27.

Time (hours)	Number of Cards
0	0
1	3
2	6
3	9

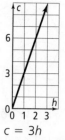

$c = 3h$

Lesson 4-2   pp. 255–261

Got It? 1.

Number of Triangles	1	2	3	4
Perimeter	10	14	18	22

Multiply the number of triangles by 4 and add 6; $y = 4x + 6$.

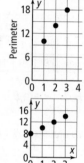

2a. Yes; the value of y is 8 more than twice the value of x; $y = 2x + 8$.

b. No; the input value 1 has more than one output value.

Lesson Check

1a. 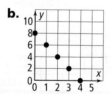 y increases by 1 for each increase of 1 for x.

b. For each increase of 1 in x, y decreases by 2.

c. 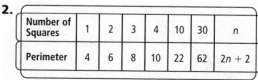 x is 3 for any value of y.

2.

Number of Squares	1	2	3	4	10	30	n
Perimeter	4	6	8	10	22	62	$2n + 2$

3. independent: number of times you brush your teeth; dependent: amount of toothpaste left in tube **4.** a and b

are functions because for each input there is a unique output, but c is not a function because there is more than one output value for the input value 3. **5.** No; the graph is not part of a line.

Exercises

7.

Number of Hexagons	1	2	3
Perimeter	6	10	14

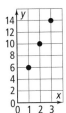

Multiply the number of hexagons by 4 and add 2; $y = 4x + 2$.

9. Start with −3 and add 5 for each increase of 1 for x; $y = 5x − 3$.

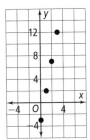

11. Yes; for each additional hour of climbing, you gain 92 ft of elevation; $y = 92x + 1127$.

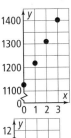

13. Yes; for every 17 mi traveled, the amount of gas in your tank goes down by 1 gallon; $y = -\frac{1}{17}x + 11.2$.

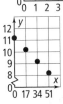

15. $y = \frac{8}{5}x$, where x is the number of gallons of water and y is the number of teaspoons of fertilizer. Or solve for x to make the gallons of water a function of the teaspoons of fertilizer used.

x	y
0	0
5	8
10	16
15	24
20	32

Yes, because there is a unique y for each x.

17. Gear A will make one-half turn for 1 complete turn of Gear B; $y = \frac{1}{2}x$.

23.

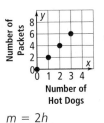

24.

Number of Hot Dogs	Number of Packets
0	0
1	2
2	4
3	6

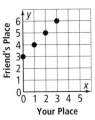

$m = 2h$

25.

Your Place	Friend's Place
0	3
1	4
2	5
3	6

$y = x + 3$

Lesson 4-3   pp. 262–269

Got It?

1a.

nonlinear

b. No; you can always multiply a number by $\frac{1}{2}$. The denominator of the fraction will get larger and larger, so the value of the fraction will approach 0 but never reach it.

2. The number of branches is 3 raised to the xth power; $y = 3^x$; 81, 243.

3. $y = x^2$

Lesson Check

1.

linear

2. $y = 3x - 2$ **3.** C **4a.** linear function **b.** nonlinear function **5.** Only the first two pairs fit this rule. The rule that fits all the pairs is $y = x^2 + 1$.

Exercises

7.

nonlinear

9.

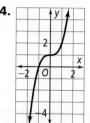

nonlinear

11.

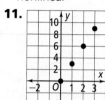

linear

13. $y = 4x^2$ **15.** $y = 2x^3$ **17.** Answers will vary. Sample: $y = (-1)^x$ **19.** $A = 4r^2 - \pi r^2$

23. The value of y is 3 more than twice x; $y = 2x + 3$.

24. −24, −3, 14.5 **25.** −11, 1, 11 **26.** −18, 0, −12.5

Lesson 4-4   pp. 270–277

Got It?

1.

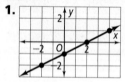

2a.

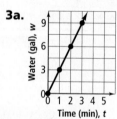

b. 700 lb; when $g = 0$, the spa is empty, and $W = 700$.

3a.

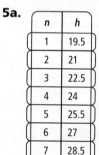

continuous because you can have any amount of water

b.

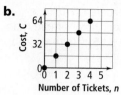

discrete because you can only have a whole number of tickets

4.

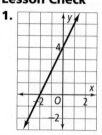

Lesson Check

1.

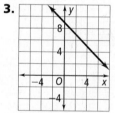

2.

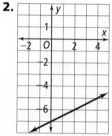

3.

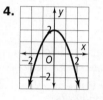

4.

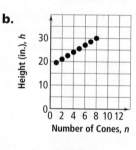

5a.

n	h
1	19.5
2	21
3	22.5
4	24
5	25.5
6	27
7	28.5
8	30

b.

Height (in.), h vs. Number of Cones, n

6. discrete **7.** continuous **8.** The graph should be continuous: connect the points with a line.

Exercises

9.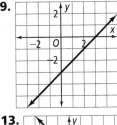

11.

13.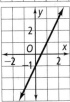

15.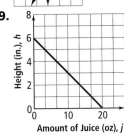

17.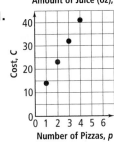

19.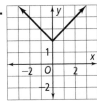

After you drink 20 oz of juice, the height is 0, so the interval $0 \le j \le 20$ makes sense. The height goes from $0 \le h \le 6$; continuous, because you can have juice in any amount.

21.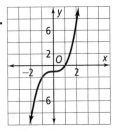

The number of pizzas can be any whole number except zero, so $0 < p$. 1 delivered pizza costs $14, so $14 \le C$.

23.

25.

27.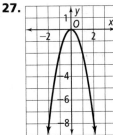

29.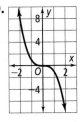

31. No; the graph is still continuous over the appropriate values of d and t.

33.  Continuous; lengths and areas can be any positive number.

35a.

b	0	1	2	3
a	0	15	30	45

Discrete; you can only have whole numbers of basketballs.

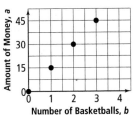

b. 8 **37.** between 2 and 3 s **42.** nonlinear **43.** linear
44. $-2, 12$ **45.** $-7, 1$ **46.** 1, 13 **47.** $-31, 9$
48. no solution **49.** $-4, 4$ **50.** $-2, 4$ **51.** no solution
52. $-3, 1$ **53.** Let x = number of cones purchased at $4. Then $14 = 4x - 2$; 4. **54.** Let x = cost of each yard of mulch. Then $200 = 35 + 5x$; $33.

Lesson 4-5   pp. 280–285

Got It? 1. $W = 50{,}000 + 420m$ **2a.** $C = 12 + 15n$; $162 **b.** No; making the stay shorter only halves the daily charge, not the bath charge. **3.** $A = b^2 + 2b$; 288 in.^{2}
Lesson Check 1. $C = 3.57p$ **2.** $f = \frac{h}{12}$ **3.** $y = x + 2$
4. $V = (d + 1)^3$ **5.** dependent, a; independent, b **6.** You can't add holes and minutes. The correct rule is $t = 15n$.
7. Continuous; side length and area can be any positive real numbers.
Exercises 9. $C = 8 + \frac{1}{2}n$ **11.** $\frac{h}{3} + 2.5 = w$
13. $p = 6.95 + 0.95t$ **15.** $a = 8 - \frac{1}{6}b$
17. $d = -10 - 50t$; -160 ft **19.** $A = \frac{3}{2}h + \frac{5}{2}h^2$; 99 cm^2 **20.** $V = \pi r^2(3 + 4r)$; 44π in.^{3}, or about 138.23 in.^{3} **23.** $d = -3.5 - 108m$; -435.5 m

25a.

Cost of Meal	$15	$21	$24	$30
Money Left	$37.75	$30.85	$27.40	$20.50

b. $m = 55 - 1.15c$

c.
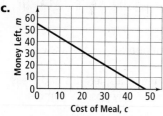
Money Left, m vs Cost of Meal, c

27a. $b = 42.95d + 45.60$ **b.** $432.15

32. 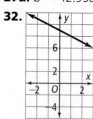 **33.**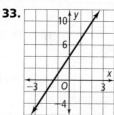

34. 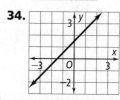 **35.**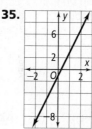

36. 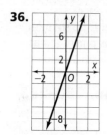 **37.**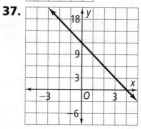

38. 132 oz **39.** 4.5 m **40.** 51 ft **41.** 1.5 min **42.** 9 days
43. 9500 m **44.** −36 **45.** 21 **46.** 111.6 **47.** −9
48. 14 **49.** 1 **50.** $\frac{5}{3}$ **51.** $\frac{21}{16}$

Lesson 4-6, Part 1　　　pp. 286–290

Got It?
1a. domain: {4.2, 5, 7}; range: {0, 1.5, 2.2, 4.8}.

not a function

b. domain: {−2, −1, 4 7}; range: {1, 2, −4, −7}.

function

2a. function **b.** not a function **3.** 1500 words
Lesson Check
1. domain: {−2, −1, 0, 1}, range: {3, 4, 5, 6}.

function

2. yes **3.** 9 **4.** $f(x) = 2x + 7$ **5.** Answers may vary.
Sample: Both methods can be used to determine whether
there is more than one output for any given input. A
mapping diagram does not represent a function if any
domain value is mapped to more than one range value.
A graph does not represent a function if it fails the vertical
line test. **6.** No; there exists a vertical line that intersects
the graph in more than one point, so the graph does not
represent a function.

Exercises 7. domain {3}, range {−2, 1, 4, 7, 8}; no
9. domain {0, 1, 4}, range {−2, −1, 0, 1, 2}; no **11.** not
a function **13.** about 5,580,000 mi **15.** not a function
19. Answers may vary. Sample given: any value except 1
and −7

Lesson 4-6, Part 2　　　pp. 291–294

Got It? 4. {−8, 0, 8, 16} **5a.** domain: $0 \le q \le 7$, range:
$0 \le A(q) \le 700$ **b.** The least amount of paint you can use
is 0 quarts. The greatest amount you can use is 3 quarts.
Lesson Check 1. {−2, −1, 0, 1, 2}
Exercises 3. {−11, −9, −7, −5, −3}
5. {0, 0.04, 1.44, 16}
7. $0 \le c \le 16$, $0 \le D(c) \le 1568$

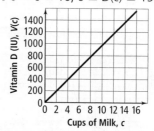
Vitamin D (IU), $V(c)$ vs Cups of Milk, c

9a. c is the independent variable and p is the dependent
variable. **b.** Yes; for each value of c, there is a unique
value of p. **c.** $p = 5c - 34$ **d.** $0 \le c \le 40$, $0 \le p \le 166$
14. $E = 5h + 7$ **15.** $a = 4.5s + 10$

16a. time and distance

b.

A Trip to the Mountains

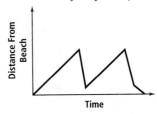

17. 9, 12, 15, 18 **18.** 8, 15, 22, 29
19. 0.4, −2.6, −5.6, −8.6

Lesson 4-7   p. 295

Got It? 1a. Add 6 to the previous term; 29, 35.
b. Multiply each previous term by $\frac{1}{2}$; 25, 12.5. **c.** Multiply
each previous term by −2; 32, −64. **d.** Add 4 to the
previous term; 1, 5. **2a.** not an arithmetic sequence
b. arithmetic sequence; 2 **c.** arithmetic sequence; −6
d. not an arithmetic sequence **3a.** $A(n) = 100 − (n − 1)$;
1.75; $73.75 **b.** 57
Lesson Check 1. Add 8 to the previous term; 35, 43.
2. Multiply the previous term by −2; 48, −96. **3.** not an
arithmetic sequence **4.** arithmetic sequence; 9
5. $A(n) = 9 − 2(n − 1)$; −3 **6.** −6; the pattern is "add −6
to the previous term." **7.** The formula $A(n) = 4 + 8n$
was used instead of $A(n) = 4 + 8(n − 1)$. $A(10) =$
$4 + (10 − 1)8 = 76$. **8.** Yes; $A(n) = A(1) +$
$(n − 1)d = A(1) + nd − d$ by the Distributive Property.
Exercises 9. Add 7 to the previous term; 34, 41.
11. Add 4 to the previous term; 18, 22. **13.** Add −2
to the previous term; 5, 3. **15.** Add 1.1 to the previous
term; 5.5, 6.6. **17.** Multiply the previous term by 2; 72,
144. **19.** not an arithmetic sequence **21.** not an
arithmetic sequence **23.** yes; 1.3 **25.** not an arithmetic
sequence **27.** yes; −0.5 **29.** not an arithmetic sequence
31. $A(n) = 50 − 3.25n$; $11 **33.** 2, 12, 47
35. 17, 33, 89 **37.** −2, 8, 43 **39.** −3.2, −5.4, −13.1
41. Yes; the common difference is −4; $A(n) = −3 +$
$(n − 1)(−4)$. **43.** No; there is no common difference.
45. Yes; the common difference is −0.8; $A(n) = 0.2 +$
$(n − 1)(−0.8)$. **47.** Answers may vary. Sample:
$A(n) = 15 + 2(n − 1)$ **49.** 350, 325, 300, 275,
250, 225; you owe $225 at the end of six weeks.
51a. 1, 6, 15, 20, 15, 6, 1 **b.** 1, 2, 4, 8, 16; 64
53a. 11, 14 **b.**

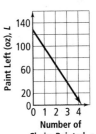

c. The points all lie on a line. **58.** {12, 4.8, 0, −4, −40}
59. {13, 5.8, 1, −3, −39} **60.** {27, 4.32, 0, 3, 300}

61. {−2.5, 8.84, 11, 9.5, −139} **62.** {−19, −2.8, 8,
17, 98} **63.** {−7.25, −5.9, −5, −4.25, 2.5}
64. 480 gal/h **65.** 132 ft/s **66.** $5.25

Chapter Review   pp. 303–306

1. independent variable **2.** linear **3.** discrete **4.** range
5. Answers may vary. Sample:

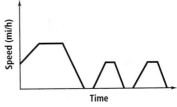

6. Answers may vary. Sample:

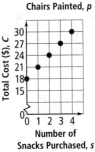

7. chairs painted, paint left; each
time p increases by 1, L decreases
by 30; $L = 128 − 30p$.

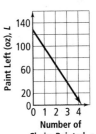

8. Snacks purchased, total cost;
for each additional snack, total
cost goes up by 3; $C = 18 + 3s$.

9. Independent n, dependent E;
the elevation is 311 more than
15 times the number of flights
climbed; $E = 15n + 311$.

10. 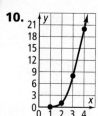 nonlinear

11. 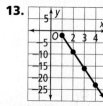 linear

12. 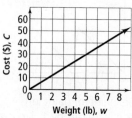 nonlinear

13. 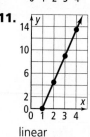 linear

14. 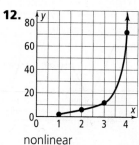 continuous because w can take on any nonnegative value

15. 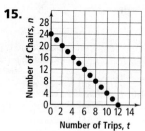 discrete because the number of trips must be a whole number

16. 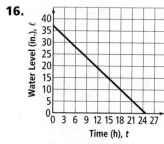 continuous because t can take on any nonnegative value

17.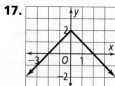

18. $V = 243 - 0.2s$ **19.** $C = 200 + 45h$ **20.** not a function **21.** function **22.** -4; 6 **23.** 53; 33 **24.** {7.2, 1.12, -4.2, -34.6} **25.** Multiply each previous term by 5; 625, 3125. **26.** Add -3 to the previous term;

-14, -17. **27.** Add 2.5 to the previous term; 14, 16.5. **28.** Multiply the previous term by -2; 32, -64. **29.** arithmetic; 1.2 **30.** arithmetic; 10 **31.** not an arithmetic sequence **32.** not an arithmetic sequence

Chapter 5

Get Ready! p. 311

1. yes **2.** no **3.** yes **4.** $y = \frac{1}{2}x + 2$ **5.** $y = 3x - 2$
6. $y = -x - 2$ **7.** boat **8.** bean plant
9.

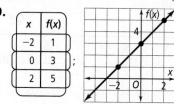

10.

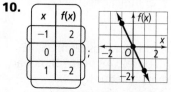

11.

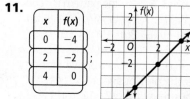

12. $A(n) = 2 + (n - 1)3$ **13.** $A(n) = 13 + (n - 1)(-3)$
14. $A(n) = -3 + (n - 1)2.5$ **15.** the steepness of the line
16. Two lines are parallel if they lie in the same plane and do not intersect. **17.** A y-intercept is the y-coordinate of the point where the line crosses the y-axis.

Lesson 5-1 pp. 314–320

Got It? 1. Yes; the rate of change is constant. **2a.** $\frac{2}{5}$
b. $-\frac{1}{3}$ **c.** yes **3.** $-\frac{4}{3}$ **4a.** undefined **b.** 0

Lesson Check 1. Yes; the rates of change between any two points is the same. **2.** $-\frac{5}{3}$ **3.** Slope; slope is the ratio of vertical change to horizontal change. **4.** The slope of a horizontal line is 0. **5.** Answers may vary. Sample: Both methods give the same result. You need the graph to count the units of change. You need the coordinates of the points to use the slope formula.

Exercises 7. Yes; -500; the plane is descending at a rate of 500 ft/min. **9.** $\frac{1}{3}$ **11.** $\frac{5}{6}$ **13.** $\frac{1}{2}$ **15.** -6 **17.** 2
19. $-\frac{1}{3}$ **21.** undefined **23.** positive; 9 **25.** positive; 12
27. independent: number of people; dependent: cost; $12/person **29.** 0 **31.** 0 **33.** No; the line could intercept the y-axis at any point and still have a slope of 1.
35. Check students' work. **37.** 0 **39.** -6 **44.** 5, 9, 21

45. 1, 13, 49 **46.** 15, 21, 39 **47.** {2, 4} **48.** {3} **49.** {8}
50. {2, 3, 4, 5, 6, 7, 8, 10} **51.** {1, 2, 3, 4, 5, 7, 8}
52. 7.5 **53.** 20 **54.** 5 **55.** −10 **56.** 81

Lesson 5-2 pp. 321–327

Got It? 1a. yes; $-\frac{4}{5}$ **b.** no **2.** $y = -5x$; 75

3a. $y = 0.166x$

b. 0.38; the slope is the coefficient of the x-term.

4. yes; $y = -0.75x$

Lesson Check 1. yes; 3 **2.** $y = 10x$ **3.** 30 muffins
4. always **5.** never **6.** sometimes

Exercises 7. no **9.** yes; −2 **11.** yes; $\frac{7}{3}$ **13.** $y = \frac{5}{2}x$; 30

15. $y = \frac{5}{2}x$; 30 **17.** $y = -\frac{56}{3}x$; −224

19. 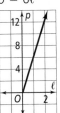 **21.**

23. $p = 6\ell$

25. yes; $y = 1.8x$

27. $y = \frac{1}{6}x$ **29.** $y = -\frac{36}{25}x$

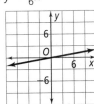 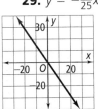

31. about 5 qt **33.** Yes; as the number of ounces increases, the number of Calories increases. When the number of ounces is 0, the number of Calories is 0.
35. Yes; as the side length increases, the perimeter increases. When the side length is 0, the perimeter is 0.

37a. 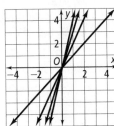 **b.** The graphs get steeper.
c. less steep than $y = x$

39a. The value of y is doubled. **b.** The value of y is halved. **45.** 1 **46.** 0 **47.** 6 **48.** $-\frac{5}{3}$ **49.** 15 **50.** −11
51. 6 **52.** −7

Lesson 5-3, Part 1 pp. 329–333

Got It? 1a. $-\frac{1}{2}$, $\frac{2}{3}$ **b.** The graph moves down 3 units; the equation of the line changes to $y = -\frac{1}{2}x + \frac{2}{3} - 3 = -\frac{1}{2}x - \frac{7}{3}$. **2.** $y = \frac{3}{2}x - 1$ **3a.** $y = -x + 2$ **b.** No; the slope is constant, so it is the same between any two points on the line. **4.** $y = \frac{1}{2}x - \frac{7}{2}$

Lesson Check 1. $y = 6x - 4$ **2.** $y = -x + 1$ **3.** Yes; it is a horizontal line with a y-intercept of 5. **4.** Sometimes; answers may vary. Sample: $y = 3x$ represents direct variation, but $y = 3x + 1$ does not.

Exercises 5. 3, 1 **7.** 2, −5 **9.** 5, −3 **11.** 0, 4
13. $\frac{1}{4}$, $-\frac{1}{3}$ **15.** $y = 3x + 2$ **17.** $y = 0.7x - 2$
19. $y = -2x + \frac{8}{5}$ **21.** $y = 2x - 3$ **23.** $y = -2x + 4$
25. $y = \frac{1}{2}x + 3$ **27.** $y = -x + 2$ **29.** $y = \frac{1}{2}x$
31. $y = -\frac{5}{7}x + \frac{5}{7}$ **33.** $-\frac{1}{2}$, 0 **35.** $\frac{3}{2}$, 3 **37.** c, d
39. −3, −2n **41.** Answers may vary. Samples: graph the line, determine whether the equation can be rewritten in the form $y = mx + b$.

Lesson 5-3, Part 2 pp. 334–337

Got It?

5a. 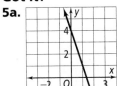 **b.**

6. $y = 35x + 65$

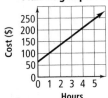

Lesson Check

1a. 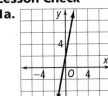 **b.**

2. Answers may vary. Sample: You can plot points or you can use the slope-intercept form to plot the y-intercept and then use the slope to find a second point; check students' work.

Exercises

3.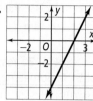

5.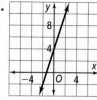

7.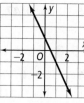

9.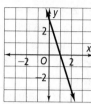

11.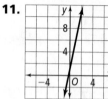

13. $y = 7.5x - 5$

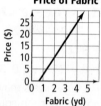

Price of Fabric

15. 2030

17a. $y = 35x + 50$

b.

c. The amount of time the repair takes and the cost must be positive.

19.

21.

23.

25a. $y = 10x + 175$　　**b.** 675 pieces

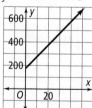

31. $y = 5x$; 50　**32.** $y = 2x$; 20　**33.** $y = 3x$; 30
34. $t = -9$　**35.** $q = 27$　**36.** $x = 7$　**37.** $-3x + 15$
38. $5x + 10$　**39.** $-\frac{4}{9}x + \frac{8}{3}$　**40.** $1.5x + 18$

Lesson 5-4, Part 1　　pp. 338–340

Got It? 1. $y + 4 = \frac{2}{3}(x - 8)$

2.

Lesson Check 1. $\frac{4}{9}$; $(-7, 12)$　**2.** $y + 8 = -2(x - 3)$

3.

4. the slope m of the line and a point (x_1, y_1) on the line
5. yes; $1 - 4 = 3(-2 + 1)$

Exercises 7. $y - 2 = -\frac{5}{3}(x - 4)$　**9.** $y = -1(x - 4)$

11.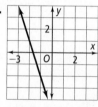

13.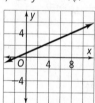

15.

17. The student graphed the point $(2, 0)$ instead of $(0, 2)$.

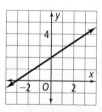

Lesson 5-4, Part 2　　pp. 341–344

Got It? 3a. $y + 3 = \frac{7}{3}(x + 2)$　**b.** They are both equal to $y = \frac{7}{3}x + \frac{5}{3}$; you can use any point on a line to write an equation of the line in point-slope form. **4a.** Answers may vary. Sample: $y - 3320 = 1250(x - 2)$; the rate at which water is being added to the tank, in gallons per hour **b.** $y = 1250x + 820$; the initial number of gallons of water in the tank

Lesson Check 1. Answers may vary. Sample: $y + 2 = 2(x + 1)$ **2.** Yes; answers may vary. Sample: $y - a = m(x - b)$, $y = mx - mb + a$, $y = mx + (a - mb)$

Exercises 3–5. Answers may vary. Samples are given.
3. $y - 3 = \frac{4}{3}(x - 1)$ **5.** $y - 2 = \frac{3}{4}(x - 1)$
7. Point-slope forms may vary. Sample:
$y - 4 = 2(x - 2)$; $y = 2x$ **9.** $y = -12x + 80$;
the slope -12 represents the change in the amount of
paint in gallons per day; the y-intercept 80 represents
the initial number of gallons of paint. **11.** Answers
may vary. Sample: $C - 10 = \frac{5}{9}(F - 50)$; 15°C
13. $b = -0.0018a + 212$; 207.5°F **18.** 1, 4 **19.** 6, 0
20. $-1, -13$ **21.** $y = \frac{z}{7x}$ **22.** $y = \frac{7b + 3}{a}$ **23.** $y = \frac{6x - c}{6}$

Chapter Review for Part A pp. 345–346

1. rate of change **2.** point-slope form **3.** -1 **4.** 0
5. 3 **6.** undefined **7.** 3 **8.** $-\frac{1}{2}$ **9.** $y = -2x$; -14
10. $y = \frac{5}{2}x$; $\frac{35}{2}$ **11.** $y = \frac{1}{3}x$; $\frac{7}{3}$ **12.** $y = -x$; -7 **13.** no
14. yes; $y = -2.5x$ **15.** $y = 4$ **16.** $y = x - 5$
17. $y = \frac{2}{3}x + 1$ **18.** $y = -x - 1$

19.

20.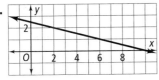

21.

22.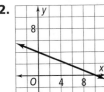

Lesson 5-5 pp. 349–356

Got It? 1a. 12; -10 **b.** 4; 3

2.

3a.   **b.**

c. **d.**

4. $x + 3y = 0$ **5a.** $x + 15y = 60$ **b.** domain:
nonnegative integers less than or equal to 60; range:
$\{0, 1, 2, 3, 4\}$

Lesson Check 1. 3, $-\frac{9}{4}$

2.

3. horizontal line **4.** $x - 2y = -6$ **5.** $10x + 25y = 285$;
answers may vary. Sample: 1 \$10 card and 11 \$25 cards,
6 \$10 cards and 9 \$25 cards, 11 \$10 cards and 7 \$25 cards
6a. point-slope form **b.** slope-intercept form
c. point-slope form **d.** standard form **7.** Answers may
vary. Sample: slope-intercept form; it is easy to find the
y-intercept and calculate the slope from the graph.

Exercises 9. 9, 9 **11.** -5; 4

13.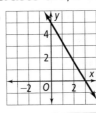

15.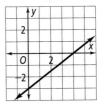

17.

19.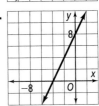

21.

23. vertical **25.** vertical

27.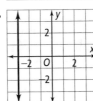

29.

31. $2x - y = -5$ **33.** $2x + y = 10$
35. $5j + 2s = 250$

Points

Answers may vary. Sample: 50 jewels and 0 stars,
48 jewels and 5 stars, 42 jewels and 20 stars

37. When you have a slope and the *y*-intercept, use the slope-intercept form. When you have two points or a slope and a point, use the point-slope form. When you have the standard form, it is easy to graph.

39.

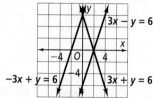

Two lines have the same slope but different *y*-intercepts. Two lines have the same *y*-intercept but different slopes.

41. The student did not subtract 1 from each side of the equation. The correct equation is $4x - y = -1$.

43.

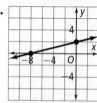

45.

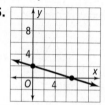

47.

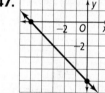

49. 4, 3; $3x + 4y = 12$ **51.** −3, −3; $x + y = -3$
53. 10, $-\frac{10}{3}$ **55.** 6, 6 **57.** 4, $-\frac{8}{5}$ **64–66.** Point-slope forms may vary. Samples are given. **64.** $y + 1 = -\frac{5}{8}(x - 5)$;
$y = -\frac{5}{8}x + \frac{17}{8}$ **65.** $y + 2 = \frac{4}{3}x$; $y = \frac{4}{3}x - 2$
66. $y + 1 = x + 2$; $y = x + 1$
67. $-2 < t \le 3$

68. $1.7 \le y < 12.5$

69. $x \le -1$ or $x > 3$

70. 2 **71.** 3 **72.** 0

Lesson 5-6   **pp. 357–362**

Got It? 1. $y = \frac{2}{3}x - 3$ **2a.** Neither; the slopes are not equal or opposite reciprocals. **b.** Parallel; the slopes are equal. **3.** $y = -\frac{1}{2}x + \frac{17}{2}$ **4.** $y = -\frac{2}{3}x + 10$
Lesson Check 1. $y = 6x$ and $y = 6x - 2$ are parallel;
$y = -\frac{1}{6}x$ and $y = 6x$, $y = -\frac{1}{6}x$ and $y = 6x - 2$ are perpendicular **2.** $y = -4x + 11$ **3a.** yes **b.** no **c.** no
5. In both cases, you compare the slopes of the lines. If the slopes are equal, then the lines are parallel. If the slopes are opposite reciprocals, the lines are perpendicular.

Exercises 7. $y = 3x$ **9.** $y = \frac{2}{3}x$ **11.** Perpendicular; the slopes are opposite reciprocals. **13.** Parallel; the slopes are equal. **15.** Perpendicular; one line is vertical and the other line is horizontal. **17.** $y = -2x - 1$
19. $y = -\frac{1}{5}x - \frac{9}{5}$ **21.** $y = -\frac{1}{2}x + \frac{5}{2}$ **23.** $y = 2x + 4$
25. Sometimes; a horizontal line has the same slope as the *x*-axis. If the horizontal line is not $y = 0$, then it is parallel to the *x*-axis. **27.** Never; two lines with the same slope are parallel. **29.** $x = 3$ **31.** $y = -100x + 600$, $y = -100x + 1000$; parallel; the slopes are the same.

35.

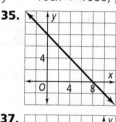

36.

37.

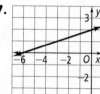

38. $y = 3x - 2$ **39.** $y = -\frac{2}{5}x + \frac{29}{5}$
40. $y = 0.25x + 1.875$ **41.** $y = -\frac{40}{7}x + \frac{660}{7}$

Lesson 5-7   **pp. 363–370**

Got It?
1a.

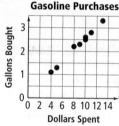

positive correlation

b. No correlation; the length of a city's name and the population are not related.

2a. Answers may vary. Sample:

Body Length of a Panda

$y = 2.23x + 8.8$; about 24.4 in.

b. No; an adult panda does not grow at the same rate as a young panda.

3. about $9964 **4a.** There may be a positive correlation, but it is not causal because a more expensive vacation does not cause a family to own a bigger house. **b.** There is a positive correlation and a causal relationship. The more time you spend exercising, the more Calories you burn.

Lesson Check

1. Average Maximum Daily Temperature in January for Northern Latitudes

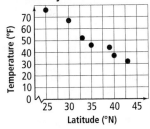

negative correlation

2–3. Answers may vary. Samples are given.
2. $y = -2x + 120$ **3.** about 20°F **4.** You use interpolation to estimate a value between two known values. You use extrapolation to predict a value outside the range of the known values. **5.** Both the trend line and the line of best fit show a correlation between two sets of data. The line of best fit is the most accurate trend line.
6. If y decreases as x decreases, then there is a positive correlation because a trend line will have a positive slope.

Exercises

7. Jeans Sales

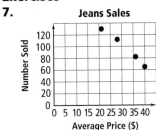

negative correlation

9. Answers may vary. Sample:

Attendance at U.S. Theme Parks

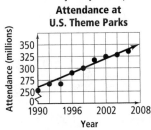

$y = 5x - 9690$; about 335 million

11. $y = 21.4x - 41557$; 0.942; 1542.6 million tickets
13. no correlation likely **15.** There is likely a correlation and a possible causal relationship, because the higher the price of hamburger, the less people are likely to buy.
19. about 7 cm
21a. $y = 10.5x + 88.2$ **b.** 10.5; the sales increase by about 10.5 million units each year. **c.** 88.2; the estimated number of units sold in the year 1990 **26.** $y = 5x - 13$
27. $y = -x + 5$ **28.** $y = -\frac{2}{3}x + \frac{10}{3}$

29.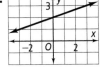

30.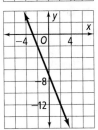

31.

32.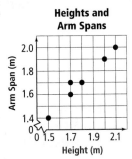

Chapter Review for Part B pp. 373–374

1. interpolation **2.** opposite reciprocals **3.** line of best fit
4. $y = 5x - 11$ **5.** $y = 9x - 5$ **6.** Parallel; the slopes are equal. **7.** Neither; the slopes are not equal or opposite reciprocals. **8.** $y = \frac{1}{3}x + 4$ **9.** $y = -\frac{1}{8}x + \frac{21}{2}$
10. negative correlation **11.** no correlation **12.** positive correlation

13a. Heights and Arm Spans

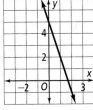

b–d. Answers may vary. Samples are given.
b. $y = 0.96x - 0.01$
c. about 1.5 m
d. about 2.1 m

Chapter 6

Get Ready! p. 379

1 identity **2.** 1 **3.** no solution **4.** 3 **5.** 1.5 **6.** no solution
7. $x < 3$ **8.** $r \le 35$ **9.** $t > -13$ **10.** $f \ge -2$ **11.** $s > \frac{5}{23}$
12. $x \ge -18$ **13a.** $2x - 1$ **b.** $A = \frac{1}{2}x(2x - 1)$
c. 248 cm^2

14.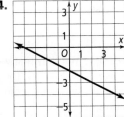

15.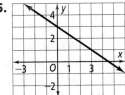

16.

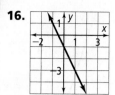

17. deletes

Lesson 6-1   pp. 382–387

Got It? 1. (−2, 0) **2.** 5 months **3a.** no solution
b. infinitely many solutions
Lesson Check 1. (6, 13) **2.** (16, 14) **3.** (−1, 0)
4. (−1, −3)
5a. $c = 10t + 8$ **b.** (4, 48); the cost is the same
     $c = 12t$ whether you buy 4 tickets for a
                  cost of $48 online or at the door.
6. A, III; B, II; C, I **7.** No; a solution to the system must be
on both lines. **8.** No; two lines intersect in no points, one
point, or an infinite number of points. **9.** The graphs of
the equations both contain the point (−2, 3).
Exercises 11. (3, 2) **13.** (1, 2) **15.** (−1, 3) **17.** 27
students; 3 students **19.** 10 classes **21.** no solution
23. no solution **25.** infinitely many solutions **27.** The
student did not show enough of the graph. If you
continue the graph to the left, the lines will intersect at
the point (−4, 7). **29a.** 100 messages **b.** the plan that
costs $40 per month and $.20 per text message
31. Infinitely many solutions; the lines are the same.
33. $b = 2.5t + 40$; 16 weeks
     $b = 5t$
37. 1 **38.** $-\frac{1}{2}$ **39.** $\frac{3}{5}$ **40.** $y = -2x + 19$
41. $y = 15 - 6x$ **42.** $y = \frac{1}{3}x - \frac{14}{3}$

Lesson 6-2   pp. 390–395

Got It? 1. (−8, −9) **2a.** (3, 4) **b.** x; $3y + x = 15$
3. 5 new games **4.** infinitely many
Lesson Check 1. $\left(25\frac{5}{11}, 6\frac{4}{11}\right)$ **2.** (3, 5) **3.** no solution
4. no solution **5.** 7 singing, 5 comedy **6.** Answers may
vary. Sample: Graphing a system can be inexact, and it is
very difficult to read the intersection, especially when
there are noninteger solutions. The substitution method
is better, as it can always give an exact answer.
7. $-2x + y = -1$ because it is easily solved for y.
8. $6x - y = 1$ because it is easily solved for y. **9.** False; it
has infinitely many solutions. **10.** False; you can use it,
but the arithmetic may be harder.
Exercises 11. (2, 6) **13.** $\left(-\frac{5}{7}, 2\frac{2}{7}\right)$ **15.** (−11, −19)
17. (−12, −5) **19.** 2 buses, 4 vans **21.** infinitely many
solutions **23.** one solution **25.** Solve $1.2x + y = 2$ for y
because then you can solve the system using substitution.
27. 6 large, 12 small **34.** one solution: (−3, −6)
35. one solution: (3, 4) **36.** no solution **37.** $-\frac{1}{3}$

38. 4 **39.** −3 **40.** −3 **41.** 2 **42.** $\frac{3}{2}$

Lesson 6-3 Part 1   pp. 396–399

Got It? 1. (2, 7) **2.** car: 20 min; truck: 30 min
Lesson Check 1. (2, 3) **2.** (4, 1) **3.** Elimination; the
objective of the elimination method is to add (or subtract)
two equations to eliminate a variable. **4.** The Addition
Property of Equality says that adding equals to equals
gives you equals. This is what you are doing in the
elimination method.
Exercises 5. (4, 5) **7.** (1, 5) **9.** (3, 5) **11.** (4, 3) **13.** 4 ft
15. (−2, −3) **17.** (−6, −4) **19.** (2, −5) **21.** $59

Lesson 6-3 Part 2   pp. 399–404

Got It? 3a. (7, −2) **b.** Answers may vary. Sample:
You could use substitution by solving the second equation
for x. **4.** (4, 2) **5.** no solution
Lesson Check 1. (1, 4) **2.** $\left(\frac{7}{25}, -\frac{2}{25}\right)$ **3.** Multiply the
first equation by 4 and then add the equations or multiply
the first equation by −3 and the second equation by 2
and then add the equations **4.** Answers may vary.
Sample: Decide which variable to eliminate, and then
multiply, if necessary, one or both equations so that the
coefficients of the variable are the same (or opposites).
Then subtract (or add) the two equations. This will result
in one equation with a single variable that you can solve.
Then substitute to find the value of the other variable.
Exercises 5. (3, 1) **7.** (3, 4) **9.** (4, 7) **11.** no solution
13. infinitely many solutions **15.** $12; $7 **17.** 660
Calories; 580 Calories **19.** (2, 0); Answers may vary.
Sample: substitution; the first equation is easily solved
for y. **21.** They both result in an equation with a single
variable to solve. Check students' work. **23.** square:
81 cm²; triangle: 15 cm² **29.** (7, 3.5) **30.** (34, 27)
31. (5, −3) **32.** $a > 1$ **33.** $x \geq 7$ **34.** $b > 0.2$
35. 2.75 h

Lesson 6-4   pp. 407–411

Got It? 1. 720 books **2.** 11.25 L of 20% alcohol; 3.75 L
of 12% alcohol
Lesson Check 1. 300 copies **2.** 1 kg of 30% gold,
3 kg of 10% gold **3.** Before the break-even point,
expenses exceed income. After the break-even point,
income exceeds expenses. **4.** Answers may vary. Sample:
elimination; neither equation is easily solved for a variable.
Exercises 5. 40 bicycles **7.** 16 kg of 20% copper, 64 kg
of 60% copper **9.** (2, −1); elimination method because
neither equation easily solves for a variable **11.** $\left(\frac{25}{6}, -\frac{23}{12}\right)$;
Explanations may vary. Sample: substitution because one
of the equations is easily solved for x **13–15.** Answers
may vary. Samples are given. **13.** Substitution; both
equations are already solved for y, so you can set them
equal. **15.** Substitution; the second equation is already

solved for *t*. **17.** 13 correctly and 7 incorrectly
21. $(-7, 6)$ **22.** $(-2, -2)$ **23.** $(4, 2.5)$ **24.** $a > 5$
25. $d \leq -2.5$ **26.** $q \leq -4$

Chapter Review for Part A pp. 412–413

1. substitution **2.** elimination **3.** system of linear
equations **4.** $(-8, -11)$ **5.** $(-2, 6)$ **6.** $(-3, -3)$ **7.** no
solution **8.** $\left(-\frac{14}{3}, -\frac{35}{3}\right)$ **9.** infinitely many solutions
10. 4 yr **11.** The lines will be parallel. **12.** $(4, 7)$
13. $(3, -10)$ **14.** no solution **15.** $(-1, -2)$ **16.** infinitely
many solutions **17.** $\left(-\frac{11}{17}, -\frac{188}{17}\right)$ **18.** \$55 **19.** no
solution **20.** $(-1, 13)$ **21.** $(-11, -7)$ **22.** $(5, 12)$
23. $(4.5, 3)$ **24.** infinitely many solutions **25.** small
centerpiece: 25 min, large centerpiece: 40 min

Lesson 6-5 Part 1 pp. 416–419

Got It? 1a. yes **b.** No; it could be on the line
$y = x + 10$.
2.

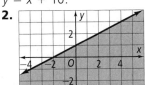

3a.

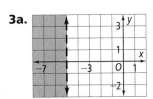

b.

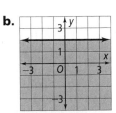

Lesson Check 1. no
2.

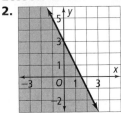

3.

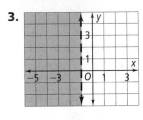

4. Answers will vary. Sample: The solutions of a linear
equation and a linear inequality are coordinates of the
points that make the equation or inequality true. The
graph of a linear equation is a line, but the graph of a
linear inequality is a region of the coordinate plane.
5. Since the inequality is already solved for *y*, the $<$ symbol
means you should shade below the boundary line. All of
these shaded points will make the inequality true.
Exercises 7. solution **9.** solution **11.** solution

13.

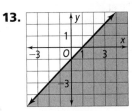

15.

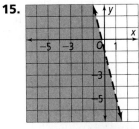

17.

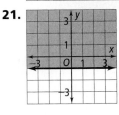

19.

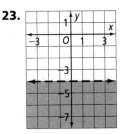

21.

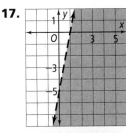

23.

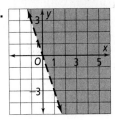

25. You could not use the point $(0, 0)$ in the case that
$(0, 0)$ lies on the boundary line. If that were the case, you
would have to choose any other point that was not on the
boundary line.

Lesson 6-5 Part 2 pp. 420–424

Got It? 4. Answers may vary.
Sample: 0 lb of peanuts and 3 lb
of cashews; 6 lb of peanuts and
0 lb of cashews; 1 lb of peanuts
and 1 lb of cashews

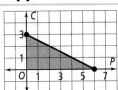

5. $y > \frac{1}{3}x - 2$
Lesson Check 1. $y < \frac{1}{2}x - 1$ **2.** $y \geq 5x + 1$
Exercises
3.

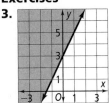

5.

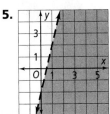

7. $2.5x + 1.75y \leq 200$

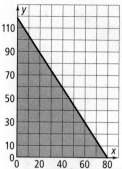

Answers may vary. Sample: 10 ft of cedar and 80 ft of pine; 20 ft of cedar and 50 ft of pine; 60 ft of cedar and 20 ft of pine

9. $y \geq -\frac{1}{3}x + 3$ **11.** $x < 3$

13a. Let x = hours at the cafe and let y = hours at the market; $10x + 8y \geq 800$

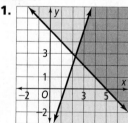

b. No; the point (30, 60) does not lie in the shaded region of the graph.

17. 96 days

18. $2 < x \leq 7$

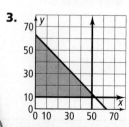

19. one solution: $(-6, -9)$ **20.** one solution: $(2, 0)$

21. no solution

Lesson 6-6   pp. 425–430

Got It?

1.

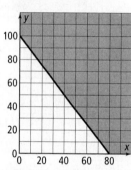

2a. $y < -\frac{1}{2}x + 1$ **b.** No; the red line is dashed,
$y \leq \frac{1}{2}x + 1$ so points on that line are not
          included in the solution.

3.

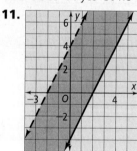

$2x + 2y \leq 126$, $x \leq 50$, $y \geq 10$

Lesson Check

1.

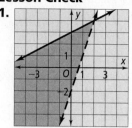

2. $y \geq 3x + 3$
$y < -x - 2$

3.

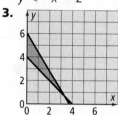

4. You can substitute the ordered pair into each inequality to make sure that it makes each true. **5.** Not necessarily; as long as there is some overlap of the half-planes, then the system will have a solution. **6.** You need to find the intersection of each of the two systems, but the intersections of lines will be a point or line and the intersections of inequalities will be a line or a planar section.

Exercises 7. yes **9.** no

11.

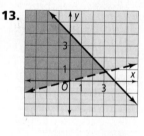

13.

15.

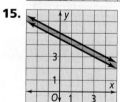

17. $y < 3x - 2$, $y \geq -2x + 2$ **19.** $x < 1$, $y < -\frac{3}{2}x + 3$

21. Let x = hours worked at mowing lawns, let y = hours worked at clothing store.

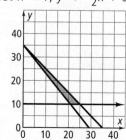

870

23. The student graphed $y \geq \frac{1}{2}x$, but he should have graphed $y \geq -\frac{1}{2}x$ and he shaded below $y = 2$, but he should have shaded above.

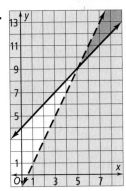

25.

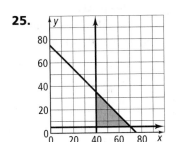

27a.

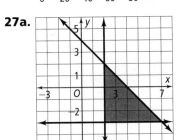

  b. right triangle
  c. (2, 2), (2, −3), (7, −3)
  d. 12.5 units^2

33.

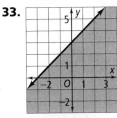

34.

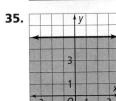

35.

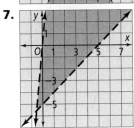

36. 12 **37.** 90 **38.** 113

Chapter Review for Part B pp. 433–434

1. solution of a system of linear inequalities **2.** linear inequality in two variables

3.

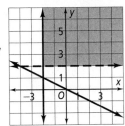

4.

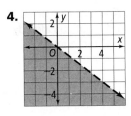

5.

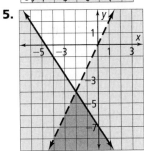

6.

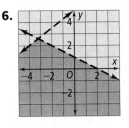

7.

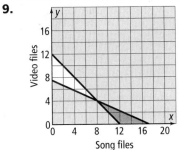

8.

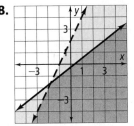

9.

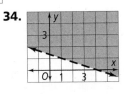

Chapter 7

Get Ready! p. 439

1. 0.7 **2.** 6.4 **3.** 0.008 **4.** 3.5 **5.** 0.$\overline{27}$ **6.** 49 **7.** 5.09
8. 0.75 **9.** 4 **10.** 16 **11.** 4 **12.** 2000 **13.** −147
14. 100 **15.** 49 **16.** 117 **17.** −31 **18.** 33% increase
19. 25% decrease **20.** 17% decrease **21.** 5% increase
22. yes; how quickly the plant grows **23.** The quantity would increase rapidly. **24.** decreasing

Lesson 7-1 pp. 442–448

Got It? 1a. $\frac{1}{64}$ **b.** 1 **c.** $\frac{1}{9}$ **d.** $\frac{1}{6}$ **e.** $\frac{1}{16}$ **2a.** $\frac{1}{x^9}$ **b.** n^3
c. $\frac{4b}{c^3}$ **d.** $2a^3$ **e.** $\frac{1}{m^2n^5}$ **3a.** $\frac{1}{16}$ **b.** $-\frac{1}{50}$ **c.** $\frac{1}{15,625}$ **d.** $-\frac{5}{2}$

e. Answers will vary. It is easier to simplify first, as once you do that you already have the answer as $1 \times 1 = 1$. **4.** 600 represents the number of insects 2 weeks before the population was measured; 5400 represents the population when it was measured; 16,200 represents the number of insects 1 week after the population was measured.

Lesson Check 1. $\frac{1}{32}$ **2.** 1 **3.** $\frac{5s^2}{t}$ **4.** $4x^3$ **5.** -2 **6.** $\frac{1}{8}$
7. division **8.** b^0 is equal to 1, not 0; $\frac{x^n}{a^{-n}b^0} = \frac{a^n x^n}{1} = a^n x^n$

Exercises 9. $\frac{1}{9}$ **11.** $\frac{1}{36}$ **13.** $\frac{1}{16}$ **15.** -1 **17.** 1 **19.** $4a$

21. $\frac{1}{9n}$ **23.** $\frac{3}{x^2y}$ **25.** $\frac{d^7}{c^5}$ **27.** $\frac{6}{ac^3}$ **29.** $\frac{1}{125}$ **31.** 9 **33.** $\frac{1}{25}$

35. 100; there were 100 visitors 4 months before the numbers of visitors was measured **37.** negative

39. negative **41.** 10^{-2} **43.** ab^2 **45.** $\frac{8c^5 d^{-4} e^2}{11}$

47.

n	3	$\frac{1}{6}$	7	$\frac{5}{8}$	2
n^{-1}	$\frac{1}{3}$	6	$\frac{1}{7}$	$\frac{8}{5}$	0.5

49. Answers may vary. Sample: Let $a = \frac{2}{3}$, then $a^{-1} = \frac{3}{2}$, $a^2 = \frac{4}{9}$, and $a^{-2} = \frac{9}{4}$.

56. 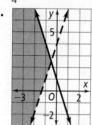 **57.**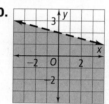

58.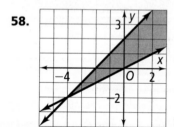

59. $y = -x + 4$ **60.** $y = 5x - 2$ **61.** $y = \frac{2}{5}x - 3$
62. 60,000 **63.** 0.07 **64.** 820,000 **65.** 0.003
66. 340,000

Lesson 7-2   pp. 449–454

Got It? 1a. No; 53 is not less than 10. **b.** yes
c. No; 0.35 is not greater than or equal to 1 and 100 is not in power form. **2a.** 6.78×10^5 **b.** 3.2×10^{-5}
c. 5.14×10^7 **d.** 7×10^{-7} **3a.** 52,300,000
b. 0.000046 **c.** 0.000209 **d.** 3,800,000,000,000 **e.** a
4. electron, proton, neutron

Lesson Check 1. 7×10^{-4} **2.** 3.2×10^7 **3.** 3,500,000
4. 0.000127 **5.** 10^{-3}, 10^{-1}, 10^0, 10^1, 10^5
6. 5×10^{-3}, 7×10^{-1}, 3×10^0, 2×10^4
7. 3.5×10^6, 3.6×10^6, 2.1×10^7, 2.5×10^7
8. Answers may vary. Sample: When numbers are very large or very small. An example of a very large distance may be the distance from Earth to the nearest star.
9. The student interpreted the negative exponent of -5 to represent the number of decimal places when it represents how many places to move the decimal point to the left; $1.88 \times 10^{-5} = 0.0000188$. **10.** No; the difference between two numbers with different powers of 10 is more significant that the difference between two numbers with the same power of 10.

Exercises 11. No; 44 is not less than 10. **13.** No; 0.9 is not greater that 1. **15.** yes **17.** 9.04×10^9
19. 9.3×10^6 **21.** 3.25×10^{-3} **23.** 1.56×10^{-2}
25. 745 **27.** 1.3 **29.** 0.0048 **31.** 2.7×10^5, 7.9×10^5, 8.1×10^5, 8.2×10^5 **33.** 5300×10^{-1}, 5.3×10^5, 0.53×10^7, 530×10^8 **35.** 8×10^{-3} **37.** 6×10^1
39. Proxima Centauri: 2.46876×10^{13} mi; Sirius: 5.11386×10^{13} mi; Vega: 1.58706×10^{14} mi; Polaris: 2.533418×10^{15} mi **45.** $\frac{c}{d^6}$ **46.** b^3

47. $\frac{9}{w^3}$ **48.** $4mn^5$ **49.** $\frac{k^5}{9}$

50. 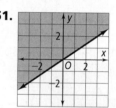 **51.**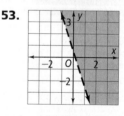

52. 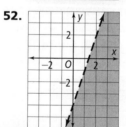 **53.**

54. t^7 **55.** $(6 - m)^3$ **56.** $(r + 2)^4$ **57.** $5^3 s^3$
58. $2^5 x^3$ **59.** $8^2(x - 1)^3$

Lesson 7-3   pp. 455–460

Got It? 1a. 8^9 **b.** $(0.5)^{-11}$ **c.** 9^5 **2a.** x^{13} **b.** $-56cd^2$
c. $\frac{12j^3}{k^2}$ **d.** Since they have like bases, you keep the same base and add the exponents; $x^a \cdot x^b \cdot x^c = x^{(a+b+c)}$
3. 2.8×10^{14} **4.** 6.7×10^{30} molecules of water
Lesson Check 1. 8^{12} **2.** $6n$ **3.** 2.4×10^{10}
4. 39,900 km **5.** No; x and y are not like bases and they do not share a common factor. **6.** Sometimes; if the product ab is greater than 10, then the number will not

be in scientific notation. **7.** No; $4 \times 3 = 12$ so the correct result is $12a^7$.

Exercises 9. $(-6)^{19}$ **11.** 2^9 **13.** m^7 **15.** $\frac{8}{t^8}$
17. $3x^4$ **19.** b^3 **21.** $-45a^4$ **23.** $45x^7y^6$ **25.** 6×10^5
27. 3.4×10^{-5} **29.** 1.5×10^{22} **31.** 2.6×10^{11}
white blood cells **33.** -4 **35.** 11 **37.** 5 **39.** 0
41. 3.42×10^{34} molecules **43.** $4x^4$ **45.** $4c^4$
47. 8×10^5 **49.** 1.2×10^{-4} **51.** 1.5×10^8
53a. Answers may vary. Sample: $y^5 \cdot y$, $y^4 \cdot y^2$, $y^3 \cdot y^3$, $y^2 \cdot y^4$ **b.** Answers may vary. Sample: $y^7 \cdot y^{-1}$, $y^8 \cdot y^{-2}$, $y^9 \cdot y^{-3}$, $y^6 \cdot y^0$ **c.** Infinitely many; there are infinitely many ways to add to get 6. **59.** 2.358×10^6
60. 4.65×10^{-3} **61.** 7×10^{-5} **62.** 5.1×10^9
63. 18, 34, 46 **64.** -1, 7, 13 **65.** -6.8, -22.8, -34.8
66. $\frac{1}{16}$ **67.** $5x$ **68.** $\frac{4n^2}{m}$ **69.** $\frac{-3x^3z^6}{y^2}$

Lesson 7-4   pp. 461–466

Got It? 1a. p^{20} **b.** p^{20} **c.** $\frac{1}{p^{20}}$ **d.** yes; $(a^m)^n = a^{mn} = a^{n(m)}$ **2a.** $\frac{1}{x^{22}}$ **b.** w^{19} **c.** r^{13} **3a.** $343m^{27}$ **b.** $\frac{1}{16z^4}$
c. $\frac{1}{9g^8}$ **4a.** $81x^4y^{20}$ **b.** $\frac{1}{81b^4c^{20}}$ **c.** $216a^3b^3$

Lesson Check 1. n^{18} **2.** $\frac{1}{b^{21}}$ **3.** $81a^4$ **4.** $81x^{20}$
5. $9a^2b^2$ **6.** $\frac{1}{16a^4}$ **7.** Answers may vary. Sample: When you raise a power to a power you multiply the exponents. When you multiply powers with the same base, you add the exponents. **8.** The first student is correct. When you raise a power to a power, you multiply the exponents, not add them. **9.** Answers may vary. Sample: x^{12}, $(x^3)^4$, $(x^6)^2$, $(x^2)^6$

Exercises 11. c^{10} **13.** $\frac{1}{w^7}$ **15.** d^{19} **17.** c^{15} **19.** $\frac{x^{10}}{m^3}$
21. $\frac{1}{49a^2}$ **23.** $\frac{1}{12g^4}$ **25.** $\frac{1}{8y^{12}}$ **27.** $r^{10}s^5$ **29.** $\frac{y^{16}}{z^{15}}$ **31.** -4
33. 0 **35.** 8 **37.** 0 **39.** 8 **41.** 1 **43.** $30x^2$ **45.** 0 **47.** 10^9
49. yes; $(7xyz)^2$ **54.** $\frac{b^4}{c^6}$ **55.** a^8b^3 **56.** $54m^5n^4$ **57.** $-4t^5$
58. $-\frac{3}{4}$ **59.** 6 **60.** $-\frac{3}{2}$ **61.** -9 **62.** $\frac{1}{4}$ **63.** 31 **64.** $\frac{2}{5}$
65. $\frac{y}{3}$ **66.** $\frac{c}{4}$

Lesson 7-5   pp. 468–474

Got It? 1a. y **b.** $\frac{1}{d^6}$ **c.** $\frac{k^5}{j^3}$ **d.** $\frac{b^5}{a^8}$ **e.** y^4z^7 **2.** 1.69×10^2
people/mi^2 **3a.** $\frac{16}{x^6}$ **b.** Answers may vary. Sample: You can simplify within the parentheses first to give you $(a^2)^3 = a^6$ or you can raise the quotient to a power first, $\left(\frac{a^{21}}{a^{15}}\right) = a^6$. **4.** $\frac{b^2}{a^2}$
Lesson Check 1. $\frac{1}{y^7}$ **2.** $\frac{x^{12}}{27}$ **3.** $\frac{n^3}{m^3}$ **4.** $\frac{y^{16}}{x^8}$ **5.** 27 cubes
6. In raising a quotient to a power, the exponent goes to

all the factors of both the numerator and the denominator and in raising a product to a power, the exponent goes to all the factors. **7a.** Answers may vary. Sample: Subtraction is not commutative so subtracting in the wrong order gives the opposite sign, which causes the same result.

Exercises 9. 1 **11.** 0 **13.** $\frac{1}{9}$ **15.** n^3 **17.** y^2 **19.** $\frac{2m^4}{n^4}$
21. $\frac{t^{11}}{27m^2}$ **23.** 4×10^{-5} **25.** 1.5×10^{-6}
27. 1×10^{-12} s **29.** about 3511 times as great **31.** $\frac{1}{a^3}$
33. $\frac{32x^5}{243y^5}$ **35.** $\frac{1}{32}$ **37.** $\frac{5}{2}$ **39.** $\frac{390,625}{x^{10}}$ **41.** 1 **43.** y^{-2}
contains a negative exponent **45.** x^0 needs to be simplified to 1. **47.** about 1.6 hours per day **49.** definition of negative exponent **51.** multiply powers with the same base **53.** $\frac{3}{2n}$ **55.** $\frac{1}{9}$ **57.** $\frac{1}{a^9}$ **59a.** The student simplified the bases of 5 instead of subtracting the exponents.
b. 125 **61.** B **63.** Answers may vary. Samples are given.

I. $\left(\frac{3}{x^2}\right)^{-3} = \left(\frac{x^2}{3}\right)^3$ Rewrite using the reciprocal
     $= \frac{(x^2)^3}{3^3}$ Raise the numerator and denominator to the third power.
     $= \frac{x^6}{27}$ Simplify

II. $\left(\frac{3}{x^2}\right)^{-3} = \frac{3^{-3}}{(x^2)^{-3}}$ Raise the quotient to a power rule
     $= \frac{3^{-3}}{x^{-6}}$ Power to a power rule
     $= \frac{x^6}{3^3}$ Definition of negative exponent
     $= \frac{x^6}{27}$ Simplify

III. $\left(\frac{3}{x^2}\right)^{-3} = \left(\frac{x^2}{3}\right)^3$ Rewrite using the reciprocal
     $= \frac{x^2}{3} \cdot \frac{x^2}{3} \cdot \frac{x^2}{3}$ Definition of an exponent
     $= \frac{x^6}{27}$ Simplify

65. $\left(\frac{m}{n}\right)^7$ **67.** $\left(\frac{3x}{2y}\right)^3$ **69a.** a^{-n} **b.** $\frac{1}{a^n}$ **c.** Since $\frac{a^0}{a^n}$ equals both $\frac{1}{a^n}$ and a^{-n}, $\frac{1}{a^n} = a^{-n}$. This is the definition of a negative exponent. **74.** $\frac{8}{m^{21}}$ **75.** $\frac{2s^6}{27}$ **76.** $\frac{1}{64c^2}$ **77.** $9r^{10}$
78. n^{15}
79. $(0, 0)$;
80. $(-4, -7)$;

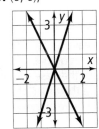
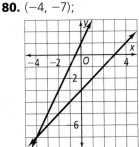

81. $(3, 5)$;

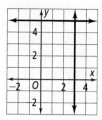

82. no solution;

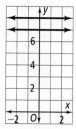

83.

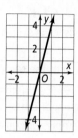

84.

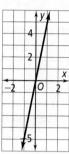

85.

86.

Lesson 7-6   pp. 475–480

Got It? 1a. No; the y-values are not multiplied by a constant amount. **b.** Yes; it is of the form $y = a \cdot b^x$.
2. 14,580 rabbits

3a.

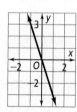

b.

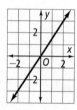

Lesson Check 1. 48 **2.** 5

3.

4.

5. Answers may vary. Linear functions have a constant rate of change, while an exponential function has a constant finite ratio. **6.** No; the value of the base cannot be negative. **7.** The student did not use the order of operations correctly. You must evaluate the exponent before you multiply. $f(-1) = 3 \cdot 4^{-1} = 3 \cdot \frac{1}{4} = \frac{3}{4}$.
Exercises 9. Not exponential; the y-values do not have a constant ratio. **11.** Not exponential; the x-value is not used as an exponent. **13.** 36 **15.** 2.5 **17.** $40,000

19.

21.

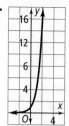

23.

25.

27. {0.16, 0.4, 1, 2.5, 6.25, 15.625}; increase
29. {0.3125, 1.25, 5, 20, 80, 320}; increase
31. {0.04, 0.4, 4, 40, 400, 4000}; increase

33. a.

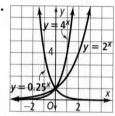

b. $(0, 1)$
c. No, the values of y are always positive
d. When $0 < b < 1$, the graph decreases to the right, but when $b > 1$, the graph rises to the right. The larger the value of b, the faster it rises.
35. $f(x) = 200x^2$ **37.** $f(x) = 100x^2$ **39.** The range of the function consists of just 500. When b equals 1, the function is a horizontal line, $y = 500$, because 1 raised to any positive integer is 1. **43.** a^4 **44.** $\frac{n^{14}}{m^{28}}$ **45.** $\frac{1}{p^{15}}$
46. $y = 5x$ **47.** $y = 3x + 1$ **48.** $y = 0.4x - 3.8$
49. 12% decrease **50.** 20% increase **51.** 31% decrease
52. 36% increase

Lesson 7-7   pp. 483–489

Got It? 1. about 36,274 people **2.** $4489.01
3a. about 55 kilopascals **b.** The decimal equivalent of 100% is 1.
Lesson Check 1. 4 **2.** 15 **3.** 0.2 **4.** 0.94
5. $32,577.89 **6.** If $b > 1$, then it is exponential growth. If $0 < b < 1$, then it is exponential decay. **7.** The value of $n = 1$ so the formula becomes $A = P(1 + r)^t$.
8. The student did not convert 3.5% to a decimal;
$A = 500\left(1 + \frac{0.035}{4}\right)^{(4 \cdot 2)} = 500(1.00875)^8 = 536.09$.
Exercises 9. 14, 2 **11.** 25,600, 1.01 **13.** 12.76 acres **15.** $5352.90 **17.** $634.87 **19.** $13,952.30
21. 10, 0.1 **23.** 0.1, 0.9 **25.** exponential growth

27. neither **29.** about 9 years **31.** exponential growth
33. exponential decay **35.** Answers may vary. Sample: By looking at a table of values or a graph for these two accounts, I would rather have the second account if I was keeping it less than 17 years as it has more money. If I was keeping the account for more than 17 years, I would choose the first account because at that point on, it has more money in it. **37a.** $P = 400(1.05)^n$, where n is the number of years and P is the profit. **b.** $5031.16

43. **44.**

45. **46.** $x < 2$ **47.** $t \geq 12$
48. $k < 0.2$ **49.** $19t$
50. $-8k$ **51.** $11b - 6$
52. $9x^2$

Chapter Review pp. 491–494

1. scientific notation **2.** growth factor **3.** decay factor
4. exponential growth **5.** exponential decay **6.** 1

7. $\frac{1}{49}$ **8.** $\frac{4y^8}{x^2}$ **9.** $\frac{q^4}{p^2}$ **10.** 9 **11.** $\frac{9}{16}$ **12.** 1 **13.** 45 **14.** $\frac{25}{9}$

15. $-\frac{20}{9}$ **16.** No; -3 should be raised to the fourth power instead of multiplying it by 4. **17.** No; 950 is not between 1 and 10. **18.** No; 100 is not written as a power of 10. **19.** yes **20.** No; 0.84 is not between 1 and 10.
21. 2.793×10^6 **22.** 1.89×10^8 **23.** 4.3×10^{-5}
24. 2.7×10^{-9} **25.** 3.86×10^{12} **26.** 4.78×10^{-6}
27. 8 **28.** 2 **29.** 3; 6 **30.** 3 **31.** -5 **32.** 2 **33.** $2d^5$
34. $q^{12}r^4$ **35.** $-20c^4m^2$ **36.** 1.7956 **37.** 7.8×10^3
pores **38.** $\frac{1}{w^3}$ **39.** $7x^4$ **40.** $\frac{n^{35}}{v^{21}}$ **41.** $\frac{e^{20}}{c^{12}}$ **42.** 2×10^{-3}
43. 2.5×10^2 **44.** 5×10^{-5} **45.** 3×10^3
46. Answers may vary. Sample:
  1) Simplify the expression within the parentheses.
  2) Take the reciprocal of the rational expression raised to the third power.
  3) Use the quotient raised to a power rule by applying the exponent to both the numerator and denominator.
  4) Simplify the numerator.
  5) Simplify the denominator using the power rule.
47. 4, 16, 64 **48.** 0.01, 0.0001, 0.000001 **49.** 20, 10, 5
50. 6, 12, 24

51. 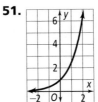 **52.**

53a. 800 bacteria **b.** about 1.4×10^{16} bacteria
54. exponential growth; 3 **55.** exponential decay; 0.32
56. exponential growth; $\frac{3}{2}$ **57.** exponential decay; $\frac{1}{4}$
58. $2697.20 **59.** 463 people

Chapter 8

Get Ready! p. 501

1. 1, 2, 3, 4, 6, 12 **2.** 1, 2, 3, 6, 9, 18 **3.** 1, 2, 4, 5, 10, 20, 25, 50, 100 **4.** 1, 3, 9, 27, 81 **5.** 1, 2, 3, 4, 6, 8, 9, 12, 18, 24, 36, 72 **6.** 1, 2, 3, 4, 5, 6, 10, 12, 15, 20, 25, 30, 50, 60, 75, 100, 150, 300 **7.** 1, 2, 5, 10, 25, 50, 125, 250 **8.** 1, 3, 9, 23, 69, 207 **9.** $x^2 - 9x$ **10.** $3d + 15$
11. $24r^2 - 15r$ **12.** $34m - 29$ **13.** $-36a^2 - 6a$
14. $-s^2 - 7s - 2$ **15.** $25x^2$ **16.** $9v^3$ **17.** $64c^6$
18. $56m^7$ **19.** $81b^6$ **20.** $36p^2q^2$ **21.** $7n^4$ **22.** $-125t^{12}$
23. p^2q^3 **24.** $5x$ **25.** $-\frac{1}{8n^5}$ **26.** $3y^2$ **27.** 3
28. A binomial is an expression with two terms.
29. b; $(x + 4)(x + 4) = (x + 4)^2$, which is a square, and $(x + 4)(x + 4) = x^2 + 8x + 16$, which is a trinomial.

Lesson 8-1 pp. 503–507

Got It? 1a. 2 **b.** 5 **c.** 0 **2a.** $5x^4$ **b.** $-5x^2y^4$
3. $8x^2 + 2x - 3$, quadratic trinomial **4.** $-12x^3 + 120x^2 - 255x + 6022$ **5.** $-4m^3 - 4m^2 - 2m + 21$
Lesson Check 1. 4 **2.** 5 **3.** $11r^3 + 11$ **4.** $x^2 - 3x - 7$
5. quadratic trinomial **6.** linear binomial **7.** The coefficient of the sum of like monomials is the sum of the coefficients. To add polynomials, you group like terms and add their coefficients. A monomial has only one term and a polynomial can have more than one term.
Exercises 9. 10 **11.** 0 **13.** no degree **15.** $9w^2x$
17. $18v^4w^3$ **19.** $-8bc^4$ **21.** $-2q + 7$; linear binomial
23. $-3c^7 + 8c^3 + c$; seventh degree trinomial
25. $13w - 3$ **27.** $7k^2 + 2k - 4$ **29.** $2g^4 - g^3 + 9g + 9$ **31.** $2n - 10$ **33.** $5h^4 + h^3$ **35.** $9x - 1$
37. The student forgot to distribute the negative sign to all the terms in the second set of parentheses.
$(4x^2 - x + 3) - (3x^2 - 5x - 6) =$
$4x^2 - x + 3 - 3x^2 - (-5x) - (-6) =$
$4x^2 - 3x^2 - x + 5x + 3 + 6 =$
$x^2 + 4x + 9$

39. No. Only a nonzero constant has a degree of 0, and a nonzero constant is a monomial. **43.** $-\frac{2}{5}$ **44.** 8 **45.** $-\frac{2}{3}$ **46.** a^5 **47.** $28x^8$ **48.** $-10t^6$

Lesson 8-2   pp. 508–512

Got It? 1. $15n^4 - 5n^3 + 40n$ **2.** $3x$
3a. $3x^2(3x^4 + 5x^2 + 4)$ **b.** $-6x^2(x^2 + 3x + 2)$
4. $9x^2(4 - \pi)$

Lesson Check 1. $12x^4 + 42x^2$ **2.** $2a^2$ **3.** $3m(2m - 5)$
4. $4x(x^2 + 2x + 3)$ **5.** B **6.** C **7.** A **8.** Answers may vary. Sample: $18x^3 + 27x^2$

Exercises 9. $7x^2 + 28x$ **11.** $30m^2 + 3m^3$ **13.** $8x^4 - 28x^3 + 4x^2$ **15.** $30b^3 + 35b^2$ **17.** $2w$ **19.** a **21.** $7z^2$
23. $3(3x - 2)$ **25.** $5(k^3 + 4k^2 - 3)$ **27.** $g^2(g^2 + 12)$
29. $25x^2(9 - \pi)$ **31.** $-10x^3 + 8x^2 - 26x$ **33.** $-60a^3 + 20a^2 - 70a$ **35.** $-t^3 + t^2 + t$ **37.** $20x^2 + 5x$;
$5x(4x + 1)$ **39.** $17xy^3(y + 3x)$ **41.** $a^5(31ab^3 + 63)$
43a. $n(n + 1)$ **b.** Always; integers are closed under multiplication and addition, so $n(n + 1)$ is always an integer. Consider two cases: (1) n is even and (2) n is odd. (1) If n is even, then $n(n + 1) =$ (even)(odd) $=$ even. (2) If n is odd, then $n(n + 1) =$ (odd)(even) $=$ even.
49. $8x^2 + 4x + 5$ **50.** $-5x^3 - 6x$
51. $y \le \frac{4}{5}x - 2$ **52.** $y \ge \frac{7}{2}x - 4$

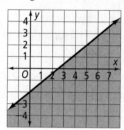 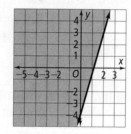

53. $y < -\frac{1}{3}x - 3$

54. $8x - 40$ **55.** $-3w - 12$ **56.** $1.5c + 4$

Lesson 8-3 Part 1   pp. 514–516

Got It? 1. $4x^2 - 21x - 18$ **2.** $3x^2 + 13x + 4$
Lesson Check 1. $x^2 + 9x + 18$ **2.** $2x^2 + x - 15$
3. $(x + 2)(x - 5) = x^2 - 3x - 10$
   $(x - 2)(x + 5) = x^2 + 3x - 10$
The trinomials are similar in that the first and last terms

are identical. They are different because the middle terms are opposites.

Exercises 5. $y^2 + 5y - 24$ **7.** $c^2 - 15c + 50$
9. $6x^2 + 13x - 28$ **11.** $x^2 + x - 20$ **13.** $w^2 + 4w - 12$ **15.** $6p^2 + 23p + 20$ **17.** $-n^3 - 3n^2 - n - 3$
19. $2m^3 + 10m^2 + m + 5$ **21.** $12z^4 + 4z^3 + 3z^2 + z$
23a. i. $x^2 + 2x + 1$, 121 **ii.** $x^2 + 3x + 2$, 132
iii. $x^2 + 4x + 3$, 143 **b.** The digits in the product of the two integers are the coefficients of the terms in the product of the two binomials.

Lesson 8-3 Part 2   pp. 517–521

Got It? 3a. $3x^2 + 2x - 8$ **b.** $4n^2 - 31n + 42$
c. $4p^3 - 10p^2 + 6p - 15$ **4.** $4\pi x^2 + 20\pi x + 24\pi$
5a. $2x^3 - 9x^2 + 10x - 3$ **b.** Answers may vary. Sample: Distribute the trinomial to each term of the binomial. Then continue distributing and combining like terms as needed.

Lesson Check 1. $x^3 + 5x^2 + 2x - 8$ **2.** $x^2 + 2x - 15$
3. $3x^2 + 11x + 8$; check students' work. **4.** The degree of the product is the sum of the degrees of the two polynomials.

Exercises 5. $a^2 + 6a - 16$ **7.** $k^2 + 2k - 48$ **9.** $5m^2 + 13m - 6$ **11.** $18h^2 - 3h - 10$ **13.** $48c^2 - 62c + 7$
15. $4\pi x^2 + 22\pi x + 28\pi$ **17.** $k^3 - 6k^2 + 11k - 6$
19. $6g^3 + 11g^2 - 31g + 14$ **21.** Check students' work.
23. 15 ft by 45 ft **28.** $2(3x - 2)$ **29.** $b(b + 8)$
30. $5t(2t^2 - 5t + 4)$ **31.** $36x^2$ **32.** $4y^2$ **33.** $9m^2$
34. $25n^2$

Lesson 8-4   pp. 522–527

Got It? 1a. $n^2 - 14n + 49$ **b.** $4x^2 + 36x + 81$
2. $(16x + 64)$ ft^2 **3.** 7225 **4a.** $x^2 - 81$ **b.** $36 - m^4$
c. $9c^2 - 16$ **5.** 2496

Lesson Check 1. $c^2 + 6c + 9$ **2.** $g^2 - 8g + 16$
3. $4r^2 - 9$ **4.** $(4x^2 + 12x + 9)$ in.^{2}. **5.** The Square of a Binomial **6.** The Product of a Sum and Difference **7.** The Square of a Binomial **8.** Answers may vary. Sample: You can use the rule for the product of a sum and difference to multiply two numbers when one number can be written as $a + b$ and the other number can be written as $a - b$.

Exercises 9. $w^2 + 10w + 25$ **11.** $4n^2 + 28n + 49$
13. $k^2 - 22k + 121$ **15.** $(10x + 15)$ units^2
17. $(36 - x^2)$ in.^{2} **19.** 6241 **21.** 162,409 **23.** $b^2 - 1$
25. $x^2 - 9$ **27.** $t^2 - 169$ **29.** 6399 **31.** 159,999
33. $4a^2 + 4ab + b^2$ **35.** $g^2 - 14gh + 49h^2$
37. $64r^2 - 80rs + 25s^2$ **39.** $4p^4 - 49q^2$
41. The middle term should be $-2(21a)$ because $(a - b)^2 = a^2 - 2ab + b^2$;

Selected Answers

876

$(3a - 7)^2 = 9a^2 - 42a + 49.$
43. $16x^2 + 160x + 400$ **47.** $6x^2 - 11x - 10$
48. $24m^2 - 34m + 7$ **49.** $5x^2 + 53x + 72$
50. increase of 25% **51.** increase of 25% **52.** decrease
of 12.5% **53.** $6x(2x^3 + 5x^2 + 7)$ **54.** $9(8x^3 + 6x^2 + 3)$
55. $7x(5x^2 + x + 9)$

Chapter Review for Part A pp. 528–529

1. binomial **2.** polynomial **3.** monomial **4.** degree of the
monomial **5.** $-9r^2 + 11r + 3$; quadratic trinomial
6. $b^3 + b^2 + 3$; cubic trinomial **7.** $8t^2 + 3$; quadratic
binomial **8.** $4n^5 + n$; fifth-degree binomial **9.** $6x + 8$;
linear binomial **10.** p^3q^3; sixth-degree monomial
11. $v^3 + 5$ **12.** $14s^4 - 4s^2 + 9s + 7$ **13.** $9h^3 - 3h + 3$ **14.** $7z^3 - 2z^2 - 16$ **15.** $-20k^2 + 15k$
16. $36m^3 + 8m^2 - 24m$ **17.** $6g^3 - 48g^2$
18. $3d^3 + 18d^2$ **19.** $-8n^4 - 10n^3 + 18n^2$
20. $-2q^3 + 8q^2 + 11q$ **21.** $4p(3p^3 + 4p^2 + 2)$
22. $3b(b^3 - 3b + 2)$ **23.** $9c(5c^4 - 7c^2 + 3)$
24. $4g(g + 2)$ **25.** $3(t^4 - 2t^3 - 3t + 4)$
26. $3h^3(10h^2 - 2h - 5)$ **27.** 30; if the GCF of p and q
is 5, then the GCF of $6p$ and $6q$ is $6(5) = 30$.
28. $w^2 + 13w + 12$ **29.** $10s^2 - 7s - 12$
30. $9r^2 - 12r + 4$ **31.** $6g^2 - 41g - 56$
32. $21q^2 + 62q + 16$ **33.** $12n^4 + 20n^3 + 15n + 25$
34. $t^2 + 6t - 27$ **35.** $36c^2 + 60c + 25$ **36.** $49h^2 - 9$
37. $3y^2 - 11y - 42$ **38.** $32a^2 - 44a - 21$
39. $16b^2 - 9$ **40.** $(3x + 5)(x + 7)$; $3x^2 + 26x + 35$

Lesson 8-5 pp. 533–538

Got It? 1. $(r + 8)(r + 3)$ **2a.** $(y - 4)(y - 2)$
b. No. There are no factors of 2 with sum -1.
3a. $(n + 12)(n - 3)$ **b.** $(c - 7)(c + 3)$ **4.** $x + 8$ and
$x - 9$
Lesson Check 1. $(x + 4)(x + 3)$ **2.** $(r - 7)(r - 6)$
3. $(p + 8)(p - 5)$ **4.** $(m + 8)(m + 4)$ **5.** $n - 7$ and
$n + 4$ **6.** positive **7.** positive **8.** negative **9.** when the
constant term is positive and the coefficient of the second
term is negative
Exercises 11. 2 **13.** 2 **15.** $(y + 5)(y + 1)$
17. $(n - 7)(n - 8)$ **19.** 9 **21.** 10 **23.** $(w + 1)(w - 8)$
25. $(z + 4)(z - 2)$ **27.** $(n + 2)(n - 5)$ **29.** $r - 4$
and $r + 1$ **31.** The sum of -4 and -6 is -10, but
their product is not -24. The factors should be
$(x + 2)(x - 12)$. **33.** $x + 6$ and $x + 9$
35. $4x^2 + 12x + 5$; $(2x + 5)(2x + 1)$ **41.** $c^2 + 8c + 16$
42. $4v^2 - 36v + 81$ **43.** $9w^2 - 49$ **44.** $\frac{ad}{b}$
45. $\frac{8d}{7}$ **46.** $mn - c$ **47.** $7x$ **48.** 6 **49.** 3

Lesson 8-6 pp. 539–544

Got It? 1a. $(3x + 2)(x + 1)$ **b.** $(3x + 5)(2x + 1)$
2. $(2x + 7)(5x - 2)$ **3.** $2x + 3$ and $4x + 5$
4. $4(2x + 1)(x - 5)$
Lesson Check 1. $(3x + 1)(x + 5)$ **2.** $(5q + 2)(2q + 1)$
3. $(2w - 1)(2w + 3)$ **4.** $3x + 8$ and $2x - 9$ **5.** There
are no factors of 20 with sum 7. **6.** 24 **7.** Answers may
vary. Sample: If $a = 1$, you look for factors of c whose sum
is b. If $a \neq 1$, you look for factors of ac whose sum is b.
Exercises 9. $(3d + 2)(d + 7)$ **11.** $(4p + 3)(p + 1)$
13. $(5z - 1)(z + 4)$ **15.** $(3t + 5)(2t - 1)$
17. $(4w + 3)(w - 2)$ **19.** $2x + 7$ and $4x + 1$
21. $4(3p - 1)(p + 2)$ **23.** $3(2s + 3)(s + 8)$
25. $2(6x + 1)(x - 4)$ **27.** $2(3d - 2)(2d + 1)$
29–33. Answers may vary. Samples are given.
29. -31, $(3v + 5)(3v - 8)$; 31, $(3v - 5)(3v + 8)$
31. 12, $(3g + 2)(3g + 2)$; 15, $(3g + 1)(3g + 4)$
33. 41, $(8r - 7)(r + 6)$; -5, $(8r - 21)(r + 2)$
35. The student should find the factors of -36 whose
sum is -16. They are 2 and -18.
$3x^2 - 16x - 12 = 3x^2 - 18x + 2x - 12 = $
$3x(x - 6) + 2(x - 6) = (3x + 2)(x - 6)$
37. $6x + 15$ **39.** $3(11k + 4)(2k + 1)$
41. $28(h - 1)(h + 2)$ **43.** $(11n - 6)(5n - 2)$
45. $(9g - 5)(7g - 6)$ **47.** 9 **52.** $(w + 4)(w + 11)$
53. $(t - 7)(t + 4)$ **54.** $(x - 5)(x - 12)$ **55.** 12.5
56. 12 **57.** 37.5 **58.** 21 **59.** $a^2 + 18a + 81$
60. $q^2 - 30q + 225$ **61.** $h^2 - 100$ **62.** $4x^2 - 49$

Lesson 8-7 pp. 545–550

Got It? 1a. $(x + 3)^2$ **b.** $(x - 7)^2$ **2.** $4m - 9$
3a. $(v - 10)(v + 10)$ **b.** $(s - 4)(s + 4)$
4a. $(5d + 8)(5d - 8)$ **b.** No; $25d^2 + 64$ is not a
difference of two squares. **5a.** $12(t + 2)(t - 2)$
b. $3(2x + 1)^2$
Lesson Check 1. $(y - 8)^2$ **2.** $(3q + 2)^2$
3. $(p + 6)(p - 6)$ **4.** $6w + 5$ **5.** perfect-square
trinomial **6.** perfect-square trinomial **7.** difference of two
squares **8.** In a difference of two squares, both terms are
perfect squares separated by a subtraction symbol.
Exercises 9. $(v - 5)^2$ **11.** $(d - 10)^2$ **13.** $(q + 1)^2$
15. $(2r + 9)^2$ **17.** $(6s - 5)^2$ **19.** $10r - 11$ **21.** $5r + 3$
23. $(a + 7)(a - 7)$ **25.** $(t + 5)(t - 5)$
27. $(2p + 7)(2p - 7)$ **29.** $(6v + 5)(6v - 5)$
31. $(4x + 11)(4x - 11)$ **33.** $2(h + 1)(h - 1)$
35. $5(4g + 3)(4g - 3)$ **37.** $8(s - 4)^2$ **39.** Answers may
vary. Sample: Rewrite the absolute value of both terms as
squares. The factorization is the product of two binomials.
The first is the sum of the square roots of the squares. The
second is the difference of the square roots of the squares.
Example 1: $x^2 - 4 = (x + 2)(x - 2)$;
Example 2: $4y^2 - 25 = (2y + 5)(2y - 5)$

41. [1] Subtract by combining like terms.
$$(49x^2 - 56x + 16) - (16x^2 + 24x + 9) =$$
$$(49x^2 - 16x^2) + (-56x - 24x) + (16 - 9) =$$
$$33x^2 - 80x + 7$$

[2] Factor each expression, then use the rule for factoring the difference of two squares.
$$(49x^2 - 56x + 16) - (16x^2 + 24x + 9) =$$
$$(7x - 4)^2 - (4x + 3)^2 =$$
$$[(7x - 4) - (4x + 3)][(7x - 4) + (4x + 3)] =$$
$$(3x - 7)(11x - 1) = 33x^2 - 80x + 7$$

43. 11, 9 **45.** 14, 6 **51.** $(6x + 7)(3x - 2)$
52. $(2x + 3)(4x + 3)$ **53.** $(4x - 7)(3x - 5)$
54. 2 **55.** $3m$ **56.** $4h^2$

Lesson 8-8   pp. 551–555

Got It? 1a. $(8t^2 + 5)(t + 2)$ **b.** Answers may vary.
Sample: In Lesson 8-6, you rewrote the middle term as the sum of two terms and then factored by grouping. In this problem, there were already two middle terms.
2. $3h(h^2 + 2)(2h + 3)$ **3.** Answers may vary. Sample: $2x$, $5x + 2$, and $6x + 1$

Lesson Check 1. $(4r^2 + 3)(5r + 2)$
2. $(3d^2 - 5)(2d + 1)$ **3.** $6(2x^2 + 3)(2x + 5)$
4. Answers may vary. Sample: $4x$, $3x + 1$, and $3x + 2$
5. No; the polynomial is a perfect square. **6.** Yes; the binomial factors are not easily evident. **7.** Yes; the polynomial has four terms **8.** No; when you factor out the GCF from each pair of terms, there is no common factor.

Exercises 9. $2z^2$, 3 **11.** $2r^2$, -5
13. $(5q^2 + 1)(3q + 8)$
15. $(7z^2 + 8)(2z - 5)$ **17.** $(2m + 1)(2m - 1)(2m + 3)$
19. $(4v^2 - 5)(5v + 6)$ **21.** $(4y^2 - 3)(3y + 1)$
23. $w(w^2 + 6)(3w - 2)$ **25.** $3q(q + 2)(q - 2)(2q + 1)$
27–29. Answers may vary. Samples are given.
27. y, $3y + 2$, and $y + 4$ **29.** $2x$, $3x - 2$, $x + 7$
31. $6y(10y^2 - 7)(y - 5)$ **33.** $5(2p - 9q)(p + 4q)$
35a. $(5x^2 + 11)(4x - 1)$ **b.** $(4x - 1)(5x^2 + 11)$
c. Answers may vary. Sample: The associative and commutative properties of addition tell us that the nonfactored polynomials in parts (a) and (b) are equivalent. **37.** Answers may vary. Sample:
$2x$, $2x + 3$, $x + 4$ **39.** Answers may vary. Sample:
$7x$, $3x + 2$, $3x - 2$ **45.** $(m + 6)^2$ **46.** $(8x - 9)^2$
47. $(7p + 2)(7p - 2)$ **48.** not a function **49.** function
50. function

51.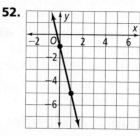

52.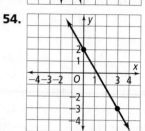

53.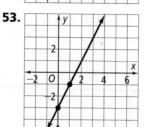

54.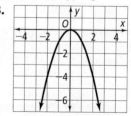

Chapter Review for Part B pp. 557–558

1. perfect-square trinomial **2.** difference of two squares
3. factoring by grouping **4.** $(r + 10)(r - 4)$
5. $(p + 6)(p + 2)$ **6.** $(t + 2)(t - 15)$
7. $(2g - 1)(g - 17)$ **8.** $(s - 10)^2$ **9.** $(4q + 7)^2$
10. $(r + 8)(r - 8)$ **11.** $(3z + 4)(3z - 4)$ **12.** $(5m + 8)^2$
13. $(7n + 2)(7n - 2)$ **14.** $(g + 15)(g - 15)$
15. $(3p - 7)^2$ **16.** $(6h - 1)^2$ **17.** $(w + 12)^2$
18. $8(2v + 1)(2v - 1)$ **19.** $(5x - 6)(5x + 6)$ **20.** No.
There are no factors of 18 that add to 15. **21.** $3n + 9$
22. It is a perfect-square trinomial. **23.** $3y^2$; 1
24. $8m^2$; 3 **25.** $2d(d + 1)(d - 1)(3d + 2)$
26. $(b^2 + 1)(11b - 6)$ **27.** $(5z^2 + 1)(9z + 4)$
28. $3(a^2 + 2)(3a - 4)$

Chapter 9

Get Ready!   p. 565

1. -13 **2.** -3.5 **3.** -9 **4.** -0.5 **5.** -23 **6.** -3
7.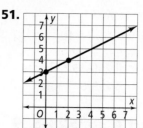

8.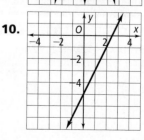

9.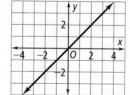

10.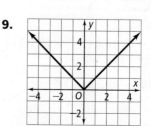

11.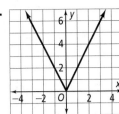

12.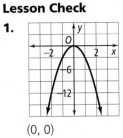

13. −108 **14.** 0 **15.** 49 **16.** 25 **17.** 24 **18.** 144
19. $(2x + 1)^2$ **20.** $(5x - 3)(x + 7)$ **21.** $(4x - 3)(2x - 1)$
22. $(x - 9)^2$ **23.** $(6y - 5)(2y + 3)$ **24.** $(m - 9)(m + 2)$
25. A quadratic function is of the form $f(x) = ax^2 + bx + c$, where $a \neq 0$. **26.** Answers will vary. Sample: You can fold the graph along the axis of symmetry and the two halves of the graph will match. **27.** A

Lesson 9-1 pp. 566–572

Got It? 1. $(-2, -3)$; minimum

2.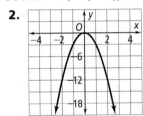

domain: all real numbers, range: $y \leq 0$

3. $f(x) = -\frac{1}{3}x^2$, $f(x) = -x^2$, $f(x) = 3x^2$

4.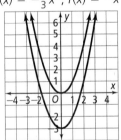

Answers will vary. Sample: They have the same shape but the second parabola is shifted down 3 units.

5a.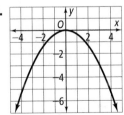

about 2 s

b. domain: $0 \leq t \leq 2.1$; range: $0 \leq h \leq 70$

Lesson Check

1.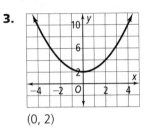

$(0, 0)$

2.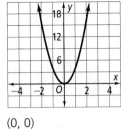

$(0, 0)$

3.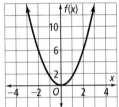

$(0, 2)$

4.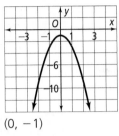

$(0, -1)$

5. If $a > 0$, the vertex is a minimum. If $a < 0$, the vertex is a maximum. **6.** Answers will vary. Sample: They have the same shape, but the second graph is shifted up 1 unit.
Exercises 7. $(2, 3)$; maximum **9.** $(2, 1)$; minimum

11.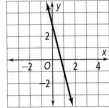

domain: all real numbers; range: $f(x) \geq 0$

13.

domain: all real numbers; range: $f(x) \geq 0$

15.

domain: all real numbers; range: $y \leq 0$
17. $f(x) = x^2$, $f(x) = -3x^2$, $f(x) = 5x^2$

19.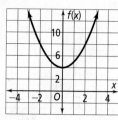

21.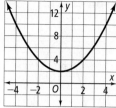

3.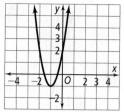

23.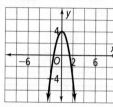

25.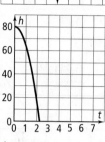

about 2.2 s

4.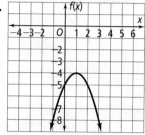

27. domain: all real numbers; range: $f(x) \geq 6$

29. domain: all real numbers; range: $y \leq -9$

31. Answers will vary. Sample: If $a > 0$, the parabola opens upward. If $a < 0$, the parabola opens downward. The vertex of the parabola is $(0, c)$. **33.** D **35.** F **37.** C

5. Answers will vary. Sample: If $a > 0$, the graph opens upward and the vertex is a minimum. If $a < 0$, the graph opens downward, and the vertex is a maximum. The greater the value of $|a|$, the narrower the parabola is. The axis of symmetry is the line $x = -\frac{b}{2a}$. The x-coordinate of the vertex is $-\frac{b}{2a}$. The y-intercept of the parabola is c.

6. First graph the vertex and then graph the y-intercept. Reflect the y-intercept over the axis of symmetry to get a third point. Then sketch the parabola through these three points.

Exercises 7. $x = 0$; $(0, 3)$ **9.** $x = -1$; $(-1, -3)$
11. $x = 1.5$; $(1.5, -4.75)$ **13.** $x = 0.3$; $(0.3, 2.45)$
15. $x = -0.5$; $(-0.5, -6.5)$ **17.** B **19.** A

39a. 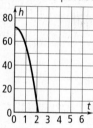 **b.** 16 ft **c.** No, from $t = 1$ to $t = 2$ the ball falls $(72 - 16)$ ft $- (72 - 64)$ ft $= 48$ ft.

21.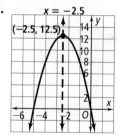

45. $3r(5r + 1)(2r + 3)$ **46.** $(3q^2 - 2)(5q - 6)$
47. $(7b^3 + 1)(b + 2)$ **48.** 0.75 **49.** -0.4 **50.** $-\frac{3}{8}$
51. $\frac{7}{20}$ **52.** $\frac{1}{8}$ **53.** -2

23.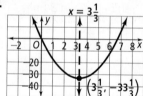

Lesson 9-2   pp. 573–578

Got It?

1.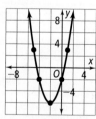

2. 2 s; 69 ft; $5 \leq h \leq 69$

25. 25 ft; 625 ft²; $0 < A \leq 625$

Lesson Check

1.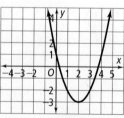

2.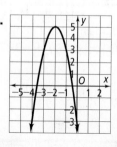

27.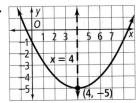

29.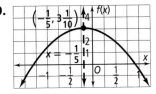

31. b is an even integer. **33.** $50

38. 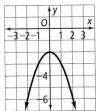 **39.**

40.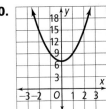

41. 5 **42.** -8 **43.** ±12 **44.** 1.1

Lesson 9-3   pp. 580–585

Got It? 1a. ±4 **b.** no solution **c.** 0 **2a.** ±6
b. no solution **c.** 0 **3.** 7.9 ft
Lesson Check 1. ±5 **2.** ±2 **3.** ±12 **4.** ±15 **5.** The
zeros of a function are the x-intercepts of the function.
Example: $y = x^2 - 25$ has zeros ±5. **6.** a and c have
opposite signs; $c = 0$; a and c have the same sign.
Exercises 7. ±3 **9.** ±2 **11.** ±3 **13.** 0 **15.** no
solution **17.** ±9 **19.** ±14 **21.** no solution **23.** ±2
25. no solution **27.** Let $x =$ length of side of a square,
then $x^2 = 169$; 13 m **29.** Let $r =$ radius, then $\pi r^2 = 90$;
5.4 cm **31.** 5.6 ft **33.** 0 **35.** 1 **37.** $n > 0$; $n = 0$; $n < 0$
39. $\pm\frac{3}{7}$ **41.** ±2.8 **43.** 144 **45.** Answers will vary.
Sample: When you *subtract* 100 from each side, you get
$x^2 = -100$, which has no solution. **47.** 6.3 ft

54.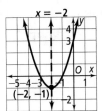

55.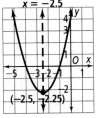

56.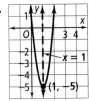

57.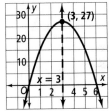

58.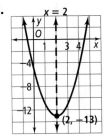

59.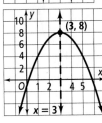

60. $(2c + 1)(c + 14)$ **61.** $(3w + 2)(w + 10)$
62. $(4g + 3)(g - 6)$ **63.** $(2r + 3)(r - 8)$
64. $(3w - 2)(w + 6)$ **65.** $(5p - 4)(p - 6)$

Lesson 9-4   pp. 586–590

Got It? 1a. $-1, 5$ **b.** $-\frac{3}{2}, 4$ **c.** $-\frac{1}{2}, -14$ **d.** $\frac{2}{7}, \frac{4}{5}$
2a. $-2, 7$ **b.** $-5, 4$ **c.** $\frac{3}{2}, 6$ **3a.** -7 **b.** The quadratic
polynomials are perfect squares. **4.** 17 in. by 23 in.
Lesson Check 1. 4, 7 **2.** $-9, 6$ **3.** $\frac{8}{3}, 3$ **4.** 2.5 ft by 4 ft
6. To solve the equation, you first factor the quadratic
expression, then set each factor equal to 0, and solve. **7.**
No, if $ab = 8$, then there are infinitely many possible
values of a and b, such as $a = 2$ and $b = 4$ or $a = -1$
and $b = -8$.
Exercises 9. $-\frac{5}{4}, -7$ **11.** 0, 2.5 **13.** $-10, -1$ **15.** 5, 9
17. $-\frac{7}{3}, 2$ **19.** $-7, -6$ **21.** $-5, -\frac{2}{3}$ **23.** 5 **25.** 10 ft by
25 ft **27.** $\{-6, -2\}$ **29.** 2 ft **31.** 2; $\pm k$ **33.** 0, 4, 6
35. 0, 3 **41.** ±12 **42.** no solution **43.** 0 **44.** ±4
45. ±7 **46.** ±3 **47.** $(y - 5)^2$ **48.** $(g - 7)^2$ **49.** $(m + 9)^2$

Chapter Review for Part A   pp. 591–592

1. parabola **2.** axis of symmetry **3.** vertex

4.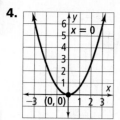

5.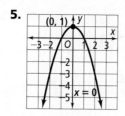

6.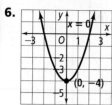

7.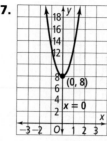

8.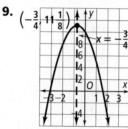

9.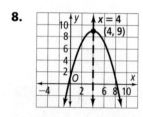

10.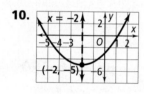

11.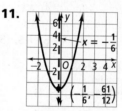

12. Answers will vary. Sample: $y = -x^2$ **13.** Answers will vary. Sample: $y = x^2$ **14.** Answers will vary. Sample: $y = x^2$ **15.** Answers will vary. Sample: $y = 0.5x^2$

16. ± 2 **17.** ± 5 **18.** 0 **19.** no solution **20.** $\pm \frac{2}{3}$ **21.** ± 4

22. 2.3 in. **23.** $-4, -3$ **24.** 0, 2 **25.** 4, 5 **26.** $-3, \frac{1}{2}$

27. $-\frac{2}{3}, \frac{3}{2}$ **28.** 1, 4 **29.** The width is 3 ft and the length is 13 ft.

Lesson 9-5   pp. 595–600

Got It? 1. 100 **2.** $-13, 19$ **3a.** $-6.79, -2.21$ **b.** No, there are no factors of 15 with a sum of 9. **4.** 5.77 ft
Lesson Check 1. $-18, 10$ **2.** $-11, 15$ **3.** $-21, 14$
4. $-9, 7.5$ **5.** Answers will vary. Samples are given.
a. factoring; $k^2 - 3k - 304 = (k - 19)(k + 16)$
b. completing the square **6.** Answers will vary. Sample: You have to know how to solve using square roots in order to solve by completing the square. There are more steps involved in completing the square.
Exercises 7. 81 **9.** 225 **11.** $\frac{289}{4}$ **13.** $-16, 9$
15. $-10.24, -5.76$ **17.** $-17, 19$ **19.** $-10.12, -1.88$

21. $-6.14, 1.14$ **23.** $-1.65, 3.65$ **25.** $-1.96, 2.56$
27. $-7, 1$ **29.** about 3.1 ft **31.** $-1.65, 3.65$ **33.** She forgot to divide each side by 4 to make the coefficient of the x^2-term 1. **43.** $-6, -5$ **44.** $\pm \frac{8}{3}$ **45.** $-\frac{1}{6}, \frac{5}{2}$ **46.** m^{12}
47. $-\frac{1}{b}$ **48.** t^{13} **49.** y^{29} **50.** 81 **51.** 0 **52.** -15

Lesson 9-6   pp. 601–607

Got It? 1. $-3, 7$ **2.** 144.8 ft **3a.** Factoring; the equation is easily factorable. **b.** Square roots; there is no x-term. **c.** Quadratic formula, graphing; the equation cannot be factored. **4a.** 2 **b.** 2; if $a > 0$ and $c < 0$, then $-4ac > 0$ and $b^2 - 4ac > 0$.
Lesson Check 1. $-4, \frac{1}{3}$ **2.** $-0.94, 1.22$ **3.** 2
4. If the discriminant is positive, there are 2 x-intercepts. If the discriminant is 0, there is 1 x-intercept. If the discriminant is negative, there are no x-intercepts.
5. Factoring because the equation is easily factorable; quadratic formula or graphing because the equation cannot be factored. **6.** If you complete the square for $ax^2 + bx + c = 0$, you will get the quadratic formula.
Exercises 7. $-1.5, -1$ **9.** $-3, 1.25$ **11.** $-11, 4\frac{2}{3}$
13. $-2.6, 12$ **15.** $-2.56, 0.16$ **17.** $-3.18, 1.68$
19. Quadratic formula, completing the square, or graphing; the coefficient of the x^2-term is 1, but the equation cannot be factored. **21.** Quadratic formula, graphing; the equation cannot be factored. **23.** 0
25. 0 **27.** 2 **29.** about 2.43 in. **31.** The next to the last line should be $25 + 48$. The discriminant is 73.
38. 1.54, 8.46 **39.** $-2, -1$ **40.** $-6.06, 0.06$

41.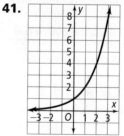

42.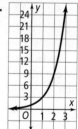

43.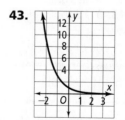

44.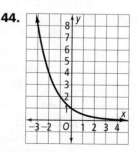

Lesson 9-7   pp. 608–613

Got It?

1. a.

exponential

b.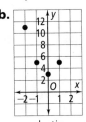

quadratic

2. exponential

3. a. exponential; $y = 6(0.2)^x$

   b. You have already used them to write the equation.

Lesson Check 1. quadratic **2.** linear **3.** exponential
4. No, a function cannot be both linear and exponential.
5. Graph the points, or test ordered data for a common
difference (linear function), a common ratio (exponential
function), or a common second difference (quadratic
function).

Exercises

7.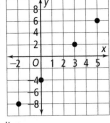

linear

9.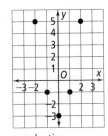

quadratic

11. quadratic **13.** exponential **15.** exponential;
$y = 5(0.4)^x$ **17.** linear; $y = 59x + 189$ **19.** Answers will
vary. Sample: $y = 53x^2 - 16x + 15$

21. a.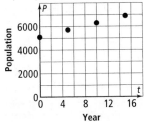

linear

   b. The population changes by 600 every 5 years; the
y-values have a common difference, so a linear
model works best.

   c. $p = 120t + 5100$ **d.** 8700

---

23. a. Check students' work.
   b. The second common difference is twice the
coefficient of the x^2-term.
   c. When second differences are the same, the data
are quadratic. The coefficient of the x^2-term is
one-half the second difference.
28. −1.5, 0.5 **29.** −3.83, 1.83 **30.** 0.13, 2.54
31. 14 **32.** $\frac{5}{7}$ **33.** 1.2 **34.** 9 **35.** 0.6 **36.** 20

Chapter Review for Part B pp. 616–618

1. discriminant **2.** quadratic formula **3.** completing the
square **4.** −6.74, 0.74 **5.** 0.38, 2.62 **6.** −2, −1.5
7. −9.12, −0.88 **8.** −1.65, 3.65 **9.** 1.26, 12.74
10. 7.6 ft by 15.8 ft **11.** 6.4 in. by 13.8 in. **12.** two
13. two **14.** −1.84, 1.09 **15.** −2.5, 4 **16.** 0.13, 7.87
17. −0.25, 0.06 **18.** ±5; square roots because there is
no x-term **19.** 3; factoring because it is easy to factor
20. 1.5 s

21.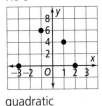

quadratic

22.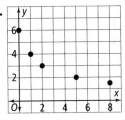

exponential

23. $y = 3x - 2$ **24.** $y = 5(2)^x$

Chapter 10

Get Ready!   p. 623

1. 10 **2.** 18 **3.** 4.5 **4.** 8 **5.** 10 **6.** 4 **7.** 12 **8.** 14
9. $-2h^2 + 5h + 12$ **10.** $9b^4 - 49$
11. $-15x^2 - 11x - 2$

12.

13.

14.   **15.** 2 **16.** 2 **17.** 0 **18.** 1 **19.**
2 **20.** 2 **21.** They both contain
the same radical expression, $\sqrt{3}$.
22. I would be rich.

Lesson 10-1   pp. 626–630

Got It? 1. 15 cm **2.** 9 **3.** no; $20^2 + 47^2 \neq 52^2$
Lesson Check 1. 39 **2.** 7 **3.** yes; $12^2 + 35^2 = 37^2$

4. If you are a student, then you study math.
5. The value of 13 should have been substituted for c since it is the hypotenuse. The correct equation is $12^2 + x^2 = 13^2$; $x = 5$.
Exercises 7. 8 **9.** 12 **11.** 15 **13.** 1.2 mi **15.** yes
17. no **19.** yes **21.** yes **23.** no **25.** 719 ft **27.** Yes; $50^2 + 120^2 = 130^2$, so the triangle formed by the forces is a right triangle.

34. 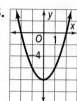 **35.**

36.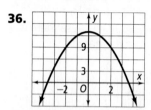

37. $45a^2 - 27a$ **38.** $12x^3 - 24x^2$ **39.** $16d^3 + 28d^4$
40. $-12m^2 - 6m^4$

Lesson 10-2, Part 1 pp. 632–635

Got It? 1. $6\sqrt{2}$ **2.** $-4m^5\sqrt{5m}$ **3a.** $18\sqrt{3}$ **b.** $3a^2\sqrt{2}$
c. $210x^3$ **d.** yes; $\sqrt{14t^2} = t\sqrt{14}$ **4.** $w\sqrt{17}$
Lesson Check 1. $7\sqrt{2}$ **2.** $4b^2\sqrt{b}$ **3.** No; 25 is a perfect-square factor of 175. **4.** A radical expression is in simplified form if the radicand has no perfect-square factors other than 1, the radicand contains no fractions, and no radicals appear in the denominator of a fraction.
Exercises 5. $3\sqrt{11}$ **7.** $8\sqrt{2}$ **9.** $-12\sqrt{13}$ **11.** $5t^2\sqrt{2t}$
13. $-63x^4\sqrt{3x}$ **15.** 16 **17.** 240 **19.** $315\sqrt{2}$ **21.** $16y^3$
23. $-126a\sqrt{a}$ **25.** $w\sqrt{37}$ **27a.** $\sqrt{18 \cdot 10} = \sqrt{180} = \sqrt{36} \cdot \sqrt{5} = 6\sqrt{5}$ **b.** Answers may vary. Sample: 4 and 45 **29.** $2\sqrt{13}$ **31.** $ab^2c\sqrt{abc}$

Lesson 10-2, Part 2 pp. 636–639

Got It? 5a. 4 **b.** $\frac{3}{a}$ **c.** $\frac{5y\sqrt{y}}{z}$ **6a.** $\frac{\sqrt{6}}{3}$ **b.** $\frac{\sqrt{10m}}{6m}$ **c.** $\frac{\sqrt{21s}}{3}$
Lesson Check 1. $12m^2$ **2.** $\frac{\sqrt{15}}{x}$ **3.** $\frac{\sqrt{15}}{3}$ **4.** $\frac{\sqrt{3n}}{n}$
5a. Yes; there are no perfect-square factors in 31, there are no fractions in the radicand, and there are no radicals in the denominator. **b.** No; there is a fraction in the radicand. **6.** Answers may vary. Sample:
$$\frac{3}{\sqrt{12}} = \frac{3}{2\sqrt{3}} \cdot \frac{\sqrt{3}}{\sqrt{3}} = \frac{3\sqrt{3}}{6} = \frac{\sqrt{3}}{2};$$
$$\frac{3}{\sqrt{12}} = \frac{3}{\sqrt{12}} \cdot \frac{\sqrt{12}}{\sqrt{12}} = \frac{3\sqrt{12}}{12} = \frac{\sqrt{12}}{4} = \frac{2\sqrt{3}}{4} = \frac{\sqrt{3}}{2}$$
Exercises 7. $\frac{7\sqrt{3}}{4}$ **9.** $-\frac{40}{27}$ **11.** $\frac{77a}{2}$ **13.** $\frac{\sqrt{10x}}{4x}$
15. $2\sqrt{11}$ **17a.** 15 mi; 18 mi; 21 mi **b.** The distance

increases rapidly at first as h increases, but then the distance does not increase as fast. A good way to see this is to look at the graph of $d = \sqrt{\frac{3h}{2}}$. **19.** not simplest form; radical in the denominator of a fraction **21.** $60\sqrt{2}$ ft, or about 85 ft **23.** $2\sqrt{15}$ **25.** $2\sqrt{6}$; Find the square root of the area; Multiplication Property of Square Roots **30.** yes **31.** yes **32.** no
33. $(8y + 3)(8y - 3)$ **34.** $(a + 9)(a - 9)$
35. $(5 + 4b)(5 - 4b)$ **36.** $6a^2 - 5a - 4$
37. $-4m^2 + 14mn - 12n^2$ **38.** $4x^2 + 16x + 15$

Lesson 10-3 pp. 640–645

Got It? 1. $7\sqrt{5}$ **2a.** $8\sqrt{7}$ **b.** $8\sqrt{2}$ **c.** No; if they are unlike and have no common factors other than 1, even if they can be simplified, they still will not be like.
3a. $2\sqrt{3} + 5\sqrt{2}$ **b.** $15 - 4\sqrt{11}$ **c.** $-6\sqrt{2} - 6$
4. $\frac{-3\sqrt{10} + 3\sqrt{5}}{5}$ **5.** $(6\sqrt{5} - 6)$ in., or about 7.4 in.
Lesson Check 1. $5\sqrt{3}$ **2.** $\sqrt{6}$ **3.** $\sqrt{21} - 2\sqrt{7}$
4. $41 - 12\sqrt{5}$ **5.** $3\sqrt{5} - \sqrt{10}$ **6.** $2\sqrt{7} - 4$
7a. $\sqrt{13} + 2$ **b.** $\sqrt{6} - \sqrt{3}$ **c.** $\sqrt{5} + \sqrt{10}$
8. $\sqrt{3} \cdot \sqrt{3} \neq 9$; $\frac{\sqrt{3} + 1}{3 - 1} = \frac{\sqrt{3} + 1}{2}$
Exercises 9. $7\sqrt{5}$ **11.** $8\sqrt{3}$ **13.** 0 **15.** $-7\sqrt{5}$
17. $-\sqrt{3}$ **19.** $2\sqrt{3} + 3\sqrt{2}$ **21.** $3\sqrt{7} - 21$ **23.** -6
25. $62 - 20\sqrt{6}$ **27.** $\frac{3\sqrt{7} + 3\sqrt{3}}{4}$ **29.** $-2\sqrt{5} - 5$
31. $\frac{7\sqrt{13} - 7\sqrt{5}}{8}$ **33.** $\frac{23\sqrt{5} - 23}{2}$ ft, or about 14.2 ft
35. $-\frac{4}{3}$; -1.3 **37.** $\frac{-1 + \sqrt{7}}{4}$; 0.4
39. $\sqrt{24} = 2\sqrt{6} \neq 4\sqrt{6}$; $3\sqrt{6}$ **41.** $6\sqrt{2} + 6\sqrt{3}$
43. $8 + 2\sqrt{15}$ **45.** $-\sqrt{2}$ **47.** $s\sqrt{3}$ **49a.** $x^{\frac{n}{2}}$
b. $x^{\frac{n-1}{2}}\sqrt{x}$ **54.** $6\sqrt{3}$ **55.** $15\sqrt{6}$ **56.** $\frac{2\sqrt{2}}{3c}$ **57.** 15
58. 8^{16} **59.** 2^{11} **60.** 5^{27} **61.** 3^3 **62.** -1 **63.** $-4, 3$
64. $-5, 3$ **65.** $-3, \frac{2}{3}$ **66.** $-2, \frac{1}{2}$ **67.** -7

Lesson 10-4 pp. 646–652

Got It? 1. 9 **2a.** 0.825 ft **b.** longer; The pendulum swings more than 7 ft in 3s so it will swing more than 7 ft in 5s. **3.** 7 **4.** -2 **5.a.** no solution **b.** The principal root of a number is never negative.
Lesson Check 1. 12 **2.** 3 **3.** 1 **4.** no solution **5.** C
6. If $x^2 = y^2$, then $x = y$; no, if $x = -1$ and $y = 1$, then $x^2 = y^2$, but $x \neq y$.
Exercises 7. 4 **9.** 36 **11.** 8 **13.** 16 **15.** -2 **17.** about 5.2 ft **19.** 4.5 **21.** 7 **23.** 4 **25.** -4 **27.** $-\frac{1}{2}$ **29.** 3
31. no solution **33.** no solution **35.** The student did not check the solutions in the original equations. Both of those solutions are extraneous, so the equation has no solution. **37a.** 25 **b.** 11.25 **39.** Add $\sqrt{y + 2}$ to each side of the equation. Square each side of the equation. Solve for y. Check each apparent solution in the original equation. **41.** 3 **43.** no solution **45a.** $V = 10x^2$

b. $x = \frac{\sqrt{10V}}{10}$ **c.** 2, 3, 4, 5, 6, 7 in. **50.** $5\sqrt{2}$ **51.** -24
52. $-\frac{2\sqrt{3} - 4\sqrt{2}}{5}$ **53.** no solution **54.** $-2, 2$ **55.** $-\frac{3}{2}$,
$-\frac{2}{3}$ **56.** $(x - 3)(x + 4)$ **57.** $(x + 2)(x + 4)$
58. $(x + 3)(x - 5)$ **59.** $(x + 3)(x + 6)$

Chapter Review   pp. 654–656

1. unlike radicals **2.** rationalize the denominator
3. conjugates **4.** 6.5 **5.** 12.5 **6.** 6.1 **7.** 84 **8.** 17.5
9. 0.7 **10.** 6.6 **11.** 2.4 **12.** yes **13.** yes **14.** no
15. yes **16.** no **17.** yes **18.** no **19.** no **20.** yes
21. $-42\sqrt{6}$ **22.** $\sqrt{3}$ **23.** $\frac{5}{2}a$ **24.** $\frac{2}{3s}$ **25.** $-\frac{28}{3}x^2\sqrt{x}$
26. $30t^4\sqrt{3}$ **27.** Answers may vary. Sample: $\sqrt{32s}$, $\frac{8s}{\sqrt{2s}}$,
$8\sqrt{\frac{s}{2}}$; they all have the s and the factor 2 under the
radical. **28.** $s\sqrt{10}$ **29.** $2\sqrt{6}$ **30.** $4 + 2\sqrt{3}$
31. $4 - 2\sqrt{10}$ **32.** $\frac{-3\sqrt{2}-9}{7}$ **33.** $-2 + \sqrt{3}$
34. $\frac{-3 + 3\sqrt{5}}{2}$ in. **35.** 169 **36.** 9 **37.** 18 **38.** 21
39. 2 **40.** 1 **41.** 1.5 **42.** $\frac{1}{2}$ **43.** 56.6 cm^3

Chapter 11

Get Ready!   p. 661

1. $2\frac{1}{30}$ **2.** $3\frac{1}{4}$ **3.** $-\frac{73}{120}$ **4.** $\frac{11}{35}$ **5.** $\frac{q^6}{p^5}$ **6.** $6\frac{30}{49}$ or $\frac{324}{49}$ **7.** $\frac{64}{729}$
8. $\frac{8yz^6}{5x^6}$ **9.** $-7, 9$ **10.** $-\frac{5}{3}, \frac{7}{4}$ **11.** -13 **12.** $0, 3$ **13.** $-\frac{4}{3}, 5$
14. $-5, -\frac{2}{3}$ **15.** $-10, -1$ **16.** $-3, 7$ **17.** $-\frac{1}{2}, \frac{5}{3}$ **18.** no
solution **19.** 1 **20.** 4 **21.** The excluded values are not
allowed. **22.** A rational expression involves a ratio.

Lesson 11-1   pp. 664–670

Got It? 1. a. $\frac{3}{a}$, $a \neq 0$ **b.** $\frac{9d^2}{2d + 4}$, $d \neq -2$ **c.** $\frac{1}{3}$, $n \neq \frac{3}{2}$
d. 13c, none **2. a.** $\frac{2}{x + 2}$, $x \neq -2$, $x \neq 4$ **b.** $\frac{a - 2}{3}$,
$a \neq 1$ **c.** $\frac{6}{2z + 3}$, $z \neq -2$, $z \neq -\frac{3}{2}$ **d.** $\frac{c - 3}{c + 3}$, $c \neq -3$,
$c \neq -2$ **3. a.** -1, $x \neq 2.5$ **b.** $-y - 4$, $y \neq 4$
c. $-\frac{3}{2d + 1}$, $d \neq -\frac{1}{2}$, $d \neq \frac{1}{3}$ **d.** $-\frac{3}{2z + 2}$, $z \neq \pm 1$
4. a. $12x + 4$ **b.** No, h must be greater than 2π in order
for the value of a to be greater than 0. If h is less than or
equal to 2π, then a will be negative, and length cannot
be negative.
Lesson Check 1. 3; $x \neq -3$ **2.** $-\frac{1}{x + 3}$; $x \neq -3$, $x \neq 5$
3. 4x **4. a.** No, the expression is not the ratio of two
polynomials. **b.** Yes, the expression is the ratio of two
polynomials. **5.** If the denominator contains a polynomial,
there may be values of the variable that make the
denominator equal to zero, and division by zero is
undefined. **6.** The only way the rational expression is not
in simplest form is if the numerator and the denominator
are equal. **7. a.** yes, $3 - x = -(x - 3)$ **b.** no, $2 - y =$
$-(y - 2)$

Exercises 9. $\frac{1}{7x}$, $x \neq 0$ **11.** $\frac{1}{2}$, $p \neq 12$ **13.** $\frac{x + 2}{x^2}$, $x \neq 0$
15. $\frac{2}{b + 4}$, $b \neq \pm 4$ **17.** $\frac{w}{w - 7}$, $w \neq \pm 7$ **19.** $\frac{m + 3}{m + 2}$,
$m \neq -4$, $m \neq -2$ **21.** $b + 3$, $b \neq -5$ **23.** -1, $n \neq \frac{5}{4}$
25. $-\frac{1}{2}$, $m \neq 2$ **27.** $w + 1$ **29.** $\frac{2r - 1}{r + 5}$, $r \neq -5$
31. $\frac{4a^2}{2a - 1}$, $a \neq 0$, $a \neq \frac{1}{2}$ **33.** $-\frac{2a + 1}{a + 3}$, $a \neq -3$, $a \neq \frac{5}{2}$
35. $\frac{x}{2x + 16}$ **37. a. i.** $\frac{2b + 4h}{bh}$ **ii.** $\frac{2r + 2h}{rh}$ **b. i.** $\frac{4}{9}$
ii. $\frac{4}{9}$ **39.** $(1 + r)^2$ **41.** $\frac{1}{4}$ **47.** $10\sqrt{2}$ **48.** $a^2b^3c^4\sqrt{b}$
49. $3x\sqrt{11}$ **50.** $\frac{\sqrt{2}}{5m^2}$ **51.** $2\sqrt{2}$ **52.** $2y\sqrt{y}$
53. $(2c + 1)(c + 7)$ **54.** $(15t - 11)(t - 1)$
55. $(3q + 2)^2$ **56.** $(2c - 1)(2c - 5)$
57. $(6t + 1)(4t - 3)$ **58.** $(3q - 7)(q + 2)$

Lesson 11-2   pp. 671–677

Got It? 1. a. $\frac{15}{y^4}$, $y \neq 0$ **b.** $\frac{x(x + 1)}{(x - 2)(x - 3)}$, $x \neq 3$, $x \neq 2$
2. a. $3x(x + 1)$ **b.** Yes, but you will have to simplify the
resulting expression. **3. a.** $(x - 7)(3x - 2)$ **b.** $(x + 1)$
$(x + 3)$ **4. a.** $\frac{1}{y}$ **b.** $\frac{6}{k + 4}$ **5.** $\frac{z - 1}{z^2 + 2}$ **6.** $\frac{1}{q^2}$
Lesson Check 1. $\frac{6}{5t^6}$ **2.** $\frac{(2x + 5)(x - 5)}{4}$ **3.** $3k^2(k + 1)$
4. $\frac{4x}{(x + 7)(2x + 3)}$ **5.** $\frac{(a - 2)^2}{3a}$ **6.** x^2 **7.** no; $\frac{b}{c} = \frac{a}{b} \div c =$
$\frac{a}{b} \cdot \frac{1}{c} = \frac{a}{bc}$, where $\frac{a}{b} = a \div \frac{b}{c} = a \cdot \frac{c}{b} = \frac{ac}{b}$ **8.** The
procedures are the same, but when you multiply rational
expressions, there may be values of the variables for which
the rational expressions are not defined. **9.** The variables
b, c, and d appear in the denominators, and division by 0
is not defined. **10. a.** Write the product of the rational
expression and the polynomial, factor, divide out common
factors, and write the product in factored form.
b. Rewrite the quotient of the rational expression and the
polynomial as the product of the rational expression and
the reciprocal of the polynomial. Factor the numerators
and denominators, divide out common factors, and write
the answer in factored form.
Exercises 11. $\frac{35x}{36}$ **13.** $\frac{40}{3a^5}$ **15.** $\frac{2x(x - 1)}{3(x + 1)}$ **17.** $\frac{2c(c + 2)}{c - 1}$
19. $\frac{1}{3}$ **21.** $\frac{3(4x + 1)}{x - 1}$ **23.** $3(2m + 1)(m + 2)$
25. $\frac{(2y + 9)(y - 2)}{4}$ **27.** $\frac{2d - 5}{-6d^2}$ **29.** $\frac{x - 1}{x + 3}$ **31.** $-\frac{1}{3}$
33. $\frac{2(x + 2)}{x - 1}$ **35.** $\frac{3}{x}$ **37.** $\frac{1}{32x}$ **39.** $(t + 2)^2$ **41.** $\frac{2(3g + 1)}{g(3g - 1)}$
43. $t + 3$ **45.** $\frac{3t - 5}{7t^2}$ **47.** \$88.71 **49.** \$518,011.65
51. The student forgot to rewrite the divisor as its
reciprocal before dividing out common factors.
$\frac{3a}{a + 2} \div \frac{(a + 2)^2}{a - 4} = \frac{3a}{a + 2} \cdot \frac{a - 4}{(a + 2)^2} = \frac{3a(a - 4)}{(a + 2)^3}$ **53.** 0, 4,
and -4 make the denominators equal 0.

55. $\frac{2m^2(m + 2)}{(m - 1)(m + 4)}$ **60.** $\frac{7}{3}$, $m \neq 2$ **61.** $\frac{1}{2a^2 - 3}$, $a \neq 0$,

$a \neq \pm\frac{\sqrt{6}}{2}$ **62.** $\frac{2c - 9}{2c + 8}$, $c \neq -4$, $c \neq 4.5$

63. $2x^2 + 10x + 12$ **64.** $-3n^2 + 11n + 20$

65. $6a^3 - 21a^2 + 2a - 7$

Lesson 11-3   pp. 679–684

Got It? 1. a. $2a + 5 + \frac{3}{2a}$ **b.** $b - \frac{3}{b} + \frac{1}{5b^3}$

c. $2c^3 + 3c + \frac{3}{2}$ **2.** $2m - 3$ **3. a.** $q^3 + q^2 + 2q + 3$

b. $h^2 - 3h + 5 - \frac{3}{h + 3}$ **4. a.** $2y - 6 + \frac{17}{3y + 4}$

b. $3a + 1 - \frac{3}{6a + 5}$ **c.** Check whether

$(2x - 3)(2x + 2) - 7$ equals $4x^2 - 10x - 1$.

Lesson Check 1. $4m + 2 - \frac{1}{m} - \frac{3}{5m^2}$

2. $20c + 43 + \frac{36}{c - 1}$ **3.** $5n^2 - 4n + 1$ **4.** $3a - 5$

5. Both processes involve dividing, multiplying, and subtracting, then "bringing down," and repeating as needed. When dividing polynomials you may need to insert a term with a coefficient of 0 as a placeholder.
6. Divide, multiply, subtract, bring down, and repeat as necessary. **7.** $-x^4 + 0x^3 + 0x^2 + 0x + 1$
Exercises 9. $3x^4 - \frac{2}{x}$ **11.** $n^2 - 18n + 3$

13. $t^3 + 2t^2 - 4t + 5$ **15.** $y - 3 + \frac{8}{y + 2}$

17. $r^2 + 5r + 1$ **19.** $b + 6 + \frac{25}{2b + 4}$

21. $2x^2 + 3x + \frac{2}{3} + \frac{-8}{3(3x - 5)}$

23. $2b^2 + \frac{1}{4}b + \frac{29}{32} + \frac{29}{32(8b - 1)}$ **25.** $2x + 2$

27. $5t^3 - 25t^2 + 115t - 575 + \frac{2881}{t + 5}$

29. $3s - 8 + \frac{29}{2s + 3}$ **31.** $m^2 + 5m + 4$ **33.** 12

35. $\frac{1}{3} + \frac{2}{3(6r + 1)}$ **40.** $n + 2$ **41.** $\frac{(t - 5)(3t + 1)(2t + 11)}{3t(2t - 55)(t + 1)}$

42. $\frac{3c + 8}{2c + 7}$ **43.** $\frac{(x + 5)(x + 4)^2}{(x + 7)(x + 8)^2}$ **44.** $\frac{2}{3}$ **45.** $-\frac{1}{12}$ **46.** x

47. $\frac{1}{2y}$

Lesson 11-4   pp. 685–691

Got It? 1. $\frac{5a}{3a - 4}$ **2. a.** $\frac{-5}{z + 3}$ **b.** $\frac{3n - 4}{5n - 2}$ **c.** $\frac{1}{q - 2}$

3. $\frac{9 + 14y^2}{21y^4}$ **4.** $\frac{c^2 - 14c + 4}{(3c - 1)(c - 2)}$ **5. a.** $\frac{45}{4r}$ **b.** $\frac{4m}{5}$; if n is the

miles per gallon when the truck is full, then $m = 1.25n$ and therefore $n = \frac{m}{1.25}$ or $\frac{4m}{5}$.

Lesson Check 1. $\frac{11}{x - 7}$ **2.** $\frac{2}{y + 2}$ **3.** $\frac{16b + 15}{24b^3}$ **4.** $\frac{10}{3r}$

5. If the expressions have like denominators, add or subtract numerators as indicated and place over the denominator. If they have unlike denominators, factor if needed, find the LCD, rewrite the expressions with the common denominator, add or subtract as indicated, and simplify. **6.** The procedure is the same. The LCD is the LCM of the denominators. **7. a.** yes **b.** No, it will give you a common denominator, but not necessarily the least common denominator.

Exercises 9. $\frac{14}{c - 5}$ **11.** $\frac{6c - 28}{2c + 7}$ **13.** $\frac{1}{n + 2}$ **15.** 2

17. $2x^2$ **19.** $7z$ **21.** $(m + n)(m - n)$ **23.** $\frac{12 - 2x}{3x}$

25. $\frac{(a + 4)(a - 3)}{(a + 3)(a + 5)}$ **27. a.** $\frac{1}{r} + \frac{1}{0.7r} = \frac{1.7}{0.7r}$ **b.** $\frac{17}{7r}$ **c.** about

0.81 h or 48.6 min **29.** Not always; the numerator may

contain a factor of the LCD. **31.** $\frac{-y^2 + 2y + 2}{3y + 1}$

33. $\frac{r - 2k - 6}{9 + p^3}$ **35.** $\frac{10x + 15}{x + 2}$ **37.** $\frac{5000r + 250,000}{r(r + 100)}$

39. $\frac{8x^2 + 1}{x}$ **41.** $\frac{-3x - 5}{x(x - 5)}$ **43.** 1 **47.** $\frac{1}{2}x^2 + 2x - 1$

48. 5b **49.** $\frac{y^2(y - 1)}{y - 3}$ **50.** 6 **51.** 3 **52.** no solution **53.** $\frac{5}{3}$

54. $\frac{6}{5}$ **55.** 1

Lesson 11-5   pp. 692–698

Got It? 1. a. -3 **b.** $\frac{37}{7}$ **2. a.** $-\frac{3}{2}, \frac{2}{3}$ **b.** $-7, -1$ **c.** The

expression $\frac{2}{x^2}$ cannot be negative. **3.** 4.8 h **4. a.** -8

b. -3 **5.** 0

Lesson Check 1. -1 **2.** 1, 5 **3.** 0 **4.** about 28 min
5. An extraneous solution of a rational equation is an excluded value of the associated rational function.

6. Answers will vary. Sample: $\frac{x^2}{x - 1} = \frac{1}{x - 1}$
7. The student forgot to first multiply both sides of the equation by the LCD, 5m.

Exercises 9. 3 **11.** $-\frac{1}{3}$ **13.** 5 **15.** $\frac{1}{3}$ **17.** -1
19. about 12.7 min **21.** ± 10 **23.** 4 **25.** Answers will

vary. Sample: $\frac{9}{x - 2} = \frac{x + 4}{3}$ **27.** 3 **29.** 0, 2 **31.** about

7.5 mi/h **33.** 20 Ω **39.** $-\frac{3}{x^2y^2z}$ **40.** $\frac{3h^2 + 2ht + 4h}{2(t - 2)(t + 2)}$

41. $\frac{-4k - 61}{(k - 4)(k + 10)}$ **42.** 1.7 **43.** 13.1 **44.** 21.15 **45.** -4.9

Chapter Review   pp. 700–702

1. excluded value **2.** complex fraction **3.** rational

expression **4.** $\frac{x + 3}{5x^2}$, $x \neq 0$ **5.** $\frac{1}{3}$, $m \neq 3$ **6.** $\frac{x + 3}{5}$,

$x \neq -3$ **7.** $\frac{2(a - 1)}{3(a + 1)}$, $a \neq -1$, $a \neq 1$ **8.** $\frac{2s + 3}{2s - 1}$, $x \neq \frac{1}{2}$,

$x \neq 4$ **9.** $-\frac{1}{2}$, $c \neq 4$ **10.** $\frac{1}{x + 2}$ **11.** $\frac{2}{3(x - 2)}$

12. $\frac{(a + 4)(a - 2)}{a^2(a + 2)}$ **13.** $(x + 5)(x + 7)$ **14.** $4x - 3 - \frac{7}{3x}$

15. $3d - 7 - \frac{8}{d + 3}$ **16.** $(2b^2 + b + 3)$ in. **17.** $\frac{8x - 3}{x + 1}$

18. $\frac{24 + 7x}{28x}$ **19.** $\frac{x^2 + 7x - 20}{(x + 2)(x - 4)}$ **20.** $\frac{-15x^2 + 23x + 27}{(3x - 1)(2x + 3)}$

21. $\frac{138,430}{59r}$ **22.** 24 **23.** 9 **24.** -14 **25.** -21 **26.** 6 min

Chapter 12

Get Ready!   p. 707

1. 1 $\frac{7}{6}$ **2.** $-\frac{1}{24}$ **3.** $\frac{47}{50}$ **4.** $\frac{5}{12}$ **5.** $\frac{13}{2}$ **6.** 3 **7.** 11
8. $6x - 42$ **9.** $2x + 3$ **10.** $-10 + 2x$ **11.** $2.5 + 2x$
12. {1, 2, 3, 5, 6, 7, 9, 10, 11, 13, 15, 16} **13.** {9}
14. {2, 6, 10, 16} **15.** {0, 1, 2, 3, 4, 5, 6, 7, 8, 9, 10, 11, 12, 13, 14, 16, 18}

16.

negative

17.

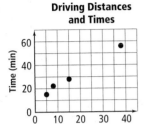

positive

18. heads or tails **19.** into two parts with an equal number of data values **20.** no

Lesson 12-1 pp. 710–715

Got It? 1. a. $\begin{bmatrix} -4 \\ 1.5 \\ -16 \end{bmatrix}$ **b.** $\begin{bmatrix} 1 & 1 \\ 2.5 & 10 \end{bmatrix}$ c. You add or subtract matrices by adding or subtracting the corresponding elements. If matrices are not the same size they will not have corresponding elements in each case.

2. a. $\begin{bmatrix} 6 & -14.2 & -10 \end{bmatrix}$ **b.** $\begin{bmatrix} -16.5 & 4.5 \\ 0 & -2.25 \end{bmatrix}$

3. Portland

Lesson Check 1. $\begin{bmatrix} -3 & 9 \\ 0 & 4 \end{bmatrix}$ **2.** $\begin{bmatrix} 2 & 3 \\ 2 & -3 \end{bmatrix}$

3. $\begin{bmatrix} 8 & 0 & 10 \\ -4 & 2 & 4 \end{bmatrix}$ **4.** $\begin{bmatrix} -30 & 0 \\ -12 & 18 \end{bmatrix}$ **5.** 9 **6.** The student added entries across the rows, but the matrices are not the same size so they cannot be added.

Exercises 9. $\begin{bmatrix} -1 & 1 \\ 0 & 0 \end{bmatrix}$ **11.** $\begin{bmatrix} 2 & -1 \\ 5 & -1 \\ 0 & 10 \end{bmatrix}$

13. $\begin{bmatrix} 24 & -12 \\ 0 & 20 \end{bmatrix}$ **15.** $\begin{bmatrix} 0 & 0 \\ 0 & 0 \end{bmatrix}$ **17.** $\begin{bmatrix} 8.1 & 12.69 \\ 0 & -8.1 \\ 15.39 & 7.29 \end{bmatrix}$

19. Factory B **21.** $\begin{bmatrix} 9 & 1 & 2 \\ -10 & 2 & 0 \end{bmatrix}$ **23.** chicken

28. $a = -25$ **29.** no solution **30.** $m = \frac{1}{3}$

31.

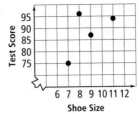

no

32.

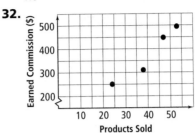

Yes; causal; the amount of sales is related to earnings.

Lesson 12-2 pp. 716–721

Got It?

1. Answers may vary. Sample:

Home Runs	Frequency
2–6	4
7–11	5
12–16	4
17–21	1

2. Answers may vary. Sample:

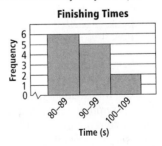

3. a.

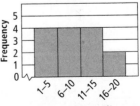

uniform

b. Answers may vary. Sample: $70 for the week; the data are fairly uniform, so on average he spends about $10 per day.

4.

Interval	Frequency	Cumulative Frequency
0–4	6	6
5–9	4	10
10–14	4	14
15–19	2	16

Lesson Check

1-3. Answers may vary. Samples are given.

1.

Battery Life

Hours	Frequency
9–12	7
13–16	2
17–20	1
21–24	2

2.

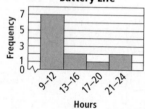

Battery Life

3.

Battery Life

Hours	Frequency	Cumulative Frequency
9–12	7	7
13–16	2	9
17–20	1	10
21–24	2	12

4. The store owner could look at the frequency column to pick out the busiest hours. **5.** A symmetric histogram has roughly the same shape if you fold it down the middle. A skewed histogram has a peak that is not in the center.
6. Add the frequency of each interval to the frequencies of all the previous intervals.

Exercises

7.

Wing Spans

Number of Centimeters	Frequency
125–134	5
135–144	4
145–154	4

9. Answers may vary. Sample:

Top Speeds

Miles per Hour	Frequency
90–109	4
110–129	4
130–149	2
150–169	3

11. Answers may vary. Sample:

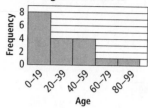

13. skewed **15.** uniform

17. Answers may vary. Sample:

Trail Lengths

Miles	Frequency	Cumulative Frequency
1–3	13	13
4–6	5	18
7–9	2	20
10–12	2	22

19. about 60

21. Answers may vary. Sample:

23. 20; fewer intervals show less variation in the data.
25. There were no numbers in the interval of 30 to 39 so the student just left out this interval. The intervals in a

frequency table should not have any gaps, so the student should have included the interval 30–39.

Interval	Frequency
20–29	6
30–39	0
40–49	5
50–59	4

27. 20–39 **29.** Nine customers spent less than $19, while 15 customers spent between $20 and $39. Thirteen customers spent between $40 and $59. Another nine customers spent between $60 and $79, and the least number of customers, four, spent between $80 and $99.

34. $\begin{bmatrix} 12 & 16 \\ 14 & 18 \end{bmatrix}$ **35.** $\begin{bmatrix} -2.1 & -5.3 \\ -6.7 & -0.5 \end{bmatrix}$ **36.** $-16, -4, 0, \frac{1}{2}, \frac{5}{4},$ 2, 13, 16 **37.** $-1, -0.2, 0, 0.1, 0.9, 1.2, 2, 5$

Lesson 12-3 pp. 722–728

Got It? 1. 112.4, 109, 104; mean **2.** 88 **3.** Stock C: 6, 4.2; Stock D: 22, 11.2; Stock C had a range of 6 and a mean of 4.2, while Stock D had a range of 22 and a mean of 10.8 for this 5-day period. So Stock D had a higher average price during the period and also had more spread out prices than Stock C. **4.** 48, 45, 35, 30 **5.** $345, $284.25, $359.25, $866.25

Lesson Check 1. 26.2, 30.5, 33; the median, since there is an outlier in this set **2.** 8.76, 8.8, no mode; the mean, since there is no outlier **3.** 14.1, 15, 15, 24 **4.** All are describing the data set by finding a representative measure of central tendency. The mean can be influenced by outliers, which can overstate or understate the measure. The median is the middle value of the ranked data, and the mode is the most commonly occurring piece of data.
5. The correct range is 8 because the range is defined as the difference between the highest and lowest values.
6. Since an outlier is either much larger or much smaller than most of the data, it causes the range to get larger.
Exercises 7. 12, 11, 10; mean **9.** 63, 52, no mode; median **11.** 5.9 **13.** 15 **15.** Set C: 3.8, 6.7; Set D: 28.3, 9.0; Set D has a greater mean and data that are more spread out. **17.** First player: .062, .300; Second player: .029, .302; the second player had a slightly higher mean over the six seasons and was more consistent as shown by the smaller range. **19.** 23.4, 24.9, 25.6, 10.6 **21.** 4.6, 5.3, 5.3, 5 **23.** 3.3, 4, 4.3, 4.1 **25.** 229.7, 144, 96 and 300, 528 **27.** 18.5, 20.4, 20.4, 13.2 **29.** All the values will be divided by the value of that nonzero number. If each data value is divided by some nonzero number n, then the sum of the original data will be divided by n. Therefore, the value of the mean will also be divided by n. $\frac{x_1}{n} + \frac{x_2}{n} + \frac{x_3}{n} = \frac{S}{n}$ The median is the middle number, so it will also be divided by n. The mode is the most

commonly occurring value in the data set, so it too will be divided by n. The range will also be divided by n, as

$$\frac{(\text{highest value})}{n} - \frac{(\text{lowest value})}{n} = \frac{\text{highest} - \text{lowest}}{n}.$$

35. Answers may vary. Sample:

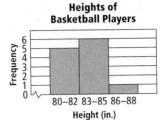

Heights of Basketball Players

36. Answers may vary. Sample:

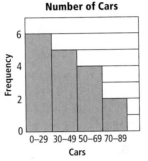

Number of Cars

37.

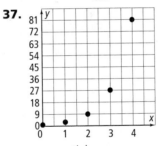

exponential

38.

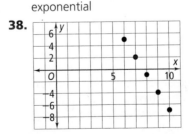

linear

39. 21, 0 **40.** 50, 22.5 **41.** 8.9, 2.1

Lesson 12-4 pp. 730–735

Got It? 1. a. 60, 75, 85, 95, 105 **b.** 5, 7, 15, 21, 53

2. Monthly Sales (millions of $)

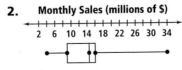

3. The median tells you the middle value of the data. So in Miami the monthly rainfall is below 4.5 in. for half the months and above 4.5 in. for half the months. For New Orleans the monthly rainfall is below about 5.3 in. for half the months and above 5.3 in. for the other half of the months. This is one indication that New Orleans gets more rain than Miami does. **4. a.** 60 **b.** No; since the percentile rank is the percent of scores that fall at or below a given score there is always at least 1 value associated with a given value. There is no 0 percentile; the lowest score is the first percentile.

Lesson Check

1. 48, 54, 100, 188, 256

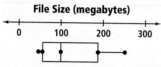

File Size (megabytes)

2. 24, 27, 29.5, 31.5, 33

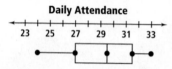

Daily Attendance

3. Class B **4.** the box **5.** 88 **6.** 75%; the third quartile is the value that divides the data so that about 75% of the data lies below and about 25% of the data lies above. **7.** No; the test is scored on point values from 0 to 100 whereas the percentile rank tells you how you did in reference to the rest of the group.

Exercises 9. 3.2, 4.2, 5, 6.15, 12 **11.** 100, 100, 101, 104, 105

13.

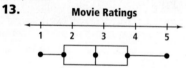

Movie Ratings

15. Sample: The fuel efficiency in mi/gal of cars goes from a low of 14.5 to a high of about 50, with the middle 50% of cars being in the range of 18 to 22 mi/gal. Trucks have a low of about 12 mi/gal to a high of about 22 mi/gal with the middle 50% being between 14 and 16 mi/gal. The range of the cars is much greater than that of the trucks. **17.** 80 **19.** The range gives the difference between the greatest and least values, while the interquartile range gives the difference between the third and first quartiles. **21.** $0 < h \leq 73.5$ **27.** 747.5, 708, 627 **28.** 43.3, 41, 41

29.

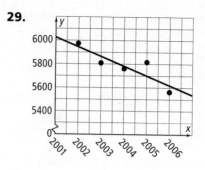

Answers may vary. Sample: $y = -81x + 167,509$; about 4300 bowling establishments

Lesson 12-5   pp. 737–743

Got It? 1. a. quantitative; numerical quantities **b.** qualitative; not numerical **2. a.** Bivariate; there are two variables. **b.** Univariate; there is only one variable. **3.** No; if you are using a stratified sampling method, you should sample at random from each group. **4.** Answers may vary. Sample: Do you prefer action movies or documentaries? **5.** Students who have e-mail may be more likely to have a cell phone.

Lesson Check 1. systematic **2.** random **3.** stratified **4.** quantitative **5.** The words delicious and plain are biased and might influence a respondent's answer. **6.** Univariate data involves one variable and bivariate data involves two variables. Check students' examples.

Exercises 7. qualitative **9.** quantitative **11.** bivariate **13.** bivariate **15.** bivariate **17.** systematic; not a good sample because it does not include randomness **19.** biased; question is influenced by the wording **21.** biased; wording of choices is biased **23.** You are asking people who are apt to have a pet because they are at a dog park. **25. a.** People at an airport are more likely to be travelers. **b.** Your question is influencing the result. Respondents might prefer "neither." **c.** The sample is biased as it includes mostly people who might prefer France. **27.** attendees at the game; random attendees; random **29.** quantitative; univariate **31.** qualitative; bivariate **33. a.** Biased; you are surveying customers who are probably bike riders. **b.** Biased; your survey is not representative of all town residents as you are excluding many. **c.** Biased; you are sampling only classmates who are not representative of the whole town. **d.** Biased; you are sampling only those residents who are customers of that shop rather than the whole town; you are probably only getting people from that particular part of town. **39.** 40 **40.** 60 **41.** $a > 1$ **42.** $x \geq -3$ **43.** $b > 0.2$ **44.** 20 **45.** 42 **46.** 6

Chapter Review for Part A   pp. 745–747

1. element **2.** frequency **3.** outlier **4.** quartile

5. $\begin{bmatrix} -12 & 7 \\ 4 & 6 \end{bmatrix}$ **6.** $\begin{bmatrix} 4.4 & 4.5 \\ 9.5 & -10.2 \\ 3.4 & -2.6 \end{bmatrix}$ **7.** $\begin{bmatrix} -12.6 & -4.62 \\ -12.6 & 8.4 \\ 4.2 & -12.18 \end{bmatrix}$

8. Sample:

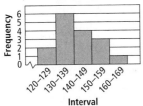

9. Sample:

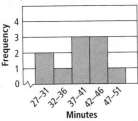

10. skewed **11.** symmetric **12.** 26.3, 26, 23 and 25 and 29, 9 **13.** 12.1, 12, 12, 2 **14.** 11.1, 11.3, 13.4; mean or median **15.** 27

16.

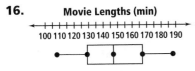

17.

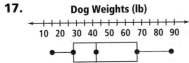

18.

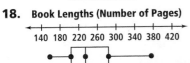

19. B; the box in A is from about 90 to 110, where the box in B is from about 75 to 125. **20.** Systematic; good sample; Do you plan on seeing more or fewer movies in the coming year? **21.** Stratified; good sample; Whom do you support for student council president?

Lesson 12-6   pp. 750–756

Got It? 1. a. 48 **b.** No; the tree diagram would be very large, so using the Multiplication Counting Principle would be easier. **2.** 40,320 ways **3.** 20,160 **4.** 455 ways
Lesson Check 1. 5040 **2.** 6,227,020,800 **3.** 120 **4.** 5040 **5.** 10 **6.** 35 **7.** 24 outfits **8.** permutations; order is important in this situation **9.** Permutations are used to count in situations where order is important. Combinations are used to count in situations where

selection, not order, is important. **10.** There is only one way to take n things, n at a time.
Also, $_nC_n = \dfrac{n!}{n!(n - n)!} = \dfrac{1}{0!} = \dfrac{1}{1} = 1$.
Exercises 11. a. 8, 10 **b.** 8×10^6, or 8,000,000 **13.** 3,628,800 **15.** 1680 **17.** 5040 **19.** 120 **21.** 1 **23.** 79,833,600 **25.** 12,144 ways **27.** 5 **29.** 21 **31.** 28 **33.** 10 **35.** 220 ways **37.** 142,506 groups **39. a.** 26×10^4, or 260,000 license plates **b.** 23,920,000 plates **41.** 6 **43.** 24 **45.** Permutation; order makes a difference. **51.** qualitative **52.** quantitative **53.** quantitative **54.** qualitative **55.** 0.81, −6.81 **56.** 6.70, 0.30 **57.** 1.46, −5.46 **58.** −1, −1.67 **59.** 32% **60.** 9% **61.** 22.5% **62.** 18%

Lesson 12-7   pp. 757–763

Got It? 1. $\frac{5}{8}$ **2.** It will be $1 - \dfrac{20}{50 + x}$, where x is the number of other samples added. The probability will increase. **3.** 3 : 1 **4.** 98% **5.** about 34,995 light bulbs
Lesson Check 1. $\frac{1}{6}$ **2.** $\frac{1}{3}$ **3.** $\frac{5}{6}$ **4.** $\frac{2}{3}$ **5.** 1 : 5 **6.** 16%
7. There are only two outcomes that are favorable, getting a 1 or a 2, therefore the probability is $\frac{2}{10}$, or $\frac{1}{5}$.
Exercises 9. $\frac{1}{2}$ **11.** $\frac{1}{6}$ **13.** $\frac{1}{2}$ **15.** $\frac{2}{3}$ **17.** 1 **19.** 1 : 1 **21.** 1 : 2 **23.** 1 : 1 **25.** 24% **27.** 15% **29.** 39% **31.** 98.4% **35.** 3 : 7 **40.** 840 **41.** 6 **42.** 30 **43.** 9 **44.** 5 **45.** {1, 4, 5, 6, 7, 10} **46.** {4, 6} **47.** {0, 2, 4, 5, 6, 7, 8, 10} **48.** {4, 10} **49.** {0, 1, 2, 4, 6, 7, 8, 10}

Lesson 12-8   pp. 765–771

Got It? 1. a. $\frac{5}{6}$ **b.** $\frac{2}{3}$ **2.** $\frac{1}{18}$ **3.** $\frac{2}{225}$ **4.** $\frac{1}{105}$ **5.** $\frac{5}{33}$
Lesson Check 1. $\frac{4}{5}$ **2.** $\frac{4}{5}$ **3.** $\frac{3}{20}$ **4.** Mutually exclusive; answers may vary. Sample: By definition, the complement of an event consists of all outcomes in the sample space that are not in the event. **5.** Because a tile can be both yellow and a letter, the formula should be
$P(\text{yellow or letter}) = P(\text{yellow}) + P(\text{letter}) - P(\text{yellow and letter}) = \frac{3}{5} + \frac{2}{5} - \frac{1}{5} = \frac{4}{5}$.
Exercises 7. $\frac{1}{5}$ **9.** $\frac{3}{5}$ **11.** $\frac{3}{5}$ **13.** $\frac{1}{4}$ **15.** $\frac{1}{6}$ **17.** $\frac{4}{81}$ **19.** $\frac{1}{9}$ **21.** $\frac{1}{8}$ **23.** $\frac{1}{12}$ **25.** $\frac{1}{12}$ **27.** $\frac{1}{25}$ **29.** Independent; the outcome of the first event does not affect the second event. **31.** about 4.7% **36.** $\frac{11}{21}$ **37.** $\frac{4}{21}$ **38.** 22 **39.** $\frac{a + 5}{5(a - 5)}$

Chapter Review for Part B pp. 773–775

1. combination **2.** independent events **3.** probability **4.** 15,120 **5.** 6 **6.** 336 **7.** 20 **8.** 360 **9.** 42 **10.** 28 **11.** 126 **12.** 10 **13.** 20 **14.** 35 **15.** 5 **16.** 10 **17.** 40,320 orders **18.** 126 outfits **19.** $\frac{1}{2}$ **20.** $\frac{1}{2}$ **21.** $\frac{1}{6}$ **22.** $\frac{5}{6}$ **23.** 0 **24.** $\frac{1}{3}$ **25.** about 93.3% **26.** $\frac{2}{7}$ **27.** $\frac{2}{7}$ **28.** $\frac{1}{36}$ **29.** $\frac{1}{4}$ **30.** Dependent; the outcome of the first event affects the outcome of the second event.
31. Independent; the outcome of the spinner does not affect the outcome of the pick.

Skills Handbook

p. 783 1. composite **3.** composite **5.** prime
7. composite **9.** prime **11.** composite **13.** 1, 2, 23, 46
15. 1, 11 **17.** 1, 3, 9, 27 **19.** 2 · 3 · 3 **21.** π3 · 3 · 3
23. 2 · 2 · 2 · 2 · 2 · 2

p. 784 1. 2 **3.** 24 **5.** 80 **7.** 33

p. 785 1–11. Answers may vary. Samples are given.
1. $350 **3.** $300 **5.** $17 **7.** 6.90 **9.** 7 **11.** $30.80

p. 786 1. $\frac{8}{14}, \frac{12}{21}, \frac{16}{28}, \frac{20}{35}, \frac{24}{42}$ **3.** $\frac{6}{16}, \frac{9}{24}, \frac{12}{32}, \frac{15}{40}, \frac{18}{48}$
5. $\frac{10}{12}, \frac{15}{18}, \frac{20}{24}, \frac{25}{30}, \frac{30}{36}$ **7.** 9 **9.** 48 **11.** 2 **13.** yes **15.** no; $\frac{1}{8}$
17. yes **19.** $\frac{1}{2}$ **21.** $\frac{2}{3}$ **23.** $\frac{3}{10}$

p. 787 1. 0.3 **3.** 0.2 **5.** 0.$\overline{714285}$ **7.** $\frac{7}{100}$ **9.** $\frac{7}{8}$ **11.** $6\frac{1}{3}$

p. 788 1. $\frac{5}{7}$ **3.** 3 **5.** $10\frac{7}{15}$ **7.** $6\frac{2}{9}$ **9.** $6\frac{7}{33}$ **11.** $9\frac{2}{3}$
13. $13\frac{7}{16}$ **15.** $\frac{3}{5}$ **17.** $1\frac{2}{7}$ **19.** $2\frac{3}{8}$ **21.** $3\frac{1}{3}$ **23.** $9\frac{4}{63}$
25. $2\frac{1}{6}$

p. 789 1. $\frac{3}{10}$ **3.** $8\frac{5}{8}$ **5.** $3\frac{1}{2}$ **7.** $25\frac{3}{10}$ **9.** $2\frac{4}{5}$ **11.** $1\frac{1}{5}$
13. $\frac{5}{7}$ **15.** $1\frac{17}{21}$ **17.** $\frac{20}{27}$ **19.** $\frac{22}{25}$

p. 790 1. 56% **3.** 602% **5.** 820% **7.** 14.3% **9.** 11.1%
11. 75% **13.** 0.07 **15.** 0.009 **17.** 0.83 **19.** 0.15
21. 0.0003 **23.** 3.65 **25.** $\frac{19}{100}$ **27.** $4\frac{1}{2}$ **29.** $\frac{16}{25}$ **31.** $\frac{6}{25}$
33. $\frac{3}{800}$ **35.** $\frac{3}{5}$

p. 791 1. 6^4 **3.** $5 \cdot 2^4$ **5.** $4^2 \cdot 3^2 \cdot 2$ **7.** 64 **9.** 141
11. 3267 **13.** $(1 \cdot 10^3) + (2 \cdot 10^2) + (5 \cdot 10^1) \cdot$
$(4 \cdot 10^0)$ **15.** $(8 \cdot 10^4) + (3 \cdot 10^3) + (4 \cdot 10^2) +$
$(0 \cdot 10^1) + (1 \cdot 10^0)$

p. 792 1. 22 cm **3.** 24 cm^2 **5.** 216 cm^3 **7.** 352 cm^3

p. 793 1. **3.**

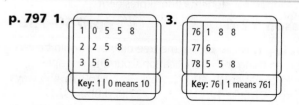

5.

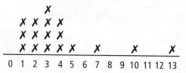

Gold Medals Won

The line plot shows that most of the countries won about 3 gold medals. The maximum number of gold medals that a country won was 13, and the minimum was 1.

p. 794 1.

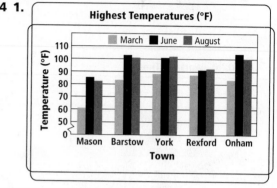

p. 795 1.

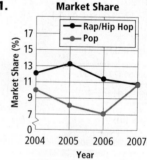

p. 796 1a.

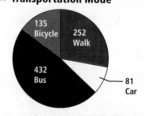

Transportation Mode

b. 48%
c. 3 times

p. 797 1.

1	0 5 5 8
2	2 5 8
3	5 6

Key: 1 | 0 means 10

3.

76	1 8 8
77	6
78	5 5 8

Key: 76 | 1 means 761

5.

Test Scores

Class A		Class B
8	6	
8 2	7	5 9
5 3 1	8	1 2 7
8 4	9	0 1
	10	0

Key:

7 | 5 means 75

2 | 7 | 5

2 | 7 means 72

Index

236, 254, 261, 268, 276, 285, 294,
301, 320, 327, 337, 344, 356, 362,
370, 387, 395, 404, 411, 424, 430,
448, 454, 460, 466, 474, 480, 489,
507, 512, 521, 527, 538, 544, 550,
555, 562, 572, 578, 585, 590, 600,
607, 613, 630, 639, 645, 652, 670,
677, 684, 691, 698, 715, 721, 728,
735, 743, 756, 763, 771

Associative Property
of addition, 26
defined, 34
of multiplication, 26

astronomy, 166, 459, 467, 472, 758

average, 722

axes, 68, 249

axis of symmetry, 566, 591

B

Bar Graphs, 794

base
defined, 11
of exponent, 456
finding, 152
multiplying powers with same,
455–458

best fit, line of. *See* line of best fit

bias
defined, 739, 747
in samples, 740
in survey questions, 739

Big Ideas
Data Collection and Analysis, 709,
749, 772, 773
Data Representation, 709, 749, 772,
773
Equivalence, 85, 129, 163, 164, 173,
209, 237, 238, 441, 490, 491, 501,
531, 556, 557, 625, 653, 654, 663,
699, 700
Functions, 246, 247, 302, 303, 313,
348, 372, 373, 441, 490, 565, 594,
615, 616
Modeling, 247, 302, 303, 313, 348,
372, 373, 381, 415, 432, 433, 615,
616
Probability, 709, 749, 772, 773
Properties, 3, 36, 75, 76, 441, 490,
491, 501, 531, 556, 557
Proportionality, 85, 129, 163, 164,
313, 348, 372, 373
Solving Equations and Inequalities,
85, 129, 163, 164, 173, 209, 237,
238, 381, 415, 432, 433, 565, 594,
615, 616, 625, 653, 654, 663, 699,
700
Variable, 3, 36, 75, 76, 173, 209, 237,
238

binomials
defined, 503
dividing polynomials by, 680
modeling multiplication of, 513
multiplying, 514–515
multiplying trinomials by, 519
squaring, 492–493, 522–524

biology, 20, 90, 119, 141, 204, 228,
365, 383, 451, 459, 494, 642, 644

bivariate, 738

box-and-whisker plot
defined, 731, 747
interpreting, 732
making, 732

braces, 20, 210

brackets, 12

break-even point, 408

C

calc key, of graphing calculator, 279,
366, 388, 575, 614

calculator, 448, 676, 753. *See also*
graphing calculator
equations in slope-intercept form, 328
exercises that use, 488, 571, 577
histograms, 717
inequality(ies), 448
linear inequalities, 431
line of best fit, 366
regressions, 614
scientific notation, 449
vertical motion model, 575

causation, 367

change
percent decrease, 158
percent increase, 158
percent of, 157–159
rate of, 225, 314

Chapter Review. *See* assessment,
Chapter Review

Chapter Test. *See* assessment, Chapter
Test

check for reasonableness, 352

chemistry, 43, 220, 411, 435, 457, 460,
644

Choose a Method exercises, 134

circle
area of, 118
circumference of, 118, 119

Circle Graphs, 796

circumference, 119
of circle, 118

classifying
data, 738
equations, 61

functions as linear or nonlinear, 263
lines, 359
numbers, 21
polynomials, 503–504
real numbers, 21

coefficient
correlation. *See* correlation coefficient
defined, 57
using percents as, 409

coins, 764

Collecting Linear Data, 371

Collecting Quadratic Data, 579

combination, 753
defined, 774

Combination Notation, 753

combining
like radicals, 640
like terms, 57, 101–102

common difference, 296, 306

common ratio, 481–482

communication. *See* Writing exercises

community service, 96

Commutative Property
of addition, 26
defined, 34
of multiplication, 26

Compare and Contrast exercises, 40,
64, 72, 120, 176, 180, 187, 228,
234, 289, 317, 355, 360, 367, 375,
403, 406, 482, 495, 505, 515, 519,
541, 569, 583, 588, 598, 638, 674,
689, 719, 740, 754

complement
of an event, defined, 758
of an event, probability of, 759

complement of a set
defined, 212, 239
finding, 212

completing the square, 617
defined, 595
by finding c, 596
when $a \neq 1$, 597

complex fraction
defined, 674
simplifying, 674

composite figures
area of, 124
perimeter of, 123

compound event, 765, 775

compound inequalities
containing *and*, 216
containing *or*, 216, 218–219
defined, 216, 239
graphing, 216–219
solving, 216–219
writing, 217–218

Index

linear parent, 329
linear vs. nonlinear, 263
modeling, 281, 335, 484
nonlinear, 262, 305
parent, 329
quadratic. *See* quadratic functions
range of, 287, 477
sequences as, 296

Functions, as Big Idea, 247, 302, 303, 313, 348, 372, 373, 441, 490, 491, 565, 594, 615, 616

G

GCF (greatest common factor), 509

geography, 451, 465

Geometric Sequences, 256, 481–482
vs. arithmetic sequences, 482
common ratio in, 481–482

geometry. *See also* area; circle; perimeter; rectangle; surface area; triangle(s); volume
exercises, 17, 25, 59, 104, 122, 128, 189, 203, 275, 325, 344, 394, 404, 414, 430, 459, 467, 473, 507, 518, 520, 526, 529, 530, 535, 540, 558, 559, 585, 589, 592, 619, 650, 651, 655, 656, 669, 677, 683, 701, 703
formulas of, 17, 118, 119, 122, 128, 200, 275, 282, 520, 562, 650.
problems, 200, 282, 535, 540, 553, 680

Get Ready!
for chapters, 1, 83, 171, 245, 311, 379, 439, 499, 563, 623, 661, 707
for lessons, 10, 18, 25, 31, 43, 51, 60, 66, 74, 93, 100, 108, 116, 122, 135, 142, 149, 156, 162, 183, 190, 196, 205, 215, 221, 229, 236, 254, 261, 268, 277, 285, 294, 301, 320, 327, 337, 344, 356, 362, 370, 387, 395, 404, 411, 424, 430, 448, 454, 460, 466, 474, 480, 489, 507, 512, 521, 527, 538, 544, 550, 555, 572, 578, 585, 590, 600, 607, 613, 630, 639, 645, 652, 670, 677, 684, 691, 698, 715, 721, 728, 735, 743, 756, 763

Glossary, 805–843

golden ratio, 284

golden rectangle, 284, 642

Got It? 5, 6, 7, 12, 13, 15, 16, 20, 21, 22, 27, 28, 29, 37, 38, 39, 40, 46, 47, 48, 53, 54, 56, 57, 61, 62, 63, 69, 70, 71, 88, 89, 90, 95, 96, 97, 101, 102, 103, 105, 106, 111, 112, 113, 118, 119, 131, 132, 133, 137, 138, 139, 144, 145, 146, 151, 152, 153, 158, 159, 175, 179, 180, 185, 186, 187, 192, 193, 194, 200, 201, 202, 211, 217, 218, 219, 223, 224, 227, 231, 232, 233, 234, 249, 251, 256, 258, 263, 264, 265, 270, 271, 273, 281, 282, 287, 288, 289, 291, 292, 296, 297, 314, 315, 316, 317, 322, 323, 330, 331, 334, 335, 339, 341, 342, 350, 351, 353, 358, 359, 360, 364, 365, 366, 367, 383, 384, 391, 392, 396, 397, 400, 408, 409, 416, 417, 421, 422, 426, 427, 443, 444, 445, 450, 451, 452, 456, 457, 458, 462, 463, 469, 470, 471, 476, 477, 484, 485, 486, 502, 503, 504, 505, 508, 509, 510, 514, 515, 518, 519, 523, 524, 525, 533, 534, 535, 540, 541, 546, 547, 548, 551, 552, 553, 567, 568, 569, 574, 576, 581, 582, 587, 588, 596, 597, 598, 602, 603, 604, 605, 609, 610, 627, 628, 633, 634, 637, 640, 641, 642, 643, 646, 647, 648, 649, 665, 666, 671, 672, 673, 674, 679, 680, 681, 685, 686, 687, 688, 693, 694, 695, 711, 712, 716, 717, 718, 723, 724, 725, 731, 732, 733, 738, 739, 740, 751, 752, 753, 758, 759, 760, 761, 766, 767, 768, 769

government, 189

graphing calculator, 67, 278–279, 328, 355, 388, 408, 431, 488, 568, 571, 575, 577. *See also* calculator
alpha key, 431
apps key, 431
calc key, 279, 366, 388, 575, 614
correlation coefficient from, 366
equation of line of best fit using, 370
finding line of best fit using, 366
graph key, 278, 279, 431
histograms, 717
INEQUAL feature, 431
of inequalities, 226–227
LINREG feature, 366
math key, 753, 764
MAXIMUM feature, 575
QUADREG feature, 614
RANDINT feature, 764
stat key, 366, 614
table key, 388
tblset key, 388
window key, 67, 278
x,t,θ,n key, 67, 279
y= key, 67, 278, 388
zoom key, 279, 328, 614

Graphing Functions and Solving Equations, 278–279

Graphing Linear Equations, 431

graph key, of graphing calculator, 278, 431

graph paper, 68, 579

graph(s)
of absolute value equations, 222–223, 226–228
of absolute value inequalities, 226–227
analyzing, 249
bar, 794
of boundary lines of linear inequalities, 417
box-and-whisker plot, 732
circle, 796
of compound inequalities, 216–219
continuous, 272–273, 305
on the coordinate plane, 68
describing relationships using, 69–70
of direct variation, 323–324
discrete, 272–273, 305
of equations, 339
estimating values in a function using, 599
of exponential functions, 477, 483, 485
finding slope using, 315
of function rules, 270–271
of geometric relationships, 256
histograms, 717–718
of horizontal lines, 351
of inequalities, 178–180, 185–186, 191–194, 216–219, 417–418, 420–422
line, 795
of linear equations, 257, 329, 334–335
of linear functions, 262–263
of linear inequalities, 417–418, 420–422, 431
line plots, 793
of a line using intercepts, 350
matching with data table, 250
misleading, 744
of nonlinear function rules, 273
of nonlinear functions, 262–263
of patterns, 71, 264
quadratic, 566–569, 573–575, 580, 581, 604, 608, 609
of a quadratic function, 574
of real numbers, 22
scatter plot, 363–364
sketching, 251
of solutions of equations, 70
of solutions of systems of linear equations, 382–384, 407
solving an equation by making a table, 67
stem-and-leaf plots, 797
of system of linear inequalities, 417–418, 420–422, 425
of systems of linear equations, 382–384
using, to describe relationships, 70
using point-slope form, 339
using slope-intercept form, 329–331
using to relate variables, 249
of vertical lines, 351

Index

Index

product(s)
of a binomial and a trinomial, 519
cross, 137, 165
of fractions, 789
of a monomial and a trinomial, 508
with multiple variables, 463
of negative numbers, 45–46
of numbers with different signs, 46
of numbers with same sign, 46
of powers with same base, 455–458
of radical expressions, 633, 641
raised to a power, simplifying, 463
of rational expression and polynomial, 672
of real numbers, 45
simplifying, 463
of a sum and difference, 524–525
of two binonmials, 513, 514–515, 518, 533–535
of two binonmials, modeling, 514

Properties, as Big Idea, 3, 36, 75, 76, 441, 490, 491, 501, 531, 556, 557

Property(ies)
Addition Property of Equality, 87
Addition Property of Inequality, 184, 185
Associative Property of Addition, 26
Associative Property of Multiplication, 26
Commutative Property of Addition, 26
Commutative Property of Multiplication, 26
Converse of the Pythagorean Theorem, 628
Cross Products Property of a Proportion, 137
Distributive Property, 53, 56, 102, 201, 514
Dividing Powers With the Same Base, 468
Division Property of Equality, 89
Division Property of Inequality, 193
Division Property of Square Roots, 636
Identity Property of Addition, 27
Identity Property of Multiplication, 27
Inverse Property of Addition, 39
Inverse Property of Multiplication, 47–48
Multiplication Property, 137
Multiplication Property of -1, 27, 54
Multiplication Property of Equality, 89
Multiplication Property of Inequality, 191, 192
Multiplication Property of Square Roots, 632
Multiplying Powers With the Same Base, 455
Raising a Power to a Power, 461
Raising a Product to a Power, 463
Raising a Quotient to a Power, 470
Reflexive Property of Equality, 197
Subtraction of Property of Equality, 87
Subtraction Property of Inequality, 186

Symmetric Property of Equality, 197
Transitive Property of Equality, 197
Transitive Property of Inequality, 197
Zero and Negative Exponents, 443
Zero-Product Property, 586
Zero Property of Multiplication, 27

Proportionality, as Big Idea, 85, 129, 163, 164, 313, 348, 372, 373

proportions
defined, 136
extremes of, 138
involving radicals, 642
means of, 138
multi-step, 138
percent, 150
rational, 695
in similar figures, 143
solving, 136–139, 695
solving using the Cross Products Property, 137–138
solving using the Multiplication Property, 137
using to find side lengths, 144
using to interpret scale drawings, 145
using to solve problems, 139

Pull It All Together, 75, 163, 237, 302, 372, 432, 490, 556, 615, 653, 699, 772

Pythagorean Theorem
converse of, 628
defined, 626, 655
using, 626–628

Q

quadrants, 68

quadratic equations
approximate solutions of, 603
choosing method for solving, 604, 608–609
choosing reasonable solutions for, 582
defined, 580
graph of, 580, 581
methods for solving, 603
modeling, 595
roots of, 580, 581
solving by completing the square, 595–598
solving by factoring, 586–588
solving by graphing, 581
solving using square roots, 581
standard form of, 580, 587
zero of, 580

quadratic formula
defined, 601, 617
using, 602

quadratic functions
defined, 566, 591
of the form $y = ax^2$, 567

of the form $y = ax^2 + bx + c$, 573–576
of the form $y = ax^2 + c$, 568
graph of, 566–569, 573–576, 604, 608, 609
parent function, 566
standard form of, 566
zero of, 586

quadratic graphs, 566–569, 573–575, 580, 581, 604, 608, 609

quadratic models
vs. exponential model, 608–609
vs. linear model, 608–609
using, 608–609

quadratic parent function, 566

QUADREG feature, of graphing calculator, 614

qualitative, 737

quantitative, 737

quantity, 4

quartile, 730

Quick Review, 33–34, 77–78, 125–127, 165–166, 206–207, 239–240, 304–306, 345–346, 374, 412–413, 434, 492–494, 528–529, 558, 591–592, 617–618, 655–656, 701–702, 745–747, 774–775

quotients
involving fractions, 789
involving rational expressions, 673
of numbers with different signs, 47
of numbers with same sign, 47
radical expressions involving, 636–637
raising to a power, 470
of real numbers, 47
sign of, 47

R

radical equations
defined, 646, 656
solving, 646–648
using, 647

radical expressions
defined, 632, 655
multiplying, 641
simplifying by multiplying, 632, 633
writing, 634

radicals
defined, 19
isolating, 646
simplifying, 632–633, 636–637

radicand, 19

Raising a Power to a Power, 461

Acknowledgments

Staff Credits

The people who made up the High School Mathematics team—representing composition services, core design digital and multimedia production services, digital product development, editorial, editorial services, manufacturing, marketing, and production management—are listed below.

Dan Anderson, Scott Andrews, Christopher Anton, Carolyn Artin, Michael Avidon, Margaret Banker, Charlie Bink, Niki Birbilis, Suzanne Biron, Beth Blumberg, Kyla Brown, Rebekah Brown, Judith Buice, Sylvia Bullock, Stacie Cartwright, Carolyn Chappo, Christia Clarke, Tom Columbus, Andrew Coppola, AnnMarie Coyne, Bob Craton, Nicholas Cronin, Patrick Culleton, Damaris Curran, Steven Cushing, Sheila DeFazio, Cathie Dillender, Emily Dumas, Patty Fagan, Frederick Fellows, Jorgensen Fernandez, Mandy Figueroa, Suzanne Finn, Sara Freund, Matt Frueh, Jon Fuhrer, Andy Gaus, Mark Geyer, Mircea Goia, Andrew Gorlin, Shelby Gragg, Ellen Granter, Jay Grasso, Lisa Gustafson, Toni Haluga, Greg Ham, Marc Hamilton, Chris Handorf, Angie Hanks, Scott Harris, Cynthia Harvey, Phil Hazur, Thane Heninger, Aun Holland, Amanda House, Chuck Jann, Linda Johnson, Blair Jones, Marian Jones, Tim Jones, Gillian Kahn, Brian Keegan, Jonathan Kier, Jennifer King, Tamara King, Elizabeth Krieble, Meytal Kotik, Brian Kubota, Roshni Kutty, Mary Landry, Christopher Langley, Christine Lee, Sara Levendusky, Lisa Lin, Wendy Marberry, Dominique Mariano, Clay Martin, Rich McMahon, Eve Melnechuk, Cynthia Metallides, Hope Morley, Christine Nevola, Michael O'Donnell, Michael Oster, Ameer Padshah, Jeffrey Paulhus, Jonathan Penyack, Valerie Perkins, Brian Reardon, Wendy Rock, Marcy Rose, Carol Roy, Irene Rubin, Hugh Rutledge, Vicky Shen, Jewel Simmons, Ted Smykal, Emily Soltanoff, William Speiser, Jayne Stevenson, Richard Sullivan, Dan Tanguay, Dennis Tarwood, Susan Tauer, Tiffany Taylor-Sullivan, Catherine Terwilliger, Maria Torti, Mark Tricca, Leonid Tunik, Ilana Van Veen, Lauren Van Wart, John Vaughan, Laura Vivenzio, Samuel Voigt, Kathy Warfel, Don Weide, Laura Wheel, Eric Whitfield, Sequoia Wild, Joseph Will, Kristin Winters, Allison Wyss, Dina Zolotusky

Additional Credits: Michele Cardin, Robert Carlson, Kate Dalton-Hoffman, Dana Guterman, Narae Maybeth, Carolyn McGuire, Manjula Nair, Rachel Terino, Steve Thomas

Illustration

Kevin Banks: 360; **Jeff Grunewald:** 254, 283, 284, 552, 572, 586, 607, 610, 612, 694; **Christopher Wilson:** 270, 286, 297, 356, 390, 414, 484, 504, 568, 676, 679, 688, 710, 714, 716, 720, 722, 750, 751, 755, 757, 765, 767; **XNR Productions:** 4, 145, 163, 182, 184, 449

Technical Illustration

GGS Book Services

Photography

Every effort has been made to secure permission and provide appropriate credit for photographic material. The publisher deeply regrets any omission and pledges to correct errors called to its attention in subsequent editions.

Unless otherwise acknowledged, all photographs are the property of Pearson Education, Inc.

Photo locators denoted as follows: Top (T), Center (C), Bottom (B), Left (L), Right (R), Background (Bkgd)

Cover
Gary Bell/Corbis

Front Matter
ix, x, xviii Stan Liu/Getty Images

3 (T) Joel Kiesel/Getty Images; **50** (BR) The Art Gallery Collection/Alamy Images; **62** (CR) Satellite Imaging Corp./GeoEye Inc.; **85** (T) Reuters/Tobias Schwarz/Landov LLC; **90** (CR) Livio Soares/BrazilPhotos, (BR) Island Effects/iStockphoto, (CC) Wildlife Bildagentur GmbH/Kimball Stock; **122** (CR) Reuters/Corbis; **146** (TR) Courtesy of the Historical and Interpretive Collections of the Franklin Institute, (CC) Ingram Publishing/SuperStock, (TC) Medi-Mation Ltd/Photo Researchers, Inc.; **173** (T) Michael Newman/PhotoEdit, Inc.; **174** (CR) Google, Inc.; **180** (TR) ©Shubroto Chattopadhyay/Corbis, (TL) Macduff Everton/Getty Images; **212** (C) acilo/iStockphoto; **237** (BR) ©DK Images, (TR) ©Ned Frisk Photography/Corbis; **247** (T) Ed Ou/©AP Images; **272** (CC) Ian O'Leary/©DK Images, (CL) iStockphoto, (CR) Taylor S. Kennedy/National Geographic Image Collection; **313** (T) Sacramento Bee/MCT/Landov LLC; **323** (TCR) Friedrich Saurer/Photo Researchers, Inc., (CR) GSFC/NASA, (BR) NASA/©AP Images; **335** (T) David Joyner/iStockphoto, (TR) Tobias Bernhard/Corbis; **381** (T) WILDLIFE GmbH/Alamy Images; **383** (TL) Ilian Animal/Alamy Images, (TR) James Carmichael Jr./Photoshot; **441** (T) Jeff Vanuga/Corbis; **447** (TR) Kevin Schafer/Photoshot; **449** (CR) Andrew Syred/Photo Researchers, Inc.; Robert Markus; **479** (CR) Biophoto Associates/Photo Researchers, Inc.; **501** (T) Stan Liu/Getty Images; **510** (TR) brt PHOTO/Alamy Images, (TCR) Paulo Fridman/Corbis; **533** (TCR) iStockphoto; **539** (TCR) iStockphoto, (CR) wingmar/iStockphoto; **546** (CR) Brandon Alms/Shutterstock; **565** (T) Bernd Opitz/Getty Images; **588** (TR) Jxpfeer/Dreamstime LLC; **599** (BR) ©DK Images; **625** (T) Roine Magnusson/The Image Bank/Getty Images; **627** (TR) Rob Belknap/iStockphoto; **630** (BR) Geoffrey Morgan/Alamy Images; **638** (TR) Laure Neish/iStockphoto; **642** (BR) Art Wolfe/Getty Images; **644** (TC) Thomas Sakoulas/Greeklandscapes; **663** (T) Peter Essick/Aurora; **676** (CR) Scott Krycia/iStockphoto; **688** (C) Theo Allofs/PhotoLibrary Group/Getty Images; **709** (T) Jamie Wilson/iStockphoto.